THE FOUNDER

The Beginning or the Founding of the Order and
the Deeds of Those Lesser Brothers
Who Were the First Companions of Blessed Francis in Religion
(1240–1241)

The Legend of the Three Companions
(1241–1247)

The Assisi Compilation
(1244–1260)

The Remembrance of the Desire of a Soul
by Thomas of Celano
(1245–1247)

The Treatise on the Miracles of Saint Francis
by Thomas of Celano
(1250–1252)

An Umbrian Choir Legend
(1253–1259)

A Letter on the Passing of Saint Francis Attributed to Elias of Assisi
(After 1253)

The Legends and Sermons about Saint Francis by Bonaventure of Bagnoregio:
The Morning and Evening Sermons, October 4, 1255
The Major Legend of Saint Francis
(1260–1263)
The Minor Legend of Saint Francis
(1260–1266)
The Evening Sermon, October 4, 1262
A Sermon, October 4, 1266
A Sermon on the Feast of the Transferal of the Body of Saint Francis, May 25, 1267
The Morning and Evening Sermons, October 4, 1267

Related Documents
(1237–1272)

A three-volume series

FRANCIS OF ASSISI: EARLY DOCUMENTS

Volume I	The Saint
Volume II	The Founder
Volume III	The Prophet

THE FOUNDER

The Beginning or the Founding of the Order and the Deeds of Those Lesser Brothers Who Were the First Companions of Blessed Francis in Religion
The Legend of the Three Companions
The Assisi Compilation
The Remembrance of the Desire of a Soul by Thomas of Celano
The Treatise on the Miracles of Saint Francis by Thomas of Celano
An Umbrian Choir Legend
A Letter on the Passing of Saint Francis Attributed to Elias of Assisi
The Legends and Sermons about Saint Francis by Bonaventure of Bagnoregio:
The Morning and Evening Sermons, October 4, 1255
The Major Legend of Saint Francis
The Minor Legend of Saint Francis
The Evening Sermon, October 4, 1262
A Sermon, October 4, 1266
A Sermon on the Feast of the Transferal of the Body of Saint Francis, May 25, 1267
The Morning and Evening Sermons, October 4, 1267
Related Documents

Volume II of:
Francis of Assisi: Early Documents

Edited by
Regis J. Armstrong, O.F.M. Cap.
J. A. Wayne Hellmann, O.F.M. Conv.
William J. Short, O.F.M.

New City Press
New York London Manila

Published in the United States, Great Britain, and the Philippines by
New City Press, 202 Cardinal Rd., Hyde Park, New York 12538
New City, 57 Twyford Ave., London W3 9PZ and
New City Publications, 4800 Valenzuela St. Sta Mesa, 1016 Manila

Cover design by Nick Cianfarani
Cover art by Domenico Ghirlandaio
The Confirmation of the Franciscan Rule by Pope Honorius, III.
in the S. Trinita, Florence, Italy.
Scala/Art Resourse, NY. Used with permission.
Maps ©1998, Franciscan Friars of California

Library of Congress Cataloging-in-Publication Data:

Francis of Assisi : early documents / edited by Regis J. Armstrong, J. Wayne Hellmann, William J. Short.
p. cm.
Includes bibliographical references and index.
Contents: v. 2. The founder.
ISBN 1-56548-113-5 (v. 2 : hardcover). -- ISBN 1-56548-112-7 (v. 2 : pbk.)
1. Francis, of Assisi, Saint, 1182-1226. 2. Christian saints--Italy--Assisi--Biography--Early works to 1800. 3. Franciscans--History--Sources. I. Francis, of Assisi, Saint, 1182-1226. Works. English. 1999. II. Armstrong, Regis J. III. Hellmann, J. Wayne. IV. Short, William J.
BX4700.F6F722 1999
271'.302--dc21
[b] 99-18776
CIP

2d printing: September 2001

Printed in Canada

Translators:

Regis J. Armstrong, O.F.M. Cap.
Paul Barrett, O.F.M. Cap
Canisius Connors, O.F.M.+
Ewert H. Cousins, Ph.D.
Eric Doyle, O.F.M.+
Edward Hagman, O.F.M. Cap.
J. A. Wayne Hellmann, O.F.M. Conv.
Claude Jarmak, O.F.M. Conv.
Timothy Johnson, S.T.D.
Dominic Monti, O.F.M.
Peter Nickels, O.F.M. Conv.
Timothy Noone, Ph.D.
Gregory Shanahan, O.F.M.
William J. Short, O.F.M.
Jaime Vidal, Ph.D.

Contributors and Consultants:

Blaine Burkey, O.F.M. Cap.
Michael Casey, O.S.C.O.
John and Vicki Chiment
Joseph Chinicci, O.F.M.
Michael Cusato, O.F.M.
Lorenzo DiFonzo, O.F.M. Conv.
Jay Hammond III, Ph.D.
Conrad Harkins, O.F.M.
Ingrid Peterson, O.S.F.
Cyprian Rosen, O.F.M. Cap.
Oktavian Schmucki, O.F.M. Cap.
Maurice Sheehan, O.F.M. Cap.
Mark Weavers, O.F.M. Conv.
William H. Winters, O.F.M. Cap.

Technical and Research Assistants:

John Isom
Noel Riggs
Robert Roddy, O.F.M. Conv.
Keith Warner, O.F.M.

Contents

General Introduction 11
Abbreviations 26
Editor's Note 27

The Beginning or Founding of the Order and the Deeds of Those Lesser Brothers Who Were the First Companions of Blessed Francis in Religion (1240–1241)

Introduction 31
[Prologue] 34
Chapter I 34
Chapter II 37
Chapter III 39
Chapter IV 41
Chapter V 42
Chapter VI 45
Chapter VII. 48
Chapter VIII 51
Chapter IX 53
Chapter X 55
Chapter XI 56
Chapter XII 57
Epilogue 58

The Legend of the Three Companions (1241–1247)

Introduction 61
[Rubric] 66
[Letter] 66
Chapter I 68
Chapter II 69
Chapter III 71
Chapter IV 74
Chapter V 75
Chapter VI 77
Chapter VII. 81
Chapter VIII 84
Chapter IX 86
Chapter X 89

Chapter XI 92
Chapter XII 95
Chapter XIII 99
Chapter XIV 100
Chapter XV 103
Chapter XVI 104
Chapter XVII 107
Chapter XVIII. 109

The Assisi Compilation (1244–1260)

Introduction 113

[1]—118; [2]—118; [3]—119; [4]—119; [5]—120; [6]—120; [7]—120; [8]—121; [9]—123; [10]—124; [11]—125; [12]—126; [13]—128; [14]—129; [15]—130; [16]—131; [17]—131; [18]—132; [19]—133; [20]—134; [21]—134; [22]—135; [23]—135; [24]—136; [25]—136; [26]—136; [27]—137; [28]—137; [29]—137; [30]—138; [31]—138; [32]—139; [33]—139; [34]—140; [35]—140; [36]—141; [37]—141; [38]—142; [39]—142; [40]—143; [41]—143; [42]—144; [43]—145; [44]—145; [45]—146; [46]—146; [47]—147; [48]—147; [49]—148; [50]—149; [51]—150; [52]—151; [53]—152; [54]—152; [55]—153; [56]—154; [57]—158; [58]—159; [59]—161; [60]—162; [61]—163; [62]—165; [63]—165; [64]—166; [65]—167; [66]—168; [67]—170; [68]—171; [69]—172; [70]—173; [71]—173; [72]—174; [73]—174; [74]—175; [75]—178; [76]—179; [77]—180; [78]—180; [79]—181; [80]—181; [81]—182; [82]—183; [83]—184; [84]—187; [85]—188; [86]—189; [87]—191; [88]—192; [89]—192; [90]—194; [91]—194; [92]—195; [93]—196; [94]—196; [95]—197; [96]—198; [97]—200; [98]—202; [99]—202; [100]—203; [101]—204; [102]—206; [103]—207; [104]—209; [105]—210; [106]—210; [107]—213; [108]—214; [109]—217; [110]—217; [111]—218; [112]—219; [113]—220; [114]—220; [115]—221; [116]—222; [117]—224; [118]—226; [119]—227; [120]—229

The Remembrance of the Desire of a Soul by Thomas of Celano (1245–1247)

Introduction 233
Prologue 239
The First Book 241
The Second Book. 263

The Treatise on the Miracles of Saint Francis by Thomas of Celano (1250–1252)

Introduction 397
Chapter I 399
Chapter II. 401
Chapter III 408
Chapter IV 411
Chapter V. 415

Chapter VI 417
Chapter VII 419
Chapter VIII 424
Chapter IX 432
Chapter X. 433
Chapter XI 436
Chapter XII 439
Chapter XIII 445
Chapter XIV 447
Chapter XV 453
Chapter XVI 454
Chapter XVII 456
Chapter XVIII. 463
Chapter XIV 468

An Umbrian Choir Legend (1253–1259)

Introduction 471
An Umbrian Choir Legend 473

A Letter on the Passing of Saint Francis Attributed to Elias of Assisi (After 1253)

Introduction 485
A Letter on the Passing of Saint Francis 489

The Legends and Sermons about Saint Francis by Bonaventure of Bagnoregio (1255–1267)

Introduction 495
The Morning Sermon on Saint Francis, 1255 508
The Evening Sermon on Saint Francis, 1255 517

The Major Legend of Saint Francis (1260–1263) 525

The Life of Blessed Francis

Prologue 525
Chapter One. 530
Chapter Two. 536
Chapter Three 542
Chapter Four 550
Chapter Five. 560
Chapter Six 569
Chapter Seven. 577
Chapter Eight 586
Chapter Nine 596

Chapter Ten . . . 605
Chapter Eleven . . . 612
Chapter Twelve . . . 622
Chapter Thirteen . . . 630
Chapter Fourteen . . . 640
Chapter Fifteen . . . 645

The Miracles Shown after His Death

Chapter I . . . 650
Chapter II . . . 655
Chapter III . . . 659
Chapter IV. . . . 663
Chapter V . . . 665
Chapter VI. . . . 668
Chapter VII . . . 670
Chapter VIII. . . . 673
Chapter IX. . . . 676
Chapter X . . . 678

The Minor Legend . . . 684
Chapter I . . . 684
Chapter II . . . 689
Chapter III . . . 694
Chapter IV. . . . 699
Chapter V . . . 704
Chapter VI. . . . 709
Chapter VII . . . 714

The Evening Sermon on Saint Francis, 1262 . . . 718
A Sermon on Saint Francis, 1266 . . . 731
A Sermon on the Feast of the Transferal of the Body, May, 1267 . . . 737
The Morning Sermon on Saint Francis, 1267. . . . 747
The Evening Sermon on Saint Francis, 1267 . . . 759

Related Documents (1237–1272)

Introduction . . . 769
Miscellaneous Franciscan Sources . . . 770
Papal Documents. . . . 774
Dominican Hagiography and Sermons . . . 782
Chronicles . . . 806

Appendix

Explanation of Maps. . . . 823
Gazetteer . . . 827
Maps . . . 833

General Introduction

Celebratory: the adjective captures the mood of the writings of the first volume of *Francis of Assisi: Early Documents.* By providing an insight into the profound simplicity of his soul, Francis's writings, the first collection of texts in that first volume, reveal the reasons for his continual joy. Even in the midst of sufferings and difficulties that most people would find overwhelming, the optimism and hope that flow spontaneously from the thirteenth century Umbrian Italian permeate every aspect of his letters, prayers, admonitions, and rules. The ever present, always new goodness of the loving triune God that gave Francis such confidence is accessible to even the most casual reader, and makes him understandably attractive.

Francis peacefully, even joyfully, died on the evening of October 3, 1226, singing the praises of God. With the song, "Most high, all powerful, all good Lord," he welcomed Sister Bodily Death. A short time later, those present at his passing indicate that they were immediately ready to acclaim Francis a saint. Two years later, the honor was given to Cardinal Hugolino di Segni, Francis's friend and confidant, now Pope Gregory IX. Gregory's enthusiasm is evident in his papal proclamation, *Mira circa nos,* issued on the occasion of his canonization. The pope's jubilation is even more obvious in the first life of the saint, Francis of Assisi, commissioned by Gregory and written by Thomas of Celano. Joy resonates throughout the liturgical pieces written by Thomas of Celano and by Julian of Speyer, and in the clever, artful verse of the papal Latinist, Henri d'Avranches. All of these texts, written within the first decade of Francis's canonization, reveal the predominantly celebratory atmosphere of the texts of *The Saint,* that is, the first volume of *Francis of Assisi: Early Documents.*

The Saint and The Pope: New Challenges

In order to understand the texts of volume two, it is helpful to appreciate that Francis's first biographers, Thomas of Celano, Julian of Speyer, and Henri d'Avranches, had a paradoxically simple yet bewildering task. Their portraits had to show to the world that Francis was indeed a saint, an assignment that was elementary when placed in the tradition of the lives of other saints such as Martin, Benedict, and Bernard. At the same time, however, these first writers bore the responsibility of defining Francis's uniqueness, a difficult challenge to meet. Francis's writings reveal a transparently and thoroughly Gospel spirituality. Yet, as history would attest, it was difficult to define its unique qualities. While some would claim Francis's call was to poverty, others would maintain it was to penance. Some would interpret his mission in terms of preaching, others would define it as one of identifying with and giving hope to the poor. Sufficiently daunting in itself, the task of those first biographers was complicated by the images with which Pope Gregory IX portrayed his canonized friend. He used terms of the Old Testament *Judges* or of the New Testament *Apocalypse*. That Thomas, Julian, and Henri succeeded can be seen, particularly in Thomas's case, in the enduring quality of their portraits. It remains difficult to understand the development of the hagiographic tradition surrounding Francis without some knowledge of *The Life of Saint Francis* by Thomas of Celano.

Different perspectives soon sowed the seeds of uncertainty and subsequent discord. Within a short time after Francis's death, questions arose concerning the interpretation of his *Rule*. The saint seemingly foresaw that this would be the case. He wrote in his *Testament:*

> I strictly command all my cleric and lay brothers, through obedience, not to place any gloss upon the Rule or upon these words saying: "They should be understood in this way." But as the Lord has given me to speak and write the Rule and these words simply and purely, may you understand them simply and without gloss and observe them with a holy activity until the end.[1]

While he was living, that request presented no difficulties.

Four years after Francis's death, however, the brothers who gathered in Assisi for the Pentecost General Chapter of 1230 seemed unable to understand the words of the *Rule* simply. Francis's brotherhood was changing too rapidly. Not simply had it exploded numerically to several thousand brothers, scattered throughout Western Christendom, but perhaps more importantly, the brothers' sense of their own vocation in the church was undergoing a radical transformation. More and more of the brothers, as well as many church leaders, especially Gregory IX himself, wished the Order to focus its energies on implementing the pastoral reform agenda of the Fourth Lateran Council. They believed the Lesser Brothers should serve the church through doctrinal preaching, combating heretical movements, and hearing the confessions of the faithful.[2] Such brothers were demanding greater flexibility in interpreting the provisions of the *Rule* to assure that they could meet these tasks effectively. Others believed that these passages should be taken literally, and Francis's *Testament* seemed to bolster their opinion. The very foundational document of the Order was becoming divisive. When the ministers could not resolve their questions, they turned to Pope Gregory IX. In the Fall of that year Gregory IX attempted to resolve the controversial issues with his papal decree, *Quo elongati*. In addition to dealing with points of poverty, the hearing of confessions, faculties for preaching, reception of postulants, participants in general chapters, and the pastoral care of the Damianites, i.e., the Sisters of Saint Clare, Gregory addressed two fundamental issues that exerted powerful influences on the life of the brothers: the authority of Francis's *Testament*, and the obligation to the Gospel.

Francis's *Testament* was the final written expression of the saint's desires for his brothers, desires that revolved around his memories of the earliest days of his conversion and of the primitive fraternity. His statement about understanding and interpreting the *Rule,* however, suggests that it was much more. The *Testament* was a document touching on the very essence of Francis's vision of the Gospel life, and, since it was written on his death bed, it reveals in a striking way the idealism and formula of his holiness.[3] To set it aside would, in a sense, undermine the authority of these words of the Founder himself. Citing his "long-standing" friendship with Francis as the source of his judgment, Gregory IX did just that: he declared that the brothers were "not bound by the *Testament.*" "For without the consent of the brothers, and especially of the ministers," *Quo elongati* maintained, "Francis could not make obligatory a matter that touches everyone."[4]

A fundamental point of Francis's vision, however, was the authority of the Gospel life. In both Rules, Francis expressed his vision that the life of the Gospel was for him and his brothers quite simply the *Rule.* Gospel life, in others words, was the equivalent of the *Rule.* If setting aside the *Testament* weakened the Gospel idealism espoused by the Founder for his brothers, compromise of this fundamental identification would do more. It also helped change the Gospel spirit and life of the *Rule* into the realm of the juridical. Once again, *Quo elongati* did just that. "You are not bound by the *Rule,*" Gregory stated, "to observe the counsels of the Gospel, other than those explicitly contained in the *Rule* to which you have committed yourselves." The fundamental endeavor, therefore, became focused on living "in obedience, without anything of their own, and in chastity." The broader and more Spirit-filled challenge of expressing Gospel life each day was assuaged.

Ironically, with one document aimed at reconciling the brothers, the pope furthered the tension between the idealists and the moderates. Admittedly, the pope was acting within his rights. With the seal of approval issued with *Solet annuere* on November 29, 1223, the *Rule* became a document of the Church and, as such, subject to its interpretation. Nonetheless, the pope unwittingly sowed among the brothers seeds of division. John R.H. Moorman[5] and Raphael Huber[6] present these early divisions within the Lesser Brothers of this period as those of the "Community" and the "Spirituals." Duncan Nimmo presents them as the "moderate" wing of the Community, the "relaxed" wing of the Community, and finally the "Spirituals."[7] Perhaps more accurately, Franz Cardinal Ehrle,[8] Livarius Oliger,[9] Lazaro Iriarte,[10] and Thaddeus MacVicar[11] prefer to call the more conservative brothers during the period of this second volume "*zelanti* [those who were zealous]." These scholars maintain that the technical or sectarian sense of the term "Spiritual" did not arise until the last quarter of the thirteenth century. Whatever labels are applied, the tensions became more pronounced during the final years of Elias's term as General Minister (1232-1239). As a result, the Lesser Brothers began considering more seriously the heritage left by Francis, the Founder of their Order. A text in the first volume, *The Sacred Exchange* (1237-1239), may well be a piece that expresses this endeavor.[12] Its biblical tapestry richly expresses the ideals of the poverty envisioned by Francis and adroitly avoids any juridical refinements.[13]

In 1239, the General Chapter of Rome, in the presence of Gregory IX, deposed Elias and in his place elected an elderly brother, Albert of Pisa.[14] When Albert died a few months later, Haymo of Faversham succeeded him. While Haymo was General Minister, the internal structures of the Order changed profoundly. Lay brothers were excluded from positions of responsibility such as local, provincial or general ministers, and were relegated to more domestic ones. Lay people were hired as servants for more menial tasks. And a monastic vocabulary became more commonplace, as the brothers introduced concepts such as "conventual mass," "regular silence," and adopted an approach to daily life that had more in common with monasticism.[15] The simplicity of Francis's Gospel vision, therefore, was slowly being replaced by a more organized and regulated way of life.

Returning to the Spirit of the Founder

Between 1240 and 1241, the first work of this second volume appeared, *The Beginning or The Founding of the Order and The Deeds of Those Lesser Brothers Who were The First Companions of Blessed Francis in Religion.* The work became more popularly called *The Anonymous of Perugia,* because its author never identifies himself. "Servants of the Lord," he states initially, "should not be ignorant of the lives and teachings of saints through which they can come to God." This opening statement immediately alluded to a serious problem: the brothers of the second generation did not have the same intimate experience of Francis as that of the primitive fraternity. The chronicles of Thomas of Eccleston and Jordan of Giano indicate that the Lesser Brothers had spread beyond the Italian peninsula to England, France, Spain, and Germany.[16] At the same time, the number of brothers in Syria, Cyprus, and Romania was growing, as was the number of brothers in Jerusalem, Bethlehem, Nazareth, and other sites in the Holy Land.[17] In 1245, John of Piancarpino set out for the Mongul Empire. Inspiring as *The Life of Saint Francis* by Thomas of Celano might be, it did not capture the excitement experienced by those first Lesser Brothers and, therefore, failed to express the fullness of the original spirit.

The aging brothers of the primitive fraternity might well have become uncomfortable with the uncontrollable growth and wary of the many organizational changes they were witnessing because of the expanding horizons of the Order. The death in 1241 of Sylvester, one of Francis's earliest followers, could have intensified their concerns and inspired some of the first followers to retell their stories. John of Perugia, a companion of Giles, Francis's third companion, seems to have been the chosen amanuensis. "For the honor of God and the edification of readers and listeners," he writes, "I, who saw their deeds, listened to their words, and also became their disciple, have compiled and recounted, as the Lord inspired me, some deeds of our most blessed father Francis and of a few of the brothers who lived at the beginning of the religion."[18] Sixty percent of *The Anonymous of Perugia* is new information and indicates sources close to the events. John's presentation is non-polemical; it conveys more of an earnest desire to communicate the first days of the fraternity. His choice to remain anonymous, that is, to avoid identifying himself, is understandable. His role was simply to articulate the remembrances of the elders, the first followers.

It is difficult to determine the impact of *The Anonymous of Perugia*. How much was the work circulated? Did it awaken among the brothers the realization that there was more to know about Francis? Did it present Francis as simply *primus inter pares*, that is, as the central figure of a much larger movement and thus diminish his role as founder? The answers to these and similar questions remain hidden. What has emerged, however, is the influence of *The Anonymous of Perugia* on the second text of this volume, a text known as *The Legend of the Three Companions*. *The Legend of the Three Companions* borrows from, adds to, and refines *The Anonymous of Perugia*.

The Request of Crescentius, New Information, and Thomas of Celano

Before noting the place of *The Legend of the Three Companions* in the development of these texts, however, it is helpful to return to the history of the Lesser Brothers. For while John of Perugia was collecting and recording the stories of Francis's early followers, the tensions continued to mount. In 1241 the "Chapter of Definitors," a new entity established by the Chapter of Rome in 1239, requested that commissions be appointed in each province to settle doubtful points of the *Rule*.[19] Thomas of Eccleston writes of such a commission in the English province.[20] Another was established in France. Its members were well-known masters of the University of Paris who produced the *Exposition of the Four Masters on the Rule of the Lesser Brothers*.[21] In it they appealed to the intention of Francis as expressed in his *Testament*, a document they quote several times. However, neither the commissions nor the *Exposition* were successful in resolving new questions, especially those concerning poverty. Thus, once again, the brothers turned to Rome: a resolution was sought from Pope Innocent IV (1243-1254). Before a response could be given, however, the leadership of the Order once again changed hands.

Four years after his election as General Minister, Haymo died. He was succeeded in 1244 by Crescentius of Iesi whose zeal Thomas of Eccleston described as "kindled by charity, informed by learning, and strengthened by perseverance."[22] According to the *Chronicle of the Twenty-four Generals*, during that Chapter of Genoa, Crescentius "directed all the brothers to send him in writing whatever they could truly recall about the life, miracles, and prodigies of blessed Francis."[23] What was Crescentius's motivation? Faced with increasing tensions among the brothers, did he hope that remembrance of Francis might heal existing divisions? Or more likely, did he simply wish to learn of more testimonials to the holiness and intercessory power of the founder of his Order whose ministries he wished to promote?[24] In any case, two highly disputed texts owe their origin to Crescentius's directive, *The Legend of the Three Companions* and *The Assisi Compilation*. In the first text, the contributors identify themselves as Brothers Leo, Angelo, and Rufino; while, in the second, they repeatedly use the formula "we who were with him."

The Legend of the Three Companions provides details and insights that confirm the claim of Leo, Angelo, and Rufino that they or their companions had personal access to Francis. Close examination of the text also reveals that they had access to the earlier texts of *The Life of Saint Francis* by Thomas of Celano and *The Anonymous of Perugia*.[25] While the authors give the impression that they are intent on clarifying Thomas of Celano's work, they seem to respect *The Anonymous of Perugia*. Taking passages from Thomas of Celano, the three abbreviate, refine or add to them. At the same time, however, they quote *The Anonymous of Perugia* almost verbatim, although, at times, they provide details or insights missing from the earlier text.

The Assisi Compilation is different. "We who were with him" offer their stories with a much more down-to-earth vocabulary. Unlike Thomas of Celano or Julian of Speyer, their Latin is simple, lacking in refinement, and bereft of quotations or allusions to the writers of Latin antiquity. In many instances, it is clear that these stories flow from warm, personal experiences with the saint and those involved. Yet the work is definitely a compilation. Different styles of writing are evident. The mood or tenor of the text shifts abruptly. Frequently paragraphs become polemical or contentious in nature.

Both texts, however, come to us in a form different from that in which they were originally written. In the case of *The Legend of the Three Companions,* a letter written by Francis's companions appears by way of introduction. Its description of the text that follows does not correspond to that introduction; that is, while claiming that the material is a collection of "some of the more beautiful flowers" presented in a haphazard way, the text at hand is actually a chronological presentation in the form of a legend. Moreover, one family of manuscripts ends abruptly, while another continues with a description of Francis's last days. Scholars see this phenomenon as an indication that one of the two is an earlier rendition of the text. *The Assisi Compilation,* meanwhile, is a complicated text also containing additional passages taken from a later text of Thomas of Celano and from writings known to have come at a later date from Leo, Francis's close companion. In both instances, however, the authors seem intent to set the record straight and to return to the primitive vision of the Founder.

Crescentius commissioned Thomas of Celano to undertake the task of re-presenting these remembrances.[26] For the third time, Thomas received a request for another portrait of Francis. The first, *The Life of Saint Francis,* was prompted by Francis's canonization. This was followed by the need for a liturgical text, *The Legend for Use in the Choir.* His confreres had received and used both with great enthusiasm. In this instance, however, his task was more daunting for it was at the behest of his brothers who, at this time, continued to be divided by fundamental questions about Francis's *Rule.*

Considering the turbulent period in which the Order existed, the task, then, given to Thomas of Celano was formidable. In addition to receiving this commission from the General Minister, not the Pope, Thomas of Celano had seen the fraternity change dramatically since his composition of *The Life of Saint Francis.* The interventions of Pope Gregory, especially that of *Quo elongati,* had only intensified ideological division among the brothers.[27] Then, as Thomas of Celano was sifting through the material entrusted to him, Innocent IV sent to Crescentius the second papal interpretation of Francis's *Rule, Ordinem vestrum*. It was dated November 14, 1245.[28] In addition to declaring that all the property of the Order belonged to the Holy See, the office of proctor was established, that is, a representative of the pope who was responsible for what technically did not belong to the Order. It is easy to understand why many interpreted this as a legal ruse enabling the Lesser Brothers to avoid the mind of Francis. As Iriarte expresses it: "All the efforts of the official side of the Order were directed toward making evangelical poverty a matter of distinguishing between possession and use; the important thing was not so much to be 'poor' and 'lesser' as to be able to claim absence of ownership of any communal poverty."[29] That, in addition to his interpretation of poverty, the pope also included in *Ordinem vestrum* other directives aimed at furthering apostolic work and studies only exacerbated the tensions.[30]

Thomas of Celano must have found himself in a quandary. Aware of the tensions within the Order, he was now witnessing new tensions between the Order and the pope. In light of the papal interpretation of Francis's *Rule*, how was Thomas of Celano to present the views of Francis as his companions remembered him? Was he to empathize with those who favored the moderation encouraged by the papal directive, or with those who were pressing for a return to the pristine life of the Francis and his first brothers?

Thomas of Celano entitled his third composition, *The Remembrance of the Desire of a Soul*. In many ways it is a work far different from his first portrait of Francis. Unlike his earlier *Life of Saint Francis*, Thomas's *Remembrance of the Desire of a Soul* avoids any extensive description of Francis's relationship with the pope. He focuses instead on the recollections of Saint Francis that had been sent to him. The influence of *The Legend of the Three Companions* is easily recognizable in details about Francis's youth and conversion, as is *The Anonymous of Perugia* in descriptions of the call of his first followers and their embrace of a Gospel life. The bulk of the work, however, is dedicated to Francis's pursuit of virtue. Here, too, Thomas relies on the reminiscences of the companions. Thus Thomas remained true to the mandate he had received from Crescentius: to re-present the responses to his directive. At the same time, Thomas appealed to the idealism of the brothers by placing Francis before them as "the holiest mirror of the holiness of the Lord."[31] But, in the same symbolic language, Thomas turned their attention to the reality of the little church of Our Lady of the Portiuncula where Francis had discovered his Gospel calling. "He wanted it," Thomas wrote, "like a mirror of the Order, always preserved in humility and highest poverty, and therefore kept its ownership in the hands of others, keeping for himself and his brothers only the use of it." It would be difficult not to recognize the distinction between "ownership" and "use." Adroitly Thomas directed the attention of his brothers to a higher plane, but he also challenged the Church to recognize in the Portiuncula's "humility and highest poverty" its own calling.

Thomas presented his new, long and complicated text, completed at least two months earlier, to the General Chapter of Lyon in 1247.[32]

Convoked by Crescentius, the General Chapter began on July 13, 1247, without him. According to the *Chronicon abbreviatum* of Peregrinus of Bononia, Crescentius requested, "because of his inadequacies," that another be elected as General Minister. Thus his enduring legacy, the commission entrusted to Thomas of Celano, was approved without Crescentius's presence. The wish Thomas uttered at the end of his Prologue went sadly unheeded: "Thus things well said will be approved by your learned opinion, and like your name, Crescentius, they will build to a crescendo . . ."

The brothers then chose John of Parma to succeed Crescentius as General Minister, a ministry he bore for ten years, 1247-1257. Thomas of Eccleston describes him well:

> One of the leading zealots of the Order, he was a lector and had read as a bachelor on the *Sentences* at Paris . . . At the University of Paris, he personally intervened to reconcile the brothers [to the faculty of theology], prevailing on them to revoke their appeal by reminding them of the simplicity of their profession. He made the ruling that the general chapter should be held alternately beyond the mountains and on this side of the mountains.[33]

Thomas of Eccleston provides this further insight into John's ministry to his brothers:

> Now this same father declared that the edifice of the Order was built upon two walls, namely, holiness of life and learning; and that the brothers had raised the wall of learning beyond the heavens and heavenly things, in that they were posing the question of whether God existed; the wall of holiness of life, however, they permitted to remain so low that it was said with great praise of a brother, "He is an untroubled brother." They therefore seemed not to be building properly. Moreover, he wished that the brothers should protect themselves against prelates and princes by reverence for their profession and by their merits before the people rather than by any apostolic privileges, and that they should be truly "lesser" among all by their humility and meekness.[34]

John of Parma appears as an experienced realist. He was no outsider to the intimidating University of Paris; in fact, according to Thomas of Eccleston, he articulated what was to become the Order's approach to learning: *pietas et doctrina* [piety and learning]. "One of the leading zealots of the Order," John was equally at home among the brothers in the hermitages. A half century later, Angelo Clareno maintained that Francis's companions declared that "in him Saint Francis lived again in spirit." *"Bene et opportune veniste, sed tarde veniste!"* Angelo puts on the lips of Giles at the news of his election: "You have come well and appropriately, but you have come late!"[35]

One of John's first tasks was to lead the brothers of the Chapter of Lyon in approving Thomas of Celano's *Remembrance of the Desire of a Soul.* According to the *Chronicle of the Twenty-four Generals,* John asked Thomas to write an orderly account of Francis's miracles; according to Thomas, however, the initiative was that of the brothers in general expressed at the chapter. "We did not set out to write these things to satisfy our vanity," Thomas writes at the conclusion of *The Treatise on the Miracles of Saint Francis.* "Nor have we plunged into this set of such differing reports of our own will. The insistence of our brothers' requests extorted it, and the authority of our prelates ordered it."[36] Thomas completed the work in 1252. Most probably it was approved by the brothers at the Chapter of Metz in 1254.[37]

John of Parma, Joachimism, and Bonaventure of Bagnoregio

While John of Parma was restoring some tranquility to the Order, new questions began to arise. In the first place both within and outside the Order, hesitancy, expressions of unbelief, or hostility toward the miracle of Francis's stigmata become pronounced.[38] As early as 1237, by order of Pope Gregory IX and Brother Elias, a list of eyewitnesses to the stigmata was drawn up. Two statements of Pope Alexander IV (1254-1261), *Benigna operatio* (October 29, 1255) and *Grande et singulare* (July 10, 1256), indicate that the doubts remained. Thomas of Eccleston tells of John of Parma's response: "Brother John of Parma, the general minister, in the general chapter at Genoa, ordered Brother Bonizo, who had been a companion of Saint Francis, to speak to the brothers concerning the truth of the stigmata, because many people throughout the world were doubting them. And he replied with tears: 'These sinful eyes have seen them; and these sinful hands touched them.'"[39]

Two documents, one authentic, the other questionable, suggest the need to re-enforce a consciousness of the importance of the stigmata. The first, *An Umbrian Choir Legend,* based on Thomas of Celano's *The Life of Saint Francis, The Remembrance of the Desire of a Soul* and *The Treatise on the Miracles of Saint Francis,* emerged at this time. Most striking is the emphasis placed on the description of the stigmata and, despite Francis's attempts to keep them hidden, the identification of those who actually saw them or who even touched the wound in his side, Elias and Rufino. One curiosity of the text is its recognition of Elias who is never mentioned by name in any of the accounts of Francis's companions or the later writings of Thomas of Celano. Elias's death on April 23, 1253, may well have prompted the anonymous author of this work to correct the silence in an attempt to restore his name.[40] It may also account for the emergence of the second document whose authenticity is still discussed: a letter of Elias announcing the death of Francis and, quite dramatically, his stigmata, "a sign that has never been heard of from the dawn of time."[41] Since the list of witnesses compiled in 1237 includes Elias himself, the letter may well have been drawn up to support the veracity of the stigmata. Its presence in the hagiographic tradition still provokes discussion.

A more serious problem, however, began to emerge: John of Parma's sympathy for the ideas of Abbot Joachim of Fiore (+1202). In addition to Joachim's theology of the Trinity, the Cistercian abbot constructed a theology of world history that intricately combined biblical, trinitarian, and apocalyptic themes. Accordingly, the year 1260 was of particular interest since, in Joachim's analysis, each biblical age would last forty generations. If that of the Old Testament, the age of the Father, ended with the birth of Jesus, the age of the Son would usher in that of the Spirit in 1260. At that point, a new order would appear at the dawning of a new age, an order having the image of and directed solely by the Holy Spirit. Joachim's accent of newness appealed to Francis's followers, who had repeatedly heard the refrain of newness throughout Thomas of Celano's writings. More powerfully, however, was the emphasis of Francis himself who summarized the life of his brothers as that of "the Spirit of the Lord and Its holy activity."[42]

The problem of these attractive thoughts came quickly to the surface in 1254, when one of the brothers, Gerard of Borgo San Donnino published his *Liber Introductorius in Evangelium Aeternum* [A Book Introducing the Eternal Gospel]. In the book Gerard went further than his master, Joachim, in presenting the abrogation of the Old and New Testaments with the advent of the Eternal Gospel of the Holy Spirit in Joachim's writings. Gerard also interpreted the apocalyptic figure of the Angel of the Sixth Seal, the one that would announce the impending destruction of the rich and powerful, as personified in Francis of Assisi. Pope Alexander IV condemned the book on October 23, 1255, but the residue of its impact was felt for years afterward, particularly as the Joachimite leanings of John of Parma became known. Salimbene de Adam's autobiographical statement about his stay in Provence expresses this best: "Then [1248] I went to live in the convent of the Friars Minor in Aix, where with the help of my companion [Brother Hugh], I made a copy of Joachim's Commentary [on the Gospels] for the general minister, John of Parma, who was also a great Joachite . . ."[43]

Iriarte maintains that "a recalcitrant minority" took advantage of this weakness of John of Parma and had no difficulty "in persuading the Pope to ask for his resignation."[44] Moorman is vague and states simply: "Complaints were made against him, and the pope was obliged to take action."[45] It is difficult to obtain a thorough, objective picture since the biased accounts of the early fourteenth century, e.g. *The History of the Seven Tribulations of the Order* by Angelo Clareno, tend to interpret these events as efforts at discrediting John of Parma. In any case, the result was very much the same. In 1257 John of Parma convened a General Chapter that was held in the newly acquired friary of the Aracoeli in Rome. John resigned. When asked to nominate his successor, he submitted the name of Bonaventure of Bagnoregio.

Bonaventure, then teaching at the University of Paris, guided the brothers from February 2, 1257, until May 20, 1273, when Pope Gregory X made him cardinal bishop of Albano. While Bonaventure's earlier writings reveal his respect for tradition and suggest that he was conservative by temperament, they also indicate his perceptive mind as well as his ability to confront the issues threatening the Order. Above all, these early writings clearly show Bonaventure's profound grasp of the mystical tradition and his sensitivity to the unique place of Francis's vision within it.[45] Within the Order, therefore, Bonaventure strove to address various crises confronting the Order, to articulate the unique character of its Gospel ideals, and to re-enkindle it among the brothers. His two surviving encyclical letters to the Order, written ten years apart, show the intensity of his efforts, the depth of his comprehension, and the simplicity of his solution: a return to the rule and life of the Lesser Brothers, that is, to the *Later Rule*.[46]

Bonaventure's Portraits of Francis

Three years after his election, the Lesser Brothers gathered for the Chapter of Narbonne, France. An important item on their agenda was the codification of the decisions made at the eleven previous general chapters. The legislative activity that preceded the Chapter of Narbonne, in 1239 after the dismissal of Elias, and in 1240 and 1242, the period of Haymo, was in need of organization. The research of Rosalind Brooke, Cesare Cenci and Dominic Monti have shown that Bonaventure inserted little that was new in the *Constitutions of Narbonne*.[47] His major contribution at that chapter was to codify the existing legislation around topical quotations from Francis's *Rule*.[48]

The Chapter of Narbonne became famous for another reason: the brothers commissioned Bonaventure to compile "one good" legend of Saint Francis based on those already in existence.[49] Even a cursory glance at *The Major Legend* reveals how faithful Bonaventure was to his mandate to compile one good legend from all the existing ones. The largest number of episodes contained in the first fifteen chapters of *The Major Legend* come from *The Life of Saint Francis* by Thomas of Celano, refined by the writings of Julian of Speyer, and from *The Remembrance of the Desire of a Soul*. The influence of *The Legend of the Three Companions* and *The Assisi Compilation* are evident, although it is difficult to determine whether or not these influences were transmitted by way of Thomas's *Remembrance of the Desire of a Soul*. For the most part, Bonaventure contributes little to the biographical data provided by his predecessors. In fact, in the second section of *The Major Legend*, the consideration of Francis's miracles, the texts come almost entirely from Thomas's *Treatise on the Miracles of Saint Francis*.[50]

Bonaventure crafted his portrait according to the overall structure of his theology. Francis had become for him a symbol of the workings of grace. To understand the unfolding of his life was to perceive the inner dynamics of the gift of the Holy Spirit. Thus Bonaventure developed the first fifteen chapters of *The Major Legend*, those that treat of Francis's life, virtues, death and canonization, in a carefully thought out manner, maintaining that the human mind works from the visible to the invisible. At the same time, however, each chapter has a structure of its own as Bonaventure articulates through the use of stories the theologies of different virtues. As a result Bonaventure crafts a brilliant synthesis of Thomas's trilogy, *The Life of Saint Francis*, *The Remembrance of the Desire of a Soul,* and *The Treatise on the Miracles,* with the refinements of Julian of Speyer's liturgical pieces and *Life of Saint Francis.*

While *The Major Legend* was read during the brothers' meals, a shorter text, *The Minor Legend,* was written at the same time. It was meant primarily for chapel and church choirs for liturgical celebrations, often in the company of the faithful. *The Minor Legend* offers a testimony to a life uniquely paradigmatic of the journey into God. Celebrative and spiritual in nature, *The Minor Legend* played a major role in diffusing this image and message of Francis as it became a salient element of the brothers' celebration of their founder.

In 1263 Bonaventure presented both of these completed works to the brothers at the General Chapter of Pisa. Three years later, the brothers gathered again at the General Chapter of Paris and, in the following words, established *The Major* and *The Minor Legends* as the definitive portraits of Francis:

> The General Chapter likewise orders under obedience that all the legends of the Blessed Francis that have been made should be removed. Wherever they find these outside the Order, let the brothers strive to remove them. For this Legend made by the General Minister has been compiled as he received it from the mouth of those who were always with blessed Francis and had certain knowledge of everything, and proven facts have been diligently placed in it.[51]

Controversial as this degree may be, it suggests that the brothers recognized the genius of Bonaventure's theological approach, one that would guarantee a more universal acceptance of Francis of Assisi. At the same time, although the critics might argue about lacuna or emphasis, *The Major Legend,* in particular, clearly reveals the brilliant mind of a theologian profoundly aware of the spiritual traditions of the Middle Ages. As in his earlier *Soul's Journey into God,* in *The Major Legend* Bonaventure identifies Francis's unique place among those traditions.[52] In both instances, he does so with his ministry of guiding his brothers, that is, of aiding them in discovering the wonder of their Founder and his vision of the world, themselves, and the God Who calls them.

As the last texts of Bonaventure in this second volume indicate, the sermons on Saint Francis that he later preached to his brothers suggest that he saw them as opportunities to explain and further many of the images in his portraits. In 1276, shortly after Bonaventure's death, the General Chapter of Padua initiated a search for new information pertaining to Francis's life, some of which later found its way into *The Major Legend.*[53] The texts that appear in the third volume of *Francis of Assisi: Early Documents* attest to the fact that Bonaventure did not resolve fundamental questions about the spirit of the Founder. He did, however, place Francis of Assisi in the larger framework of history and, in doing so, provided future writers with the image of the prophet, one sent by God with a message to tell.

Notes

1. Francis of Assisi, *The Testament* 38-39 (hereafter Test), in *Francis of Assisi: Early Documents,* Vol. 1 *The Saint,* 127 (hereafter FA:ED I, II, or III respectively).

2. As an example, see Gregory's letter, *Quoniam abundavit* (1237), FA:ED I 575-577.

3. Cf. Cajetan Esser, *The Rule and Testament of Saint Francis: Conferences for Modern Followers of St. Francis,* translated by Sr. Audrey Marie (Chicago: Franciscan Herald Press, 1977).

4. Cf. FA:ED I, 571.

5. John R.H. Moorman, *A History of the Franciscan Order: From Its Origins to the Year 1517* (London: Oxford University Press, 1968).

6. Raphael Huber, *A Documented History of the Franciscan Order from the Birth of St. Francis to the Division of the Order 1182-1517* (Milwaukee: Nowiny Publishing Apostolate, 1944).

7. Duncan Nimmo, *Reform and Division in the Medieval Franciscan Order: From Saint Francis to the Foundation of the Capuchins,* Bibliotheca Seraphico-Cappuccina 33 (Rome: Capuchin Historical Institute, 1987).

8. Franz Cardinal Ehrle, "Die Spiritualen, ihr Verhältnis zum Franziskanerorden und zu den Fraticellen," in *Archiv für Literatur und Kirchengeschichte des Mittelalters,* III (Freiburg im Breisgau, 1885-1900).

9. Livarius Oliger, "Spirituels," *Dictionnaire de Théologie Catholique,* vol. 14, ed. A. Vacant and E. Mangenot, (Paris: Librairie Letouzey et Ani, 1930), 2522-2549.

10. Lazaro Iriarte, *Franciscan History: The Three Orders of St. Francis of Assisi, trans. Patricia Ross,* with an appendix, "The Historical Context of the Franciscan Movement," by Lawrence C. Landini (Chicago: Franciscan Herald Press, 1982).

11. Thaddeus MacVicar, *The Franciscan Spirituals and the Capuchin Reform,* edited by Charles McCarron (St. Bonaventure, NY: The Franciscan Institute, 1986).

12. FA:ED I 529-554.

13. The editors debated the place of this document. On one hand, it deserves to be placed in this second volume since it reflects a tendency to focus on the ideals of the founder and the primitive fraternity. On the other hand, it does have that sense of the biblical idealism of those early days and, in spirit at least, belongs to the texts of the first volume. After much consideration—and for more practical reasons—it was placed in volume one, *The Saint.*

14. Cf. Thomas of Eccleston, *The Coming of the Lesser Brothers to England* 14, in *XIIIth Century Chronicles* (hereafter ChrTE), translated by Placed Hermann, introduction and notes by Marie-Therese Laureille (Chicago: Franciscan Herald Press, 1961), 166. All future references to this work will be to this translation.

15. Cf. Iriarte, *Franciscan History,* 36.

16. "The Chapter of 1230 split up most of the Provinces, so that there were twelve in Italy, two in Germany, five in France, three in Spain, two in British Isles, and one in the East. " Iriarte, *Franciscan History,* 79.

17. Cf. Iriarte, *Franciscan History,* 136-137.

18. John of Perugia, *The Beginning of the Founding of the Order and the Deeds of Those Lesser Brothers Who Were the First Companions of Blessed Francis in Religion* (*The Anonymous of Perugia*) 2 (hereafter AP), infra, 34.

19. "This was a democratic move, borrowed from the Dominicans, which gave the friars power to elect their own representatives or 'definitors' who were to meet during the two years when there was no meeting of the General Chapter. . . . The Definitors met for their first chapter at Montpellier in 1241, but the experiment does not seem to have been a success, and no further meetings were called. The word 'definitor' was retained; but it was applied in future either to those friars who were summoned to the General Chapter, though without power of voting, or to those who were elected by the Provincial Chapters to assist in the administration of the province." Cf. Moorman, *History,* 106. The word "definitor" entered the vocabulary of the Lesser Brothers through the Premonstratensians and the Friars Preacher who used the word to describe an officer whose task was the inquiry into misuses and their amendment. Cf. J.F. Niermayer, *Mediae Latinitatis Lexicon Minus* (Leiden, New York, Köln: Brill, 1997), 314.

20. Its members: Adam Marsh, Peter of Tewkesbury, and Henry of Buford. Cf. ChtTE, 13.

21. The four Parisian masters were: Alexander of Hales, John de La Rochelle, Odo Rigaldus, and Robert of Bascia. These Cf. *Expositio Quattuor Magistrorum super Regulam Fratruum Minorum* [1241-2], ed. Livarius Oliger (Rome: 1954) and also. FA:ED I 312.

22. ChrTE 13.

23. Cf. "Chronica XXIV Generalium," *Analecta Franciscana sive Chronica Aliaque Varia Documenta ad Historiam Fratrum Minorum* III (Ad Claras Aquas, Quaracchi: Collegium S. Bonaventurae, 1897), 262 (hereafter AF III).

24. Crescentius seems to have been a member of the liberal party which desired more concessions. Shortly after his election, he received the bull *Ordinem Vestrum* of Innocent IV, infra, 774-779.

25. Maurice Causse, "Des Sources Primitives de *La Legende des Trois Compagnons,*" *Collectanea Franciscana* 69/3-4 (1998): 469-491. Causse suggests that the authors also had access to another unknown document, possibly a copy of the canonical process investigating Francis's canonization, a document that has unfortunately been lost.

26. Salimbene de Adam notes that "Crescentius commanded Brother Thomas of Celano, who had written the first Legend of Saint Francis, to write another book, because many things about Saint Francis had been discovered which had never been written." Salimbene de Adam, *The Chronicle of Salimbene de Adam,* Medieval and Renaissance Texts and Studies, 40, ed. Joseph L. Baird, Giuseppe Baglivi, and John Robert Kane (Binghamton, NY: Center for Medieval and Early Renaissance Studies, University Center at Binghamton, 1986), 294. All future references to this work will be from this translation.

Thomas of Celano himself indicates that the choice of his role was that of the General Chapter of Genoa in 1244: "The holy gathering of the last general chapter and you, most reverend father, chose to charge us, insignificant as we are, to write down the deeds as well as the words of our glorious father Francis, for the consolation of our contemporaries and the remembrance of future generations" (2C 1).

27. Cf. FA:ED I 570-575.

28. Cf. FA:ED II 774-779

29. Iriarte, *Franciscan History,* 37. That the implications of *Ordinem vestrum,* as well as *Quo elongati,* continue to disturb the collective conscience of the Lesser Brothers can be seen in the intense preparations for and the documents of the Sixth Plenary Council of the Capuchin Friars Minor dedicated to the study of Institutional Poverty. Cf. *Analecta Ordinis Fratrum Minorum Capuccinorum* 114:3 (1998).

30. Innocent IV went further in a decree he issued on August 19, 1247. Two weeks earlier, August 6, 1247, he had issued *Cum omnis vera religio,* a Form of Life for the Order of Saint Damian, i.e., the followers of Saint Clare. Since it was not widely accepted, he issued a second decree, *Quoties a nobis,* August 23, 1247, insisting on its observance. Three years later he rescinded the universal imposition of his Form of Life and, in 1253, gave Clare, on her death bed, papal approval of her *Rule.* Cf. *Clare of Assisi: Early Documents,* 2nd ed., translated and edited by Regis J. Armstrong (St. Bonaventure NY: The Franciscan Institute, 1993), 113.

31. Thomas of Celano, *The Remembrance of the Desire of a Soul,* 26 (hereafter 2C), infra, 263.

32. Michael Bihl, *Analecta Franciscana sive Chronica Aliaque Varia Documenta ad Historiam Fratrum Minorum* X (Ad Claras Aquas, Quaracchi: Collegium S. Bonaventurae, 1926-1941), xxvi (hereafter AF X).

33. ChrTE 13. John was sufficiently strong to reconcile the subtle factions at the University and was also aware of the need to develop deeper bonds of unity among the brothers beyond the Italian peninsula. Both of these attributes made him an ideal candidate for General Minister.

34. Ibid.

35. Cf. *Archiv fur Litteratur und Kirchenheschichte des Mittelalters,* vol. II, (Freiburg im Breisgau, 1885-1900), 263.

36. Thomas of Celano, *The Treatise on the Miracles of Saint Francis* 197 (hereafter 3C). Infra.

37. Cf. Bihl, AF X xxxviii.

38. Cf. André Vauchez, "The Stigmata of Saint Francis and Its Medieval Detractors," *Greyfriars Review* 13 (1999): 61-89 (hereafter GR).

39. ChrTE 13.

40. Cf. infra, 472.

41. *A Letter on the Passing of Saint Francis* attributed to Elias of Assisi, infra.

42. Francis of Assisi, *Later Rule* X 8 (hereafter LR), FA:ED I 105.

43. Salimbene, *Chronicle,* 294.

44. Iriarte, *Franciscan History,* 39.

45. Moorman, *History,* 115.

46. Bernard McGinn notes: "Bernard of Clairvaux and Bonaventure—the *doctor mellifluous* and the *doctor seraphicus*—may be justly described as the two premier mystical teachers of the Medieval West. Both were important ecclesiastical officials who were forced to be men of action, as well as of contemplation. Both wrote on a variety of theological and church-political topics, as well as on how the soul attains God in this life." Bernard McGinn, *The Presence of God: A History of Western Christian Mysticism,* The Flowering of Mysticism (New York: The Crossroad Publishing Company, 1998), 87.

47. Both of these letters can be found in *Works of Saint Bonaventure: Writings Concerning the Franciscan Order,* edited and translated by Dominic Monti (St. Bonaventure, NY: Franciscan Institute Publications, 1994), 57-62, 225-229.

48. Monti's edition of the text not only offers an excellent translation; it provides critical apparatus that enables readers to see how the Narbonne statutes occur in the earlier edition of the constitutions produced by Cesare Cenci.

49. Cesare Cenci, "De Fratrum Minorum constitutionibus praenarbonensibus," *Archivum Franciscanum Historicum* 83 (1990): 50-95 (hereafter AFH); "The Constitutions of Narbonne" (1260), in *Writings Concerning the Franciscan Order,* Works of Saint Bonaventure V, introduction and

translation by Dominic Monti (St. Bonaventure, NY: Franciscan Institute Publications, 1994), 71-135.

50. The source of this mandate is obscure. It cannot be found in either the *Constitutions of Narbonne* nor in its *Definitiones.* Giralomo Golubovich notes that the *Ceremoniale ordinis minorum vetutissimum* or *Ordinationes divini officii* issued in 1254 during the generalate of John of Parma contains this phrase*: Item ordinetur de legenda beati Francisci, ut de omnibus una bona compiletur* [Likewise it is ordained concerning the legend of blessed Francis, that one good one be compiled from all the others]. Golubovich and Desbonnets maintained that the decision referred to the composition of *The Minor Legend* (hereafter LMn) because of difficulties in reconciling the liturgical texts with the data provided by later texts. Michael Bihl, on the other hand, was convinced that the decree was appended to the *Ceremoniale* at a later date and, in reality, was directed at the composition of *The Major Legend* (hereafter LMj). Cf. *Ceremoniale ordinis minorum vetutissimum* seu *"Ordinationes divini officii" sub Ioanne de Parma ministro generali emanatae an. 1254,* a cura di Giralomo Golubovich, in AFH 3 (1910): 76.

51. Bonaventure intersperses thirty-five of the miracles described in 3C in LMj. Bonaventure adds five new episodes to his own *Treatise on the Miracles,* the second part of LMj.

52. Cf. *Miscellanea Franciscana* 72 (1972): 247. See discussion FA:ED I 18. Duncan Nimmo offers a balanced critique of Bonaventure's work in the context of rival standpoints on observance of the Rule, cf. *Reform,* 75-78.

53. Ewert H. Cousins described Bonaventure's *Soul's Journey into God* as " a *summa,* comparable in its own sphere to the *Summa theologicae* of Thomas Aquinas, for he draws together in a comprehensive synthesis major strands of Christian spirituality." Cf. *Bonaventure: The Soul's Journey into God, the Tree of Life, The Life of Saint Francis,* translation and introduction by Ewert H. Cousins, preface by Ignatius C. Brady (New York, Ramsey, Toronto: Paulist Press, 1978), 20. In a similar vein, LMj could been seen as Bonaventure's attempt to pinpoint Francis's uniqueness in the larger spiritual tradition of Christianity and, in doing so, to identify the fundamental reason of his holiness, i.e., the mystical pursuit of God.

54. Cf. infra LMj III 9.

Abbreviations

Writings of Saint Francis

Adm	The Admonitions
BlL	A Blessing for Brother Leo
CtC	The Canticle of the Creatures
CtExh	The Canticle of Exhortation
1Frg	Fragments of Worchester Manuscript
2Frg	Fragments of Thomas of Celano
3Frg	Fragments from Hugh of Digne
LtAnt	A Letter to Brother Anthony of Padua
1LtCl	First Letter to the Clergy (Earlier Edition)
2LtCl	Second Letter to the Clergy (Later Edition)
1LtCus	The First Letter to the Custodians
2LtCus	The Second Letter to the Custodians
1LtF	The First Letter to the Faithful
2LtF	The Second Letter to the Faithful
LtL	A Letter to Brother Leo
LtMin	A Letter to a Minister
LtOrd	A Letter to the Entire Order
LtR	A Letter to Rulers of the Peoples
ExhP	Exhortation to the Praise of God
PrOF	A Prayer Inspired by the Our Father
PrsG	The Praises of God
OfP	The Office of the Passion
PrCr	The Prayer before the Crucifix
ER	The Earlier Rule (*Regula non bullata*)
LR	The Later Rule (*Regula bullata*)
RH	A Rule for Hermitages
SalBV	A Salutation of the Blessed Virgin Mary
SalV	A Salutation of Virtues
Test	The Testament
TPJ	True and Perfect Joy

Franciscan Sources

1C	The Life of Saint Francis by Thomas of Celano
2C	The Remembrance of the Desire of a Soul
3C	The Treatise on the Miracles by Thomas of Celano
LCh	The Legend for Use in the Choir
Off	The Divine Office of Saint Francis by Julian of Speyer
LJS	The Life of Saint Francis by Julian of Speyer
VL	The Versified Life of Saint Francis by Henri d'Avranches
1-3JT	The Praises by Jacopone da Todi
DCom	The Divine Comedy by Dante Alighieri
TL	Tree of Life by Ubertino da Casale
1MP	The Mirror of Perfection, Smaller Version
2MP	The Mirror of Perfection, Larger Version
HTrb	The History of the Seven Tribulations by Angelo of Clareno
ScEx	The Sacred Exchange between Saint Francis and Lady Poverty
AP	The Anonymous of Perugia
L3C	The Legend of the Three Companions
LP	The Legend of Perugia
AC	The Assisi Compilation
UChL	An Umbrian Choir Legend
1-4Srm	The Sermons of Bonaventure
LMj	The Major Legend by Bonaventure
LMn	The Minor Legend by Bonaventure
BPr	The Book of Praises by Bernard of Besse
ABF	The Deeds of Saint Francis and His Companions
LFl	The Little Flowers of Saint Francis
KnSF	The Kinship of Saint Francis
ChrTE	The Chronicle of Thomas of Eccleston
ChrJG	The Chronicle of Jordan of Giano

Other Sources

AF	Analecta Franciscana
AFH	Archivum Franciscanum Historicum
BFr	Bullarium Franciscanum
CCSL	Corpus Christianorum, Series Latina
CF	Collectanea Franciscana
CSEL	Corpus Scriptorum Eccles. Latinorum
GR	Greyfriars Review
PL	Patrologia Latina

Scripture abbreviations are from *The New American Bible*; the Psalms follow the modern numbering sequence. Scripture references accompanying non-italicized text imply *confer*, or cf. References to the other volumes in *Francis of Assisi: Early Documents* will be abbreviated FA:ED I, II, III.

Editor's Note

The editors gave this second volume of *Francis of Assisi: Early Documents* the subtitle "The Founder." The texts presented in this volume reveal the more intense focus of the Lesser Brothers on the Gospel ideals that Francis of Assisi envisioned shaping their fraternity. The endeavor to publish the texts of this second volume in a chronological order, according to the principle established for all three volumes, became a daunting challenge. The dating of the first three texts of this volume are especially controversial,[1] as is *A Letter on the Passing of Saint Francis* attributed to Elias of Assisi which recent scholarship maintains is of dubious origin and should not even appear in this volume.

The manuscript tradition of *The Legend of the Three Companions* and *The Assisi Compilation* initially moved discussions toward publishing these two texts in the third volume.[2] Further study and careful comparison of the texts, however, revealed that such a decision would reflect more on the development of the Order of Lesser Brothers than on the hagiographical tradition of Francis himself. In other words, although the manuscript tradition dates these texts in the early fourteenth century, the editors believe that the content of these manuscripts has roots in the mid-thirteenth century.[3]

A careful examination of the Latin texts of *The Anonymous of Perugia* and *The Legend of the Three Companions* revealed the dependence of one text upon the other. A relationship was found between *The Assisi Compilation* and *The Remembrance of the Desire of a Soul.* In both instances, questions arose regarding the chronological priority of these documents. For example, did *The Assisi Compilation* rely on *The Remembrance of the Desire of a Soul,* or vice versa? To resolve these questions, the editors used the critical editions of these texts, as well as their computerized analyses, *Corpus des Sources Franciscaines,* undertaken by the Centre de Traitement Électronique des Documents of the Université Catholique of Louvain.[4] In the case of *The Assisi Compilation* and *The Remembrance of the Desire of a Soul,* the editors came to the conclusion that at least some sections of *The Assisi Compilation* were earlier and served as a source for *The Remembrance of the Desire of a Soul.*

As in volume one, *The Saint,* in order to delineate the reliance of one text upon the other and thereby facilitate a chronological reading of these texts, this second volume also provides cross references in the inner margins to earlier texts. In *The Assisi Compilation,* however, the reader will note a new symbol: ↑. This indicates those portions of *The Assisi Compilation* that are taken from *The Remembrance of the Desire of a Soul* by Thomas of Celano, a later text.[5]

In addition to cross references, the reader will likewise note that specific sections of the texts are delineated by employing an emboldened font.[6] This method of identifying the different texts, although initially distracting, allows the reader to see the specific portions of the text that are literally dependent on earlier authors. The editors made efforts to assure that the translations reflect this interdependence of the Latin texts.

In the case of Bonaventure's *Major Legend,* for example, this will be particularly helpful. It will enable the reader to see what Bonaventure specifically added to the writings of Thomas of Celano or Julian of Speyer. The theological and/or poetic subtleties Bonaventure advances then become easily identifiable. Thus, the stages of hagiographical and theological tradition interpreting the legacy of Francis of Assisi become clearer. The editors hope their effort will advance a more careful and nuanced reading of these texts.

Notes

1. These texts are AP, *The Legend of the Three Companions*, and *The Assisi Compilation* (hereafter L3C, and AC respectively).

2. Cf. Introductions to these texts in which the manuscript tradition suggests their origins in the early fourteenth century.

3. The research of Raoul Manselli, Théophile Desbonnets, Giovanni Miccoli, Maurice Causse and Jacques Dalarun confirmed the decision to place these two texts in this second volume, a decision that was further confirmed in reviewing each of the translations.

4. *Corpus des Sources Franciscaines,* vol. I-VII, ed. Georges Mailleux, Jean-François Godet, (Louvain: Publications du CETEDOC, 1974).

5. AC is found in the Manuscript 1046 of Perugia's Biblioteca Comunale Augusta. Careful analysis shows that it is a compilation containing passages from "we who were with him," writings of Br. Leo, and 2C. Others have chosen to omit the Thomas of Celano passages and to entitle the work *The Legend of Perugia.* Cf. infra.

6. In their publication of the critical edition of the "official texts" of Thomas of Celano, Julian of Speyer, and Bonaventure, the Quarrachi editors facilitated the identification of texts by employing different fonts. Cf. AF X. The editors of the present volume have chosen to utilize their work in following this same procedure for these official texts. They have extended this methodology, however, by incorporating the same principle in the publication of others texts which are often referred to as "non-official."

THE BEGINNING OR FOUNDING OF THE ORDER

AND

THE DEEDS OF THOSE LESSER BROTHERS WHO WERE THE FIRST COMPANIONS OF BLESSED FRANCIS IN RELIGION

(The Anonymous of Perugia)

BY JOHN OF PERUGIA

(1240–1241)

Introduction

In 1671 the Jesuit Daniel Papebroch discovered a manuscript in the friary of San Francesco al Prato in the Italian city of Perugia.[1] The work became known as the *Anonymus Perusinus* [Anonymous of Perugia] because its only known manuscript was found in Perugia, and the identity of its author was unknown. Although *The Anonymous of Perugia* received some attention in 1675 and again in 1768, the complete text was never published until 1902 by Francis Van Ortroy, another Jesuit.[2] Even with this publication, the work never received serious attention until Lorenzo DiFonzo studied the available manuscripts and, in 1972, produced a critical edition of the text.[3] Seven years later, Pierre Beguin published a thorough study of the work, *L'Anonyme de Pérouse. Un Témoin de La Fraternité Franciscaine Primitive Confronté aux Autres Sources Contemporaines.*[4]

Undoubtedly, interest in this previously overlooked work was a result of the call of the Second Vatican Council that men and women of religious orders "return to the spirit of the founders."[5] The work's description of the first days of the primitive fraternity of Francis and his brothers may also provide an insight into its unique attraction as contemporary students of *The Anonymous of Perugia* struggle, as did those of the second generation of Francis's followers, to understand his spirit.

Di Fonzo followed the manuscript tradition and entitled the work *The Beginning or The Founding of the Order and The Deeds of Those Lesser Brothers Who Were the First Companions of Blessed Francis in Religion.* Two words in that title, *religio* [religion] and *ordo* [order], while seemingly synonymous, suggest the historical nature of the work. It is a description of the growth of the movement from the first *fraternity* of Francis and his brothers to a *religion,* a gathering of those committed to God in some way, and then into an *Order,* a group of those who follow a set rule and the same customs.[6] The distinction is simply mentioned in passing: "At that time the religion of the brothers was not yet called an order."[7]

By singling out "the first companions of Blessed Francis in religion," the ancient title and the Prologue suggest the author's interest in the dynamics that enabled that primitive fraternity to grow from its small beginnings. This is a work in which the protagonist is not Francis the Saint; the principals are the first companions of Francis. Francis, although *primus inter pares,* remains simply one of the brothers. The brotherhood becomes the context in which the Gospel ideals are discovered as Francis and his brothers strive to live together.[8]

This shift of emphasis from the saint, as found in the earlier works of Thomas of Celano and Julian of Speyer, to the fraternity focuses attention on the new material found in the work. Sixty percent of the material is new, while the remaining forty percent reflects *The Life of Saint Francis* by Thomas of Celano. New details provide particulars to incidents described by Thomas, e.g., the role of Bishop Guido of Assisi in guiding Francis and his brothers, names of some of the brothers who joined after Bernard, Peter, and Giles, the role of Cardinal John of Saint Paul, and the growing pains of the brothers as they first encountered hostility. Knowledge of such details could only have come from those involved in the events and support the claim of the author: "I, who saw their deeds, listened to their words, and also became their disciple, have compiled and recounted . . . some [of these] deeds." Since the text conveys a sense of intimacy or familiarity and, as such, a non-polemical description of the Franciscan ideals, DiFonzo and later Beguin focused their attention on the friary of San Francesco al Prato where Papebroch had discovered the manuscript. Since Brother Giles had spent considerable time and died there in 1262, it seemed logical to both DiFonzo and Beguin that *The Anonymous of Perugia* was in someway associated with him. Both men determined that its author was John of Perugia (+c. 1270), a companion of Brother Giles and an acquaintance of Brother Bernard of Quintavalle.[9]

Two events mentioned by the author suggest dates within which he wrote these reminiscences: the death of Sylvester, and the continuing presence of Hugolino who, at that time, was Pope Gregory IX. Since Sylvester did not die until March 4, 1240, and Gregory IX until August 22, 1241, it is reasonable to maintain that the work was written within that period.[10]

Notes

1. Daniel Papebroch or Papenbroch (1628-1714) was a member of a small group of Jesuits dedicated to the critical study and publication of the lives of the saints. Founded in the early 1600's by Leribert Rosweyde (1569-1629), the group's aims and methods were refined by Jean Bolland, S.J., (1596-1665) who began publishing the *Acta Santorum*. Because of his research, discovery of ancient manuscripts, and sound judgment, Papebroch became one of the most energetic, dedicated Bollandists, as they were called.

2. Cf. *Acta Sanctorum*, April III *(Vita Beati Aegidii*, April 23) introduction by Daniel Papebroch [Antwerp: 1675]: 219, nn. 2, 5-6; Cornelius Suyskens, Commentarius praevius, in *Acta Sanctorum*, October II *(Vita Sancti Francisci*, October 4) [Antwerp, 1768]: 549ab, nn.19-20; 562a, n. 88; Franciscus Van Ortroy "La Leggenda Latina di S. Francesco secondo *l'Anonimo Perugino*," *Miscellanea Franciscana* 9 (1902): 33-48. Another copy of the text had been discovered in 1765, copied by Stefano Rinaldi, in 1808, and preserved in the Friary of Dodici Apostoli in Rome. Lorenzo Di Fonzo judged this the best copy of the work and used it as the basis of his critical edition in 1972. The original was lost.

3. Lorenzo Di Fonzo, "*L'Anonimo Perugino* Tra Le Fonti Francescane del Secolo XIII: Rapporti Letterari e Testo Critico," *Miscellanea Franciscana* 72 (1972): 117-483.

4. Pierre Beguin, *L'Anonyme de Pérouse. Un Témoin de La Fraternité Franciscaine Primitive Confronté aux Autres Sources Contemporaines* (Paris: éditions Franciscaines, 1979).

5. Second Vatican Council, *Perfectae Caritatis* 2.

6. See infra, 34 a.

7. AP 19. This formula provides the inspiration of the study of Théophile Desbonnets, *From Intuition to Institution: The Franciscans*, trans. Paul Duggan and Jerry DuCharme (Chicago: Franciscan Herald Press, 1988).

8. Although the word *fraternitas* [fraternity/brotherhood] never appears in the work, *frater* [brother] appears 118 times, the most used noun in the entire work.

9. DiFonzo, *L'Anonimo* 396-409. John of Perugia is described in the terms highlighted by Beguin in the Letter introducing *The Legend of the Three Companions*, cf. infra L3C 1.

10. This is the position taken by Beguin, *L'Anonyme,* and accepted by Jacques Dalarun, *La Malavventura di Francesco d'Assisi* (Milano: Edizioni Biblioteca Francescana, 1996), 122. Dalarun comments: "*É difficile essere piú precisi* [It's difficult to be more precise]." In his 1972 study of the work, DiFonzo suggested a much later date of composition, sometime after the death of Brother Giles, i.e., after 1262, and possibly after the decree of the Chapter of Paris in 1266 mandating the removal of all earlier lives. Cf. DiFonzo, *L'Anonimo,* 378-386. However, in the initial stages of publishing *Francis of Assisi: Early Documents,* the editors consulted with Lorenzo DiFonzo who agreed with them in dating *The Anonymous of Perugia* at this earlier period.

The Beginning or Founding of the Order and the Deeds of Those Lesser Brothers Who Were the First Companions of Blessed Francis in Religion

[Prologue]

[2]Servants of the Lord should not be ignorant of the lives and teachings of saints through which they can come to God. Therefore, for the honor of God and the edification of readers and listeners, I, who saw their deeds, listened to their words, and also became their disciple, have compiled and recounted, as the Lord inspired me, 1C Prol
some deeds of our most blessed Father Francis and of a few of the brothers who lived at the beginning of the religion.[a]

Chapter I
How blessed Francis began to serve God

[3]On the sixteenth of April, after one thousand two hundred and seven years had been completed since the Incarnation of the Lord,[b] God saw that His people, whom He had redeemed by the precious blood of His only begotten Son, had forgotten His commandments and were ungrateful for His goodness. Although they deserved
Ez 33:11 death, He had been merciful toward them for a long time, *desiring not the death* of the sinner, *but that he be converted and live.* Impelled by His
Mt 9:38 most bountiful mercy, God willed *to send workers into His vineyard.*

He enlightened a man who was in the city of Assisi, Francis by 1C 1
name, a merchant by trade, and a very vain spendthrift of worldly wealth.

[4]One day he was in the shop where he customarily sold cloth, to- 1C 17
tally absorbed in business, when a poor man came in, begging alms for the Lord's sake. Preoccupied with thoughts of wealth and care of

a. This translation is based on the critical edition published in 1972, which begins numbering the text with 2. See Lorenzo Di Fonzo, "*L'Anonimo Perugino* Tra Le Fonti Francescane del Secolo XIII: Rapporti Letterari e Testo Critico," *Miscellanea Franciscana* 72 (1972):117-483.

The Latin reads *religionis* [of the religion]. Throughout this and subsequent texts *religio* means "a religious way of life" in which persons bound themselves by vow or promise to serve God in a certain way. *Ordo* [Order], on the other hand, at that time referred to those who followed the same authorized rule and/or customs.

b. Therefore, on April 16, 1208.

the business, Francis sent him away without giving him alms. After the poor man left, touched by divine grace, he began to accuse himself of great rudeness,[a] saying: "If the poor man had asked in the name of a count or a powerful baron, you would have granted him his request. How much more should you have done this for the King of Kings and the Lord of all?"

Because of this incident, he resolved in his heart, from then on, never to refuse a request from anyone asking in the name of so great a Lord. He called the poor man back and gave him a generous alms.

O heart, I say, full of all grace, fruitful and enlightened!
O unswerving and holy resolve,[b]
followed by that wonderful and unexpected omen for the future!
We should not be surprised,
for the Holy Spirit said through Isaiah:
When you will pour out your soul to the hungry Is 58:10
and will refresh the afflicted soul,
your light shall rise for you in the darkness,
and the gloom shall be for you like midday.
And
If you bestow your bread on the hungry, Is 58:7
then your light shall break forth like the dawn,
and your justice will go before your face.

[5]After a while, a marvelous thing happened to this blessed man which in my estimation should not be passed over in silence. One night when he was asleep in his bed, someone appeared to him calling him by name. He led him into a palace of unspeakable beauty, filled with military arms, its walls covered everywhere with shining shields emblazoned with crosses.

He inquired to whom these brightly shining arms and this beautiful palace belonged. "All these things, including the palace," said the guide, "belong to you and your knights."

Upon awakening, he began to interpret this in a worldly way, like someone who had not yet fully tasted God's Spirit. He thought he would become a magnificent prince. After giving the matter much thought, he decided to become a knight to obtain this princely power. After having as expensive a wardrobe as possible made for

a. Whereas Thomas of Celano notes that Francis's deed was "contrary to his custom, since he was very polite," the phrase *magna rusticitas* [great rudeness] highlights an action contrary to the requirements of chivalry.

b. The word used here is *propositum* [resolve]. Cf. FA:ED I 189 d.

himself, he arranged to join up with a noble count in Apulia, to be knighted by him.[a]

Everyone marveled that he was happier than usual, and when they asked him the reason why, he answered: "I know that I am going to be a great prince."

[6]After obtaining a squire, he mounted his horse and rode toward Apulia.

It was night when he arrived in Spoleto and, anxious about his trip, he retired for the night. Half asleep, he heard a voice asking him where he intended to go. He outlined to him his whole plan.[b] The voice then asked him: "Who can do more for you, the lord or the servant?" "The lord," he answered. "Then why are you abandoning the lord for the servant, and the patron for the client?" To which Francis
Acts 9:6; Gn 32:9 responded: *"Lord, what do you want me to do?" "Go back,"* it said, *"to your own land to do what the Lord will tell you."*

It seemed to him that divine grace had suddenly made him a different man.

[7]But when it was morning, he returned home as he had been told. 1C 8

And when, on the way back, he reached Foligno,[c] he sold the horse he was riding as well as the wardrobe with which he had equipped himself for the expedition to Apulia, and put on cheaper clothing.

While he was returning from Foligno to Assisi, carrying the 1C 9
money he had obtained from these things, he approached a church built in honor of Saint Damian. He found the poor resident priest, named Peter,[d] and gave him that money for safekeeping. Not having
2 Kgs 6:9, 10 a safe place to keep it, the priest refused the money. When *the man of God,* Francis, heard this, he threw the money on the windowsill of that church for he considered it worthless. Led by God's Spirit, he resolved to use the money to rebuild its structure, seeing that the church was poor and on the verge of collapse. He decided to reside

a. The Latin text reads: "*unde disposuit ad comitem gentilem* [he arranged to join up with a noble (or gentle) count]." In the understanding of the author of the AP, *gentilem* is used as an adjective referring to this person, not as a proper name. Cf. Pierre Beguin, *L'Anonyme de Pérouse: Un Témoin de la Fraternité Franciscaine Primitive* (Paris: éditions Franciscaines, 1979), 29; Jacques Dalarun, *La Malavventura di Franceso d'Assisi* (Milano: Edizioni Biblioteca Francescana, 1996), 134.

b. Once again the word used is *propositum*, cf. FA:ED I 189 d.

c. The Latin text reads *Et iter faciens, cum Fulgineum devenisset* . . . Lorenzo DiFonzo interprets this passage in light of the previous sentence. Thus he sees Francis going from Spoleto to Assisi; and afterwards going to Foligno. Pierre Beguin, however, interprets this passage that Francis stopped at Foligno on the way back from Spoleto. The *et* at the beginning of this sentence, links it to the immediately preceding verse and seems to support the interpretation that Francis stopped at Foligno while on the way back from Spoleto. Cf. Beguin, *L'Anonyme*, 29.

d. This is the only source for this priest's name.

there and do something to help its impoverished condition. After a while, with God's approval, he completed the undertaking.

1C 13-14 [8]When his father learned of this, he began to vent his rage against him, for he loved him in a worldly way and was longing for the money. He abused Francis with insults, demanding he return the money.

1C 14-15 In the presence of the bishop of Assisi, he promptly gave back to his father the money and clothes he was wearing. He stood there naked under the cloak of the bishop, who embraced him.

1C 36 Without any worldly possessions, dressed in cheap and very miserable clothing, he went back to that church to stay there. The Lord enriched the poor and contemptible man. Filling him with His Holy Spirit, He put into his mouth the words of life that he might preach and announce to the people judgment and mercy, punishment and glory and to recall to their minds the commandments of God they
had forgotten. The Lord made him *the prince over a multitude of nations* Gn 17:4
which God had gathered into one from the whole world through him.

The Lord led him *on a straight* and narrow *path.* Desiring *to possess* Wis 10:10; Mt 10:9
neither *gold* nor *silver, nor money* nor any other thing, he followed the Lord in humility, poverty, and the simplicity of his heart.

[9]Walking about barefoot, he wore a contemptible habit with a wretched belt.

And whenever his father met him, overwhelmed with great sorrow, he would curse him. The blessed man, however, took with him a poor old man named Alberto[a] and asked him for a blessing.

Many people used to laugh at him, insulting him with spiteful
1C 11 words. Almost everyone considered him mad. But he did not care, nor did he answer them; instead, he strove with all eagerness to fulfill the task God had shown him. He walked not *in the learned words of* 1 Cor 2:4
human wisdom, but in the display and *the power of the Spirit.*

Chapter II

The First Two Brothers Who Followed Blessed Francis

[10]When they saw and heard these things, two men from Assisi, inspired by divine grace, humbly approached him. One of these was

a. This is the only source to name this man. Beguin suggests that Alberto may have been the unknown first follower of Francis mentioned in 1C 24. Cf. Beguin, *L'Anonyme*, 123 ff.

Brother Bernard, and the other, Brother Peter.[a] They told Francis simply: "We wish to live with you from now on and do what you are doing. Tell us, therefore, what we should do with our possessions." Overjoyed at their coming and their resolve he answered them kindly: "Let us go and seek counsel from the Lord."

So they went to one of the city's churches. Upon entering it, they fell on their knees and humbly prayed: "Lord, God, Father of glory, we beg you in your mercy, show us what we are to do." After finishing the prayer, they asked the priest of the church who was there: "Sir, would you show us the Gospel of Our Lord Jesus Christ."

11And, since before this happened none of them knew how to read very well,[b] when the priest opened up the book, they immedi-
Mk 10:21 ately found the passage *If you wish to be perfect, go, sell everything you pos-*
sess and give to the poor, and you will have a treasure in heaven.[c] Opening up
Mt 16:24 the book a second time, they discovered: *Whoever wishes to come after*
me . . . . When they opened up the book for the third time, they came
Lk 9:3 upon: *Take nothing for the journey* . . . When they heard this, they were filled with great joy and exclaimed: "This is what we want, this is what we were seeking." And blessed Francis said: "This will be our rule." Then he told both of them: "Go and may you fulfill the Lord's counsel as you heard it."

Then Brother Bernard, who was rich, sold all his possessions, acquiring a large sum of money from the transaction. Brother Peter, on the other hand, who was poor in worldly goods, now became rich in spiritual goods. Therefore, he also did as the Lord's counsel would have it. Summoning the city's poor people, they gave them the money acquired from the sale of their goods.

12While they were doing this, and blessed Francis was present, a priest named Sylvester came. Blessed Francis had purchased stones from him for the repair of the church of San Damiano where he had lived before he acquired brothers.

When the priest saw them giving away so much money, consumed by a burning passion of greed, he craved to be given some of

a. Thomas of Celano, in his *Life of Saint Francis*, does not identify this second disciple (1C 25). This is the first source to give his name, and, on this basis, many biographers of Francis have assumed this to be Peter of Catanio, who became the first vicar of Francis and died on March 10, 1221.

b. In light of this text, it seems highly unlikely that this early disciple was Peter of Catanio. Jordan of Giano, a contemporary, affirms that he was an "expert in the law," and, therefore, quite literate. Cf. Jordan of Giano, *The Chronicle* 11 (hereafter ChrJG).

c. While this passage has frequently been identified as Mt 19:21, Gebhard C.P. Voorvelt and Bertulf P. Van Leeuwen argue that this passage was actually Mk 10:21, and base their arguments on an examination of the Missal containing the Gospel texts consulted by Francis and his companions. Matthew's version of the passage cannot be found in it. This Gospel Book is presently preserved at the Walters Art Gallery in Baltimore, Maryland. Gebhard C.P. Voorvelt and Bertulf P. Van Leeuwen, "L'Evangéliaire de Baltimore: Étude critique sur le missel que saint Françoise aurait consulté," *Collectanea Franciscana* 59 (1989): 271-73 (hereafter CF).

that money. "Francis," he said, "you did not pay me well for the stones which you bought from me." When blessed Francis, who had renounced all greed, heard him complaining unjustly, he approached Brother Bernard and putting his hand into his cloak where the money was, took out a handful of coins and gave them to the priest. He put his hand into the cloak a second time, pulled out some coins, as he had done before, and gave them to the priest. "Do you now have full payment?" he asked. "I have it fully," he replied. Overjoyed the priest returned home.

[13]A few days later, the priest, inspired by the Lord, began to reflect on what blessed Francis had done. "Am I not miserable?" he said to himself. "Old as I am, don't I still covet and desire the things of this world, and doesn't this youth despise and scorn them for the love of God?"

The following night he saw in a dream an immense cross whose top reached to the heavens, while its base rested in the mouth of blessed Francis. The arms of the cross reached from one part of the world to the other.

Upon awakening, the priest then believed that blessed Francis was indeed God's friend and that the religion he had founded would spread all over the world. From that time on, he began to fear God and do penance in his own home. And after a little time had passed, he entered the Order of the brothers where he lived well and ended gloriously.[a]

Chapter III

THE FIRST PLACE WHERE THEY STAYED AND PERSECUTION BY THEIR RELATIVES

[14]Once Brother Bernard and Brother Peter sold their possessions and gave the money to the poor, as we mentioned, they dressed like the man of God, blessed Francis, and became his companions.

Having no place to stay, they went and found a poor and nearly abandoned church called Saint Mary of the Portiuncula. There they built a small dwelling where they all lived together.

After eight days a man from that city, Giles, came to them. He was a very dedicated and faithful man, on whom God bestowed many

a. According to Arnaldo Fortini, Sylvester was a canon of San Rufino whose conversion began shortly after that of Bernard and Peter. He was the first priest to join the primitive fraternity, although he was not one of the original twelve who accompanied Francis to Rome for the approval of the *propositum vitae*. He joined them upon their return to Assisi in 1209/10. Since he died March 4, 1240, this passage indicates that this text was begun sometime afterwards. Cf. Arnaldo Fortini, *Nova Vita di San Francesco* II, (Santa Maria degli Angeli: Tipografia Porzioncula, 1959), 280-281.

graces.[a] On his knees, he begged blessed Francis with great devotion and reverence to accept him into his company. When he heard and saw this, Blessed Francis was filled with joy and received him enthusiastically with open arms. And so the four of them had boundless joy and exceptionally great spiritual joy.

[15]Blessed Francis then took Brother Giles with himself to the Marches of Ancona, while the other two remained behind. As they were going along, they rejoiced not a little in the Lord. Francis, the man of God, reveled in a very loud voice, singing out in French, praising and blessing the Lord.

Indeed they were filled with great joy, as if they had just acquired an immense treasure. They were able to rejoice so much because they had forsaken so much, and considered as dung the things over which people usually grieve. They regarded as bitter what people of the world consider desirable, things that bring about much misery and grief.

Then blessed Francis told his companion, Brother Giles: "Our religion will be like a fisherman who casts his nets into the water, catching a great number of fish. Seeing the large number of fish, he puts the big ones in his baskets, leaving the small ones in the water." Giles was astonished at the prophecy that the saint uttered, for he knew how few the brothers were. 1C 28

The man of God did not yet preach to the people. But while they were going through towns and villages, he would encourage men and women to fear and love the Creator of heaven and earth and to do penance for their sins.[b] Brother Giles would respond: "What he says is very good. Believe him."

[16]Those who heard them would say to each other: "Who are these men, and what are these words they're saying?"

Some of them used to say that they seemed to be fools or drunkards, while others would say: "The words coming out of their mouths are not those of fools." One of them said: "Either they are clinging to the Lord for the sake of the highest perfection, or they have gone mad, for their physical life seems reckless. They walk barefoot, wear cheap clothing, and eat very little." Yet there was no one who followed them at that time. Young women, seeing them at a distance, would run away fearing they would be taken in by foolishness. Even though hardly anyone followed them, people remained nevertheless

a. For biographical information on Giles of Assisi, cf. FA:ED I 204 b.

b. This is an example of early Franciscan popular or penitential preaching, as found in the *Earlier Rule* XXI (hereafter ER), cf. FA:ED I 78.

in awe at the holy way of life with which they seemed to be marked for the Lord's sake.

After they had traveled around that province, the brothers returned to Saint Mary of the Portiuncula.

17After a few days had elapsed, three other men from Assisi, Brother Sabbatino,[a] Brother John[b] and Brother Morico the Short,[c] came to them, humbly begging Blessed Francis to admit them into his company. He received them kindly and eagerly.

However, when they went about the city begging alms, scarcely anyone was willing to give to them; instead they would tell them: "You got rid of your own possessions, and now you want to eat those of others." Thus, they suffered extreme want. Even their relatives and families would persecute them. Others from that city—great and small, men and women—would scorn and ridicule them as senseless and stupid, except for the city's bishop to whom the blessed Francis frequently went to seek counsel.[d]

The reason their families and relatives used to persecute them, while others ridiculed them, was because at that time you could not find anyone who would abandon all his possessions and go begging from door to door.

One day when the blessed Francis had gone to that bishop, the bishop told him: "It seems to me that your life is very rough and hard, not having or possessing anything in this world." The saint of God answered: "Lord, if we had any possessions, we would need arms to protect them because they cause many disputes and lawsuits. And possessions usually impede the love of God and neighbor. Therefore we do not want to possess anything in this world."

And this answer pleased the bishop.

Chapter IV
How He Admonished the Brothers and Sent Them Throughout the World

1C 26 18Saint Francis, since he was already filled with the grace of the
1C 29 Holy Spirit, predicted what would happen to his brothers. And

a. Luke Wadding maintains that Sabbatino was of unknown parentage; he was "unable to find anything credible written about him." Luke Wadding, *Annales Minorum* I (Ad Claras Aquas, Quaracchi: Collegium S. Bonaventurae, 1931), 56, xvii.

b. Although Brother John is commonly identified as John of Cappello or John of Cappella, the author of this text does not identify him further. Cf. L3C 35, infra, 88 a.

c. Beyond the fact that he is from Assisi, this Morico is not clearly identified.

d. For further information on the influence of the Bishop of Assisi on the developing fraternity and its way of life, see Michael Robson, "Assisi, Guido II and Saint Francis," GR 12:3 (1998): 225-287.

calling together his six brothers in the woods next to the church of Saint Mary of the Portiuncula where they often went to pray, he told them: "My dear brothers, let us consider our calling because God has mercifully called us not only for our own good but also for the salvation of many. Therefore, let us go through the world, encouraging and teaching men and women by word and example to do penance for their sins and to remember the Lord's commandments, which they have forgotten for such a long time."

Lk 12:32 He also told them: *"Do not be afraid, little flock,* but have confidence 1C 29
in the Lord. And do not say among yourselves 'We are simple and illiterate men, how should we preach?' But be mindful of the Lord's
Mt 10:20 words to his disciples: *'You yourselves will not be the speakers; the Spirit of your Father will be speaking in you.'* For the Lord Himself will give you spirit and wisdom to encourage and preach to men and their wives the way and deeds of the commandments. You will find, however, faithful people—meek, humble and kind—who will receive you and your words with joy and love. You will find others—unfaithful, proud, and blasphemous—resisting and criticizing you and your words. Therefore, resolve in your hearts to bear all these things with patience and humility."

When the brothers heard these words, they were afraid. Realizing 1C 27
Mk 16:6 that they were frightened, he told them: *"Do not be frightened.* Keep in mind that within a short time many learned, prudent and noble men will be with us. They will preach to nations and peoples, to kings and princes, and many people will be converted to the Lord. And the Lord will make His family grow and increase throughout the entire world."

After saying this, Francis blessed them and they went on their way.

Chapter V
THE PERSECUTIONS WHICH THE BROTHERS ENDURED AS THEY WENT THROUGHOUT THE WORLD

19 Wherever these devout servants of the Lord walked along and 1C 45
came upon a church, whether in use or abandoned, or upon some
cross alongside the road, they would pray devoutly: "We adore you, Test 5
O Christ, and we bless you, and in all your churches throughout the whole world, because by your holy cross you have redeemed the world." And they believed and felt that they had found a place of the Lord.

Those who saw them were amazed: "We have never seen religious dressed like this." They seemed to differ from all others by their habit and lifestyle, like wild men. When they entered a city, town or a home, they would announce peace. Whenever they saw men or women on the streets or in the piazzas, they would encourage them to fear and love the Creator of heaven and earth, to remember His commandments that they had forgotten, and to strive to fulfill them.

Some people willingly and joyfully listened to the brothers; others, however, jeered at them. Many people repeatedly questioned them, and it was extremely wearisome to answer so many questions because new situations often gave rise to new questions. Some asked them: "Where do you come from?" While others asked: "To which Order do you belong?" They answered simply: "We are penitents and were born in Assisi." At that time the religion of the brothers was not yet called an order.[a]

[20]Many who saw and heard them considered them impostors or fools. Someone among them remarked: "I wouldn't care to invite them into my house; they would probably steal my belongings." And because of this, any number of insults were inflicted on them in many places. Therefore they very frequently sought lodging in the porticos of churches or houses.

About this time two brothers[b] were in the city of Florence, going throughout the city in search of a place to stay, but were unable to find any. When they found a house with a portico containing a bread-oven, they said to each other: "We can stay here." They therefore asked the lady of the house if she would please welcome them into her home. When she instantly refused, they begged her at least to let them spend that night near the oven.

She let them do this. However, when her husband came home, and saw the brothers on the porch near the oven, he said to her: "Why did you offer lodging to these two rogues?" She answered: "I didn't want to offer them hospitality in the house, but gave them permission to stay on the porch where they couldn't steal anything from us except the firewood." On account of this distrust, they did not want to give the brothers anything to cover themselves, although the weather was severely cold.

---

a. Cf. supra, 31 a, in this edition. This subtle distinction suggests the development of the primitive fraternity. Further insights can be found in Théophile Desbonne, *From Intuition to Institution: The Franciscans,* translated by Paul Duggan and Jerry Du Charme (Chicago: Franciscan Herald Press, 1988); Jacques Dalarun, *La Malavventura di Francesco d'Assisi: Per Un Uso Storico delle Leggende Francescane* (Milano: Edizioni Biblioteca Francescana, 1996), 122-123.

b. According to the *Vita S. Bernardi* 3, these brothers were Bernard and Giles. Cf. *Vita Fr. Bernardi* 3 in AF III, 37-38.

During that night the brothers got up for matins and went to the nearest church.

[21]When morning came, the lady went to church to hear Mass and saw them remaining devoutly and humbly in prayer. She said to herself: "If these men were evildoers, as my husband claimed, they would not be praying so reverently."

While she was thinking these things, a man named Guido was going around the church distributing alms to the poor. When he approached the brothers, he attempted to give each one a coin, as he had done to the others, but they refused to take it. He told them: "Why don't you accept coins like the other poor people, for I see that you are just as poor and needy?" One of them, Bernard, answered him: "While it is true that we are poor, our poverty is not as burdensome for us as it is for the other poor, for we have become poor by the grace of God and in fulfillment of His counsel."

[22]Astonished, the man asked them if they had ever possessed anything in the world. They told him that they in fact had, but for the love of God had given their belongings to the poor.

When that woman considered that the brothers had refused the coins, she approached them and said: "Christians, if you want to come back to my hospitality, I will gladly receive you into my home." The brothers answered her with humility: "May the Lord reward you." When that man realized that the brothers were unable to find lodging, he took them to his own house and told them: "Look, this is the lodging that the Lord has prepared for you. Stay here as long as you want." The brothers thanked God for showing them His mercy and for hearing the cries of the poor. They stayed with him several days. Because of their words and good example, he was afterwards very generous to the poor.

[23]Although they were treated by this man with kindness, others considered them good-for-nothings, so much so that many, the
small and the great, treated them and spoke to them "as masters LR X 5
with their servants." Although the brothers wore the poorest and ER II 14; LR II 16
cheapest clothes, for amusement many people still took these away
from them. And so, even though they were left naked, for they had
Lk 6:29 only one tunic, the brothers nevertheless always observed the form ER XIV 6
of the Gospel by not demanding back what was taken from them. However, if motivated by piety, the people returned the tunic, they willingly accepted it.

People threw mud at the heads of some of the brothers; to others they shoved dice in their hands, inviting them to play. One brother was carried by the capuche across someone's back, for as long as he pleased.[a] These things, as well as many others, were inflicted on them. But we will not go on about these things, for it would unduly prolong our words. In a word, people considered them most despicable; that is why they nonchalantly and brazenly persecuted them as if they were criminals. In addition, they endured a great deal of hardship and suffering from hunger and thirst, from cold and nakedness.

1C 29 They suffered all these things with constancy and patience, as blessed Francis had counseled them. They did not become dejected or distressed, but exalted and rejoiced in their misfortunes like men
LR X 10 placed at a great advantage. They fervently prayed for their persecu- Mt 5:44
tors.

24When people saw them rejoicing in their tribulations and enduring them patiently for the Lord, unceasing in very devout prayer, neither accepting nor carrying money like other indigent poor people did, possessing such a great love for one another that they were known to be the Lord's disciples, many of them, by the kindness of the Lord, experienced a change of heart. They came to them, begging forgiveness for their offenses against them. Those men forgave them from their hearts and joyfully told them: "May the Lord forgive you." And so, from then on, the people willingly listened to them.

1C 30 Some asked them to receive them into their society. And they accepted many of them,[b] for, at this time, because of the small number of the brothers, each one had received from blessed Francis authority to admit whomever he wished. At the established time, they came back to Saint Mary of the Portiuncula.

Chapter VI
THE BROTHERS' MANNER OF LIVING AND THE LOVE THEY HAD FOR ONE ANOTHER

25Each time they saw one another, the brothers were filled with such delight and spiritual joy that they forgot all the adversity and the extreme poverty they had suffered.

---

a. The Latin *caputium* [capuche] was the pointed hood worn by the brothers as part of the habit, cf. ER II 13, FA:ED I 65; LR II 9, FA:ED I 101.

b. Lorenzo DiFonzo suggests that it is doubtful that *plurimi* [many] were received during the mission of the six early companions. Either the superlative *plurimi* is a mistake, or the author is looking at the entire period from 1208 to 1217. For the subsequent return of the six companions "at the established time," see 1C 30. Cf. Lorenzo Di Fonzo, "*L'Anonimo Perugino* tra Le Fonti Francescane del Secolo XIII: Rapporti Letterari e Testo Critico," *Miscellanea Franciscana* 72 (1972): 448, note 42.

Every day they were conscientious about prayer and working with their hands to avoid all idleness, the enemy of the soul. At night, they were equally conscientious about rising in the middle of the night according to that passage of the Prophet: *At midnight I rise to give you thanks* and they prayed devoutly with frequent tears. 1C 39, 40; ER VII 10-12; Test 20-21; Ps 119:62

They loved one another from the heart and each one served and took care of the other, as a mother serves and cares for her son. The fire of love burned so intensely in them, that they would have willingly sacrificed their lives not only for the name of our Lord Jesus Christ, but also for one another. 1C 38, 39; ER IX 11

26 One day, two brothers were walking along a road when suddenly a simpleton began throwing stones at them. One of them, seeing that a stone was about to strike his brother, ran directly in front of him. Because of ardent mutual love, he preferred that the stone strike him rather than his brother. They frequently did these and similar things.

They were rooted and founded in love and humility, and one would respect the other as if he were his master. Whoever among them excelled because of a position or gifts of grace, seemed even more humble and self-effacing than the others. 1C 38

They all dedicated themselves wholeheartedly to obedience: the moment the one giving an order opened his mouth, their feet were ready to go, their hands set to carry it out. Whatever they were ordered, they considered to be to the Lord's will. Thus it was pleasant and easy for them to fulfill everything. 1C 39, 45; Adm III

They abstained from carnal desires and, in order to avoid being judged, they judged themselves carefully. 1C 41

27 If one unwittingly uttered a word that could possibly give offense to another, his conscience reproached him so much that he could find no peace until he confessed his fault. Then, lying flat on the ground, he made the other—no matter how unwilling he was—put his foot on his mouth. If the other refused to do this, then, should the one who uttered the offensive word be a prelate, he would command him to do it; otherwise he would have a prelate command him.[a] They did these things to rid themselves of ill will and to preserve perfect love with each other at all times. And so they strove to combat each vice with a corresponding virtue.

Whatever they had, a book or a tunic, was used in common and no one called anything his own, just as it was done in the primitive church of the Apostles. Acts 4:32

a. For an understanding of the word *praelatus* [prelate], see FA:ED I 130 a.

Although extreme poverty abounded in them, they were always generous, and spontaneously shared the alms given them with all who asked for the love of God.

[28]When they went along and came upon poor people begging from them, some of the brothers would give them some of their clothing, since they had nothing else to give. One of them even tore the capuche from his tunic and gave it to a poor beggar;[a] while an-
1C 17 other tore off a sleeve and gave it away; and still others gave away a
part of their tunic to observe that Gospel passage: *Give to all who ask of* Lk 6:30
you.

One day a poor man came to the church of Saint Mary of the Portiuncula where the brothers were staying and asked for alms. There was a cloak there that one of them had while he was still in the world. Blessed Francis told the brother, whose cloak it was, to give it to the poor man.[b] He freely and quickly gave it to him. And immediately, because of the reverence and dedication that the brother had in donating the gift, it seemed to him that the alms rose up to heaven and he felt himself filled with a new spirit.

[29]When the rich of this world went out of their way to visit them, they received them quickly and kindly, and would invite them to call them back from evil, and prompt them to do penance.

At that time, the brothers would eagerly beg not to be sent to where they had been raised so that, in this way, they would avoid association and dealings with their relatives and observe the words of
the Prophet: *I have become an outcast to my brothers, a stranger to my* Ps 69:9
mother's sons.

They rejoiced most in their poverty, for they desired no riches ex-
ER VIII 6 cept those of eternity. They never possessed gold or silver, and, although they despised all wealth of this world, it was money especially that they trampled under foot.

[30]One day while the brothers were staying at Saint Mary of the Portiuncula, some people came for a visit. They entered the church and placed some money on the altar without their knowledge. Then, one of the brothers, entering the church, took the coins he had found, and put them on the church's windowsill. Another brother, when he found the money where the other one left it, took it to Saint Francis.

---

a. *The Life of Brother Giles* 4 identifies Br. Giles as the one who gave his capuche to a poor man during a pilgrimage to Santiago de Compostella "and for twenty days he went about without a capuche." Cf. *Scripta Leonis, Rufini et Angeli Sociorum S. Francisci* [The Writings of Leo, Rufino and Angelo Companions of St. Francis], edited and translated by Rosalind B. Brooke (Oxford: Oxford at The Clarendon Press, 1970), 325.

b. *The Life of Brother Giles* 2 tells of Br. Giles as the one who gave away his cloak the same day he joined Francis on April 23, 1208, cf. Brooke, 323.

When blessed Francis heard this, he diligently asked which one of the brothers had placed the money there. When he found out who it was, he ordered him to come to him. "Why did you do this?" he said. "Didn't you know that I want the brothers not only to avoid using money, but also not even to touch it?" When the brother heard this, he bowed his head, confessed his fault on his knees, and asked that a penance be given him. Francis then ordered him to carry the money out of the church in his mouth and, when he came upon some ass's dung, to place the money upon it. The brother very diligently fulfilled this. Then Francis admonished the brothers that whenever they found money, they should scorn it and consider it worthless. ER VIII 3

They were constantly rejoicing, for they had nothing that could disturb them. The more they were separated from the world, the more were they united to God. These men entered upon a narrow and rough trail. They broke up the rocks, trampled upon the thorns, and so have left us, their followers, a smooth path.

Chapter VII
How They Traveled to Rome and How the Lord Pope Granted Them a Rule and the Office of Preaching

31 As he realized that the Savior's grace was increasing his brothers in number and merit, blessed Francis told them: "Brothers, I see that the Lord intends to make of us a large congregation. Therefore, let us go to our mother, the Roman Church, and inform the Supreme Pontiff about what the Lord is doing through us so we may continue doing what we have begun by his will and command." Since what Francis said pleased the rest of the brothers, he took the twelve with him, and they went to Rome.[a]

While they were on the way, he told them: "Let us make one of us the leader and consider him the vicar of Jesus Christ for us. Wherever he wants to go, we will go; when he wants to rest, we will rest." They chose Brother Bernard, who was the first to be received by the blessed Francis, and they did as he said.

They made their way rejoicing and spoke about the words of the Lord. No one dared to say anything unless it pertained to the Lord's praise and glory or to the benefit of their souls, and they spent time in

a. Thomas of Celano does not specify the number of brothers who accompanied Francis to Rome (1C 32), while Julian of Speyer indicates that they were twelve in number— Francis and eleven brothers (*The Life of Saint Francis* 21 [hereafter LJS]). In examining this passage of AP that specifies twelve brothers who accompanied Francis, Beguin suggests that the author, in order to highlight the similarity between Christ and his twelve disciples, is also taking into account the presence of Albert, the poor man identified in AP 9. Cf. Beguin, *L'Anonyme*, 120-128.

prayer. The Lord, on the other hand, prepared lodging and food for them as the need arose.

1C 32 [32]When they arrived in Rome, they met the bishop of the city of Assisi who was then staying in the City.[a] When he saw them, he welcomed them with immense joy.

Now, the bishop was acquainted with one of the cardinals, the Lord John of St. Paul, a good and religious man, who loved servants of the Lord very much.[b] The bishop of Assisi familiarized him with the proposal and life of blessed Francis and his brothers. After he heard these things, he had a strong desire to meet blessed Francis and some of the brothers. When he heard that they were in the City, he sent for them and had them come to him. Seeing them, he welcomed them with eagerness and love.

[33]Even though they stayed with him for only a few days, he came to love them from the depths of his heart, because he saw shining forth in their actions all he had heard about them. He told blessed Francis: "I commend myself to your prayers and, from now on, I want you to consider me as one of your brothers. Therefore, tell me, why did you come?" Then blessed Francis made known to him his whole proposal: how he wanted to speak to the Apostolic Lord and, with his approval and mandate, to continue what he was doing. To which the cardinal responded: "I want to be your procurator at the Curia of the Lord Pope."

Thus it was that he went to the Curia and told the Lord Pope Innocent the Third: "I found a most perfect man who wishes to live according to the form of the holy Gospel and to observe evangelical perfection. Through him, I believe the Lord intends to renew His church in the entire world." When he heard this, the Lord Pope was amazed and told him: "Bring him to me."

[34]On the following day, therefore, he brought him to the pope. Blessed Francis laid his whole proposal before the Lord Pope, just as he had previously done to the cardinal.

The Lord Pope answered him: "Your life is too hard and severe, if you wish to found a congregation possessing nothing in this world. For where will you obtain the necessities of life?" Blessed Francis re-

---

a. The Latin text reads *in Urbe* [in the City]. As early as the writings of Cicero (106-43 B.C.), *Urbs* [the City] referred specifically to the city of Rome. Cf. *Oxford Latin Dictionary*, ed. P.G.W. Glare (Oxford: The Clarendon Press, 1982), 2105. This is the first instance of this use in this volume. It occurs throughout the L3C 47, 53, 60; the AC 8, 117, 120; 2C 96, 104, 119, 148; 3C 37, 181; LMj VI 10; VIII 7. The editors have chosen to use both translations, i.e., "Rome" and "the City."

b. For further information on the role of Bishop Guido in the search of Francis and his companions to have their *propositum vitae* approved, cf. Michael Robson, "Assisi, Bishop Guido II and Saint Francis," GR 12 (1998): 255-287. For biographical information on Cardinal John of St. Paul, O.S.B. (+1215), cf. FA:ED I: 210 b.

sponded: "My Lord, I trust in my Lord Jesus Christ. Since He has promised to give us life and glory in heaven, He will not deprive us of our bodily necessities when we need them on earth." "What you say is true, son," the pope replied, "but human nature is weak and never remains in the same state.[a] But, go and pray to the Lord with all your heart, so that He may show you what is better and more beneficial for your souls. Come back and tell me and I will then grant it."

[35]Francis withdrew to pray. With a pure heart, he prayed to the Lord that in His ineffable piety He would reveal this to him. While he was engaged in prayer, with his whole heart focused on the Lord, the word of the Lord came into his heart and spoke to him figuratively. "There lived in the realm of a great king a very poor but beautiful woman, who caught the king's eye and by whom he fathered many sons. One day that woman began to think to herself: 'What am I to do, a poor woman with so many sons? I have no possessions to provide them with a livelihood!' While she was pondering all these things in her heart, her face became sad. When the king arrived, he said to her 'What is the matter? I see that you are lost in thought and sad.' With her whole heart she told him all her thoughts. The king told her: 'Do not be afraid of your dire poverty, nor of the sons you have, and the many you will have. If the many hired hands in my house have their fill of food, I certainly do not want my own sons to die of hunger. No, I want them to have even more than the others.'"

The man of God, Francis, immediately understood that the poor woman symbolized him.[b] As a result, the man of God strengthened his resolve to observe most holy poverty in the future.

[36]Getting up at that very hour, he went to the Apostolic Lord, and told him all that the Lord had revealed to him.

On hearing this, the Lord Pope was greatly amazed that the Lord had revealed His will to so simple a man. And he realized that he was
1 Cor 2:4 not proceeding according to human wisdom, *but in the display* and *power of the Spirit.*

Then blessed Francis bowed down and humbly and devotedly promised obedience and reverence to the Lord Pope. And the other brothers, because they had not yet promised obedience, likewise promised obedience and reverence to blessed Francis according to the precept of the Lord Pope. ER Prol 3; LR I 2-

a. Before becoming pope, Innocent III had published *De miseria humanae conditionis* [On The Misery of the Human Condition], edited by Donald R. Howard and translated by Margaret Mary Dietz (Indianapolis: Bobbs-Merrill, 1969).

b. Even before this text was written, Odo of Cheriton told a similar story about Francis in one of his sermons, cf. FA:ED I 590-591.

The Lord Pope approved the rule for him and his brothers, both present and future.[a] He also gave him authority to preach everywhere as the grace of the Holy Spirit was given him and that the other brothers were also to preach, provided that blessed Francis gave them the office of preaching.

From then on, blessed Francis began preaching to the people in the cities and villages, as the Spirit of the Lord revealed to him. The Lord placed in his mouth uncompromising, honey-flowing, and very sweet words, so that hardly anyone ever tired of listening to him.

Because of his great love for the Brother,[b] that cardinal had all twelve of them given the tonsure.[c]

ER XVIII Afterwards, Blessed Francis ordered that a chapter be held twice a year, on Pentecost and on the feast of Saint Michael in the month of September.

Chapter VIII

HOW HE ORDERED THAT A CHAPTER BE HELD AND THE MATTERS TO BE TREATED AT THE CHAPTER

[37]On Pentecost all the brothers used to gather for a chapter near the church of Saint Mary of the Portiuncula. At the chapter they would discuss how they could better observe the *Rule.* They appointed brothers who would preach to the people throughout each of the provinces, and assigned brothers in their province.[d]

ER IV 2

a. It is difficult to determine with precision when this initial approval was granted. It is generally held that the approval was granted in the spring of 1209, before May 25, when Innocent III left to spend the summer in Viterbo. For an in-depth study of the problem, see Omer Englebert, *Saint Francis of Assisi: A Biography*, 2nd ed., trans. Eve Marie Cooper, revised and augmented by Ignatius Brady and Raphael Brown (Chicago: Franciscan Herald Press, 1965), 377-383.

b. This designation of Francis as "the Brother" is unique. Jordan of Giano highlights the fact that, when recognizing Francis at a Chapter, Elias would refer to him simply as "the Brother." Cf. ChrJG 17 infra.

c. The Latin of this passage reads: *"Dictus autem Cardinalis . . . omnibus illis duodecim fratribus clericam fecit dari* [The said cardinal had a *clericam* given to all twelve brothers]." This passage is fraught with difficulties. In the first place, the nature of the act, *clericam fecit dari* [had a *clericam* given], is not clear. Although the term *clerica,* which the editors have rendered "tonsure," is used, it is not clear if it means that (1) the brothers had received the "tonsure" and thus became "clerics;" or (2) they had been recognized as lawful preachers, a permission granted in a previous paragraph; or (3) they could be publicly recognized as religious. Secondly, in this text the author seems to contradict what he said above (AP 31), that there were twelve brothers in addition to Francis. AP seems to present it as an act of kindness on the part of the cardinal to help the brothers to be accepted as preachers.

d. ER IV 2 prescribes that the ministers of each province have the responsibility of assigning the brothers. This present text is describing an earlier practice, before the division of the brothers into provinces at the chapter of 1217, cf. AP 40, infra, 53. Here the word "province" has the more generic sense of "region." The brothers were assigned at the annual Pentecost chapter. The texts suggests two types of assignment: (1) of certain brothers to the office of preaching, and (2) of all brothers to and within a specific region.

Saint Francis used to give the brothers admonitions, corrections and precepts, as it seemed best to him, after consulting the Lord.[a] Everything, however, that he said in word, he would first, with eagerness and affection, show them in deed.

He used to revere prelates and priests of the holy Church. He would respect the elderly, and honored the noble and the wealthy. He loved the poor intimately and showed compassion to them. In a word, he showed himself to be subject to all.

Adm XXVI; 1C 62

Although he was more exalted than all other brothers, he still appointed one of the brothers staying with him as his guardian and master. He humbly and devoutly obeyed him, in order to avoid any occasion of pride. Among people this saint lowered his head even to the ground, and for this the Lord lifted him on high among the saints and elect in heaven.

Test 27-28

1C 53

Adm XXIII

He zealously used to admonish them to observe the holy Gospel and the *Rule* conscientiously as they had promised; and especially to be reverent toward ecclesiastical offices and regulations; to be attentive and devoted when hearing Mass, and when they saw the Body of our Lord Jesus Christ. They were to have reverence toward priests who handle these tremendous and greatest sacraments and, whenever they encountered them, they were to bow their heads to them and kiss their hands. If they found them on horseback, they were to make a sign of reverence, kissing not only the hands of a priest, but, out of reverence for their power, even the hooves of their horses.

Adm I 9

Adm XXVI; Test

38 He also admonished them not to judge or look down upon anyone, not even those who drink and eat and dress extravagantly, as stated in the *Rule*. "Their Lord is also our Lord. He who called us can call them, and He who willed to justify us can also justify them."

ER XI 10-12; LR I

ER XI 9; LR II 17

He would say: "And I wish to honor them as my brothers and masters. They are my brothers, because we are all from the one Creator; they are my masters because they help us to do penance, providing us with necessities of life." He also told them: "Let your way of life among the people be such that whoever sees or hears you will glorify and praise our heavenly Father."

His great desire was that he and his brothers would perform deeds through which the Lord would be praised. He used to tell them: "As you announce peace with your mouth, make sure that you have greater peace in your hearts, thus no one will be provoked to anger or scandal because of you. Let everyone be drawn to peace and kindness

a. The author is undoubtedly referring not only to the *Admonitions* (hereafter Adm) of Francis, cf. FA:ED I 128-137, but also to those passages of ER that have a distinctly personal tone, e.g. ER IX, XVII, XXII, cf. FA:ED I 63-86.

through your peace and gentleness. For we have been called to this: to cure the wounded, to bind up the broken, and to recall the erring. Many who seem to us members of the devil will yet be disciples of Christ."

1C 40 [39]On the other hand, he used to reprove them for the great austerity which they brought upon their bodies, for the brothers were then exerting too much effort in fasts, vigils, and bodily mortification in order to repress within themselves every urge of the flesh. They would inflict so much discomfort on themselves that it seemed they hated themselves. When he heard and saw this, blessed Francis reprimanded them, as we said, and ordered them not to act excessively. He was so filled with the Savior's grace and wisdom, that he would make his admonition with kindness, his reprimand with reason, and his command with gentleness.

Among the brothers assembled at chapter, not one of them dared to discuss worldly matters with anyone. Instead, they spoke about the lives of the holy fathers, or about the holiness of one of the brothers, or how they could better attain the grace of our Lord.

If any of the brothers gathered at chapter experienced temptations of the flesh or the world, or some other kind of trial, the temptations would go away either on hearing blessed Francis who would speak fervently and sweetly, or on seeing his presence. For he spoke to them compassionately, not as a judge, but as a father to his children and a doctor to his patient, so that, the words of the Apostle were fulfilled in him: *Who is weak that I am not affected by it? Who is scandalized that I am not aflame with indignation?* 2 Cor 11, 29

Chapter IX
How the Brothers Were Sent Throughout All the Provinces of the World

[40]Once a chapter had ended, he would bless all the brothers at chapter and designated each of them throughout the provinces, as he wished.[a] Whoever of them had the spirit of God and the eloquence for preaching—cleric or lay—to him he would give permission and an obedience to preach. They received his blessing with great happiness and joy in the Lord Jesus Christ. They went through the world as

a. This passage contradicts AP 37 in which the ministers assigned the brothers. The wording of both paragraphs, however, is confusing. In AP 37 the brothers *constituebant* [appointed] those who would preach and *collocarent* [assigned] each one in his province. In this paragraph, Francis is the one who *destinabat* [designated] them *per provincias* [throughout the provinces]. Both paragraphs reflect the evolving process of assigning brothers to the newly formed provinces or jurisdictions of the fraternity.

1 Pt 2:11 *strangers and pilgrims,* taking nothing for the journey, except the books in which they could say their Hours. Test 24

Whenever they met a priest, whether rich or poor, they bowed to him, as blessed Francis had taught them, and paid their respect. When it was time to seek lodging, they preferred to stay with them, rather than with secular persons. 1C 62

[41]When they could not find lodging with priests, they would inquire who in that locality was a good and God-fearing person with whom they could be more suitably welcomed. After a while, the Lord inspired one such God-fearing person in each of the cities and towns they were prepared to visit to prepare a lodging for them, until, after a while, they built their own dwellings in the cities and towns.

The Lord gave the brothers the words and spirit suited to the time, to speak with incisive words, penetrating the hearts of many, but especially the young more than the elderly. Those who abandoned mother and father, and all their possessions, put on the habit of the holy religion. At that time and particularly in that religion, the word of the Lord in the Gospel was fulfilled: *Do not suppose that my mission on earth is to spread peace. My mission is to spread not peace, but division. I have come to set a man at odds with his father and a daughter with her mother.* Those whom the brothers accepted, they brought to the blessed Francis to invest them. 1C 23 Mt 10:34-35

In the same way, many women, virgins and those without husbands, hearing their preaching, would come to them with contrite hearts, saying: "And we, what are we to do? We cannot stay with you. So tell us what we can do to save our souls." In response, they established, in every city they could, reclusive monasteries for doing penance.[a] They also appointed one of the brothers their visitator and corrector.[b]

Similarly, married men said: "We have wives who will not permit us to send them away. Teach us, therefore, the way that we can take

a. The Latin text reads *monasteria reclusa ad paenitentiam faciendam* [reclusive monasteries for doing penance], a passage that clearly suggests the life of Saint Clare and the Poor Ladies. Nonetheless, *reclusa* [reclusive] suggests the flexibility of religious movements of women at this time, i.e., women recluses, who embraced perpetual seclusion from the surrounding environment, lived differently than enclosed women, who entered into a stable environment, the enclosure, separated from the world. Cf. Mario Sensi, "The Woman's Recluse Movement in Umbria during the 13th and 14th Centuries," GR 8 (1994): 319-345.

b. The role of a visitator had its origins with the Cistercian *Charter of Love* in which the abbot was bound to visit the monasteries entrusted to his care. Very often the abbot assigned another monk to this task, especially when the monastery involved was one of nuns. The first visitator of the Poor Ladies was a Cistercian, Ambrose, who held that position from 1218-1219. He was succeeded by Brother Philip the Tall. Cf. Vincentius Hermans, *Commentarium Cistercense: Historico-Practicum in Codicis Canones de Religiosis* (Rome: Tipografia Pio X, 1961), 168.

more securely." The brothers founded an order for them, called the Order of Penitents, and had it approved by the Supreme Pontiff.[a]

Chapter X

When the Cardinals Became Kindly Disposed Toward the Brothers and Began to Counsel and Offer Them Assistance

42The venerable father, the Lord Cardinal, John of Saint Paul, who frequently offered counsel and protection to blessed Francis, would praise the merits and deeds of blessed Francis and all of his brothers to all the other cardinals. When they heard him, their hearts were moved to loving the brothers and each of them desired to have some brothers in his Curia, not for receiving service from them, but because of the devotion and love that they had toward the brothers.

One day when blessed Francis came to the Curia, particular cardinals asked him for some brothers; and he graciously acceded to their request.

Lord John of St. Paul, the man who loved the holy poor men, died and rested in peace.[b]

43After this, the Lord inspired one of the cardinals, Hugolino, the bishop of Ostia, who loved blessed Francis and his brothers very much, not merely as a friend, but even more as a father. When blessed Francis heard of his reputation, he approached him. When the cardinal saw him, he received him with joy and said: "I offer myself to you for counsel, assistance, and protection as you wish, and I want you to have me remembered in your prayers."

Blessed Francis gave thanks to the Most High for inspiring that man's heart to offer advice, assistance, and protection, and told him: "I gladly want to have you as the father and lord of me and of all my brothers. And I want all my brothers to be bound to pray to the Lord for you." Then he invited him to come to the chapter of the brothers at Pentecost. He agreed and came each year.

Whenever he came, all the brothers gathered at the chapter would go in procession to meet him. As they were coming, he would dismount from his horse and go on foot with the brothers to the church because of the devotion he had for them. Afterward he would preach

a. Cf. Raoul Manselli, "Francis of Assisi and Lay People Living in the World: Beginning of the Third Order," GR 11 (1997): 41-48. For a comparative treatment of the origins of the Third Order, now known as the Secular Franciscan Order, see Octavian Schmucki, "The Third Order in the Biographies of St. Francis," GR 6 (1992): 81-107.

b. He died in the summer of 1215, a few months before the Fourth Lateran Council.

to them and celebrate Mass during which blessed Francis would chant the Gospel.[a]

Chapter XI

How the Church Protected the Brothers from Persecutors

44 After eleven years had passed since the founding of the religion and the number of brothers had increased, ministers were elected and sent with some of the brothers throughout almost all the provinces of the world where the Catholic faith was practiced.[b]

In some of the provinces they were received, but were not allowed to build houses. From others they were expelled, because people feared that the brothers were not faithful Christians, for the brothers did not as yet have a rule confirmed by the pope, but one merely allowed by him.[c] For that reason, after they had endured many trials (1C 40) from clerics and laity and had been stripped by thieves, they returned to blessed Francis very embittered and depressed. And these trials beset them in Hungary, Germany, and other provinces beyond the Alps.

The brothers informed the Lord Cardinal of Ostia about these situations. Once he called blessed Francis to himself, he took him to the Lord Pope Honorius—because the Lord Innocent had already died,[d] had another rule written for him, and had it confirmed and strengthened with the force of the papal seal.

In this rule he extended the time between chapters to avoid hardship for the brothers who lived in faraway places.

45 Blessed Francis petitioned the Lord Pope for one of the cardinals (LR XIII 3) who would be the governor, protector, and corrector of this religion, as stated in the *Rule*. And he granted him the Lord of Ostia.

Now that he had this commission from the Lord Pope, the Lord Bishop of Ostia, raising his hand to protect the brothers, sent a letter

---

a. For information on the role of Francis as a deacon, i.e., the one who "would chant the Gospel," see FA:ED I 256 b.

b. That is, at the chapter of 1217. In his reckoning of time here, the author dates "the foundation of the religion" to Francis's break with his father, also see infra AP 46. In what follows in the remainder of AP 44 and AP 45, the author conflates in a rather facile way a number of events which took place over a period of some six years, from the first sending of the brothers outside Italy in 1217 to the confirmation of the *Rule* in 1223.

c. The Latin contrasts *confirmatam* [confirmed] and *concessam* [allowed], thus highlighting the "temporary" nature of the *Regula non bullata* [Rule without the Papal Seal, the *Earlier Rule*] and the need for the *Regula bullata* [the Rule with the Papal Seal, the *Later Rule*].

d. Pope Innocent III died on July 16, 1216. Due to the desecration of his body in Perugia's cathedral, his successor, Honorius III was quickly elected two days later.

to many bishops in the dioceses where they experienced hardships.[a] He did this so that they would not be opposed to the brothers, but rather give them advice and assistance in preaching and living in their provinces, as good and religious men approved by the Church. Many other cardinals likewise sent letters concerning this.

And so, in another chapter in which blessed Francis gave the ministers permission to receive brothers into the Order, the brothers were again sent to those provinces, carrying the confirmed *Rule* and the letters, as we have said, of the cardinal. Once the prelates saw the *Rule*, confirmed by the Supreme Pontiff, as well as the endorsement of the brothers by the Lord Cardinal of Ostia and the other cardinals, they permitted the brothers to build, live, and preach in their provinces.

After this happened and the brothers lived and preached there, many people, seeing their humble way of life, upright conduct, and their very pleasant words, came to the brothers and put on the habit of holy religion.

1C 100 Seeing the trust and love that the Lord of Ostia had for the brothers, blessed Francis loved him from the depths of his heart, and when he would write to him, he would say: "To the venerable father in Christ, Bishop of the entire world."

After a short time had passed, the Lord of Ostia was elected to the Apostolic See, according to the prophecy of blessed Francis, and is called Pope Gregory the Ninth.[b]

Chapter XII

THE DEATH OF BLESSED FRANCIS, HIS MIRACLES AND CANONIZATION

[46]When twenty years had passed since blessed Francis had embraced evangelical perfection, the merciful God willed that *he should* Rv 14:3
rest from his labors, for he had labored greatly in vigils, in prayers and 2 Cor 6:5
fasting, in supplications, in sermons, in journeys, in concerns, and in compassion for his neighbors. He had given his whole heart to God, his creator, and loved Him with all his heart and his whole being. For he carried God in his heart, praised Him with his lips, and glorified

a. This seems to be a reference to the papal documents *Cum dilecti* (1219) and *Pro dilectis* (1220) of Pope Honorius III, which were most likely requested on the brothers' behalf by Hugolino, cf. FA:ED I 558-559. The author appears to be magnifying the role of Hugolino, who was still alive—and pope—while he was writing.

b. Since Gregory died on August 22, 1241, this passage indicates that this text was completed before that date.

Him with his deeds. When someone mentioned God's name, he
Phil 2:10 would say: *"At* this *name, heaven and earth* must bow."

Wanting to show the love He had for him, the Lord impressed on his members and his side the stigmata of His most beloved Son. And
Ps 25:8 because the servant of God, Francis, wanted to go to His *house* and *the dwelling place of His glory,* the Lord called him to Himself, and so he gloriously passed over to the Lord.

After this, many signs and miracles appeared among the people, so that the hearts of many who were stubbornly against believing what the Lord had manifested in his servant were moved to admit:
Wis 5:4-5 *His life we accounted madness, and his death dishonored. See how he is accounted among the sons of God; how his lot is with the saints!*

[47]The venerable lord and father, the Lord Pope Gregory, who loved the saint during his life, also paid tribute to him after his death. Coming with the cardinals to the place where the body of the holy man had been buried, he enrolled him in the catalog of the saints.

On that account many important and noble men, forsaking everything, have converted to the Lord with their wives, sons and daughters, and their whole family. Wives and daughters have enclosed themselves in monasteries. Husbands and sons have put on the habit of the Lesser Brothers.

Thus that word is fulfilled which he once predicted to his broth- AP 18
ers: "After not much time, many learned, prudent, and noble men will come to us, and will dwell with us."

Epilogue

[48]I beg you, most beloved brothers, meditate earnestly on the things we have recorded about our most beloved fathers and brothers, understand them correctly, and strive in deed to fulfill them, so we may deserve to share with them in the glory of heaven.

May our Lord Jesus Christ lead us to this glory.

THE LEGEND OF THE THREE COMPANIONS

(1241–1247)

Introduction

In 1244 the brothers buried Haymo of Faversham, the first English General Minister and the first academician, then gathered in Genoa on October 4, and elected Cresentius of Iesi his successor. Thomas of Eccleston provides a description of the character of the man chosen to guide the Order during this tumultuous period:

> Brother Haymo was succeeded by Brother Crescentius, a famous physician and the provincial minister of Verona,[1] whose zeal was kindled by charity, informed by learning, and strengthened by perseverance.[2]

According to Thomas, the choice of Crescentius was not without some hesitation or reluctance. As Provincial Minister of the Lesser Brothers in the Province of Le Marche, his reputation among some of his brothers was not as positive as that of Thomas. "For in his own province," he writes,

> there were brothers so opposed to him that on the very night before the general chapter in which he was elected, after he had lodged a complaint against them before the zealous brothers of the order concerning the rebellion of his brothers,[3] one of the brothers [at the chapter] saw him in a vision, with his head shaved and a beard flowing down to his cord, and heard a voice coming from heaven upon him, saying: "This is Mordechai."[4] Now, when Brother Ralph of Rheims heard of this vision, he immediately said: "Assuredly, he will be elected general today."

Beyond his election, there is little recorded about the Chapter that elected him, only an initiative of Crescentius himself. According to the *Chronicle of the Twenty-Four Generals:* "In that chapter the same General directed all the brothers to send him in writing whatever they could truly recall about the life, miracles, and prodigies of blessed Francis."[5] The author does not provide any reasons for this decision, nor can any be found in any other early document. Engelbert Grau suggests that the considerations must have revolved around the fact that many of the sayings, episodes, and events of the saint had been handed down orally, that is, they were preserved neither in *The Life of Saint Francis* by Thomas of Celano nor in that of Julian of Speyer.[6] But Crescentius may simply have recognized the fact that Francis's followers were dying at the same time that the Order was growing dramatically. In the wake of many of the reforms of his predecessor, Haymo of Faversham, he may have realized that a return to the initial ideals of the primitive fraternity could only be achieved by a re-acquaintance with the memory of the Founder's life and holiness.

Two highly disputed texts, *The Legend of the Three Companions* and *The Assisi Compilation,* reflect the contributions of the three friars who identify themselves in the first text as Brothers Leo, Angelo, and Rufino and in the second text as "we who were with him." Both texts provide facts about and insights into Francis not found in the earlier lives and, as such, are indispensable in knowing the details of his life and vision.

"In its present condition," Paul Sabatier wrote in 1894, "*The Legend of the Three Companions* is the finest piece of Franciscan literature, and one of the most delightful productions of the Middle Ages . . . As it has come down to us, this document is the only one worthy from the point of view of history to be placed beside the *The Life of Saint Francis* by Celano."[7] The controversial Frenchman was merely echoing the eighteenth century Bollandists who, in 1768, incorporated *The Legend of the Three Companions* into the *Acta Sanctorum* together with Thomas's *Life of Saint Francis* and Bonaventure's *Major Legend.*[8] His position as an "outsider"—Sabatier was neither a Catholic nor a friar—may have contributed to the storm that his judgment created. François Van Ortroy soon characterized *The Legend of the Three Companions* as "a bad parody of official legends," and questioned Sabatier's dating of the document maintaining that it came "from the last part of the thirteenth century, and even from the first quarter of the fourteenth." [9] Sabatier's defense, in 1901, served to highlight the text further and to raise what became known as the "Franciscan Question," the question regarding the authenticity of this work, the date of its composition, and the identity of its author.

A problem of manuscripts immediately complicates a simple answer to the questions surrounding the text. Two families of manuscripts emerge: the "traditional," containing nineteen examples, most of which come from the second half of the fourteenth century;[10] and the "Sarnano," containing three examples, one from the early 1300's, the others from 1405, all of which, unfortunately, are incomplete.[11] The relationship between these two families of manuscripts is difficult to determine. In 1939 Giuseppe Abate argued that the "traditional" family depended on that of Sarnano, an argument proposed in a similar vein by Théophile Desbonnets in his 1972 study.[12] That same year, in a thorough study of the *The Legend of the Three Companions,* Sophronius Clasen took a contrary position.[13] Not until his 1974 critical edition of the *The Legend of the Three Companions* was Desbonnets able to prove his position and, at the same time, to show the close bond existing between it and *The Anonymous of Perugia.*[14] Since that time, Maurice Causse has furthered Desbonnets's findings by meticulously examining the earlier Sarnano and later traditional versions of *The Legend of the Three Companions,* together with *The Life of Saint Francis* by Thomas of Celano, and *The Anonymous of Perugia.*[15] Focusing on nine chapters of the *Legend,* Causse maintains that these chapters represent earlier texts contemporaneous with the lost "process of canonization." In light of these arguments, *The Legend of the Three Companions,* at least in the first sixty-seven paragraphs or sixteen chapters, can be dated between 1241 and 1247. The first of possibly many editions would have occurred sometime after August 11, 1246, the date of the letter introducing the work.

In many of the manuscripts a rubric or explanatory note introduces this letter: "These are certain writings of three companions of blessed Francis about his life and manner of living while he was in the attire of the world, about his marvelous and perfect conversion, and about the perfection of the origin and foundation of the Order in him and in the first brothers." The statement's intent is clearly to underscore the source of the text, that is, three companions of Francis. The rubric's vocabulary, however, rightfully evokes reminiscences of earlier texts, especially *The Life of Saint Francis* by Thomas of Celano that accentuates Francis's life, *conversatio* [manner of living] and *conversio* [conversion], and *The Anonymous of Perugia* with its description of the *origo* [origin] and *fundamentum* [foundation] of the Order.

The letter that follows immediately identifies the three companions, Leo, Angelo, and Rufino, and those with whom they spoke, Philip, Illuminato, Masseo, and John. Moreover, it presents the reason for their undertaking this project, that is, the command of the General Chapter, held in Genoa in 1244, to forward information about Francis to the General Minister.[16] However, the letter presents this disclaimer: "We do not intend to write a legend, since other legends about his life and the miracles that the Lord worked through him have been written some time ago; rather, we have picked, as it were, from a field of flowers those we have judged the more beautiful. We are not following a chronological order, and are omitting many things which have already been related eloquently and accurately in other legends already mentioned." Be this a rhetorical expression, a gesture of humility, or an honest declaration of what would have followed the original letter, it raises serious questions. In point of fact, the text of *The Legend of the Three Companions* forms a *legend,* that is, a life to be read, one presented in a chronological order.[17]

Some have argued in favor of placing this controversial letter as an introduction to the information sent to Crescentius of Iesi in 1246.[18] Were it not for a simple observation of Desbonnets, that judgment would seem correct. The fact is, he notes, none of the manuscripts of *The Legend of the Three Companions* omits the letter.[19] This phenomenon raises more questions: was the letter attached only to this text or to some other text? Or, was the letter attached to the legend much later? If so, for what reason? The answers continue to evade scholars.

As already noted, Causse's study clearly identifies the strong dependency of *The Legend of the Three Companions* on the earlier texts of Thomas of Celano and *The Anonymous of Perugia.*[20] Making the same observation, Jacques Dalarun proposes a three-fold breakdown of the text: one third taken from *The Life of Saint Francis* by Thomas of Celano, another from *The Anonymous of Perugia,* and another from an unknown earlier source.[21] Both men maintain that the "three companions" use passages from Thomas of Celano's work which they shorten, refine, or clarify, and, at the same time, take passages from *The Anonymous of Perugia* which, for the most part, they refine but do not change. In the first instance, the "companions" seem intent on clarifying the record set down by Thomas of Celano, such as information concerning Francis's youth and conversion. This material Thomas of Celano later incorporates into his second portrait of the saint. In the second instance, the authors tweak the data of the *The Anonymous of Perugia* either to clarify or to examine it from a different perspective.[22]

The Legend of the Three Companions provides insights into Francis, his youth, struggles with his father, and the emerging consciousness of his call that Thomas of Celano and the author of *The Anonymous of Perugia* do not have. In addition to his behavior while in a Peruguian prison (L3C 4), *The Legend of the Three Companions* tells of Francis's central place among his friends, both as their prodigal host and as their fun-loving leader (L3C 7). The scene before the Crucifix of San Damiano (L3C 13), as well as Pietro di Bernardone's appeal to the civil authorities of Assisi (L3C 19) are introduced, adding to the drama unfolding between son and father. And Francis's enigmatic "precursor" is brought into the story, who anticipated the saint by walking through Assisi's streets crying *"Pax et bonum!"* (L3C 26) When this new information is examined together with the nuances added to both *The Life of Saint Francis* and *The Anonymous of Perugia,* the role of those intimately involved in Francis's life, possibly from Assisi itself, becomes clear.

It may well be that the rubric attributing this text to "three companions of blessed Francis" and the letter introducing it were added to bolster its authority. Since the earlier remembrances of John of Perugia, as found in *The Anonymous of Perugia,* remain more or less intact, singling him out as a companion of Giles and associated with Bernard is significant. John's contributions add to the historical veracity of the legend and root it firmly in the tradition of Francis's companions. From this perspective, *The Legend of The Three Companions* emerges as a companion piece of *The Anonymous of Perugia,* both aiming at retelling the story of the evolution of the primitive fraternity. Nevertheless, the two texts examine the events from different perspectives: *The Anonymous of Perugia* embraces Francis and his first companions collectively, while *The Legend of the Three Companions* focuses on Francis himself, the founder of the fraternity.

Notes

1. He was a native of Iesi in the Marches of Ancona and elected at a general chapter in Genoa, May 22, 1244. Crescentius had been provincial minister of the Marches; perhaps Verona is a copyist's error for Ancona.
2. Thomas of Eccleston, ChrTE 33.
3. As minister of the Marches, Crecentius had difficulties with "zealous" friars who did not want to accommodate themselves to current directions in the Order and therefore refused to obey his commands. He apparently lodged a complaint about this to those friars of the general chapter who shared their views.
4. A reference to the guardian of the Old Testament Esther.
5. Cf. *Chronica XXIV Generalium,* AF III, 262.
6. Cf. Engelbert Grau, "Thomas of Celano: Life and Work," GR 8 (1994): 187.

7. Paul Sabatier, *Life of Saint Francis,* translated by Louise Seymour Houghton (New York: Charles Scribner's Sons: 1906), 374, 378.

8. "Appendix inedita ad *'Vitam primam,'* auctoribus tribus ipsius sancti Francisci sociis," *Acta Sanctorum,* Octobris, t. II, 723-742.

9. François Van Ortroy, "La Légende de S. François d'Assise dite *'Legenda trium sociorum,'*" *Analecta Bollandiana* 19 (1900): 119-197.

10. Only the manuscript preserved in the Friary of Saint Isidore in Rome, codex 1/25, comes from the first half of the fouteenth century, two others come from the second half of that century. The majority of the remaining manuscripts come from the fifteenth century.

11. The Sarnano manuscript, cod E n 60, was discovered by Giuseppe Abate in 1939 in the Biblioteca Commune of Sarnano, Italy, and was missing the last two chapters, paragraphs 68 to 73 of the present edition. Cf. Giuseppe Abbate, "Nuovi studi sulla Legenda di S. Francesco dette dei 'tre compagni,'" *Miscellanea Franciscana* 39 (1939): 645. The other two manuscripts, those of Barcelona, Biblioteca Central, Cod. 665, and of Fribourg, Bibliothèque des Cordeliers, Cod. 23 J 60, come much later, 1405 and 1406. Cf. Théophile Desbonnets, "*Legenda trium Sociorum:* Edition critique," AFH 67 (1974): 38-144.

12. Théophile Desbonnets, "*La Légende des trois compagnons.* Nouvelles recherches sur la généalogie des biographies primitives de saint François," AFH 65 (1972): 66-106.

13. Sophronius Clasen, *Die Dreigefährtenlegende des heilgen Franziskus* (Werl: 1972), 1-168.

14. Théophile Desbonnets, "*Legenda trium Sociorum:* Edition critique," AFH 67 (1974): 38-144.

15. Maurice Causse, "Des Sources Primitives de *La Legende des Trois Compagnons,*" CF 68/3-4 (1998): 469-491.

16. The request of the General Chapter of Genoa is known only from this letter, although Arnald of Sarrant described it in 1365 in his *Chronicle of the Twenty-four Generals.* Arnald of Sarrant, "Chronica generalium ministrorum ordinis fratrum minorum cum pluribus appendicibus inter quas excellit hucusque ineditus *Liber de laudibus s. Francisci* fr. Bernardi a Bessa," AF III, 1-575.

17. This became a central issue in the debate between Sabatier and Van Ortroy. On the one hand Sabatier argued that L3C, in its present state, is only a fragment of the original. Van Ortroy dismissed Sabatier's thesis completely and, because he found no logical connection between the Legend and the Letter, dismissed the L3C.

18. For example, *Scripta Leonis, Rufini et Angeli Sociorum S. Francisci: The Writings of Leo, Rufino and Angelo, Companions of St. Francis,* edited and translated by Rosalind B. Brooke (Oxford: The Clarendon Press, 1970). Brooke offers an explanation for her insertion of this letter on pages 69-72.

19. Only the manuscript of the Vatican 7339 and that of Barcelona 665 omit the letter. It must be remembered that the Sarnano manuscript has the initial pages missing, although some scholars believe that it was also present in that manuscript. Cf. Luigi Pellegrini, "Introduzione," "Legenda Trium Sociorum," *Fontes Franciscani,* a cura di E. Menestò, S. Brufani, G. Cremascoli, E. Paoli, L. Pellegrini, Stanislao da Campagnola. Apparato critico di G.M. Boccali (Sta. Maria degli Angeli: Edizioni Portiuncula, 1995),1361.

20. Causse, Sources Primitives 469-475.

21. Jacques Dalarun, *La Malavventura,* 130-140.

22. An example of the *Legend's* attempt at clarification can be found in the description of Francis's proposal to join the count in Apulia. AP 5 states: *disposuit ad comitem gentilem . . . proficisci* [he arranged to join up with a noble count]; L3C 5 changes the adjective *gentile* to a proper name, Gentile, i.e., *quidam comes Gentilis nomine* [a certain count, Gentile by name]. On the other hand, while AP 31 describes Francis proposing to *eis* [them] to go to Rome for approval of their way of life, L3C 46 states: *Dixit illis undecim, ipse duodecimus dux et pater eorum* [he said to the eleven, he being the twelfth, their leader and father]. Thus L3C is more precise in identifying Francis's position but sensitive to avoiding any Christological comparison by pointing out that he is one of the twelve.

The Legend of Three Companions

[Rubric][a]

These are certain writings of three companions of blessed Francis about his life and manner of living while he was in the attire of the world, about his marvelous and perfect conversion, and about the perfection of the origin and foundation of the Order in him and in the first brothers.

[Letter][b]

[1]To the Reverend Father in Christ, Brother Crescentius, by the grace of God General Minister,[c] Brother Leo,[d] Brother Rufino,[e] and

a. This translation is based on the critical edition of Théophile Desbonnets, "*Legenda Trium Sociorum:* Edition Critique," AFH 67 (1974): 38-144. This title or rubric, missing in some of the manuscripts, is a synthesis of L3C. It suggests that the document ends with Chapter Sixteen. The last two chapters, which treat of the stigmata and the death of Francis, clearly break with the preceding chapters, and seem to have been added at a later date.

b. Rosalind B. Brooke argues that this letter belongs more appropriately at the beginning of the "flowers" sent by Leo, Angelo, and Rufino and, therefore, places it at the beginning of her edition of that information, *Scripta Leonis, Rufini et Angeli Sociorum S. Francisci: The Writings of Leo, Rufino and Angelo, Companions of St. Francis*, translated and edited by Rosalind B. Brooke, (Oxford: Oxford at The Clarendon Press, 1970), 69-70. Persuasive as her arguments may be, the letter is found only in the manuscripts of the *Legend of the Three Companions*, cf. Desbonnets, Edition Critique, 86-89.

Since the end of the thirteenth or beginning of the fourteenth century, this letter has been traditionally attached to the beginning of L3C. The letter was meant to accompany material sent in response to the request of the General Chapter of Genoa articulated by Crescentius of Iesi for more information about Francis. According to this letter, the companions intended not to write a life but to make contributions, previously unpublished, that "gather some of the more beautiful flowers . . . from a pleasant meadow." However, it is clearly at odds with a document that follows a strict chronological order. Scholars are not in agreement about where the material that accompanied this letter is actually found, cf. AC, Introduction, infra 114.

c. Crescentius of Iesi (1244-47), formerly provincial minister of the Marches of Ancona, was elected general minister after the death of Haymo of Faversham. He was elected at the Chapter of Genoa in 1244, held the position until 1247, and died in 1262.

d. Leo appears throughout Franciscan literature as the confessor, secretary, and constant companion of Francis. Arnaldo Fortini notes that AC and the *Mirror of Perfection* (hereafter 1 or 2 MP) identify Leo as coming from Assisi but observes: "the only Leo in Assisi records is a Domino Leone—a title sometimes used for priests—who is mentioned in one of the documents dealing with the liberation of serfs" (*Archivum Cathedrale*, fasc. 8, no. 3). "This," Fortini concludes, "is perhaps our Brother Leo." Cf. Arnaldo Fortini, *Francis*, 324. Leo spent his last years in Assisi where Salimbene, James of Massa, and Angelo of Clareno visited him. He died in Assisi in 1278 and is buried near the tomb of Saint Francis.

e. Brother Rufino was a cousin of Clare of Assisi. Although there is no record of the date of his entrance into the Order, Thomas of Eccleston maintains he was at La Verna in 1224, cf. ChrTE 13. Rufino spent most of his years in the Carceri where he died in 1270. He is buried near the tomb of Saint Francis in Assisi.

Brother Angelo,[a] one-time companions, although unworthy, of the blessed father Francis, express their dutiful and devout reverence in the Lord.

By command of the last general chapter, and of yourself, the brothers are bound to forward to Your Paternity such signs and wonders of our blessed father Francis which they know or can ascertain. We who, though unworthy, lived for a long time in his company, thought it opportune to recount truthfully to Your Holiness a few of his many deeds. We ourselves have seen or heard about them from other holy brothers, in particular from Brother Philip, the Visitator of the Poor Ladies,[b] Brother Illuminato of Arce,[c] Brother Masseo of Marignano,[d] and a companion of the venerable father, Brother Giles, Brother John,[e] who gathered these things from that holy Brother Giles, and from Brother Bernard of blessed memory, the first companion of blessed Francis.

We[f] do not intend merely to relate miracles, which demonstrate, //1C 70
but do not cause sanctity. Our intention is to point out some striking aspects of his holy manner of life and the intention of his pious desires, for the praise and glory of almighty God and of the holy father Francis, and for the edification of those who desire to follow in his footsteps.

We do not intend to write a legend, since other legends about his life and the miracles that the Lord worked through him have been written some time ago; rather, we have picked, as it were, from a field of flowers those we have judged the more beautiful. We are not following a chronological order, and are omitting many things which have already been related eloquently and accurately in other legends already mentioned.

---

a. The identity of Angelo is controversial. Whereas Fortini argues that this was Angelo of Rieti, the same friar who was present at the Process of Canonization of Clare (cf. *Process*, Introduction), others argue that this was Angelo Tancredi, a knight of Assisi and one of Francis's first twelve followers. For a discussion of his identity and different positions, see Brooke, *Scripta*, 11-12.

b. For information on Brother Philip, cf. FA:ED I 204 c.

c. Illuminato was a native of Arce, a district of Assisi on the plain near the Portiuncula. He entered the fraternity about 1210 and, according to an old tradition, died about 1266 either in Assisi or Toulouse. Cf. Omer Englebert, *Saint Francis of Assisi: A Biography*, 2d ed., trans. Eve Marie Cooper, revised and augmented by Ignatius Brady and Raphael Brown (Chicago: Franciscan Herald Press, 1965), 434.

d. According to Fortini, Masseo was born in Marignano not far from Assisi, joined Francis in 1210 and frequently traveled with him. He also spent much of his later life in the Carceri and at the Hermitage of Cibóttola, west of Perugia. He died in Assisi in 1280 and is also buried near the tomb of Saint Francis in Assisi. Arnaldo Fortini, *Nova Vita di San Francesco* (Assisi: Tipografia Porziuncola, 1959) II, 298; III, 461.

e. Because of his closeness to Br. Giles, John of Perugia is considered the "anonymous" of Perugia.

f. Passages or paragraphs reflecting those of earlier texts, in this instance 1C in FA:ED I 180-308, will be indicated by //. Verbatim reliance on these earlier texts will be indicated by a simple cross reference, the text will be in an emboldened font.

If you deem it expedient, you may insert these few things we have written into the other legends. For we believe that if these things had been known to the venerable men who wrote those legends, they would in no way have passed them by; rather they would have embellished them with their own polished style as best they could, and thus transmitted them to posterity.

May your Paternity always be well in the Lord Jesus Christ, in whom we commend ourselves to your holiness as your devoted sons.

Given at Greccio, August 11, in the year of Our Lord 1246.

Chapter I[a]

His Birth, Vanity, Frivolity and Prodigality, how he became generous and charitable to the poor

[2]Francis was raised in the city of Assisi, which is located in the //1C 1
boundaries of the valley of Spoleto. His mother at first called him John; but when his father, who had been away when he was born, returned from France, he later named him Francis.

When he grew up, endowed with clever natural abilities, he pursued his father's profession, that of a merchant. He was, however, vastly different from his father. He was more good-natured and generous, given over to revelry and song with his friends, roaming day and night throughout the city of Assisi. He was most lavish in spending, so much so that all he could possess and earn was squandered on feasting and other pursuits.

Because of this his parents often reprimanded him, telling him that he spent so much money on himself and others that he seemed to be the son of some great prince rather than their son. But since his parents were wealthy and loved him very much, they tolerated all these things to avoid upsetting him. When neighbors commented on his extravagance, his mother replied: "What do you think of my son? He will still be a son of God through grace."

He was lavish, indeed prodigal, not only in these things, but also in spending more money on expensive clothes than his social position warranted. He was so vain in seeking to stand out that some-

a. Some manuscripts (Foligno, Sarnano) begin the text of L3C with the following prologue: "Francis was seen to rise as a kind of new light, resplendent as the dawn and as the morning star, or even as the rising sun, setting the world alight, cleansing it, and giving it fertility. Like the sun, he shone by his words and works upon a world lying torpid amid winter's cold, darkness and sterility, lighting it up with radiant sparks, illuminating it with the rays of truth, and setting it afire with charity, renewing and embellishing it with the abundant fruit of his merits, and enriching it wonderfully with various fruit-bearing trees in the three Orders he founded. Thus did he bring the world to a kind of season of spring."

times he had the most expensive material sewed together with the cheapest cloth onto the same garment.

[3]He was naturally courteous in manner and speech and, following his heart's intent, never uttered a rude or offensive word to anyone. Moreover, since he was such a light-hearted and undisciplined youth, he proposed to answer back those speaking to him rarely in a brusque manner. His reputation, because of this, became so widespread throughout almost the entire region, that many who knew him said that, in the future, he would be something great.

From these stepping stones of natural strengths, he was brought to that grace that prompted him to look within himself: "You are generous and courteous to those from whom you receive nothing except passing and worthless approval. Is it not right that, on account of God who repays most generously, you should be courteous and generous to the poor?" From that day he looked on poor people generously and provided them affluently with alms. Although a merchant, he was a very **flamboyant squanderer** of wealth.

AP 3; //1C 2

AP 4; //1C 17

One day when he was in the shop where he was selling **cloth, totally absorbed in business** of this sort, **a poor man** came in, begging **alms** for the love of God. Preoccupied with thoughts **of wealth** and **the care** of business, he did not give him **alms. Touched by divine grace,** he accused himself **of great rudeness,** saying: "If that **poor** man **had asked** something from you **for a great count or baron,** you would certainly have granted him his request. **How much more should you have done this for the King of kings and the Lord of all!"**

Because of this incident, he resolved in his heart, from then on, not to deny **a request to anyone asking in the name of so great a Lord.**

Chapter II

How he was imprisoned in Perugia and the two visions he had while he wanted to become a knight

[4]At that time, war broke out between Perugia and Assisi.[a] Together with many of his fellow citizens, Francis was captured and

a. The war between Assisi and Perugia lasted intermittently from 1202 to 1209. It was sparked when Assisi's popular class rose against the noble class, which in turn sought assistance from Perugia. Francis was captured in a battle that seems to have occurred in 1202, in the vicinity of Collestrada and Ponte San Giovanni, several miles from Perugia. On August 31, 1205, a fragile peace was reached, after prisoners had already been freed in 1203. Francis would have been in prison about a year. Cf. Fortini, *Francis,* 151ff.

confined in Perugia, yet, because of his noble manners, he was imprisoned with the knights.

One time when his fellow prisoners were depressed, he, who was naturally cheerful and jovial, not only was not dejected but actually seemed to be happy. One of the prisoners rebuked him as insane for being cheerful in prison. Francis replied vigorously: "What do you think will become of me? Rest assured, I will be worshiped throughout the whole world."

One of the knights who was imprisoned with him had injured a fellow prisoner, causing all the others to ostracize him. Francis alone not only acted in a friendly way toward him, but also urged the other prisoners to do the same.

After a year, when peace was restored between those cities, Francis and his fellow prisoners returned to Assisi.

5 A few years later, a nobleman from the city of Assisi was preparing himself with knightly arms to go to Apulia in order to increase his wealth and fame. When Francis learned of this, he yearned to go with him to that same place, and to be knighted by that count, Gentile by name.[a] He prepared clothing as expensive as possible, since even though he was poorer in riches than his fellow citizen, he was far more extravagant. 1C 4; AP 5

He was completely preoccupied in carrying this out, and was burning with desire to set out, when, one night, the Lord visited him in a dream. Knowing his desire for honors, He enticed and lifted him to the pinnacle of glory by a vision. That night while he was sleeping, someone appeared to him, a man *calling* him *by name*. He led him into a beautiful bride's elegant palace filled with knightly arms and on its walls hung glittering shields and other armor of knightly splendor.[b] Overjoyed, he wondered what all this meant and asked to whom these brightly shining arms and this beautiful palace belonged. He was told that all these, including the palace, belonged to him and his knights. (Gn 4:17)

Awakening in the morning, he got up with great joy. Since he had not yet fully tasted the spirit of God, he thought in a worldly way that he must be singled out magnificently, and he considered the vision a portent of future good fortune. He resolved then to undertake the journey to Apulia to be knighted by the count. He was even more cheerful than usual, prompting many people to wonder. When they

a. Cf. AP 5, p. 36 a. L3C 5 changes the adjective, *gentile*, into a proper name, Gentile.

b. L3C 5 describes Francis's dream as a consequence of his decision to join the Count Gentile. This inverts the order found in AP 5. Further, L3C 5 introduces the image of the beautiful bride, a phrase not found in many of the manuscripts of this text. This may be an allusion to 1C 7.

asked him the reason why he was beaming with joy, he answered: "I know that I will become a great prince."

[6]The day before the vision occurred, the promise of great chivalry and nobility was so strong in him, that it may be believed that the vision itself may have provided the motive. On that day, in fact, he donated all the refined and expensive clothes he had recently acquired to a poor knight.

AP 6 **When** he set out for Apulia, he got as far as **Spoleto,** where he began to feel a little ill. No less anxious about the trip, as he was falling to sleep, half awake, he heard someone asking him where he wanted to go. When Francis **revealed to him his entire plan,** the other said: **"Who can do more good for you? The lord or the servant?"** When [Francis] answered **him: "The lord,"** he again said to him: **"Then why are you abandoning the lord for the servant, the patron for the client?"** And **Francis** said: ***"Lord, what do you want*** *me* ***to do?" "Go back*** Acts 9:6; Gn 32:9
to your land," he said, ***"and what you are to do will be told to you.*** You must Acts 9:7
understand in another way the vision which you saw."

When he woke up, he began to think very carefully about this vision. Just as the first vision had caused him to be almost completely carried away with great joy in a desire for worldly prosperity, the second made him completely introspective, causing him to marvel at and consider its strength, so that he was unable to sleep any more that night.

AP 7 Therefore **when it was morning,** buoyant and happy, **he** quickly **returned** to Assisi, expecting that the Lord, who had revealed these things to him, would show him His will and give him counsel about
IC 6 salvation. **Changed in mind, he now refused to go to Apulia** and desired to conform completely to the divine will.

Chapter III

How the Lord visited Francis's heart for the first time filling it with marvelous tenderness that gave him strength to begin to progress spiritually in looking down on himself and all vanities, in prayer, almsgiving, and poverty

[7]A few days after he returned to Assisi, one evening his friends chose him to be in charge so that, according to his whim, he would pay their expenses. He made arrangements for a sumptuous banquet, as he had done so often in the past.

When they left the house bloated, his friends walked ahead of him, singing throughout the city. Holding in his hand the scepter of his office as their leader, he fell slightly behind them.[a] He was not singing, but was deeply preoccupied. Suddenly he was visited by the Lord who filled his heart with so much tenderness that he was unable to speak or move. He could only feel and hear this marvelous tenderness; it left him so estranged from any sensation that, as he himself said later, even if he had been completely cut to pieces, he would not have been able to move.

When his companions glanced back and saw him so removed
1 Sm 10:6 from them, they went back surprised at seeing him already *changed into another man.* They asked him: "What were you thinking about that you did not follow us? Were you perhaps thinking about taking a wife?"

He answered in an unequivocal voice: "You are right! I was think- 1C 7
ing **about taking a wife more noble, wealthier, and more beautiful**
Mt 9:24; Lk 16:14; 23:35 **than you have ever seen."** *They laughed at him.* For he said this not of his own accord, but because he was inspired by God. In fact, the bride was the true religion that he later embraced, a bride more noble, richer and more beautiful because of her poverty.[b]

8 From that very hour **he began to consider himself of little value** 1C 4
and to despise those things **which he had previously held in love.** Since he was not entirely detached from worldly vanities, this
change was not yet perfect. **He retired for a short time from the tu-** 1C 6
mult and business of the world and was anxious to keep Jesus Christ in his inmost self, and, *after selling all he had,* **he desired to buy** *the pearl,* **concealing it from the eyes of mockers.** Often, almost daily, he withdrew secretly to pray. He was inclined to do so by that same tenderness he had tasted earlier, which now visited him ever more frequently, driving him to prayer in the piazza and in other public places.

Although he had been for some time a benefactor of the poor, **he** 1C 17
Ps 14:1; Acts 5:4 proposed *in his heart,* from then on, **never to deny** alms to any poor person **begging from him for God's sake,** but rather to give more willingly and abundantly than usual. When away from home, if he could, he always gave money to any poor person requesting alms. If he had no money, he gave him his hat or belt, making sure never to send him away empty-handed. If he lacked even these things, he would go to a deserted place, take off his shirt, and give it to the poor

a. Fortini believes that this is a reference to the celebration of the second patron of Assisi, Saint Victorinus, for which the Compagnia di San Vittorino, or the Compagnia del Bastone, was organized. Its leader carried a large staff to show his office and, on the day of his election, his companions swore him allegiance by touching his staff. Cf. Fortini, *Francis,* 132.

b. Although this is a reference to 1C 7, L3C underscores the identity of the noble, richer bride as being such because of poverty.

man, begging him to take it for the love of God. He would even purchase furnishings for adorning churches, and would secretly send them to poor priests.

[9]When his father was away and he was at home alone with his mother, although only two of them took their meals, he filled the table with loaves of bread as if he were preparing for an entire family. When his mother asked why he put so much food on the table, he answered that it would be *given as alms* for the poor, since he had resolved to give to anyone begging alms for God's sake. Because his mother loved him more than the other children, she tolerated him in such matters, noticing the things he did and admiring in his heart many more. Lk 6:30

For he was so accustomed to setting his heart on joining his companions when they called him, and was so captivated by their company, that he would frequently leave the table even if he had eaten only a little. In this way he would upset his parents by his thoughtless flight. Now, however, his whole heart was intent on seeing the poor, listening to them, and giving them alms.

[10]He was so changed by divine grace that, although he was still in secular attire, he yearned to be in another city where, as someone unknown, he would take off his own clothes and, in exchange, put on the rags of a poor man. And he would try begging alms for the love of God.

At this time he happened to go to Rome on pilgrimage. As he was entering the church of Saint Peter,[a] he noticed the meager offerings made by some, and said to himself: "Since the Prince of the Apostles should be greatly honored, why do they make such meager offerings in the church where his body rests?" With great enthusiasm, he took a handful of coins from his money pouch, and threw them through a grating of the altar, making such a loud noise that all the bystanders were astonished at his generosity.

As he was leaving and passed the doors of the church, where there were many poor people begging alms, he secretly exchanged clothes with one of those poor people and put them on. Standing on the steps of the church with the other poor, he begged for alms in French, because he would speak French spontaneously, although he did not do so correctly.[b]

---

a. Pilgrimages to the tomb of Saint Peter in Rome were important events in the Middle Ages. The first recorded pilgrimage was that of Albercius, Bishop of Hierapolis in Phrygia in 216. The church of Saint Peter described in the text was the basilica begun by Constantine c. 324 and completed by his son, Constantius, c. 354. Cf. Jonathan Sumption, *Pilgrimage: An Image of Mediaeval Religion*, (Totowa, NJ: Rowman and Littlefield, 1975), 217-231.

b. For Francis's use of French, see FA:ED I 194b.

After taking off the beggar's clothes and putting on his own, he returned to Assisi, and began to pray that the Lord would direct his way. He did not share his secret with anyone; nor did he seek counsel from anyone, except from God alone, and, periodically, from the bishop of Assisi. For at that time no one possessed the real poverty that he desired more than anything else in this world, in which he yearned to live and die.

Chapter IV
HOW HE BEGAN TO OVERCOME HIMSELF BY HIS DEALING WITH LEPERS, AND TO CONSIDER SWEET WHAT WAS PREVIOUSLY BITTER

[11]One day, while he was praying enthusiastically to the Lord, he received this response: "Francis, everything you loved carnally and desired to have, you must despise and hate, if you wish to know my will. Because once you begin doing this, what before seemed delightful and sweet will be unbearable and bitter; and what before made you shudder will offer you great sweetness and enormous delight."

He was overjoyed at this and was comforted by the Lord. One day he was riding his horse near Assisi, when he met a leper. And, even though he usually shuddered at lepers, he made himself dismount, and gave him a coin, kissing his hand as he did so. After he accepted a kiss of peace from him, Francis remounted and continued on his way. **He then began to consider himself less and less, until,** by 1C 17
God's grace, **he came to complete victory over himself.**

After a few days, he moved to a hospice of lepers, taking with him a large sum of money. Calling them all together, as he kissed the hand of each, he gave them alms. When he left there, what before Test 3
had been bitter, that is, to see and touch lepers, was turned into sweetness. For, as he said, the sight of lepers was so bitter to him, that he refused not only to look at them, but even to approach their dwellings. If he happened to come near their houses or to see them, even though he was moved by piety to give them alms through an intermediary, he always turned away his face and held his nose. With the help of God's grace, he became such a servant and friend of the lepers, that, as he testified in his *Testament,* he stayed among them Test 1-3
and served them with humility.

[12]Changed into good after his visit to the lepers, he would take a companion, whom he loved very much, to secluded places, telling him that he had found a great and precious treasure. **The man was** 1C 6
not a little **overjoyed, and gladly went with him whenever he was summoned.** Francis often led him **to a cave** near Assisi, and, while

he went alone inside, he left his companion outside, eager for the treasure. **Inspired by a new and extraordinary spirit, he would pray to** ***his Father in secret,*** wanting **no one to know what was happening** Mt 6:6
within except **God alone,** whom he consulted about acquiring heavenly treasure.

The enemy of the human race, observing him, strove to lure him from the good he had begun by striking fear and dread in him. There was in Assisi a deformed, hunchbacked woman, whom the devil, appearing to the man of God, recalled to him. He threatened to inflict him with her deformity unless he reneged on the plan he had conceived. But the very brave *knight of Christ,* shunning the devil's 2 Tm 2:3
threats, prayed all the more fervently within the cave that God would direct his path.

1C 6 **He endured great suffering** and mental anxiety, **unable to rest until he accomplished in action what he had conceived in mind. Different thoughts followed one after the other, and their relentlessness disturbed him** even more severely. For **he was burning inwardly with a divine fire, unable to conceal outwardly the flame kindled in his soul. He repented that he had sinned so grievously. While his past and present transgressions no longer delighted him, he was not yet fully confident of refraining from future ones. This is why, when** he emerged from the cave, **he seemed to his companion** to have changed into a different man.

Chapter V

HOW THE CRUCIFIX SPOKE TO HIM FOR THE FIRST TIME AND HOW HE HENCEFORTH CARRIED THE PASSION OF CHRIST IN HIS HEART UNTIL DEATH

1C 7 13 **One day, when** he was more passionately **begging for the Lord's mercy, the Lord showed him** that he would be told in the near future **what he must do.** From that moment on, **he was filled with such great joy, that, failing to restrain himself in the face of happiness, he carelessly mentioned** some of his secrets **to others. He nevertheless spoke cautiously and in riddles, saying that he did not want to go to Apulia, but that** he would accomplish **great and noble deeds at home.**

His companions noticed the change in him, indeed he was already estranged from them in his thoughts, even though he sometimes joined their company. And so they asked him as a joke: **"Francis, do you want to get married?" He replied** to them in a riddle, as we mentioned above.

//1C 8

A few days had passed when, while he was walking by the church of San Damiano, he was told in the Spirit to go inside for a prayer. Once he entered, he began to pray intensely before an image of the Crucified,[a] which spoke to him in a tender and kind voice: "Francis, don't you see that my house is being destroyed? Go, then, and rebuild it for me." Stunned and trembling, he said: "I will do so gladly, Lord." For he understood that it was speaking about that church, which was near collapse because of its age. He was filled with such joy and became so radiant with light over that message, that he knew in his soul that it was truly Christ crucified who spoke to him.

Upon leaving the church, he found a priest sitting nearby[b] and, putting his hands into the pouch, he offered him a handful of coins. "My Lord," he said, "I beg you, buy some oil and keep the light before the Crucified burning continually. When this money runs out, I will again give you as much as you need."

[14]From that hour, therefore, his heart was wounded and it melted when remembering the Lord's passion. While he lived, he always carried the wounds of the Lord Jesus in his heart. This was brilliantly shown afterwards in the renewal of those wounds that were miraculously impressed on and most clearly revealed in his body.

From then on, he inflicted his flesh with such fasting that, whether healthy or sick, the excessively austere man hardly ever or never wanted to indulge his body. Because of this he confessed on his death bed that he had greatly sinned against "Brother Body."

Once he was walking by himself near the church of Saint Mary of the Portiuncula, weeping and wailing loudly. A spiritual man, overhearing him, thought he was suffering some sickness or pain. Moved by piety for him,[c] he asked why he was crying. "I am crying because of the Passion of my Lord," he said, "for whom I should not be ashamed to go throughout the world crying in a loud voice." That man, in fact, likewise began to cry with him in a loud voice.

Frequently, even when he got up from prayer, his eyes seemed full of blood because he was crying with such bitterness. But, in memory of the Lord's passion, not only did he afflict himself in tears, he also did so by abstaining from food and drink.

---

a. At this point, two of the oldest manuscripts of this text, the Barcelona (1405) and Fribourg (1406) manuscripts, present the text of the *Prayer Before the Crucifix* (hereafter PrCr), FA:ED I 40. For information on the Crucifix of San Damiano, which is mentioned for the first time in this passage, see Marc Picard, *The Icon of the Christ of San Damiano* (Assisi: Casa Editrice Francescana, 1989).

b. If this is the priest of San Damiano, AP 7 names him as Peter.

c. For the frequent use of the word *pietas* [piety] and the difficulty of capturing its meaning, cf. FA:ED I 189 c.

[15]Whenever he would eat with seculars, and they would give him some delicious food, he would eat only a little of it, offering some excuse so that it would not seem he was refusing it because of fasting. When he ate with his brothers, he often sprinkled ashes on the food he was eating, telling a brother, as a cover for his abstinence, that "Brother Ash" was chaste.[a]

Once, when he sat down to eat, a brother remarked that the Blessed Virgin was so poor that when it came time to eat, she had nothing to give to her son. When he heard this, the man of God sighed deeply with great sorrow and, after he left the table, he ate bread off the bare ground.

Many times, in fact, having sat down at table, he had barely begun to eat when he would stop eating and drinking, absorbed in meditation on heavenly things. Then he did not want to be disturbed by any conversation. Sighing loudly from the depths of his heart, he would tell the brothers that, whenever they heard him sighing this way, they should always praise God and pray for him faithfully.

We have told these things about his crying and abstinence in an incidental way to show that, after that vision and the message of the image of the Crucified, he was always conformed to the passion of Christ until his death.

Chapter VI

How he escaped from the persecution of his father and relatives, living with the priest at the church of San Damiano where he threw the money on the window

IC 8 [16]Overjoyed by the vision and hearing the words of the Crucified
Christ, he got up, **fortifying himself with the sign of the cross**. And
AP 7 **mounting his horse and** taking **cloth** of different colors, he arrived
at a city named Foligno and, after **selling there** the horse and **everything he was carrying**, he returned immediately to the church of San Damiano.

IC 9 **After he found a poor priest there, he kissed his hands with great faith** and devotion; he **offered him the money he was carrying, and explained his purpose in great detail. The priest, astounded** and surprised **at his sudden conversion, refused to believe** this, and, **thinking he was being mocked, refused to keep his money. But stubbornly persisting, he endeavored to create confidence in his**

a. The Latin text is *fratrem cinerem* [Brother Ash].

words, and he begged the priest more emphatically to allow him to stay with him.

Finally the priest agreed to let him stay but, out of fear of his parents, did not accept the money. And so the true scorner of money, throwing it on a windowsill, cared for it as much as he cared for dust.

While he was staying there, his father, like a diligent spy, went 1C 10; //AP 8
around seeking to learn what might have happened to his son. And when he heard that he was so changed and was living in that place in such a way, he was touched inwardly with sorrow of heart and deeply disturbed by the sudden turn of events. Calling together his friends and neighbors, he ran to him.

Because he was a new knight of Christ, as he heard the threats of his pursuers and knew beforehand of their coming, he left room for his father's anger; and, going to a secret cave[a] which he had prepared for this, he hid there for a whole month. That cave was known to only one person in his father's house. He would eat the food that, from time to time, was secretly brought to him there, praying all the
Ps 142:7 while with flowing tears *that the Lord would free* him from destructive persecution, and that he could favorably fulfill his fervent wishes.

Jl 2:12 [17]And so he begged the Lord relentlessly *in fasting and weeping.* 1C 10
Ps 55:23 Lacking confidence in his own effort and strength, *he cast* his hope completely on the Lord, who filled him with an inexpressible happiness and enlightened him with a marvelous light, even though he still remained in darkness.

Glowing with this inner radiance, after he left the pit, he made his
way to Assisi, lighthearted and happy. Strengthened with Christ's 1C 11
armor of confidence, and burning with divine fervor, he blatantly exposed himself to the threats and blows of his persecutors, accusing himself of laziness and groundless fear.

Those who knew him earlier, seeing him now, reproached him harshly. Shouting that he was insane and out of his mind, they threw mud from the streets and stones at him. For they saw him so changed from his earlier ways and so weakened by starving his body, that they blamed everything he did on starvation and madness. But, as he passed through their midst deaf to all these things, neither broken nor changed by any wrong, the knight of Christ gave thanks to God.

a. The Latin text is *occultam caveam* [hidden cave] which the Sarnano text renders *occulta fovea* [hidden pit]. In the following paragraph, the critical text published by Théophile Desbonnets refers to Francis leaving the *fovea* [pit]. In light of the modern archeological excavations underneath San Damiano, scholars differ on the interpretation of the nature and location of this "cave" or "pit."

1C 12; //AP 8 When rumor of this sort spread *through the streets and quarters of the city,* it finally reached his father. After he heard that the townspeople had done such things to him, he instantly arose to look for him, not to free him, but rather to destroy him. With no restraint, he ran like a wolf after a lamb, and, glaring at him wild-eyed and savagely, he mercilessly took him in tow. Confining him to home and locking him up in a dark prison for several days, he strove, by words and blows, to turn his spirit to the vanities of this world. Sg 3:2

1C 12 18 But, since he was neither moved by words, nor exhausted by chains or blows, he endured all these things patiently, more fit and eager to carry out his holy plan.

1C 13 When his father had to leave home on a pressing need, his mother remained at home alone with him. Since she did not approve of her husband's action, she spoke to her son in gentle words. When she realized she could not dissuade him from his holy intention, moved by her deep feeling for him, she removed the chains, and let him go free.

Thanking Almighty God, he returned to the place where he had been before, now enjoying greater freedom, since he passed the devil's temptations and had been taught by the lessons of temptation. More self-confident because of the injuries he had received, he made his way more freely and with an even greater heart.

In the meantime his father returned, and not finding his son, he turned on his wife in abuse, heaping sin upon sin.

19 Then the father hurried to the palace of the commune complaining to the city magistrates about his son and asking them to make him return the money he had taken from the house. When the magistrates saw how distraught he was, they sent a messenger to summon Francis to appear before them. He told the messenger that he had been made free by God's grace and, since he was a servant of almighty God alone, was no longer bound by the magistrates. The magistrates, unwilling to force the issue, told his father: "Because he is in the service of God, he no longer falls within our power."[a]

Realizing that he could accomplish nothing with the magistrates, he made the same complaint before the bishop of the city. The bishop, a discerning and understanding man, duly called him to appear in order to respond to his father's complaint. [Francis] answered the messenger: "I will appear before the lord bishop, because he is the father and lord of souls."

---

a. In his *Nova Vita di San Francesco*, Fortini notes that, given the nature of his accusations, Pietro was bringing criminal charges against his son. Fortini presents the steps that he took as those outlined in the statutes for bringing criminal proceedings and the course followed by the consuls. Cf. *Fortini, Nova Vita* II, 223-237; also Fortini *Francis*, 222-227.

1C 15; AP 8

Then he came before the bishop and was received by him with great joy. "Your father," the bishop said to him, "is infuriated and extremely scandalized. If you wish to serve God, return to him the money you have, because God does not want you to spend money unjustly acquired on the work of the church. [Your father's] anger will abate when he gets the money back. My son, have confidence in the Lord and act courageously. Do not be afraid, for He will be your help and will abundantly provide you with whatever is necessary for the work of his church."[a]

AP 8

[20]Then the man of God got up, joyful and comforted by the bishop's words, and, as he brought the money to him, he said: "My Lord, I will gladly give back not only the money acquired from his things, but even all my clothes." And going into one of the bishop's rooms, he took off all his clothes, and, putting the money on top of them, came out naked before the bishop, his father, and all the bystanders, and said: "Listen to me, all of you, and understand. Until now I have called Pietro di Bernardone my father. But, because I have proposed to serve God, I return to him the money on account of which he was so upset, and also all the clothing which is his, wanting

Mt 6:9

to say from now on: *'Our Father who are in heaven,'* and not 'My father, Pietro di Bernardone.'" At that moment, the man of God was found to be wearing under his colored clothes a hair shirt next to his skin.

Then his father, overcome with unbearable pain and anger, took the money and all the clothing. While he was carrying these home, those who were present at this spectacle were indignant at him, for he left nothing for his son to wear. Moved by piety, they began to weep over him.

1C 15

The bishop, focusing his attention on the man of God's **frame of mind** and enthusiastically admiring **his fervor and determination, gathered him into his arms,** covering **him with his mantle.** For he **clearly** understood his deeds **were prompted** by divine counsel, and realized that what he had seen **contained** no small **mystery.** And so,

Ps 30:11; Col 3:12

from that moment, ***he became*** his ***helper,*** exhorting, encouraging, loving, and **embracing him with the depths of his charity.**

a. For a thorough discussion of this "trial," see Richard C. Trexler, *Naked Before the Father: The Renunciation of Francis of Assisi, Humana Civilitas:* Sources and Studies Relating to the Middle Ages and Renaissance, vol. 9 (New York: Peter Lang, 1989), 31-69.

Chapter VII
THE HARD WORK AND FATIGUE INVOLVED IN RESTORING THE CHURCH OF SAN DAMIANO AND HOW HE BEGAN TO OVERCOME HIMSELF BY GOING OUT FOR ALMS

1C 15 [21]Therefore, Francis, the servant of God, stripped of **all that is of the world,** is free for **divine justice** and, **despising his own life,** he gives himself to divine service in every way he can.[d]

//AP 8 Returning to the church of San Damiano, joyful and eager, he made a hermit's habit for himself, and comforted the priest of that church with the same words with which the bishop had comforted him.

Then, getting up and going back to the city, he began to praise the Lord throughout the piazzas and neighborhoods, like one inebriated with the Spirit. When he finished praising the Lord in this way, he turned to obtaining stones for the repair of the church. "Whoever gives me one stone," he would say, "will have one reward. Whoever gives me two, will have two rewards. Whoever gives me three, will have that many rewards."

//AP 8 Thus, burning with enthusiasm, he also made many other simple statements. Because he was unlettered and simple,[b] the man chosen by God did not speak in the learned words of human wisdom, but in
//AP 9 everything was quite simple. Many ridiculed him thinking he was mad, while others, prompted by piety, were moved to tears seeing how quickly he had come from such pleasure and worldly vanity to such an intoxication of divine love. Disregarding their scorn, he thanked God with burning enthusiasm.

It would be long and difficult to relate how he worked on the project, for he, who had been very refined in his father's house, hauled stones on his own shoulders, afflicting himself greatly in the service of God.

[22]The priest judged the work to be beyond his strength, even though he was offering himself so enthusiastically to divine service. Although poor himself, he obtained special food for Francis, for he knew that, while he was in the world, he had lived rather delicately. Of course, as the man of God later admitted, he would frequently enjoy delicacies and sweets, and refrain from disagreeable foods.

---

d. The author momentarily breaks his historical narrative style by moving into the present tense.

b. This description of Francis as *idiota et simplex* [unlettered and simple] reflects Francis's own way of speaking of himself, cf. *A Letter to the Entire Order* 13 (hereafter LtOrd), Test 29. The phrase occurs exactly as it appears in this text in *True and Perfect Joy* 11 (hereafter TPJ).

One day, when he noticed what the priest was preparing for him, he said to himself: "Will you find a priest like this wherever you go who will offer you such human kindness? This is not the life of the poor that you have chosen. As a beggar, going from door to door, you should carry a bowl in your hand, and, driven by necessity, you should collect the scraps they give you. This is how you must live willingly, out of love for him who was born poor, lived very poorly in this world, remained naked and poor on the cross, and was buried in a tomb belonging to another."

As a result, one day he took a bowl and, entering the city, he went door-to-door begging alms. Whenever he put various scraps in his bowl, many who knew what a pampered life he had lived were astonished at how marvelously changed he was, seeing that he held himself in such contempt. But when he wanted to eat the mixed food offered him, he felt revulsion because he was not accustomed not only to eating such things, but even at looking at them. At last overcoming himself, he began to eat, and it seemed to him that no delicacy had ever tasted so delicious.

Then his heart rejoiced in the Lord so much that his flesh, although weak and afflicted, was strong enough to endure joyfully for the Lord anything harsh or bitter. Above all, he gave thanks to God that He had changed the bitter into the sweet, and that He had comforted him in so many ways. Then he told the priest not to prepare or obtain any food for him in the future.

[23]When his father saw him in such disgrace, he was filled with unusual pain. Because he loved him dearly, he was ashamed and felt great sorrow for him. Seeing his flesh half-dead from excessive affliction and cold, he would curse him whenever he came upon him. //AP 9

Aware of his father's curses, the man of God chose a poor and looked-down-upon man to take the place of his father,[a] and told him: "Come with me, and I will give you some of the alms that were given to me. When you see my father cursing me, I will also say to you: 'Bless me, father.' You will then make the sign of the cross over me, and bless me in his place." The next time this happened and the beggar was blessing him, the man of God said to his father: "Don't you believe that God can give me a father to bless me against your curses?"

Afterwards, many of those who mocked him and saw how patiently he endured every abuse marveled with great astonishment. One winter morning, while he was at prayer, dressed in poor clothes,

a. AP 9 names this beggar Alberto.

his carnal brother was passing by,[a] and remarked sarcastically to his companion: "You might tell Francis to sell you a penny's worth of his sweat." When the man of God heard this, filled with a wholesome joy, he answered enthusiastically in French: "I will sell that sweat to my Lord at a high price."

24While he was working steadily at restoring the church, he wanted to have a lamp burning continually in the church, so he went through the city begging for oil. But when he was approaching a certain house, he saw a group of men gathered for a game. Ashamed to beg in front of them, he backed away. Mulling it over, he accused himself of having sinned. Hurrying back to the place where they were playing, he told everyone standing around his fault, that he was ashamed to beg because of them. And, in fervor of spirit, he entered that house and, for the love of God, begged in French for oil for the lamps of that church.

While laboring with others in that work, he used to cry to passers-by in a loud voice, filled with joy, saying in French: "Come and help me in the work of the church of San Damiano which, in the future, will be a monastery of ladies through whose fame and life our heavenly Father will be glorified throughout the church."[b]

See how, filled with the spirit of prophecy, he truly foretold the fu-
1C 18 ture! **For this is that sacred place where the glorious religion and most excellent Order of Poor Ladies and** sacred **virgins had its happy beginning about six years after the conversion of blessed**
1C 20 **Francis and through the same blessed** Francis. **Their wondrous life and renowned practices** were fully approved **by the Lord Pope Gregory** IX, of holy memory, **at that time the Bishop of Ostia,** and confirmed by the authority of the Apostolic See.[c]

---

a. Basing his arguments on the research of Arnaldo and Gemma Fortini, and Leone Bracaloni, Trexler argues that this is Angelo, who was actually Francis's half-brother, the son of Pica by an earlier marriage. Cf. Trexler, *Naked Before the Father*, 7-21.

b. The manuscripts of Barcelona, Fribourg, and Sarnano all state: " . . . the monastery of San Damiano in which there will be handmaids of Christ the Lord through whose fame and deeds . . . " These manuscripts are thus more in accord with Clare's own *Testament*, cf. Clare of Assisi, *Testament* 13-14, in *Clare of Assisi: Early Documents*, trans. and ed. Regis J. Armstrong (St. Bonaventure: Franciscan Institute Press, 1993), 57.

c. Cf. "Form and Manner of Life," in *Clare of Assisi: Early Documents*, 89-100. Pope Gregory IX died on August 22, 1241, that is, before at least this part of the text was written.

Chapter VIII
Hearing and Understanding the Counsels of Christ in the Gospel, He Immediately Changed His External Garb and Put on a New Habit of Internal and External Perfection

[25]While he was completing the church of San Damiano, blessed LJS 15
Francis wore **the habit of a hermit: a staff in his hand, shoes on his feet, and a leather belt around his waist.**
Then, **one day at Mass, he heard those things which Christ tells** the disciples **who were sent out to preach,** instructing them to carry no
Mt 10:9-10; Lk 9:3; 10:4 *gold* or *silver, a wallet* or *a purse, bread, walking stick,* or *shoes,* or *two tunics.*
After **understanding this more clearly because of the priest, he was filled with indescribable joy. "This," he said, "is what** I want to do with **all** my strength."

And so, after committing to memory **everything he had heard, he joyfully fulfilled them,** removed his second garment without delay,
Mt 10:9-10 and from then on **never used** ***a walking stick, shoes, purse,*** **or** ***wallet.*** He made for himself a very **cheap and plain tunic,** and, throwing the belt away, he girded himself with a cord.

Applying all the care of his heart to observe the words **of new grace as much as possible,** he began, inspired by God, to be a messenger of evangelical perfection and, in simple words, to preach penance in public. His words were **neither hollow nor ridiculous, but filled with the power of the Holy Spirit, penetrating the marrow of the heart,** so that listeners were turned to great **amazement.**

[26]**As he later testified, he learned a greeting of this sort by the** 1C 23; //LJS 16; T
Nm 6:26; 2 Thes 3:16 **Lord's revelation:** ***"May the Lord give you peace!"*** Therefore, **in all his preaching, he greeted the people at the beginning** of his sermon **with a proclamation of peace.**

It is certainly astonishing, if not miraculous, that this greeting of peace was used before his conversion by a precursor who frequently went through Assisi greeting the people with "Peace and good! Peace and good!"[a] It seems plausible that, as John heralded Christ but withdrew when Christ began his mission of preaching, so too, like another John, this man preceded Francis in using the greeting of peace, but disappeared when he appeared.

Immediately, therefore, filled with the spirit of the prophets, the LJS 16
man of God, Francis, after that greeting, **proclaimed peace,**

a. The Latin text reads *Pax et bonum* [Peace and good], a difficult phrase offering a variety of interpretations. *Bonum* [good] could refer to "good things" or to a state of well-being. If it is indeed Francis who is using this greeting, a point which is not clear from this text, then *bonum* [good] would refer to the very source of all good, God, the Good, cf. PrsG 3.

preached salvation, and, according to a prophetic passage, **by his salutary admonitions**, brought **to true peace** many **who had previously lived at odds with Christ and far from salvation.**

LJS 17 [27]**As both the truth of blessed Francis's simple teaching as well as that of his life became known to many,** two years after his con-
AP 10 version, **some men began to be moved to do penance by his example**[a] **and, leaving all things, they joined him in life and habit.** The first of these was Brother Bernard of holy memory.[b]

He knew well how luxuriously blessed Francis had lived in the world; now he observed his constancy and zeal in the divine service, how, in particular, he was restoring dilapidated churches with a great deal of work, and what an austere life he was leading. He planned wholeheartedly to give everything he possessed to the poor, and, with determination, to join him in life and garb.

Therefore, one day approaching the man of God in secret, he disclosed his plan to him, and arranged to have him come that evening to his home. Thanking God, for he did not then have a companion, blessed Francis was overjoyed, especially since Lord Bernard was a person of great stature.

[28]On the appointed evening, blessed Francis came to his house, his heart filled with great joy, and spent that whole night with him. Among many things, Lord Bernard said to him: "If, for many years, someone holds on to the possessions, many or few, he has acquired
//AP 10 from his lord, and no longer wishes to keep them, what is the better thing for him to do with them?" Blessed Francis answered that he must give back to the lord what was received from him. And Lord Bernard said: "Then, brother, I want to give away all my worldly goods for the love of my Lord who gave them to me, as it seems best to you." The saint told him: "We will go to the church early in the morning and, through the book of the Gospels, we will learn how the Lord instructed his disciples."

//AP 10 Rising at daybreak, then, together with another man named Peter, who also wanted to become a brother, they went to the church of San Nicolò next to the piazza of the city of Assisi.[c] They entered for prayer, but, because they were simple, they did not know how to find the passage in the Gospel about renunciation. They prayed devoutly that the Lord would show them his will on opening the book the first time.

---

a. AP 10 mentions only two—not some or several—men, Bernard and Peter.

b. Bernard died between 1241 and 1246, that is, sometime before at least this passage was written. Cf. Fortini, *Nova Vita* II, 273-276.

c. The Church of San Nicolò, the patron of merchants, was erected about the year 1000 in the Mercato or Market Square of Assisi.

[29]Once they had finished prayer, blessed Francis took the closed book and, kneeling before the altar, opened it.[a] At its first opening, //AP 11
Mk 10:21 the Lord's counsel confronted them: *If you wish to be perfect, go, sell everything you possess and give to the poor, and you will have a treasure in heaven.*

Blessed Francis was overjoyed when he read this passage and thanked God. But since he was a true worshiper of the Trinity, he desired it to be confirmed by a threefold affirmation. He opened the book a second and a third time. When he opened it up the second
Lk 9:3 time he saw: *Take nothing for your journey,* etc., and at the third opening:
Mt 16:24 *If any man wishes to come after me, he must deny himself,* etc.

Each time he opened the book, blessed Francis thanked God for confirming his plan and the desire he had conceived earlier. After the third divine confirmation was pointed out and explained, he said to those men, Bernard and Peter: "Brothers, this is our life and rule and that of all who will want to join our company. Go, therefore, and fulfill what you have heard."

Then Lord **Bernard**, who **was** very **rich, after selling all** he had AP 11
and acquiring a large sum of money, went and distributed it all to the city's poor. Peter likewise followed the divine counsel according to his means.

After getting rid of everything, they both received the habit which //AP 14
the saint had adopted after he put aside the habit of a hermit; and, from that hour, they lived with him according to the form of the holy Gospel as the Lord had shown them. This is why blessed Francis said in his *Testament:* "The Lord Himself revealed to me that I should live Test 14
according to the form of the holy Gospel."

Chapter IX
THE VOCATION OF BROTHER SYLVESTER AND THE VISION HE HAD BEFORE ENTERING THE ORDER

[30]As we have said, while Lord Bernard was giving all his posses- AP 12
sions to the poor, blessed Francis was at his side assisting him, glorifying and praising the Lord in his heart, in awe at the astounding work of the Lord. **A priest named Sylvester, from whom the blessed Francis had purchased stones** for the repair **of the church of San Damiano, came**. Seeing so much money being given away on the man of God's advice, he was consumed by a burning passion of greed, and said to him: **"Francis, you did not completely pay me** for

a. The absence of the priest in this passage offers a different perspective on this event from that of AP 11.

the stones which you bought from me." The scorner of greed, hearing him complaining unjustly, approached Lord Bernard, and putting his hand into his cloak where the money was, in great fervor of spirit, filled it with a handful of coins, and gave them to the disgruntled priest. He filled his hand with money a second time, and said to him: "Do you now have full payment, Lord Priest?" "I have it completely, brother," he replied. Overjoyed, he returned home with his money.

AP 13 31 But after a few days that same priest, inspired by the Lord, began to reflect on these things blessed Francis had done, and he said to himself: "Am I not a miserable man? Old as I am, don't I still covet and desire the things of this world? And this young man despises and scorns them all for the love of God!"

The following night he saw in a dream an immense cross. Its top reached to the heavens, its base rested fixed in the mouth of the blessed Francis, and its arms stretched from one part of the world to the other.

When he woke, therefore, the priest understood and resolutely believed that Francis was indeed Christ's friend and servant, and the religion which he founded would spread all over the world. From then on he began to fear God and to do penance in his own home. At last, after a little while, he entered the Order in which he lived excellently and ended gloriously.

//AP 14 32 The man of God, Francis, accompanied by his two brothers, had no place to stay, so he moved with them to a poor little abandoned church, which was called Saint Mary of the Portiuncula. And there they built a little hut in which they would live from time to time.

AP 14 After a few days, an Assisian, named Giles, came to them and, on his knees, begged the man of God with great reverence and devotion to accept him into his company. When the man of God saw how unusually faithful and devout the man was, realizing that he was able to obtain great grace from God, as later became clear by his success, he received him with open arms. These four, united in immense happiness and the joy of the Holy Spirit, separated for greater spiritual advantage.

AP 15 33 Blessed Francis, taking Brother Giles with him, went into the Marches of Ancona; the other two went into another area. While going to the Marches, they rejoiced enthusiastically in the Lord; the holy man, however, sang with a loud and clear voice, in French, the praises of the Lord, blessing and glorifying the goodness of the Most High. There was as much happiness in them as if they had found a great treasure in the evangelical field of Lady Poverty, for whose love they gladly and willingly disdained all worldly things as dung.

The saint told Brother Giles: "Our religion will be like a fisherman who casts his nets into the water catching a great number of fish, and, leaving the small ones in the water, he puts the large ones into his basket." Thus he prophesied that the Order would expand.

Even though the man of God did not yet fully preach to the people, when he went through cities and towns, he encouraged everyone to fear and love God and to do penance for their sins. Brother Giles, on the other hand, exhorted his listeners to believe him because he gave them the best advice.

[34]Those who heard them would say: "Who are these men?" and "What are these words they're saying?" For, at that time, love and fear of God were non-existent almost everywhere, and the way of penance was not only completely unknown, but it was also considered folly. Lust for the flesh, greed for the world, and pride of life was so widespread, that the whole world seemed to be engulfed in these three malignancies. AP 16

There was a diversity of opinions about these evangelical men. Some declared that they were fools or drunkards, while others maintained that such words did not come from fools. One of those listening said: "Either they cling to the Lord for the sake of the highest perfection, or they are demented for sure, because their life seems reckless: they use little food, walk barefoot, and wear wretched clothes."

Although some among them were struck with fear at seeing the form of their holy way of life, others would not as yet follow them. Instead, young ladies seeing them would run far away and tremble at perhaps being carried away by foolishness and madness.

After they had traveled around that province, they returned to the place called Saint Mary's.

[35]After a few days had elapsed, however, three other men from Assisi, Sabbatino, Morico, and John de Capella,[a] came to them, begging blessed Francis to receive them as brothers. He received them humbly and kindly. AP 17

When they were begging alms throughout the city, hardly anyone would give to them; instead they denounced them for disposing of their possessions so that they could live off others and, therefore,

a. While AP 17 identifies this disciple of Francis as simply "John," this text is more specific, i.e., John of Capella. Fortini maintains that he belonged to the same noble family as the notary Lord Pietro Giovani of Capella mentioned in a document of 1297, cf. Fortini, *Nova Vita* II 283. Giuseppe Abate connects the name with the place of origin of the architect of the Basilica of Saint Francis in Assisi, Filippo da Campello, cf. Giuseppe Abate, *Nuovi studi sull'ubicazione della casa paterna di. S. Chiara d'Assisi* (Assisi, 1954), 12, n. 2.

they suffered extreme want. **Even their own relatives and families would persecute** those men, and others in the city mocked them as **senseless and stupid, because no one at** that **time** would abandon what was his to go begging **alms from door to door.**

The bishop of the city of Assisi, to whom the man of God **would frequently** go for counsel, receiving him kindly, **told him: "It seems to me that your life is very rough and hard,** especially, in not possessing **anything in this world." To which the saint** said: **"Lord, if we had possessions, we would need arms** for our protection. **For disputes and lawsuits usually arise out of them, and,** because of this, **love of God and neighbor are** greatly **impeded.** Therefore, **we do not want to possess anything in this world."** The man of God's response greatly **pleased** the **bishop.** For Francis scorned all worldly goods, but money most of all; so much so, that in all his rules he most forcefully commended poverty and repeated that the brothers be eager to avoid money.

For he composed several rules and tested them, before writing that which he ultimately left to the brothers.[a] In one of them he ex-
ER VIII 5-6 pressed his scorn of money: "May we who have left all things, then, be careful of not losing the kingdom of heaven for so little. If we find coins anywhere, let us pay no more attention to them than to the dust we trample underfoot."

Chapter X

HOW HE PREDICTED TO HIS SIX COMPANIONS ALL THAT WOULD HAPPEN TO THEM ON THEIR JOURNEYS THROUGHOUT THE WORLD EXHORTING THEM TO PENANCE

AP 18 36 Calling together the six brothers, **Saint Francis, since he was**
1C 26, 28 **full of the grace of the Holy Spirit,** predicted to them what was about to happen. **"Dearest brothers,"** he said, **"let us consider our vocation,** to which **God has mercifully called us, not only for our own good, but for the salvation of many.** We are to **go throughout the world,** encouraging everyone, more **by deed** than **by word,** to do **penance for their sins** and to recall **the commandments** of God. **Do not be afraid** that you seem few and uneducated. With confidence, simply proclaim penance, trusting in the Lord, who conquered the world. Because by his Spirit, He is speaking through and in you,

a. In addition to ER and *A Rule for the Hermitages* (hereafter RH), this reference may shed light on the various fragments to which Thomas of Celano, Hugh of Digne, and the manuscript in the library of the Worchester Cathedral allude, cf. FA:ED I 61-62, 63-86, 87-96.

encouraging everyone to be converted to him and to observe his commandments.

"You will find some faithful people, meek and kind, who will receive you and your words with joy. You will find many others, faithless, proud, and blasphemous, who will resist and reject you and what you say. Therefore, resolve in your hearts to bear these things with patience and humility."

When the brothers heard this, they began to be afraid. The saint told them: "Do not fear, because after not much time many learned and noble men will come to us, and will be with us preaching to kings and rulers and great crowds. Many people will be converted to the Lord, Who will multiply and increase His family throughout the entire world."

37 And when he had said these things and blessed them, the men AP 18
of God went on their way devoutly observing his warnings. When- AP 19
ever they came upon a church or a cross, they bowed in prayer and
said with devotion: "We adore you, Christ, and we bless you in all 1C 45; Test 5
your churches throughout the whole world, because, by your holy cross, you have redeemed the world." For they believed they would find a place of God wherever they found a cross or a church.

Those who saw them, however, were greatly amazed that they differed from all others by their habit and life and seemed almost like wild men. In fact, whenever they entered especially a city, estate, town, or home, they announced peace, encouraging everyone to fear and love the Creator of heaven and earth and to observe the commandments.

Some people listened to them willingly; others, on the other hand, mocked them; and many tired them out with questions by saying to them: "Where do you come from?" Others wanted to know which was their Order. Although it was tiresome answering so many questions, they responded simply that they were penitents originally from the city of Assisi.[a] At that time their religion was not yet called an order.

38 In fact, many judged them impostors or fools, and were unwill- AP 20
ing to receive them into their homes lest, as thieves, they might slyly take their belongings. Therefore, in many places, after they had suffered a number of insults, they sought lodging in the porticos of churches and homes.

About this time, there were two of them in Florence, unable to find lodging as they were begging throughout the city. When they

a. AP 19 contains a similar expression, "We are penitents and were born in the city of Assisi." In both instances, this was literally true for those identified as Francis's followers were natives of Assisi.

came upon a house having a portico and, in the portico, a bread-oven, they told each other: "We can stay here." Therefore, asking the lady of the house to accept them into her home and having her make an excuse, they humbly said that she at least might let them spend that night near the oven.

She allowed them to do this. When her husband came and found them in the portico, he called his wife and told her: "Why did you offer lodging to those two scoundrels in our portico?" She answered that she did not want them inside the house, but she did let them stay outside in the portico where they could steal nothing but firewood. Considering them scoundrels and thieves, he was opposed to giving them any kind of shelter, although the weather was bitterly cold.

That night, they rested near the oven in a sound sleep, warmed only by the glow of divine love and covered with the blanket of Lady Poverty. In the morning they went to the nearest church to hear the office of matins.

AP 21 [39]When morning came, the woman went to the same church and, seeing those brothers devoutly steadfast in prayer, she said to herself: "If these men were scoundrels and thieves, as my husband claimed, they would not be persevering in prayer so reverently." While she was thinking these things, a man, named Guido, was distributing alms to the poor who were in the church. When he came to the brothers and wanted to give money to each one of them, as he had done to the others, they refused the money and did not want to accept it. But he said to them: "Since you are poor, why don't you accept the coins like the others?" Brother Bernard answered: "While it is true that we are poor, poverty is not burdensome for us as it is for other poor people. For, by the grace of God, we have willingly
AP 22 made ourselves poor. It is His counsel we fulfilled." Astonished at these things and asking if they had ever possessed anything, he heard from them that they had indeed possessed much. For the love of God, though, they had given everything to the poor. The one who answered in this way was Brother Bernard, the first disciple of blessed Francis, whom today we truly believe to be a most holy father. He was the first to run after the holy one of God, embracing the delegation of peace and penance. Selling everything he possessed and giving to the poor, according to the counsel of Gospel perfection, he persevered to the end in most holy poverty.

When that woman reflected that the brothers did not want the coins, she approached them and told them that she would gladly receive them into her home if they wanted lodging there. The brothers answered humbly: "May the Lord reward you for your good will." That man, however, hearing that the brothers were unable to find lodging, took them to his house, saying: "Look, this is the lodging the Lord has prepared for you. Stay in it according to your pleasure." Giving thanks to God, they stayed with him several days, edifying him in the fear of the Lord, more by example than by word. Afterwards, he gave much to the poor.

40 Although they were treated kindly by that man, they were con- AP 23
sidered good-for-nothings, so that many, the small and the great, abused and harmed them, at times taking away from them even the cheapest clothing they had. Whenever the servants of God re-
Lk 6:29 mained naked, because they wore only one tunic, according to the ER XIV 6
pattern of the Gospel, they did not demand back what had been taken from them. If some, moved by piety, did want to return what was taken from them, they willingly accepted.

They did these and similar things to them, regarding them as so worthless that they brazenly afflicted them as they chose. In addition, they endured immense hardship and suffering from hunger and thirst, from cold and nakedness. Suffering all these things steadfastly and patiently, as blessed Francis had admonished them, they did not become dejected or disturbed, nor did they curse those who brought evil upon them. On the contrary, as perfectly evangelical men, placed at a great advantage, they greatly exulted in the Lord, considering it pure joy when they fell into temptations and trials of this sort. According to the word of the Gospel, they prayed carefully and enthusiastically for their persecutors.

Chapter XI

THE RECEPTION OF FOUR OTHER BROTHERS AND THE MOST BURNING CHARITY THEY HAD FOR EACH OF THE FIRST BROTHERS, OF THEIR EAGERNESS IN WORKING AND PRAYING AND THEIR PERFECT OBEDIENCE

41 People then saw that the brothers rejoiced in their tribulations, AP 24
persisted in prayer with eagerness and devotion, neither accepted nor carried money, and possessed a great love for one another; and through this they were known to be really the Lord's disciples. Many came to them with heartfelt sorrow, asking pardon for the offenses they had committed against them. They forgave them from their hearts, saying: "May the Lord forgive you," and encouraged them soundly about their eternal salvation.

Some asked those brothers to receive **them into their company.** And because of the small number of the brothers—all six of them possessed authority from blessed Francis to receive others into the Order—they accepted some of them into their company. After they were received, they all **returned** at a predetermined time **to Saint Mary of the Portiuncula.**

AP 25 **When they saw one another again, however, they were filled with such delight and joy,** as if **they didn't remember anything** of what they had endured at the hands of the wicked.

ER VII 10-12; LR V 2; Test 21 **Each day they were conscientious in prayer and working with their hands to avoid all idleness, the enemy of the soul.** They rose **conscientiously in the middle of the night,** and prayed most devoutly with copious **tears** and sighs. **They loved each other deeply,** served one another, and **took care** of each other as **a mother** for an only and beloved **child. Charity burned so ardently in them** that it seemed easy for them to give their bodies to death, **not only for the love of Christ,** but also for the salvation of the soul or the body of their confreres.

AP 26 [42]**One day, when two** of the brothers were walking along, **they came across a simpleton** who began to throw **rocks** at them. One of them, noticing that **stones were being thrown** at the other, ran directly in front of him, preferring that **the stones strike him rather than** his brother. **Because of the mutual charity** with which they burned, they were prepared to lay down their life in this way, one for the other.

They were so **rooted and grounded in humility and love, that one respected** the other as father and **master,** while those who **excelled** by way of **the office** of prelate or some **grace, seemed humble and more self-effacing than the others. They all dedicated themselves wholeheartedly to obedience,** ever prepared for the will of **the one giving orders.** They did not distinguish between a just and an unjust command **because they considered whatever they were ordered to be the Lord's will.** Fulfilling commands, therefore, **was pleasant and easy for them. They abstained from carnal desires, judging themselves carefully** and taking care that in no way would one offend the other.

AP 27 [43]If it ever happened that **one uttered an annoying word to another, his conscience** troubled him, **so much so that he could not rest until he admitted his fault.** He would humbly prostrate himself **on the ground,** so that his brother would place his **foot over his mouth.** If the brother who was offended refused to do this, then the brother who offended him, **if he were a prelate, would order** him to do so. If he were a subject, he would have a prelate give the order. In this way, with the grace of Jesus Christ anticipating and helping them, they strove to banish all ill will and malice from their midst, to preserve among them always perfect love, and, to combat, as far as possible, each vice by practicing a corresponding virtue.

Moreover, they did not appropriate anything as their own, but used books or other items in common according to the pattern handed down and observed by the apostles. Although there was real poverty in and among them, they were generous and openhanded with everything given them for God's sake. The alms freely given to them out of His love, they gave to all those who begged from them, especially to the poor.

[44]In fact, if they were traveling along the road and found the AP 28
poor begging from them for the love of God, when they had nothing to offer them, they would give them some of their clothing even though it was shabby. Sometimes they gave their capuche, tearing it from the tunic; at other times they gave a sleeve, or tore off a part of
Lk 6:30 their habit, that they might fulfill that Gospel passage "Give to all who beg from you." One day, however, a poor man begging alms came to the church of Saint Mary of the Portiuncula, near where the brothers sometimes stayed. There was a cloak there that a brother wore while in the world. When blessed Francis told him to give it to that poor man, he gave it to him freely and quickly. And immediately, because of the reverence and devotion which that brother had in giving the cloak to the poor man, it seemed to him that the alms rose up into heaven and he felt himself inundated by a new happiness.

[45]When, in fact, the rich of this world would go out of their way AP 29
for them, they received them quickly and kindly, striving to call them from evil and prompting them to do penance. They also eagerly sought not to be sent to the lands where they had been raised, that they might avoid association and dealings with their relatives
Ps 69:9 and could observe the prophetic word: *"I have become an outcast to my brothers, a stranger to my mother's sons."*

They rejoiced most in poverty, because they did not desire riches, but spurned everything transitory that can be desired by
those enamored of this world. Above all, they trampled upon money AP 30
as if it were dirt under their feet, and, as they had been taught by the saint, considered it as equal in worth and weight to the dung of an ass.

They constantly rejoiced in the Lord, not having within themselves nor among themselves anything that could make them sad.

For the more they were separated from the world, the more they were united to God. As they advanced **on the way** of the cross and the paths of justice, they cleared all hindrances from the narrow path of penance and of the observance of the Gospel, that they might make a smooth and safe path for the future.

Chapter XII
How Blessed Francis with his eleven companions went to the papal curia that he might inform him of their proposal and have the Rule that he had written confirmed

AP 31 [46]**Seeing that** the Lord would increase **his brothers in number and merit,** since there were already twelve most perfect men expressing the same belief, **blessed Francis said** to the eleven, he being the twelfth, their leader and father: **"Brothers, I see that the Lord mercifully** wants **to increase** our **congregation. Then, going to our mother, the** holy **Roman Church, let us inform the Supreme Pontiff what the Lord** has begun to do **through us, that, with** his **will and command,** we may continue doing what we have undertaken."

And since the proposal of their father pleased the other brothers, and they had embarked together with him on the journey to the Curia, he said to them: **"Let us make one of us our leader and consider** that man **a kind of vicar of Jesus Christ,** so that wherever he wants **to go, we will go, and whenever he wants to rest, we will rest." And they chose Brother Bernard,** the first after blessed Francis, and, as the father said, they served him.

They, then, **made their way rejoicing and spoke about the words of the Lord,** not daring to say anything except for **the praise and glory** of God and **the benefit** of the soul, and **they** frequently **spent time in prayer. The Lord, on the other hand, prepared lodging for them,** doing what was necessary to minister to them.

AP 32 [47]**When they arrived in Rome** and found **the bishop of the city of Assisi** there, they were received **with immense joy,** for he honored
//IC 32 blessed Francis and all the brothers with special affection. Not knowing the reason for their arrival, he began to be apprehensive, fearing that they might want to leave their native land, where the Lord had begun to do marvelous things through them. For he rejoiced to have in his diocese such men whose life and conduct he greatly appreciated. After he learned their purpose and understood their plan, however, he was overjoyed and promised them his counsel and help.

The bishop was known to the cardinal bishop of Sabina, named
Lord John of Saint Paul, a man truly full of God's grace, who loved, in
particular, servants of God.[a] The bishop of Assisi made **the life of** AP 32
blessed Francis and his brothers clear to him. On this account, he
was eager to meet the man of God and some of his brothers. Hearing
that **they were in the City, he sent for** those men and welcomed
them with great reverence and love.

48 **During the few days** they were staying **with** that man, they so AP 33
edified him with their holy words and example, that, seeing what he
had heard about them to shine in deed, he commended himself
humbly and devoutly to their prayers. He even asked them, as a special grace, to be considered one of their brothers. Then asking blessed
Francis the reason why he came and hearing from him their entire
proposal and intention, he offered to be their procurator at the Curia.

That cardinal then went **to the Curia** and **told the Lord Pope In-**
nocent III: "I found a most perfect man, who wishes to live accord-
ing to the form of the holy Gospel, and to observe evangelical
perfection in all things. **I believe that the Lord wills, through him,**
to reform **the faith of the holy Church** throughout the world." Hearing this, **the lord pope was** greatly **amazed** and had the cardinal
bring blessed Francis to him.

49 **On the following day,** therefore, the man of God was presented AP 34
by that cardinal to the pope, to whom he revealed **his entire** holy **pro-**
posal. The pope, a man of extraordinary discernment, in due fashion
assented to Francis's request, and encouraged him and his brothers
in many ways. He blessed them saying: **"Go with the Lord, brothers,** 1C 33
and as He will see fit to inspire you, preach penance to everyone.
When almighty God increases you in number and **grace, come back**
to us. We will grant you more, and entrust you with a greater
charge."

Before the saint left his presence, the Lord Pope wanted to know
whether what had been, and what would be conceded, was according to the Lord's will. And so, he said to him and his companions:
"My dear young sons, **your life** seems to Us exceptionally **hard and** AP 34
severe. While We believe there can be no question about your living
it because of your great zeal, We must take into consideration those
who will come after you lest this way of life seem too burdensome."

The pope saw that their constancy of faith and the anchor of their
hope were so firmly grounded in Christ, that they did not want to be
shaken from their enthusiasm. So he said to blessed Francis: "My
son, go and pray that God will reveal to you whether what you ask

a. See FA:ED I 210 b.

proceeds from His will. In this way, knowing the Lord's will, We may accede to your desires."

//AP 35 [50]Once God's saint had prayed, as the Lord Pope suggested, the Lord spoke figuratively to him in spirit: "There was a little, poor and beautiful woman in a desert, whose beauty fascinated a great king. He wanted to take her as his wife, because he thought that, from her, he would have handsome sons. After the marriage was celebrated and consummated, there were many sons born and raised. Their mother spoke to them in this way: 'My sons, do not be ashamed, for you are sons of the king. Therefore, go to his court and he will provide for all your needs.' When they went to see the king, he was struck by their good looks, and noticing a resemblance to himself in them, he asked them: 'Whose sons are you?' When they answered that they were the sons of the little poor woman living in the desert, the king embraced them with great joy. 'Do not be afraid,' he said, 'for you are my sons. If strangers are fed at my table, how much more will you, who are my lawful sons.' He then ordered the woman to send to his court all of the children she had borne to be fed."

When these things had been shown to blessed Francis while he was praying, the man of God understood that the poor woman signified him.

[51]After he completed his prayer, he presented himself to the Supreme Pontiff and narrated point-by-point the story that the Lord had revealed to him. "My lord," he said, "I am that little poor woman whom the loving Lord, in His mercy, has adorned, and through whom He has been pleased to give birth to legitimate sons. The King of kings had told me that He will nourish all the sons born to me, because, if He feeds strangers, He must provide for His own. For if God gives temporal goods to sinful men out of love for providing for His children, how much more will He give to Gospel men who deserve these things out of merit."

On hearing this, the pope was greatly amazed, especially since, before blessed Francis's arrival, he had seen in a vision the church of Saint John Lateran threatening to collapse, and a religious, small and of shabby appearance, supporting it on his own shoulders.[a] When he awoke, stunned and shaken, as a discerning and wise man,

a. This same dream is recounted in the third *Life of St. Dominic* by Constantius Medici written around 1244-45. According to Constantius Medici, this vision took place in 1215 when Dominic arrived in Rome with Bishop Fulcone of Toulouse for the IV Lateran Council, that is, before Dominic received approval from Honorius III on December 22, 1216. See Quetif-Echard, *Scriptores Ordinis Praedicatorum*, 1 (Paris 1721), 2. A second version of this same incident can be found in *Chronica Ordinis* in *Monumenta Ordinis Fratrum Praedicatorum Historica (Vitae Fratrum Ordinis Praedicatorum Necnon Cronica Ordinis ab Anno MCCIII usque ad MCCLIV)*, ed. Fr. Benedictus Reichert, O.P. (Rome, 1897), 323.

he pondered what this vision meant to tell him. A few days later, //AP 36
blessed Francis came to him, made known his proposal, as we have said, and asked him to confirm the rule he had written in simple words, using the words of the holy Gospel, for whose perfection he fully longed. As he was reflecting on how enthusiastic blessed Fran- //1C 32
cis was in God's service, and comparing his vision with that shown to the man of God, he began to say to himself: "This is indeed that holy and religious man through whom the church of God will be sustained and supported."

So he embraced him and approved the rule he had written. He //AP 36
also gave him and his brothers permission to preach penance everywhere, with the stipulation that the brothers who preach obtain permission from blessed Francis. Afterwards he approved this in a consistory.[a]

52 Therefore, after obtaining these favors, blessed Francis thanked ER Pr 3; LR I 2; //AP 36
God, and on bended knees, promised obedience and reverence to the Lord Pope humbly and devoutly. The other brothers, in accordance with the precept of the Lord Pope, promised obedience and reverence to blessed Francis in a similar way.

After receiving a blessing from the Supreme Pontiff and visiting the tombs of the Apostles, blessed Francis and the other eleven brothers were given the tonsure, as the lord cardinal had arranged, wanting all twelve of them to be clerics.[b]

53 As he was leaving the City, the man of God, with his brothers, set out into the world, greatly surprised at how easily his desire had been granted. He was growing each day in the hope and trust of the Savior, who had earlier shown him by holy revelations what was to happen.

For before he had obtained these things, **one night when he had** 1C 33
gone to sleep, it seemed to him that he was making his way **down a road beside which** there was **a lovely, strong and thick tree that was exceedingly high.** As **he approached and stood under it, marveling** at its height and **beauty, the holy man** suddenly **rose to so great a height, that he touched the top of the tree and very easily bent it** even **to the ground.**

a. In some of the manuscripts, the Latin word, *consistorio* [consistory], a solemn assembly of all cardinals present in Rome, becomes *consilio* [council], possibly a reference to the Fourth Lateran Council (1215).

b. In contrast to a similar passage in AP 36, L3C employs a different vocabulary in describing this event. In this instance the word *clerica* becomes *tonsura*, and the reason for its reception is clearly stated, i.e., so that they would be clerics.

It really happened this way, when the Lord Innocent, a very high, lovely, and strong **tree in the world, bent himself so kindly to his wish and request.**

Chapter XIII

THE EFFICACIOUS PREACHING OF BLESSED FRANCIS AND THE FIRST PLACE HE HAD HOW THE BROTHERS STAYED THERE AND HOW THEY LEFT

//AP 36 [54]From then on, blessed **Francis,** *going around the cities* **and vil-** Mt 9:35
lages, began *to preach* more widely and more perfectly **proclaiming**
the kingdom of God with confidence, *not in the persuasive words of* 1 Cor 2:4
human wisdom, but in the **learning and** *power of the Holy Spirit.*

1C 36 Strengthened by apostolic authority, he was a forthright preacher of truth, **not using fawning words** or seductive flattery, because **he first convinced himself by action and then convinced others by word,** so that he spoke the truth with the greatest fidelity. Even a very great number of learned and well-educated people marveled at his power and truth, which no human had taught, and they hurried to see and hear him as if he were a person of another age.

1C 37 Drawn **by divine inspiration, many people, well-born and lowly, cleric and lay,** began to cling to blessed Francis's footsteps, and, after they had abandoned the concerns and vanity of this world, to live under his discipline.

1C 42 [55]The blessed father with his sons were staying in a place **near Assisi called Rivo Torto** where there was a hut abandoned by all. The place was so cramped that **they could barely sit or rest.** Very often for lack of bread, their only food was the turnips that **they begged in their need,** here and there.

1C 44 The man of God would write the names of the brothers on the beams of that hut, so that anyone wishing to rest or pray would know his place, and so that any unusual noise would not disturb the mind's silence in such small and close quarters.

One day while the brothers were staying in that place, a peasant came with his donkey, wanting to stay in that hut with it. And so that he would not be driven away by the brothers, on walking into the hut, he said to his donkey: "Go in, go in, **because we will do well in this place."**

When the holy father heard the peasant's words and realized his intention, he was annoyed at him, most of all because he made quite an uproar with his donkey, disturbing all the brothers who were then immersed in silence and prayer. Then the man of God said to his brothers: "I know, brothers, that God did not call us to prepare a lodging for a donkey, nor to have dealings with men. While we are preaching the way of salvation to people and are giving them wise counsel, we should dedicate ourselves most of all to prayer and thanksgiving."

They left that hut for the use of poor lepers, moving to a small dwelling near Saint Mary of the Portiuncula where they stayed from time to time before acquiring that church.

56 Afterwards blessed Francis, in accordance with God's will and inspiration, obtained it from the abbot of the monastery of Saint Benedict on Mount Subasio near Assisi.[a] The saint, in a special and affectionate way, commended this place to the general minister and to all the brothers, as the place loved by the glorious Virgin more than any other place or church in this world.

A vision one of the brothers had, while in the world, contributed much to the commendation and love of this place. Blessed Francis loved this brother with unique affection as long as he was with him, by showing him extraordinary affection. This man, wanting to serve God—as he later did so faithfully in religion—saw in a vision that all the people of the world were blind and were kneeling in a circle around the church of Saint Mary of the Portiuncula with their hands joined and their faces raised to heaven. In a loud and sobbing voice, they were begging the Lord in his mercy to give them sight. While they were praying, it seemed that a great light came from heaven and, resting on them, enlightened all of them with its wholesome radiance.

On awakening, the man resolved to serve God more faithfully, and, shortly thereafter, leaving the world with its seductions, he entered religion where he persevered in the service of God with humility and dedication.

Chapter XIV
The Chapter that was held twice a year at Saint Mary of the Portiuncula

57 After **blessed Francis** had obtained that place of Saint Mary AP 36
from the abbot of Saint Benedict, he **ordered that a chapter be held** ER XVIII

a. It is difficult to understand what the author means when using *acquisivit* [acquired] or *obtinuit* [obtained], since there is no record of the transaction between Francis and the abbot of the monastery of Saint Benedict.

there twice a year, that is, on Pentecost and on the Dedication of Saint Michael.[a]

AP 37 At Pentecost, all the brothers used to gather at the church of Saint Mary and discuss how they could better observe the *Rule*. They appointed brothers throughout the various provinces who would preach to the people, and assigned other brothers in their provinces. Saint Francis, however, used to give admonitions, corrections, and directives as it seemed to him to be according to the Lord's counsel. Everything that he said to them in word, however, he would show them in deed with eagerness and affection.

He used to revere prelates and priests of the holy Church, and honored the elderly, the noble, and the wealthy. Moreover, he intimately loved the poor, suffering deeply with them, and he showed himself subject to all.

Although he was more elevated than all the brothers, he still appointed one of the brothers staying with him as his guardian and master. He humbly and eagerly obeyed him, in order to avoid any occasion of pride. For in the presence of people, he lowered his head even to the ground; so that now in the presence of God's saints and chosen ones, he merits to be exalted in the divine sight.

He zealously used to admonish the brothers to observe the holy Gospel and the *Rule* which they had firmly promised; and particularly to be reverent and devoted about divine services and ecclesiastical regulations, hearing Mass devotedly, and adoring the Body of the Lord even more devotedly. He wanted priests who handle the tremendous and greatest sacraments to be honored uniquely by the brothers, so that wherever they met them, as they bowed their heads to them, they would kiss their hands. And if they found them on horseback, he wanted them not only to kiss their hands but, out of reverence for their power, even the hooves of the horses upon which they were riding.

3; ER XI; LR II 17 58 He also admonished the brothers not to judge anyone, nor to look down upon those who live with refinement and dress extravagantly or fashionably. For, he would say, their God is ours, the Lord Who is capable of calling them to Himself and justifying those called. He also used to tell them he wanted the brothers to show reverence to these people as their brothers and lords. They are brothers, because we were all created by one Creator; they are lords, because they

a. At the time, there were two feasts of Saint Michael, May 8, which commemorated the apparition of the angel at his renowned sanctuary on Monte Gargano or Monte Sant'Angelo in Southern Italy; and September 29, the Dedication of the Basilica of Saint Michael, six miles north of Rome on the Via Salaria. This latter feast, September 29, was celebrated as a holy day of obligation in the Middle Ages and was abolished by the eighteenth century.

help the good to do penance by providing them with the necessities of life. He added: "The brothers' way of life among the people should be such that whoever hears or sees them glorifies and praises the heavenly Father with dedication."

For his great desire was that he, as well as his brothers, would abound in such good deeds for which the Lord would be praised. He used to tell them: "As you announce peace with your mouth, make sure that greater peace is in your hearts. Let no one be provoked to anger or scandal through you, but may everyone be drawn to peace, kindness, and harmony through your gentleness. For we have been called to this: to heal the wounded, bind up the broken, and recall the erring. In fact, many who seem to us to be members of the devil will yet be disciples of Christ."

59 Moreover, the pious father used to reprove his brothers who to AP 39
him were too austere, exerting too much effort in those vigils, fasts and corporal punishments. Some of them afflicted themselves so harshly to repress within them every impulse of the flesh, that they seemed to hate themselves. The man of God forbade them, admonishing them with kindness, reprimanding them with reason, and binding up their wounds with the bandages of wholesome precepts.

Among the brothers who had come to the chapter, no one dared to discuss worldly matters, but they spoke of the lives of the holy fathers, and how they could better and more perfectly find the grace of the Lord Jesus Christ. If some of the brothers who came to the chapter experienced any temptation or tribulation, upon hearing blessed Francis speaking so sweetly and fervently, and on seeing his penance, they were freed from their temptations and were miraculously relieved of the tribulations. For, while suffering with them, he spoke to them, not as a judge, but as a merciful father to his children, or a good doctor to the sick, knowing how to be sick with the sick and afflicted with the afflicted. Nevertheless he duly rebuked all delinquents, and restrained the obstinate and rebellious with an appropriate punishment.

When a chapter had ended, he would bless all the brothers and AP 40
assign each of them to individual provinces. To anyone possessing the Spirit of God and an eloquence suitable for preaching, whether cleric or lay, he gave permission to preach. When those men received his blessing with great joy of spirit, they went throughout the world as pilgrims and strangers, taking nothing on their way except the books in which they could say their Hours. Whenever they found a priest, rich or poor, good or bad, bowing humbly they

paid him their respect. When it was time to seek lodging, they more willingly stayed with priests rather than with secular.

AP 41 [60]When they were unable to stay with priests, they would seek more spiritual and God-fearing persons with whom they could more suitably be welcomed. After this, in each city and town that the brothers wanted to visit, the Lord inspired some God-fearing people to offer them hospitality, until some places were built for them in cities and towns.

The Lord gave them the word and the spirit, according to need of the time, to speak with most incisive words, penetrating the hearts of the young—as well as the elderly—who, abandoning fathers and mothers and all they had, followed the brothers, by putting on the habit of religion. Then, indeed, a sword of separation was sent to the earth, when the young came to religion, leaving behind their parents in the dregs of sin. Those whom they received to the Order they led to blessed Francis, that they might receive from him the habit of religion with humility and dedication.

Not only were men converted to the Order; but also many virgins and widows, struck by their preaching, on their advice secluded themselves in cities and towns in monasteries established for doing penance.[a] One of the brothers was appointed their visitator and corrector.[b] Similarly, both married men and women given in marriage, unable to separate because of the law of matrimony, committed themselves to more severe penance in their own homes on the wholesome advice of the brothers. And thus, through blessed Francis, a perfect worshipper of the Holy Trinity, the Church of God was renewed in three orders, just as the earlier repair of the three churches foreshadowed. Each one of these orders was in its time approved by the Supreme Pontiff.

Chapter XV

The Death of Lord John, the First Protector of the Order and How the Lord Hugolino of Ostia Assumed the Role of Father and Protector of the Order

AP 42 [61]The venerable father, the Lord Cardinal John of Saint Paul, that cardinal who more frequently offered counsel and protection

a. See AP 41 note. The Latin in this instance reads: *monasteriis ordinatis recludebant se ad poenitentiam faciendam* [secluded themselves in monasteries established for doing penance]. The use of *ordinatis* [established] may indicate a development in the somewhat fluid movements of women religious at this time. Cf. Mario Sensi, "The Women's Recluse Movement in Umbria during the 13th and 14th Centuries," GR 8 (1994): 319-345.

b. See AP 40, p. 54 b.

to blessed Francis, commended the life and accomplishments of the saint and his brothers to the other cardinals. Their minds were moved to love the man of God with his brothers, so that each one of them wanted to have brothers in his own household, not for any service they might provide, but because of their holiness and the dedication with which they burned for them.

After the Lord Cardinal John of Saint Paul had died, **the Lord in-** AP 43
spired one of the cardinals, **Hugolino,** at that time **the bishop of Ostia, to cherish,** protect, and support **Francis and his brothers.** With burning intensity, he held them in awe as if he were the father of them all. What is more, more than the love of a carnal father reaching out naturally to his own sons, the love of this man overflowed spiritually on the man of God and his brothers, loving and supporting them in the Lord.

The man of God heard of this man's glorious reputation, for among the cardinals he was famous, and with his brothers approached him. Receiving them with joy, he told them: **"I am offering you myself for advice, assistance** and **protection,** ready to give myself according to **your** good pleasure. I only **ask that,** for God's sake, **you have me remembered in your prayers."**

Then **blessed Francis, thanking God, told** that lord cardinal: "My lord, **I gladly want to have you as the father** and protector of our religion, and **I want all my brothers** to have **you** always remembered in their prayers." Then blessed Francis asked him **to be** present **at the chapter of the brothers at Pentecost.** He immediately agreed graciously, and, from then on, was present every year at their chapter.

When he came to the chapter, all **the brothers who had gathered at the chapter would go in procession to meet him. As they were approaching, he would dismount from his horse and go on foot with them to the church** of Saint Mary. Afterward **he preached** to them **and celebrated Mass,** during which the man of God, **Francis, would chant the Gospel.**

Chapter XVI
THE ELECTION OF THE FIRST MINISTERS AND HOW THEY WERE SENT THROUGHOUT THE WORLD

62**Eleven years after the founding of the religion** when the broth- AP 44
ers had increased in number and merit, ministers were chosen and sent with some of the brothers throughout nearly the entire world in which the Catholic faith was practiced and observed. They were received in some of the provinces, but were not permitted to build

houses. On the other hand, **they were expelled from others** for fear they might be non-believers, because, although the Lord Pope Innocent III had approved the Order and the *Rule,* nonetheless, he did not confirm this by letter, and the brothers, therefore, suffered **many adversities from clerics and lay people.** The brothers were then forced to flee from various provinces, and so, persecuted, afflicted, even set upon by thieves who stripped and beat them, they returned to blessed Francis with great bitterness. For they had suffered this **in** almost **every** region **beyond the Alps, in Germany, Hungary,** and in many **other regions**.

When this had been made known to the Lord Cardinal, he called blessed Francis to him and took him to the Lord Pope Honorius, since the Lord Innocent was now dead.[a] He had another rule—composed by blessed Francis as he was taught by Christ—confirmed by the same Lord Honorius with a seal solemnly affixed. In this rule, the time between the chapters was prolonged to avoid hardship for the brothers living in remote areas.

63**Blessed Francis** proposed to ask the Lord Pope Honorius, therefore, that **one of the cardinals** of the Roman Church be a sort of pope of his Order, that is, the Lord of Ostia, to whom the brothers could have recourse in their dealings.

For blessed Francis had had a vision which led him to ask for the cardinal, and to entrust the Order to the Roman Church. He saw a hen that was small and black, with feathered legs and the feet of a domestic dove. It had so many chicks that it was unable to gather them all under its wings, and so they wandered all around her in circles.

Waking from sleep, he began to think about this vision and, immediately, he perceived by means of the Holy Spirit that that hen symbolized him. "I am that hen," he said, "short in stature, and dark by nature. I must be simple like a dove, flying up to heaven with the feathered strokes of virtue. The Lord in his mercy has given, and will give me, many sons whom I will be unable to protect with my own strength. I must, therefore, commend them to the holy Church who will protect and guide them under the shadow of her wings."

64A few years after this vision, he came to Rome and visited the Lord of Ostia who obliged blessed Francis to go with him to the Curia the following morning. He wanted him to preach before the Lord Pope and the cardinals, and to commend his religion to them with

a. Innocent III died on July 16, 1216, and, because of the desecration of his body that evening in Perugia's Duomo, Cencio Savelli was quickly elected as his successor on July 18, 1216, and took the name Honorius III.

devotion and eagerness. Although blessed Francis excused himself, claiming he was simple and stupid, he nevertheless had to accompany that man to the Curia.

When blessed Francis presented himself before the Lord Pope and the cardinals, they saw him with boundless joy. Getting up, he preached to them, prepared only by the Holy Spirit's anointing. After he finished speaking, he commended his religion to the Lord Pope and to all the cardinals. The Lord Pope and lord cardinals had been greatly edified by his preaching, and their hearts were moved to a more burning love of the religion.

[65]Afterwards blessed Francis told the Supreme Pontiff: "Lord, I am suffering with you over the worry and continuing labor with which you must watch over God's Church, and I am greatly ashamed that you must have such solicitude and care for us lesser brothers. For, since many nobles, rich people, as well as many religious, are unable to come to you, we, who are surely poor and looked down upon by some religious, must have great fear and shame not only to have access to you, but even to stand at your door and to presume to knock at the tabernacle of Christian virtue. Therefore, I humbly and resolutely beg your Holiness to give us the Lord of Ostia as pope, so that, at a time of need, the brothers may have recourse to him, always saving your pre-eminent dignity."

//AP 45 The Lord Pope was pleased with the petition, and he granted blessed Francis that Lord of Ostia, appointing him a most fitting protector of his religion.

AP 45 [66]**With the mandate of the Lord Pope,** as a good protector, he extended **his influence to protect the brothers,** writing to many prelates who were persecuting the brothers. He did this so that they would no longer **oppose** them, **but would rather give them advice and assistance in preaching and living in their provinces, as good and holy religious approved by the authority** of the Apostolic See. Many other cardinals likewise sent their own letters for the same reason.

In the following chapter, **after blessed Francis gave the ministers permission to receive brothers into the Order,** he sent them to those provinces, **carrying the letters** of the cardinals as well as the *Rule* confirmed by the apostolic seal. Once the prelates saw all of these, and recognized the endorsements shown by the brothers, **they permitted** the brothers **to build, live, and preach in their provinces.**

And after the brothers lived and preached in this way in those provinces, **many people, seeing their humble** and holy **way of life,** and hearing **their very pleasant words,** moving and inflaming minds to love of God and to doing penance, they came to them and humbly accepted **the habit of holy religion.**

AP 45 [67]**Seeing the trust and love that the Lord of Ostia had for the brothers,** blessed Francis loved him most affectionately from the depths of his heart. And because he knew, through an earlier revelation of God, that he would be the future Supreme Pontiff, he predicted this in the letters he wrote to him, calling him the father of the whole world. For **he wrote** to him in this manner: **"To the venerable father of the whole world in Christ** . . . "

Shortly afterwards, after the death of the Lord Pope Honorius III, that **Lord of Ostia was elected** the Supreme Pontiff, **named Pope Gregory IX,** who, until the end of his life was a remarkable benefactor and protector of the brothers as well as of other religious, and above all, of Christ's poor.[a] For this reason, he is believed to be numbered deservedly in the gathering of the saints.[b]

Chapter XVII
THE DEATH OF BLESSED FRANCIS AND HOW TWO YEARS EARLIER HE RECEIVED THE STIGMATA OF OUR LORD JESUS CHRIST

[68]After twenty years of clinging most perfectly to Christ, and of
1C 88 following the life and footsteps of the apostles, **in the one thousandth, two hundredth, and twenty-sixth year of the Incarnation of the Lord, on the fourth of October, a Sunday,** Francis, that apostolic man, most joyfully passed to Christ, winning eternal rest after many labors, and fittingly entering into the presence of the Lord.

1C 110 **One of his followers,** renowned for his sanctity, **saw his soul like a star as big as the moon with the brilliance of the sun,** rising up above the great waters, and borne up to heaven by a brilliant cloud.

//AP 46 For he had worked intensely in the Lord's vineyard, eager and fervent in his prayers, fasts, vigils, sermons, and wholesome journeys, in care and compassion for his neighbor, and in disregard of himself. From the beginning of his conversion to the day of his passing to Christ, he had loved Him with his whole heart, constantly keeping the memory of Him in his mind, praising Him with his mouth, and

a. Honorius III died on March 18, 1227, and was succeeded on March 19, 1227, by Hugolino who took the name Gregory IX. This passage, indicating that Gregory IX's death, on August 22, 1241, had already occurred, provides an insight that this text was completed sometime thereafter.

b. Two of the earliest manuscripts, that of the Biblioteca Central in Barcelona, Cod. 665, and that of the Biblioteca Communale in Sarnano, Cod. E n 60, conclude at this point. This has led scholars to maintain that the following two chapters were added at a much later date. Comparison of the contents of these final chapters indicate the influence of 2C and LMj, influences that are missing in the first sixteen chapters of L3C.

glorifying Him with his fruitful deeds. For he loved God with such enthusiasm from the depths of his heart that, on hearing His name, completely melting within, he would burst forth saying that heaven and earth must bow at the Lord's name.

[69]While he was still alive in the flesh, the Lord adorned him with a //AP 46
wonderful prerogative of a unique privilege, wishing to show the whole world the fervor of love and the incessant memory of the Passion of Christ which he carried in his heart.

For when he was taken above in the seraphic ardor of desires into God and into Him, he who, by a boundless love, wanted to be crucified, was transformed by a compassionate sweetness. One morning, around the feast of the Exaltation of the Holy Cross,[a] while he was absorbed in prayer on a slope of Mount LaVerna, two years before his death, a seraph with six wings appeared to him. Within its six wings there was the form of a very beautiful, crucified man, whose hands and feet were extended after the manner of a cross, and whose features were clearly those of the Lord Jesus. Two wings covered his head, two, the rest of his body down to the feet, and two were extended as if for flight.

When the vision disappeared, a marvelous glow of love remained in his soul, but, even more marvelous, an impression of the stigmata of our Lord Jesus Christ appeared in his flesh. Until his death, the man of God, unwilling to divulge God's sacrament, concealed it to the best of his ability, although he was unable to cover it completely since it became known to at least his intimate companions.

[70]After his most happy passing, all the brothers who were present, as well as many seculars, clearly saw his body unmistakably adorned
with the wounds of Christ. They saw in his hands and feet, **not just** 1C 113
the holes of the nails, but the nails themselves formed by his own
flesh, taking shape from it, and showing **the dark color of iron. His** 1C 95
right side appeared **as if pierced with a lance,** covered with a red scar from a very real and very visible wound, which, even while he was living, frequently poured out sacred blood.

The undeniable truth of those stigmata appeared most brilliantly through sight and contact not only in his life and in death, but also after his death, the Lord revealed their truth even more brilliantly by many miracles shown in different parts of the world. Through these miracles, the hearts of many who did not look kindly on the man of God and doubted the stigmata were also moved to a great assurance of faith. Thus, those who had been his detractors, by God's active

a. That is, September 14.

goodness and the undeniable weight of evidence, became faithful heralds and promoters of his fame.

Chapter XVIII
His Canonization

[71]In various parts of the world blessed Francis was becoming resplendent because of the light of new miracles. And from far and wide, those who, through his merits, enjoyed unique and extraordinary benefits from the Lord, hurried to reverence his holy remains. After consulting the cardinals and many other prelates, and approving the miracles which the Lord wrought through his intercession, the Lord Pope Gregory enrolled him in the catalog of saints, ordering
LCh 17 **that his feast be solemnly celebrated on the day of his death.**
1C 126 **These things happened in the city of Assisi,** in the presence of many prelates of the Church, an exceptionally large representation of rulers and barons, and a vast crowd of people from all parts of the world whom the Lord Pope had invited. This took place in the year one thousand two hundred and twenty-eight, the second year of the Lord Pope's pontificate.

[72]The Sovereign Pontiff, who loved the saint very much during his lifetime, not only honored him through an extraordinary canonization, but also laid the first stone of the church to be built in his honor, enriching it with sacred gifts and precious appointments. To this new church, two years after his canonization, the saint's most sacred body was solemnly transferred from the place where it was first buried.

LCh 17 He sent to the church a **golden cross, decorated with precious gems** and containing **wood from the Lord's cross.** He also sent appointments, vessels, and many other furnishings for the service of the altar, together with many precious and solemn vestments.

Exempting the church from any inferior jurisdiction, the Sovereign Pontiff, by apostolic authority, proclaimed it "the Head and Mother" of the whole Order of Lesser Brothers, as is clear in an official public document that was undersigned by all the cardinals.

[73]It would mean little to honor the saint of God with material things, had not the Lord willed to work through him, physically dead but spiritually alive in glory, numerous miracles of conversion and healing. After his death, both men and women, through his interces-
//AP 47 sion, were converted to the Lord. Many nobles and their sons put on the habit of his Order, and their wives and daughters entered the monasteries of the Poor Ladies.

Many learned and exceptionally educated men, some laymen, //1C 120
others holding ecclesiastical offices, wholeheartedly renounced the allurements of the flesh, the absence of piety, and the lust of this world. They entered the Order of the Lesser Ones, obliging themselves to follow, according to the particular grace given them by God, the poverty and the footsteps of Christ and his most blessed servant Francis.

What was written of Samson can fittingly be said of him who lives
Jg 16:30 a life of glory: *those he killed at his death were more than those he had during his lifetime.* Through the merits of our most holy father Francis, may He who lives and reigns forever bring us to this same glory. Amen.

THE ASSISI COMPILATION

(1244–1260)

Introduction

The second text resulting from the request of Cresentius, *The Assisi Compilation,* presents anecdotes about Francis that could only have come from day-to-day association with him. "We who were with him" offer stories of his practice of virtue, his dealings with the brothers, and his struggles with those who found his Gospel vision difficult to understand. In scattered recollections that lack any plan or structure, *The Assisi Compilation* provides details of incidents that took place not in the piazzas or papal households, but in the remote and hidden places of the brothers, and offers insights into the daily life of the primitive fraternity. Very quickly the reader of these reminiscences becomes aware that they flow from personal and intimate experiences with the saint.

Unlike the manuscript tradition of *The Legend of the Three Companions,* that of *The Assisi Compilation* is quite simple. The text is found in a handsome fourteenth century binding, Manuscript 1046 of the Biblioteca Comunale Augusta in Perugia. It appears to have been written by different scribes, one of whom numbered all the sections in a distinctive way indicating that they were bound up shortly after they were written.[1] The very first folio describes the contents of the entire codex and indicates the presence of the *Legenda major et antiqua sancti Francisci* [A Major and An Ancient Legend of Saint Francis]. The manuscript was brought to modern attention in 1922 when Ferdinand Delorme published an edition of the text and, two years later, an in-depth study. Because the parchment includes a papal decree of March 23, 1310, by Pope Clement V,[2] Delorme maintained that the manuscript had to have been written after that date. Most scholars accept the date of 1311, the year when Ubertino da Casale mentions his awareness of its existence.[3] Unfortunately, the manuscript Delorme discovered was missing sections XI, XII, and XV, and so he was left with many questions. While sections XI and XII lacked the beginning and end of Bonaventure's *Legenda Major* [Major Legend] section XV more seriously lacked the *incipit* or introductory statement to the other work. Taking his cue from the first folio of Codex 1046, Delorme entitled the work *Legenda antiqua Sancti Francisci.*[4]

A primary difficulty with this text, however, had always been its title. Since Delorme's initial edition, the manuscript was unfortunately published in different forms and with different titles: *Legenda Antiqua* [Ancient Legend], *I Fiori dei Tre Compagni* [The Flowers of the Three Companions],[5] *Scripta Leonis, Rufini et Angeli Sociorum S. Francisci* [The Writings of Leo, Rufino and Angelo, Companions of St. Francis],[6] *Legenda Perugina* [The Legend of Perugia][7] and *Compilatio Assisiensis* [The Assisi Compilation].[8] These titles have certainly added to the controversial nature of the text and influenced its interpretation.

In his study of Codex 1046, Delorme noted that the text had been divided into three sections, each of which began with illuminated initials. In addition to some previously unknown material (AC 4-14), the first section consisted of passages taken from *The Remembrance of the Desire of a Soul* by Thomas of Celano (AC1-3), written in 1247, and Leo's *Verba Sancti Francisci* [Words of Saint Francis] (AC 15-20).[9] The second section was taken entirely from Thomas's *Remembrance* (AC 23-49). Because the third section began with the largest of the illuminated initials, Delorme maintained that it contained the most important material. Therefore he arranged this material into three subdivisions of anecdotes or remembrances of "we who were with him" (AC 50-100, 107-120) and put Leo's *Intentio Regulae* [The Intention of the Rule] in the last section (AC 101-106).[10] However, Delorme published part of the first section of his discovery and all of the third, that is, the three subdivisions, arguing that the other sections, those containing passages of Thomas, were already known.

Discussions of the merits of Delorme's publication have since influenced twentieth-century approaches to Francis of Assisi. In 1967, Jacques Cambell examined the material presented in the 1920's. Not only did Cambell re-order the material but, to suggest its authorship, he gave it a new title: *I fiori dei tre compagni* [The Flowers of the Three Companions].[11] Three years later, Rosalind Brooke published her own edition of the same Perugia manuscript.[12] Like Delorme, she omitted some passages arguing that they could be found elsewhere. In her arrangement of the material, Brooke took the same approach as Cambell, however, by identifying "we who were with him" with Brothers Leo, Rufino, and Angelo, the companions of Saint Francis. She based her argument on the letter traditionally found at the beginning of *The Legend of The Three Companions,*[13] maintaining that it offered a more accurate description of what was contained in the final three sections of Codex 1046. Thus Brooke published the letter at the beginning of the Perugia manuscript.

Marino Bigaroni in 1975 attempted to correct the problems associated with this text. In the first place, he "reclaimed" the work for Assisi,[14] arguing that the manuscript had been written in Assisi, not Perugia. More importantly, Bigaroni gave the work the more appropriate title of a "compilation." In doing so, however, he introduced another problem: the manner of treating this compilation. Bigaroni was undoubtedly aware of the approach originally taken by Delorme, and later by Cambell and Brooke, that is, to untangle the documents that make up the compilation and to study them chronologically.[15] Nevertheless, Bigaroni chose to publish the entire manuscript 1046 simply as a compilation of different texts written at different times, all of which were transcribed about 1311. By publishing the manuscript as he found it and giving it a new title, *The Assisi Compilation,* he avoided any attempts to re-arrange or interpret it.

As the initiatives of Cambell, Brooke, and Bigaroni were unfolding, Raoul Manselli was studying texts associated with Francis's companions. The result was *Nos Qui Cum Eo Fuimus,* which Manselli subtitled: *Contributo alla Questione Francescana* [Contribution to the Franciscan Question].[16] He called for a more critical, objective study of the sources for understanding Francis of Assisi. Manselli viewed Bigaroni's edition critically as a major contribution because it made the entire text of the Perugia manuscript accessible.[17] In 1992 Bigaroni eventually published a second edition of the *Compilatio Assisiensis,* correcting many of the errors or oversights of his first work and addressing the criticisms of scholars.[18] This final work forms the basis of this translation.

In light of the principle of the chronological order established at the outset,[19] determination of the place of *The Assisi Compilation* in *Francis of Assisi: Early Documents* was difficult. As noted, most scholars agree with 1311 as the date for the composition of Codex 1046. Bigaroni correctly called the work a "compilation" containing the material sent to Crescentius between 1244 and 1245, statements of Leo that Brooke maintains were written much later, and parts of *The Remembrance of the Desire of a Soul* by Thomas of Celano written between 1245 and 1247. Publishing only the earliest sections, following the examples of Delorme and Brooke, would settle the problems of chronology and of confusion about its title, and *The Legend of Perugia* could still be used. Such a decision, however, would overlook Bigaroni's contribution of identifying the work as a compilation.

In order to resolve these difficulties, the editors chose, in the first place, to acknowledge the Bigaroni text and to publish the entire *Assisi Compilation.* It is placed in this volume before *The Remembrance of the Desire of a Soul* to acknowledge the earlier composition of those reminiscences of Francis's companions. A meticulous comparison of the Latin texts of *The Assisi Compilation* with *The Remembrance of the Desire of a Soul* by Thomas of Celano revealed exact parallels. These verbatim parallels are indicated in *The Assisi Compilation* by means of a marginal note [2C↑] in which the arrow points to a future text. *The Remembrance of the Desire of a Soul* will indicate these passages by use of an emboldened font and the customary marginal reference [AC]. In both instances, the translation of each passage is the same. Furthermore, the editors chose to use marginal references to refer to *The Legend of Perugia* [LP] published by Ferdinand Delorme in his 1926 edition and translated in *St. Francis of Assisi: Omnibus of Sources.*

The Assisi Compilation remains a puzzling text. The opening paragraphs offer an insight into the overall text which is lacking in chronological or thematic order. The frequent use of the phrase "we who were with him" suggests that the text is a more immediate experience of Francis. Nevertheless, it is uneven and, at times, contradictory. On one hand, the text presents Francis as tolerant of many practices undertaken by the brothers, even as one who favors a greater liberty in certain ascetical practices. In many other passages, however, the saint appears harsh, judgmental, and abrupt.[20] At times "we who were with him" come across as acerbic, sharp, and opinionated; at others almost intimidated by the gentle, warm-hearted brother whom they champion.

Even a cursory reading of the *Assisi Compilation* gives the impression that, as early as the 1240's, its authors were disgruntled at events within the Order and eager to return to its primitive beginnings as they remembered them. Although it is difficult to date the *Words of Saint Francis* (AC 15-20) and the *Inten-*

tion of the Rule (AC 101-106), if, as Brooke suggests, those sections were written after 1247 and before 1260, they express the increasingly strident attitude of those friars who opposed developments within the Order. It is significant that all these texts, that is, the *Words*, the *Intention*, as well as the recollections of Francis's companions, were gathered and compiled at the turn of the century. The association of these texts with Ubertino da Casale and Angelo Clareno suggests that the *Assisi Compilation* involved more than furthering knowledge of Francis of Assisi. It took advantage of that knowledge to promote a cause, that of the Spirituals. As such, the *Assisi Compilation* is a document that represents three stages of Franciscan history: its earliest stage, then its early growing pains, and, finally, that of the clearly delineated division within the Order.

Notes

1. A complete description of the contents of the manuscript can be found in *Scripta Leonis, Rufini et Angeli Sociorum Sancti Francisci* [The Writings of Leo, Rufino and Angelo, Companions of Saint Francis], ed. and trans. by Rosalind B. Brooke (Oxford: Oxford University Press, 1970), 26-32.

2. See Brooke, *Scripta* 27, note 2.

3. Cf. Ubertino da Casale, *Declaratio fratris Ubertini de Casale et sotiorum eius contra falsitates datas per fratrem Raymundum procuratorem et Bonagratiam de Pergamo,* a cura di F. Ehrle, *Zur Vorgeschichte des Concils von Vienne,* "Archiv für litteratur-und kirchen-Geschichte des Mitellalters" 3 (1887), 162-195.

4. See Felice Accrocca, "La *Compilatio Assisiensis* nella 'Questione Francescana,' " AFH 86 (1993): 105-110; A. Gattucci, "dalla '*Legenda antiqua S. Francisci*' alla '*Compilatio Assisiensis*': storia di un testo piú prezioso che fortunato," *Studi Medievali* 20 (1979): 790-807.

5. *I Fiori dei Tre Compagni. Testi francescani latini ordinati, con introduzione e note,* edited by Jacques Cambell; Versione italiana a fronte di Nello Vian (Milan, 1966); translated into English by the title *We Were With Saint Francis: An Early Franciscan Story,* edited and translated by Salvator Butler (Chicago: Franciscan Herald Press, 1976).

6. See supra, n. 1.

7. *Légende de Pérouse,* translation and notes by Damien Vorreux, introduction by Théophile Desbonnets, in *Saint François d'Assise: Documents, écrits et Premières Biographies,* rassemblés et présentés par Théophile Desbonnets et Damien Vorreux. English translation, *Legend of Perugia,* translated by Paul Oligny from the annotated French version by Damien Vorreux, with an Introduction by Théophile Desbonnets in *Saint Francis of Assisi Writings and Early Biographies: English Omnibus of the Sources for the Life of Saint Francis,* edited by Marion A. Habig (Chicago: Franciscan Herald Press, 1973), 975-1091.

8. *"Compilatio Assisiensis" dagli Scritti di fr. Leone e Compagni su s. Francesco d'Assisi. Dal Ms. 1046 di Perugia. Il edizione integrale reveduta e correta con versione italiana a fronte e variazioni.* Edited by Marino Bigaroni (Assisi: Publicazioni della Biblioteca Francescana di Chiesa Nuova, 1992).

9. In 1901, Leonard Lemmens published the *Verba S. Francisci* which he had discovered in manuscrupt 1/73 in the library of St. Isidore Friary, Rome. It paralleled a text of Angelo Clareno, the *Expositio Regulae Fratrum Minorum* at the beginning of the fourteenth century. Cf. *Documenta Antiqua Franciscana,* vol I, ed. Leonardus Lemmens (Ad Aquas Claras, Quaracchi: Collegium S. Bonaventurae, 1901-1902), 83-99.

10. Ubertino da Casale cites *The Intention of the Rule* in his *Arbor Vitae.* It was also discovered in manuscript 1/73 of St. Isidore Friary in Rome. Cf. *Documenta Antiqua Franciscana,* vol I, ed. Leonardus Lemmens (Ad Aquas Claras, Quaracchi: Collegium S. Bonaventurae, 1901-1902), 100-106.

11. Supra, n. 5. For an assessment of Cambell's work, see the review of Edith Pásztor, *Studi Medievali* (1968): 252-264.

12. Supra, n. 1.

13. L3C 1, supra, 67-68

14. Théophile Desbonnets entitled the work the *Compilation of Perugia* and the text published by Delorme, *The Legend of Perugia.* The *Legend* was later republished by Desbonnets himself and Damien Vorreux in *Saint François d'Assise: Documents.* The French text was then translated into English and published in *St. Francis of Assisi: Writings and Early Biographies, English Omnibus of the Sources*

for the Life of St. Francis, edited by Marion A. Habig (Chicago: Franciscan Herald Press, 1973), 957-1101.

15. Cf. Jacques Dalarun, *La Malavventura di Francesco d'Assisi: Per Un Usuo Storico delle Legende Francescane* (Milano: Edizioni Biblioteca Francescana, 1996) 140-150.

16. Raoul Manselli, *Nos Qui Cum Eo Fuimus: Contributo alla Questione Francescana,* Bibliotheca Seraphico-Capuccina, 28 (Roma: Istituto Storico dei Cappuccini, 1980).

17. Cf. Raoul Manselli, "Introduction," in *Speculum Perfectionis (minus),* a cura di Marino Bigaroni (Assisi: 1983), XI-XII.

18. *"Compilatio Assisiensis" dagli Scritti di frate Leone e Compagni su S. Franceso d'Assisi. Dal Ms. 1046 di Perugia. Il edizione integrale riveduta e corretta con versione italiana a fronte e varianti, a cura di M. Bigaroni* (Assisi, 1992).

19. If the date given to the manuscript by Delorme is correct, the text says a great deal about the tensions existing in the first decades of the fourteenth century.

20. Cf. AC 62, 70, 74, etc. In light of these passages, it becomes easier to understand the challenges facing Thomas of Celano in writing the *Remembrance,* and Bonaventure in his *Legends.*

The Assisi Compilation

[1][a]
[FRANCIS DOES NOT WANT COMMANDS UNDER OBEDIENCE TO BE GIVEN LIGHTLY]

[His opinion was that only rarely should something be commanded under obedience, for the weapon of last resort should not be the first one used. As he said, "The hand should not reach quickly for the sword." He who does not hurry to obey what is commanded under obedience neither *fears God nor respects man.* Nothing could be truer. For what is command in a rash leader, but a sword in the hands of a madman? 2C 153↑

Lk 18:4

And what could be more hopeless than a religious who despises obedience?][b]

[2]
[HE FORETELLS THE FUTURE OF THE ORDER]

Ez 7:12 [Saint] Francis [also said: *"A time will come* when the religion loved by God will have such a bad reputation because of bad examples that it will be embarrassing to go out in public. Whoever comes to enter the Order at that time will be led only by the working of the 2C 157↑
Mt 16:17; Sir 11:23 Holy Spirit; *flesh and blood* will put no *blot on them;* they will be truly
Ps 114:5 *blessed by the Lord.* Although they will not do works of merit, for the love that makes saints work fervently will have grown cold, still they will undergo temptations; and whoever passes the tests of that time

a. The translation of this text is based on the critical edition of Marino Bigaroni, *"Compilatio Assisiensis" dagli Scritti di fr. Leone e Compagni su S. Francesco d'Assisi. Dal Ms. 1046 di Perugia. II edizione integrale revduta e correta con versione italiana a fronte e variazioni*, ed. Marino Bigaroni (Assisi: Pubblicazioni della Biblioteca Franciscana Chiesa Nuova, 1992).

Bigaroni numbered the paragraphs by taking into account paragraph beginnings marked by capital letters. Since there are no rubrics within the Manuscript 1046 of Perugia, Bigaroni considered the only criterion suggesting divisions of the text were those understood by the compiler or transcriber. "Even this criterion," he notes, "entails inconsistencies; but for a transcription of the Manuscript, it seems to me the only one that can be adopted." Cf. Bigaroni, *Compilatio* xi. Chapter headings are those of the editor of this translation. The numbers, as well as the titles of the chapters are bracketed to indicate that these have been added by Bigaroni or by the editors.

b. Bracketed sections of the text indicate those passages of AC which the editor of Manuscript 1046 of Perugia—dated 1310-1312—has taken verbatim from 2C, written between 1245-1247. Thus, although the bulk of this text was undoubtedly written by "we who were with him" before Thomas's second portrait of Francis, sections of the mauscript borrow from that later work. Cross references to these later passages of Thomas of Celano will be indicated in the inner margins as 2C↑. The translation that follows is based on the edition of Marino Bigaroni that assiduously follows the Perugia manuscript and delineates the Thomas passages.

will be better than those who came before. But woe to them who congratulate themselves over the appearance of a religious way of living, those numbed by idleness, those who do not firmly resist the temptations which are permitted to test the chosen! Only those who are *tested will receive the crown of life,* those who in the meantime are disturbed by the malice of the wicked."] Jas 1:12

[3]

[THE LORD SHOWS HIM WHEN HE IS BEING A TRUE SERVANT OF GOD]

2C 159↑ "Brothers," he would also say, ["*I prayed to the Lord* that he might 2 Cor: 12:8
deign to show me when *I am his servant* and when I am not, for I want Ps 119:125
to be nothing except his servant. And now the gracious Lord himself in his mercy is giving me this answer: 'Know that you are in truth my servant when you think, speak, and do things that are holy.' And so I have called you brothers because I want to be shamed in front of you if ever I am not doing any of those three"].

LP 98 [4][a]

[A BROTHER TELLS HIM THAT HIS BODY WILL BE HONORED AFTER HIS DEATH]

One day when blessed Francis lay sick in the palace of the bishop of Assisi,[b] one of the brothers, a spiritual and holy man, smiling and playfully, said to him: "You will sell all your sackcloth to the Lord for a good price! Many canopies and silk coverings will hang over this body of yours now clothed in sackcloth." At the time Saint Francis, on account of his illness, wore a fur cap covered with sackcloth as well as a tunic of sackcloth. With great fervor of spirit and joy blessed Francis—not himself, but the Holy Spirit through him—answered: "You're right because that's how it will be."

a. The cross reference indicated here refers to Ferdinand Delorme's ordering of the text. Cf. supra, 115.

b. A recurrent theme of AC is consideration of his illnesses. It occurs in AC 3, 4, 5, 7, 12, 22, 30, 44, 50, 51, 59, 66, 70, 71, 79, 80, 81, 83, 84, 85, 86, 90, 91, 96, 99, 100, 106, 117, 119, and 120. For thorough studies of Francis's illnesses, see Octavian Schmucki, "The Illnesses of Saint Francis of Assisi before His Stigmatization," GR 4 (1990) 31-61; "The Illnesses of Francis During the Last Years of His Life," GR 13 (1999), esp. 42-46.

[5] LP 99

[HE BLESSES ASSISI AS HE IS BEING CARRIED TO SAINT MARY OF THE PORTIUNCULA]

While he was staying in that palace, blessed Francis, realizing that he was getting sicker by the day, had himself carried on a litter to the church of Saint Mary of the Portiuncula, since he could not ride horseback because of his severe illness. When those who were carrying him passed by the hospital along the road, he asked them to place the litter on the ground. Since he could hardly see because of the serious and prolonged eye-disease, he had the litter turned so that he would face the city of Assisi. Raising himself up slightly on the litter, he blessed the city of Assisi. "Lord," he said, "just as I believe that at an earlier time this city was the abode of wicked and evil men, with a bad reputation throughout all this region; so now I realize that, because of Your abundant mercy and in Your own time, You have shown an abundance of mercies to it. Now it has become the abode of those who acknowledge You, give glory to Your name, offer the fragrance of good life, doctrine, and good reputation to the whole Christian people. I ask you, therefore, Lord Jesus Christ, Father of mercies, not to consider our ingratitude. May it always be mindful of the abundant mercies which You have shown to it, that it always be an abode for those who acknowledge You, and glorify Your name blessed and glorious throughout the ages. Amen."

After saying these things, he was carried to Saint Mary of the Portiuncula.

[6] LP 100

[AT THE NEWS OF HIS COMING DEATH HE HAS THE BROTHERS SING THE CANTICLE OF BROTHER SUN, WITH A NEW VERSE FOR SISTER DEATH]

From the time of his conversion till the day of his death, blessed Francis, whether healthy or sick, was always concerned to know and follow the will of the Lord.

[7] LP 100

One day a brother said to blessed Francis: "Father, your life and manner of living were and are a light and a mirror not only for your brothers but also for the entire Church of God, and your death will be the same. Although for the brothers and many others your death will mean great grief and sorrow, for you it will rather be a great consolation and infinite joy. You will pass from great toil to the greatest rest, from many sorrows and temptations to infinite happiness, from your great poverty, which you always loved and carried from the beginning of your conversion till the day of your death, to the greatest, true, and infinite riches, from death in time to life in eternity. There you will forever behold face to face the Lord your God whom you have contemplated in this world with so much desire and love."

After saying these things he said to him openly: "Father, you should know the truth: unless the Lord sends his own remedy from heaven to your body, your sickness is incurable and, as the doctors already said, you do not have long to live. I told you this to comfort your spirit, that you may always rejoice in the Lord, inside and out; especially so that your brothers and others who come to visit you may find you rejoicing in the Lord, since they know and believe that you will die soon. Thus, as they see this and, after your death, others hear about it, your death, like your life and manner of living, may be held in remembrance by all."

Although racked with sickness, blessed Francis praised God with great fervor of spirit and joy of body and soul, and told him: "If I am to die soon, call Brother Angelo and Brother Leo that they may sing to me about Sister Death."

CtC 1-11 Those brothers came to him and, with many tears, sang the *Canticle of Brother Sun* and the other creatures of the Lord, which the Saint himself had composed in his illness for the praise of the Lord and the consolation of his own soul and that of others. Before the last stanza he added one about Sister Death:

CtC 12-13 "Praised be You, my Lord, through our Sister Bodily Death,
from whom no one living can escape.
Woe to those who die in mortal sin.
Blessed are those whom death will find in Your most holy will,
for *the second death* shall do them no harm."

LP 101

[8]
[Lady Jacoba, inspired in prayer, comes from Rome to provide for his burial]

One day blessed Francis called his companions to himself: "You know how faithful and devoted Lady Jacoba dei Settesoli was and is to me and to our religion. Therefore I believe she would consider it a great favor and consolation if you notified her about my condition. Above all, tell her to send you some cloth for a tunic of religious cloth the color of ashes, like the cloth made by Cistercian monks in the region beyond the Alps.[a] Have her also send some of that confection which she often made for me when I was in the City. This confection, made of almonds, sugar or honey, and other things, the Romans call *mostacciolo.*

That spiritual woman was a holy widow, devoted to God. She belonged to one of the more noble and wealthy families of the entire City.[b] Through the merits and words of blessed Francis she had obtained such grace from God that she seemed like another Magdalene, always full of tears and devotion for love of God.

After the letter was written, as dictated by the holy father, while one brother was looking for another one to deliver the letter, there was a knock at the door. When one of the brothers opened the gate, he saw Lady Jacoba who had hurried from the City to visit blessed Francis. With great joy the brother immediately went to tell blessed Francis that Lady Jacoba had come to visit him with her son and many other people. "What shall we do, Father," he said, "shall we allow her to enter and come in here?" He said this because blessed Francis a long time ago had ordered that in that place no women should enter that cloister out of respect and devotion for that place. Blessed Francis answered him: "This command need not be observed in the case of this lady whose faith and devotion made her come here from so far away." And in this way, she came in to see blessed Francis, crying many tears in his presence.

It was amazing: she brought with her shroud-cloth, that is, gray-colored cloth, for a tunic, and all the other things that were written in the letter. This made the brothers greatly marvel at the holiness of blessed Francis.

"While I was praying," Lady Jacoba told the brothers, "a voice within me said 'Go, visit your father, blessed Francis, without delay, and hurry, because if you delay long you will not find him alive.

a. The Cistercians adopted a habit of unbleached wool at the time of the second abbot, Alberic, in the first decade of the twelfth century. It was rhetorically called white, but was in fact a dirty gray, so that the monks were frequently called the "gray monks." Cf. Vincentius Hermans, *Commentarium Cisterciense: Historico-Practicum in Codicis Canones de Religiosis* (Roma: Tipografia Pio X, 1961), 402.

b. Jacoba (or Giacoma) dei Settesoli was of a noble Roman family of high rank, the descendant on her father's side of the Norman knights who had conquered Sicily. Her husband, Graziano, was a member of one of Rome's great families, the Frangipani. They were believed to be the descendants of Flavius Anicius, who in 717 A.D. saved the people of Rome from famine by giving them bread and so was given the name *Frangens panem.* (or "Frangipani," "breaking bread"). The family also traced its descent from Aeneas, son of Anchises, the Trojan hero whose emigration to Italy is told in Virgil's *Aeneid.* The name Settesoli came from the Septizonium, the imposing structure that the Frangipani acquired in 1145 from Camaldolese monks.

Moreover, take such and such cloth for his tunic, as well as the ingredients for making that particular confection. Take with you also a great quantity of wax and incense.'" Blessed Francis did not have incense written in the letter, but the Lord Himself willed to inspire that lady as a reward and consolation for her soul. In this way we would more easily recognize the great holiness of that saint, that poor man, whom the heavenly Father wished to honor so greatly in the days he was dying. He inspired the Kings to travel with gifts to honor the child, His beloved Son, in the days of His birth and His poverty. So too He willed to inspire this noble lady in a faraway region to travel with gifts to honor and venerate the glorious and holy body of His servant the saint, who loved and followed the poverty of His beloved Son with so much fervor and love in life and in death.

One day that lady made that confection the holy father wanted to eat. He ate only a little of it, however, since he was near death, and daily his body was becoming weaker on account of his illness.

She also had many candles made which would burn around his holy body after his death. From the cloth she had brought for his tunic, the brothers made him the tunic in which he was buried. He himself ordered the brothers to sew pieces of sackcloth on the outside of it as a sign and example of most holy humility and poverty. It happened, as it pleased God, that during the same week that Lady Jacoba arrived, blessed Francis passed to the Lord.

LP 102

[9]

[HE WANTS HIS BROTHERS TO SERVE LEPERS AS A SIGN OF HUMILITY AND POVERTY]

From the beginning of his conversion blessed Francis, with God's help, like a wise man, established himself and his house, that is, the religion, upon a firm rock, the greatest humility and poverty of the Son of God, calling it the religion of "Lesser Brothers."

On the greatest humility: thus at the beginning of the religion, after the brothers grew in number, he wanted the brothers to stay in hospitals of lepers to serve them. At that time whenever nobles and commoners came to the religion, they were told, among other things, that they had to serve the lepers and stay in their houses.

LR VI 2 On the greatest poverty: as stated in the *Rule,* let the brothers re-
LR VI 6 main as strangers and pilgrims in the houses in which they stay. Let
them not seek to have anything under heaven, except holy poverty, by which, in this world, they are nourished by the Lord with bodily food and virtue, and, in the next, will attain a heavenly inheritance.

He established himself on the greatest poverty and humility, because, although he was a great prelate in the church of God, he wanted and chose to be lowly not only in the church of God, but also among his brothers.

[10] LP 103

[HIS HUMILITY TOWARD THE BISHOP OF TERNI "I MAY YET HAVE SONS AND DAUGHTERS"]

One day he was preaching to the people of Terni in the piazza in front of the bishop's residence. The bishop of that city, a discerning and spiritual man, attended that sermon. When the sermon was over, the bishop stood up and, among the other words of God that he spoke to them, he said: "From the beginning, when the Lord planted and built His church, He always beautified it with holy men who would improve it by word and example. Now, in this final hour, God has beautified his Church with this little poor man, lowly and unlettered," pointing all the while to blessed Francis. "And because of this," he continued, "you should love and honor the Lord and avoid
Ps 147:20 sin *'for He has not done this for every nation.'* "

After the sermon, blessed Francis came down from the place where he was preaching, and together the Lord Bishop and blessed Francis entered the bishop's church. Then blessed Francis bowed down before the Lord Bishop and fell down at his feet, saying to him: "I tell you the truth, my Lord Bishop: no person in this world has yet honored me as much as you have today. Other people say: 'That man is a saint!' They attribute glory and holiness to the creature, not to the Creator. You, however, like a discerning man, have separated what is precious from what is vile."

Often when blessed Francis was honored and people said, "This LP 104
man is a saint," he would respond to such expressions by saying: "I'm still not sure that I won't have sons and daughters." And he would say: "If at any moment the Lord wanted to take back the treasure He has loaned to me, what would I have left except just body and soul, which even non-believers have? I must believe, rather, that if the Lord had granted a thief and even a non-believer as many gifts as He has given me, they would be more faithful to the Lord than I."

He continued: "As in a painting of the Lord and the Blessed Virgin on wood, it is God and the Blessed Virgin who are honored, and God and the Blessed Virgin are held in memory. The wood and the paint attribute nothing to themselves because they are merely wood and paint. In the same way, a servant of God is a painting, that is, a creature of God, in whom God is honored because of His goodness. Like wood or paint, he must not attribute anything to himself, but give all honor and glory to God. He should not attribute anything to himself while he is alive except shame and trouble, because, while he is alive, the flesh is always opposed to God's gifts."

LP 105

[11]
[He resigns from office in the Order and always wants to have a guardian]

Blessed Francis wanted to be humble among his brothers. To preserve greater humility, a few years after his conversion he resigned the office of prelate before all the brothers during a chapter held at Saint Mary of the Portiuncula. "From now on," he said, "I am dead to you. But here is Brother Peter di Catanio: let us all, you and I, obey him." Then all the brothers began to cry loudly and weep profusely, but blessed Francis bowed down before Brother Peter and promised
ER Prol 4 him obedience and reverence.

LP106 From that time on, until his death, he remained a subject, like one of the other brothers. He wished to be subject to the general minister and the provincial ministers, so that in whatever province he stayed or preached, he obeyed the minister of that province. What is more, a long time before his death, for the sake of greater perfection and humility, he said to the general minister: "I ask you to put one of my companions in your place regarding me, so that I may obey him as I would obey you. For the sake of good example and the virtue of obedience, in life and in death I always want you to be with me."

From that time until his death, he always had one of his companions as a guardian whom he obeyed in place of the general minister.[a] One time he said to his companions: "Among other favors, the Most High has given me this grace: I would obey a novice who entered our religion today, if he were appointed my guardian, just as readily as I would obey him who is the first and the eldest in the life and religion of the brothers. A subject should not consider his prelate, a human being, but God, for love of Whom he is subject to him." He likewise said: "There is no prelate in the whole world who would be as feared by his subjects and brothers as the Lord would make me feared by my brothers, if I wished. But the Most High gave me this grace: that I want to be content with all, as one who is lesser in the religion."

a. For an explanation of the word *guardianus* [guardian], see FA:ED I 98a.

We who were with him[a] witnessed this often with our own eyes. Frequently, when some of the brothers did not provide for his needs, or said something to him that would ordinarily offend a person, he would immediately go to prayer. On returning, he did not want to remember it by saying "Brother so and so did not provide for me," or "He said such and such to me."

The closer he approached death, the more careful he became in complete perfection to consider how he might live and die in complete humility and poverty.

[12] [As he is dying he blesses Brother Bernard and predicts his holy death]

LP 107

The day Lady Jacoba prepared that confection for blessed Francis, the father remembered Bernard. "Brother Bernard likes this confection," he said to his companions. Calling one of his companions, he told him: "Go, tell Brother Bernard to come to me immediately." The brother went at once and brought him to blessed Francis. Sitting next to the bed where blessed Francis was lying, Brother Bernard said: "Father! I beg you, bless me and show me your love. I believe that, if you show me your love with fatherly affection, God Himself and the other brothers of the religion will love me more."

Blessed Francis was not able to see him, since many days earlier he had lost his sight. Extending his right hand, he placed it on the head of Brother Giles, the third of the first brothers, who at that moment was sitting next to Brother Bernard. He thought he was placing it on the head of Brother Bernard. Feeling the head of Brother Giles, like a person going blind, he immediately recognized him by the Holy Spirit, and said, "This is not the head of my Brother Bernard."[b]

Brother Bernard immediately drew closer to him. Blessed Francis, placing his hand on his head, blessed him. "Write what I tell you," he then said to one of his companions. "Brother Bernard was the first brother the Lord gave me. He began first and most perfectly fulfilled the perfection of the holy Gospel, distributing all his goods to the

a. Raoul Manselli, *Nos Qui Cum Eo Fuimus: Contributo alla Questione Francescana*, Bibliotheca Seraphico-Capuccina, 28 (Roma: Istituto Storico dei Cappuccini, 1980), 44-57.

b. This blessing of Bernard is in contradiction to that of Elias, see 1C 108. It suggests the shifting portrait of Elias that undoubtedly changed with the vicissitudes of history. Thorough studies of this incident can be found in Raoul Manselli, "L'Ultima Decisione di S. Francesco. Bernardo di Quintavalle e la benedizione di s. Francesco morente," in *Bolletino dell'Istituto Storico Italiano per il Medio Evo e Archivio Muratoriano* 78(1967) 137-153; Jacques Dalarun, "La dernière volonté de saint François. Homage à Raoul Manselli," in *Bolletino dell'Istituto Storico Italiano per il Medio Evo e Archivio Muratoriano* 94 (1988), 329-366.

poor. Because of this and his many other prerogatives, I am bound to love him more than any other brother in the whole religion. As much as I am able, it is my will and command that whoever becomes general minister should love and honor him as he would me. Let the other provincial ministers and the brothers of the whole religion hold him in my place."[a] Because of this, Brother Bernard was greatly consoled as were the other brothers who saw this.

LP 108 Another time, considering the outstanding perfection of Brother Bernard, blessed Francis prophesied about him in the presence of some of the brothers: "I tell you, some of the greatest and most cunning devils have been sent to test Brother Bernard. They will send him many trials and temptations. The merciful Lord, however, will deliver him toward the end of his life from all troubles and temptations, internal and external. And He will place his spirit and body in such peace, quiet, and consolation that all the brothers who see or hear of this will be greatly astonished, and consider it a great miracle. In this peace, quiet, and consolation of both body and soul, he will pass from this world to the Lord."

The brothers who heard this from blessed Francis were greatly astonished, since everything he predicted about him through the Holy Spirit came true, to the letter, point by point. In his last illness Brother Bernard was in such great peace and quiet of spirit that he did not want to lie down. And if he lay down, he lay in a sitting position so that not even the lightest mist of humors would reach his head, inducing fantasies or dreams, rather than thoughts of God. And if this happened, he would immediately get up and strike himself, saying "What was that? Why was I thinking that way?" For relief, he gladly used to smell rose water, but as he drew closer to death, he refused to do even this, for the sake of constant meditation on God. He would say to anyone offering it: "Don't distract me."

In order to die more freely, peacefully, and quietly, he deprived himself of care for his body, putting himself in the hands of one of the brothers who was a doctor and who was taking care of him. "I do not wish to be concerned about eating or drinking," he would say, "but I entrust myself to you. If you give me something, I'll take it. If you don't, then I won't."

When he began to grow weaker, he wanted to have a priest brother with him at all times, until the hour of his death. Whenever

a. In his critical edition of the writings of Saint Francis, Kajetan Esser placed this passage among the "Dictates," cf. *Opusucla Sancti Patris Francisci Assisiensis*, Bibliotheca Franciscana Ascetica Medii Aevi, t. XII, ed. Caietanus Esser (Grottaferrata, Roma: Editiones Collegii S. Bonaventurae Ad Claras Aquas, 1978), 319-320.

any thought entered his mind for which his conscience reproached him, he immediately confessed it and then said his penance.

After his death, his flesh became white and soft and he seemed to be smiling, so that he appeared more handsome after death than before. Whoever gazed on him experienced more delight in seeing him this way than when he was alive, because he looked like a saint who was smiling.

[13]

LP 109

[BEFORE DYING HE SENDS A LETTER TO LADY CLARE, PROMISING THAT SHE WILL SEE HIM AGAIN]

During the week in which blessed Francis died, Lady Clare was seriously ill. She was the first plant of the Order of Sisters, the abbess of the Poor Sisters of the monastery of San Damiano in Assisi, who emulated Saint Francis in observing always the poverty of the Son of God.[a] She feared that she would die before blessed Francis. She wept in bitterness of spirit and could not be comforted, because she would not be able before her death to see her only father after God, that is, blessed Francis, her comforter both internally and externally, and her first founder in God's grace.[b]

She sent word of this to blessed Francis through one of the brothers. Blessed Francis heard this and was moved to piety,[c] since he loved her and her sisters with fatherly affection because of their holy manner of living, and especially because, a few years after he began to have brothers, she was converted to the Lord through his advice, working with the Lord. Her conversion not only greatly edified the religion of the brothers, but also the entire Church of God. Blessed Francis considered that what she desired, that is, to see him, could not be done then since they were both seriously ill. To console her, he wrote his blessing in a letter and also absolved her from any failings, if she had any, regarding his commands and wishes or the com-

a. While none of the early sources for Clare's life provides information on the nature of her illness at this time, the Poor Ladies living with her at San Damiano "marveled at how her body survived" due to her prolonged and strict fasts. Lady Pacifica testified: "She kept such abstinence that she developed a certain illness so Saint Francis together with the Bishop of Assisi commanded her to eat a half roll of bread, about one and a half ounces on those three days, i.e., Monday, Wednesday and Friday when she did not eat anything." Cf. "Process of Canonization" I:7-8, in *Clare of Assisi: Early Documents,* 138.

b. Rosalind B. Brooke, in her *Scripta Leonis*, adds a variant at this point: "*ab ipso glorioso domino sibi collata, ante eius conversionem, et in eius sancta conversatione* [granted her by the Lord before her conversion and in her holy manner of living]."

c. As in earlier texts, *pietas* [piety] appears as a frequent motive. The phrase *motus est ad pietatem* [moved to piety] or variations appears throughout this text. In fact various forms of the word *pietas* appear 29 times throughout the text. See FA:ED I 189 c.

mands and wishes of the Son of God.[a] Moreover, so that she would put aside all her grief and be consoled in the Lord, he, or rather the Spirit of God speaking through him, spoke to the brother she had sent. "Go and take this letter to Lady Clare, and tell her to put aside all her grief and sorrow over not being able to see me now. Let her be assured that before her death, both she and her sisters will see me and will receive the greatest consolation from me."

Soon afterwards blessed Francis passed away during the night. In the morning, all the people of the city of Assisi, men and women, with all the clergy, took the holy body from the place where he had died. With hymns and praises, all carrying tree branches, they carried him to San Damiano at the Lord's will, in order to fulfill that word which the Lord had spoken through His saint to console His daughters and servants.

The iron grille was removed from the window through which the servants of Christ usually receive communion and sometimes hear the word of God. The brothers lifted his holy body from the stretcher and, raising him in their arms, they held him in front of the window for over an hour. By then Lady Clare and her sisters had received the greatest consolation from him, although they wept profusely and were afflicted with great grief, because, after God, he was their one consolation in this world.[b]

LP 110

[14]

[A FLOCK OF LARKS SING ABOVE THE HUT WHERE HE IS DYING]

Saturday evening before nightfall, after vespers, when blessed Francis passed to the Lord, many birds called larks flew low above the roof of the house where blessed Francis lay, wheeling in a circle and singing.

We, who were with blessed Francis, and who wrote these things about him, bear witness that we often heard him say: "If I ever speak to the emperor, I will beg him, for the love of God and by my entreaties, to enact a written law forbidding anyone to catch our sister larks or do them any harm. Likewise, all mayors of cities and lords of castles and villages should be bound to oblige people each year on the Nativity of the Lord to scatter wheat and other grain along the roads outside towns and villages, so that all the birds, but especially our sister larks, may have something to eat on such a solemn feast. Also,

a. In *Die Opuscula*, 320, Esser also placed this passage among the "Dictates."

b. There are significant differences between this account of the body of Francis being brought to San Damiano and that of Thomas's *Life of Saint Francis*, cf. 1C 116-117.

out of reverence for the Son of God, whom His Virgin Mother on that night laid in a manger between an ox and ass, everyone should have to give brother ox and brother ass a generous portion of fodder on that night. Likewise, on the Nativity of the Lord, all the poor should be fed their fill by the rich."

For blessed Francis held the Nativity of the Lord in greater reverence than any other of the Lord's solemnities. For although the Lord may have accomplished our salvation in his other solemnities, nevertheless, once He was born to us, as blessed Francis would say, it was certain that we would be saved. On that day he wanted every Christian to rejoice in the Lord and, for love of Him who gave Himself to us, wished everyone to be cheerfully generous not only to the poor but also to the animals and birds.

Concerning larks, blessed Francis used to say, "Our Sister Lark, has a capuche like religious, and is a humble bird, who gladly goes along the road looking for some grain. Even if she finds it in the animals' manure, she pecks it out and eats it. While flying, she praises the Lord, like good religious who look down on earthly things, and whose life is always in heaven. Moreover, her clothes, that is, her feathers, resemble earth, giving an example to religious not to wear clothes that are colorful and refined, but dull, like earth." And because blessed Francis considered all these things in sister larks, he loved them very much and was glad to see them.

[15][a]

LP 111

[TAKING ALMS CAN ROB THE POOR]

Blessed Francis often said these words to the brothers: "I have never been a thief, that is, in regard to alms, which are the inheritance of the poor. I always took less than I needed, so that other poor people would not be cheated of their share. To act otherwise would be theft."

a. Paragraphs 15-20 contain the *Verba Sancti Francisci* [The Words of Saint Francis] which were quoted by Angelo Clareno in his *Expositio Regulae Fratrum Minorum*, edited by Livarius Oliger (Quaracchi, Florence: 1912), 126-130. They were also identified by Leonard Lemmens in his 1901 edition of manuscript 1/73 of the College of Saint Isidore in Rome, cf. *Documenta Antiqua Franciscana* (Quaracchi: Ad Aquas Claras, 1901-1902). Rosalind Brooke writes: "We may conclude . . . that the *Verba*, which has not impinged on 2 Celano and shows signs of being later than the original collection made by the Three Companions, would appear to be a group of stories added to their original collection after 1247, but well before 1311, most probably before 1260," Cf. Brooke, *Scripta*, 63.

LP 112

[16]
[THE MINISTERS AND POVERTY]

When the brother ministers urged him to allow the brothers to have something at least in common, so that such a great number would have some resources, Saint Francis called upon Christ in prayer and consulted Him about this. Christ immediately responded that He would take away everything held individually or in common, saying that this is His family for whom He was always ready to provide, no matter how much it might grow, and He would always cherish it as long as it would put its hope in Him.[a]

LP 113

[17]
[HE RESPONDS TO BROTHER ELIAS AND THE MINISTERS WHO OBJECTED TO THE RULE HE WAS WRITING AT FONTE COLOMBO]

When blessed Francis was on a mountain with Brother Leo of Assisi and Brother Bonizo of Bologna to make the *Rule*,[b]—because the first, which he had written at Christ's instruction, was lost[c]—a great many ministers gathered around Brother Elias, who was the vicar of blessed Francis. "We heard that Brother Francis is making a new rule," they told him, "and we fear that he will make it so harsh that we will not be able to observe it. We want you to go to him and tell him that we refuse to be bound to that *Rule*. Let him make it for himself and not for us."

Brother Elias replied to them that he did not want to go because he feared the rebuke of Brother Francis. When they insisted that he go, he said that he refused to go without them; so they all went.

When Brother Elias, with those ministers, was near the place where blessed Francis was staying, he called him. Blessed Francis responded and, seeing those ministers, he said: "What do these brothers want?" "These are ministers," Brother Elias answered, "who heard that you are making a new rule. They fear that you are making it very harsh, and they say, and say publicly, that they refuse to be bound by it. Make it for yourself and not for them."

a. This is the first passage that portrays Christ as speaking directly to Francis concerning the direction of the brothers.

b. Little is known about Bonizo (Bonizzo) of Bologna. Arnaldo Fortini calls him "a gifted jurist of the University of Bologna," although he provides no source for that information, cf. Fortini, *Francis*, 524. Rosalind B. Brooke is undoubtedly more accurate when she describes Bonizzo as simply "an obscure figure," cf. Brooke, *Scripta* 60.

c. There has been long-standing speculation and controversy about this loss and the reasons for it.

Then blessed Francis turned his face to heaven and spoke to Christ in this way: "Lord! Didn't I tell you they wouldn't believe you?" The voice of Christ was then heard in the air, saying "Francis, nothing of yours is in the *Rule*: whatever is there is all mine. And I want the *Rule* observed in this way: to the letter, to the letter, to the letter, and without a gloss, without a gloss, without a gloss."[a] And He added: "I know how much human weakness is capable of, and how much I want to help them. Those who refuse to observe it should leave the Order." Then blessed Francis turned to the brothers and said: "Did you hear? Did you hear? Do you want me to have you told again?" Then the ministers, confused and blaming themselves, departed.

[18]

LP 114

[His response to Cardinal Hugolino and to the brothers about taking an existing monastic rule]

When blessed Francis was at the general chapter called the Chapter of Mats, held at Saint Mary of the Portiuncula, there were five thousand brothers present. Many wise and learned brothers told the Lord Cardinal, who later became Pope Gregory, who was present at the chapter, that he should persuade blessed Francis to follow the advice of those same wise brothers and allow himself to be guided by them for the time being. They cited the *Rule* of blessed Benedict, of blessed Augustine, and of blessed Bernard, which teach how to live in such order in such a way.[b]

Then blessed Francis, on hearing the cardinal's advice about this, took him by the hand and led him to the brothers assembled in chapter, and spoke to the brothers in this way: "My brothers! My brothers! God has called me by the way of simplicity and showed me the

a. Although the phrase *ad litteram* [to the letter], repeated three times for emphasis, appears in 1C 22, in the context of living the Gospel, this is the first instance of its use in this context, concerning the literal observance of the *Rule*. Gregory IX used it in *Quo elongati* 4 in attempting to resolve conflicts in interpreting the *Rule*: *vix vel numquam omnia posse ad litteram observari* [it is only with difficulty, if at all, that they can observe everything to the letter]. The phrase has its origins in the Cistercian tradition where it is used in the *Exordium Magnum* 3, and represents language linked with reformist monasticism from 1050-1150. Cf. Examples in PL 182:887; 185:1008; 188:640; 202:1309. The same may be said of the thrice emphasized phrase *sine glossa* [without gloss], which is also found in the *Exordium Magnum* 3. In his *Testament*, however, Francis forbids the brothers to place any gloss upon the *Rule* or his writings (Test 38), and encouraged them to understand the *Rule* and *Testament* "simply and without gloss" (Test 39). To place these phrases in a fuller context, see Duncan Nimmo, *Reform and Division in the Franciscan Order: From Saint Francis to the Foundation of the Capuchins*, Bibliotheca Seraphico-capuccina 33 (Rome: Capuchin Historical Institute, 1987), esp. 104-108.

b. The text may also be rendered: "which teach living in such and such a way, with order"; or "which teach living in this way, and in such an orderly manner"; or even, "which teach how to live in such and such a way, like an Order."

way of simplicity. I do not want you to mention to me any *Rule*, whether of Saint Augustine, or of Saint Bernard, or of Saint Benedict.[a] And the Lord told me what He wanted: He wanted me to be a new fool in the world. God did not wish to lead us by any way other than this knowledge, but God will confound you by your knowledge and wisdom. But I trust in the Lord's police that through them He will punish you, and you will return to your state, to your blame, like it or not."

The cardinal was shocked, and said nothing, and all the brothers were afraid.

[19]

[HIS EXPLANATION OF THE BROTHERS' RELATIONSHIP TO CLERICS]

2C 146↑ [Although] blessed Francis [wanted his sons *to keep peace with all* Rom 12:18
and to behave as little ones toward everyone, he taught them to be particularly humble toward clerics by his word and showed them by his example.

He used to say: "We have been sent to help clerics for the *salvation* 1 Pt:9
of souls so that we may make up whatever may be lacking in them.[b]
Each shall receive a reward, not *on account of* authority, but because *of the* 1 Cor 3:8
work done. Know then, brothers, that the] profit or [good of souls is
what pleases God the most, and this is more easily obtained through
peace with the clergy than fighting with them. If they should stand
in the way of the people's salvation, *revenge is* for God, *and he will repay* Dt 32:35
them *in due time.* So, be subject to prelates so that, as much as *possible* Rom 12:18
on your part no jealousy arises. *If you are children of peace,* you will win Lk 10:6
over both clergy and people for the Lord, and *the Lord* will judge that 1 Pt 2:5
more *acceptable* than only winning over the people, while scandalizing the clergy. Cover up their failings, make up for their many defects, and *when you have done* this, be even more humble."] Lk 17:10

a. For a synthesis of the different paradigms of religious life expressed in these three traditions, i.e., the Benedictine, Cistercian, and Augustinian, see David Knowles, *From Pachomius to Ignatius: A Study of the Constitutional History of the Religious Orders* (Oxford: Oxford at The Clarendon Press, 1966), 1-41; Herbert Grundmann, *Religious Movements in the Middle Ages*, trans. Steven Rowan with introduction by Robert E. Lerner (Notre Dame, London: University of Notre Dame Press, 1995), 31-67.

b. This statement echoes Canon 10 of the IV Lateran Council which ordered bishops to ordain suitable persons for assistance. Cf. Herbert J. Schroeder, *Disciplinary Decrees of the General Councils* (St. Louis: Herder and Herder, 1938), 252.

[20]

[His refusal to request privileges from the Roman Curia]

LP 115

Some of the brothers told blessed Francis: "Father, don't you see that sometimes bishops do not permit us to preach, allowing us to remain idle in an area for many days before we can preach to the people? It would be better if you arranged for the brothers to get a privilege from the Lord Pope: it would be the salvation of souls."

He answered them with a stern rebuke, telling them: "You, Lesser Brothers, you do not know the will of God, and will not allow me to convert the whole world as God wills. For I want to convert the prelates first by humility and reverence. Then, when they see your holy life and your reverence for them, they will ask you to preach and convert the people. These will attract the people to you far better than the privileges you want, which would lead you to pride. And if you are free of all avarice, and lead the people to give the churches their due, they will ask you to hear the confessions of their people. Although you should not be concerned about this, for if they are converted, they will easily find confessors.

For my part, I want only this privilege from the Lord: not to have any privilege from any human being, except to show reverence to all, and, by the obedience of the holy *Rule*, to convert everyone more by example than by word."[a]

[21]

[Christ complains to Brother Leo about the ingratitude of the] brothers

LP 116

One time the Lord Jesus Christ said to Brother Leo, the companion of blessed Francis: "I have a complaint about the brothers." "About what, Lord?" Brother Leo replied. And the Lord said: "About three things. They do not recognize My gifts which, as you know, I generously bestow on them daily, since they neither sow nor reap. All day long they are idle and complain. And they often provoke one another to anger, and do not return to love, and do not pardon the injury they receive."

a. This is the last of the *Verba Sancti Francisci*, cf. AC 15, supra, 130 a.

LP 117

[22]

[HE BLESSES THE BROTHERS AND SHARES BREAD WITH THEM WHEN HE WAS VERY ILL]

One night blessed Francis was so afflicted with the pains of his illness that he could barely rest or sleep that night. In the morning, when his pain eased a bit, he had all the brothers staying in that place called to him, and when they were seated around him, he considered them and regarded them as representatives of all the brothers.

Beginning with one brother, he blessed them, placing his right hand on the head of each one, and he blessed all who were in the religion and all who were to come until the end of the world.[a] He seemed to feel sorry for himself because he was not able to see his sons and brothers before his death.

Afterwards he ordered loaves of bread to be brought to him and he blessed them. Unable to break them because of his illness, he had them broken into many little pieces by one of the brothers. Taking them, he offered each of the brothers a little piece, telling them to eat all of it. Just as the Lord desired to eat with the apostles on the Thursday before His death, it seemed to those brothers that, in a similar way, blessed Francis, before his death, wanted to bless them and, in them, all the other brothers, and that they should eat that blessed bread as if in some way they were eating with the rest of their brothers.

And we can consider this obvious because, while it was a day other than Thursday, he told the brothers that he believed it was Thursday.

One of the brothers kept a piece of that bread, and after the death of blessed Francis some people who tasted it were immediately freed from their illnesses.

[23]

[THE DWELLINGS OF THE BROTHERS SHOULD BE POOR; ABOUT FURNISHINGS, BOOKS, AND BEDS]

2C 56↑ [He taught his] brothers [to make poor little dwellings out of wood, and not stone, and how to build these huts according to a crude sketch].

a. In contrast with the earlier account of this final blessing, no brother in particular is mentioned, i.e., neither Bernard of Quintavalle nor Elias. Cf. AC 12, supra, 126 a.

[He did not want the brothers to live in any place unless it had a definite owner who held the property rights. He always wanted to have the law of pilgrims for his sons].[a] 2C 59↑

[24]

[This man not only hated pretense in houses; he also abhorred having many or fine furnishings in them. He disliked anything, in tables or dishes, that recalled the ways of the world. He wanted everything to sing of exile and pilgrimage]. 2C 60↑

[25]

Ps 19:8 [He taught that in books *the testimony of the Lord,* not value, should be sought, edification rather than elegance. He wanted few books kept, and these should be available to the brothers who needed them]. 2C 62↑

[26]

[Finally, beds and coverings abounded in such plentiful poverty that if a brother had a ragged sheet over some straw he considered it a bridal couch]. 2C 63↑

a. Marino Bigaroni notes a reference to Exodus 12:49 which speaks of the law for anyone who is a pilgrim among the Hebrews. The law in question refers to what is demanded of a pilgrim wishing to celebrate the Passover with the Hebrew community, i.e., circumcision. Francis's use of the term seems more appropriately to refer to the laws established for pilgrims to the Holy Land, Rome, and Compostella because of abuses that had developed. Many of these laws or required practices were described in guidebooks and differed from shrine to shrine. In this instance, however, Francis may well be referring to the medieval requirements of wearing special clothes reminiscent of a penitent, of putting one's affairs in order, traveling poorly and depending on the alms of others, and of obtaining permission from a bishop or religious superior. Cf. Jonathan Sumption, *Pilgrimage: An Image of Medieval Religion* (Totowa, NJ: Rowman and Littlefield, 1975); Steven McMichael, "Francis of Assisi as Medieval Pilgrim," *Holy Land Quarterly* (1984): 3-10; E.R. LaBande, "Pilgrimages: 3. Medieval and Modern," *New Catholic Encyclopedia* XI (Washington, D.C.: Catholic University of America, 1967), 365-372.

[27]
[HE REBUKES A BROTHER WHO TOUCHED COINS LEFT AT THE PORTIUNCULA]

2C 65↑ [While this true friend of God completely despised all worldly things, he detested money above all. From the beginning of his conversion, he despised money particularly and encouraged his followers to flee from it always as from the devil himself. He gave his followers this observation: money and manure are equally worthy of love.

Now it happened one day that a layman came to pray in the church of Saint Mary of the Portiuncula and placed some money by the cross as an offering. When he left, one of the brothers simply picked it up with his hand and threw it on the windowsill. What the brother had done reached the saint, and he, seeing he had been caught, ran to ask forgiveness, threw himself to the ground, and offered himself to be whipped.

The saint rebuked him and reprimanded him severely for touching coins. He ordered him to pick up the money from the windowsill with his own mouth, take it outside the fence of that place, and with his mouth to put it on the donkey's manure pile. While that brother was gladly carrying out this command, fear filled the hearts of the rest who heard it. From then on, all of them held in even greater contempt what had been so equated with manure and were encouraged to despise it by new examples every day].

[28]
[HIS EXHORTATIONS ABOUT AVOIDING SOFT CLOTHING AND ENDURING LACK OF NECESSITIES]

2C 69↑ [Clothed with power this man was warmed more by divine fire on the inside than by what covered his body on the outside].

[29]

2C 69↑ [He detested those in the Order who dressed in three layers of clothing or who wore soft clothes without necessity. As for "necessity" not based on reason but on pleasure, he declared that it was a
sign of a *spirit* that was *extinguished.* "When the spirit is lukewarm," 1 Thes 5:19
he said, "and gradually growing cold as it moves from grace, flesh and blood inevitably seek their own interests. When the soul finds no delight, what is left except for the flesh to look for some? Then the

base instinct covers itself with the excuse of necessity, and the mind of the flesh forms the conscience."

And he added:][a]

[30]

["Let's say one of my brothers encounters a real necessity: he is af- 2C 69↑
Gn 29:15 fected by some need. If he rushes to satisfy it, *what reward will he get?*
He found an occasion for merit, but clearly showed that he did not like it." With these and similar words he pierced those who would not tolerate necessity. He taught that not bearing patiently with
Nm 14:2-4 need is the same as *returning to Egypt*. He did not want the brothers to have more than two tunics under any circumstances, and these he allowed to be mended with patches sewn on them. He ordered the brothers to shun fine fabrics, and those who acted to the contrary he rebuked publicly with biting words. To confound them by his example, he sewed sackcloth on his own rough tunic and at his death he asked that the tunic for his funeral be covered in cheap sackcloth. But he allowed brothers pressed by illness or other necessity to wear a soft tunic next to the skin, as long as rough and cheap clothing was kept on the outside. For he said: "A time will come when strictness will be relaxed, and tepidity will hold such sway, that sons of a poor father will not be the least ashamed to wear even velvet cloth, just changing the color].[b]

[31]
[HE GIVES AWAY A MANTLE TO A POOR WOMAN]

[In Celano at winter time, Saint Francis was wearing a piece of 2C 86↑
folded cloth as a cloak, which a friend of the brothers had lent him. While he was at the palace of the bishop of the Marsi,[c] an old woman
Acts 3:2 came up to him *begging for alms.* He quickly unfastened the cloth from his neck, and, although it belonged to someone else, he gave it to the

a. Following manuscript 1046 of Perugia, Marino Bigaroni breaks the narration of this incident in his critical edition. As indicated, it remains one complete paragraph in the 2C 69.

b. While *scarulaticus* [velvet] only denotes, in modern usage, a shade of red; in the Middle Ages it meant an expensive material, velvet or silk, usually dyed a rich shade of red.

c. The diocese of Marsi, i.e., the diocese of Celano, takes its name not from the residence of the bishop but from the geographic area of the ancient Marsi people. The bishop did not have a permanent residence, but he did use the church of Santa Sabina in San Benedetto dei Marsi as his cathedral. At the time this event took place, in winter of 1220, the bishop was residing in Celano.

poor old woman, saying: "Go and make yourself a tunic; you really need it."

The old woman laughed; she was stunned—I don't know if it was out of fear or joy—and took the piece of cloth from his hands. She ran off quickly, so that delay might not bring the danger of having to give it back, and cut it with scissors. But when she saw that the cut cloth would not be enough for a tunic, she returned to the saint, knowing his earlier kindness to a degree,[a] and showed him that the material was not enough. The saint turned his eyes on his companion, who had just the same cloth covering his back. "Brother," he said, "do you hear what this old woman is saying? For the love of God, let us bear with the cold! Give the poor woman the cloth so she can finish her tunic." He gave his; the companion offered his as well; and both were left naked, so the old woman could be clothed].

[32]

[Returning from Siena he gives a mantle to a poor man]

2C 87↑ [Another time, when he was coming back from Siena, he met a poor man, and said to his companion: "We must give back to this poor man the mantle that is his. *We accepted* it *on loan* until we should Lk 6:34; Prv 22:7
happen to find someone poorer than we are." The companion, seeing the need of his pious father, stubbornly objected that he should not provide for someone else by neglecting himself. But he said to him: "I do not want to *be a thief;* we will be accused of theft if we do not give to Jn 12:6
someone in greater need." So his companion gave in, and he gave up the mantle].

[33]

[At the "Le Celle" di Cortona the brothers have to ransom his mantle from a poor man]

2C 88↑ [A similar thing happened at "Le Celle" of Cortona.[b] Blessed Francis was wearing a new mantle that the brothers had gone to some trouble to find for him. A poor man came to the place weeping for his dead wife and his poor little family that was left desolate. The

a. *Ex parte experta* ("experienced to a degree") may be a copyist's error, a repetition, since the two words are similar.

b. "Le Celle" is a name that existed before Francis and his brothers came there in 1211. It was most likely derived from the presence of some small huts or "cells" near the mills situated along the stream coming down from the nearby mountain. Cf. Teobaldo Ricci, *Historical Background and Spirituality of "Le Celle" of Cortona* (Cortona: Editrice Grafica L'Etruria, 1994).

saint said to him: "I'm giving you this cloak for the love of the Son of God, but on the condition that you do not hand it over to anyone unless they pay well for it." The brothers immediately came running to take the mantle away and prevent this donation. But the poor man, taking courage from the father's look, clutched it with both hands and defended it as his own. In the end the brothers had to redeem the mantle, and the poor man left after getting his price].[a]

[34]
[He gives a mantle to a poor man, on the condition that he pardon his master]

[Once when he was at Colle[b] in the county of Perugia, Saint Fran- 2C 89↑
cis met a poor man whom he had known before in the world. He asked him: "Brother, how are you doing?" The man] malevolently [began to heap curses on his lord, who had taken away everything he
Rv 1:8; Gn 5:29 had. "Thanks to my lord, *may the Almighty Lord curse* him, I'm very bad off!"

Blessed Francis felt more pity for the man's soul, rooted in mortal hatred, than for his body. He said to him: "Brother, forgive your lord
Est 4:13 for the love of God, so you may *set your soul free,* and it may be that he will return to you what he has taken. Otherwise you will lose not only your property but also your soul." He replied: "I can't entirely forgive him unless he first gives back what he took." Blessed Francis had a mantle on his back, and said to him: "Here, I'll give you this cloak, and beg you to forgive your lord for the love of the Lord God." The man's mood sweetened, and, moved by this kindness, he took the gift and forgave the wrongs].

[35]
[He explains a passage from Ezechiel to a brother preacher]

[While he was staying in Siena, someone from the Order of 2C 103↑
Preachers happened to arrive; he was a spiritual man and a Doctor of Sacred Theology. He visited blessed Francis, and he and the holy man enjoyed a long and sweet conversation about the words of the Lord].

a. The reference to *redemere* [redeem], that is, to buy back, is curious, considering that the brothers had little with which to buy it back.

b. Now known as Collestrada, on the plain between Perugia and Assisi.

[36]

2C 103↑ [This teacher asked him about the words of Ezekiel: *If you do not* Ez 3:18-20; 33:7-9
warn the wicked man about his wickedness, I will hold you responsible for his
soul. I'm acquainted with many people, good father, who live in mortal sin, as I'm aware. But I don't always warn them about their wickedness. Will I then be held responsible for their souls?"

Blessed Francis then said that he was an unlettered man, and it
would be better for him to be taught by the other rather than to answer a question about Scripture. But that humble teacher replied:
"Brother, it's true I have heard these words explained by some wise
men; still, I'd be glad to hear how you understand it." So blessed
Francis said to him: "If that passage is supposed to be understood in
a universal sense, then I understand it to mean that a servant of God
should be burning with life and holiness so brightly, that by the light
of example and the tongue of his conduct, he will rebuke all the
wicked. In that way, I say, the brightness of his life and the fragrance
of his reputation will *proclaim their wickedness* to all of them." Ez 3:19

That man went away greatly edified, and said to the companions
of blessed Francis: "My brothers, the theology of this man, held aloft
by purity and contemplation, is a soaring eagle, while our learning
crawls on its belly on the ground"]. Gn 3:14

[37]
[A PARABLE ABOUT IMMODEST GLANCES]

2C 113↑ [He used to pierce eyes that are not chaste *with this parable.* "A 1 Cor 13:12
powerful] and pious [king sent two messengers to his queen, one af-
ter the other. The first returned and simply reported her words verbatim. Truly *the eyes of the wise man* stayed *in his head* and did not dart Eccl 2:14
elsewhere. The other returned and, after reporting in brief words,
launched into a long story about the lady's beauty. 'Truly, my lord, I
saw a lovely woman; happy is he who enjoys her!' And the king said,]
'You [evil servant, you cast your shameless eyes on my wife? It is
clear that you would like to buy what you inspected so carefully!' He
then called back the first messenger and asked: 'What did you think
of the queen?' And he answered: 'I thought very highly of her, for she
listened] gladly [and then replied wisely.' 'And don't you think she's
beautiful?' the king said. 'My lord,' he said, 'this is for you to see; my
job was simply to deliver messages.'

And the king then pronounced his sentence: 'You, chaste of eyes, even more chaste in body, stay in my chamber. Let that other man leave my house, so he does not defile my marriage bed.' "]

He used to say: [Who would not fear to look at the bride of Christ?] 2C 114↑

[38]

[SOMETIMES HE BROKE OUT SINGING IN FRENCH, ENDING IN ECSTASY]

[Sometimes he used to do this: a sweet melody of the spirit bubbling up inside him would become on the outside a French tune; the *thread of a divine whisper* which *his ears heard secretly* would break out in a French song. 2C 127↑ Jb 4:12

Other times—as I saw with my own eyes—he would pick up a stick from the ground and put it over his left arm, while holding a bent bow in his right hand, drawing it over the stick as if it were a viola, performing all the right movements, and in French would sing] about God.

[All of this dancing often ended in tears, and the cry of joy dissolved into compassion for Christ's suffering. Then the saint would sigh without stopping and sob without ceasing. Forgetful of lower things he had in hand, he was caught up to heaven].

[39]

[HIS PRAYER FOR THE ORDER]

[In order to preserve the virtue of holy humility, a few years after his conversion, at a chapter,[a] he resigned the office of prelate before all the brothers of the religion, saying: "From now on, I am dead to you. But here you have Brother Peter of Catanio; let us all, you and I, obey him." And bowing down immediately, he promised him obedience and reverence. 2C 143↑ ER Prol 4

The brothers were weeping, and sorrow drew deep groans from them, as they saw themselves orphaned of such a father. As blessed Francis got up, he joined his hands and, lifting his eyes to heaven, said: "Lord, I give back to You the family which until now You have entrusted to me. Now, sweetest Lord, because of my infirmities, which You know, I can no longer take care of them and I entrust them to the ministers. If any brother should perish because of their

a. This was the Pentecost Chapter held at the Portiuncula in September, 1220, shortly after Francis's return from the East. Thus, "a few years after his conversion" cannot be taken literally.

negligence, or example, or even harsh correction, let them be bound to render an account for it before You, Lord, on the day of judgment."

From that time on, he remained subject until his death, behaving more humbly than any of the others].[a]

[40]

[HE REFUSES TO HAVE COMPANIONS CHARGED WITH CARING FOR HIM]

2C 144↑ [Another time he consigned all his companions to his vicar, saying: "I don't want to seem singular because of this privilege of freedom; any brothers can go with me from place to place 'as the Lord inspires them.'" And he added: "Why, I have seen a blind man who had no guide for his journey except one little dog." This indeed was his glory: he gave up any appearance of being singular or important, so that *the power of Christ might dwell in him*]. 2 Cor 12:9

LR 2:7

[41]

[GOOD BROTHERS PUNISH THEMSELVES FOR AN OFFENSE AGAINST CHARITY]

2C 155↑ [He used to affirm that the Lesser Brothers had been sent from the Lord in these last times to show forth examples of light to those wrapped in the darkness of sins. He would say that he was filled with the sweetest fragrance and anointed with strength from precious ointment whenever he heard of the great deeds of holy brothers in faraway lands.

It happened that a brother once threw out an insulting word at another brother in the presence of a nobleman of the island of Cyprus. But when he saw that his brother was rather hurt by the impact of that word, he took some donkey manure and, burning with rage against himself, put it into his mouth to chew, saying: "Let the tongue that spat the poison of anger on my brother now chew manure!"

At seeing this,] that man [was thunder-stuck, and went away greatly edified; from that time on, he put himself and all he had at disposal of the brothers.

All the brothers observed this custom without fail: if any of them spoke an upsetting word to another, he would immediately fall to the ground and embrace the feet of the one he had offended, even if

a. As the brackets indicate, this passage is identical with 2C 143, therefore among the passages from 2C later incorporated into Manuscript 1046 of Perugia. This same passage is similar to AC 11 which is, however, less developed than 2C 143. This may suggest that AC 11 is the source used by Thomas to write the account in 2C 143.

unwilling, with holy kisses. The saint rejoiced over such behavior, when he heard the examples of holiness that his sons themselves produced, and he would heap blessings worthy of full acceptance on those brothers, who, by word or deed, led sinners to the love of Christ. Zeal for souls, which filled him completely, made him want his sons to resemble him as a true likeness].

[42]
[A DESCRIPTION OF THE GENERAL MINISTER]

[As he neared the end of his call to the Lord, a brother] said to 2C 184↑
him: ["Father, you will pass on, and the family of your followers will
Ps 84:7 be left behind *in this vale of tears.* Point out someone in the Order, if you know one, on whom your spirit may rest, and on whom the weight of the general ministry may safely be laid." Saint Francis, drawing a sigh with every word, replied as follows: "Son, I find no one adequate to be the leader of such a varied army, or the shepherd of such a widespread flock. But I would like to paint one for you to show clearly what kind of person the father of this family should be.]

["He must be a person of very dignified life, of great discernment, 2C 185↑
and of praiseworthy reputation. He must be without personal favorites, lest by loving some more than others, he create scandal for all. He must be a committed friend of holy prayer, who can distribute some hours for his soul and others for the flock entrusted to him. He must put the sacrament of the Mass first, early in the morning, and with prolonged devotion commend himself and his flock to divine protection.

"After prayer, he must make himself available for all to pick at him, and he should respond to all and provide for all with meekness.
Rom 2:11 He] is [someone who does not create sordid *favoritism toward persons,* but will take as much care of the lesser and simple brothers as of the learned and greater ones. Even if he should be allowed to excel in gifts of learning, he should all the more bear in his behavior the image of holy simplicity and nourish this virtue. He should loathe money, the principal corrupter of our profession and perfection. As the head of] our [religion, offering himself to others as someone to be imitated, he must never engage in the abuse of using any money pouch."]

[43]

2C 185↑ ["For his needs," he said, "a habit and a little book should be enough for him and, for the brothers' needs he should have a pen case and seal. He should not be a book collector or too intent on reading, so he does not take away from his duties what he spends on his studies. Let him be someone who comforts the afflicted, and *the final* Ps 32:7; 46:2 *refuge of the distressed,* so that the sickness of despair does not overcome the sick because he did not offer healing remedies. In order to bend rebels to meekness, let him lower himself and let go of some of his rights *that he may gain a soul for Christ.* As for runaways from the Phil 3:8; Mt 16:26 Order, let him not *close the heart of mercy* to them, for they are like *lost* 1 Jn 3:17; Lk 15:4 *sheep;* and he knows how overpowering the temptations can be which can push someone to such a fall."]

2C 186↑ ["I want all to honor him as standing in Christ's place, and to be provided for in everything with all the kindness] of Christ. [He must not enjoy honors, nor delight in approval more than insults. If he should need more substantial food, he should not eat it in secret but in a public place, so that others may be freed from embarrassment at having to provide for their weak bodies.

It especially pertains to him to discern what is hidden in consciences and to draw out the truth from its hidden veins]. Let him [never weaken the manly norm of justice, and he must feel such a great office more a burden than an honor. And yet, excessive meekness should not give birth to slackness, nor loose indulgence to a breakdown of discipline, so that, loved by all, he is feared nonetheless, by *those who work evil.* Prv 10:29

I would like him to have companions endowed with honesty, who], with him, [*show themselves an example of all good works,* strong Ti 2:7 against difficulties, and yet friendly in the right way, so that they receive all who come to them with holy cheerfulness.

There," he concluded, "the general minister of the Order should be like this"].

[44]
[He responds to a brother asking why he abandoned governing the Order]

2C 188↑ [Once a brother asked him why he had renounced the care of all the brothers and turned them over into the hands of others, as if they did not belong to him. He replied: "Son, I love the brothers as I can, but if they would *follow my footsteps* I would surely love them more, 1 Pt 2:21

and would not make myself a stranger to them. For there are some among the prelates who draw them in a different direction, placing before them the examples of the ancients and paying little attention to my warnings. But what they are doing will be seen in the end."

A short time later, when he was suffering a serious illness, he raised himself up in bed in an angry spirit: "Who are these people? They have snatched out of my hands my religion and that of the brothers. If I go to the general chapter, I'll show them what is my will."]

[45]
[He was not ashamed to beg even meat for sick brothers]

Blessed Francis [was not embarrassed to go through the city's 2C 175↑
public places to find some meat for a sick brother. However, he also advised the sick to be patient when things were lacking and not stir up a scandal if everything was not to their satisfaction.

Because of this he had these words written in one of the *Rules*: "I ER X 4
beg all my sick brothers that in their illness they do not become angry or upset at] the Lord or [the brothers. They should not anxiously seek medicines, nor desire too eagerly to free the flesh that is soon to die
1 Thes 5:18 and is an enemy of the soul. *Let them give thanks for all things* and let them desire to be however God wills them to be. For God teaches
Acts 13:48 with the rod of punishments and sicknesses those whom *he has des-*
Rv 3:19 *tined to eternal life* as he himself has said: *'Those whom I love I correct and chastise.'* "]

[46]
[Praise of the *Rule*]

[He burned with great zeal for the common profession and *Rule*, 2C 208↑
and endowed those who were zealous about it with a special blessing. He called it their Book of Life, the hope of salvation, the marrow of the Gospel, the way of perfection, the key of Paradise, the pact of an eternal covenant. He wanted all to have it, all to know it, in all
Wis 8:9 places to let it speak to the inner man, as *encouragement in weariness* and as a reminder of a sworn oath. He taught them to keep it always before their eyes as a reminder of the life they should lead, and, what is more, that they should die with it.

This teaching was not forgotten by a certain lay brother whom we believe should be venerated among the martyrs, since he gained the palm of glorious victory. When he was taken by the Saracens to his

martyrdom, he held the *Rule* in his uplifted hands, and kneeling
humbly, said to his companion: "Dear brother I proclaim myself
guilty before *the eye's of Majesty* of everything I ever did against this Is 3:8
holy *Rule*!" The stroke of the sword followed this short confession,
and with his martyrdom he ended his life, and afterwards shone
with *signs and wonders*. This brother had entered the Order so young 2 Cor 12:12
that he could hardly bear the *Rule*'s fasting, yet even as a boy he wore
a harness next to his skin.

Oh happy child, who began happily to end even happier!].

[47]
[The Brothers and Study]

2C 195↑ [It grieved] the blessed Father [when brothers sought learning
while neglecting virtue, especially if they did not *remain in* that *calling* 1 Cor 7:20, 24
in which they were first *called*. He said: "Those brothers of mine who are
led by curiosity for knowledge will find themselves *empty-handed* on Sir 35:4
the day of reckoning. I would prefer that they grow strong in virtue,
so that when *the times of tribulation* arrive they may have the Lord with Ps 37:39
them *in their distress*. For," he said, *"a tribulation is approaching*, when 2 Chr 15:4 Ps 22:12; Prv 1:27
books, useful for nothing, shall be thrown into cupboards and closets!"

He did not say these things out of dislike for the study of Scriptures, but to draw all of them back from excessive concern for learning, because he preferred that they be good through charity rather than be dilettantes through curiosity.

Besides, he could smell in the air that a time was coming, and not too far away, when he knew learning would be an occasion of ruin. After his death he appeared in a vision to one of the companions who was once tending toward preaching, and he forbade it, commanding him to walk on the way of simplicity].

[48]
[He Detested Laziness and Wanted All the Brothers to Work]

2C 161↑ [He used to say that the lukewarm who do not apply themselves
constantly to some work, would quickly be *vomited out of the Lord's* Rv 3:16
mouth. No idler could appear in his presence without feeling the
ER VII; LR V sharp bite of his criticism. This exemplar of every perfection always
worked, and worked with his hands, not allowing the great gift of
Test 20-21 time to go to waste. And so he would often say: "I want all my brothers to work and keep busy, and those who have no skills to learn

some so that we may be less of a burden to people, and that in idleness the heart and tongue may not stray." But he would not have profit or payment for work left to the whim of the worker, but entrusted it to the guardian or the family].

[49]
[SAINT FRANCIS AND SAINT DOMINIC ARE GUESTS OF CARDINAL HUGOLINO]

[Those two bright lights of the world,] namely, [Saint Francis and Saint Dominic,[a] were once in the City with the Lord of Ostia, who later became Supreme Pontiff. As they took turns pouring out honey-sweet words about the Lord, the bishop finally said to them: "In the early Church the Church's shepherds were poor, and men of charity, not on fire with greed. Why don't we make bishops and prelates of your brothers who excel in teaching and example." 2C 148↑

There arose a disagreement between the saints about answering, neither wishing to go first, but rather each deferring to the other. Each urged the other to reply. Each seemed superior to the other, since each was devoted to the other. At last humility conquered Francis as he did not speak first, but it also conquered Dominic, since in speaking first, he humbly obeyed Francis. Blessed Dominic therefore answered the bishop, "My lord, my brothers are already raised to a good level, if they will only realize it, and as much as possible I would not allow them to obtain any other] appearance [of dignity." As this brief response ended, Blessed Francis bowed to the bishop and said: "My lord, my brothers are called 'lesser' precisely so they
Mt 20:26 will not presume to *become 'greater.'* They have been called this to
1 Pt 2:21 teach them to stay down to earth, and to *follow the footprints of Christ's* humility, which in the end will exalt them above others in the sight
Jn 15:2,8; Phil 3:6 of the saints. If you want them *to bear fruit in the Church of God,* keep them in the status in which they were called and hold them to it. Bring them back down to ground level even against their will. Never allow them to rise to become prelates" These were the replies of the saints.]

[When they finished their replies, the Lord of Ostia was greatly 2C 150↑
Acts 27:35 edified by the words of both and gave unbounded *thanks to God.* And as they left that place, blessed Dominic asked Saint Francis to be

a. Dominic Guzman was born in Caleruega (Diocese of Osma, Old Castile) in 1170. In 1196 he became a canon in the chapter of the cathedral of Osma, and in 1206 he began the life of an itinerant preacher to preach against heresy. By 1217 he had a band of followers, and they, with the Rule of Saint Augustine, received the approval of Pope Honorius III. From that time onward, until his death in Bologna on August 6, 1221, Dominic often spent his winters in Rome. Gregory IX canonized him on July 3, 1234. This incident has not been recorded in early Dominican sources.

kind enough to give him the cord he had tied around him. Francis was slow to do this, refusing out of humility what the other was requesting out of charity. At last the happy devotion of the petitioner won out, and he devoutly put on the gift under his inner tunic. Finally they clasped hands and commended themselves to each other with great sweetness. And so one saint said to the other: "Brother Francis, I wish your Order and mine might become one, so we could share the same form of life in the Church."

At last, when they had *parted from each other,* Saint Dominic said to Acts 15:39
the many bystanders: *"In truth I tell you,* the other religious should Lk 4:25
follow this holy man Francis, as his holiness is so perfect"].

LP 1 [50]

[HE EATS WITH A BROTHER WHO CLAIMS HE IS DYING OF HUNGER; AUSTERE WITH HIMSELF, HE WAS COMPASSIONATE WITH OTHERS]

One time in the very beginning, that is, at the time when blessed Francis began to have brothers, he was staying with them at Rivo Torto. One night, around midnight, when they were all asleep in their beds, one of the brothers cried out, saying: "I'm dying! I'm dying!" Startled and frightened all the brothers woke up.

Getting up, blessed Francis said: "Brothers, get up and light a lamp." After the lamp was lit, blessed Francis said: "Who was it who said, 'I'm dying?' "

"I'm the one," the brother answered.

"What's the matter, brother?" blessed Francis said to him. 'Why are you dying?"

"I'm dying of hunger," he answered.

So that that brother would not be ashamed to eat alone, blessed Francis, a man of great charity and discernment, immediately had the table set and they all ate together with him. This brother, as well as the others, were newly converted to the Lord and afflicted their bodies excessively.

After the meal, blessed Francis said to the other brothers: "My brothers, I say that each of you must consider his own constitution, because, although one of you may be sustained with less food than another, I still do not want one who needs more food to try imitating him in this. Rather, considering his constitution, he should provide his body with what it needs. Just as we must beware of overindulgence in eating, which harms body and soul, so we must beware of excessive abstinence even more, because the Lord desires mercy and not sacrifice."

And he said: "Dearest brothers, great necessity and charity compelled me to do what I did, namely, that out of love for our brother we ate together with him, so he wouldn't be embarrassed to eat alone. But I tell you, in the future I do not wish to act this way because it wouldn't be religious or decent. Let each one provide his body with what it needs as our poverty will allow. This is what I wish and command you."

The first brothers and those who came after them for a long time mortified their bodies excessively, not only by abstinence in food and drink, but also in vigils, cold, and manual labor. Next to their skin, those who could get them wore iron rings and breastplates and the roughest hair shirts, which they were even better able to get. Considering that the brothers could get sick because of this, and in a short time some were already ailing, the holy father therefore commanded in one of the chapters that no brother wear anything next to the skin except the tunic.

We who were with him bear witness to this fact about him: from the time he began to have brothers, and also during his whole lifetime, he was discerning with the brothers, provided that in the matter of food and other things, they did not deviate at any time from the norm of the poverty and decency of our religion, which the early brothers observed. Nevertheless, even before he had brothers, from the beginning of his conversion and during his whole lifetime, he was severe with his own body, even though from the time of his youth he was a man of a frail and weak constitution, and when he was in the world he could not live without comforts.

One time, perceiving that the brothers had exceeded the norm of poverty and decency in food and in things, he said in a sermon he gave, speaking to a few brothers, who stood for all the brothers: "Don't the brothers think that my body needs special food? But because I must be the model and example for all the brothers, I want to use and be content with poor food and things, not fine ones."

[51] LP 2

[HE PERSUADES THE BROTHERS TO GO JOYFULLY BEGGING FOR ALMS]

When Francis began to have brothers, he was so happy about their conversion and that the Lord had given him good company, that he loved and revered them so much that he did not tell them to go for alms, especially because it seemed to him that they would be ashamed to go. Rather, sparing them shame, he himself would go alone for alms every day. His body was worn out by this, especially since in the world he had been a refined man, and of a weak constitution; and he had become weaker from the day when he left the world because of the excessive fasting and suffering he endured.

He considered that he could not bear so much labor, and that they were called to this, even though they would be ashamed, and did not fully understand; but neither had they been discerning enough to tell him: "We want to go for alms." So he talked to them. "My dearest
LR VI 3 brothers and sons, don't be ashamed to go for alms, because *the Lord* 2 Cor 8:9
for our sake made Himself poor in this world. Therefore, because of His example, we have chosen the way of the most genuine poverty and that of His most holy Mother.[a] This is our inheritance, which the Lord Jesus Christ acquired and bequeathed to us and to all who want to live in holy poverty according to His example." And he told them: "I tell you the truth: many of the noblest and wisest of this world will come to this congregation and they will consider it a great honor to go for alms. Therefore, go for alms confidently with joyful hearts with the blessing of the Lord God. And you ought to go begging more willingly and with more joyful hearts than someone who is offering a hundred silver pieces in exchange for a single penny, since you are offering the love of God to those from whom you seek alms. Say to them: 'Give alms to us for the love of the Lord God: compared to this, heaven and earth are nothing!'"

They were still few in number so that he could not send them out two by two, so he sent each one separately through the towns and villages. When they returned, each one showed blessed Francis the alms he had collected, one saying to the other, "I collected more alms than you!"

This gave blessed Francis reason to rejoice, seeing them so happy and cheerful. From then on each of them more willingly asked permission to go for alms.

[52] LP 3

[HE DOES NOT WANT THE BROTHERS TO THINK ABOUT TOMORROW, FOLLOWING THE GOSPEL]

At that time, as Blessed Francis was with his brothers whom he had then, he was of such purity that, from the hour the Lord revealed
to him that he and his brothers should live according to the form of ER Prol 1
the holy Gospel, he desired and strove to observe it to the letter during his whole lifetime.

a. The word order is odd, and implies following, not the example of "His most holy Mother," but her "most genuine poverty."

Therefore he told the brother who did the cooking for the brothers, that when he wanted the brothers to eat beans, he should not put them in warm water in the evening for the next day, as people usually do. This was so the brothers would observe the words of the holy
Mt 6:34 Gospel: *"Do not be concerned about tomorrow."* So that brother used to
put them in water to soften after the brothers said matins.

Because of this, for a long time many brothers observed this in a great many places where they stayed on their own, especially in cities. They did not want to collect or receive more alms than were enough for them for one day.

[53] LP 4

[He eats grapes with a sick brother]

One time when blessed Francis was at that same place, a certain brother, a spiritual man, an elder in religion, was staying there. He was very sick and weak. Considering him, blessed Francis was moved to piety toward him. The brothers back then, sick and healthy, with cheerfulness and patience took poverty for abundance. They did not take medicines in their illnesses, but more willingly did what was contrary to the body. Blessed Francis said to himself: "If that brother would eat some ripe grapes early in the morning, I believe it would help him."

One day, therefore, he secretly got up early in the morning, and called that brother and took him into the vineyard which is near that same church. He chose a vine that had grapes that were good and ready for eating. Sitting down with that brother next to the vine, he began to eat some grapes so that the brother would not be ashamed to eat alone, and while they were eating them, that brother praised the Lord God. As long as he lived, he always recalled among the brothers, with great devotion and flowing tears, the mercy the holy father had done to him.

[54] LP 6

[A surprising visit from the bishop of Assisi]

One time when blessed Francis was at that same place, he stayed at prayer in the cell that was in the back, behind the house. One day while he was staying in it, the bishop of Assisi came to see him. It happened that as he came into the house, he knocked on the door to approach blessed Francis. He opened the door himself, and immediately entered the cell in which there was another small cell made of mats where blessed Francis stayed. And because he knew that the holy father treated him with friendliness and love, he entered without hesitation, and opened for himself the little cell of mats to see him. As he quickly stuck his head inside the little cell, all of a sudden, by the will of the Lord, because he was not worthy to see him, he was forcefully pushed outside, willy-nilly, stumbling backwards. He immediately came outside the cell, trembling and stunned, and told the brothers his fault, and said he was sorry for coming there that day.

LP 7

[55]

[HIS FRIENDSHIP FREES A BROTHER FROM DEPRESSION]

There was a certain brother, a spiritual man, an elder in religion, and close to blessed Francis. It happened one time that for many days he suffered the most severe and cruel suggestions of the devil, so that he was almost cast into the depths of despair. And even though he was tormented daily, he was ashamed to confess it every time. And, because of this, he afflicted himself with fasting, with vigils, with tears, and with beatings.

While he was being tormented daily for many days, blessed Francis came to that place by divine guidance. And when blessed Francis was walking one day not too far from that place with one brother and with the brother who was so tormented, he left the other brother behind and walked with the one who was being tempted. He said to him: "My dearest brother, I wish and tell you that from now on you are not bound to confess these suggestions and intrusions of the devil to anyone. Don't be afraid, because they have not harmed your soul. But I give you my permission just to say seven *Our Father's* as often as you are troubled by these suggestions."

That brother was overjoyed at what he said to him, that he was not bound to confess those things, especially because, since he would have had to confess daily, he was quite upset, and this was the main reason for his suffering. He marveled at the holiness of the holy father, how he knew his temptations through the Holy Spirit, since he had not confessed to anyone except priests. And he would frequently switch priests because of shame, since he was ashamed that one priest would know all his weakness and temptation.

From the very moment blessed Francis spoke to him, he was immediately freed both in spirit and body from that great trial which he endured for such a long time. And, through the grace of God and the merits of blessed Francis, he remained in great serenity and peace of soul and body.

[56] LP 8

[He receives the Portiuncula from the Abbot of the Monastery of Saint Benedict; he tries to destroy a house built there; special norms for brothers who live there]

Seeing that the Lord willed to increase the number of brothers, blessed Francis told them: "My dearest brothers and sons, I see that the Lord wants us to increase. Therefore, it seems good and religious to me to obtain from the bishop, or the canons of San Rufino, or from the abbot of the monastery of Saint Benedict, some small and poor little church where the brothers can say their Hours and only have next to it a small and poor little house built of mud and branches where they can sleep and care for their needs. This place is not suitable, and this house is too small for the brothers to stay in, since it pleases the Lord to increase them, especially because here we do not have a church where the brothers can say their Hours. And, should any brother die, it would not be proper to bury him here or in a church of the secular clergy." This speech pleased the other brothers.

So blessed Francis got up and went to the bishop of Assisi. The same speech he made to the brothers he made to the bishop. "Brother," the bishop answered him, "I do not have any church that I can give you." Then he went to the canons of San Rufino and said the same thing to them. But they gave him the same answer as the bishop. He went, therefore, to the monastery of Saint Benedict on Mount Subasio, and made the same speech to the abbot he had made to the bishop and the canons, informing him also of how the bishop and the canons had responded. The abbot was moved to piety and took counsel with his brothers about this.

As it was the will of God, they granted blessed Francis and his brothers the church of Saint Mary of the Portiuncula as the poorest little church they had. In fact, it was also the poorest little church in the area around the city of Assisi, something blessed Francis had desired for a long time.

"Brother, we have granted your request," the abbot told blessed Francis. "But, if the Lord increases your congregation, we want this place to be the head of all your places." And this speech pleased blessed Francis and his brothers.

Blessed Francis was overjoyed at the place granted to the brothers, especially because of the name of this church of the Mother of Christ, and because it was such a poor little church, and because of the surname it had, for it was surnamed: "of the Portiuncula." This name foreshadowed that it was to be the mother and head of the poor Lesser Brothers. It was called "Portiuncula" after the neighborhood where that church was built, which from earliest times was called "Portiuncula." Blessed Francis used to say: "This is why the Lord willed that no other church be granted to the brothers, and why the first brothers would not build any completely new church, and would not have any other but this one. For this church was a prophecy that has been fulfilled in the coming of the Lesser Brothers." And although it was poor and almost in ruins already for a long time, the people of the city of Assisi and its neighborhood had always held the church in great devotion and hold it in even greater devotion today.

As soon as the brothers went to stay there, almost daily the Lord increased their number; and their fame and reputation spread throughout the whole valley of Spoleto. From old times, it was named Saint Mary of the Angels, and called by the local people Saint Mary of the Portiuncula. But after the brothers began to repair it, the men and women of that region would say: "Let's go to Saint Mary of the Angels."

Although the abbot and the monks had freely granted that church to blessed Francis and his brothers without any payment or annual tax, blessed Francis, a good and experienced teacher who wished to build his house on solid rock, that is, his congregation on great poverty, every year used to send the abbot a basket full of small fish called *"lasche."* He did this as a sign of greater humility and poverty, so that the brothers would not have any place of their own, and would not remain in any place that was not owned by others, and thus they in no way had the power to sell it or give it away. Each year, when the brothers brought the little fish to the monks, they in turn, because of the humility of blessed Francis, who had done this of his own will, gave him and his brothers a jar filled with oil.

LP 9 We who were with blessed Francis bear witness that he spoke of that church with great conviction, because of the great preference that the Lord indicated there and revealed to him in that place, namely that among all the other churches of this world the blessed Virgin loves that church. Therefore, during his whole lifetime, he had the greatest reverence and devotion toward it. And so that the brothers would always keep its remembrance in their hearts, at his death he wanted it written in his *Testament* that the brothers do likewise.

About the time of his death, in the presence of the general minister and the other brothers, he said:

"I want to leave and bequeath to the brothers the place of Saint Mary of the Portiuncula as a testament, that it may always be held in the greatest reverence and devotion by the brothers. Our old brothers did this: for although the place itself is holy, they preserved its holiness with constant prayer day and night and by constant silence. And if, at times, they spoke after the time established for silence, they discussed with the greatest devotion and decorum matters pertaining to the praise of God and the salvation of souls. If it happened, and it rarely did, that someone began to utter useless or idle words, immediately he was corrected by another. They used to mortify the flesh not only by fasting, but also by many vigils, by cold, nakedness and manual labor. In order not to remain idle, they very frequently went and helped poor people in their fields, and sometimes these people would give them some bread for the love of God.

"By these and other virtues, they used to sanctify themselves and the place; and others who came after them for a long time did the same, although not as much. Afterwards, however, a great number of brothers and others would come to that place more than was usual, especially when all the brothers of the religion had to visit there, as well as those who intended to join the religion. Moreover, the brothers are colder in prayer and other good works than in the past, and are more careless about exchanging idle and useless words and even worldly news. Therefore, the brothers who stay there and other religious do not hold that place in such great reverence and devotion as is proper and as I would wish.

"Therefore I want it always to be under the jurisdiction of the gen- LP 10
eral minister, that he may show greater concern and care in providing for it, especially in placing a good and holy family there. The clerics should be chosen from among the holiest and most upright brothers of the entire religion and who know how to say the office best. In this way, not only other people, but also the brothers will gladly listen to them with great devotion. And some holy lay brothers, discerning and upright men, should also be chosen, who may serve them.

"I also wish that none of the brothers or any other person enter that place except the general minister and the brothers who serve him. And they may not speak to anyone except the brothers who serve them and to the minister when he visits them.

"I likewise want the lay brothers who serve them to be bound not to pass on to them any word or news of the world which they have heard which is not useful to the soul. And that is the reason why I particularly want no one else to enter that place, so that they may better preserve their purity and holiness, and not exchange in that place any idle words, useless to the soul. Rather, the entire place should be kept and held pure and holy in hymns and praises of the Lord. And when any of these brothers passes, let the general minister have another holy brother come there, no matter where he is staying, to replace the one who died. If some day the brothers and the places where they stay stray from the purity and holiness and decency befitting them, I want this place to be a mirror and a good example for the entire religion, a candelabra before the throne of God and before the blessed Virgin. Thus may the Lord have mercy on the faults and failings of the brothers and always preserve and protect this religion, His little plant."[a]

LP 11 One time, close to a chapter that was to be held—which in those days was held annually at Saint Mary of the Portiuncula—the people of Assisi considered that, by the Lord's grace, the brothers had already increased and were increasing daily. Yet, especially when they all assembled there for a chapter, they had nothing but a poor, small hut covered with straw, and its walls were built with branches and mud, as the brothers had built when they first came to stay there. After a general meeting, within a few days, with haste and great devotion, they built there a large house with stone-and-mortar walls without the consent of blessed Francis while he was away.

When blessed Francis returned from another region and came to the chapter, and saw that house built there, he was amazed. He considered that, seeing this house, the brothers would build or have built large houses in the places where they now stayed or where they would stay in the future. And especially because he wanted this place always to be a model and example for all the places of the brothers, before the chapter ended he got up one day, climbed onto the roof of that house, and ordered the brothers to climb up. And, intending to destroy the house, he, along with the brothers, began to throw the tiles covering it to the ground.

The knights of Assisi saw this, as well as others who were there on behalf of the city's Commune to protect that place from secular people and outsiders who were outside the place, arriving from all over to see the brothers' chapter. They saw that blessed Francis and the other brothers wanted to destroy that house. They immediately approached them and said to blessed Francis: "Brother, this house belongs to the Commune of Assisi and we are here on behalf of the same Commune, and we're telling you not to destroy our house." "If the house belongs to you," answered blessed Francis, "I don't want to touch it." He and the brothers who were with him immediately came down. That is why for a long time the people of the city of Assisi

a. Raoul Manselli considers this commendation of Saint Mary of the Portiuncula another "testament" that Francis left his brothers at the time of his death. Cf. Raoul Manselli, "From the Testament to the Testaments of St. Francis," GR 2 (1988): 91-99.

decreed that every year their podestà, whoever he is, is obliged to have it roofed and repair it if necessary.

Another time the general minister wanted to build a small house LP 12
there for the brothers of that place where they could sleep and say their Hours. At that time especially, all the brothers of the religion, and those who were coming to the religion, were coming and going to that place. For this reason those brothers were being worn out almost daily. And because of the large number of brothers gathering in that place, they had no place where they could sleep and say their Hours, since they had to give up the places where they slept to others.

Because of this they frequently endured a lot of trouble because, after so much work, they could hardly provide for the necessities of their own bodies and the good of their own souls.

When that house was already almost finished, blessed Francis returned to that place. While he was sleeping in a small cell one night, at dawn he heard the noise of the brothers who . . .[a] were working there. He began to wonder what this could be. "What is that noise?" he asked his companion. "What are those brothers doing?" His companion told him the whole story.

Blessed Francis immediately sent for the minister and said to him: "Brother, this place is a model and example for the entire religion. And it is my will that the brothers of this place endure trouble and need for the love of the Lord God, so that the brothers of the whole religion who come here will take back to their places a good example of poverty, rather than have these brothers receive satisfaction and consolation. Otherwise, the other brothers of the religion will take up this example of building in their places. They will say: "At Saint Mary of the Portiuncula, which is the first place of the brothers, such and such buildings are built, so we can certainly build in our own places, because we do not have a suitable place to stay."

[57] LP 13

[He refuses to stay in a cell specially prepared for him]

One of the brothers, a spiritual man, to whom blessed Francis was very close, was staying in a hermitage. Considering that if blessed Francis came there at some time he would not have a suitable place to stay, he had a little cell built in a remote place near the place of the brothers, where blessed Francis could pray when he came. After a few days, it happened that blessed Francis came. When the brother

a. There is a lacuna in the manuscript here, suggesting that a phrase is missing.

led him to see it, blessed Francis said to him: "This little cell seems too beautiful to me. But, if you want me to stay in it for a few days, have it covered inside and out with ferns and tree-branches."

That little cell was not made of stonework but of wood, but because the wood was planed, made with hatchet and axe, it seemed too beautiful to blessed Francis. The brother immediately had it changed as blessed Francis had requested.

For the more the houses and cells of the brothers were poor and religious, the more willingly he would see them and sometimes be received as a guest there. As he stayed and prayed in it for a few days, one day, outside the little cell near the place of the brothers, a brother who was at that place came to where blessed Francis was staying. Blessed Francis said to him: "Where are you coming from, brother?" He told him: "I am coming from your little cell." "Because you said it is mine," blessed Francis said, "someone else will stay in it from now on: I will not."

We who were with him often heard him repeat the saying of the holy Gospel: *Foxes have dens and the birds of the air have nests; but the Son of Man has nowhere to lay his head.* Mt 8:20; Lk 9:58

And he would say: "When the Lord stayed in solitude where he prayed and fasted for forty days and forty nights, He did not have a cell or a house built there, but He sheltered under the rocks of the mountain." And so, after His example, he did not want to have a house or cell in this world, nor did he have one built for him. Moreover, if he ever happened to say to the brothers: "Prepare this cell this way," he would refuse afterwards to stay in it, because of that saying of the holy Gospel: *"Do not be concerned."* Lk 12:22; Mt 6:31, 34

Shortly before his death, he wanted it written in his *Testament* that all the cells and houses of the brothers ought to be built only of mud and wood, the better to safeguard poverty and humility.[a]

LP 14

[58]

[HIS WISHES ABOUT HOW THE BROTHERS' PLACES SHOULD BE BUILT]

Once when he was in Siena for treatment of the disease of his eyes, he was staying in a cell, where after his death a chapel was built out of reverence for him. Lord Bonaventure, who had donated to the brothers the land where the brothers' place had been built, said to him: "What do you think of this place?" Blessed Francis answered

a. Test 24 does speak of the poverty of buildings, but there is no directive as specific as this. For a discussion of this passage, cf. Raoul Manselli, "From the Testament to the Testaments of St. Francis," GR 2 (1988): 91-99.

him: "Do you want me to tell you how the places of the brothers should be built?" "I wish you would, Father," he answered.

And he told him: "When the brothers go to any city where they do not have a place, and they find someone who wants to give them enough land to build a place, have a garden, and whatever is necessary for them, they must first consider how much land is enough for them, always considering the holy poverty we have promised, and the good example we are bound to offer to others."

The holy father said this because he did not want the brothers for any reason to go beyond the norm of poverty either in houses or churches, in gardens or in other things they used. And he did not want them to possess the right of ownership to these places, but al-
1 Pt 2:11 ways to stay in them *as pilgrims and strangers.* For this reason, he did Test 24
not want the brothers to have to be assigned to places in large groups, because it seemed to him that it was difficult to observe poverty fully. From the beginning of his conversion until the end, at his death, this was his will: that holy poverty be observed to its fullest.

Afterwards they should go to the bishop of that city and say to LP 15
him: "Lord, for the love of the Lord God and the salvation of his soul, such and such a person wants to give us enough land so that we can build a place there. Therefore we have recourse to you first, because you are the father and lord of the souls of the entire flock entrusted to you, as well as our souls and those of the other brothers who will stay in this place. Therefore, with the blessing of the Lord God and yours, we would like to build there."

The saint would say this because the good of souls the brothers want to produce among the people was better achieved by peace with prelates and clerics, winning them and the people, rather than by scandalizing prelates and clerics, even though they might win the people.

"The Lord," he used to say, "has called us to help His faith and the prelates and clerics of holy Mother Church. This is why we are always bound to love, honor, and revere them as much as we can. For this reason let them be called Lesser Brothers because, in name as well as example and deed, they should be humbler than all other people of this world. From the beginning of my conversion, when I separated myself from the world and father in the flesh, the Lord put His word in the mouth of the bishop of Assisi so he could counsel me well in the service of Christ and comfort me. On account of this, as well as many other excellent qualities that I consider in prelates, not only in bishops, but in poor priests as well, I want to love them, revere them and regard them as my lords.

LP 16 "After receiving the bishop's blessing, let them go and have a big ditch dug around the land which they received for building the place, and as a sign of holy poverty and humility, let them place a hedge there, instead of a wall. Afterwards they may have poor little houses built, of mud and wood, and some little cells where the brothers can sometimes pray and where, for their own greater decency and also to avoid idle words, they can work.

"They may also have churches made; however, the brothers must not have large churches made, in order to preach to the people there or for any other reason, for it is greater humility and better example when the brothers go to other churches to preach, so that they may observe holy poverty and their humility and decency."

"And if prelates and clerics, religious or secular, should sometimes visit their places, their poor house, little cells, and churches in that place will preach to them and edify them."

"The brothers often have large buildings made, breaking with our holy poverty, resulting in complaints and bad example to their neighbor. Afterwards, they abandon those places and buildings for the sake of better or healthier places, prompting those who gave alms there, as well as others who see or hear about this to be scandalized and greatly upset. It is, therefore, better that the brothers have small and poor places built, observing their profession, and giving their neighbor good example, rather than making things contrary to their profession and offering bad example to others. For, if it should ever happen that the brothers leave their little places and poor buildings for the sake of a more decent place, that would be very bad example and scandal."

LP 17

[59]
[He dictates his first testament at Siena]

During those days and in the same cell where blessed Francis spoke about these things to Lord Bonaventure, one evening he wanted to vomit because of the disease of his stomach.[a] Because of the strain he put on himself in vomiting, he vomited up blood all night until morning.

When his companions saw him already almost dying from weakness and the pain of his illness, they said to him with great sorrow

a. Three possible explanations have been offered to explain this sudden attack: (a) a gastric ulcer aggravated by malnutrition and stress; (b) a malignant tumor, a cancer of the stomach; or (c) a recurring malarial infection that reached the point of malarial cachexia. Cf. Octavian Schmucki, "The Illnesses of Francis During the Last Years of His Life," GR 13 (1999): 42-46.

and flowing tears: "Father, what shall we do? Bless us and the rest of your brothers. In addition leave your brothers some remembrance of your will, so that, if the Lord wants to call you away from this world, your brothers may always keep it in their memory and say: 'Our father left these words to his sons and brothers at his death.' "

He then told them: "Call me Brother Benedict of Piratro."[a] He was a brother priest, discerning and holy, an elder in religion. He sometimes celebrated for blessed Francis in that cell, since, although he was sick, he always wanted, gladly and devoutly, to hear Mass whenever he was able. And when he had come, blessed Francis told him: "Write that I bless all my brothers, those who are and who will be in the religion until the end of the world."

For when the brothers gathered in chapter, it was always blessed Francis's custom in the brothers' chapters, when the brothers were called together at the end of the chapter, to bless and absolve all the brothers present and the others who were in the religion. And he would also bless all those who were to come to this religion. He would bless all the brothers in the religion and those to come, not only in chapters, but also many other times.

And blessed Francis told him: "Since I cannot speak much because of weakness and the pain of my illness, I am showing my will to my brothers briefly in these three words: as a sign of remembrance of my blessing and my testament, may they always love each other; may they always love and observe our Lady Holy Poverty; and may they always remain faithful and subject to the prelates and all the clerics of holy Mother Church."[b]

He used to warn the brothers to fear and beware of bad example. Furthermore he cursed all those who by their wrong and bad example caused people to blaspheme the religion and life of the brothers and the holy and good brothers, who, because of this, were ashamed and distressed.

[60] LP 18

[He carries a broom to clean churches]

At one time while blessed Francis was staying at Saint Mary of the Portiuncula, and there were still only a few brothers, blessed Francis

a. Nothing further is known of him beyond this mention of his presence here in Siena. The place of his origin appears in different forms throughout the tradition, i.e., of Prato, of Piratio, of Piaroco.

b. In his critical edition of the writings of Saint Francis, Kajetan Esser placed this passage among the "Dictates," cf. *Opusucla Sancti Patris Francisci Assisiensis*, Bibliotheca Franciscana Ascetica Medii Aevi, t. XII, ed. Caietanus Esser (Grottaferrata, Roma: Editiones Collegii S. Bonaventurae Ad Claras Aquas, 1978), 323-324.

sometimes used to go through the villages and churches in the area around the city of Assisi, proclaiming and preaching to the people that they should do penance. And he would carry a broom to sweep the churches.

For blessed Francis was very sad when he entered some church and saw that it was not clean. Therefore, after preaching to the people, at the end of the sermon he would always have all the priests who were present assembled in some remote place so he could not be overheard by secular people. He would preach to them about the salvation of souls and, in particular, that they should exercise care and concern in keeping churches clean, as well as altars and everything that pertained to the celebration of the divine mysteries.

LP 19

[61]

[Brother John the Simple joins the brothers; and how he imitates Francis]

One day blessed Francis went to a church in a village of the city of Assisi and began to sweep it. Immediately talk about this spread through that village, especially because those people enjoyed seeing and hearing him.

A man named John heard it, a man of amazing simplicity, who was ploughing in a field of his near the church, and he immediately went to him. Finding him sweeping the church, he said to him: "Brother, give me the broom because I want to help you." Taking the broom from him, he swept the rest.

When they sat down, he said to blessed Francis: "Brother, it's a long time now that I've wanted to serve God, especially after I heard talk about you and your brothers, but I did not know how to come to you. Now that it pleased God that I see you, I want to do whatever pleases you."

Considering his fervor, blessed Francis rejoiced in the Lord, especially because he then had few brothers, and because it seemed to him that, on account of his pure simplicity, he would make a good religious. So he said to him: "Brother, if you wish to belong to our life and company, you must rid yourself of all your things that you can get without scandal, and give them to the poor according to the counsel of the holy Gospel, because my brothers who were able to do so have done this."

As soon as he heard this, he immediately went into the field where he had left the oxen and, untying them, brought one of them back to blessed Francis. "Brother," he said to him, "I have served my father and everyone in my household for many years. Although my portion of the inheritance is small, I want to take this ox as my share and give it to the poor, as you think best according to God."

But when his parents and brothers, who were still small, saw that he wanted to leave them, they and the entire household began to cry so bitterly and wail so loudly that blessed Francis was moved to piety, especially because the family was large and penniless. Blessed Francis said to them: "Prepare and serve a meal so we can all eat together, and don't cry, because I will make you happy." So they prepared it at once, and all of them ate with great joy.

After the meal blessed Francis said to them: "This son of yours wants to serve God, and you should be glad and not sad about this. This will be counted an honor and advantage to your souls and bodies, not only according to God but also according to the world, because God will be honored by your own flesh and blood, and all our brothers will be your sons and brothers. And because he is a creature of God and wishes to serve his Creator, and to serve Him is to reign, I cannot and should not return him to you. But in order that you receive and keep some consolation from all this, I want him to rid himself of this ox by giving it to you, although, according to the counsel of the holy Gospel, it ought to be given to other poor people." They were all consoled by the words of blessed Francis, and they rejoiced especially that the ox was returned to them, since they were poor.

Because blessed Francis greatly loved and was always pleased by pure and holy simplicity in himself and in others, he immediately dressed him in the clothing of the religion and took him as his companion. He was a man of such simplicity, that he believed he was bound to do everything blessed Francis would do.

So, whenever blessed Francis was in some church or in some other place to pray, he wanted to watch and observe him so that he could imitate all his gestures. If blessed Francis knelt, or joined his hands toward heaven, or spat, or coughed, he would do the same. With great joy, blessed Francis began to reprove him for these kinds of simplicity. But he answered: "Brother, I promised to do everything you do. Therefore I want to do everything you do."

And blessed Francis marveled and rejoiced, seeing him in such purity and simplicity. For he began to be perfect in all virtues and good habits, so that blessed Francis and the other brothers greatly marveled at his perfection. A short time afterwards he died in that holy perfection. Therefore, with great inner and outer joy, blessed Francis used to tell the brothers about his manner of living and would call him not "Brother John," but "Saint John."

LP 20

[62]

[HE REJECTS A MAN WHO GAVE AWAY HIS POSSESSIONS TO HIS RELATIVES]

Once blessed Francis went preaching throughout the province of the Marches. While he was preaching one day to the people of one village, a man happened to come to him. "Brother," he said to him, "I want to leave the world and enter your religion." Blessed Francis told him: "Brother, if you wish to enter the religion of the brothers, you must first distribute all your goods to the poor, according to the counsel of the holy Gospel, and then renounce your will in all things."

When he heard these things, the man left hurriedly, and, led by the love of the flesh, he distributed all his goods to his relatives. He returned to blessed Francis, and told him: "Brother, I have expropriated myself of all my goods."

Blessed Francis asked him: "How did you do it?"

The man told him: "Brother, I gave all my goods to some of my relatives who needed them."

Through the Holy Spirit, blessed Francis immediately knew that the man was of the flesh, and told him: "Go on your way, Brother Fly, because you have distributed your goods to your relatives, and you want to live on alms among the brothers."

Refusing to distribute his goods to other poor people, he immediately went on his way.

LP 21

[63]

[HE IS FREED FROM A LONG-LASTING TEMPTATION]

At that time, while blessed Francis was staying in that same place of Saint Mary, it happened that a very serious temptation of the spirit was inflicted on him for the benefit of his soul. He was tormented inside and out, in body and spirit, so much that he sometimes withdrew from the close company of the brothers, especially since he could not be his usual cheerful self because of that temptation. He inflicted upon himself not only abstinence from food, but also from talking. He would often go to pray in the woods near the church, so that he could better express his pain and could more abundantly pour out his tears before the Lord, so that the Lord who is able to do all things, would be kind enough to send him a remedy from heaven for this great trial.

He was troubled by this temptation day and night for more than two years. One day while he was praying in the church of Saint Mary,

Mt 17:19 he happened to hear in spirit that saying of the holy Gospel: *"If you have faith like a mustard seed, and you tell* that *mountain to move* from its place *and move* to another place, it will happen." Saint Francis replied: "What is that mountain?" He was told: "That mountain is your temptation." "In that case, Lord," said blessed Francis, "be it done to me as you have said."

Immediately he was freed in such a way that it seemed to him that he never had that temptation.

[64] LP 22

[He criticizes Brother James the Simple and as a penance eats with a leper]

Once when blessed Francis had returned to Saint Mary of the Portiuncula, he found there Brother James the Simple with a leper covered with sores who had come there that day. The holy father had entrusted this leper to him, and especially all the other lepers who had severe sores. For in those days, the brothers stayed in the leper hospitals. That Brother James was like the doctor for those with severe sores, and he gladly touched, changed, and treated their wounds.

As if reproving Brother James, blessed Francis told him: "You should not take our Christian brothers about in this way since it is not right for you or for them." Blessed Francis used to call lepers "Christian brothers."

Although he was pleased that Brother James helped and served them, the holy father said this because he did not want him to take those with severe sores outside the hospital. This was especially because Brother James was very simple, and he often went with a leper to the church of Saint Mary, and especially because people usually abhorred lepers who had severe sores.

After he said these things, blessed Francis immediately reproached himself, and he told his fault to Brother Peter of Catanio, who was then general minister, especially because blessed Francis believed that in reproving Brother James he had shamed the leper. And because of this he told his fault, to make amends to God and to the leper. Blessed Francis said to Brother Peter: "I tell you to confirm for me the penance I have chosen to do for this and do not oppose me in any way."

Brother Peter told him: "Brother, do as you please."

Brother Peter so venerated and feared blessed Francis and was so obedient to him, that he would not presume to change his obedience, although then, and many other times, it hurt him inside and out.

Blessed Francis said: "Let this be my penance: I will eat together with my Christian brother from the same dish."[a]

While blessed Francis was sitting at the table with the leper and other brothers, a bowl was placed between the two of them. The leper was completely covered with sores and ulcerated, and especially the fingers with which he was eating were deformed and bloody, so that whenever he put them in the bowl, blood dripped into it.

Brother Peter and the other brothers saw this, grew very sad, but did not dare say anything out of fear of the holy father.

The one who wrote this, saw it and bore witness to it.

LP 23

[65]

[The vision of Brother Pacifico in a church at Bovara]

At one time blessed Francis was going through the valley of Spoleto together with Brother Pacifico, from the Marches of Ancona, who in the world had been known as "King of Verses," a nobleman and courtly master of singers.[b] They stayed in the lepers' hospital at Trevi.

Blessed Francis said to Brother Pacifico: "Let's go to the church of Saint Peter in Bovara, because I wish to stay there tonight."

That church was not too far from the hospital, and no one was staying there, because at that time the town of Trevi had been destroyed, so that no one lived in the town or the village.

On the way there, blessed Francis said to Brother Pacifico: "Go back to the hospital because I would like to remain here alone tonight. Come back to me at dawn tomorrow."

So blessed Francis remained there by himself. After he said compline and other prayers, he wanted to rest and sleep, but could not do so, and his soul grew afraid and he began to feel diabolical suggestions. He immediately got up, went outside the house, signed himself, and said: "On behalf of Almighty God, I tell you, demons, do whatever the Lord Jesus Christ has permitted you, to harm my body. I am prepared to endure anything, because the greatest enemy I have

a. Eating "from the same dish" is not allowed for brothers at table with women, cf. ER XII 2.

b. Background information on Brother Pacifico can be found in Fortini, *Francis*, 389-392 whose sources are Umberto Cosmo, *Con Madonna Povertà* (Bari: 1940), 59-81; and Ciro Ortolani, (Ciro da Pesaro), "Fra Pacifico re dei versi," *Picenum Seraphicum* 4 (1918): 121-169. Another treatment is that of Octave D'Angers, "Du frère cithariste qui, à Rieti, se récusa," *Études Franciscaines* 44 (1932): 549-556.

Lk 18:3 is my body. Therefore, *you will be avenging me on my opponent and enemy.*"

Those suggestions stopped immediately and, when he returned to the place where he had been lying, he rested and slept peacefully.

When morning came Brother Pacifico returned to him. Blessed Francis was standing in prayer in front of the altar inside the choir. Brother Pacifico stood and waited for him outside the choir, in front of the crucifix, praying to the Lord at the same time. As he began to
Rv 4:12 pray, Brother Pacifico was taken up into an ecstasy, *whether in the body or out of the body, God knows,* and he saw many thrones in heaven, one of them higher than the others, glorious, resplendent adorned with every precious stone. As he admired its beauty, he began to wonder what kind of throne it was and whose it might be. All at once he heard a voice telling him: "This was Lucifer's throne and blessed Francis will sit on it in his place."

As he came back to himself, blessed Francis came out to him. He immediately prostrated himself in the form of a cross at the feet of blessed Francis. Because of the vision he saw about him, he considered blessed Francis as if he were already in heaven, and said to him: "Father, forgive me my sins, and ask the Lord to forgive me and have mercy on me." Extending his hand, blessed Francis lifted him up, and he realized that he had seen something in prayer.

He appeared almost totally changed and spoke to blessed Francis not as if he were living in the flesh, but as if he were already reigning in heaven. Afterwards, as if on another point, because he was unwilling to speak about the vision to blessed Francis, Brother Pacifico asked him: "What do you think of yourself, brother?"

Blessed Francis responded: "It seems to be that I am a greater sinner than anyone in this world."

And immediately Brother Pacifico was told this in his heart: "In this you can know that the vision you saw is true. For as Lucifer was cast down from that throne because of his pride, so blessed Francis will merit to be exalted and to sit on it because of his humility."

[66] LP 24

[He hears the music of a lute in the house of Teobaldo Saraceno in Rieti]

Once, when blessed Francis was in Rieti because of the disease of his eyes, he was staying for a few days in a room of Teobaldo Saraceno. One day he said to one of his companions, who while in the world knew how to play a lute: "Brother, the children of this world do not understand divine things. Contrary to the will of God, they use instruments such as lutes, the ten-stringed harps, and other instruments, for the sake of vanity and sin, which in times past were used by holy people to praise God and offer consolation to souls. Therefore, I would like you to obtain secretly from some upright person a lute on which you could play for me a decent song and, with it, we will say the words and praises of the Lord, especially because my body is tormented with disease and pain. So I wish by this means to change that pain of my body to joy and consolation of spirit."

For, during his illness, blessed Francis composed some *Praises of the Lord* which he had his companions recite sometimes for the praise of God, the consolation of his spirit, and also for the edification of his neighbor.

"Father," the brother answered him, "I would be embarrassed to get one, especially because the people of this city know that I played the lute when I was out in the world. I fear they will suspect me of being tempted to play the lute again."

Blessed Francis told him: "Then, brother, let's let it go."

The following night, around midnight, blessed Francis was keeping vigil. And behold, around the house where he was staying he heard the sound of a lute playing a melody more beautiful and delightful than he had ever heard in his life. The one playing it would go some distance away so that he could barely be heard, and then returned, but was always playing. And he did this for over an hour.

Blessed Francis, considering that it was the work of God and not of any human being, was overjoyed, and with an exultant heart with deep feeling he praised the Lord who was so kind as to console him with such a great consolation.

When he arose in the morning he said to his companion: "My brother, I asked you for something and you did not grant it. But the Lord, who consoles His friends in their sufferings, was kind enough to console me last night."

He then told him everything that had happened.

The brothers were amazed and considered this a great miracle. And they knew that it was truly a work of God for the consolation of blessed Francis, especially since, by a decree of the podestà, no one dared go about the city, either at midnight or even after the third ringing of the bells. And because, as blessed Francis said, it came and went in silence, without a word or a noise from its mouth, for more than an hour to console his spirit.

[67] [His visitors trample a priest's vineyard in Rieti and it is miraculously restored]

LP 25

Because of the disease of his eyes, blessed Francis at that time was staying in the church of San Fabiano near the same city, where there was a poor secular priest. At that time the Lord Pope Honorius and other cardinals were in the same city. Many of the cardinals and other great clerics, because of the reverence and devotion they had for the holy father, used to visit him almost every day.

That church had a small vineyard next to the house where blessed Francis was staying. There was one door to the house through which nearly all those who visited him passed into the vineyard, especially because the grapes were ripe at that time, and the place was pleasant for resting.

And it came about that for that reason almost the entire vineyard was ruined. For some picked the grapes and ate them there, while others picked them and carried them off, and still others trampled them underfoot.

The priest began to be offended and upset. "I lost my vintage for this year!" he said. "Even though it's small, I got enough wine from it to take care of my needs!"

When blessed Francis heard of this, he had him called and said to him: "Do not be disturbed or offended any longer. We can't do anything about it. But trust in the Lord, because for me, His little servant, He can restore your loss. But, tell me, how many measures of wine did you get when your vineyard was at its best?"

"Thirteen measures, father," the priest responded.

"Don't be sad over this any more," blessed Francis told him, "and don't say anything offensive to anyone because of it, or argue with anyone about it. Trust the Lord and my words, and if you get less than twenty measures of wine, I will make it up to you."

The priest calmed down and kept quiet. And it happened by divine dispensation that he obtained twenty measures and no less, just as blessed Francis had told him. Those who heard about it, as well as the priest himself, were amazed. They considered it a great miracle due to the merits of blessed Francis, especially because not only was it devastated, but even if it had been full of grapes and no one had taken any, it still seemed impossible to the priest and the others to get twenty measures of wine from it.

We who were with him bear witness that whenever he used to say: "This is the way it is . . . or this is the way it will be . . .", it always happened as he said. We have seen many of these fulfilled not only while he was alive but also after his death.

LP 26

[68]

[AT FONTECOLOMBO THE DOCTOR HAS DINNER WITH THE BROTHERS AND THE LORD PROVIDES THE FOOD]

At that same time, blessed Francis stayed in the hermitage of the brothers at Fonte Colombo near Rieti because of the disease of his eyes. One day the eye doctor of that city[a] visited him and stayed with him for some hours, as he often used to do. When he was ready to leave, blessed Francis said to one of his companions: "Go and give the doctor a good meal." "Father," his companion answered, "we're ashamed to say that, because we're so poor now we'd be ashamed to invite him and give him anything to eat." Blessed Francis told his companions: "O you of little faith! Don't make me tell you again!"

The doctor said to blessed Francis and his companions: "Brother, it is because the brothers are so poor that I am happy to eat with them." The doctor was very rich and, although blessed Francis and his companions had often invited him, he had refused to eat there.

The brothers went and set the table. With embarrassment, they placed the little bread and wine they had as well as the few greens they had prepared for themselves.

When they had sat down at the table and eaten a bit, there was a knock on the door of the hermitage. One of the brothers rose, went and opened the door. And there was a woman with a large basket filled with beautiful bread, fish, crabcakes, honey, and freshly-picked grapes, which had been sent to brother Francis by a lady of a town about seven miles away from the hermitage.

After they saw this and considered the holiness of blessed Francis, the brothers and the doctor were greatly amazed. "My brothers," the doctor told them, "neither you nor we sufficiently recognize the holiness of this saint."

a. The Latin reads *medicus oculorum* [doctor of the eyes]. According to A. Sacchetti Sassetti, this doctor may have been "Magister Nicolaus medicus," whose name appears in many documents in the archives of Rieti between 1203-1233. See A. Sacchetti Sassetti, *Anecdota Franciscana Reatini*, 40-43. Since ophthalmology did not exist as a special branch of medicine before the end of the thirteenth century, it is difficult to imagine that a small city as Rieti employed such an expert. See the discussion in Octavian Schmucki, "The Illnesses of Saint Francis of Assisi before His Stigmatization," GR 4 (1990): 31-61; "The Illnesses of Francis During the Last Year of His Life," GR 13 (1999): 37-40.

[69] LP 27

[He tells a Lady of Limisiano that Her Husband will be Converted]

One time blessed Francis was going to "Le Celle" of Cortona and was following the road that passes at the foot of a fortified town called Limisiano, near the place of the brothers at Pregio. A noble woman of the town happened to come with great haste to speak to blessed Francis. When one of his companions saw this woman, extremely tired, hurrying after them, he ran to tell blessed Francis. "Father, for the love of God, let us wait for the lady who is following us, since she is quite exhausted from her desire to speak with us."

Blessed Francis, as a man full of charity and piety, waited for her. When he saw her exhausted and coming to him with great fervor and devotion, he said to her: "What is it, please, my lady?"

The lady answered: "Father, please, bless me."

Blessed Francis asked her: "Are you bound to a man or single?"

"Father," she said, "for a long time the Lord has given me the will to serve him. I had and still have a strong desire to save my soul. But I have a husband so cruel that he is an antagonist to me and to himself in the service of Christ. Because of this, my soul is tormented to death with great sorrow and anguish."

Blessed Francis was moved by piety for her, considering the burning spirit she had, and especially because she was a young girl and was delicate according to the flesh. He blessed her and said to her, "Go, and you will find your husband at home. Tell him for me that for the love of the Lord who endured the passion of the cross to save us, I beg both you and him to save your souls in your own home."

When she returned and entered the house, she found her husband at home, just as blessed Francis had told her.

Her husband said to her: "Where are you coming from?"

"I'm coming from seeing blessed Francis who blessed me," she answered, "and his words have consoled and gladdened my soul in the Lord. Moreover, he told me to tell you on his behalf and to beg you that we should both save our souls in our own home."

After she said this, the grace of God immediately came down on him, through the merits of blessed Francis. Suddenly changed anew by the Lord, he answered her with great kindness and meekness: "My lady, from now on, as it will please you, let us serve Christ and save our souls, as blessed Francis said."

His wife told him: "My lord, it seems to me that it would be good for us to live in chastity, because it is very pleasing to the Lord and is a virtue with great reward."

"Lady," her husband answered, "what pleases you, pleases me. For in this, as in other good deeds, I want to unite my will to yours."

And from then on, for many years, they lived in chastity, giving many alms to the brothers and to other poor people. Not only seculars, but also religious marveled at their holiness, especially since this man, who once was very worldly, so quickly became spiritual. Persevering till the end in all these things and other deeds, both of them died within a few days of each other. Because of the fragrance of their good life, there was great mourning over these two who had given all the time of their lives to praising and blessing the Lord who had given them graces, sincerity, and harmony during life in His service. Even in death they were not separated, because one died right after the other. Their memory, like that of the saints, is recalled to this day by those who knew them.

LP 28

[70]

[HE REFUSES ENTRANCE TO THE ORDER TO A YOUNG NOBLEMAN FROM LUCCA]

At a time when no one was received into the life of the brothers without the permission of blessed Francis, the son of a nobleman of this world from Lucca, together with others who wished to enter the religion, came to see blessed Francis. At the time he was sick and was staying at the palace of the bishop of Assisi. When the brothers presented them to blessed Francis, the son of the nobleman bowed before blessed Francis and began to cry aloud, begging to be received.

Looking at him, Blessed Francis said: "O wretched and fleshly man! Why are you lying to the Holy Spirit and to me? You are crying in the flesh and not in the spirit!"

After he said these things, his relatives suddenly arrived outside the palace on horseback, wanting to seize him and take him back home. When he heard the clatter of horses, he looked out a window of the palace, and saw his relatives. He immediately got up, and went outside to them. He returned to the world with them, just as blessed Francis had known through the Holy Spirit. The brothers, and others who were there, marveled, magnified, and praised God in his saint.

LP 29

[71]

[HE WANTS TO EAT SOME FISH AND IT IS PROVIDED IN A WONDERFUL WAY]

Once when he was very sick and staying in the same palace, the brothers begged and encouraged him to eat. But he answered them:

"My brothers, I don't have the wish to eat; but if I had a bit of that fish called *squalo,* perhaps I would eat some."

Once he said this, someone came carrying a basket in which there were three large and well-prepared *squali* and crabcakes. The holy father gladly ate these. These were sent to him by Brother Gerardo, the minister at Rieti.

As they considered his holiness, the brothers were amazed and praised the Lord who had provided for his servant, especially because it was winter and such things were not available in that area.

[72] LP 30

[He knows the thoughts of a critical brother]

Once blessed Francis was travelling with a spiritual brother from Assisi who came from a great and powerful family. Because he was weak and ill, blessed Francis rode on a donkey. Feeling tired from walking, that brother began to think to himself: "His parents were never at the same level as mine, and here he is riding, while I'm worn out, walking behind him, prodding the beast."

While he was thinking this, blessed Francis got off the donkey and said to him: "No, brother, it's not right or proper for me to ride while you go on foot, for in the world you were nobler and more influential than I." The brother, stunned and ashamed, fell down at his feet and, in tears, confessed his thought and then said his penance. He was greatly amazed at his holiness, for he immediately knew his thought.

In fact, when the brothers petitioned the Lord Pope Gregory and the cardinals in Assisi to canonize blessed Francis, he testified to this before the Lord Pope and the cardinals.

[73] LP 31

[He blesses a brother at Greccio, knowing his wish at a distance]

A brother, a spiritual man and a friend of God, was living in the place of the brothers of Rieti. One day he got up and came with great devotion to the hermitage of the brothers of Greccio, where blessed Francis was then staying, out of a desire to see him and receive his blessing. Blessed Francis had already eaten and had returned to the cell where he prayed and rested. Because it was Lent he did not leave the cell except at mealtime and returned to the cell immediately afterward. The brother did not find him and grew very sad, attributing this to his sins, especially because he had to return that day to his own place.

The companions of blessed Francis consoled him, and he had not gone more than a stone's throw away from the place when, by the will of the Lord, blessed Francis came out of his cell and called one of his companions, who was travelling with him as far as Fonte del Lago. He said to him: "Tell that brother to look back toward me." And when he turned his face to blessed Francis, he made the sign of the cross and blessed him. That brother, rejoicing both in body and spirit, praised the Lord who fulfilled his desire. His consolation was so much the greater because he saw that it was the will of God that the saint bless him without being asked by him or others.

The companions of blessed Francis, and the other brothers of the place, were amazed, considering it a great miracle since no one had told blessed Francis about the arrival of that brother. And neither the companions of blessed Francis, nor any other brother would have dared approach him unless he had called them. This was true not only there but everywhere blessed Francis stayed to pray, for he wanted to remain so removed, that no one would go to him without being called.

LP 32

[74]

[HE CORRECTS THE BROTHERS OF GRECCIO FOR AN ELEGANT TABLE-SETTING; THE VISIT OF CARDINAL HUGOLINO TO THE PORTIUNCULA; PRAISE FOR THE PEOPLE OF GRECCIO]

One day a minister of the brothers came to blessed Francis who was then staying in that same place, in order to celebrate the feast of Christmas with him. It happened that the brothers of that place on Christmas day itself prepared the table elaborately because of that minister, covering it with lovely white tablecloths which they obtained for the occasion, and vessels of glass for drinking.

Blessed Francis came down from the cell to eat, and when he saw the table set on a dais and finely prepared, he went secretly and took the hat of a poor man who had arrived there that very day, and the staff he carried in his hand. He called one of his companions in a whisper and went outside the door of the hermitage, unnoticed by the other brothers of the house.

Meanwhile the brothers came to the table, especially because it was sometimes the custom of the holy father that, if he did not arrive immediately at mealtime, and the brothers wanted to eat, he wanted them to go to the table and eat.

His companion closed the door, remaining next to it on the inside. Blessed Francis knocked on the door and he immediately opened it for him. He entered with his hat on his back and with staff in hand, like a pilgrim. When he came to the door of the house where the brothers were eating, he called out to the brothers like a poor man: "For the love of the Lord God, give alms to this poor, sick pilgrim."

That minister and the other brothers recognized him at once. The minister told him: "Brother, we are also poor, and because we are so many, we need these alms we are eating. But, for the love of that Lord you invoked, come into the house, and we will give you some of the alms which the Lord has given us."

When he came in and stood in front of the brothers' table, the minister gave him the bowl from which he was eating and some bread. Taking it, he sat down on the floor beside the fire, facing the brothers who sat at the elevated table. Sighing he said to the brothers: "When I saw the table finely and elaborately prepared, I considered that this was not a table of poor religious, who go door-to-door each day. For more than other religious, we should follow the example of poverty and humility in all things, because we have been called to this and have professed this before God and people. So, now it seems to me I'm seated like a brother."

The brothers were ashamed at this, considering that blessed Francis was speaking the truth. Some of them began to weep loudly, considering how he was seated on the ground, wishing to correct them in such a holy and simple way.

He told the brothers that they have a humble and decent table so LP 33
as to edify secular people. And if the brothers invite a poor person he should sit with them, and not have the poor man sit on the ground and have the brothers sit on high.

When the Lord Pope Gregory was the bishop of Ostia, he came to the place of the brothers at Saint Mary of the Portiuncula, with many knights, monks, and other clerics. He entered the house of the brothers to see their dormitory and, when he saw that the brothers lay on the ground, with nothing underneath except a little straw, no pillows, and some poor coverings, torn and threadbare, he began to weep profusely before them all. "Look where the brothers sleep," he said. "But we, wretched creatures, enjoy such a surplus. What will become of us?" Both he and the others were greatly edified. He did not see a table there because the brothers ate on the ground. From the very beginning, that place, once it was built, was visited by the brothers of the entire religion more than any other place, for everyone who entered religion was invested there. No matter whether they were few or many, the brothers always used to eat on the ground. As long as the holy father lived, after his example and will, the brothers who lived there used to sit on the ground to eat.

LP 34 For blessed Francis found the hermitage of the brothers at Greccio to be becoming and poor and the inhabitants, although poor and simple, were more pleasing to him than those of the rest of the region. For this reason he rested and stayed there, especially because there was a poor cell, very isolated, in which the holy father would stay.

Many of these people, with the grace of God, entered religion because of his example and preaching and that of his brothers. Many women preserved their virginity and, remaining in their own homes, dressed in the clothing of religion. And although each remained in her own home, each of them lived the common life decently, afflicting her body with fasting and prayer. Thus it seemed to the people and to the brothers that their manner of living was not among seculars and their relatives, but among holy and religious people who had served the Lord a long time, despite their youthful age and simplicity. That is why, with joy, blessed Francis often said to the brothers about the men and women of this town: "Even in a large city not as many people have been converted to penance as in Greccio, which is only a small town."

For frequently, when the brothers of that place used to praise the Lord in the evening, as the brothers at that time were accustomed to do in many places, the people of that town, both the great and the small, would come outside. Standing on the road in front of the town, they would respond to the brothers in a loud voice: "Praised be the Lord God!" Even children, who could not yet speak, when they saw the brothers, would praise the Lord as best they could.

In those times they endured an awful scourge which they had suffered for many years. Huge wolves would eat people, and every year hailstorms would destroy their fields and vineyards. One day when blessed Francis was preaching, he said to them: "To the praise and honor of God, I tell you that, if each one of you turns away from sin, and turns to God with whole heart, firm resolve, and will to persevere, I trust in the Lord Jesus Christ that, in His mercy, He will soon deliver you from the scourge of the wolves and of the hail from which, for so long a time, you have been suffering. He will make you grow and increase in both spiritual and temporal things. I also tell you if you return to your vomit, this scourge and pestilence will return, and more and worse disasters will afflict you."

Through divine providence and the merits of the holy father, it happened that, from that hour and time, this scourge ceased. Moreover, it was a great miracle when hail came down and destroyed their neighbors' fields, but did not touch their fields that were next to them. And for sixteen to twenty years they began to increase and abound in spiritual and temporal things.

Afterwards, however, they began to grow fat and proud, to hate each other, to strike one another with swords even to the point of death, to kill animals secretly, stealing and pillaging at night, and to commit many other evils. When the Lord saw that their works were evil and that they did not observe what was told them by His servant, blessed Francis, His anger flared up and He withdrew the hand of His mercy from them. The scourge of wolves and hail returned, as the holy father had said, and many other even worse calamities befell them. The town was entirely burned and, after losing everything they had, they escaped only with their lives. Then the brothers and others who had heard what blessed Francis said, how he predicted prosperity and adversity for them, were amazed at his holiness, seeing all his words fulfilled to the letter.

[75] LP 35

[He preaches in the piazza of Perugia and foretells a civil war]

Once blessed Francis was preaching in the piazza at Perugia to a large crowd gathered there. All of a sudden some knights of Perugia began racing their horses around the piazza, jousting with their weapons, and thus disturbing the preaching. Although the men and women, who were intent on listening to the sermon, reprimanded them, they did not stop. Blessed Francis turned to them and, with a fiery spirit, said: "Listen and understand what the Lord is telling you through me, His servant, and don't say, 'This one is from Assisi!'" Blessed Francis said this because of a long-standing enmity between the people of Assisi and those of Perugia.[a]

"The Lord has exalted and elevated you above all your neighbors," he said. "Because of this, you must acknowledge your Creator all the more, and humble yourselves not only before almighty God but also before your neighbors. But your heart is puffed up by arrogance in your pride and might. You attack your neighbors and kill many of them. Because of this I tell you, unless you quickly turn to Him and compensate those whom you have injured, the Lord, who leaves

a. Civil strife erupted in Perugia in 1214 and flared up again in 1217. In this instance, however, Assisi took advantage of Perugia's internal weakness in order to claim the road from Assisi to Perugia by occupying the castle of Postignano. In 1222, another outbreak of civil strife divided Perugia and, once again, Assisi took advantage by moving against the commune of Bettona. Thus Francis would be looked down upon by the knights of Perugia, hostile to Assisians. Cf. Arnaldo Fortini, *Francis of Assisi*, translated by Helen Moak (New York: Crossroad, 1981), 569-574.

nothing unavenged, to your greater punishment and disgrace, will cause you to rise up against each other. You will be torn apart by sedition and civil war, suffering by a far greater calamity than your neighbors could ever inflict on you."

In his preaching blessed Francis was not silent about people's vices, through which they publicly offended God and their neighbor. The Lord had given him such grace, that everyone who saw or heard him, small or great, feared and revered him because he had such an abundance of grace from God. As a result, no matter how much he reprimanded them, even to the point of shaming them, they were edified. Indeed, sometimes, for this reason, and so that he would pray to the Lord more intently for them, they would turn to the Lord.

A few days later, by divine consent, a scandal broke out between the knights and the people. The people drove the knights out of the city. The knights, supported by the Church, destroyed many of their fields, vineyards and trees, doing as much harm to them as they could. The people likewise destroyed the knights' fields, vineyards and trees. And thus, that people was afflicted with greater punishment than all of their neighbors whom they had offended.

In this way everything that blessed Francis predicted about them was fulfilled to the letter.

LP 36

[76]

[HE MEETS A DEVOUT ABBOT, WHO FEELS THE POWER OF HIS PRAYER]

When blessed Francis was going through one region, he met an abbot of a monastery who had a great love and veneration for him. Dismounting from his horse, the abbot spoke to him for over an hour about the salvation of his soul. When the time came for them to part, the abbot asked blessed Francis with great devotion to pray to the Lord for his soul. "I will gladly do that," blessed Francis told him.

The abbot had gone a short distance from blessed Francis when blessed Francis said to his companion: "Wait for me a little while, brother, for I want to pray for that abbot, as I promised." And he prayed for him.

It was customary for blessed Francis, whenever anyone out of devotion requested him to pray to the Lord for his soul, to offer a prayer as soon as possible, so that he would not forget afterwards.

The abbot was still on his way, not very far from blessed Francis, when suddenly the Lord visited him in his heart. A gentle warmth filled his face, and, for a brief moment, he was raised in ecstasy of spirit. When he came to himself, he immediately knew that blessed

Francis had prayed for him. He began to praise God and to rejoice both in body and soul. From that time on, he had an even greater devotion to the holy father, considering in him the greatness of his holiness. As long as he lived he held this to be a great miracle, and he often related to the brothers and others what had happened to him.

[77] LP37

[He overlooks his own illnesses out of love for the Passion of the Lord]

For a long time and even until the day of his death, blessed Francis suffered ailments of the liver, spleen, and stomach. From the time when he was overseas to preach to the Sultan of Babylon and Egypt, he had a very severe eye disease, caused by the hardship and fatigue of travel, as he endured the extreme heat both in coming and going.[a] Because of the fervent spirit he had from the moment of his conversion to Christ, he refused to be concerned about treatment for any of his ailments despite the request of his brothers and many others, moved by piety and compassion for him. What was bitter to his body he accepted and considered sweet on account of the sweetness and compassion that he drew daily from the humility and footprints of the Son of God. Because of the sufferings and bitter experiences of Christ, which He endured for us, he grieved and afflicted himself daily in body and soul to such a degree that he did not treat his own illnesses.

[78]

[He is seen walking and crying over the Passion of Christ]

Once, a few years after his conversion, he was walking alone one day along the road not too far from the church of Saint Mary of the Portiuncula, crying loudly and wailing as he went. As he was walking along, a spiritual man met him, someone we know and from whom we learned about this incident, who had shown him great mercy and consolation, both before he had any brothers and afterwards. Moved by piety toward him, he asked him: "Brother, what's wrong?" He thought that blessed Francis was suffering some painful illness. But he answered: "I should go through the whole world this way, without any shame, crying and bewailing the Passion of my

a. For a thorough study of the early illnesses of Francis's life, see Octavian Schmucki, "The Illnesses of Saint Francis of Assisi before His Stigmatization," GR 4(1990): 31-61, especially 35-38.

Lord." At this, the man began to weep and cry aloud together with him.

LP 38

[79]

[HE REPLIES TO A BROTHER WHO ENCOURAGED HIM TO HAVE SCRIPTURE READ TO COMFORT HIM]

On another occasion, at the time of his eye disease, he endured such pain that one day a minister said to him: "Brother, why don't you have one of your companions read to you from the prophets or other passages of Scripture? In that way, *your spirit will rejoice in the* Lk 1:47
Lord and receive great consolation." He knew that he rejoiced greatly in the Lord whenever he heard the divine Scriptures read to him.

"Brother," he answered him, "every day I find so much sweetness and consolation in my memory from meditating on the humility of the footprints of the Son of God that, if I were to live till the end of the world, I'd have no great need to hear or meditate on other passages of Scripture."

He often called to mind and afterward spoke to the brothers this verse of David: *"My soul refuses to be consoled."* For this reason, as he fre- Ps 77:3
quently told the brothers, because he had to be a model and example to all the brothers, he refused to take, not only medicines, but even necessary food in his illnesses. Because he took these things into consideration, he was severe with his body, not only when he appeared healthy, although he was always weak and ill, but also when he was ailing.

LP 39

[80]

[HE AVOIDS HYPOCRISY, CONFESSING WHAT HE HAS EATEN DURING AN ILLNESS]

One time when he had recovered somewhat from a very serious illness, after some consideration, it seemed to him that he had received some little delicacies during that illness, although he ate only a little, since with his many, diverse, and serious illnesses he was not able to eat.

One day, although still sick from a quartan fever,[a] he had the people of Assisi called to the piazza for a sermon. When he had finished preaching, he requested that no one leave until he returned.

a. The Latin text reads *de febre quartana* [from a quartan fever], a type of malaria in which the symptoms occur every fourth day. Cf. Octavian Schmucki, "The Illnesses of St. Francis of Assisi before His Stigmatization," GR 4 (1990): 49-52.

Together with Brother Peter of Catanio, whom he chose as the first general minister, and with a few other brothers, he entered the church of San Rufino, going into the *confessio*.[a] He ordered Brother Peter to obey and not contradict whatever he wanted to say and do to himself. And Brother Peter said to him: "Brother, in what concerns you and me, I cannot, and should not want anything else except what pleases you."

Taking off his tunic, blessed Francis ordered Brother Peter to lead him naked with a rope tied around his neck in front of the people. He ordered another brother to take a bowl full of ashes and, mounting the place from where he had preached, to throw them and sprinkle them on his head. But moved by piety and compassion towards him, the brother did not obey him. Brother Peter got up and, weeping bitterly with the other brothers, led him out as he had been ordered to do.

In this way he came back in front of the people naked, to the place where he had preached, and said: "You believe me to be a holy man, as do others who, following my example, leave the world and enter the religion and life of the brothers. But I confess to God and to you that during my illness I ate meat and broth flavored with meat."

Almost all the people began to weep out of piety and compassion for him, especially since it was wintertime and was very cold and he had not yet recovered from the quartan fever. They struck their breasts, accusing themselves. "This holy man," they said, "whose life we know, accuses himself with such shame over a just and manifest necessity. Yet because of excessive abstinence and the severity with which he treats his body from the moment of his conversion to Christ, we see him living in flesh that is almost dead. What shall we do, wretches that we are, we who all our life have lived, and wish to live, according to the will and desires of the flesh?"

[81] LP 40

[He abhors hypocrisy both in eating and in clothing]

Likewise, at another time, he was staying in a hermitage for the Lent of Saint Martin.[b] Because of his illness, the brothers cooked the food they gave him to eat in lard, because oil was very bad for him in

a. That is, the crypt below the sanctuary, where the relics of the saints were preserved and venerated.

b. Toward the end of the fifth century, a custom arose in the diocese of Tours, France, in which the feast of Saint Martin, November 11, initiated a fast that was observed three days of the week. The custom spread so that a penitential season prior to Christmas began on November 11, "the Fast of Saint Martin."

his illnesses. When the forty days had ended and he was preaching to a large crowd of people, gathered not far from that hermitage, in the opening words of his sermon he told them: "You came to me with great devotion and believe me to be a holy man. But I confess to God and to you that during this Lent in that hermitage, I have eaten food flavored with lard."

Indeed, if the brothers or the friends of the brothers, with whom he would eat, occasionally prepared a special dish for him because of his illnesses or the obvious need of his body, it frequently happened that he would immediately tell this to the brothers or lay people who did not know about it, whether inside the house or outside, saying publicly: "I ate such and such foods." He did not wish to conceal from people what was known to God.

Moreover, if his soul were ever tempted to vainglory, pride, or any vice, no matter where he was, or in whose presence, whether they be religious or lay, he would immediately and openly confess it to them, without concealing anything. That is why he told his companions one day: "I want to live before God, in hermitages and other places where I stay, just as the people see and know me. If they believe that I am a holy man and I do not lead a life becoming a holy man, I would be a hypocrite."

Thus one time in winter, one of the companions, who was his guardian, acquired a piece of fox fur because of the illness of the spleen and the cold of his stomach. He asked him to permit him to have it sewn under his tunic next to his stomach and spleen, especially because it was then extremely cold. But from the moment he began to serve Christ until the day of his death, in any weather, he did not want to wear or have anything but a single patched tunic.

Blessed Francis answered him: "If you want me to wear that fur under the tunic, allow me to sew a piece of the fur on the outside of my tunic as an indication to people that I have a piece of fur underneath." And this is what he had done; and, although it was a necessity on account of his illnesses, he did not wear it long.

LP 41

[82]

[HE ACCUSES HIMSELF OF VAINGLORY, NOT WISHING TO BE A HYPOCRITE]

Another time, he was going through the city of Assisi and many people went with him. A poor old woman asked him for alms for the love of God and he immediately gave her the mantle he had on his back. And, at once, he confessed before everyone that on that account he felt vainglory.

We who were with him saw and heard many other examples similar to these but we cannot tell them because it would take too long to write or recount them.

Blessed Francis's highest and principal concern was that he should not be a hypocrite before God. Although he needed special food for his body because of his infirmity, nevertheless, he thought that he must always offer good example to the brothers and to others, so that he might take away from them any reason for complaining and bad example. He preferred to endure bodily needs patiently and willingly, and he did endure them until the day of his death, rather than satisfy himself, even though he could have done so according to God and good example.

[83] LP 42

[Brother Elias and Cardinal Hugolino ask him to accept medical help He composes the Canticle of Brother Sun at San Damiano]

The Bishop of Ostia, who later became the apostolic bishop,[a] seeing how blessed Francis was always severe with his body, and especially because he was rapidly losing his eyesight because he refused to have himself treated, admonished him with great kindness and compassion. He told him: "Brother, you do not do well in not allowing yourself to be helped with your eye disease, for your health and your life are of great value not only to yourself but also to others. If you have compassion for your sick brothers, and have always been and still are merciful to them, you must not be cruel to yourself in such a serious and manifest need and illness. I therefore order you to allow yourself to be helped and treated."

Likewise, two years before his death, while he was already very sick, especially from the eye disease, he was staying at San Damiano in a little cell made of mats.

The general minister, seeing and considering how tormented he was with the eye disease, ordered him to let himself be treated and helped. He also told him that he wanted to be present when the doctor began the treatment, especially so that he could more effectively arrange for him to be cared for and comforted, since he was suffering a great deal from it. At that time it was very cold, and the weather was not conducive to treatment.

a. That is, pope, bishop of the "Apostolic See" of Rome.

LP 43 Blessed Francis lay there for more than fifty days, and was unable to bear the light of the sun during the day or the light of a fire at night. He stayed in the dark in the house, inside that little cell. In addition, day and night he had great pains in his eyes so that at night he could scarcely rest or sleep. This was very harmful and was a serious aggravation for his eye disease and his other illnesses.[a]

Sometimes he did want to rest and sleep, but there were many mice in the house and in the little cell made of mats where he was lying, in one part of the house. They were running around him, and even over him, and would not let him sleep. They even disturbed him greatly at the time of prayer. They bothered him not only at night, but also during the day, even climbing up on his table when he was eating, so much so that his companions, and he himself, considered it a temptation of the devil, which it was.

One night as blessed Francis was reflecting on all the troubles he
was enduring, he was moved by piety for himself. "*Lord,*" he said to Jn 21:25
himself, "*make haste to help me* in my illnesses, so that I may be able to bear them patiently." And suddenly he was told in spirit: "Tell me, brother, what if, in exchange for your illnesses and troubles, someone were to give you a treasure? And it would be so great and precious that, even if the whole earth were changed to pure gold, all stones to precious stones, and all water to balsam, you would still judge and hold all these things as nothing, as if they were earth, stones and water, in comparison to the great and precious treasure which was given you. Wouldn't you greatly rejoice?"

"Lord," blessed Francis answered, "this treasure would indeed be great, worth seeking, very precious, greatly lovable, and desirable."

"Then, brother," he was told, "be glad and rejoice in your illnesses and troubles, because as of now, you are as secure as if you were already in my kingdom."

The next morning on rising, he said to his companions: "If the emperor were to give a whole kingdom to one of his servants, shouldn't he greatly rejoice? But, what if it were the whole empire, wouldn't he rejoice even more?" And he said to them: "I must rejoice greatly in my illnesses and troubles and be consoled in the Lord, giving thanks always to God the Father, to His only Son, our Lord Jesus Christ, and to the Holy Spirit for such a great grace and blessing. In His mercy He

a. Francis seems to have suffered from trachoma or contagious conjunctivitis granulosa, which is characterized by abundant teary secretions, progressive corneal complications, sensitivity to light, and consequent impaired vision. In Francis's case, it was aggravated by his frequent malarial fevers and habitual malnutrition. A graphic description of Francis's trachoma is presented by Henri d'Avranches, *The Versified Life of Saint Francis* XII 70-84 (hereafter VL), see FA:ED I 510-511. Cf. Octavian Schmucki, "The Illnesses of Francis During the Last Year of His Life," GR 13 (1999): 30-31.

has given me, His unworthy little servant still living in the flesh, the promise of His kingdom.

"Therefore for His praise, for our consolation and for the edification of our neighbor, I want to write a new *Praise of the Lord* for his creatures, which we use every day, and without which we cannot live. Through them the human race greatly offends the Creator, and every day we are ungrateful for such great graces, because we do not praise, as we should, our Creator and the Giver of all good."

Sitting down, he began to meditate and then said: "Most High, CtC
all-powerful, good Lord." He composed a melody for these words and taught it to his companions so they could repeat it. For his spirit was then in such sweetness and consolation, that he wanted to send for Brother Pacifico, who in the world was called "The King of Verses," and was a very courtly master of singers. He wanted to give him a few good and spiritual brothers to go through the world preaching and praising God.

He said that he wanted one of them who knew how to preach, first to preach to the people. After the sermon, they were to sing the *Praises of the Lord* as minstrels of the Lord. After the praises, he wanted the preacher to tell the people: "We are minstrels of the Lord, and this is what we want as payment: that you live in true penance."

He used to say: "What are the servants of God if not His minstrels, who must move people's hearts and lift them up to spiritual joy?" And he said this especially to the Lesser Brothers, who had been given to the people for their salvation.

The *Praises of the Lord* that he composed, that is, "Most High, CtC
all-powerful, good Lord," he called *"The Canticle of Brother Sun,"* who is more beautiful than all other creatures and can be most closely compared to God.

He used to say: "At dawn, when the sun rises, everyone should praise God, who created it, because through it the eyes are lighted by day. And in the evening, when it becomes night, everyone should praise God for another creature, Brother Fire, because through it the eyes are lighted at night."

He said: "For we are all like blind people, and the Lord lights up our eyes through these two creatures. Because of this, we must always praise the glorious Creator for these and for His other creatures which we use every day."

He did this and continued to do this gladly, whether he was healthy or sick. And he encouraged others to praise the Lord. Indeed, when his illness grew more serious, he himself began to say the *Praises of the Lord,* and afterwards had his companions sing it, so that in reflecting on the praise of the Lord, he could forget the sharpness of his pains and illnesses. He did this until the day of his death.

LP 44

[84]

[He makes peace between the bishop and mayor of Assisi, adding a verse to the Canticle]

At that same time when he lay sick, the bishop of the city of Assisi at the time excommunicated the podestà. In return, the man who was then podestà was enraged, and had this proclamation announced, loud and clear, throughout the city of Assisi: no one was to sell or buy anything from the bishop, or to draw up any legal document with him. And so they thoroughly hated each another.

Although very ill, blessed Francis was moved by piety for them, especially since there was no one, religious or secular, who was intervening for peace and harmony between them. He said to his companions: "It is a great shame for you, servants of God, that the bishop and the podestà hate one another in this way, and that there is no one intervening for peace and harmony between them."

And so, for that reason, he composed one verse for the *Praises:*

CtC 10-11 Praised be by You, my Lord, through those who give pardon for Your love,
and bear infirmity and tribulation.
Blessed are those who endure in peace
for by You, Most High, they shall be crowned.

Afterwards he called one of his companions and told him: "Go to the podestà and, on my behalf, tell him to go to the bishop's residence together with the city's magistrates and bring with him as many others as he can."

And when the brother had gone, he said to two of his other companions: "Go and sing the *Canticle of Brother Sun* before the bishop, the podestà, and the others who are with them. I trust in the Lord that He will humble their hearts and they will make peace with each other and return to their earlier friendship and love."

When they had all gathered in the piazza inside the cloister of the bishop's residence, the two brothers rose and one of them said: "In his illness, blessed Francis wrote the *Praises of the Lord* for His creatures, for His praise and the edification of his neighbor. He asks you, then, to listen to them with great devotion." And so, they began to sing and recite to them. And immediately the podestà stood up and, folding his arms and hands with great devotion, he listened intently, even with tears, as if to the Gospel of the Lord. For he had a great faith and devotion toward blessed Francis.

When the *Praises of the Lord* were ended, the podestà said to everyone: "I tell you the truth, not only do I forgive the lord bishop, whom I must have as my lord, but I would even forgive one who killed my brother or my son." And so he cast himself at the lord bishop's feet, telling him: "Look, I am ready to make amends to you for everything, as it pleases you, for the love of our Lord Jesus Christ and of his servant, blessed Francis."

Taking him by the hands, the bishop stood up and said to him: "Because of my office humility is expected of me, but because I am naturally prone to anger, you must forgive me." And so, with great kindness and love they embraced and kissed each other.

And the brothers marveled greatly, considering the holiness of blessed Francis, that what he had foretold about peace and harmony between them had been fulfilled, to the letter. All the others who were present and heard it took it for a great miracle, crediting it to the merits of blessed Francis, that the Lord had so quickly visited them, and that without recalling anything that had been said, they returned to such harmony from such scandal.

Therefore we who were with blessed Francis bear witness that al- AC 67
ways whenever he would predict "such-and-such a thing is or will be this way," it happened almost to the letter. We have seen with our own eyes what would be too long to write down or recount.

[85] LP 45

[He composes another song to console Clare and her sisters]

Likewise, in those same days and in the same place, blessed Francis, after he composed the *Praises of the Lord* for his creatures, also CtExh
composed some holy words with chant for the greater consolation of the Poor Ladies of the Monastery of San Damiano. He did this especially because he knew how much his illness troubled them.

And since he was unable to console and visit them personally because of that illness, he wanted those words to be proclaimed to them by his companions. In these words, he wanted to reveal his will to them briefly, for then and for always, how they should be of one mind and how they should live in charity toward one another. He wanted to do this because they were converted to Christ by his example and preaching when the brothers were still few. Their conversion and manner of living is the glory and edification not only of the religion of the brothers, whose little plant they are, but also of the entire Church of God.

Therefore, since blessed Francis knew that from the beginning of their conversion they had led, and were still leading, a strict and poor life by free choice and by necessity, his spirit was always moved to piety for them.

With these words, then, he begged them that, as the Lord had gathered them as one from many different regions in holy charity, holy poverty, and holy obedience, so in these they should live and die. And he begged them particularly to provide for their bodies with discernment from the alms which the Lord would give them, with cheerfulness and thanksgiving. And he especially asked them to remain patient: the healthy, in the labors which they endure for their sick sisters; and the sick in their illnesses and the needs they suffer.

LP 46

[86]

[He is taken to Fonte Colombo to have his eyes cauterized; the kindness of Brother Fire]

It happened that, when the season conducive to healing of the eyes arrived, blessed Francis left that place, even though his eye disease was quite serious. He was wearing on his head a large capuche the brothers had made for him, with a piece of wool and linen cloth sewn to the capuche, covering his eyes. This was because he could not look at the light of day because of the great pain caused by his eye disease. His companions led him on horseback to the hermitage of Fonte Colombo, near Rieti, to consult with a doctor of Rieti who knew how to treat eye diseases.

When that doctor arrived there, he told blessed Francis that he wanted to cauterize from the jaw to the eyebrow of the weaker eye.[a] Blessed Francis, however, did not wish the treatment to begin until Brother Elias arrived.

He waited for him, and he did not come because, on account of many engagements he had, he could not come. So he was in doubt about beginning the treatment. But, constrained by necessity, and especially out of obedience to the Lord Bishop of Ostia and the general minister, he proposed to obey, although it was difficult for him to have any concern about himself, and that is why he wanted his minister to do this.

a. On cauterization, cf. Schmucki, "The Illnesses of Francis During the Last Years of His Life," GR 13 (1999): 39-41.

Afterwards, one night when the pain of his illness prevented him LP 47
from sleeping, he had pity and compassion on himself. He said to his companions: "My dearest brothers and sons, do not grow weary or burdened because of your care for me in my illness. The Lord, on my behalf, His little servant, will return to you, in this world and the next, all the fruit of the good work that you are unable to do because of your care for me in my illness. In fact, you will obtain an even greater profit than those who assist the whole religion and life of the brothers. You should even tell me: 'We're paying your expenses, but the Lord, on your behalf, will be our debtor.' "

The holy father spoke in this way because he wanted to help them and lift them up in their faint-heartedness and weakness. He did this so that they would not be tempted to use this work as an excuse to say: "We can't pray and we can't put up with all this work"; and so that they would not become weary and faint-hearted, and thus lose the fruit of their labor.

One day the doctor arrived with the iron instrument used for cau- LP 48
terizing in eye diseases. He had a fire lit to heat the iron, and when the fire was lit, he placed the iron in it.

To comfort his spirit so it would not become afraid, blessed Francis said to the fire: "My Brother Fire, noble and useful among all the creatures the Most High created, be courtly to me in this hour. For a long time I have loved you and I still love you for the love of that Lord who created you. I pray our Creator who made you, to temper your heat now, so that I may bear it." And as he finished the prayer he made the sign of the cross over the fire.

We who were with him, overcome by piety and compassion for him, all ran away, and he remained alone with the doctor.

When the cauterization was finished, we returned to him. "You, faint-hearted, of little faith," he said to us, "why did you run away? I tell you the truth: I felt no pain or even heat from the fire. In fact, if it's not well cooked, cook it some more!"

The doctor was greatly amazed, and noting that he did not even move, considered it a great miracle. "My brothers," the doctor said, "I tell you, and I speak from experience: I doubt that a strong man with a healthy body could endure such a severe burn, much less this man, who is weak and sick."

The burn was a long one, extending from the ear to the eyebrow, because, day and night for years fluid had been accumulating in his eyes. This is the reason, according to the advice of the doctor, for cauterizing all the veins from the ear to the eyebrow, although, according to the advice of other doctors, it would be very harmful. And this proved to be true, since it did not help him at all. Similarly, another doctor pierced both his ears, but to no avail.

LP 49 It is not surprising that fire and other creatures sometimes showed him reverence because, as we who were with him saw, he loved and revered them with a great feeling of charity. He took great delight in them and his spirit was moved to so much piety and compassion toward them that he was disturbed when someone did not treat them decently. He used to speak with them with joy, inside and out, as if they could hear, understand, and speak about God. And for that reason he was often caught up in the contemplation of God.

Once when he was sitting close to a fire, without being aware of it, his linen pants next to the leg caught fire. He felt the heat of the fire and his companion saw that the fire was burning his pants and ran to put out the flame. Blessed Francis told him: "No, dearest brother, do not hurt Brother Fire." And he did not permit him to extinguish it. So the brother ran to the brother who was his guardian and brought him to blessed Francis and, against his wishes, he began to put it out.

He was moved with such piety and love for it that he did not want to blow out a candle, a lamp, or a fire, as is usually done when necessary. He also forbade a brother to throw away fire or smoldering wood, as is usually done, but wanted him simply to place it on the ground, out of reverence for Him who created it.

LP 50

[87]
[He will not help to put out a fire at La Verna]

Another time, while he was keeping a lent on Mount La Verna, his companion lit a fire at mealtime one day in the cell where he ate. Once the fire was lit, he went to blessed Francis, who was in the cell where he usually prayed and slept, to read him the holy Gospel that was read in the Mass of that day. Whenever blessed Francis was unable to hear Mass, he always wanted to hear the Gospel of the day before he ate.

When blessed Francis came to eat in the cell where the fire was lit, the flames had already reached the roof of the cell and were burning it. His companion tried his best to extinguish it, but could not do it by himself. But Blessed Francis did not want to help him: he took the hide that he used to cover himself at night, and went into the forest.

The brothers of the place, although they stayed some distance from the cell, since the cell was far from the place of the brothers, seeing that the cell was burning, came and extinguished it. Afterwards, blessed Francis returned to eat. After the meal, he said to his companion: "From now on, I don't want this hide over me since, because of my avarice, I did not want Brother Fire to consume it."

[88] LP 51

[HIS LOVE FOR ALL CREATURES]

When he washed his hands, he chose a place where the water would not be trampled underfoot after the washing. Whenever he had to walk over rocks, he would walk with fear and reverence out of love for Him who is called "The Rock."

Ps 61:3 Whenever he recited the verse of the psalm, *"You have set me high upon the rock,"* he would say, out of great reverence and devotion: "You have set me high at the foot of the rock."

He also told the brother who cut the wood for the fire not to cut down the whole tree, but to cut in such a way that one part remained while another was cut. He also ordered the brother in the place where he stayed to do the same.

He used to tell the brother who took care of the garden not to cultivate all the ground in the garden for vegetables, but to leave a piece of ground that would produce wild plants that in their season would produce "Brother Flowers." Moreover, he used to tell the brother gardener that he should make a beautiful flower bed in some part of the garden, planting and cultivating every variety of fragrant plants and those producing beautiful flowers. Thus, in their time they would invite all who saw the beautiful flowers to praise God, for every creature announces and proclaims: "God made me for you, o people!"

We who were with him saw him always in such joy, inwardly and outwardly, over all creatures, touching and looking at them, so that it seemed his spirit was no longer on earth but in heaven. This is evident and true, because of the many consolations he had and continued to have in God's creatures. Thus, shortly before his death, he composed the *Praises of the Lord* by His creatures to move the hearts of his listeners to the praise of God, and that in His creatures the Lord might be praised by everyone.

[89] LP 52

[HE HELPS A POOR WOMAN FROM RIETI SUFFERING FROM AN EYE DISEASE]

At that time a poor woman from Machilone came to Rieti with an illness of her eyes. One day when the doctor came to visit blessed Francis, he said to him: "Brother, a woman with eye trouble came to see me. But she is so poor that I have to help her for the love of God and give her expenses."

When blessed Francis heard this, moved by piety for her, he called one of the companions, who was his guardian, and said to him: "Brother Guardian, we have to give back what belongs to someone else." "And, what is that, brother?" he said. "That mantle," he replied, "which we received as a loan from that poor woman with eye trouble. We must give it back to her." "Do what you think best, brother," the guardian answered.

With joy, blessed Francis called a spiritual man, who was extremely close to him, and said to him: "Take this mantle and a dozen loaves of bread with you, and go to that poor and sick woman whom the doctor, who is taking care of her, will point out to you. Say to her: 'The poor man to whom you lent this mantle thanks you for the loan of the mantle which you made with him. Take what is yours.' "

He went then and told her everything as blessed Francis had told him. Thinking he was joking, she replied with fear and embarrassment: "Leave me in peace. I don't know what you are talking about!" He placed the mantle and the dozen loaves of bread in her hands. When the woman reflected that he had spoken the truth, she accepted everything with trembling and her heart filled with joy. Then, fearful that he would take it back, she secretly got up during the night and joyfully returned to her home.

Moreover, blessed Francis also told his guardian that every day, for the love of God, he should give her food for as long as she stayed there.

We who were with blessed Francis bear witness that, sick or well, he displayed such charity and piety, not only to his brothers, but also toward the poor, whether healthy or sick. Thus, he deprived himself of the necessities of his body that the brothers procured for him with great devotion and solicitude. At first coaxing us not to worry, with great inner and outer joy, he would then offer to others things he had denied his own body, even though they were extremely necessary for him.

And that is why the general minister and his guardian ordered him not to give his tunic to any brother without their permission. Because the brothers, out of the devotion they had for him, would occasionally ask him for his tunic, and he would immediately give it to them. Or he himself, if he saw a sickly or poorly clad brother, would at times cut his habit in half, giving one part to him and keeping the other for himself, for he wanted to have and to wear only one tunic.

[90] LP 53

[He would give away the tunic he was wearing to help the poor]

Once when he was traveling through a certain region preaching, two brothers from France happened to meet him. From this they enjoyed great consolation. Finally, out of the great devotion they had toward him, for the love of God they asked for his tunic. As soon as he heard "the love of God," he immediately took off his tunic, remaining naked for almost an hour.

For it was blessed Francis's custom when someone said to him "for the love of God, give me your tunic or cord," or anything else that he had, he would immediately give it to them out of reverence for that Lord who is called Love. Furthermore he would be greatly displeased, and would reprimand the brothers when he heard them invoking the love of God needlessly. For he would say: "The love of God is so very exalted that it should be mentioned with great reverence rarely and only in dire necessity." Then one of the brothers took off his tunic and gave it to him.

Very often he endured great need and hardship when he gave away his tunic or a part of it to someone, because he could not quickly find or have another one made. This was true especially since he always wished to have and to wear a poor tunic made of bits and pieces, and occasionally he wanted it patched on inside and out. Because he rarely, if ever, wanted to have or wear a tunic made from new cloth, but would acquire one worn by a brother for a long time, and sometimes he would even accept one part of his tunic from one brother and the rest from another. But, because of his many illnesses and the cold, he would occasionally patch it on the inside with new cloth.

He held and observed this kind of poverty in his clothing until the year when he returned to the Lord. For a few days before his death, because he was suffering from dropsy, he was almost completely dehydrated and weakened by many of the other sicknesses he had, the brothers made several tunics for him, so that they could change his tunic night and day as was necessary.

[91] LP 54

[He tries to give a piece of his tunic to a poor man]

Another time a poor man with poor clothing came to a hermitage of the brothers and, for the love of God, asked for some cloth from the brothers. Blessed Francis told a brother to look around the house and, if he found some, to give it to him. And going around the whole house, that brother told him that he did not find any. So that the poor man would not go away empty-handed, blessed Francis went out secretly, so that his guardian would not forbid him. He took a knife, and sitting in a hidden place, he began to cut away a piece of his tunic, which was sewed on the inside of the tunic, wanting to give it to the poor man in secret. But immediately, since the guardian sensed what he wanted to do, he went to him and forbade him to give it away, especially since the weather was then very cold, and he was extremely sick and cold.

Blessed Francis told him: "If you do not want me to give it to him, you must make sure that some piece is given to the poor brother." And so, at the prompting of blessed Francis, the brothers gave the poor man some cloth from their own clothes.

When the brothers loaned him a mantle—or when he was traveling through the country preaching and he became sick and could no longer go on foot, he would occasionally ride a donkey, since he did not want to ride on a horse unless compelled by the greatest necessity. And such was the case shortly before his death when he became seriously ill.[a] When he was staying in some place, he did not want to accept it unless, in some way, he could give it to a poor person he might meet or who would come to him if his spirit were convinced that the person was in evident need.

LP 55

[92]

[He asks Brother Giles to give his mantle to a poor man]

At the beginning of the religion, when he was staying at Rivo Torto with only two brothers whom he had at that time, the one who was the third brother, came from the world to receive his life. When he had stayed there for a few days, still wearing his secular clothes, a poor man happened to come to the place asking alms of blessed Francis. Blessed Francis said to him who was the third brother: "Give the poor brother your mantle." Immediately, with great joy, he took it off his back and gave it to him. It then seemed to him that, at that moment, the Lord immediately had infused new grace into his heart because he had given the poor man his mantle with joy.

a. The account of the mantle loaned to Francis continues at this point.

[93] LP 56
[He has a New Testament at the Portiuncula given to the poor mother of two brothers]

Another time while he was staying at Saint Mary of the Portiuncula, a poor old woman who had two sons in religion, came to that place seeking some alms of blessed Francis because that year she did not have enough to live.

Blessed Francis said to Brother Peter of Catanio, who was the general minister at the time: "Have we anything to give our mother?" For he used to say that the mother of any brother was his own and that of all the brothers in the religion. Brother Peter told him: "We do not have anything in the house that we can give her, especially since she wants such alms as would provide for her corporal needs. In the church we only have one New Testament for reading the lessons at matins." At that time, the brothers did not have breviaries and not many psalters.

Blessed Francis responded: "Give our mother the New Testament, so she can sell it for her needs. I firmly believe that the Lord and the Blessed Virgin, His Mother, will be pleased more by giving it to her than if you read in it." And so he gave it to her.

For it can be said and written about blessed Francis, what was
Jb 31:18 said and written about Job: *Mercy grew up with me and it came out with me from my mother's womb.*

For us, who were with him, it would take a long time to write and recount not only what we learned from others about his charity and piety toward the poor, but also what we saw with our own eyes.

[94] LP 57
[A cattle disease at Sant'Elia is cured by water used to wash the stigmata]

At the same time when blessed Francis was staying in the hermitage of Saint Francis (!) at Fonte Colombo,[a] a cattle disease, commonly called *basabove,*[b] from which none usually escapes, happened

a. Manuscript 1046 of Perugia contains this identification of the hermitage of Fonte Colombo suggesting that at an early date, c. 1240, it was closely identified with Saint Francis. In ancient times the hermitage was called Monte Rainerio. The editorial comment (!) is found in the manuscript.

b. *Basabove,* also known as "falling disease," brought about the sudden death of cattle and was attributed to exercise induced heart failure. The primary cause, a dietary deficiency of copper, was not recognized until the 1930's. Cf. T.S.G.A.M. Van den Ingh and C. Lenghaus, "Myocardfibrose: een geval van falling disease," *Tijdschr Diergeneeskd* (1975) 327-329; S.W. Casteel and James R. Turk, "Collapse/Sudden Death," *Large Animal Internal Medicine,* 2nd ed., ed. Bradford P. Smith (St. Louis, London, Sydney: Mosby, 1996), 288-298.

to spread among the cattle of Sant'Elia, not too far from the hermitage. So that all the cattle became sick and died.

One night it was said that a certain spiritual person of that town had a vision in which he was told: "Go to the hermitage where blessed Francis is staying and get the water with which he washed his hands and feet. Sprinkle it upon all the oxen, and they will immediately recover."

That man got up early in the morning, went to the hermitage, and told all of this to the companions of blessed Francis.

At meal time they put the water for washing his hands in a jar, and, in the evening, they asked him to allow them to wash his feet, without telling him about the matter. And so, afterwards, they gave the man the water blessed Francis used to wash his hands and feet. The man took it and with it, as if it were holy water, sprinkled the cattle stretched out on the ground almost dead and also all the others. And immediately, through the grace of God and the merits of blessed Francis, all of them were cured. At the time blessed Francis already had scars in his hands, feet, and side.

LP 58

[95]

[THE HEALING OF A CLERIC, GEDEONE, OF RIETI AND HIS MISERABLE END]

In those days, when blessed Francis was suffering from the disease of his eyes and was spending a few days in the bishop's palace in Rieti, a cleric of the curia of Rieti named Gedeone, a very worldly man, lay sick for a long time with a very serious illness with pains in his back.[a] He could not move or turn around in bed without help and could not get up and walk without help from several people. When he was carried, he went about stooped and almost bent over because of the pain in his back, and he could no longer stand upright.

One day he had himself carried before blessed Francis. He threw himself at his feet and tearfully begged him to make the sign of the cross on him.

Blessed Francis said to him: "How can I make the sign on you, when you live according to the desires of the flesh, without reflecting on and fearing the judgments of God?"

Seeing him afflicted with so much sickness and pain, blessed Francis was moved by piety for him and told him: "I sign you in the name of the Lord. But if it pleases the Lord to cure you, beware that

a. Gedeone, a priest, administered the holdings of the cathedral in Rieti from 1213-1216. He is named as a witness in different documents of Rieti in the years 1201, 1208, 1212, 1213, 1222, and 1236. He died sometime after that last document.

you do not return to your vomit. Because, in truth, I assure you that should you return to your vomit, things worse than the first will come upon you. And you will incur a very harsh judgment because of your sins, ingratitude, and disregard of the kindness of the Lord."

After blessed Francis made the sign of the cross over him, he immediately stood up and got up, completely healed. When he stood up, you could hear the bones in his back cracking like dry wood in your hands.

A few years later he returned to the vomit and did not observe what the Lord had said to him through his servant Francis. One day it happened that . . .[a]

[96]

LP 59

[Knights from Assisi Learn How to Beg before Bringing Him Back from Nocera]

After returning from Siena and from "Le Celle" at Cortona, blessed Francis came to Saint Mary of the Portiuncula, and later went to stay at Begnara, north of Nocera, where the brothers were staying in a house that had recently been constructed for them. He stayed there for many days. And because his feet, and even his legs, began swelling up because of dropsy, he began to be seriously ill.

When the people of Assisi heard that he was sick there, they quickly sent some knights of Assisi to that place to bring him back to Assisi, fearing that he would die there and others would claim his most precious remains.

While they were bringing him back, they stopped in a small town belonging to the Commune of Assisi, wanting to have dinner there. Blessed Francis and his companions rested in the house of a man who received him with joy and charity. The knights, however, went about the town, attempting to buy things for their corporal needs, but did not find anything. And they returned to blessed Francis, saying to him as a joke: "Brother, you must give us some of your alms, because we can find nothing to buy."

Blessed Francis, with great intensity of spirit, told them: "You didn't find anything because you trust in your flies, that is, in your coins, and not in God. But go back to the houses where you went when you were looking for things to buy, and do not be ashamed,

a. Since there is a lacuna in the manuscript, the remainder of the story is taken from 2C 41: "he dined at the house of one of his fellow canons, and slept there that night. Suddenly the roof of the house collapsed on them. Others who were there escaped with their lives, and only that wretch was trapped and killed."

and ask them for alms for the love of God. The Holy Spirit will inspire them and you will find abundance."

So they went and begged alms, as the holy father told them to do. With the greatest joy, those men and women offered them generously whatever they had. Overjoyed, they came back to blessed Francis telling him what had happened to them.

They held this as a great miracle, considering that what he told them had come true to the letter.

LP 60 For blessed Francis held that to beg for alms for the love of the Lord God was of very great nobility, dignity, and courtesy before God and before the world. He held this because, everything that the heavenly Father has created for a human's use, after the sin, He has given freely, as alms, both to the worthy and the unworthy on account of the love of His beloved Son.

Therefore blessed Francis would say that a servant of God must beg alms for the love of God with greater freedom and joy than someone, who, out of courtesy and generosity, wants to buy something, and goes around saying: "Whoever will give me a penny, I will give him a hundred silver pieces, nay, a thousand times more." Because a servant of God offers the love of God which a person merits when he gives alms; in comparison to which, all things in this world and even those in heaven are nothing.

Therefore, before the brothers became numerous—and even after they grew in number—when blessed Francis went through the world preaching, and some noble and wealthy person invited him to eat and lodge with him, since as yet there were no places of residence of the brothers in many cities and towns, he would always go begging for alms at mealtime. He did this, even though he knew that his host had abundantly prepared everything he needed for the love of God, to give a good example to the brothers and because of the nobility and dignity of Lady Poverty. Sometimes he would say to his host: "I do not want to renounce my royal dignity, my heritage, my vocation, and my profession and that of my brothers, that is, to go begging alms. Even if I were to bring no more than three alms, I always want to exercise my responsibility."

And so he used to go begging alms,[a] and, the one who invited him would unwillingly sometimes go with him. The alms that Francis acquired, he would accept and place them as relics out of his devotion.

He who writes has seen this many times, and bears witness to it.

a. The Latin reads: *et sic nolente, ibat pro helemosinis* [literally: And thus with one unwilling, he went for alms]. A variant in one manuscript adds *nolente ipso* [that man unwilling], presumably the host. In light of this the editors have taken the liberty of placing *nolente* in the following sentence, as an adverb accompanying the host's action.

[97] LP 61
[He goes for alms before dinner while a guest of the Bishop of Ostia; the story of Brother Fly]

Moreover, one time, when he was visiting the Lord Bishop of Ostia, who later was pope, he went out for alms at mealtime, secretly as it were, because of the Lord Bishop. And when he returned, the Lord Bishop was sitting at table and eating, particularly since he had invited to dinner some knights who were his relatives. Blessed Francis put his alms on the bishop's table and came to the table next to the bishop, because the Lord Bishop always wanted blessed Francis, whenever he was with him, to sit next to him at mealtime. The Lord Bishop was somewhat embarrassed that blessed Francis went begging alms, but said nothing to him particularly because of those at table.

After blessed Francis had eaten a little, he took some of his alms and sent a little on behalf of the Lord God to each one of the knights and chaplains of the Lord Bishop. They all accepted them with great devotion. Some ate them, others kept them out of devotion for him. Moreover, because of devotion for Saint Francis, they even took off their emblems when they accepted the alms. From then on, the Lord Bishop was greatly amazed at their devotion, especially since those alms did not consist of wheat bread.

After the meal, the Lord Bishop got up and went to his room, taking blessed Francis with him. Lifting up his arms, he embraced blessed Francis with utmost joy and told him: "Why, my simple little brother,[a] did you shame me in my own house, which is also the home of your brothers, by going out as you did for alms?"

"On the contrary, Lord Bishop," blessed Francis answered, "I paid you a great honor. Because when a subject exercises and fulfills his duty and the obedience of his lord, he does honor both to the lord and to his prelate."

Then he said to him: "I must be a model and example of your poor. Especially because I know that in the life and religion of the brothers there are and will be Lesser Brothers, in name and in deed, humble in all things, obedient, and of service to their brothers. They are and will be such because of the love of the Lord God and by the anointing of the Holy Spirit, who teaches and will teach them in all things. There also are and will be those among them who, held back by shame and because of bad habit, are and will be scorned by humbling them-

a. The Latin reads: *frater mi simpliçone* [my simple little brother], which is difficult to translate with the warmth and affection contained in *simpliçone*.

selves, by demeaning themselves by begging alms, and by doing this kind of servile work. Therefore, I must teach by deed those who are or who will be in religion, that they might be without excuse in the eyes of God in this age and in the future.

"While I am with you, who are our Lord and Pope, and with other great and wealthy people in the eyes of the world, who for the love of the Lord God and with great kindness, not only receive me into their houses, but even compel me to do so, I do not want to be ashamed to go for alms. Indeed I want to have and hold it as a sign of great nobility, as the highest dignity and an honor to that most exalted King, who though He was Lord of all, willed for our sake to become the servant of all and, although he was rich and glorious in majesty, came as one poor and despised in our humanity. So I want all who are and will be brothers to know that I hold it a greater consolation for both soul and body when I sit at a poor little table of the brothers and see before me the meager alms they begged from door to door for the love of the Lord God, than when I sit at your table and that of other lords, set abundantly with all kinds of food, even though they are offered to me with great devotion. For the bread offered as alms is holy bread which the praise and love of God have hallowed, because when a brother goes out begging, he must first say: 'Praised and blessed be the Lord God!' Afterwards he must say: 'Give us alms for the love of the Lord God.' "

The Lord Bishop was greatly edified by the holy father's words of instruction.[a] He said to him: "My son, do what seems good in your eyes, for the Lord is with you and you with Him."

LP 62 For the will of blessed Francis, as he often said, was that no brother should procrastinate in going for alms, so that he not be ashamed to go later on. Indeed, the greater and nobler a brother had been in the world, so much the more pleased and happy was he when he went for alms and did servile work of this sort because of good example. Thus it was in the early days.

At the religion's beginning, when the brothers were staying at Rivo Torto, there was a brother among them who prayed little, did not work, and did not want to go for alms because he was ashamed; but he would eat heartily. Giving the matter some thought, blessed Francis knew through the Holy Spirit that the man was carnal. He therefore told him: "Go on your way, Brother Fly, because you want to feed on the labor of your brothers, but wish to be idle in the work of

a. The Latin reads: *in collatione verborum suorum*, which could also be rendered as "a conference," like the "collation" given by an abbot before the light meal, also called the "collation," taken in the morning.

God, like Brother Drone that does not want to gather or work, yet eats the work and gain of the good bees."

So he went his way. And because he lived according to the flesh, he did not ask for mercy.

[98] LP 63

[HE GOES TO MEET A BROTHER RETURNING FROM BEGGING AND KISSES HIS SHOULDER]

Another time a holy brother was coming back from Assisi with a bag of alms one day, while blessed Francis was at Saint Mary of the Portiuncula. When he came to the road near the church, he began to praise God in a loud voice with great joy.

Hearing him, blessed Francis immediately went out and met him on the road. He ran up to him and, with great joy, kissed the shoulder on which he was carrying the bag with the alms. Taking the bag from his shoulder, he put it on his own shoulder and carried it to the home of the brothers. He said to the brothers: "This is how I want a brother of mine to go for alms and to return happy and joyful."

[99] LP 64

[HE AWAITS DEATH AT THE BISHOP'S PALACE IN ASSISI; HIS COMPANIONS SING THE CANTICLE FOR HIM]

When blessed Francis lay gravely ill in the palace of the bishop of Assisi, in the days after he returned from Bagnara, the people of Assisi, fearing that the saint would die during the night without them knowing about it, and that the brothers would secretly take his body away and place it in another city, placed a vigilant guard each night around the palace's walls.

Blessed Francis, although he was gravely ill, to comfort his soul and ward off discouragement in his severe and serious infirmities, often asked his companions during the day to sing the *Praises of the Lord* which he had composed a long time before in his illness. He likewise had the *Praises* sung during the night for the edification of their guards, who kept watch at night outside the palace because of him.

When Brother Elias reflected that blessed Francis was so comforting himself and rejoicing in the Lord in such illness, one day he said to him: "Dearest brother, I am greatly consoled and edified by all the joy which you show for yourself and your companions in such affliction and infirmity. Although the people of this city venerate you as a saint in life and in death, nevertheless, because they firmly believe that you are near death due to your serious and incurable sickness, upon hearing praises of this sort being sung, they can think and say to themselves: 'How can he show such joy when he is so near death? He should be thinking about death.'

"Do you remember," blessed Francis said to him, "when you saw the vision at Foligno and told me that it told you that I would live for only two years? Before you saw that vision, through the grace of the Holy Spirit, who suggests every good in the heart, and places it on the lips of his faithful, I often considered day and night my end. But from the time you saw that vision, each day I have been even more zealous reflecting on the day of my death."

He continued with great intensity of spirit: "Allow me to rejoice in the Lord, Brother, and to sing His praises in my infirmities, because, by the grace of the Holy Spirit, I am so closely united and joined with my Lord, that, through His mercy, I can well rejoice in the Most High Himself."

LP 65

[100]
[A DOCTOR NAMED JOHN TELLS HIM HE WILL DIE SOON: "WELCOME, MY SISTER DEATH!"]

Another time during those days, a doctor from the city of Arezzo, named Good John, who was known and familiar to blessed Francis, came to visit him in the bishop's palace. Blessed Francis asked about his sickness saying: "How does my illness of dropsy seem to you, Brother John?"

For blessed Francis did not want to address anyone called "Good"
by their name, out of reverence for the Lord, who said: *No one is good* Lk 18:19
but God alone. Likewise, he did not want to call anyone "father" or
"master," nor write them in letters, out of reverence for the Lord,
who said: *Call no one on earth your father nor be called masters,* etc. Mt 23:9-10

The doctor said to him: "Brother, by the grace of the Lord, it will be well with you." For he did not want to tell him that he would die in a little while.

Again blessed Francis said to him: "Tell me the truth. How does it look to you? Do not be afraid, for, by the grace of God, I am not a coward who fears death. With the Lord's help, by His mercy and grace, I am so united and joined with my Lord that I am equally as happy to die as I am to live."

The doctor then told him frankly: "According to our assessment, your illness is incurable and you will die either at the end of September or on the fourth day before the Nones of October."[a] Blessed Francis, while he was lying on his bed sick, with the greatest devotion and reverence for the Lord stretched out his arms and hands with great joy of mind and body and said to his body and soul: "Welcome, my Sister Death!"

[101][b] LP 66

[HE TELLS BROTHER RICCERIO HIS LAST WISHES; THE MEANING OF "LESSER BROTHERS."]

Brother Riccerio of the Marches of Ancona, noble by birth and more noble by holiness, was loved by blessed Francis with great affection. One day he came to visit blessed Francis in that palace. Among other points he discussed with blessed Francis about the state of the religion and observance of the *Rule*, he asked him: "Tell me, Father, when you first began to have brothers, what was your intention? And what is it today, and what do you believe it will be until the day of your death? Because I want to be sure of your intention and of your first and last wish, so that we, cleric brothers who have many books, may keep them although we will say that they belong to the religion?"

Blessed Francis told him: "I tell you, brother, that it has been and is my first and last intention and will, if the brothers would only heed it, that no brother should have anything except a tunic as the *Rule* allows us, together with a cord and underwear."

Another time, blessed Francis said: "The religion and life of the Lesser Brothers is a little flock, which the Son of God in this very last hour has asked of His heavenly Father, saying: 'Father, I want you to make and give me a new and humble people in this very last hour, who would be unlike all others who preceded them by their humility and poverty, and be content to have me alone.' And the Father said to His beloved Son: 'My Son, Your request has been fulfilled.'"

This is why blessed Francis would say: "Therefore, the Lord has LP 67
willed that they be called Lesser Brothers, because they are the people whom the Son of God asked of the Father. They are the ones of

a. For an understanding of the "fourth day before the Nones of October," see FA:ED I 258 c.

b. The following five paragraphs (AC 101-106) contain a collection of stories entitled the *Intentio Regulae* [Intention of the *Rule*] that are focused on Francis's attitude toward poverty, especially in books and buildings. In 1305 Ubertino da Casale quoted these paragraphs in his *Arbor Vitae Crucifixae Jesu* and attributed them to Leo, cf. Ubertino da Casale, *Arbor Vitae Crucifixae Jesu* V. 5 (Venice: 1485).

whom the Son of God speaks in the Gospel: *Do not be afraid, little flock,* Lk 12:32
for it has pleased your Father to give you the kingdom; and again: *What you* Mt 25:40
did for one of these, the least of my brothers, you did it for me. For, although the Lord may be understood to be speaking of all the spiritually poor, he was nevertheless predicting the religion of the Lesser Brothers that was to come in His Church."

Therefore, as it was revealed to blessed Francis that it the was to be called the Religion of the Lesser Brothers, he had it so written in the first *Rule*, when he brought it before the Lord Pope Innocent III, and he approved and granted it, and later announced it to all in the Council.[a] Likewise, the Lord also revealed to him the greeting that
Test 23 the brothers should use, as he had written in his *Testament:* "The Lord revealed a greeting to me that we should say 'May the Lord give you peace.' "

At the beginning of the religion, when blessed Francis would go with a brother who was one of the first twelve brothers, that brother would greet men and women along the way as well as those in their field, saying: "May the Lord give you peace."

And because people had never before heard such a greeting from any religious, they were greatly amazed. Indeed, some would say almost indignantly: "What does this greeting of yours mean?" As a result that brother began to be quite embarrassed. Then he said to blessed Francis "Let me use another greeting."

Blessed Francis told him: "Let them talk, for they do not grasp what is of God. But do not be embarrassed, for one day the nobles and princes of this world will show respect to you and the other brothers because of a greeting of this sort." And blessed Francis said: "Isn't it great that the Lord wanted to have a little people among all those who preceded them who would be content to have Him alone, the Most High and most glorious?"

LP 68 If any brother wanted to ask why blessed Francis in his own time did not make the brothers observe such a strict poverty as he told Brother Riccerio, and did not order it to be observed, we who were with him would respond to this as we heard from his mouth. Because he told the brothers this and many other things, and also had written down in the *Rule* what he requested from the Lord with relentless prayer and meditation for the good of the religion, affirming that it was completely the Lord's will.

Afterwards when he showed them, they seemed *harsh and unbear-* Mt 23:4
able, for they did not know what was going to happen to the religion after his death. And because he feared scandal for himself and for the

a. Regarding consistory/Council, cf. supra, 98 a.

brothers, he did not want to argue with them; but he complied with their wish, although not willingly, and excused himself before the Lord. But, that the word of the Lord, which He put in his mouth for the good of the brothers, would not return to Him empty, he wanted to fulfill it in himself, so that he might then obtain a reward from the Lord. And at last he found peace in this and his spirit was comforted.

[102] LP 69

[A MINISTER ASKS ABOUT BOOKS; THE MINISTERS REMOVE THE CHAPTER IN THE RULE ABOUT POVERTY]

At the time when he returned from overseas, a minister spoke with him about the chapter on poverty. He wanted to know his will and understanding, especially since at the time a chapter had been
Lk 9:1-6 written in the *Rule* from prohibitions of the holy Gospel: *Take nothing with you on the journey,* etc.

And blessed Francis answered: "I want to understand it in this way, that the brothers should have nothing except a tunic with a cord and underwear, as contained in the *Rule,* and those compelled by necessity, may have shoes." And the minister said to him: "What shall I do, for I have so many books worth more than fifty pounds?"

He said this because he wanted to hold on to them with a clear conscience, most especially because he had a qualm of conscience about keeping so many books when he knew blessed Francis strictly interpreted the chapter on poverty.

"Brother," blessed Francis said to him, "I cannot and must not go against my own conscience and the perfection of the holy Gospel which we have professed." Hearing this, the minister became sad. Seeing how disturbed he was, blessed Francis said to him with intensity of spirit, intending this for all the brothers: "You, Lesser Brothers, want to be seen as and called observers of the holy Gospel, but in your deeds you want to have money bags."

Although the ministers knew that, according to the *Rule* of the brothers they were bound to observe the holy Gospel, they nevertheless had that chapter of the *Rule* where it says "Take nothing for your journey, etc." removed, believing, despite it, that they were not obliged to observance of the perfection of the holy Gospel.

Knowing this through the light of the Holy Spirit, blessed Francis said in the presence of some brothers: "The brother ministers think they can deceive God and me." Then he said: "Indeed, that all the brothers may know that they are bound to observe the perfection of the holy Gospel, I want it written at the beginning and at the end of the *Rule* that the brothers are bound to observe the holy Gospel of our Lord Jesus Christ. And that the brothers may always be without an excuse before God, I want to show with these deeds and always observe, with God's help, what God has placed in my mouth for the welfare and usefulness of my soul and those of my brothers."

Therefore, he observed the holy Gospel to the letter from the day he began to have brothers until the day of his death.

LP 70

[103]

[THE NOVICE WHO WANTED TO HAVE A PSALTER; A DESCRIPTION OF HIS HOLY BROTHERS]

Likewise, there was once a brother novice who could read the psalter, but not very well. And because he enjoyed reading, he sought permission from the general minister to have a psalter and the minister granted it to him. But he did not wish to have it unless he first had permission from blessed Francis, especially since he had heard that blessed Francis did not want his brothers to be desirous of learning and books, but wanted and preached to the brothers to be eager to have and imitate pure and holy simplicity, holy prayer, and Lady Poverty, on which the holy and first brothers had built. And he believed this to be the more secure path for the soul's well-being.

Not that he despised or disdained holy knowledge. On the contrary, he revered with great feeling those who were knowledgeable in religion, and all knowledgeable persons, as he himself says in his
Test 13 *Testament:* "We must honor all theologians and those who minister the divine words and respect them as those who minister to us spirit and life."

But, foreseeing the future, he knew through the Holy Spirit and even repeated it many times to the brothers, that many brothers, under the pretext of edifying others, would abandon their vocation, that is, pure and holy simplicity, prayer, and our Lady Poverty. And it will happen that, because they will afterwards believe themselves to be more imbued with devotion and enflamed with the love of God because of an understanding of the Scriptures, they will occasionally remain inwardly cold and almost empty. And so, they will be unable to return to their first vocation, especially since they have wasted the time for living according to their calling; and I fear that even what they seem to possess will be taken away from them, because they have lost their vocation.

LP 71 "There are many," he used to say, "who, day and night, place all their energy and care in knowledge, losing their holy vocation and devout prayer. And when they have preached to others or to the people,[a] and see or learn that some have been edified or converted to penance, they become puffed up or congratulate themselves for someone else's gain. For those whom they think they have edified or converted to penance by their words, the Lord edified and converted by the prayers of holy brothers, although they are ignorant of it. This is the will of God so that they do not take notice of it and become proud.

"These brothers of mine are my knights of the round table,[b] the brothers who hide in deserted and remote places, to devote themselves more diligently to prayer and meditation, weeping over their sins and those of others, whose holiness is known to God, and is sometimes ignored by the brothers and people. And when their souls will be presented to the Lord by the angels, the Lord will then reveal to them the fruit and reward of their labors, that is, the many souls saved by their prayers, saying to them: 'My sons, behold these souls

Mt 25:21 have been saved by your prayer, and *since you were faithful in little things, I will set you over many.*' "

Because of this, blessed Francis used to say about this passage:

1 Sm 2:5 *The barren one has given birth to many children and the mother of many languishes:* the barren one is the good religious who edifies himself and others by his holy prayers and virtues.

He often said these words in a talk in the presence of the brothers, especially during a chapter of the brothers at Saint Mary of the Portiuncula in the presence of the ministers and the other brothers. He therefore instructed the brothers, the ministers as well as preachers, about work, telling them, because of the office of ministry or of their zeal for preaching, that they should not abandon holy and devout prayer, go for alms, and work with hands like the other brothers, for good example and for the benefit of their souls as well as others.

He said: "The brothers who are subjects will be very edified when their ministers and preachers devote themselves freely to prayer, bow down, and humble themselves."

Therefore that faithful disciple of Christ, while he was in good health, practiced what he taught the brothers.

a. The Latin, *Et cum aliquibus vel populo praedicaverint* [when they have preached to others and to the people], is cryptic. It probably refers to preaching to one another, that is, to the brothers themselves, and, in another instance, to the people.

b. A reference to the celebrated table of King Arthur around which he and his knights sat. According to the story, Arthur had the table made round so that none of his knights could claim precedence over the other.

LP 72 When that brother novice described above was staying in a certain hermitage, blessed Francis one day happened to come there. That brother said to him: "Father, it would be a great consolation for me to have a psalter. But, although the general minister has given me permission to have it, I still want to have it with your knowledge."

Blessed Francis gave him this sort of response: "The Emperor Charles, Roland, and Oliver, and all the paladins and valiant knights who were mighty in battle, pursuing unbelievers with great toil and fatigue even to death, had a glorious and memorable victory for themselves, and, finally, died in battle fighting as holy martyrs for the faith in Christ. And there are many who want to receive honor and praise by only relating what they did."

And because of this he wrote the meaning of these words in his
Adm VI 3 *Admonitions,* saying: "The saints have done these deeds, and we want to receive honor and glory by recounting and preaching about them," as if to say: "Knowledge puffs up, but charity builds." 1Cor 8:1

LP 73

[104]

[The same novice asks again: "A breviary, a breviary!"]

Another time, when blessed Francis was sitting near a fire, warming himself, the same one spoke to him again about a psalter. And blessed Francis told him: "After you have a psalter, you will desire and want to have a breviary; after you have a breviary, you will sit in a fancy chair, like a great prelate telling your brother: 'Bring me the breviary.'" And speaking in this way with great intensity of spirit, he took some ashes in his hand, put them on his head rubbing them around his head as though he were washing it, saying: "I, a breviary! I, a breviary!" He spoke this way many times, passing his hand over his head. The brother was stunned and ashamed.

Afterwards blessed Francis said to him: "Brother, I was likewise tempted to have books. But, in order to know God's will about this, I took the book, where the Lord's Gospels are written, and prayed to the Lord to deign to show it to me at the first opening of the book. After my prayer was ended, on the first opening of the holy Gospel this verse of the holy Gospel came to me: *To you it is given to know the mystery* Mk 4:11
of the kingdom of God, but to the others all things are treated in parables."

And he said: "There are many who willingly climb to the heights of knowledge; that person be blessed who renounces it for the love of God."

[105] LP 74

[THE SAME NOVICE ASKS HIM AGAIN ABOUT A PSALTER, AND HE IS UPSET]

Many months later, when blessed Francis was at the church of Saint Mary of the Portiuncula, at a cell behind the house on the road, that brother spoke to him again about the psalter. And blessed Francis said: "Go and do as your minister tells you." When he heard this, that brother began to go back by the same road he had come.

Blessed Francis remained on the road, and began to think over what he said to that brother. Suddenly he yelled after him: "Wait for me, brother, wait!" He went up to him and said: "Come back with me and show me the place where I told you to do with the psalter what your minister tells you." When they returned to the spot where he had said this, blessed Francis bent over in front of the brother and, kneeling, said to him: "*Mea culpa,* brother, *mea culpa.* Whoever wishes to be a Lesser Brother must have nothing but the tunics, a cord, and short trousers the *Rule* allows him; and for those forced by necessity or illness, shoes."

Whenever brothers came to him to ask advice about such things, he would give them the same answer. For this reason he used to say: "A person is only as learned as his actions show; and a religious is only as good a preacher as his actions show;" as if to say, "A good tree is known only by its fruit."

[106] LP 75

[HE REPLIES TO A BROTHER WHO ASKED HIM WHY HE DID NOT CORRECT ABUSES IN THE ORDER; AND THE PORTIUNCULA AS AN EXAMPLE]

One day while blessed Francis was staying in that palace, one of his companions there said to him: "Father, excuse me, because what I want to say to you, many have already thought. You know," he said "how formerly through the grace of God, the whole religion flourished in the purity of perfection, that is, how all the brothers fervently and zealously observed holy poverty in all things, in small and poor dwellings, in small and poor furnishings, in small and poor books, and in poor clothing. And as in these things, as well as in other exterior things, they were of one will, concerned about observing everything that had to do with our profession and calling and good example. In this way they were of one mind in the love of God and neighbor.

"But now for a little while, this purity and perfection have begun to change into something different, though the brothers make lots of excuses saying that, because of large number, this cannot be observed by the brothers. In fact, many brothers believe that the people are more edified by these ways than by those mentioned, and, it seems to them, more fitting to live and behave according to these ways. Therefore, they consider worthless the way of simplicity and poverty, which were the beginning and foundation of our religion. Thinking this over, we believe that they displease you, but we really wonder why, if they displease you, you tolerate them and do not correct them."

LP 76 "May the Lord forgive you," blessed Francis said to him, "for wanting to be against me and opposed to me and involve me in these things that do not pertain to my office." And he said: "As long as I held office for the brothers, and they remained faithful to their calling and profession, and, although I was ill from the beginning of my conversion to Christ, with a little of my care, I satisfied them by my example and preaching. But afterwards I realized that the Lord multiplied the number of the brothers daily and that through tepidity and lack of spirit they began to turn away from the straight and sure way on which they used to walk and take, as you said, a broad way, without paying attention to their profession and calling and good example, or would not give up the journey that had already begun despite my preaching and my example. I entrusted the religion to the Lord and to the ministers. When I renounced and gave up among the brothers, I excused myself before the brothers at the general chapter saying that, because of my illness I could not take care of them and care for them. And yet, if the brothers had walked and were still walking according to my will, for their consolation I would not want them to have any other minister except me until the day of my death. As long as a faithful and good subject knows and observes the will of his prelate, then the prelate has to have little concern about him. Rather, I would be so happy at the goodness of the brothers and be so consoled, both on their account and my own, that even if I were lying sick in bed, it would not be considered a burden to me to satisfy them."

He said: "My office, that is, a prelacy over the brothers, is spiritual, because I must overcome vices and correct them. Therefore, if I cannot overcome and correct them by preaching and example, I do not want to become an executioner who beats and scourges, like a power of this world. I trust in the Lord; invisible enemies, the Lord's police, who punish in this world and in the next those who transgress the commandments of God, will take revenge on them, having corrected men of this world, and thus they will return to their profession and calling.

"Nevertheless, until the day of my death, I will not cease teaching the brothers by example and action to walk by the path which the Lord showed me, and which I showed and explained to them. Thus, they will have no excuse before the Lord, and I will not be bound to render any further account about them or about myself before the Lord."

Thus he had it written in his *Testament* that all houses of the broth- LP 77
ers should be built of mud and wood, as a sign of holy poverty and humility, and the churches constructed for the brothers must be small. In fact, he wanted reform on this matter, that is, houses constructed of wood and mud, and in every other good example to begin in the place of Saint Mary of the Portiuncula. This was the first place where, after they settled there, the Lord began to multiply the brothers, and it should be an external reminder to the other brothers who are in religion and those who will come to it.[a]

But some told him it did not seem good to them that the houses of the brothers had to be constructed of mud and wood because in many places and provinces wood is more expensive than stone. But blessed Francis did not wish to argue with them because he was very sick and close to death, and, he lived only a short time afterwards.

This is the reason he wrote in his *Testament:* "Let the brothers be Test 24
careful not to receive in any way churches or dwellings or any other things built for them, unless they are according to the poverty we have promised in the *Rule,* as pilgrims and strangers let them always be guests there."

We who were with him when he wrote the *Rule* and almost all his other writings bear witness that he had many things written in the *Rule* and in his other writings, to which certain brothers, especially prelates, were opposed. So it happened that on points where the brothers were opposed to blessed Francis during his life, now, after his death, they would be very useful to the whole religion. Because he greatly feared scandal, he gave in, although unwillingly, to the wishes of the brothers. But he often repeated this saying: "Woe to those brothers who are opposed to what I know to be the will of God for the greatest good of the religion, even if I unwillingly give in to their wishes."

He often said to his companions: "Here lies my pain and grief: those things which I received from God by His mercy with great effort of prayer and meditation for the present and future good of the religion, and which are, as He assures me, in accordance with His

a. For a discussion of this passage, cf. Raoul Manselli, "From the Testament to the Testaments of St. Francis," GR 2 (1988): 91-99.

will, some of the brothers on the authority and support of their knowledge nullify and oppose me saying: 'These things must be kept and observed; but not those!' "

But, as was said, because he feared scandal so much that he permitted many things to happen and gave in to their will in many things that were not according to his will.

LP 78

[107]
[He corrects idle words among the brothers at the Portiuncula]

When our most holy father Francis was staying at the church of Saint Mary of the Portiuncula, it was his daily custom after the meal to work at some task with his brothers to avoid the vice of idleness. Thinking of himself and his brothers, lest they lose, because of useless and idle words after prayer, the good they earned with the help of the Lord during the time of prayer, he ordered the brothers to observe avoid falling into useless and idle words. And he established the following: If any brother, while walking or working at something, utters any useless or idle word, he must say one *Our Father* with the *Praises of God* at the beginning and end of this prayer, with this condition: if perhaps he is the first to notice it and accuses himself of what he did, let him say the *Our Father* for his own soul together with *The Praises of God* as was said. But if another brother corrected him first, he is bound to say the *Our Father* in the way mentioned for the soul of the brother who corrected him. If after being corrected, he offers an excuse, refusing to say the *Our Father,* he is bound to say two *Our Father's,* as above, for the soul of the brother who corrected him, whose testimony, or perhaps that of another brother, will prove that it is true that he said that useless or idle word.

He shall say the *Praises of God,* as mentioned, at the beginning and end of that prayer loud enough and clear enough for the brothers staying there to understand and hear, and while he is saying them, the brothers must be quiet and listen. If one of them keeps silent about this, he shall be bound to say one *Our Father* in the same way with the *Praises of God* for the soul of the brother who spoke.

When any brother enters a cell, a house, or any place and finds a brother or brothers there or anywhere, he should always earnestly praise and bless God. It was the custom of the most holy father always to say those *Praises,* and it was his fervent wish and desire that the other brothers be similarly careful and devout in saying them.

[108] LP 79

[He sends the brothers on mission from the Portiuncula; how he decides to go to France; his devotion to the Body of Christ; Brother Sylvester casts out demons at Arezzo; Cardinal Hugolino sends him back from Florence]

At the time of the general chapter celebrated in that same place, in which the brothers were sent for the first time to regions overseas, when the chapter had ended, blessed Francis staying in that same place with a few brothers, said to them: "Dearest brothers, I must be a model and example to all the brothers. If therefore I send my brothers into far distant countries where they will endure toil, shame, hunger, and many other types of need, it seems to me to be just and good that I also go to some far distant region, especially so that the brothers may be able to bear their needs and trials more patiently when they hear that I am also undergoing the same thing."

And he said to them: "Therefore go and ask the Lord that He may allow me to choose that region which will give more praise to the Lord and for the profit and salvation of souls and good example to our religion."

It was the custom of our most holy father to pray to the Lord, and to send his brothers to pray, not only when he was going to a far away region to preach, but also when he went to nearby regions, so that the Lord might direct his heart to go wherever it seemed best to God.

The brothers, therefore, went off to pray and when their prayer was finished they returned to him. He said to them: "In the name of our Lord Jesus Christ, of his glorious Virgin Mother and of all the saints, I choose the region of France, in which there is a Catholic people, especially because of the other Catholics of the holy Church. They show great reverence to the Body of Christ, which pleases me very much. Because of this, I will gladly live among them."

Now blessed Francis had such reverence and devotion to the Body LP 80
of Christ, that he wanted it written in the *Rule* that the brothers in the regions where they stay should take care and be concerned about this, and should admonish and preach about this to clerics and priests, so that they place the Body of Christ in a good and fitting place ; and, if they did not do so, he wanted the brothers to do so.

In fact one time he wanted to send some brothers through every region with pyxes and wherever they found the Body of Christ placed illicitly, they were to place It honorably in them. Out of reverence for the most holy Body and Blood of the Lord Jesus Christ, he wanted it LtOrd 35-37
placed in the *Rule* that, wherever the brothers find the written words and name of the Lord by which the most holy sacrament is confected,

not well kept, or carelessly thrown around in some place, let them gather them up, honoring in the words the Lord *Who spoke them.* 1 Kgs 2:4 Many things are made holy *by the words of God,* and the sacrament of 1 Tm 4:5 the altar is celebrated in the power of the words of Christ.

Although he did not write this in the *Rule,* particularly because it did not seem good to the brother ministers that the brothers should take this as a command, nevertheless, the holy father wanted to leave the brothers in his *Testament* and in his other writings his will about these things.

He also wanted to send other brothers throughout every region with good and beautiful wafer irons for making hosts.

When blessed Francis had chosen from those brothers the ones he wished to take with him, he said to them: "Go, in the name of the Lord, two by two along the way, decently, in the greatest silence from dawn until after terce, praying to the Lord *in your hearts.* And let no Col 3:16 idle or useless words *be mentioned among you.* Although you are travel- Eph 5:3 ing, nevertheless, let your behavior be as decent as if you were staying in a hermitage or a cell because wherever we are or wherever we travel, we have a cell with us. Brother Body is our cell, and the soul is the hermit who remains inside the cell to pray to God and meditate. So if the soul does not remain in quiet and solitude in its cell, a cell made by hands does little good to a religious."

LP 81 When they arrived at Arezzo, there was a great scandal and war night and day throughout almost the entire city, because of two factions who had hated each other for a long time. Blessed Francis heard all the noise and cries night and day; since he received hospitality in a hospice in a neighborhood outside the city, it seemed to him that the demons were overjoyed by this and were inciting the people to destroy their city with fire and other dangerous means.

Moved by piety over that city, he said to Brother Sylvester, the priest, a man of God, of great faith and admirable simplicity and purity, whom the holy Father venerated as a saint: "Go in front of the city gate and in a loud voice command all the devils that they all leave this city." Brother Sylvester got up, went in front of the city gate crying out in a loud voice: "Praised and blessed be the Lord Jesus Christ. On behalf of Almighty God and in virtue of holy obedience of our most holy father Francis, I command all the devils that they all leave this city!"

Through the mercy of God and the prayer of blessed Francis, it so happened that, without any preaching, shortly afterwards, they returned to peace and unity. Since blessed Francis was not able to preach to them at that time, when he once preached to them later, he said to them in the first words of his sermon: "I speak to you as to those in demons' chains. You bound and sold yourselves like animals in the market because of your wretched state. You betrayed yourselves into the hands of the demons when you placed yourselves at the will of those who have destroyed and continue to destroy themselves, and want to destroy you and the whole city. But you are wretched and ignorant people and ungrateful for the favor of God who, although unknown to many of you, at one time freed this city through the merits of a most holy brother, Sylvester."

When blessed Francis reached Florence, he found there Lord LP 82
Hugolino, the bishop of Ostia, who later became pope. He had been sent by Pope Honorius as a legate for the Duchy of Tuscany, and Lombardy, and the Marches of Treviso as far as Venice. The Lord Bishop greatly rejoiced at his arrival, but when he heard from blessed Francis that he wanted to go to France, he prohibited him from going, telling him: "Brother, I do not want you to go beyond the mountains, because there are many prelates and others who would willingly block the religion's interests in the Roman Curia. The other cardinals and I, who love your religion, can protect and help it more willingly if you stay within the confines of this region."

But blessed Francis said to him: "Lord, it is a great shame to me, if I remain in these regions when I send my brothers to remote and far away regions." The Lord Bishop, however, said to him as if rebuking him: "Why did you send your brothers so far away to die of hunger
Rv 19:10 and to so many other trials?" In great fervor of spirit and in *the spirit of prophecy,* blessed Francis answered him: "Lord, do you think or believe that the Lord sent the brothers only for these regions? But I tell you in truth that the Lord chose and sent the brothers for the benefit and salvation of the souls of all people in the whole world and they should be received not only in the land of believers, but also in that of non-believers. As long as they observe what they promised the Lord, the Lord will minister to them in the land of non-believers as well as in the countries of believers."

The Lord Bishop marveled at his words and admitted that he spoke the truth. But the Lord Bishop did not allow him to go to France. Instead blessed Francis sent Brother Pacifico there with other brothers, and he returned to the valley of Spoleto.

LP 83

[109]

[BEFORE A CHAPTER AT THE PORTIUNCULA HE TALKS ABOUT BEING A TRUE LESSER BROTHER WHEN INSULTED]

Once when the time for the chapter of the brothers was approaching, to be held at the church of Saint Mary of the Portiuncula, blessed Francis said to his companion: "It seems to me that I am not a Lesser Brother unless I have the attitude I will tell you." And he said: "The brothers come to me with great devotion and veneration, invite me to the chapter, and, touched by their devotion, I go to the chapter with them. After they assemble, they ask me to proclaim the word of God among them and I rise and preach to them as the Holy Spirit instructs me.

"After the sermon, suppose that they reflect and speak against me: *'We do not want* you *to rule over us*. You are not eloquent and you are Lk 19:14
too simple. We are very ashamed to have such a simple and contemptible prelate over us. From now on, do not presume to call yourself our prelate.' And so, with insults, they throw me out.

"It seems to me that I am not a Lesser Brother unless I am just as happy when they insult me and throw me out in shame, refusing that I be their prelate, as when they honor and revere me, if in both cases the benefit to them is equal. If I am happy about their benefit and devotion when they praise and honor me, which can be a danger to the soul, it is even more fitting that I should rejoice and be happy at my benefit and the salvation of my soul when they revile me as they throw me out in shame, which is profit for the soul."

LP 84

[110]

[HE IS CONSOLED AT THE PORTIUNCULA BY SISTER CRICKET]

One time during summer blessed Francis was at that same place, and he stayed in the last cell next to the hedge of the garden behind the house, where, after his death, Brother Raineri, the gardener, stayed. It happened that one day, as he came down from that little cell, there was a cricket within on the branch of the fig tree next to that cell, and he could touch it. Stretching out his hand, he said: "Sister Cricket, come to me." The cricket immediately climbed onto the fingers of his hand, and with a finger of his other hand, he began to touch it, saying: "Sing, my Sister Cricket." It obeyed him at once and began to chirp. This consoled blessed Francis greatly and he praised God. He held it in his hand that way for more than an hour. Afterwards he put it back on the branch of the fig tree from which he had taken it.

And in the same way, for eight days constantly, when he came down from the cell, he found it in the same place. And daily he would take it in his hand, and as soon as he told it to sing, touching it, it sang. After eight days, he said to his companions: "Let us give permission to our sister cricket to go where she wants. She has consoled us enough; and the flesh might vainglory from this." As soon as it had received permission, the cricket went away and never appeared there again. His companions admired how obedient and tame she was to him.

Blessed Francis found so much joy in creatures because of love of the Creator, to console him in his inner and outer self, that the Lord made even those that are wild to people become tame to him.

[111] LP 85

[HE ENDURES THE COLD IN A HERMITAGE NEAR RIETI BECAUSE HE WANTS TO BE A MODEL TO THE OTHER BROTHERS]

At one time blessed Francis was staying at the hermitage of Sant' Eleuterio, near the town of Condigliano in the district of Rieti. Since he was wearing only one tunic, one day because of the extreme cold, and out of great necessity, he patched his tunic and that of his companion with scraps of cloth on the inside, so that his body began to be comforted a little. A short while afterwards, when he was returning from prayer one day, he said with great joy to his companion: "I must be the form and example of all the brothers; so, although it is necessary for my body to have a tunic with patches, nevertheless I must take into consideration my brothers who have the same need, but perhaps do not and cannot have this. Therefore, I must stay down with them, and I must suffer those same necessities they suffer so that in seeing this, they may be able to bear them more patiently."

We who were with him could not say how many and how great were the necessities that he denied his body in food and clothing, to give good example to the brothers and so that they would endure their necessities in greater patience. At all times, especially after the brothers began to multiply and he resigned the office of prelate, blessed Francis had as his highest and principal goal to teach the brothers more by actions than by words what they ought to do and what they ought to avoid.

LP 86

[112]

[HE IS SADDENED BY THE BROTHERS' BAD EXAMPLE; THE LORD ASKS: "TELL ME, WHO FOUNDED THE ORDER OF THE BROTHERS?"]

Noticing and hearing at one time that some brothers were giving a bad example in religion and that the brothers were turning aside from the highest summit of their profession, moved inwardly with sorrow of heart, one time he said to the Lord in prayer: "Lord I give back to you the family You gave me."

And the Lord said to him: "Tell me, why are you so upset when one of the brothers leaves religion and when others do not walk the way I showed you? Also tell me: Who planted the religion of the brothers? Who makes a man convert and to do penance in it? Who gives the strength to persevere in it? Is it not I?"

And it was said to him in spirit: "I did not choose you as a learned or eloquent man to be over my family, but I chose you, a simple man, so that you and the others may know that I will watch over my flock.
But *I have placed you as a sign* to them, so that the works that I work in Hg 2:24
you, they should see in you, emulate, and do them. Those who walk in my way have me and will have me more abundantly. Those who refuse to walk in my way, that which they seem to have will be taken away from them. Therefore, I tell you, don't be so sad; do what you do, work as you work, for I have planted the religion of the brothers in everlasting love. Know that I love it so much that if any brother, returning to his vomit, dies outside religion I will replace him with another in religion who will have his crown in his place, and supposing that he has not been born, I will have him born. And so that you know that I love the life and religion of the brothers, suppose that in the whole life and religion of the brothers only three brothers remained: I would never abandon it."

LP 87 These words greatly comforted the mind of blessed Francis, for he was immensely saddened when he heard anything about bad example regarding the brothers.

Although he could not totally restrain himself from becoming sad when he heard of something evil, nevertheless, after being comforted by the Lord in this way, he remembered this and spoke to his companions about it.

Therefore blessed Francis often used to say to the brothers in chapters and also in his words of instruction: "I have sworn and declared to observe the *Rule* of the brothers and all the brothers also pledged the same. For this reason, after I resigned the office among the brothers, because of my illnesses and for the greater good of my soul and those of all the brothers, from now on I am bound in regard to the brothers only to show good example.

"I learned that from the Lord and know in truth that even if my illness had excused me, the greatest help I can render to the religion of the brothers is to spend time in prayer to the Lord for it everyday, that He govern, preserve, protect, and defend it. I have pledged myself to this, to the Lord and to the brothers, that if any one of the brothers perishes because of my bad example, I will be held to render an account to the Lord."

And even though from time to time a brother would tell him that he should occasionally put himself forward in the affairs of the religion, he used to reply with words like these: "The brothers have their *Rule*, and furthermore have sworn to it. And so that they have no excuse, after it pleased the Lord to decide that I would be their prelate, I also swore to it in their presence and I want to observe it to the end. So, since the brothers already know what they should do and what to avoid, the only thing left for me to do is to teach them by actions, because this is why I have been given to them during my life and after my death.

[113] LP 88

[HE IS ASHAMED TO MEET SOMEONE POORER THAN HIMSELF]

It happened once when blessed Francis was going about preaching in some region he met a poor man. Noticing his dire poverty, he said to his companion: "This man's poverty brings great shame on us; it passes judgment on our poverty."

"How so, brother?" his companion replied. "I am greatly ashamed," he answered, when I find someone poorer than myself. I chose holy poverty as my Lady, my delight and my riches of spirit and body. And the whole world has heard this news, that I professed poverty before God and people. Therefore I ought to be ashamed when I come upon someone poorer than myself."

[114] LP 89

[HE CORRECTS A BROTHER WHO RASHLY JUDGED A POOR MAN]

When blessed Francis went to a hermitage of the brothers near Rocca di Brizio to preach to the people of that region, it happened that on the very day that he was to preach, a poor sick man came to him. When he saw him and noticed his poverty and illness, he was moved to piety for him and he began to speak to his companion about the man's nakedness and illness. "It is true, brother," his companion said to him, "that he is poor, but perhaps there is no one in the whole province who desires riches more."

Blessed Francis rebuked him for not speaking well and he admitted his fault. Blessed Francis told him: "Do you want to do the penance I will tell you?" "Willingly" he replied. "Go, *strip off your tunic,*" he said, "and go to that poor man naked, throw yourself at his feet, and tell him how you sinned against him, how you slandered him, and ask him to pray for you that God may forgive you." Bar 5:1

So he went and did everything blessed Francis had told him. When he finished, he got up, put on his tunic, and returned to blessed Francis. And blessed Francis said to him: "Do you want me to tell you how you sinned against him, and even against Christ?"

And he said: "Whenever you see a poor person you ought to consider Him in whose name he comes, that is, Christ, who came to take on our poverty and weakness. This man's poverty and weakness is a mirror for us in which we should see and consider lovingly the poverty and weakness of our Lord Jesus Christ which He endured in His body for the salvation of the human race."

LP 90

[115]
[A STRATEGY FOR CONVERTING THE ROBBERS OF BORGO SAN SEPOLCRO]

At one time robbers used to come sometimes to the hermitage of the brothers above Borgo San Sepolcro to ask the brothers for bread.[a] They hid in the thick forest of that region, coming out from time to time to rob travelers on the streets and footpaths. Some of the brothers of that place said: "It is not right to give them alms because they are robbers and they do many very great evil things to people." Others, taking into consideration that they begged humbly and were compelled by great necessity, used to give them alms sometimes, always admonishing them to be converted to penance.

Meanwhile blessed Francis arrived at that place. The brothers asked him whether they should give them bread, or not. "If you do as I tell you," blessed Francis told them, "I trust in the Lord that you will win their souls. Go get some good bread and good wine and take it to them in the woods where you know they are staying, and cry out: 'Come, Brother Robbers, come to us, because we are brothers and we are bringing you some good bread and good wine.' They will immediately come to you. Then you spread out a table cloth on the ground,

a. That is, the hermitage of Monte Casale.

placing the bread and wine on it, and, while they are eating, humbly and joyfully wait on them. After the meal, speak to them some words of the Lord. Finally, for the love of the Lord ask them for this first request: make them promise you that they will not strike anyone or injure anyone's person. Do not ask for everything all at once, or they will not listen to you. Because of the humility and charity you show them, they will at once make you this promise. The next day, get up and, because of the promise they made to you, besides eggs and cheese, bring them the bread and wine, and take these to them, and wait on them while they eat. After the meal, say to them: 'Why do you stay here all day long, dying of hunger, suffering many evil things and in your actions doing many evil things for which you will lose your souls unless you are converted? It is better to serve the Lord, who will both supply your bodily needs in this world and save your souls in the end.' Then the Lord in His mercy will inspire them to convert and they will be converted because of the humility and charity you show them."

So the brothers got up and did everything as blessed Francis told them. And by the mercy of God and His grace which descended on them, those men listened and observed to the letter point by point all the requests which the brothers asked of them. Further, because of the friendliness and charity the brothers showed them, they began carrying wood on their shoulders to the hermitage. By the mercy of God, through the charity and friendliness that the brothers showed them, some entered religion, others embraced penance, promising in the hands of the brothers no longer to commit these evil deeds, but to live by the work of their hands.

The brothers and others who heard or knew about this, were quite amazed, as they reflected on the holiness of blessed Francis, how he had predicted the conversion of these men who had been perfidious and wicked, and how quickly they converted to the Lord.

[116] LP 91

[He reveals that a brother considered a saint is an impostor]

There was a brother of a decent and holy way of living, who concerned himself with prayer day and night. He observed constant silence so that when he went to confession to a brother priest, he confessed with signs, not with words. He appeared so devout and fervent in the love of God, that sometimes when he sat down with the brothers, although he did not speak, he rejoiced so much internally and externally on hearing some good words that he moved all the brothers and others who saw him in devotion to God. He was willingly considered a saint by the brothers and others.

After he had been living this way for several years, it happened that blessed Francis came to that place where he was staying. When he heard the brothers tell him about this brother's way of life, he said: *"Know for a truth* that this is diabolical temptation and deception, because he does not want to confess." Mt 22:16

In the meantime the general minister came there to visit blessed Francis and began to praise this brother in front of blessed Francis. "Believe me, brother," blessed Francis told him, "this brother is led and deceived by an evil spirit."

The general minister replied to him: "I find it amazing and almost unbelievable that a man who shows so many signs and works of holiness, can be what you say he is."

"Test him then," blessed Francis replied. "Tell him to go to confession twice or even once a week. If he does not listen to you, *you will know what I told you is true."* Jn 5:32

One day when the general minister was speaking to this brother, he told him: "Brother, I want you to confess twice or at least once a week."

He put a finger to his lips and shook his head, showing by signs that he would in no way do that. The minister, however, fearing that he would scandalize him, let him go. A few days later he left the religion of his own will, and returned to the world wearing secular clothing.

One day while two companions of blessed Francis were walking along some road, they met him. He was walking alone like a very poor pilgrim. Feeling compassion for him, they said: "You wretch, where is your holy and upright life? You used to love the solitary life so much that you did not want to show yourself to your brothers nor speak to them. And now you go wandering through the world like a man who does not know God or his servants."

He began to speak to them, often swearing on his faith like secular people.

"Wretched man," the brothers told him, "why do you swear on your faith like secular people? When you were in religion, you abstained not only from idle words, but from even good ones." He told them: "It can't be different."

They left him. And a few days later, he died.

The brothers and others were quite amazed, as they reflected on the holiness of blessed Francis who had predicted his fall at a time when he was considered a saint by the brothers and others.

[117] LP 92
[He is beaten by demons while staying in a tower of Cardinal Leo of Santa Croce]

Blessed Francis once went to Rome to visit the Lord Hugolino, the bishop of Ostia, who later became pope, and stayed with him a few days, and with his permission he visited Lord Leo, Cardinal of the Santa Croce, who was a very kind and courtly man.[a] He was happy to see blessed Francis whom he greatly revered. With great devotion, he asked him to spend a few days with him, especially because it was winter and very cold and almost every day there was heavy wind and rain, as happens during that season.

"Brother," he said to him, "this weather is unsuitable for traveling. If it is agreeable to you, I want you to stay with me until there is good weather for travel. Since I feed a number of poor people in my house, you will receive food from me in place of one poor person." The Lord Cardinal said this, knowing that blessed Francis, because of his humility, always wanted to be received wherever he lodged as a poor person. And yet his holiness was so outstanding that the Lord Pope, the cardinals, and all the mighty of this world who knew him venerated him as a saint. And he added: "I will give you a good remote house where you can pray and eat if you wish."

Brother Angelo Tancredi, one of the first twelve brothers, was staying with the cardinal. He said to blessed Francis: "Brother, near here there is a beautiful tower on the city walls, quite ample and spacious on the inside, with nine chambers where you can stay as removed as in a hermitage."

"Let us go to see it," blessed Francis told him. On seeing it, he liked it, and returning to the Lord Cardinal said to him: "Lord, perhaps I will stay with you a few days." The Lord Cardinal was pleased.

So Brother Angelo went and prepared it so blessed Francis could stay there night and day with his companion. Blessed Francis did not wish to come down day or night as long as he was staying with the Lord Cardinal. Brother Angelo suggested that he bring food for blessed Francis and his companion each day, leaving it outside, for neither he nor any other was supposed to enter.

Blessed Francis went to stay there with his companion. But when he wanted to sleep there on the first night, demons came and beat him severely. He immediately called his companion who was staying some distance away: "Come to me." He got up at once and came to

a. Leo Brancaleone was cardinal deacon of Santa Lucia from 1200 to 1202 and cardinal priest of the Roman Basilica of Santa Croce in Gerusalemme from 1202 to 1230.

him. "Brother," blessed Francis told him, "the demons have beaten me severely so I want you to stay next to me because I am afraid to stay here alone." His companion stayed by him the whole night for blessed Francis trembled all over like a man suffering a fever. Both of them remained awake that whole night.

During that time, blessed Francis talked with his companion: "Why did the devils beat me? Why has the Lord given them the power to harm me?"

And he began to say: "The devils are the police of our Lord. Just as the podestà sends his police to punish a wrong-doer, in the same way, the Lord punishes and corrects those whom He loves through the demons, who are His police and act as His ministers in this office.

"Even a perfect religious very often sins in ignorance. Consequently if he does not realize his sin, he is punished by the devil so that he may see and carefully reflect internally and externally because of that punishment how he may have offended. For in this life the Lord leaves nothing unpunished in those whom He loves tenderly. By the mercy and grace of God, I do not know if I have offended Him in any way which I have not corrected by confession and satisfaction. Indeed the Lord in His mercy granted me this gift. He makes me understand through prayer any way in which I please or displease Him.

"It seems to me that it could be that the Lord punished me through His police because, although the Lord Cardinal gladly does this mercy to me and my body needs to accept, and I can accept it from him confidently, nevertheless, my brothers, who go through the world suffering hunger and many hardships, and other brothers who stay in poor little houses and hermitages, may have an occasion for grumbling against me when they hear that I am staying with the lord cardinal: 'We are enduring so many hardships while he is having his comforts,' I am bound always to give them good example; because I was given to them, especially for this. For the brothers are more edified when I stay in poor little places among them rather than in other places. When they hear and know that I am bearing the same trials, they endure theirs with greater patience."

Blessed Francis was always sickly. Even in the world he was by nature a frail and weak man, and he grew more sickly until the day of his death, yet he considered that he should show a good example to the brothers and always take away from them any occasion for complaining about him, so the brothers could not say: "He has all he needs, but we don't."

Whether he was healthy or sick, until the day of his death, he wanted to endure so much need, that if any of the brothers who knew this, as we did, we who were with him for some time until the day of his death, and if they brought this back to mind, they would not be able to restrain their tears; and when they suffer some need or troubles, they would bear them with greater patience.

Very early in the morning, blessed Francis came down from the tower, and went to the Lord Cardinal, telling him all that had happened and everything that he said to his companion. And he added: "People have great faith in me and think that I am a holy man, and as you see the devils have driven me from the cell." He wanted to stay there as if in a remote cell, not speaking to anyone except his companion.

The Lord Cardinal was very happy with him. Nevertheless, since he knew and venerated him as a saint, he was satisfied with his decision not to stay there any longer.

Thus, blessed Francis with permission returned to the hermitage of Saint Francis at Fonte Colombo near Rieti.

[118] LP 93

[He has a vision of the winged seraph during the Lent of Saint Michael on La Verna][a]

One time blessed Francis went to the hermitage of Mount La Verna and because that place is very remote, he liked it very much, and he wanted to do a Lent in honor of Saint Michael. He went there before the feast of the Assumption of the glorious Virgin Mary, and he counted the days from the feast of Saint Mary to the feast of Saint Michael, which are forty days, and he said: "I want to make a Lent here, in honor of God, the Blessed Virgin Mary, His mother, and blessed Michael, the prince of angels and of souls."

And it happened as he entered his cell where he was to stay constantly, he asked the Lord on the first night to show him in some way how he could know if it were His will for him to remain there.

When blessed Francis stayed constantly in a place to pray, or when he went through the world preaching, he was always anxious to know the will of the Lord, about how he could please Him better. He was sometimes afraid that, under the pretext of remaining in prayer in a remote place, the body wanted to rest, refusing the labor of going through the world preaching, for which Christ came down from heaven into this world. Indeed he would ask those he consid-

a. Francis seems to have adopted the practice of keeping a special period of forty days of fasting from the Assumption (August 15) to the Feast of Saint Michael the Archangel (September 29). There is no evidence that his confreres joined him in this practice. Cf. Fortini, *Francis*, 553i.

ered beloved by the Lord to ask Him to show them His will, whether he should go through the world preaching or stay for a while in a remote place to pray.

In early morning at dawn, while he stood in prayer, birds of various kinds came over the cell where he was staying. They did not come altogether, but first one would come and sing its sweet verse, and then go away, and another one come and sing and go away. They all did the same.

Blessed Francis was very happy at this and received great consolation from it. But when he began to meditate on what this might be, the Lord told him in spirit: "This is a sign that the Lord will do good for you in this cell and give you many consolations."

This was really true. Among all the consolations, hidden and manifest, which the Lord granted him, there was shown to him by the Lord a vision of a Seraph, from which, for the whole time of his life, he had great consolation in his soul between himself and the Lord. And it happened that while his companion brought him food that day, he told him everything that happened to him.

And, although he had many consolations in that cell, demons also gave him many trials at night, as he himself told his companion. That is why he once said: "If the brothers knew how many trials the demons cause me, there would not be one of them who would not have great piety and compassion for me."

As a result, as he often said to his companions, he was unable by himself to satisfy the brothers or sometimes to show them the friendliness which the brothers desired.

LP 94

[119]

[He is tormented by a demon in a feather pillow at Greccio]

At one time blessed Francis was staying in the hermitage of Greccio. He remained in prayer day and night in the last cell, behind the large cell. One night, during the first sleep, he called his companion who was sleeping near him in the old, large cell. The brother got up immediately and went to him, and entered the yard of that little cell, next to the door, where blessed Francis was lying inside.

Blessed Francis said to him: "Brother I couldn't sleep this whole night, or remain upright and pray; my head and my knees are shaking as if I had eaten bread made from rye grass."

His companion talked with him, trying to console him. Blessed Francis said: "I believe there's a devil in this pillow I have for my head."

He had received that pillow that was filled with feathers the day before from Lord John of Greccio, whom the saint loved with great affection and to whom he showed great friendliness during his whole lifetime. After he left the world, blessed Francis did not want to sleep on a mattress nor have a feather pillow for his head, when he was sick or for any other reason. This time the brothers forced him to accept it, against his will, because of his very serious eye disease. He threw it at his companion. His companion got up and picked it up in his right hand, threw it over his left shoulder, and holding it there with his right hand, he left that yard. He suddenly lost the power of speech, could not move from that place, nor could he move his arms or hands to throw away that thing. There he stood, stiff, it seemed to him that he was like a man outside of himself, sensing nothing in himself or others. He stood like this for about an hour, until through the mercy of God blessed Francis called him. Immediately he returned to himself and threw the pillow behind him. He returned to blessed Francis and told him everything that happened to him.

Blessed Francis said to him, "Last night as I was saying compline, I sensed when the devil had come into my cell." After he realized it was true that it was the devil who had prevented him from sleeping or standing up to pray, he began to tell his companion, "The devil is very cunning and subtle. Because by the mercy and grace of God he cannot harm me in my soul, he wanted to disturb the need of the body by preventing me from sleeping and standing up to pray, in order to stifle the devotion and joy of my heart so that I will complain about my sickness."

LP 95 For many years blessed Francis suffered from serious illness of his stomach, spleen, and liver, as well as from a disease of the eyes.[a] Yet, he was so devout and prayed with so much reverence, that during times of prayer, he refused to lean against a wall or partition, but always stood erect, without a capuche over his head, and sometimes on his knees, especially when he spent the greater part of the day and night in prayer.

When he went through the world on foot, he always would stop walking in order to say his Hours. If he was riding on horseback, because he was always sickly, he would get down to say his Hours.

a. Cf. AC 4, supra, 119 b.

LP 95 ## [120]

[His devout way of praying the Divine Office and his efforts to preserve joy of spirit]

One time, when he was returning from the City, after staying with the Lord Cardinal Leo for a few days, it rained the whole day as he was leaving the City. Since he was very sick, he was riding on horseback, but he got off his horse to say his Hours, standing on the roadside despite the rain which completely soaked him.

He said: "If the body wants to eat its food in peace and quiet, and both it and the body eventually will become food for worms, in what peace and quiet should the soul receive its food, which is God Himself!"

LP 96 And he used to say: "The devil is delighted when he can extinguish or prevent devotion and joy in the heart of a servant of God which spring from clean prayer and other good works. For if the devil can have something of his own in a servant of God, he will in a short time make a single hair into a beam, always making it bigger, unless the servant of God is wise, removing and destroying it as quickly as possible by means of contrition and confession and works of satisfaction."

He said: "In eating, sleeping, and other necessities, the servant of God must satisfy the body with discernment, so that Brother Body cannot grumble, saying: 'Because you do not satisfy me, I cannot stand up straight and persevere in prayer, or rejoice in tribulations, or do other good works.' "

He also used to say: "If a servant of God, with discernment, has satisfied his body well enough and as decently as he could, but Brother Body wants to be lazy, negligent, and sleepy in prayer, vigils, and other good works, then he should punish it like any wicked and lazy beast of burden, because it wants to eat but refuses to work or carry its weight.

"If, however, Brother Body cannot have its needs fulfilled whether healthy or sick, because of want or poverty, and after requesting them decently and humbly for the love of God from his brother or his prelate they are not given to him, then let him patiently bear this for the love of God and it will be credited it to him as martyrdom. And because he did what is his to do, making his needs known, he would be excused from sin, even if the body only on this account would become very sick."

LP 97 Blessed Francis had this as his highest and main goal: he was always careful to have and preserve in himself spiritual joy internally and externally, even though from the beginning of his conversion until the day of his death he greatly afflicted his body. He used to say that if a servant of God always strives to have and preserve joy internally and externally which proceeds from purity of heart, the devils can do him no harm. They would say: "Since the servant of God has joy both in tribulation and in prosperity, we do not know where to find an entrance to enter him and do him harm."

One day he reproved one of his companions who looked sad and long-faced. He told him: "Why are you sad and sorrowful over your offenses? It is a matter between you and God. Pray to Him, that by His mercy He may grant you the joy of His salvation. Try to be joyful always around me and others, because it is not fitting that a servant of God appear before his brother or others with a sad and glum face.

"I know that the devils envy me because of the gifts which the Lord has granted me in His mercy. Because they cannot harm me through myself, they try to hurt me through my companions. If they cannot do harm either through me or my companions, they withdraw in great confusion. Indeed, whenever I feel tempted and depressed and I look at the joy of my companion, because of that joy I turn away from the temptation and depression and toward inner joy."

THE REMEMBRANCE
OF THE DESIRE OF A SOUL

(The Second Life of Saint Francis)

BY

THOMAS OF CELANO

(1245–1247)

Introduction

The Chronicles of Salimbene degli Adami, written between 1283 and 1288, notes that Crescentius ordered Thomas of Celano to undertake the task of re-presenting the remembrances sent to him.[1] Thomas himself indicates that the choice of his role was that of the chapter itself: "The holy gathering of the last general chapter and you, most reverend father, chose to charge us, insignificant as we are, to write down the deeds as well as the words of our glorious father Francis, for the consolation of our contemporaries and the remembrance of future generations."[2] The result of Thomas's endeavor was a new, long and complicated text, completed shortly before the General Chapter of Lyons in July of 1247. Thomas entitled his third composition, *The Remembrance of the Desire of a Soul.*

The task, then, given to Thomas was formidable. In addition to receiving this commission from the General Minister, not the Pope, Thomas was now fifteen years older and had seen the fraternity change. The tumultuous years of Elias's term as General Minister (1232-1239), the sudden death of his successor, Albert of Pisa (1239), the sweeping changes of Haymo of Faversham (1239-1244), and his sudden death all had left their impressions. The interventions of Pope Gregory, moreover, especially that of *Quo elongati,*[3] had debilitating effects. Thomas's purposes, therefore, were quite different. *The Remembrance of the Desire of a Soul* is neither a continuation nor a complement to his earlier work, *The Life of Saint Francis*. The questions underlying the composition of *The Remembrance of the Desire of a Soul* were not so much about the life of Francis but about the way of life he founded.

Sources

"This work," Thomas states, "contains some marvelous details about the conversion of Saint Francis not included in earlier legends written about him because they were never brought to the author's attention." Besides traces from *The Life of Saint Francis,* in Book One Thomas takes advantage of material from *The Anonymous of Perugia* and *The Legend of the Three Companions.*[4] In these he was confronted with new information not only about Francis's youth and conversion, but also the beginnings of the primitive fraternity. This can be seen, for example, in the accentuation of Francis's Baptismal name, John, in the experience of the Crucified in San Damiano, and in his dealings with both Popes Innocent III and Honorius III. He incorporates the information offered in *The Anonymous of Perugia* and *The Legend of the Three Companions,* as well as presenting a new chronological order.

In Book Two Thomas shifts his attention from specifically biographical information to a more thematic presentation of ideals. "We will attempt," he proposes in his Prologue, "to express and carefully state the good, pleasing, and perfect will of our most holy father. This concerns both himself and his followers, the exercise of heavenly discipline and that striving for highest perfection which he always expressed in love for God and in living example for others." To accomplish this, Thomas relies heavily on *The Assisi Compilation*. Even a cursory examination of incidents found in both *The Assisi Compilation* and *The Remembrance of the Desire of a Soul* reveals subtle differences but general dependency. *The Assisi Compilation* offers simple, colloquial, and immediate presentations of these incidents. To these Thomas brings his eloquent and literary style as well as his facility with Scripture to re-present the same stories within the framework of his specific purposes.[5] Many times, he omits the details of *The Assisi Compilation,* especially geographical ones that are not pertinent.[6] Sometimes he changes certain details in order to accentuate his themes;[7] at others, he shortens descriptions to develop more clearly their theological significance.[8]

While a more precise, in-depth comparison of *The Anonymous of Perugia, The Legend of the Three Companions, The Assisi Compilation,* and *The Remembrance of the Desire of a Soul* needs to be done, the inter-dependence of these texts is evident. The letter at the beginning of *The Legend of the Three Companions* attests to a block of information sent in response to Crescentius's request. That could easily have been the data of *The Legend of the Three Companions* edited to include much of the *The Anonymous of Perugia,* as well as that of *The Assisi Compilation.* In the final analysis, Thomas's work reflects the input of Francis's companions, crafted, however, according to Thomas's own design. Little wonder, then, that Thomas concludes his work with a prayer of the saint's companions. It adroitly omits any mention of "we who were with him," and so it may be seen as a prayer of Thomas himself as well as of any of Francis's companions.

Vision

Aside from the Prologue (2C 1-2) and the lengthy concluding prayer (2C 221-224), Thomas divides this work into two disproportionate sections. Book One is made up of only twenty-three paragraphs (2C 3-25) that, as noted, are biographical in nature. Book Two, on the other hand, contains one hundred and ninety-nine paragraphs (2C 26-220) presented in a thematic vein. Of these, six numbers (2C 114-220) describe Francis's death and, in two manuscripts, his canonization.

Two contemporary interpretations of *The Remembrance of the Desire of A Soul* exist. In that of François DeBeer, Thomas centered his material around the theme of conversion and, from that starting-point organized into two books to address two themes: initial conversion and the lifetime embrace of conversion.[9] The other is of Engelbert Grau who cites a passage in Thomas's introduction to Book Two for his interpretation: "I consider blessed Francis the holiest *mirror* of the holiness of the Lord, the *image of his* perfection."[10] "It is the intention of the author," Grau maintains, "to hold up a 'mirror of perfection' of Francis's exemplary life to the friars of the second generation who had not personally experienced or known him in his lifetime."[11] Both perspectives offer an understanding of the biographical material in Book One portending the thematic material of Book Two. In other words, the first provides insights into the nature and the foundation of Gospel life, while the second addresses practical attitudes and behaviors that can assist or impede the living out of the Gospel.

Thomas adjusts and nuances the information of the Companions to present a new perspective on Francis's vocation, its prophetic dimension. His baptism is a call to a prophetic generosity that embraces fellow prisoners, a poor knight, the beggars before Saint Peter's, and, most challenging of all, lepers. It is a call to overcome temptations, to reject the worldly career of knighthood, and to see beyond his carousing friends to Christ. Only then is Francis led by the Spirit to enter the church of San Damiano where "with the lips of the painting, the image of Christ crucified spoke to him . . . calling him by name"[12] From Christ, he receives a command that will direct him the rest of his life.[13] It takes him before the bishop where he proclaims God as his Father, pledges to go to the Lord naked· and begins serving the common Lord of all and begging leftovers from door to door. Thus Thomas interprets these events teaching the nature of Francis's prophetic vocation as rooted in baptism. As he opens himself in generosity to others, his vocation is to allow himself to be moved by the Spirit in Christ to the Father.

Thomas moves quickly in narrating Francis's prophecy concerning the virgins who would live in San Damiano, his example in attracting Bernard of Quintavalle and others, and his discourse before the pope. Curiously, Thomas devotes significant time to describing the role of the Portiuncula (2C 18-20) and the vision of the small black hen and her unruly chicks. In doing so, he provides two symbols that guide his thought in Book Two: the Portiuncula that represents the Church in which the Gospel life is discovered and lived, and the small black hen referring to Francis himself unable to defend with his wings.

Book Two moves to many particulars and examples of what this vocation in prophetic baptismal grace can mean for the brothers in the course of everyday life. The material from which Thomas drew offered him memories of everyday events in Francis life, experienced for the most part in intimate and private settings known particularly to "we who were with him." This second book has its own introduction, but almost every delineated thematic section also has its own introduction.[14] These are key to understanding Thomas's theological perception of events remembered about Francis. In *The Remembrance of the Desire of a Soul,* unlike in his *Life of Saint Francis,* Thomas seems more interested in showing the power of God's intervening and prophetic grace that begins in baptism and progressively develops through life. This grace of conversion is not a private matter, but is shared grace to be further developed among brothers who in dialogue mutually listen to the Gospel and entrust themselves to the Church. This is the foundation for the life of the Lesser Brothers, and in Francis's vocation the brothers can find their own call.

Thus a dynamic exchange takes place between the two books in which a theme developed in the second book can be found in seminal form in the first. Book One begins with Francis in comparison to John the Baptist (2C 3-4), while Chapter I of Book Two begins describing Francis's spirit of prophecy (2C 27-54). The correspondence continues as Thomas highlights the image of Martin of Tours (2C 5-6) and develops the theme of poverty (2C 55-93). His new spiritual energy (2C 7) finds inspiration in prayer (2C 94-101), his Catholic faith (2C 8) in Sacred Scriptures (2C 102-111); his religious spirit overcoming both temptation and himself (2C 9) in varied temptations (2C 112-124); and his service of lepers (2 C 9) in his true spiritual joy (2C 125-134). Finally, there is his response to Christ's command and his new family of brothers (2 C 7-17) which prompts a consideration of the virtues of the new fraternity: humility (2C 139-150), obedience (2C 151-154), simplicity (2C 189-203), special devotions (2C 196-203) and care for the Poor Ladies (2C 204-207).

Although Thomas constructed Book Two according to a thematic, not without relationship to Book One, he never had far from his mind the central concern of the brothers of his day, the problem of interpreting provisions of the *Rule*.[15] There is no rupture with the past, but rather in the past the future is already gestating. The foundation, however, is Christ in the grace of baptism, becoming every more present and finally giving to each person his or her own *mandatum* within the deepest recesses of the soul. This is the lesson he wishes to communicate to his brothers who struggle with the identity of their vocation in the tumultuous period of the 1240's.

Thomas concludes Book Two with a description of Francis's death. It is the one place in *The Remembrance of the Desire of a Soul* that Thomas extensively uses what he had earlier written in *The Life of Saint Francis*. This indicates that Thomas took his new task seriously, to write about Francis from the memories of others and to present them in a new way for a new time. In Book One, even in our day, he reveals the ever-increasing gift of grace deep in the heart of the baptized, and in Book Two he motivates the grace-filled believer into action. In both books, however, remembrance of Saint Francis stirs the desire of every soul, eternal life.

Conclusion

The Remembrance of The Desire of a Soul: the title is provocative. Thomas's work is undoubtedly one of remembrance, a collage of the memories of Francis's companions stitched together in Thomas's unique style. Nonetheless, is it not difficult and, at the same time, intriguing to determine the soul possessing such desire? Is the desire of the companions? Of Thomas? Of Francis himself? Or did Thomas see his work as a means of stirring the memories of those who would read his work and, in so doing, re-enkindling the desire deep in their own souls?

In the final analysis, *The Remembrance of the Desire of a Soul* is a piece of spiritual literature that resonates deeply with those attempting to define the spirituality of Francis of Assisi. As it embraces a profoundly theological approach by seeing baptismal grace as the lynchpin of Francis's life, it also provides an anthropological dimension that provides insight into the saint's human nature and experience, or, as Ewert Cousins expresses it, "the inner dimension of the person . . . [where] ultimate reality is experienced."[16] While it must be read in the context of the historical milieu of the middle of the thirteenth century, Thomas's accentuation of the rich symbols that fill its history make it a text of contemporary relevance.

Notes

1. Salimbene degli Adami, *Chronicle,* 166: "In the year of the Lord 1244, Brother Haymo of England, general minister of the Order of Lesser Brothers, died, and elected in his place was Brother Crescentius of the March of Ancona, who was an old man. Crescentius then commanded Brother Thomas of Celano, who had written the first Legend of Saint Francis, to write another book, because many things about Saint Francis had been discovered which had never been written. And so Thomas of Celano wrote a very beautiful book about the miracles, as well as the life of Saint Francis, which he entitled the 'Remembrance of the Blessed Francis in the Desire of the Soul.' "

2. 2C 1.

3. Cf. FA:ED I 570-575; cf. supra, 15-18.

4. Jacques Dalarun notes that in 2C there are three episodes taken from 1C, five from AP, thirty-four from L3C, and eighty-seven from AC. One hundred one are without earlier recognizable sources, thus giving the text a total of 230 narrative episodes. Cf. Jacques Dalarun, *La Malavventura di Francesco d'Assisi: Per Un Uso Storico delle Leggende Francescane* (Milano: Edizioni Biblioteca Francescana, 1996), 92. The editors of this volume have assiduously studied the Latin texts of these works and attempted to bring the translations of each into uniformity so that their interdependence is obvious.

5. The simple statement found in AC 68 *Nolite facere amplius dicere* [Don't make me tell you again] is changed in 2C 44 to *Quid vultis ut iterum dicam?* (Mt 20:32; Jn 9:27) [Do you want me to say it again?]

6. E.g. 2C 31, 37, 40, 44, 75, 91, 122, 126, 181.

7. For example, in 2C 45 Thomas changes "a certain brother" (AC 73) to "two brothers" travelling to Greccio to catch a glimpse of Francis. "Two brothers" travelling together is more in accord with the Gospel injunction (Lk 10:1) and Thomas's earlier reiteration of it in 1C 29. In another instance, Thomas changes the occasion of Francis's appearing as a poor, humble pilgrim before the brothers at Greccio from Christmas (AC 74) to Easter (2C 61). This allows him to place greater emphasis on the example of Francis as a pilgrim, an important point in LR VI 2.

8. E.g. 2C 21-22, 59, 64, 73, 100, 151, 165. In 2C 21-22, the story of the brother dying of hunger, Thomas recasts AC 50 in order to accentuate Francis's image as a shepherd in caring for his sheep. In 2C 38, the story of the young woman coming to Francis with a complaint about her cruel husband, Thomas re-orders AC 69. In Thomas's rendering, Francis is sensitive to the "delicate and tender" woman who dies on the same day as her husband. In this way, Thomas emphasizes their celibate lives as a sacrificial offering, the "one as a morning holocaust, and the other as an evening sacrifice."

9. François De Beer, *La Conversion de Saint François selon Thomas de Celano* (Paris: Éditions Franciscaines, 1963).

10. 2C 26.

11. Engelbert Grau, "Thomas of Celano: Life and Work," GR 8:2 (1994): 190.

12. Cf 2C 10.

13. The Latin word *mandatum* [command] is significant in 2C where it is used far more than in 1C. See infra 2C 5, 245 a.

14. Cf. 2C 27 For specific introductions to the various individual narratives in which Thomas theologically contextualizes the various memories of Saint Francis, see the following: 2C 27 (prophecy), 55 (poverty), 94 (prayer), 102 (Scripture), 115 (temptation), 125 (spiritual joy),135 (hiding the stigmata), 140 (humility), 151 (obedience), 159 (idleness), 165 (love for creatures),

172 (charity), 189 (simplicity), 201(devotion to Eucharist), 202 (devotion to relics), 203, (devotion to the cross), and 204 (the Poor Ladies).

15. Throughout Book Two, Thomas makes many allusions or direct references to LR, the Rule confirmed by Pope Honorius III with the papal decree, *Solet annuere,* cf. FA:ED I, 99-106. Cf. 2C 58, 66, 69, 72, 80, 81, 91, 131, 152, 175.

16. Ewert Cousins, "Preface to the Series." *Christian Spirituality.* Vol I. Origins to the Twelfth Century. Ed. Bernard McGinn, et al., (New York: Crossroad, 1985), xiii.

The Remembrance of the Desire of a Soul

Prologue

IN THE NAME OF OUR LORD JESUS CHRIST. AMEN.

TO THE GENERAL MINISTER OF THE ORDER OF THE LESSER BROTHERS
HERE BEGINS THE PROLOGUE

[1]The holy gathering of the last general chapter and you, most reverend father,[a] chose to charge us, insignificant as we are, to write down the deeds as well as the words of our glorious father Francis, for the consolation of our contemporaries and the remembrance of future generations.

We, more than others, learned these things through constant living together and mutual intimacy with him over a long time.[b] We hastened with humble devotion to obey this sacred command: it would be wrong to neglect it in any way. But on further considering the weakness of our capacities we are struck with a justified fear that such a worthy topic, handled in an unworthy manner, should be tainted by our efforts and become distasteful to others. We fear that, like food full of *delicious flavors,* it may be rendered tasteless by incom- Wis 16:20

a. For information on the request for information on Francis of the previous General Chapter of Genoa and the General Minister, Crescentius of Iesi, in 1244, see supra, 15-18. This text of *The Remembrance of the Desire of a Soul* was presented to Crescentius of Iesi before the General Chapter of 1247, when John of Parma was elected in his place. The translation is based on the critical text of the AF X, 129-268.

b. This first number echoes the letter dated August 11, 1246, from Greccio attached to L3C, cf. L3C 1, supra 67-68. See conclusion of the whole work, 2C 221-224, infra, 392-393 the *Prayer of the Companions*.

petent servants, and that our efforts will be criticized as presumption, rather than obedience.

Blessed father, if the results of so much labor were to be examined only by your kind self, and did not have to be presented to a public audience, we would gladly be instructed by your correction and rejoice in your approval. Who can examine closely and balance carefully such diverse words and deeds, so that *all* listeners would *be of one mind?* We simply want to benefit each and everyone. So we beg those who read this to interpret it kindly and to bear with or correct the simplicity of the narrator so that reverence for the person who is our subject may remain intact. Our memory, like that of ignorant people, is blunted by the passage of time and cannot attain the heights of his profound words or due praise for his marvelous deeds. Even a quick and well-trained mind could hardly grasp these things, even if directly confronted with them. By your authority, you repeatedly ordered us to write. Now, pardon us publicly for our clumsy mistakes.

2 Mc 14:20

[2]In the first place, this work contains some marvelous details about the conversion of Saint Francis not included in earlier legends written about him because they were never brought to the author's attention. Then we will attempt to express and carefully state the *good, pleasing and perfect will* of our most holy father. This concerns both himself and his followers, the exercise of heavenly discipline, and that striving for highest perfection which he always expressed in love for God and in living example for others. Here and there, according to the opportunity, we have included a number of his miracles. We describe in a plain and simple way things that occur to us, wishing to accommodate those who are slower and, if possible, also to please the learned.

Rom 12:2

We beg you, therefore, kind father, consecrate with your blessing this small gift of our work—small, but not to be despised—which we gathered with no small labor. Correct its errors. Trim away the superfluous.

Thus things well said will be approved
by your learned opinion, and
like your name,
Crescentius,
they will build to a crescendo
and everywhere *increase and multiply in Christ.*

Gn 1:22,28; Acts 12:24; Eph 2:20-21

Amen.

Here ends the Prologue

The First Book

The Remembrance of the Desire of a Soul[a]
THE DEEDS AND WORDS
OF OUR MOST HOLY FATHER

His Conversion

Chapter I
How he was at first called John, and later Francis; what his mother prophesied about him, what he himself predicted would happen to him, and his patience while in chains.

3 "Francis"
was the name of this servant and friend of the Most High.
Divine Providence gave him this name,
unique and unusual,
1C 120 that the fame of his ministry should spread even more rapidly
throughout the whole world.
He was named *John* by his own mother
when, being, *born again through water and the Holy Spirit*[b] Jn 3:5
he was changed from a *child of wrath* Eph 2:3
into a child of grace.[c]

a. This title, *Memoriale in Desiderio Animae* [The Remembrance of The Desire of a Soul], is inspired by the Vulgate version of Is 26:8: *nomen tuum et memoriale tuum in desiderio animae* [your name and your memory are the desire of the soul]. This is how the editors have chosen to entitle this whole work in order to capture its nature as a work of remembrance of Francis rather than as a life of Francis. This passage serves as a means of approaching the text since Book One (2C 1-25) begins by concentrating on the name, Francis, as a means of indicating the saint's vocation; while Book Two (2C 26-224) does so by reflecting on the importance of remembrance as a tool of honor and of love (2C 26).

b. This is the first reference to Francis's baptism. Since there is no record of it, scholars conjecture that it took place in the church of Santa Maria del Vescovado. Since the Duomo of San Rufino was being repaired, Santa Maria del Vescovado became the pro-cathedral. The baptismal font was later transferred back to San Rufino where it remains to this day. Cf. Omer Englebert, *Saint Francis of Assisi: A Biography*, trans. Eve Marie Cooper, 2nd Edition revised and augmented by Ignatius Brady and Raphael Brown (Chicago: Franciscan Herald Press, 1965), 405-406.

c. In contrast with 1C, Thomas now accents baptismal grace as operating within Francis from the very beginning. His baptismal name of *John* is actually more significant because it identifies this grace as prophetic.

This woman was
a friend of all complete integrity,
with some of the virtue of Saint *Elizabeth,*
of whom we read in Scripture,
she was privileged to resemble and act,
Lk 1:57-63 both in the *name* she gave her *son*
and in her prophetic spirit.[a]
For when her neighbors were admiring 1C 2; L3C 2
Francis's greatness of spirit and integrity of conduct
she asked them,
as if prompted by divine premonition,
Lk 1:66 *"What do you think* this **son of mine** *will become?*[b] L3C 2
You will see
Mt 5:9, Lk 20:36 that he shall merit to become a *son of God!"*
In fact this was the opinion of many,
whom Francis pleased, by his very fine efforts, as he grew older.
He completely rejected
anything that could sound insulting to anyone.
No one felt a young man of such noble manners
could be born of the stock
of those who were called his parents.

The name *John,*
refers to the mission which he received;[c]
the name *Francis*
to the spread of his fame which quickly reached everywhere,
once his turning to God was complete.[d]
Thus,
he used to keep the feast of John the Baptist
more solemnly than the feasts of all other saints,
because the dignity of this name

a. In 1C 13, Francis's mother tried by "gentle words" to dissuade "her son from his intention," and, although unsuccessful, she "broke his chains and let him go free." In this text, Francis's mother is much more positive about his call. She is thus presented in the classical role of a saint's mother, e.g. the mothers of Saints Bernard and Dominic.

b. In this text, as in AP, L3C, AC, paragraphs paralleling earlier texts are indicated in the margins by a reference to the text. Where a verbal dependence on an earlier text is present, the text is emboldened and the reference is found in the margin.

c. The Hebrew name *John* was translated by Saint Jerome as *"the grace of the Lord,"* or *"grace is his."* In this context, Thomas sees his baptismal name as referring to Francis's prophetic mission. Cf. Jerome, *Liber de Interpretatione de Nominibus Hebraicis* 8,7; 9:25; *Corpus Christianorum Latinum* 3, 1972, 20.

d. For an understanding of the name *Francis,* see 1C 120, as well as FA:ED I 290 b.

marked him with a trace of mystical power.[a]
This observation is worthy of note:
among all those born of women Mt 11:11
there has never been one greater than John
and among all the founders of religious communities
there has never been one more perfect than Francis.

[4]John
prophesied enclosed within the hidden confines
of his mother's womb. Lk 1:41
Francis,
still unaware of God's guidance
foretold things to come
while held in an earthly prison.

L3C 4 Once there was a great massacre in a war between the citizens of Perugia and Assisi.[b] Francis was captured along with many others, and, chained with the rest of them, endured the squalor of prison. His fellow captives were overcome with sadness, weeping bitterly over the fact of their imprisonment, but Francis *rejoiced in the Lord,* Ps 35:9 laughing and making fun of his chains. His unhappy companions rebuked him as he reveled in his chains, and thought he was out of his mind. Francis answered them prophetically: "What do you think makes me so happy? I'm thinking about something else: some day **the whole world will worship me** as a saint!" And now that is true; everything he said has been fulfilled.

L3C 4 Among the others who were then imprisoned with him there was an arrogant and utterly unbearable knight. Everyone else decided to avoid him but he could not wear down Francis's patience; he tolerated the intolerable man and restored the others to peace with him.

What a *chosen vessel of all virtues;* Sir 24:25; Acts 9:15
able to contain *every grace*!
Already he pours out charisms in all directions!

a. The frequent use of the adverb *iam* [already] and expressions such as *ab initio* [from the beginning] indicate important differences between Thomas's portrayals of Francis's conversion. In 1C, the conversion moves gradually with numerous new beginnings, but in 2C his conversion moves decisively from one beginning. Thomas not only highlights the prophetic dimension of Francis's baptismal name, but also the "mystical power" associated with it.

b. For background information on the war between Assisi and Perugia see L3C 4, supra, 69 a.

Chapter II
HOW HE CLOTHED A POOR KNIGHT
AND HOW HE SAW A VISION OF HIS CALLING WHILE STILL IN THE WORLD

5After a short time
freed from his chains,
he became more generous to the needy.
Already he resolved 1C 17; L3C 3
Tb 4:7; Sir 4:5 never to *turn his face away from any poor person*
who asked anything "for the love of God."

One day he met a poor, half-naked knight, and moved by piety, for love of Christ, he generously gave him the finely tailored clothes he was wearing. Did he do any less than the great Saint Martin?[a] They did the same thing, with the same purpose, though in different ways.

Francis first gave away his clothes,
then everything else;
Martin gave away everything else[b]
and then gave away his clothes.
Is 16:14 Both lived *poor and humble* in this world
and both *entered heaven rich.*[c]
Martin was poor, but a knight,
and clothed a poor man with part of his clothes.
Francis was rich, but not a knight, L3C 6
and he clothed a poor knight with all of his clothes.
Both of them,

---

a. Cf. Sulpicius Severus describes the generosity of Saint Martin of Tours (+397) in the following manner: "Accordingly, at a certain period, when he had nothing except his arms and his simple military dress, in the middle of winter, . . . he happened to meet at the gate of Amiens a poor man destitute of clothing. . . . He had nothing except the cloak in which he was clad, for he had already parted with the rest of his garments for similar purposes. Taking, his sword therefore he cut his cloak into two equal parts, and gave one part to the poor man, while he again clothed himself with the remainder." *The Life of Martin* 3. [This and other quotations from *The Life of Martin* and from the *Letters* have been taken from: "The Works of Sulpicius Severus," translated with Preface and Notes by Alexander Roberts, in *A Select Library of Nicene and Post-Nicene Fathers of the Christian Church*, Second Series, Volume XI, (New York: The Christian Literature Company, 1894).]

b. Sulpicius Severus, *Life of Martin* 3: "He had nothing except the cloak in which he was clad, for he had already parted with the rest of his garments for similar purposes."

c. Sulpicius Severus, *Letter III*: "Martin, poor and insignificant on earth, has a rich entrance granted him into heaven." This famous phrase, *pauper et humilis caelum dives ingreditur* [poor and humble he entered heaven rich] appears twice in the Office of Saint Martin. See Responsory VIII at Matins and Antiphon V at Lauds. With a change of name, it is also used for the Alleluia verse in a Mass of Saint Francis. See *Second Mass*, Gradual versicle as found in the Liturgical Texts, cf. FA:ED I 349.

having carried out Christ's command[a]
1C 5 deserved to be visited by Christ in a vision.[b]
Martin was praised for his perfection
and Francis was graciously invited to what was still missing.

1C 5, 7; LJS 3; AP 5; L3C 5

[6] A little later, he saw in a vision a beautiful palace, and there he saw various suits of armor and a lovely bride.[c] In that same dream Francis was *called by name* and was attracted by the promise of all these things. He therefore tried to go to Apulia[d] in order to gain knighthood, and richly outfitted, he hastened to achieve the honors of knightly rank. The spirit of the flesh prompted him to give an interpretation of the flesh to the vision. In fact, in the *treasury of God's wisdom* something even more magnificent was hidden there. Gn 4:17 Col 2:2-3

AP 6; //L3C 6

As he slept one night, someone spoke to him a second time in a vision and asked him with concern where he was going. He explained his plan and said he was going to Apulia to become a knight. The other *questioned him anxiously* **"Who can do more for you, the servant or the lord?" "The lord!"** said Francis. "Then why do you seek **the servant** instead **of the lord?"** Francis then asked: **"Lord, what do you want me to do?"** And the Lord said to him: **"Go back to the land** *of your birth* because I will fulfill your dream in a spiritual way." Lk 7:4 Acts 9:6 Gn 32:9

He turned back without delay
becoming even now *a model* of obedience. 1 Pt 5:3
Giving up his own will
he changed from Saul to Paul.
Paul was thrown to the ground
and his stinging lashes bore fruit in soothing words;[e]

---

a. This text emphasizes Christ's *mandatum* [command], a word used thirteen times in 2C, while it is used only four times in 1C. Moreover, Francis is "called by name" in this text. Thus Francis's conversion is connected to his encounter with Christ. This differs from 1C in which more emphasis is placed on the initiative of Francis's *propositum* [proposal], a word that appears twenty-two times in that earlier text and only eight times in 2C. On *propositum*, see FA:ED I 189 d.

b. Sulpicius Severus, *The Life of Martin* 3: "In the following night, when Martin had resigned himself to sleep, he had a vision of Christ arrayed in that part of his cloak with which he had clothed the poor man. . . . After this vision the sainted man was not puffed up with human glory, but, acknowledging the goodness of God in what had been done, and being now of the age of twenty years, he hastened to receive baptism." In this text Thomas puts more emphasis on knighthood, a theme also found in AP 6 and L3C 5.

c. Thomas builds on information supplied by the Three Companions (cf. L3C 5) which introduces the presence of a bride into the dream. In doing so, he introduces the theme of an espousal that he accentuates in describing Francis's commitment to Lady Poverty. This theme was quite prominent in the spiritual literature of the time, cf. Jean Leclercq, *Monks and Love in Twelfth-Century France: Psycho-Historical Essays* (Oxford: Oxford at The Clarendon Press, 1979); and Ann W. Astell, *The Song of Songs in the Middle Ages* (Ithaca and London: Cornell University Press, 1990), 73-104.

d. For information on Apulia, see FA:ED I 185 d.

e. A word play: *verbera dura verba dulcia* [stinging lashes . . . soothing words].

while Francis turned his fleshly weapons into spiritual ones,
and, instead of knightly glory,
received a divine rank.[a]
To the many who marveled at his unusual joy, L3C 5
he said that he was going **to become a great prince.**

Chapter III
How a crowd of young people chose him as their lord so that he would feed them, and how he changed.

Eph 4:13 [7]He started to change into the *perfect man,*
and became a different person.[b]
When he returned home,
Ez 23:17 the *sons of Babylon* followed him,
and dragged him, though unwilling, in one direction
while he was heading in another.

Earlier he had been the ringleader of Assisi's frivolous young 1C 2; L3C 7
crowd. They still invited him to their dinner parties, in which the
suggestive and vulgar were always served. They chose him as their
leader, since they had often experienced his generosity, and knew for
sure he would pay all their expenses. They made themselves obedi-
Lk 15:16 ent so they could *fill* their *bellies,* and made themselves subject so they
could gorge themselves. Not wanting to seem stingy, Francis did not
reject the honor. Even while meditating on sacred things, he maintained his courtly manners. He set out a sumptuous dinner, with
Is 28:8; Prv 26:11 double portions of the most elegant food, and *stuffed to the point of*
Gn 10:11 *vomiting,* they dirtied *the streets of the town* with their drunken songs.
Gn 38:18; Ex 12:11 As their lord, *bearing a staff in his hands,* Francis followed them. But
gradually he withdrew bodily as he had already mentally turned deaf
1 Chr 23:30 to those things, while he *sang to the Lord* in his heart.

So much divine sweetness poured over him—as he later re- L3C 7
counted—that he was struck dumb and could not move. A burst of
spiritual energy rushed through him, snatching him into the un-

a. The Latin reads: *divinum praesidatum* [a divine rank], the only time the word *praesidatum* appears in the works of Thomas of Celano. It may be interpreted as Francis's becoming a feudal lord over a conquered territory, that is, over himself.

b. In 2C 6 Francis is "changed from Saul to Paul." In this passage, another change is highlighted, i.e. into "the perfect man." All of these transformations lead to the "mysterious change" that occurs in Francis in 2C 10.

seen.[a] It was so powerful it made him consider earthly things unimportant and utterly worthless.

What amazing generosity of Christ!
To those who do small things
He *gives the greatest gifts.* 2 Pt 1:4
In the flood of many waters Ps 32:6
He *saves* and lifts up *His own.* Jn 17:10-12
Christ *feeds the crowds with loaves and fishes* Mt 14:15-21; Mk 6:33-44; Lk 9:12-17; Jn 6:5-13
and does not drive away sinners from his table.
When they *seek to make him king,* Mt 9:10-13; Lk 5:29-32, 15:2
He flees and *goes up the mountain to pray.* Mt 14:23; Jn 6:15
These are *mysteries of God* toward which Francis reaches, Col 2:2
and he is lead to unknowingly *perfect knowledge.* Jb 22:2

Chapter IV

How he dressed in poor garments and ate with the poor in front of the church of Saint Peter, and the gift he offered there

[8]Already he was an outstanding lover of the poor
and his sacred beginning gave a glimpse
of what would be fulfilled in the future.
He often stripped himself to clothe the poor.
Although he had not yet made himself one of them
he strove to be like them with his *whole heart.* Mt 22:37; Lk 10:27

L3C 10 Once on pilgrimage to Rome, out of love for poverty he took off his fine clothing and dressed himself in a poor man's clothes. He happily settled among the poor in the square in front of the church of Saint Peter, a place where the poor are abundant. Considering himself one of them, he eagerly ate with them. If his embarrassed friends had not restrained him, he would have done this many times.

L3C 10 When he approached the altar of the Prince of the Apostles, he was surprised that people gave such small gifts. He threw in a whole handful of money, showing that the one God honored above others should be honored by all in a special way.

st 6-10; L3C 8, 57 Showing *due honor,* he often gave liturgical vestments to poor priests, even to those of the lowest rank. Rom 13:7

a. The Latin text *sed ipsum ad invisibilia raptans* is an allusion to the Preface of Christmas: "In him we see our God made visible and so are caught up in the love of the God we cannot see."

As he was to be entrusted 1C 33, 36, 43; LJS 28, 46
with the mission of an apostle, Off Vesp 1 1
he was completely Catholic in faith.
From the very beginning
he was full of reverence
for God's ministers and ministries.

Chapter V
How the Devil Showed Him a Woman While He Was Praying and the Answer Which God Gave Him, and What He Did for Lepers

[9]Under his worldly clothing
he wore a religious spirit;
leaving public places
he sought places of solitude,
where he was often instructed by visits of the Holy Spirit.
He was drawn away,
lured by that remarkable delight
that from the very beginning flowed over him abundantly
and never left him as long as he lived.

As he began to visit hidden places conducive to prayer, the devil 1C 6; LJS 4
struggled to drive him away with an evil trick. He made Francis think L3C 12
of a horribly hunchbacked woman who lived in town and whose looks scared everyone. The devil threatened that he would become like her if
Eph 6:10 he did not turn back sensibly from what he had begun. But, *strengthened by the Lord,* he rejoiced at a response of healing and grace. "Fran-
Mt 22:43 cis," God said to him *in spirit* "you have traded what you loved in a
Prv 27:7 fleshly, empty way for things of the spirit, *taking the bitter for the sweet*. If you want to come to know Me, despise yourself. For when the order is reversed, the things I say will taste sweet to you even though they seem the opposite." He was moved to obey immediately the divine command, and was led through experience to the truth of these things.

Among all the awful miseries of this world Francis had a natural horror of lepers, and one day as he was riding his horse near Assisi he 1C 17; LJS12; L3
met a leper on the road. He felt terrified and revolted, but not wanting to transgress God's command and break the sacrament[a] of His word, he dismounted from his horse and ran to kiss him. As the leper
Est 8:4; Acts 3:5; Gn 43:21 *stretched out his hand, expecting something,* he *received* both *money* and a

a. The Latin text reads *sacramentum* [sacrament], a word that appears fourteen times in Thomas's portraits of Francis and with a variety of meanings. At times it refers to the stigmata (1C 90, 114; 2C 203), to the Eucharist (2C 185, 201; 3C 28, 40), and, at other times, to actions or deeds containing a deeper symbolic meaning as in this instance (2C 9, 68, 126).

kiss. Francis immediately *mounted his horse* and although the field Ps 75:7
was wide open, without any obstructions, when he looked around he
could not see the leper anywhere.[a]

Filled with joy and wonder at this event, 2 Cor 7:4
within a few days he deliberately tried to do something similar.
1C 17 He made his way to the houses of the lepers[b]
and, giving money to each,
he also *gave a kiss on the hand* and mouth. Sir 29:5
Test 3; L3C 11 Thus he *took the bitter for the sweet* Prv 27:7
and courageously prepared to carry out the rest.

Chapter VI

THE IMAGE OF THE CRUCIFIED WHICH SPOKE TO HIM, AND THE HONOR THAT HE GAVE TO IT.

1C 6 [10]With his heart already completely changed—soon his body was
3,9; LJS 6; L3C 13 also to be changed—**he was walking** one day **by the church of San**
Damiano,[c] which was abandoned by everyone and almost in ruins.
Led by the Spirit he went in to pray and knelt down devoutly before the Mt 4:1
crucifix. He was shaken by unusual experiences and discovered that
he was different from when he had entered. As soon as he had this
feeling, there occurred *something unheard of in previous ages*: with the Jn 9:32
lips of the painting, **the image of** Christ **crucified spoke to him.**
"Francis," it said, *calling him by name*, **"go rebuild My house;** as you Is 40:26
see, **it is** all being **destroyed."** Francis was more than a little stunned,
trembling, and stuttering like a man out of his senses. He prepared
himself to obey and pulled himself together to carry out the command. He felt this mysterious change in himself, but he could not de-
L3C 14 scribe it. So it is better for us to remain silent about it too. From that
time on, compassion for the Crucified was impressed into his holy
soul. And we honestly believe the wounds of the sacred Passion were
impressed deep in his heart, though not yet on his flesh.

[11]What an admirable thing,
unheard of in earlier ages! Jn 9:32
Who would not be amazed at this?
Who ever heard of anything like it?

a. Gregory the Great relates the story of the monk Martirio (or Martino) who carried Christ, disguised as a leper, on his shoulders. When the monk tries to detain him, he disappears. Cf. Gregory the Great, *Homilia in Evangelium* II, 39: 10 (PL 76: 1300).

b. See FA:ED I 195 b for information on the leper colonies of Assisi during Francis's time.

c. For background on the church of San Damiano, see FA:ED I 189 b.

Who could ever doubt that Francis,
as he returned to his homeland,
already appeared crucified?
Christ spoke to him from the wood of the cross
in a new and unheard of miracle,[a]
even when to all appearances,
he had not yet completely forsaken the world.
From that very hour
Sg 5:6 his *soul melted*
as the Beloved spoke to him.
A little while afterward 1C 94, 95
his heart's love
showed in the wounds of his body.

From then on, he could not hold back his tears, even weeping loudly over the Passion of Christ, as if it were constantly before his eyes. He filled the roads with his sobbing, and, as he remembered the wounds of Christ, he would take no comfort. Once, upon meeting a close friend, he explained the reason for this sorrow, moving him also to bitter tears. LCh 10; L3C 14; A

He does not forget to care for that holy image
nor hesitate to carry out the command. L3C 13
Lk 19:15 He *gives* the priest *money* to buy a lamp and some oil,
lest the sacred image lack, even for a moment, the honor of light.
He then runs quickly to fulfill the rest, 1C 18; LJS 13; L3
working tirelessly to rebuild that church.
Gn 15:1 Although *the divine word spoken* to him
was really about that Church
Acts 20:28 *which* Christ *acquired with* His own *blood*,[b]
he did not immediately reach that level,
Rom 8:9 but moved gradually *from flesh to spirit*.

a. In 2C 11 Christ's speaking to Francis from the cross is described as an "unheard-of miracle." In 1C 112 Thomas writes of the stigmata as "a new miracle." This is an example of how references in 1C to later events in Francis's life are linked to earlier events in 2C.

b. Another example of Thomas's developing ecclesiology and theology of renewal that permeate his writings. Cf. Regis J. Armstrong, "Clare of Assisi, The Poor Ladies, and Their Ecclesial Mission in the *First Life* of Thomas of Celano," GR 5:3 (1991): 389-424.

Chapter VII

HOW HIS FATHER AND HIS BROTHER IN THE FLESH PERSECUTED HIM.

1C 10, 12; LJS 7, 8 [12]But, now that he was set upon *works of piety,* his father in the 1 Tm 2:10
flesh began to persecute him. *Judging it madness* to be a servant of Wis 5:4
AP 9; L3C 23 Christ, he would lash out at him with curses wherever he went. The
servant of God then called a lowly, rather simple man to help him.
Substituting him for his father, he asked him for a blessing whenever his father cursed him. He turned into deeds the words of the
prophet, revealing the meaning of that verse: *Let them curse; you give* Ps 109:28
your blessing.

1C 14-15; LJS 9; AP 8; L3C 19 The *man of God* gave back to his father the money he wanted to 1 Kgs 3:1
spend for work on the church. He did this on the advice of the bishop
of the town,[a] a very devout man, because it was wrong to spend
L3C 20 ill-gotten gain for sacred purposes.[b] Within earshot of *many who had* Acts 10:27
gathered about, he declared: *"From now on I will say* freely:[c] ***'Our Father*** Jn 13:19; Mt 6:9
who art in heaven', **and not 'My father, Pietro di Bernardone.'** Look,
not only do I return his money; I give him back all my clothes. I will
L3C 21 go to the Lord naked."

Oh how free is the heart of a man for whom Christ is already Phil 3:8; 1:21
enough!

L3C 20 **The *man of God* was found to be wearing a hair shirt under his** 1 Sm 2:27
clothes, rejoicing in the reality of virtue rather than in its appearance.

His brother in the flesh, just like his father, hounded him with
L3C 23 poisoned words.[d] One winter's morning, when he saw Francis praying, covered with pitiful rags and shivering with cold, that wicked
man said to a neighbor: "Tell Francis that now he should be able to
sell you a penny's worth of sweat!" When the *man of God* heard this, 1 Sm 2:27
he was very happy, and answered with a smile: "Actually, **I'll sell it**
at a higher price to my Lord!"

Nothing could have been closer to the truth!
He not only *received*
a hundredfold in this life,
but even a thousand times more,

a. For information concerning the bishop of Assisi, Bishop Guido II, see AP 17, supra, 41 d.

b. Cf. Gratian, *Decretum, C.* 14, q. 5, c. 1-5. Thomas's statement can be taken in two ways. (a) Francis should not use for sacred purposes what he has taken from his father without his consent; or, (b) Francis should not dedicate to a sacred purpose money that his father had acquired by cheating customers and sharp business practice. In either case, it is tainted money.

c. Thomas adds *libere* [freely] to this phrase, which he omits in 1C 15, prompting some to speculate that he echoes his description of Francis as *liber et liberalis* [free and freeing] found in 1C 120.

d. Cf. L3C 23, supra 83 a.

Mt 19:29 and in the world to come *eternal life*
not only for himself,
but also for many others.

Chapter VIII
HOW HE OVERCAME FEELINGS OF SHAME, AND HIS PROPHECY ABOUT THE POOR VIRGINS

13 He struggled to turn his earlier, luxurious way of life in a different direction, and to lead his unruly body back to its natural good-
1 Sm 2:27 ness.[a] One day the *man of God* was going through Assisi begging oil to L3C 24
fill the lamps in the church of San Damiano, which he was then rebuilding. He saw a crowd carousing by the house he intended to enter. Turning bright red, he backed away. But then, turning his noble
Jas 3:1 spirit toward heaven, he rebuked his cowardice and *called himself to*
account. He went back immediately to the house, and frankly ex-
Jer 23:9; Acts 2:13, 15 plained to all of them what had made him ashamed. Then, *as if drunk*
in the Spirit,[b] he spoke in French, and asked for oil, and he got it.[c] He 1C 18; LJS 13
Gn 23:10 fervently encouraged everyone to help repair that church, and *in front*
of everyone he cried out in French that some day that place would be a L3C 24
monastery of Christ's holy virgins.[d]

Whenever he was
Is 4:4 filled with *the fire of the* Holy *Spirit*
he would speak in French,
Ps 45:1 *bursting out in* fiery *words,*
for he could foresee
that he would be honored
with special reverence by that people.

---

a. In this passage Thomas accents a theme found in Athanasius's *Life of Anthony* 20, that the return to natural goodness highlighted that the Lord "may recognize his work as being just the same as he made it." Athanasius, *Life of Anthony and The Letter to Marcellinus*, translation and introduction by Robert C. Gregg, preface by William A. Clebsch (New York, Ramsey, Toronto: Paulist Press, 1980), 47.

b. See the Ambrosian hymn *Splendor Paternae Gloriae*, for Monday Lauds in the Roman Office: *laeti bibamus sobriam ebrietatem Spiritus* [as joyful people, let us drink the sober drunkenness of the Spirit].

c. For the use of French see FA:ED I 194 b. Although this incident is found in L3C 24, Thomas emphasizes the role of the Holy Spirit in prompting Francis to burst into French.

d. Curiously, Clare's *Testament* refers to this same prophecy of Francis, but suggests that it was already a monastery. Cf. Clare, *Testament* 13 in *Clare of Assisi: Early Documents*.

Chapter IX

HOW HE BEGGED FOOD FROM DOOR TO DOOR.

14Once he began serving
the common Lord of all,
he loved doing what was common,
and avoided singularity in everything,
which reeks of every vice.[a]

He continued the sweaty work of repairing that church as Christ had commanded him, and from being over-delicate he changed into
L3C 22 a rough and work-worn man. The priest who had that church saw him worn out with constant labor and, moved to piety, began to serve him each day some of his own food, although nothing very tasty, since he was poor. Francis appreciated the priest's concern and welcomed his kindness, but said to himself: **"You won't find a priest** like this everywhere, always bringing you food! **This is not the life for someone** professing **poverty;**[b] you'd better not get used to this, or you'll slowly return to what you've rejected, and you'll drift back to your easy ways! Get up, stop being lazy, and beg scraps from door to door!"

L3C 22 **He went** through Assisi **begging** leftovers **from door to door.** When he saw his bowl filled with all kinds of scraps, he was at first
struck with revulsion; but he *remembered God* and, overcoming himself, Jb 7:4; Ps 77:4
ate it with spiritual relish.

Love softens all,[c]
st 3; L3C 11; 2C 9 and changes the bitter to sweet.

Chapter X

HOW BROTHER BERNARD GAVE AWAY HIS PROPERTY

1C 24; L3C 27 15Bernard from the town of Assisi, who later became a son of perfection, planned to reject the world perfectly, thanks to the example

a. *Singularitas* [singularity] is difficult to translate. In Thomas's use, it means being eccentric or odd, behaving in a way that draws attention to one's self. It does not speak against being an individual, as much as addressing individualism. It appears again in this text as a vice to be avoided, cf. 2C 14, 28, 29, 144, 162. It is a word that frequently appears in monastic writings in both positive and negative senses, cf. Jean Leclercq, *Études sur Le Vocabulaire Monastique du Moyen Âge* (Rome: Herder, 1961).

b. This is the first time that this specific, more canonical phrase, *paupertatem profitens* [professing poverty], is applied to Francis in the literature, and suggests a shift in emphasis from the practice of a virtue to a more canonical or juridical sense.

c. This echoes, by way of antithesis, the saying of Vergil: *Omnia vincit amor.* [Love conquers all], cf. Vergil, *Ecologues* X: 69.

1 Sm 2:27 of the *man of God*.[a] He humbly sought advice: "Father, **if someone** L3C 28
had held a certain lord's possessions for a long time, and **no longer**
1 Sm 2:27 **wishes to keep them, what would be** the best thing to do?" The *man*
of God replied that all those things should be returned to the lord who
gave them. Bernard said to him: "I know that everything I have was
Rom 15:15 *given to me by God* and on your advice I am now ready to return all to
Him." The saint replied: "If you want to prove your words with
deeds, let us go into the church tomorrow at dawn, take up the Gos-
Mt 27:1 pel Book, and seek the counsel of Christ." *When morning had broken* AP 10; AP 11; L3C
they went into the church and, after preparing with a devout prayer,
2 Chr 10:6 **they opened the book of** the Gospel, ready to act on **whatever coun-**
sel should first come to them. When they opened the book, **Christ** 1C 24,92,93
Mt 9:21 **openly** gave them His counsel: *If you wish to be perfect, go and sell* **all**
you own, and give to the poor.[b]

Lk 9:3 They repeated this **a second time, and found:** *Take nothing for your*
Lk 9:23; Mt 16:24 *journey*. They tried **a third time,** and found: *If anyone would follow me,*
let him deny himself. Bernard immediately carried out all these things,
without neglecting a single iota of this counsel. In a short time, many Off Vesp I IV
turned away from the weary cares of the world toward an infinite
Gn 30:25 Good, *returning to their homeland* with Francis as their guide. It would
Phil 3:14 take too long to describe how each of them attained *the prize of their*
heavenly calling.

Chapter XI

HOW HE TOLD A PARABLE IN THE PRESENCE OF THE LORD POPE

16 When he presented himself and his followers before Pope Innocent to request a rule for his life,[c] it seemed to the pope that their proposal for a way of life was beyond their strength. A man of great discernment, he said to Francis: "My son, pray to Christ that through you he may show us his will, so that, once we know it, we may confidently approve your holy desire." The saint accepted the command of the supreme shepherd and hurried to Christ. He prayed intently, and devoutly exhorted his companions to appeal to God. 1C 32-33; //LJS 2

a. Cf. FA:ED I 203 d.

b. The AP 10, L3C 28 describe two men going with Francis to consult the Gospels, Bernard and Peter. In this text, Thomas mentions only Bernard that underscores his role as the first-born and the exemplar of the brothers.

c. The Latin text, *ad petendam regulam* [to seek a rule], refers to seeking recognition or approval of his proposal. *Regula* [rule] in this context does not refer to either the *Earlier Rule* or the *Later Rule*. Furthermore, Francis is not asking for a rule as much as a ruling on his proposal.

Acts 13:26; Mt 13:3

What next? In praying, the answer came to him and he told his sons the *news of salvation*. Thus, Christ's familiar speaking *in parables* is recognizable.[a]

AP 35; //L3C 50

"Francis," He said, "say this to the pope: 'Once upon a **time there was a poor but lovely woman who lived in a desert. A king** fell in love with her because of her great **beauty;** he gladly betrothed her and with her had lovely children. When they had grown up, having been nobly raised, their mother said: **"Dear children, do not be ashamed** because you are poor, for **you are all children of a great king. Go** joyfully **to his court,** and ask him **for what you need."** Hearing this they were amazed and overjoyed. At the thought of being royalty, their spirits were lifted. Knowing they would be the king's heirs, *they reckoned* all their poverty *riches*. They presented themselves boldly to the king: they were not afraid to look at him since they bore his very image. When the king saw **his likeness in them,** he was surprised, and asked whose sons they might be. When they said they were **the children of the poor woman who lived in the desert, the king embraced them. "You are my** *heirs,*" he said, "*and my sons; have no fear!* **If strangers are fed at my table,** it is only right that I feed you; for by law my whole inheritance belongs to you." **The king then sent orders to the woman to send all his sons to be fed at his court.'"** This parable made the saint happy, and he promptly reported this holy message to the pope.[b]

Tb 5:25

Rom 8:17; Mt 14:27; 17:7

1C 36, 37

17 Francis himself was this woman, not because he was soft in his deeds,[c] but because he was fruitful and bore many children. The desert was the world, which was then wild and sterile, with no teaching of virtue. The many beautiful children were the large number of brothers, *clothed with* every *virtue*. The king was the Son of God, whom they resemble by their holy poverty. They were fed *from the king's table,* refusing to be ashamed of their lowliness, when, in imita-

2 Mc 3:26

Dn 1:8

a. The story or "exemplum" of Odo of Cheriton in 1219 is similar to this story, as it is to AP 34. Each instance, however, has its own nuances, prompting scholars to suggest that the story was passed by word of mouth and adapted to fit the circumstances in which it is told. Cf. FA:ED I 590-591; AP 34, infra p. 50; Jacques Dalarun, *La Malavventura di Francesco d'Assisi* (Milano: Edizioni Biblioteca Francescana, 1996), 61-63.

b. Cf. AP 35, supra 50 b.

c. The Latin reads: *non factorum mollitie* [not soft in deeds]. Isidore of Seville (+636) taught in *Etymologies*, XI:2,18, *Mulier a mollitie, tamquam mollier, detracta littera . . . appellatur est* [Woman is taken from the word softness, as she is called soft]; and *Etymologies* X, 180 *Mollis . . . quasi mulier molliatur* [Woman as if a woman were softened]. In light of this, Thomas does a word play: *mulier . . . mollitie*.

tion of Christ,[a] they were content to live on alms and realized that because of the world's contempt they would be blessed.

Mt 13:24 The lord pope was amazed at *the parable presented* to him, and recognized without a doubt that Christ *had spoken in* this *man*. He remembered a vision he had seen only a *few days earlier*, and *instructed by the Holy Spirit*, he now believed it would come true in this man. *He saw in a dream* the Lateran basilica almost ready to fall down. A religious man, *small and scorned*, was propping it up with his own bent back so it would not fall.[b] "I'm sure," he said, "he is the one who will hold up Christ's Church by what he does and what he teaches!" Because of this the lord pope easily bowed to his request; from then on, filled with devotion to God, he always loved *Christ's servant* with a special love.[c] He quickly granted what was asked and promised even more. L3C 51

Acts 23:9; Acts 25:13; Lk 12:12; Gn 28:12; Is 16:14; 53:3; Rom 1:1; Jas 8:31; 1C 33; L3C 49

Mt 9:35 Visiting *towns and villages*, 1C 62
Francis began, with the authority now granted him,
to preach passionately
and to scatter the seeds of virtue.

Chapter XII
Saint Mary of the Portiuncula
How the Saint Loved This Place, How the Brothers Lived There, and How the Blessed Virgin Loved It

2 Chr 29:9 18Francis, *the servant of God*,
Is 16:14; Mt 11:29; Lk 9:48 was *small* in stature, 1C 83
humble in attitude,
and *lesser* by profession.
While living in the world 1C 38; AC 56
Jn 15:19 he *chose* a little portion *of the world*

a. The Latin text reads: *in imitatione Christi*, the only reference to this theme of spirituality found in the writings of Thomas of Celano. In 1C 25, Francis is described as "an imitator of those whom the Jewish leaders considered ignorant and without learning." In 2C 109 Sylvester becomes "a perfect imitator of the man of God," i.e. Francis. For its importance, see Alfonso Marini, "'*Vestigia Christi Sequi*' or '*Imitatio Christi*': Two Different Ways of Understanding Francis of Assisi's Gospel Life," GR 11:3 (1997), 331-358. For development of this Christological theme in Thomas, see Duane Lapsanski, *Evangelical Perfection: An Historical Examination of the Concept in the Early Franciscan Sources* (St. Bonaventure, NY: Franciscan Institute Publications, 1977), 103-105; 135-138.

b. The Latin text, *proprio dorso submisso, ne caderet, sustentabat* [propping it up with his own bent back so it would not fall], includes the notion of submission in order to hold up. In the next sentence, the pope bows to Francis's request. Compare 1C 33 where Thomas writes that Innocent, "a very high and lofty tree in the world, bent himself so kindly to his wish and request."

c. See L3C 51, supra, 97 a. The Quaracchi editors note that in Thomas's text, there is an addition to the Dominican text that Francis is "small and scorned" and will hold up the Church "by what he does and by what he teaches." Cf. AF X 141, note 8.

for himself and his followers,
since he could not serve Christ
unless he had something of this world.
1C 21,22; LJS 14 Since ancient times, prophetically,
this place was called "the Little Portion,"[a]
since it was the *lot ceded* Jos 17:8
to those who wished to hold nothing of this world.
In this place
there was a church built for the Virgin Mother,
who by her unique *humility* Lk 1:48
deserved, after her Son, to be the head of all the saints.
1C 44, 57 It is here the Order of Lesser Ones
had its beginning.
As their numbers increased,
there "a noble structure arose
1C 38 *upon* their solid *foundation.*" Eph 2:20-21
The saint loved this place more than any other.[b]
1C 106; LJS 68 He commanded his brothers
to venerate it with special reverence.
He wanted it, like a mirror of the Order,[c]
always preserved in humility and *highest poverty,* 2 Cor 8:2
and therefore kept its ownership in the hands of others,
keeping for himself and his brothers only the use of it.[d]

1C 39-41; 51-54 [19]There the most rigid discipline was kept in all things: as much in silence and in labor as in other religious observances.[e] The entrance there was not open except to specially selected brothers, gathered from every region, whom the saint wanted to be truly devoted to God and perfect in every respect. Similarly, entrance was completely

a. Cf. FA:ED I 201b; AC 56.

b. This description of the Portiuncula is first found in L3C 13, "this is the place which the glorious Virgin loved more than any other church in the world." A similar passage is also found in AC 56. In this passage, however, it is Francis, not the Virgin, who loves the church more than any other.

c. The use of *speculum* [mirror] is significant. Medieval authors saw the mirror as signifying a tableau, a portrait, or a description upon which a bystander could gaze and receive information or norms for everyday life. In 1C 90, it is Francis who is identified as a mirror for those who wish to "learn all perfection." In this passage it is the Portiuncula that is placed as the mirror of the Gospel life. See Margo Schmidt, "Mirroir," *Dictionnaire de spiritualité ascétique et mystique, doctrine et histoire* XII (Paris: Beauchesne, 1986), 1290-1303; Ritamary Bradley, "Backgrounds of the Title *Speculum* in Medieval Literature," *Speculum* (1954): 100-115.

d. This paragraph reflects the later juridical vocabulary used by Pope Gregory IX in *Quo elongati* in 1230, which introduced the juridical distinction between "ownership" and "use," cf. FA:ED I 570-575. In another papal bull, *Ordinem Vestrum* (1245) of Innocent IV (1243-1254), the Pope assumed ownership of all moveable and immovable goods of the Order, except in those cases where the donors reserved the right of ownership explicitly to themselves, cf. infra 774-779.

e. This text focuses on rigorous discipline and, as such, introduces a theme more reflective of the tensions of the fraternity of the 1240's than that of 1210.

forbidden to any secular person. He did not want the brothers dwelling there—always kept below a certain number—to have their *ears itching* for worldly news and, interrupting their contemplation of heavenly things, to be dragged down to dealing with lower things by the talk of gossips. No one was allowed to speak *idle words* there, nor to repeat those spoken by others. And, if anyone happened to do this, punishment taught him to avoid *further harm* and not to repeat this *in the future. Day and night, without interruption,* those living in the place were engaged in the praises of God and, scented with a wonderful fragrance, they led the life of angels.[a] This was only right! According to the stories of the old neighbors, that church used to be called *by another name,* "Saint Mary of the Angels." As the blessed Father used to say, God revealed to him, that among all other churches built in her honor throughout the world, the blessed Virgin cherished that church *with special affection.* For that reason the saint also *loved it more than all others.*

2 Tm 4:3; Mt 12:36; 1 Sm 27:4; Eccl 4:13; Acts 12:5; 1 Thes 2:13; 5:17; Gn 48:7; L3C 56; 1 Pt 1:22; 2 Cor 12:13; Gn 37:4

Chapter XIII
A VISION

[20]Before his conversion, a brother dedicated to God had a vision about this church which is worth telling. He saw countless people sadly *stricken with blindness, on their knees* **in a circle around** this church, **with their faces raised to heaven.** All of them, with sobbing voices and *upraised hands,* were *crying out to God* begging for mercy and **light.** Then a great light came down from heaven and, diffusing itself through them, gave each the sight and health they desired.

L3C 56; Gn 19:11; 2 Chr 6:13; 2 Mc 14:34; Ps 55:17; 1C 106

THE WAY OF LIFE OF SAINT FRANCIS AND THE BROTHERS

Chapter XIV
THEIR STRICT DISCIPLINE

[21]The resolute *knight of Christ* never spared his body. As if it were a stranger to him, he exposed it to every kind of injury, whether in word or deed. If anyone tried to enumerate everything this man underwent, the list would be longer than that passage where the apostle recounts the tribulations of the saints.

2 Tm 2:3; AC 50; 2 Cor 11:23-29; Hb 11:33-38

a. For reference to "angelic life," cf. FA:ED I 273 a.

Those enrolled in that first school also subjected themselves to every discomfort. It was even considered criminal to seek any *consolation* Acts 9:31
1C 40 *except that of the spirit*. Wearing iron belts and breastplates they grew weak from constant *fasting* and *frequent vigils*. They would have 2 Cor 11:27
collapsed many times, were it not for their devoted shepherd's constant warnings that made them relax the rigors of their self-denial.

Chapter XV
THE DISCERNMENT OF SAINT FRANCIS[a]

AC 50 22 **One night** while all were sleeping, **one** of his flock **cried out:** "Brothers! **I'm dying! I'm dying** of hunger!" At once that extraordinary shepherd got up, and hurried to treat the sick lamb with the right medicine. He ordered them to set the table, although filled with everyday fare. Since there was no wine—as often happened—they made do with water. Francis started eating first. Then, he invited the rest of the brothers to do the same, for charity's sake, so their brother would not be embarrassed.

Once *they had taken their food in the fear of the Lord*, so that nothing Acts 2:46, 9:31
would be lacking in this act of charity, the father wove for his sons a long parable about the virtue of discernment. He ordered them to *season with salt every sacrifice to God*. With concern he reminded them that Lv 2:13
in offering *service to God each one should consider his own strength*. Jn 16:12

He insisted that it was just as much a sin to deprive the body without discernment of what it really needed as, prompted by gluttony, to offer it too much. And he added: "Dear brothers, realize that, what I just did by eating was not my own choice, but an exception,[b] demanded by fraternal charity. Let the charity, not the food, be an example for you, for the latter feeds the belly while the former feeds the spirit."

---

a. The Latin word *discretio* is translated as discernment. Benedicta Ward notes: "Since the eighteenth century, 'discretion' has been increasingly used in connection with good behavior, especially in speech, but earlier it was synonymous with 'discernment', both coming from *'discretio'* the Latin form of *'diakresis.'* " Cf. Benedicta Ward, "Discernment: A Rare Bird," in *The Way Supplement* 64 (1989): 10-18.

b. The Latin word *dispensatio* [*exception*] is used in a sense close to *epikeia*, exceptions to a rule that in itself is good.

Chapter XVI

How he foresaw the future and how he commended the Order to the Roman Church and of a vision he had

[23]As the holy father advanced in virtue and merit of life 1C 37, 89, 100
his large crop of children
increased everywhere in number and grace.
With an amazing abundance of fruit,
Ez 17:6,7; Ps 19:5 their *branches extended to the farthest ends of the earth*.

Ps 144:12 But he often worried about those *new plants*, how they could be
Eph 4:3 cared for and helped to grow, tied together in a *bond of unity*. He saw 1C 74
Mt 7:15; Lk 12:32; Dn 13:52 that many people howled *like wolves* at that *little flock*. Those *grown old in wickedness* would take every opportunity to hurt it just because it was new. He could foresee that even his sons might do things opposed to holy peace and unity. He feared that some might turn into
Col 2:18 rebels, as often happens among the chosen, *puffed up by their self-importance*, ready for battle and prone to scandals.

1 Kgs 13:1; Dn 10:7 [24]Mulling over these things, the *man of God saw this vision*. As he L3C 63
slept one night, **he saw a small black *hen*, similar to a common**
Mt 23:37; Lk 13:34 **dove, with feathered legs and feet.** She had countless *chicks*, and they kept running around her frantically, but she could not ***gather* all**
1 Kgs 13:1; Mt 1:24 **of them *under her wings*.** The *man of God woke up*, remembering his
Dn 8:27 concerns, *interpreted* his own *vision*. "**I am the hen,**" he said, "**small in size and dark by nature,** whose innocence of life should serve dove-like simplicity, which is as rare in this world as it is swift in flight **to heaven.** The chicks are the brothers, multiplied in number and grace. The strength of Francis is not enough to defend them
Ps 31:21 from *human plotting* and *contradicting tongues*.

"Therefore, I will go and entrust them to the holy Roman Church. L3C 63
Mt 5:9 The evil-minded will be struck down by the rod of her power. The *sons*
Col 2:19; Gal 4:31 *of God* will enjoy *complete freedom*, which will help to increase eternal salvation everywhere. From now on, let the children acknowledge their mother's sweet favor, and always follow her holy footprints
1 Kgs 5:4 with special devotion. With her protection, *nothing evil* will happen to
Dt 13:13; 1 Sm 2:12; 25:17; Is 5:17 the Order, and no *son of Belial* will trample the *vineyard of the Lord* unpunished. She, that holy one, will emulate the glory of our poverty and will prevent the praises of humility from being obscured by

clouds of pride. She will *preserve* intact among us the *bonds of charity* Col 3:14; Eph 4:3
and peace, striking dissidents with harsh punishments. In her sight the sacred observance of the purity of the Gospel will constantly flourish and she will not allow the *sweet fragrance of* their *life* to vanish 2 Cor 2:15
even *for an hour.*" Sir 33:9; 2 Cor 7:8

This was the saint's full intent in embracing this submission; this is precious proof of the man of God's foreknowledge of the need for this protection in the future.

Chapter XVII
How he asked for the lord of Ostia to be his own pope

[25]When the *man of God* came to Rome, the Lord Pope Honorius Jdgs 13:6
and all the cardinals received him with great respect. For what his reputation proclaimed shone forth in his life and resounded in his speech and, when he was present, there was no room for anything
1C 73; L3C 64 but devotion. With conviction and passion he preached before the pope and the cardinals, letting whatever the Spirit moved him to say
pour out from the *fullness* of his heart. Those *mountains were moved*[a] at Ps 45:2; Ps 18:8; Is 54:10
his words and, sighing *from the depths* they washed their *inner selves* Ps 130:1; Rom 7:22; Eph 3:16
with tears.

When he had finished preaching, he exchanged a few brief and
L3C 65 friendly words with the lord pope. Finally he made this request: "As you know, my lord, it is not easy for poor and unimportant men to gain access to such majesty. You hold the world in your hands, and the pressure of important business does not allow you time to look after little things. For this reason, my lord," he said," I beg your holiness to give us **the lord of Ostia as pope.** That way, **while always saving your preeminent dignity,** the brothers can turn to him *in their* Sir 8:12
hour of need, to benefit from his protection and direction."

1C 100; AP 45 The pope *looked with pleasure* on this holy request. He immediately 2 Kgs 10:30
set Lord Hugo, then bishop of Ostia, over the religion, as the *man of* Jdgs 13:6
AP 43 *God had requested.* That holy cardinal embraced the flock entrusted to

---

a. Medieval exegesis often interpreted the "mountains" as symbols of the apostles, e.g. Augustine, ". . . we understand the mountains to represent certain illustrious people, great spiritual men in the Church, people who are great because of their massive worth; they are the prophets, the evangelists, the good teachers." Augustine, *Exposition of Psalm 39,* 6; see also, *Exposition on Psalm 35, 9*; *Exposition on Psalm 45,* 6. Augustine, *Exposition on The Psalms,* translated by Maria Boulding (Hyde Park: New City Press, 2000).

him. He became its diligent foster father and, to the day of his blessed passing,[a] he remained both its shepherd and its foster child.

Because of this unique submission, the holy Roman Church never ceases to show its preferential love and concern for the Order of Lesser Ones.

Here ends the first book.

a. Cardinal Hugolino, Pope Gregory IX, died on August 22, 1241.

The Second Book

Introduction to the Second Book[a]

[26]To preserve the great deeds of ancestors for the remembrance of their children, gives honor to the former, and shows love in the latter. The ancestors, separated by the passage of time, offer their children a memorable witness. Those who did not know them in their bodily presence are at least spurred to do good by their deeds and encouraged to do better. The first benefit we receive—and a great one—is knowledge of our own smallness. We see their merits abound while ours can hardly be found.

1C 90 I consider blessed Francis the holiest *mirror* of the holiness of the
Lord,[b] the *image of his* perfection. I think everything about him, both Wis 7:26
his words and deeds, is fragrant with God's presence. Anyone who
studies them humbly and diligently, will quickly be filled with the
1C 91 teaching of salvation, ready for the saint's highest philosophy.

1C Prol I will recount a few things about him in a brief and simple style. I think it may be appropriate to mention a few of the many things that will honor the saint and rouse our dozing hearts.

Chapter I
The Spirit of Prophecy which Blessed Francis Possessed

[27]Elevated above what is of the world, our blessed father,
with a wonderful power,
had everything on earth subject to him.
His mind's eye was always fixed
on the highest Light.
1C 26-27 He not only knew by divine revelation what was going to happen
and foretold many things
in the spirit of prophecy; Rv 19:10
1C 48 he even probed *the secrets of the heart,* 1 Cor 14:25
knew events from afar,

a. See 2C 3, supra, 241 a.

b. Cf. 2C 18, footnote on mirror, supra, 257 c.

foresaw, and foretold things to come.[a]
These examples will prove what we say. 1C 30,49-50

Chapter II
HOW HE KNEW SOMEONE CONSIDERED HOLY WAS A FRAUD

28There was a brother who, to all appearances, led a life of extraor- AC 116
1 Cor 7:5 dinary holiness, but who stood out for his singular ways.[b] He *spent all*
his time in prayer, and kept such strict silence that he used to make his
confession by gestures instead of words. He took in the words of
Scripture with such great fervor that on hearing them he gave signs
of feeling great sweetness. What more shall I say? Everyone considered him holy three times over.

It happened that the blessed father came to that place to see and
Lk 4:15 hear this holy brother. While *everyone* was commending and *praising*
the man, our father replied: "Brothers, stop! Don't sing me the
Mt 22:16 praises of his devilish illusions. *You should know the truth.* This is diabolical temptation, deception and fraud. I am sure about this. And
the fact that he won't go to confession proves it."

Gn 21:11 The brothers *took this very hard,* especially the saint's vicar.[c] "How
can this be true?" they asked. "How can lies and such deception be
disguised under all these signs of perfection?" "Tell him to go to confession twice or even once a week," the father said. "If he doesn't do
Jn 5:32 it, you will know what I said is true."

Lk 9:10 The vicar *took* the brother *aside.* He first chatted pleasantly with
Jb 21:5, 29:9 him, finally telling him to go to confession. He spat back, put his *fin-*
ger to his mouth, and shook his head, showing he would never make
his confession. The brothers were speechless, fearing the scandal of a
false saint. A few days later he left religion on his own, turned back
Prv 26:11, 2 Pt 2:22 to the world and *returned to his vomit.* Finally, after doing even worse
things, he was deprived of both repentance and life.

a. The first section of this Second Book, The Spirit of Prophecy (27-54), greatly expands on 1C 26-28. While the prophet may more generally be defined as any "inspired person who believes that he has been sent by God with a message to tell," the medieval Christian tradition understood that person differently, as "one who foretells the future, or the one who seeks to correct a present situation in the light of an ideal past or glorious future." In the apocalyptic milieu of his times, it is understandable that Thomas presents Francis in this light. Cf. Bernard McGinn, *Visions of the End: Apocalyptic Traditions in the Middle Ages* (New York: Columbia University Press, 1979), esp. 1-36.

b. Cf. 2C 14, supra, 253 a.

c. The "saint's vicar" is Elias who is named ten times in 1C and not once in 2C or 3C. Since these two works were written after Elias had fallen out of the brothers' favor and was subsequently deposed as General Minister in 1239, it is understandable that Thomas would not place him in a prominent position in his later writings. Cf. Rosalind B. Brooke, *Early Franciscan Government: From Elias to Bonaventure* (Cambridge: Cambridge University Press, 1959).

Beware of singularity:
it is nothing but a beautiful abyss.[a]
Experience shows that many who seem so unique
rise up to the heavens,
and then fall into the depths. Ps 107:26
Realize the power of a good confession.
It is both a cause and sign of holiness.

Chapter III
AGAINST SINGULARITY
A SIMILAR CASE

29 Something similar happened with another brother named Thomas of Spoleto. Everyone had a good opinion of him, firmly convinced of his holiness. Our holy father considered him wicked; and his later apostasy confirmed this. He did not remain long, for no false show of virtue can last. He left religion, and when he died outside it, he must have realized then what he had done.

Chapter IV
HOW HE FORETOLD THE MASSACRE OF CHRISTIANS AT DAMIETTA

1C 57; LJS 36 30 When the Christian army was besieging Damietta,[b] the *holy* 2 Kgs 2:4
man of God was there with his companions,[c] since they had crossed
the sea in their fervor for martyrdom. When the holy man heard that
our forces *were preparing* for war, *on the day of battle* he grieved deeply. Prv 21:31
He said to his companion: "If the battle happens on this day *the Lord* 2 Kgs 8:10
has shown me that *it will not go well* for the Christians. But *if I say* this, Nm 14:41; Jb 16:7
they will take me for a fool, and *if I keep silent* my conscience won't
leave me alone. What do you think I should do?" His companion *re-* Lk 3:16
1C 11 *plied:* "Father, don't give *the least* thought *to how people judge you.* This 1 Cor 4:3
wouldn't be the first time people took you for a fool. Unburden your
conscience, and *fear God rather than men.*" Lk 12:4-5; Acts 5:29

The saint leapt to his feet, and rushed to the Christians crying out warnings to save them, forbidding war and threatening disaster. But they took the truth *as a joke.* They *hardened* their *hearts* and refused to Tb 3:4; Ex 4:21; Jn 12:40

a. 2C 14, supra, 253 a.

b. The siege took place on August 29, 1219 during the Fifth Crusade. Francis had left for the Orient in early June, arriving there before August 29. See 1C 57, FA:ED I 231.

c. Jordan of Giano identifies the companions as Elias, Peter of Catanio, and Caesar of Speyer among his companions, cf. infra ChrJG 11, 12 14; Bonaventure also identifies Illuminato as one of these companions, LMj IX 8, infra, 602.

turn back. They charged, they attacked, they fought, and then the enemy struck back.

In that moment of battle, filled with suspense, the holy man made his companion *get up to look.* The first and the second time he got up, he saw nothing, so Francis told him to look a third time. What a sight! The whole Christian army was in *retreat fleeing* from the battle carrying not triumph but shame. The massacre was so great that between the dead and the captives the number of our forces was diminished by six thousand. Compassion for them drove the holy man, no less than regret, for what they had done overwhelmed them. He wept especially for the Spaniards: he could see their boldness in battle had left only a few of them alive.[a]

Nm 22:20-1; Jer 49:24

1 Chr 28:21; Ps 19:5 *Let the princes of the whole world take note* of this,
and let them know:
Sir 46:8 *it is not easy to fight against God,*
2 Cor 8:5 that is, against *the will of the Lord.*
Stubborn insolence usually ends in disaster.
It relies on its own strength,
thus forfeiting the help of heaven.
If victory is to be expected from on high,
then battles must be entrusted to the divine Spirit.

Chapter V
HOW HE KNEW SECRETS OF A BROTHER'S HEART

31As the holy man was returning from overseas, with Brother Leonard of Assisi as his companion, **he rode on a donkey** for a while, because he was weak and *tired from his journey.* His companion walked behind, and was also quite tired. *Thinking in human terms,* he *began to say to himself*: "His parents and mine did not socialize as AC 72

Jn 4:6; Rom 6:19; Lk 7:39

a. The bull, *Supplicasti nobis*, Honorius III of March 15, 1219, to the Archbishop of Toledo, identifies the role of the Spaniards in this Crusade. "Since many of those who throughout Spain had taken upon themselves the sign of the Cross in support of the Holy Land, could be of no or little help there in comparison to the help that they would lend in Spain fighting against the Moors; you asked us that you be allowed to relieve such persons of their apostolic obligations. Consequently, by the authority of the present document, we allow you to relieve such persons freely of their vows concerning the aforesaid undertaking, however, with the exception of the lords and knights whom we, until a certain point in time, do not want to be relieved of the vows that they have made in support of the Holy Land, unless perhaps some would be so frail or poor that their journey to the Holy Land would seem useless: whom you can nevertheless relieve of their vows, provided that they designate some of their goods, in accordance with your judgment and advice, as well as according to their own capacities, for the purpose of supporting the Holy Land. Given at the Lateran on the Ides of March, in the third year of our Pontificate." Cf. AFH 16 (1923): 245-246.

equals[a], and here he is riding while I am on foot leading this donkey." *As he was thinking this,* the holy man immediately **got off the** Mt 1:20
donkey. "No, brother," he said. "It is not right that **I should ride**
while you **go on foot, for in the world you were more noble and in-**
fluential than I." The brother was *completely astonished,* and *overcome* Est 7:6; Nm 12:14
with embarrassment: he knew the saint had caught him. **He fell down** Est 8:3
at his feet and, *bathed* **in tears,** he exposed his naked thought and Lk 7:38, 44
begged forgiveness.[b]

Chapter VI

How he saw a devil over a brother, and against those who draw away from unity

[32]There was another brother esteemed by the people for his good reputation. Because of his holiness, he was even more esteemed before God. The father of all *envy* was jealous of his virtue. He planned Wis 2:24
to *cut down this tree* which already *touched the heavens* and to snatch the Dn 4:11; Gn 28:12
crown from his hands. He scavaged, searched, shredded, and sifted everything about that brother, looking for the right way to make him stumble. He stirred up in him, under the appearance of greater perfection, a yearning to isolate himself. Then that jealous one could swoop down on him while he was alone and quickly make him fall.
SC 11 And *if someone falls while alone, there is no one to lift him up.* Eccl 4:10

What happened?

Separating himself from the religion of the brothers, he went
LR VI 2; Test 24 about the world *as a guest and a pilgrim.* He wore a short tunic made Heb 11:13
from his habit and a hood not sown to the tunic; and, in this way, he
wandered the countryside, despising himself in all things. *As he went* Lk 8:42
about in this way, *it came to pass,* that all divine comfort was taken Lk 2:1
from him. Soon he was awash in the waves of temptation. *The waters* Ps 69:2
climbed up into his soul. Desolate in body and spirit, he marched on *like* Prv 7:23
a bird that hurries toward a snare. Already near the abyss he was driven
to the brink. Then *for his own good, the eye* of fatherly Providence *looked* Sir 11:13
mercifully on this miserable man. *In his panic* he regained Is 28:19

a. The Latin text reads: *Non ludebat de pare parentes huius et mei* [His parents and mine did not socialize as equals]. Thomas's allusion seems to be to Horace's *Satires* Book II, satire 3, line 248, where children are said to play *par impar,* which seems to refer to a game called "odds and evens," but which could also be rendered "equal with unequal." Leonard obviously must have come from the kind of family that would not have let its children play with such as Francis's social class, mere merchants.

b. In light of AC 73, the story may have been given as testimony to the pope and cardinals during a canonical process on the holiness of Francis. In AC 73, the narration of this story concludes: "Indeed when the brothers in Assisi petitioned the Lord Pope Gregory and the cardinal to canonize blessed Francis, the brothers gave witness to this incident before the Lord Pope and the cardinals."

Acts 12:11 *understanding. Coming to his senses,* he said: "Oh, miserable one! Go
Ps 35:3 back to religion! That's where *your salvation* is." Immediately he
jumped up and ran to his mother's lap.

[33]He went to the brothers' place in Siena, and Saint Francis was
Phil 2:23 staying there. *As soon as* he *saw* that brother—and this is extraordi-
Mk 14:52 nary—the saint *ran away from him* and quickly closed himself in a
cell. The brothers were thrown into confusion and wondered why he ran away. "Why are you surprised that I ran away?" the saint asked. "Didn't you see the cause? I fled to the protection of prayer to set free the one who strayed. I saw in my son something that displeased me, and rightly so. But now, by the grace of my Christ, the whole delusion has vanished."

The brother fell on his knees and declared with shame that he was guilty. "May God be kind to you, brother," the saint said to him. "But I warn you: Never again separate yourself from religion and your brothers, under some pretext of holiness." From then on that brother
Prv 18:24 became a *friend of company* and camaraderie. He was especially de-
voted to those groups where regular observance flourished.[a]

Ps 111:1-2 *Great are the works of the Lord*
in the gathering and the assembly of the just!
Wis 3:5; Ps 145:14 There *the shaken* are held,
the fallen are lifted
and the lukewarm are roused;
Prv 27:17 there *iron sharpens iron*
Prv 18:19 and a *brother helped by his brother,*
stands *like a strong city.*
And even if you cannot see Jesus because of
Lk 19:3 *the* worldly *crowds,*
the heavenly crowd of angels[b]
will never block your view.
Just do not run away!
Rv 2:10 *Be faithful unto death*
and you will receive the crown of life.

---

a. Thomas does not write of *regularis observantia* [regular observance] except in this passage. The phrase connotes the exact and conscientious observance of the *regula* [rule]. It was frequently used in the context of the Cistercian reform in which the authentic or regular observance of the *Rule of Saint Benedict* was a burning issue. Cf. Louis J. Lekai, *The Cistercians: Ideals and Reality* (Kent State: Kent State University Press, 1977).

b. Cf. Easter Proclamation: *Exultet iam angelica turba caelorum* [Let the angelic crowd of heaven now rejoice]. References to the Easter Proclamation are also found in 1C 85, 119, 126.

ANOTHER SIMILAR CASE

[34]A little time later something similar happened to someone else. One of the brothers would not submit to the saint's vicar, but followed a different brother as his master. The saint was there at the time, and sent him a warning by means of a messenger. The brother at once cast himself at the feet of the vicar and, rejecting his earlier master, obeyed the one whom the saint had made his prelate.[a] The saint took a deep breath and said to the companion who had been sent as his messenger: "Brother, I saw the devil perched on the back of that disobedient brother holding him tightly by the neck. With a rider like that on him, he spit out the bit of obedience, and gave free rein to his own will. But when *I prayed to the Lord* for that brother, sud- 2 Cor 12:8
denly all confused the devil retreated."

This man was full of insight. His eyesight for physical things was weak, for spiritual things it was very sharp. Is it any wonder that one who refused to carry the *Lord of majesty* was burdened by this filthy Is 3:8
baggage?

I tell you: there is no middle ground.
Either carry the *burden that is light* Mt 11:30
—which rather carries you—
or *evil will sit upon you like a lead weight,* Zec 5:7-8
like *a millstone*[b] *hung around your neck.* Mt 18:6

Chapter VII
HOW HE FREED THE PEOPLE OF GRECCIO FROM ATTACKS BY WOLVES AND FROM HAILSTORMS

[35]The saint used to enjoy staying in the brothers' place at Greccio. He found it rich in poverty and there, in a remote little cell on a cliff,
1C 84-86 he could give himself freely to heavenly things. This is the place where he had earlier recalled the birth of the *Child of Bethlehem*, be- 1 Sm 16:18
coming a child with the Child.

Now, it happened that the people there had been stricken by multiple disasters. A pack of raging wolves devoured not only animals,
AC 74 but even people. And every year hailstorms destroyed their wheat

a. The term *praelatus* [prelate] is used more extensively in 2C where it appears seventeen times. In 1C, the term appears only four times. Cf. FA:ED I 130 a.

b. The Latin reads: *molla asinaria* [millstone] and refers to the stone of a mill turned by the labor of an ass.

fields and **vineyards.** One day, while preaching to them, blessed
Wis 7:25 Francis said: "**To the praise and honor of** *Almighty* **God,** listen to the
Ps 30:10; 1 Jn 1:9 *truth* which I *proclaim* to you. If each of you *will confess your sins,* and
Lk 3:8 *bear worthy fruit of genuine repentance,* I swear to you that all these di-
Ex 14:24; Ps 11:4 sasters will cease, and *the Lord looking down upon you, will multiply your*
Jer 28:17; Acts 17:3 *earthly goods. But also hear this,*" he said. "***I tell you*** again, **if you** are un-
Prv 26:11; 2 Pt 2:22 grateful for these gifts, and ***return to your vomit,*** the disasters will re-
Jos 22:18 turn, the punishment will double, and greater *wrath* will *rage* against
you."

[36]And so **it happened: at that very hour** the disasters **ceased,** and AC 74
through the merits and prayers of our holy father, all dangers van-
Dn 3:50 ished.[a] The wolves and hailstorms *caused no more harm.* And even
more remarkable, whenever the hail, falling on neighboring fields,
reached the boundaries of Greccio, either it would stop or move off in
a different direction.

Wis 11:4; Ps 107:38; Tb 12:3 So they *received relief, increased greatly,* and *overflowed* with earthly
Jb 15:27; 21:24 *goods.* But prosperity had its usual effect: either *their faces grew bloated,*
Tb 2:10 or *the dung* of earthly riches *blinded them* even more. They fell back to
Ps 106:21 ways worse than before, *forgetting the God who had saved them.* But they
did not go unpunished. Divine justice punishes one who falls less se-
Sir 36:6 verely than one who repeats an earlier fall. *The wrath* of God *flared up*
against them. The evils which had departed returned. The sword of
human violence was now added, and a decree of death from heaven
Rv 8:7 devoured them. In the end the whole town *was burned to the ground* by
flames of vengeance.

It is only just
that those who turned their backs on such gifts
should come to destruction.

Chapter VIII

How he foretold civil war among the people of Perugia when he preached to them, and how he recommended unity

[37]Some days later, as our blessed father was coming down from AC 75
that cell, he complained to the brothers who were with him: "The
people of Perugia have done many evil things to their neighbors, and
Jer 8:11; Ez 28:2-6 *to* their *disgrace* their *heart has grown proud.* But now there comes the
Jer 46:10; Jer 15:2 *vengeance of God,* whose hand is already *upon the sword.*"

a. Thomas repeats part of Responsory VIII of *The Rhymed Office of Saint Anthony* by Julian of Speyer: "*Pereunt pericula, cessat et necessitas*" [Dangers vanish and necessity ceases].

After a few days had passed, with his soul on fire, he got up and set out for the city of Perugia.

The brothers clearly thought that he had seen some vision in his
cell. Arriving in Perugia he began to preach to *the people gathered* there. Dt 31:12
But **the knights,** as usual, **racing their horses** and **jousting with**
their weapons, drowned out *the word of God.* The saint *turned to them* Lk 11:28; Lk 9:55; Mk 7:34
and *groaned.* "Oh, the miserable madness of miserable men!" he said.
"You neither consider nor fear the *judgment of God!* Hear what the Rom 2:3
Lord *tells you* through me, a little *poor man. The Lord has exalted* you Jn 16:13; Is 66:2; Ps 37:34
above all *around you.* Because of this you should be kinder to your Ez 5:7, 11:12
neighbors and more grateful to God. But you are ungrateful for these
gifts, and fully armed you attack your neighbors: you kill and pillage.
I tell you, *this will not go unavenged.* God will punish you severely: you Mt 23:38; Jb 24:12
will destroy yourselves in a civil war; in a general uprising one will
rise up against the other. Wrath will teach you what kindness did
not."

Not many days passed before **a** *scandal* **arose among them,** they took Lk 15:13; Acts 1:5
up arms against their neighbors. The common people attacked
knights, and nobles drew their swords on the lower classes.[a] Things
at last turned to such cruelty and slaughter that even the neighboring towns they had oppressed were moved to piety.

Judgment worthy of praise!
Since they had moved away from
the One, the Most High,
it followed that they lost their own oneness.
A state can have no stronger bond
than a devout love for God
with a true and *sincere faith.* 1 Tm 1:5

Chapter IX
HOW HE PREDICTED TO A WOMAN HER EVIL HUSBAND WOULD BECOME A GOOD ONE

AC 69 [38]In those days, *the man of God* **was traveling to "Le Celle" of** 1 Sm 2:27
Cortona. A noble woman from a village called Volusiano heard of
this and hurried to see him. Exhausted from the long journey since
she was very refined and delicate, she finally reached the saint. Our holy Dt 28:56
father was moved with compassion on seeing her exhausted and
gasping for breath. **"What pleases you, my lady?"** he asked. **"Father,** Gn 27:38

a. See AC 75, p. 179 a in this editon.

please bless me," she said. The saint asked: "Are you married or single?" She replied: "Father, **I have a husband,** a very **cruel man, an antagonist to my service of Jesus Christ.** He stops me from putting into action the **good will the Lord** has inspired in me; and this is my greatest sorrow. So I beg you, holy man, pray for him, that divine mercy will *humble his heart.*" The father was amazed at virility in a female, an aging spirit in a child.[a] Moved by piety, he said to her: "**Go,** *blessed daughter,* and, regarding your husband, know that you will soon have consolation." And he added: "**You may tell him** for God and **for me,** that *now is the time of salvation,* and later it will be the time for justice."

Jn 4:17; 2 Cor 5:8; Dn 5:22; Jdt 12:32; Sir 4:28, 40:7; 2 Cor 6:2

After receiving his blessing, the lady returned home, found her husband and relayed the message. Suddenly *the Holy Spirit came upon him,* and he was changed from the old to the new man, prompting him to reply *very meekly:* "My lady, *let us serve the Lord* and *save our souls* in our own house."[b] And his wife replied: "**It seems to me** that continence should be placed in the soul as its *foundation,* and the other virtues *built upon it.*" "This," he said, "**pleases me as it pleases you.**" They lived a celibate life for many years until, on the same day, both departed happily—one as a *morning holocaust,* and the other as an *evening sacrifice.*

Acts 10:44; Eph 4:2; Jos 22:27; Gn 19:19; Eph 2:20; 2 Kgs 16:15; Ps 141:2

What a fortunate woman!
She softened her lord for the sake of life![c]
In her was fulfilled that text from the Apostle:
The unbelieving husband will be saved by his believing wife.
But today
—to use a common saying—
you can count people like that on your fingers.[d]

1 Cor 7:14

a. Three Latin words are used in this paragraph: *mulier* [woman], *domina* [lady], and *femina* [female], all of which impact on Thomas of Celano's descriptions of Francis's attitudes toward women. Cf. 2C 112-114, infra, 321-323.

b. For background information on the "domestic" living of the Franciscan ideals by seculars, see Raoul Manselli, "Francis of Assisi and Lay People Living in the World: Beginnings of the Third Order?" GR 11 (1997): 41-48.

c. Another instance in which Thomas plays with the words: *mulier, mollitia* [woman, softness], cf. 2C 17, supra 255 c.

d. Pliny, *Natural History*, XXXIV:19, 38.

Chapter X
How he knew through the Spirit that one brother scandalized another, and foretold that the former would leave religion

[39]Once two brothers were traveling from Terra di Lavoro, and the older one had seriously scandalized the younger one. I would say he was not a companion but a tyrant. The younger brother, because of God, endured all of this in remarkable silence. When they reached Assisi the younger one went to see Saint Francis, for he knew him well, and among other things the saint asked: "How did your companion behave toward you during the trip?" "Well enough, really, dear father," the brother answered. But the saint said to him: "Be careful, brother: don't lie under the pretext of humility! I know how he behaved toward you; but just wait a bit and you'll see." The
brother was quite amazed that he knew, *through the Spirit,* such far Acts 21:4
away events. *Just a few days later* the one who *had scandalized his brother,* Lk 15:13; Rom 14:13; Mt 5:22
having turned against religion, was cast out.

Without a doubt,
to share the same road with a good companion
and not to share his good will,
shows a *lack of understanding* Sir 19:21
and is a mark of wickedness.

Chapter XI
How he knew that a young man who entered religion was not led there by the Spirit of God

AC 70 [40]About the same time **a noble boy from Lucca** came to Assisi,
wishing **to enter religion.** When he was presented to Saint Francis,
he *fell on his knees* and *with tears begged* the saint to receive him. The 2 Chr 6:13; Heb 5:7
man of God, looking intently at him, knew at once *through the Spirit* that 1 Sm 2:27; Acts 3:4
the boy was not *led by the Spirit,* and said to him: **"Wretched and car-** Acts 21:4; Rom 8:14
nal as you are, why do you think **you can lie to me and the Holy** Acts 5:3-4
Spirit? Your tears come from the flesh, and *your heart is not* with *God.* Acts 8:21
Get out! You have no taste for things of the spirit!" **As he was saying this,** Mk 8:33
word came that the boy's **relatives** *were at the door,* **looking to seize** Jn 18:16; Lk 11:54
their son, and **take him back home.** He *went out to them,* and in the Jn 18:29
end agreed to return home. The brothers were amazed and *praised the* Ps 150:1
Lord **in his saint.**

Chapter XII
How he healed a cleric and foretold that because of his sins he would suffer even worse things

[41]While our holy father lay sick **in the bishop's palace in Rieti,** a 1C 99; AC 95
canon named Gedeone—a lustful, **worldly man**—was seized by a
painful illness.[a] And, with pains throughout his body, he was bedridden. He had himself carried to Saint Francis, and **tearfully begged
him to mark him with the sign of the cross.** But the saint said to
him: **"How can I sign you with the cross, when you once lived ac-**
Gal 5:16 **cording to the** ***desires of the flesh*** and with no fear of the *judgements of*
Sir 17:24 *God?"* But he made the sign of the cross on him, saying: **"I will sign**
Acts 4:10 **you in the name of** *Christ*; but you must know you will suffer worse
Prv 26:11 things if once set free **you** *return to your vomit."* And he added: "The
Mt 12:45; Lk 11:26 sin of ingratitude always brings on **new ills** *worse than the first."*

**When he made the sign of the cross over him, immediately the
man** who was lying crippled **got up** restored to health, and bursting
with praise cried: "I am free!" Many people there **heard the bones of
his hips cracking,** as when someone snaps dry twigs with his hands.
Jgs 3:7 But after a short time the canon, *forgetting God,* turned his body back
to its unchaste ways. One evening he dined at the house of one of his fellow canons, and slept there that night. Suddenly the roof of the house collapsed on all of them. Others who were there escaped with their lives, and only that wretch was trapped and killed.

It is no wonder that,
as the saint told him,
Mt 12:45 *worse evils* follow *the first ones.*
Gratitude must be shown for forgiveness received,
and a crime repeated doubles displeasure.

Chapter XIII
A brother who was tempted

Jn 11:6 [42]While the saint *was staying in that same place,* a brother, a spiritual
man, from the custody of Marsico, tormented by serious tempta-
Ps 14:1 tions, *said in his heart:* "Oh, if only I had something from Saint Francis, even the fingernail parings, I believe this whole storm of temptations would break up, and by the grace of God calm would return!" After receiving permission, he went to the place where Francis

a. See AC 95, supra 197 a.

was, and explained his purpose to one of our holy father's companions. But this brother answered him: "I'm afraid it won't be possible for me to give you his nail parings, for even though we do sometimes trim his nails, he commands us to throw the parings away, and forbids us to save them."

At that very moment the brother was called away and told to go to the saint, who was looking for him. "Would you look for some scissors for me, son," said the saint, "so you can *cut* my *nails* right away." Dt 12:12
The brother brought out the scissors which he had already picked up for that very purpose, and saving the clippings, gave them to the brother who had asked for them. He received them with devotion and preserved them even more devoutly, and was immediately set free from all his struggle.

Chapter XIV

A MAN WHO OFFERED A PIECE OF CLOTH WHICH THE SAINT HAD EARLIER REQUESTED

1C 76 [43]While living at this same place, the *father of the poor* was dressed Jb 29:16
in an old tunic. One day he said to one of his companions, whom he had made his guardian: "Brother, if possible, I wish you would find me material for a tunic." On hearing this, the brother started turning over in his mind how he could get the necessary cloth so humbly requested. The next day at the break of dawn he went to the door, on his way to town for the cloth. There he found a man sitting on the doorstep and wishing to speak to him. This man said to the brother: "For the love of God, please accept this cloth, enough for six tunics; keep one for yourself and distribute the rest as you please for the good of my soul."

The brother was exhilarated, and returned to Brother Francis, announcing to him the gift sent from heaven. And our father said: "Accept the tunics, for this man was sent to care for my need in this way." And he added: "Thanks be to him who seems to be the only one *concerned for us!*" 1 Sm 9:5; Ps 40:18

Chapter XV
HOW HE INVITED HIS DOCTOR TO LUNCH WHEN THE BROTHERS LACKED EVERYTHING, AND HOW THE LORD SUDDENLY PROVIDED FOR THEM IN ABUNDANCE; AND GOD'S PROVIDENCE FOR HIS OWN

44While the holy man was staying in a hermitage **near Rieti, a** AC 68
doctor used to visit him every day to treat his eyes. One day the saint
said to his brothers: "Invite the doctor, and **give him the best to eat."**
Lk 14:9 The guardian **answered him: "Father,** *we're embarrassed* to say this,
but we're ashamed to invite him, because right now **we're so poor."**
Mt 20:32; Jn 9:27 But the saint answered: *"Do you want me to tell you again?"* And **the**
doctor, who was nearby, **said:** "Dear brothers, I would consider it a
treat to share in your poverty."

The brothers hurried to place the whole contents of their store-
2 Chr 18:20 room on the table: **a little bread**, and not much wine, and, to make
the meal more lavish, the kitchen provided a few beans. Meanwhile,
Mal 1:7; Lk 13:25 *the table of the Lord* took pity on the table of his servants. *Someone* Test 22
knocked **at the door,** and they answered immediately. **There was a** 1C 34
woman offering a basket filled with beautiful bread, loaded **with**
fish and crabcakes, and with **honey** and **grapes** heaped on top. The
table of the poor rejoices at this sight, the cheap food is put away, and
the delicacies are eaten immediately.

The doctor heaved a sigh and spoke to them: **"Neither you, brothers, as you should, nor we** lay people, **realize the holiness of this man." They would not have been sufficiently filled if the miracle had not fed them even more than the food.**

Prv 30:17 A father's *eye*
never *looks down on* his own,
but rather feeds beggars with greater care
the needier they are.
The poor enjoy a more generous meal than a prince's,
as God is more generous than humans.

HOW HE SET BROTHER RICCERIO FREE FROM A TEMPTATION[a]

44aThere was a brother called Riccerio, noble in birth and behav- 1C 49, 50; LJS 31
ior. He placed such trust in the merits of blessed Francis that he believed that anyone who enjoyed the gift of the saint's affection would

a. This paragraph is missing from a number of manuscripts, possibly because of its similarity with 1C 49 and 50. Nevertheless editors of the critical edition found in AF X published it as part of this text, see AF X, 158 n. 13.

be worthy of divine grace; any without it would deserve God's wrath. He therefore anxiously longed to obtain the benefit of his intimacy, but *he was very fearful* that the saint might discover in him some hid- Jdt 8:8
den fault and then he would actually be further away from the saint's good will.

These deep fears tormented that brother every day, and he did not reveal his thoughts to anyone. One day, worried as usual, he approached the cell where Saint Francis was praying. The *man of God* 1 Sm 13:1
knew of both his coming and his state of mind and called him kindly to himself. "My son," he said, "let no fear or temptation disturb you any more, for you are very dear to me, and among all those who are dearest to me I love you with a special love. Come to me confidently whenever you want, and leave me freely whenever you want." The brother was extremely shocked and overjoyed at the words of the holy father. From that time on, knowing he was loved, he grew—as he believed—in *the grace of the Savior.* Ti 2:11

Chapter XVI

HOW HE LEFT HIS CELL TO BLESS TWO BROTHERS, KNOWING THROUGH THE SPIRIT WHAT THEY DESIRED

AC 73 45 Saint Francis usually passed the whole day in an isolated cell, returning to the brothers only when pressed by necessity to take some food. He did not leave it for dinner at the assigned time because his hunger for contemplation was even more consuming, and often completely overpowered him.

Now it happened one time that two brothers, with a way of life worthy of God, came to the place at Greccio from far away.[a] The only reason was to see the saint and to receive his blessing, which they had long desired. When they arrived, they *did not find him,* for he had al- Lk 2:45
ready left the common area for a cell. They were greatly saddened. Since an uncertain outcome demanded a long stay, they left completely discouraged, believing their failure was caused by their faults.

Blessed Francis's companions accompanied them, comforting them in their discouragement. But when they had walked *about a* Lk 22:41
stone's throw away from the place, the saint suddenly called after them, and said to one of his companions: "Tell my brothers who came here to look back toward me." And when those brothers turned their faces to him, he made the sign of the Cross over them and affectionately blessed them. They became so joyful at receiving

a. AC 73 tells of one brother coming to see the saint. Thomas, however, writes of two. In both instances the brothers are not identified.

Lk 24:53 both their wish and even a miracle, that they returned home *praising and blessing the Lord.*

Chapter XVII

How he brought forth water from the rock by prayer and gave it to a thirsty peasant

[46]Once blessed Francis wanted to travel to a certain hermitage so
that he could more freely spend time in contemplation. Because he
was very weak, he got a donkey to ride from a poor man. It was sum-
Jos 2:16; I Kgs 13:14, 21 mer, and as the peasant *went up the mountain* following the *man of*
Jn 4:6 *God,* he was *worn out from the journey* over such a rough and long road.
And before they came to the place, he was exhausted, fainting with a
Dt 13:17 burning thirst. He urgently cried out after the saint, begging him *to*
have pity on him. He swore he would die if he was not revived by some-
Lk 4:34 thing to drink. *The holy one of God,* always compassionate to the dis-
tressed, immediately leaped down from the donkey, knelt down on
Col 1:9 the ground, and raised his hands to heaven, *praying unceasingly* until
he sensed he had been heard. "Hurry now," he said to the peasant,
Is 48:21 "and over there you will find living *water* which at this very hour
Christ *has* mercifully *brought forth from the rock for you to drink.*" How
amazingly kind God is, so easily bowing to his servants! By the power
Ps 78:16 of prayer a peasant drinks *water from the rock* and draws refreshment
Dt 32:13; Ps 1:3 *from the hard flint.*[a] There was no *flow of water* there before this; and
even after a careful search, none was found there afterwards.

Why should we be surprised
that this one,
Lk 4:1 so *filled with the Holy Spirit,*
re-enacts the marvelous deeds of all the just!
If one is joined to Christ
by a gift of special grace,
is it not wonderful that he,
like other saints,
Mk 7:13 should do *similar things.*

a. Gregory the Great describes a similar incident in the life of Saint Benedict. Cf. Gregory the Great, *Dialogue* II 5, PL 66:144. See Saint Gregory the Great, *Dialogues,* translated by Odo John Zimmerman (New York: Fathers of the Church, Inc., 1959), 67-68.

Chapter XVIII

THE LITTLE BIRDS HE FED, ONE OF WHICH DIED BECAUSE OF ITS GREED

[47]One day when blessed Francis was sitting at table with the brothers, little birds, a male and a female, came over and took some *crumbs from* the saint's *table* as they pleased. They did this every day, anxious to feed their newly hatched chicks. The saint rejoiced over them, and caressed them, as was his custom, and offered them a reward for their efforts. One day the father and mother offered their children to the brothers, as if they had been raised at their expense; and once they entrusted their fledglings to the brothers, they were never seen again in that place. The chicks grew tame with the brothers and used to perch on their hands. They stayed in the house, not as guests but as members of the family. They hid at the sight of people of the world, showing they were the foster children of the brothers alone.

Mt 15:27; Mk 7:28

The saint noticed this, surprised, and invited the brothers to rejoice: "See," he said, "what our brothers the robins[a] have done, as if they were endowed with reason! They have said to us: 'Brothers, we present to you our babies, who have been fed by your crumbs. Do with them as you please; we will go off to another home.' "

The young birds became completely tame with the brothers, and all ate together peacefully. But greed broke up this harmony, for a bigger one grew arrogant and harassed the smaller ones. When the big one had already eaten his fill, he still pushed the others away from the food. "Look now," said the father, "at what this greedy one is doing! He's full to bursting, but he's still jealous of his hungry brothers. He will die an evil death." The punishment followed soon after the saint's word. The one who disturbed his brothers climbed on the edge of a water pitcher to take a drink, and suddenly fell into it and drowned; not a cat or any other animal was found that dared touch that one cursed by the saint.

When so punished in birds,
is not avarice an evil to be feared
when found in mortals!
And is not the judgment of the saint to be feared
when punishment ensues with such ease!

a. *Pectusrubei*, literally redbreasts; *pettirosso* is still the Italian for "robin."

Chapter XIX
How all the things which he foretold about Brother Bernard were fulfilled

[48]Another time he spoke prophetically about Brother Bernard, 1C 24; AC 12
who was the second brother in the Order, saying: **"I tell you, Brother**
Mt 12:45 **Bernard has been given the most cunning devils to test him,** *the*
worst among all the other evil spirits. They constantly strive to make this
Rv 6:13, 9:1; Ru 3:18; 2 Mc 13:13 *star fall from heaven*, but the *outcome* will be something else. He will be
troubled, tormented, and harassed, but in the end he will triumph
over all." And he added: "Near the time of his death, with every
storm calmed, every temptation overcome, he will enjoy wonderful
Acts 20:24; 2 Tm 4:7 tranquillity and peace. *The race finished* he will pass over happily to
Christ."

And in fact it happened just like that: his death was lit up with
1 Kgs 13:31-32 miracles, and everything happened exactly as the *man of God foretold*.
Gn 42:8 That is why the brothers said when he died: "This brother *was not* really *recognized* while he lived!" But we leave to others the task of telling Bernard's praises.

Chapter XX
A brother who was tempted and wanted to have something written by the hand of the saint

[49]While the saint was secluded in a cell on Mount La Verna, one of his companions was yearning with great desire to have something encouraging from the words of our Lord, commented on briefly by Saint Francis and written with his own hand. He believed that by this means he would be set free from, or at least could bear more easily, a serious temptation which oppressed him, not in the flesh but in the spirit. Though growing weary with this desire, he feared to express it to the
1 Cor 2:10 most holy father. But what man did not tell him, *the Spirit revealed.* One
2 Jn 12 day Saint Francis called this brother and said: "Bring me *paper and ink*,
because I want to write down the words of the Lord and his praises
Ps 77:7 upon which *I have meditated in my heart.*" What he had asked for was
quickly brought to him. He then wrote down with his own hand the PrsG
Praises of God and the words he wanted and, at the end, a blessing for BlL
Gn 28:2 that brother, saying: "*Take* this paper *for yourself* and keep it carefully to
your dying day." The whole temptation disappeared immediately. The letter was preserved; and later it worked wonders.[a]

a. The inscription of *The Praises of God*, cf. FA:ED I 108-112, indicates it is the text written by Francis on this occasion. The companion was Leo.

Chapter XXI

How He Gave His Tunic to the Same Brother Who Wanted It

1C 108 [50]Another wonder of our holy father was manifested for that
same brother. When the saint lay sick in the palace at Assisi, that
brother *thought to himself*: "Now our father is close to death, and *my* Wis 2:1, Mt 16:7, Lk 12:17; Ps 77:3
soul would be comforted so much if I could have the tunic of my father 2 Kgs 2:13
after his death." As if that *desire of the heart* had been spoken with his Ps 21:3
lips, Saint Francis called him shortly after and said: "I am giving you
this tunic. Take it. From now on it is yours. Even though I wear it
while I still live, at my death it should be returned to you." Amazed at
his father's insight, the brother was consoled and accepted the tunic.
Out of holy devotion, this tunic was carried to France.

Chapter XXII

The Parsley Found at His Command Among Wild Herbs at Night

[51]At the time of his last illness, and in the dark of night, he wanted
to eat some parsley and humbly asked for it.[a] The cook was called so
he could bring it, but he replied that he could not pick any in the garden at that time. "I've been picking parsley every day," he said, "and
I've cut off so much of it that even in broad daylight I can hardly find
any. Even more so now that darkness has fallen, I won't be able to
distinguish it from the other herbs." "Brother" the saint replied,
"don't worry, bring me the first herbs your hand touches." The
brother went into the garden, unable to see anything, and tore up the
first wild herbs he came upon, and brought them back into the
house. The brothers looked at the wild herbs, and sorting through
them carefully, they found a leafy, tender stock of parsley in the middle of them. The saint then ate a bit of it and felt much better. Then
the father said to the brothers: *"Dear brothers,* do what you're com- Phil 4:1
manded the first time you're told, and don't wait for it to be repeated.
Don't pretend that something is impossible; for even if what I command is beyond your strength, obedience will find the strength."
Thus to a high degree the Spirit entrusted to him the *spirit of prophecy*. Rv 19:10

---

a. Parsley was used to give new strength to the dying, a belief that sprang from the ancient myth in which a snake bit Opheltes, the child of Hypsipyle, Queen of Lemmos. Since the boy, buried with the name "Archemorous," the forerunner of death, had been sitting on a parsley-bed when bitten, the herb became associated with dying. Cf. Michael Grant and John Hazel, "Hypsipyle," *Gods and Mortals in Classical Mythology* (Springfield, MA: G.&.C. Merriam Company, Publishers: 1973), 240.

Chapter XXIII
THE FAMINE WHICH HE FORETOLD WOULD COME AFTER HIS DEATH

52Holy men are sometimes forced by the prompting of the Holy
Spirit to say some remarkable things about themselves. Either the
2 Sm 3:7 glory of God demands that they *reveal the word* or else the order of
1 Cor 14:3 charity calls for it for the *edification* of their neighbor. This was why
Jn 19:20 the blessed Father one day turned to a brother *he loved very much, and*
1 Mc 15:32 *spoke this word, which* he had brought from the audience hall of God's
majesty, which he knew so well. "Today there is a servant of God
Gn 1:11; Gn 26:1; Jos 22:18; Jer 14:5 *upon this earth,*" he said, "and for his sake the Lord will not allow *hun-*
ger to rage against people as long as he is alive."

There was no vanity here but rather a holy pronouncement spo-
1 Cor 13:5; Ps 45:2 ken by that *charity which is not self-seeking*, in modest and holy *words* for
our edification. Neither should this favor of such a special love of
Christ for his servant have been concealed by useless silence. All of us
Jn 3:11 *who saw* these days *know well* how quietly and peacefully those times
passed, as long as the servant of Christ was alive, and what rich
Am 8:11 abundance there was of all good things. There was no *famine of the*
word of God, for the word of preachers in those days was especially full
2 Tm 2:15 of power, and the hearts of all their listeners were *worthy of God's ap-*
proval. Examples of holiness were shining brightly in religious life,
Mt 23:27-28 and the hypocrisy of *whitened sepulchers* had not yet infected so many
2 Cor 11:13-15 holy people, nor had the teaching of *those who disguise themselves* excited so much curiosity. No wonder material goods were so abun-
dant, when eternal goods were so truly loved by all!

53But once he had been taken away, the order of things was com-
Lk 21:9 pletely reversed and everything changed. *Wars and insurrections*
sprang up everywhere, and the carnage of death in many forms suddenly spread through many regions.[a] A frightful famine spread far
and wide, and many indeed were devoured by its cruelty, painful beyond anything else.[b] Sheer necessity turned all things into food, and

a. Thomas's description applies primarily to central Italy where, between 1227 and 1230, there was strife between Pope Gregory IX and Emperor Frederick II. In 1227 Gregory excommunicated him for postponing too long his departure for the Crusade. As Frederick was finally leaving for the Holy Land, in 1228, some of his imperial forces attacked the Marches of Ancona and the Duchy of Spoleto, under papal control. In retaliation the papal forces, in 1229, invaded the imperial territory of the Kingdom of Naples, and hostilities continued to spread. Cf. Riccardo di S. Germano, "Chronicon," in *Monumenta Germaniae Historica* XIX, 349 ff. See AF X,163, n.15.

b. This famine is described in contemporary chronicles, e.g. the *Chronicon Parmense*, 1138-1338: "In that year [1227] there was a great famine in all of Italy. From the month of May, a six-measure of grain cost 20 imperial soldi and spelt was six soldi. And in the city of Bologna a basket of grain cost 20 imperial soldi," in Muratori, *Rerum Italicarum Scriptores*, IX, 765; so also the *Corpus Chronicarum Bononiensium*, "In that year [1227] there was a great famine in Bologna and various regions," in Muratori, XVIII (2nd ed.) II, 92; and Riccardo di S. Germano, "1227, in the month of January there was such a famine in the city of Rome that the senate could hardly get a ruble of wheat for 20 soldi," in *Monumenta Germaniae Historica* XIX, 347.

human teeth bit into what animals would normally reject. Bread was made from nut shells and tree bark. Hunger became so compelling that parental piety was unmoved—to put it gently—by the death of their own children, as one of them admitted.

The blessed father Francis clearly revealed to that same brother, to whom, while he was yet living, he had foretold the future disasters, that he himself was that servant of God. He did this so that we would clearly know who that *faithful servant* was, for whose love the divine punishment held back its hand from vengeance, only a few days after his death. For one night as the brother was sleeping, he *called him* in a loud voice, *saying:* "Brother, *a famine* is now coming which, while I was living, the Lord did not allow to come *upon the earth.*" The brother woke up when he heard the voice, and later recounted it all from beginning to end. On the third night after this, the saint appeared to him again and repeated the same words.

Mt 24:45

Jn 11:28; Ps 105:16

Chapter XXIV
The Saint's Clear Sight and Our Ignorance

[54]It should not seem strange to anyone that this prophet of our own time should shine with such great privileges. Truly freed from the darkness of earthly things and not subjected to the lusts of the flesh, free, his understanding flew up to the heights; pure, it stepped into the light.

Thus,
illumined by the flashes of light eternal,[a] Wis 7:26
he drew from the Word what echoed in words.
Ah, how different we are today!
Wrapped in darkness Jb 37:19
we are ignorant even of what we need to know.
And what do you think is the reason for this?
Are we not also friends of the flesh,
wallowing in the dust of worldly things?
Surely,
if we would only *raise our hearts as well as our hands to heaven,* Lam 3:41
if we would choose to depend on the eternal,
maybe we would know what we do not know:
God and ourselves.
Mired in mud, we see only mud.

a. Cf. *Easter Proclamation: tellus . . . irradiata fulgoribus et aeterni regis splendore illustrata* [illumined by flashes of the eternal king].

For the eye fixed on heaven,
it is impossible not to see heavenly things.

POVERTY

Chapter XXV
THE PRAISE OF POVERTY

Ps 84:6-7 55 *Placed in a vale of tears*
the blessed father scorned
Ps 31:20 the usual riches of the *children of men* as no riches at all[a]
and, eager for higher status,
Sir 47:10 *with all his heart,* he coveted poverty.
Realizing that she was a close friend[b]
Heb 7:3 of the *Son of God,*
Est 9:28 but nowadays an outcast throughout *the whole world,*
Jer 31:3 he was eager to espouse her *in an everlasting love.*
Wis 8:2 He *became the lover of her beauty*
Gn 2:24; Mt 19:5; Mk 10:7; Eph 2:18 and not only *left his father and his mother*
but gave up everything he owned
so that he might *cling to his wife* more closely,
and *the two might be in one spirit.*
He held her close in chaste embraces
and could not bear to cease being her husband
Gal 2:5 *and even for an hour.*
He told his sons that she is the way of perfection.
She is the pledge and guarantee of eternal wealth.
No one coveted gold as avidly as he coveted poverty;
no one was as careful to guard a treasure
Mt 13:45-46 as he was to watch over this *pearl* of the Gospel.
In this especially would his sight be offended:
if he saw in the brothers
—whether at home or away from it—

a. Thomas again plays on words; in this instance *opes* [riches] *inopes* [no riches], which, in the Latin text, immediately strikes the ear since the two words are placed next to one another.

b. Cf. 1C 35, 39, 51. In contrast to the allegorical references on poverty found in 1C, this reflection on poverty develops the explicit spousal imagery found in earlier texts such as SC 3-5, 7-22. Its origins are clearly within the psycho-historical circumstances of the twelfth century during which spirituality struggled with the "difficult and dangerous discussion of love," as Origen described it. Cf. Ann W. Astell, *The Song of Songs in the Middle Ages* (Ithaca and London: Cornell University Press, 1990), 2. For a thorough study of this image, cf. Dominique Gagnon, "Typologie de la pauvreté chez saint François d'Assise: l'espouse, la dame, la mère," *Laurentianum* 19 (1977): 462-552.

anything that was contrary to poverty.
Truly, from the beginning of his religious life until his death,
Test 16-17 his entire wealth was a single tunic,
cord and breeches;
he had nothing else.
His poor clothing showed
where he stored his riches.
This was the reason he was happy;
he was carefree.
He was ready for the race.
He was glad to exchange perishable treasure
for the *hundredfold.* Mt 19:29

POVERTY OF HOUSES

Chapter XXVI

AC 23 [56]**He taught his own to build poor little dwellings out of wood, and not stone, and how to build these according to a crude sketch.** Often, when he spoke to the brothers about poverty, he would insist on that saying of the Gospel: *"The foxes have holes and the birds of the air have nests, but the Son of God has no place on which to rest his head."* Mt 8:20; Lk 9:58

Chapter XXVII

THE HOUSE NEXT TO THE PORTIUNCULA THAT HE BEGAN TO PULL DOWN

[57]Once, there was going to be a chapter at Saint Mary of the Portiuncula. *The time was* already *close at hand,* and the people of Assisi could see that there was no house there. So in a great rush they built a house for the chapter, while the *man of God* was away and unaware of this. When the father finally returned, he saw the house and was annoyed. He complained, and not gently. Immediately, wanting to dismantle the building, he was the first to get up; he *climbed up to the roof* and started tearing out slates and *tiles with a mighty hand.* He ordered the brothers also to climb up and to tear down completely that monstrosity against poverty. He said that this would quickly spread throughout the Order, and everyone would take for an example any sign of pretension they saw in that place. He would have destroyed that house right to the foundations, but some knights standing

2 Tm 4:6 · 2 Kgs 4:42 · Lk 5:19 · Ez 20:34

nearby dampened his fiery spirit. They told him that the building belonged to the town, not to the brothers.

Chapter XXVIII
THE HOUSE IN BOLOGNA WHERE HE THREW OUT THE SICK

58 At another time, when he was returning from Verona and wished to pass through Bologna, he heard that a new house of the brothers had been built there. And just because he heard the words "house of the brothers," he changed course and went by another route, avoiding Bologna. Furthermore, he commanded the brothers to leave the house quickly. For this reason the house was abandoned; and even the sick could not stay, but were thrown out with the rest of them. And they did not get permission to return there until Lord Hugo, who was then Bishop of Ostia and Legate in Lombardy, declared while preaching in public that this house was his. And *he who writes this and bears witness to it* was at that time thrown out from that house while he was sick.[a]

Jn 21:24; 19:35

Chapter XXIX
HOW HE REFUSED TO ENTER A CELL BECAUSE IT WAS CALLED HIS

AC 23

59 **He did not want the brothers to live in any place unless it had a definite owner who held the property rights. He always wanted the laws of pilgrims for his sons:** to be sheltered under someone else's roof, to travel in peace, and to thirst for their homeland.[b] Once at the hermitage of Sarteano, one brother asked another brother where he was coming from. "I'm coming from Brother Francis's cell," he answered. The saint heard this and replied: "Since you have put the name 'Francis' on the cell making it my property, go and look for someone else to live in it. From now on I will not stay there. When the Lord stayed in a cell[c] where he prayed and *fasted for forty days,* he

AC 57

Mt 4:1-2; Mk1:12-13; Lk 4:2

a. This event occurred between 1219 and 1221. It is not clear if Hugolino was present in Bologna at the time the house was abandoned. The one thrown out in this story is most probably not Thomas, but rather one of his informants, who would have given him the story in writing and mentioned that he was one of the sick.

b. For comment on the "laws of pilgrims," see AC 23, supra, 136 a.

c. The Latin reads *stetit in carcere* [stayed in a cell], but the context is clearly Christ in the desert. While *carcer* means literally prison, it took on the sense of voluntary but temporary incarceration. Thus the Franciscan hermitage on Subasio in Assisi, the Carceri, takes its name from the eremitical breaking away or separation from the world, an incarceration. Cf. Marcella Gatti, "A Historical Look at the Carceri in the Pre-Franciscan and Early Franciscan Period," *Franciscan Solitude*, ed. Andre Cirino and Josef Raischl (St. Bonaventure: Franciscan Institute Publications, 1995), 128-138. Information on the meaning of *carcer* can be found in Octavian Schmucki, "Place of Solitude: An Essay on the External Circumstances of the Prayer Life of Francis of Assisi," GR 2 (1988): 103-106.

did not have a cell made for him or any kind of house, but stayed beneath a rock on the mountainside. We can follow him in the way pre-
LR VI 1; Test 24 scribed: holding nothing as our own property, even though we
cannot live without the use of houses."

Chapter XXX
POVERTY OF FURNISHINGS

AC 24 [60]**This man not only hated pretense in houses; he also abhorred
having many or fine furnishings in them. He disliked anything, in
tables or dishes, that recalled the ways of the world. He wanted everything to sing of exile and pilgrimage.**

Chapter XXXI
AN EXAMPLE OF THE TABLE SET ON EASTER DAY AT GRECCIO, HOW HE PRESENTED HIMSELF AS A PILGRIM AFTER THE EXAMPLE OF CHRIST

[61]On a certain Easter Day[a] the brothers in the hermitage of
Greccio set the table more carefully than usual, with white clothes
AC 74 and glassware. The Father came down from his cell and went to the
table. He saw that it was elevated and elaborately decorated, but he
did not smile at all at that smiling table. He secretly tiptoed away, put
on his head **the hat** of a poor man who was there at the time, and
with a staff in hand, *went outside.* He waited *outside, at the door,* until Ps 41:7; Jn 18:16
the brothers had started eating. They were accustomed not to wait
for him when he did not come at the usual signal.

As they began to eat, that true *poor man cried out* at the door: **"For** Ps 34:7;
the love of the Lord God, *give alms* to this poor, sick pilgrim!" And Mt 6:2
the brothers replied: "Come in, man, **for the love of Him you invoked."** He quickly came in, and showed himself to those dining.
You can imagine the surprise the pilgrim provoked in those home-
bodies! The beggar **was given a bowl** and, sitting on the ground by
himself, placed his dish on the ashes. "Now," he said, "I am sitting
IX 1,4; LR VI 3; LtOrd 29 like a Lesser Brother!" And he said to the brothers: "The *examples of* Jn 5:25; 13:15
the Son of God's poverty should move us more than other religious. I
saw here **a table all prepared** and decorated, and recognized it as not
the table of poor men who go door to door."

The chain of events proves that he was
like that other *pilgrim* Lk 24:18

a. Thomas changes the text of AC 74 in which this event takes place on Christmas Day, not Easter.

who was alone in Jerusalem on that same day.
And he certainly made
Lk 24:32 *the hearts* of his disciples *burn as he spoke.*

Chapter XXXII
AGAINST EAGERNESS FOR BOOKS

Ps 19:8 [62] **He taught that in books *the testimony of the Lord,* not value, should be sought, and edification rather than elegance.** AC 25 Nevertheless, **he wanted few books kept, and these were to be available to the brothers who needed them.** And so, when a Minister asked him IC 189; AC 102 for permission to keep some elegant and very expensive books, he got this reply: "I refuse to lose the Book of the Gospel that I promised 2 Sm 24:12 for these books of yours! *Do as you please,* but don't use my permission for a trap."

POVERTY OF BEDS

Chapter XXXIII
THE EXAMPLE OF THE LORD OF OSTIA AND IN PRAISE OF HIM

[63] **Finally, beds and coverings abounded in such plentiful poverty that, if a brother had a ragged sheet over some straw he considered it a bridal couch.** AC 26

It happened that the Lord of Ostia, with a great crowd of clerics AC 74 and knights, came to visit the brothers at the time they were holding a chapter at Saint Mary of the Portiuncula. When he saw how **the** Jdt 14:15 **brothers** *lay on the ground,* and had a good look at their beds, which you might think were animals' dens, he began to weep loudly, and Mt 19:27 said in front of everyone: **"Look where the brothers sleep!** *What will become of us,* who are wasteful with **our surplus?"** And all those present were moved to tears, and left the place greatly edified.

This was that man of Ostia IC 99-101
1 Cor 16:9 who eventually became *the great door* of the Church,
a door which always held hostile powers at bay
until his blessed soul returned to heaven as a sacred offering.[a]
Oh, holy soul and heart of charity!

a. Thomas plays on the name of Hugolino's diocese of Ostia, connecting it with *ostium* [door], *hostibus* [enemies] and *hostia* [sacrificial victim, or host].

Placed in an exalted position,
he grieved at not having exalted merits.
In fact, he was loftier in virtue than by status.

Chapter XXXIV

WHAT HAPPENED TO HIM ONE NIGHT BECAUSE OF A FEATHER PILLOW

AC 119 [64]Since we have mentioned beds, an incident comes to mind which may be useful to retell. From the time when this holy man *had turned to Christ* and *cast the things of this world into oblivion,* he never Acts 11:21; Lam 2:6; 1 Cor 7:33-34 wanted to lie on a mattress or place his head on a feather pillow. He never broke this strict resolution, even when he was sick or receiving the hospitality of strangers. But it happened that while he was staying at the hermitage of Greccio his eye disease became worse than usual, and he was forced against his will to use a small pillow. The first night, during the morning vigil, the saint called his companion and said to him: **"Brother, I couldn't sleep this whole night, or remain upright and pray.** My head was spinning, my knees were giving way, and the whole framework of my body was shaking **as if I had eaten bread made from ryegrass.**[a] **I believe,"** he added, **"there's a devil in this pillow I have for my head.** Take it away, because I don't want the devil by my head any more."

The brother, sympathizing with the father's complaint, caught the pillow thrown at him to take away. But as he was leaving, **he suddenly lost the power of speech.** Struck by terror and paralyzed, he could not move his feet from where he stood **nor could he move his arms.** After a moment, the saint recognized this and called him. He was set free, came back in and told him what he *had suffered.* The Heb 5:8 saint said to him: **"Last night as I was saying compline** I knew for certain that the devil had come **into my cell.** Our enemy," he added, **"is very cunning and subtle;** when he can't harm you inside, in your soul, he at least gives you cause for complaint in your body."

Let those listen Ez 13:18
who prepare *little pillows on every side*
so that wherever they fall
they will land on something soft!
The devil gladly follows luxury;

a. The Latin text reads: *uti comedissem panem de lolio* [as if I had eaten bread made from ryegrass]. *Lolium* [darnel or ryegrass] is a wheat-like weed (the "cockle" of Mt 13:25) which is particularly susceptible to ergot, a fungus which can cause convulsions and altered states of consciousness in those who eat bread made from flour infected by it.

he delights in standing by elegant beds,
especially where necessity does not demand them
and profession forbids them.
On the other hand
Rv 12:9 the *ancient serpent* flees from a naked man,
either because he despises the company of the poor
or because he fears the heights of poverty.
If a brother realizes
that the devil is underneath feathers
he will be satisfied with straw under his head.

EXAMPLES AGAINST MONEY

Chapter XXXV
THE SEVERE CORRECTION OF A BROTHER WHO TOUCHED MONEY WITH HIS HANDS

1 Cor 7:33-34 [65]While this true friend of God completely despised all *worldly* 1C 9; L3C 45; AC
things he detested money above all. From the beginning of his conversion, he despised money particularly and encouraged his followers to flee from it always as from the devil himself. He gave his ER VIII 6; LR IV
followers this observation: money and manure[a] are equally worthy of love.

Gn 39:11 Now, *it happened one day* that a layman came to pray in the church of Saint Mary of the Portiuncula, and placed some money by the cross as an offering. When he left, one of the brothers simply picked it up with his hand and threw it on the windowsill.[b] What the brother had done reached the saint, and he, seeing he had been caught ran to ask forgiveness, threw himself to the ground and offered himself to be whipped. The saint rebuked him and reprimanded him severely for touching coins. He ordered him to pick up the money from the windowsill with his own mouth, take it outside the fence of that place, and with his mouth to put it on the donkey's manure pile. While that brother was gladly carrying out this command, fear filled the hearts of all of those who heard it. From then on, all of them held in even greater contempt what had been so equated with manure and were encouraged to despise it by new examples every day.

a. In 1C 9, Thomas uses the image of money as dust. In this text, money is even more despicable.

b. Cf. 1C 9 where Francis does the same after the priest at San Damiano refuses his money.

Chapter XXXVI

THE PUNISHMENT OF A BROTHER WHO ONCE PICKED UP A COIN

[66]Once two brothers were walking together and as they approached a hospital for lepers, they noticed a coin on the roadway. They stopped and began to discuss what to do with that manure. One of them laughed at the scruples of his brother and went to pick the coin up to give it to those responsible for the expenses of lepers. Seeing he was deceived by false piety, his companion told him to
ER VIII 6 stop. He reminded his reckless brother of a passage in the *Rule,* which clearly teaches that when a coin is found it should be trampled underfoot like dirt. But that brother, who had always been *stiff-necked,* Ex 32:9; 33:3
hardened his heart against these warnings. In contempt of the *Rule* he bent down and picked up the coin, but he did not escape the judgment of God. He immediately lost the power of speech; he *gnashed his* Ps 35:16
teeth, but could not manage to speak. Thus the punishment showed his insanity; and vengeance taught the proud man to obey the laws of the father. At last, he threw away the stinking thing, and his *un-* Is 6:5
clean lips[a] now washed by the waters of repentance were set free to give praise. There is an old proverb: "Correct a fool and he will be Prv 28:23; Eccl 20:17
your friend."

Chapter XXXVII

THE REBUKE OF A BROTHER WHO WANTED TO KEEP MONEY UNDER THE PRETEXT OF NECESSITY

[67]Brother Peter of Catanio,[b] the saint's vicar, saw that great crowds of brothers from other places visited Saint Mary of the Portiuncula, and that the alms received were not sufficient to provide for their needs. He told Saint Francis: "Brother, *I don't know what* Jn 15:15
to do; I don't have enough to provide for all the crowds of brothers pouring in from all over. I beg you, please allow some of the goods of those entering as novices to be kept so that we can have recourse to these for expenses *in due season.*" But the saint replied: "May that pi- Ps 145:15
ety be elsewhere, my dear brother, which treats the *Rule* with impiety for the sake of anyone." "Then, what should I do?" asked Peter. "Strip the Virgin's altar and take its adornments when you can't care for the needy in any other way. Believe me, she would be happier to

a. See the hymn of Second Vespers for the feast of the Nativity of Saint John the Baptist written by Paul the Deacon. It prompted Guido of Arezzo to name the notes of the scale: . . . *solve polluti labii reatum, Sancte Ioannes*. [Loosen the bonds that hold our unclean lips, blessed John].

b. Information on Peter of Catanio can be found in FA:ED I 204 a.

have her altar stripped and the Gospel of her Son kept than have her altar decorated and her Son despised. The Lord will send someone to return to his Mother what He has loaned to us."

Chapter XXXVIII
The Money that Turned into a Snake

[68]Once traveling with a companion through Apulia near Bari, the
Jgs 13:6, 8 *man of God* found a large bag lying on the road. It was the kind merchants call a "fonda" or sling, and it was bursting with coins. The saint's companion alerted him, and strongly urged him to pick the purse up from the ground and distribute the money to the poor. While he praised piety for the needy and extolled the mercy shown in giving them alms, the saint flatly refused to do it. He declared it was a trick of the devil. "My son," he said, "it isn't right to take what belongs to someone else. Giving away someone else's property deserves punishment as sin, not honor as a good deed."

Jgs 19:14 They left that place and hurried to finish the *journey* they had *begun*. But that brother, deluded by empty piety, was not yet at peace;
he kept insisting on the misdeed. The saint agreed to return to the
Nm 15:18; Dn 2:29 place, not to *fulfill the* brother's *desire* but to *reveal divine mystery* to the
Jn 4:6 fool. He called over a young man who happened to be *sitting on a wall*
Mt 18:16 along the road, so that *by word of two or three witnesses* the sacrament of the Trinity might be evident. When the three of them had returned to the "fonda," they saw it was bursting with money, but the saint forbade either of them to approach it that by the power of prayer the devil's deceit might be revealed.

Lk 22:41 He withdrew *about a stone's throw* from there, and concentrated on holy prayer. He returned from praying, and ordered the brother to pick up the bag, which, after his prayer, now contained not money but a snake. The brother trembled. He was stunned. I don't know what he sensed, but something out of the ordinary was going through his mind. The fear of holy obedience made him cast all hesitation from his heart, and he grasped the bag in his hands. A large snake slid out of the bag, and showed him the diabolical deceit. Then the saint said to him: "Brother, to God's servants money is nothing but a devil and a poisonous snake."

POVERTY IN CLOTHING

Chapter XXXIX

HOW THE SAINT REBUKED BY WORD AND EXAMPLE THOSE WHO WEAR FINE SOFT CLOTHES

AC 28 69 Clothed with power from on high, Lk 24:49
this man was warmed more by divine fire on the inside
than by what covered his body on the outside.

AC 29 He detested those in the Order who *dressed* in three layers of Mt 11:8
clothing or who wore soft clothes without necessity. As for "necessity" not based on reason but on pleasure, he declared that it was a
sign of a *spirit* that was *extinguished*. 1 Thes 5:19

"When the spirit is lukewarm," he said, "and gradually growing
cold as it moves from grace, flesh and blood inevitably *seek their* Phil 2:21
own interests. When the soul finds no delight, what is left except for
the flesh to look for some? Then the base instinct covers itself with
the excuse of necessity, and the *mind of the flesh* forms the con- Col 2:18
AC 30 science." And he added: "Let's say one of my brothers encounters
a real necessity: he is affected by some need. If he rushes to satisfy
it, *what reward will he get?* He found an occasion for merit, but Gn 29:15
clearly showed that he did not like it." With these and similar
words he pierced those who would not tolerate necessity. He
taught that not bearing patiently with need is the same as *returning* Nm 14:2-4
to Egypt.

ER II 13-14; LR II 14-15 He did not want the brothers to have more than two tunics under any circumstances, and these he allowed to be mended with
patches sewn on them. He ordered the brothers to shun fine fabrics, and those who acted to the contrary he rebuked publicly with
biting words. To confound them by his example he *sewed sackcloth* Jb 16:16
on his own rough tunic and at his death he asked that the tunic for
his funeral be covered in cheap sackcloth.

But he allowed brothers pressed by illness or other necessity to wear a soft tunic next to the skin, as long as rough and cheap clothing was kept on the outside. For, he said: "A time will come when strictness will be relaxed, and lukewarmness will hold such sway, that sons of a poor father will not be the least ashamed to wear even velvet cloth, just changing the color."[a]

a. Cf. AC 30, supra, 138 b.

Father!
[Ps 18:46] We are *children who are strangers*
[Ps 27:12] and, it is not you whom we *deceive,*
but our own *iniquity deceives itself*!
This is obvious, clear as day,
and increases day by day.

Chapter XL
He declares that those who withdraw from poverty will be corrected by want

70The holy man would often repeat this: "As far as the brothers will withdraw from poverty, that far the world will withdraw from [Rv 9:6; Mt 7:8; Lk 11:10; Jn 7:34] them; *they will seek,*" he said, "*but will not find*. But if they would only embrace my Lady Poverty, the world would nourish them, for they [Phil 1:19] are given to the world *for its salvation*." He would also say: "There is an exchange[a] between the brothers and the world: they owe the world good example, and the world owes them the supply of necessities of life. When they break faith and withdraw their good example, the world withdraws its helping hand, a just judgment."

[2 Kgs 1:9] Concerned about poverty, the *man of God* feared large numbers: they give the appearance, if not the reality, of wealth. Because of this [Mk 14:35; Gal 4:15] he used to say: "Oh, *if it were possible,* I wish the world would only rarely get to see Lesser Brothers, and should be surprised at their small number!" Joined by an unbreakable bond to Lady Poverty, he expected her dowry in the future, not in the present. He also sang with warmer feeling and livelier joy the psalms that praise poverty, [Ps 9:19; Ps 69:33] such as, "*The patience of the poor will not perish in the end*" and, "*Let the poor see this and rejoice.*"

---

a. The Latin text reads: *Commercium est inter mundum et fratres* [there is an exchange between the brothers and the world]. See FA:ED I, 214 b. The concept of *commercium* is incorporated into the title of the *Sacrum Commercium Sancti Francisci cum Domina Paupertate* [The Sacred Exchange of Saint Francis with Lady Poverty]. In addition to this text, it is found only twice more in Thomas's writings, 1C 35, 2C 19, always in the sense of an exchange but evoking ideas of contract and covenant.

SEEKING ALMS

Chapter XLI

HIS RECOMMENDING THE SEEKING OF ALMS

71 The holy Father was much happier to use alms begged from
ER IX 3-8; 2-3 door to door rather than offerings. He used to say that being
ashamed to beg was an enemy of salvation, asserting that shame
while begging, which does not hang back, was holy. He praised the
blush spreading over a sensitive face, but not the kind that means being overcome by embarrassment. *Using these words,* he would often Sir 20:8
exhort his followers to seek alms: "Go, for in *this last hour* the Lesser 1 Jn 2:18
Brothers *have been given* to the world so that the elect may carry out 1 Sm 1:28
for them what the divine Judge will praise: What *you did for one of my* Mt 25:40
lesser brothers, you did for me." Because of this he used to say that this
religion was privileged by the *Great Prophet,* who had so clearly ex- Lk 7:16
pressed the *title of its name.*[a] He therefore wanted the brothers to dwell 2 Sm 18:18
not only in cities, but also in the hermitages, so that people everywhere might be given the opportunity for merit, and the dishonest
might be stripped of *the veil of an excuse.* Jn 15:22; 2 Cor 2:16

Chapter XLII

THE SAINT IS AN EXAMPLE IN SEEKING ALMS

72 So that he might never offend his holy bride even a single time,
this *servant of the Most High God* would do as follows: whenever he was Acts 16:17
invited by some lord and was to be honored by a more lavish dinner,
he would first beg *some pieces of bread* at the neighboring houses, and Mt 15:36-37
then, *enriched by poverty* he would hurry to the table. Sometimes peo- 2 Cor 8:9
ple asked why he did this, and his answer was that he would not give
up a permanent inheritance for a fief granted for an hour.[b] "Pov-
LR VI 4 erty," he said, "not your false riches, makes us *heirs* and kings *of the* Jas 2:5; Rom 8:17; Mt 13:24
kingdom of Heaven."

---

a. Thomas places these comments on poverty in an eschatological context, introduced by the apocalyptic phrase of "this last hour." It continues with the more feudal concepts of "privilege" and "title," implying notions of exemption as well as inheritance. The canonical "title" of poverty entitled one to a claim to God's care, cf. FA:ED I 198 c.

b. A lord granted a vassal land in "fief," i.e. in *fidelitas* [fidelity] for as long as he fulfilled the obligations prescribed. Feudalism, the political and economic system of medieval western Europe, was based on the institutions of vassalage and fief-holding; that is, the humble sought out a powerful lord and agreed to render services in return for protection and a piece of land. In this case, Francis understands poverty as a permanent inheritance, in contrast to land held under a conditional arrangement.These feudal allusions are continued in 2C 73 with its references to "a royal dignity and an outstanding nobility," and 2C 74 with its mention of "the down payment of a heavenly inheritance."

Chapter XLIII

THE EXAMPLE HE GAVE AT THE COURT OF THE LORD OF OSTIA, AND HIS RESPONSE TO THAT BISHOP

[73]Saint Francis once visited Pope Gregory of venerable memory, at that time holding a lesser office. When it was time for dinner, **he went out for alms,** and on his return he placed some crusts of black bread on the bishop's table. When the bishop saw this he was rather embarrassed, especially since there were dinner guests he had invited for the first time. The father, however, with a smile on his face, distributed the alms he had received to the knights and chaplains who were his table companions, and **they all accepted them with** remarkable **devotion. Some ate the crusts,** while others saved them out of reverence. AC 97

When the meal was over **the bishop got up** from the table and, taking the man of God aside to a private place, **lifting up his arms he**
Gn 33:4 *embraced* him **"My brother,"** he said, **"why did you shame me in a house, which is yours and your brothers', by going out for alms?"** The saint replied: **"I showed you honor** instead, while I honored a
Ps 68:17 greater Lord. For *the Lord is pleased by* poverty, and especially when one freely chooses to go begging. As for me, I consider it a royal dig-
Mt 19:21; Lk 18:22; 2 Cor 8:9 nity and an outstanding nobility *to follow* that *Lord* who, *though he was rich, became poor for our sake."* And he added: "I get greater delight from a poor table, set with some little alms, than from a great table
Ps 40:13 with so many dishes that they *can* hardly *be numbered."*
1 Sm 3:18; Jos 1:9 **The bishop, greatly edified, said** to the saint: **"Son,** *do what seems good in your eyes, for the Lord is with you."*

Chapter XLIV

HOW HE ENCOURAGED BY WORD AND EXAMPLE THE SEEKING OF ALMS

[74]At first he often used to go for alms by himself, both to train himself and to spare embarrassment for his brothers. But seeing that many of them were not giving due regard to their calling, **he** once **said:** "My AC 51
Phil 4:1; Mt 4:3; 2 Cor 8:9 *dearest brothers,* the Son of God was more noble than we are, and yet *for*
Ps 119:30 *our sake he made himself poor in this world.* For love of him we have *chosen* LR VI 3
the way of poverty. So we should not be ashamed to go for alms. The
Jas 2:5 heirs of the kingdom should not at all be embarrassed by the down
Mt 5:22; 1 Cor 1:26 payment of a heavenly inheritance![a] *I say to you* **that** *many noble and*

a. The Latin text reads: *Arrham caelestis hereditatis* [the down payment of a heavenly inheritance]. The word, *arrha,* is difficult to translate. In English, the word means "earnest money," and refers to a pledge of an eventual fuller gift or payment. The *arrha* gives the recipient an actual right to this fuller gift. By the time of Thomas of Celano it had come to designate those gifts that were given at the time of a betrothal. For a fuller discussion of the word, see Kevin Herbert, "Introduction," in Hugh of St. Victor, *Soliloquy on the Earnest Money of the Soul,* translated from the Latin with an introduction by Kevin Herbert (Milwaukee: Marquette University Press, 1956), 11.

learned men will join our company and will consider it an honor to go
begging for alms. You, who are the *first fruits* of such men: *rejoice and be* 1 Cor 15:16; Ps 32:11; Mt 5:12
glad! Do not refuse to do what you must hand on to those holy men."

Chapter XLV

THE REBUKE OF A BROTHER WHO REFUSED TO BEG

[75]Blessed Francis would often say that a true Lesser Brother should not go for long periods without seeking alms. "And the more noble my son is," he said, "the more eager he should be to go, because in that way merits for him are increased."

AC 97 In a certain place there was a brother who was no "one" for begging, but was "many" for eating. The saint observed this friend of the
belly, who shared in the fruits but not in the labor, and said to him
once: "Go on your way, Brother Fly, because you want to feed on
the sweat of your brothers but wish to be idle in the *work of God*.[a] 1 Cor 15:58
You are just like Brother Drone, who wants to be the first to eat the
honey without doing the work of the bees." This *man of the flesh* real- 1 Cor 3:3
ized that his gluttony had been discovered, and he went back to the
world, which he had never left. He left religion. And he who was no
"one" for begging, now was no brother; he who was many "ones" for
eating, became even more for the devil.

Chapter XLVI

HOW HE RAN TO MEET A BROTHER CARRYING ALMS AND KISSED HIM ON THE SHOULDER

AC 98 [76]Another time at the Portiuncula a certain brother was returning
from Assisi with alms, and as he approached the place he broke into
song, and began in a loud voice to *praise the Lord*. When the saint Ps 135:1
heard him, he suddenly jumped up and ran outside. He kissed the
brother on the shoulder, and took the sack on his own shoulder, saying: "Blessed be my brother who goes willingly, begs humbly, and *re-* Lk 10:17
turns joyfully!"

Chapter XLVII

HOW HE GOT SOME SECULAR KNIGHTS TO GO SEEKING ALMS

AC 96 [77]When blessed Francis, suffering every kind of illness, was already close to his end, the people of Assisi through their formally

a. In the *Rule of Saint Benedict*, *Opus Dei* [the work of God] refers to the celebration of the Divine Office or Liturgy of the Hours. In this instance, the meaning includes the sacred work of begging for alms.

appointed representatives sought him out in the place at Nocera, so as *not to give their glory to others,* that is, the body of the *man of God.* As knights carried him reverently on horseback, they came to a very poor village called Satriano.[a] Their hunger and the time of day called for food, but they went through the whole place and *found nothing* for sale. So the knights came back to blessed Francis and said: **"You must give us some of your alms, because we can find nothing** here **to buy."** The saint *replied and said:* **"You didn't find anything because you trust your flies** more than **in God."** He used to call coins "flies." **"But go back,"** he said, **"to the houses** you have visited, offering **the love of God** instead of money, and humbly beg for alms! Don't be embarrassed. After sin everything is bestowed as alms, for the Great Almsgiver gives to the worthy and the unworthy with kind piety." The knights overcame their embarrassment and promptly went begging alms, and they bought more with the love of God than with money. In fact everyone eagerly gave with good humor, and hunger could not have its way where lavish poverty held sway.

Chapter XLVIII
A PIECE OF A CAPON TURNED INTO FISH AT ALESSANDRIA

78 In almsgiving he sought profit for souls
rather than support for the body,
and *he made himself an example* for others
no less in *giving*
than in *receiving* alms.

Once he came to Alessandria in Lombardy *to preach the word of God,* and was devoutly welcomed as a guest by a *godfearing man* of praiseworthy reputation. This man asked him to *eat* of everything *set before him,* in observance of the holy Gospel. Overcome by the graciousness of his host, he graciously agreed. The host then hurried off and prepared a fat, seven-year-old capon for the *man of God* to eat.[b] As the Patriarch of the Poor[c] was sitting at table with the joyful family, a *son of*

a. Fortini maintains that Satriano was a castello northeast of Assisi, in a valley beyond Mount Subasio. It is mentioned in the records of the Commune of Assisi in 1030 in which property in Satirano was given to the abbot of the monastery of Farfa. See Fortini, *Francis* 591j.

b. A belief existed that certain precious stones could be found in the entrails of a capon that had reached seven years, cf. Philippe de Thaon, *Les Lapidaires Francais au Môyen Age,* ed. L. Pannier (Paris, 1882). A French proverb maintained: Capon of eight months, a feast for a king, cf. Le Roux de Lincy, *Le Livres de Proverbs Francais,* t. I (Paris, 1842), 155.

c. This is only instance of Thomas's use of this title.

Belial[a] suddenly appeared at the door, poor in grace, but pretending
to be poor in necessities of life. He cleverly invoked the love of God as
he begged for alms, and in a tearful voice requested help for God's
2:17, 19; Rom 9:5 sake. The saint acknowledged the *Name which is blessed above all* and
s 14:18; Ps 19:11 which was to him *sweeter than honey*. He gladly took a piece of the bird
that was being served, put it on a piece of bread,[b] and gave it to the
beggar.

What else? The wretch saved the gift so as to discredit the saint!

Jn 1:43; 12:12 79 *The next day* the people gathered and, as usual, the holy man was
ts 13:5; Gn 27:34 *proclaiming the word of God*, when that wicked man suddenly *cried out*,[c]
Acts 4:10 trying to show the piece of capon to *all the people*. "Look," he yelled,
"see what kind of man this Francis is. He preaches; you revere him as
a holy man! Look at the meat he gave me, which he was eating last
night!" They all turned on that wicked man, and accused him of being possessed by the devil, for what he insisted was a piece of capon
appeared to all of them as a fish. The wretched man himself was astounded at the miracle, and he was compelled to admit what the oth-
Jos 7:15 ers said. Finally, his *crime discovered*, blushing with shame, the
miserable man wiped it away by penance. He begged the saint's for-
Is 46:8 giveness in front of everyone, confessing his evil intention. After *the
rebel turned back* to his senses, the meat returned to its original nature.

THOSE WHO RENOUNCE THE WORLD

Chapter XLIX

THE EXAMPLE OF A MAN WHO GAVE TO HIS RELATIVES RATHER THAN TO THE POOR AND HOW THE SAINT REBUKED HIM

80 The saint taught those coming to the Order
Mt 5:31; Is 50:1; Jer 3:8 that, before giving to the world a *bill of divorce*
they should first offer what was theirs outwardly
Heb 9:14 and then *offer themselves* inwardly *to God*.

a. The term, "son of Belial," (cf. 2C 24) refers to one taken over by evil. In this case, it probably refers to a Cathar heretic, since the Cathars condemned the eating of flesh meat. For background information on the Cathars, see Herbert Grundmann, *Religious Movements in the Middle Ages*, translated by Steven Rowan with an introduction by Robert E. Lerner (Notre Dame, London: University of Notre Dame Press, 1995).

b. Slices or flat rolls of bread were often used instead of plates in the Middle Ages. Since the beggar could take the "plate" home and not have to return it, this custom would fit well in these circumstances.

c. The word *irrugit*, [cried out] appears only once in the Vulgate version of the Bible, i.e. in this passage of Gn 27:34, the plea of the frustrated Esau, the first born son, after Isaac bestowed his blessing on the younger son, Jacob.

He would admit to the Order
only those who had given up everything
and kept nothing,
Mt 19:21 both because of the words of the holy Gospel ER II 4; LR II 5
and because they should not cause scandal
Jn 12:6 by keeping *a money bag*. ER VIII 7; Adm IV

[81]It happened once in the March of Ancona after the saint had AC 62
been preaching, that a man came to him humbly requesting to enter
Jas 2:5 the Order. And the holy man said to him: "If you want to join *God's*
1 Cor 13:3 *poor*, first *distribute* what you have to the *poor* of the world." When he
Ps 112:9 heard this, the man went off and, **led by the love of the flesh,** *distrib-*
uted **his goods to his relatives** and not to the *poor*. When he came
back and told the saint about his open-handed generosity, the father
laughed at him: "**Go on your way, Brother Fly,**" he said, "for you
Gn 12:1; Acts 7:3 have not yet *left your home* and *family*. You gave what you had to your
Sir 34:24-25 relatives and *cheated the poor*. You are not worthy of the holy poor. You
Wis 4:3 began with flesh, and *laid down* a crumbling *foundation* for a spiritual
1 Cor 2:14; Lk 6:30 building!" And so this *carnal man* returned to his own, and *demanded*
back his goods: refusing to leave them to the poor; he soon left his proposal of virtue.

Today, this kind of stingy distribution fools
many setting out on a blessed life with a worldly beginning.
Jgs 16:17 Nobody *consecrates* himself *to God*
Prov 10:22 to *make* his relatives *rich*,
Rom 2:7; Phil 1:22 but to *acquire life by the fruit of good work*,
redeeming his sins
Ex 13:13 *by the price* of piety.

He often taught that if the brothers were in want, it was better to have recourse to others than to those who were entering the Order, primarily for the sake of example and also to avoid any appearance of base interests.

A Vision about Poverty

Chapter L

82At this point I would like to tell about a memorable vision the saint had.

One night, after praying for a long time, he gradually grew drowsy and fell asleep. Then his holy soul was brought into *the sanctuary of God*, and, among other things, he saw *in a dream* a lady who looked like this: *Her head* seemed to be *of gold, her breast and arms of silver, her belly* was crystal, and her lower parts of *iron. She was tall in stature, slim and harmonious in form. But that very beautiful* lady was covered by a filthy mantle. When the blessed Father *got up the next morning* he told this vision to the holy man, Brother Pacifico, but without explaining what it meant.

Ps 73:17; Gn 20:3; Dn 2:31-33; Ez 23:23; Gn 24:54

Many have interpreted it as they please, but I do not think it out of place to keep to the interpretation of Pacifico, which *the Holy Spirit suggested* to him as he was hearing it. "This very beautiful lady," he said, "is the beautiful soul of Saint Francis. Her golden head is his contemplation and wisdom about things of eternity; her silver breast and arms are *the words of the Lord meditated in the heart* and *carried out in deeds.* The hardness of the *crystal* is his sobriety, its *sparkle* is his chastity, and iron is his steadfast perseverance. Finally, consider the filthy mantle as the little and despised body covering his *precious soul.*"

Jn 14:26; Ps 11:7; Ps 118:11; Gn 11:6; Sir 43:22; Rv 4:6; Rv 22:1; Prv 6:26

However, many others who also *have the Spirit of God* understand this Lady, as the father's bride, Poverty. "The reward of glory made her golden," they say, "the praise of fame made her silver; profession made her crystal, because she was internally and externally the same, without a money-pouch; and perseverance until the end made her iron. But the opinion of *carnal men* has woven a filthy garment for this exceptional lady."

Dn 4:5; 1 Cor 7:40; 1 Cor 2:14

Many also apply this vision to the Order, following the successive periods of Daniel.[a] But it is evident that the vision is principally about the father, since to avoid vanity he absolutely refused to interpret it. Surely if it had touched on the Order, he would not have passed over it in total silence.

Dn 2:36-45

a. Daniel's interpretation of King Nebuchadnezzar's dream of the golden, silver, brass, and iron statue was considered a prophetic announcement of the course of the history. Cf. Bernard McGinn, *Visions of the End: Apocalyptic Traditions in the Middle Ages* (New York: Columbia University Press, 1979), 94-116.

SAINT FRANCIS'S COMPASSSION TOWARD THE POOR

Chapter LI
HIS COMPASSION TOWARD THE POOR AND HOW HE ENVIED THOSE POORER THAN HIMSELF

[83]What tongue could
tell of this man's compassion for the poor?
He certainly had an inborn kindness,
doubled by the piety poured out on him.
Therefore,
Sg 5:6 Francis's *soul melted* for the poor,
and to those to whom he could not extend a hand,
he extended his affection.
Any need, Off I V
any lack he noticed in anyone,
with a rapid change of thought, he turned back to Christ.
In that way
he read the Son of our Poor Lady in every poor person.
As she held Him naked in her hands
so he carried Him naked in his heart.
1 Pt 2:1 Although he had driven away *all envy* from himself,
he could not give up his envy of poverty.
If he saw people poorer than himself, 1C 76
he immediately envied them and,
contending with a rival for poverty
was afraid he would be overcome.

Gn 39:11;1 Sm 2:27 [84]*It happened* one day when the *man of God* **was going about** AC 113
preaching he met a poor man on the road. Seeing the man's nakedness, he was deeply moved and, turning **to his companion, said: "This man's need brings great shame on us; it passes** a harsh **judgment on our poverty." "How so, brother?" his companion replied.** The saint answered in a sad voice: "I chose Poverty for my riches and for my Lady, but look: She shines brighter in this man. Don't you know that **the whole world has heard** that we are the poorest of all for Christ? But this poor man proves it is otherwise!"

Oh enviable envy!
Oh rivalry to be rivaled by his children!
This is not the envy
that is distressed by the good fortune of others;

nor that which grows dim in the sun's rays,
opposed to piety and tormented by spite.
Do you think that Gospel poverty
has nothing worth envying?
She has Christ himself,
and through him has *all in all.* 1 Cor 12:6
Why do you pant after stipends,
clerics of today?
Tomorrow you will know Francis was rich
when you find in your hand
the stipend of torments.

Chapter LII

HOW HE CORRECTED A BROTHER WHO CRITICIZED A POOR MAN

AC 114 85 Another day, when he was preaching, a sick poor man came to
the place. Taking pity on the man's double misfortune—that is, his
need and his illness—he began to speak about poverty with his companion. And since suffering with the suffering, he had moved beyond *to the depths of his heart,* when the saint's companion said to Ps 73: 7
him: "My brother, it is true that he is poor, but it could be that in
the whole province there is no one who desires riches more!" At
once the saint rebuked him, and as the companion acknowledged
his fault, said to him: *"Quickly now, strip off* your tunic; throw yourself Is 5:19; Bar 5:1
down at the poor man's feet and confess your fault! And, don't just
ask his pardon, but also beg for his prayers!" The brother obeyed,
made his amends and returned. The saint said to him: "Brother,
X 5; 2LtF 5; 2C 83 whenever you see a poor person, a mirror of the Lord and his poor
Mother is placed before you. Likewise in the sick, look closely for the
infirmities which He accepted *for our sake."* Mt 8:17; Is 53:4

Ah!
Always *a bundle of myrrh* abided in Francis.[a] Sg 1:13
Always *he gazed upon the face of* his *Christ.* Ps 84:10, Vg
Always he caressed the *Man of Sorrows, familiar with suffering.*[b] Is 53:3

---

a. Because myrrh was a bitter spice used in embalming, the verse, *My beloved is to me as a bundle of myrrh which rests on my bosom* (Sg 1:13), was interpreted mystically as meaning that the Passion of Christ should always be in the Christian's heart. See William of St-Thierry, *Commentary on the Song of Songs,* 80-83, and Bernard, *Homilies on the Song of Songs,* 43:3-5.

b. Francis's embrace of the Suffering Christ is developed in 1C 84, 92-93, 97-98, 102, 103. For the impact of Francis's continued gaze on Christ, see Octavian Schmucki, "The Passion of Christ in the Life of St. Francis of Assisi: A Comparative Study of the Sources in the Light of Devotion to the Passion Practiced in His Time," GR 4 (1990): 61-85.

Chapter LIII
THE MANTLE GIVEN TO AN OLD WOMAN IN CELANO

86 In Celano at winter time Saint Francis was wearing a piece of folded cloth as a cloak, which a man from Tivoli, a friend of the brothers, had lent him. While he was at the palace of the bishop of the Marsi,[a] an old woman came up to him *begging for alms*. He quickly unfastened the cloth from his neck, and, although it belonged to someone else, he gave it to the poor old woman, saying: "Go and make yourself a tunic; you really need it." The old woman laughed; she was stunned—I don't know if it was out of fear or joy—and took the piece of cloth from his hands. She ran off quickly, so that delay might not bring the danger of having to give it back, and cut it with scissors. But when she saw that the cut cloth would not be enough for a tunic, she returned to the saint, knowing his earlier kindness, and showed him that the material was not enough. The saint turned his eyes on his companion, who had just the same cloth covering his back. "Brother," he said, "do you hear what this old woman is saying? For the love of God, let us bear with the cold! Give the poor woman the cloth so she can finish her tunic." He gave his, the companion offered his as well, and both were left naked so the old woman could be clothed.

AC 31; Acts 3:2

Chapter LIV
ANOTHER POOR PERSON TO WHOM HE GAVE ANOTHER MANTLE

87 Another time when he was coming back from Siena he met a poor man, and the saint said to his companion: "Brother, we must give back to this poor man the mantle that is his. *We accepted* it *on loan* until we should happen to find someone poorer than we are." The companion, seeing the need of his pious father, stubbornly objected that he should not provide for someone else by neglecting himself. But the saint said to him: "I do not want to *be a thief*; we will be accused of theft if we do not give to someone in greater need." So his companion gave in, and he gave up the mantle.

AC 32; Lk 6:34; Prv 22:7; Jn 12:6

a. See AC 31, supra 138 c.

Chapter LV

HE DOES THE SAME WITH ANOTHER POOR MAN

AC 33 [88]A similiar thing happened at "Le Celle" of Cortona. Blessed
Francis was wearing a new mantle which the brothers had gone to
some trouble to find for him. A poor man came to the place weeping for his dead wife and his poor little family which was *left deso-* Ps 10:14
late. The saint said to him: "I'm giving you this cloak for the love of
God, but on the condition that you do not hand it over to anyone
unless they pay well for it." The brothers immediately came running to take the mantle away and prevent this donation. But the
poor man, *taking courage* from the father's look, clutched it with 2 Chr 17:6
both hands and defended it as his own. *In the end* the brothers had 2 Mc 5:5
to redeem the mantle, and the poor man left after getting his price.

Chapter LVI

HOW HE GAVE HIS MANTLE TO A CERTAIN MAN SO THAT HE WOULD NOT HATE HIS LORD

AC 34 [89]Once when he was at Colle in the county of Perugia Saint
Francis met a poor man whom he had known before *in the world.* He Ti 2:12
asked him: "Brother, how are you doing?" The man malevolently
began to *heap curses* on his lord, who had taken away everything he Nm 5
had. "Thanks to my lord, *may the Almighty Lord curse* him, I'm very Rv 1:8, Gn
bad off!" Blessed Francis felt more pity for the man's soul, rooted
in mortal hatred, than for his body. He said to him: "Brother, forgive your lord for the love of God, so you may *set your soul free,* and it Est 4:13
may be that he will *return* to you *what he has taken.* Otherwise you Ex 22:12
will *lose* not only your property but also your *soul.*" He replied: "I Lk 9:24
can't entirely forgive him unless he first gives back what he took."
Blessed Francis had a mantle on his back, and said to him: "Here,
I'll give you this cloak, and beg you to forgive your lord for the love
of *the Lord God.*" The man's mood sweetened, and, moved by this Is 42:5
kindness, he took the gift and forgave the wrongs.

Chapter LVII

HOW HE GAVE THE HEM OF HIS TUNIC TO A POOR MAN

[90]Once, when a poor man asked him for something, he had nothing at hand, so he unstitched the hem of his tunic and gave it to the poor man. More than once in the same situation he took off his trousers.

Col 3:12 With such *depths of piety*
he knew no bounds for the poor;
with such depths of feeling he followed
I Pt 2:21 the *footprints of* the poor *Christ.*

Chapter LVIII

How he had the first New Testament in the Order given to the poor mother of two of the brothers

[91]The mother of two of the brothers once came to the saint, confi- AC 93
Acts 3:2 dently *asking for alms*. Sharing her pain the holy father said to Brother
Peter of Catanio: "Can we **give** some alms **to our mother?"** He used
to call **the mother of any brother his** mother and the mother **of all**
Lk 11:41 **the brothers.** Brother Peter replied: "There is *nothing left* in the house
which we could *give* her." Then he added: **"We do have one New Testament, for reading the lessons at matins,** since we don't have a breviary." Blessed Francis said to him: **"Give our mother the New Testament so she can sell it to care for her needs,** for through it we are reminded to help the poor. **I believe that** God **will be pleased more by the giving** than by the reading."[a] So the book was given to the woman, and the first Testament in the Order was given away though this sacred piety.

Chapter LIX

How he gave his mantle to a poor woman with an eye disease

[92]At the time when Saint Francis was staying at the palace of the AC 89
bishop of Rieti to be treated for his eye disease, **a poor woman from Machilone** who had the same disease as the saint came to see the doctor.[b]

Then the saint, speaking familiarly to his guardian,[c] nudged him a bit: **"Brother Guardian, we have to give back what belongs to someone else."** And he answered: "Father, if there's such a thing with us, let it be returned." And he said: "Yes, there is this **mantle,**
Lk 6:34 **which we** *received as a loan* **from that poor woman;** we should give it
back to her, because she has nothing in her purse for her expenses."

a. A similar incident occurs in the tradition of the desert when the monk Serapion sells his copy of the Gospels to help the poor, and says: "I have sold the book which told me to sell all that I had and give to the poor." Cf. Thomas Merton, *The Wisdom of the Desert: Sayings from the Desert Fathers* (New York: New Directions, 1960), 37.

b. Cf. Octavian Schmucki, "The Illnesses of Saint Francis of Assisi before His Stigmatization," GR 4 (1990): 31-61.

c. Cf. FA:ED I 98 a.

The guardian replied: "Brother, this mantle is mine, and nobody lent it to me! Use it as long as you like, and when you don't want to use it any longer, return it to me." In fact the guardian had recently bought it because Saint Francis needed it. The saint then said to him: "Brother Guardian, you have always been courteous to me; now, I beg you, show your courtesy." And the guardian answered him: "Do as you please, father, as the *Spirit suggests* to you!" The saint called a very devout layman and told him: **"Take this mantle and twelve loaves of bread,** and *go say* **to that poor woman 'The poor man to whom you lent this mantle thanks you for the loan,** but now **take what is yours!'"** The man went and said what he was told, but the woman thought *she was being mocked,* and **replied to him,** *all embarrassed:* ***"Leave me in peace,*** you and your mantle! ***I don't know what you're talking about!"*** The man insisted, and put it all in her hands. She saw that this was in fact no deception, but fearing that such an easy gain would be taken away from her, she left the place by night and returned home with the mantle, not caring about caring for her eyes.

Jn 14:26

Ez 3:1

Mt 20:14

Gn 27:12; Lk 14:9

1 Sm 20:13; Mt 26:70

Chapter LX
How Three Women Appeared to Him on the Road, and How They Disappeared After a Novel Greeting

[93]I will tell in a few words something marvelous, doubtful in interpretation, most certain in truth. When Francis, the poor man of Christ, was traveling from Rieti to Siena for the treatment of his eyes, he passed through the plain near Rocca Campiglia, taking as a *companion on the journey* a doctor who was very devoted to the Order. Three poor women appeared by the road as Saint Francis was passing. They were so similar in stature, age, and face that you would think they were a three-part piece of matter, modeled by one form.[a] As Saint Francis approached, they reverently bowed their heads, and hailed him with a new greeting, saying: "Welcome, Lady Poverty!" At once the saint was *filled with* unspeakable *joy,* for he had in himself nothing that he would so gladly have people hail as what these women had chosen. And since he thought at first that they really were poor women, he turned to the doctor who was accompanying him, and said: "I beg you, for God's sake, give, so that I can give something to these poor women." The doctor immediately took out

Gn 33:12

Ps 126:2

a. Thomas is using a comparison from Aristotelian physics, according to which "matter" by itself is amorphous, but takes its shape and characteristics from the "substantial form" which is impressed on it.

some coins, and leaping from his horse he gave some to each of them.
They then went on for a short way, and suddenly the doctor and the
brothers glanced back and saw no women at all on that whole plain.
Ps 107: 8, 15 They were utterly amazed and counted the event *as a marvel of the*
Wis 5:11 *Lord,* knowing these were not women who had *flown away* faster *than*
birds.

Saint Francis's dedication to prayer

Chapter LXI
The time, place and the intensity of his praying

2 Cor 5:6 [94]A *pilgrim* while *in the body, away from the Lord,*
2 Kgs 5:8 Francis, the *man of God,*
1 Cor 5:3 strove to keep himself *present in spirit* to heaven,
and, being already made a fellow-citizen of the angels,
he was separated from them
only by the wall of the flesh.
Ps 63:2 With all his *soul* he *thirsted for* his Christ:
to him he dedicated not only his whole heart
but also his whole body.
We will tell only a few things, to be imitated by posterity
1 Cor 2:9 —to the extent that they can be told *to human ears*—
Sir 17:11 about the *wonders* of his prayer,
things we have *seen* with our own eyes.

He turned all his time into a holy leisure[a]
Sir 45:31 in which to engrave *wisdom on his heart,*
so that, if he did not always advance,
he would not seem to give up.
If visits from people of the world 1C 96
or any kind of business intruded,

a. This is Thomas's only use of the rich monastic phrase *otium sanctum* [holy leisure]. *Otium* is an ambivalent word that could mean the post-Classical *otiositas* [laziness] and was seen as the antithesis of *negotium* [employment]. Medieval monasticism saw *otium sanctum* as the field for contemplation and frequently saw it in conjunction with *vacatio, quies or sabbatum,* all signifying rest. Bernard of Clairvaux maintained that wisdom is the product of leisure and lamented that the time of "holy leisure is not of sufficient length," cf. Bernard of Clairvaux, Sermon 85, *On the Song of Songs,* translated by Irene M. Edmonds, introduction by Jean Leclercq (Kalamazoo, MI: Cistercian Publications, 1980), 203; Sermon 58:1, *On the Song of Songs,* translated by Kilian Walsh and Irene M. Edmonds, introduction by Emero Stiegman (Kalamazoo, MI: Cistercian Publication, 1979), 108. See Hermann Josef Sieben, "Quies" et "Otium," *Dictionnaire de la Spiritualité Ascetique et Mystique* XI (Paris: Beauchesne, 1982), 2746-2756; Jean Leclercq, *Otia Monastica: Études sur La Vocabulaire de La Contemplation au Moyen Âge* (Rome: Herder, 1963), 26-41.

he would cut them short
rather than finish them,
and hurry back to the things that are within.
The world had no flavor to him,
fed on the sweetness of heaven,
and divine delicacies had spoiled him
for crude human fare.
1C 6, 71, 91, 103 He always sought out a *hidden place* Mt 6:4
where he could join to God
not only his spirit
but every member of his body.
When it happened that he was suddenly overcome in public
by a *visitation of the Lord* Lk 1:68
so as not to be without a cell,
he would make a little cell out of his mantle.
Sometimes, when he had no mantle,
he would cover his face with his sleeve
to avoid revealing the *hidden manna.* Rv 2:17
He would always place something between himself and bystanders
so they would not notice *the Bridegroom's touch.* Sg 5:4
1C 55; 2C 30 Even when crowded in the confines of a ship,[a]
he could pray unseen.
Finally, when none of these things was possible,
he made a temple out of his breast.
Forgetful of himself
he did not cough or groan;
and being absorbed in God
took away any hard breathing or external movement.

95 Thus it was at home.
But when praying in the woods or solitary places
he would fill the forest with groans,
water the places with tears,
strike his breast with his hand,
and, as if finding a more secret hiding place,
he often conversed out loud with his Lord.
There he replied to the Judge,
there he entreated the Father;
there he conversed with the Friend,
there he played with the Bridegroom.

a. The Latin text *navis plurimis insertus* [crowded in the confines of a ship] may have more than one meaning. *Navis* is translated here as ship. It could also be translated as the nave of a church.

Indeed, in order to make
Ps 66:15 all the marrow of his heart a holocaust in manifold ways,
Ps 101:3 he would place *before his eyes*
Wis 7:22 *the One who is manifold and supremely simple.*
Sg 7:9 He would often *ruminate* inwardly with unmoving *lips,*
and, drawing outward things inward,
he raised his spirit to the heights.
Thus he would direct all his attention and affection
Ps 27:4 toward the *one thing* he *asked of the Lord,*
not so much praying as becoming totally prayer.
How deeply would you think he was pervaded with sweetness,
as he grew accustomed to such things?
Jb 28:23 *He knows.*
I can only wonder.
Those with experience
will be given this knowledge;
but it is not granted to those with no experience.
Jb 41:22; Wis 7:22 His *spirit kindled,* with *boiling heat,*
his whole expression,
Sg 5:6 and his whole *soul melting.*
He was already dwelling in the highest homeland,
2 Tm 4:18 the *heavenly kingdom.*
The blessed Father usually
neglected no visitation of the Spirit,
but, whenever offered,
he would follow it;
1 Cor 16:7 and for as long as *the Lord allowed,*
he enjoyed the sweetness thus offered him.
When he was pressed by some business
or occupied with travel,
as he began to feel the touch of grace
he would enjoy brief tastes,
of the sweetest manna here and there.
Even on the road,
with his companions going on ahead,
he would stop in his tracks,
as he turned
a new inspiration into something useful.
2 Cor 6:1 *He did not receive grace in vain.*

Chapter LXII

How the Liturgy of the Hours Should Be Devoutly Fulfilled

96 He celebrated the canonical hours with no less awe than devo-
AC 119 tion. Although he was suffering from diseases of the eyes, stomach,
AC 120 spleen, and liver,[a] he did not want to lean against a wall or partition
when he was chanting the psalms. He always fulfilled his hours
standing up straight[b] and without a hood, without letting his eyes
wander and without dropping syllables.

AC 119 When **he was travelling the world on foot, he always would stop
walking in order to say the Hours,** and when he was on horseback
AC 120 **he would dismount to be on the ground.** So, one day **when he was
returning from Rome** and it was raining constantly, **he got off his
horse to say** the Office, and, standing for quite a while, he became
2LtF 85 **completely soaked.** He would sometimes say: "If the body calmly
eats its food, which along with itself will be food for worms, the soul
should receive its food, which is its God, in great peace and tranquillity."

Chapter LXIII

How He Would Chase Away the Heart's Imaginings While Praying

97 He thought he committed a serious offense if he was disturbed by empty imaginings while he was at prayer. When such a thing would happen, he did not fail to confess it and immediately make amends. He had made such a habit of this carefulness that he was rarely bothered by this kind of "flies."

One Lent he had been making a small cup, so as not to waste any
spare time. But one day as he was devoutly saying terce, his eyes ca-
sually fell on the cup and he began to look at it, and he felt his *inner* Rom 7:22
self was being hindered in its devotion. He grieved that the cry of his
heart to the divine ears had been interrupted, and when terce ended
he said, so the brothers could hear: "Alas, that such a trifle had such
power over me as to bend my soul to itself! I will sacrifice it to the
Lord, whose sacrifice it had interrupted!" Saying this he grabbed the
cup and *burned it in the fire*. "Let us be ashamed," he said, "to be seized Ez 22:20
by petty distractions when we are speaking with the *Great King* at the Ps 95:3
time of prayer."

a. For other references to Francis's specific illnesses, see AC 4, supra, 119 b.

b. In the Eastern and Western Churches it was the custom to chant the psalms standing, and listen to the readings while sitting down. Medieval choir stalls had a small projection or shelf called a "misericord," which would allow the singer some support while standing up. Francis did not even take advantage of the misericord.

Chapter LXIV
AN ECSTASY

[98]Many times he was often suspended in such sweetness of contemplation that he was carried away above himself and experienced things beyond human understanding, which he would not reveal to anyone.

However, one incident that did become known shows us how frequently he was absorbed in heavenly sweetness. One time he was riding on a donkey and had to pass through Borgo San Sepolcro, and when he stopped to rest at the dwelling of some lepers, many found
2 Kgs 5:14 out about the visit of the *man of God*. Men and women came running
from every direction to see him, and with their usual devotion wanting to touch him. What then? They touched and pulled him, cut off bits of his tunic, but the man seemed not to feel any of this. He noticed as much of what was happening as if he were a lifeless corpse. They finally came to the place, and were long past Borgo, when that
Dt 13:14 contemplator of heaven, as returning from somewhere else, *anxiously*
inquired when they would be reaching Borgo.

Chapter LXV
HOW HE ACTED AFTER PRAYING

[99]When he returned from his private prayers, in which he was
1 Sm 10:6 *changed* almost *into a different man*, he tried his best to resemble the
others; lest, if he appeared glowing, the breeze of favor might cancel what he had gained.

2 Chr 24:9 Often he would say to those close to him: "When a *servant of God* is
Lk 1:68 praying, and is *visited by the Lord* in some new consolation, he should
Jn 6:5; Lk 18:13 *lift his eyes up to heaven* before he comes away from prayer, fold his
1 Pt 1:12 hands and say to the Lord: 'Lord, you have *sent* this sweetness and
Lk 18:13 consolation *from heaven* to *me, an* unworthy *sinner*, and I send it back
Gn 27:36 to you so you may *save it for me*, because I am a thief of your treasure.'
Eph 1:21 And also, 'Lord, take away your gift from me *in this world*, and keep it
for me *in the next*.' This is the way it should be," he said. "When one Adm XXI, XXVIII
comes away from prayer he should appear to others a poor sinner, who had not obtained any new grace." He also used to say: "It happens that one loses something priceless for the sake of a small reward, and may easily provoke the giver not to give again."

Finally, his custom was to be so secret and quiet in rising for prayer that none of his companions would notice his rising or praying. But in the evening he made a good loud noise in going to bed, so that everyone would hear him as he went to rest.

Chapter LXVI

How a Bishop Found Him Praying and Was Deprived of Speech

AC 54 100 Once when Saint Francis was praying in the place at the
Portiuncula, the bishop of Assisi happened to come for a friendly
visit, as he often did. As soon as he entered the place, he went rather
boldly to the saint's cell without being invited, knocked on the little
door and was about to barge in. But when he stuck his head inside,
he saw the saint praying, and suddenly he was *struck with trembling,* Jb 21:6
his limbs froze, and he lost his voice. *By the Lord's will,* he was quickly Acts 21:14; Ps 51:20
pushed outside by force and dragged backwards a long way. I be-
lieve he was either unworthy of seeing something so secret, or that
Francis was worthy of holding longer onto what he had. The bishop,
stunned, returned to the brothers, and, at the first word confessing
his fault, he regained his speech.

Chapter LXVII

How an Abbot Felt the Power of His Prayer

AC 76 101 Another time the abbot of the monastery of San Giustino in the
diocese of Perugia happened to meet Saint Francis, and quickly dismounting from his horse, conversed for a short time with him about
the salvation of his soul. Finally, as he left him, he humbly asked him
to pray for him, and Saint Francis replied: "My Lord, I will willingly
pray." Now, when the abbot had ridden away a short distance, the
saint said to his companion: "Wait for me a little while, brother, for
I want to pay that debt I promised." For this was always his custom,
that when he had a request for prayer he never did *toss* it *behind his* Is 38:17
back, but rather *fulfilled his promise* quickly. As the saint entreated Prv 25:14
God, the abbot suddenly *felt in spirit* unusual warmth and sweetness Rom 8:5
like nothing he felt before, and carried *into ecstasy,* he seemed to faint Acts 11:5
away. This lasted for a short time, and then he *returned to his senses* and Lk 15:17
realized the power of Saint Francis's prayer. From that time on he always burned with ever greater love for the Order, and told many
about this miraculous event.

These small gifts are the kind
that servants of God should give each other;
among them,

Phil 4:15 this is the proper *communion* of *giving* and *receiving*.
This holy love, sometimes called "spiritual,"
is content with the fruit of prayer:
charity holds earthly gifts in low esteem.
To help and be helped in spiritual warfare,
to commend and be commended
2 Cor 5:10 *before Christ's judgement seat*,
that is what I believe is characteristic of holy love.
How far do you think Francis rose in prayer,
if he could raise up someone else this way by his merits?

THE SAINT'S UNDERSTANDING OF SACRED SCRIPTURE AND THE POWER OF HIS WORDS

Chapter LXVIII
HIS KNOWLEDGE AND MEMORY

102 Although this blessed man
was not educated in scholarly disciplines,
Col 3:1-3; Jas 1:17 still he learned from God *wisdom from above*
and, enlightened by the splendors of eternal light,
he understood Scripture deeply.
His genius, pure and unstained,
Col 1:26 penetrated *hidden mysteries*.
Where the knowledge of teachers is outside,
the passion of the lover entered.
He sometimes read the Sacred Books,
and whatever he once put into his mind,
Rom 2:15; 2 Cor 3:2 he *wrote* indelibly *in his heart*.
His memory took the place of books,[a]
Because, if he heard something once,
it was not wasted,
as his heart would mull it over with constant devotion.
He said this was the fruitful way to read and learn,
rather than to wander through a thousand treatises.
He considered a true philosopher
the person who never set anything ahead

a. Athanasius writes of Anthony: "For he paid such close attention to what was read that nothing from Scripture did he fail to take in, rather he grasped everything, and in him the memory took the place of books." Cf. Athanasius, *The Life of Antony* 3, in *Athanasius: The Life of Antony and The Letter to Marcellinus*, translation and introduction by Robert C. Gregg, preface by William A. Clebsch (New York, Ramsey, Toronto, Paulist Press, 1980), 31-32. For an in-depth study on the importance of the memory for a medieval person, see Mary J. Carruthers, *The Book of Memory: A Study of Memory in Medieval Culture* (New York: Cambridge University Press, 1990).

of the desire for eternal life.
He affirmed that it was easy to move
from self-knowledge to *knowledge of God* Prv 2:5
for someone who searches Scripture intently
with humility and not with presumption.
He often untangled the ambiguities of questions.
Unskilled in words, 2 Cor 11:6
he spoke splendidly with understanding and power.

Chapter LXIX

HOW HE EXPLAINED A PROPHET'S WORDS AT THE REQUEST OF A BROTHER PREACHER

AC 35 103 While he was staying in Siena someone from the Order of
Preachers happened to arrive; he was a *spiritual man* and a Doctor Hos 9:7
of Sacred Theology. He visited blessed Francis, and he and the holy
man enjoyed a long and sweet conversation about the *words of the* Jn 3:34
AC36 *Lord*. This teacher asked him about the words of Ezekiel: *If you do* Ez 3:18-20; 33: 7-9
not warn the wicked man about his wickedness, I will hold you responsible
for his soul. "I'm acquainted with many people, good Father, who
live in mortal sin, as I'm aware. But I don't always *warn them* about
their *wickedness*. Will I then be held *responsible for their souls?"* Ez 3:18
Test 19 Blessed Francis then said that he was an unlettered man, and it
would be better for him to be taught by the other rather than to answer a question about Scripture. But that humble teacher replied:
"Brother, it's true I have heard these words explained by some
wise men, still, I'd be glad to hear how you understand it." So
blessed Francis said to him: "If that passage is supposed to be understood in a universal sense, then I understand it to mean that a
servant of God should be burning with life and holiness so brightly, Dn 6:20
that by the *light* of *example* and the tongue of his *conduct*, he will re- Jn 5:35; 1 Tm 4:12
buke all the wicked. In that way, I say, the brightness of his life and
the fragrance of his reputation will *proclaim their wickedness* to all of Ez 3:19
them." That man went away greatly edified, and said to the companions of blessed Francis: "My brothers, the theology of this
man, held aloft by purity and contemplation, is a *soaring eagle*,[a] Jb 9:26
while our learning *crawls on its belly on the ground*." Gn 3:14

---

a. An allusion to the well-known characteristics attributed to the eagle in the medieval bestiaries. The eagle could soar close to the sun, and its eyes were not blinded by looking directly upon it, but were rather fed and strengthened by it. Cf. *The Book of Beasts: A Translation from a Latin Bestiary of the Twelfth Century*, trans. and ed. T.H. White (New York: G.P. Putnam, 1954), 105-106.

Chapter LXX
THINGS HE EXPLAINED WHEN ASKED BY A CARDINAL

[104]Another time, when he was in Rome at the home of a cardinal,
Wis 6:24 he was asked about some obscure passages, and he *brought* to light their depths in such a way that you would think he was constantly studying the Scriptures. The Lord Cardinal said to him: "I'm not ask-
1 Cor 7:40 ing you as a scholar, but as a person who *has the Spirit of God*, and so I
Jn 15:26; Mt 4:4 gladly accept the meaning in your answer, because I know it *comes from God alone*."

Chapter LXXI
WHAT HE TOLD A BROTHER HE KNEW WHEN URGED TO CONCENTRATE ON SOME READINGS

[105]Once when he was sick and full of pain all over, his companion AC 79
said to him: "Father, you have always taken refuge in the Scriptures, and they always have offered you relief from pain. Please, have something from the prophets also read to you now, and maybe your
Lk 1:47 *spirit will rejoice in the Lord*." The saint said to him: "It is good to read the testimonies of Scripture, and it is good to seek the Lord our God in them. But I have already taken in so much of Scripture that I have more than enough for meditating and reflecting. I do not need more,
1 Cor 2:2 son; *I know Christ*, poor and *crucified*."

Chapter LXXII
THE SWORDS THAT BROTHER PACIFICO SAW GLEAMING FROM THE SAINT'S MOUTH

[106]In the March of Ancona there was a man of the world who had forgotten himself and did not know God, and who had prostituted himself entirely to vanity. He was known as the "King of Verses," because he was prince of bawdy singers and creator of worldly ballads.[a] To be brief I will just say worldly glory had raised the man so high that he had been pompously crowned by the Emperor himself.[b]
Jn 8:12; Is 9:1; Is 5:18 While in this way, he was *walking in darkness* and *in the harness of vanity*

a. This is a reference to Brother Pacifico, cf. AC 65, supra 167 b.

b. In the belief that this had been the custom in classical Rome, thirteenth-century custom introduced the formal crowning of poets with laurel by the hand of a civil authority. It is difficult to know which Emperor is referred to in the text, since there is no certain knowledge of the poet's age at the time of his conversion, or how long he had been an outstanding poet. Henry VI (1190-97) is known to have written love songs in German, Otto IV (1198-1214) may have known some Aquitanian troubadors in the court of Richard the Lion Hearted, who was his uncle, and Frederick II (King of Sicily in 1198, Emperor in 1215) was a patron of poets and writers; all three spent much time in Italy.

pulling iniquity, the divine piety had pity on him and *decided to call back* 2 Sm 14:14
the miserable man, *so the outcast would not perish.* By God's providence blessed Francis and this man met each other at a monastery of poor enclosed women;[a] the blessed father had come there with his companions to visit his daughters, while that man had come with many of his comrades to see one of his women relatives.

Then *the hand of the Lord came upon* him, and, with his bodily eyes, Ps 80:18
he saw Saint Francis marked with two bright shining swords intersecting in the shape of a cross. One of them stretched from his head to his feet, and the other across his chest from one hand to the other.

He did not know blessed Francis, but once when he had been pointed out by such a miracle, he recognized him immediately. Struck at once by what he saw, he began to promise to live better at some future date. But although the blessed Father at first preached generally to everyone there, he pointed the *sword of God's word* on that Heb 4:12
man. He took him aside and gently reminded him about the vanity of society and contempt of the world, and then pierced his heart warning him about divine judgement. At once the man replied: "What's the point of piling up any more words? Let's move on to deeds! Take me away from people, and give me back to the Great Emperor!" The next day the saint invested him, and, since he had been brought back to the *peace of the Lord,* named him Brother Pacifico. His conversion Is 26:12, Ps 85:9
was all the more edifying to many because the crowd of his vain comrades had been so widespread.

Enjoying the company of the blessed father, Brother Pacifico began to experience anointings he had never felt before. Repeatedly he was allowed to see what was veiled to others. For, shortly after that, he saw the great *sign of the Tau*[b] *on the forehead* of blessed Francis, Ez 9:4,6
which displayed its beauty with the multi-colored circles of a peacock.

---

a. Possibly the monastery of San Salvatore di Copersito in the city of San Severino in the March of Ancona. See 1C 78 and Fortini, *Francis*, 389-392.

b. The *Tau* (τ) is a letter of the Hebrew and Greek alphabet. The origin of its use as a sign is found in Ez 9:4: "Pass through the city [through Jerusalem] and mark a τ on the foreheads of those who moan and groan over all the abominations that are practiced within it." When Pope Innocent III opened the IV Lateran Council on November 11, 1215, he preached on this text. The pope set forth the Tau as the sign of penance and renewal in Christ. Francis embraced this sign as an expression of Christ's cross. He drew it on walls and he signed his name with it. An example of Francis's signature as a τ is found on the original parchment containing *The Praises of God and the Blessing*. For further information, see Damien Vorreux, *A Franciscan Symbol: The Tau,* translated by Marilyn Archer and Paul Lachance (Chicago: Franciscan Herald Press, 1977); and Octavian Schmucki, "The Passion of Christ in the Life of St. Francis of Assisi: A Comparative Study of the Sources in the Light of Devotion to the Passion Practiced in His Time," GR 4 (1990) Supplement: 13-21.

Chapter LXXIII
THE POWER OF HIS WORDS, AND THE WITNESS GIVEN TO THIS BY A PHYSICIAN

107 Although the evangelist Francis
preached to the simple,
in simple, concrete terms,
since he knew that virtue
is more necessary than words,
still, when he was among spiritual people
with greater abilities
he gave birth to life-giving and profound words.
With few words he would suggest
what was inexpressible,
and, weaving movement with fiery gestures,
he carried away all his hearers toward the things of heaven.
He did not use the keys of distinctions,[a]
for he did not preach about things he had not himself discovered.
1 Cor 2:1-2, 4-5 *Christ,* true *Power and Wisdom,*
Ps 68:34 *made his voice a voice of power.*

A physician, a learned and eloquent man, once said: "I remember the sermons of other preachers word for word, only what the saint, Francis, says eludes me. Even if I memorize some of his words, they
Sg 4:11 don't seem to me like those that originally *poured from his lips.*"

Chapter LXXIV
HOW THE POWER OF HIS WORD CHASED THE DEVILS OUT OF AREZZO THROUGH BROTHER SYLVESTER

108 The words of Francis were powerful not only when he was
Is 55:11 present; but even when they were transmitted by others *they did not return to him empty.*

Once when he happened to come to the city of Arezzo, the whole AC 108
city was shaken by a civil war which threatened its imminent de-
1 Sm 9:7 struction. Thus the *man of God* received hospitality in a neighborhood outside the city walls. He saw demons above that land leaping for joy, fanning the flames of mutual destruction among its citizens.

a. At the time of Thomas, distinctions, techniques used in art of logic for clarifying and developing an argument, were in vogue in medieval scholastic theology. Since the human person was endowed with a special faculty for making distinctions, that ability became the trait defining the human being and enabling one to unlock the mysteries of creation. Thus medieval preaching was frequently characterized by a plethora of logical distinctions.

Calling **Brother Sylvester** by name, a *man of God,* of admirable sim- 1 Sm 9:7
plicity, *he gave him this command*: **"Go in front of the city gate** and on Gn 28:1
behalf of *Almighty God* **command the devils to leave the city** at once!" Wis 7:25

Devout simplicity hurried to carry out the obedience, and *caught* Ps 95:2
up in praise before the face of the Lord, he *boldly cried out* in front of the Dn 3:4
gate: "On behalf of God, and by the command of our father Francis, get away from here, all you demons!" Shortly afterwards, the city returned to peace, and the people in it safeguarded civil law in great tranquility.

Because of this, when blessed Francis was later preaching to them, he said as he began to preach: **"I speak to you** as people once subjugated to the devil **in demons' chains,** but now, I know, you have been liberated through the prayers of a poor man."

Chapter LXXV

THE CONVERSION OF THAT SAME BROTHER SYLVESTER AND A VISION HE HAD

AP 12; L3C 30-31 109 I do not think it would be out of place to link to the preceding
story the conversion of that same Brother Sylvester, how the Holy Spirit moved him to enter the Order. This Sylvester was a secular
priest of the city of Assisi. The *man of God* once bought from him some 2 Kgs 1:10
stones for repairing a church. At that time, this man Sylvester, inflamed with consuming greed, saw Brother Bernard—who was the
first small sprout of the Order of Lesser Ones after the *holy one of God,* Lk 4:34
perfectly giving up what he had, *and giving it to the poor.* He lodged a com- Mt 19:21, 29
plaint with the *man of God* that the price of stones he once sold to him 2 Kgs 1:10
had not been paid in full. Francis smiled when he saw that the priest's mind was infected with the poison of avarice. Wishing to offer something to cool that man's cursed heat, he filled his hands with money, without even counting it. The priest Sylvester rejoiced at this gift, but even more he was amazed at the generosity of the giver. When he returned home, he kept thinking about what happened. Under his breath he grumbled a contented complaint that, although
he was already getting old, he still *loved this world;* it was amazing that 1 Jn 2:15
that younger man despised it all. At last, he was filled with a *pleasant* 2 Cor 2:15
fragrance, and Christ opened the bosom of His mercy.

He showed him *in a vision* how much the deeds of Francis were Acts 18:9
worth; how eminently they shone in His presence; how magnificently they filled the frame of the whole world. *He saw in a dream* a
golden cross coming out from Francis's mouth. *"Its top touched the* Gn 28:12
heavens,"[a] its outstretched arms circled the world on every side with

a. Matins for *Dedication of a Church,* 2nd nocturn, 2nd antiphon: *Vidit Jacob scalam summitas eius caelos tangebat* . . . [Jacob saw a ladder, its top touched the heavens . . .].

their embrace. Struck to the heart by what he saw, the priest cast off harmful delay, left the world and became a perfect imitator of the
2 Kgs 1:10 *man of God*. He began perfectly his life in the Order, and by the grace of Christ completed it more perfectly.[a]

Is it surprising
that Francis appeared crucified
when he was always so much with the cross?
Is it any wonder
that the wondrous cross,
taking root inside him,
Mt 13:8, 23 and sprouting in such *good soil*
should bear remarkable flowers, leaves, and fruit?[b]
Nothing of a different kind
could come to be produced by such soil,
which that wonderful cross from the beginning claimed entirely for itself.

But now we must return to our subject.

Chapter LXXVI

A BROTHER FREED FROM THE ATTACK OF A DEMON

110 A certain brother happened to be vexed for a long time by a temptation of the spirit, which is worse and more subtle than prompting of the flesh. At last he came to Saint Francis, and humbly
Mt 15:30 *threw himself at his feet;* overflowing with bitter tears, he could say nothing, prevented by deep sobs. The father was moved with piety
Jn 15:14; 1 Cor 2:5 for him, realizing that he was tormented by wicked impulses, *"I command you,"* he said,*"by the power of God,* from this moment demons, stop attacking my brother, as you have dared to do up to now." At
2 Pt 2:17 once the *gloom of darkness* scattered and the brother rose up free, no 1C 46, 101
more bothered than if it had never happened.

a. Brother Sylvester had already died in 1240 before the writing of this text.

b. See the third verse of the hymn by Venantius Fortunato (530-609), *Lustra sex qui iam peregit,* Laudes during the season of Lent: *Crux fidelis, inter omnes/Arbor una nobilis:/Silva talem nulla profert/Fronde, flore, germine:/Dulce ferrum, dulce lignum,/dulce pondus sustinent* [Faithful Cross! above all other,/One and only noble Tree!/None in foliage, none in blossom,/None in fruit thy peers may be;/Sweetest Wood and sweetest Iron!/Sweetest Weight is hung on thee]. *The Hymns of the Breviary and Missal,* edited with introduction by Matthew Britt, preface by Hugh T. Henry (New York, Cincinnati, Chicago: Benziger Brothers, 1922), 53.

Chapter LXXVII
THE VICIOUS SOW THAT DEVOURED A LAMB

1C 58-61 111 His word had marvelous power even on brute beasts, as shown
clearly elsewhere. I will touch on one instance that I have at hand.
One night, when the *servant of the Most High* was a guest at the monas- Acts 16:17
tery of San Verecondo in the diocese of Gubbio, a little sheep gave
birth to a baby lamb.[a] There was a cruel sow there, which did not
spare the life of the innocent but killed it with a ravenous bite. *In the* Mk 16:9
morning, when the people were *rising*, they found the little lamb
dead, and they *knew surely* that the sow was guilty of that vicious Jn 17:8
deed. When the pious father heard this, he was moved to remarkable
compassion, and, remembering that other Lamb, lamented for the
1C 77-79 dead baby lamb, *saying in front of everyone*: "Alas, brother lamb, inno- Gal 2:14
cent animal, always displaying to people what is useful! *Cursed be* the Jb 24:18
pitiless one who killed you, and neither man nor beast shall eat of Gn 3:17
her!" It is amazing to tell. Immediately the vicious sow began to get
sick and, after paying the punishment of torments for three days, finally suffered an avenging death. She was thrown in the monastery's ditch, and laying there for a long time, dried up like a board,
and did not become food for any hungry creature.

AGAINST FAMILIARITY WITH WOMEN

Chapter LXXVIII
AVOIDING FAMILIARITY WITH WOMEN AND HOW HE SPOKE WITH THEM

112 He ordered avoiding completely honeyed poison, that is, familiarities with women, by which *even* holy men *are led astray*.[b] He feared Mt 24:24
that in this the weak spirit would quickly be broken, and the strong
spirit often be weakened. He said that avoiding contagion when Ez 21:7

---

a. An allusion to this same event is found in the *Passion of San Verecondo*, infra 806-807.

b. This narrative of 2C 112, unlike many other narratives in Book Two, is not found in any earlier source. Notice the contrast between the harshness of this number with the earlier story in 2C 38, also found in AC 69, that highlights Francis's warmth upon "seeing" the "very refined and delicate" noble lady from Volusiano. For other examples of Francis's response to women, see 2C 53, 59, 60, 86, 92, 95,132, 155, 157. It seems that in 2C 112 issues of the 1240's are attributed to Francis. Although echoing monastic encouragement of caution and respect regarding relationships with women, this negative attitude is not evident in his writings or in other earlier texts. For one who in his writings never even mentions Eve in his accounts of the Fall, the above narrative of 2C 112 is not consistent.

Jas 1:12; Prv 6:28 conversing with them,[a] except for *the most well-tested,* was as easy as
walking on live coals without burning his soles, as Scripture has it. But in
Ti 2:7 order to speak by action, *he showed himself an exemplar of virtue.*

Indeed the female even troubled him so much that you would be-
lieve this was neither caution nor good example,[b] but fear or terror.
When their inappropriate chattering made for competition in speak-
Dn 10:15; Rom 9:28 ing, *with face lowered* with a humble and *brief word,* he called for si- LR IX 3
Acts 7:55 lence. Sometimes, with his eyes *looking up to heaven,* he seemed to
Is 29:4 draw from there what he replied to those who *were muttering from the*
ground. Women in whose minds the urging of holy devotion had
made a home for Wisdom, he taught in wonderful but brief conver-
sations.

When he spoke with a woman, he would speak out in a loud voice so that all could hear. He once said to his companion: "I'll tell you the truth, dear brother, I would not recognize any woman if I looked at her face, except for two.[c] I know the face of this one and that one, but any other, I do not know."

Well done, father! For looking on them makes no one holy. Well
done, I say, for that brings no gain, but rather, much loss, at least of
time. They are an obstacle to those who want to undertake the hard
Est 15:17 journey, and look on the *face full of grace.*[d]

Chapter LXXIX
A PARABLE ABOUT LOOKING AT WOMEN

Ps 119:120; 1Cor 13:12 113 However, he used to *pierce* eyes that are not chaste *with this* AC 37
parable: "A powerful king sent two messengers to his queen, one
after the other. The first returned and simply reported her words
Eccl 2:14 verbatim. Truly *the eyes of the wise man* stayed *in his head* and did not
dart elsewhere. The other returned and, after reporting in brief
words, launched into a long story about the lady's beauty. 'Truly,
my lord, I saw a lovely woman; happy is he who enjoys her!' And
Mt 18:32 the king said, *'Evil servant,* you cast your shameless eyes on my

a. The Latin is: *harum contagionem evadere conversantem cum eis* [avoiding contagion when conversing with them].

b. The Latin text uses *femina* [female] instead of *mulier* [woman] in expressing this negative attitude. While Thomas uses femina in 1C 36, 62, 138, he does so in 2C 9, 38, 47, 93, 112, 207. In two instances of 2C, he uses the word to contrast the masculine and feminine (2C 38, 47); in two other instances, he uses the word in a negative sense (2C 9, 112). For further development on this issue see, Jacques Dalarun, *Francesco: un passaggio—Donna e donne negli scritti e nelle leggende di Francesco d'Assisi* (Roma: Viella Libreria Editrice, 1994), 88-93.

c. The originator of this story had to allow two exceptions. Francis's relationships with Clare and Jacopa di Settesoli was well known.

d. This is an allusion to King Ahasuerus who looked upon Esther with a glance of gracious kindness. It is here used allegorically to refer to the countenance of Christ.

wife? It is clear that you would like to buy what you inspected so carefully!' He then called back the first messenger and asked: 'What did you think of the queen?' And he answered: 'I thought very highly of her, for she listened in silence and then replied wisely.' 'And don't you think she's beautiful?' the king said. 'My lord,' he said, 'this is for you to see; my job was simply to deliver messages.' And the king then pronounced his sentence: 'You, chaste of eyes, even more chaste in body, stay in my chamber. Let that other man leave my house, so he does not defile my marriage bed!' "

The blessed father used to say: "When one is too secure, one is less wary of the enemy. If the devil can hold on to one hair of a person, he will soon make it grow into a plank. And if for many years he cannot pull down the one he's tempting, he doesn't complain about the delay, as long as that one gives in to him in the end. This is his work, day and night. He isn't concerned about anything else."

Chapter LXXX
THE SAINT'S EXAMPLE AGAINST EXCESSIVE FAMILIARITY

114 Once as Saint Francis was going to Bevagna he was so weak
from fasting that he could not reach the village. His companion sent
a messenger to a certain spiritual lady to ask humbly for some bread
and wine for the saint. When she heard this, she hastened to the
saint with her daughter, a virgin dedicated to God,[a] carrying what
was needed. When the saint had eaten and regained some strength,
he in turn fed the mother and daughter with the word of God. But
while he was preaching to them, he *looked* at neither of them *in the*
face. When they left, his companion said to him: "Brother, why didn't Ps 84:10
you look at the holy virgin, who came to you with such devotion?"
The father answered: "Who would not fear to look at the bride of
AC 37 Christ? And if preaching is done with the eyes and the face, she may
look at me, but I do not look at her."

Many times, when he spoke about this matter, he declared that all
conversation with women was unnecessary except for confession, or
as often happens, offering very brief words of counsel. And he used
to say: "What business does a Lesser Brother have with a woman, ex-
ER XII 3-4 cept when she religiously makes a request of holy penance or advice
about a better life?"

a. The Latin text reads: *virgo Deo devota* [a virgin dedicated to God]. This implies she lived at home under a private vow of chastity, most probably as a lay woman penitent. See 2C 34.

THE TEMPTATIONS HE ENDURED

Chapter LXXXI
THE SAINT'S TEMPTATIONS AND HOW HE OVERCAME ONE TEMPTATION

[115]As the merits of saint Francis increased,
Rv 12:9 his quarrel with the *ancient serpent* also increased.
1 Cor 12:31 The *greater his gift,*
the more subtle the serpent's attempts,
and the more violent his attacks on him.
Although he had often shown himself to be
Is 3:2 *a mighty warrior*
Gal 2:5 who had not *yielded* in the struggle even for an hour,
still the serpent tried to attack
the one who always won.

At one time a very serious temptation of spirit came upon the holy AC 63
Heb 11:37 father, surely to embellish his crown. Because of it he was *filled with anguish and sorrow*; he *afflicted* and chastised his body, he prayed and wept bitterly. He was under attack in this way for several years, until one day while praying at Saint Mary of the Portiuncula, he heard in
Mt 17:19 spirit a voice: "Francis, **if you had faith like a mustard seed, you would tell the mountain to move from here, and it would move**." The saint replied: "Lord, **what is the mountain** that I could move?" And again he heard: "The **mountain is your temptation**." And he
Lk 1:38 said, sobbing: *"Lord,* **be it done to me as you have said**!" At once the whole **temptation** was driven away. He was set free and inwardly became completely calm.

Chapter LXXXII
HOW THE DEVIL CALLED HIM AND TEMPTED HIM TO LUST AND HOW THE SAINT OVERCAME IT

[116]In the brothers' hermitage at Sarteano that evil one who al-
Rom 5:2 ways envies the progress of *God's children* dared to attempt something
Rv 22:11 against the saint. Seeing that *the holy man was becoming even holier,* and
Jas 4:13; 1 Cor 7:5 not overlooking *today's profit* because of *yesterday's,* as the saint *gave*
1 Sm 3:8 *himself one night to prayer* in his cell, the evil one *called* him *three times*:
Mk 9:37; Mt 20:21 "Francis! Francis! Francis!" And he *replied saying*: *"What do you want?"*
The reply was: "There is no sinner in the world whom the Lord will
Ez 33:9 not forgive *if he is converted*. But if anyone kills himself by hard pen-
Dn 3:39; Gal 1:12; Sir 1:6 ance, for all eternity *he will find* no *mercy*." At once *by a revelation,* the

saint *recognized* the enemy's *cunning*, how he was trying to call him
back to being lukewarm. What then? The enemy did not give up. He
tried a new line of attack. Seeing that he had not been able to hide
this *snare*, he prepared a different one, namely, an urge of the flesh. Ps 140:6
But to no use, since the one who detected a clever trick of the spirit
could not be fooled by the flesh. The devil sent into him a violent
temptation to lust, but as soon as the blessed father felt it, he took off
his clothes and lashed himself furiously with the cord, saying:
"Come on, Brother Ass, that's the way you should stay under the
whip! The tunic belongs to religion: no stealing allowed! If you *want* Is 40:4; 1 Sm 30:13
to leave, leave!"

117 However, when he saw that the temptation did not leave even
after the discipline, though he painted welts all over his limbs black
and blue, he opened the cell, *went out* to the garden, and threw him- Mk 14:68
self naked into the deep snow. Taking snow by the handful he
packed it together into balls and *made seven piles*. Showing them to Jb 38:38
himself, he began to address his body: "Here, this large one is your
wife, and those four over there are your two sons and your two
daughters; the other two are your servant and your maid who are
needed to serve them. So hurry" he said, "get all of them some
clothes, because they're freezing to death! But if complicated care of
them is annoying, then take care to *serve one Master!"* At that the devil Mt 4:10
went away in confusion, and the saint *returned* to his cell *praising God.* Lk 2:20

A certain spiritual brother was *giving himself to prayer at that time,* 1 Cor 7:5
and he saw it all in the bright moonlight. When the saint later learned Jb 31:36
that the brother had seen him that night, he was very disturbed, and
ordered him not to reveal it to anyone *as long as he lived in the world*. Ti 2:12

Chapter LXXXIII

HOW HE FREED A BROTHER FROM TEMPTATION AND THE BENEFITS OF TEMPTATION

118 Once a brother who was tempted was sitting alone with the
saint and said to him: *"Pray for me,* kind father, for I firmly believe if 1 Kgs 13:6; 1 Thes 5:25
you should be good enough to pray for me, I'll be freed from *my temp-* Lk 22:28
tation immediately. I really am tormented beyond my strength, and I
know this is not hidden from you." Saint Francis said to him: *"Believe* Jn 4:21
me, son, I believe you are even more a *servant of God* because of this. Acts 16:17
And you should know the more you're tempted, the more I will love
you." He added: "I tell you the truth, no one should consider himself
a servant of God until he has *passed through temptations and tribulations*. Jdt 8:23
A temptation overcome is like a ring with which the Lord betroths

Ps 86:4 the *soul of his servant*. Many flatter themselves over their many years of merit and rejoice at never having suffered any temptations. But sheer fright would knock them out before a battle even started. So they should know that the Lord has kept in mind their weakness of spirit. Hard fights are rarely fought except by those with the greatest strength."

HOW DEMONS STRUCK HIM

Chapter LXXXIV

HOW DEVILS BEAT HIM AND THAT COURTS ARE TO BE AVOIDED

Lk 22:31 [119]Not only was this man *attacked by Satan* with temptations, he AC 117
even had to struggle with him hand to hand. On one occasion Lord Leo, the Cardinal of Santa Croce,[a] invited him to stay with him for a little while in Rome. He chose to stay in a detached tower, which offered nine vaulted chambers like the little rooms of hermits. The first
2 Chr 6:19 night, when he had *poured out his prayer to God* and wanted to go to
Lk 4:34 sleep, demons came and fiercely attacked the *holy one of God*. They
Lk 10:30 beat him long and hard, and finally *left him half dead*. When they left and he had caught his breath, the saint called his companion who was sleeping under another vault of the roof. When he came over he said to him: "Brother, I want you to stay by me, because I'm afraid to be alone. A moment ago demons were beating me." The saint was trembling and quaking in every limb, as if he had a high fever.

[120]They spent a sleepless night, and Saint Francis said to his companion: "Demons are the police[b] of our Lord, whom he assigns to punish excesses. It is a sign of special grace that he does not leave anything in his servant unpunished while he still lives in the world. I AC 119
Rom 12:1 do not recall my offense which, *through God's mercy,* I have not washed away by reparation. For He has always acted toward me with such fatherly kindness, that in my prayer and meditation He shows me what pleases or displeases Him. But it could be that He allowed His police to burst in on me because my staying at the courts of the great doesn't offer good example to others. When my brothers who stay in poor little places hear that I'm staying with cardinals, they
Lk 7:25 might suspect that I am *living in luxury*. And so, brother, I think that
Jb 17:6; Prv 28:27 one who is *set up as an example* is better off avoiding courts,

a. For information on the identity of Leo, Cardinal of Santa Croce, see AC 117, supra, 224 a.

b. The Latin *castaldus* [police] or *gastaldus* designates in the Lombard dialect a *praefectum* [prefect] with authority to police and, if necessary, punish citizens.

strengthening those who suffer want by putting up with the same things." So *in the morning they went* to the cardinal, told him the whole Mk 16:2
story, and said goodbye to him.

Let those in palaces[a] be aware of this,
and let them know that they are *aborted,* 1 Cor 15:8
torn *from their mother's womb.* Mk 16:2
I do not condemn obedience;
but ambition, idleness, and luxuries
I denounce.
Finally, I put Francis
ahead of all obediences.
We have to endure what *displeases God,* Eccl 5:3; Ps 53:6
seeing that it *pleases men.*[b]

Chapter LXXXV
A RELEVANT EXAMPLE

121 Something now comes to mind which I don't think should be overlooked. There was a brother who, seeing some other brothers dwelling in a certain court, was seduced by I don't know what vanity. He longed to become a palace man along with them. When he was inquiring about the court, one night he *saw in a dream* those brothers Gn 31:4
put outside the place of the brothers and cut off from their company. He saw besides that they were eating out of a filthy and disgusting trough for pigs, where they ate chickpeas mixed with human excrement. The brother was stunned by what he saw, and when he *rose at* Mk 1:35
dawn he had lost all interest in court.

Chapter LXXXVI
THE TEMPTATIONS HE SUFFERED IN A SOLITARY PLACE AND A BROTHER'S VISION

AC 65 122 The saint once arrived with a companion at a church located far from any inhabited area. He wanted *to offer* solitary *prayer,* and so he Tb 12:12
notified his companion: "Brother, I would like to spend the night

a. At the time of the composition of this text, 1247, some brothers were serving as chaplains, counselors or clerks in the households of nobles or important prelates.

b. There is a sense of deep irony in this passage directed at those who enjoy the hospitality of royal courts because it pleases their hosts. All the while it displeases God.

here alone. Go to the hospice[a] **and come back to me at dawn."** When
Ps 142:3; Mt 23:14 he was alone, he *poured out long* and devout *prayers to the Lord*. Finally
Mt 8:20 he looked around for a *place to lay his head* so he could sleep. Suddenly
Jn 13:21; Mk 14:33 he was *disturbed in spirit* and *began to feel fear and loathing*, and to shake
in every part of his body. He clearly felt diabolical attacks against him
and heard packs of devils running across the roof of the house with a
Mt 26:75 great clatter. He quickly got up, *went outside*, traced the sign of the
cross on his forehead and said: **"On behalf of Almighty God I tell**
you, demons, do to my body **whatever** is permitted to you: I will SalV 14
gladly bear it. I have no **greater enemy** than the body, **so you will be**
Lk 18:3; Nm 33:4 ***avenging me on my opponent*** when you *exercise vengeance* on it in my
place." And so those who had gathered to terrify his spirit discovered
Mt 26:41; Ps 71:13 a *willing spirit in weak flesh* and quickly vanished in *shame and confu-*
sion.

Jn 21:4 123 **When** ***morning came*** his companion returned to him, and find- AC 65
1 Kgs 8:31 ing the saint lying prostrate *before the altar*, **waited for him outside**
the choir, praying fervently before the cross. He passed **into an ec-**
Rv 4:1-2 **stasy! He saw many** ***thrones in heaven*****, and one of them was** more no-
Est 15:9 ble than the rest, **adorned with** ***precious stones*** and glittering with
Dn 4:16 great glory. He wondered *within himself* about that noble throne, and
Acts 9:4 *silently thought* about whose it might be. Then *he heard a voice saying to*
Is 14:9-15 *him:* **"This throne** belonged to one of those who fell, and now it is re-
Acts 12:11 served **for** the humble **Francis."** Finally the brother *came back to him-*
self, and saw the blessed Francis coming away from prayer.
Immediately he prostrated himself **in the form of a cross** and spoke
to him as if he were already reigning in heaven, not still living in the
Ps 32:2; world: "Father, pray for me to the Son of God, that he may *not consider*
Mt 14:31; 1 Kgs 13:4; Acts 3:7 *my sins!"* **Extending his hand the man of God lifted him up,** realizing
that something must have been shown him in prayer. As they were
leaving the brother asked blessed Francis: "Father, what is your own
opinion about yourself?" And he replied: "I see myself as the greatest
of sinners. For if God had pursued any criminal with so much mercy,
he would be ten times more spiritual than I am." At this point the
Dn 8:26 Spirit said within that brother's heart: "Now you know that *the* **vi-**
sion was **true**. Humility will lift the humblest one to the seat that was
lost by pride."

a. The Latin *hospitale* refers to a hospice or asylum where travelers and the poor could lodge. Here it refers to the hospice for lepers at Trevi.

Chapter LXXXVII
A BROTHER FREED FROM TEMPTATION

AC 55 124**A certain brother, a spiritual man, an elder in religion,** was afflicted with a great *tribulation of the flesh*, and seemed to be *swallowed* 1 Cor 7:28; Ps 69:16
into the depth of despair. His sorrow doubled daily, as his conscience,
more delicate than discerning, made him go to confession over nothing. Certainly there is no need to confess having a temptation, but
only giving in to it, even a little. But he was so shamed that he was
afraid to reveal the whole thing, even though it was nothing, to a single priest. Instead, dividing up these thoughts, he confided different
pieces to different priests. One day as he was walking with blessed
Francis, the saint said to him: "Brother, I tell you that from now on
you do not have to **confess** your tribulation to anyone. ***Do not be*** Gn 15:1; Mt 1:20
afraid. Whatever happens to you that is not your doing will not be to
your blame, but to your credit. Whenever *you are troubled*, **I give you** Ps 107:6
my permission just to say seven *Our Fathers*." The brother wondered how the saint could have known about this; *smiling and over-* Prv 15:13
joyed, he got over the temptation in a short time.

TRUE SPIRITUAL JOY

Chapter LXXXVIII
SPIRITUAL JOY AND ITS PRAISE AND THE EVILS OF ACEDIA[a]

AC 120 125This holy man insisted that spiritual joy was an infallible remedy against a thousand *snares* and *tricks* of the enemy. He used to say: Eph 6:11; 2 Cor 11:3
"The devil is most delighted when he can steal the *joy of spirit* from a Gal 5:22
servant of God. He carries dust which he tries to throw into the tiniest openings of the conscience, to dirty a clear mind and a clean life.
But if spiritual joy fills the heart, the serpent *casts its poison in vain*. The Prv 23:32
devils cannot harm a servant of Christ when they see him *filled* with
holy *cheerfulness*. But when the spirit is teary-eyed, feeling aban- Acts 2:28; Ps 16:11
doned and sad, it will easily be *swallowed up in sorrow*, or else be car- 2 Cor 2:7
ried away toward empty enjoyment." The saint therefore always
strove to keep a joyful heart, to preserve the anointing of the spirit
and the *oil of gladness*. Ps 45:8

---

a. *Acedia* is one of the capital sins, described by monastic authors as one of the most enervating in the spiritual life. A type of spiritual discouragement that saddens the soul, it causes a loss of interest in the spiritual life. For an overview of considerations of *acedia*, see G. Bardy, "Acedia," *Dictionnaire de Spiritualité Ascétique e Mystique, Doctrine et Histoire* I (Paris: Beauchenes, 1936), 166-169.

He avoided very carefully the dangerous disease of *acedia,* so that when he felt even a little of it slipping into his heart, he quickly rushed to prayer. For he used to say: "When a servant of God gets disturbed about something, as often happens, he must get up at once to
Ps 51:14 pray and remain before the most High Father until he *gives back to him*
Hab 2:3 *the joy of* his *salvation*. But *if he delays,* staying in sadness, that Babylonian sickness will grow and, unless scrubbed with tears, it will produce in the heart permanent rust."[a]

Chapter LXXXIX

THE ANGELIC LUTE HE HEARD

126 In the days when he was staying at Rieti[b] for the treatment of AC 66
his eyes, he called **one of the companions,** who in the world had
Lk 16:8 been a lute player, and said to him: **"Brother,** ***the children of this world***
Wis 2:22 **do not understand** ***the divine*** sacraments.[c] Human lust has turned musical **instruments,** once assigned to the divine praises, into enjoyment for their ears. But **I would like you,** brother, to borrow **a lute secretly** and bring it here and to play some **decent song** to give some consolation to Brother Body, which is filled with pain." But the brother answered: **"I would be** quite **embarrassed** to do this, father, for I fear people **will suspect me of being tempted** to my old levity." And the saint said to him: **"Then, brother, let's let it go!** It is good to let go of many things to avoid offending people's opinion."

The following night, as the holy man was keeping vigil and meditating on God, suddenly a lute was playing with wonderful harmony
Sir 40:21; Ez 10:13 an extraordinarily *sweet melody*. He could see no one, but the *changes in his hearing* suggested that the lute player was moving back and forth
Jb 34:14 from one place to another. At last, with his *spirit turned to God,* he enjoyed such delight in that sweet-sounding song that he thought he had exchanged this world for the other.

Gn 28:18 **When he** ***arose in the morning,*** the saint called the brother in ques-
Est 15:9 tion and told him *everything from beginning to end,* adding: "The Lord,
2 Cor 1:4 who *consoles* the afflicted, has never left me without *consolation*. See, since I could not hear the lutes of humans, I have heard a more delightful lute."

---

a. An allusion to Ezechiel's allegory of the destruction of Jerusalem in 588 B.C., cf. Ez 24:3-14. Written during the siege of the city, the prophet describes the fate of remaining in Jerusalem in terms of a pot in which the best cuts of meat are placed to be boiled. Eventually everything, the pot and its contents, will be consumed. Thomas places this unique reference on the lips of Francis describing the similar fate of the one who broods in sadness, the rust of the heart.

b. This event took place when the Roman Curia was residing in Rieti. See 1C 99.

c. Thomas employs a broad notion of *sacramentum* [sacrament]. Cf. supra 2C 9, supra, 248 a.

Chapter XC

HOW THE SAINT USED TO SING IN FRENCH WHEN EXHILARATED IN SPIRIT

AC 38 **127 Sometimes he used to do this: a sweet melody of the spirit
bubbling up inside him would become a French tune on the out-
side; the *thread of a divine whisper* which *his ears heard secretly* would Jb 4:12
break out in a French song of joy. Other times—as I saw with my
own eyes[a] —he would pick up a stick from the ground and put it
over his left arm, while holding a bow bent with a string in his right
hand, drawing it over the stick as if it were a viola, performing all
the right movements, and in French *would sing* about the Lord. All Ps 13:6
this dancing often ended in tears, and the song of joy dissolved
into compassion for Christ's suffering. Then the saint would sigh
without stopping, and sob without ceasing. Forgetful of lower
things he had in hand, he was caught up to heaven.**

Chapter XCI

HOW HE REBUKED A SAD BROTHER AND TOLD HIM HOW TO BEHAVE

AC 120 128 Once he saw a companion with a sad and depressed face and,
not taking it kindly, said to him: "It is not right for a *servant of God* to Is 42:2
show himself to others *sad and upset*, but always pleasant. Deal with
your offenses *in your room*, and weep and moan *before* your *God*. But Eccl 10:20; Gn 6:8
when you come back to your brothers, put away your sorrow and
conform to the others." A little later he added: "Those who envy the
salvation of humankind bear a grudge against me, and when they
cannot disturb me, they try to do it among my companions."

He so loved the man filled with spiritual joy, that at one chapter he
ER VII 16 had these words written down as a general admonition: "Let them
be careful not to appear outwardly as sad and gloomy hypocrites but
show themselves *joyful*, cheerful, and consistently gracious *in the* Is 61:6
Lord."

Chapter XCII

HOW THE BODY SHOULD BE TREATED THAT IT WILL NOT COMPLAIN

AC 120 129 The saint also said on one occasion: "Brother Body should be
cared for with discernment, so that it won't raise the storm of *acedia*.
We must take away from it the occasions for complaining, so it won't
get weary keeping vigil and *staying* reverently *at prayer*. Otherwise it Lam 2:19

a. The narrator here is not Thomas, but the one who submitted the story.

will say: *'I'm dying of hunger*. I can't hold up the load of your exercises.' Now, if it grumbles that way after it has gobbled down a sufficient ration, then you will know that lazy ass needs a good kick, and 2C 116
the reluctant donkey is waiting for the stick."

This was the only teaching in which the most holy father's actions were not in harmony with his words. For he tamed his innocent body
Prv 23:29 with flogging and privation, covering it with *wounds for no reason*. For 1C 97
the burning of his spirit had already refined his body so much that
Ps 63:2 his most holy *flesh thirsted for God in many ways, just as did his soul*.

FALSE JOY

Chapter XCIII
AGAINST VAINGLORY AND HYPOCRISY

[130]While he embraced spiritual joy, he carefully avoided the false kind, knowing that what perfects should fervently be loved, but
Gal 5:26 what corrupts should be carefully avoided. He strove to uproot *empty*
1 Sm 29:7 *boasting* as it sprouted, not allowing anything *that would displease the eyes of* his *Lord* to survive even for a moment. Many times it happened, as he was being highly praised, he felt pain and grief, instantly turning the feeling into sadness.

One winter his holy little body was covered with only a single tu- AC 81; ER II 14; LR II 16; Test 16
nic. It was mended with cheap patches. **His guardian, who was also his companion, acquired a piece of fox fur** and brought it to him, saying: "Father, you're suffering illness **in your spleen and stomach;** so I'm begging your charity in the Lord to allow this skin to be sewn inside your tunic. And if you don't want the whole skin, at least take some of it to cover your stomach." **The blessed Francis** answered **him: "If you want** me to put up with this under my tunic, have another piece of the same size sewn on the outside, telling people that a piece of **fur is** hidden **underneath."** The brother heard, but did not agree; he insisted, but got nowhere. At last his guardian gave in, and one piece was sewn on top of the other, so that Francis should not appear differently on the outside than he was on the inside.

Oh, the same in word and life!
The same outside and inside!
The same as subject and as prelate!
1 Cor 1:31 You, who would always *boast in the Lord,*
loved nothing of outward glory,

nothing of personal glory!
But, please I do not wish to offend
those covered in furs,
if I say: *"skin for skin!"* Jb 2:4
After all,
we know those stripped of innocence
needed *tunics made of skins!* Gn 3:21

Chapter XCIV

How he accused himself of hypocrisy

AC 81 [131]**Once at the hermitage** of Poggio about the time of the Lord's nativity a large crowd assembled for the sermon, which he began with this opening: **"You all believe me to be a holy man,** and that is why **you came to me with great devotion.** But I declare to you that this whole Lent I **have eaten food flavored with lard.**" In this way he often blamed pleasure for what was, in fact, a concession to illness.

Chapter XCV

How he accused himself of vainglory

AC 82 [132]With the same fervor, whenever his spirit was moved to vanity, he displayed it naked before everyone with a confession. Once as he was going **through the city of Assisi, an old woman** met him and *asked him for something*. As *he had nothing* except his **mantle,** he offered Mt 20:20; 2 Cor 6:10
it with quick generosity. But then he felt an impulse of empty con-
1C 52 gratulations, and **at once he confessed before everyone that he felt vainglory.**

Chapter XCVI

His words against those who praise themselves

AC 10 [133]He strove to hide the *good things of the Lord* in the secrecy of his Ps 27:13
heart, not wanting to display for his own glory what could be the cause of ruin. **Often, when many** were calling him blessed, **he would reply** *with these words*: "Don't praise me as if I were safe; I can **still** Gn 39:10
have sons and daughters! No one should be praised as long as his end is uncertain. Whenever something is on loan and the lender wants it back, all that's left is **body and soul—and even non-believers** have that much!" This he would say to those who praised him. But he would say to himself: "If the Most High had

given so much to a thief, he would be more grateful than you, Francis!"[a]

Chapter XCVII
FURTHER WORDS AGAINST THOSE WHO PRAISE THEMSELVES

134 He would often say to the brothers: "No one should flatter himself with big applause for doing something a sinner can do. A sinner can fast," he said, "he can pray, he can weep, he can mortify his flesh. But this he cannot do: remain faithful to his Lord. So this is the only Adm V
Sir 35:10; Jn 9:24 reason for boasting: if we *return to God the glory* that is his; if we serve him faithfully and credit him for what he has given us.

"A person's worst enemy is the flesh; it does not know how to remember what it should regret and it doesn't know how to foresee what it should fear. All its concern is how to squander the present. What is worse," he said, "it claims for itself and takes credit for what was given not to it, but given to the soul. It grabs the praise for virtues and outsiders' applause for vigils and prayers. It leaves nothing for the soul, and even expects to be paid for its tears."

THE HIDING OF THE STIGMATA

Chapter XCVIII
HOW HE ANSWERED THOSE WHO ASKED ABOUT THEM AND THE CARE WITH WHICH HE HID THEM

135 It would not be right to pass over in silence 1C 95-96
the marks of the Crucified,
worthy of the reverence of the highest spirits.
How thickly he covered them!
How carefully he concealed them!
Is 8:23 From the *very first*,
when true love of Christ
2 Cor 3:18 *transformed* the lover *into his very image*,[b]

a. This is an echo of the sentiment found in 2C 123, cf. supra 328.

b. See Augustine, tenth treatise *On the First Epistle of John*, ch. 4, n. 9 (PL 35, 2051) and Hugh of St. Victor, *Ea vis amoris est, ut talem esse necesse sit, quae illus est quod amas, et qui per affectum conjungeris, in ipsius similitudinem ipsa quodammodo dilectionis societate transformaris* [This is the force of love, that it is necessary for you to be such as the one you cherish. Somehow by the association of love you are transformed to the likeness of the very one to whom you are joined by affection]. Hugh of St. Victor, *De arrha animae*, PL 176, 954; *Soliloquy on the Earnest Money of the Soul*, translated with introduction by Kevin Herbert (Marquette: Marquette University Press, 1956), 16.

he began to hide and conceal the treasure with such care
that, for quite *a long time,* Wis 4:13
even those closest to him were not aware of them.
But Divine Providence did not want them to be forever hidden,
never meeting the eyes of those dear to him.
In fact, they were on parts of the body that were plainly visible
and could not be hidden.

One time a companion saw the marks on his feet, and said to him: "What is this, good brother?" But he replied: *"Mind your own business!"* Sir 41:15; Jas 1:25

136 Another time the same brother asked him for his tunic in order to clean it, and noted the blood. When he returned it, he said to the saint: "Whose blood is this that has stained your habit?" The saint put a finger to his eye and said to him: "Ask what this is, if you don't know it's an eye!"

He rarely washed his hands completely; he would only wash his fingers, so as not to allow those standing nearby to see the wounds. He washed his feet very infrequently, and no less secretly than rarely. When someone would ask to kiss his hand, he offered it halfway, putting out only his fingers; sometimes instead of the hand he offered his sleeve.

He began to wear woolen socks so his feet could not be seen, placing a piece of leather over the wounds to soften the wool's roughness. And while the holy Father was not able to hide completely the stigmata on his hands and feet from his companions, he was vexed if someone stared at them. So even his close companions, filled with *prudence of spirit*, would *avert their eyes* when he had to uncover his hands or feet for any reason. Ex 28:3; Ps 119:37

Chapter XCIX

How someone saw them by a pious ruse

137 When the *man of God* was staying at Siena,[a] a brother from Brescia happened to come there. He was very anxious to see the stigmata of our holy Father, and insistently asked Brother Pacifico for a chance to do so. He answered: "When I take my leave, I'll ask to kiss his hands, and when he offers them, I'll signal to you with *a wink*, and you will get a look." When they were ready to leave, the two of them went to the saint and Brother Pacifico *on bended knee* said to Jdg 13:6 Prv 10:10 Eph 3:14

a. In April or May of 1226.

Saint Francis: "Give us your blessing, my dearest mother,[a] and give me your hand to kiss!" He kissed the hand, offered reluctantly, and signaled the brother to look. Then he asked for the other hand too, kissed it and showed it to the other. After they had left, the father suspected a holy trick had been played on him, and judging that pious curiosity to be impious, he at once called Brother Pacifico back and said to him: "The Lord forgive you, brother. You sometimes
2 Cor 2:4; Jdt 9:1 make *a lot of trouble* for me!" Pacifico immediately *prostrated himself* and humbly asked: "What trouble have I caused you, dear mother?" But blessed Francis made no answer, and the incident ended in silence.

Chapter C
How someone looked at the wound in his side

[138]Although the very location of the wounds on the hands and feet in such exposed parts of the body allowed some to see them, no one was worthy to see the wound in his side while he still lived, with only one exception, and he saw it only once.

Whenever he had his tunic shaken out, he covered the wound on the side with his right arm, though occasionally he would conceal that blessed cut by applying his left hand to his pierced side.

When a companion was rubbing him, his hand fell on the wound, 1C 95
causing him acute pain. Another brother was straining with eager curiosity to see what was hidden from the others, and one day said to the holy father: "Father, would you like us to shake out your habit?" And
Ps 18:21, 25 the saint replied: *"The Lord reward you* brother, because it really does need it." As Francis stripped, that brother spied him with *watchful eyes,*
Lam 4:17 and he saw the wound plainly marked on his side. He alone saw it during his life. None of the others did until after his death.

Chapter CI
Hiding virtues

[139]In this way this man rejected any glory
which did not *recall* Christ:
Phil 3:19 in this way he inflicted everlasting anathema on human favor.

a. For an understanding of the title "mother," see RH, FA:ED I 61-62. Carolyn Walker Bynum also notes the practice of addressing abbots in a similar way among the Cistercians. See Carolyn Walker Bynum, *Jesus as Mother: Studies in the Spirituality of the High Middle Ages* (Berkeley, Los Angeles, London: University of California Press, 1982), 110-116.

He realized that the price of fame
is to lose privacy of conscience,
and that misusing virtues is much more harmful
than not having them.
He knew that protecting what you have
is as virtuous as seeking what you lack.[a]
Ah! Vanity inspires us more than charity;
and the world's approval prevails over the love of Christ.
We do not discern initiatives;
we do not *test the spirits*. 1 Jn 4:1
And so, when vanity drives us to do something
we imagine it was prompted by charity.
Furthermore, if we do even a little good,
we *cannot bear its weight*, Jb 31:23
while we are living we keep unloading it,
and let it slip away as we approach the final shore.
We can patiently accept not being good.
What we cannot bear
is not being considered good, not appearing good.
And so we live only for *human praise*, Rom 2:29
since *we are* only *human*. Mt 8:9

HUMILITY

Chapter CII
SAINT FRANCIS'S HUMILITY IN MANNER, OPINION AND CONDUCT AND AGAINST HOLDING ONTO OPINIONS

140Humility is
the guardian and embellishment
of all virtues.
Any spiritual building without this foundation
may appear to rise higher
but is headed for ruin.
So that this man,
adorned with so many gifts,
should lack nothing,
this gift *filled* him more *abundantly*. Ps 65:12
In his own opinion

a. A paraphrase of Ovid's *Ars Amatoria* II:213. *Nec minor est virtus quam quaerere parte tueri* [No less is it a virtue to see what parts are to be protected].

he was nothing but a sinner,
though he was the beauty and splendor
of every kind of holiness.

It was on this
that he strove to build himself,
Heb 6:1 to *lay the foundation*
Mt 11:29 as he had learned from Christ.
Mt 25:16,17 Forgetting what *he had gained*,
Ps 101:3 he *kept before his eyes* only what he lacked,
considering that more was lacking in him than present.
Not satisfied with his first virtues,
his only ambition was to become better
and to add new ones.
Humble in manner,
he was more humble in opinion,
and most humble in his own estimation.
Gn 23:6 This *prince of God*
could not be identified as a prelate,
except by this sparkling gem:
he was the least among the lesser.
This virtue, this title, this badge pointed him out
as general minister.
There was no arrogance in his mouth,
no pomp in his gestures,
no conceit in his actions.
Sir 16:24; Wis 9:18 He *learned* by revelation
the meaning of many things,
but when he was conversing among others
he put the opinions of others ahead of his own.
He considered the opinions of his companions safer than his own
and the views of others better than his own.
He would say
Mt 19:27 that a man had not yet *given up everything* for God
as long as he held on to the moneybag
of his own opinions.
Ps 31:14 He would rather *hear himself blamed* than praised,
since the former moved him to change
while the latter pushed him to fall.

Chapter CIII

His humility to the bishop of Terni and a peasant

AC 10 [141]Once, when he was preaching **to the people of Terni,** the bishop[a] of that city commended him to everyone at the end of the sermon, saying: *"In this last hour* God **has honored** his Church **by means of this** *little, poor, and* **looked down upon** *man,* simple and **unlettered. And because of this** we should always *praise the Lord,* realizing that *he has not done this for every nation."* 1 Jn 2:18 Is 53:3, 66:2 Ps 147:1 Ps 147:20

When the saint heard this, he accepted it with deep feeling, for the bishop had so expressly referred to him as a contemptible man. Entering **the church,**[b] *he fell down at* the bishop's *feet,* **saying: "My Lord Bishop,** *in truth* **you have done me** great **honor,** for you alone have kept safe for me what is my own, while others take it away. *You have distinguished between what is precious from what is vile,* like **a discerning man,** *giving God the glory* and me the scorn." Mk 5:22 Ps 111:8 Jer 15:19 Lk 18:43

[142]The *man of God* not only showed himself humble to the great, but also to his peers and to the lowly, more willing to be admonished and corrected than to admonish others. For example, one day he was riding a donkey, since he was too weak and sickly to walk, and he passed through the field of a peasant who was working there. The peasant ran to him and asked anxiously if he were Brother Francis. When the *man of God* humbly answered that he was, the peasant said: "Try hard to be as good as everyone says you are, because many people put their *trust in you*. So I'm warning you; don't ever be different from what people expect!" When the *man of God,* Francis, heard this, he got down from the donkey on to the ground, and *prostrate* before the peasant, humbly *kissed his feet, thanking him* for being so kind to admonish him. Jdg 13:6 Jdg 13:6 Heb 6:9 Jdg 13:6 Lk 7:38 Tb 11:7

Although so famous that many considered him a saint, he thought himself vile *in the sight of God and people.* He did not feel proud of his great fame or the holiness attributed to him: not even of the many holy brothers and *sons* given *to him* as the down payment of a *reward* for his merits. Rom 12:17 2 Cor 6:13,18

a. Terni had been without a bishop for almost five hundred years. In 1218 Honorius III nominated bishop Rainerio (+1253).

b. It seems the bishop's sermon was preached outside in the open piazza, as often happened when the church could not hold the crowds. The bishop may have spoken from a balcony or loggia on the church's façade.

Chapter CIV
How he resigned as prelate at a chapter, and his prayer

[143]In order to preserve the virtue of holy humility, a few years af- AC 39; AC 11, 3
ter his conversion, at a chapter,[a] he resigned the office of prelate before all the brothers of the religion, saying: "From now on, I am dead
to you. But here you have Brother Peter of Catanio; let us all, you and
I, obey him." And bowing down immediately, he promised him ER Pr 3; LR I 2
"obedience and reverence." The brothers were weeping, and sorrow
drew deep groans from them, as they saw themselves orphaned of
such a father.

Jn 17:1 As blessed Francis got up, he joined his hands and, lifting his *eyes
to heaven*, said: "Lord, I give back to you the family which until now
you have entrusted to me. Now, sweetest Lord, because of my infir-
Lk 10:35 mities, which you know, I can no longer *take care of them* and I entrust
them to the ministers. If any brother should perish because of their ER IV 6
negligence, or example, or even harsh correction, let them be bound
Mt 12:36 *to render an account* for it before You, Lord, on the *Day of Judgment*."

**From that time on, he remained subject until his death, behav- Test 27-29
ing more humbly than any of the others.**

Chapter CV
How he gave up companions

**[144]Another time he consigned all his companions to his vicar, AC 40
saying: "I don't want to seem singular because of this privilege of
freedom; any brothers can go with me from place to place 'as the LR II:7
Lord inspires them.' " And he added: "Why, I have seen a blind
man who had no guide for his journey except one little dog." This
indeed was his glory: he gave up any appearance of being singular
2 Cor 12:9 or important, so that *the power of Christ might dwell in him.***

Chapter CVI
His words against those who loved being prelates and the description of a lesser brother

[145]Seeing how some were panting for prelacies, an ambition AC 109
which even by itself made them unworthy of presiding, he said that
Gal 5:4 they were not Lesser Brothers, but that *they had fallen away from glory*

a. Cf. AC 39, supra, 142 a.

by forgetting *the vocation to which they were called.* He criticized the Eph 4:1
wretched few who were upset when removed from office; they were
looking for honors, not burdens.

He once said to his companion: "I would not consider myself a
Lesser Brother unless I had the attitude which I will describe to
you." And he said: "Here I am, a prelate of the brothers, and I go to
the chapter. I preach to the brothers and admonish them, and, in the
end, they speak against me: 'An uneducated and despicable man is
not right for us; *we do not want* you *to rule over us.* You cannot speak; Lk 19:14
TPJ 11 you are *simple and ignorant.*' So in the end I'm thrown out in dis- Acts 4:13
grace, looked down upon by everyone. I tell you, unless I hear these
words with the same expression on my *face,* with the same *joy* in my Ps 16:9
heart, and with the same resolution for holiness, then I am in no
sense a Lesser Brother." And he would add: "In a prelacy there is a
fall; in praise, a precipice; in the humility of a subject, profit for the
soul. Why, then, do we pay attention to danger more than profits,
while we have time for making profit?"

Chapter CVII

THE SUBMISSION HE WANTED HIS BROTHERS TO SHOW TO CLERICS, AND WHY

AC 19 146 Although he wanted his sons *to keep peace with all,* and to be- Rom 12:18
have as little ones toward everyone, he taught them to be particularly humble toward clerics by his word and showed them by his
example. He used to say: "We have been sent to help clerics for the
salvation of souls[a] so that we may make up whatever may be lacking 1 Pt 1:9
in them. *Each shall receive a reward,* not *on account of* authority, but 1 Cor 3:8
because of the *work* done. Know then, brothers, that the *good of* Wis 3:13
souls is what pleases God most, and this is more easily obtained
through peace with the clergy than fighting with them. If they
should stand in the way of the people's salvation, *revenge is* for God, Dt 32:35
and he will repay them *in due time.* So, be subject to prelates so that
as much as *possible on your part* no jealousy arises. *If* you *are children* Rom 12:18; Lk 10:6
of peace, you will win over both clergy and people for the Lord, and
the Lord will judge that more *acceptable* than only winning over the 1 Pt 2:5
people while scandalizing the clergy. Cover up their failings, make
up for their many defects, and *when you have done* this, be even more Lk 17:10
humble."

a. Cf. AC 19, supra, 133 b.

Chapter CVIII
THE RESPECT HE SHOWED TO THE BISHOP OF IMOLA

147 When Saint Francis came to Imola, a city of Romagna, he presented himself to the bishop of that region[a] and asked him for permission to preach. LR IX 1 But the bishop said: "Brother, I preach to my people and that is enough."[b] Saint Francis bowed his head and humbly *went outside*, but less than an hour later he *came back in*. Mt 26:75, 58 "What do you want now, brother?" the bishop asked. "What else do you want?" Blessed Francis replied: "My Lord, if a father throws his son out by one door, he should come back in by another!" The bishop, overcome by his humility, embraced him with a smile, saying: "From now on you and your brothers have my general permission to preach in my diocese. Holy humility earned it!"

Chapter CIX
HIS HUMILITY TO SAINT DOMINIC, AND VICE VERSA, AND THEIR MUTUAL CHARITY

Gn 1:16 148 Those two *bright lights* of the world, Saint Dominic and Saint Francis, AC 49 were once in the City with the Lord of Ostia, who later became Supreme Pontiff. As they took turns pouring out honey-sweet words about the Lord, the bishop finally said to them: "In the early Church the Church's shepherds were poor, and men of charity, not on fire with greed. Why don't we make bishops Ti 2:7 and prelates of your brothers who excel more than others *in teaching* and *example?*"

Lk 22:24 There *arose a disagreement* between the saints about answering —neither wishing to go first, but rather each deferring to the other. Each urged the other to reply. Each seemed superior to the other, since each was devoted to the other. At last humility conquered Francis as he did not speak first, but it also conquered Dominic, since in speaking first, he humbly obeyed.

Blessed Dominic therefore answered the bishop: "My Lord, my brothers are already raised to a good level, if they will only realize it, and as much as possible I would not allow them to obtain any other mark of dignity."

As this brief response ended, Blessed Francis bowed to the bishop and said: "My Lord, my brothers are called 'lesser' precisely

a. Mainardo Aldigheri was bishop of Imola from 1207 to 1249.

b. The bishop was the "ordinary minister" for preaching in his own diocese or city. This early tradition had recently been reiterated at the Fourth Lateran Council in 1215.

so they will not presume to *become 'greater.'* They have been called Mt 20:26
this to teach them to stay down to earth, and to *follow the footprints* 1 Pt 2:21
of Christ's humility, which in the end will exalt them above others *in* Wis 3:13
the sight of the saints. If you want them *to bear fruit in the Church of* Jn 15:2,8; Phil 3:6
God, keep them in the status in which they *were called* and hold 1 Cor 7:20
them to it. Bring them back down to ground level even against
their will. And so I beg you, Father, never allow them to rise to become prelates, otherwise they will just be prouder because they're poorer, and treat the others arrogantly." These were the replies of those blessed men.

149 What do you say, *sons of the saints? Your jealousy and envy* show Tb 4:12; 1 Mc 8:16
you are degenerates, and your ambition for honors proves you are illegitimate. *You bite and devour each other,* and these *conflicts and disputes* Gal 5:15; Jas 4:1
arise only because of *your cravings. Your struggles* must be *against* the Eph 6:12
forces *of darkness,* a *hard struggle* against armies of demons—and in- Wis 10:12
stead you turn your weapons against each other!

Your fathers, *full of knowledge, look at each other* as friends, *their faces* Rom 15:14; Ex 25:20
turned to the Mercy Seat,[a] but their sons are *full of envy,* and find it *hard* Rom 1:29; Wis 2:15
even to see each other! What will the body do, if its *heart* is *divided*? Hos 10:2
Surely the teaching of piety would flourish more *throughout the whole* 2 Mc 3:12
world if the *ministers of God's word* were more closely joined by the *bond* Acts 6:4; Col 3:14
of charity! What we say or teach becomes suspect especially because
evident signs show the leaven of hatred in us. I know this is not about 2 Mc 14:15
the good men on both sides, but about the bad ones who, I believe, should be rooted out so they will not infect the holy ones.

Finally, what should I say about those concerned with higher matters? It was by way of humility, not by haughtiness, that the fathers *reached the Kingdom;* but their sons *walk in circles* of ambition and Lk 23:42; Ps 12:9
do not ask the way to an inhabited town. What should we expect? If we do Ps 107:4
not follow their way, we will not reach their glory! *Far be it from us,* Jos 24:16
Lord! Make the disciples humble under the wings of their humble masters. Make those who are brothers in spirit kind to each other,
and *may you see your children's children. Peace upon Israel!*[b] Ps 128:6

a. In this context, Exodus 25:20, Francis and Dominic are portrayed as the two golden cherubim placed on the ark of the covenant. The Mercy Seat is as a symbol of Christ.

b. This encouragement to peace and harmony reflects an encyclical letter of John the German, O.P., Prior General between 1241-1252, sent to the followers of Saint Dominic in 1246. "Show kindness above all to the Lesser Brothers. Show yourselves affable and kind to them, for the Church conceived twins in her womb and, at almost the same time, gave them birth in the light of the nations. Beware more diligently of every offensive gesture, take away any cause of anger, and should anything be annoying, while safeguarding the laws of our Order, be careful to remove it. "Litterae Encylicae Magistrum Generalium," *Monumenta Ordinis Fratrum Praedicatorum Historica* V (Rome: 1900), 7-9.

Chapter CX
HOW EACH ENTRUSTED HIMSELF TO THE OTHER

150 When the servants of God finished their replies, narrated AC 49
above, the Lord of Ostia was greatly edified by the words of both,
Acts 27:35 and gave unbounded *thanks to God*. And as they left that place,
blessed Dominic asked Saint Francis to be kind enough to give
him the cord he had tied around him. Francis was slow to do this,
refusing out of humility what the other was requesting out of charity. At last the happy devotion of the petitioner won out, and he devoutly put on the gift under his inner tunic. Finally they clasped
hands, and commended themselves to each other with great
sweetness. And so one saint said to the other: "Brother Francis, I
wish your Order and mine might become one, so we could share
Acts 15:39 the same form of life in the Church." At last, when they had *parted*
Lk 4:25 *from each other*, Saint Dominic said to the many bystanders: *"In*
truth I tell you, the other religious should follow this holy man Francis, as his holiness is so perfect."

OBEDIENCE

Chapter CXI
HOW HE ALWAYS HAD A GUARDIAN FOR THE SAKE OF TRUE OBEDIENCE

151 In order to make a profit in every possible way,
Jer 6:29 and *melt down* all the present time into merit,
this very shrewd businessman chose to do everything
under the harness of obedience
and to submit himself to the rule of another.

He not only resigned the office of general, but also, for the greater
good of obedience, he asked for a special guardian to honor as his
personal prelate. And so he said to Brother Peter of Catanio, to whom
he had earlier promised obedience: "I beg you for God's sake to entrust me to one of my companions, to take your place in my regard
and I will obey him as devoutly as you. I know the fruit of obedience,
Sir 51:26 and that no time passes without profit for one who *bends his neck to the*
Phil 2:8 *yoke* of another." His request was granted, and *until death* he re- Test 27-29
mained a subject wherever he was, always submitting to his own
guardian with reverence.

One time he said to his companions: "Among the many things AC 11
which God's mercy has granted me, he has given me this grace, that I

would readily obey a novice of one hour, if he were given to me as my **guardian,** as carefully as I would obey the oldest and most discerning. **For a subject should not consider his prelate a human being,** but rather the One **for love of whom** he is subject. And the more contemptibly he presides, the more pleasing is the humility of the one who obeys."

Chapter CXII
HOW HE DESCRIBES ONE WHO TRULY OBEYS, AND THREE SORTS OF OBEDIENCE

152 Another time, when he was sitting with his companions, blessed Francis let out a sigh: "There is hardly a single religious in the whole world who obeys his prelate perfectly!" His companions, disturbed, said to him: "Tell us, father, what is the perfect and highest obedience?" And he replied, describing someone truly obedient using the image of a dead body:[a] "Take a lifeless corpse and place it wherever you want. You will see that it does not resist being moved, does not complain about the location, or protest if left. Sit it on a throne, and it will look down, not up; dress it in purple and it will look twice as pale. This," said he, "is someone who really obeys: he doesn't argue about why he's being moved; he doesn't care where he's placed; he doesn't pester you to transfer him. When he's raised to an office, he keeps his usual humility, and the more he's honored, the more he considers himself unworthy."

On another occasion, speaking about this same matter, he said that things granted because of a request were really "permissions," but things that are ordered and not requested he called "holy obediences." He said that both were good, but the latter was safer.
But he believed that the best of all, in which *flesh and blood* had no Mt 16:17
R XV 3; LR XII 1 part, was the one by which one goes "among the non-believers, by
divine inspiration" either for the good of one's neighbor or from a desire for martyrdom. He considered this request very *acceptable to God.* Phil 4:18

a. The concept of obedience as a form of death may well have its origin in the thought of John Cassian who saw death to the world as a form of obedience, cf. John Cassian, *De coenobiorum institutionum* XII 32 (PL 47, 475). Although Thomas places this saying on his lips, Francis's writings convey a different impression of "loving obedience," cf. SalV 14, that is re-inforced by his concept of prelate as a "minister and servant" of his brothers. To see the contrasts between Francis's theology of obedience and that of others, see Jean-Marie R. Tillard, "Obéissance," *Dictionnaire de Spiritualité Ascetique et Mystique, Doctrine et Histoire* XI (Paris: Beauchesne, 1982), 535-563.

Chapter CXIII

THAT COMMANDS UNDER OBEDIENCE SHOULD NOT BE GIVEN LIGHTLY

153 His opinion was that only rarely should something be commanded under obedience, for the weapon of last resort should not be the first one used. As he said, "The hand should not reach quickly for the sword." He who does not hurry to obey what is commanded under obedience neither *fears God nor respects man.* Nothing could be truer. For, what is command in a rash leader, but a sword in the hands of a madman? And what could be more hopeless than a religious who despises obedience? AC 1

Lk 18:4

Chapter CXIV

A BROTHER WHOSE HOOD HE CAST INTO THE FIRE BECAUSE, THOUGH DRAWN BY DEVOTION, HE CAME WITHOUT AN OBEDIENCE

154On a certain occasion he took off the hood from a brother who had come alone and without an obedience,[a] and ordered that it be cast into a great bonfire. No one kicked the hood out of the fire, for they were scared by the upset expression on the father's face, and the saint ordered it to be pulled out of the flames, and it was unharmed.

Of course this may have been caused by the merits of the saint. But possibly that brother also was not without merit, for he had been overcome by his dedication to seeing the most holy father, even though he had been lacking in discernment, which is the only charioteer of the virtues.[b]

a. An "obedience" is a formal directive expressed by one in authority and, in many cases, could be communicated in writing.

b. A reminiscence of Plato's analogy of the soul as the charioteer who must control the two horses of emotion and desire (*Phaedrus*, 246, 253-6), Aristotle's doctrine that prudence must regulate all the other virtues (*Nicomachean Ethics*, VI:13), and Bernard of Clairvaux, Sermon 49:5, *On the Song of Songs,* translated by Kilian Walsh and Irene M. Edmonds, introduction by Emero Stiegman (Kalamazoo, MI: Cistercian Publications), 1979) 25. For a thorough study, cf. André Cabassut, "Discrétion," *Dictionnaire de Spiritualité Ascetique et Mystique, Doctrine et Histoire* III (Paris: Beauchesne, 1957), 1311-1330.

THOSE WHO GIVE GOOD OR BAD EXAMPLE

Chapter CXV
THE GOOD EXAMPLE OF ONE OF THE BROTHERS AND A CUSTOM OF THE EARLY BROTHERS

1C 36-37; AC 41 [155] **He used to affirm that the Lesser Brothers had been *sent from* Jn 1:6
***the Lord* in *these last times* to show forth examples of light to those** Jude 18 Mt 5:15-16; Eph 5:8
wrapped *in the darkness* of sins.[a] **He would say that he was filled** Prv 7:9
with the sweetest fragrance and anointed with strength from *pre-* Ex 29:18; Jn 12:3 Mt 26:7
***cious ointment* whenever he *heard of the great deeds* of holy brothers in** Acts 2:11
faraway lands.

It happened that a brother named Barbaro once *threw out* an in- Jb 18:2
sulting *word* at another brother in the presence of a nobleman of the island of Cyprus.[b] But, when he saw that his brother was rather hurt by the impact of that word, he took some donkey manure, and, burning with rage against himself, put it into his mouth to chew, saying:
"Let the tongue which *spat the poison* of anger upon my brother now Prv 23:32
chew manure!" The knight was thunderstruck at seeing this, and went away greatly edified; from that time on, he freely put himself and all he had at the disposal of the brothers.

All the brothers observed this custom without fail: if any of them
spoke an upsetting word to another, he would immediately *fall to the* 2 Mc 10:4
ground and embrace the feet of the one he had offended, even if unwilling, with holy kisses.

The saint rejoiced over such behavior, when he heard the examples of holiness which his sons themselves produced, and he
would heap blessings *worthy of full acceptance* on those brothers, 1 Tm 1:15
who, by *word or deed,* led sinners to the love of Christ. *Zeal* for souls, Col 3:17; Acts 5:17
which *filled him* completely, made him want his sons to resemble him as a true likeness.

---

a. This passage echoes that of Gregory the Great: "*cum per bona opera proximis lucis exempla monstramus* [since we show by good deeds done for our neighbors examples of light]" which was used in Third Nocturn of the Common of Confessors. Cf. Gregory the Great, *Homilia in Evangelium* XIII 1 (PL 76: 1124).

b. At that time Cyprus was under the Latin dynasty of the Lusignans, who had been kings of Jerusalem, and still claimed that title. Others propose the reading "island of Scipio," or Limisiano (Limigiano), near Assisi.

Chapter CXVI
SOME WHO HAVE BAD EXAMPLE, THE SAINT'S CURSE ON THEM, AND HOW PAINFUL THIS WAS TO THEM

2 Pt 2:8 [156]So also, anyone who violated sacred religion by *evil deeds* or bad example incurred the heavy penalty of his curse.

One day he was told how the bishop of Fondi[a] had told two brothers who came to him who, under the pretext of greater self-contempt, let their beards grow longer: "Watch out that the beauty of your religion is not disfigured by this bold search for novelties." At
2 Mc 14:34 this the saint immediately got up, *stretched out his hands to heaven,* his face streaming with tears, broke out into words of prayer, or rather a curse:

"Lord Jesus Christ, you chose twelve Apostles, though one fell,
Eph 2:18 the rest clung to you, and filled with *one Spirit,* preached the Holy Gospel.

1 Jn 2:18; Ps 89:50 "You, Lord, in this *last hour, remembering your ancient mercies,* have planted the religion of the brothers as a support for your faith, and that the mystery of your Gospel through them might be fulfilled. Who, then, will make satisfaction for them before you, if they not
Rom 13:12 only fail to show examples of Light to all, but, rather, display *works of darkness?*

"By you, most holy Lord, and by the whole court of Heaven, and by me, your little one, may they be cursed who break up and destroy by their bad example what you earlier built up, and do not cease to build up, through holy brothers of this religion!"

Where are they now, those who proclaim themselves happy because of his blessing, and boast about having been as close to him as they wished? If, God forbid, they should be found without repen-
Rom 13:12 tance showing in themselves *works of darkness* endangering others,
Jude 11 *woe to them!* Woe of eternal damnation!"[b]

[157]He used to say: "The best brothers are confounded by the deeds of the bad ones; they *bear* being judged by the example of the wicked,
Lam 5:7 although they themselves have not *sinned*. They are stabbing me with a sharp sword, twisting it in my bowels all day long." It was principally because of this that he withdrew from the company of the

a. Fondi is a city near Gaeta, near what was the border between the Papal States and the Kingdom of Naples; its bishop at the time was Robert (1210-1217), a Cistercian monk.

b. This may be an allusion to Brother Elias, who had been an intimate friend of Francis and had received a personal blessing from the dying saint (Cf. 1C 107). At the time of this writing Elias had already been deposed (1239) by Pope Gregory XI and had fled to Pisa to the court of the excommunicated emperor Frederick II, thus incurring the same penalty.

brothers, so that he would not happen to hear some evil report about any of them, and so renew his pain.

AC 2 He also said: "A *time will come* when the religion loved by God Ez 7:12
will have such a bad reputation because of bad examples that it
will be embarrassing to go out in public. Whoever comes to enter
the Order at that time will be led only by the working of the Holy
Spirit; *flesh and blood* will put no *blot* on them; they will be truly Mt 16:17; Sir 11:23
blessed by the Lord. Although they will not do works of merit, the *love* Ps 114:5
which makes saints work fervently *will have grown cold*, still they
will undergo temptations; and whoever passes the tests of that
time will be better than those who came before. But woe to those
who congratulate themselves over the appearance of a religious
way of living, those numbed by idleness, those who do not firmly
resist the temptations which are permitted to test the chosen! Only
those who are *tested will receive the crown of life*, those who, in the Jas 1:12
meantime, are disturbed by the malice of the wicked."

Chapter CXVII

A Revelation Made to Him by God About the State of the Order and That the Order Will Never Die Out

AC 112 [158]He was greatly consoled, however, by *God's visitations* which re- 1 Pt 5:6
assured him that the foundations of the religion would always re-
main unshaken. He was also promised that the number of those
being lost would undoubtedly be replaced by those being chosen.
One time he was disturbed by some bad examples. In his disturbance
he turned to prayer and received a scolding from the Lord: "Why are
you so upset, little man? Have I set you up as shepherd over my religion so that you can forget that I am its main protector? I have entrusted this to you, a simple man, so that the things that I work in
you for others to imitate may be followed by those who want to fol-
low. *I have called; I will preserve, and I will pasture;* and I will raise up oth- Is 48:15; Rv 10:3
ers to make up for the fall of some, so that, even if they *have not been* Mt 26:24
born, I will have them born! So do not be upset, but *work out your sal-* Phil 2:12
vation, for even if the religion should come to number only three, by
my gift it will still remain forever unshaken."

From that time on he used to say that the virtue of a single holy person overwhelms a great crowd of the imperfect, just as the deepest darkness disappears at a single ray of light.

AGAINST IDLENESS AND THE IDLE

Chapter CXVIII

A REVELATION HE RECEIVED ABOUT WHEN HE WAS A SERVANT OF GOD AND WHEN HE WAS NOT

[159]From the time in which this man gave up transitory things and
Zec 13:7 began to *cling to the Lord,* he allowed hardly a second of time to be
Dn 1:2 wasted. Although he had brought *into the treasury of the Lord* a great
abundance of merits he remained always new, always ready for spir-
Rom 9:11 itual exercise. He thought it a grave offense not *to be doing something
good,* and he considered not going forward going backward.

Once, when he was staying in a cell near Siena, he called his companions one night while they were sleeping and said to them: AC 3
2 Cor 12:8 **"Brothers, *I prayed to the Lord* that he might deign to show me when
Ps 119:125 *I am his servant* and when I am not, for I want to be nothing except
his servant. And now the gracious Lord himself in his mercy is giving me this answer: 'Know that you are in truth my servant when
you think, speak, or do things that are holy.' And so I have called
you brothers, because I want to be shamed in front of you if ever I
am not doing any of those three."**

Chapter CXIX

THE PENANCE AGAINST IDLE WORDS AT THE PORTIUNCULA

2 Tm 3:17 [160]Another time, **at Saint Mary's of the Portiuncula,** the *man of* AC 107
Mt 12:35 *God* began to consider how the benefit of prayer is lost through *idle
words.* And so **he established** the following remedy: "Whenever a
Mt 12:35, 36 brother ***utters a useless* or idle *word,* he must admit** his fault at once,
and for each idle word he must say **one *Our Father*.** Further, if he accuses himself of what he did, **let him say the *Our Father* for his own
soul, but if someone else corrected him first, let him say it for the
soul of the one who corrected him."**

Chapter CXX

HOW, WORKING HIMSELF, HE DESPISED THE IDLE

[161]He used to say that the *lukewarm,* who do not apply them- AC 48
Rv 3:16 **selves constantly to some work, would be quickly *vomited out of the
Lord's mouth.* No idler could appear in his presence without feeling
the sharp bite of his criticism. This exemplar of every perfection al-**

ways worked, and *worked with his hands,* not allowing the great gift 1 Cor 4:12 1 Thes 4:11
Test 20-21 of time to go to waste. And so he would often say: "I want all my brothers to work and keep busy, and those who have no skills to learn some." And he gave this reason: "That we may be less of a burden to people, and that in idleness the heart and tongue may not stray into what is forbidden." But he would not have profit or payment for work left to the whim of the worker, but entrusted it to the guardian or the family.[a]

Chapter CXXI
A COMPLAINT TO HIM ABOUT THE IDLE AND GLUTTONS

162 Allow me today, holy father, to raise a complaint up to heaven about those who claim to be yours! The exercises of virtues have become hateful to many who want to rest before they work, proving they are sons of Lucifer, not of Francis.

We have a more abundant supply of invalids than soldiers, even though they were *born to work* and should consider *life warfare.* They Jb 5:7; Jb 7:1
do not like to contribute through action, and are incapable of doing so through contemplation. They upset everyone by their singularity, and work more with their jaws than with their hands. *They hate him* Am 5:10
who corrects them at the gate, and will not allow themselves to be touched even with a fingertip.

I am even more amazed at their lack of shame, to use the words of blessed Francis: if they had stayed home they would have lived only *by their own sweat,* but now, without working, they feed themselves on Gn 3:19
the sweat of the poor. How clever! They do nothing, but you'd think they're always busy. They know the time for meals, and if they ever feel hungry, they complain that the sun fell asleep. Can I believe, good father, that these monsters of men are worthy of your glory? They're not worth your tunic!

You always taught that in this slippery, fleeting time we should seek the riches of merit so that in the future age we should not have to beg. But these men are not now enjoying the heavenly fatherland, and in the future life will have to go into exile. This sickness spreads in the subjects because the prelates ignore it, as if it were possible for them to put up with their vice and not earn their painful punishment.

---

a. This is the only instance in which *familia* [family] is applied to a local fraternity. Elsewhere the word is used to indicate the entire Order, 1C 73, 100; 2C 143, 184, 192; AC 48.

The Ministers of God's Word

Chapter CXXII
What a Preacher Should Be Like

Acts 6:14; 17:13 163 He wanted *ministers of the word of God* to be intent on spiritual study and not hindered by other duties. He said that these men were heralds chosen by a great king to deliver to the people the decrees received from his mouth. For he used to say: "The preacher must first secretly draw in by prayer what he later pours out in sacred preaching; he must first of all grow warm on the inside, or he will speak frozen words on the outside." He said that this office was worthy of reverence and that those who exercised it should be revered by all. As he said, "They are the life of the body, the opponents of demons, the
Mt 5:14 *lamp of the world.*"

He considered doctors of sacred theology to be worthy of even greater honor. Indeed he once had it written as a general rule that "we should honor and revere all theologians and those who minister Test 13
Jn 6:64 to us the words of God, as those who minister to us *spirit and life.*" And once, when writing to blessed Anthony, he had this written at the beginning of the letter: "To brother Anthony, my bishop." LtAnt 1

Chapter CXXIII
Against Those Longing for Empty Praises, and an Explanation of a Prophetic Saying

164 He felt deeply sorry for those preachers who often sell what AC 103
they do for the price of some empty praise. He would sometimes treat the swelling of such people with this antidote: "Why do you boast about people being converted? My simple brothers converted them
1 Sm 2:5 by their prayers!" And then he would explain the saying *while the barren one has given birth to many children* in this sense: "*the barren one* is my poor little brother who does not have the duty of producing children in the Church. At the Judgement he will *give birth to many children,* for then the Judge will credit to his glory those he is converting now by
1 Sm 2:5 his secret prayers. But *the mother of many will languish,* because the preacher who rejoices over many as if they were born through his power will then discover that he has nothing of his own in them."

He had little love for those who would rather be praised as orators than as preachers or for those who speak with elegance rather than feeling. He said that they divided things badly, putting everything in preaching and nothing in devotion. But he would praise that preacher who takes time to taste and eat a bit himself.

THE CONTEMPLATION OF THE CREATOR IN CREATURES, ANIMATE AND INANIMATE

Chapter CXXIV
THE SAINT'S LOVE FOR CREATURES ANIMATE AND INANIMATE

[165]This happy traveler,
hurrying to leave the world
as the exile of pilgrimage,
was helped, and not just a little,
by what *is in the world.* Jn 17:11, 16
Toward *the princes of darkness,* Eph 6:12
he certainly used it as a field of battle.
Toward God, however, he used it
as the clearest *mirror of goodness.* Wis 7:26
In art
he praises the Artist;
Off I V whatever he discovers in creatures
he guides to the Creator.
He rejoices in all the works of the Lord's hands, Ps 92:5
and through their delightful display
he gazes on their life-giving reason and cause.
1C 80, 81 In beautiful things he discerns Beauty Itself;
all good things cry out to him: Gn 1:31
"The One who made us is the Best." Ps 100:3
Following the *footprints* imprinted on creatures,
he *follows his Beloved* everywhere; Jb 23:11; Sg 5:17; Mt 12:18
out of them all he makes for himself a *ladder* Gn 28:12-13
by which he might reach the Throne. Jb 23:3

He embraces all things
with an intensity of unheard devotion,
speaking to them about the Lord
1C 58-61; 77-79 and exhorting them to praise Him.

He spares lanterns, lamps, and candles unwilling to use his hand to put out their brightness which is a sign of the *eternal light.*

He walked reverently over rocks, out of respect for Him **who is** 1C 58-61, 77-79 AC 88
1 Cor 10:4; Ps 61:3 **called** *the Rock*. When he came **to the verse "You have set me high upon the rock,"** in order to express it more respectfully, **he would**
Ps 18:39 **say: "You have set me high** *under the feet* **of the Rock."**

When the brothers are cutting wood he forbids them to cut down the whole tree, so that it might have hope of sprouting again.

He commands the gardener to leave the edges of the garden undisturbed, so that in their season the green of herbs and the beauty of
Eph 4:6 flowers may proclaim the beautiful *Father of all.* He even orders that within the garden a smaller garden should be set aside for aromatic and flowering herbs so that those who see them may recall the memory of eternal savor.

He picks up little worms from the road so they will not be trampled underfoot. 1C 80

That the bees not perish of hunger in the icy winter, he commands that honey and the finest wine should be set out for them.

He calls all animals by a fraternal name, although, among all kinds of beasts, he especially loves the meek. 1C 77

Sir 18:2 *Who is capable of describing* all of this?
Truly, that fountain-like goodness,[a]
1 Cor 12:6 which will be *all in all,*
already shone clearly in all for this saint.

Chapter CXXV
HOW CREATURES RETURNED HIS LOVE AND THE FIRE THAT DID HIM NO HARM

166 All creatures, therefore, 1C 58-61
strive to return the saint's love,
and to respond to his kindness with their gratitude.
They smile at his caress,
his requests they grant,
they obey his commands.

It may be good to tell of a few cases. At the time of an eye disease, he is forced to let himself be treated by a physician. A surgeon is 1C 98, 101 called to the place, and when he comes he is carrying an iron instrument for cauterizing. He ordered it to be placed in the fire until it became red hot. But the blessed Father, to comfort the body, which was

a. Cf. Pseudo Dionysius, *Celestial Hierarchy* IV:1 and *Divine Names* IV:1, 20.

AC 86 struck with panic, spoke to the fire: **"My brother Fire,** your beauty is
the envy of all creatures, the *Most High created* you strong, beautiful Sir 1:8, 9
and **useful.** ***Be gracious to me*** **in this hour; be courteous! For a long** Gn 33:10
time I have loved you in the Lord. **I pray** the *Great Lord* **who created** Ps 48:2; Dt 32:6
you to temper now your heat that I may bear your gentle burning."

**When the prayer is finished, he makes the sign of the cross over
the fire** and then remains in place unshaken. The surgeon takes in
his hands the red-hot glowing iron. The brothers, overcome by human feeling, run away. The saint joyfully and eagerly offered himself
to the iron. The hissing iron sinks into tender flesh, and the burn is
extended slowly straight from the ear to the eyebrow. How much
pain that burning caused can best be known by the witness of the
saint's words, since it was he that felt it. For when the brothers who
had fled return, the father says with a smile: **"Oh, you** *weak souls of* 1 Thes 5:14; Mt 14:31
little heart; **why did you run away?** ***Truly I say to you,*** I did not feel the Lk 4:25
fire's heat, **nor any pain** in my flesh." And turning to the doctor, he
says: "If the flesh isn't well cooked, try again!" The doctor had experienced quite a different reaction in similar situations, exalts this as a
divine miracle, saying: "I tell you, brothers; *today I have seen wonderful* Lk 5:26
things!" I believe he had returned to primeval innocence, for when he
wished, the harshest things grew gentle.

Chapter CXXVI
A LITTLE BIRD NESTLING IN HIS HANDS

[167]Heading to the hermitage of Greccio, blessed Francis was
crossing the lake of Rieti in a small boat. A fisherman offered him a
little water-bird so he might rejoice in the Lord over it. The blessed
Father received it gladly, and with open hands, gently invited it to fly
away freely. But the bird did not want to leave: instead it settled
down in his hands as in a nest, and the saint, his eyes lifted up, remained in prayer. *Returning to himself* as if after a long stay in another Acts 12:11
place, he sweetly told the little bird to return to its original freedom.
And so the bird, having received permission with a blessing, flew
away expressing its joy with the movement of its body.

Chapter CXXVII
A FALCON

[168]When blessed Francis, fleeing, as was his custom, from the
sight of human company, came to stay in a certain hermitage place, a
falcon nesting there bound itself to him in a great covenant of

friendship. At nighttime with its calling and noise, it anticipated the
hour when the saint would usually rise for the divine praises. The
Lk 4:34 *holy one of God* was very grateful for this because the falcon's great
concern for him shook him out of any sleeping-in. But when the
saint was burdened more than usual by some illness, the falcon
2 Tm 3:17 would spare him, and would not announce such early vigils. As if *in-*
structed by God, it would ring the bell of its voice with a light touch
about dawn.

It is no wonder that other creatures revere
the greatest lover of the Creator.[a]

Chapter CXXVIII
BEES

Dn 14:36 169 Once a little cell was made on a certain mountain. In it the *ser-*
vant of God did penance rigorously for a period of forty days. After that
span of time was over he left that place, and the cell remained in its
lonely location without anyone taking his place. The small clay cup
from which the saint used to drink was left there. Now, some people
one time went to that place out of reverence for the saint, and they
found that cup full of bees. With wonderful skill they had constructed the little cells of their honeycomb in the cup itself, certainly
Mk 1:24 symbolizing the sweetness of the contemplation which the *holy one of*
God drank in at that place.

Chapter CXXIX
A PHEASANT

170 A nobleman from the area of Siena sent a pheasant to blessed Francis while he was sick. He received it gladly, not with the desire to eat it, but because it was his custom to rejoice in such creatures out of love for their Creator. He said to the pheasant: "Praised be our Creator, Brother Pheasant!" And to the brothers he said: "Let's make a test now to see if Brother Pheasant wants to remain with us, or if he'd rather return to his usual places, which are more fit for him." At the saint's command a brother carried the pheasant away and put

a. "For if a man faithfully and wholeheartedly serves the maker of all created things, it is no wonder though all creation should minister to his commands and wishes." Cf. Bede, *Vita S. Cuthberti* XXI, in *Two Lives of Saint Cuthbert: A Life by an Anonymous Monk of Lindisfarne and Bede's Prose Life*, texts, translation, and notes by Bertram Colgrave, (New York: Greenwood Press, Publishers, 1969), 224-225.

him down in a vineyard far away. Immediately the pheasant returned at a brisk pace to the father's cell.

The saint ordered it to be carried out again, and even further away, but with great stubbornness it returned to the door of the cell, and as if forcing its way, it entered under the tunics of the brothers who were in the doorway. And so the saint commanded that it should be lovingly cared for, caressing and stroking it with gentle words. A doctor who was very devoted to the *holy one of God* saw this, Mk 1:24
and asked the brothers to give it to him, not because he wanted to eat it, but wanting rather to care for it out of reverence for the saint. What else? The doctor took it home with him, but when separated from the saint it seemed hurt, and while away from his presence it absolutely refused to eat. The doctor was amazed, and at once carried the pheasant back to the saint, telling him in order all that happened. As soon as it was placed on the ground, and saw its father, it threw off its sadness and began to eat with joy.

Chapter CXXX
A CRICKET

AC 110 171 A cricket lived in a fig tree by the cell of *the holy one of God* at the Mk 1:24
Portiuncula, and it would sing frequently with its usual sweetness. Once the blessed father stretched out his hand to it and gently called it to him: "My **Sister Cricket, come to me!**" And the cricket, as if it had reason, **immediately climbed onto his hand.** He said to it: **"Sing, my sister cricket,** and with joyful song praise the Lord your Creator!" The cricket, obeying without delay, **began to chirp,** and did not stop singing until the *man of God,* mixing his own songs with its 2 Kgs 4:9
praise, told it to return to its usual place. There it remained **constantly for eight days,** as if tied to the spot. Whenever the saint would come down from the cell he would always touch it with his hands and command it to sing, and it was always eager to obey his commands. **And the saint said to his companions: "Let us give permission to our sister cricket** to leave, who has up to now made us so happy with her praises, so that our *flesh may not boast* vainly *in any* 1 Cor 1:29
way." **And as soon as it had received permission,** the cricket went away **and never appeared there again. On seeing all this, the brothers were quite amazed.**

Charity

Chapter CXXXI
His charity
and how he showed himself an example of perfection for the salvation of souls

[172]The power of love
had made him
a brother to other creatures;
2 Cor 5:14 no wonder *the charity of Christ*
made him even more a brother to those marked
with the image of the Creator.

1 Pt 1:9 He would say that nothing should be placed ahead of the *salvation of souls* and would often demonstrate this with the fact that the
Jn 3:18 *Only-begotten Son of God* saw fit to hang on the cross for the sake of souls. From this arose his effort in prayer, his frequent travel in preaching and his extraordinary behavior in giving example.

Jn 15:14-15; 1 Jn 4:21 He would not consider himself a *friend of Christ* unless he *loved* the souls which *He loved.* For him this was the principal cause for revering
Rom 16:9 the doctors of theology: they are the *helpers of Christ,* who carry out
Ez 25:6 with Christ this office. With all the *unbounded affection* of the depths of his heart, he embraced the brothers themselves as fellow members
Gal 6:10; Heb 9:15 in *the household of the* same *faith,* united by a share in an *eternal inheritance.*

[173]Whenever somebody criticized him for the austerity of his life,
Dt 32:11 he would reply that he was given to the Order as an example, *as an eagle that prompts her young to fly.* His innocent flesh, which already submitted freely to the spirit, had no need of the whip because of any
Ps 17:4 offense. Still he renewed its punishments because of example, *staying on hard paths* only *for the sake* of others. And he was right.

Sir 28:19, 20; Jdt 13:7 In prelates what *the hand* does is *noticed* more than what *the tongue* says. By your deeds, Father, you convinced more gently; you per-
1 Cor 13:1-3 suaded more easily, you proved things more certainly. For *if* they *were to speak in the tongues of men and angels, but without* showing examples of *charity,* it *profits* little; they *profit nothing*. For if the one who gives correction is not feared, and gives his will as the reason to act,[a] will

a. An allusion to a verse of Juvenal, *Sic volo, sic iubeo, sit pro ratione voluntas* [Thus I will, thus I command; the fact that I will, it is argument enough!] *(Satires*, VI: 223).

the trappings of power suffice for salvation?[a] Still, what they thunder about should be done: as water flows to the gardens in empty canals. Meanwhile, let the rose be gathered from thorns, that *the greater may serve the lesser.* Gn 25:23; Rom 9:12

Chapter CXXXII
His concern for subjects

[174]But who now takes on himself Francis's concern for subjects? He always *raised his hands to heaven* for the *true Israelites,* attending first to his brothers' health and often forgetting his own. Casting himself at the feet of Majesty he offered *sacrifice of spirit* for his sons, urging God to give generous gifts. Ex 17:11-13; Jn 1:47 Ps 51:19

For the *little flock* which he drew behind him he felt compassion and love filled with fear, that after losing the world, they would also come to lose heaven. He thought he would be without future glory unless he could make those entrusted to him glorious along with him. His *spirit* had *given birth* to them *with greater labor pains* than a mother feels within herself. Lk 12:32 Gal 4:19

Chapter CXXXIII
His compassion for the sick

[175]Great was his compassion towards the sick and great his concern for their needs. If lay people's piety sent him tonics he would give it to the others who were sick even though he had greater need of them. He had sympathy for all who were ill and when he could not alleviate their pain he offered words of compassion. He would eat on AC 45 fast days so the weak would not be ashamed of eating, and he was not embarrassed to go through the city's public places to find some meat for a sick brother.

However, he also advised the sick to be patient when things were lacking and not stir up a scandal if everything was not done to their satisfaction. Because of this he had these words written in ER X 4 one of the rules: "I beg all my sick brothers that in their illness they do not become angry or upset at God or the brothers. They should not anxiously seek medicine, or desire too eagerly to free the flesh, that is soon to die and is an enemy of the soul. *Let them give thanks* 1 Thes 5:18

a. The Latin text reads: . . . *satis ad salutem sigilla sufficiunt* [will the trappings of power suffice for salvation]. *Sigilla* refers to the seals or official stamps to make an order or a document official and binding. It can also refer to the symbols to express authority of an office.

for all things and let them desire, however, to be as God wills them to be. For God teaches with the rod of punishment and sicknesses
Acts 13:48 those whom *he has destined to eternal life* as he himself has said:
Rv 3:19 *'Those I love, I correct and chastise.'"*

176 He once realized that a sick brother had a craving to eat grapes, AC 53
1 Mc 4:4 so he took him into the vineyard and, *sitting under a vine,* in order to encourage him to eat, began to eat first himself.

Chapter CXXXIV

THE COMPASSION HE SHOWED TO THOSE WHO WERE SICK IN SPIRIT, AND THOSE WHO DO THINGS CONTRARY TO THIS

177 With even greater mercy and patience he would bear with and
Eph 4:14 comfort those sick brothers whom he knew were like *wavering chil-*
Ps 77:4 *dren,* agitated with temptations and *faint in spirit*. Avoiding harsh cor-
Prv 13:24; 1 Mc 13:5 rections when he saw no danger he *spared the rod* so as to *spare the soul.*
He would say that it was proper for a prelate, who is a father, not a tyrant, to prevent occasion for failure and not allow one to fall who,
Ps 145:14 once *fallen* can be *lifted up* only with difficulty.

Woe to the pitiful madness of our age!
Not only do we not lift up or even hold the tottering,
but often enough we push them to fall!
We consider it nothing
to take away from that greatest shepherd,
one little lamb
for whose sake
Heb 5:7 *he offered loud cries and tears* on the cross.

On the contrary you, holy father, preferred to correct the strays rather than lose them. We know that in some the disease of self-will is so deeply rooted that they need cauterizing, not salve. It is clear
Ps 2:9 that for many it is healthier to be *broken with a rod of iron than to be*
Eccl 3:1; Lk 10:34 *rubbed down with hands.* Still, *to every thing there is a season; oil and wine;*
Ps 23:4 *rod and staff;* zeal and pity, burning and salving, prison and womb. All
Ps 94:1; 2 Cor 1:3 of these are demanded by *the God of vengeance,* and *Father of mercies,*
Mt 9:13 who desires *mercy* more *than sacrifice.*

Chapter CXXXV
THE BROTHERS IN SPAIN

178 This most holy man sometimes *went out of the mind to God* in a 2 Cor 5:13
wondrous manner, and was overflowed with joy in the spirit, whenever the *sweet fragrance* of his sons reached him. 2 Cor 2:15

Once a Spaniard, a devout cleric, happened to enjoy some time
seeing and talking with Saint Francis. Among other news about the
brothers in Spain, he made the saint happy with this report: "Your
brothers in our country stay in a poor hermitage. They have set up the
following way of life for themselves: half of them take care of the
RH 10 household chores and half remain free for contemplation. In this
manner each week the active half moves to the contemplative, and
the repose of those contemplating returns to the toils of labor.[a] One
day, the table was set and a signal called those who were away. All
the brothers came together except one, who was among those contemplating. They waited a while, and then went to his cell to call him
to table, but he was being fed by the Lord at a more abundant table.
For they saw him *lying on his face* on the ground, stretched out in the Tb 12:16
form of a cross, and showing no signs of life; not a breath or a motion.
At his head and at his feet there flamed twin candelabra, which lit up
the cell with a wonderful golden light. *They left* him *in peace* so as not Lk 2:29
to disturb his anointing[b] or *awaken the beloved until she wished.* The Sg 2:7
brothers peeked through the openings in the cell, *standing behind the* Sg 2:9
wall and peering through the lattice. What else? *While the friends listened for* Sg 8:13
her who waited in the gardens, suddenly the light disappeared and the
brother returned to his human self. He got up at once, came to the table, and confessed his fault for being late. That's the kind of thing,"
said the Spaniard, "that happens in our country."

Saint Francis could not restrain himself for joy; he was so pervaded by *the fragrance of his sons.* He suddenly rose up to give praise, as Gn 27:27
if his only glory was this: hearing good things about the brothers. He
burst out from the depths of his heart: "*I give you thanks* Lord, Lk 18:11
Sanctifier and Guide of the poor, you who have gladdened me with
this report about the brothers! Bless those brothers, I beg you, with a
most generous blessing, and sanctify with a special gift all those who
make their profession fragrant through good example!"

---

a. See Kajetan Esser, "The *Regula Pro Eremitoriis Data* of St. Francis of Assisi," in *Franciscan Solitude*, ed. André Cirino and Josef Raischl (St. Bonaventure, NY: Franciscan Institute Publications, 1995)147-205; Octavian Schmucki, "Place of Solitude: An Essay on the External Circumstances of the Prayer Life of St. Francis of Assisi," GR 2 (1988): 77-132.

b. *Unctioni* [anointing] indicate an elevated state of contemplation.

Chapter CXXXVI
AGAINST THOSE WHO LIVE INCORRECTLY IN HERMITAGES, AND HOW HE WANTED ALL THINGS TO BE IN COMMON

[179]Although we learn from these things the love which made the saint rejoice in the successes of those he loved, we believe this is also a great criticism of those who live in hermitages in a very different way.

Many turn the place for contemplation into a place for laziness, and turn the way of life in the hermitage, established for perfection of souls, into a cesspool of pleasure. This is the norm of those modern anchorites for each one to live as he pleases.[a] This does not apply to
Gal 2:20 all; we know saints *living in the flesh* who live as hermits by the best of rules. We also know that the fathers who went before us stood out as solitary flowers.

May the hermits of our times not fall away
from that earliest beauty:
may the praise of its justice remain forever!

[180]As Saint Francis exhorted all to charity, he encouraged them to show a friendly manner and a family's closeness. "I want my broth- ER IX 11; LR VI 7
ers," he said, "to show they are sons of the same mother, and that if one should ask another for a tunic or cord or anything else, the other should give it generously. They should share books and any pleasant thing; even more, one should urge the other to take them."

And so that, even in this,
he might not speak of anything
that Christ has done through him,
he was the first to do all these things.

Chapter CXXXVII
TWO FRENCH BROTHERS TO WHOM HE GAVE HIS TUNIC

[181]Two French brothers, men of great holiness, happened to meet AC 90
Saint Francis. This made them incredibly happy, and their joy was doubled because they had carried this desire a long time. After ex-

a. Cf. Jerome, *Letter to Eustochium*, XXII, 34 (PL 22,419); in *The Letters of St. Jerome*, translated by Charles Christopher Mierow, introduction and notes by Thomas Comerford Lawler (Westminster, MD: The Newman Press, 1963), 169-170; John Cassian, *The Conferences*, Eighteenth Conference VII-VIII, translated and annotated by Boniface Ramsey (New York, Mahwah: Paulist Press, 1997), 640-643.

changing affectionate gestures and pleasant words, their ardent devotion led them to ask Saint Francis for his tunic. He quickly took off the tunic and remaining naked gave it to them devoutly; in a pious exchange, he put on the poorer tunic he received from one of them.[a]

He was ready to give not only things like this,
but even himself,
and whatever he was asked for
he gave away with gladness.

SLANDER

Chapter CXXXVIII

HOW HE WANTED SLANDERERS TO BE PUNISHED

182Finally, since a spirit filled with charity will hate those *hateful to God,* this was upheld in Saint Francis. He had a horrible loathing for slanderers, more than any other kind of vicious people, and used to say that they had *poison* in their *tongues*, with which they infect others. And so he avoided rumormongers like biting fleas, and when they spoke he turned away his ears—as we ourselves have seen—so they would not be contaminated by hearing them. Rom 1:30 Jas 3:8

One time, when he heard one brother blackening the reputation of another, he turned to brother Peter of Catanio, his vicar, and threw out these terrifying words: "Danger threatens religion if it doesn't stop slanderers. Unless the *mouths* of stinking men *are closed,* soon enough the *sweet smell* of many *will stink*. Get up! Get up! Search thoroughly; and if you find the accused brother innocent, make the accuser known publicly by a severe punishment. If you can't punish him yourself, throw him to the Florentine boxer!" (Brother John of Florence was a man of great height and tremendous strength, and so he used to call him "the boxer.") "I want you and all the ministers," he said, "to take extreme care that this foul disease does not spread." Est 13:14 Lev 1:13; Ex 5:21

More than once he decided that a brother should be stripped of his tunic if he had stripped his brother of his good reputation, and that he could not *raise his eyes* up to God until he had given back what he had stolen. Because of this the brothers of those days had a special abhorrence for this vice, and set up a firm rule among themselves carefully to avoid anything that might take away the honor of another. That was right and good! For what is a slanderer? If not the Lk 18:13

a. This brother may have been Lawrence of Beauvais, one of the first to go to England. Cf. ChrTE 1.

bile of humanity, the yeast of wickedness, the shame of the earth! What is a backbiter? If not the scandal of the Order, the poison of the
Ex 10:5 cloister, a breaker of unity! Ah, the *surface of the earth* is crawling with these poisonous animals, and it is impossible for the righteous to avoid the fangs of the envious! Rewards are offered to informers, and after innocence is undermined, the palm of victory often enough goes to falsehood. Where a man can not make a living by reputable means, he can always earn his food and clothing by devastating the reputation of others.

[183]About this Saint Francis often used to say: "These are the words of the slanderer: 'My life is far from perfect, and I don't have at my disposal any supply of learning or special grace, and so I cannot
Lk 16:4; Sir 11:33 find a position with God or men. *I know what I will do: let me put a stain on the chosen,* and so I'll win the favor of the great. I know my prelate
Jgs 9:15 is human; he sometimes uses my same method: cut down the *cedars* so only the *buckthorn* can be seen in the forest.'

"You wretch! Go ahead and feed on human flesh; since you can't survive otherwise, gnaw at your brothers' entrails! That type strives to appear good, not to become good; they point out vices; they do not give up vices. They only praise people whose authority they want for protection. Their praises go silent if they think they will not be reported to the person they praised. They sell for the price of pernicious
Mt 6:16; 1 Cor 14:37 praise the pallor of their *fasting faces, that they may appear to be spiritual*
1 Cor 2:15 *men who can judge all, and may be judged by none.* They rejoice in the reputation, not the works of holiness, in the name, not in the virtue of 'angels.'"

A DESCRIPTION OF THE GENERAL MINISTER AND OF THE OTHER MINISTERS

Chapter CXXXIX

HOW HE SHOULD BEHAVE WITH HIS COMPANIONS

[184] **As he neared the end of his call to the Lord, a brother** who AC 42
was always concerned about the things of God, asked him a question out of piety for the Order. **"Father, you will pass on, and the family**
Ps 84:7 **of your followers will be left behind *in this vale of tears*. Point out someone in the Order, if you know one, on whom your spirit may rest, and on whom the weight of the general ministry may safely be laid."**

Saint Francis, drawing a sigh with every word, replied as follows: "Son, I find no one adequate to be the leader of such a varied army, or the shepherd of such a widespread flock. But I would like to paint one for you, or make one by hand, as the phrase goes, to show clearly what kind of person the father of this family should be.

185 "He must be a very dignified person, of great discernment, and of praiseworthy reputation. He must be without personal favorites, lest by loving some more than others, he create scandal for all. He must be a committed friend of holy prayer, who can distribute some hours for his soul and others for the flock entrusted to him. *Early in the morning,* he must put first the sacrament of the Mt 20:1 Mass, and with prolonged devotion commend himself and his flock to divine protection. After prayer, he must make himself available for all to pick at him, and he should respond to all and provide for all with meekness. He must be someone who does not create sordid *favoritism toward persons,* but will take as much care of Rom 2:11 the lesser and simple brothers as of the learned and greater ones. Even if he should be allowed to excel in gifts of learning, he should all the more bear in his behavior the image of holy simplicity, and nourish this virtue.

"He should loathe money, the principal corrupter of our profession and perfection; as the head of a poor religion, offering himself to others as someone to be imitated, he must never engage in the AC 43 abuse of using any money pouch. For with his needs," he said, "a habit and a little book should be enough, and, for the brothers' needs, he should have a pen case and seal. He should not be a book collector, or too intent on reading, so he does not take away from his duties what he spends on his studies.

"Let him be someone who comforts the afflicted, and *the final* Ps 32:7; 46:2 *refuge of the distressed,* so that the sickness of despair does not overcome the sick because he did not offer healing remedies. In order to bend rebels to meekness, let him lower himself, let go of some of his rights *that he may gain a soul for Christ.* Phil 3:8; Mt 16:26 As for runaways from the Order, let him not *close a heart of mercy* to them, for they are like *lost* 1 Jn 3:17; Lk 15:4, 6 *sheep;* and he knows how overpowering the temptations can be which can push someone to such a fall.

AC 43 186 "I want all to honor him as standing in Christ's place, and I wish that all his needs be provided for with every kindness. He should not enjoy honors, or delight in approval more than insults. If he should need more substantial food when he is sick or tired, he should not eat it in secret but in a public place, so that others may

be freed from embarrassment at having to provide for their weak bodies. It especially pertains to him to discern what is hidden in consciences and to draw out the truth from its hidden veins, not lending an ear to gossips. Finally, he must be one who would never allow the desire for preserving honor to weaken the strong figure of justice, and he must feel such a great office more a burden than an honor. And yet, excessive meekness should not give birth to slackness, nor loose indulgence to a breaking down of discipline, so
Prv 10:29 that, loved by all, he is feared, nonetheless, by *those who work evil.*

"I would like him to have companions endowed with honesty,
Ti 2:7 who, like him, *show themselves an example of all good works*: stern against pleasures, strong against difficulties, and yet friendly in the right way, so that they receive all who come to them with holy cheerfulness. There," he concluded, "that is the kind of person the general minister of the Order should be."

Chapter CXL
THE PROVINCIAL MINISTERS

187 The blessed Father also demanded all these things in provincial ministers, though each ought to stand out even more in the general minister. He wanted them to be friendly to the lesser ones, and peaceful and kind so that those who committed faults would not be afraid to entrust themselves to their affection. He wanted them to be moderate in commanding, gracious when offended, more willing to bear injuries than to inflict them; enemies of vice but healers of the vice-ridden. In short, he wanted them to be men whose life would be a mirror of discipline for others. He would have them honored and loved in every way, as those who bear the burden of cares and labor. He said they deserved the highest rewards before God if they rule the souls committed to them according to this model and this law.

Chapter CXLI
THE ANSWER THAT THE SAINT GAVE WHEN HE WAS ASKED ABOUT THE MINISTERS

188 Once a brother asked him why he had renounced the care of AC 44
all the brothers and turned them over into the hands of others as if they did not belong to him. He replied: "Son, I love the brothers as I
1 Pt 2:21 can, but if they would *follow my footsteps* I would surely love them more, and would not make myself a stranger to them. For there are some among the prelates who draw them in a different direction,

placing before them the examples of the ancients[a] and paying little attention to my warnings. But what they are doing will be seen in the end."

A short time later, when he was suffering a serious illness, he raised himself up in bed in *an angry spirit*: "Who are these people? Ps 48:8
They *have snatched out of my hands* my religion and that of the broth- Jn 10:28
ers. If I go to the general chapter, then I'll show them what my will is!" And that brother asked him: "Won't you also change those provincial ministers who for a long time have abused their freedom?" And our father answered, sobbing, with this terrible word: "Let them live any way they want, for there is less harm in the damnation of a few than in the damnation of many!"

He did not say this about all, but because of some who had been prelates for such a long time that they seemed to have laid claim to their positions by right of property. He always commended this in all kinds of religious prelates: not to change behavior except for the better; not to beg to win favors; not to exercise power, but fulfill a duty.

HOLY SIMPLICITY

Chapter CXLII
THE NATURE OF TRUE SIMPLICITY

189Holy *Simplicity,* Wis 1:1
the daughter of grace,
the sister of wisdom,
the mother of justice,
with careful attention he showed in himself
and *loved* in others.
It was not just any kind of simplicity that he approved,
but only that
which, content with her God
scorns everything else.[b]
This is she
who *glories in the fear of God,* Sir 9:16
who does not know how to do evil

a. That is, Saints Benedict, Augustine, or Bernard. Cf. AC 18, supra 132.

b. Traditionally simplicity is seen as one of the most salient virtues of the spiritual life, cf. "Simplicité," *Dictionnaire de Spiritualité Ascétique et Mystique* (Paris: Beauchesne, 1990), 892-921; in particular, Vincent Desprez, "Il Monchisme Ancien et Médiéval," 903-910.

or speak it.
This is she
who examines herself
Jn 8:16 and *condemns no one* by her judgment;
who grants due authority to her betters
and seeks no authority for herself.
This is she
who does not
2 Mc 4:15 *consider the best glories of the Greeks*
Acts 1:1 and would rather *do*,
than *teach* or learn.
This is she
who, when dealing with all the divine laws,
leaves all wordy wanderings,
fanciful decorations,
shiny trappings,
showy displays and odd curiosities,
who seeks not the rind but the marrow,
not the shell but the kernel,
not the many, but the much,
supreme and enduring good.

She was what the most holy father demanded in the brothers,
learned and lay; not believing she was the contrary of wisdom but
rather, her true sister, though easier to acquire for those poor in
knowledge and more quickly to put into use. Therefore, in the *Praises* SalV 1
of the Virtues which he composed, he says: "Hail, Queen Wisdom! May
the Lord protect you, with Your Sister holy pure Simplicity!"

Chapter CXLIII
BROTHER JOHN THE SIMPLE

190 Once, when Saint Francis was passing by a village near Assisi, AC 61
a certain John, a very simple man, **was plowing in the field.** He ran
Acts 14:3; Mt 6:24 to him, saying: "I want you to make me a brother, *for a long time* now I
have wanted *to serve God*." The saint rejoiced noticing the man's simplicity, and responded to his intention: "Brother, **if you want** to be
Mt 19:21 our companion, *give to the poor* if you have anything, and once rid of ER I 2; II 4; LR II
your property, I will receive you." He immediately unyoked the oxen
and offered one to Saint Francis saying: "Let's give this ox to the
Lk 15:12 poor! I am sure I deserve to get this much as my *share of my father's*
things." The saint smiled, but he heartily approved his sense of sim-

plicity. Now, when the parents and younger brothers heard of this, they hurried over in tears, grieving more over losing the ox than the man. The saint said to them: "*Calm down!* Here, I'll give you back the ox and only take away the brother." And so he took the man with him, and, dressed in the clothing of the Order, he made him his special companion because of his gift of simplicity. Bar 4:27

Whenever Saint Francis stayed in some place to meditate, simple John would immediately repeat and copy whatever gestures or movements the saint made. If he spat, John would spit too, if he coughed, he would cough as well, sighing or sobbing along with him. If the saint *lifted up his hands to heaven,* John would raise his too, and he watched him intently as a model, turning himself into a copy of all his actions. The saint noticed this, and once asked him why he did those things. He replied: "I promised to do everything you do. It is dangerous for me to leave anything out." The saint delighted in this pure simplicity, but gently told him not to do this anymore. Shortly after this the simple man departed to the Lord in this same purity. The saint often proposed his life as worth imitating and merrily calling him not Brother John, but Saint John. Dt 32:40

Note that it is typical of holy simplicity
to live by the norms of the elders
and always to rely
on the example and teaching of the saints.
Who will allow human wisdom to follow him, Jb 6:8; 1 Cor 2:4
now reigning in heaven,
with as much care as holy simplicity
conformed herself to him on earth!
What more can I say?
She followed the saint in life,
and went before the saint to Life.

Chapter CXLIV
How he fostered unity among his sons and spoke about it in a parable

[191]His constant wish and watchful concern
was to foster among his sons *the bond of unity* Eph 4:3
so that those *drawn by the same Spirit* Jb 34:14
and *begotten by the* same *father* Prv 23:22
should be held peacefully
on the lap of the same mother.

He wanted to unite the greater to the lesser,
to join the wise to the simple in brotherly affection,
and to hold together those far from each other
with the glue of love.

He once presented a moral parable, containing no little instruction. "Imagine," he said, "a general chapter of all the religious in the
Acts 4:13 Church. Because the literate are present along with those *who are unlettered,* the learned, as well as those who, without learning, have
Heb 11:6 learned *how to please God,* a sermon is assigned to one of the wise and
Mt 16:17 another to one of the simple. The wise man, because he is wise, *thinks
to himself*: 'This is not the place to show off my learning, since it is full
of understanding scholars. And it would not be proper to make myself stand out for originality, making subtle points to men who are
even more subtle. Speaking simply would be more fruitful.'

Est 10:11; Est 8:11; Ps 11:1 "*The appointed day* dawns, *the gathering of the saints gathers as one,*
Jn 3:5 thirsting to hear this sermon. The learned man comes forward *dressed
Lam 2:10 in sackcloth,* with *head sprinkled with ashes,* and to the amazement of
Rom 9:28 all, *he spoke briefly,* preaching more by his action. 'Great things have
we promised ,' he said, 'greater things have been promised us; let us
observe the former and yearn for the latter. Pleasure is short and
Mt 20:16 punishment is eternal; suffering is slight and glory infinite. *Many are
Gn 43:30 called; few are chosen,* all are repaid.' The hearts of the listeners *were
pierced,* and they *burst into tears,* and revered this truly wise man as a
saint.

Ps 14:1 " 'What's this?' the simple man says *in his heart*. 'This wise man
Lk 16:4 has stolen everything I planned to do or say! But *I know what I will do*. I
know a few verses of the psalms; I'll use the style of the wise man,
since he used the style of the simple.' The next day's meeting arrives
and the simple brother gets up, and proposes a psalm as his theme.
Then, inspired with the divine Spirit, he preaches by the inspired gift
Acts 3:10 of God with such fire, subtlety and sweetness that all are *filled with
Prv 3:32 amazement* and say: 'Yes, *He speaks with the simple!*' "

1 Kgs 13:1 192 The *man of God* would then explain the moral parable he told:
"Our religion is a very large gathering, like a general council gathered
together from every part of the world under a single form of life. In it
the learned can draw from the simple to their own advantage when
they see the unlettered seeking the things of heaven with fiery vigor
Acts 11:28; Mt 16:23 and those not taught by men knowing *spiritual things by the Spirit*. In it Off 17 II
even the simple turn to their advantage what belongs to the learned,
Sir 44:1, 2 when they see outstanding men, who could live with great *honor*
anywhere *in the world,* humble themselves to the same level with
themselves. Here," he said, "is where the beauty of this blessed fam-

ily shines; a diverse beauty that gives great pleasure to the father of the family."

Chapter CXLV
How the Saint Wanted to be Shaved

193Whenever Saint Francis was being shaved, he would always say to the one who shaved him: "Be careful: don't give me a big tonsure! I want my simple brothers to *have a share in* my head!"[a] Jb 31:2

Really he wanted the Order to be held in common by the poor and illiterate and not just by the learned and rich. *"With God,"* he would Rom 2:11
say, *"there is no respecting of persons,* and the Holy Spirit, the general minister of the religion, rests equally upon the poor and simple." He really wanted to put these words in the *Rule,* but the papal seal already given to the rule precluded it.

Chapter CXLVI
How He Wanted "Eminent Clerics" Who Entered the Order to Give up Their Property

194Once he said that if an "eminent cleric"[b] were to join the Order, he should in some way renounce even learning, so that having renounced even this possession, he might offer himself naked to the arms of the Crucified.[c] "Learning," he would say, "makes many hard to teach, not allowing them to bend something rigid in them to humble disciplines. And so I wish an educated man would first *offer* me Heb 5:7
this *prayer*: 'Look, Brother; I have *lived* for a long time *in the world* and Ti 1:12
have *not* really *known* my *God*. Grant me, I pray you, a place removed Jn 1:10
from the noise of the world, where *I may recall my years in* sorrow and Is 38:15
where I may gather the *scattered bits of* my *heart* and turn my spirit to Ps 147:2; Lk 1:51
better things.' What do you think will become," he asked, "of someone who begins in this way? He will emerge an unchained lion, strong enough for anything, and the blessed sap which he tapped in the beginning will grow in him through constant progress. To him at last the true *ministry of the word* will be given safely, for he will pour Acts 6:4
out what bubbles up in his heart."

---

a. The lay brothers at that time wore small tonsures, while the clerics wore large ones. Cf. AP 36, supra, 51 c, and L3C 51, supra 98 b, on tonsure.

b. A *magnus clericus* [eminent cleric] is a person of great learning. Cf. Lothar Hardick, "Gedanken zu Sinn und Tragweite des Begriffes Clericus," AFH 50 (1957): 7-26.

c. For a study of this phrase, see FA:ED I 194 a.

What a holy teaching! What is more necessary, for someone returning from the land of unlikeness,[a] than to scrape and wash away, by humble exercises, worldly feelings stamped and ground in for a long time? Whoever enters the school of perfection will soon reach perfection.

Chapter CXLVII
HOW HE WANTED THE BROTHERS TO STUDY, AND HOW HE APPEARED TO A COMPANION OF HIS WHO WAS INTENT ON BEING A PREACHER

**195 It grieved him when brothers sought learning while neglect- AC 47
1 Cor 7:20, 24 ing virtue, especially if they did not *remain in that calling in which
they were first *called*. He said: "Those brothers of mine who are led
Sir 35:4 by curiosity for knowledge will find themselves *empty-handed* on
Hos 9:7 the *day of reckoning*. I wish they would grow stronger in virtue, so
Ps 37:39 that when the *times of tribulation* arrive they may have the Lord with
2 Chr 15:4; Ps 22:12 Prv 1:27 them *in their distress*. For," he said, "a *tribulation is approaching*,
when books, useful for nothing, shall be thrown into cupboards
and into closets!" He did not say these things out of dislike for the
study of the Scriptures, but to draw all of them back from excessive
concern for learning, because he preferred that they be good
through charity, than dilettantes through curiosity.**

Besides, he could smell in the air that a time was coming, and not too far away, when he knew learning would be an occasion of ruin, while dedication to spiritual things would serve as a support to the spirit.

**A lay brother who wanted to have a psalter asked him for per- AC 104
mission: he offered him ashes instead of a psalter.**

**After his death he appeared in a vision to one of the companions AC 47
who was once tending toward preaching, and he forbade it, com-
Rom 1:9 manding him to walk on the way of simplicity.** *As God is his witness,*
he felt such a sweetness after this vision that for many days it seemed
the dew of the father's words was still dropping into his ears.

a. The "land of unlikeness" is a very common image in the writings of St. Bernard and the Cistercian school of spirituality; its origin is in the thought of St. Augustine and ultimately in Plato's *topos tes anomoiotetos*, a land which is not the soul's true country. See Amédée Hallier, OCSO, *The Monastic Theology of Aelred of Rievaulx* (Spencer, Mass: Cistercian Publications, 1969), 12.

THE SAINT'S SPECIAL DEVOTIONS

Chapter CXLVIII
HOW HE WAS MOVED WHEN HE HEARD "THE LOVE OF GOD"

[196]Perhaps it would be useful and worthwhile to touch briefly on the special devotions of Saint Francis. Although this man was devout in all things, since he enjoyed the *anointing of the Spirit,* there Lk 4:18
were special things that moved him with special affection.

Among other expressions used in common speech, he could not hear "the love of God" without a change in himself. As soon as he heard "the love of God" he was excited, moved, and on fire, as if these words from the outside were a pick strumming the strings of his heart on the inside.

He used to say that it was a noble extravagance to offer such a treasure for alms, and that those who considered it less valuable than
1C 17 money were complete fools. As for himself, he kept until his death the resolution he made while still entangled in the things of this world: he would never refuse any poor person who asked something "for the love of God."

AC 91 Once a poor man begged something of him "for the love of God," and since he had nothing, he secretly picked up scissors and hurried to cut his small tunic in two. And he would have done just that, except that he was caught by the brothers and they had the poor man supplied with a different compensation.

He said:
"The love of him who loved us greatly
is greatly to be loved!"

Chapter CXLIX
HIS DEVOTION TO THE ANGELS, AND WHAT HE DID OUT OF LOVE FOR SAINT MICHAEL

[197]He venerated the angels with the greatest affection, for they
are with us in battle, and *walk* with us *in the midst of the shadow of death.* Ps 23:4; Is 9:2
He said that such companions should be revered everywhere, and invoked as protectors. He taught that their gaze should not be offended, and no one should presume to do in their sight what he
would not do *in the sight of others.* And since in choir one *sings* the Rom 12:17; Ps 138:1
psalms *in the presence of the angels,* he wanted all who were able to
gather in the oratory and *sing psalms wisely.* Ps 47:8

He often said that Blessed Michael should be especially honored because his duty is presenting souls to God.[a] In honor of Saint Michael he would fast with great devotion for forty days between the Feast of the Assumption and St. Michael's feast day. For he used to
Mt 5:23-24 say: "Each person should *offer God* some special praise or *gift* in honor
of such a great prince."

Chapter CL
His devotion to Our Lady to whom he especially entrusted the Order

198 He embraced the Mother of Jesus with inexpressible love, since
Ps 29:4; Is 2:10 she made *the Lord of Majesty* a brother to us. He honored her with his SalBVM
own *Praises*, poured out prayers to her, and offered her his love in a
way that no human tongue can express. But what gives us greatest
joy is that he appointed her the Advocate of the Order, and placed
Ps 17:8 *under her wings* the sons to be left behind, that she might *protect* and
cherish them to the end.

Oh Advocate of the Poor!
Gal 4:2 Fulfill towards us your duty as *protectress*
until the time set by the Father!

Chapter CLI
His devotion to the Lord's nativity and how he then wanted all to receive assistance

199 He used to observe the Nativity of the Child Jesus with an im- 1C 84-86
mense eagerness above all other solemnities, affirming it was the
Feast of Feasts, when God was made a little child and hung on human breasts. He would kiss the images of the baby's limbs thinking
of hunger, and the melting compassion of his heart toward the child
also made him stammer sweet words as babies do. This name was to
Ps 19:11; Prv 16:24 him like *honey and honeycomb* in his mouth.

When there was discussion about not eating meat, because it was
on Friday, he replied to Brother Morico: "You sin, brother, when you
Is 9:6 call 'Friday' the day when *unto us a Child is born*. I want even the walls
to eat meat on that day, and if they cannot, at least on the outside
they be rubbed with grease!"

a. Cf. *Roman Breviary*, third antiphon for Lauds on the feast of St. Michael: *Archangele Michael, constitui te principem super omnes animas suscipiendas* [Archangel Michael, I have set you as prince over all the souls who are to be presented to me].

AC 14 [200]He wanted the poor and *hungry to be filled* by the rich, and *oxen* 1 Sm 2:5
and asses to be spoiled with extra feed and hay. **"If ever I speak with the Emperor,"** he would say, **"I will beg him** to issue a general decree that all who can should throw **wheat and grain along the roads,** so that on the day of such a great solemnity the birds may have an abundance, especially our sisters the larks."

L3C 15 He could not recall without tears the great want surrounding the
2C 83, 85 little, poor Virgin on that day. One day when he was sitting down to
dinner a brother mentioned the poverty of the blessed Virgin, and reflected on the want of Christ her Son. No sooner had he heard this than
he *got up from the table,* groaning with sobs of pain, and bathed in tears 1 Sm 20:34
ER IX 5; 2LtF 5 ate the rest of his bread on the naked ground. He used to say this must
be a royal virtue, since it shone so remarkably in a King and Queen.

When the brothers were debating in a gathering about which of the virtues made one a greater friend to Christ, he replied, as if opening the secret of his heart: "My sons, know that poverty is the special
way to salvation; its fruits are many, and known only to a few." Acts 16:17

Chapter CLII
HIS DEVOTION TO THE BODY OF THE LORD

[201]Toward the sacrament of the Lord's Body
he burned with fervor to his very marrow,
and with unbounded wonder
of that loving condescension
and condescending love.
He considered it disrespectful
not to hear, if time allowed, at least one Mass a day.
He received Communion frequently
and so devoutly
that he made others devout.
Following that which is so venerable with all reverence
he offered the sacrifice of all his members,
and receiving *the Lamb that was slain* Rv 5:12; 1 Pt 1:19
he slew his own spirit
in the *fire* which *always burned* Lv6 6:5, 6
upon the altar of his heart.

Because of this he loved France as a friend of the Body of the Lord,[a] and even wished to die there, because of its reverence for sacred things.

a. The Latin, *Francia*, would mean the *Ile de France* or northern France, including the Low Countries. This love for the Eucharist was in contrast to southern France where the Albigensian heresy was widespread. Francis could have been informed of this devotion by James of Vitry, later a cardinal, who was ordained bishop of Akon in Perugia on July 31, 1216. For the situation in *Francia*, see Miri Rubin, *Corpus Christi: The Eucharist in Late Medieval Culture* (Cambridge: Cambridge University Press, 1991).

Jn 3:16 He once wanted to *send* brothers *throughout the world* with pre- AC 108
cious pyxes, so that wherever they should find the price of our re- 1LtCl 11; 2LtCl 1 1LtCus 4; Test 1
demption in an unsuitable place they might put it away in the very
best place.

He wanted great reverence shown to the hands of priests, since
they have the divinely granted authority to bring about this mystery.
He often used to say: "If I should happen at the same time to come
Jn 3:31; Gal 1:8 upon any saint *coming from heaven* and some little poor priest, I would
Rom 12:10 *first show honor* to the priest, and hurry more quickly to kiss his hands.
1 Jn 1:1 For I would say to the saint: 'Hey, Saint Lawrence,[a] wait! His *hands*
may *handle the Word of Life*, and possess something more than human!' "

Chapter CLIII
His devotion to relics

Sir 45:1 [202]This *beloved one of God*
showed himself greatly devoted to divine worship
Mt 22:21 and left nothing *that is God's*
dishonored through carelessness.

When he was at Monte Casale in the province of Massa he commanded the brothers to move with all reverence the holy relics from
an abandoned church to the place of the brothers. He felt very bad
that they had been robbed of the devotion due them for a long time.
When, for an urgent reason, he had to go somewhere else, his sons,
forgetting the command of their Father, disregarded the merit of
obedience. But one day the brothers wanted to celebrate, and when
as usual they removed the cloth cover from the altar they discovered
some beautiful and very fragrant bones. They were stunned at this,
since they had never seen them there before. Shortly afterwards the
Lk 4:34 *holy one of God* returned, and he took care to inquire if his orders about
the relics had been carried out. The brothers humbly confessed their
fault of neglecting obedience, and won pardon together with a pen-
Ps 18:47 ance. And the saint said: *"Blessed be the Lord my God,* who himself carried out what you were supposed to do!"

Consider carefully Francis's devotion,
Ps 69:14 pay attention to *God's good pleasure* towards our dust;
Ps 69:31 *magnify the praise* of holy obedience.

a. Saint Lawrence (+258) was a deacon and a Roman martyr.

For when humans did not heed his voice
God obeyed his prayers.

Chapter CLIV
HIS DEVOTION TO THE CROSS AND A CERTAIN HIDDEN SACRAMENT

[203]Finally, who can express,
or who can understand,
how it was *far from him to glory* Gal 6:14
except in the cross of the Lord?
To him alone is it given to know,
to whom alone it is given to experience.
Without a doubt, even if
we were to perceive it in some sense in ourselves,
words would be unable to express such marvels,
soiled as they are by cheap and everyday things.
For this reason perhaps
it had to appear in the flesh, 1 Tm 3:16
since it *could not be explained in words*. Eccl 1:8
Therefore,
let silence speak, where *word falls short*, Sir 43:29
for symbol cries out as well, where sign falls short.
This alone intimates to human ears
what is not yet entirely clear:
why that *sacrament appeared* in the saint.[a] 1 Tm 3:16
For what is revealed by him
draws understanding and purpose from the future.
It will be true and worthy of faith,
to which nature, *law* and *grace* Jn1:17
will be witnesses.

THE POOR LADIES

Chapter CLV
HOW HE WANTED THE BROTHERS TO HAVE DEALINGS WITH THEM

[204]It would not be right to pass over in silence
the memory of a spiritual building,

a. See 2C 9, supra, 248 a.

much nobler than that earthly one,
that the blessed father established in that place
Is 63:14 with the Holy *Spirit leading*
for the increase of the heavenly city,
after he had repaired the material church.
We should not believe
that for the sake of repairing a crumbling and perishable building,
that Christ spoke to him from the wood of the Cross
and in such an amazing way
2 Mc 12:22 that it *strikes fear* and inflicts pain
upon anyone who hears of it.
But, as earlier foretold by the Holy Spirit,
an Order of holy virgins was to be established there
to be brought one day
1 Pt 2:5 as a polished collection of *living stones*[a]
for the restoration of the heavenly house.
The virgins of Christ
had begun to gather in that place,
assembled from diverse regions of the world,
professing the greatest perfection
2 Cor 8:2 in the observance of the *highest poverty*
Jdt 10:4 and *the beauty of every virtue*.
Though the father gradually withdrew
2 Cor 10:10 his *bodily presence* from them,
Mt 3:11 he still offered *in the Holy Spirit*,
his affection to care for them.
The saint recognized that they were marked
with many signs of the highest perfection,
and that they were ready to bear any loss
Phil 1:29 and undergo any labor *for Christ*
Ps 119:21 and did not ever want to *turn aside*
from the holy *commandments*.
Therefore, he firmly promised them,
and others who professed poverty
in a similar way of life,
that he and his brothers
would perpetually offer them help and advice.
And he carried this out carefully
as long as he lived,

a. This line alludes to the hymn *Urbs beata Ierusalem*, from the Common of the Dedication of a Church: "Living stones are planed and polished / by the hammer's buffets / at the builder's hand, and fitted / to their proper places; / thus arranged, they stand forever / joined into one building."

and when he was close to death
he commanded it to be carried out without fail always,
saying that
one and the same Spirit 1 Cor 12:11
had led the brothers and those little poor ladies
out of this world. Gal 1:4

[205]The brothers were sometimes surprised that he did not often
visit such holy handmaids of Christ in his *bodily presence*, but he Col 2:5
would say: "Don't imagine, dear brothers, that I don't love them
fully. For if it were a crime to cherish them in Christ, wouldn't it be
even worse to have joined them to Christ? Not calling them would
not have been harmful, but not to care for them after calling them
would be the height of cruelty. But *I am giving you an example, that as I* Jn 13:15
do, so should you also do. I don't want one volunteering to visit them,
but rather command that those who are unwilling and very reluctant
should be assigned to their service, as long as they are *spiritual men* Hos 9:7
tested by a longstanding, worthy way of life."

Chapter CLVI

How he reproved some of the brothers who went freely to monasteries

[206]On one occasion a brother who had two daughters of a very holy life in a certain monastery said that he would gladly bring to that place a poor little gift which the saint was sending. But the saint scolded him harshly, indeed, using words which are best not repeated here, and sent the gift with someone else who had refused, although not to the point of obstinacy.

Another brother went to a monastery in winter, for reasons of compassion, unaware of the saint's prohibition about going. When the saint found out about this, he made him walk naked for many miles in the snow and bitter cold.

Chapter CLVII

Preaching more by example than by word

[207]While the holy father was staying at San Damiano, he was pestered by his vicar with repeated requests that he should present the *word of God* to his daughters, and he finally gave in to his insistence. The Ladies gathered as usual to *hear the word of God,* but no less to see their father, and he *raised his eyes to heaven,* where he always had his

Mt 6:21 *heart,* and began to pray to Christ. Then he had ashes brought and
1 Mc 3:47 made a circle with them round himself on the floor, and then *put the
rest on his own head.*

As they waited, the blessed father remained in silence within the circle of ashes, and real amazement grew in their hearts. Suddenly
Ps 51:3 he got up, and to their great surprise, recited the *"Have mercy on me,
God,"* instead of a sermon. As he finished it, he left quickly. The handmaids of God were so filled with contrition by the power of this mime that they were flowing with tears, and could hardly restrain their hands from punishing themselves. By his action he taught them to consider themselves ashes, and that nothing else was close to his heart except what was in keeping with that view.

This was his way of behaving with holy women;
this was his way of visiting them
rare and constrained, but very useful!
This was his will for all the brothers,
whom he wanted to serve
Col 3:24 for the sake of *Christ, whom they serve*:
Prv 1:17; Ps 69:23 that they might always, like *winged* creatures,
beware of *the nets before them.*

EXTOLLING THE RULE OF THE BROTHERS

Chapter CLVIII
EXTOLLING THE RULE OF SAINT FRANCIS, AND A BROTHER WHO ALWAYS CARRIED IT WITH HIM

208 **He burned with great zeal for the common profession and** AC 46
***Rule,* and endowed those who were zealots about it with a special
blessing.**

Sir 24:32; Rv 3:5; 1 Thes 5:8 **He called it their** ***Book of Life, the hope of salvation,*** **the marrow of** 1C 32
Gn 17:13 **the Gospel,** the way of perfection, the key of Paradise, *the pact of an
eternal covenant.* **He wanted all to have it, all to know it, in all places** ER XXIV; Test 3
Rom 7:22; Wis 8:9 **to let it speak to the** *inner man* **as** *encouragement in weariness* **and as a
reminder of a sworn oath.**

He taught them to keep it always before their eyes as a reminder of the life they should lead and, what is more, that they should die with it.

This teaching was not forgotten by a certain lay brother whom we believe should be venerated among the martyrs, since he gained the palm of glorious victory.[a] **When he was taken by the Saracens to his martyrdom, he held the *Rule* in his uplifted hands, and kneeling humbly, said to his companion: "Dear brother, I proclaim myself guilty before *the eyes of Majesty* of everything that I ever did against this holy *Rule!*" The stroke of the sword followed this short confession, and with this martyrdom he ended his life, and afterward** Is 3:8 **shone with *signs and wonders*. This brother had entered the Order so** 2 Cor 12:12 **young that he could hardly bear the *Rule's* fasting, yet even as a boy he wore a harness next to his skin. Oh happy child, who** began happily, that he might finish more happily!

Chapter CLIX
A VISION EXTOLLING THE RULE

209The most holy Father once saw by heavenly revelation a vision concerning the *Rule.* It was at the time when there was discussion among the brothers about confirming the *Rule,* and the saint was extremely anxious about this matter. This is what was shown to him *in a dream:* It seemed to him that he was gathering tiny bread crumbs Mt 1:20 from the ground, which he had to distribute to a crowd of hungry brothers who stood all around him. He was afraid to give out such little crumbs, fearing that such minute particles might slip between his fingers, when a *voice cried out* to him from above: "Francis, make one Dn 6:20 host out of all the crumbs, and give it to those who want to eat." He did this, and whoever did not receive it devoutly, or showed contempt for the gift received, soon appeared obviously infected with leprosy.

In the morning the saint recounted all this to his companions, regretting that he did not understand the *mystery of the vision.* But Dn 2:19 shortly afterward, as he *kept vigil in prayer,* this *voice came down* to him Tb 3:11; 2 Pt 1:17-18 *from heaven:* "Francis, the crumbs you saw last night are the words of the Gospel; the host is the *Rule,* and the leprosy is wickedness."

The brothers of those times
did not consider this promise which they had sworn
either hard or harsh;
they were always more than ready

a. This was Brother Electus, who was executed by the Muslims, probably at Tunis, before 1246, and quite possibly during the lifetime of Francis.

Lk 10:35 *to give more* than required in all things.[a]
For there is no room for apathy or laziness
where the goad of love is always urging to greater things.

The illnesses of Saint Francis

Chapter CLX
How he conversed with a brother about care of the body

210Francis, the herald of God,
Jos 3:13 *put* his *footprints* on the ways of Christ
through innumerable labors and serious diseases,
and he did not retreat
Lk 14:30 until he had more perfectly *completed*
what he had perfectly *begun*.
Jgs 16:16 When *he was exhausted*
and his whole body completely shattered,
he never stopped on the race of his perfection
and never allowed relaxing
the rigor of discipline.
For even when his body was already exhausted
he could not grant it even slight relief
without some grumbling of conscience.

So, when even against his will it was necessary to smear medical remedies on his body, which exceeded his strength, he spoke kindly one day with a brother whom he knew was ready to give him advice: "What do you think of this, dear son? My conscience often grumbles about the care of the body. It fears I am indulging it too much in this illness, and that I'm eager for fine lotions to help it. Actually, none of this gives it any pleasure, since it is worn out by long sickness, and the urge for any savoring is gone."

211The son replied attentively to his father, realizing that the words of his answer were given to him by the Lord. "Tell me, father, if you please, how attentively did your body obey your commands while it was able?" And he said:

a. *Supererogare* [to give more] is used only once in the Old and New Testaments, that is, in this passage of Luke's Gospel treating of the Good Samaritan. It is also the only use of the word in Thomas's writings suggesting an obvious connection in his thought, the promise of the Good Samaritan and that of the brothers.

"I will bear witness to it, my son, Jn 5:31
for it was *obedient in all things.* Col 3:20
It did not spare itself in anything,
but almost rushed headlong
to carry out every order.
It evaded no labor,
it turned down no discomfort,
if only it could *carry out commands.* Jgs 9:54
In this it and I were in complete agreement:
that *we should serve the Lord Christ* Col 3:24
without any objection."

The brother said: "Well, then, my father, where is your generosity? Where is your piety and your great discernment? Is this a repayment worthy of *faithful friends*: to accept favors gladly but then not Sir 6:14-16
give anything in return in time of need? To this day, what service could you offer to Christ your Lord without the help of your body? Haven't you admitted that it exposed itself to every danger for this reason?"

"I admit, son," said the father, "this is nothing but the truth."

And the son replied: "Well, is it reasonable that you should desert
a *faithful friend* in great need, who risked himself and all that he had Gn 18:25
for you, even to the point of death? *Far be it from* you, father, you who Gn 18:25
are the help and support of the afflicted; *far be it from you to sin against* 1 Sm 12:23
the Lord in such a way!"

"Blessed are you also, *son,"* he said, "you have wisely given me a 1 Sm 26:25
drink of healing medicine for my disquiet!" And he began to say jok-
2C 116, 129 ingly to his body: "Cheer up Brother Body, and *forgive me*; for I will Jb 7:16
now gladly do as you please, and gladly hurry to relieve your complaints!"

But, what could delight this little body already so ruined?
What could uphold it,
already broken in every way?
Francis *was* already *dead to the world,* Gal 2:19-20; 6:14
but *Christ lived in* him.
The delights of the world were a cross to him,
since he carried the *cross of Christ* rooted in his heart. Gal 6:14
And that is why the stigmata
shone outwardly in his flesh,
because inwardly that root was growing
deep in his spirit.

Chapter CLXI
WHAT THE LORD PROMISED HIM FOR HIS SUFFERINGS

212 Worn out with sufferings on all sides, it was amazing that his strength could bear it. But in fact he did not call these tribulations by the name of "pains," but rather "Sisters." There is no question that they came from many causes. Truly, in order that he might become more famous through victories, the Most High not only entrusted to him difficult tasks during his early training but also gave him occasions for triumph while he was a veteran.

In this too the followers have him for an example,
for he never slowed down because of age
or became more self-indulgent because of his illness.
And there was a reason that his purgation was complete
Ps 84:7 *in this vale of tears:*
Mt 5:25 so he might *repay up to the last penny,*
if there was anything to burn left in him,
so at the end completely cleansed
he could fly quickly to heaven.
But I believe the principal reason for his sufferings was,
as he affirmed about others,
Ps 19:11 that *in* bearing *them there is great reward.*

213 One night, when he was more worn out than usual because of
various serious discomforts from his illnesses, he began to feel sorry
Mt 26:41 for himself in the depths of his heart. But, lest his *willing spirit* should
give in to the flesh in a fleshly way even for a moment, unmoving he
held the shield of patience by praying to Christ.

Lk 22:43; Heb 10:36; Jn 6:68 And as he *prayed* in this *struggle,* he *received a promise of eternal life*
Is 40:12 through this comparison: "If the whole *mass of the earth* and fabric of
the universe were made of the most precious gold, and you with all
pain gone were given as the reward for the hard suffering you're
Wis 7:9 bearing a treasure of such glory that all this *gold* would be as nothing
in comparison to it,—not even worth mentioning—wouldn't you rejoice, and gladly bear what you're bearing at the moment?" "I'd be
2 Cor 4:17 happy to," said the saint, "I'd be *immeasurably happy.*"

"Rejoice, then," the Lord said to him, "for your illness is the
Wis 7:23 pledge of my Kingdom; by merit of your patience you can be *firm and*
Eph 5:5 *secure* in expecting the *inheritance of this Kingdom.*"

Can you imagine the joy felt by one
blessed with such a happy promise?

Can you believe the great patience,
and even the charity,
he showed in embracing bodily discomforts?
He now knows it perfectly,
but then it was impossible for him to express it.
However, as he could, he told a little to his companions.
C; 1C 80; AC 83 It was then that he composed
the *Praises about Creatures,*
rousing them in any way
to praise of the Creator.

THE PASSING OF OUR HOLY FATHER OUT OF THIS WORLD

Chapter CLXII

HOW AT THE END HE ENCOURAGED AND BLESSED HIS BROTHERS

214 *At a human's end,* says the wise man, Sir 11:27-28
comes the disclosing of his works,
and we see this gloriously fulfilled in this saint.
Running eagerly *on the road of God's commandments,* Ps 119:32
he scaled the steps of all the virtues
until he reached the very summit.
Like a malleable metal,
he was brought to perfection
under the hammering blows of many tribulations,
and *saw the end of all perfection.*[a] Ps 119:96
Then his wonderful work shone all the brighter,
and it flared out in *the judgement of truth* Ps 111:7
that everything he lived was divine.
He trampled on the allure of mortal life
and escaped free into the heights.
For he considered it dishonor to live for the world,
loved his own to the very end, Jn 13:1
and welcomed Death singing.
When he approached his final days
—when *light eternal*[b] was replacing
the limited light that had been removed—

a. This refers to a medieval technique for purifying and strengthening metals by hammering. Therefore the blacksmith who worked with iron, but also gold-and-silver smiths.

b. Entrance Antiphon for the Requiem Mass, taken from the apocryphal book of 4 Ezra, 2:35.

he showed by his example of virtue
that he had nothing in common with the world.

As he was wasted by that grave illness which ended all his sufferings, he had himself placed naked on the naked ground, so that in 1C 110
that final hour, when the Enemy could still rage, he might wrestle
naked with the naked.[a] The fearless man awaited triumph and, with
2 Tm 4:8; Jb 20:4 hands joined, held the *crown of justice.* Placed *on the ground* and
Jb 11:15 stripped of his sackcloth garment, he *lifted* up his *face to heaven* as
Acts 7:55 usual, and, totally *intent* upon that *glory,* he covered the wound on his
right side with his left hand, so no one would see it. Then he said to
1 Kgs 19:20; Eph 4:21 his brothers: "I have done *what is mine; may Christ teach* you what is
yours!"

215 Seeing this, his sons wept streams of tears, drawing sighs from deep within, overwhelmed by sorrow and compassion.

Meanwhile, as their sobs somewhat subsided, his guardian, who
by divine inspiration better understood the saint's wish, quickly got
up, took the tunic, underwear and sackcloth hood, and said to the father: "I command you under holy obedience to acknowledge that I
am lending you this tunic, underwear and hood. And so that you
know that they in no way belong to you, I take away all your author-
Sg 3:11 ity to give them to anyone." The saint rejoiced, and his *heart* leaped
Mt 10:22 for *joy* seeing that he had kept faith *until the end* with Lady Poverty.
For he had done all of this out of zeal for poverty, not wanting to have
at the end even a habit of his own, but one borrowed from another.
He had been wearing a sackcloth cap on his head to cover the scars he
had received in the treatment of his eyes; what was really needed for
this was a smooth cap of the softest and most expensive wool.

2 Chr 6:13 216 After this the saint *raised his hands to heaven*
and glorified his Christ;
free now from all things, he was going to him free.

1 Cor 4:16 But in order to show himself in all things a true *imitator of Christ,* AC 22
Jn 13:1 his God, *he loved to the very end* the brothers and sons *he had loved* from
the beginning. **He had them call to him** all the brothers present
Zec 1:13 there, and, comforting them about his death with *words of consolation,*
he exhorted them to the love of God with fatherly affection. He spoke

a. See Gregory the Great, *Homilia in Evangelium,* 32:2. "All of us who come to the wrestling ground of Faith are to wrestle with the evil spirits. Now, the evil spirits possess nothing in this world, and therefore it behooves us to wrestle naked with naked adversaries. For if a clothed man should wrestle with a naked man, he will soon be thrown down, for his adversary will have something by which to take hold of him." This passage became a common quotation in medieval ascetical literature. See also FA:ED I 194 a.

at length about patience, about preserving poverty, and about placing the Holy Gospel ahead of all other observances.

As all the brothers sat around him *he stretched out his right hand over* Gn 48:14-22
them and, beginning with his vicar, *he placed it on* each of *their heads*
saying:

1C 108 "Good bye, my sons,
live in the *fear of the Lord* Acts 9:31
and remain in it always!
A great trial and tribulation is at hand!
Happy are they who will persevere
in the things they have begun!
I am hurrying to God,
to whose grace I commend all of you!"

He then blessed in those who were there, all the other brothers
who *were living* anywhere *in the world,* and those who *were to come after* 2 Cor 1:12; Jn 1:15
them *unto the end of all ages.* Dn 7:18

Let no one claim this blessing as his own
for he pronounced it for those absent through those present.
As written elsewhere
it sounded like something for an individual;[a]
instead it should be redirected to the office.

Chapter CLXIII

His Death and What He Did Before It

AC 22 217 As the brothers shed bitter tears and wept inconsolably, the
holy father had *bread brought* to him. He *blessed and broke* it, and gave Mt 14:17, 18; Mt 26:26
each of them a piece to eat.

1C 110 He also ordered a Book of the Gospels to be brought and asked
that the Gospel according to Saint John be read to him starting from
that place which begins: *Before the feast of Passover.*[b] He was remember- Jn 13:1
ing that most sacred Supper, the last one the Lord celebrated *with his* Mt 26:20
disciples. In reverent memory of this, to show his brothers how much
he loved them, he did all of this.

a. In 1C 108-109, the blessing could be interpreted as given to Brother Elias personally. Here the author interprets the blessing as designated for the one who holds the office of Vicar.

b. Here, in contrast to 1C 110, Thomas corrects the confusion about the starting point for the reading of the Gospel. See FA:ED I 278 a.

The few days that remained to him before his passing he spent in 1C 109
praise of God, teaching his beloved companions how to praise Christ
Ps 142, 2-8 with him. As best he could, he broke out in this psalm, *With my voice I*
cried to the Lord, With my voice I beseeched the Lord. He also invited all 1C 108
creatures to the praise of God, and exhorted them to love by some
words which he had composed earlier.[a] Even death itself, terrible
Jgs 19:3 and hateful everyone, he exhorted to praise, and *going to meet her joy-*
fully, invited her to be his guest, saying: "Welcome, my Sister Death!"
And to the doctor he said: "Be bold, Brother Doctor, foretell death is
near; for to me she will be the gate of Life!" But to the brothers he
said: "When you see I have come to my end put me out naked on the
ground as you saw me naked the day before yesterday,[b] and once I
am dead, allow me to lie there for as long as it takes to walk a leisurely mile."

Jn 4:21 The *hour came.*
Col 4:3 All *the mysteries of Christ*
were fulfilled in him,
and he happily flew off to God.

How a Brother Saw the Passing of the Holy Father's Soul

217a One of his disciples, a brother of no small fame, saw the soul of 1C 110, 112, 113
Sir 50:6; Jos 8:20 the most holy father *like a star ascending to heaven,* having the immen-
Ps 29:3 sity of the moon and the brightness of the sun, extending *over many*
Rv 14:14 *waters* carried by *a little white cloud.*

Acts 21:30; Lk 2:20 Because of this *a great crowd of many peoples* gathered, *praising and*
glorifying the name of the Lord. The whole city of Assisi rushed down in
Acts 2:11 a body and the whole region hurried to see the *wonderful works of God,*
Lk 2:15 which the *Lord* had *displayed* in his servant. The sons lamented the
loss of such a father and displayed their hearts' tender affection by
tears and sighs.

But a new miracle turned their weeping into jubilation and their mourning into cries of joy. They saw the body of their holy father adorned with the wounds of Christ. Not the holes of the nails but the nails themselves in the middle of his hands and feet, made from his own flesh, in fact grown in the flesh itself retaining the dark color of iron and his right side stained red with blood. His skin, naturally

a. This refers to the *Canticle of the Creatures,* see FA:ED I 113-114

b. Thomas does a word play here: *sicut me nudiustertius nudum vidistis.*

dark before, now shining bright white promised the rewards of the blessed resurrection.

Finally, his limbs had become soft and pliable; not rigid, as usual with the dead, but changed to be like those of a boy.

Chapter CLXIV

The Vision Brother Augustine Saw as He Was Dying

[218]At that time the minister of the brothers of Terra di Lavoro was Brother Augustine. He was in his last hour, and had already for some
time lost his speech when, in the hearing of those *who were standing* Acts 23:4
by, he suddenly cried out and said: "Wait for me, father, wait! Look, I'm Lk 9:39
coming with you!" The amazed brothers asked him to whom he was speaking, and he responded boldly: "Don't you see our father Francis going to heaven?" And immediately his holy soul, released from the flesh, followed his most holy father.

Chapter CLXV

How the Holy Father Appeared to a Brother after His Passing

[219]At the very same hour that evening the glorious father appeared to another brother of praiseworthy life, who was at that moment absorbed in prayer. He appeared to him clothed in a purple dalmatic[a] and followed by an innumerable crowd of people. Several
separated themselves from the crowd and said to that brother: *"Is* Jn 7:26
this not *Christ,* brother?" And he replied: *"It is he."* Others asked him Mt 26:48
again, saying: "Isn't this Saint Francis?" And the brother likewise replied that it was he. For it really seemed to that brother, and to the whole crowd, as if Christ and Saint Francis were one person.

And this will not seem at all like a rash statement to those who
rightly understand it, for whoever *clings to God,* becomes *one spirit* 1 Cor 6:17
with Him, and that *God* will be *all in all.* 1 Cor 12:6

Finally the blessed father and the crowd arrived at a very beautiful place, watered with the clearest waters, flourishing with the beauty of flowers and full of every delightful sort of tree. There, too, was a palace of amazing size and singular beauty. The new inhabitant of heaven entered it eagerly. He found inside many brothers sitting at a splendidly set table loaded with various delicacies and with them he delightfully began to feast.

a. The dalmatic is the liturgical vestment proper to deacons. The color of the dalmatic is probably meant to be a royal purple.

Chapter CLXVI
THE BISHOP OF ASSISI'S VISION OF THE HOLY FATHER'S PASSING

[220]At that time the bishop of Assisi[a] had been at the church of
Saint Michael[b] because of a pilgrimage. He was returning from there,
and was lodging at Benevento, when the blessed father Francis appeared to him in a vision on the night of his passing, and said to him:
Jn 16:28; Gn 24:54 "See, my father, *I am leaving the world and going to Christ!" When he rose
in the morning,* the bishop told his companions what he had seen, and
summoning a notary, had the day and hour of the passing noted. He
was very saddened about this, and flowing with tears he regretted
Mt 2:12 having lost such an outstanding father. And so *he returned to his own
Acts 27:35 country* and told it all in order, giving unending *thanks to the Lord* because of his gifts.

THE CANONIZATION AND TRANSFER OF SAINT FRANCIS

1 Cor 6:11 [220a]*In the name of the Lord Jesus.* Amen. 1C 88, 119-126
In the twelfth hundredth twenty sixth year of the Incarnation,
on the fourth day before the Nones of October,
the day he had foretold,
having completed twenty years
from the time he perfectly adhered to Christ,
1 Pt 2:21 *following in the footsteps*
and the life of the Apostles,
the apostolic man Francis,
freed from the fetters of mortal life,
departed happily to Christ.
He was buried in the city of Assisi
and began to shine with so many wonders
and with diverse miracles in every region,
that,
in a short time,
he had led most of the earth
to admire the new age.

Since in the new light of miracles, he was already shining in many parts of the world and those who rejoiced in being saved from disasters by his favor were hastening from everywhere, the Lord Pope

a. Bishop Guido, who was bishop of Assisi throughout the whole of Francis's religious life.

b. At Monte Gargano in southern Italy.

Gregory, who was then in Perugia with all the cardinals and other prelates of the Church, began to discuss with them the issue of his canonization. All of them, with one accord, gave the same opinion. They read and approved the miracles which the Lord had worked through his servant, and extolled the life and behavior of the blessed father with the highest praises.

The *princes of the earth* were called first to this great solemnity, and on the appointed day a great number of prelates along with an infinite multitude of people entered with the blessed Pope into the city of Assisi, for it was there that the canonization was to be held, for greater reverence of the saint. Ps 148:11

And so, when all had come to the place which had been prepared for such a solemn gathering, Pope Gregory preached first to *all the people* and announced with honey-flowing affection *the wonderful works of God*. He also praised the holy father Francis with the most noble sermon, and as he spoke of the purity of his way of life he was wet with tears. Then, when his sermon was over, Pope Gregory *lifted his hands to heaven* and cried out with a loud voice . . . [a] Heb 9:19 Sir 18:5 2 Mc 3:20

a. Number 220a is only in one manuscript, the *Codex of Marseille*, and it breaks off at this point. Cf. AF X, p. 258, note 1.

A PRAYER OF THE SAINT'S COMPANIONS TO HIM

Chapter CLXVII

221 Behold, our blessed father, the efforts of our simple capacities have attempted to praise your wondrous deeds to the best of our ability, and to tell at least a few of the countless virtues of your holiness for your glory. We know that our words have much diminished the splendor of your outstanding deeds, since they have been found unequal to expressing the great deeds of such perfection.

We ask you, and also those who read this, to keep in mind our affection and our effort, and to rejoice that the heights of your life are beyond the best efforts of human pens. For who, oh outstanding
Is 4:4 saint, could be able to bring into himself the burning *ardor of your spirit* or to impress it on others? Who would be able to conceive those inexpressible feelings which flowed uninterruptedly between you and God? But we wrote these things delighting in your sweet memory which, while we still live, we try to express to others even if it is by stammering.

Ps 81:17 You who once were hungry, now *feed upon the finest wheat;* you who
Ps 36:9 once were thirsty, now *drink of the torrent of delight.* But we do not be-
Ps 36:9 lieve that you are so far *inebriated with the abundance of God's house,* as to
Hos 4:6; Ps 115:12 have *forgotten your own children* when he who is your very drink *keeps us in mind.*

Sg 1:3 *Draw us,* then, to *yourself,*
that we may run after the fragrance of your perfumes,
for, as you can see, we have become
lukewarm in apathy,
listless in laziness,
half-dead in negligence!
Lk 12:32 This *little flock* is stumbling
along in your footprints;
the weakness of our eyes cannot bear
the shining rays of your perfection.
Lam 5:21 *Give us such days as we had of old,*
oh mirror and exemplar of the perfect!
Do not allow that those
who are like you by profession
be unlike you in life.

[222]At this point we *lay down* the prayer of our lowliness before the merciful kindness of the *eternal Majesty* for Christ's servant, our minister, the successor of your holy humility, and emulator of your true poverty, who, for *the love of your Christ,* shows diligent *care for* your *sheep* with gentle affection.

Dn 9:18
Ps 72:19
Rom 8:35; Gn 46:32

We ask you, oh holy one,
so to encourage and embrace him that,
by constantly adhering to your footprints,
he may attain forever *the praise and glory* Phil 1:11
which *you have achieved.* 1 Tm 4:6

[223]We also pray with all our heart's affection, oh kind father, for that son of yours who now and earlier has devoutly written your praises. He, together with us, offers and dedicates to you this little work which he put together, not in a manner worthy of your merit but at least devoutly, and as best he could.

From every *evil* Mt 6:13
mercifully preserve
and *deliver* him.
Increase holy merit in him,
and, by your prayers,
join him forever to the company of the saints.

[224]Remember all your children, father.
You, most holy one, know perfectly how,
lost in a maze of mystifying perils,
they *follow your footprints* Gn 33:14
from how great a distance.
Give them strength, that they may resist.
Purify them, that they may shine radiantly.
Fill them with joy, that they may delight.

Pray that
the spirit of grace and of prayer may inundate them Zec 12:10
that they may have the true humility you had;
that they may cherish the poverty you embraced;
that they may be filled with the love
with which you always loved
Christ crucified. 1 Cor 1:23
Who with the Father and the Holy Spirit
lives and reigns forever and ever. Rv 11:15
Amen.

THE TREATISE ON THE MIRACLES OF SAINT FRANCIS

BY

THOMAS OF CELANO

(1250–1252)

Introduction

In *The Life of Saint Francis, The Legend for Use in the Choir* based on it, and *The Remembrance of the Desire of a Soul,* Thomas of Celano wrote of the miracles of Francis of Assisi. In each of these works, Thomas saw these miracles as signs through which God had authenticated the holiness of his subject and, at the same time, as extraordinary deeds attesting to God's power working through him.[1] When John of Parma, the newly elected General Minister, approached the now aging writer to treat of them in one collection, he was implicitly asking for the completion of a trilogy in which each work had its own unique focus and its own contribution to the entire portrait.

Written between 1250 and 1252, *The Treatise on the Miracles of Saint Francis* is made up of 198 paragraphs. Fifty-four of these are taken from *The Life of Saint Francis,* one from *The Legend for Use in the Choir,* and nine from *The Remembrance of the Desire of a Soul.* In other words, for one third of his work, Thomas relies on his earlier portraits of Francis. The remaining paragraphs come from different sources. *The Assisi Compilation* is easily identifiable and suggests that "we who were with him," as Francis's companions write of themselves, contributed to Thomas's awareness of the miracles. Other paragraphs come from an unknown source, prompting speculation about the existence of a "process of canonization" in which an official or notary would have written down the testimonies of witnesses to these miracles. Throughout, however, the hand of Thomas is obvious as he orders, sculpts and refines the material given to him into the portrait of Francis the Thaumaturgist, the Miracle Worker.

Thomas divided his work into nineteen chapters. One manner of approaching these chapters is to see them simply in terms of those miracles performed while Francis lived, that is, the first six chapters, and those performed, through his intercession, after his death, that is, the final thirteen. However, the first six chapters deal with miracles that touch more on the inner dynamic of Francis himself or on that of his brothers: the founding and growth of the fraternity, the stigmata, the miraculous power he had over creatures, and the arrival of Lady Jacoba at his death. These far more reflective and theological chapters reveal Thomas at his inspirational best, never hesitating to add his own interpretation of an incident or to draw a moral from it. The remaining chapters, with the exception of the conclusion, i.e., chapter nineteen, are far more historical and ordered giving the impression that Thomas was following a predetermined order. From considerations of Francis's miraculous raising of the dead to his healing of broken bones, Thomas presents one hundred and fifty-seven miracles. In doing so, he deftly paints a portrait of this "new man," Francis, through whom the Creator makes all things new (3C 1).

The first printed edition of the Latin text of *The Treatise on the Miracles of Saint Francis* appeared only in 1899 when François van Ortroy published it in the *Acta Bollandiana*.[2] In his edition of the complete corpus of Thomas of Celano in 1906, Édouad d'Alençon also published it, as did the editors of the tenth volume of the *Analecta Franciscana*.[3] The latest publication of the text is that of the *Fontes Franciscani* in 1995.[4]

Translating this lengthy list of miracles, however, seems to have been a daunting enterprise, and, because of its repetitious nature, one that was tedious and tiring. That translators and publishers gave little attention to Thomas's last work is verified by the fact that there have been no complete translations of the work. The Spanish, French, and American editions either printed selected paragraphs or nothing at all.[5] Thus, little attention has been given to the work until the Italian *Fonti Francescane* published *The Treatise on the Miracles of Saint Francis* in its entirety, prompting six studies that began to shed light on its richness.[6] The authors of these essays examined aspects such as the sites of the miracles, the sociological backgrounds of the recipients, the information the incidents provide concerning the daily life of those involved, and Thomas's changing image of Francis.

Notes

1. For a thorough study of the medieval understanding and appreciation of miracles, see Benedicta Ward, *Miracles and the Medieval Mind: Theory, Record and Event, 1000-1215* (Philadelphia: University of Pennsylvania Press, 1982). For background information on Thomas of Celano's approach to miracles in *The Life of Saint Francis,* see Roberto Paciocco, "Miracles and Canonized Sanctity in the 'First Life of St. Francis,'" GR 5(1991): 251-274.

2. François van Ortroy, "Traité des miracles des François d'Assise par le b. Thomas de Celano," *Analecta Bollandiana* 18 (1899): 81-179.

3. Eduardus Alenconiensis, *Sancti Francisci Assiensis Vita et Miracula, additis opusculis liturgicis auctore Fr. Thoma de Celano,* (Romae, 1906), 341-432; "Tractatus de Miraculis," *Analecta Franciscana* X (Ad Claras Aquas, Quaracchi: Collegium S. Bonaventurae, 1926-1941), 269-331.

4. *Fontes Franciscani,* ed. Enrico Menestó, Stefano Brufani, Giuseppe Cremascoli, Emore Paoli, Luigi Pellegrini, and Stanislao da Campagno (Sta. Maria degli Angeli, Assisi: Edizioni Porziuncula, 1995).

5. The Spanish edition, *San Francisco de Asis. Sus escritos. Las Florecillas. Biografías del santo por Celano, san Buenaventura y los Tres Compañeros. Espejo de Perfección.* 5 ed. (Madrid: BAC, 1951), ignored the work completely. The French edition, *Saint François d'Assise: Documents, écrits et premières biographies.* (Paris: éditions Franciscaines, 1968), was limited to only the titles. The American edition, *Saint Francis of Assisi, Writings and Early Biographies: English Omnibus of The Sources for the Life of Saint Francis* (Chicago: Franciscan Herald Press, 1972), published only certain paragraphs, i.e., those that had already been translated.

6. *Fonti Francescane. Scritti e biografie di san Francesco d'Assisi. Cronache e altre testimonianze del primo secolo francescano. Scritti et biografie di santa Chiara.* 2 Volumes. (Assisi: Movimento Francescano, 1977).

Mariano D'Alatri, "Da Una Rilettura del 'Tratatto dei miracoli' di Fra Tommaso da Celano," *I'Italia Francescana* 53 (1978): 29-40; Jacques Paul, "L'Image de Saint François dans Le Traite 'De Miraculis' de Thomas de Celano," in *Francesco d'Assisi nella Storia, Secoli XIII-XV,* a cura di Servus Gieben (Roma, 1983): 251-274; Roberto Paciocco, *Da Francesco ai 'Catologi Sanctorum.' Livelli Istituzionali e Immagini Agiografiche nell'Ordine Francescano (Secoli XIII-XIV)* (Assisi: 1990); Maria Antonietta Romano, "Tractatus de Miraculis B. Francisci," *Hagiographica 2* (1996): 187-221; and Jacques Dalarun, "Il Tractatus de Miraculis, Vertice dell'Opera Celaniana," in *La Malavventura di San Francesco: Per Un Uso Storico delle Leggende Francescane* (Milano: Edizioni Biblioteca Francescana, 1996), 97-119.

The Treatise on the Miracles of Saint Francis

Chapter I
THE BEGINNING OF HIS RELIGION WAS MIRACULOUS

[1]We have undertaken to write down
the miracles of our most holy father Francis;
and we have decided to note in first place in this account,
before all the others,
that sacred miracle by which the world was warned,
by which it was roused, and by which it was frightened.
2, 31, 36-7, 62, 89; LCh 9 That miracle was the beginning of the religion:
the sterile made fruitful,
giving birth to a varied people.
People observed
1C 8 that the old world was growing *filthy* with a mange of vices, Rv 22:11
that Orders were slipping away from the footprints of the apostles,
that *the night* of sinners had reached *mid-course in its journey,* Wis 18:14-15
and *silence* had been imposed on sacred studies.

Just then, suddenly, there *leapt upon the earth* Eph 2:15
a new man;
a new army quickly appeared;
1C 89 and the peoples marveled *at the signs* of an apostolic newness.[a] Ps 65:9; Mk 16:20
Quickly there *came to light* Jb 28:11
the long-buried perfection of the primitive Church:
the world read of its marvels,
but did not see any examples of it.
Why, therefore, should *the last* not be called the *first,* Mt 19:30; 20:16
since now *the hearts of fathers are* wondrously *turned to their children* Mal 4:6
and the hearts of children to their fathers?
1C 37-8, 18-20 Sould *the mission* of the two Orders,[b] 2 Cor 5:20
so well-known and famous,

a. Thomas returns to a theme found throughout his earlier works, that of newness. While it is most prominent in 1C in which *novus* [new] appears thirty-nine times, it is proportionately less so in 2C where it appears twenty-four times. In this work, it appears thirteen times. In this instance, the theme of the "newness" found in the "new man" appears to indicate the wonders brought by the saint and the "new Orders" founded by him. Cf. FA:ED I 196 c.

b. A reference to the Order of Friars Minor and that of Saint Damian, the Poor Ladies. *Solet annuere*, the papal decree of Pope Honorius III confirming the Later Rule with a papal seal (cf. FA:ED I 99-106), declared the Lesser Brothers an Order. In the papal document, *Cum omnis vera religio* (August 6, 1247), Pope Innocent IV called the Poor Ladies, the followers of Clare of Assisi (+1253), the "Order of Saint Damian." It was not called the Order of Saint Clare until the papal decree of Pope Urban IV in 1256. Thomas omits mention of the Third Order, the Order of Penitents.

be considered unimportant,
and not a portent of great things to come?
Never since the time of the apostles was there
such an outstanding, such an amazing warning to the world!

Wonderful, its sterile fruitfulness.
Sterile, I say, and dried out this poor little Religion:
the moisture of earthly things remains far from it.
Mt 6:26 Sterile indeed the one who *neither reaps nor gathers into barns,*
Lk 9:3; 10:4 Acts 18:25 nor *carries a* bulging *wallet on the way of the Lord.*
Rom 4:18 And yet this saint *believed, hoping against hope,*
Rom 4:19 that *he would inherit the world,*
Jb 4:13; Gn 11:30 *not thinking his own body as good as dead*
and the womb of Sarah sterile.
God's power brought forth from her the Hebrew people.
He was not sustained
Lk 12:24; Is 39:2 by full *cellars,*
by overflowing *storehouses,*
or bountiful possessions;
but the same poverty that makes him worthy of heaven
marvelously nourished him in the world.
1 Cor 1:25 *O weak one of God, stronger than men,*
you both bring glory to our cross
and also sustain our poverty with plenty!
We then saw that vine spreading, in the briefest time, 1C 36-7, 89
Ez 17:6-7; 47:17; Ps 80:12 extending its fruitful branches from sea to sea.
People came running from everywhere,
the crowds swelled,
1 Pt 2:5 and were quickly joined *as living stones*

Mk 13:1 to the grand *structure of* this marvelous *temple.*
Not only do we see it multiply with children in a short time;
we also see it become famous,
for we know that many of those it bore
have obtained the palm of martyrdom,[a]
and we venerate many others enrolled in the catalog of saints[b]
as confessors of most perfect holiness.
But let us turn now to him who is the head of them all.

---

a. This is a reference to Brothers Berard, Otto, Peter, Adjutus, and Accursius, who were put to death in Morocco on January 16, 1220. Cf. AF III, 579-96; AF IV 322-3; Jordan, *Chronicle* 7-8. Thomas writes of another unnamed brother martyred by the Saracens, cf. 2C 208. Brother Daniel and seven companions were killed in Ceuta, Mauritania, present day Morocco, on October 10, 1227; cf. AF III 613-6; IV, 296f. Brothers John of Perugia and Peter of Sassoferrato were put to death by Moors in 1231 (certainly not before 1225); see AF III, 186-7; IV, 324.

b. Anthony of Lisbon, who died in Padua on June 13, 1231, was proclaimed a saint by Gregory IX with the papal decree, *Cum dicat Dominus,* June 12, 1232. Cf. *Bullarium Franciscanum* I (hereafter BFr), ed. Joannis H. Sbaraleae, 79-84; 1C 48; 2C 163. In the *Catalogo Sanctorum Fratrum Minorum* ed. Leonard Lemmens (Rome: 1903), 9; AF IV, 235.

Chapter II
THE MIRACLE OF THE STIGMATA
AND THE MANNER IN WHICH THE SERAPH APPEARED TO HIM

[2]*The new man,* Francis, Eph 4:24
became famous for a new and stupendous miracle.
112, 114; 2C 11 By a singular privilege, not granted in previous ages,
he appeared marked,
adorned with the sacred stigmata,
and *conformed in this body of death* Phil 3:10, 21; Rom 7:24
to the body of the Crucified.

Whatever human speech can say about this will be less than the praise it deserves. No explanation should be demanded, because it was a wonder. No example should be sought, because it was unique.[a]
2C 109, 203; 1C 45, 115 All the striving of this *man of God,* whether in public or in private, 1 Sm 9:6
revolved around the cross of the Lord. From the earliest days when he began his knightly service for the Crucified, various mysteries of the cross shone around him. At the beginning of his conversion, when he had decided to take leave of the allurements of this life, Christ spoke to him from the wood of the cross while he prayed.
2C 10 From the mouth of Christ's image a voice declared: "Francis, go, rebuild my house, which, as you see, it is all being destroyed." From that moment the memory of the Lord's passion was stamped on his heart with a deep brand-mark, and as conversion reached his deep-
1C 22 est self, his soul began *to melt, as his beloved spoke.* And he also enclosed Sg 5:6
himself in the cross itself when he put on the habit of a penitent, bearing the image of the cross.

Though for him the more the habit reflected poverty,
the more appropriate it would be to his plan,
the saint approved in it even more the mystery of the cross,
because just as, internally, his mind *had put on* the crucified Lord, Gal 3:27
so, externally, his whole body put on *the cross of Christ.* Gal 6:14
And, in the sign
by which God had vanquished the powers of the air
his army would battle for God.

2C 109 [3]Brother Sylvester, one of his brothers, a man of the greatest discipline in everything, saw coming forth from the saint's mouth a

a. The prominence given to the stigmata at the beginning of this work reflects the hesitancy on the part of some within the Order, as well as some in the larger Christian community, to put credence in the miracle. Cf. infra, *An Umbrian Choir Legend*, introduction, infra 471-472, (hereafter UChL).

golden cross whose extended arms wonderfully indicated the whole
Mt 4:4 world. *It is written,* and verified by trustworthy report, that Brother 1C 48
Monaldo, who was famous for his life, behavior and deeds, saw, in
bodily fashion, blessed Francis crucified, while blessed Anthony was
preaching about the inscription on the cross. It was his custom, es- 1C 45
tablished by a holy decree also for his first sons, that wherever they
saw the likeness of the cross they would give it honor and due rever-
Ez 9:4, 6 ence. He favored the sign of the Tau over all others.[a] With it alone he BIL; 2C 106
signed letters he sent, and painted it on the walls of cells everywhere.
1 Kgs 13:1, 5, 6 That *man of God,* Pacifico, seer of heavenly visions, saw with his 2C 106
bodily eyes a great sign of the Tau on the forehead of the blessed father. It was many-colored and flashed with the brightness of gold.

How worthy then of reasonable human conviction
and of catholic credence
that one who so wonderfully excelled in love of the cross
should also so wonderfully become a wonder in honor of the cross!
Nothing therefore is more appropriate to him
than what is preached about the stigmata of the cross.

[4]This was the manner of the apparition. **Two years prior to the** 1C 94
time that he returned his spirit **to heaven, in the hermitage called**
LaVerna, which is in the province of Tuscany, he was wholly intent
on heavenly glory in the recesses of devout contemplation.

1 Tm 2:10; Ez 8:2, 3 **He saw in a vision** a Seraph upon a cross, **having six wings,** ex-
Is 6:2; Ez 1:5-14, 22-25 tended **above him, arms and feet affixed to a cross.** *Two of his wings*
were raised up over his head, two were stretched out as if for flight, **and** *two*
covered his whole body. Seeing this, **he was filled with the greatest**
awe, but as he did not know **what this vision meant for him, joy**
mixed with **sorrow** flooded his heart. **He greatly rejoiced at the gra-**
cious look that he saw the Seraph give him, but the fact that it was
fixed to the cross terrified him. With **concern** his mind pondered
what this revelation **could mean,** and the search for some **meaning**
made **his spirit anxious.** But understanding came from discovery:
while he was searching outside himself, the meaning was shown to
him in his very self.

At once **signs of the nails began to appear on his hands and feet,** 1C 94
just as he had seen them a little while earlier on the crucified man
in the air **over him. His hands and feet seemed to be pierced** 1C 95
through the middle by nails, with the heads of the nails appearing
on the inner part of his hands and on the upper part of his feet, and

a. Cf. 2C 107, supra, 317 b.

1C 113 **their points protruding on opposite sides.** The heads of the nails **in his hands and feet were round** and black, while their points were **oblong and flattened,** rising from the flesh itself, and **extended beyond the flesh around them. His right side was marked with an oblong** red **scar as if pierced by a lance, and,** since **this often dripped blood, his tunic and undergarments were stained with his holy blood.**

LJS 63; 2C 138 **Rufino,** that *man of God* of angelic purity, **one time rubbed** the holy father with the affection of a son; and **his hand slipped and he** physically **touched** the wound. **The holy one of God felt great pain and pushed Rufino's hand away, crying out** *for the Lord to spare him*. 1 Tm 3:17; Gn 19:16

2C 217a [5]When, after two years' time, with a blessed ending, he at last exchanged the valley of misery for the blessed homeland, the amazing announcement of this extraordinary thing reached peoples' ears.

A crowd of people came together praising and glorifying the name of the Lord. The whole city **of Assisi rushed down as a group and** *the entire region* **hurried,** eager to see that new wonder that God newly displayed *in this world*. **The novelty of the miracle changed their weeping to jubilation,** and swept up their bodily sight toward amazement and ecstasy. They observed the blessed body adorned with the stigmata of Christ, not the holes of the nails, but the nails themselves, in the middle of his hands and feet, marvelously fashioned by divine power from his own flesh, in fact, grown in the flesh itself. From whatever point they were pressed, simultaneously, as if a single tendon, they pulsed at the opposite end. They also saw his side stained red with blood. Acts 21:30; Mi 5:7, 8; Lk 2:13, 20; Ps 86:9; Mt 8:34; Mt 3:5; 2 Cor 1:12

We who say these things
have seen these things; 1 Jn 1:1, 4; Jn 3:11
we have touched with our hands
what we are writing by hand.
With tears in our eyes,
we have sketched what we profess with our lips,
and what we once swore, Ps 89:36
while touching sacred things,
we declare for all time.

1C 113 Many brothers besides us saw it[a] while the saint was alive;
at his death, more than fifty of them with countless lay people
venerated it.

a. It is not clear from this use of the first person plural whether Thomas is speaking for himself, or is speaking for other authors or eyewitnesses.

Let there be no room for ambiguity:
let no one doubt this outpouring of everlasting goodness!
[1 Cor 12:12] If only *the many members* were joined
[Eph 1:22] in that same seraphic love *to Christ their head!*
[Eph 6:11] If only they were to be found worthy of such *armor* in a similar battle,
[Rv 1:9] and be raised to the same rank in the Kingdom!
[Mk 5:15] Who *of sane mind* would not attribute this to the glory of Christ?
But let the punishments already inflicted on unbelievers repay the irreverent
and make the reverent even more confident.

[6]In Potenza, a city in the kingdom of Apulia, there was a cleric named Ruggero, an honorable man and a canon of its major church. He was weakened by a long illness, and one day he entered a church to pray for his health. In the church there was a painted image of blessed Francis, showing the glorious stigmata. He approached, knelt down before the image and prayed with sincere devotion. However, as he fixed his eyes on the saint's stigmata, he turned his thoughts to useless things, and did not repel by force of reason the creeping sting of doubt. With the old enemy deceiving him, his heart torn, he began to say to himself: "Could this be true, that this saint could be singled out for such a miracle, or was this a pious fraud of his followers? Was this," he asked, "a sham discovery, perhaps a deception invented by the brothers? This goes beyond common sense, and is far from reasonable judgment."

The madness of the man! Fool! You should rather have humbly venerated that divine work all the more, the less you could comprehend it. You should have known, if your reason was working, that it is the easiest thing for God to renew the world always with new miracles, [1 Cor 4:12] always *to work in us* for His glory things He has not done in others.

What happened? A severe wound was inflicted by God on the one [Heb 5:8] thinking empty thoughts, so that he might *learn from the things he suffers* not to blaspheme. He was instantly struck in the palm of his left hand (he was left-handed) as he heard a noise like an arrow shot [1 Mc 14:45] from a bow. Instantly, as he was *injured by the wound* and stunned by the noise, he took off the glove from his hand, since he was wearing gloves. Though there had previously been no mark in his palm, he now saw a wound in mid-hand, as if struck by an arrow. So much heat was coming from it that he thought he would pass out. What a wonder! There was no mark on the glove, so the pain of the hidden wound corresponded to the hidden wound of his heart.

[7]He cried out and roared, afflicted with terrible pain for two days, and unveiled his unbelieving heart to all. He declared that he believed that the sacred stigmata were truly in Saint Francis, and swore
to affirm that all shadow of doubt was gone. He humbly prayed *the* Mk 1:24
holy one of God to come to his aid through his sacred stigmata, and he seasoned his many prayers with the sacrifice of tears.

Amazing! His unbelief discarded, bodily healing followed the healing of the spirit: all the pain calmed, the fever cooled, and no sign of the wound remained. He became a man humble before God, devoted to the saint, and subject in lasting friendship to the brothers of the Order.

The miraculous nature of this incident was attested by a signed oath, fully corroborated by the bishop of the place. In all things, blessed be the wonderful potency of God, which in the city of Potenza He magnificently demonstrated![a]

[8]It is the custom of noble Roman matrons, whether widowed or married, especially those whose wealth preserves the privilege of generosity, and on whom Christ pours out his love, to have in their own homes small chambers or a bedroom set apart for prayer. There they would have some painted icon, and the image of the saint they especially venerated.

A certain lady[b] of upright life and noble family chose Saint Francis
for her advocate. She had his image in *the secluded chamber,* where she Jdt 8:5
prayed to the Father in secret. One day while she was praying devoutly, Mt 6:6
her eyes searched intently for those sacred signs, but could not find them at all: she was sad and very surprised. No wonder they were not in the painting: the painter left them out! For several days the
woman kept this *in her heart* and told no one. Often she gazed at the Lk 2:51
image, and always with sadness. Suddenly, one day those wonderful signs appeared in the hands, just as they are usually painted in other images. Divine power supplied what human art had neglected.

[9]The woman was shaken, astonished, and quickly called her daughter, who followed her mother in a holy way of life. The mother
showed her what had happened, *inquiring diligently* whether she had Lk15:8
seen the image before then without the stigmata. The daughter affirmed and swore that before it was without the stigmata, but now truly appeared with the stigmata.

But since the human mind sometimes stumbles over itself, and calls the truth into doubt, harmful doubts again entered the

a. Here Thomas engages again in word play, praising the wonderful potency or power (*potentia*) of God demonstrated in the city of Potenza (*potentia*).

b. She must be distinguished from two other (named) Roman ladies, Jacoba dei Settesoli and Prassede, mentioned below in 3C 37-39 and 3C 181.

woman's heart: perhaps the image had those marks from the beginning.
Acts 8:10 So the *power of God* added a second miracle, so that the first would not be denied. Suddenly the marks disappeared and the image remained denuded of those privileged signs. Thus the second sign became proof of the first. (I met this married and virtuous woman. I declare that I saw in secular clothing a spirit consecrated to Christ the Lord.)[a]

10 Still, human reason from the very moment of birth is ensnared by the stirring of the senses and crass illusions. It is sometimes driven by the waves of imagination to call into doubt anything that is supposed to be believed. As a consequence, only with difficulty do we believe the marvelous deeds of the saints, and frequently faith itself struggles with many obstacles in matters of salvation.

A certain brother, Lesser by Order, preacher by office, religious by life, was firmly convinced of the holy stigmata. But, either from force of habit or from excessive marvel, he began to be irritated by a scruple of doubt about the saint's miracle. Imagine the battle going on in his spirit, with reason defending the side of truth, and fantasy always pushing on the opposing side! Reason posited, with many supporting arguments, that it was just as it was said to be, and when other evidence was lacking, it relied on the truth believed by holy church. On the opposing side the senses' shadows conspired against
1 Jn 9:32 the miracle: it seemed contrary to all of nature, and *unheard-of in all the ages*. 2C 10

One evening, worn out by this wrestling-match, he entered his bedroom, carrying with him a weakened reason and a strengthened, bold imagination. As he slept, Saint Francis appeared to him, with muddy feet, humbly stern and patiently irritated. And he spoke: "Why all these conflicting struggles in you? Why these filthy doubts?
Jn 20:27 *See my hands* and my feet!" He saw the pierced hands, but he did not see the stigmata on the muddy feet. Francis said, "Remove the mud
Jn 20:25 from my feet and examine *the place of the nails*." He took hold of the
1 Jn 1:1 saint's feet, and it seemed to him the mud washed away, and he *touched with* his *hands the places of the nails*. Then suddenly, as the brother awoke, he was flooded with tears, and he cleansed himself of his earlier muddy feelings by public confession.

1 Tm 2:3 11 Those sacred stigmata of the invincible *soldier of Christ* should not be considered lacking in great power, besides being a sign of special grace and a privilege of supreme love which the whole world does not cease to admire.

a. It must be Thomas of Celano himself who speaks here.

How those signs are also powerful weapons for God can be understood through a novelty and evident miracle that happened in Spain, namely in the Kingdom of Castile. There were two men who for a long time had been quarreling with each other with deep hostility. There was no rest for their bitterness; there could be no enduring relief for their violent enmity, nor for *even a moment* any cure for the an- Gal 2:5
imosity they harbored, unless one were to die the cruelest death at the hand of the other. So each of them, fully armed, with many comrades, set up frequent ambushes for his adversary, because the crime could not be committed in public.

One evening, in the deepening dusk, a man of honest life and praiseworthy reputation happened to pass by on the road where there was concealed an ambush of one for the death of the other. This man was hurrying on his way to pray, as he usually did, after the hour of compline at the church of the brothers, for he had given himself with deep devotion to Saint Francis. The *sons of darkness* rose up 1 Thes 5:5
against the *son of light,* and they believed him to be that rival of theirs whom they had long sought to kill. Stabbing him with deadly blows from every side, they left him half-dead. But at the last moment the cruelest enemy thrust a sword deeply into the man's throat, and, unable to remove it, left it in the wound.

[12]People rushed from everywhere, and with cries to heaven the whole neighborhood wailed at the death of the innocent. Because *the living spirit* was still in the man, the advice of doctors prevailed: that Wis 15:11
the sword not be removed from his throat. (Perhaps they did this for the sake of confession, so that he might be able to confess at least by some sign.) The doctors worked the whole night until the hour of matins to wipe away the blood and close the wounds, but because of the multiple, deep stab wounds, they could do nothing and ceased treatment. Some Lesser Brothers stood by the bed with the doctors, filled with grief, awaiting the departure of their friend.

Then the brothers' bell rang for matins. The man's wife heard the bell and, groaning, ran to the bed and cried: "My Lord, *rise quickly,* go Acts 12:7
to matins, your bell is calling you!" Immediately, the one believed to be dying, with a groaning rumble of the chest, struggled to stammer some wheezing words. And raising his hand toward the sword stuck in his throat, he seemed to be motioning for someone to remove it. A miracle! The sword immediately sprang from its place, and in the sight of them all it flew over to the door of the house as if launched by the hand of a very strong man. The man got up, unharmed and in perfect health, as if rising from sleep, and *recounted the wonderful deeds* Ps 26:7
of the Lord.

Lk 5:9; Acts 1:24 [13]Such great amazement *seized the hearts of all* that they all seemed
out of their minds. They thought they were seeing a fantastic vision.
Lk 2:10 But the one who was healed said, "*Do not be afraid!* Do not believe that
what you see is false, because Saint Francis, to whom I was always devoted, has just left this place and has cured me completely of every wound. He placed those most holy stigmata of his over each of my wounds, and he rubbed all of my wounds with their gentleness. By their touch, as you see, he wondrously knit together everything that was broken. When you heard the rattle of my rumbling chest, the other wounds were already healed with great gentleness. Then the most holy father seemed to be leaving, with the sword left in my throat. Since I could not speak, I signaled to him with my weak hand to extract the sword, the one threat of imminent death. Immediately he took hold of it, as you all saw, and threw it with a powerful hand. And thus, as before, with the sacred stigmata he stroked and rubbed my throat. He so perfectly healed it that the flesh that was cut and what was still intact both appear the same."

Who would not marvel at these things? Who would pretend anything different from what is preached about the stigmata as something wholly divine?

Chapter III

THE POWER FRANCIS HAD OVER INANIMATE CREATURES: FIRST, FIRE[a]

[14]At the time of an eye disease, he is forced to let himself be 2C 166
**treated. A surgeon is called to the place, and when he comes he is
carrying an iron instrument for cauterizing. He ordered it to be
placed in the fire until it became red hot. But the blessed Father, to
comfort the body, which was struck with panic, spoke to the fire:**
Sir 1:8, 9 **"My brother Fire, your beauty is the envy of all creatures, the *Most***
Gn 33:10 ***High created* you strong, beautiful and useful. *Be gracious to me* in**
this hour; be courteous! For a long time I have loved you in the
Ps 48:2; Dt 32:6 **Lord. I pray the *Great Lord who created you* to temper now your heat**
that I may bear your gentle burning."

When the prayer is finished, he makes the sign of the cross over the fire and then remains in place unshaken. The surgeon takes in his hands the red-hot, glowing iron. The brothers, overcome by human feeling, run away. The saint joyfully and eagerly offers himself to the iron. The hissing iron sinks into tender flesh, and

a. In the following paragraphs, passages taken verbatim from earlier works are identified by an emboldened font. In this instance, it is helpful to see how Thomas has edited the text of AC, that material submitted by "we who were with him," that is, Francis's companions.

the burn is extended slowly from the ear to the eyebrow. How much pain that burning caused can best be known by the witness of the saint's words, since it was he that felt it. For when the brothers who had fled return, the father says with a smile: "Oh, you *weak souls of little heart;* why did you run away? *Truly I say to you,* I did not feel the fire's heat, nor any pain in my flesh." And turning to the doctor, he says: "If the flesh isn't well cooked, try again!" The doctor, who had experienced quite a different reaction in similar situations, exalts this as a divine miracle, saying: "I tell you, brothers; *today I have seen wonderful things!*"

I Thes 5:14; Mt 14:31
Lk 4:25
Lk 5:26

I believe
he had returned to primeval innocence,
for when he wished the harshest things grew gentle.[a]

2C 46

[15]Once blessed Francis wanted to travel to a certain hermitage so that he could more freely spend time in contemplation. Because he was very weak he got a donkey to ride from a poor man. It was summer, and as the peasant *went up the mountain* following the *man of God*, he was *worn out from the journey* over such a rough and long road. And before they came to the place, he was exhausted, fainting with a burning thirst. He urgently cried out after the saint, begging him *to have pity on him.* He swore he would die if he was not revived by something to drink. *The holy one of God,* always compassionate to the distressed, immediately leaped down from the donkey, knelt down on the ground, and raised his hands to heaven, *praying unceasingly* until he understood he had been heard. "Hurry now," he said to the peasant, "and over there you will find living *water* which at this very hour Christ *has* mercifully *brought forth from the rock* for you to drink." How amazingly kind God is, so easily bowing to His servants! By the power of prayer a peasant drinks *water from the rock* and draws refreshment *from the hard flint.* There was no *flow of water* there before this; and even after a careful search, none was found there afterwards.

Jos 2:16
I Kgs 13:14, 21
Jn 4:6
Dt 13:17
Lk 4:34
Col 1:9
Is 48:21
Ps 78:16; Dt 32:13
Ps 1:3

[16]Gagliano is a populous and noble town in the diocese of Valva.[b] A woman named Maria lived there who, through the difficult ways of this world, was *converted to God* and she subjected herself completely to the service of Saint Francis.

Acts 14:15

a. The place of this episode as the first example of Francis's power over inanimate creatures, found at the end of 2C, exemplifies Thomas's understanding of Francis as a new Adam. Thomas, therefore, places Francis in a new perspective, i.e., that of primeval innocence.

b. Now Gagliano-Aterno, a town east of Celano, in the diocese of Sulmona. In Monte Canale, above Gagliano-Aterno, the fountain mentioned is said to flow near the remains of a chapel of Saint Francis. Cf. A. Chiappini, *L'Abruzzo Francescano nel secolo XIII* (Rome, 1926), 23.

One day she went out to a mountain that was totally deprived of water to prune maple trees, and she forgot to take water along with her. The heat was unbearable and she began to faint from thirst. When she could no longer work and was lying nearly lifeless on the ground, she began intently to call upon her patron, Saint Francis. In her exhaustion she drifted off to sleep. And there was Saint Francis,
Is 40:26 who *called her by name.* "Get up," he said, "and drink the water that is provided by divine gift for you and for many!" At the sound the woman yawned but, overcome by drowsiness, fell back asleep. She was called again, but fell back on the ground in her weariness. But the third time, strengthened by a command of the saint, she got up. She grabbed a fern next to her and pulled it from the earth. When she saw that its root was all wet, she began to dig around it with her finger and a twig. Immediately the hole was filled with water and the
Est 10:6 *little* puddle *grew into a spring.* The woman drank, and when she had had enough, she washed her eyes. They were clouded by a long
Sm 14:27n illness, and she could see nothing clearly. *Her eyes were enlightened,* their old roughness removed, and were flooded as if with new light.

The woman ran home and told everyone about the great miracle,
Mt 9:26 to the glory of Saint Francis. *News* of the miracle *spread* and reached
Mk 1:34; Jn 5:4 the ears of everyone, even in other regions. *Many troubled by various*
1 Pt 1:9 *diseases* came running from every direction, and putting the *health of their souls* first, through confession, they were then freed of their illnesses. The blind recovered their sight, the lame their walk, the swollen grew slim, and for various illnesses their appropriate remedy was offered. That clear spring still flows, and a chapel in honor of Saint Francis has been built there.

[17]**At the hermitage of Sant'Urbano he was suffering from a se-** 1C 61
vere illness, when with a weak voice he requested some **wine.** The response was that there was no wine there to give him. He ordered some water to be brought, and when it was brought he blessed it with the sign of the cross. Immediately the element was transformed to another use; it lost its own taste and took on another. What had been pure water became excellent wine. What poverty could not provide, holiness furnished. **Once he tasted it, he recovered easily.** That marvelous conversion was the cause of his marvelous healing, and the marvelous healing a proof of the marvelous conversion.

[18]In the province of Rieti a serious plague broke out, destroying
Jb 1:1 cattle so cruelly that almost none remained.[a] A certain *God-fearing man* was instructed in a dream to go quickly to the hermitage of the

a. In this and the following paragraph, Thomas shifts his attention to the more "indirect" influence of Francis upon inanimate creatures. Thus, the water he once used, or the bread he blessed, the cord he wore, or the straw he used in Greccio.

brothers and to collect some water used to bathe the hands or feet of blessed Francis, who was then staying there. On getting it, he was to sprinkle all the cattle with it. *Rising early,* anxious for his own benefit, Mk 16:9 he came to the place, and unknown to the saint, he pilfered some of the wash water with the help of some brothers. With it he sprinkled all the cattle as he had been commanded. From that moment, *by the grace of God,* Rom 5:15 the contagious pestilence ceased and never again returned to that region.

1C 63 [19]In many places the fervent devotion of many people led them to offer bread and other food for Francis to bless. These they kept for a long time, preserved from spoiling by divine gift; when they were eaten bodily illnesses were healed. It has even been shown that such foods had the power to ward off violent thunderstorms and hailstorms.

1C 120; 63 Many claim that through the cord that he wore and patches from his clothes illnesses were put to flight, fevers ceased, and long-sought health returned.

1C 84-86 On the day of the Lord's Nativity when he celebrated the memory of the manger of the Child of Bethlehem, he mystically repeated all the events that once surrounded the child Jesus. God manifested
1C 87 many wonders there. Among them, the hay taken from the manger was for many a health remedy, especially for women with difficulties in childbearing, and for all infected animals. After offering these samples concerning insensible creatures, let us include a few words about the obedience of sensible creatures.

Chapter IV

HIS MASTERY OVER SENSIBLE CREATURES

2C 166 [20]Creatures themselves strove to repay Saint Francis for his love and to respond to his kindness with their gratitude.

1C 58 One time as he was passing through the Spoleto valley, he came upon a place near Bevagna, in which a great multitude of birds of various kinds had assembled. When *The holy one of God* saw them, Lk 4:34 because of the outstanding love of the Creator with which he loved all creatures, he ran swiftly to the place. He greeted them in his usual way, as if they shared in reason. As the birds did not take flight, he went to them, going to and fro among them, touching their heads and bodies with his tunic. Meanwhile his joy and wonder increased as he carefully admonished them to listen to the Word of God: "My brother birds, you should greatly praise your Creator and love Him always. He clothed you with feathers and gave you wings for flying. Among all His creatures He made you free and

Lk 12:4 gave you the purity of the air. You neither *sow nor reap*, He nevertheless governs you without your least care." At these words, the
birds gestured a great deal, in their own way. They stretched their
necks, spread their wings, opened their beaks and looked at him.
They did not leave the place until, having made the sign of the cross,
he blessed them and gave them permission. On returning to the
brothers he began to accuse himself of negligence because he had
not preached to the birds before. From that day on, he carefully exhorted birds and beasts and even insensible creatures to praise and
love the Creator.

[21]Once he went to a village called Alviano to preach. The people 1C 59
gathered and he called for silence. But some swallows nesting there
were shrieking so much that he could not be heard at all. In the
Tb 12:20 hearing of all, he spoke to them: "My sister swallows, now *it is time*
Ez 6:3 for me also to speak, since you have already said enough. Hear the
1 Chr 36:21 word of God and stay quiet until *the word of the Lord is completed*." As
if capable of reason, they immediately fell silent, and did not leave
from that place until the whole sermon was over. All who saw this
Acts 3:10; Mt 9:8 were *filled with amazement* and *gave glory to God.*

[22]In the city of Parma there was a scholar who was so annoyed by
the inconsiderate chattering of a swallow that he could not stay in
the place he needed for meditation. Rather provoked, he began to
say, "This swallow was one of those we read about,[a] who once would
Mt 22:34 not allow Saint Francis to preach until he *imposed silence* on them."
And turning to the swallow he said, "In the name of Saint Francis I
command you to let me catch you." Without hesitation the bird flew
to his hands. The surprised scholar gave it back its original freedom,
and never again heard its chattering.

[23]Heading to the hermitage of Greccio, blessed Francis was
crossing the lake of Rieti in a small boat. A fisherman offered him a
little water-bird so he might rejoice in the Lord over it. The blessed
Father received it gladly, and with open hands, gently invited it to
fly away freely. But the bird did not want to leave: instead it settled
down in his hands as in a nest, and the saint, his eyes lifted up to
Acts 12:11 heaven, remained in prayer. *Returning to himself* as if after a long
stay in another place, he sweetly told the little bird to return to its
original freedom. And so the bird, having received permission with
a blessing, flew away expressing its joy with the movement of its
body.

a. Doubtless in 1C 59 or LJS 38.

1C 61 [24]Another time he was travelling by boat on the same lake. When he arrived at the port, someone offered him a large fish that was still alive. Calling it "brother" in his usual way, he put it back next to the boat. The fish kept playing in the water in front of the saint, which made him very happy, and he praised Christ the Lord. The fish did not leave the spot until it was commanded by the saint.

2C 168 [25]When blessed Francis, fleeing, as was his custom, from the
sight of human company, came to stay in a certain hermitage, a falcon nesting there bound itself to him in a great covenant of friendship. At nighttime with its calling and noise, it anticipated the
hour when the saint would usually rise for the divine praises. The
holy one of God was very grateful for this because the falcon's great Lk 4:34
concern for him shook him out of any lazy sleeping-in. But when
the saint was burdened more than usual by some illness, the falcon would spare him, and would not announce such early vigils.
As if *instructed by God*, it would ring the bell of its voice with a light 1 Tm 3:17
touch about dawn.

It is no wonder that other creatures revered
the greatest lover of the Creator.

2C 170 [26]A nobleman from the area of Siena sent a pheasant to blessed Francis while he was sick. He received it gladly, not with the desire to eat it, but because it was his custom to rejoice in such creatures out of love for their Creator. He said to the pheasant: "Praised be our Creator, Brother Pheasant!" And to the brothers he said: "Let's make a test now to see if Brother Pheasant wants to remain with us, or if he'd rather return to his usual places, which are more fit for him." At the saint's command a brother carried the pheasant away and put him down in a vineyard far away. Immediately the pheasant returned at a brisk pace to the father's cell.

The saint ordered it to be carried out again, and even further away, but with great stubbornness it returned to the door of the cell, and as if forcing its way, it entered under the tunics of the brothers who were in the doorway. And so the saint commanded that it should be lovingly cared for, caressing and stroking it with gentle words.

Mk 1:24 A doctor who was very devoted to the *holy one of God* saw this, and asked the brothers to give it to him, not because he wanted to eat it, but wanting rather to care for it out of reverence for the saint.

What else? The doctor took it home with him, but when separated from the saint it seemed hurt, and while away from his presence it absolutely refused to eat. The doctor was amazed, and at

once carried the pheasant back to the saint, telling him in order all
that happened. As soon as it was placed on the ground, and saw its
father, it threw off its sadness and began to eat with joy.

Mk 1:24 27 A cricket lived in a fig tree by the cell of *the holy one of God* at the 2C 171
Portiuncula, and it would sing frequently with its usual sweet-
ness. Once the blessed father stretched out his hand to it and
gently called it to him: "My Sister Cricket, come to me!" And the
cricket, as if it had reason, immediately climbed onto his hand. He
said to it: "Sing, my sister cricket, and with joyful song praise the
Lord your Creator!" The cricket, obeying without delay, began to
1 Kgs 4:9 chirp, and did not stop singing until *the man of God,* mixing his own
songs with its praise, told it to return to its usual place. There it remained constantly for eight days, as if tied to the spot. Whenever
the saint would come down from the cell he would always touch it
with his hands and command it to sing, and it was always eager to
obey his commands. And the saint said to his companions: "Let us
give permission to our sister cricket to leave, who has up to now
1 Cor 1:29 made us so happy with her praises, so that our *flesh may not boast*
vainly *in any way."* And as soon as it had received permission, the
cricket went away and never appeared there again. On seeing all
this, the brothers were quite amazed.

28 While he was staying in a poor place the holy man used to 2C 169
drink from a clay cup. After his departure, with wonderful skill
bees had constructed the little cells of their honeycomb in it, wonderfully indicating the divine contemplation he drank in at that
place.

29 In Greccio a little hare, live and unharmed, was given to Saint 1C 60
Francis. When it was put down, free to run away where it pleased, at
the saint's call it leapt quickly into his lap. The saint gently took it
and kindly warned it not to let itself be caught again. He then gave it
his blessing and ordered it to return to the woods.

30 Something similar happened with another little rabbit, a wild 1C 60
one, when he was on the island in the Lake of Perugia.

31 Once when the man of God was on a journey from Siena to the
valley of Spoleto he passed a field where a sizeable flock of sheep
were grazing. He greeted them kindly as he usually did, and they all
Lk 21:28 ran to him, *raised* their *heads* and returned his friendly greeting with
loud bleating. His vicar took careful note of what the sheep had done
and, following at a slower pace with the other companions, said to
Jb 1:1 the rest, "Did you see what these sheep did for the holy father? *He is*
truly *great* whom the dumb animals revere as their father, and those
lacking reason recognize as a friend of their Creator."

[32]Larks are birds that are the friends of light and dread the shadows of dusk. But in the evening when Saint Francis passed from this world to Christ, when it was already twilight of nightfall, they gathered above the roof of the house, where they circled about noisily for a long while. Whether they were showing their joy or their sadness with their song, we do not know. They sang with tearful joy and joyful tears, either to mourn the orphaned children, or to indicate the father's approach to eternal glory. The city watchmen who were guarding the place with great care were amazed and called others to admire this.

Chapter V
Divine Mercy was always responsive to Francis's requests

[33] Not only did creatures offer this man their services at his wish, but even the providence of the Creator everywhere consented to do his pleasure. That fatherly mercy anticipated his wishes and ran, as it were, to foresee his needs. His lack and its filling were one, his wish and its fulfillment.

1C 55 In the sixth year of his conversion, **burning with the desire for holy martyrdom, he wished to take a ship to the region of Syria. But after he had boarded a ship to go there, contrary winds started blowing, and he found himself with his fellow travelers on the shores of Slavonia.**

When he realized that he had been cheated of what he desired, after a while he begged some sailors going to Ancona to transport **him with them. But the sailors stubbornly refused to do so since he could not pay them. The holy one of God, trusting God's goodness, secretly boarded the ship with his companion. Immediately, by divine providence, a man arrived**—no one knew him—**who brought the food needed. He called over a person from the ship,** ***a God-fearing man.*** "***Take with you*** **all these things," he said, "and in their** ***time of need*** **faithfully give them to those poor men hiding in your ship."** Jb 1:1; Tb 11:4 Sir 8:12

A great storm arose and they had to spend many days ***laboring at the oars.*** **They had used up all their food. Only the food of the poor Francis remained. Owing to divine grace and power, his food multiplied so much that, although there were still many days of sailing remaining, it fully supplied the needs of them all until they reached the port of Ancona. When the sailors realized that they had escaped the dangers of the sea through God's servant Francis, and** that they received through him what they had denied to him, they Mk 6:48

Sir 50:19 gave thanks *to almighty God,* who is always revealed through his
servants as awesome and loving.

34 Saint Francis became gravely ill while returning from Spain after failing to reach Morocco as he had wished.[a] Suffering from want
and weariness, he was expelled from his lodging by a rude host and
lost his speech for three days. When he had recovered his strength a
bit, while walking along the road he said to Brother Bernard that he
would have eaten a bit of a bird if he had one. Just then a horseman
came riding across the field carrying an exquisite bird. He said to
blessed Francis, "Here, servant of God, take gladly what divine
Tb 7:1 mercy sends you." He *accepted* this gift *with joy* and, seeing how Christ
Tb 13:1; 1 Thes 5:23 cared for him, *he blessed Him for everything.*

Jb 29:16 35 While he lay sick in the bishop's palace at Rieti, the *father of the* 2C 41; 2C 43
poor was dressed in an old tunic. One day he said to one of his companions, whom he had made his guardian: "Brother, if possible, I
wish you would find me material for a tunic. "On hearing this, the
brother started turning over in his mind how he could get the nec-
Jas 4:13 essary cloth so humbly requested. *The next day* at the break of dawn
Lk 22:10 he went to the door, on his way to town for the cloth. *There* he
found *a man* sitting on the doorstep and wishing to speak to him.
This man said to the brother: "For the love of the Lord, brother,
please accept this cloth, enough for six tunics; keep one for yourself and distribute the rest as you please for the good of my soul."
The brother was overjoyed, and returned to Brother Francis, announcing to him the gift sent from heaven. And our father said:
"Accept the tunics, for this man was sent to care for my need in this
way." And he added: "Thanks be to him who seems to be the only
1 Sm 9:5; Ps 40:18 one *concerned for us.*"

36 While the holy man was staying in a hermitage near Rieti, a 2C 44
physician used to visit him every day to treat his eyes. One day the
saint said to his brothers: "Invite the doctor, and give him a good
Lk 14:9 meal." The guardian answered him: "Father, *we're embarrassed* to
say this, but we're ashamed to invite him, because right now we're
Mt 20:32, Jn 9:27 so poor." But the saint answered: *"Do you want me to tell you again?"*
And the doctor, who was nearby, said: "Dear brothers, I would
consider it a treat to share in your poverty." The brothers hurried to
1 Chr 18:20 place the whole contents of their storeroom on the table: *a little
bread,* and not much wine, and, to make the meal more lavish, the
Mal 1:7 kitchen provided a few beans. Meanwhile, *the table of the Lord* took Test 22
Lk 13:25 pity on the table of his servants. *Someone knocked at the door,* and

a. The failed attempt to reach Morocco and illness are mentioned in 1C 56, but the other events appear here for the first time.

they answered immediately. There was a woman offering a basket filled with beautiful bread, loaded with fish and crabcakes, and with honey and grapes heaped on top.

The table of the poor rejoices at this sight,
and, the cheap food is put away,
the delicacies are eaten today.
The doctor heaved a sigh and spoke to them:
"Neither you, brothers,
as you should,
nor we lay people,
realize the holiness of this man."
They would not have been sufficiently filled
if the miracle had not fed them even more than the food.
A father's *eye* Prv 30:17
never *looks down on* his own,
but rather feeds beggars with greater care
the needier they are.

Chapter VI
Lady Jacoba dei Settesoli [a]

AC 8 [37]Jacoba dei Settesoli, equal in fame and holiness in the city of Rome, earned the privilege of special love from the saint. It is not for me to repeat, in praise of her, her noble lineage, family honor, and ample wealth, nor the great perfection of her virtues and long, chaste widowhood.

The saint was bedridden with that illness by which, putting off all his weariness, he was about to *complete* the *race* with a blessed end- 1 Tm 4:7
ing. A few days before his death he decided to send for Lady Jacoba in Rome, telling her that if she wanted to see the one whom she so loved so warmly as an exile, she should come with all haste, because he was about to return to his homeland. A letter was written; a messenger noted for his swiftness was sought and, once found, was outfitted for the journey. Just then there was heard at the door the sound of horses, the commotion of knights, the crowd of an escort. One of the companions, the one who had given instructions to the messenger, went to the door and found there present the one whom he sought because absent. He was struck with wonder and ran very quickly to the saint. Unable to restrain himself for joy, said, "I have

a. Although much of the material of this chapter can be found in AC 8, its last section, i.e., the outcome of Lady Jacoba's pilgrimage, is new.

good news for you, father." Without a pause the saint immediately
Ps 66:20 replied, "*Blessed be God,* who has brought our Brother Lady Jacoba to us! Open the doors and bring her in. The decree about women is not to be observed for Brother Jacoba!"[a]

38 There was great rejoicing among the noble guests, but their spiritual delight was mingled with flowing tears. To make the miracle complete, it was discovered that the holy woman had brought with her everything that the letter just written had requested for the father's burial. God had supplied everything that the spirit of this man wanted: she brought some ash-colored cloth to cover the little body of the one who was departing; many candles; a cloth for his face; a cushion for his head; and a special dish[b] the saint had a longing for.

But I want to narrate the outcome of this pilgrimage, so that I do not leave the noble pilgrim without consolation. A great crowd of people, especially the devout inhabitants of the city, expected the saint's birth through death very shortly. But he seemed to be strengthened by the arrival of the devout Roman lady, and there was a glimmer of hope that he would recover. So the lady gave orders that the rest of her escort should leave: she alone with her children and a few attendants would remain. But the saint said to her, "No, don't! I will depart on Saturday, and on Sunday you and all the others will return." And so it happened. At the predicted time, he who had fought valiantly in the Church militant entered the Church triumphant. I omit here[c] the crowds of people, the shouts of rejoicing, the ringing of bells, the streams of tears. Likewise I leave out the mourning of his sons, the sobbing of those dear to him, the lament of his companions. I want to recount only how this pilgrim, deprived of the solace of her father, was consoled.

39 All wet with tears, she was brought in private and alone, and the body of her friend was placed in her arms. "Here," said his vicar, "hold, even in death, the one you loved when alive!" Her warm tears bathed his body, and with sobs and sighs she kept hugging and kissing him, and pulled back the veil to see him unveiled. What did she
Prv 20:15 see? She gazed on that *precious vessel* that hid a precious treasure adorned with five pearls.[d] She beheld those engravings that the hand of the Almighty alone had produced for the whole world to admire. Then she was refreshed with unusual joy over the death of her friend.

a. See the prohibitions about entry to the Portiuncula in 2C 19, supra, 257-258.

b. According to AC 8, the pastry called *mostacciolo*, made of almonds, sugar or honey, and other ingredients.

c. Cf. 1C 112, 113, 116-118.

d. Namely the stigmata. Cf. 1C 112-13.

Right then she counseled that such an unheard-of miracle should not be disguised or hidden any further. Rather, she wisely advised it should be displayed for all to see with their own eyes. All ran eagerly to see this sight.[a] They were able to verify for themselves that God *had not done thus for any other nation* and stood in awe. Ps 147:20

Here I will put down my pen rather than stammer over something I cannot explain. Giovanni Frigia Pennate,[b] who was then a boy, and afterwards a Roman proconsul and count of the Sacred Palace, freely swears and declares, against all doubts, that at that time he was with his mother, and that he *saw with* his own *eyes* and *touched* it *with* his *hands*. The lady pilgrim may now return to her homeland,[c] comforted by this privilege of grace. Let us now turn to events after the saint's death. Jb 13:1; Gen 27:12; 1 Jn 1:1

Chapter VII
THE DEAD RAISED THROUGH THE MERITS OF BLESSED FRANCIS[d]

40 I turn now to those who were raised from the dead through the merits of the confessor of Christ. I ask the attention of listeners and readers alike. For the sake of brevity I will omit many of the circumstances, and will keep silent about the account of the amazed witnesses, recounting only the extraordinary events themselves.

There was a woman, noble by birth and nobler in virtue, in Monte Marano near Benevento. She clung to Saint Francis with special devotion and offered him her reverent service. She took sick and her end seemed near: she was going *the way of all flesh*. She died at sundown, but burial was delayed to the following day to allow her many dear ones to gather. The clergy came at night with their psalters to sing the wake and vigils. There was a gathering of *many of both sexes* for prayer. Suddenly, in the sight of all, the woman sat up in bed and Jos 23:14 1 Chr 31:18

a. Cf. 1C 113.

b. His is another form of the family surname (also rendered *Frangipani*). Cf. AC 8, note. Giovanni was the eldest son of Lady Jacoba; in 1226 he would have been a young man, rather than a boy.

c. That is, to Rome, or possibly to heaven.

d. Although there are no miracles of resurrection described in Thomas's earlier works, the accounts given here reflect the tendencies of the late thirteenth and fourteenth centuries. André Vauchez explains: "This should probably be seen as a consequence of the development of the canonization procedure rather than of a change of attitude on the part of the faithful toward the saints. Aware that it was difficult to get a favorable decision out of the papacy and that the Curia was very demanding with regard to miracles, the promoters of a cause were tempted to raise the threshold of the miraculous to prove the sanctity of their candidates." Vauchez, *Sainthood in the Later Middle Ages*, translated by Jean Birrell (Cambridge, New York, Melbourne: Cambridge University Press, 1997), 467. A thorough study of the understanding of miraculous phenomena in the Middle Ages can be found in Benedicta Ward, *Miracles and the Medieval Mind: Theory, Record and Events, 1000-1215* (Philadelphia: University of Pennsylvania Press, 1982).

called to one of them, a priest who was her godfather, "I want to confess, Father, hear my sin! I have indeed died, and was destined for a harsh prison because I had never confessed the sin I will reveal to you. But Saint Francis prayed for me as I was always devoted to him. I have now been permitted to return to my body so that after confess-
Gn 4:13 ing my sin I might *merit forgiveness.* So now, as all of you watch, after I reveal that to you I will hurry off to my promised rest." She then shakily confessed to the shaken priest, received absolution, com-
Acts 7:60 posed herself peacefully on the bed and happily *fell asleep in the Lord.*

Who can adequately praise Christ's mercy? Who can sufficiently sing the praises of the power of confession and of the saint's merits?

41Confession is a marvelous gift of God which ought to be wholeheartedly embraced by all; and in Christ's presence this saint always enjoyed special merit. These things can be amply demonstrated by recounting events of his life on earth, and even more clearly proven by what his Christ did in his regard after death.

When the blessed father Francis once went to Celano to preach,[a] a knight invited him insistently, with humble devotion, to dine with him. After much refusing and declining, he finally gave in to the insistent pressure. He arrived at dinnertime and a splendid table was prepared. The devout host was overjoyed, and his whole family was delighted at the arrival of their poor guests. Blessed Francis stood
Dn 4:31 and *raised his eyes to heaven,* then called his host aside privately. "Look," he said, "brother host, I was overcome by your requests, and
Lk 7:44 *I have entered your home* to eat. Do quickly what I tell you, for you shall
1 Jn 7:44 not eat here but elsewhere! *Confess* your *sins* with devotion and contrition; leave nothing within you unconfessed. The Lord will repay
1 Tm 6:3 you today for receiving His poor with such devotion." The man *agreed to* the saint's *words* without delay. He called the companion of Saint Francis, who was a priest, and told all his sins in a good confession.
Is 38:1 *He put his house in order* and without any doubts waited for the saint's word to be fulfilled. Then they went to the table and began to eat. After marking his breast with the sign of the cross, the knight reached with his hand—it was shaking—for the bread. But before he could
Jn 19:30 draw back his hand, he *bowed his head* and breathed forth his *spirit.*

O, how the confession of sins should be cherished!
See how the dead are revived in order to confess.
Jn 10:28 And so that the living should not *perish forever*
they are set free by benefit of confession.

a. This is the author's birthplace, but he unfortunately did not reveal the name of the soldier. Celano is again mentioned as a place for miracles in 3C 51.

[42]A barely seven-year-old son of a notary of the city of Rome wanted in his childish way to follow his mother who was going to the church of San Marco[a] to hear a preacher. He was turned back by his mother and her refusal upset him. By some diabolical impulse—I do not know why—he threw himself from the window of the building and, shaking with a last tremor, he came to know the passing of death, the common lot of all. The mother had not gone far, and the sound of someone falling made her suspect the fall of her treasure. She quickly returned home and saw her son lifeless. She turned avenging hands on herself; her neighbors rushed out at her screams; and doctors were called to the dead boy. But could they *raise the dead?* Acts 26:8 The time for prognoses and prescriptions was past. He was in the hands of God: that much the doctors could determine, but could not help. Since all warmth and life were gone, all feeling, movement and strength, the doctors determined he was dead.

Brother Rao, of the Order of Lesser Brothers and a well-known preacher in Rome, was on his way to preach there. He approached the boy and, full of faith, spoke to the father. "Do you believe that Francis, the saint of God, is able to raise your son *from the dead* because of the love he always had for the *Son of God, the Lord Jesus Christ?*" Acts 17:31; Acts 8:37; 11:17 The father replied, "I firmly believe and confess it. I will be his lasting servant, and I will regularly visit his holy place." That brother knelt with his companion in prayer and urged all those present to pray. With that the boy began to yawn a little, lift his arms and sit up. His mother ran and embraced her son; the father was beside himself for joy. All the people, filled with wonder, marveled and, shouting, praised Christ and His saint. In the sight of all the boy immediately began walking, restored to full life.

[43]The brothers of Nocera asked a man named Peter for a certain cart that they needed for a short time. He foolishly replied, "I would rather skin the two of you, and Saint Francis too, rather than loan you a cart." The man immediately regretted his blasphemous words, slapped his mouth, and asked forgiveness. He feared revenge, and it came soon after.

At night he *saw in a dream* his home full of men and women dancing with loud jubilation. Gn 28:12 His son, named Gafaro, soon took sick and shortly afterwards gave up his spirit. The dances he had seen were turned into a funeral's mourning, and the jubilation to lament. He recalled the blasphemy he had uttered against Saint Francis. His punishment showed how serious was his fault. He rolled about on

a. Probably the very ancient church of San Marco in Via Lata. It was incorporated in 1477 into the Palazzo Veneto, on what is today the Piazza Venezia in the heart of Rome.

the ground and called out to Saint Francis again and again, saying,
1 Sm 24:17 "*It is I who have sinned*; you were right to punish me. Give me back,
dear saint, the one you took from this wicked blasphemer, for now I
have repented. I surrender myself to you; I promise you lasting service, and will always offer you all the first fruits."

Amazing! At these words the boy arose, called for a halt to the wailing, and spoke about his experience of death. "When I had died," he said, "blessed Francis came and led me along a very dark and long road. Then he put me in a garden so beautiful and delightful that the whole world can't be compared to it. Then he led me back along the same road and said to me, 'Return to your mother and father; I do not want to keep you here any longer.' And, as he wished, I have returned."

[44]In the city of Capua a lad was playing carelessly with his friends LCh 15
on the bank of the river Volturno. From the bank of the river he fell
Ps 46:5 into the deep. The *force of the river* quickly swallowed him up and buried him, dead, beneath the sand.

The children who had been playing near the river with him shouted, and many men and women ran quickly to the spot. When they learned what happened they cried out tearfully, "Saint Francis, return the boy to his father and grandfather: they are sweating in your service!" Indeed the boy's father and grandfather were working as hard as they could on building a church in honor of blessed Francis. All the people were humbly and devoutly invoking the merits of blessed Francis.

Some distance away a swimmer heard their cries and approached
them. He learned that a good hour had passed since the boy fell into
Acts 22:16 the river. He *invoked the name* of Christ and the merits of blessed Francis, then taking off his clothes flung himself naked into the river. Since he did not know where the boy had fallen in, he began to search back and forth along the banks and on the bottom. Finally by the will of God he found the place where mud had covered over the boy's cadaver like a tomb. He dug and dragged him out, and was saddened to find him dead. Though the crowd saw that the youth was dead, they nevertheless wept and cried out, "Saint Francis, give the father back his child!" The same phrase was also said by the Jews who had come, moved by natural piety: "Saint Francis, give the father back his child!" Blessed Francis, moved by the people's prayers and devotion (as is clear from what happened) quickly raised the dead boy. They all marveled and rejoiced. When the boy got up, he begged to be taken to the church of blessed Francis, swearing he had been revived thanks to him.

LCh 15 [45]In the city of Sessa, in the neighborhood called "Le Colonne," the devil, destroyer of souls and killer of bodies, destroyed and leveled a house. He tried to destroy many children who were playing their children's games near that house, but trapped only one youth who was instantly killed by the falling house. Men and women heard the crash of the house and came running from all around. Raising beams here and there, they succeeded in restoring the dead son to his poor mother. She tore at her face and hair, sobbed bitterly, shed rivers of tears, and cried out as best she could, "Saint Francis, Saint Francis, give me back my son!" She was not alone: all the men and women there wept bitterly and cried, "Saint Francis, give this poor mother back her son!" After an hour of this pain the mother caught her breath, recovered her senses, and made this vow: "O Saint Francis, give back to me in my misery my beloved son! I will wreathe your altar with silver thread; I will cover it with a new altar cloth; and I will encircle your whole church with candles!" Since it was night, they placed the cadaver on a bed, waiting to bury him the following day. But about midnight the young man began to yawn; warmth returned to his limbs; and before daybreak he was fully revived and burst into shouts of praise. When all the people and the clergy saw him healthy and unharmed, they too rendered thanks to blessed Francis.

[46]In the village of Pomarico, in the mountains of Apulia, a mother and father had an only daughter, tender of age and tenderly loved. And since they did not expect any future offspring, she was the object of all their love, the motive for all their care. When she became deathly ill, the girl's mother and father considered themselves dead. Day and night they kept anxious watch over the child's care, but one morning they found her dead. Perhaps they had been negligent, overcome by sleep or the strain of their vigil. The mother, deprived of her daughter and with no hope of other offspring, seemed to die herself.

Friends and neighbors gathered for a very sad funeral and prepared to bury the lifeless body. The unhappy mother lay grief-stricken, and the depth of her sorrow kept her from noticing what was going on. In the meantime, Saint Francis with one companion visited the desolate woman and spoke these comforting words, "*Do not weep,* I will rekindle the light of your *quenched lamp*!" Lk 7:13; 2 Sm 21:17
The woman jumped up, told everyone what Saint Francis had told her, and would not allow the body of the deceased to be carried away. Then the mother turned to her daughter, invoked the saint's name, and lifted her up safe and sound. We leave it to others to describe the

wonder that filled the hearts of the bystanders and the rare joy of the girl's parents.

47In Sicily, a young man named Gerlandino, from Ragusa, went LCh 15
out with his parents to the vineyard at harvest-time. He crawled into a wine vat beneath the press to fill some skins. The wooden supports shifted, and the huge stones used to press the grape skins[a] instantly struck his skull a deadly blow. The father hurried over to his son, but he could not help him; he left him under the weight where it had fallen. Other vineyard workers rushed to the scene when they heard the loud wail and cry. Pitying the pitiful father, they pulled his son from the ruin. They took the lifeless body aside and wrapped it, concerned only about his burial. But the father defiantly fell at the feet of Jesus Himself. He implored Him to give him back his only son through the merits of Saint Francis, whose feast day was coming soon. He groaned his prayers, he promised works of piety, and promised to visit the holy man's bones very soon. A little while later the boy's mother arrived and fell madly upon her dead son; her wailing moved the others also to wail. Then suddenly the boy stood up, told them to stop crying, and rejoiced that he had been brought back to life through the help of Saint Francis. All the people who had gathered raised their cries of praise on high, to the One who through His saint had freed the boy from the cords of death.

48He raised another dead person in Germany: the Lord Pope Greg- LCh 15
ory recounted this event in his apostolic letter on the occasion of the translation of blessed Francis.[b] Through it he informed and gladdened all the brothers who had gathered for the translation and the chapter. I did not write the account of this miracle because I did not know of it, believing that papal testimony is a proof that surpasses any other assertion.

Let us now go on to others whom he snatched from the jaws of death.

Chapter VIII
Those Francis Brought Back to Life from the Jaws of Death

49A certain Roman nobleman named Rodolfo had a tower of considerable height, and, as is usual, had a guard in the tower. One night

a. That is, the *vinaccia* [pulp].

b. The "translation" is the official moving of a saint's body: here, the moving of Francis's body to the Basilica dedicated to him. The letter is the bull *Mirificans*, promulgated by Gregory IX on May 16, 1230, cf. BFr I, 64-65.

the guard was sleeping soundly at the very top of the tower. He lay upon a pile of wood on the top edge of the wall. Then the pulley either came loose or broke at its base and, in a flash, he fell along with the planks onto the roof of the palace, and from there to the ground. The loud crash awoke the whole family and, suspecting hostile action, the knight got up and went out armed. He shook his drawn sword over the prone man, intending to strike the sleeping man, since he did not recognize him as the guard. But the wife of the knight feared that this might be her brother—her husband hated him to death, so she stopped him from wounding the man, throwing herself upon the prostrate man in loyal defense. What an amazing sleeping potion! The sleeping man never woke, either at his double fall nor at the loud noise.

Finally he was shaken awake with a gentle hand, and as if deprived of pleasant rest he said to his lord, "Why are you disturbing my sleep now? I have never rested so easily; I was sleeping sweetly in the arms of blessed Francis."

When he learned from the others about his fall, and he saw himself on the ground, not up above where he was lying, he was amazed that he had not felt what had happened. He then promised publicly to do penance, and his master gave him permission to set out on a pilgrimage. The lady sent a beautiful priestly vestment to the brothers staying in her hometown outside the City, out of reverence and honor for the saint. The Scriptures promise a great reward for hospitality, and examples confirm it. For the lord in question had that night given hospitality to two Lesser Brothers, out of reverence for Saint Francis. They had also been among those who ran out when that servant fell.

[50]In the town of Pofi, located in Campagna, a priest named Tommaso went with many others to repair a mill belonging to his church. Below the mill was a deep gorge, and the raised channel flowed rapidly. The priest carelessly walked along the edge of the channel, and accidentally fell into it. In an instant he was thrust by force against the wooden blades that turned the mill. There he remained, pinned against the wood, unable to move at all. Because he was lying face down the flow of water pitiably muffled his voice and blocked his sight. But his heart, if not his tongue, was free to call plaintively on Saint Francis.

He remained there a long time, and his companions, rushing back to him, nearly despaired of his life. "Let's turn the mill by force in the opposite direction," said the miller, "so it will release the corpse." With a struggle they turned the mill in reverse, and they saw the trembling body thrown into the water.

The priest, still half-alive, was being rolled around in the pool, when suddenly there appeared a Lesser Brother in a white tunic bound with a cord.[a] With great gentleness he drew the unfortunate man by the arm out of the water, and said, "I am Francis, the one you called." The man was stunned to be freed in this way and began to run here and there saying, "Brother, Brother!" and asking the bystanders, "Where is he? Which way did he go?" But they were terri-
Nm 14:5; Lk 2:20 fied: they *fell prostrate to the ground and gave glory to God* and to his saint.

[51]Some children from the town of Celano in the Capitanata region went out together to cut grass. In those fields there was an old well: its opening was covered with plant growth; and it held water with a depth of four paces. While the children ran about on their own, one accidentally fell into the well. But while he suffered earthly disaster, he invoked heavenly aid. "Saint Francis," he said as he fell, "help
1 Kgs 18:45 me!" The others *turned around this way and that,* and when they no-
Gn 37:30 ticed that the other *boy was missing* they went in search of him, shouting and crying. Finally they came to the opening of the well. Seeing the grass just springing back from being stepped on, they realized that the boy had fallen in. They ran crying back to the village, gathered a crowd of people, and returned to the spot, though everyone thought it hopeless. A man was lowered by a rope into the well and he found the boy floating on the surface of the water totally unharmed. When the boy was lifted out of the well, the boy said to all who had gathered, "When I suddenly fell, I called for Saint Francis's protection, and he instantly arrived while I was still falling. He reached out his hand and gently held me and did not leave until, along with you, he pulled me from the well."

[52]The treatment of a young girl of Ancona, worn out by a deadly illness, had been terminated, and for her passing funeral arrangements had already begun. Blessed Francis came to her when her last
Mt 9:22 breath was near and said to her, "*Courage, daughter,* for through my
Mt 8:4 favor you are completely healed. *Tell no one* until evening about your
Mt 20:8 health, which I am restoring." *When evening came* she suddenly raised
Mk 14:70 herself up in bed, stunning *the bystanders,* who fled. They thought that a demon had invaded the body of the dying girl: when her own soul had left, a perverse spirit had replaced it. The girl's mother dared to come closer, and breathing oaths against what she thought was a devil, she tried to get the girl to lie down on the bed. But the daughter said, "Mother, please don't think it's the devil. At the third hour

a. The apparition of Francis in this garb appears again in 3C 52 . He is further described as "glorious," (3C 105, 106) is accompanied with one or more brothers, or on a most beautiful throne (3C 152), or together with the Blessed Virgin and the Apostles (3C 158). All of these images suggest new dimensions to the cult of the saint and accentuate his place as a "miracle worker."

blessed Francis healed me of all the sickness, and ordered me to tell no one until this hour." The name of Francis was cause for surprise and joy for them, just as the devil was cause for flight. They encouraged the girl right away to eat some chicken, but shaking her head she refused to eat because it was the Great Lent. "*Do not be afraid,*" she said. "Don't you see Saint Francis dressed in white? He is commanding me not to eat meat because it is Lent, and to offer the funeral tunic to a certain woman in prison. Look, you can see him leaving!" Mt 17:7

[53]In Nettuno, there were three women in a house. One of them was devoted to the brothers and most devoted to Saint Francis. A great *wind* shook *the house,* demolished it, and *crushed,* killed, and buried two of them. Blessed Francis quickly arrived at a silent request, and did not allow the one devoted to him to suffer any harm. For the wall to which she clung remained intact to her height; a beam fell on it from above in such a way that it bore all the weight of the falling debris. People heard the crash of the collapse and came running. For the two deceased there were tears; for the surviving friend of the brothers all gave thanks to Saint Francis. Jb 1:19

[54]Corneto[a] is a powerful and not an unimportant town in the diocese of Viterbo. There a bell of no small size was to be cast at the brothers' place, and many of the brothers' friends had gathered to contribute their help to the project. When the casting was completed, with great rejoicing a grand banquet began. Then an eight-year-old boy named Bartolomeo, whose father and uncle had worked devotedly on the casting, carried in a gift for those at the banquet. All of a sudden a *great wind came up and shook the house*; with great force it blew down the large, heavy door of the house onto the boy. It was feared that its weight pressing upon him had crushed him to death. He was so completely buried under its weight that nothing of him could be seen from the outside. The work of the foundry turned into confounding,[b] and the lament of mourners replaced the *festivity of the banquet.* Jb 1:19 Jude 12

Everyone rushed from the table; the uncle dashed with some others to the door, calling on Saint Francis. The father, however, could not move, his limbs frozen *from grief.* Vowing out loud, he offered his son to Saint Francis. The deadly weight was lifted off the boy, and there he was! The one they thought was dead appeared cheerful, like someone waking from sleep, with no sign of injury. After the Is 65:14

a. More recently named "Tarquinia."

b. Another of Thomas's play on words: *fusioni confusio* [the foundry turned into] . . . *succedit* [confounding].

Lk 1:14; Gn 15:1 confusion, there was an infusion of joy,[a] and *great gladness* followed the interrupted banquet. The boy himself reported to me[b] that no feeling of life remained in him as he lay beneath that weight. When he reached the age of fourteen he became a Lesser Brother and later became a learned man and an eloquent preacher in the Order.

55 A little boy of the same town swallowed a silver buckle that his father had placed in his hand. It so blocked all the passages of his throat that he was completely unable to breathe. The father wept bit-
Mk 9:20 terly and *rolled on the ground* in a frenzy because he considered himself his son's murderer. His mother tore at her hair and her whole body, wailing at the sad news. All their friends shared their grief, that a healthy youth was snatched by such sudden death.

The father invoked the merits of Saint Francis and offered a vow to the saint to save his son. Then suddenly the boy spat the buckle from his mouth and joined the others in blessing the name of Saint Francis.

Jgs 15:18 56 A man named Niccolò from the town of Ceprano one day *fell into the hands* of cruel enemies. With beastly rage they heaped blow upon blow on him, and did not stop their cruelty until they thought him
Lk 10:30 dead or soon to die. They left him *half dead* and went away spattered with blood. When the first blows fell on him, Niccolò started calling out in a loud voice, "Help me, Saint Francis! Save me, Saint Francis!" Many heard his voice from far away but could not help him. When he had been carried home drenched with his own blood, he claimed that he was not about to die and did not feel any pain, because Saint Francis had come to his aid and begged the Lord that he be allowed *to*
Mk 6:12 *do penance.* So, cleansed of blood and contrary to any human hope, he was rescued.

57 Some men of Lentini[c] cut a huge stone from a mountain. It was to be set over the altar of the church of blessed Francis which was soon to be consecrated. A good forty men strained to load the stone on a cart, but after several attempts the stone fell on one man and covered him like a tomb. In their mental confusion they did not know what to do: most of the men left in despair. The ten who remained plaintively invoked Saint Francis not to allow this man who was in his service to die so hopelessly. The man lay buried, half-dead,
Wis 15:11 but *the living spirit* in him sighed for the help of Saint Francis. With renewed courage, those men then so easily removed the stone that no

a. Another play on words: *successit confusioni refusio* [after the confusion, there was an infusion].

b. No doubt Thomas himself.

c. In the Sicilian province of Siracusa where, at the time of Thomas, the brothers had built a convent. See AF IV, 533.

one doubted that the hand of Francis was involved. The man stood up unharmed; he who was almost *dead revived* completely. He recovered his eyesight as well, which earlier had been dimmed: further proof to all of the power of Francis in desperate cases. Lk 15:24

[58]A similar incident worth remembering happened at San Severino in the Marches. A huge stone from Constantinople was being transported to Assisi for the construction of a fountain in honor of Saint Francis. With the efforts of many it was being dragged along at a rapid pace when a man fell beneath it. He appeared to be not just dead, but totally crushed.

At once Saint Francis arrived, as it seemed to him and as it turned out to be true, lifting the stone and thrusting it aside without any injury to him. So it happened that what looked horrible turned into something astonishing to all.

[59]Bartolomeo, a citizen of Gaeta,[a] was hard at work on the construction of the church of Blessed Francis. He was trying to position one of the building's beams, but the beam, poorly positioned, fell and crushed his neck severely. He was bleeding profusely, and with trembling breath he asked one of the brothers for Viaticum. The brother was not immediately able to find it, and thinking he would die at any moment, he quoted to him the words of blessed Augustine, "Believe, and you have eaten."[b]

That night blessed Francis appeared to him with eleven brothers; he carried a little lamb between his breasts. He approached the bed, *called him by name,* and said, "Do not fear, Bartolomeo, the enemy *will not prevail against you.* He wanted to keep you from my service, but you will arise in good health! Here is the lamb you asked for: you have received it because of your good desire. That brother gave you good advice!" Then drawing his hand across the wounds, he told him to return to the work he had begun. Gn 4:17; Jer 1:19

The man got up very early the next morning, and the workers who had left him half-dead were shocked and amazed when he appeared, healthy and unharmed. Because there seemed to be no hope for his recovery, *they thought* they were seeing a *ghost,* neither man nor flesh, but a spirit. (Since there has been mention of the construction of buildings in honor of this saint, I thought it only right to include here another extraordinary miracle.) Mk 6:49

[60]Two Lesser Brothers once undertook to build a church in honor of the holy father Francis in the town of Peschici in the diocese of

a. On the Tyrrhenian Sea, between Rome and Naples. By this time the friars had also buit a friary in Gaeta, see AF IV, 529.

b. From his commentary on the Gospel of John: *In Joh. Evang.* 25: 12, in *PL* 35, 1602.

Siponto.[a] They had a very fatiguing task, and lacked the means necessary to complete the construction. One night when they had *risen* Jgs 16:14
from sleep to offer lauds, they began to hear the sound of falling and
crashing stones. Each encouraged the other to go look, and when *they* Mt 10:14
went outside they saw a great crowd of people competing to gather
stones. They all came and went in silence, and all were dressed in
white clothing. The great pile of stones gathered was proof that this
was not an illusion: these did not run out until the work was finished. The suspicion that this was accomplished by men *living in the* Gal 2:20
flesh was removed when a diligent search turned up no one who
would have planned such a thing.

[61]The son of a nobleman of Castel San Gimigniano suffered from
a severe illness; all hope was abandoned and he seemed near the end.
A stream of blood trickled from his eyes, like the flow of blood from
the severed vein of an arm. Other signs of death's approach appeared
in the rest of his body, and he seemed already gone. His friends and
family, as is usual, gathered for mourning and arranged the funeral.
All that remained was the burial. Meanwhile, his father, surrounded
by the crowd of mourners, remembered a vision he had previously
heard of. He rushed off to the church of Saint Francis, which had
been built in that same town.[b] With a cord hanging around his neck
he humbly *threw himself on the ground.* He *made a vow* and *prayed repeat-* Jdt 10:23
edly. With sighs and groans, he gained Saint Francis as his patron 1 Sm 1:11; Jb 4
with Christ. As the father returned quickly to his son and found him
restored to health, his *mourning turned into joy.* Lam 5:15

[62]A certain young man of the village of Piazza in Sicily had already
had his soul commended in the last rites of the church. He was
brought back from the threshold of death through the holy father's
intercession after his uncle made a vow to him.

[63]In the same neighborhood a young man called Alessandro was
tugging a rope with some companions on a high cliff. The rope broke,
and he fell from the cliff; he was carried away, presumed dead. His
father, with tears and sobs vowed to the saint of Christ, and got him
back safe and sound.

[64]A woman of the same town suffered from typhus and was nearing her end. The commendation of her soul had already been performed, but those around her invoked the most holy father and she
was instantly *restored to health.* Mt 12:13

a. Near Manfredonia in Apulia, Peschici is on the northern side of Monte Gargano. Concerning the church of Saint Francis, see AF IV, 531. This incident is recounted in *Dialogus de gesti sanctorum fratrum minorum,* ed. Frederick Delorme (Ad Claras Aquas, Quaracchi: Collegium S. Bonaventurae, 1923), 253.

b. Concerning the church there, see AF IV, 518.

[65]In Rete of the diocese of Cosenza two boys of that town got into a brawl at school, and one wounded the other in the abdomen so severely that the stomach was torn and undigested food came out through the wound. He was unable to retain any nourishment and he could not digest food, nor hold it in. It all came out undigested through the wound. Doctors could offer him no help. He and his parents finally, at the suggestion of one of the brothers, first forgave the one who had inflicted the wound, then made a vow to blessed Francis. If he would snatch from the jaws of death the mortally wounded boy, who was given no hope by the doctors, they would send him to his church and ring it with candles. On making their vow, the boy was so completely and wonderfully healed that doctors from Salerno[a] called it no less a miracle than if he had been raised from the dead.

[66]At Monte near Trapani[b] two men arrived together on business
when one of them suddenly became ill *to the point of death*. Doctors Ps 68:21
were called and came quickly to help him, but they could do nothing
to cure him. His healthy companion *made a vow* to Saint Francis. If Ps 132:2
the sick man should receive healing through the saint's merits, he would observe his feast every year with a solemn Mass. After making his vow, he returned to the house where he had left his companion speechless and motionless, thinking him already doomed to destruction. There he found him restored to his former health.

1C 139 [67]**A boy from the city of Todi lay on his bed for eight days as if** Mt 9:2
dead. His mouth was tightly shut, and there was no light in his eyes. The skin of his face, hands and feet turned black as a pot. No one held out hope for his recovery, but as a result of his mother's vow he recovered with amazing speed. Though he was just an infant and *could not speak* he said, lisping, that he was saved by blessed Jer 1:6
Francis.

1C 140 [68]**A young man who had been up on a very high place fell from**
there and lost the use of all his limbs as well as his ability to speak.
For *three days he neither ate nor drank* nor felt anything, so that they Mt 11:18; Acts 9:9
thought he was dead. His mother, without even seeking the aid of a doctor, asked blessed Francis to cure him. After she had made a vow the young man was restored to her, alive and sound, and she began to praise the all-powerful Creator.

1C 140 [69]**A boy from Arezzo by the name of Gualtiero was suffering from prolonged fever and so tormented by multiple abscesses that**

a. Doctors from the school at Salerno, near Naples, were considered outstanding at that time.

b. Now Monte San Giuliano. Probably the ancient Erycinum, in Sicily.

all the doctors gave up hope for him. But his parents made a vow to blessed Francis, and he recovered the health they so longed for.

Chapter IX
Cases of dropsy and paralysis

70 In the city of Fano a man suffering from dropsy obtained a 1C 141
complete cure of his illness through the merits of blessed Francis.

71 A woman in the city of Gubbio lay paralyzed in bed; after she 1C 142
invoked the name of blessed Francis three times for her healing she was freed from her infirmity and cured.

72 A girl from Arpino in the diocese of Sora was beset by a paralytic illness. She was deprived of all human functions, and her limbs were so uncontrolled and twisted by nerves that she appeared more harassed by a demon than animated by a human spirit. She was so tormented by this infirmity that she seemed to have regressed to the cradle. Finally, her mother, by divine inspiration, took her to the church of blessed Francis in Vicalvi.[a] She carried her in a cradle, and after many tearful prayers the girl was freed from every danger of illness and was restored to her former age and health.

73 A young man of the same town was bound by a paralysis that held his mouth shut and distorted his eyes. His mother took him to the church mentioned above. She prayed fervently for him, and whereas he had been completely unable to move, he recovered his original health before they reached their home.

74 In Poggibonsi a girl named Ubertina suffered from falling sickness,[b] as severe as it was incurable. Her parents despaired of any human remedy, and strenuously demanded the help of blessed Francis. By common agreement they vowed to the saint that they would fast on the vigil of the most blessed father's feast and provide food for the poor on the day of his solemnity every year if he would free their daughter from such an unusual affliction. After making their vow, the girl totally recovered and never again suffered any harm from that hurtful illness.

75 Pietro Mancanella, a citizen of Gaeta,[c] lost the use of an arm and hand to paralysis, and his mouth was twisted back to his ear. When he submitted to the advice of doctors, he lost both his sight and his hearing. Finally he humbly dedicated himself to blessed Francis, and

a. On this church, see AF IV, 529.

b. That is, epilepsy.

c. See 3C 59, supra, 429 a.

was thus completely freed from his affliction through the merits of that most blessed man.

76 A citizen of Todi suffered from such an acute arthritic condition that he could not lie down at all. It seemed he would become entirely helpless; and as he received no relief from doctors, in the presence of a priest he called on Saint Francis. Having made his vow, he regained his former health. 1C 141

77 A man by the name of Bontadoso suffered such pain in his feet that he was absolutely unable to move about. He was losing both his sleep and his appetite. A woman encouraged him to vow himself humbly to Saint Francis but, beside himself with pain, he replied that he did not believe him to be a saint. The woman nevertheless stubbornly persisted, and finally he vowed himself in this way: "I vow myself to Saint Francis, and I believe he is a saint if he frees me from this illness in three days." He immediately got up, to his own surprise, with the health that had left him now fully restored. 1C 141

1C 141 78 A woman was confined to bed for many years by illness, unable to turn or move at all. She was healed by blessed Francis and resumed her usual duties.

1C 141 79 A young man in the city of Narni was in the grip of a very serious illness for ten years; his whole body was so swollen no medicine could treat it. His mother vowed him to Saint Francis, and he immediately received from him the relief of health.

1C 141 80 In the same city there was a woman who for eight years had a withered hand with which she could do no work. Blessed Francis appeared to her *in a vision,* and stretching her hand made it able to work as well as the other. Dn 4:10

Chapter X
THOSE SAVED FROM SHIPWRECK

81 Some sailors were placed in grave danger at sea when a fierce storm came up while they were ten miles out from the port of Barletta. Anxious for their lives, they let down the anchors. But the *stormy wind* swelled the sea more violently, breaking the ropes and releasing the anchors. They were tossed about the sea on an unsteady and uncertain course. Ps 11:6

Finally at God's pleasure the sea was calmed, and they prepared with all their strength to recover their anchors, whose lines were floating on the surface. So they put their full effort into retrieving the

anchors. They invoked the help of all the saints and were worn down
by their exertion, but could not recover even one after a whole day.

One of the sailors was named Perfetto, though he was perfectly
Mt 22:21 good for nothing. He despised everything *that belongs to God.* With
malice he scoffed and said to his companions, "You have invoked the
aid of all the saints, and as you see not one of them has helped. Let's
call that Francis. He's a new saint; let him dive into the sea with his
capuche and get our anchors back. We can give an ounce of gold to
his church, which is just being built in Ortona, if we decide he
helped." The others fearfully agreed with the scoffer, but they rebuked him by making a vow. At that very moment the anchors were
suddenly floating on the water with no support, as if the nature of
iron had been changed into the lightness of wood.

82 A pilgrim, feeble in body, and not quite sound in mind because
of a bout of madness he had suffered, was traveling with his wife by
ship from regions overseas.[a] He was not completely free of his illness
and was troubled by a burning thirst. As the water had run out, he
began to shout loudly, "Go confidently, pour me a cup! Blessed Francis has filled my flask with water!" What a wonder! The flask they
Gn 1:2 had left *void and empty* they now found filled with water.

Some days later a storm came up and the boat was being *swamped*
Mt 8:24 *by the waves* and shaken by strong winds so that they feared they
would be shipwrecked. That same sick man suddenly began to shout
around the ship, "Get up, everyone, come to meet blessed Francis. He
Jn 9:38 is here to save us!" And with a loud voice and tears he *bowed down to*
worship. As soon as he had seen the saint the sick man recovered his
Mt 8:26 full health; and, on *the sea, calm* ensued.

83 Brother Giacomo of Rieti was a passenger on a small boat making a river crossing. At the shore, his companions disembarked first,
and he prepared to get out last. But the boat's small raft accidentally
overturned, and while the pilot could swim, the brother was plunged
Mt 18:6 *into the depths.* The brothers on shore with tender cries called on
blessed Francis and tearfully insisted that he save his son. The
drowning brother too, in the belly of a great whirlpool, could not call
with his mouth, but called out from his heart as well as he could. See!
With the help of his father's presence he walked across the depths as
if on dry land. He caught hold of the overturned little boat and
reached the shore with it. More wonderful still, his clothes were not
wet: not a drop of water clung to his tunic.

84 Two men and two women with one child were travelling by boat
across the Lake of Rieti. The little boat accidentally shifted to one side

a. The Holy Land, also called *Outremer*, "beyond the sea," i.e., the Mediterranean.

and was quickly filled with water; they seemed to be heading for death. All shouting, convinced they were going to die, one of the women cried out with very great trust, "Saint Francis, you favored me while still *living in the flesh* with the kindness of your friendship. Phil 1:22
Now from heaven give your help to us who are going to perish!" The saint was there as soon as he was called and carefully escorted the boat full of water to shore. Someone had brought a sword aboard the boat, and it miraculously floated among the waves following the boat.

85Some sailors from Ancona were caught in a violent storm and knew they were in danger of sinking. In desperation for their lives they humbly invoked Saint Francis. A great light appeared on the sea, and with the light a heaven-sent calm. To fulfill their vow they offered a splendid curtain and countless expressions of thanks to their rescuer.

86A brother named Bonaventure was crossing a lake with two men when a side of the boat split, and, with the force of the water rushing in, they sank. "From the deep lake"[a] they called on Saint Francis, and shortly the water-filled boat reached the shore with them in it.

Similarly a brother from Ascoli was saved by the merits of Saint Francis when he fell into a river.

87A man from the parish of Saints Cosmas and Damian in Pisa confirmed by his testimony that he was at sea with many others when the ship was driven by a great storm toward collision with a mountain. The sailors saw this and built a sort of raft out of ropes and planks as a refuge for themselves and others on board. But the man from Pisa lost his balance on the raft, and a strong wave *threw him* Mt 21:21
into the sea. He did not know how to swim and could not be helped by the others, so he headed desperately toward the depths of the sea. He was unable to speak, but in his heart he devoutly commended himself to blessed Francis. He was quickly raised from the depths as if by some hand and carried back to the raft, and was saved from shipwreck with the others. The ship, though, hit the mountain and was completely demolished.

a. *De profundo lacu* [from the deep lake]: from the Offertory of the Mass for the dead.

Chapter XI
THE BOUND AND IMPRISONED

[88]In Romania[a] it happened that a Greek servant of a certain lord was falsely accused of theft. His lord ordered him to be shut in a narrow prison and heavily chained; after final sentencing he was to have a foot cut off. The wife of the lord was concerned to free the innocent man, but her husband remained firm and rejected her request. The lady turned humbly to Saint Francis and, by a vow, commended the innocent man to his compassion. Quickly the helper of the afflicted was present. He took the imprisoned man by the hand, loosened his chains, broke open the jail, and led the innocent man out. "I am the one to whom your mistress devoutly commended you," he said. The man shook with fear as he wandered at the edge of a precipice, looking for a way to descend from the very high cliff. Suddenly he found himself on level ground without knowing how.

He returned to his lady and told her his miraculous story. She immediately made a wax image because of her vow, and hung it before
Prv 16:29 the saint's picture for all to see. The *unjust man* was upset, and when he struck his wife with his hand he fell gravely ill. He was not able to heal until he had confessed his fault and rendered sincere praise to the Saint of God, Francis.

[89]In Massa San Pietro a poor fellow owed a certain knight a sum of money. Since he had no means of paying the debt, the knight had him confined as a debtor. He humbly asked for mercy and, interjecting prayers, requested a deferral for love of Saint Francis. He thought the knight respected this famous saint. The knight haughtily scorned his prayers; he stupidly mocked the love of the saint as something stupid. He obstinately replied, "I will lock you up in such
Gn 41:10 a place and *put you in* such a *prison* that neither Francis nor anyone else will be able to help you." And he attempted to do what he said. He found a dark prison and threw the chained man into it.

A short time later Saint Francis arrived and broke open the prison; he shattered the man's leg-irons and led him to his own home unharmed. Afterward the man brought his chains to the church of blessed Francis in Assisi. In them he had experienced the mercy of the father; now they would become a demonstration of his marvelous power. Thus the strength of Francis plundered the proud knight
Mt 6:13; 2 Tm 4:18 and *delivered from evil* the captive who had made himself his subject.

a. That is, the Latin Empire of the East, "Roman" territory. There are two other miracles performed in Romania, 3C 118, 194, suggesting that devotion to Saint Francis had begun to spread to this part of Europe.

[90]Five officials of a great prince were arrested under suspicion. They were not only sturdily chained together but also confined to a very narrow prison. When they heard that blessed Francis was shining through miracles everywhere, they devoutly entrusted themselves to him. One night Saint Francis appeared to one of them and promised them the favor of freedom. The one who saw the vision was overjoyed and told his fellow captives about the promised favor. Though still in the dark, they both wept and rejoiced. They *made their vows* and *prayed repeatedly.* One of them immediately began to scratch the thick wall of the tower with a bone; its mortar gave way so easily that it seemed a mixture of ashes. When the wall was breached he tried to pass through, and with their chains broken, one after the other they reached freedom. There was still a steep drop that blocked their escape. But Francis, their bold leader, gave them the boldness to climb down. So they went off unharmed and got away safely; they became great heralds of the mighty works of this saint.

1 Sm 1:11

Jb 40:27

[91]Alberto of Arezzo was being held tightly in chains for debts unjustly charged to him. He humbly placed his innocence before Saint Francis. He greatly loved the Order of the brothers and venerated Francis with special affection among all the saints. His creditor had made the blasphemous statement that neither God nor Francis would be *able to deliver him from his hands.*

Dn 3:17

On the vigil of the feast of Saint Francis the bound man had eaten nothing, but out of love for the saint had given his meal to someone in need. As night fell, Saint Francis appeared to him during his vigil. At the saint's entry, the *chains fell from his hands* and his feet. The doors *opened by themselves* and the boards on the roof fell down; the man got away free and returned to his home. From then on he kept his vow to fast on the vigil of Saint Francis and to make an annual offering of a candle, to which each year he added an extra ounce.

Acts 12:7

Acts 12:10

[92]A young man from the region of Città di Castello[a] was accused of arson. As he lay shackled in a harsh prison, he humbly entrusted his case to Saint Francis. One night, as he was restrained by both chains and guards, *he heard a voice saying to him, "Get up quickly* and go where you like, for your chains are loosed!" He lost no time in obeying the command, and once outside the jail he took the road to Assisi to offer to his liberator a *sacrifice of praise.*

Acts 9:4;12:7

Ps 50:14

[93]When the Lord Pope Gregory IX[b] was occupying the see of blessed Peter there arose an inevitable persecution of heretics. A

a. See FA:ED I 242 a.

b. Pope from 1227 to 1241. See 1C 1 Prologue, FA:ED I 180 b.

certain Pietro from Alife[a] was among those accused of heresy, and he was arrested in Rome. The Lord Pope Gregory handed him over to the bishop of Tivoli for safekeeping. Fearing the threat of losing episcopal office, the bishop took him and bound him in leg irons. But because Pietro's simplicity indicated innocence, he was granted less careful watch.

Some nobles of the city, it is said, had a long-standing hatred of the bishop and were eager to see him incur the punishment decreed by the Pope. So they secretly advised Pietro to escape. He agreed with them; he escaped one night and soon fled far away.

When the bishop heard this, he took it seriously: he feared the expected punishment and he was no less pained to see his enemies' wish fulfilled. So he took every precaution and sent out searchers in every direction. When the poor fellow was found, considering him ungrateful, he put the man in the strictest custody for the future. He had a dark jail cell prepared, surrounded with thick walls. Inside he had the man confined between thick planks and fastened with iron
Ps 149:8 nails. He had him bound in *fetters of iron* weighing many pounds, and
Ez 4:16 provided him food *by weight* and drink *by measure.*

Because all other hope of freedom was now cut off, God, who does
Jb 4:7 not allow the *innocent to perish,* soon came with His mercy to help him. That poor man, with much weeping and praying, began to call on blessed Francis to take pity on him. He had heard that the vigil of his solemnity was near. The man had great faith in Saint Francis because, as he said, he had heard that heretics railed furiously against him.[b] On the night before his feast, around dusk, blessed Francis mercifully came down into the prison, called him by name, and or-
1 Chr 10:4 dered him to stand up. The man asked *in great fear* who was calling him, and heard that it was blessed Francis. He jumped up, called the
Gn 45:3 guard and said, "I am *very afraid,* someone is here ordering me to get up, and he says he is Saint Francis." "Lie down, wretch," the guard replied, "sleep in peace! You're out of your mind because you didn't eat well today." But when, toward midday, the saint of God still ordered him to get up, he saw the chains on his feet break and fall suddenly to the ground. Looking about the cell, he saw the timbers opened with their nails sprung outward: there was a clear path for his escape.

Once free, he was so astounded that he did not know enough to flee. Instead, he let out a cry and frightened all the guards. When the bishop was told that the man had been freed from his chains, he

a. In the province of Caserta.

b. For examples of Francis and heretics, see 1C 62; 2C 78-79.

thought that he had fled. Since he had not yet heard of the miracle, he was struck with fear and, since he was ill, fell from where he had been sitting. But once he understood what had happened, he devoutly went to the prison, and openly *acknowledging the power of God,* he there *worshiped the Lord.* Mk 5:30 Gn 24:26

Later the chains were sent to the Lord Pope and the cardinals: on *seeing what had happened,* with much wonder *they blessed God.* Lk 23:47; Dn 13:60

[94]Guidalotto of San Gimignano was falsely accused of poisoning a man, and further that he had intended to kill the man's son and the whole family with the same poison. He was arrested by the local podestà, who had him heavily chained and thrown into a ruined tower. The podestà thought about what punishment he could inflict on him, to obtain a confession of the crime through torture. He finally ordered him suspended from a revolving rack. He weighed him down with weights of iron until he fainted. Several times he ordered him let down and raised up again with the hope that one torment after another would more quickly bring him to confess his crime. But the man's face seemed joyful in an innocent way, showing no sign of sorrow in his pain. Then a rather large fire was lit beneath the man, but not a hair of his head was harmed while his head hung toward the ground. Finally, burning oil was poured over him, but he laughed through it all, because he was innocent and from the beginning had entrusted himself to blessed Francis. The night before he was to be punished, he had been visited by Saint Francis. He was surrounded by an immense bright light, and he remained in its light until morning, *filled with joy* and great confidence. *Blessed be God,* who does not allow the *innocent to perish,* and even in a *flood of many waters* is present to those who hope in Him. Ps 126:20; Ps 66:20 Jb 4:7; Ps 32:6

Chapter XII

THOSE FREED FROM THE DANGERS OF CHILDBIRTH AND THOSE WHO FAIL TO KEEP HIS FEAST

[95]A certain countess of Slavonia,[a] illustrious in nobility and a friend of goodness, had an ardent devotion to Saint Francis and a sincere affection for the brothers. She suffered severe pains at the time of childbirth; she was so overcome with pain that it appeared that the expected birth of the child would mean the demise of the mother. She seemed incapable of bringing the child into life unless she departed from life; and, by this effort, not to give birth but to

a. Used for Dalmatia and, more generally, Croatia; cf. 1C 55, FA:ED I 229 b.

Rv 19:1 perish. But the fame of Francis, his *glory and might,* sustained her heart. Her faith aroused, her devotion kindled, she turned to the effective helper, the trusted friend, the comforter of those devoted to Phlm 12 him, the refuge of the afflicted. "Saint Francis," she said, *"all my heart* cries out to your mercy, and I vow in spirit what I cannot say aloud." O the speed of mercy! The end of her speaking was the end of her suffering, and the end of her labor was the beginning of giving birth. Just as soon as the pains ceased, she safely gave birth to a child. Nor did she forget her vow or run away from her promise. She had a beautiful church built and, once it was built, donated it to the brothers in honor of the saint.

[96]A certain Beatrice from the region of Rome was close to giving birth. For four days she had been carrying a dead fetus in her womb. She was much distressed and beset by deadly pain. The dead fetus was causing the mother's death, and still the obvious threat to the mother did not bring forth the abortive offspring. The help of doctors Ps 127:1 proved fruitless; every human remedy *labored in vain.* Thus did the Jer 20:17 ancient curse fall heavily upon the unfortunate woman. Her *womb* Jb 3:21, 22 *became a grave,* and she certainly *awaited the grave* soon. Finally, by means of messengers, she entrusted herself with great devotion to the Lesser Brothers. She humbly requested in great faith some relic of Saint Francis. By divine consent a piece of a cord was found, one that the saint had once worn. As soon as the cord was placed on the suffering woman, all her pain was relieved with ease. The dead fetus, cause of death, was released and the woman was restored to her former health.

[97]Giuliana, wife of a nobleman of Calvi, passed a number of years in mourning over the death of her children: she constantly mourned those unhappy events. All the children she had borne were consigned to the earth; the axe cut down each new shoot. So when she Mt 1:23 was four months *with child,* she was moved more by sorrow than joy, because she feared that deceptive joy over birth would be changed later to mourning over death.

Mt 1:20 Then one night as she slept, a woman *appeared* to her *in a dream.* The woman carried a beautiful infant in her hands and joyfully offered him to her saying, "Take this child, my lady; Saint Francis sends him to you!" But she was reluctant to accept something that would soon perish, so she refused. "Why should I want this child," she said, "when I know it will soon die like all the others?" "Take it," Ez 18:9, 19 was the reply, "because the one Saint Francis sends you *shall surely live!"* They spoke this way three times before the lady took the child in her hands. She immediately awoke from her sleep and told her husband about the vision. Both of them were thrilled with joy and increased their vows for having a child. The *time for delivery arrived* and the woman *gave birth* to a son. He thrived to a lively age and made up for the grieving over those who had died. Lk 1:57

[98]A woman was near to childbirth in Viterbo, but perhaps nearer to death. She had severe abdominal pains and suffered the misfortunes that befall women. Doctors were consulted and the midwives summoned. They had no success, and only despair remained. The afflicted woman called upon blessed Francis, and promised, among other things, that she would celebrate his feast as long as she lived. She was immediately healed and joyfully finished giving birth.

But when she got what she wanted, she forgot what she promised. In fact, she did not so much forget her vow as despise it, since she went out to wash clothes on the feast of Saint Francis. Instantly an extraordinary *pain fell upon her* and, warned by the pain, she returned home. Jb 20:22

But the pain passed, and because she was one of those who changes her mind ten times an hour, when she saw her neighbors at work, she foolishly set to work more strenuously than before. Suddenly she was unable to draw back the right arm she had extended to work; it was rigid and withered. When she tried to raise it with her other arm, that too withered with a similar curse. The pitiful woman now had to be fed by her son, and was unable to do any other tasks by herself. Her husband was puzzled and searched for the cause of what had happened; he concluded that her false faith toward Saint Francis was the cause of her torment. Both the man and his wife were *struck with fear* and without delay reaffirmed the vow. So the saint *had* Acts 10:4; Bar 3:2
mercy because *he was* always *merciful;* he restored the limbs to the one who repented, just as he had disabled them when she despised her vow. The woman's punishment made her sin known; she became an example to all who fail to keep their vows, and put fear into those who would presume to violate the feasts of the saints.

[99]The wife of a judge in the city of Tivoli burned *with great fury,* Est 1:12
since she had borne six daughters. She decided to stay away from her husband. Why should she continue to plant when she was so thoroughly displeased with the fruit? The woman bristled at always producing females, was worn out by the desire of the male sex, and even questioned God's will. But one should not bear reluctantly the judgment that the laws of *almighty God* impose on humans. In any case, Rv 16:14
she angrily remained separated from her husband for a year. A little later, *led to repentance,* she was told to be *reconciled to her husband.* The Mt 27:3 Mt 27:3; 1Cor 7:11
confessor persuaded her to request a son from blessed Francis, and to name it Francis because she would have the child through his merits. Not long after, the woman conceived and the one she had implored

allowed her to bear twin boys, even though he had been asked for only one. One was named Francesco and the other Biagio.

[100]A noble woman of the city of Le Mans[a] had a lowly servant girl
Lv 23:7 whom she forced to do *servile work* on the feast of Saint Francis. But the girl was of nobler mind and refused, out of reverence for the feast. Human fear, however, prevailed over fear of God, and the girl
Prv 31:19 did as she was told, even if unwillingly. *She put her hand* to the distaff, *her fingers plied the spindle.* But immediately her hands stiffened with pain and her fingers burned unbearably. The punishment revealed the fault as the sharpness of the pain made silence impossible. The girl hurried to the sons of Saint Francis,[b] revealed her offense, showed her punishment, and asked forgiveness. So the brothers marched in procession to the church and begged Saint Francis's mercy for the girl's health. As the sons begged their father she was healed, though a trace of the burning remained on her hands.

[101]A similar thing happened in Campania.[c] A certain woman was frequently rebuked by her neighbors for not abstaining from work on the saint's feast. On the vigil of blessed Francis she obstinately continued to work into the evening without ceasing. But after her work she was suddenly struck with pain and shock; a weakness in her hands kept her from even ordinary tasks. She soon arose and declared that the feast she had despised should be revered. In the hands of a priest she solemnly vowed that she would forever observe the saint's feast with reverence. After her vow she was taken to a church built in honor of Saint Francis. There, after many tears, she recovered her health.

[102]In the village of Olite[d] a neighbor warned a certain woman to observe the feast of Saint Francis, and not to do any work. But the woman impudently replied, "If there were one saint for every trade, the number of saints would be more than the number of days." At her foolish words she immediately fell ill by divine vengeance. For many days she lost her mind and memory until, through the prayers of many to blessed Francis, her madness subsided.

[103]In the town of Piglio in the province of Campania[e] a woman busily went about her work on the feast of Saint Francis. A noblewoman sternly rebuked her for this, since everyone should observe

a. In France, north of Tours.

b. On the brothers' presence there see AF IV, 307, 543.

c. Either the Champagne region of France or the Campagna (Terra di Lavoro) in Italy. Cf. AF IV, 307, n. 3.

d. This site has not been identified with certainty: perhaps Olite in the custody of Navarre or Vallodolid in the province of Castille (AF IV, 536, 537).

e. Roman Campagna (AF IV, 249, 345, 517).

the feast out of divine reverence. She answered, "I only have a little of my work left to finish: *Let the Lord see* whether I'm doing wrong!" 1 Chr 24:22 She soon saw the harsh judgment, in her daughter, who was sitting nearby. The girl's mouth twisted back to her ears and her eyes bulged, pitifully distorted. Women gathered quickly from all around and cursed the mother's ungodliness on account of the innocent daughter. The mother was overcome with sorrow and fell to the ground, promising to observe the feast annually, and further to feed the poor on that day out of reverence for the saint. Her daughter's troubles subsided without delay, once the mother had repented of her offense.

104 Matteo of Tolentino had a daughter named Francesca. He was quite upset when the brothers moved to another place, and he took to calling his daughter Mattea, depriving her of Francis's name. Soon she lost her health as well as her name. Because his action involved contempt for the father and hatred for his sons, his daughter fell gravely ill to the point of being in danger of death. Thereupon the man suffered bitter sorrow over the passing of his daughter. When his wife rebuked him for his hatred of the servants of God and his contempt of the saint's name, he quickly returned devoutly to the first name and reinstated to the daughter the title of which she had been deprived. Then, with fatherly tears, he took his daughter to the place of the brothers where she recovered her health as well as her name.

105 A woman of Pisa, unaware that she was pregnant, put in a hard day of work on a church of Saint Francis being built in that city. Saint Francis, led by two brothers carrying candles, *appeared* to her *in the* 2 Chr 1:7
night and said, "Daughter, *behold: you have conceived and are bearing a son.* Lk 1:31
You will rejoice over him if you give him my name." When her *time for* Lk 1:57
delivery arrived, she gave birth to a son. "He will be named Enrico," said her mother-in-law, "after one of our relatives." *"No,"* said his Lk 1:60
mother, *"he is to be called* Francesco." The mother-in-law scoffed at this noble name as if it were for peasants. A few days later when the baby was to be baptized, he became weak almost to the point of death. The whole household was saddened, their *joy turned into sor-* Jas 4:9
row. The mother's distress kept her awake that night. Saint Francis came with the two brothers as before and, as if disturbed, said to her, "Did I not tell you that you would not rejoice over this son unless you gave him my name?" She began to shout and swear that she would give him no other name. In the end the boy, graced with the name Francesco, was both baptized and healed. The boy was given the grace of not crying; his infant years passed happily.

106 A woman from the region of Arezzo in Tuscany bore the pains
of labor through seven days, and was turning black. In her death
throes, when everyone had despaired of her, she made a vow to Saint
Francis and called on his aid. When she had made her vow, she
quickly fell asleep, and Saint Francis appeared to her. He called her
by her name, "Adelasia," and asked her whether she recognized his
face. She replied, "Yes, father, I do recognize you." The saint went on,
"Can you recite the *Salve Regina?*" "Yes, father," she answered.
"Start," said the saint, "and before you finish you will safely give
Mt 27:46 birth." Then the saint *cried out in a loud voice* and disappeared. At that
cry, the woman woke up and anxiously began *"Salve regina . . ."*
When she reached the words *"illos misericordes oculos,"* before she had
finished, she suddenly gave birth to a beautiful child in joy and good
health.

107 Although she knew that it was the solemn feast day of blessed
Lv 23:7 Francis, a woman in Sicily nevertheless failed to abstain from *servile
work*. She took a baker's mixing bowl, put in some flour and, with
bare arms, she began to knead it. Right away the dough appeared to
be flecked with blood. When the stunned woman saw this, she began to call her neighbors. The more the spectators gathered, the more
the trickles of blood increased in the dough. The woman repented of
Ps 132:2 what she had done, and *swore a vow* never again to do servile work on
his feast. Once her promise was confirmed, the flow of blood left the
dough.

108 While the saint was still living in the flesh, **a woman in the** 1C 63
**Arezzo area was pregnant and at the time of childbirth she was in
labor for several days** with extraordinary distress. **Blessed Francis
was on his way to a hermitage, and was on horseback because of
Acts 28:6 the weakness of his body.** ***They were*** all ***waiting*** **for him to pass by
the place where the woman was suffering.** But the saint was al-
ready staying in the hermitage, and a brother was returning through
that village **with the horse on which the saint had ridden.** When the
Tb 10:3 inhabitants of the place realized that **he was not Saint Francis,** *they
Lk 22:23 were greatly saddened* **and they began to inquire among themselves if
they could find some item that the servant of God had touched
with his own hand. Discovering the bridle reins, which he had held
in his hands, they quickly pulled the bridle from the horse's
mouth.** And when the woman felt **the reins placed upon her, she
gave birth in great joy and good health.**

Chapter XIII
RUPTURES REPAIRED

[109]Brother Giacomo of Iseo, a man of considerable fame and renown in our Order,[a] *testifies of himself* and gives thanks to God's saint for the grace of his health to the glory of our father. When he was a tender youth in his parental home his body suffered a serious rupture. With great suffering from the injury, the body's inner parts poured out: things that nature had placed inside were now in a place that was not theirs. His father and family, who were aware of the cause, were concerned and repeatedly sought medical help, but to no avail. Inspired by the divine Spirit the youth began to reflect *about his salvation* and to seek with a sincere mind the God *who heals the brokenhearted and binds up their wounds.* He thus devoutly entered the Order of Saint Francis without revealing to anyone the infirmity that troubled him. After *he stayed* in the Order a short time, the brothers became aware of his infirmity; and they intended to make the painful decision to send him back to his parents.[b] But the boy's determination was strong enough to overcome this unpleasant decision. The brothers took the youth into their care until, *strengthened by grace,* his sound way of life proved him a good man. He undertook the care of souls among them and was praiseworthy for his religious discipline.

Jn 1:15 · 1 Pt 1:9 · Ps 147:3 · Mt 25:5 · Lk 2:40

It happened that when the body of blessed Francis was transferred to its place,[c] this same brother was among the many who joyfully celebrated the translation. He approached the tomb in which the body of the most holy father rested and prayed at length for his long-standing infirmity. His inner parts suddenly and wonderfully returned to their proper place and he felt himself healed. He laid aside his truss and was from then on totally free of his pain.

[110]A man from Pisa suffered bitter pain and terrible shame because he eliminated all the *hidden things of his bowels* by way of his private parts, and he contemplated diabolical action against himself: in the depth of his despair he resolved to end his life by hanging himself. But before that, the sting of his not yet deadened conscience led him to impress on his memory the name of Saint Francis and, however weakly, to invoke him with his mouth. He soon experienced a

Prv 20:27

a. He served as Minister of the Roman province of the Order: cf. Salimbene, *Chronicle*, 67-8.

b. This reflects the legislation concerning those entering the Order which became more refined as the fraternity grew. For information on these developments, see Saint Bonaventure, *Writings Concerning The Franciscan Order*, introduction and translation by Dominic Monti (St. Bonaventure, NY: Franciscan Institute Publications, 1994): 76-77.

c. That is, on May 25, 1230; see 3C 48, supra, 424 b.

speedy conversion from his damnable intention and a full cure of his great misfortune.

[111]The son of a man from the town of Cisterna in Marittima[a] was horribly burdened with a rupture of the genitals and no device could hold back his intestines. For the truss, which usually supports such ruptures, caused many new ones. His parents were tormented, and the horrible spectacle provided their friends and neighbors with ample grounds for tears. They tried every remedy and cure with no success whatever. Finally his father and mother vowed their son to Saint Francis.

On the feast day of Saint Francis they took him to the church at
Velletri built in his honor. They laid him out before the saint's image
and, making their vows along with a crowd of many others, offered
many tears for him. When the gospel was being sung, at the words
Mt 11:25 *"what you have hidden from the learned you have revealed to the merest children,* his truss suddenly broke, and the useless remedies fell away. A
scar quickly formed and the full health desired was restored. A great
Lk 2:13 cry went up from those *praising the Lord* and venerating his saint.

[112]A sacristan named Niccolò one morning was entering his
Ez 26:16 church in Ceccano, a town in Campania, when he took *a sudden fall.*
The sad result was that all his intestines poured out at his private parts. The clergy and other neighbors rushed to him, lifted him and carried him to his bed. He lay motionless for eight days, unable even to rise for his natural functions. Doctors were called and they applied their remedies, but his pain only increased: his illness was not healed, but heightened. His monstrous organs remained in their unnatural position with such pain that the poor fellow was unable to eat for eight days. The man was now desperate and destined for death. Then he turned to the help of blessed Francis.

Acts 10:1 He had a daughter who was *religious and God-fearing*; he asked her
Jn 18:29; Ru 3:10 to beg the aid of Saint Francis for him. *The blessed daughter went out* a
short distance and with many tears gave herself to prayer. She
prayed to the father for her own father. O the power of prayer! Her father suddenly called out to her while she was still praying and joy-
Wis 5:2 fully informed her of his *unexpected healing.* Everything returned to its
proper place, and the man felt in better condition now than before his fall. He vowed then that blessed Francis would always be his patron, and that he would annually observe his feast day.

[113]A man from the village of Spello **suffered for two years from** 1C 144
such a severe rupture that it seemed that all his bowels **protruded through the side of his body. He could not keep them in place for**

a. Today, Cisterna di Latina, in Lazio

any length of time, nor was the attention of doctors able to put them back into their proper place. When he **gave up hope in the help of doctors, he turned to divine help.** When he devoutly **called upon the merits of blessed Francis,** he experienced with wondrous speed that what was broken was made whole, what was deformed was restored.

[114]A young man named Giovanni from the diocese of Sora was afflicted by a severe intestinal hernia and could not be helped by any doctor's medicine. One day his wife happened to go to a church of blessed Francis. While she was praying, one of the brothers, a simple soul, said to her, "Go tell your husband to vow himself to blessed Francis, and to make the sign of the cross on his rupture!" She went home and told her husband. The man vowed himself to blessed Francis, signed the place of his injury, and his intestines immediately returned to their proper place. The man was amazed at the *suddenness of his unexpected healing,* and to test whether the healing he so suddenly enjoyed was real, he tried a number of exercises. Wis 5:2

Once when this same man had a high fever, blessed Francis *appeared in a dream, called* him *by name and said, "Do not fear,* Giovanni, for you will be *healed of your sickness."* The trustworthiness of this miracle was confirmed when blessed Francis appeared to a certain religious man named Roberto. When the man asked who he was, he replied, "I am Francis who came to heal a friend of mine." Mt 1:20 Is 40:26; Lk 5:10; 13:12

[115]In Sicily he wondrously freed a man named Pietro, who was suffering from a rupture of the genitals, after the man had promised to visit the saint's tomb.

Chapter XIV
THE BLIND, THE DEAF AND THE MUTE

[116]A brother named Roberto of the residence[a] of the brothers in Naples had been blind for many years. Excess flesh grew in his eyes and impeded the movement and use of his eyelids. Many brothers from other places had gathered there on their way to different parts of the world. The blessed father Francis, that mirror and exemplar of holy obedience, in order to encourage them on their journey with a

a. This first appearance of the Latin word *conventus* [convent] indicates a change in vocabulary. Previously the words *locus* [place] and *eremitorum* [hermitage] were used to refer to the places where brothers stayed. While Thomas uses *conventus* elsewhere (1C 123, 124), he does so in his reference to the sacred gathering of the pope and cardinals. Niermeyer indicates that in the twelfth and thirteenth centuries *conventus* referred to a general assembly, synod, or church council. Its interpretation as a gathering place—*con-venire*—appears only sporadically to an assembly of monks. Cf. Jan Frederik Niermeyer, *Mediae Latinitatis Lexicon Minus* (Leiden, New York, Köln, E.J. Brill, 1976), 270. This the only instance of the word's use in these hagiographical documents.

new miracle, healed the aforesaid brother in their presence in this way.

One night Brother Roberto lay deathly ill and his soul had already been commended, when suddenly the blessed father appeared to him along with three brothers, perfect in holiness, Saint Anthony,[a] Brother Agostino,[b] and Brother Giacomo of Assisi.[c] Just as these three had followed him perfectly in their lives, so they readily accompanied him after death. Saint Francis took a knife and cut away the excess flesh, restored his sight and snatched him from the jaws of death, saying, "Roberto, my son, the favor I have done for you is a sign to the brothers on their way to distant countries that I go before
Ps 40:3 them and *guide their steps.* May they go forth joyfully and fulfill the charge of obedience with enthusiasm! Let the sons of obedience rejoice, who have left their own land, forgetting their earthly homeland: they have an active leader and caring forerunner!"

117 In Zancato, a village near Anagni,[d] a knight named Gerardo had entirely lost his sight. It happened that two Lesser Brothers arriving from abroad sought out his home for hospitality. The whole household received them with honor and treated them with every kindness. The brothers gave no notice to the blindness of their host. After their stay, the two brothers journeyed to the brothers' place six miles away and stayed there eight days. One night blessed Francis
Mt 2:13 *appeared* to one of the brothers *in a dream* with the command: "*Get up,* hurry with your companion to the home of your host. He honored me through you and on account of me was so graciously kind! Show your thanks for your delightful reception and repay honor to the honorable! For the man is sightless and blind, and that is what he de-
Jb 3:5 serves for the sins he has not yet confessed. The *shadows of* eternal *death* await him, and unending torture is his lot. He is bound to this by the misdeeds he has not let go."

When the father had gone, the son got up stunned and hurried with his companion to carry out the command. Both of the brothers returned to their host together, and the one related what he had seen
Est 15:9 *all in order.* The man was quite astonished as he confirmed the truth of all he heard. He broke out in tears, freely made his confession and promised amendment. As soon as the inner man was thus renewed, he recovered the outer light of his eyesight. The greatness of this

a. Anthony of Padua; cf. 3C 1, supra 400 b; 3C 3.

b. See 2C 218.

c. According to *The Book of Praises* by Bernard of Besse 1 (hereafter BPr), he is the brother mentioned in 1C 110 and 2C 217a.

d. On the presence of the brothers in Anagni, see AF IV, 517.

miracle spread everywhere and encouraged all who heard of it to extend the gift of hospitality.

118A blind woman of Thebes in Romania,[a] spent the vigil of Saint Francis fasting on bread and water, and was led by her husband at early dawn of the feast to the church of the brothers.[b] During the celebration of the Mass, at the elevation of the Body of Christ, she opened her eyes, saw clearly, and devoutly adored. In the very act of adoration she broke into a loud cry, "Thanks be to God and to his saint," she cried, "I see the Body of Christ!" All those present broke *into cries of gladness*. After the Mass the woman *returned to her home* using her own sight. Ps 47:2; Lk 1:56

Christ was a light to Francis while he lived,
and just as then he attributed all of his wonders to Christ,
so now he wishes that all glory be given to His Body.

119A fourteen-year-old boy from the village of Pofi in Campania[c] suffered a sudden attack and completely lost use of his left eye. The acuteness of the blow thrust the eye out of its socket so that it hung by a weak, inch-long strip of flesh; after eight days it had nearly dried up. Cutting it off seemed the only choice when medical remedies proved hopeless. Then the boy's father turned his *whole mind* to the help of blessed Francis, and the tireless helper of the afflicted did not fail the prayers of his petitioner. He marvelously returned the dried eye to its socket and restored its former vigor with the rays of light so longed for. Mk 12:30

120In the same province, at Castro dei Volsci, an immense beam fell from a high place and crushed the skull of a priest, blinding his left eye. Flat on the ground, he began to cry out mournfully to Saint Francis, "Help me, holy father, so that I can go to your feast as I promised your brothers!" It was the vigil of the saint's feast. He quickly got up fully recovered and broke into shouts of praise and joy. And all the bystanders who were lamenting his accident were amazed and jubilant. He went to the feast and there told everyone how he had experienced the power and mercy of the saint. This was a lesson to all that they should devoutly venerate the saint whom they know will so readily assist them.

---

a. See 3C 88, supra, 436 a.

b. Concerning the church, see AF IV, 533.

c. The same village appears in 50, above. This incident is briefly mentioned in *The Legend for Use in the Choir* 15 (hereafter LCh).

121 While blessed Francis was still alive, **a woman** of Narni, **af- 1C 67**
flicted with blindness, miraculously **received the sight** she had lost
when the man of God **made the sign of the cross over her eyes.**

122 A man named Pietro Romano from Monte Gargano[a] was working in his vineyard and while he was cutting wood with a blade
struck his own eye and sliced it in half, so that part of the pupil was
hanging out. Since the danger was desperate and he despaired that
human help could save him, he promised that he would eat nothing
on the feast of Saint Francis if the saint would help him. Right then
the saint of God replaced the man's eye to its proper place, closed the
wound and restored his earlier sight.

Jn 9:1 123 The son of a nobleman *was born blind* and obtained the sight he
longed for through the merits of blessed Francis. He was called Illuminato,[b] named for the event. When he was old enough he joined
the Order of Saint Francis and finally fulfilled a holy beginning with
an even holier ending.

124 Bevagna is a noble town in the valley of Spoleto. In it there 2C 114
lived a holy woman with an even holier daughter, a virgin, and a
niece very devoted to Christ. Saint Francis several times enjoyed
their hospitality, for the woman had a son in the Order, a man of outstanding virtue. One of them, however, the niece, was deprived of
bodily sight, though her inner sight, which sees God, was sharp and
clear. Saint Francis was once asked to take pity on the girl's infirmity
Jn 9:1 and to consider all their hard work. He *smeared the eyes* of the blind girl
with his *saliva* three times in the name of the Trinity, and thus restored to her the sight she desired.

125 **In Città della Pieve there was** a young man, **a beggar who was** 1C 147-8
Jn 9:1 **deaf and mute** *from birth*. **His tongue was so short and stubby that,**
to those who many times examined it, it seemed to be completely
cut out. A man named Marco received him as a guest for God's sake.
When the youth saw the good will shown him, he stayed on with
him.

One evening that man was dining with his wife, while the boy
stood by. He said to his wife, "I would consider it the greatest mira-
cle if blessed Francis were to give back to this boy his hearing and
Ps 132:2 **speech. I vow to God," he added, "that if Saint Francis in his good-**
ness will do this, for the love of him I will support this boy as long
as he lives." **A marvelous promise indeed! Suddenly the boy's**
Gn 8:15 **tongue grew, and he spoke, saying, "Long live Saint Francis! I see**
him standing above me, and he has granted me speech and

a. Site of the important pilgrimage sanctuary of Saint Michael, in Apulia.

b. That is, "enlightened."

hearing! **What will I tell the people?"** His foster father replied, **"You shall praise God, and you shall save many people."** The people of that region, who had known the youth previously, were filled with the greatest wonder. Ps 69:31; 36:70

[126]A woman in the region of Apulia had long ago lost the ability to speak and to breathe freely. One night while she slept the Virgin Mary appeared to her and said, "If you want to be cured, go to the church of Saint Francis in Venosa; there you will receive the cure you desire." The woman got up, and since she could neither breathe nor speak, she indicated by signs to her relatives that she wanted to travel to Venosa. Her relatives agreed and accompanied her to the place. When the woman entered the church of Saint Francis, she poured out her heartfelt request, and immediately she vomited a mass of flesh and was marvelously healed in the sight of all.

[127]A woman in the diocese of Arezzo had been mute for seven years. She continually sent her wish to the ears of God, that He would see fit to loose her tongue. Amazing! While she slept two brothers dressed in red appeared and gently instructed her to vow herself to Saint Francis. She willingly took their advice and vowed in her heart, since she could not speak. She was soon roused, and on waking her speech returned.

[128]People were amazed when a judge named Alessandro, who had belittled the miracles of blessed Francis, was deprived of speech for more than six years. Great repentance overcame him, when he recognized that a man *is tormented by the very things through which he sins,* Wis 11:16
and he was sorry that he had ridiculed the saint's miracles. So the saint's anger did not last, and he restored his favor by repairing the man's speech, since he was repentant and humbly invoked him. From then on the judge dedicated his blasphemous tongue to praise of the blessed father. His suffering greatly increased his devotion.

[129]Since we have mentioned blasphemy, another event deserves mention. A knight named Gineldo from Borgo in the province of Massa shamelessly dismissed the works and miraculous signs of blessed Francis. He taunted the pilgrims on their way to observe the saint's feast, and he publicly babbled foolishness against the brothers.

One day while he was playing dice, in his madness and disbelief he said to the bystanders, "If Francis is a saint, let's see the dice roll eighteen!" On the next roll the dice showed three 6's, and for the next nine rolls, three 6's appeared each time. But the madman persisted; he added sin upon sin and piled blasphemy upon blasphemy. "If it's true that this Francis is a saint," he cried, "let my body fall by the sword today, and if he's not a saint, I'll be unharmed!" Scarcely

Ps 78:21, 31; Ps 109:7 had the *anger of God risen* than by divine judgment *his prayer was turned to sin*! As the game ended, he insulted his nephew, and the latter drew his sword and bloodied it with his uncle's bowels. The accursed
1 Thes 5:5 man died the same day and became a slave of hell and a *son of darkness*.

Let blasphemers beware! Words do not fly off with the wind, and there is One who avenges insults to the saints.

[130]**A woman named Sibilla suffered from blindness in her eyes** 1C 136
for many years. She was led to the tomb of the man of God, blind and dejected. She recovered her sight and, rejoicing and exulting, returned home.

[131]In the village of Vico Albo in the diocese of Sora, a girl who had been born blind was taken by her mother to an oratory of blessed Francis. Invoking the name of Christ, and through the merits of blessed Francis, she deserved to receive the sight that she never had.

[132]In the city of Arezzo, in the church of blessed Francis built near the city, a woman who had not been able to see for seven years recovered the sight she had lost.

[133]In the same city the son of a poor woman was granted sight by blessed Francis when she vowed him to the saint.

[134]**At the tomb of the holy body, a blind man from Spello recov-** 1C 136
ered his sight, which he had lost long before.

[135]In Poggibonsi of the diocese of Florence there was a blind woman who, because of a revelation, began to visit an oratory dedicated to blessed Francis. When she was brought there and lay pitiably before the altar, she suddenly received her sight and found her way home without a guide.

[136]**Another woman, from Camerino, was totally blind in her** 1C 136
right eye. Her parents covered the damaged eye with a cloth that the blessed Francis had touched. After making a vow, they gave thanks to the Lord God and Saint Francis for restoring her sight.

[137]A similar thing **happened to a woman of Gubbio who, after** 1C 136
making a vow, rejoiced on recovering her vision.

[138]**A citizen of Assisi was blind for five years. While the blessed** 1C 136
Francis was still living, he was friendly to him, so whenever he prayed to the blessed man, he would recall their former friendship. He was cured as soon as he touched his tomb.

[139]**Albertino from Narni was totally blind for about a year, for his** 1C 136
eyelids hung down over his eyes. Vowing himself to the blessed Francis, his sight was immediately restored; then he prepared himself and went to his glorious tomb.

1C 149 140 A young man named Villa could neither walk nor speak. His mother made a wax image for him and carried it with great reverence to the resting place of the blessed father Francis. When she returned home, she found her son walking and talking.

1C 149 141 There was a man in the diocese of Perugia who was unable to utter a word. His mouth was always open, and he gaped and gasped horribly, for his throat was swollen and inflamed. When he came to the place where the most holy body rested and started going down the steps to the tomb, he vomited much blood. And he was entirely cured and began to speak, opening and closing his mouth in a normal way.

1C 150 142 A woman had a stone in her throat. Due to a violently feverish condition, her tongue stuck to her palate. She could neither speak nor eat, nor drink. After many medicines were tried she felt no comfort or relief. She made a vow to Saint Francis in her heart, and suddenly the flesh opened and she spat the stone from her throat.

143 Bartholomew from the village of Arpino in the diocese of Sora had been deaf for seven years and recovered his hearing by invoking the name of blessed Francis.

144 A woman from the village of Piazza in Sicily was deprived of her speech. When she prayed to Saint Francis with the tongue of her heart she regained the desired gift of speech.

145 In the town of Nicosia, a priest arose as usual for matins and when asked by the lector for the usual blessing, he uttered some barbarous threat. He was then confined at home, out of his mind, and totally lost his speech for a month. At the suggestion of some man of God he vowed himself to Saint Francis, and was freed of his madness and regained his speech.

Chapter XV
Lepers and Hemorrhagics

1C 146 146 At San Severino there was a young man named Atto who was covered with leprosy. All his limbs were stretched and swollen; he looked at everything with an unpleasant expression. Spending all his time in misery on his sickbed, he brought great sorrow to his parents. One day his father came to him and suggested that he dedicate himself to blessed Francis. The youth happily agreed, so the father had the wick of a candle brought, and with it he measured his son's height. The youth then vowed each year to bring a candle of this length to blessed Francis. Having made his vow, he immediately rose from his bed, cleansed of his leprosy.

[147]Another man, **named Buonuomo, from the city of Fano was a** 1C 146
leper and paralytic. His parents brought him to the church of blessed Francis, and there **he recovered his health completely** of both illnesses.

[148]A noblewoman named Rogata, from the diocese of Sora, had LCh 16
Mt 9:20 *suffered from hemorrhages* for twenty-three-years. One day she heard a boy singing in Roman dialect a song about the miracles that God had worked in those days through blessed Francis.[a] Sadness over-
Lk 11:38 whelmed her, and as she broke into tears her faith moved her *to say within herself:* "O blessed father Francis, so many miracles radiate from you: if only you would see fit to free me of my illness! You have not yet done such a great miracle." For the flow of blood was so great that it often appeared that the woman would soon breathe her last, and whenever the flow of blood was stopped, her whole body swelled up. What happened? A few days later she felt herself freed through the merits of blessed Francis.

Her son Mario, who had a withered arm, after a single vow was cured by the saint of God.

[149]Blessed Francis, Christ's standard bearer, also **healed** a woman LCh 16
from Sicily who was worn out by suffering **a flow of blood for seven years.**

Chapter XVI
THE INSANE AND POSSESSED

[150]**There was a man from Foligno named Pietro, who went one** 1C 137
time on a pilgrimage to the shrine of blessed Michael; he drank from a fountain, when he saw himself drinking up demons. From then **he was possessed for three years,** was physically run down, vile in speech, and dreadful in expression. Finally, as soon as **he touched the tomb of the** blessed **father** and humbly invoked his power, **he was marvelously delivered from the demons** that so **cruelly** tormented him.

Mt 2:13 [151]Saint Francis appeared *in a dream* to a woman in the city of 1C 138
Narni who was possessed by a devil and commanded her to make **the sign of the cross.** In her mental state the woman did not know how, so the blessed father **made the sign of the cross on her** and released her from the devil's control.

a. Such songs have not been preserved.

[152]A woman in the Marittima[a] had lost her mind for five years and was unable to see or hear. She tore her clothes with her teeth and had no fear of the dangers of fire or water. And lately she suffered terribly from falling sickness she had contracted.

One night, as divine mercy prepared to show her mercy, she drifted into a healing sleep. She saw blessed Francis *seated on a* beau- Is 6:1
tiful *throne,* and prostrate before him she humbly begged for her health. As he still had not granted her request, she made a vow, promising for love of him never to refuse alms, as long as she had them, to anyone who asked. The saint immediately recognized the same pact he had once made with God,[b] and signing her with the sign of the cross he restored her to full health.

[153]A girl of Norcia appeared listless for some time and it was eventually clear she was troubled by a devil. For she would often gnash her teeth and tear at herself. She would not avoid dangerous heights, nor did she fear any hazard. Then she lost her speech and was deprived of the use of her limbs, and became totally irrational.

Her parents were tormented by the confusion of their offspring; they tied her on a stretcher mounted on a draft animal and took her to Assisi. During the celebration of Mass on the feast of the Lord's Circumcision, she lay prone before the altar of Saint Francis. Suddenly she vomited some damnable thing—I can't say what—and then got up on her feet. She kissed the altar of Saint Francis, and now fully free of her illness she shouted, *"Praise the Lord* and *His holy one!"* Ps 150:1

[154]The son of a nobleman was tormented by falling sickness, no less horrible than painful. He foamed at the mouth and he looked at everything with a wild expression, and from his abused limbs he would spit out—I can't say what—something diabolical. His parents cried out to the saint of God, begging a cure, and offering their pitiful son to his feelings of pity. So the friend of mercy appeared one night to the mother while she slept and said to her, "See, I have come now to save your son." The woman was awakened by his voice and got up trembling, and found her son fully cured.

[155]What great power Francis demonstrated over demons in his lifetime, should not, in my judgment, be kept secret.

1C 69 One time the man of God was proclaiming the good news of the
kingdom of God **in a village of San Gemini. He received hospitality** Lk 8:1; Mt 5:20
from a God-fearing man whose wife was troubled by a demon, as Acts 10:1-2
all were aware. When blessed Francis was asked to help her, he re- Mt 15:22
fused, because he feared the peoples' applause. **Since so many**

a. See 3C 111, supra, 321 a.

b. Cf. 1C 17; 2C 5.

people kept asking, he set the three brothers who were with him in
Jdt 6:16 three corners, and he went to the fourth to pray. When *the prayer was*
finished Francis confidently approached the woman, who was
Acts 3:6 twisting miserably, and ordered the demon to depart *in the name* of
1 Kgs 4:9, 16 Jesus Christ. It left with such swiftness at his command that the
man of God thought he was deceived, and for this reason he left
that place, ashamed.

That is why when he passed through that same place on an-
Mt 15:23 other occasion, that woman ran down the street and cried out after
Est 13:13 him. She kissed his footprints asking him to speak to her. Reas-
sured by many of her deliverance, he finally acceded to the many
who asked him to speak with her.

156 Another time, at Città di Castello, there was a woman who 1C 70
Lk 4:33 *had a demon.* She was led to the house where he was staying and
Jn 20:11 stood outside, gnashing her teeth, disturbing everyone with her
barking. Many people had in fact humbly asked the saint of God to free her, since they had for so long been disturbed by her madness. Blessed Francis sent out to her the brother who was with him, since he wished to check whether it was a demon or the woman's deception. But she knew that he was not the holy man, Francis, so she mocked and belittled him. The holy father was inside praying, and once his prayer was finished, he came outside to the woman. She could not bear his presence, and she shook and rolled on the ground. God's saint commanded the demon to leave her by virtue of obedience. It departed immediately and left the woman unharmed.

Chapter XVII
THE CRIPPLED AND LAME

157 In the county of Parma a man had a son born with a foot reversed, that is, with the heel forward and the toes at the back. The man was poor, but devoted to Saint Francis. He complained daily to Saint Francis about his son who was born to be ridiculed, constantly adding to his poverty. He had thought about forcibly returning the tender boy's foot to its proper place, and with the nurse's permission he prepared to do just that while the boy's limbs were softening in the bath. But before he could attempt anything so rash, as the boy was being unswaddled he was found, through the merits of Saint Francis, as sound as if he had never been deformed.

158 At Scoppito in Amiterno[a] a man and wife had but one son, but he was the cause of daily lament, a sort of disgrace to their family

a. The place is thought to have been near the ancient Amiterno, a town above Aquila.

line. For he appeared to be more monster than human, for, contrary to the order of nature, his forward limbs were twisted to the back. His forearms were joined to his neck, his knees to his chest, and his feet joined to his buttocks, making him appear more like a ball than a body. He was kept out of the sight of relatives and neighbors so they could not see him: his parents certainly acted out of sadness, but even more out of shame. In his sorrow the husband reproached his wife for not producing children like other women, but monsters worse than any dumb brutes. He perversely blamed his wife's sin for this judgment of God. The wife was downcast and filled with shame. She constantly poured out her sorrow to Christ, and invoked the help of Saint Francis, to see fit to lift her from her unhappy and shameful condition.

One night, while she was overcome with sad sleep because of her sad state, Saint Francis appeared to her and kindly addressed these soothing words to her: "Get up and take the boy to the place nearby dedicated to my name.[a] There bathe the boy in the water of the well. As soon as you pour that water over the boy, he will be restored to full health." The woman failed to carry out the saint's command about the boy, so Saint Francis appeared a second time with the same orders, but the woman still did not comply. The saint kindly took pity on her simplicity and found a marvelous way to *increase his mercy.* He Hos 1:6
appeared to her a third time, this time accompanied by the glorious Virgin and the noble band of the holy Apostles. He took her, together with her son, and in an instant transported them to the door of that place.

Dawn was breaking and the bodily vision had completely disappeared. The woman was stunned and wondering beyond belief as she knocked at the door. Her story aroused no little wonder among the brothers, since she was totally confident of a cure for her son: it was promised three times through an oracle. Then a group of noble women from the area arrived there out of devotion, and when they heard what had happened they too were in awe. They immediately drew some water from the well, and the noblest among them bathed the child with her own hands. The boy instantly appeared healthy, with all his limbs in their proper place. The greatness of this miracle aroused wonder in them all.

159 In the village of Cori of the diocese of Ostia, a man had so totally lost the use of a leg that he could not walk or move at all. He was thus confined in bitter agony and had lost hope in any human assistance.

a. Probably the church at Aquila; cf. AF IV, 530.

One night he began to spell out his complaint to blessed Francis as if he saw him there present. "Help me, Saint Francis! Think of all my service and devotion to you. I carried you on my donkey; I kissed your holy hands and feet. I was always devoted to you, always gracious, and, as you see, I am dying of the torture of this harsh suffering." The saint was moved by his complaint and gratefully recalled his good deeds and devotion. Along with one brother he appeared to the man keeping vigil, saying that he had come to him because he had been called, and that he brought the means of healing with him. He touched the source of the pain with a small stick bearing the figure of the "Tau." The abscess healed quickly, his full health was restored, and to this day the sign of the "Tau" remains on the spot.[a]

Saint Francis signed his letters with this sign whenever charity or necessity led him to send something in writing.

160 A young girl was brought to his tomb who, for over a year, 1C 127
had suffered a deformity in her neck so hideous that her head rested on her shoulder and she could only look sideways. She put her head for a little while beneath the coffin in which the precious body of the saint rested, and through the merits of that most holy man she was immediately able to straighten her neck, and her head was restored to its proper position. At this the girl was so overwhelmed at the sudden change in herself that she started to run away and to cry. There was a depression in her shoulder where her head had been when it was twisted out of position by her prolonged affliction.

1C 128 161 In the district of Narni there was a boy whose leg was bent back so severely that he could not walk at all without the aid of two canes. He had been burdened with that affliction since his infancy; he had no idea who his father and mother were; and had become a beggar. This boy was completely freed from his affliction by the merits of our blessed father Francis so that he could freely go where he wished without a cane.

1C 129 162 A certain Niccolò, a citizen of Foligno, was so crippled in his left leg that it caused him extreme pain; as a result he spent so much on doctors in his endeavor to restore his health that he went more deeply into debt than he could ever hope to pay. Finally, when the help of physicians had proven worthless, he was suffering such extreme pain that his neighbors could not sleep at night because of his moaning cries. Then dedicating himself to God and to Saint Francis, he had himself carried to the tomb of the saint.

a. Cf. 2C 106, supra, 317 b; 3C 3.

After spending a night in prayer at the saint's tomb, his crippled leg was cured and, overflowing with joy, he returned home without a cane.

1C 130 [163]A boy had one leg so deformed that his knee was pressed against his chest and his heel against his buttocks. He was carried to the tomb of the blessed Francis, while his father was mortifying his own flesh with a hair shirt and his mother was performing severe penance for him. Suddenly the boy had his health fully restored.

1C 131 [164]In the city of Fano there was a man who was crippled with his legs doubled up under him. They were covered with sores that gave off such a foul odor that the hospice staff refused to take him in or keep him. But then he asked the blessed father Francis for mercy and, through his merits, in a short time he rejoiced in being cured.

1C 132 [165]There was also a little girl in Gubbio; her hands and all her limbs were so crippled that for over a year she was totally unable to use them. Carrying a wax image, her nurse brought her to the tomb of the blessed father Francis to seek the favor of a cure. After she had been there for eight days, on the last day all her limbs were restored to their proper functions so that she was considered well enough to return to her activities.

1C 133 [166]There was another boy from Montenero lying for several days in front of the doors of the church where the body of Saint Francis rested. He could not walk or sit up, since he was completely paralyzed from the waist down. One day he got into the church and touched the tomb of the blessed father Francis. When he came back outside, he was completely cured. Moreover, the young boy himself reported that while he was lying in front of the tomb of the glorious saint, a young man was there with him clothed in the habit of the brothers, on top of the tomb. The young man was carrying some pears in his hands, and he called the boy. Offering him a pear, he encouraged him to get up. The boy took the pear from the young man's hand, and answered: "See, I am crippled and cannot get up at all!" He ate the pear given to him, and then started to put out his hand for another pear that the young man offered him. The young man again encouraged him to stand up, but the boy, feeling weighed down with his illness, did not get up. But while the boy reached out his hand, the young man holding out the pear took hold of his hand and led him outside. Then he vanished from sight. When the boy saw that he was cured, he began to cry at the top of his voice, telling everyone what had happened to him.

1C 134 [167]**After another citizen from Gubbio brought his crippled son on a stretcher to the tomb of the glorious father, he received him back whole and sound, though before he had been so crippled and deformed that his legs were completely withered and drawn up under him.**

[168]In the diocese of Volterra a man named Riccomagno could scarcely drag himself along the ground with his hands. His own mother had abandoned him on account of his monstrous swelling. He humbly vowed himself to blessed Francis and was instantly healed.

[169]Two women named Verde and Sanguigna, from the same diocese, were so crippled that they could not move about unless carried by others. They had stripped the skin from their hands attempting to move themselves. By their vow alone were they restored to health.

[170]A certain Giacomo from Poggibonsi was so pitiably bent and crippled that his mouth touched his knees. His widowed mother took him to an oratory of blessed Francis and poured out her prayer to the Lord for his recovery; she brought him home healthy and whole.

[171]A woman from Vicalvi with a withered hand had it restored to match the other through the merits of the holy father.

[172]In the city of Capua a woman vowed to visit in person the tomb of blessed Francis. Because of the press of household matters she forgot her vow, and suddenly lost the use of her right side. On account of pinched nerves she was unable to turn her head or arm in any direction. She had so much pain that she wore her neighbors out with her constant wailing. Two of the brothers happened to pass by her home, and at a priest's request they stopped to visit the pitiful woman. She confessed to them her unfulfilled vow, and when she received their blessing she at once arose healthy. And now that she was made wiser by punishment, she fulfilled her vow without delay.

1C 135 [173]**Bartolomeo, from Narni, was sleeping in the shade of a tree**
when a diabolical seizure left him without use of **a leg** and **a foot.**
Since he was **a very poor man,** he did not know where to turn. But
that **lover of the poor, Francis,** Christ's standard bearer, *appeared to* Mt 2:13
him in a dream and **ordered** him to go to a certain place. **He set out to**
drag himself there, but had left the direct route when **he heard a**
voice saying to him: *"Peace be with you! I am the one to whom you vowed* Acts 9:4; Dn 10:19
yourself." Then leading him to the spot, it seemed that **he placed one**
hand upon his foot and the other upon his leg, and thus restored his
crippled limbs. This man *was advanced in years* and **had been crippled** Jos 13:1
for six years.

[174]He also performed many such powerful signs while he was still living in the flesh.

Thus when he was once passing through the diocese of Rieti he came to a village where a tearful woman carried her eight year old son in her arms and laid him at his feet. The boy for four years had been so hugely swollen that he could not see his legs. The saint took him kindly and passed his truly holy hands over his abdomen. The swelling went down at his touch and the boy was soon healthy. He joined his joyous mother in giving boundless thanks to God and to his saint.

1C 65 [175]**A knight of the city of Tuscanella took in blessed Francis as
his guest.** The man *had only one son, who was lame and had no bodily* Lk 7:12
*strength. Although the young boy was no longer being breast fed, he was
still sleeping in a cradle. The knight humbly* **fell down at his feet, beg-** Ru 3:7-8
ging him for his son's health. The saint considered himself unworthy of such grace, and said so, **but at last was overcome by the persistence of the father's entreaties, he prayed,** he signed the boy **and blessed him. Immediately the boy stood up and, with the onlookers rejoicing, began to walk all around.**

1C 66 [176]Another time when **he came to Narni, a man of that city named Pietro was bedridden as a paralytic. Hearing that God's saint had come to Narni, he sent a message to the bishop of the city requesting him to send the servant of the most high God** to heal **him. This man had been so deprived of the use of all his members, that he could only move his tongue and blink his eyes. The blessed Francis came to him, made the sign of the cross over him from head to toe, and, as the affliction vanished, immediately restored him to his earlier health.**

1C 67 [177]**At Gubbio, there was a woman with both hands so crippled that she was unable to handle anything with them.** When she knew that the man of God **had entered the city, she immediately ran to him. With a sad and mournful face, she showed him her crippled hands and begged him to touch them. He was moved by great pity. He touched her hands and healed them. The woman immediately returned home full of joy, made a cheesecake with her own hands, and offered it to the holy man. He kindly took a little of that cake** because of the woman's friendly devotion **and told her to eat the rest of it with her family.**

[178]One time Francis went to stay as a guest in the city of Orte. There a boy named Giacomo, who had lain curled up for a long time, came to him with his parents and begged a healing from the saint. After his long infirmity the boy's head was bent to his knees and

some of his bones were broken. As soon as Saint Francis made a sign of blessing over him, he began to uncoil. He straightened up fully and was completely cured.

[179]A neighbor from that same city had a tumor the size of a large loaf of bread between his shoulders. When he was blessed by Saint Francis he was instantly so fully cured that not a trace of his tumor remained.

[180]There was a young man whom everyone knew in the hospital at Città di Castello. He had been crippled for seven years and dragged himself along the ground like an animal. His mother implored Saint Francis for him many times, asking him to restore her snake-like son to a normal walk. When the saint heard the mother's mournful plea and accepted her vow, he immediately loosed the horrible bonds and restored her son to his natural freedom.

[181]Prassede was among the best known religious women in the City and in Roman circles. From her tender infancy she had, for love of her eternal Spouse, withdrawn for nearly forty years to a narrow cell. She earned the favor of a special friendship with Saint Francis. He did for her what he did for no other woman: he received her to obedience,[a] and with pious devotion gave her the habit of the Religion, that is, the tunic and cord.

One day in the course of her tasks, under some imaginary impulse, she went up to the attic of her cell, and by a cruel accident fell to the ground. Her foot and leg were both broken and her shoulder was totally separated from its joint. This virgin of Christ had for many years been withdrawn from the view of everyone, and she firmly intended to remain so. But she now lay on the ground like a tree trunk without anyone to help her, and she did not know where to turn. She had been advised by religious persons and ordered by a cardinal to break her confinement and to accept the assistance of some religious women, and thus to guard against the danger of death that could occur from negligence or neglect. She steadfastly refused to do this, and resisted every way she could to avoid breaking her vow even slightly. She thus cast herself with urgency at the feet
Mk 6:47 of divine mercy, and *as evening drew on* she poured out her pious complaints to the blessed father Francis. "My holy father, you so kindly respond anywhere to the needs of so many whom you did not know while you were in the flesh, why do you not help me in my misery since I merited your sweet favor while you were alive? As you can see, blessed father, I must either change my promised way of life or submit to a death sentence." While she repeated these expressions with

a. Cf. ER XII 4, where this is prohibited.

her heart and mouth, and expressed her miserable condition with
rising sobs, she was suddenly overcome by sleep and fell *into a trance.* Acts 11:5

Behold, her kindly father, clothed in white, *in glorious garments,* Is 52:1
came down into her dark cell and began to speak to her in sweet
words, "Get up, *beloved daughter, get up and do not fear!* Receive the sign Ru 3:10; Lk 6:8. 1:30
of complete healing and keep your promise intact!" Then *he took her* Mk 9:27
by the hand and lifted her up, and disappeared. She turned here and
there in the cell, not realizing what the servant of God had done for
her. She still thought she was *seeing a vision.* Acts 12:9

Finally she went to the window and made the usual sign. A monk
came right away, and marveling beyond belief said to her, "What
happened, mother, to enable you to get up?" But she still thought she
was dreaming and that it was not really he, so she told him to light
the fire. When the lamp was brought, she *recovered her senses.* She felt Acts 12:11
no pain and proceeded to recount *in order all* that had happened. Est 15:9

Chapter XVIII
Various Miracles

182 An eighty year old woman from the diocese of Sabino had two
daughters. When one of them died, her infant son was given to the
other to nurse. Then when this one conceived a child with her husband, the milk in her breasts stopped. No one could be found to help
the orphaned child, no one to provide a drop of milk for the thirsty
baby. The fretful old woman was distressed over her grandson, but
since she was extremely poor, she did not know where to turn. As the
boy grew weaker and faded, the compassionate grandmother was
dying with him. The old woman *went about through streets and houses* Sg 3:2
and no one could escape her cries.

One night she put her withered breast in the boy's mouth to alleviate his squalling, and tearfully begged for the help and advice of blessed Francis. The lover of the age of innocence was immediately there, to show his usual mercy to the miserable. "Woman," he said, "I am Francis whom you called with so many tears. Put your breasts in the baby's mouth, for the Lord will give you milk in abundance." The old woman did what she was told, and straightaway her eighty year old breasts filled with milk.

This became known to all who saw with their own eyes, to their amazement, that the bent old woman glowed with the warmth of youth. Many came to see; among them was the count of that province, who had to admit from experience what he doubted about the rumor. When the count arrived and was investigating everything that happened, the wrinkled old woman squirted a stream of milk on him, and chased him away with this sprinkling.

Ps 103:20; 136:4 Therefore, let *everyone bless the Lord, who alone does great wonders,* and venerate with eager homage His servant Saint Francis. The boy grew quickly on this marvelous nourishment and soon outgrew his need for it.

183 A man named Martino took his oxen far from home to find pasture. The leg of one ox was accidentally broken so badly that Martin could think of no remedy. He was concerned about getting the hide, but since he had no knife, he returned home and left the ox in the care of Saint Francis, lest wolves devour it before his return. Early next morning he returned to the ox with his skinning knife, but found the ox grazing peacefully; its broken leg could not be distin-
Jn 10:11; Lk 10:34 guished from the other. He thanked *the good shepherd* who *took* such loving *care* of him, and procured the remedy.

184 Another man from Amiterno had three years earlier lost one of his draft animals by theft, and he took his complaint to Saint Francis and threw himself lamenting before him.

One night, when he had fallen asleep, he heard a voice saying to
Acts 11:7 him: "Get up, go to Spoleto[a] and bring back your animal from there." When he woke up, he wondered about the voice, and went back to sleep. When he was called again and had the same vision, he turned to ask who it was. "I am," he said, "that Francis whom you requested." He still feared that it was all an illusion, so he put off doing what he was told. But when he was called a third time he devoutly obeyed the reminder.

He went to Spoleto; he found the animal, which was generously returned to him in good health, and he led it home. He told everyone everywhere about the incident and became a lasting servant of Saint Francis.

185 A man of Antrodoco bought a beautiful bowl and gave it to his wife to treasure. One day the wife's maid took the bowl and put clothes in it with lye for washing. But the heat of the sun and the caustic lye broke the bowl to pieces and made it useless. The trembling maid took the bowl to her lady and showed her what had happened, more with tears than with words. The wife too was shaken; she feared her husband's anger and expected a beating. For the time being she carefully hid the bowl and called on the merits of Saint Francis, asking his favor. At the saint's command the broken parts came together, the cracks were sealed and the bowl was intact. The

a. The town here and below should probably be "Scopleto," which is about five miles or nine kilometers from Amiterno, not "Spoleto," which is too far away to go looking for an ox.

neighbors who had first feared for the woman now rejoiced with her, and the wife was the first to tell the news of the amazing event to her husband.

186 A man from Monte dell'Olmo[a] in the Marches one day was attaching the iron blade to his plow when the blade broke into several pieces. The man was saddened by the broken blade and even more by the loss of produce. So he cried, "O Blessed Francis, help me who trusts in your mercy! I will give your brothers an annual share of the grain, and I will do jobs for them, if I might now experience your favor that so many others have experienced." When he finished his prayer, the iron was rejoined and the blade was whole. Not a trace of the fracture remained.

LCh 16 187 A cleric from Vicalvi named Matteo *drank* some *deadly poison*. He Mk 16:18
was obviously ill, and was so afflicted that he could not speak at all; he awaited only his end. Even a priest who encouraged him to confess could not pry a single word from him. But he humbly prayed to
Christ *in his heart,* to save him through the merits of blessed Francis. Ps 14:1
Soon after, he tearfully pronounced the name of blessed Francis, and with witnesses present, he vomited up the poison.

188 Lord Trasmondo Anibaldi was a consul of the Romans. When he exercised his office in Siena in Tuscany,[b] he had by his side an assistant named Niccolò who was dear to him and always ready for household tasks. When a sudden deadly disease invaded Niccolò's jaw, doctors predicted death was near. The Virgin Mother of Christ appeared while he slept and instructed him to vow himself to Saint
Francis and to visit his tomb without delay. When *he got up in the* Gn 24:54
morning, he recounted the vision to his lord. That lord was amazed and hurried to put it into practice. So the lord accompanied him to Assisi, and before the tomb of Saint Francis he got his friend back quickly healed.

This recovery of health was wonderful;
even more wonderful the kindness of the Virgin
who both stooped so kindly to help a sick man
and also raised up the merits of our saint.

189 This saint knew how to help *all who called upon* him, and he Ps 145:18
never considered anyone's needs beneath him.

a. Cf. AF IV, 514.

b. That is, in 1234; cf. *Annales Senenses,* in Muratori, *Rerum Italicarum Scriptores* XV (1729), 25; in *Monumenta Germaniae Historica Scriptum* XIX, 229.

In the Spanish town of San Facondo[a] a man had a cherry tree in
Lk 2:52;Wis 15:12 his garden; it annually bore *abundant fruit* that *produced a profit* for the
gardener. Then the tree dried up and withered from its roots. The
Lk 13:7 master wanted to *cut it down,* so it would not *clutter the ground* any longer, but a neighbor suggested that he put it under blessed Francis's
Rom 4:18 care, and the man agreed. In marvelous fashion, *against hope,* it re-
Lk 21:30 vived, produced leaves, blossomed, and *produced fruit* in its time, just
as before. In thanks for this miracle the owner annually gave its fruit
to the brothers.

190 Around Villesilos an infestation of worms was devastating the
vineyards. The townspeople asked the advice of a member of the Order of Preachers about a remedy for the pestilence. He told them to
choose any two saints, whomever they wished, and to select one of
them by lot and make him their advocate to eradicate the pest. They
Acts 1:26 chose Saint Francis and Saint Dominic. The *choice fell to* Saint Francis,
and the people directed their prayers to him, and the pest suddenly and totally disappeared. The people consequently held him in special reverence, and have great affection for his Order. In thanksgiving for the miracle in the vineyards, they each year send a special alms of wine to the brothers.

191 Near Palencia[b] a priest owned a barn for storing grain, but to the priest's loss it was annually full of weevils, the worms found in grain.[c] The priest was upset with his loss, and searching for a remedy, he assigned blessed Francis to guard the storehouse. Shortly thereafter he found all the weevils dead and heaped outside the barn, and he no longer had to put up with such a pest. The priest felt himself blessed for being heard, and was quite grateful for the favor: for love of Saint Francis he provided an annual ration of grain for the poor.

192 Some time back, when a plague of locusts devastated the kingdom of Apulia, the lord of the castle of Pietramala humbly put his
land under the care of blessed Francis. That land remained, through
the merits of the saint, totally unharmed by the vile plague, while the
Jer 21:14 same pestilence devoured *all its surroundings.*

193 A noble lady of the castle of Galete[d] suffered from an ulcer between her breasts, and it afflicted her both with its pain and its stench. She could find nothing to restore her health. One day by

a. Today Sahagún.

b. In Old Castile, where there was a friary; cf. AF IV, 536.

c. Classical authors had already identified these *curculiones*; cf. Vergil, *Georgics* I, 186; Pliny, *Historia Naturalis* XVIII, 73, 2.

d. The site cannot be identified; many villages and places in central and southern Italy have similar names.

chance she stopped to pray in the church of the brothers. There she caught sight of a booklet containing the life and miracles of Saint Francis,[a] and she looked through it carefully. When she learned the truth of its contents, she tearfully took it and spread it over the diseased area. "As the things written about you on this page are true, Saint Francis," she said, "may I now be freed of my affliction through your holy merits!" She continued her weeping and praying for awhile, then removed her bandages. She was so completely healed that not even a trace of a scar could be detected.

[194]A similar thing happened in the area of Romania [b] where a father stormed Saint Francis with his humble prayers for his son, who was sick with a serious ulcer. "Saint of God," he prayed, "if all those marvelous things said of you around the world are true, let me experience to the praise of God the kindness of your mercy in my son." Suddenly the bandage was torn away from above, and in the sight of all, pus spurted from the wound, and the boy's flesh appeared intact, so that no sign of his former illness remained.

[195]While blessed Francis was still living in the flesh, a brother suf- 1C 68
fered from a terrible affliction, because of which he would often fall. He would often have an attack in which all of his limbs were bent into a circle. Sometimes he would be all stretched out and rigid, with his feet level with his head, and then would be lifted up as high as a man stands, then suddenly bounce back to the
ground, where he would *roll around foaming* at the mouth. The holy Mk 9:20
father took pity on him, prayed, and with the sign of the cross healed him, and he was never again troubled by that illness.

1C 145 [196]After the blessed father's death, another brother had a painful ulcer in his side, so serious that all hope of a cure had been given up. When the brother asked permission of his minister to visit the tomb of blessed Francis, the minister would not give permission, for fear he would incur greater danger from the hardships of the journey. The brother was saddened by this, but blessed Francis one night stood by him and said, "My son, do not be sad any more. Take off the fur you are wearing, and remove that dressing from
your wound. Obey your *Rule,* and you will soon be healed." Early *the* Gn 19:27
next morning he rose and did as the saint commanded, and was immediately healed.

1C 143 [197] A man was seriously wounded in the head by a metal arrow. He could get no relief from doctors, because the arrow had gone through his eye socket and was embedded in his head. He turned

a. Likely Celano's own 1C, or at least his LCh.

b. See 3C 88, supra, 436 a.

humbly and devoutly to blessed Francis, and while he was resting
Gn 31:24 a bit and sleeping, he heard blessed Francis say *to him in a dream,*
that he should have the arrow pulled out through the back of his
Sir 13:17 head. The next day he did what he had *heard* in the dream and
without great difficulty he obtained relief.

Chapter XIV
Conclusion of the miracles of Blessed Francis

Lk 2:11; Acts 15:11 198 The boundless piety of *Christ the Lord* has confirmed as true
Jn 20:30 *what has been written* and published about His saint and our father,
Mk 16:20 *through the signs which accompanied* them.
I Cor 4:3 Thus it truly seems absurd to submit *to human judgment*
what has been approved by divine miracle.
I, a humble son of the same father,
humbly beg everyone to receive them kindly,
and to hear them reverently.
Though some may not be worded worthily,
still they are in themselves most worthy
of being treated with reverence.
Do not look down on the author's awkwardness,
but consider his faith, his dedication, and his labor.
We cannot forge something new every day,
nor square circles,
nor bring to agreement
the innumerable variety of times and wishes
that we received in a single block.
We did not set out to write these things to satisfy our vanity.
Nor have we plunged into this set of such differing reports
of our own will.
The insistence of our brothers' requests extorted it,
and the authority of our prelates ordered it.
Rom 1:7 We expect our reward from *Christ the Lord;*
from you, brothers and fathers, we ask grace and love.
So let it be!
Amen.

At the end of this book,
To Christ be praise and glory.

AN UMBRIAN CHOIR LEGEND

(1253–1259)

Introduction

Among the least known and the more puzzling early texts about Francis of Assisi is a brief two-part piece entitled quite simply: *An Umbrian Choir Legend.*[1] Designated a liturgical piece, it is unique in the way it treats the events of the last two years of Francis's life, death and burial, canonization, and the transferal of his body to the newly built basilica in his honor; and, in the second section, in the way it presents twenty-three miraculous events in such a haphazard way.

The author of the work is unknown, as is his audience. Although there are two manuscript collections of the fourteenth century in which it can be found, only the manuscript found in the Biblioteca Communale in Terni, in the Province of Umbria, Italy, contains the entire work. Since that manuscript also contains statutes for the Province of Friars Minor in Umbria, as well as a list of its hermitages, the work became identified as "An Umbrian Choir Legend."

The presence in the text of the Thomas of Celano "Trilogy," that is, the *The Life of Saint Francis, The Remembrance of the Desire of a Soul,* and *The Treatise on the Miracles of Saint Francis,* means that the work must have been written after 1253 or May 31, 1254 when the friars at the Chapter of Metz approved *The Treatise of the Miracles of Saint Francis.* It would have been completed before the Chapter of Narbonne in 1260 when the friars asked Bonaventure to compile a new, definitive legend. Placing *An Umbrian Choir Legend* in this span prompts questions about the motivation behind it. Two major themes suggest possible reasons.

A careful examination of the first two paragraphs of *An Umbrian Choir Legend* reveals the presence of earlier descriptions of the events on LaVerna, those of Thomas of Celano and Julian of Speyer. Most striking is the emphasis placed on the description of the stigmata and, despite Francis's attempts to keep them hidden, the identification of those who actually saw or touched the wound in his side, Elias and Rufino. This emphasis might not seem significant were it not for the hesitation of many within the Order to believe in the miracle, a hesitation that became more pronounced as the direct witnesses began to die.[2] A thirteenth century Assisi manuscript contains a list, drawn up in 1237, of those who saw the stigmata during and after the death of the saint.[3] In *The Treatise on the Miracles of Saint Francis,* 10, Thomas of Celano mentions a brother beset by doubts about the stigmata, and shortly thereafter Thomas of Eccleston tells of Brother Bonizio at the Chapter of Genoa in 1254 telling the brothers of the stigmata.[4] By 1259, six papal documents had been promulgated denouncing those who denied the stigmata, all of whom were outside the Order.[5] *An Umbrian Choir Legend* may have been written against the background of this skepticism and, while presenting in a succinct way the events of LaVerna and a description of the wounds, it provided details bolstering the belief of those brothers in Umbria who may have been wavering.

Another striking characteristic of *An Umbrian Choir Legend* is its positive regard of Elias. Francis's vicar from 1221 to 1227, and again from 1232 to 1239, Elias was always controversial.[6] His excommunication in 1239 because of his relationship with Frederick II placed him in no better light. *An Umbrian Choir Legend,* however, overlooks these negative aspects. Not only is he introduced as the one for whom Francis had "a special love," Elias touches the saint's wounds, exchanges a tunic with him, and cheers and consoles him. (LChL 2) While the earlier descriptions of Francis's final blessing vacillate between identifying Elias, Bernard or an unknown brother symbolizing each and every brother, this text highlights Francis's praise of his controversial vicar: "You took my burdens on your shoulders and have courageously met the needs of the brothers." Elias's death on April 23, 1253, may well have prompted the anonymous author of this work to correct Thomas of Celano's silence in *The Remembrance of the Desire of a Soul* and *The Treatise on the Miracles of Saint Francis*.

An Umbrian Choir Legend adds little to knowledge of Francis of Assisi. It does, however, provide insights into the milieu preceding the Chapter of Narbonne in 1260 in which the brothers asked the newly elected Bonaventure of Bagnoregio to compile a new legend in honor of the saint and the Chapter of Paris in 1266 in which the brothers mandated the deletion of all legends other than one of the two legends submitted by him.[7]

Notes

1.The translation of this anonymous work is based on the text found in the AF X, 543-554. It is part of seven documents entitled "Some Minor Legends of St. Francis of Assisi Based on the Lives of Thomas of Celano:" a liturgical legend of St. Francis of a "Minorite" breviary in the Vatican, 531-532; an ancient liturgical legend of the Order of Preachers, 533-535; a shorter version of the previous piece, 535-536; a very brief liturgical legend taken from this last piece, 537; a choir legend of Chartres, 538-540; a work of Bartholomew of Trent, O.P., 540-543; and this piece.

2. See André Vauchez, "The Stigmata of St. Francis and Their Medieval Detractors," GR 13 (1999): 61-89.

3. Michael Bihl, "De quodam elencho Assisiano testum oculatorum S. Francisci stigmatum," AFH XIX (1926): 931-936.

4. ChrTE, 13.

5. Gregory IX wrote three denunciations: *Confessor Domini,* April 5, 1237, to the faithful of Germany; *Usque ad terminos,* April 2, 1237, to the Cistercian Robert of England, the Bishop of Olomouc, Bohemia; and *Non minus dolentes,* April 2, 1237, to the Dominican Everhardus (Euchard/ Ebehard). Alexander IV wrote three papal documents on the same theme: *Benigna operatio,* October 29, 1255, to all bishops, cf. infra, 779-781 ; *Grande et singulare,* July 10, 1256, also to all bishops; and *Quia longum,* July 28, 1259, to the bishops of Castille and Leon.

6. Cf. Giulia Barone, "Brother Elias Revisited," GR 13 (1999): 1-18.

7. Cf. Bonaventure of Bagnoregio, Introduction, infra, 503.

An Umbrian Choir Legend

61; 1C 94; //3C 4 [1]Indeed, the friend of God, Francis, two years before he returned
his soul to heaven, in the hermitage called LaVerna, saw in a vision
a single Seraph in the air, having six wings spread above him with
hands and feet attached to a cross. Two wings were raised above
his head, two were stretched out for flight, and two covered his
LJS 61; 3C 4 whole body. The holy man was deeply stunned at this sight, but
1C 94 was unaware what to make of the meaning of this vision. Joy and
grief alternated with concern in his heart. He rejoiced in the pleasant regard with which the Seraph seemed to look at him; its beauty
LJS 61 was beyond measure. But the crucifixion terrified him. Concerned,
he kept thinking about what this vision might mean, and his spirit
LJS 61 was anxious to discern a sensible meaning from the vision. Nevertheless, he was unable to understand anything from it clearly, until
he later saw in himself that most glorious miracle of Christ unheard of in former times.

1C 94 From that moment signs of the nails began to appear on his
hands and feet, just as he had seen them a little while earlier in the
1C 95 man crucified hovering over him. His hands and feet seemed to be
pierced through the middle by nails, with the heads of the nails appearing on the inner part of his hands and on the upper part of his
feet, and their points protruding *on the opposite.* For the marks on the Mk 15:39
inside of his hands were round, but oblong on the outside, and small pieces of flesh were visible, like the points of nails, bent over and flattened, extending beyond the flesh around them. On his feet, the marks of the nails were stamped in the same way and raised above the surrounding flesh. His right side too was marked with an oblong scar, as if pierced by a lance, and this often dripped blood, so that his tunic and undergarments were frequently stained with his sacred blood. It frequently discharged blood so that his cloak and drawers were oftentimes spattered with his precious blood.

LJS 62 [2]Therefore, with such pearls radiant within him, the man of
God strove to keep hidden from the eyes of all living beings that
1C 96 most precious treasure, so that he would not inflict *damage on the* Rom 12:3
great grace given to him by reason of familiarity with someone. He always carried in his heart and often had on his lips the saying of

Ps 119:11 **the prophet:** *"I have hidden your words in my heart to avoid any sin*
against you."

Thus, although many saw the signs in his hands and feet, while IC 95
Gal 2:20 the friend of the Crucified *lived in the flesh,* no one was able to see the
wound in his side, except **Brother Elias** who, because **of the special** IC 96
love the saint had for him,[a] put the saint's tunic on him one time and
gave him his own in exchange. **Brother Rufino, when allowed to** LJS 63
scratch him, felt it palpably with his hand, but only by chance. As IC 95
soon as he touched it, the holy one of God felt great pain and
Gn 19:16 **pushed his hand away, crying out** ***for the Lord to spare him.***

[3]**Six months before the day of his death, while he was staying in** IC 105
Siena, his stomach trouble outweighed **the eye disease, his whole** LJS 67
body wasted away more gravely than previously, and he seemed IC 105
close to death. Brother Elias quickly came to him. **He** cheerfully **re-**
covered at his arrival and left **with him for "Le Celle" of Cortona.**
When his illness became even worse there, he had himself **taken to** LJS 67; IC 105
Est 8:15 **Assisi.** *The city exulted at* **his** *arrival* **and everyone unanimously re-** LJS 67
joiced hoping that such a very precious **treasure was being put back**
close among them.

While he was **in the palace of the bishop of Assisi, since his ill-** IC 108; IC 107
ness grew worse, he lost all bodily strength and, deprived of his
powers, he began to be atrociously tormented in every part of his LJS 68
body. When **he was asked what** he thought **of the** bodily **suffering** IC 107
he was undergoing, he responded that he would more easily undergo
Jer 32:27 **any sort of martyrdom.** But **"The Lord's will,"** he said, "makes every
difficulty light."

[4]Indeed, when he saw his final day was drawing near, as **he had** IC 108; LJS 68
learned two years before from Brother Elias to whom the Lord had
Mk 3:13 deigned **to reveal** the father's passing, ***he called to him*** **the brothers** IC 108
and sons whom ***he chose.*** **He blessed each one as it was given to him**
from above, just as Jacob of old. When Brother Elias sat down on his
left side with the other sons sitting around him, crossing his ***hands,***
he placed his right upon his ***head.*** But **he had lost the sight and use of**
his bodily eyes, so he asked: "Over whom am I holding my right
hand?" "Over Brother Elias," they replied. "And this is what I wish
Eph 4:6 **to do," he said. "I bless you, son,** *in all and through all.* You took my
burdens on your shoulders and have courageously met the needs of
the brothers.[b] **And just as the Most High has increased** and pre-

a. In Thomas's *Life of Saint Francis,* this phrase, "special love," is not applied to Elias, but in general to those close to Francis. Thus it becomes one of the comments of the author revealing his prejudice in favor of the controversial General Minister.

b. Another indication of the special place of Elias in the mind of the author.

served them in your hands, so too upon you and in you, I bless
them all. *May God*, the king of all, *bless you in heaven and on earth.* I Ps 112:6; Tb 9:9
bless you as I can and more than I can, and what I cannot do may
the One who can do all things, do in you. *May God remember* your Dn 14:37
work and labors and may a place be reserved for you *among the rewards of the just.* Heb 2:2
May you receive every blessing you desire and may
your every worthy request be fulfilled.

"Goodbye, all my sons. Live *in the fear of the Lord* and remain in Eccl 9:22
Him always. And because a future test and tribulation is drawing
near, happy are those who will persevere in what they have begun.
2C 216 For now I am hurrying to the Lord to whose grace I commend you
all."

1C 108 [5]After that he commanded that he be brought to Saint Mary of
the Portiuncula, that he might give back his soul to God where he
first came to know perfectly *the way of truth.* This place he had Ps 19:30
learned from experience was full of grace and filled with visits of
LJS 68 heavenly spirits. This place he always wanted to be guarded by the
1C 74 brothers with honor, because the new seedling of the religion,
sprouting first from there, filled the whole world.

1C 109 After resting a few days in the place he longed for, he knew the
time of his approaching death was at hand, he called Brother
LJS 69 Angelo and Brother Leo, the dearest of all to him,[a] and ordered them
to sing loudly *The Praises of the Lord* for his nearing death.

LJS 69 [6]He himself, as much as he could, broke forth into this psalm:
With my voice I cried to the Lord, with my voice I have beseeched the Lord.
2C 217 And immediately ordering the Book of the Gospels to be brought
he asked that the Gospel according to John be read to him from
1C 109 that place which begins: *Before the feast of Passover.* And turning to a Jn 13:1
certain brother whom he loved, he said: "You will bless my brothers for me, the present as well as the absent. I forgive all their faults
and offenses, and I absolve them insofar as I am able."

1C 110; JLS 69 Finally, when he was covered with sackcloth and sprinkled
with ashes, with his sons and brothers standing around him weeping,
1C 110 that most holy soul was released from the flesh, and as it was
2C 217a absorbed into the abyss of light, his body fell *asleep in the Lord.* One Acts 7:59
of his disciples, one of no small fame, saw the soul of the most holy
father *like a star ascending to heaven,* having the immensity of the Sir 50:6; Jos 8:20
moon and the brightness of the sun, extending *over many waters* carried Ps 29:3
by *a little white cloud.* Rv 14:14

a. This identification of the "two brothers, his special sons," whom Thomas mentions were asked by the dying Francis to sing *The Praises of the Lord,* is a new piece of information.

Acts 21:30; Lk 2:20 7 Because of this, *a great crowd of many people gathered, praising and* 2C 217a
Mt 8:34 *glorifying the name of the Lord. The* whole *city* of Assisi rushed down
Mt 3:5; Acts 2:11 in a body and *the whole region* hurried to see *the wonderful works of*
Lk 2:15 *God,* which *the Lord had* gloriously *displayed* in his servant. The sons
lamented the loss of such a father and displayed their hearts' tender affection by tears and sighs. But a new miracle turned their weeping into joy and their mourning into cries of jubilation.

They saw the body of the holy father decorated with the stig- 1C 71
mata of Christ. Not the holes of the nails but the nails themselves 2C 217a
in the middle of his hands and feet, made from his own flesh, in fact grown in the flesh itself retaining the dark color of iron and his right side stained red with blood. His skin, naturally dark before, now shining bright white, promised the rewards of the blessed resurrection. Finally, his limbs had become soft and pliable; not rigid, as usual with the dead, but changed to be like those of a boy.

His sons therefore cried for joy of heart and kissed the marks of LJS 71
the most high King on their father.

Ez 27:33 Then the brothers and sons assembled with the *whole multitude* 1C 116
of people from the neighboring cities. They spent that entire night of the holy father's parting in the divine praises. The sweet sound of jubilation and the brightness of the lights made it seem that angels were keeping vigil.

Jn 21:4 8 *When day was breaking,* the crowds that had gathered, taking 1C 116
branches of olive and other trees, brought the sacred body to the
Jos 6:20 city of Assisi with many lights, *the blowing of horns,* and with hymns
and praises. When the sons had carried the pious father and arrived at the place where he first planted the religion of the Poor Ladies, they halted for a while in the church of San Damiano. The small window was opened, the one used by these servants of
2 Sm 24:15 Christ *at the appointed time* to receive the sacrament of the Lord's
body. Behold the Lady Clare, who was truly brilliant in the holiness of her merits, the first mother of the others, because she was the first plant of that holy Order, came with her daughters to see the body of the most gentle father.

Ps 38:9 They looked upon him, groaning and weeping with great *an-* 1C 117
Jos 3:3 *guish of heart.* "Father! O father, what shall we do?" *they began to cry*
out. "Why are you abandoning us poor women? To whom are you entrusting us? All our consolations ebb away along with you, just as no solace remains for us buried to the world." Then kissing his hands that glittered with precious gems and the most exquisite pearls, they endured with much wailing. Once he was taken away,
Mt 25:10 *the door was closed* to them.

1C 118 Finally all reached the city and, *with great joy and gladness,* laid Bar 3:35; Ps 45:16
LJS 72 the most holy body in a sacred place. In this place he first learned his letters as a little boy, there he later preached for the first time, with the result that it was clear that a happy beginning to the height of glory would be followed by a happier ending of even greater glory.

2C 220a [9]So, in the twelve hundredth twenty-sixth year of the Incarna-
JLS 73; 2C 220a tion, on the fourth day before the nones of October, a Sunday, having completed twenty years from the time he perfectly adhered to
Christ, *following in the footsteps* and the life of the Apostles, the apos- 1 Pt 2:21
tolic man Francis, freed from the fetters of mortal life, departed happily to Christ and was buried in that place. He began to shine with so many wonders and with diverse miracles in every region, that in a short time he had led most of the earth to admire the new age. Since in the new light of miracles, he was already shining in many parts of the world and those who rejoiced in being saved from disasters by his favor were hastening from everywhere; the Lord Pope Gregory, who was then in Perugia, began to discuss his canonization with all the cardinals and other prelates of the Church. All of them, with one accord, gave the same opinion. They read and approved the miracles which the Lord had worked through his servant, and extolled the life and behavior of the
blessed father with the highest praises. Then *the princes of the earth* Ps 148:11
were called first to this great solemnity, and on the appointed day a great number of prelates along with an infinite multitude of people entered with the blessed Pope into the city of Assisi. When they had come to the place prepared for such a solemn gathering, Pope
Gregory preached first *to all the people* and announced with Heb 9:19
1C 125; 2C 220a honey-flowing affection the praises of God. He also praised the holy father Francis with a most noble sermon and, as he spoke of the purity of his way of life, he was wet with tears.

2C 220a [10]Then, when his sermon was over, Pope Gregory *lifted his hands* 2 Mc 3:20
1C 126 *to heaven* and cried out in a loud voice: "To the praise and glory of God almighty, Father, Son, and Holy Spirit, the glorious Virgin Mary, the blessed Apostles Peter and Paul, to the honor of the glorious Roman Church! On the advice of our brothers and other prelates, we decree that the most blessed father Francis, whom the Lord has gloried in heaven and we venerate on earth, shall be enrolled in the catalogue of saints, and his feast is to be celebrated solemnly on the day of his death."

At this announcement, the reverend cardinals began to sing the *Te Deum laudamus* in a loud voice with the Pope. And there rises the

cry of all peoples and, with the clanging bells and the blare of trumpets, the earth resounds. The air is filled with jubilation and the IC 126
ground is soaked with tears. The day is breaking, colored with radiant sunbeams. There are green branches of olive and fresh
boughs of other trees. There all are dressed in festive clothing,
shining brightly, while the blessing of peace gladdens the spirits.
Pope Gregory comes down from the throne, and with his blessed
Jb 40:22; Is 1:15 lips kisses the tomb holding the sacred body dedicated to God. *He
offers many prayers* and celebrates the sacred mysteries. All the people
Lk 18:43 echo *the praises of God* and offer gifts of thanks to His saint. These
things happened in the twelve hundredth twenty-eighth year of the LJS 74
Incarnation, in the second year of the pontificate of the Lord Pope
Gregory, on the seventeenth day of the calends of August.

[11] Two years after these events the body of the most holy father LJS 75
was transferred from the place where it was first buried to the
church newly constructed in his honor outside the city walls. For
there was also a general chapter being celebrated there for such
great solemnities and the greatest crowd of brothers gathered there
from all parts of the world. Such a great crowd of people had gath- LJS 76
ered there from different parts of the world that the city was not able
to contain them, and they filled the surrounding fields and roads.

But the Lord Pope Gregory was prevented from attending such LJS 75
great solemnity because of other urgent business of the Church,
and sent nuncios for the purpose with a personal letter explaining
the causes of his absence.

He also sent the Basilica of Blessed Francis a gold cross adorned LCh 17; LJS 75
with precious stones, in which there was enclosed wood from the
Lord's cross. He also sent ornaments and several vessels pertaining to the ministry of the altar, including some ceremonial vestments that were very expensive.

He exempted the church itself, in which he had placed the first LJS 75; LCh 17
foundation stone, from all jurisdiction lower than his own.

Thanks be to God.
Amen.

The Miracles of Saint Francis

LCh 14 [1]Therefore, Blessed Francis, standard bearer of the Eternal King, on the very day he was buried worked his first miracle.

3C 160 A young girl was brought to his tomb who, for over a year, had suffered a deformity in her neck so hideous that her head rested on her shoulder and she could only look sideways. She put her head for a little while beneath the coffin in which the precious body of Christ's servant rested, she was immediately able to straighten her neck and her head was restored to its proper position. At this the girl was so overwhelmed at the sudden change in herself that she began to run away and cry. There was a depression in her shoulder where her head had been when it was twisted out of position by her prolonged affliction.

3C 161; //1C 127 [2]In the district of Narni there was a boy whose leg was bent back so severely that he could not walk at all without the aid of two canes. He made his living from begging; he had been burdened with that affliction for many years, and he had no idea who his father or mother were. This boy was completely freed from his affliction by the merits of the blessed Francis so that he could walk about freely without any support from canes.

3C 166; //1C 133 [3]There was another boy from Montenero lying for several days in front of the doors of the church where the body of Saint Francis rested. He could not walk or sit up, since he was completely paralyzed from the waist down. One day he got into the church and touched the tomb of the most blessed father Francis. When he came back outside, he was completely cured. Moreover, the young boy himself reported that while he was lying in front of the tomb of the glorious saint, a young man was there with him clothed in the habit of the brothers on top of the tomb. The young man was carrying some pears in his hands, and he called the boy. Offering him a pear, he encouraged him to get up. The boy took the pear from the young man's hand, and answered: "See, I am crippled and cannot get up at all!" He ate the pear given to him, and then started to put out his hand for another pear that the young man offered him. The young man again encouraged him to stand up, but the boy, feeling weighed down with his illness, did not get up. But while the boy reached out his hand, the young man holding out the pear took hold of his hand and led him outside. Then he vanished from sight.

When the boy saw that he was cured, he began to cry at the top of his voice, telling everyone what had happened.

[4]In the city of Capua a woman vowed to visit the tomb of 3C 172
blessed Francis in person. Because of the press of her household matters, she forgot her vow and suddenly lost the use of her right side. On account of pinched nerves she was unable to turn her head or arm in certain directions. So overrun with pain was she that she wore her neighbors out with her constant wailing. Two of the brothers happened to pass by her home, and at a priest's request they stopped to visit the pitiful woman. She confessed to them her unfulfilled vow, and when she received their blessing, she right away arose healthy. And now that she was wiser, for her penance, she fulfilled her vow without delay.

[5]Bartholomew of Narni was sleeping in the shade of a tree when 3C 173; //1C 173
a diabolical seizure left him without use of a leg and a foot. Since he was a very poor man, he knew not where to turn. But that lover of
Mt 2:13 the poor, Francis, God's standard bearer, *appeared* to him in a
dream and ordered him to go to a certain place. He set out to drag
Acts 9:4; Dn 10:19 himself there, but had left the direct route when *he heard a voice saying to him: "Peace be with you!* I am the one to whom you vowed yourself." Then leading him to the spot, that he might be seen by him, he placed one hand upon his foot and the other upon his leg, and
Jos 13:1 thus restored his crippled limbs. This man was *advanced in years* and had been crippled for six years.

[6]In the city of Capua a lad was playing carelessly with his 3C 44
friends on the bank of the river Volturno. From the bank he fell into
Ps 46:5 the deep. *The force of the river* quickly swallowed him up and buried him dead beneath the gravel. The children who had been playing with him shouted, and many men and women ran quickly to the spot. When they heard the children's story they cried out in mourning, "Saint Francis, return the boy to his father and grandfather: they are your hard-working servants!" Indeed the boy's father and grandfather had contributed all they could to build a church in honor of Saint Francis. Everyone was beseeching and invoking the patronage of Saint Francis. Some distance away a swimmer heard their cries and approached them. He learned that a
Acts 22:16 good hour had passed since the boy fell into the river. *He invoked the name* of Christ and the merits of Saint Francis, then undressed and flung himself naked into the river. Since he did not know where the boy had fallen in, he began to search back and forth from banks to depths. Finally by the grace of God he found the place where mud had covered over the cadaver like a grave. He dug and dragged

him out, and was saddened to find him dead. Though the crowd saw that he was dead, they wept and cried out, "Saint Francis, give the father back his child!" Some Jews who had gathered, moved by natural piety, said the same thing: "Saint Francis, give the boy to his father!"[a] It was as if blessed Francis had appeared in response to the people's prayers and devotion, he was there to raise the boy up. The crowd marveled and rejoiced. When the boy had risen, he asked kindly to be brought to the church of blessed Francis. At this all praised God who had deigned to work such wonders through his servant.

3C 45 7 In the city of Sessa, in the quarter called "Ad Columnas," the devil, destroyer and slayer of flesh, destroyed and leveled a home. . . . When the people and clergy saw him healthy and unharmed, they too rendered thanks to blessed Francis.[b]

3C 196 22 A brother had a serious ulcer in his groin, so serious that he had despaired entirely of any cure. When the brother asked permission of his minister to visit the tomb of Saint Francis, the minister refused, lest he incur greater danger from the exertion of the journey. The brother was saddened by this. Saint Francis appeared to him one night and said: "Don't worry any more, my son, but take off the truss you are wearing and remove the bandage from your wound. Obey your *Rule,* and you will be healed." Rising in the morning, he did everything commanded him, and received a quick healing.

23 When Gregory IX was on the throne of Peter, there arose an inevitable persecution of heretics. A certain Peter from Alife was among those accused of heresy, and he was arrested in Rome . . . Later the chains were brought to the Lord Pope and the cardinals. Upon seeing what had happened, with much wonder they blessed God.[c]

24 Bartholomew, a citizen of Gaeta, was hard at work on the construction of a church dedicated to Saint Francis. He was intending to place a beam of the building, but the beam was misplaced; it fell

a. This sentence is missing from the early 1300's Marseille manuscript of Thomas of Celano's *Treatise on the Miracles* from which this incident is taken. It is present in the manuscript of the same period found in the Biblioteca Communale in Terni, Italy.

b. The next sections of this text follow the AF X 543-554, i.e., only the references to the writings of Thomas of Celano are indicated in the manuscripts. Thus the remainder of this paragraph is taken from 3C 45. The subsequent 14 numbers are quoted as follows: the entire text of number 8 is that of 3C 47; number 9 is that of 3C 48; number 10 is that of 3C 62; number 11 is that of 3C 63; number 12 is that of 3C 64; number 13 is that of 3C 66; number 14 is that of 3C 139; number 15 is that of 3C 140; number 16 is that of 3C 69; number 17 is that of 3C 148; number 18 is that of 3C 149; number 19 is that of 107; number 20 is that of 3C 187; number 21 is that of 1C 143.

c. The editors have again followed the manuscripts by indicating that, although there are minor verbal discrepancies, the remainder of this paragraph is that of 3C 93.

and severely crushed his neck. . . . The man got up early the next morning, and the workers who had left him half dead were amazed and puzzled when he appeared healthy and sound. Because there seemed to be no hope for his recovery, they thought they were seeing a ghost.[a]

[25]A religious woman, who from her tender infancy had, for love of her eternal Spouse, withdrawn for nearly thirty years, earned the comfort of the friendship of blessed Francis while he lived. One day in the course of her tasks she went up to the sun from her cell, by some phantom impulse, by dreadful accident she fell to the ground. . . . She felt no pain and proceeded to recount everything that happened step by step.[b]

[26]Here we conclude this narration, and impose silence on the number of miracles to be written.

Thanks be to God.
Amen.

a. The editors have again followed the manuscripts by indicating that, although there are minor verbal discrepancies, the remainder of this paragraph is that of 3C 59.

b. The editors have again followed the manuscripts by indicating that the text is taken from 3C 181.

A LETTER

ON THE PASSING OF SAINT FRANCIS

ATTRIBUTED TO

ELIAS OF ASSISI

(AFTER 1253)

Introduction

One of the most enigmatic texts of Franciscan literature is a letter announcing to the Provincial Minister and all the brothers of France the death of Saint Francis and the discovery of his stigmata. If such a letter was written, which seems likely, its author wrote it shortly after the evening of Francis's death. Its author, more than likely, would have been someone with the responsibility to do so, such as Francis's vicar, Brother Elias. As scholars examine both the external and internal evidence to prove the authenticity of this text, however, the questions increase.[1] The manuscript tradition is extremely weak, in fact, non-existent. And the letter's contents, beginning with the identification of its author, raise a variety of historical difficulties that, at the present state of scholarship, are difficult to resolve.

External Evidence: A Lack of Manuscripts

The text first appeared in 1620 in the *Speculum vitae beati Francisci et sociorum ejus* [The Mirror of Life of Blessed Francis and His Companions] published by William Spoelberch. "In the friary of the Friars Minor Recollect in Valenciennes, Belgium," he wrote, "there is a beautiful document of Brother Elias from when he was General. It is the original letter he sent to the Minister of the Province of France on the death of Saint Francis."[2] Curiously, Spoelberch never wrote that he saw that "original letter." In other words, he provides no information about a manuscript of the text he published as Elias's letter. The archives of the Valenciennes did produce the manuscript of the only known letter we have of Elias, one transcribed by James of Guisia (+1399), the archivist of the Valenciennes friary. In his *Annales historiae illustrium principum Hannoniae,* James makes no mention of a second letter by Elias, that is, the one discovered by Spoelberch.[3] The absence of such an important text prompts scholars to wonder about the precise nature of Spoelberch's letter.

Shortly after the publication of Spoelberch, Luke Wadding published a refined edition of the letter in his *Annales Minorum.*[4] At this juncture, in 1625, this previously unknown text entered circulation. It is strange that such an important letter has no manuscript foundation.

Internal Evidence: Three Problems

The contents of the Spoelberch Letter raise more questions. In the first place, its biblical typology suggests an advanced reflection on the stature of Francis. The biblical imagery of the Spoelberch Letter is similar to that of Pope Gregory IX's proclamation of Francis's sainthood and Thomas of Celano's *Life of Saint Francis*.[5] Did the pope and Francis's biographer borrow from this text, or vice versa? It is impossible to determine. While the images of Francis as another Moses, Jacob, or John the Baptist are understandable even in 1226, those that portray him as another Christ are not. The Christological imagery develops slowly, it is indicative of a much later date of composition. As Stanislao da Campagnola maintains: "in the years 1246-47 a celebration of Francis as an *alter Christus* must have seemed audacious and rash."[6]

The same quandary is encountered in comparing the descriptions of Francis's stigmata provided by Thomas of Celano with those of the Spoelberch Letter. In his careful analysis of the texts, Felice Accrocca suggests that the more traditional hypothesis that Thomas used the letter of Elias is doubtful.[7] The contrary seems more reasonable, that is, that the author of this letter used Thomas's *Life*. ". . . To imagine that Thomas had filled out what he would have found in the letter of 'Elias,'" Accrocca maintains, "adding new particulars and exposing all in a coherent and plain form, is much more difficult than to explain the passages in which the letter recalls *The Life of Saint Francis* by way of summary and sometimes awkward extrapolations."[8] This too would suggest a later date of composition, certainly one later than the publication of Thomas's portrait in the late 1220's.

Finally, the last paragraph of the Spoelberch Letter, i.e., the prescription for offering suffrages for the deceased Francis, raises further questions. "Let each priest say three Masses," the author directs, "each cleric the Psalter, and the lay brothers five *Our Fathers*. Let the clerics also recite in common the vigil office." Shortly before his death, Francis encouraged his brothers "to celebrate only one Mass a day . . . But," he concluded, "if there is more than one priest there, let the other be content at hearing the celebration of the other priest."[9] Not only do the suffrages of the Spoelberch Letter seem disproportionate, that is, the clerical brothers are burdened more than the lay; they betray a distinctly clerical emphasis that seems somewhat premature. Only after Haymo of Faversham had presented his *Ordinationes* to the Chapter of 1243 was it possible to enjoy what was becoming the common practice of the Roman Church, i.e., private celebration of the Eucharist.[10] In 1260 the Constitutions of Narbonne incorporated in an earlier statute a papal decree concerning suffrages for a general minister who dies in office, including an obligation of each priest to offer three Masses.[11] This decree is the same as that in the Spoelberch letter. Once again, however, a question of reliance arises: are the earlier Constitutions based on the Spoelberch Letter, or vice versa? Accrocca argues that the Letter relies on the Constitutions since "the *Rule* of Francis didn't give precise dispositions in this regard, while on the celebration of Masses Francis had been quite clear."[12]

Toward a Resolution

The Chronicle of Jordan of Giano makes it clear that Elias wrote an encyclical letter to do what this letter purports: to announce the death of Saint Francis and his stigmata.

> After the death of Blessed Francis, Brother Elias, who was his vicar, addressed a letter of consolation to the brothers throughout the Order who were dismayed over the death of so great a father. He announced to one and all, as Blessed Francis had commanded him, that he blessed them all on his behalf and absolved them from every fault. Furthermore, he made known to them the stigmata and the other miracles which the Most High God had deigned to perform through Blessed Francis after his death.[13]

The question remains, however: whatever happened to the manuscripts of such an important, encyclical letter? It is reasonable to expect some trace of the important letter Elias sent "to the brothers throughout the Order." None has been found.

The text produced by William Spoelberch in 1620 seems to be, in the words of Felice Accrocca, one that was " 'constructed' *ex novo* after the time of Elias, or it is a later redaction with significant rewriting of the original text."[14]

The editors discussed the merits of publishing this text. Recent scholarship provides reasons justifying its omission. Nevertheless, since Spoelberch's discovery and, perhaps more influentially, Luke Wadding's publication, the text has become part of the Franciscan tradition. The editors, therefore, decided to publish the text in *Francis of Assisi: Early Documents.*

A second discussion centered on its place in the chronological order of the three volumes. Two arguments persuaded the editors to place the Spoelberch Letter after *An Umbrian Choir Legend.* The first of these is the evidence present in the letter of much later developments in the tradition, e.g. the Christological typology, the liturgical prescriptions. In light of these a date late after the *Ordinationes* of Haymo of Faversham, i.e., 1243, possibly after the promulgation of the Constitutions of Narbonne, i.e., 1260, seemed advisable. The pro-Elias stance of *An Umbrian Choir Legend,*[15] however, suggested a reasonable yet undefined association of the two documents. This, of course, leaves the question of manuscript evidence unanswered. The open-ended suggestion, "After 1253," leaves determination of the date of composition unresolved. Arguments may be developed suggesting the letter's composition in the thirteenth century or in any other prior to Spoelberch's discovery in 1620.

In the final analysis, the Spoelberch Letter expresses images and sentiments rooted deeply in the soil of the Franciscan literary tradition and since the seventeenth century has become part of it.

Notes

1. The most thorough study of this text is that of Felice Accrocca, "Is the 'Encyclical Letter of Brother Elias on the *Transitus* of Saint Francis' Apocryphal?" GR 13 (1999): 19-63.
2. William Spoelberch, *Speculum vitae b. Francisci et sociorum ejus* II (Antwerp: 1620), 102, n. 2.

3. Cf. *Monumenta Germaniae Historica,* Scriptores XXX, 78-334. The lack of any reference to this letter is odd given James's concern for the authenticity of the stigmata and the "Spoelberch Letter's" detailed description of them.

4. Luke Wadding, *Annales Minorum* ad annum 1226, n. 45, t. II (Ad Claras Aquas, Quaracchi, 1931), 167-169.

5. Cf. FA:ED I 180-308, 565-569.

6. Stanislao da Campagnola, *"L'angelo del sesto sigillo e l'alter Christus." Genesi e sviluppo di due temi francescani nei secoli XIII-XIV,* Studi e ricerche 1, (Roma, 1971), 142.

7. Accrocca, Encyclical, 30-38.

8. Accrocca, Encyclical, 38.

9. LtOrd 30-31.

10. Cesare Cenci, "De Fratrum Minorum constitutionibus praenarbonensibus," AFH 83 (1990): 50-95.

11. *The Constitutions of Narbonne* (1260), in *Writings Concerning the Franciscan Order,* Works of Saint Bonaventure V, introduction and translation by Dominic Monti (St. Bonaventure, NY: Franciscan Institute Publications, 1994), 71-135.

12. Accrocca, Encyclical, 39-40.

13. Jordan of Giano, *Chronicle* 50, in *XIIIth Century Chronicles,* trans. by Placid Herman, introduction and notes by Marie-Therese Laureilhe (Chicago: Franciscan Herald Press, 1961), 57.

14. Accrocca, Encyclical, 46.

15. Cf. supra, 472 a.

A Letter on the Passing of Saint Francis Attributed to Elias of Assisi

1 To Gregory, his beloved brother in Christ, the minister of the brothers who are in France,[a] together with all his brothers and ours, Brother Elias, a sinner, sends greetings.[b]

2 *Before* I begin to speak, *I sigh,* and rightly so. My groans *gush forth* Jb 3:24:25
like waters in a flood. For what I feared has overtaken me and has over-
taken you. *And what I dreaded has happened* to me and to you. *Our con-* Lam 1:16; Hos 11:3; Lk 1:41; 15:5
soler has gone away from us and *he who carried us in his arms like lambs has* Mt 21:33
gone on a journey to a far off country. He who was beloved of God and of man, Lk 19:12; Sir 45:1
who taught Jacob the law of life and of discipline, and *gave to Israel a cove-* Sir 45:6; Is 45:30,6
nant of peace has been received into the most resplendent dwellings.
We would rejoice exceedingly on his account, yet for our own part we
must mourn, since in his absence darkness *surrounds us* and *the* Eccl 23:26; Ps 43:20
shadow of death covers us. It is a loss for all, yet it is a trial singularly my
own,[c] for he has left me *in the midst of darkness,* surrounded by many Dt 5:23
anxieties and pressed down by countless afflictions. For this reason I
implore you. Mourn with me, brothers, for I am *in great sorrow* and, Zec 9:5
with you, in pain. For *we are orphans without our father* and bereaved *of* Lam 5:3; Ps 37:11
the light of our eyes.

3 In truth, in very truth, the presence of our brother and father
Francis *was a light,* not only *for us who were near,* but *even to those who* Ps 111:4; Eph 2:17
were far from us in calling and in life. *He was a light shed by the true light to* Jn 1:8,9; Lk 1:79
give light to those who were in darkness and sitting in the shadow of death, to
guide our feet into the way of peace. He did this because *the true Daystar* Lk 1:78
from on high shone upon his heart and enkindled his will with the fire
of His love. By *preaching the kingdom of God* and *turning the hearts of fa-* Mk 1:14-15; Lk 1:17; Mk 14:9
thers to their children and the rebellious *to the wisdom of the just, he pre-*
pared for the Lord a new *people in the world.* His name reached distant Eccl 47:18
coasts and *all lands* were in awe *at his marvelous deeds.* Ps 138:14; Gn 13:9

4 For this reason, sons and brothers, do not mourn beyond mea-
sure. *God, the father of orphans, will give us comfort by his* holy *consolation.* Ps 67:6; 2 Cor 7:6-7
And if you weep, brothers, *weep for yourselves* and not for him. For "in Lk 23:26

a. A reference to Brother Gregory of Naples, the minister of the brothers in France between 1223-1233.

b. A similar phrase, "Brother Elias, a vile and fallen sinner," appears in Elias's letter to the Lesser Brothers of Valenciennes, cf. *Monumenta Germaniae Historica, Scriptores* XXX, 294, edited by O. Holder-Egger (Hanover, 1905-13).

c. This phrase is reminiscent of that of Bernard of Clairvaux at the death of his brother Gerard, cf. *On the Song of Songs* 26:3.

Jn 5:24 the midst of life, we are caught in death,"[a] while *he has passed from*
2 Kgs 2:9; cf. Gn 14:1-32 *death to life*. Rejoice, for, like another Jacob, he blessed all his sons *be-*
fore he was taken from us and forgave them all the faults which any one
of us might have committed, or even thought of committing, against
him.[b]

Lk 2:10 [5]And now, after telling you these things, *I announce to you a great joy*
Mt 12:39; Jn 9:32 and the news of a miracle.[c] Such *a sign* that *has never been heard of from*
Mt 16:16; 26:63; Lk 2:11 *the dawn of time except in the Son of God, who is Christ the Lord.*

Not long before his death, our brother and father appeared cruci-
Gal 6:17; Jn 20:25 fied, *bearing in his body* the five wounds which are truly *the marks of*
Christ. His hands and feet had, as it were, the openings of the nails
and were pierced front and back revealing the scars and showing the
Jn 19:31 nails' blackness. His side, moreover, seemed opened by a lance and
Sir 24:21 often *emitted* blood.[d]

Is 53:2-4, 4-5 [6]As long as his spirit lived in the body, *there was no beauty in him for*
his appearance was that of a man despised.[e] No part of his body was without great suffering. By reason of the contraction of his sinews, his
limbs were stiff, much like those of a dead man. But after his death,
1 Sm 16:12; 17:42 his appearance was *one of great beauty* gleaming with a dazzling white-
ness and giving joy to all who looked upon him. His limbs, which had
been rigid, became marvelously soft and pliable, so that they would
be turned this way and that, like those of a young child.

Tb 12:6 [7]Therefore, brothers, *bless the God of heaven and praise Him before all,*
Phil 1:11 *for He has shown His mercy to us*. Hold fast *the memory* of our father and
Jdt 13:35; Ps 90:15 brother, Francis, *to the praise and glory* of Him *Who made him so great*
Lk 12:8, 9 among people and gave him glory *in the sight of angels*. Pray for him, as
he begged us, and pray to him that God may make us share with him
in his holy grace. Amen.

[8]On the fourth day before the nones of October, the Lord's day, at
the first hour of the preceding night, our father and brother went to
Christ. I am sure, dearest brothers, that when this letter reaches you,
Gn 13:14 you will *follow the footprints* of the people of Israel as they mourned the

a. This is the first verse of an antiphon attributed to Notkero Balburo OSB (+912), a monk of Saint Gall. It was frequently sung during the Middle Ages.

b. The comparison of Francis to Jacob reflects that of Thomas of Celano especially in 1C 109: "Look, my son, I am being called by God. I forgive all my brothers, present and absent, all their faults and offenses, and I absolve them insofar as I am able." Cf. 1C 108, 109.

c. The following description of Francis's stigmata has provoked controversy over the date of this letter. It is difficult to determine if Thomas of Celano took his description from this piece or vice versa (Cf. 1C 112). Whereas the editors of AF X maintain that this letter is authentic and, therefore, that Thomas borrowed from it, subsequent studies hold the opposite opinion.

d. Similar passages can be found in 1C 95, and LJS 62.

e. A similar description can be found in 1C 112.

loss of their great leaders, Moses and Aaron. Let us, by all means, give Nm 20:30; Dt 5-8
way to tears for we are deprived of so great a father.

9 Indeed, it is in keeping with our love for him that we rejoice with
Francis. Still, it is right to mourn him! It belongs to us to rejoice with
Francis, for he has not died *but gone* to the fair in heaven, *taking with* Prv 7:19-20
him a bag of money and will not return until the full moon.

At the same time it is right for us to weep for Francis. *He who came* 1 Kgs 18:16
and went among us, as did Aaron, who *brought forth from his storehouse* Heb 5:5; Mt 13:52
both the new and the old and *comforted us in all our afflictions, has been* 2 Cor 1:4; 1 Cor 5:2
taken from our midst.[a] Now we are like *orphans without a father*. Yet, be- Lam 5:3
cause it is written, "the poor depend on you and you are the helper of Ps 10:14
orphans" all of you, dearest brothers, *must earnestly pray that, though* Jer 19:1; Is 10:33
this earthen jar has been broken in the valley of Adam's children, the Most
High Potter will deign *to repair and restore* another of similar honor, Jer 19:11
who will rule over the multitude *of our race* and go before us into bat- 1 Mc 6:29-30; 4-21
tle like a true Maccabee.

10 And, because *it is not useless to pray for the dead, pray to the Lord* for 2 Mc 12:44; Ps 5:4
his soul. Let each priest say three Masses, each cleric the Psalter, and
the lay brothers five Our Fathers. Let the clerics also recite in common the vigil office.[b] Amen.

Brother Elias, Sinner.

---

a. Peter of Blois writes in a similar vein in his letter announcing the death of Thomas of Becket, Archbishop of Canterbury, December 29, 1171. Cf. PL 207:93.

b. This kind of prescription or rubric for prayers for deceased friars did not occur in the Order's legislation until 1260 in the *Constitutions of Narbonne* XII 3, although Cesare Cenci suggests that similar legislation can be found in the Prenarbonian Constitutions, cf. Cesare Cenci, "De Fratrum Minorum Constitutionibus Praenarbonensibus," AFH 83 (1990): 81.

THE LEGENDS AND SERMONS ABOUT SAINT FRANCIS

BY

BONAVENTURE OF BAGNOREGIO

(1255–1267)

Introduction

In 1260 the Lesser Brothers gathered for a General Chapter in Narbonne, France. An important item on their agenda was the codification of the decisions made at the eleven previous general chapters. This resulted in a legal document that became known as the *Constitutions of Narbonne.*[1] The Chapter became famous, however, for another reason: the brothers mandated Bonaventure of Bagnoregio, the general minister whom they had elected three years earlier, to compile a new legend of Saint Francis based on those already in existence. Nothing in the *Definitiones* or decisions of the Chapter record indicates the reasons for this mandate. Only the brothers' decision to correct the liturgical antiphon *Hic vir in vanitatibus nutritus indecenter* suggests the need to bring uniformity to the voluminous material forming around the Founder.[2]

According to his own testimony, Bonaventure was hesitant. "I feel," he writes in the Prologue to the *Major Legend,* "that I am unworthy and unequal to the task of writing the life of a man so venerable and worthy of imitation. I would never have attempted it if the fervent desire of the brothers had not aroused me, the unanimous urging of the General Chapter had not induced me, and the devotion which I am obliged to have toward our holy father had not compelled me."[3] History confirms the legitimacy of the brothers' intuition. Six years later, the decision of the brothers at the Chapter of Paris effectively recognized Bonaventure's portraits of Francis as a "hagiographical and theological masterpiece."[4]

Bonaventure was born Giovanni di Fidanza, in the small town of Bagnoregio about 1221. Although he never claims to have met Francis, the devotion to which he felt obligated undoubtedly came from a cure he enjoyed because of the saint's intercession. "When I was just a child," he declares in the *Major Legend,* "and very seriously ill, my mother made a vow on my behalf to the blessed Father Francis. I was snatched from the very jaws of death and restored to the vigor of a healthy life."[5] That Francis's influence rested on the boy is verified in Bonaventure's entrance into the Order of Lesser Brothers in 1243, probably in Paris where, eight years earlier, he had gone to study.

As a young student brother in the Parisian Couvent des Cordeliers, the friary of the "Cord-bearers," as the brothers were known, established in 1231, Bonaventure's formation was strongly influenced by four great Franciscan "masters:" John de la Rochelle (+1245), Odo Rigaldus (+ 1275), William of Middleton (+1260), and, above all, Alexander of Hales (+ 1245). In 1250, now enjoying the title "Master of Arts," Bonaventure began his commentary on *The Sentences of Peter Lombard,* a mandatory exercise introduced by Alexander into the curriculum of the Parisian brothers. Four years later, the General Minister, John of Parma (+1272), granted him the license to teach theology. He immediately became engrossed in a dispute with William of Saint-Amour (+ 1272) of the University of Paris over the principles governing the Lesser Brothers and the Friars Preacher. The dispute brought such notoriety to Bonaventure and his Dominican colleague, Thomas of Aquino (+ 1274), that Pope Alexander IV urged the Parisian masters to incorporate both men into their ranks. This incorporation was achieved in August, 1257, six months after the brothers had elected Bonaventure their General Minister.

The Chapter of Ara Coeli, Rome lasted one day, February 2, 1257. Pope Alexander IV, the former Cardinal Rainaldo, the Cardinal Protector of the Order, had asked for and obtained the resignation of the General Minister, John of Parma. In his place, the brothers turned to Bonaventure. Their choice was understandable for the saintly John of Parma had been accused of being sympathetic to and of promoting certain tenets of Joachim of Fiore (+ 1202). Joachim, a Cistercian abbot, had proposed a theology in which an understanding of the Trinity, revelation and history were all entwined. His followers, including one of the Lesser Brothers, Gerardo of Borgo San Donnino, promoted his millenarian vision and his references to the coming age of the Holy Spirit heralded by the Angel of the Sixth Seal. In 1254 William of Saint-Amour and other Parisian masters condemned Gerardo, proposing him as another example of the distorted understanding of evangelical life expounded by the brothers. Alexander IV condemned Gerardo's *Introductorius in Evangelium Eternum* in 1255. The following year he condemned William of Saint-Amour's *Tractatus de periculis novissimorum temporum*, and, to cleanse the Lesser Brothers of any suggestion of Joachimite influences, urged John of Parma to resign.

Understandably the quickly developing Order, now grown to thirty thousand brothers spread throughout Europe, Africa and Asia, was in need of direction. The brothers were becoming gradually more divided in their interpretations of the Founder's ideals and their day-to-day expression.[6] Since the death of Francis, the brothers had seen a succession of General Ministers: Elias (1226-1227), John Parenti (1227-1232), Elias again (1232-1239), Albert of Pisa (1239), Haymo of Faversham (1239-1244), Crescentius of Iesi (1244-1247), and John of Parma (1247-1257).

No stranger to controversy, Bonaventure guided the brothers from February 2, 1257 until May 20, 1273 when Pope Gregory X made him Cardinal Bishop of Albano. While Bonaventure's earlier writings reveal his respect for tradition and suggest that he was conservative by temperament, they also indicate his perceptive mind as well as his ability to confront the issues threatening the Order. Above all, these early writings clearly show Bonaventure's profound grasp of the mystical tradition and his sensitivity to the unique place of Francis's vision within it.[7] Within the Order, therefore, Bonaventure strove to address various crises confronting the Order, to articulate the unique character of its Gospel ideals, and to re-enkindle it among the brothers. His first two letters, written ten years apart, show the intensity of his efforts, the depth of his comprehension, and the simplicity of his solution: a return to the rule and life of the Lesser Brothers, that is, to the *Later Rule.*[8]

Early Writings about Saint Francis

By the time he had begun to honor the request of the brothers assembled at the Chapter of Narbonne, Bonaventure had already written a considerable amount. Surprisingly, beyond the *Soul's Journey into God,* little is concerned with Francis of Assisi. Occasional references can be found in Bonaventure's commentaries on the *Sentences* of Peter Lombard and the Gospel of Luke. Were these his only references, the judgment of John H.R. Moorman may be justified: Bonaventure "never really understood the Franciscan ideal."[9] His letter to an unknown master, however, provides an insight into his understanding of his call to be Francis's follower.

> Do not be disturbed, that the brothers were simple and illiterate men in the beginning; this should confirm your faith in the Order even more. I confess before God that it is this that made me love the life of blessed Francis above all, because it is similar in its beginning and perfection to that of the Church, which began with simple fishermen and grew to include the most illustrious and learned doctors. And so you will see in the Order of blessed Francis, as God displays, that it was not invented by human discernment but by Christ.[10]

While it is difficult to date this letter, this passage suggests it was written during the same period as two sermons he delivered on the Feast of Saint Francis, October 4, 1255, five years before the brothers commissioned Bonaventure to compile the new legend. All three, the letter and the morning and evening sermons of October 4, touch on aspects of the same theme: "the essence of true discipleship of Jesus Christ, which was singularly realized and shone in Saint Francis."[11]

The sermons of 1255 are Bonaventure's first known writings dedicated principally to Saint Francis. Although they do not have the depth that can be found in his later Franciscan works, they nevertheless reveal seminal ideas that come to fruition in the *Major* and *Minor Legends.* Bonaventure reveals in the morning sermon his struggle with the meaning of "conversion" in the Christian life of the young Francis, his cultivation, even at an early age, of solitude, and the differing shades and meanings of his embrace of poverty. In a milieu in which Francis's stigmata were being challenged,[12] Bonaventure subtly crafts a theology of signs maintaining that the stigmata were "signs of consummate love." "Such is the power of love," Bonaventure reminds his listeners in the words of Hugh of St. Victor, "that it transforms the lover into the Beloved."[13] Throughout, Bonaventure displays his awareness of the literary heritage left by Thomas of Celano. His use of many of Thomas's images, undoubtedly controversial in the anti-Joachimite milieu of the University of Paris, indicate how sensitive Bonaventure was to their implications.

The evening sermon takes a somewhat different approach as Bonaventure explores the significance of his calling, and that of his brothers, to be a Lesser Brother. While the morning sermon was dedicated to Christ's words (Mt 11:29), "Learn from me," the evening sermon developed the remaining part of the verse, ". . . for I am meek and humble of heart." "To be meek is to be a brother to everybody," he declares, "to be humble is to be less than everybody. Therefore, to be meek and humble of heart is to be a true lesser brother."[14] Thus, in the evening sermon, Bonaventure lays the foundations of the universality of the fraternal relations he describes in the eighth chapter of *The Major Legend.*

Valuable as these insights into Bonaventure's Franciscan thought may be, those provided by his *Itinerarium mentis in Deum* [The Soul's Journey Into God] are even more so. The *Itinerarium* is the fruit of Bonaventure's stay on LaVerna where Francis had received the stigmata. At the opening of the work, the meditative General Minister writes:

> Inspired by the example of our most blessed father, Francis, I wanted to seek after this peace with yearning soul, sinner that I am and all unworthy, yet the seventh successor as Minister to all the brothers in the place of the blessed father after his death. It happened that, thirty-three years after the death of the saint, about the time of his passing, moved by a divine impulse, I withdrew to Mount La Verna, as to a place of quiet, there to satisfy the yearning of my soul for peace. While I dwelt there, pondering on certain spiritual ascents to God, I was struck among other things, by that miracle which in this very place had happened to the blessed Francis, that is, the vision he received of the winged seraph in the form of the Crucified. As I reflected on this marvel, it immediately seemed to me that this vision might suggest the rising of Saint Francis into contemplation and point out the way by which that state of contemplation may be reached.[15]

On the cliffs of La Verna, it became clear to him that Francis's mystical experience was not only the goal of his vocation and that of his brothers, but also the road to it. A sermon Bonaventure delivered on Holy Saturday reveals his reflections on three ways of ascending into God: that of Bernard of Clairvaux,[16] another of Richard of St. Victor,[17] and, finally, that of Giles of Assisi, the companion of Francis himself.[18] His first letter to the brothers, April 23, 1257, suggests that he may have returned to these reflections as a means recalling the Order from the paths onto which it had strayed and of finding consolation for his soul. On La Verna, however, Bonaventure, like Francis, seems himself to have had a mystical experience. His understanding of the saint deepened; his insight into the rapture of Francis's experience on La Verna and its result, the stigmata, left an indelible mark on Bonaventure's genius. The vision of a six-winged Seraph re-enforced his conviction that the crucified Christ was at the very heart of Christian life, the center around which all else revolved.

> The six wings of the Seraph, can be rightly understood as signifying the six levels of uplifting illuminations by which, as if by steps or stages, the soul is disposed to pass over to peace through ecstatic transport of Christian wisdom. The road to this peace is through nothing else than a most ardent love of the Crucified, the love of which so transformed Paul into Christ when he (2 Cor 12:2) *was carried up to the third heaven* that he could say: (Gal 2:20) *With Christ I am nailed to the cross. I live, now not I, but Christ lives in me.* And this love also so absorbed the soul of Francis that his spirit shone through his flesh the last two years before his death when he carried in his body the sacred marks of the passion.[19]

Bonaventure then proceeds to articulate his own understanding of the vision. In doing so, however, the figure of Francis becomes that of the Christian soul, the one who enters through the Crucified, who washes in the blood of the Lamb, who becomes inflamed with desire.

> The figure of the six wings of the Seraph, therefore, brings to mind the six steps of illumination which begin with creatures and lead up to God, Whom no one rightly enters save through the Crucified. (Jn 10:1) *For he who enters not by the door, but climbs up another way, is a thief and a robber* (Jn 10:9) *But if anyone enter* by this door, *he shall go in and out and shall find pastures.* For this reason Saint John says in the Apocalypse: (Rv 22:14) *Blessed are they who wash their robes in the blood of the Lamb, that they may have a right to the tree of life and that by the gates may enter into the city.* That is to say, no one can enter by contemplation into the heavenly Jerusalem unless he enters through the blood of the Lamb as through a door. For no one is in any way disposed for divine contemplations that lead to spiritual transports unless, like Daniel he is also (Dn 9:23) *a man of desires.* Now, such desires are enkindled in us in two ways, to wit, through the outcry of prayer, which makes one sigh (Ps 37:9) from *anguish of heart,* and through *the refulgence of speculation* by which the mind most directly and intently turns itself toward the rays of light.[20]

Those "signs of consummate love," as Bonaventure described the stigmata in his 1255 sermon on Saint Francis, now provided for those who would follow Francis's lead on the path into God. And, as Bonaventure articulated in his final work, *The Collations on the Six Days,* they provided one of the underlying principles of the *Major Legend:* the *impressed* stigmata were *expressed* signs.[21]

The stigmatized Francis became for Bonaventure someone whose life provided a road map of perfection, one that could be followed not only because of internal evidence, but, more so, because of these external signs of God's approbation.

The Major Legend

Even a cursory glance at the *Major Legend* reveals how faithful Bonaventure was to his mandate to compile one good legend from all the existing ones.[22] The largest number of episodes contained in the first fifteen chapters of the *Major Legend* come from Thomas of Celano's *Life of Saint Francis*, refined by the writings of Julian of Speyer, and *The Remembrance of the Desire of a Soul*. The influence of the *Legend of the Three Companions* and the *Assisi Compilation* are certainly evident, although it is difficult to determine whether or not these influences were transmitted by way of Thomas's *Remembrance*. For the most part, Bonaventure contributes little to the biographical data provided by his predecessors. In fact, in the second section of the *Major Legend*, the consideration of Francis's miracles, the texts come almost entirely from Thomas's *Treatise on the Miracles*.[23]

Bonaventure's contribution consists in setting these earlier materials in a new framework. "From the visible to the invisible," he teaches in his *Commentary on John's Gospel*. Thus, the historical, observable events of Francis's life led Bonaventure to understand more concretely the mysterious, hidden designs of God. The opening lines of the Prologue reveal immediately this appreciation of Francis's life. "The grace of God our Savior," Bonaventure declares at the outset, "has appeared in his servant Francis . . ." The sanctity of Francis, as that of every Christian, consists in the unfolding of grace, that gift of the Holy Spirit that, according to the *Breviloquium*, purifies, illumines, and perfects.[24] In a rich mosaic of biblical passages, Bonaventure elegantly outlines his portrait of the "hierarchic man" in a framework that resonates with the threefold approach found throughout his writings.[25]

Undoubtedly Bonaventure was influenced in this approach by the writings of the Pseudo-Dionysius and Thomas Gallus (+1246), both of whom described growth in the spiritual life as growth through the successive stages of purgation, illumination, and unification.[26] For Francis's disciple, Bonaventure, however, growth in virtue consisted in more than this hierarchical progress. Francis's *Canticle of Brother Sun* opened a new horizon and showed that the saint had discovered God in the most simple gifts of creation. This dimension of the mystic Francis challenged Bonaventure, his follower, to re-think the hierarchical vision. The *ordo amoris* [the ordering of love], as he described virtue in the first of the *Disputed Questions on Evangelical Perfection*, demands a clear sense of direction. His view of creation sees a "twofold order of things, one within the universe, and another with regard to their end."[27] By the time of his compilation of Thomas and Julian, Bonaventure had produced a well-developed theology in which he envisioned God having written for humanity three books: the Book of Creation, the Book of Scripture, and the Book of Life. Had Adam not sinned, he maintains, the Book of Creation would have been efficacious in leading human beings to discover the power, wisdom, and goodness of God. Because of sin, that Book had become obscured prompting God to provide the Book of Scripture. In it, a human can discover the triune God and, enlightened by grace, a human can discover the Book of Life and in it the fullness of life.[28] Bonaventure's portrait of the "hierachic man" Francis is also that of the individual whom grace teaches to see correctly and to interact with the created world in which he lives.

At the very heart of this vision is the cross. As in all his other writings, Bonaventure places the mystery of the crucified Christ at the very center of his understanding. After the manner of John the Evangelist, he accentuates six manifestations or signs pointing to a seventh, that is, six apparitions of the cross, all of which are in the first four chapters, pointing to the reception of the stigmata in the thirteenth. Then, in Chapter Nine, at the very heart of the nine chapters treating the virtues of Francis, Bonaventure describes the saint's burning desire to be identified with Christ crucified. The evening sermon that he preached on October 4, 1262, while he was writing *The Major Legend*, focuses on Matthew 24:30: *Then will appear the sign of the Son of man in heaven.* Reading that sermon now, it is obvious that it was a key to Bonaventure's portrait of Francis. His reception of the stigmata was not only the supreme moment of contemplative ecstasy, it was the vindication of his entire life. "The cross of Christ is the sign of God's perfect works and of all his wonderful deeds," Bonaventure reminds his brothers in Paris. "And because Saint Francis can be likened to the heavens in all he did, we should expect to find the cross imprinted on him, so that by this sign he would be raised on high."[29]

While it is important to understand the overall structure of Bonaventure's portrait of Francis, the *Major Legend,* each chapter has a structure of its own. In some of these, the theology of the Parisian master is more obvious than in others. Linear in some, it is concentric in others. Chapter Six, for example, begins describing the foundations of Francis's humility before God and continues with its exercise before his brothers, especially in the practice of obedience. The second half of the chapter is dedicated to God's response to this practice of virtue, providing by way of examples a balanced picture of the pursuit of virtue. Chapter Eight, on the other hand, describes Francis's practice of piety through a pattern of concentric circles in which his devotion to God after the example of Christ is at its very heart. Bonaventure then continues with the saint's relations with his brothers, his fellow human beings, especially with the poor and the sick, and proceeds to his relations with animals. In each instance, Bonaventure respectfully uses the texts of Thomas of Celano and Julian of Speyer to craft his image of Saint Francis.

As he describes Francis's life in visible detail, Bonaventure underscores the invisible strokes of God's grace. The result is a remarkable piece of literature, written in much the same way as the artisans and craftsmen of those recently built Gothic structures that surrounded his Parisian friary.[30] To understand the aesthetics of his portrait of Francis, it is as important to comprehend the architectonic lines of his thought as to concentrate on the nuances of his delicately crafted tableaux. Like any gifted architect living in close contact with the sculptors, glass painters, and wood carvers, Bonaventure focused his attention on the details of Thomas of Celano, Julian of Speyer, and those who knew Francis, and studied their writings attentively that he might gracefully incorporate them into his own design.

The Minor Legend

The second commission Bonaventure received was to write a work similar to Thomas of Celano's Legend for the Use in Choir. *The Minor Legend* for official use during the Octave of the Feast of Saint Francis ensured the eradication of Thomas of Celano and Julian of Speyer's earlier liturgical-hagiographical memories of Francis. The possible insertion of this concise theological reflection on Francis's life into the portable breviaries[31] also encouraged the broad diffusion of Bonaventure's text throughout Europe.[32]

The Minor Legend emerged as the brothers promoted Francis's spirituality in the midst of an on-going interpretation of their identity and mission. Architects and artists assisted in these efforts as they designed and decorated the Basilica of Saint Francis in Assisi and other large urban churches.[33] In surprisingly spacious and stunningly beautiful liturgical environs,[34] men and women were reminded through paintings, preaching, and praying of God's incredible condescension in the Crucified Christ[35] and Francis's response to this divine initiative. Present in image and word, Francis's life revealed a paradigmatic conformity to Christ invoking and inviting people everywhere, regardless of social or ecclesial standing, to follow him, in union with the Crucified, into the mystery of God.[36] *The Minor Legend,* celebrative and spiritual in nature,[37] played a major role in diffusing this image and message of Francis as it became a salient element of the celebration of the Founder.[38]

The liturgical celebration of Francis's spiritual journey focused on the Feast of Saint Francis which was celebrated throughout the Roman Church on October 4th. The opening chapter of *The Minor Legend* was read during the solemn office on that day, and the remaining chapters throughout the Octave of the Feast of Saint Francis culminating on October 11th when the first chapter was repeated. The nine lessons of each chapter were divided among the nocturnal hours.[39]

The liturgical nature of *The Minor Legend* underscores the relationship between the text of Francis's story and the context of Bonaventure's personal dedication to prayer. It also offers a hermeneutic insight into how to read *The Major Legend.* As both theologian and General Minister, Bonaventure had urged his brothers to pray unceasingly with the entire Church and recognize, in prayer, the opportunity to encounter the Crucified Christ manifested in the stigmatized flesh of Francis.[40] An echo of Bonaventure's devotion is heard at the conclusion of *The Major Legend.* At the opening of *The Major Legend,* Bonaventure links the miracle of his childhood healing through Francis's intercession with a formal recognition of a literary debt owed to the saint. In *The Minor Legend* of Saint Francis, however, the memory of Francis's intercession evokes a prayer of gratitude and an accompanying plea for the Franciscan minor fraternity to come together in the prayerful remembrance of the Poor Man, now venerated as the saint from Assisi.

Approval

In 1263 Bonaventure presented his completed legends to the brothers at the General Chapter of Pisa. It is not difficult to imagine that, as Michael Bihl suggests, thirty-four manuscripts of the text were prepared, one for each Province of the Order.[41] There is no evidence of these manuscripts, nor is there any statement of the Chapter's approval of the work. The brothers gathered at the General Chapter of Paris in 1266 may well have mandated that each friary have a manuscript of the text, but their decision to establish the *Major Legend* as the definitive portrait of Francis remains its far more important contribution. "The General Chapter likewise orders under obedience that all the legends of the Blessed Francis that have been made should be removed. Wherever they find these outside the Order, let the brothers strive to remove them. For this Legend made by the General Minister has been compiled as he received it from the mouth of those who were always with blessed Francis and had certain knowledge of everything, and proven facts have been diligently placed in it."[42]

In light of Bonaventure's prologue to the *Constitutions of Narbonne* in which he states that "the highest governing authority of the Order resides in the general chapter,"[43] it is difficult to imagine that he would be so presumptuous as to mandate his portrait of Francis as definitive and to order the destruction of all others. In reaction to the autocratic administration of Elias and following the example of the Friars Preacher, the Lesser Brothers decided that the chapter determined policy; the responsibility of the general minister was to execute it.[44] Nevertheless, the results of the decree were drastic. The editors of the *Analecta Franciscana* discovered less than twenty manuscripts of Thomas's *Life of Saint Francis* and most of these were in the possession of the Cistercians. There were only two of Thomas's *Remembrance of the Desire of A Soul.*

Thus Bonaventure's work became the fundamental, primary portrait of Francis and, next to his *Rule* and *Testament,* the principal interpreter of his vision. By the middle of the next century, there were one thousand five hundred and thirty manuscripts of the *Major Legend* in friaries throughout Europe and at least another four hundred in the monasteries of the Poor Clares. Sadly, the Order had begun to fragment at this time and Bonaventure and his interpretation of Francis became a highly contested point. Nevertheless, Arnaud of Sarrant eloquently compared Bonaventure's portrait in terms of John's Gospel:

> The fourth author was like another John the Eagle, Brother Bonaventure. His knowledge was like that of an eagle lifted ever high. And when he was general minister, it was as if he were the king of all fowl. This man, more clearly than the others, de-

> scribed the rapture and ecstasy of Francis, and recounted that vision and appearance of the Seraph more brilliantly than the rest.[45]

Undoubtedly, it was that mystical dimension of Bonaventure's work that made it such a reservoir of spirituality to the second generation of Francis's followers. As the spiritual climate changed at the end of the thirteenth century, so did the appeal of Bonaventure's portrait.

The final judgment of the scope of his portrait, however, is best left to Bonaventure himself. At the conclusion of his *Soul's Journey into God,* he wrote:

> . . . In a transport of contemplation on the mountain height, there appeared to Blessed Francis the six-winged Seraph fastened to a cross, as I and many others have heard from the companion who was then with him at that very place. Here he passed over into God in a transport of contemplation. He is set forth as an example of perfect contemplation, just as previously he had been of action, like a second Jacob-Israel. And thus, through him, more by example than by word, God would invite all truly spiritual persons to this passing over and this transport of soul.[46]

Later Writings

Bonaventure was to dedicate four more sermons to Saint Francis, all of which he preached to his brothers at the University of Paris. All of these, the sermon of October 4, 1266, that commemorating the transferral of Francis's body to the new basilica built in Assisi in his honor, that is, the sermon of May 27, 1267, and the morning and evening sermons of October 4, 1267, seem to be outlines. The first of these, in particular, is quite brief and proceeds in an orderly fashion, numbering each point that it might easily be remembered. Although it is somewhat longer, the same manner of presentation is obvious in the second of these sermons. Only the last two pieces show the same in-depth, carefully developed composition that can be seen in Bonaventure's first sermon on Saint Francis, October 4, 1255.

It is important to note, however, Bonaventure used these sermons to explain or deepen images or biblical passages present in his legends. The third sermon, for example, revolves around Haggai 2:23, I will take you, O Zerubbabel my servant . . . and make you like a seal. "For as Zerubbabel," Bonaventure explains, "whose name means 'leader of the exodus,' led the people out of Babylon and rebuilt the Temple, so Saint Francis brought many people from the disorder of sin to Christ and, he founded a religious Order." The sermon becomes a brilliant elaboration of the seal that Bonaventure's new Zerubbabel, Francis, had become: "refashioned, transformed, imprinted and declaratory."[47] In the Sermon on the Feast of the Transferral, Bonaventure elaborates on the images of Jacob and Moses, both present in the *Major Legend*, and offers a new one as he applies the image of Mordecai, the guardian of Esther, to Francis.

The final sermon, that of October 4, 1267, reveals Bonaventure at his biblical best. His theme is Isaiah 42:1, *Behold my servant whom I uphold*... Zerubbabel, Job, Elijah, Paul, the wise servant of Luke's Gospel, Jesus Himself: all become images of Francis and reminders of what it means to be a Lesser Brother. Bonaventure offers new insights into persons who appear in his legends, Gregory IX, Pacifico, Saint Clare and her Sisters: each of these reveals a dimension of Francis's story portrayed in passages from Scripture, and authors such as Augustine, Anselm, Bernard, and Francis himself. This final sermon is, in a sense of *tour-de-force*, a commentary on Bonaventure's developing appreciation for the saint he knew as a boy, Francis of Assisi.

Notes

1. Cesare Cenci, "De Fratrum Minorum constitutionibus praenarbonensibus," AFH 83 (1990): 50-95; The Constitutions of Narbonne (1260), in *Writings Concerning the Franciscan Order*, Works of Saint Bonaventure V, introduction and translation by Dominic Monti (St. Bonaventure, NY: Franciscan Institute Publications, 1994), 71-135.

2. Julian of Speyer, following the biographical material presented by Thomas of Celano, wrote *Hic vir in vanitatibus nutritus indecenter/Plus suis nutritoribus, Se gessit insolenter* [This man was raised in vanities/And shameful was his rearing;/Outstripping those that nurtured him,/His ways were overbearing.] The Chapter changed the last phrase of the antiphon to: *Divinis charismatibus/Praeventus est clementer* [Through divine gifts/He was mercifully delivered.] Cf. FA:ED I 332 c.

3. Cf. LMj Prol 3.

4. Bernard McGinn, *The Flowering of Mysticism: New Men and Women in the New Mysticism–1200-1350*, The Presence of God: A History of Western Christian Mysticism, Vol. III (New York: The Crossroad Publishing Company, 1998), 94-95. McGinn's judgment reflects that of contemporary scholarship and at odds with those of A.G. Little, "Guide to Franciscan Studies," in *Études franciscaines* 40 (1928): 517-533; (1929): 64-68; John H.R. Moorman, *The Sources of the Life of Saint Francis* (Manchester: University Press, 1940), 141; and Anthony Mockler, *Francis of Assisi: The Wandering Years* (Oxford: Phaedon, 1976).

5. LMn VII 8.

6. For an understanding of these divisions, see Duncan Nimmo, *Reform and Division in the Franciscan Order (1226-1538)*, (Rome: Capuchin Historical Institute, 1987), 51-108.

7. Bernard McGinn notes: "Bernard of Clairvaux and Bonaventure–the *doctor mellifluous* and the *doctor seraphicus*–may be justly described as the two premier mystical teachers of the Medieval West. Both were important ecclesiastical officials who were forced to be men of action, as well as of contemplation. Both wrote on a variety of theological and church-political topics, as well as on how the soul attains God in this life." Bernard McGinn, *The Presence of God: A History of Western Christian Mysticism*, The Flowering of Mysticism (New York: The Crossroad Publishing Company, 1998), 87.

8. Both of these letters can be found in Monti, *Writings*, 57-62, 225-229.

9. Moorman, *Sources*, 141.

10. Bonaventure of Bagnoregio, *Doctoris Seraphici S. Bonaventurase opera omnia*. 10 volumes, in folio. (Ad Claras Aquas, Quaracchi: Collegium S. Bonaventurae, 1882-1902), VIII, 336. This work is referred to by the traditional method, citing Roman numeral for volume, Arabic for page. A translation of the entire *Letter to an Unknown Master* can be found in Monti, *Writings*, 39-56.

11. Cf. Sermon 1 on Saint Francis by Bonaventure of Bagnoregio, 1 (hereafter 1-4 Srm).

12. Cf. André Vauchez, "The Stigmata of St. Francis and Its Medieval Detractors," GR 13 (1999): 61-89.

13. cf. 1Srm, infra, 515 a.

14. cf. 1Srm, infra, 517.

15. Bonaventure, *The Journey of the Mind into God*, Prologue 2, translated by Philotheus Boehner, edited, with Introduction and notes by Stephen F. Brown (Indianapolis/Cambridge: Hackett Publishing Company, 1993), 1.

16. Cf. Bernard of Clairvaux, *Five Books on Consideration: Advice to a Pope*, V 14:32, translated by John D. Anderson and Elizabeth T. Kennan (Kalamazoo, MI: Cistercian Publications, 1976), 139.

17. Richard of St. Victor, *The Mystical Ark (Benjamin Major)*, III 6, in *Richard of St. Victor: The Twelve Patriarchs, The Mystical Ark, Book Three of The Trinity,* translation and introduction by Grover A. Zinn, preface by Jean Châtillon (New York, Ramsey, Toronto: Paulist Press, 1997), 231-232.

18. Cf. LMj III 4, infra, 544 a.

19. Bonaventure, *Journey*, 2.

20. Bonaventure, *Journey*, 2.

21. Cf. Bonaventure, *Collationes in Hexaëmeron* XXII 23: *illa apparitio Seraph . . . quae fuit expressiva et impressa* [that apparition of the Seraph . . . that was expressed and impressed]; LMj XIII 10.

22. As noted in the text, the source of this mandate is obscure. It cannot be found in either the *Constitutions of Narbonne* nor in its *Definitiones*. Golubovich notes that the *Ceremoniale ordinis minorum vetutissimum* or *Ordinationes divini officii* issued in 1254 during the generalate of John of Parma contains this phrase: *Item ordinetur de legenda beati Francisci, ut de omnibus una bona compiletur* [Likewise it is ordained concerning the legend of blessed Francis, that one good one be compiled from all the others]. Golubovich and, later, Desbonnets maintained that the decision referred to the composition of LMn because of difficulties in reconciling the liturgical texts with the data provided by later texts. Michael Bihl, on the other hand, was convinced that the decree was appended to the *Ceremoniale* at a later date and, in reality, was directed at the composition of LMj. Cf. *Ceremoniale ordinis minorum vetutissimum* seu *"Ordinationes divini officii" sub Ioanne de Parma ministro generali emanatae an. 1254,* a cura di G. Golubovich, in AFH 3 (1910): 76.

23. In LMj Bonaventure intersperses thirty-five of the miracles described in 3C. Bonaventure adds five new episodes to his own *Treatise on the Miracles*, the second part of LMj.

24. Bonaventure, *Breviloquium* V 1:1 (V 222): "Grace is a gift that cleanses, enlightens, and perfects the soul; that vivifies, reforms, and strengthens it; that lifts it up, makes it like to God, and unites it with Him, thus rendering it acceptable to Him."

25. Bonaventure, *Commentary of Luke's Gospel* XIII 21: 47 (VII 349). Bonaventure develops this concept of the "hierarchical man" in his Prologue of his *De Triplici Via:* "This threefold understanding, moreover, corresponds to a threefold hierarchical activity, which is purgative, illuminative, and perfective. Purgation, in fact, leads to peace, illumination to truth, perfection to love. Once it has perfectly mastered these [activities], the soul becomes blessed and, as it behaves in these ways, grows in merit. The entire knowledge of Sacred Scripture as well, the reward of eternal life depends upon knowing these three activities." Cf. Also, *Itinrarium* IV 4-8; *Collationes in Hexaëmeron* XXII.

26. Cf. McGinn, *Flowering* 78-87.

27. Cf. *Questiones Disputatae de Perfectione Evangelica,* q. I, concl. (V 123); *Commentarius in Libros Sententiarum* I., dist. XLIV, a.1, q.3, ad 2 (I, 786).

28. See K. Foster, *"Liber Vitae* bei Bonaventura: Ein begriffsgeschichtlicher Aufriss," *Theologie in Geschichte und Gegenwart. Michael Schmaus, zum 60. Geburtstag dargebracht* (Munchen, 1957); W. Rauch, *Das Buch Gottes: Eine systematische Untersuching des Buchbegreffes bei Bonaventura* (Munchen: Hueber, 1961); Grover A. Zinn, Jr., "Book and Word. The Victorine Background of Bonaventure's Use of Symbols," *S. Bonaventura 1274-1974* (Sta. Maria degli Angeli: Tipografia Porziuncula, 1973): 143-169.

29. Cf. 2Srm, infra, 730. Cf. Noel Muscat, *The Life of Saint Francis in Light of Saint Bonaventure's Theology of the Verbum Crucifixum,* (Floriana, Malta: Edizzjoni Tau, 1989); Zachary Hayes, "The Theological Images of Saint Francis of Assisi in the Sermons of St. Bonaventure," *Bonaventuriana: Miscellanea in onore di Jacques Guy Bougerol, ofm,* edited by Francisco de Asis Chavero Blanco,. 2 Vols. (Rome: Edizioni Antonianum, 1288): 1:323-45

30. Cf. Edwin Panofsky, *Gothic Architecture and Scholasticism,* Wimmer Lecture, 1948 (Latrobe, PA: The Archabbey Press, 1951).

31. "Praefatio" in AF X, LXXIV. On the development of hagiographic texts, portable breviaries, and travel, see: Eric Palazzo, *A History of Liturgical Books from the Beginning to the Thirteenth Century,* trans. Madeleine Beaumont (Collegeville, Minnesota: The Liturgical Press, 1998): 156-158 and 169-172.

32. Stanislao da Campagnola, "La *Legenda maior* e la *Legenda minor sancti Francisco di Bonaventura da Bagnoregio"* in *Fontes Franciscani: Introduzioni critiche* (S. Maria degli Angeli: Edizioni Porziuncola, 1997) 64-65.

33. On this theme, see: Dieter Blume, *Wandmalerei als Ordenspropaganda. Bildprogramme im Chorbereich franziskanischer Konvente Italiens bis zur Mitte des 14. Jahrhunderts* (Worms: Werner'sche V.-G, 1983).

34. Franciscan churches offered a unique integration of theology, art, architecture, and social awareness to the medieval worshiper, see: Gennaro Bove, "Luogo" in *Dizionario Francescano* (Padua: Edizioni Messaggero, 1983) 914-918. Light, as the privileged metaphor for God's grace, was a theological concept germane to this architectronic-artistic synthesis. On light in Bonaventure's writings, see: Emma Thérèse Healy, *On the Reduction of the Acts to Theology* (St. Bonaventure, N.Y: The Franciscan Institute, 1955) 45-110; and with reference to Gothic architecture, see: Remigus Boving, *Bonaventura und die französische Hochgotik* (Wel/Westfallen: Franziskus Drukerei, 1930) 85-96.

35. On the theological significance of divine condescension, see: Alexander Gerken, Theologie des Wortes (Düsseldor: Patmos Verlag, 1963) 328-329 and Zachary Hayes, *The Hidden Center: Spirituality and Speculative Christology in St. Bonaventure* (Ramsey, N.J.: Paulist Press, 1981): 136-137. On the image of the Crucified in Franciscan art and architecture, see: Pasquale Magro, "Il Cristo crocifisso dei minori" in *Città di Vita*, 35 (1980): 17-29.

36. The representation of Francis of Assisi in early Franciscan writings and art is delineated in Ruth Wolff, *Der heilige Franziskus in Schriften und Bildern des 13. Jahrhunderts* (Berlin: Gebr. Mann Verlag, 1996). On the relationship between the Giotto cycle in the Upper Basilica of Saint Francis and *The Minor Life of Saint Francis*, see: 224-225; 282.

37. Jacques Guy Bougerol, *Francesco e Bonaventura: La Legenda Major* (Vicenza: Edizioni L.I.E.F., 1984) 109.

38. Stanislao da Campagnola, "La *Legenda maior* e la *Legenda minor sancti Francisco di Bonaventura da Bagnoregio*" in *Fontes Franciscani: Introduzioni critiche*, 62-63.

39. Jacques Guy Bougerol, *Francesco e Bonaventura: La Legenda Major*, 109.

40. On prayer in Bonaventure's theology, see: Timothy Johnson, *Iste Pauper Clamavit: Bonaventure's Mendicant Theology of Prayer* (Frankfurt am Main: Peter Lang Verlag, 1990); especially 137-148 in regard to unceasing prayer and the Liturgy of the Hours.

41. Michael Bihl, "Praefatio," AFH X, lxxii.

42. Cf. *Miscellanea Franciscana* 72 (1972): 247. See discussion FA:ED I 18.

43. Cf. Monti, *Writings* 75.

44. Monti, *Writings* 29.

45. Arnald of Sarrant, *De cognatione S. Francisci*, in F. M. Delorme, "Pages Inédites sur S. François, Écrites vers 1365 par Arnaud de Sarrant Min. Prov. d'Aquitaine," *Miscellanea Franciscana* 126.

46. Bonaventure, *Journey* VII.

47. Cf. 3Srm, infra, 731.

The Morning Sermon on Saint Francis
Preached at Paris, October 4, 1255

Scholars have traditionally considered this sermon coming not earlier than 1269.[a] However, there are no parallels with the *Major Legend* and there is no evidence in the sermon that Saint Bonaventure was acquainted with the papal document of Pope Alexander IV on the stigmata, *Benigna operatio,* published on October 19, 1255.[b] Rather than Gerard of Abbeville's attack on the mendicant way of life, this sermon is concerned especially in its first part to refute the onslaught of William of Saint Amour, made in 1255. The sermon is to be dated, therefore, October 4, 1255.[c]

Mt 11:29 *Learn from me, for I am meek and humble of heart.*

These words from Saint Matthew's Gospel were spoken by the greatest follower of Christ, Saint Francis, and they are taken from the gospel which is read on his feast day. But whether on the lips of Christ or Saint Francis, they are a short and succinct saying,[d] which in concise and plain terms expresses the sum total of gospel perfection. The saying is concise, so that nobody can claim ignorance of it because of scarcity of books, and plain, so that nobody may be excused from understanding it through lack of schooling. Mass I

The saying has two parts: a preliminary statement and a word of instruction. The first is to encourage the hearers, the second to inspire them. To encourage us he says: *Learn from me,* and to inspire us he adds: *for I am meek and humble of heart.* In other words, be meek and humble like me.

---

a. Sophronius Clasen, *Franziskus Engel des Sechsten Siegels. Sein Leben nach den Schriften des heligen Bonaventura* (Werl/West, 1962), 160.

b. Cf. infra 779-781.

c. Ignatius C. Brady, "The Authenticity of Two Sermons of Saint Bonaventure," *Franciscan Studies* 28 (1968), 12; "The Writings of Saint Bonaventure Regarding the Franciscan Order," *San Bonaventura Maestro di vita francescana e di sapienza cristiana.* Atti del Congresso Internazionale per il VII Centenario di San Bonaventura I (Roma, 1976), 95; "Saint Bonaventure's Sermons on Saint Francis," *Franziskanische Studien* 58 (1976), 139-140.

d. The Latin reads: "*est verbum abbreviaturn et consummatum,*" *Opera Omnia* IX, 590. The Vulgate text of Romans 9:28: "*Verbum enim consummans, et abbrevians in aequitate, quia verbum breviatum faciet Dominus super terram* [For completing the word, and cutting it short in justice, the Lord made his word short while on earth]."

Learn from me . . .

The words *Learn from me* have two meanings, both of which can give encouragement: Take me as your model of discipleship and embrace my teaching. Both can be applied to Saint Francis, the first on account of the life he led as a result of his conversion, the second because he attained perfection. The former made him a true disciple, and the latter an excellent teacher.

Because of the life he embraced at his conversion, Saint Francis can say: *Learn from me,* that is, take me as your model of discipleship, for I am a true disciple. The essence of true discipleship of Jesus Christ, which was singularly realized and shone in Saint Francis, consists first of all in separating oneself from the company of evil people, as Proverbs says: *A friend of fools shall become like them.* This is Prv 13:20
the meaning of those words about Christ that *privately to his own disci-* Mk 4:34
ples he explained everything where "privately" signifies well removed from wicked people and away from the crowds. This shows that the disciple of Christ must keep away from evil and divisive company.

Realizing this, Saint Francis, under God's inspiration, immediately left the company of the young people who had been his com-
1C 5; LJS 3 rades in sin, for it was evil company. He also stopped associating with merchants, which was worldly company, and went off alone to a secluded place, knowing that *Christ explained everything to his own disciples privately.* That is what anyone must do who desires to be a perfect disciple of Christ: he must withdraw from evil and worldly company. At the least one must withdraw from evil company, which the call to perfection demands, even if one has no desire to relinquish worldly company. We are told of the Israelites: *They mingled with the nations* Ps 106:35-36
and learned to do as they did. They served their idols which became a snare to them. "The nations" in this text refer to those who lead an ungodly life and "to mingle with them" means to associate with them in such a way as of necessity to copy their evil ways. The Book of Sirach tells us: *Whoever touches pitch will be defiled and whoever associates with a proud* Sir 13:1
man will become like him. Proverbs advises us: *Make no friendship with a* Prv 22:24-25
man given to anger, nor go with a wrathful man, lest you learn his ways and entangle yourself in a snare; and the Psalmist warns us: *With the perverse* Ps 17:26
you will be perverted.

Second, it is essential for true discipleship to free oneself from useless cares in the affairs of life. Anyone who is anxious about useless things cannot give attention to those that are profitable. As Saint Matthew's Gospel says: *the cares of the world and the delight in riches* Mt 18:22
choke the word and it proves unfruitful. Thus it is recorded by Saint Luke: *Whoever of you does not renounce all that he has cannot be my disciple.* The Lk 14:33

Lord says this not because there is sin in having possessions, but because it is sinful to be anxiously concerned about them. In any case, it is impossible, or at least very difficult, to have great possessions without being preoccupied with them. And so the Lord stipulates: *Whoever of you does not renounce all that he has cannot be my disciple.*

Taking this to heart, Saint Francis on hearing God's voice at once gave everything away to the extent that he did not even keep back a stitch to cover his nakedness. As in his heart he despised all possessions, so outwardly he gave away everything he had. This is what
Mt 19:21 anyone must do who desires to be a perfect disciple of Christ: *he must go, sell everything he has and give to the poor.* If one does not have the will to do that, one must at least keep oneself from the cares, anxieties, and vanities that go with possessions; otherwise, one will be a disci-
Mt 6:24 ple, not of Christ, but of the devil. It is impossible to serve God and mammon at the same time. As it says in the First Epistle to Timothy:
1 Tm 6:9 *Those who desire to be rich fall into temptation, into many senseless and hurtful desires that plunge men into ruin and destruction.* Not all learn the
Ez 19:3 teaching of Christ; some learn to catch prey as Ezechiel has it: *She brought up one of her whelps; he became a young lion, and he learned to catch prey; he devoured men.*

Third, the true disciple must rid himself of inordinate attach-
1 Cor 2:14 ments to his loved ones. As Saint Paul teaches, the sensual or *unspiritual man does not receive the gifts of the Spirit of God,* and Saint Luke
Lk 14:26 records: *If anyone comes to me and does not hate his own father and mother and wife and brothers and sisters, yes, and even his own life, he cannot be my disciple.* The Lord does not forbid us to love our father and mother, for the Decalogue commands that we honor them; what he does forbid is to be inordinately attached to our parents, because inordinate attachment rejects the teaching of Christ.

Understanding this, Saint Francis hated his father and mother, and having broken the ties of natural attachment, he abandoned them completely. Anyone who desires to attain perfect discipleship
Ps 45:10 of Christ must *forget his father's house* and hate *his own life,* that is, his
Jer 12:7 natural affections, in order to imitate Christ who gave *his dear soul into the hands of her enemies.* But if a man does not wish to hate or sacrifice natural affections for his parents altogether, he must at least sacrifice them in regard to women; otherwise, he will not be able to attain
2 Tm 3:6-7 knowledge of the truth. As Saint Paul writes to Timothy: *For among them are those who make their way into households and capture weak women, burdened with sins and swayed by various impulses who will listen to anybody and can never arrive at a knowledge of the truth.*

Fourth, the true disciple of Christ must purify his heart of all that militates against the practice of virtue. As the Book of Wisdom says:

Wisdom will not enter a deceitful soul, nor dwell in a body enslaved to sin and Wis 1:4
as Isaiah admonishes: *Cease to do evil, learn to do good.* In other words, Is 1:16
you will not be able to learn holiness from Christ unless you have resolved to eradicate its opposite, sinfulness, just as knowledge cannot be acquired unless satisfaction with its opposite, ignorance, has been uprooted.

Acknowledging this, Saint Francis strove with constant sighs of sorrow to root out vice and sin totally from the field of his heart. Nor did he cease to lament up to the moment when he was found worthy
to hear from God: *Your sins are forgiven.* In the same way, anyone who Lk 7:48
desires to be a perfect disciple of Christ, must *every night drench his* Ps 6:7
couch with weeping, just as Saint Francis did. If one cannot follow that advice which leads to perfection, then one must at least cease to do evil if one wishes to become Christ's disciple. Therefore, anyone who does not resolve to abandon his evil ways cannot learn virtue, as Jeremiah reflects: *Can the Ethiopian change his skin or the leopard his spots?* Jer 13:23
Then also you can do good who are accustomed to do evil. Here the Prophet is addressing those who from long habit have become stubborn in their malice so that it is well nigh impossible to root it out. They cannot learn virtue because they learned evil habits well enough in their youth.

Saint Francis, then, can rightly say: *Learn from me,* that is, take me as your model of discipleship, for I am a true disciple of Christ.

Likewise he can say to us *Learn from me* in the second sense, namely, embrace my teaching, because by being a true disciple, he became an authentic teacher. There are four grounds on which he can address these words to us.

First of all, he taught what he himself had learned without error
because of the truth of God's revelation. As Scripture tells us: *God is* Rom 3:4
true, and every man a liar. Therefore, the teaching which anyone receives from revelation cannot be other than true. It is from having learned in this way that Saint Paul commends his teaching to the
Galatians: *For I would have you know, brethren, that the gospel which was* Gal 1:11-12
preached by me is not man's gospel. For I did not receive it from man, nor was I taught it, but it came through a revelation of Jesus Christ.

Saint Francis learned his teaching in the same way. Indeed, one may well wonder at his teaching. How was he able to teach others what no human had taught him? Did he come by this knowledge of himself? Be assured he did not. The evidence of that is found in the
1C 73; LJS 58 account of his life. When he was instructed by another human or had to prepare something himself, he had absolutely nothing to say. In that, however, he is more to be praised and wondered at than imitated. Hence it is not without reason that his sons attend the schools.

To arrive at knowledge without a human teacher is not for everyone, but the privilege of a few. Though the Lord himself chose to teach Saint Paul and Saint Francis, it is his will that their disciples be taught by human teachers.

Second, he taught what he had learned without guile due to his fervent love, which directs the whole heart to grasp what is being taught. Speaking of wisdom Solomon glories that he himself learned
Wis 7:13 in this way: *I learned without guile and impart without grudging; I do not hide her wealth.* That is to say, as ardent love brought me to learn without guile, so it moves me to share without jealousy or grudging envy what I have learned.

That is precisely how Saint Francis learned and taught. He so
Wis 7:8-9; Sg 8:7 loved what he learned that he *accounted wealth as nothing in comparison with that; gold as but little sand and silver as clay; he gave up all the wealth of his house and scorned it as nothing.* He learned with such diligence that
Wis 1:1 he became the teacher of many disciples whom he taught to *think of the Lord with uprightness and seek him with sincerity of heart, because he is found by those who do not put him to the test, and manifests himself to those who do not distrust him.* He manifested himself to Saint Francis who, because he had learned without guile, shared what he had learned without envy.

Third, he taught what he had learned without forgetting it, be-
Jas 1:25 cause he put it into practice *being no hearer that forgets but a doer that acts,* and because of that he was an excellent teacher. On observing
Mt 5:19 the commandments Saint Matthew records: *He who does them and teaches them shall be called great in the kingdom of heaven.* Sirach praises
Sir 34:9 this method of learning when he says: *A man who has much experience knows many things,* which he will think on with composure and without blame; *and one who has learned many things will speak with understanding,* because he did not acquire his knowledge by reflecting in general terms on a limited number of truths, but by individual experience over a wide range of life.

That is how Saint Francis learned, but by experiencing sufferings not joys. We can say of him what Saint Paul says of his own Teacher:
Heb 5:8 *He learned obedience through what he suffered.* At the outset of his conversion Saint Francis experienced derision, beatings, fetters, imprisonment, destitution, nakedness, and adversity. Like Saint Paul he
Phil 4:11 learned to be content in his sufferings: *For I have learned, in whatever state I am, to be content. I know how to be abased and I know how to abound; in any and all circumstances I have learned the secret of facing plenty and hunger, abundance and want.* And because the teaching of a true disciple is recognized by his patience, Saint Francis is to be praised and imitated in his teaching and we should learn from him.

Fourth, he taught what he had learned without doubting because of the trustworthy signs he was given. He knew by those signs with absolute certitude that the teaching he had learned was saving truth. Therefore, he held to it firmly as Saint Paul advised Timothy: *But as for you continue in what you have learned and have firmly believed, knowing from whom you learned it.* Saint Paul exhorted Timothy to remain steadfast in what he had learned because he knew and was certain through signs and miracles that the teaching he had learned was for salvation. 2 Tm 3:14, 39; Mk 16:20

In the same way Saint Francis was established in what he had learned and so like the Apostles he *went forth and preached everywhere, while the Lord worked with him and confirmed the message by the signs that attended it.* Mk 16:20

Moreover, it pleased the Lord to endorse and confirm the teaching and *Rule* of Saint Francis, not only by miraculous signs, but also by the marks of his own stigmata, so that no true believer could possibly call them into question on external or internal evidence.[a] It pleased God in his goodness to affix his own seal to the *Rule* and teaching of Saint Francis, for Saint Francis would never have dared to teach or write down other than what he received from the Lord. As he himself testifies, God revealed to him the entire *Rule*. As it is the Pope's practice to endorse documents with his seal, so Christ, having recognized the teaching of Saint Francis as his own, affixed the seal of his stigmata to his body, and thereby irrevocably confirmed his teaching. Test 14

His teaching could not have had its lasting character, in the eyes of others, from Saint Francis himself, for he was an uneducated merchant and no learned doctor. Therefore, it was the Lord's good pleasure to confirm it by manifest signs in the form of an awe-inspiring seal from on high, so that none of the learned could dare despise his teaching and *Rule* as only the efforts of an uneducated man. This shows us clearly how we ought to marvel at the depth of God's judgments, which Christ indicates at the beginning of today's Gospel when he says: *I thank you, Father, Lord of heaven and earth, that you have hidden these things from the wise and understanding and revealed them to little ones.* Mt 11:25

Consequently, anyone who doubts that the doctrine and *Rule* of Saint Francis are a most perfect way to reach eternal life, when these have been confirmed by such great signs, must be exceedingly hard of heart. And particularly so, when it is abundantly evident from the

a. Bonaventure is using an argument from Aristotle, one that he seems to have been taken from Boethius's translation of Aristotle's *Organon*, cf. *In Librum Aristotelis de Interpretatione, edtio secunda, seu majora commentaria, liber primus* (PL 64, 422), and in *I Sent.*, d. viii, p. I, a.viii, q. 2, (I, 155).

great number of witnesses, their authority, and their holiness, that God wondrously imprinted these signs on his body.

The great number of witnesses furnishes definite assurance. Many trustworthy lay people actually saw the stigmata of Saint Francis and more than a hundred clerics confirmed it by their own
Mt 18:16 testimony. And if *every word is confirmed by the evidence of two or three witnesses,* how much more by the evidence of a hundred?

The authority of the witnesses strengthens the minds of believers with certainty. The fact of the stigmata was established and confirmed by the Roman Curia which possesses the highest authority on earth. Should any contradict this, they are by this same authority to be cut off from the communion of the faithful, as they have estranged themselves from the faith.

The holiness of the witnesses totally dispels all doubt. His companions are men of outstanding holiness, upright life, and manifest virtue. They affirm, not in timid defense, but unhesitatingly by steadfast oath, that they themselves saw those wonderful signs with their own eyes and touched them with their own hands.

The whole world, therefore, ought to give thanks to the Most High Creator for this sublime gift, that by the stigmata imprinted on Saint Francis, he deigned not only to reveal the way of truth, but to establish it in a wondrous way and for readily intelligible reasons.

It happened in a wondrous way indeed when considered in terms of natural causes. The stigmata were imprinted in a way outside usual experience, contrary to nature's laws and above human powers. They were outside usual experience, for whoever heard of such precious gems appearing on a human body? They were also contrary to nature's laws, for there was a wound in his side from which his holy blood flowed, yet without applying bandages to it, the saint of God went on living and continued untiringly in his works; and they were above human powers: for his hands had no open wounds nor were they injured, which would have been the case had iron or wooden instruments been used. On the contrary, the nails came up out of the flesh, the heads on one side and the points bent over on the other, quite above the surface of the skin and distinct from the rest of the flesh of his hands and feet. It was so remarkable that no believer could possibly doubt that these signs were imprinted other than by an unparalleled miracle.

If we raise our minds a little and consider the stigmata in terms of supernatural causes, we discover they were imprinted for readily understandable reasons. This miracle was made necessary under the law of divine providence, for the needs of the church in this final age and because of Saint Francis's eminent holiness.

The law of divine providence required it because God willed to make this cloth merchant a fisher of men, and the leader of those who imitate Christ perfectly. Therefore, he handed over to him his own ensign, namely, the marks of the Crucified Lord.

Further, it was made necessary by the needs of the church in these last times. At the beginning of the Church unbelief held sway; as it developed heresy reigned and at the end wickedness will prevail, for then *most men's love will grow cold.* So at the beginning of the church, Mt 24:12 the Lord granted powerful miracles to drive out idolatry. Later on he endowed learned men with proofs of wisdom to root out heresy. In these latter times, he bestowed the signs of goodness and mercy on Saint Francis to enkindle love, and what are the signs of consummate love except the marks of the passion which God chose to endure for us out of measureless love?

Third, this miracle was made necessary because of Saint Francis's eminent holiness which found expression in his most fervent love of the Crucified Lord. For the sake of that love he so weakened his eyes by tears of compassion that he lost his sight. Hugh of Saint Victor tells us: "Such is the power of love, that it transforms the lover into the Beloved."[a] Love of the Crucified Lord was supremely and gloriously aflame in his heart, and so the Crucified himself, in the form of the Seraph, an angelic spirit burning with the fire of love, appeared before his saintly eyes and imprinted the sacred stigmata on his body.

We should not consider this impossible to believe or less than reasonable, for it is recorded that something similar happened to Saint Ignatius of Antioch.[b] When he was ordered by the tyrant to deny Christ, he replied that Christ could not be taken from his lips. Then the tyrant threatened that he would cut off his head and so remove Christ from his lips. Saint Ignatius answered that though Christ might be taken from his lips, he could never be removed from his heart. Then consumed with fury to prove the Saint of God wrong, the tyrant had his head cut off and ordered his heart to be torn from his body. When it was done his heart was found to have written on it the name of Jesus Christ in gold letters. How fitting that was, for he had

a. *Ea vis amoris est, ut talem esse necesse sit, quae illus est quod amas, et qui per affectum conjungeris, in ipsius similitudinem ipsa quodammodo dilectionis societate transformaris* [This is the force of love, that it is necessary for you to be such as the one you cherish. Somehow by the association of love you are transformed to the likeness of the very one to whom you are joined by affection]. Hugh of St. Victor, *De arrha animae*, PL 176, 954; *Soliloquy on the Earnest Money of the Soul*, translated with introduction by Kevin Herbert (Marquette: Marquette University Press, 1956), 16.

b. Ignatius of Antioch (+c. 110) was martyred in Rome during the reign of Trajan. According to an ancient account of his death, the *Martyrium Ignatii*, the "tyrant" mentioned by Bonaventure is Trajan himself. Cf. PG V 37-473. B. Mombritius, *Sanctuarium seu vitae sanctorum* (Paris, 1910), 10:45, 46-53; *Acta Sanctorum*, die 1 Feb, Commentarium praevius (Antwerp, 1658), 14.

Sg 8:6 *set* Christ *as a seal upon his heart, as a seal upon his arm.* Because Saint
Sg 8:6 Francis *set* Christ crucified *as a seal upon his arm,* the precious gems of the stigmata of Jesus Christ appeared visibly on his body. This took place for understandable reasons by the glorious power of God.

Mt 20:15 Let no one begrudge God's generosity, but let everyone listen to and learn the teaching of Christ, indeed, of Saint Francis, that good teacher who taught others what he had learned without error, without guile, without forgetfulness, and without doubting. Saint Francis, therefore, can rightly say: *Learn from me,* to encourage others, and equally, *for I am meek and humble of heart,* to inspire them.

The Evening Sermon on Saint Francis
Preached at Paris, October 4, 1255

Learn from me, that is, be meek and humble after my example. A person is meek by loving his brothers, humble by loving lowliness or "minority." To be meek is to be a brother to everybody; to be humble is to be less than everybody. Therefore, to be meek and humble of heart is to be a true lesser brother. Saint Francis can say to us: Learn from me to be meek and humble, that is, to be Lesser Brothers.[a] Although it is not for everyone to take the habit and profess the *Rule* of the Lesser Brothers, it is necessary for everyone who wants to be saved to be a lesser brother in the sense of being meek and humble. As the Lord himself teaches: *Unless you turn and become like children, you will never enter the kingdom of heaven.* Mt 18:3

As the easier of the two, he mentions meekness first. While it is no effort for a soul that is well-disposed, it is nevertheless both necessary and profitable to the spiritual life: to the pursuit of truth for beginners, in the practice of virtue for the advanced, to make right judgments by those in authority, and to attain eternal life by those tending toward it. Meekness, in fact, pertains to every form and state of life.

First, then, meekness is necessary to the pursuit of truth both in those learning and those who teach. Those learning have to be meek in order to grasp the truth, as Sirach says: *Be meek to hear the word, that you may understand.* As an image is reflected only in peaceful waters, so the word of doctrine is received only by meek minds. Also those who teach have to be meek because "anger hinders the mind from perceiving the truth."[b] As the *Gloss* on Matthew 5:4 explains: "He is meek whom neither anger nor spitefulness, harshness nor bitterness, disturbs."[c] Saint Paul writes to Timothy: *The Lord's servant must not be quarrelsome but kindly to everyone, an apt teacher, forbearing, correcting his opponents with gentleness.* How much more gently ought he to listen to those who are seeking the truth. Sir 5:13 2 Tm 2:24

---

a. The English rendering cannot have the impact of the Latin in which Bonaventure plays with words: *unde esse mitem, hoc est esse omnium fratrem; esse humilem, hoc est esse omnibus minorem: esse ergo mitem et humilem corde, hoc est esse vere fratrem minorem; discite igitur a me esse mites et humiles, hoc est esse fratres minores,* (IX, 594).

b. *Catonis disticha* II, 4 in *The Distichs of Cato: A Famous Medieval Textbook,* University of Wisconsin Studies in the Social Sciences, vol. 7, translated by Wayland Chase (Madison: University of Wisconsin Press, 1922).

c. *Glossa ordinaria* in Mt 5:4 in *Biblia sacra cum glossa ordinaria . . . et Postilia Nicolai Lirani . . .* vol. v (Antwerp, 1634), f. 1gr.

Second, meekness is necessary for the inward and outward practice of virtue so that one may remain serene in conscience and be well pleasing in the judgment and minds of one's neighbors. Sirach urges
Sir 10:31 us to acquire interior meekness: *My son, keep your soul in meekness and give it honor according to its desert.* To keep one's soul in meekness and give it honor according to its desert is to let it not be troubled except on account of sin. He exhorts us to outward meekness with the
Sir 3:19 words: *My son, perform your tasks in meekness, then you will be loved by those whom God accepts.* Everybody loves a meek man because he epitomizes natural human goodness and is naturally blessed with a fondness for company.

Third, meekness is necessary to make right judgments, for without it others are not corrected, but destroyed. Saint Paul asks the Co-
1 Cor 4:21 rinthians: *What do you wish? Shall I come to you with a rod, or with love in a spirit of gentleness?* That is to say: I will come with both, because there can be no truly equitable judgment if meekness is not coupled with the rod and *vice versa.* Without the rod, meekness is a defect in a
1 Sm 2:22-25; Zep 2:3 prelate, as it was in Eli. Zephaniah tells us: *Seek the Lord all you meek of the earth, you that have wrought his judgment.* Likewise, the rod without
Ps 2:3 meekness destroys, it brings no correction. The Psalmist says: *For mildness is come upon us and we shall be corrected.* A good prelate does not rage against a subject as if he were an enemy, but corrects him as a
Sir 4:35 friend and companion. As Sirach advises: *Do not be like a lion in your home, terrifying the members of your household, and oppressing those under you.*

Finally, meekness is necessary to attain eternal life. The Gospel
Mt 5:5 tells us: *Blessed are the meek for they shall inherit the earth,* and the Psalm
Ps 37:11 says: *the meek shall possess the land and shall delight in abundance of peace.* Because they lived on this earth in goodness and peace even when unjustly oppressed by harsh people, by God's just judgments *the meek*
Ps 27:13 *shall inherit the land,* not this earthly land, but *the land of the living,* and the harsh will be rejected. The land of the living will be assigned and awarded to them in the future judgment, just as the kingdom of heaven will be awarded to the poor who, having set their hearts on heavenly treasures, willingly give up earthly possessions. We read in
Is 11:4 Isaiah: *With righteousness he shall judge the poor,* which means God will grant them the kingdom of heaven; the text continues: *and decide with equity for the meek of the earth,* which is to say, he will give them the land of the living.

We ought to learn meekness, which is utterly necessary, from Saint Francis. He cherished an extraordinary meekness not only toward other people, but also toward dumb animals. He called all animals by the name "brother" and we read in the account of his life

that even wild animals came running to him as their friend and com-
1C 58; LJS 37 panion. And so what is said of Moses in the Book of Numbers, may
well be sung in praise of him: *The man Moses was very meek, more than* Num 12:3
all men that were on the face of the earth. Like another Moses, Saint Francis can say: *Learn from me for I am meek of heart.*

He can also say to us: *Learn from me for I am humble of heart.* Learn,
that is, to have true, not counterfeit, humility as hypocrites cun-
ningly humble themselves. Of these Sirach says: *There is one who hum-* Sir 19:23
bles himself wickedly and inwardly he is full of deceit, and Saint Paul writes
to the Colossians: *Let no one disqualify you, insisting on self-abasement* Col 2:18
*and worship of angels, taking his stand on visions, puffed up without reason
by his sensuous mind.* He is not encouraging us to that sort of humility,
but to humility of heart on which Saint Bernard writes: "The truly
humble man wants to be considered despicable rather than to be
proclaimed a humble man."[a]

Saint Francis possessed this humility supremely. He loved and Wis 8:2
sought it, from the origin of his religious life until his death. For this
he left the world, ordered that he be dragged naked through a city,
ministered to lepers, told his own sins while preaching and even
commanded others to pour scorn on him. We ought to learn this virtue especially from him.

That we may desire it let us look at the fruits which make it so attractive, the manner in which it is acquired and the means by which
it is maintained.

The fruits of humility are manifold. First, it calms the anger of
God, while moving him to suspend judgment due to guilt. This is
well exemplified in the Book of Kings where the Lord says to Elijah:
Have you seen how Ahab has humbled himself before me? Because he has 1 Kg 21:29
humbled himself before me, I will not bring the evil in his days. What extraordinary power humility has, that it can contain the hand of God!
The Psalmist tells us: *The Lord is the keeper of little ones: I was humbled,* Ps 114:6
and he delivered me, and Saint James says: *God opposes the proud, but gives* Jas 4:6
grace to the humble. He protects and guards them. *The haughty he knows
from afar, but the lowly he* does not cease to regard from near at hand,
nor can he despise them, as the Psalmist says: *The sacrifice acceptable to* Ps 50:19
*God is a broken spirit; a contrite and humbled heart, O God, you will not de-
spise.*

The second fruit of humility is that it finds grace. Just as anyone
looking for water must dig down into the earth, so anyone longing to

a. Bernard of Clairvaux, Sermon 16:10, *On the Song of Songs* I, The Works of Bernard of Clairvaux, vol. II, translated by Kilian Walsh and introduction by M. Corneille Halflants (Spencer, MA: Cistercian Publications, 1971), 121.

Jn 4:10 find *living water* has to dig a well of humility inside himself. As Sirach
Sir 3:20; Jas 4:6 says: *The greater you are, the more you must humble yourself and you will
find grace before God.* It was on account of her humility that the Blessed
Lk 1:30 Virgin Mary *found grace with God,* as she herself testifies in Saint
Lk 1:48 Luke's Gospel: *He has regarded the low estate of his handmaiden.* That is
hardly to be wondered at because humility prepares a dwelling place for love and clears the mind of vanity. That is why Saint Augustine writes: "The more we rid ourselves of the canker of pride, so much the more are we filled with love."[a] As water flows into valleys, so the grace of the Holy Spirit comes down on the humble; or again, the higher water rises, the further it descends, so it is with prayer coming from a humble heart. It rises up to God and resounds in his ears to
Sir 35:17 implore his grace. Thus Sirach tells us: *The prayer of the humble pierces
the clouds and he will not be consoled until it reaches the Lord,* and the
Ps 145:19 Psalmist says that the Lord *fulfills the desire of all who fear him, he also
hears their cry and saves them.*

The third fruit of humility is that it brings righteousness to perfec-
Mt 3:15 tion. The Lord said to John the Baptist: *Let it be so now; for thus it is fit-
ting for us to fulfill all righteousness,* "that is," according to the *Gloss* on this text, "perfect humility, which is perfect righteousness."[b] Total righteousness consists in perfect humility, and humility, the greatest
Prv 15:5 virtue, in total righteousness, as we read in Proverbs: *In total righ-
teousness there is the greatest virtue.* Perfect humility is the greatest virtue both because it makes us perfect in God's sight and because by it uniquely God is revered and honored to the utmost, as Sirach says:
Sir 3:20 *For great is the might of the Lord: he is glorified by the humble* alone. Only
the humble revere God, for the rest seek to glorify themselves, not God. Thus, if all our righteousness and the sum total of the Christian religion consist in honoring God, then it is obvious that total righteousness lies in humility and the greatest virtue in total righteousness. To Dioscorus, seeking to know the summit of gospel perfection, Saint Augustine replied in a way similar to a certain philosopher when asked what should be taught in rhetoric. When asked the first time, he replied: "eloquence;" the second time, again he replied: "eloquence," and the same the third time. Saint Augustine answered likewise: "If you were to ask me what is the summit of gospel perfection, I would answer: humility. Should you ask me a second and

a. Augustine, *De Trinitate,* VIII, c. 8, n. 12, *Corpus Christianorum, Series Latina* (Collected Works of Christian Writers, Latin Series) (hereafter CCSL) 50, 287; *The Trinity,* translated with introduction and notes by Edmund Hill, edited by John Rotelle (Brooklyn: New City Press, 1991), 253.

b. *Glossa ordinaria* in Mt 3:15, in *Bibl. sac. cure glossa Lirani* v, f. 15r.

third time, I would still answer: humility."[a] When one of the holy fathers was asked "What is human perfection?" he replied: "Humility."[b] And the Lord himself, when asked by the disciples to increase in them the grace of faith, answered: *"When you have done all that is commanded you, say 'We are unworthy servants, we have only done what was our duty.'"* Lk 17:10

The fourth fruit of humility is that it leads to eternal glory, its last and perfect fruit. Job says of this: *He who has been humbled shall be in glory: and he who shall bow down his eyes, he shall be saved.* That is to say, through humility every evil is avoided and all good is obtained. How right it is when the text says *he shall be in glory,* for by fair recompense the more humble one is here, the higher and more sublime will be one's place in glory. The more lowly and humble a person is on earth, the closer is he to Christ who sits *in the lowest place.* And the closer one is to Christ in this world, the closer must one be to him in heaven. It is manifest that Christ is raised above all others, and it is therefore entirely proper that his servant be honored among all others, for where Christ is, there shall his servant be also. The more a person cultivates lowliness, the less is he tainted with vainglory. Therefore, as he received no reward whatever in this world, how much greater and more splendid must he appear in that true glory of heaven on which alone his heart is set and to which he is pledged unconditionally! Jb 22:29 Lk 14:19

We should embrace humility with our whole heart in order to obtain these four fruits. Though outwardly humility seems like a useless, hard old shell, inside it holds a precious kernel. And further, as the farmer sows corn seed in the ground and leaves it there to die while he waits for it to bear fruit, so ought we cheerfully to long to be despised. Saint James writes: *Let the lowly brother boast in his exaltation.* Jas 1:9

Second, let us look at how this noble virtue is acquired. There are four pathways that lead to it. The first is meditation on God. This is a road leading directly to humility for anyone who duly attends to God. We must meditate on God as the author of every good and the one who rewards us according to our deeds. As the author of all good we are obliged to call out to him: *O Lord you have wrought for us all our works,* and so to ascribe every good to him and nothing to ourselves. And that makes us humble. The First Letter of Saint Peter advises us: *Humble yourselves under the mighty hands of God,* and we should keep in mind that it is not by our power or the might of our hands that we have achieved the good that is ours, but *it is the Lord that made us and* Is 26:12 1 Pt 5:6 Dt 8:17 Ps 100:3

a. Augustine, *Epistola* 118, n. 22, PL 33, 442; *Saint Augustine: Letters*, vol. 2, The Fathers of the Church, vol. 18, translated by Wilfrid Parsons (New York: Fathers of the Church, 1953), 282.

b. Anonymous, *De vitis Patrum*, V, lib. 15, n. 77, PL 73, 966.

Dt 32:27 *not we ourselves.* This rids us of pride which trumpets: *Our hand is triumphant, the Lord has not wrought all this.*

We must also keep before our minds that God will deal with us most justly according to our deeds. God is so strictly just that he remits no punishment. On the contrary, for only one evil act of the will he cast the most noble angelic spirits out of heaven forever. Thus
Sir 7:17 Sirach advises us: *Humble yourselves greatly, for the punishment of the ungodly is fire and worms.*

The second pathway to humility is remembrance of Christ. We should call to mind that Christ was humbled even to the most horrible form of death as the price of our salvation and the pattern of our
Is 53:4 life. He was the price of our salvation as we read in Isaiah: *We esteemed him stricken, smitten by God, and afflicted.* If Christ humbled himself for our salvation, surely we ought to humble ourselves for his glory. Moreover, he humbled himself as the pattern for our life, as Saint
Jn 13:15 John records: *For I have given you an example, that you also should do as I*
Jn 13:13; Mt 10:24 *have done to you.* Therefore, because he is our *Teacher and Lord,* and *a disciple is not above his teacher nor a servant above his Lord,* and we are the servants of Christ, then we ought to be humble and self-effacing.
Phil 2:5, 8 Saint Paul exhorts us to this in Philippians: *Have this mind among yourselves which was in Christ Jesus,* and he continues: *he humbled himself and became obedient unto death, even death on a cross.* How lukewarm
Ps 131:10 is the believer who, seeing his Lord humbled and despised, lifts up his heart and occupies himself with things great and marvelous above him.

The third pathway to humility is just assessment of oneself. A person makes a just estimate of himself when he not only examines his present condition, but also has before his mind the two poles of his life, namely, where he is going and whence he came. Then he reflects on himself in the midst of his afflictions. As we read in the Prophet
Mi 6:14 Micah: *Your humiliation shall be in the midst of you.*

Bear in mind where you came from. You were rescued from the heap of the damned, created out of the dust and slime of the earth,
Jn 9:34 *you were born in utter sin,* you became sinful and now you are in exile from the glory of paradise. Thoughts such as these drive off and keep away the spirit of pride to the extent that one begins to cry out with
Dn 3:14 the three young men in the Book of Daniel: *We are brought low today in all the world because of our sins.*

Consider attentively also the end of your life, that is, where you are going. You are moving toward disintegration and decay. As Gen-
Gn 3:19 esis tells us: *You are dust, and to dust you shall return;* and as Sirach asks:
Sir 10:9 *How can he who is dust and ashes be proud?* Today you are alive, tomorrow you may be dead; healthy and strong today, sick and weak to-

morrow; today a rich man, tomorrow perhaps a beggar; wise today, possibly you will become foolish tomorrow. Who, then, could dare to be proud, surrounded by such adversity? Nobody, except perhaps the person who makes no just assessment of himself, but rivets his attention on present prosperity and says what we read in the Book of Revelation about the proud: *For you say, I am rich in natural gifts; I have* Rv 3:17 *prospered in spiritual graces; and I need nothing* of worldly goods. But examine yourself well and you will realize that *you are wretched and pitiable* for lack of natural gifts; *poor and blind* for want of spiritual graces; *and naked* in possessing nothing of this world's goods. For as Job realized: *Naked I came from my mother's womb, and naked shall I return,* and Jb 1:21 Saint Paul reminds us: *For we brought nothing into the world and we cannot take anything out of the world.* 1 Tm 6:7

The fourth pathway to humility is respect for one's neighbor. It consists in respecting one's neighbor outwardly, as Saint Peter writes: *Clothe yourselves, all of you, with humility toward one another,* and 1 Pt 5:5 this especially toward one's superiors. There is also inner respect which is found when a person reckons others better than himself. Each one ought to do this, as Saint Paul advises: *In humility count others better than yourselves.* Phil 2:3 Undoubtedly, we should all have this inner respect for others, because anyone of our neighbors is blessed with hidden or manifest graces for which we ought to count him better than ourselves. Elijah was reproached for thinking he was the only servant of the Lord left in Israel: *I will leave seven thousand in Israel, all* 1 Kgs 19:18 *the knees that have not bowed to Baal.* Each one knows his own sins better than the sins of others.

Finally, we come to consider the means by which humility is maintained and there are four. Anyone who desires to safeguard humility unfailingly must make his own the means which protect it.

First of all he must maintain a heartfelt sorrow for his sins. We read in the Book of Proverbs: *Grief in a man's heart shall bring him low.* Prv 12:25 Grief over sins deflates the puffed up spirit, and constant sorrow does not allow one word of praise which would flatter the spirit, to re-echo in the heart. This clearly is what is meant by the words in Job: *No one spoke a word to him, for they saw that his suffering was very* Jb 2:13 *great.* Intense sorrow which springs from heartfelt lament turns the attention of the soul wholly toward God, empties the soul of vanity and fills it with humility. As the Psalmist says: *I am afflicted and hum-* Ps 37:9 *bled exceedingly: I roared with the groaning of my heart.*

Secondly, he must observe silence because this protects humility. The Psalmist says: *I was dumb and was humbled and kept silence from* Ps 38:3 *good things.* Humility is safeguarded by silence, not about one's sins, but about one's virtues. For a person ought not to parade his virtues,

but his vices, as beggars are accustomed to show their afflictions in
Sir 18:21 public. As Sirach advises: *Humble yourself before you are sick and when
you have sinned make known your regret.* We do that by honest and accurate confessions of sins.

Third, he must train himself to hard work and discipline, for these
Est 14:2 protect humility. Scripture tells us that Esther *humbled her body, and
every part that she loved to adorn she covered with her tangled hair.* That is
how one ought constantly to maintain atoning humility in oneself,
Ps 34:13 as the truly penitent Psalmist says: *I humbled myself with fasting.* Consequently, anyone who desires to keep humility intact must persevere in chastising his flesh continually by fasts and vigils, prayers
and penance.

Fourth, he must learn to despise being honored. One achieves this
by striving to be considered worthless, which people generally de-
2 Sm 6:21-22 spise. This is what King David did: *I will make merry before the Lord. I
will make myself yet more contemptible than this and I will be abased in your
eyes.* The same is true of Saint Francis who had himself dragged na- 1C 17, 52; 2C 9
ked like a silly drunkard through a city, and who also took care of lepers.

And so because he left us an outstanding example of humility,
with every right he says to us: Learn from me to be not only meek but
also humble of heart, for I am most meek and humble. Therefore,
Sir 11:12-13 these words from Sirach apply to him: *There is a man who is slow and
needs help,* because of his severe penance; *who lacks strength and
abounds in poverty,* because of the extreme poverty and indigence he
embraced; *but the eyes of the Lord have looked upon him for his good,* by be-
stowing upon him the gifts of grace; *and lifted him out of his low estate
and raised up his head,* by delivering him from the miseries of this life
and leading him to the heights of glory.

May the only begotten Son of God, the Lord Jesus Christ, through the prayers of Saint Francis lead us to those same heights. Amen.

The Major Legend of Saint Francis

(1260-1263)

Prologue

HERE BEGINS THE PROLOGUE TO THE LIFE OF BLESSED FRANCIS

[1]*The grace of God our Savior has appeared* Ti 2:11
in these last days Acts 2:17; Heb 1:2
in his servant Francis
to all who are truly humble and lovers of holy poverty,[a]
who, while venerating in him God's superabundant mercy,
learn by his example
to reject wholeheartedly *ungodliness and worldly passions,* Ti 2:12
to live in conformity with Christ
and to thirst after *blessed hope* with unflagging desire. Ti 2:13

In an outpouring of kindness,
the Most High God looked upon him, Jb 36:22
a little, poor, and contrite man, Is 66:2
so that He not only *lifted the needy man* 1Kgs 2:8

---

a. With this opening sentence, Bonaventure places Francis within the framework of the history of salvation. Paul's Letter to Titus 2:11, which appears frequently in Bonaventure's sermons, not only underscores the gift of grace, but also articulates the dimensions of the revelation of the Word, cf. IX 52, 114, 129, 141, 187, 270, 480. While reflecting an Augustinian approach to history, Bonaventure's use of Acts 2:17 and Hebrews 1:2 shows the influences of the formulations of Rupert of Deutz (1070-c.1135) and the controversial Joachim of Fiore (c. 1130-1202), cf. Bernard McGinn, *Visions of the End: Apocalyptic Traditions in the Middle Ages* (New York: Columbia University Press, 1979); Joseph Ratzinger, *The Theology of History in Saint Bonaventure,* translated by Zachary Hayes, (Chicago: Franciscan Herald Press, 1971); Gerhart Ladner, *The Idea of Reform: Its Impact on Christian Thought and Action in the Age of the Fathers* (New York, Evanston, and London: Harper and Row, 1967). Thus, Francis appears as a symbolic representation of grace, one that is perceived best by the lowly and the poor.

from the dust of a worldly life;
Is 49:6 but also gave him as a light for believers,
a practitioner, a leader, and a herald of Gospel perfection,
Jn 1:7 that by *bearing witness to the light*
Lk 1:76,79 he might *prepare for the Lord a way* of light *and peace*
to the hearts of his faithful.

Shining with the splendor of his life and teaching,
Sir 50:6 *like the morning star in the midst of clouds,*
by his resplendent rays he guided into the light
Lk 1:79 those sitting in *darkness and in the shadow of death,*
Sir 50:8 and like *the rainbow shining among clouds of glory*
he made manifest in himself
Gn 9:13 *the sign* of the Lord's *covenant.*

Rom 10:15 *He preached* to people
the Gospel of peace and salvation,
Is 33:7 being himself *an angel of true peace.*
Like John the Baptist,
he was destined by God
Is 40:3 *to prepare in the desert a way* of the highest poverty
Lk 24:47 and to *preach repentance* by word and example.

First endowed with the gifts of divine grace,
he was then enriched
by the merit of unshakable virtue;
Lk 1:67 and *filled with the spirit* of prophecy,
he was also assigned an angelic ministry
and was totally aflame with a Seraphic fire.

Like a hierarchic man,[a]
2 Kgs 2:11 lifted up on *a fiery chariot,*
it may be reasonably accepted as true
Lk 1:17 that he came *in the spirit and power of Elijah,*

a. The Latin text reads: *vir hierarchicus* [hierarchic man] a technical term through which Bonaventure refers to the process that restructures the soul according to its place in God's design and to its true image, that is, among other creatures above and below it, and within itself. This approach has its roots in the writings of the Psuedo-Dionysius which had an enormous influence on the writers of the Middle Ages due to the translations of John Scotus Erigena (c. 810-c. 877) and, closer to the time of Bonaventure, Thomas Gallus (+1246). See Bernard McGinn, *The Flowering of Mysticism: Men and Women in the New Mysticism,* Volume III of *The Presence of God: A History of Western Christian Mysticism* (New York: Crossroad, 1998) 93-100. Bonaventure sees this hierarchical dimension of Francis's life, as that of any Christian, as flowing from the presence of grace, that gift "that purges the soul, enlightens and perfects it; gives it life, reforms and stabilizes it; elevates, assimilates, and joins it to God." Cf. *Breviloquium* VI 1 (V 252).

as will appear quite clearly in the course of his life.
And so in the true prophecy
of that other *friend of the Bridegroom,* Jn 3:29
John the Apostle and Evangelist,
he is considered not without reason
to be like the angel ascending from the rising of the sun
bearing the seal of the living God.
For *"at the opening of the sixth seal,"* Rv 6:12
John says in the Apocalypse,
"I saw another Angel Rv 7:2
ascending from the rising of the sun,
having the sign of the living God."[a]

[2]If we consider the height of his extraordinary sanctity
we can come to the conclusion, without any doubt,
that this messenger of God
—worthy of love by Christ,
imitation by us,
1C Prol 2 and admiration by the world—
was God's servant, Francis.
In this, while living among humans,
he was an imitator of angelic purity
and was placed as an example for the perfect followers of Christ.

This conviction should be faithfully and devotedly
in the forefront of our minds:
not only does this advance the mission he held Is 22:12
of calling to weep and mourn,
to shave one's head and wear sackcloth,
and to sign the Tau Ez 9:4
on the foreheads of those moaning and grieving[b]
with a sign
of a penitential cross,
and of a habit conformed to the cross;
even more,
it confirms with the irrefutable testimony of truth that
the seal of the likeness of the living God, Ez 28:12

---

a. The identification of this angel became a controversial point in the apocalyptic traditions of the Middles Ages. It reached its apogee in the Franciscan tradition with Bonaventure's description of Francis. Cf. Bernard McGinn, *Visions; Stanislao da Campagnola, L'Angelo del Sesto Sigillo e l'Alter Christus* (Rome, 1971); Joseph Ratzinger, *The Theology of History in Saint Bonaventure*, translated by Zachary Hayes, (Chicago: Franciscan Herald Press, 1971).

b. 2C 106, supra, 317 b.

Ez 28:12 that is, of *Christ crucified,*
was imprinted on his body,
not by natural forces or human skill,
2 Cor 3:3 but by the wondrous power *of the Spirit of the living God.*

[3]I feel that I am unworthy and unequal to the task of writing the
life of a man so venerable and worthy of imitation.[a] I would never 1C Prol 2
have attempted it if the fervent desire of the brothers had not
aroused me, the unanimous urging of the General Chapter had not
induced me,[b] and the devotion which I am obliged to have toward
our holy father had not compelled me. For when I was a boy, as I still
vividly remember, I was snatched from the jaws of death by his invocation and merits. So if I remained silent and did not sing his praises,
I fear that I would be rightly accused of the crime of ingratitude. I
recognize that God saved my life through him, and I realize that I
have experienced his power in my very person. Although I cannot accomplish this fully, this is my principal reason for undertaking this
Jn 6:12 task: that I may *gather together* the accounts of his virtues, actions and
words—like so many *fragments,* partly forgotten and partly scattered—*that they may not be lost* when those who lived with this servant
of God die.

[4]In order to have a clearer and more certain grasp of the authentic
facts of his life, which I was to transmit to posterity, I visited the sites
of the birth, life, and death of this holy man. I had careful interviews
with his companions who were still alive, especially those who had
intimate knowledge of his holiness and were his outstanding followers. Because of their acknowledged truth and proven virtue, they can 1C Prol 1
be trusted beyond any doubt. In describing what God graciously accomplished through his servant, I decided that I should avoid a cultivated literary style, since the reader's devotion profits more from
simple rather than ornate expression. To avoid confusion I did not al- 1C Prol 2
ways weave the story together in chronological order. Rather, I
strove to maintain a more thematic order, relating to the same theme

a. This reference to the Prologue to *The Life of Saint Francis* by Thomas of Celano (hereafter 1C) suggests a difference between the two works. Whereas Thomas underscores the veneration, admiration, and love due to the newly canonized Francis, Bonaventure adds that he is also "worthy of imitation." Bonaventure's portrait is a presentation of how that imitation might be accomplished.

b. The Latin reads *me fratrum fervens incitasset affectus, generalis Capituli concors induxisset instantis* [the fervent desire of the brothers had aroused me, the unanimous urging of the General Chapter induced me]. The brothers gathered at the General Chapter of Narbonne, 1260, were the force behind the composition of this text, undoubtedly motivated by a variety of reasons, not the least of which was the need for a liturgical text with a more universal appeal.

events that happened at different times, and to different themes events that happened at the same time, as seemed appropriate.

[5]The life of Francis—in its beginning, progress, and end—is described in the following fifteen chapters:

Chapter One: his manner of life while in the attire of the world.

Chapter Two: his perfect conversion to God and his restoration of three churches.

Chapter Three: the foundation of the Order and the approval of the Rule.

Chapter Four: the progress of the Order under his hand and the confirmation of the Rule.

Chapter Five: the austerity of his life and how creatures provided him comfort.

Chapter Six: his humility and obedience and God's condescension to his slightest wish.

Chapter Seven: his love of poverty and the miraculous fulfillment of his needs.

Chapter Eight: his affectionate piety and how irrational creatures were affectionate toward him.

Chapter Nine: the fervor of his charity and his desire for martyrdom.

Chapter Ten: his zeal for prayer and the power of his prayer.

Chapter Eleven: his understanding of Scripture and his spirit of prophecy.

Chapter Twelve: the efficacy of his preaching and his grace of healing.

Chapter Thirteen: his sacred stigmata.

Chapter Fourteen: his patience and his passing in death.

Chapter Fifteen: his canonization and the solemn transferal of his body.

Finally, there is appended an account of miracles which took place after his happy death.

Here Ends the Prologue

HERE BEGINS THE LIFE OF BLESSED FRANCIS

Chapter One

SAINT FRANCIS'S MANNER OF LIFE IN THE ATTIRE OF THE WORLD[a]

Jb 1:1 [1] *There was a man* 1C 1
in the city of Assisi,
named **Francis**
Sir 45:1 *whose memory is held in benediction,*
because God graciously
Ps 21:4 *preceded him with blessings of sweetness,*
mercifully snatching him from the dangers of the present life,
and richly filling him with gifts of heavenly grace.

Ps 62:9 For **at a young age,** he lived among *foolish children of mortals* and was 1C 3
brought up in foolish ways. After acquiring a little knowledge of reading and writing, he was assigned to work in a lucrative merchant's 1C 2
business. Yet with God's protection, although he indulged himself in
pleasures, even among **wanton youths,** he did not give himself over to 2C 7
the drives of the flesh; not even among greedy merchants *did he place his*
Sir 31:8 *hope in money or treasures,* although he was intent on making a profit.

Jb 31:18 There was to be sure, *growing* with him *from his infancy,* a generous 1C 17
care for the poor divinely implanted in the heart of the young Francis.[b] It had so filled his heart with kindness that, even at that time, **he** 2C 5
Lk 6:30 **resolved** not to be **a deaf hearer of the Gospel**[c] but *to give to everyone* 1C 22
who begged, especially if he asked out of **"divine love."** 2C 5

On one occasion, however, **when** he was caught up in the pressures of business, **contrary to his usual manner of acting,** he sent away

a. The Latin title reads: *De conversatione sancti Francisci in habitu saeculi* [Saint Francis's manner of living in the Attire of the World] referring to the earlier monastic concept of the life embraced by a religious upon entrance into the monastery, this is, after a conversion. In his *Commentary on Ecclesiastes,* Bonaventure describes *conversatio* as the life-style of a person who is unworldly and, therefore, concerned with a virtuous manner of living. In this context, this title reflects the changed understanding of Francis's youth that had been generally accepted at Bonaventure's time, and alludes to and anticipates the description of Francis's "perfect conversion" in the following chapter. Cf. Philibert Schmitz, "Conversatio morum," *Dictionnaire de la Spiritualité Ascetique et Mystique, Doctrine et Histoire* III (Paris: Beauchesne, 1963), 2206.

b. Bonaventure uses *miseratio* [care or pity], the word employed by Jerome in the Vulgate translation of Job, to describe this characteristic of Francis. It has the sense of an act of kindness towards those in need, *miseratio,* and is used five times in this work (I 1; II 2; IV 7; VIII 1–2x). This is also the first of six manifestations of the cross (I 3, 5; II 1; III 3-6; IV 9,10) during Francis's life leading to the seventh, that of LaVerna where he received the stigmata (XIII).

c. Cf. FA:ED I 202c.

empty-handed **a poor man who had begged alms for the love** of God.
Immediately turning back *to his heart,* he ran after him, and, gently Ps 85:9
with extravagant alms, he promised God that from that moment,
while he had the means, he would not refuse those who begged from
2C 196 him for the love of God. **He observed this** with untiring piety **until his
death** and merited an abundant increase of grace and love for God.[a]
For afterwards, when he had perfectly *put on Christ,* he would say that Gal 3:27
even while he was in secular attire, he could scarcely ever **hear** any
mention of the divine **love without being deeply moved** in his heart.

1C 2 At the same time, the sensitivity of his gentleness, together with a
refined set of manners, a patience and affability beyond human decorum, and a generosity beyond his means singled him out as a
young man of flourishing natural disposition. This seemed to be a
prelude to the even greater abundance of God's blessings that would
be showered on him in the future. Indeed a certain exceptionally
simple man of Assisi, whom, it is believed, God had instructed,
whenever he chanced to meet Francis going through the city, used to
take off his cloak and *spread the garment* under his feet, claiming that Lk 19:36
1C 4 Francis was worthy of reverence, since he was destined to do great
things in the near future and would be magnificently honored by the
entire body of the faithful.[b]

2C 4 [2]However, up to this time, Francis **was ignorant** of *God's counsel* for Jb 15:8
him. For this reason, drawn in several directions to the external by the demand of his father as well as forced down to the inferior by the corruption of his natural origin,[c] he had not yet learned how to contemplate the celestial nor had he become accustomed to savor the divine.

And because *affliction can enlighten* spiritual *awareness,* Is 28:19
1C 2 *the hand of the Lord was upon him,* Ez 1:3
and *a change of the right hand of the Most High,* Ps 76:11

---

a. This is Bonaventure's first use of *pietas*, a word that appears forty-two times in LMj. The third book of his *Commentary on the Sentences of Peter Lombard* reveals that, prior to LMj, he had a well-developed theology of *pietas* and perceived that through it God was worshipped and neighbor served. Cf. *III Sent,* Dist. VI, art 1, q. 6. As noted in previous passages of *Francis of Assisi: Early Documents,* the word is not easily translated into English, cf. supra FA:ED I 189c.

b. In one of its liturgical prescriptions, the friars at the Chapter of Narbonne (1260) had changed Julian of Speyer's first antiphon for Matins to *Hic vir in vanitatibus nutritus indecenter/divinis charismatibus preventus est clementer, cf.* FA:ED I 332c. Thus, they accepted the revision of Thomas of Celano's *Remembrance* portraying the young Francis whom Baptism had changed "from a child of wrath to a child of grace" (2C 3).

c. Bonaventure is struggling with the effects of original sin, thus his description of Francis as *distractus* [drawn in several directions] and *depressus* [forced down] by nature and by original sin. For a succinct theology of the creation, fall, and restoration of the human, see Bonaventure's "Prologue to the Second Book of Sentences," in *Bonaventure: Mystic of God's Word,* introduced and edited by Timothy Johnson (Hyde Park: New City Press, 1999), 59-64.

afflicting his body with **prolonged illness** LJS 2
in order to prepare his soul for the anointing of the Holy Spirit.

And **when the strength** of his body **was restored,** dressed as usual in his fine **clothes, he met a knight** who was of noble birth, but **poor** and badly clothed. Moved by a pious impulse of care for his poverty,[a] he took off his own garments and clothed the man on the spot. At one and the same time he fulfilled the two-fold duty of piety by covering over the embarrassment of a noble knight and relieving the want of a poor human being. 1C 3; LJS 2; 2C 5

[3]The following **night,** when he had fallen **asleep,** the divine kindness showed him a large and **splendid palace** with **military arms** emblazoned with the insignia of Christ's cross. Thus it vividly indicated that the mercy he had exhibited to a poor knight for love of the supreme King would be repaid with an incomparable reward.[b] When he asked to whom these belonged, the response he received from on high was **that all these things were for him and his knights.** Therefore, **on waking up in the morning,** since he was not yet disciplined in penetrating the divine mysteries and did not know how to pass through the visible appearance[c] to contuit[d] the invisible truth, he 1C 5; 2C 6; 1C 5; 1C 17; 1C 5; LJS 3

a. The Latin reads: *pio affectu* [a pious impulse]. *Affectus* is one of the more difficult words to translate since Bonaventure's use is very much influenced by that of Bernard of Clairvaux, especially in his treatise *On Loving God*. Cf. "Affectio, Affectus," *Lexique Saint Bonaventure*, edited by Jacques-Guy Bougerol, (Paris: Éditions Franciscaines, 1969), 15-16; Bernard of Clairvaux, *On Loving God with An Analytical Commentary*, by Emero Stiegman (Kalamazoo: Cistercian Publications Inc.,1995), 88-98. The adjective *pius*, closely related to *pietas*, is also difficult to translate in contemporary English in which it takes on the sense of one "having or showing religious devotion." Thus the contemporary English translation of *pius* overlooks the richer nuance of *pietas*.

b. At this point Bonaventure introduces the word *misericordia* which appears twelve times in the text (I 3; II 8; III 1; V 4; IX 3; XI 4; XII 11; XXI 5–3x; XXIII 2,3,4. Whereas *miseratio* has the sense of an act of pity or kindness, *misericordia* has the sense of "heart sensitive to misery," *compassio* the ability to suffer with another. Bonaventure's sermons suggest that this text reflects his rich theology of *misericordia*.

c. The Latin text reads: *per visibilum species transire ad contuendam invisibilem veritatem* [to pass through the visible appearance to contuit the invisible truth]. In this phrase Bonaventure proposes his understanding of the spiritual journey from the visible to the invisible, a journey articulated in his *Journey of the Soul into God*, see *Bonaventure: The Journey of the Soul into God, The Tree of Life, The Life of St. Francis*. Translated and Introduction by Ewert H. Cousins, Preface by Ignatius Brady (New York: Paulist Press, 1978).

d. The Latin word, *contuitus*, is used nine times by Bonaventure in LMj, and can be translated as "concomitant gaze or insight." The most important discussion of the teaching that the divine reason is "contuited by us" along with created reason in every act of certain knowledge is found in *Questiones Disputatae de Scientia Christi* q.4, concl. (V:22b-24b). See also *De reductione artium ad theologiam* 18 (V:32a), *Sermo Chrisus unus omnium magister* 7-19 (V:569a-572a), and *III Sent.* D. XXXV, a.1, q.3, conc. (III, 778). For a succinct presentation of the significance of *contuitio* in Bonaventure's mysticism, see Ewert H. Cousins, "Bonaventure's Mysticism of Language," in *Mysticism and Language*, edited by Steven T. Katz (New York, Oxford: Oxford University Press, 1992), 236-253. After a discussion of the journey through the visible to the invisible, Cousins concludes: "This innate awareness of God can be awakened by the excessive contuition through the technique of contemplative *reductio*, and it can be brought to ecstatic awareness by divine grace." Cf. Rossano Zas Friz De Col, "La Contuizione de Simbolo Secondo San Bonaventura," *Collectanea Franciscana* 69 (1999): 43-78.

assessed the unusual vision to be a judgment of great prosperity in the future. For this reason, **still** ignorant of the divine plan, he set out
2C 6 to join a generous count **in Apulia,** hoping in his service to obtain the glory **of knighthood,** as his vision foreshadowed.

Shortly after he had embarked on his journey and had gone as far as the neighboring city, he heard the Lord speaking to him during **the night** in a familiar way: "Francis, **who** can **do more** for you, a **lord or a servant,** a rich person or one who is poor?" **When Francis** replied that **a lord** and a rich person could do more, he was at once asked: **"Why, then, are you abandoning the Lord for a servant** and the rich God for a poor mortal?" **And Francis replied:** *"Lord, what do* Acts 9:6
you want me to do?" And the Lord answered him: "Go back to your own Gn 32:9
land, **because the vision** which you have seen prefigures a **spiritual** outcome which will be accomplished in you not by a human but by a divine plan."

When morning came, then, **he returned** in haste to Assisi, free of Jn 21:4
care and filled with joy, and, **already** made an exemplar **of obedience,** he awaited the Lord's will.

LJS 3 [4]From that time on, **as he was removing himself from the pressure of public business,** he would eagerly beg the divine kindness to
1C 6 show him what he should do. When the flame of heavenly desire intensified in him by the practice of frequent prayer, and already, out of his love for a heavenly home, he *despised* all earthly things *as noth-* Sg 8:7
ing; he realized that he had found a *hidden treasure,* and, like a wise Mt 13:44-46
merchant, planned to buy *the pearl he had found by selling everything.*

Nevertheless,
how **he should do** this, he did not yet know;
except that it was suggested to his spirit
that a spiritual merchant must begin with contempt for the world
and a knight of Christ with victory over one's self.

2C 9 [5]One day, therefore, **while he was riding his horse** through the plain that lies below the city **of Assisi, he met a leper.** This unforeseen encounter struck him **with not a little horror.** Recalling the plan of perfection he had already conceived in his mind, and remembering that he must first conquer himself if he wanted to become *a* 2 Tim 2:3
knight of Christ, **he dismounted from his horse and ran to kiss him. As the leper stretched out his hand as if to receive something, he gave him money with a kiss. Immediately mounting his horse,** however, **and turning** all around, **even though the open plain stretched clear in all directions, he could not see the leper**

2 Cor 7:4 **anywhere.** He began, therefore, *filled with wonder and joy,* to sing
praises to the Lord, while proposing, because of this, to embark always on the greater.

He then began to seek out **solitary places,** favorable to grieving, 2C 9
Rom 8:26 where, with *unutterable groans,* he concentrated incessantly on meriting to be heard by the Lord after the long perseverance of his prayers.

One of those days, withdrawn in this way, while he was praying
and all of his fervor was totally absorbed in God, Christ Jesus ap- 2C 10-11
Sg 5:6 peared to him as fastened to a cross.[a] His *soul melted* at the sight, and
the memory of Christ's **passion was so impressed on** the innermost 3C 2
recesses of his **heart. From** that **hour,** whenever **Christ's** crucifixion 2C 11
came to his mind, he could scarcely **contain** his tears and sighs, as he
later revealed to his companions when he was approaching the end
of his life. Through this the man of God understood as addressed to
Mt 16:24 himself the Gospel text: *If you wish to come after me, deny yourself and
take up your cross and follow me.*

[6]From then on he clothed himself with a spirit of poverty, a sense 1C 17; 2C 9
of humility, and an eagerness for intimate piety. For previously not
only had association with lepers horrified him greatly, so too did
even gazing upon them **from a distance.** But, now because of Christ LJS 12
crucified, who according to the text of the prophet appeared despised 1C 17
Is 53:3 *as a leper,* he, in order to **despise himself** completely, showed deeds of
humility and humanity to lepers with a gentle piety. He visited their 2C 9
houses frequently, generously distributed alms to them, and with a
great drive of compassion **kissed their hands** and their mouths.[b]

To **poor** beggars he even wished to give not only his possessions but his very self, sometimes taking off his clothes, at others altering them, at yet others, when he had nothing else at hand, ripping them in pieces to give to them.

To poor priests he also provided help, reverently and piously, especially **in the appointments** of the altar, and, in this way, he both became a participant in the divine worship and provided assistance for the need of its celebrants.

With religious devotion he visited at this time the shrine **of the Apostle Peter.** When he saw a large number **of the poor** before the entrance **of the church,** led partly by the gentleness of his piety,

a. This is the first of many ecstatic experiences described in Bonaventure's portrait, cf. I 5; II 1; III 6; VIII 10; IX 2; X 1-4; XI 13; XII 1. It is clear that, for Bonaventure, Francis was a model of the Christian caught in ecstasy.

b. Bonaventure now introduces the word *compassio* [compassion] that appears five times (I 6; VIII 1,5,6; XIV 4) suggesting more than *miseratio* [an act of kindness] or *misericordia* [a heart sensitive to suffering]. Compassion *(com-passio)* has the sense of suffering with another.

encouraged partly by the love of poverty, he gave his own clothes to
1C 16 one of the neediest among them. Dressed in his rags, he spent that day in the midst of the poor with an unaccustomed joy of spirit, in order to spurn worldly glory and to arrive, by ascending in stages, at Gospel perfection.

He was more attentively vigilant
to mortifying his flesh
so that he might carry externally in his body
the cross of Christ
which he carried internally in his heart.
The man of God, Francis,
did all these things
while not yet withdrawn from the world
in attire and way of life.

Chapter Two

His Perfect Conversion to God and His Repair of Three Churches[a]

[1]Because the servant of the Most High 1C 8
had no other teacher in these matters
except Christ,
His kindness visited him once more 2C 9
in the sweetness of grace.

Gn 24:63 For **one day** when Francis *went out to meditate in the fields,* **he** 2C 10
walked near the church of San Damiano which was threatening to 1C 8
collapse because of age. Impelled by the Spirit, **he went inside to**
pray. Prostrate before an image **of the Crucified,** he was filled with
no little consolation as he prayed. While his tear-filled eyes were gazing at the Lord's cross, he heard with his bodily ears **a voice coming** 3C 2
from that cross, telling him three times: "Francis, go and repair my
house which, as you see, is all being destroyed."

Trembling, Francis was stunned at the sound of such an aston- 2C 10
ishing voice, since he was alone in the church; and as he absorbed the
power of the divine words into his heart, he fell into an ecstasy of
mind. At last, coming back to himself, **he prepared himself to obey**
and pulled himself together to carry out the command of repairing
the material church, although the principal intention of the words
Acts 20:28 referred to that which *Christ purchased with his own blood,* as the Holy 2C 11
Spirit taught him and as he himself later disclosed to the brothers.

Then, after fortifying himself with the sign of the cross, he 1C 8
arose, and **taking cloth to sell,** he hurried off **to a city** called **Foligno.** LJS 6
There, after selling everything he had brought with him, even the
horse he was riding, the successful merchant quickly returned 1C 9
with the price he had obtained. Returning **to Assisi,** he **reverently** LJS 6
entered the church he had received the command to repair. **When he**
found the poor priest there, he showed him fitting **reverence,** LJS 6

a. This title also provides insight into Bonaventure's interpretation and must be seen in light of the title of the previous chapter. Whereas the earlier monastic tradition envisioned a *conversio* [conversion] anticipating a *conversatio* [a virtuous manner of living], Bonaventure reverses the order, and does so by adding the adjective *perfecta* [perfect] to it.

Off 11 II offered him money for the repair of the church and for the use of the
poor, and humbly requested that he be allowed to stay with him for
a time. The priest agreed to his staying there but, out of fear of his
parents, would not accept the money that the true scorner of
wealth had thrown on a windowsill, valuing it no more than if it
were dust.

1C 10 [2]When he learned that the servant of God was *spending time* with Mt 25:5
this priest, his disturbed father ran to the place. But because [Fran-
cis] was still a new athlete of Christ, when he heard the threats of
his pursuers and learned in advance of their coming, wanting to
leave room for their anger, he hid himself in a secret pit. There he re- Rom 12:19
mained in hiding for some days, imploring the Lord incessantly with
flowing tears to *deliver him from the hands of those who were persecuting* Ps 31:16; 109:31; 142:7
his soul and to fulfill the fervent wishes he had inspired. He was then
1C 11 filled with an excessive joy and began to accuse himself of cowardice. He cast aside his fear, abandoned the pit, and took the road to
the city of Assisi.

When the townspeople saw his unkempt face and his changed
LJS 8 mentality, they thought he had gone out of his senses. They threw
mud and stones from the streets, and shouted insults at him, as if
1C 11; LJS 8 he were insane and out of his mind. But the Lord's servant passed
through it as if he were deaf to it all, neither broken nor changed by
1C 12; LJS 8 any wrong. When his father heard the shouting, he ran to him at
LJS 8 once, not to free him but rather to destroy him. With no pity, he
dragged him home and badgered him first with words, then with
blows and chains. But as a result of this he became more fit and eager to carry out what he had begun, recalling that Gospel passage:
Blessed are they who suffer persecution for justice' sake, for theirs is the king- Mt 5:10
dom of heaven.

1C 13 [3]After a little while, when his father had left the country, his
LJS 8 mother, who did not approve what her husband had done and had
no hope of being able to soften her son's inflexible determination,
released him from his chains and permitted him to leave.

1C 13; LJS 8 He gave thanks to the Almighty Lord and went back to the place
LJS 8 he had been before. Returning and not finding him at home, his father reviled his wife with a bitter tongue-lashing and raced to that
place shaking so that, if he could not call him back, he might at
least drive him from the neighborhood. But strengthened by God,
Francis went out on his own to meet his furious father, crying out
loudly that binding and beating lead to nothing. In addition, he

declared he would gladly suffer anything for the name of Christ.
When the father, therefore, saw that he could not recall him, he 1C 14; LJS 8
turned his attention to recovering the money. When he finally
found it on the windowsill, his rage was dampened a little, and his
thirsty greed was somewhat quenched by gulping down the money.

[4]Thereupon the father of the flesh worked on leading the child of 1C 13
grace, now stripped of his money, before the bishop of the city that
he might renounce his family possessions into his hands and return everything he had. The true lover of poverty showed himself
eager to comply and went before the bishop without delaying or 1C 15
hesitating. He did not wait for any words nor did he speak any, but
immediately took off his clothes and gave them back to his father.
Then it was discovered that the man of God had a hair shirt next to 2C 12
his skin under his fine clothes. Moreover, drunk with remarkable 1C 15
fervor,[a] he even took off his trousers, and was completely stripped
naked before everyone. He said to his father: "Until now I have 2C 12
called you father here on earth, but now I can say without reserva-
Mt 6:9 tion, *'Our Father who art in heaven,'* since I have placed all my treasure
and all my hope in him." The bishop, recognizing and admiring such 1C 15
intense fervor in the man of God, immediately stood up and in tears
drew him into his arms, covering him with the mantle that he was
wearing. Like the pious and good man that he was, he bade his ser- LJS 10
vants give him something to cover his body. They brought him a
poor, cheap cloak of a farmer who worked for the bishop, which he
accepted gratefully and, with his own hand, marked a cross on it
with a piece of chalk, thus designating it as the covering of a crucified
and half-naked poor man.

Thus the servant of the Most High King
was left naked
that he might follow
his naked crucified Lord, whom he loved.[b] 1C 15
Thus the cross strengthened him
to entrust his soul
to the wood of salvation
Wis 14:1-7 that would save him from the shipwreck of the world.

a. Bonaventure describes spiritual inebriation as the fourth of six steps in the love of God in his *De Triplici Via* II 10: "Inebriation consists in those who love God with such love that they not only find solace burdensome, but even take delight in and seek suffering instead of solace and, out of love of Him whom they love, delight in pain, abuse, and scourging as did the Apostle" (cf. 2 Cor 12:5,10).

b. For a thorough history of spiritual nudity and the uniqueness of Bonaventure's use of the term in this instance, cf. Jean Châtillon, "*Nudum Christum Nudus Sequere:* A Note on the Origins and Meaning of the Theme of Spiritual Nakedness in the Writings of St. Bonaventure." GR 10:3 (1996): 293-340.

1C 16 [5]Released now from the chains of all earthly desires,
this scorner of the world left the town
and in a carefree mood
1C 91; 2C 214 sought the secret of solitude[a]
that alone and in silence
he would hear the mystery of the divine eloquence.

While Francis, the man of God, was making his way through a certain forest, singing with glee praises to the Lord in French, robbers suddenly rushed upon him from an ambush. When they asked who he was, the man of God, filled with confidence, replied in a prophetic voice: "I am the herald of the great King!" But they beat him and threw him into a ditch filled with snow, saying: "Lie there, you stupid herald of God!" After they left, he jumped out of the ditch, and exhilarated with great joy, he began in an even louder voice to make the woods resound with praises to the Creator of all.

Off 14 IV; LJS 11 [6]And coming to a certain neighboring monastery,[b] he asked for alms like a beggar and received it like someone unknown and despised. Setting out from there, he moved to Gubbio, where he was recognized and welcomed by an old friend and clothed with a poor
LJS 11 little tunic, like one of Christ's little poor.

From there the lover of profound humility
moved to the lepers and lived with them,
serving them all most diligently for God's sake.
He washed their feet,
bandaged sores,
drew pus from wounds
and wiped away filth.
He who was soon to be a physician of the Gospel Lk 10:30-37
even kissed their ulcerous wounds
out of his remarkable devotion.
As a result, he received such power from the Lord
that he had miraculous effectiveness
in healing spiritual and physical illnesses.

I will cite one case among many, which occurred after the fame of the man of God became more widely known.

a. For a thorough study of the role of solitude and the meaning of this phrase "*secretum solitudin*is [the secret of solitude]" cf. Octavian Schmucki, "Place of Solitude: An Essay on the External Circumstances of the Prayer Life of St. Francis of Assisi," GR 2:1 (1988) 77-132.

b. Bonaventure employs the word used by Julian, *coneobium*, to describe Thomas's *claustrum monachorum*.

There was a man in the neighborhood of Spoleto whose mouth and cheek were being eaten away by a certain horrible disease. He could not be helped by any medical treatment and went on a pilgrimage to implore the intercession of the holy apostles. On his way back from visiting their shrines he happened to meet God's servant. When out of devotion he wanted to kiss his footprints, that humble man, refusing to allow it, kissed the mouth of the one who wished to kiss his feet. In his remarkable piety Francis, the servant of lepers, touched that horrible sore with his holy mouth, and suddenly every sign of the disease vanished and the sick man recovered the health he longed for. I do not know which of these we should admire more: the depth of his humility in such a kind kiss or his extraordinary power in such an amazing miracle.

[7]Grounded now in the humility of Christ, Francis recalled to mind 2C 13
the obedience enjoined upon him **from the cross, to repair the church of San Damiano.** As a truly obedient man, he returned **to Assisi** to obey the divine command at least by begging. Putting aside all **embarrassment** out of love of the poor Crucified, **he begged** from those among whom he was accustomed to have plenty, and he
loaded stones upon his frail body that **was weakened by fasting.** 2C 14
With God's help and the devoted assistance of the citizens, he com- 1C 21
pleted repairs on **that church.**

After this work, to prevent his body from becoming sluggish with laziness, he set himself to repair a certain church of Blessed Peter a further distance from town, because of the special devotion which, in his pure and sincere faith, he bore to the prince of the apostles.

[8]When he finally completed this church, he came **to a place** called 1C 21
the Portiuncula **where there stood a church of the most Blessed Vir-**
gin Mother of God, built in ancient times but now deserted and no LJS 14
one was taking care of it. When the man of God saw it so abandoned, **he began to stay** there **regularly** in order to repair it, **moved**
by the warm devotion he had toward the Lady of the world. Sensing 1C 106
that angels **often visited** there, according to the name of that church, 2 C 18
which from ancient times was called **Saint Mary of the Angels,** he 1C 19
stayed there out of his reverence for the angels and his special love for the mother of Christ.

This place 1C 18
the holy man loved more than other places in the world;
for here he began humbly,
here he progressed virtuously,

here he ended happily.
This place
he entrusted to his brothers at his death
as the the most beloved of the Virgin.

1C 20 **Before his conversion, a certain brother, dedicated to God, had a vision about this church which is worth telling. He saw countless people who had been *stricken with blindness, on their knees* in a circle** Gn 19:11; 2 Chr 6:13
around this church, with their faces raised to heaven. All of them, with tearful voices and *uplifted hands, were crying out to God,* begging Ps 55:17
for mercy and light. Then a great light came down from heaven and, diffusing itself through them, gave each the sight and health they desired.

2C 18 **This is the place**
where the Order of Lesser Brothers
was begun by Saint Francis
under the prompting of divine revelation.
For at the bidding of divine providence
which guided Christ's servant in everything,
LJS 14 he **built up three** material **churches**
before he preached the Gospel
and began the Order not only
to ascend in an orderly progression
from the sensible to the intelligible,
from the lesser to the greater,
but also
to symbolize mystically
in external actions perceived by the senses
what he would do in the future.[a]
For like the three buildings he built up,
so the Church
—where there is victory
for the triple army of those being saved—
was to be renewed in three ways
under his leadership:
1C 37 **by the form, rule, and teaching** of Christ
which he would provide.
And now we see
that this prophecy has been fulfilled.

a. Bonaventure may well be alluding to an interpretation of progress in the spiritual life offered by Richard of Saint Victor, who, in his *Mystical Ark*, described the different stages of the spiritual life in similar terms. Cf. *Richard of Saint Victor: The Twelve Patriarchs, The Mystical Ark, Book Three of The Trinity*, trans. and intro by Grover A. Zinn, preface by Jean Châtillon (New York, Ramsey, Toronto: Paulist Press, 1979), 34-35.

Chapter Three

THE FOUNDING OF THE RELIGION[a] AND THE APPROVAL OF THE RULE

[1]In the church of the Virgin Mother of God, 1C 21
Mt 25:5 her servant Francis *lingered*
and, with continuing cries,
insistently begged her
who had conceived and brought to birth
Jn 1:14 *the Word full of grace and truth,*[b]
to become his **advocate.** 2C 198
Through the merits of the Mother of Mercy,
he conceived and brought to birth
the spirit of the Gospel truth.

One day while **he was** devoutly **hearing** a Mass of the Apostles, 1C 22
the Gospel was read in which Christ sends **out his disciples to** LJS 22
Mt 10:9 **preach** and gives them the Gospel form of life, that they *may not keep*
gold or silver or money in their belts, nor have a wallet for their journey, nor
may they have two tunics, nor shoes, nor staff. Hearing, understanding,
and committing this to memory, this friend of apostolic poverty was
then overwhelmed with an **indescribable** joy. **"This is what** I want," LJS 15; 1C 22
Ex 5:24 he said, **"this is what I desire with all my heart!"** Immediately, ***he***
took off the shoes from his feet, put down his staff, denounced his wallet
and money, **and, satisfied with one tunic, threw away** *his leather belt* LJS 15
and put on a piece of rope for a belt. He directed all his heart's desire
to carry out what he had heard and to conform in every way to the
rule of right living given to the apostles.

---

a. The Latin is *religio* which Bonaventure uses in the title of this chapter to contrast it with that of the fourth. While *religio* and *ordo* tended to be synonyms in the twelfth and thirteenth centuries, *religio* had a more generic sense of religious life, while *ordo* designated those who followed the same customs or prescriptions, e.g. different monasteries. Bonaventure uses these words, as do the earlier texts, to show the development of the primitive fraternity, cf. AP 19, L3C 37.

b. The use of this passage of John's Gospel reflects Bonaventure's theology of Christ as the Word "full of grace and truth," cf. *III Sent,* Dist. XIII, art 1, q. iii, spoken that we might participate in a life of virtue, I (III, 281), *Breviloquium* IV 5 (V, 246). In his *Itinerarium mentis in Deum* I 7, Bonaventure sees reception of the Word full of grace and truth as the means needed for rectifying sinful human nature (V, 298). Two references to this scriptural passage in Bonaventure's *Commentarius in Evangelium Lucae* (I 47; XI 60) place it in a Marian context, that is, she who is the receptacle as well as the means of bringing into the world the Incarnate Word (VII, 22, 296).

LJS 16 [2]Through divine prompting the man of God began to become a
1C 23 model of evangelical perfection and to invite others to penance. His
statements were neither hollow nor worthy of ridicule, but filled
with the power of the Holy Spirit, they penetrated the marrow of
the heart, so that they moved those hearing them in stunned
1C 24 amazement. In all his preaching, he announced peace by saying:
"May the Lord give you peace."[a] Thus he greeted the people at the begin- Mt 10:12; Lk 10:5
Test 5 ning of his talk. As he later testified, he had learned this greeting by
the Lord revealing it to him.

Thus it happened that,
filled with the spirit of the prophets
and according to a prophetic passage, Is 52:7
he proclaimed peace,
preached salvation,
and, by counsels of salvation,
brought to true peace
many who had previously lived at odds with Christ
and far from salvation.

LJS 17 [3]Therefore
as the truth of the man of God's simple teaching and life
became known to many,
some men began to be moved to penance
and, abandoning all things,
joined him in habit and life.
1C 24 The first among these was
Bernard, a venerable man,
who was made a *sharer* in the divine *vocation* Heb 3:1
and merited to be the firstborn son of the blessed Father,[b]
both in priority of time and in the gift of holiness.

2C 15 For this man, as he was planning to reject the world perfectly after his example, once he had ascertained for himself the holiness of Christ's servant, sought his advice on how to carry this out. On

a. The significance of this greeting can be seen in the opening paragraph of the Prologue of Bonaventure's *Journey of the Soul into God.* Cf. Bonaventure, *The Journey of the Mind to God,* translated by Philotheus Boehner; edited, with introduction and notes by Stephen F. Brown (Indianapolis/Cambridge: Hackett Publishing Company, 1993), 40, n.5.

b. Bonaventure's identification of Bernard as the *primogenitus* [first born] introduces an important theme of this chapter, one to which Bonaventure alludes in his twice-used phrase "conceived and brought to birth" (III 1). This may possibly be an allusion to the image of Odo of Cheriton, who quotes Francis as declaring "he was the woman whom the Lord had impregnated with his word, and that he had borne these spiritual sons" cf. FA:ED I 590-591. But it is also consistent with Bonaventure's theology of the interiorization and proclamation of the Word.

hearing this, God's servant was filled with the consolation of the Holy Spirit over the conception of his first child. "This requires **counsel** that is from God," he said.

Mt 27:1 ***When morning had broken* they went into the church** of Saint
Nicholas, and, after they had prepared with a prayer, Francis, a wor-
shiper of the Trinity, opened **the book of the Gospels** three times Off 3 IV-VI
asking God to confirm Bernard's plan with a threefold testimony. **At**
Mt 19:21 **the first opening of the book** this text appeared: *If you will be perfect,* 1C 92
Lk 9:3 *go, sell all that you have, and give to the poor.* **At the second:** *Take nothing*
Mt 16:24 *on your journey.* **And at the third:** *If anyone wishes to come after me, let him*
deny himself and take up his cross and follow me. "This is our life and
rule," the holy man said, "and that of all who wish to join our com-
Mt 19:21 pany. Go, then, if you wish to be perfect, and carry out what you have
heard."

[4]Not long afterwards five other men were called by the same 1C 25
Spirit, and **the number** of Francis's sons **reached** six. The third among them was the holy father **Giles,** a man indeed filled with God and worthy of his celebrated reputation.[a] Although he was **a simple** and unlearned man, he later became famous for his practice of heroic virtue, as God's servant had prophesied, and was raised to the height of exalted **contemplation.** For through the passage of time, he was continually intent on elevations; [b] and he was so often rapt into God in ecstasy, as I myself have observed as an eyewitness, that he seemed to live among people more like an angel than a human being.

[5]Also at that time **a priest of the town of Assisi, Sylvester,** a man 2C 109
of an upright way of life, was **shown a vision** by the Lord which should not be passed over in silence. Reacting in a purely human way, he had an abhorrence for the bearing and the way of Francis and his brothers. But then he was visited by grace from heaven in order to save him from the danger of rash judgment. **For he saw in a**
Dn 14:22 **dream** the whole town of Assisi encircled by *a huge dragon* which,

a. He died near Perugia on April 22, 1262, while Bonaventure was writing the present work. In his *Commentary on Luke's Gospel,* Bonaventure draws attention to the seven degrees of contemplation articulated by Giles. "Although in words that are simple but not scientific, Brother Giles, who was frequently known to be in rapture, distinguished the degrees in this way. There are seven degrees of contemplation. The first is fire; the second, unction; the third, ecstasy; the fourth, contemplation; the fifth, taste; the sixth, rest; and the seventh, glory. Beyond these nothing remains except eternal happiness." Cf. Bonaventure, *Commentarius in Evangelium Lucae* IX 48 (VII, 231-232).

b. The Latin read *sursumactionibus incessanter intentus* a word he frequently uses in the context of the spiritual life as a continuing ascent into God, e.g. *Itinerarium mentis in Deum* I 1, where prayer is seen as the mother and origin of all *sursum-actio* (V 297); *Collationes in Hexaëmeron* XIX 27, XXII 22 (V 24, 440). In general, Bonaventure sees it as the passive elevation of the soul toward ecstatic love. Sylvester is described here and also in LMj VI 9 and LMj XII 2 as a man of "dove-like simplicity" and great prayer.

because of its enormous size, seemed to threaten the entire area with destruction. Then he contuited[a] issuing **from Francis's mouth a golden cross whose** *top reached the heavens* **and whose arms** Gn 28:12 **stretched far and wide** and seemed to extend to the ends of the world. At the sight of its shining splendor, the foul and hideous dragon was put to flight. When he had seen this vision for the third time and realized that it was a divine revelation, he told it point by point **to the man of God** and his brothers. Not long afterwards, **leaving the world,** he clung to the footsteps of Christ with such perseverance that his life **in the Order** confirmed the authenticity of the vision which he had had in the world.

1C 26 [6]On hearing of this vision,
the man of God was not carried away by human glory;
but recognizing God's goodness in his **gifts,**
he was more strongly inspired to put to flight
our ancient enemy with his cunning
and to preach the glory of the cross of Christ.
One day,
while he was weeping in a solitary place
as he looked back over his past *years in bitterness,* Is 38:15
the **joy** of the Holy Spirit came over him
and he was assured of the complete **forgiveness of all of his sins.**
Then he was caught up above himself
LJS 18 **and totally engulfed in a** wonderful **light,**
and, with his inmost soul opened wide,[b]
he clearly saw what would transpire for him and his sons
in the future.

1C 27 After this **he returned to the brothers** and said: **"Be strong,** my beloved ones, **and** *rejoice in the Lord.* **Do not be sad because you** are Eph 6:10; Phil 3:1, 4:4 **so few,** nor afraid because **of my simplicity or yours. For as the Lord has shown me in truth that He will make us grow into a great multitude and will spread us in countless ways by the grace of his blessing."**

a. In this instance Bonaventure changes the verb used in 2C 109, *videt* [he sees] to the stronger, more "Bonaventurian" verb, *contuebatur* [he contuited]. *Contuebatur*, cf. LMj I 2, supra, 532 d. By doing so, he underscores the conviction arising in Sylvester from the evidence of the dream that could only be accounted for by divine intervention. This vision of Sylvester becomes important in understanding the significance of the stigmata, cf. LMj XIII 10, infra, 638.

b. The Latin reads: *raptus deinde supra se et in quoddam mirandum lumen totus absorptus, dilatato sinu mentis* [Then he was taken above himself and totally engulfed in a wonderful light, with his inmost soul opened wide] is reminiscent of the language of Gregory the Great and later mystics. Cf. Bernard McGinn, *The Growth of Mysticism: Gregory the Great through the 12th Century*. The Presence of God: A History of Western Christian Mysticism, Volume II (New York: Crossroad, 1996).

7 At the same time, another good man entered the religion, 1C 29
bringing the number of the man of God's blessed offspring to seven. Then the pious father called all his sons to himself and, as he told them many things about the kingdom of God, contempt for the world, the denial of their own wills, and the chastising of their bodies, he revealed his proposal to send them to the four corners of the LJS 19
world.

For the poor and sterile simplicity of our holy father
1 Sm 2:5 had already *brought* seven *to birth*
and now he wished to bring to birth in Christ the Lord
all the faithful of the world called to cries of penance.

"Go," the gentle father said to his sons, "while you are announc-
Mk 1:4; Lk 3:3 ing peace to the people, *preach repentance for the forgiveness of sins*. Be
patient in trials, watchful in prayer, strenuous in work, moderate in speech, reserved in manner, and grateful for favors, for because of all these things an eternal kingdom is being prepared for you." As
they humbly prostrated themselves on the ground before God's LJS 19
servant, they accepted the command of obedience with a spirit of
Ps 55:23 joy. Then he spoke to each one individually: *"Cast your care upon the Lord, and he will sustain you."* He was accustomed to saying this
phrase whenever he sent a brother under obedience. LJS 19

Knowing he should give himself as an example to others, he too 1C 30
then set out with one companion for one part of the world that he might first practice rather than preach. The remaining six he sent to three other parts of the world, thus forming the pattern of a cross.

After a short time had passed,
the kind father, LJS 20
longing for the presence of his dear children,
since he could not bring them together as one by himself,
prayed that this be done
by the One
who *gathers the dispersed of Israel.* Ps 146:2
So it happened that,
after a short time,
without any human summons,
they all came together according to his desire,
quite unexpectedly and much to their amazement,
through the working of divine kindness.
During those days four upright men joined them,
LJS 20 increasing their number to twelve.

LJS 21; 1C 32 8 **Seeing that the number of brothers was gradually increasing,** Christ's servant **wrote for himself and his brothers a form of life in simple words** in which, after he had placed the observance **of the holy Gospel** as its unshakable foundation, **he inserted a few other things that** seemed **necessary** for a uniform way of life. **As he desired to have what he had written** approved by the **Supreme** Pontiff, he decided to go with his band of simple men before the presence of the Apostolic See, placing his trust solely in God's guidance. As God was looking from *on high* upon their desire, He strengthened the Lk 1:78
companions' frame of mind, terrified at the thought of their simplicity, by showing the man of God a vision of this sort.

1C 33 **It seemed** to him that he was walking along **a road beside which stood a tree of great** height. When **he approached and stood under it, he marveled at** its **height. Suddenly** he was lifted **so** high by divine power **that he touched the top of the tree** and **easily** bent it down to the ground. The man, filled with God, understanding the portent of this vision to refer to the condescension of the Apostolic See, was overjoyed and, after he had comforted his brothers, set out with them on the journey.

1C 33 9 When **he arrived** at the Roman Curia and was brought into the
LJS 21 presence of the Supreme Pontiff, **he explained his proposal,** humbly and urgently imploring him to approve that rule of life. The Vicar of
1C 33 Christ, **the Lord Innocent III, a man** thoroughly **brilliant** with wisdom, admiring in the man of God remarkable purity and simplicity of heart, firmness of purpose, and fiery ardor of will, **gave his assent** to the pious request. Yet he hesitated to do what Christ's little poor
2C 16 man asked because **it seemed** to some of the cardinals to be some-
1C 32 thing novel and difficult **beyond** human **powers.**

Among the cardinals there was a most venerable man, **the lord John of St. Paul, Bishop of Sabina, a lover** of holiness, and helper of Christ's poor. Inspired by the Holy Spirit, he said to the Supreme Pontiff and his brother cardinals: "If we refuse the request of this poor man as novel or too difficult, when all he asks is to be allowed to lead the Gospel life, we must be on our guard lest we commit an offense against Christ's Gospel. For if anyone says that there is something novel or irrational or impossible to observe in this man's desire to live according to the perfection of the Gospel, he would be guilty of blasphemy against Christ, the author of the Gospel." At this observation, the successor of the Apostle Peter turned to the poor man of
2C 16 Christ and said: **"My son, pray to Christ that through you He may**

show us His will, so that once we know it with more certainty, we may confidently approve your holy desire."[a]

> [10]The servant of Almighty God, 2C 16
> giving himself totally to prayer,
> obtained through his devout prayers
> both what he should say outwardly
> and what the pope should hear inwardly.

For when he told a parable, as he had accepted it from God, about a rich king who gladly betrothed a poor but lovely woman who bore him children with the king's likeness, and, for this reason were fed at his table, he added his own interpretation. "The sons and heirs of the eternal King should not fear that they will die of hunger. They have been born of a poor mother by the power of the Holy Spirit in the image of Christ the King, and they will be begotten by the spirit of poverty in our poor little religion. For if the King of heaven prom-
2 Pt 1:11; Mt 19:28 ises his followers an *eternal kingdom,* he will certainly supply them
Mt 5:45 with those things that he gives to *the good* and *the bad* alike."

While the Vicar of Christ listened attentively to this parable and 2C 17
its interpretation, he was quite amazed and recognized without a doubt that Christ had spoken in this man. But he also confirmed a vision he had recently received from heaven, that, as the Divine Spirit indicated, would be fulfilled in this man. He saw in a dream, as he recounted, the Lateran basilica almost ready to fall down. A little poor man, small and scorned, was propping it up with his own back bent so that it would not fall. "I'm sure," he said "he is the one who will hold up Christ's Church by what he does and what he teaches." Because of this, filled with exceptional devotion, he bowed to the request in everything and always loved Christ's servant with special love. Then he granted what was asked and
promised even more. He approved the rule, gave them a mandate to LJS 21

a. The following paragraph, except for the first sentence, was added to Bonaventure's text by Jerome of Ascoli, Minister General of the Order, 1274-1279, and later Pope Nicholas IV. He learned of it from Cardinal Riccardo degli Annibaldi, a relative of Innocent III; cf. Arnold of Saurrant, "Chronicle of the Twenty-Four Generals," in AF III, 365: "When 'he arrived' ["LJS 21] at the Roman Curia and was led into the presence of the Supreme Pontiff, 'he explained his proposal,' asking with humility and persistence that that rule of life be approved. The Vicar of Christ was in the Lateran Palace, walking in a place called the Hall of the Mirror, occupied in deep meditation. Knowing nothing of Christ's servant, he sent him away indignantly. Francis left humbly, and the next night God showed the Supreme Pontiff the following vision. He saw a palm tree sprout between his feet and grow gradually until it became a beautiful tree. As he wondered what this vision might mean, the divine light impressed upon the mind of the Vicar of Christ that this palm tree symbolized the poor man whom he had sent away the previous day. The next morning he commanded his servants to search the city for the poor man. When they found him near the Lateran at Saint Anthony's hospice, he ordered him brought to his presence without delay."

preach penance, and had small tonsures given to all the lay brothers, who were accompanying the servant of God, so that they could freely preach *the word of God.*[a] Lk 11:28

a. The Latin reads *coronas parvulas* [small tonsures], a phrase much different from those of AP 36 (see p. 51 c) *(clericam)* and L3C 51 (see p. 98 b) *(tonsuram)*. In this instance, it is the pope who has this imposed upon the lay brothers; the earlier texts state that it was due to the influence of the cardinal, John of Saint Paul, and that it was imposed on all the brothers. Furthermore, this is imposed "so that they could freely preach the word of God." Bonaventure's reference to Lk 11:28, the conclusion to the praise of "the womb that bore you . . . ," may be a fitting thematic conclusion to this chapter in which generative power of the Word and the image of the woman are so central.

Chapter Four

THE PROGRESS OF THE ORDER UNDER HIS HAND AND THE CONFIRMATION OF THE RULE

[1]Relying on divine grace and papal authority, 2C 17
with great confidence,
Francis took the road to the Spoleto valley, 1C 34
Acts 1:1 that *he might fulfill and teach* Christ's Gospel.
On the way **he discussed with his companions**
how they might sincerely keep the rule they had accepted,
Lk 1:75 **how** they might advance *in* all *holiness* and *justice* before God,
how they should improve themselves LJS 22
and be **an example for others.**

The hour was already late as they continued their long discussion. Since they were **exhausted** from their prolonged **activity, the** LJS 22
hungry men stopped in **a place** of solitude. When there seemed to be
no way for them to get the food they needed, God's **providence im-**
mediately came to their aid. For **suddenly a man carrying bread in** LJS 22
his hand appeared, which **he gave** to Christ's little poor, and then
suddenly disappeared. They had no idea where he came from or
where he went.

From this the poor brothers realized
that while in the company of the man of God
they would be given assistance from heaven,
and so they were refreshed more by the gift of divine generosity
than by the food they had received for their bodies.
Moreover, 1C 35
filled with **divine consolation,**
they firmly **decided**
and irrevocably **resolved never**
to withdraw from the promise to **holy poverty,**
be it from starvation or from **trial.**

[2]When they arrived in **the Spoleto valley,** going back to their holy 1C 35
proposal, **they began to discuss whether they should live among** LJS 23

the people or go off to solitary places. But Christ's servant Francis,
putting his trust in neither his own efforts nor in theirs, sought the
pleasure of the divine will in this matter by the fervor of prayer. Enlightened by a revelation from heaven, he realized that he was sent
by the Lord to win for Christ the souls which the devil was trying to
LJS 23 snatch away. Therefore he chose to live for everyone rather than for
himself alone, drawn by the example of the one who deigned *to die* 2 Cor 5:15
for all.

1C 42 [3]The man of God then gathered with his companions in an abandoned hut near the city of Assisi, where they kept themselves alive
according to the pattern of holy poverty in much labor and want,
drawing their nourishment more from *the bread of tears* than of de- Ps 79:6
lights.

1C 40 They spent their time there praying incessantly, directing their effort mentally rather than vocally to devoted prayers, because they
did not yet have liturgical books from which to chant the canonical
hours. In place of these they had the book of Christ's cross which
they studied continually day and night, taught by the example and
words of their father who spoke to them constantly about the cross
of Christ.

When the brothers asked him to teach them to pray, he said: LJS 27; 1C 45
Lk 11:2 "When you pray, say 'Our Father . . .' and 'We adore you, O Christ, Test 5
in all your churches throughout the whole world, and we bless
you, for by your holy cross you have redeemed the world.' " He also
taught them to praise God in all and with all creatures,[a] to honor 1C 80; 1C 62
priests with a special reverence, and to believe with certainty and to
confess with simplicity the truth of the faith, as the holy Roman
Church holds and teaches. They observed the holy father's teaching LJS 41
in every detail, and prostrated themselves humbly before every 1C 45
church and crucifix which they were able to see from a distance, LJS 27
praying the formula he had taught them.

[4]While the brothers were still staying in the place already mentioned, one Saturday the holy man entered the city of Assisi to preach in the cathedral on Sunday morning, as was his custom. In a hut situated in the garden of the canons, away from his sons in body,

a. This description of the prayer-life of the primitive fraternity and, in particular, Francis's teaching about it, is thoughtfully crafted. As the cross-references indicate, Bonaventure carefully uses the texts of Thomas of Celano, Julian of Speyer, and Francis himself. His addition of *et ex omnibus* [and with all] to Francis's encouragement "to praise God in all creatures" (1C 80) underscores Bonaventure's appreciation for the role of creation in the adoration of God. Cf. infra LMj IX 1. *The Oxford Latin Dictionary* offers twenty-one nuances to the preposition *ex* suggesting that God is praised in and because of, or in accordance with. In light of CtC 3, the preposition is translated "with."

the man devoted to God spent the night in his customary way, in the
prayer of God. About midnight, while some of the brothers were 1C 47
2 Kgs 2:11-14 resting and others were persevering in prayer, behold, *a fiery chariot*
of wonderful brilliance entering the door of the house moved *here*
and there through the little house three times. On top of it sat a
bright globe that looked like the sun, and it made the night bright
as day. *Those who were awake* were dumbfounded, while those
sleeping were disturbed and, at the same time, terrified; they
sensed the brightness with their hearts as much as with their bodies, while the conscience of each was laid bare to the others by the LJS 29
power of that marvelous light.

As they looked into each other's hearts,
they all understood together that the holy father,
1 Cor 5:3 *while away from them in body,*
was present in spirit
transfigured in such an image
radiant with heavenly brilliance
and inflamed with burning ardor
2 Kgs 2:11 in a glowing *chariot of fire,*
as the Lord had shown him to them
Jn 1:47 that they might follow him as *true Israelites.*
Like a second Elijah,
God had made him
2 Kgs 2:12 *a chariot and charioteer* for spiritual men.
Certainly we can believe
Jn 9:32 that *He opened the eyes*
of these simple men at the prayers of Francis
Acts 2:11; Sir 18:5 that they might see *the wonders of God*
just as he had once opened the eyes of a child
2 Kgs 6:17 *to see the mountain full of horses and chariots of fire*
round about Elisha.
When the holy man returned to the brothers,
he began to probe the secrets of their consciences, LJS 29
to draw courage for them from this wonderful vision
and to make many predictions about the growth of the Order.
When he disclosed many things 1C 48
that transcended human understanding,
the brothers completely realized
Is 11:2 *the Spirit of the Lord had come to rest* upon him in such fullness
that it was absolutely safe for them
to follow his life and teaching.

[5]After this,
under the guidance of heavenly grace,
the shepherd Francis led
LJS 21 *the little flock* of those **twelve brothers** Lk 12:32
to St. Mary of the Portiuncula,
that where the Order of Lesser Brothers had had its beginning
by the merits of the mother of God,
it might also begin to grow with her assistance.
1C 36 There, also,
having become a herald of the Gospel,
he went about the cities and towns Mt 9:35; Lk 9:60
proclaiming the kingdom of God
not in words taught by human wisdom, 1 Cor 2:4, 13
but in the power of the Spirit.
To those who saw him,
he seemed to be a person of another age as,
with his mind and face always intent on heaven,[a]
he tried to draw them all on high.
1C 37 As a result,
the vineyard of Christ **began**
to produce buds with the sweet smell of the Lord Sir 24:23
and, when it had produced
flowers *of sweetness, of honor, and of respectability,*
to bring forth abundant *fruit.*

[6]For set on fire by the fervor of his preaching, a great number of people bound themselves by new laws of penance according to the rule which they received from the man of God. Christ's servant decided to name this way of life the Order of the Brothers of Penance. As the road of penance is common to all who are striving toward
LJS 23 heaven, so this way of life admits **clerics and lay, virgins and married of both sexes.** How meritorious it is before God is clear from the numerous miracles performed by some of its members.

Virgins, too, were drawn
to perpetual celibacy,
among whom was the virgin
especially dear to God,
Clare.

a. "Always intent on heaven" is a phrase taken from the fourth antiphon of Lauds in the Office of Saint Martin of Tours, as well as from the *Third Letter*, n. 14, of Sulpicius Severus, (PL 20, p. 182).

As **the first tender sprout,**[a] 2C 109
she gave forth a fragrance
like a lustrous untouched flower
that blossoms in springtime,
and she shone
like a brilliant star.
Now she is glorified in heaven
and fittingly venerated by the Church on earth,
she who was the daughter in Christ
of our holy father Francis, the little poor man,
and the mother of the Poor Ladies.

7 **Many people** as well, not only **driven** by devotion but also in- 1C 37
flamed by a desire for the perfection of Christ, once they had condemned the emptiness of everything worldly, followed the footsteps
of Francis. Their numbers increased daily and quickly reached even
Ps 18:15 *to the ends of the earth.*

Holy poverty, 1C 39
which was all they had to meet their expenses,
made them prompt for every **obedience,**
robust for work,
and free for travel.
And since they had nothing earthly
they loved nothing and feared losing **nothing.**
They were safe wherever they went,
held back by no fear, **distracted by no cares;**
they lived with untroubled minds,
and, without any anxiety,
looked forward to the morrow
and to finding a lodging for the night.

In different parts of the world 1C 40
many insults were hurled against them
as persons unknown and looked down upon,
but true love of the Gospel of Christ
had made them so **patient,**
that they sought
to be where they would suffer physical persecution

a. Curiously, Bonaventure takes Thomas's reference to Bernard of Quintavalle (2C 109) and applies it to Clare.

rather than where their holiness was recognized
and where they could glory in worldly favor.

1C 41 Their very poverty
seemed to them overflowing abundance
since, according to the advice of the Wise Man,
a little pleased them Sir 29:30
instead of much.

When some of the brothers went to the lands of non-believers, a certain Saracen, moved by piety, once offered them money for the food they needed. When they refused to accept it, the man was amazed, seeing that they were without means. Realizing they did not want to possess money because they had become poor out of love of God, he felt so attracted to them that he offered to *minister to all their* 1 Kgs 4:7
needs as long as he had something to give.

O ineffable value of poverty,
whose marvelous power moved
the fierce heart of a barbarian
to such sweet pity!
What a horrible and unspeakable crime
that a Christian *should trample upon* Mt 7:6
this noble pearl
which a Saracen held in such veneration!

8At that time a certain religious of the Order of the Crosiers, Morico by name, was suffering from such a grave and prolonged illness in a hospital near Assisi that the doctors had already despaired of his life. In his need, he turned to the man of God, urgently entreating him through a messenger to intercede for him before the Lord. Our blessed father kindly consented and said a prayer for him. Then he took some bread crumbs and mixed them with oil taken from a lamp that burned before the altar of the Virgin. He made a kind of pill out of them and sent it to the sick man through the hands of the brothers, saying: "Take this medicine to our brother Morico. By means of it, Christ's power will not only restore him to full health, but will make him a sturdy warrior and enlist him in our forces permanently." When the sick man took the medicine, prepared under the inspiration of the Holy Spirit, he was cured immediately. God gave him such strength of mind and body that when a little later he entered the holy man's Order, he wore only a single tunic, under which for a long time he wore a hair shirt next to his skin. He was satisfied with uncooked food such as herbs, vegetables, and fruit; and for many years, never tasted bread or wine, yet remained strong and in good health.

[9]As the merits of the virtues increased in Christ's little poor,
the fragrance of a good reputation spread everywhere
and attracted a great number of people
from different parts of the world
to come and see our holy father.

Among them was **a certain** refined **composer of worldly songs,** 2C 106
who, because of this, had been crowned by the Emperor and was, therefore, called **the "King of Verses."** He decided to visit the man of God, who despised the things of the world. When he found him
Ez 1:3 preaching in a monastery in the village of San Severino, *the hand of the Lord came upon him.* **He saw** Francis, the preacher of Christ's cross, **marked with two bright shining swords intersecting in the shape of a cross. One of them stretched from his head to his feet, and the other across his chest from one hand to the other. He did not know** Christ's servant by sight, **but once he had been pointed out by such a miracle, he recognized him immediately. Stunned at once by what he saw,** he began to resolve to do better. He was struck in his conscience by the power of his words, as if pierced by a spiritual sword coming from his mouth. He completely despised his worldly **displays** and joined the blessed father by profession. When the holy man saw that he had been completely converted from the restlessness of the world **to** the **peace** of Christ, he called him **Brother Pacifico.** Afterwards this man advanced in holiness; and, before he went to France as provincial minister—indeed he was the first to hold that office there, he merited **again to see a great Tau on Francis's forehead, which** displayed a variety of different **colors** that caused his face to glow with wonderful beauty.

The holy man venerated this symbol with great affection,
often spoke of it with eloquence,
and signed it with his own hand **in the letters he sent,**
as if his whole desire were,
according to the prophetic text,
Ez 9:4 *to mark with a Tau* LMj Prol 2
the foreheads of those moaning and grieving,
of those truly converted to Jesus Christ.

[10]With the passing of time when the number of brothers had increased, the watchful shepherd began to summon them to a general chapter at Saint Mary of the Portiuncula to allot to each a portion of
obedience *in the land of* their *poverty,* according to *the measuring cord of* Gn 41:52; Ps 78:54
divine *distribution.* Although there was a complete lack of all necessities and sometimes the number of the brothers was more than five thousand, nevertheless with the assistance of divine mercy, they had adequate food, enjoyed physical health and overflowed with spiritual joy.

Because he could not be physically present at the provincial chapters, he was present in spirit through his solicitous care for governing, fervor of prayer, and effectiveness of blessing, although, he did sometimes appear visibly by God's wonderful power.

1C 48 For the outstanding preacher, who is now a glorious confessor of Christ, Anthony, **was preaching to the brothers at the chapter** of
Arles on the inscription on the cross: ***Jesus of Nazareth, King of the*** Jn 19:19
***Jews.* As he glanced at the door** of the chapter, a **brother** of proven **virtue, Monaldo by name,** moved by a divine reminder, **saw with his bodily eyes blessed Francis lifted up in the air with his arms extended as if on a cross, blessing the brothers. All** the brothers felt themselves **filled with a consolation of spirit,** so great and so un-
usual, that it was certain to them that the Spirit *was bearing witness* **to** Jn 1:7
the true **presence of the** holy **father** among them. This was later confirmed not only by the evidence of signs, but also by the external testimony of the words of the holy father himself.

It must be clearly believed that the almighty power of God,
which allowed the holy bishop Ambrose
to attend the burial of the glorious Saint Martin
and to honor that holy prelate with his holy presence,[a]
also allowed his servant Francis to be present
at the preaching of his true herald Anthony,
in order to attest to the truth of his words,
especially those concerning Christ's cross,
of which he was both a carrier and a minister.

[11]When the Order was already widely spread and Francis was considering having the rule which had been approved by Innocent

a. In the first of his four books describing the miracles of Saint Martin of Tours (+397), Gregory of Tours (+594) writes that Saint Ambrose (+397), while people thought he was dozing at Mass, was present at Martin's funeral that was celebrated at the same time. Cf. Gregory of Tours, *De miraculis sancti Martini Episcopi,* I 5 (PL 71, 918ff).

permanently confirmed by his successor Honorius, he was advised by the following revelation from God.

It seemed to him that he was gathering tiny bread crumbs from the ground, which he had to distribute to a crowd of hungry brothers who stood all around him. He was afraid to give out such little crumbs, fearing that such minute particles might slip between his fingers, when a voice said to him from above: "Francis, make one host out of all the crumbs, and give it to those who want to eat." He did it, whoever did not receive it devoutly, or showed contempt for the gift received, soon appeared obviously covered with leprosy. 2C 209

In the morning the holy man told all this to his companions, re-
Dn 2:19 gretting that he did not understand *the mystery of the vision.* On the
Tb 3:11 following day, while *he kept vigil in prayer,* he heard this voice coming down from heaven: "Francis, the crumbs of last night are the words of the Gospel; the host is the rule and the leprosy is wickedness."

Since he therefore wanted the Rule that had been taken from a more widespread collection of Gospel passages to be confirmed, he went up to a certain mountain led by the Holy Spirit, with two of his companions, to condense it into a shorter form as the vision had dic-
Dt 9:9 tated. There he fasted, content with only *bread* and *water,* and dictated the rule as the Holy Spirit suggested to him while he was praying.[a] When he came down from the mountain, he gave the rule to his vicar to keep. After a few days had elapsed, the vicar claimed that it had been lost through carelessness. The holy man went off
Dt 10:3 again to the place of solitude and rewrote it *just as before,* as if he were
Dt 10:4 taking *the words* from the mouth of God. And he obtained confirmation for it, as he had desired, from the lord Pope Honorius, in the eighth year of his pontificate.

Fervently exhorting the brothers to observe this rule,
Francis used to say
that nothing of what he had placed there
came from his own efforts
but that he dictated everything
just as it had been revealed by God.
To confirm this with greater certainty by God's own testimony,
when only a few days had passed,

a. The allusions to Deuteronomy in this and the following passages suggest that Bonaventure may have been comparing the events surrounding the writing of the Rule to those of Moses' reception of the Ten Commandments. Thus Fonte Colombo may be seen as another Sinai, Francis's fasting on bread and water is similar to that of Moses, as is his vicar, the unnamed Elias, to Aaron who, in Deuteronomy, is also unnamed; and his return to the mountain's top to receive, again, the words of God.

the stigmata of our Lord Jesus were imprinted upon him
by the finger *of the living God,* Rv 7:2
as the seal of the Supreme Pontiff, Christ,
for the complete confirmation of the rule
and the commendation of its author,
as will be described below,
after our exposition of his virtues.

Chapter Five

THE AUSTERITY OF HIS LIFE AND HOW CREATURES PROVIDED HIM COMFORT

[1]When the man of God, Francis, saw
that many were being inspired
by his example
to carry the cross of Christ with fervent spirit,
he himself, like a good leader of Christ's army,
Rv 7:9 was encouraged to reach the palm of victory
through the height of heroic virtue.[a]
He directed his attention to this text of the Apostle:
Gal 5:24 *Those who belong to Christ*
have crucified their flesh
with its passions and desires.[b]
To carry in his own body the armor of the cross,
he held in check his sensual appetites with such a rigid discipline
that he scarcely took what was necessary
for the sustenance of nature.

He used to say that it would be difficult **to satisfy the necessity** of 1C 51
the body without giving in to the earthbound inclinations of the

a. Pages 81-90 of the Index to Bonaventure's *Commentarius in Quatuor Libros Sententiarum* establish his well-articulated theology of virtue. The *ordo amoris* [the ordering of love], as he calls virtue in the first of the *Disputed Question on Evangelical Perfection*, demands a clear sense of direction since his view of creation sees a "twofold order of things, one within the universe, and another with regard to their end." Cf. *Questiones Disputatae de Perfectione Evangelica*, q. I, concl. (V 123); *Commentarius in Libros Sententiarum* I., dist. XLIV, a.1, q.3, ad 2 (I, 786). While the earlier *legendae* and lives of Saint Francis describe his virtues, especially 2C, they do so in a somewhat unclear fashion. To be true to his own theology of virtue, Bonaventure develops an approach that is well-defined and carefully delineated. Cf. Regis J. Armstrong, "Towards an Unfolding of the Structure of St. Bonaventure's *Legenda Major*" *The Cord* 39 (1989): 3-17.

b. Curiously *austeritas* [austerity] is seldom used in Bonaventure's writings; aside from the chapter headings, it appears only three times in this work (LMj VI 2; IX 4; XIII 2). Francis is described only twice as *austerus* [austere] in this work (LMj V1, 7). The same may be said of the earlier descriptions of Francis: the word does not appear in any form in Thomas of Celano, and only once in AP 39 and twice in L3C 39, 61. His *Commentary of Luke's Gospel* and his sermons reveal Bonaventure's appreciation for the word. Austerity is seen as (a) the "beginning of human reparation" (IX, 208); (b) the means of freeing us "from the disturbances of sin" (IX, 466); (c) that which enables us to enter the gate of heaven (VII, 350); and (d) that which identifies us with Christ (VII, 16, 228). In commenting on this passage, Gal 5:24, Bonaventure writes: "Austerity is a sign of an interior holiness . . ." (V, 16).

senses.[a] Therefore when he was in good health, he **hardly ever allowed** himself **cooked food; and on the rare occasion when he did so, he either sprinkled it with ashes** or added **water** to make it extremely insipid. **What shall I say about wine, when he would** scarcely **drink** even **enough water** while **he was burning with** a fierce **thirst?** He discovered more effective methods of abstinence and daily improved in their exercise. Although he had already attained the height of perfection, nevertheless always beginning, he was innovative in punishing the lust of his flesh with afflictions.[b]

When he went out among people, he conformed himself to his
IX 13; LR III 14 hosts in the food he ate **because of the text of the Gospel.** But when Lk 10:7
he returned home, he kept strictly his sparse and rigid abstinence. Thus he was austere toward himself but considerate toward his neighbor. Making himself obedient to the Gospel of Christ in everything, he gave an edifying example not only when he abstained but also when he ate.

1C 52; LJS 31 More often than not, **the naked ground was a bed for his** weary **body; and he would often sleep sitting up, with a piece of wood or a**
LJS 31 **stone** positioned **for his head.** Clothed in a single poor little **tunic,** he
served the Lord in *cold and nakedness.* 2 Cor 11:27

[2]Once when he was asked how he could protect himself against the bite of the winter's frost with such thin clothing, he answered with a burning spirit: "If we were touched within by the flame of desire for our heavenly home, we would easily endure that exterior cold." In the matter of clothes, he had a horror for softness and loved
coarseness, claiming that John the Baptist had been praised by the Mt 11:8; Lk 7:25
Lord for this. If he felt the softness of a tunic that had been given to him, he used to sew pieces of cord on the inside because he used to
Mt 11:8 say, according to the word of Truth itself, that we should look for soft ER II 14
clothes not in the huts of the poor but in the palaces of princes. For his own certain experience had taught him that demons were terrified by harshness, but were inspired to tempt one more strongly by what is pleasant and soft.

a. The changes made to Thomas's text are important for obtaining a correct understanding of austerity. Bonaventure changes "it is impossible" (1C 51) to "it is difficult." More importantly, while Thomas adds ". . . without bowing to pleasure," Bonaventure states: "without giving into earthbound inclination of the senses." Thus he directs the readers attention to the larger questions of the significance of the human body in the plan of God, and the role of the senses.

b. Bonaventure uses *libido* [lust] in this passage, a word that appears rarely in these documents. Francis never uses the word, Thomas of Celano once (2C 126), and Bonaventure only three times and only in this chapter (LMj V 1,3,4). Bonaventure's homilies deal with the word sporadically. Following Augustine, he defines it as "the love of those things that someone unwilling can lose," cf. Sermon II on the Purification (IX, 646), and identifies twelve "masks" used by the devil in its promotion, e.g. riches, laziness, luxury, etc, cf. Sermon VI and the XXII Sunday after Pentecost.

One **night**, contrary to his **accustomed** manner, he had allowed a 2C 64
feather pillow to be placed **under his head** because of **an illness** in
his head and **eyes.** The devil got into it, gave him no rest until the
hours **of matins,** and in many ways disturbed him from the fervor **of**
holy **prayer,** until, after he had called a companion, he had him **take**
the pillow with the devil far away out of his cell. But when the
brother went out of the cell **with the pillow, he lost** the strength and
use of his limbs, until **at the voice of the holy** father, **who was aware**
of this in spirit, his former strength of heart and body was fully restored to him.

Is 21:8 [3]**Unbending in discipline** *he stood upon his guard,* taking the great- 1C 42
est care to preserve purity of both soul and body.[a] Near the beginning
of his conversion, **in wintertime he would** frequently **immerse him-** LJS 24
self in a ditch filled with icy water in order to perfectly subjugate the
enemy within and preserve the white robe of modesty from the
flames of voluptuousness. He used to say that it should be incomparably more tolerable for a spiritual man to endure great cold in his
flesh rather than to feel even slightly the heat of carnal lust in his
heart.

1 Cor 7:5 [4]**One night** while *he gave himself to prayer* **in a cell at the hermitage** 2C 116
1 Sm 3:8 **of Sarteano,** the ancient enemy *called* **him** *three times:* **"Francis,**
Francis, Francis!" When **he replied** to him, he asked **what** he
wanted. And that one continued deceitfully: **"There is no sinner in**
the world whom God **will not forgive if he is converted. But if any-**
Dt 3:39 **one kills himself by hard penance,** *he will find no mercy* for all eternity." **At once by a revelation,** the man of God **recognized the**
enemy's treachery, **how he was trying to call him back to being**
lukewarm. This was surely shown by what followed. For immedi-
Jb 41:12 ately after this, at the whim of him *whose breath sets coals afire,* **a seri-**
ous temptation of the flesh seized him. When that lover of chastity
felt it coming, after **he took off his clothes,** he began **to lash himself**
very strenuously **with a cord,** saying: **"Come on, Brother Ass, that's**
the way you should stay under the whip! The tunic has given up on

a. This passage of Isaiah 21:8 appears frequently in Bonaventure's writings. In his *Commentary on Luke's Gospel,* his three references are specifically directed to the struggles of the spiritual life (XII 58; XVII 7; XXI 59), most specifically to the temptations of the contemplative life. A reference in *The Exposition on the Rule of the Friars Minor* IV centers on the roles of the Minister and Custodian which Bonaventure sees in terms of vigilance or keeping guard. *The Treatise on Twenty-Five Points to Remember* 23 employs the same language as this passage of LMj in speaking of the ancient enemy that attacks both the inner and outer man. The Latin has *utriusque hominis puritate servanda* [preserving purity of both persons], a difficult phrase to translate literally. It's soul and body. Cf. VII 326, 427, 539; VIII 419, 517.

religion; it presents a symbol of holiness. It is not lawful for a lustful person to steal it. *If you want to leave, leave!"* Is 40:4; 1 Sm 30:13

2C 117 Even more inspired by a wonderful fervor of spirit, once he opened the cell, went out into the garden and, throwing his poor still naked body into the deep snow, began to pack it together by the handful into seven mounds. Showing them to himself, he spoke as if to another person: "Here, the larger one is your wife; those four over there are your two sons and two daughters; the other two are a servant and a maid who are needed to serve them. Hurry, then, and get them some clothes because they are freezing to death! But if the complicated care of them is annoying, then take care to serve one Master!" At that the tempter went away conquered. And the holy man returned to the cell in victory, because while he froze outwardly as penance, he so quenched the fire of lust within, that he hardly felt anything of that sort from that time on.

A certain brother, who *was giving himself to prayer* at the time, 1 Cor 7:5
saw *in the bright moonlight* all these things. When the man of God Jb 31:36
learned that he had seen this that night, while giving him an account of the temptation, he ordered him to reveal to no living being what he had seen as long as he himself lived.

1C 43 [5]He taught not only that the vices of the flesh must be mortified and its prompting checked, but also that the exterior senses, through which death enters the soul, should be guarded with the greatest care.[a]

2C 112 He solicitously commanded the avoidance of familiarities with women by sight or by conversation, for many are an occasion of ruin; and he maintained that, through these, a weak spirit would be broken and a strong spirit often weakened. He said that avoiding this contagion when conversing with them, except for the most
well-tested, was as easy as *walking* in fire *and not burning one's feet.* Prv 6:28
He himself so *turned aside his eyes, lest they see vanity* of this kind, that, Ps 119:37
as he once said to a companion, he almost recognized no woman by her face. For he did not think it was safe to drink into one's interior such images of woman's form, which could either rekindle the fire in
2C 114 an already tamed flesh, or stain the brightness of a pure heart. He even used to declare that a conversation with a woman was unnec-
ER XII 3,4 essary except only for confession or very brief instruction, as their

a. *Exteriores sensus* [the exterior senses]: while Bonaventure uses the words of Thomas (1C 43), his theology of the spiritual senses suggests that he perceives much more. The already noted change of Thomas's text in which Bonaventure articulates a different purpose in the practice of austerity, LMj V 1, describes the result of sin as bringing about the "earthbound inclination of the senses." Thus the demand for austerity, i.e., to direct the senses "heavenward" or, in the terminology of this text, "life-giving."

salvation requires and respectability allows. **"What business,"** he asked, **"should** a religious **have with a woman, except when she religiously makes a request for holy penance or for counsel concerning a better life? When one is too secure, one is less wary of the** 2C 113
enemy. If the devil can hold onto one hair of a person, he will soon make it grow into a plank."

[6]He taught the brothers to flee with all their might from idleness, ER VII 11; LR V 2; Test 21
the cesspool of all evil thoughts;[a] and he demonstrated to them by his own example that they should master their rebellious and lazy flesh by constant discipline and useful work. Therefore he used to 2C 129
call his body **Brother Ass,** for he felt it should be subjected to heavy labor, beaten frequently with whips, and fed with the poorest food.

If he saw **someone idle** and vagrant, wanting to eat **the labors** of 2C 75
others, he thought he should be called "**Brother Fly,"** because he did nothing good himself but poisoned the good done by others and so rendered himself useless and obnoxious to all. On account of **this he** 2C 161
once said: "I want my brothers to work and be kept busy, so that, given **to idleness, they stray into what is forbidden with heart and tongue."**

He strongly wanted the brothers to observe the silence recommended by the Gospel, so that they particularly abstain at all times 2C 160
Mt 12:37 from *every idle word,* since they would have *to render an account on the*
day of judgment But if he found a brother accustomed to shallow talk, ER XI; RH; Adm; LR III
he would reprimand him bitterly, affirming that a modest silence was the guardian of a pure heart and no small virtue itself, in view of
Prv 18:21 the fact that *death and life* are said to be *in the hands of the tongue,* not so much by reason of taste as by reason of speech.

[7]Although he energetically urged the brothers to lead an austere
Col 3:12 life, he was not pleased by an intransigent severity that did not *put on*
a heart of piety and **was not seasoned with the salt of discernment.**[b] 2C 22

---

a. Bonaventure introduces *otium* [idleness] into his discussion of austerity and, in doing so, describes it in words similar to those of his first letter to the entire Order in 1257: "Certain brothers have succumbed to idleness, that cesspool of every vice, where they have been lulled into choosing a monstrous kind of state somewhere between the active life and the contemplative, while cruelly feeding on the blood of living souls." Cf. *Epistolae Officiales* I 2 (VIII, 469), translation is that of Dominic Monti, *Works of Saint Bonaventure V: Writings Concerning the Franciscan Order* introduction and translation by Dominic Monti (St. Bonaventure, NY: The Franciscan Institute, 1994), 59. The theme returns frequently in Bonaventure's writings, especially those to the friars, *Instruction for Novices* IX 1-2; *Constitutions of Narbonne* VI, and the *Defense of the Mendicants* XII 17 (VIII 321, 455, 484, 502).

b. Bonaventure's concept of *discretio* is more in keeping with the contemporary English word, discernment. In his *Commentarius in Ecclesiasten,* C. IX he writes of *discernendum* [distinguishing or discerning] between what is bad and good (VI, 75), a process he maintains in his *Commentarius in Ioannem,* C. XI, coll. XIi, a. 38; coll. XIii, 7, that is clouded by the sleep of sin (VI, 587, 589). In his *Commentarius in Evangelium Lucae* C. II, v. 45, he describes the time of *discretionis* [discernment] as that of turning to good (VII, 66).

One night, when one of the brothers was tormented with hunger
2C 21 because of his excessive fasting, he was unable to get any rest. **The pious shepherd** understood the danger threatening his sheep, called the brother, put some bread before him, and, to take away **his embarrassment, he started eating first** and gently **invited** him to eat. The brother put aside his embarrassment, **took the food,** overjoyed that, through the discerning condescension of his shepherd, he had both avoided harm to his body, and received an edifying example of no small proportion.

When morning came, after the man of God had called the brothers together and recounted what had happened during the night, he added this reminder: **"Brothers, in this incident let charity, not food, be an example for you."** He taught them, moreover, to follow **discernment** as the charioteer of the virtues,[a] not that which the flesh recommends, but that taught by Christ, whose most sacred life expressed for us the exemplar of perfection.

8Encompassed by the weakness of the flesh,
a human cannot follow
the spotless crucified Lamb so perfectly
as to avoid contacting any filth.
Therefore he taught
those who strive after the perfect life
to cleanse themselves daily
with streams of tears.
Although he had already attained extraordinary purity
of heart and body,
he did not cease to cleanse the eyes of his soul
with a continuous flood of tears,
unconcerned about the loss of his bodily sight.[b]
When he had incurred a very serious eye illness
from his continuous weeping,
and a doctor advised him to restrain his tears
if he wanted to avoid losing his sight,
the holy man answered:
"Brother doctor,
we should not stave off

a. The Latin here is *aurigam virtutum* [the charioteer of the virtues]. The phrase comes from Bernard of Clairvaux, *On The Song of Songs*, Sermon 49:5, translated by Kilian Walsh and Irene M. Edmonds (Kalamazoo, MI: Cistercian Publications, 1962), 25.

b. In a passage comparing the tears of Mary Magdalene with those of St. Monica and St. Ambrose, Bonaventure notes: "The blessed Francis wept so much that the doctors told him to stop weeping, otherwise he would be blind. And, because of his tears, he did go blind. Cf. *Sermon 1 on St. Mary Magdalene* ii (IX, 557).

a visitation of heavenly light even a little
because of love of the light
that we have in common with flies.
For the body receives the gift of light
for the sake of the spirit
and not the spirit for the sake of the body."
He preferred to lose his sight
rather than to repress the devotion of his spirit
and hold back the tears
which cleansed his interior vision
so that he could see God.[a]

[9]Once he was advised by doctors, and was strongly urged by the brothers, to undergo the process of cauterization. The man of God agreed humbly because he realized that it would be at the same time salutary and harsh. **The surgeon who had been summoned** then 2C 166
came and placed an iron instrument in the fire for cauterizing. But the servant of Christ, **comforting his body, which was struck with panic, spoke to the fire** as a friend: **"My brother Fire, your beauty is the envy of all creatures, the Most High created you strong, beautiful and useful. Be gracious to me in this hour; be courteous! I pray the Great Lord who created you to temper now your heat that I may bear your gentle burning."**

With the prayer finished, he traced **the sign of the cross** over the iron instrument **glowing in the fire, and waited unafraid. The hissing iron was sunk into tender flesh, and the burn is extended straight slowly from the ear to the eyebrow.** How much pain that burning caused, that holy man expressed: "Praise the Most High," he said **to the brothers, "because I tell you truly, I felt neither the heat of the fire nor any pain in my flesh." And turning to the doctor, he said: "If my flesh isn't well cooked, then try again!"** The experienced doctor was amazed at the powerful strength of spirit in his weak body, and proclaimed it a divine miracle, saying: "I say to you,
Lk 5:26 brothers, *I have seen wonderful things today*."

a. This carefully crafted paragraph, a bridge between the more negative section of LMj V 1-7 and the more positive (LMj V 9-12), needs to be understood in light of Bonaventure's theology of the spiritual senses, the "fullest account" of which, according to Karl Rahner's thorough study, "is to be found in the mystical theology of Saint Bonaventure," cf. Karl Rahner, "The Doctrine of the Spiritual Senses in the Middle Ages," *Theological Investigations* XIV 7 (New York: Crossroad-Seabury, 1979) 104-134. Clearly the result of grace, Bonaventure understands this as one of challenges of spiritual growth. Thus the following paragraphs of Bonaventure's portrait of Francis touches on the "spiritualization" of his senses of touch, taste—and smell which is implied, hearing, and sight.

For he had reached such purity
LJS 64 that his **flesh was in** remarkable **harmony**
with his spirit
and his spirit with God.
As a result God ordained
that *creation which serves its Maker* Wis 16:24
should be subject in an extraordinary way
to his will and command.

3C 17 [10]**For, at another time when** the servant of God **was suffering from a severe illness at the hermitage of Sant'Urbano,** he was feeling the weakness of his nature, **and requested a drink of wine. He was told that there was no wine that** they could **give him; so he ordered some water and when it was brought, he blessed it with the sign of the cross. At once what had been brought as pure water became excellent wine; and what the poverty** of a deserted place **could not provide,** the purity **of the holy** man obtained.

At its taste,
he immediately **recovered with such ease,**
that the newness **of taste**
and the renewal **of health,**
supernaturally renewing the tasted and the taster,
confirmed by a twofold witness,
that he had perfectly stripped away *the old man* Col 3:9-10
and put on *the new*.

1C 61 [11]Not only did **creation** serve God's servant
at his nod,
but even the Creator's providence condescended everywhere
to his pleasure.

For one time when his body was weighed down by many forms of
2C 126 illness, he had a desire to hear some music to arouse the joy of his
spirit. But since it seemed inappropriate that this should be done by a
human ministry, the deference of angels came to indulge the holy
man's pleasure. **One night, as he was keeping vigil and meditating**
about the Lord, **suddenly a lute was playing some wonderful har-**
mony and *a very sweet melody*. **No one was seen,** but *the changes in his* Sir 40:21; Ez 10:13
hearing **suggested that the lute player was moving back and forth**
from one place to another. With *his spirit turned to God,* there was Jb 34:14
such delight in that sweet sounding song, that he thought he had
exchanged this world for the other.

This did not remain hidden from the brothers who were close to him, who, by clear signs, would often see him *visited by the Lord* with such overwhelming and frequent consolation, that he was incapable of keeping them hidden.

Lk 1:68; 7:16

[12]At another time when the man of God and a companion were walking on the banks of the Po while on a journey of preaching between Lombardy and the Marches of Treviso, they were overtaken by the darkness of night. The road was exposed to many great dangers because of the darkness, the river and some swamps. His companion said to the holy man: "Pray, father, that we may be saved from these threatening dangers!" Full of confidence, the man of God answered him: "*God is powerful,* if it pleases him in his sweetness, to disperse this darkness and give us the benefit of light." Scarcely had he finished speaking when, behold, such a great light began to shine around them with a heavenly radiance that they could see in clear light not only the road, but also many other things all around, although the night remained dark elsewhere. By the guidance of this light they were led physically and comforted spiritually; singing hymns of praise to God they arrived safely at their lodging, which was a long way off.

Lk 3:8

Consider that,
at his nod,
that man of admirable purity and great virtue
tempered the heat of fire,
changed the taste of water,
brought comfort with angelic melody
and was led by divine light,
so that, in this way, it might be proved
that the entire fabric of the universe
came to the service
of the sanctified senses of the holy man.[a]

a. It is helpful to read the first two chapters of Bonaventure's *Journey of the Soul into God* in order to appreciate his attempts to theologize on the uniqueness of the purification of a human's senses to the extend of returning to the order established by God.

Chapter Six

His Humility and Obedience and the Divine Condescensions Made to Him at His Nod

2C 140 [1]**Humility,**
the guardian and embellishment of all the virtues,
had filled the man of God **with abundance.**
In his own opinion
he was nothing but a sinner,
2C 26 **though** in truth **he was a mirror**
and the splendor of every kind of holiness.
As he had learned from Christ,
he strove to build himself upon this
Cor 3:10; Heb 6:1 *like a wise architect laying a foundation.*[a]
He used to say that it was for this reason
that the Son of God came down
from the height of his Father's bosom
to our lowly estate
so that our Lord and Teacher might teach humility
1C 53 in both **example** and **word.**

1C 4 Therefore as Christ's disciple, he strove **to regard himself** as **worthless** in his own eyes and those of others, recalling what had been said by his supreme Teacher: *What is highly esteemed among mortals is an abomination before God.* He used to make this statement frequently: "What a person is before God, that he is and no more." Lk 16:15
Adm XIX 2 Therefore, judging that it was foolish to be elated by worldly **favors,** he rejoiced in insults and was saddened by praise. If nothing else, *he* **would rather** *hear himself blamed* **than praised, knowing that the** former would lead **him to change his life, while the latter would push him to a fall.** And so **frequently** when people extolled the merits of his holiness, he commanded **one of the brothers to impress** upon his ears words that were, on the contrary, insulting. **When the**

2C 140 · Ps 31:14 · 1C 53 · LJS 33

a. Bonaventure's theology of humility is clearly stated in his *Disputed Questions on Evangelical Perfection*, Question I, in which he proposes it as "the foundation of all virtue," cf. *Quaestiones Disputatae de Evangelica Perfectione* (V, 117-124). Throughout those writings directed to the friars he continually returns to the theme and repeatedly describes it as virtue's "guardian" and "beauty" or "embellishment," whose primary model is Christ.

brother, though unwilling, called him a boor and a mercenary, un**skilled and useless, he would reply,** exhilarated in mind and face: **"May the Lord bless you,** my beloved son, **for** it is **you** who **are really telling the very truth and what the son of Peter Bernardone needs to hear."**

[2]**In order** to make **himself** looked down upon by **others,** 1C 54
he did **not** spare himself **the shame** of bringing up his own faults
in his preaching before all the people.

Once **it happened, because he was ill,** he somewhat relaxed the 1C 52
rigor of his abstinence in order to recover his health. **When his physi-**
cal strength returned, the authentic scorner of himself was inspired
to insult his own flesh. "It is not right," he said, "that people should
believe I am abstaining while, in fact, I eat meat secretly." He got up,
inflamed with the spirit of true humility, and after he had called the
people together in the piazza **of the city of Assisi,** he solemnly entered the principal church with many of the brothers whom he had
brought with him. **He commanded that he be dragged** before the
eyes of all, **with a cord tied around his neck** and stripped to only his
underwear, to the stone where criminals received their punishment.
Climbing upon the stone, although he had a fever and was weak and
the weather was bitter cold, he preached with much vigor and spirit.
He asserted to all his hearers that he should not be honored as a spiritual man but rather he should be despised by all as a carnal man and
a glutton. Therefore those who had gathered there were amazed **at**
so great a spectacle. They were well aware of his austerity, and so
their hearts were struck with compunction; but they professed that
his humility was easier to admire than to imitate. Although this inci-
Is 20:3 dent seemed to be more *a portent* like that of a prophetic utterance
than an example, nevertheless it was a lesson in true humility instructing the follower of Christ **that he must condemn** the fame of 1C 53
transitory praise, suppress the arrogance of bloated bragging, and reject the lies of deceptive pretense.

[3]**He more often did many things in this way,** LJS 33
Ps 30:12 **that** outwardly he would become *like a discarded utensil*
while inwardly he would possess the spirit of holiness.

Ps 27:13 **He strove to hide** *the good things of his Lord* **in the secrecy of his** 2C 133
heart, not wanting to display for his own glory what could be the
cause of ruin. For often, when many were calling him blessed, he
would utter **words of this sort: "Don't praise me as if I were safe! I**

can still have sons and daughters. No one should be praised as long as his end is uncertain." This he would say to those who praised him; but to himself: "Francis, if the Most High had given so much to a thief, he would be more grateful than you!"

2C 134 He would often say to the brothers: "No one should flatter himself for big applause for doing anything a sinner can do. A sinner," he said, "can fast, pray, weep, and mortify his flesh. This one thing he cannot do: be faithful to his Lord. So this is the only reason for boasting: if we return to the Lord the glory that is his, if we serve him faithfully, and credit Him for what he has given us."

2C 151 [4]That this Gospel merchant
would profit in many ways
and *melt down* all the present time into merit, Jer 6:29
he chose not only to be under, rather than above
but also to obey, rather than command.

Therefore, resigning the office as general, he asked for a guardian whose will he would obey in all things. He maintained that the fruit of holy obedience was so abundant, that, for those who submit their necks to its yoke, no time passes without profit. Therefore he always promised obedience to the brother who customarily was with him when travelling. Once he said to his companions: "Among the many other things that divine piety has bestowed upon me, it has granted me this grace: that I would obey a novice of one hour, if he were given to me as my guardian, as diligently as I would obey the oldest and most discerning brother. A subject," he said, "must not consider in his prelate a human being, but rather Him for love of Whom he is a subject. The more contemptibly he presides, the more pleasing is the humility of the one who obeys."

2C 152 One time, when they asked him who should be judged truly obedient, he suggested as an example the likeness of a dead body. "Take a lifeless corpse," he said, "and place it wherever you want! You will see that it does not resist being moved, nor complain about location, nor protest if left. Sit it on a throne, and it will look down, not up; dress it in purple, and it looks twice as pale. This," he said, "is someone truly obedient, who doesn't argue about why he's being moved; he doesn't care where he's placed, he doesn't pester you to transfer him. When raised to an office, he keeps his usual humility; the more he's honored, the more he considers himself unworthy."[a]

a. See 2C 152, infra, 345 a.

5 **He once said to his companion: "I wouldn't consider myself a Lesser Brother unless I had the attitude I will describe to you. Suppose, as a prelate of the brothers, I go to the chapter, preach and admonish the brothers, and, at the end, they speak against me: 'You are not suitable for us, because you are uneducated, inarticulate, unlettered, and simple!' So, in the end, I am thrown out in disgrace, looked down upon by everyone. I tell you, unless I hear these words with the same expression on my face, with the same joy, and with the same resolution for holiness, I am in no sense a Lesser Brother!" And he added: "In a prelacy there is a fall, in praise a precipice, in the humility of a subject profit for the soul. Why, then, do we pay more attention to dangers than to profits, while we have time for profit?"** 2C 145

For this reason, 1C 38
Francis,
the pattern of humility,
wanted his brothers **to be called Lesser** ER I 6-7; LRI II 1
and the prelates of his Order to be called ministers,
Mt 25:45 that he might use the words of the Gospel
he had promised to observe,
and that his followers
might learn from this very name
that they had come to the school
of the humble Christ
to learn humility.
The teacher of humility,
Jesus Christ,
to instruct his disciples in true humility,
said:
Mt 20:26-2 *"Whoever wishes to become great among you,* ER V 11-12
let him be your servant;
and whoever wishes to be first among you
will be your slave."

When the Lord of Ostia, the chief protector and promoter of the Order of Lesser Brothers—who afterwards, as the holy man **had foretold,** was elevated to the honor of the supreme pontificate, and was called Gregory IX—asked him whether he would allow his brothers to be promoted to ecclesiastical offices, he responded: **"My Lord, my brothers are called 'lesser' precisely so they will not presume** *to become 'greater.'* **If you want them** to bear *fruit in the Church of* 2C 148 LJS 65 Mt 20:26; Jn 15:2, 8; Phil 3:6

God, keep them and preserve them in the status in which *they were* 1 Cor 7:20
called, and do not permit them to rise to ecclesiastical prelacies."

[6]And because he preferred humility to honor
both in himself and in all his subjects,
God, the lover of the humble,
judged him worthy of higher honors
as a heavenly vision revealed to one brother,
a man of outstanding virtue and devotion.

2C 122 For when he was in the company of the man of God and was pray-
2C 123 ing fervently with him in a deserted church, he passed into ecstasy,
and saw *among the many thrones in heaven* one more noble than the Rv 4:1-2
rest, adorned with precious stones and glittering with great glory.
He wondered within himself at the splendor of the lofty throne, and Est 15:9
thought quietly about whose it might be. *Then he heard a voice saying* Dn 4:16; Acts 9:4
to him: "This throne belonged to one of *those who fell,* and now it is Is 14:9-15; Rv 12:7
reserved for the humble Francis." Finally, when the brother *came* Acts 12:11
back to himself from the flight of prayer, he followed the blessed man
as he proceeded to act in his usual manner.

2C 123 As they went along the road, talking to one another about God,
that brother, not unmindful of his vision, skillfully asked him what
he thought of himself. The humble servant of Christ said to him: "I
see myself as the greatest of sinners." When the brother said, to the
contrary, that he could neither say nor feel this with a good conscience, [Francis] continued: "If Christ had pursued so great a criminal with such mercy, I surely think he would be much more
grateful to God than I." At hearing such remarkable humility, the
brother was convinced of the truth of the vision, knowing from the Mt 23:12; Lk 1:52
sacred testimony of the Gospel that the truly humble will be exalted
to the height of glory from which the proud have been cast out.

2C 202 [7]Another time, when he was praying in a deserted church at Monte Casale in the province of Massa, he realized through the spirit that sacred relics had been left there. When he sadly reflected that they had been robbed of the honor due them for a long time, he ordered the brothers to bring them with reverence to the place. But when, for an urgent reason he had gone away, his sons, forgetting the father's order, disregarded the merit of obedience. One day when they wanted to celebrate the sacred mysteries, after they had removed the cover from the altar, they discovered—not without great wonder—some very beautiful and very fragrant bones. They were gazing upon the relics which had been brought there not by human hands, but by the power of God.

A little later, when he had returned, the man devoted to God diligently began to inquire if his orders about the relics had been carried out. The brothers humbly confessed their fault of neglecting obedience, and won pardon together with a penance. And the holy
Ps 18:47 man said: *"Blessed be the Lord my God* who himself carried out what you were supposed to do."

Consider carefully
the care of divine providence for our dust,
and ponder
the excellent virtue of the humble Francis
in the eyes of God!
Whose commands a human did not heed,
whose wishes God obeyed.[a]

8 One time when he came to Imola, he went to the bishop of the 2C 147
city and humbly asked, according to his pleasure, to be able to call the people together to preach to them. The bishop replied harshly to him: "Brother, I preach to my people and that is enough!" The gen-
Mt 26:75, 58 uine humble man bowed his head and *went outside,* but less than an hour later *he came back in*. At this, since the bishop was annoyed, he asked him what he was looking for a second time. He responded with a humility of heart as well as of voice: "My lord, if a father throws his son out by one door, he should come back by another." The bishop, overcome by humility, embraced him with a smile, saying: "From now on, you and all your brothers have my general permission to preach in my diocese, because your holy humility has earned it."

9 It happened once that he came to Arezzo at a time when the 2C 108
whole city was shaken by a civil war that threatened its destruction. Given hospitality in the outskirts, he saw demons over the city leaping for joy and arousing the troubled citizens to mutual slaughter. In order to put to flight those seditious spiritual powers, he sent Brother Sylvester, a man of dove-like simplicity, before him as a herald, saying: "Go in front of the city gate and, on behalf of Almighty God, command the devils to leave at once!" The genuine

a. In his commentary on the healing of the centurian's son, Bonaventure comments on the power of humility in prompting God to bow to human needs and desires. Thus this sentence provides a transition from the pursuit of humility as a self-emptying to a means of drawing the Almighty to human needs. *Commentary on Luke's Gospel* VII 18 (VII, 170).

obedient man hurried to carry out his father's orders and, caught up in *praise before the face* of the Lord, he began to cry out boldly in front of the city gate: "On behalf of Almighty God and by the command of his servant Francis, get away from here, all you demons." At once the city returned to peace and all the citizens reformed their civil law with great tranquility. Ps 94:2

Once the raging pride of the demons,
which had surrounded the city like a siege,
had been driven out,
as the wisdom of a poor man entered in,
that is, the humility of Francis,
it brought back peace and saved the city.
For by his lofty virtue of humble obedience,
he had gained such powerful control
over those rebellious and obstinate spirits
that he could repress their ferocious brashness
and drive back their savage violence.

2C 119 [10]The proud demons flee from the lofty virtues of the humble,
unless occasionally the divine goodness allows them
to be buffeted to protect their humility, 2 Cor 12:7
as the Apostle Paul writes about himself,
and as Francis learned through experience.

On one occasion he was invited by Lord Leo, the Cardinal of Santa Croce, to stay with him for a little while in the City, and he humbly accepted out of respect and affection. The first night, when he wanted to rest after his prayer, demons came upon the soldier of Christ, attacking him fiercely. After they beat him long and hard,
Lk 10:30 they finally *left him half-dead*. When they left, the companion he had called came. The man of God told him what had happened, adding: "Brother, I believe that the devils can do nothing, unless God's providence allows it. Therefore, they have now attacked me fiercely in this way, because my staying at the court of the great doesn't offer good example. My brothers, who stay in poor places, hearing that I am staying with cardinals, might suspect perhaps that I am involved in
Lk 7:25 worldly affairs, puffed up by honors and *living in luxury*. And so, I think that one who is set up as an example is better off avoiding courts and living humbly among the humble in humble places, that
Prv 28:27 he might bring about *a strengthening of those who suffer* want, by putting up with the same things." In the morning, then, they went to the cardinal, offered a humble excuse, and said good-bye.

[11]The holy man abhorred
pride, the source of all evil,
and disobedience, its worst offspring,
but he welcomed the humility of repentance
with no less intensity.

It happened once that **a brother, who** had done something against the law **of obedience,** was brought to him to be punished according to justice. Seeing that the brother showed clear signs of being truly sorry, the man of God was drawn to be easy on him out of love of humility. However, so this easy forgiveness might not be an incentive for others to fail in their duty, **he ordered that the brother's hood be taken off and thrown** into the midst of a fire, so that all could see what and how harsh a punishment the offense of disobedience deserved. When **the hood** had been within the fire for a while, he ordered that **it be pulled out of the flames** and returned to the humbly repentant brother. What a marvel! The hood was pulled out of the middle of the flames, showing no trace of a burn. This was done so that, with this one miracle, God might so commend both the holy man's virtue and the humility of repentance. 2C 154

Therefore,
worthy of being followed
is the humility of Francis
that obtained such marvelous honor even on earth
that, at his mere nod,
it inclined God to his wish,
changed the attitude of a human being,
repulsed the obstinacy of demons at his command,
and restrained the greed of flames.
In truth,
as it exalts its possessors,
this is what
wins honor from all,
while it exhibits reverence to all.

Chapter Seven

HIS LOVE OF POVERTY
AND THE MIRACULOUS FULFILLMENT OF NEEDS

1 Among the gifts of charisms[a]
which Francis obtained from the generous Giver,
he merited,
as a special privilege,
to grow in the riches of simplicity
LR VI 6; 2C 55 through his love of the highest poverty.
The holy man,
realizing that she was a close friend of the Son of God,
yet was nowadays an outcast throughout almost the whole world,
was eager to espouse her *in an everlasting love.* Jer 31:3
For her sake,
he not only *left his father and mother,* Gn 2:24; Mk 10:7
but also scattered
everything he could have.
No one coveted gold as he coveted poverty;
no one was as careful of guarding a treasure
as he was of this pearl of the Gospel. Mt 13:45-46
In this especially would his sight be offended:
if he saw in the brothers
anything which did not accord completely with poverty.
Truly, from the beginning of his religious life until his death,
his wealth was
a tunic, a cord, and underwear,
1C 76 with these he was content.
2C 200 He frequently brought to mind with tears
the poverty of Jesus Christ and his mother,
claiming that she was the queen of the virtues
because she shone so remarkably

a. The Latin reads *inter cetera charismatum dona* [among the gifts of charisms]. *Charismata* is a word that does not frequently appear in Bonaventure's writings. Beyond its use here and in the conclusion to Francis's miracles (LMj M X 8), it appears in the *Commentary of Luke's Gospel* I 114 (VII, 370) and the *Commentary on John's Gospel* XVII, Collation LXII 2 (VI, 611). The Lucan Commentary refers to Is 26:8, "Your name and remembrance are the desire of the soul . . ." as Bonaventure suggests that remembrance leads us to charisms that must be sought.

1 Tm 6:15; Rv 19:16 **in the *King of Kings***
and in the Queen, his mother.

For when the brothers were seeking **at a gathering about which of the virtues makes one a greater friend of Christ, he replied, as if opening the secret of his heart: "You know,** brothers, **that poverty is the special way to salvation,** as the stimulus of humility and the root of perfection, **whose fruit is many,** but hidden. For this is the
Mt 13:44 *hidden treasure of the* Gospel *field;* to buy it, everything must be sold,
and, in comparison, everything that cannot be sold must be spurned."

2"Whoever desires to attain this height," he said, "must renounce 2C 194
in some way not only worldly wisdom but also the expertise of
Ps 70:15-16 knowledge, **that, having renounced even this possession,** he *might*
enter into the mighty works of the Lord and **offer himself naked to the**
arms of the Crucified. For in vain does one perfectly renounce the 2C 140
world, who keeps **the money bag of his own opinions** in the hidden recesses of his heart."[a]

Often when he spoke to the brothers about poverty, he would 2C 56
Mt 8:20; Lk 9:58 **insist on the saying of the Gospel:** ***The foxes have their holes and the***
birds of the air have nests, but the Son of Man ***has nowhere to lay his head.***
Because of this, **he taught** the brothers **to build,** like the poor, **poor**
1 Pt 2:11 **little houses,** which they should inhabit not as their own but, like *pil-* LR VI 2
grims and strangers, as belonging to others. For he would say that **the** 2C 59
laws of pilgrims was to be **sheltered under someone else's roof, to thirst for their homeland, and to travel in peace.**[b] Sometimes he ordered the brothers to tear down houses they had built, or to move out
of them, if he noticed in them something **contrary to gospel poverty** 2C 55
because it was appropriated or sumptuous.

This, he used to say, was the foundation of his Order,
on which primary substratum the structure of religion rests,
so that it is strengthened by its strength,
and weakened by the weakness of its base.

3In the same way he would teach, 2C 80
as he learned from a revelation,
that entering the sacred religion should begin

a. Whereas Thomas places the curious statement, "the moneybag of his own opinion," in a more general context, Bonaventure inserts it into this description of the poverty demanded of a scholar.

b. Cf AC 23, supra 136 a.

from that Gospel passage:
LR II 5; Test 16 *If you wish to be perfect,* Mt 19:21
go, sell all *that you have,*
and give to the poor.
Therefore,
only those who had given up everything and kept nothing
would he admit to the Order,
ER II 4; LR II 5 both because of the words of the holy Gospel
and because they should not cause scandal
VII 7; Adm IV 3 by keeping a money bag. Jn 12:6; 13:29

2C 81 Thus when someone asked to be received into the Order in the
2C 78 Marches of Ancona, the true patriarch of the poor replied: "If you
want to join Christ's poor, distribute what you have to the poor of
the world." When he heard this, the man went off and, led by love
of the flesh, left his goods to his relatives, and nothing to the poor.
When the holy man heard him tell of this, he reproached him
harshly: "Go on your way, Brother Fly, for you have not yet *left your* Gn 12:1
home and your family. You gave what you had to your relatives, and
cheated the poor; you are not worthy of the holy poor. You began Sir 34:24-25
with the flesh; you laid down a crumbling foundation for a spiritual building." The *carnal man* returned to his own and demanded 1 Cor 2:14
back his goods; refusing to give them to the poor, he soon left his
proposal of virtue.

2C 67 [4]Another time, in the place of Saint Mary of the Portiuncula, the destitution was so great, that it was not possible to provide for the brothers coming as guests according to their needs. His vicar went to the man of God, pointing out the indigence of the brothers and asking permission to save some of the goods of those entering as
novices to which the brothers could have recourse *in due season*. Not Ps 145:15
ignorant of heavenly guidance, the man of God said to him: "Far be it from us, dearest brother, to treat without piety what is in the *Rule* for the sake of anyone. I prefer that you strip the altar of the glorious Virgin, when necessity requires it, than to use something or even a little that is contrary to the vow of poverty and the observance of the Gospel. For the Blessed Virgin will be happier to have her altar stripped and the counsel of the holy Gospel kept perfectly, than to have her altar decorated and her Son's counsel, as promised, neglected."

2C 68 [5]One time as the man of God was traveling with a companion through Apulia near Bari, he found a large bag lying on the road;

the kind they call a *fonda,*[a] apparently bursting with coins. His companion alerted the poor man of Christ and urged him to pick the purse up from the ground and distribute the money to the poor. The man of God refused, declaring there was a trick of the devil in this purse they had found, and that the brother was recommending something sinful rather than meritorious, that is, to take what belonged to another and give it away. They left the place and hurried
Jgs 19:14 to finish *the journey* they had *begun*. But the brother was not yet at peace, deluded by empty piety, bothering the man of God as if he had no concern to relieve the destitution of the poor. The gentle man agreed to return to the place, not to carry out the brother's wish, but to uncover the devil's trickery. So he returned to the *fonda* with the brother and a young man who was on the road, and after they had prayed, he ordered his companion to pick it up. The trembling brother was dumbfounded, sensing beforehand a diabolical omen. Nevertheless, because of the command of holy obedience, as he was casting out hesitation from his heart, he stretched out his hand toward the bag. Behold, a large snake slid out of the bag and, suddenly disappearing along with it, showed the brother the diabolical deceit. After the enemy's trickery and cunning were grasped, the holy man said to his companion: "To God's servants, brother, money is nothing but a devil and a poisonous snake."

[6]After this something marvelous happened to the holy man 2C 93
while he was going to the city of Siena for some urgent reason. Three poor women, who were exactly alike in height, age, and appearance, met him on the great plain between Campiglia and San Quirico and offered him a small gift of a new greeting. "Welcome, Lady Poverty!" they said. When he heard this, the true lover of poverty was filled with unspeakable joy, for he had in himself nothing that he would so gladly have people hail as what these women had chosen.

Once they had abruptly disappeared,
considering
the remarkable novelty
of the likeness among them,
of the greeting,
of the meeting
and of the disappearance,
the brothers accompanying him weighed,

a. The Latin term *fonda* literally means a sling and might be translated as *money belt*.

not without reason,
what the mystery meant about the holy man.
Clearly,
it would seem that through those three poor women
so alike in appearance,
offering such an unusual greeting,
and disappearing so quickly,
the beauty of Gospel perfection,
consisting in poverty, chastity, and obedience
was fittingly revealed
to be shining perfectly in the man of God
in an equal way.
Nonetheless,
he had chosen to glory above all
in the privilege of poverty
which he was accustomed to call
his mother, his bride, and his lady.
In this
he desired to surpass others
because he had learned from her
to regard himself inferior to all.

2C 83 Therefore if he saw someone dressed **poorer than himself, imme-**
diately criticizing himself, he set out to be similar, as if contending
2C 84 with **a rival for poverty and afraid to be overcome. It happened one**
day that he met a poor man on the road. When he saw the man's
nakedness, his heart **deeply moved, he said to his companion** in a
sad voice: **"This man's need brings great shame on us,** for we **have**
chosen poverty for its great **riches; and see, it shines more clearly in**
him."

[7]For love of holy poverty,
the servant of almighty God
used the alms he had begged from door to door more gladly
than those offered spontaneously.[a]
2C 72 For if **he were invited by** distinguished persons
and honored by a more lavish dinner,

a. At this juncture, Bonaventure shifts his considerations of Francis's poverty (1-6) to the acceptance of begging (7-10). In doing so, he follows the approach he had taken in his *Disputed Questions on Evangelical Perfection*, Question II, which is divided into three articles: (i) poverty as renunciation; (ii) poverty as begging; (iii) poverty and manual labor. Cf. V, 124-165. In this shift, Bonaventure is laying the groundwork for the last section of this chapter devoted to God's miraculous fulfillment of the brothers' needs (11-13).

he would first seek **some pieces of bread at the neighboring houses**
and then, enriched by poverty, sit down at table.

And once he did this, **when he** was invited by the Lord Bishop of 2C 73
Ostia, who held Christ's poor man in special affection. After **the**
bishop complained that he had disparaged his honor as would be expected when a dinner guest goes out for alms, God's servant replied:
"My lord, **I showed you** great **honor while I have honored a greater**
Ps 68:17 **Lord.** ***For the Lord is pleased*** **by poverty and especially when one**
freely chooses to go begging for Christ. This is **the royal dignity**
2 Cor 8:9 which **the Lord** Jesus assumed when he *became poor* **for us** that he
Mt 5:3 might enrich us by *his want* and *would* make us truly *poor in spirit,* ***as*** LR VI 4; 2C 72
heirs **and kings of** ***the kingdom of heaven.*** **I do not wish to relinquish**
this royal dignity for a fief of false riches granted for only an hour."

[8]**Sometimes, as he encouraged** the brothers **to beg for alms, he** 2C 71
1 Jn 2:18 **would use words** such as these: **"Go, for** ***in this last hour*** **the Lesser**
Brothers have been given to the world so that the elect may carry
out for them what will be commended by the Judge as they hear
Mt 25:40 those most sweet words: *As long as you have done it for one of my lesser*
brothers, you did it for me." Then he would say that it was a delight **to**
beg with the title of Lesser Brothers, which the Teacher of Gospel
truth had so clearly expressed by his own mouth in rewarding the
just. When there was an opportunity, he used to go begging even on
the principal feasts, saying that, in the holy poor, the prophecy is ful-
Ps 77:25 filled: *Man will eat the bread of angels.*

He used to say
that bread is clearly angelic,
which holy poverty gathers from door-to-door,
which is sought out of God's love
and is given out of His love
by the blessed prompting of angels.

[9]Once, on a holy **Easter Sunday,** while he was staying **at a hermit-** 2C 61
age that was so far from any houses that he could not conveniently
go begging, he begged **alms** from the brothers, like **a pilgrim and**
Lk 24:13 **beggar,** mindful of him who *that day* appeared in the guise *of a pilgrim*
to his disciples travelling on the road to Emmaus.

When he had humbly received it,
he taught them with sacred eloquence
to continually celebrate the Lord's Passover,

in poverty of spirit
that is,
his passing *from this world to the Father,* Jn 13:1
passing through the desert of the world
LR VI 2 like *pilgrims and strangers* 1 Pt 2:11
and, like true Hebrews.[a]
And because,
when begging alms,
he was motivated
not by greed for profit but by liberty of spirit,
God, *the Father of the poor,* Jb 29:16
seemed to have a special care for him.

2C 77 [10]Once when the Lord's servant was gravely **ill at Nocera,** he was brought back to **Assisi by formally appointed representatives** sent for that purpose out of devotion by the people of Assisi. As they carried Christ's servant back, **they came to a poor little village called Satriano where, since their hunger and the hour called for food, they went out, and finding nothing for sale, returned** empty-handed. The holy man told them: **"You didn't find** anything, **because you trust more in those flies of yours than in God." For he used to call coins "flies." "But go back," he said, "to the houses which you have visited and, offering the love of God** as a reward, **humbly** ask **for an alms.** Do not consider this shameful or cheap out of false esteem, **for after sin everything is bestowed as alms, for that great Almsgiver, out of his** abundant **piety, gives to both the worthy and the unworthy."**

The knights overcame their embarrassment, readily **begged for alms, and bought more with the love of God than with money.** Since their hearts were struck with compunction by the divine nod, the poor villagers generously gave not only what was theirs, but also themselves. And so it happened that Francis's wealthy poverty supplied the need which money could not alleviate.

2C 44 [11]**At the time when** he was lying **ill in a hermitage** near Rieti, a **doctor** visited him often to care for him. Since the poor man of Christ was unable to pay him adequately for his services, the most generous

a. This is clearly a reference to Francis's role in preparing "in the desert a way of the highest poverty," cf. LMj Prol 1. It further accentuates the biblical and eschatological dimensions of a poverty closely linked to the Paschal or *transitus* that permeates Bonaventure's thought. Cf. Jacques-Guy Bougerol, "Transitus," in *Lexique Saint Bonaventure* (Paris: Éditions Franciscaines, 1969), 127-128; Werner Hülsbusch, "Die Theologie des *Transitus* dei Bonaventura," in *S. Bonaventura 1274-1974,* Vol. IV (Grottaferrata, Rome: Collegio S. Bonaventura, 1974), 533-565; André Ménard, "Spiritualité du *Transitus,*" in *S. Bonaventura 1274-1974,* Vol. IV (Grottaferrata, Rome: Collegio S. Bonaventura, 1974), 607-635.

God made up for the poor man and repaid the doctor for his devoted
care with the following favor, so that he would not go without payment in the present life. The doctor's new house, which he had just
spent all his money building, was threatened with collapse because
Mt 27:51 of a wide crack in the wall, which reached *from the top to the bottom,* a
collapse which seemed unavoidable by human means. Fully trusting
in the merits of the holy man and out of the devotion of his great
faith, he asked his companions to give him something which the
man of God had touched with his hands. After many requests he obtained a small amount of his hair which he placed one evening in the
crack in the wall. When he rose in the morning, he found that the
crack had been so firmly closed that he could not pull out the hairs he
Wis 5:10 had placed there nor could he *find* any *trace* of the crack. And so it
happened that because he had dutifully ministered to the body of
God's servant in its state of collapse, he avoided the danger of the collapse of his house.

[12]**Another** time as the man of God **wanted** to go **to a hermitage to** 3C 15
spend more time in contemplation, because he was weak, he rode
on **a donkey belonging to a certain poor man. As it was summer-
time,** that man **climbed up a mountain following** Christ's servant.
Worn out from the long **and grueling journey, and weakened further by a burning thirst,** he began **to cry out urgently after the saint:**
"Look, **I'll die** of thirst if I don't get a drink **immediately!" Without
delay** the man of God **leaped down from the donkey, knelt on the
ground, raised his hands to heaven and prayed unceasingly until
he understood that he had been heard.** After he had finished his
prayer, **he told** the man: **"Hurry over there to the rock and you will
find living water which at this very hour Christ has mercifully**
Ps 78:16; Dt 32:13 *brought forth water from the rock* **for you to drink."**

How amazingly kind God is,
so easily bowing to his servants!
Ps 78:16; Ex 17:1-7 A thirsty man drank *water from the rock*
by the power of another's prayer
Dt 32:13 and took a drink from *the most solid rock.*
There was no stream of water there before,
nor could any be found since,
even after a careful search.

[13]How Christ **multiplied** food at sea 1C 55
through the merits of his poor man will be noted below.
Here let it suffice to mention

that with only a small amount of food
that he had been given as alms,
LJS 34 he saved sailors for a number of days
from starvation and the danger of death.
From this one could clearly see
that just as the servant of Almighty God was
like Moses in drawing *water from the rock,* Ps 78:16; Ex 17:1-7
like Elisha in the multiplication of provisions. 2 Kgs 41

Therefore, let every lack of confidence be far from Christ's poor!
For if the poverty of Francis was so abundantly sufficient
that, by a marvelous power,
it supplied
the destitution of those who came to his aid,
providing food, drink, and housing
when money, skill, and natural means were lacking,
how much more will it merit
those things that are given to all
in the usual plan of divine providence.
If a dry rock gave drink abundantly
to a poor man who was thirsty
at the word of another poor man,
nothing at all
will refuse its service
to those who have left all
for the Creator of all.

Chapter Eight

THE DRIVE OF PIETY
AND
HOW IRRATIONAL CREATURES
SEEMED MOVED TOWARD HIM

1 Tm 4:8

[1]True *piety,*[a]
which according to the Apostle
gives power to all things,
had so filled Francis's heart
and penetrated its depths
that it seemed to have claimed the man of God
completely into its dominion.
This is what,
through devotion, lifted him up into God;
through compassion, transformed him into Christ;
through self-emptying,[b] turned him to his neighbor;
through universal reconciliation with each thing,
refashioned him to the state of innocence.[c]

Through this virtue
he was moved with piety to all things,
especially to souls redeemed by the precious blood of Jesus Christ.
When he saw them being stained by the filth of sin,
he grieved with such tender care

a. To place this chapter into a proper historical context, it would be helpful to read André Méhat, Aimé Solignac, Irénée Noye, "Piété," *Dictionnaire de Spiritualité Ascetique et Mystique, Doctrine et Histoire XII* (Paris: Beauchesne, 1986), 1694-1743.

b. The Latin is *condescensionem* [condescension], a word that has negative overtones in contemporary English. In this sense, it implies the stooping of one who is actually exalted in power, rank and dignity, i.e., Christ, so as to accommodate himself to others. Cf. *Webster's Dictionary of Synonyms*, first edition (Springfield, MA: G.& C. Merriam Co., Publishers, 1951), 791.

c. In his *Third Book of Commentary on the Sentences of Peter Lombard*, Bonaventure quotes Augustine's *The City of God* X, c.1, n.3: "The word 'piety' (*eusebeia* in Greek) is generally understood as referring particularly to the worship of God. But this word also is used to describe a dutiful attitude towards parents; while in popular speech it is constantly used in connection with acts of compassion . . . From this application comes the application of the epithet *pius* to God himself." Augustine, *The City of God*, translation by Henry Betterson, introduction by John O'Meara (London, New York, Victoria, Ontario, Auckland: Penguin Books, 1972), 373. Cf. *III Sent.* D. 35, au., q.6, concl. (III, 785b). In this passage, however, Bonaventure extends the meaning of piety to embrace reconciliation with all creation, thus introducing the Franciscan dimension of the word and extending its meaning.

that he seemed like a mother
who was daily bringing them to birth in Christ.
2C 172 **And this was the principal reason for revering**
ministers of God's word:
they raise up *seed for their deceased brother,*[a] Dt 25:5
Christ, crucified particularly for sinners,
and, with pious concern for their conversion,
they guide them with concerned piety.

He maintained that a service of this kind of care was more acceptable to *the Father of mercies* than every sacrifice, especially if it were 2 Cor 1:3
undertaken with the eagerness of perfect charity. Thus it should be done more by example than by word, more by tear-filled prayer than by long-winded sermons.

2C 164 [2]In the same way **he said that a preacher must be wept over,** as over someone without real piety, who in preaching seeks not the salvation of souls, but his own **praise,** or who destroys with the depravity of his life what he builds up with the truth of teaching. He said that a **simple** tongue-tied **brother** must be preferred who challenges others to good by his good example. And so **he would explain that passage** *So that the barren has borne many* **in this sense: "The barren** I Sm 2:5
one," he said, **"is the poor little brother who does not have the duty of producing children in the Church. At the judgment he will** ***give birth to many children,*** **for then the Judge will credit to his glory those he is converting now** to Christ **by his secret prayers.** ***She who*** I Sm 2:5
has many children will languish, **because** the vain and long-winded preacher, **who rejoices over many** now as if **they were born through his power, will discover then that he has nothing of his own in them."**

[3]*Therefore,*
he yearned with heartfelt piety
and burned with ardent zeal
for the salvation of souls.
2C 155 **He would say**
that he ***was filled with the sweetest fragrance*** Ex 29:18
and as if anointed **with** ***precious ointment*** Jn 12:3
whenever he heard
of many people being converted to the way of truth

a. An allusion to the Levirate law through which, in order to perpetuate a family name, a widow who has no son is taken to wife by her brother-in-law.

by the fragrant reputation of holy brothers in faraway lands.
He rejoiced in spirit upon hearing of such brothers,
1 Tm 1:15 and would heap blessings on those brothers
worthy of full acceptance
who, by word or deed, led sinners to the love of Christ.

2 Pt 2:8 So also, those who violated sacred religion by evil deeds incurred the very heavy penalty of his curse. "By you," he said, "most holy Lord, and by the whole court of Heaven, and by me, your little one, may they be cursed who break up and destroy by their bad example what you earlier built up and do not cease to build up through holy brothers of the Order!" 2C 156

He was often so deeply saddened by scandal given to the weak, that he felt he would be overcome unless he had been bolstered by the consolation of the divine mercy. 2C 157

One time when he was disturbed by some bad examples, he anxiously prayed to the merciful Father for his sons, and brought back a response of this sort from the Lord: "Why are you so upset, poor little man? Have I set you up as a shepherd over my religion so that you can forget that I am its main protector? I have entrusted this to you, a simple man, so that the things that I work in you
Is 48:15; Rev 10:3 would be attributed not to human industry, but to divine grace. *I have called, I will preserve, and I will pasture,* and I will raise up others to make up for the fall of some. So that, even if they have not been born, I will have them born! No matter how severely this poor little religion is shaken, it will always remain safe by my gift." 2C 158

4He hated the vice of detraction like a snakebite, as a foe to the source of piety and grace. He firmly held it to be the most atrocious plague and abominable to the most pious God, because the detractor
Ps 56:4 feeds on the blood of the souls which he kills with *the sword of his tongue.*

One time, when he heard one brother blackening the reputation of another, he turned to his vicar and said: "Get up! Get up! Search thoroughly; and if you find the accused brother innocent, make the accuser known publicly by a severe punishment." More than once he decided that a brother should be stripped of his habit if he had stripped his brother of the glory of his reputation, and that he
Lk 18:13 could not raise his eyes up to God until he first did his best to give back what he had stolen. "To the degree that the impiety of detractors is greater than that of thieves," he would say, "so much more does the law of Christ, fulfilled in the observance of piety, oblige us to desire the well-being of souls rather than of bodies." 2C 182

[5]Emptying himself
through a wonderful tenderness of compassion
for anyone with a bodily affliction,
in the sweetness of his pious heart,
2C 83 **he turned back to Christ**
any need, any lack he might notice in anyone.
He certainly had an inborn kindness[a]
doubled by the piety of Christ poured out on him.
Therefore his **soul melted for the poor** and the infirm; Sg 5:6
to those to whom he could not extend a hand
he extended his affection.

1C 76 Once it happened that one of the brothers responded more gruffly
to a poor man begging alms at an inconvenient time. **When the pi-**
2C 8 **ous lover of the poor heard this, he ordered the brother to strip na-**
2C 85 **ked,** prostrate **himself at that poor man's feet, confess his fault, and**
beg for his prayers and forgiveness. When he had done this with humility, the father added gently: "Brother, as long as **you see a poor**
person, a mirror of the Lord and his poor Mother is placed before
you. Likewise in the sick, look closely for the infirmities which He Mt 8:17; Is 53:4
accepted."

In all the poor
that most Christian poor man also saw before him
a portrait of Christ;
he not only gave freely to those he met
the necessities of life, if these had even been given to him,
but he also resolved they should be returned,
as if they truly belonged to them.

2C 87 It happened once that **a poor man** met him on his return **from**
Siena, when, because of an illness, he was wearing a short mantle
over his habit. When his kind eye observed the man's misery, he said
to his companion: "We must give back to this poor man his mantle,
for it is his! For **we accepted it on loan until we should happen**
upon someone poorer than we are." But **his companion, seeing the**
need of his pious father, objected to this stubbornly, lest by provid-
2C 77 **ing for someone else, he neglect himself.** But he said: **"The great**
Almsgiver will **accuse me of theft if I do not give** what I have to
someone in greater need."

a. Cf. Lmj I 1.

Therefore of all that was given him to relieve the needs of his body,
he was accustomed to ask the permission of the donors
so that he could give it away
should he meet someone in greater need.
He spared nothing at all,
neither mantles nor tunics,
neither books nor even appointments of the altar:
all these he gave to the poor, when he could,
to fulfill his obligation of piety.
Frequently,
whenever he met poor people burdened with heavy loads, 1C 76
he would carry their burdens on his own weak shoulders.

6 From a reflection on the primary source of all things, 1C 80
filled with even more abundant piety,
he would call creatures, 1C 81
no matter how small,
by the name of "brother" or "sister,"
because he knew they shared with him the same beginning.
However, 1C 77
he embraced more affectionately and sweetly
those which display
the pious meekness of Christ in a natural likeness
and portray him in the symbols of Scripture.
He often paid to ransom lambs that were being led to their death, 1C 79
remembering that most gentle Lamb
Is 53:7 who willed *to be led to slaughter* to pay the ransom of sinners.[a]

One night when the servant of God was a guest at the monastery 2C 111
of San Verecondo in the diocese of Gubbio, a little sheep gave birth to a baby lamb. There was a very cruel sow there, which did not spare the life of the innocent, but killed it with her ravenous bite. When the pious father heard this, he was moved to remarkable compassion and, remembering the Lamb without stain, lamented for the dead baby lamb, saying in front of everyone: "Alas, brother lamb, innocent animal, always displaying Christ to people! Cursed be the pitiless one who killed you, and neither man nor beast shall eat of her!" It is amazing to tell! Immediately the vicious sow began to get sick and, after paying the bodily punishment for three days, finally suffered an avenging death. She was thrown into the mon-

a. The reference to *agnus* [lamb] is obviously to the images of the New Testament: Jn 1:29, 36; Acts 8:32; 1 Pt 1:19; Rv 5:8, 12, 13; 6:1, 16; 7:9, 10, 14, 17; 12:11; 13:8; 14:1, 4, 10, etc.

astery's ditch and, laying there for a long time, **dried up like a board, and did not become food for any hungry creature.**

Therefore,
let human impiety pay attention
to how great a punishment might at last be inflicted on it,
if such animal cruelty is punished with so horrible a death.
Let also the devotion of the faithful weigh
how the piety in God's servant
was of such marvelous power and of such abundant sweetness
that even the nature of animals acknowledged it
in their own way.

3C 31 [7]When he **was on a journey** near the city **of Siena, he passed a** large **flock of sheep grazing** in a pasture. **He greeted them kindly, as usual. After they left the pasture, they all ran to him, lifted their heads,** fixed their eyes on him. They gave him such **a loud bleating** that the shepherds and the brothers were amazed to see the lambs and even the rams frisking about him in such an extraordinary way.

Another time at Saint Mary of the Portiuncula the man of God was offered a sheep, which he gratefully accepted in his love of that innocence and simplicity which the sheep by its nature reflects. The pious man admonished the little sheep to praise God attentively and to avoid giving any offense to the brothers. The sheep carefully observed his instructions, as if it recognized the piety of the man of God. For when it heard the brothers chanting in choir, it would enter the church, genuflect without instructions from anyone, and bleat before the altar of the Virgin, the mother of the Lamb, as if it wished to greet her. Besides, when the most sacred body of Christ was elevated during the Solemnity of the Mass, it would bow down on its knees as if this reverent animal were reproaching the irreverence of those who were not devout and inviting the devout to reverence of the Sacrament.

Once in Rome he had with him a little lamb out of reverence for the most gentle Lamb of God. At his departure he left it in the care of the noble matron, the Lady Jacoba of Settesoli.[a] Now the lamb went with the lady to church, standing reverently by her side as her inseparable companion, as if it had been trained in spiritual matters by the saint. If the lady was late in rising in the morning, the lamb rose and nudged her with its horns and woke her with its bleating, urging her with its nods and gestures to hurry to the church. On account of this,

a. Cf. AC 8, supra, 122 b.

the lamb, which was Francis's disciple and had now become a master of devotion, was held by the lady as an object of wonder and love.

[8]Another **time at Greccio a small live hare was given** to the man 3C 29
of God, **which he put down on the ground free to run away where it**
pleased. At the call of the kind father, it leapt quickly into his lap.
He fondled it with the pious affection of his heart and seemed to pity
it like a mother. **After warning it with gentle** talk not to let itself be
caught again, **he let it** go **free. But as often as he placed it on the** 1C 60
ground to run away, it always came back to the father's **bosom**, as if
it perceived with some hidden sense of its heart the piety he had for
it. **Finally, at the** father's **command, the brothers** carried it away **to a**
safer place of solitude.

In the same way, **on the island in the Lake of Perugia, a little rab-** 3C 30
bit was caught and offered to the man of God. Although it fled from
everyone else, it entrusted itself to his hands and his heart as if to
natural security.

When he was hurrying **across the Lake of Rieti to the hermitage** 3C 23
of Greccio, out of devotion **a fisherman offered him a little wa-**
ter-bird. He **received it** gladly **and, with open hands, invited it** to go
away, but it did not want to go. **He remained in prayer for a long**
time with his eyes lifted to heaven. Returning to himself as if after
no more than an hour **stay in another place, he gently** ordered **the**
little bird to go away to praise the Lord. **And so the bird, having re-**
ceived permission with a blessing, flew away expressing its joy in
the movements of its body.

On the same lake in a similar way **he was offered a large fish that** 3C 24
was still alive. Calling it **by name** in his usual **brotherly way, he put**
it back in the water next to the boat. The fish kept playing in the
water in front of the man of God; and as if it were attracted by his
love, it would in no way leave the boat until it received from him his
permission with a blessing.

[9]Another time when he was walking with a brother through the
marshes of Venice, he came upon a large flock of birds singing
among the reeds. When he saw them, he said to his companion: "Our
Sister Birds are praising their Creator; so we should go in among
them and chant the Lord's praises and the canonical hours." When
they had entered among them, the birds **did not move from the** 3C 20
place; and on account of the noise the birds were making, they could
not hear each other saying the hours. The saint turned to the birds
and said: "Sister Birds, stop singing until we have done our duty of

praising God!" At once they were silent and remained in silence as long as it took the brothers to say the hours at length and to finish their praises. Then the holy man of God gave them permission to sing again. When the man of God gave them permission, they immediately resumed singing in their usual way.

3C 27 **Near the cell of the man of God** at Saint Mary of the Portiuncula, **there was a cricket living and singing on a fig tree.** With its song, it frequently aroused the Lord's servant **to the** divine praises, for he had also learned to marvel at the Creator's magnificence even in insignificant creatures. One day, after he called it, **it flew upon his hand** as if taught from heaven. He said to it: **"Sing, my Sister Cricket, and with your joyful song praise the Lord Creator!" Obeying without delay, it began to chirp;** nor did it stop **until** at the father's command **it flew back to its** own **place. There it remained for eight days,** coming each day, singing and returning at his **command.** Finally **the man of God said to his companions:** "Let us give permission to our sister cricket now, for **while making us so happy with her singing,** she has aroused us to the praises of God over the space of eight days." **As soon as it received permission, the cricket went away and never appeared there again,** as if it did not dare to disobey his command in the slightest way.

3C 26 10**When he was sick at Siena, a nobleman sent him** a live **pheas-**
//2C 170 **ant** he had recently caught. The moment it saw and heard the holy man, it was drawn to him with such affection that it would in no way allow itself to be separated from him. For many times **it was put down** outside the **brothers'** place **in the vineyard** so that it could go away if it wanted. But every time it ran right back to the father as if it had always been reared by him. Then it was given to a man who used to visit God's servant out **of devotion** but it absolutely refused to eat, as if it were upset at being out of the sight of the devoted father. It was finally brought back to God's servant, and as soon as it saw him, showed signs of joy and **ate** heartily.

When he went to the hermitage of La Verna to observe a forty-day fast in honor of the Archangel Michael, birds of different kinds flew around his cell, with melodious singing and joyful movements, as if rejoicing at his arrival. They seemed to be inviting and enticing the devoted father to stay. When he saw this, he said to his companion: "I see, brother, that it is God's will that we stay here for some time, for our sisters the birds seem so delighted at our presence."

3C 25 **When** he extended his stay there, **a falcon nesting there bound itself to him in a great covenant of friendship with him. For at the** hour of the night when the holy man usually rose for the divine office, it anticipated him with its noise and song. This pleased God's servant very much because such great concern for him shook out of him all sluggish laziness. But when Christ's servant was more than usually burdened with illness, the falcon would spare him and would not announce such early vigils. As if instructed by God, at about dawn it would ring the bell of its voice with a light touch.

In the joy of the different kinds of birds
and in the song of the falcon,
there certainly seems to have been a divine premonition
of when this praiser and worshiper of God
would be lifted up on the wings of contemplation
and then
would be exalted with a seraphic vision.

[11]Once while he was staying in the hermitage at Greccio, the 2C 35
people of that place had been stricken by multiple disasters. A pack of raging wolves devoured not only animals, but even people. And every year hailstorms destroyed their wheat field and vineyards. When the herald of the holy Gospel preached to those afflicted in this way, he said to them: "To the praise and honor of Almighty God, I assure you that all the disasters will cease, and the Lord looking down upon you, will multiply your earthly goods. If you believe me, show mercy to yourselves. Once you have made a sincere
Mt 3:8 confession, *bring forth fruits worthy of repentance.* I tell you again, if
Prv 26:11; 2 Pt 2:22 you are ungrateful for these gifts, and *return to your vomit,* the disas-
Jos 22:18 ters will return, punishment will double, and even greater *wrath will rage* against you."

From that hour, therefore, once the people did penance at his ex- 2C 36
hortation, the disasters ceased, the dangers vanished, and neither
Dn 3:50 the wolves nor the hailstorms caused *any more harm.* And even more remarkable, whenever the hail, falling on neighboring fields, reached the boundaries of Greccio, either it would stop or move off in a different direction.

The hail kept the pact of God's servant
as did the wolves;
nor did they try to rage anymore contrary to the law of piety
against people converted to piety,
as long as, according to their agreement,
the people did not act impiously
against God's most pious laws.

Therefore, we should respond piously
to the piety of the blessed man,
which had such remarkable gentleness and power
that it subdued ferocious beasts,
tamed the wild,
trained the tame,
and bent to his obedience
the beasts that had rebelled against fallen humankind.
Truly this is the virtue
that binds all creatures together,
and *gives power to all things* I Tm 4:8
having the promise of the life,
that now is and,
is yet to come.

Chapter Nine

THE ARDOR OF CHARITY
AND THE DESIRE FOR MARTYRDOM

[1]Who would be competent to describe the burning charity 1C 80
Jn 3:29 with which Francis, *the friend of the Bridegroom,* was aflame?
Like a thoroughly burning coal,
he seemed totally absorbed in the flame of divine love.
For as soon as he heard "the love of the Lord," 2C 196
he was excited, moved, and on fire
as if these words from the outside
were a pick strumming the strings of his heart on the inside.
He used to say that it was a noble extravagance
to offer such a treasure for alms
and that those who considered it less valuable than money
were complete fools,
because the priceless price of divine love alone
was sufficient to purchase the kingdom of heaven,
and
the love of him who loved us greatly
is greatly to be loved!

Aroused by everything to divine love, 2C 165
Ps 91:4 he *rejoiced* in all *the works of the Lord's hands*
and through their delightful display
he rose into their life-giving reason and cause.
In beautiful things he contuited Beauty itself[a]
and through the footprints impressed in things
Jb 23:11; Sg 5:17 he followed his Beloved everywhere,
Gn 28:12-13 out of them all making for himself *a ladder*
through which he could climb up to lay hold of him
Sg 5:16 *who is utterly desirable.*[b]
With an intensity of unheard devotion

a. Once again the Latin is *contuebatur,* cf. supra 532 d.

b. The Latin here is *consurgebat* [he rose], *contuebatur* [he contuited], and *conscenderet* [he would climb up], all words which Bonaventure adds to the text of Thomas of Celano who writes *intuetur* [gazes upon] *cognoscit* [discerns] and *perveniatur* [reaches].

he savored
in each and every creature
—as in so many rivulets—
that fontal Goodness,
and discerned
an almost celestial choir
in the chords of power and activity
given to them by God,
and, like the prophet David, Ps 148
he sweetly encouraged them to praise the Lord.[a]

[2]Jesus Christ crucified
always *rested like a bundle of myrrh in the bosom* of his soul,[b] Sg 1:12
into Whom
he longed to be totally transformed
through an enkindling of ecstatic love.
And as a sign of his special devotion to him,
he found leisure[c]
from the feast of the Epiphany through forty successive days
—that period when Christ was hidden in the desert— Mt 4:1-11; Mk 1:12-13; Lk 4:1-13
resting in a place of solitude,
shut up in a cell,
with as little food and drink as possible,
fasting, praying, and praising God without interruption.[d]
He was borne aloft into Christ
with such burning intensity,
but *the Beloved* repaid him with such intimate love Sg 1:12
that it seemed to that servant of God
that he was aware
of the presence of that Savior before his eyes,
like a yoke,
as he once intimately revealed to his companions.

---

a. Bonaventure seems to be alluding here to Francis's *Canticle of the Creatures*, cf. FA:ED I 113-114.

b. The reference to myrrh from the Song of Songs is reminiscent of Bernard of Clairvaux's *Forty-second Sermon on the Song of Songs* 11 in which he writes that under the name of myrrh, the beloved includes "all the bitter trials she is willing to undergo through love of her beloved." Cf. Bernard of Clairvaux, *On the Song of Songs* II, translated by Kilian Walsh, introduction by Jean Leclercq (Kalamazoo, London and Oxford: Cistercian Publications, 1976, 1976), 219.

c. The Latin is *vacabat* [he found leisure], a word difficult to translate but one rich in the contemplative tradition, where it has the sense of vacationing or taking a holiday in God. A thorough study of the word can be found in Jean Leclercq, *Otia Monastica: Études sur Le Vocabulaire de La Contemplation au Moyen Âge* (Rome: "Orbis Catholicus," Herder, 1963), 42-49.

d. The Rules (ER III 11; LR III 6) suggest this extra Lent as a commendable, but optional, practice. It is reckoned from the Epiphany because Christ was taken by the Spirit to the desert immediately after his baptism, which is commemorated on that feast. Cf. 2C 59.

Toward the sacrament of the Lord's Body 2C 201
he burned with fervor to his very marrow,
marveling **with unbounded wonder**
at that loving condescension and condescending love.
He received Communion frequently
and so devoutly
that he made others devout,
1 Pt 1:19 for at the sweet taste of *the spotless Lamb*
he was often rapt in ecstasy as if drunk in the Spirit.[a]

[3]**He embraced the mother of the Lord Jesus** 2C 198
with an inexpressible love
since she made the Lord of Majesty a brother to us
1 Pt 2:10 and, through her,
we *have obtained mercy.*

In her, after Christ, he put all his trust **and made her the advocate** of him and his brothers and, in her honor, he used to fast with great devotion from the Feast of the Apostles Peter and Paul to the Feast of the Assumption.[b]

He was joined in a bond of inseparable love 2C 197
to the angels
who burn with a marvelous fire
to pass over into God
and to inflame the souls of the elect.

Out of devotion to them he used to spend **the forty days after the Feast of the Assumption** of the glorious Virgin **in fasting** and continual prayer. Because of the ardent zeal he had for the salvation of all, he was more devoted with a special love **to blessed Michael** the Archangel **in view of his duty of presenting souls to God.**

Ez 28:14, 16 From remembering all the saints like *fiery stones,*
he was re-enkindled into a godlike fire,
embracing with the greatest devotion
all the apostles,
especially Peter and Paul,
because of the burning love they had toward Christ.
Out of reverence and love for them

a. Cf. Lmj II 4, supra, 538 a.
b. From June 20 to August 15.

he dedicated to the Lord a special fast of forty days.
The poor man of Christ
had nothing other than *two small coins,* Mk 12:42
namely his body and his soul,
which he could give away in generous charity.
But for the love of Christ
he offered them so continuously
that he seemed to be constantly immolating
his body through the rigor of fasting,
and his spirit through the ardor of his desire,
without, sacrificing a *holocaust* in the courtyard, Ex 30:1, 27-28
and within, burning *incense* in the temple.[a]

[4]The exceptional devotion of his charity
so bore him aloft into the divine
that his loving kindness was enlarged
and extended to those who shared with him nature and grace.
2C 172 Since the piety of his heart had made him
a brother to other creatures,
no wonder *the charity of Christ* 2 Cor 5:14
made him
even more a brother to those who are marked
in the image of their Creator
and *redeemed with the blood* of their Author! Rv 5:9

For he would not consider himself a friend of Christ, unless he cared for the souls whom He had redeemed. He used to say that nothing should be preferred to the salvation of souls, demonstrating this forcefully with the fact that *the Only-begotten Son of God* saw Jn 3:18
fit to hang on the cross for the sake of souls.

From this arose
his effort in prayer,
his travel in preaching,
and his excess in giving example.

2C 173 Therefore, whenever somebody criticized him for the excessive austerity of his life, he would reply that he was given as an exam-

a. The vocabulary in this passage is reminiscent of *The Soul's Journey into God* in which Bonaventure continually returns to the images of the courtyard and the temple to describe the soul's journey into the Holy of Holies. Cf. *Bonaventure: The Soul's Journey into God, The Tree of Life, The Life of Saint Francis,* translation and introduction by Ewert H. Cousins (New York, Ramsey, Toronto: Paulist Press, 1978), 53-116.

ple. For although **his innocent flesh, which was already submitting freely to the spirit, had no need of the whip because of any offense, he still renewed its punishment** and burdens **because of example,**
Ps 17:4 *staying on the hard paths only* **for the sake of others.** For he used to say:
1 Cor 13:1-3 "*If* I *speak in the tongues of men and angels,* **but without charity** and do not show examples of the virtues to my neighbors, it is little use to others, nothing to myself."

[5]In the **fervent** fire of his charity 1C 55
he strove to emulate
the glorious triumph of the holy martyrs
in whom
the flame of love could not be extinguished,
nor courage weakened.
Set on fire, therefore,
1 Jn 4:18 by that perfect charity *which drives out fear,*
he desired to offer to the Lord
Rom 12:1 *his own life* as *a living sacrifice* in the flames of martyrdom
so that he might repay Christ, who died for us,
and inspire others **to divine love.**

In the sixth year of his conversion, burning with the desire for martyrdom,[a] he decided **to take a ship to the region of Syria in order to preach the Christian faith and penance to the Saracens and** LR XII 1
other non-believers. When he had boarded **a ship to go there,** he was driven **by contrary winds to land on the shores of Slavonia.**[b] He LJS 34
spent **a little while** there and could not find a ship that would cross the sea at that time. Feeling that **he had been cheated of** his **desire, he begged some sailors going to Ancona to take him with them** for the love of God. When **they stubbornly refused because he could not pay them,** the man **of God, completely trusting the Lord's goodness, secretly boarded the ship with his companion. A man arrived,** sent by God for his poor man, as it is believed, who **brought**
Jb 1:1; Tb 11:4 **with him the food needed. He called over a person from the ship, a God-fearing man,** and spoke to him in this way: "Keep **all these things faithfully for the poor** brothers **hiding on your ship** and distribute them in a friendly fashion **in their time of need."** And it so

a. The theology of the desire for martyrdom is succinctly expressed in Bonaventure's *De Triplici Via* II 8: ". . . we are crucified for the world when we choose to die for everyone that they might please God as well. We do not reach this perfect love of neighbor unless we first reach that perfect love of God because we love our neighbor who would not be lovable were it not for God." (VIII 9-10) In his *Apologia Pauperum* IV 1, he maintains that the desire for martyrdom is the perfection of love (VIII, 252).

b. Cf. FA:ED I 229 b.

happened that, when the crew was unable to land anywhere for
many days because of the force of the winds, they used up all their
food. Only the alms given from above to the poor Francis remained.
Since this was only a very small amount, by God's power it was multiplied so much that while they were delayed at sea for many days by
the relentless storm, it fully supplied their needs until they reached
the port of Ancona. When the sailors realized that they had es-
LJS 34 caped many threats of death through God's servant, as those who
had experienced the horrifying dangers of the sea and *had seen the* Ps 107:24
wonderful *works of the Lord in the deep,* they gave thanks to almighty
God, who is always revealed through his friends and servants as
awesome and lovable.

1C 56 [6]When he left the sea, he began to walk the earth and to sow in it
the seed of salvation, reaping fruitful harvests. But, because the fruit
of martyrdom had attracted his heart to such an extent, he desired a
precious death for the sake of Christ more intensely than all the merits of the virtues. So he took the road to Morocco to preach the Gospel of Christ to the Miramamolin and his people,[a] hoping to attain in
this way the palm of martyrdom he so strongly desired. He was so
LJS 35 carried away with desire that, although he was physically weak, he
1C 56 would race ahead of his companion on the journey and hurry to
carry out his purpose, flying along, as if intoxicated in spirit. But after he had gone as far as Spain, by the divine design, which had other
things in store for him, he was overtaken by a very grave illness
LJS 35 which hindered him from achieving what he desired.

Realizing, then,
that his physical life was still necessary
for the children he had begotten,
the man of God,
while he considered death as *gain* for himself, Phil 1:21
returned *to feed the sheep* entrusted to his care. Jn 21:17

[7]But with the ardor of his charity
urging his spirit on toward martyrdom,
he tried yet a third time to set out to the non-believers,
hoping to shed his blood
for the spread of the faith in the Trinity.

a. Cf. FA:ED I 230 b.

In the thirteenth year of his conversion, he journeyed to the re- 1C 57
gions of Syria, constantly exposing himself to many dangers in order
to reach the presence **of the Sultan** of Babylon.[a] For at that time there
was a fierce war **between the Christians** and the Saracens,[b] with
their camps situated in close quarters opposite each other in the
field, so that there was no way of passing from one to the other without danger of death. A cruel edict had been issued by the Sultan that
whoever would bring back the head of a Christian would receive as a
reward a gold piece.[c] But Francis, the intrepid knight of Christ, hoping to be able to achieve his purpose, decided to make the journey,
not terrified by the fear of death, but rather drawn by desire for it. Af-
1 Sm 30:6 ter praying, *strengthened by the Lord,* he confidently chanted that pro-
Ps 23:4 phetic verse: *"Even if I should walk in the midst of the shadow of death, I
shall not fear evil because you are with me."*

8**Taking a companion with him, a brother** named Illuminato, a
virtuous and enlightened man, after he had begun his journey, he
came upon two lambs. Overjoyed to see them, the holy man said to
Sir 11:22 his companion: *"Trust in the Lord,* brother, for the Gospel text is being
Mt 10:16 fulfilled in us: *Behold, I am sending you forth like sheep in the midst of
wolves."* When they proceeded farther, the Saracen sentries fell upon
them like wolves swiftly overtaking sheep, savagely seizing the servants of God, and cruelly and contemptuously dragging them away,
treating them with **insults, beating** them with whips, and putting 1C 57
them in chains.

Finally, after they had been maltreated in many ways and were exhausted, by divine providence they were led **to the Sultan,** just as the man of God wished. When that ruler inquired by whom, why, and how they had been sent and how they got there, Christ's servant, Francis, answered with an intrepid heart that he had been sent not by man but by the Most High God in order to point out to him and his people the way of salvation and to announce the Gospel of truth.

He preached to the Sultan
the Triune God and the one Savior of all, Jesus Christ,
with such **great firmness,**

a. *Syria* was often used as a general name for the Levant. The *soldan of Babylon* was actually the ruler of Egypt *(Babylon* was the name given to modern Cairo) whose power extended over the Holy Land except for the small enclaves still held by the Crusaders.

b. The fifth Crusade, which for tactical reasons attacked Egypt rather than Palestine. The Crusaders were at this time besiging Damietta, on the delta of the Nile. Cf. FA:ED I 231c.

c. In the original *Byzantinum arueum.* The gold *byzant* or *bezant* was a current coin all over Christendom and Islam.

such **strength of soul,**
and such fervor of spirit
that the words of the Gospel appeared
to be truly fulfilled in him:
I will give you utterance and wisdom Lk 21:15
which all your adversaries will not be able to resist or answer back.

For the Sultan, perceiving in the man of God a fervor of spirit and a courage that had to be admired, willingly listened to him and invited him to stay longer with him. Inspired from heaven, Christ's servant said: "If you wish to be converted to Christ along with your people, I will most gladly stay with you for love of him. But if you hesitate to abandon the law of Mohammed for the faith of Christ, then command that an enormous fire be lit and I will walk into the fire along with your priests so that you will recognize which faith deserves to be held as the holier and more certain." "I do not believe," the Sultan replied, "that any of my priests would be willing to expose himself to the fire to defend his faith or to undergo any kind of torment." For he had seen immediately one of his priests, a man full of authority and years, slipping away from his view when he heard Francis's words.

"If you wish to promise me that if I come out of the fire unharmed," the saint said to the Sultan, "you and your people will come over to the worship of Christ, then I will enter the fire alone. And if I shall be burned, you must attribute it to my sins. But if God's power protects me, you will acknowledge *Christ the power and wisdom of God* as *the true God* and the *Savior* of all." (1 Cor 1:24; Jn 17:3, 4:42) The Sultan replied that he did not dare to accept this choice because he feared a revolt among his people. (57; LJS 36; 1C 57) Nevertheless **he offered** him **many precious gifts,** which the man of God, greedy not for worldly possessions but the salvation of souls, spurned as if they were dirt. Seeing that the holy man so completely **despised** worldly possessions, the Sultan **was overflowing with admiration,** and developed an even greater respect for him. Although he refused, or perhaps did not dare, to come over to the Christian faith, he nevertheless devoutly asked Christ's servant to accept the gifts and give them to the Christian poor or to churches for his salvation. But, because he was accustomed to flee the burden of money and did not see a root of true piety in the Sultan's soul, Francis would in no way accept them.

[9]When he saw that he was making no progress
in converting these people
and that he could not *achieve his purpose,* 2 Tm 3:10

namely martyrdom,
he went back to the lands of the faithful,
as he was advised by a divine revelation.
Thus by the kindness of God
and the merits of the virtue of the holy man,
it came about,
mercifully and remarkably,
that the friend of Christ
sought with all his strength to die for him
and yet could not achieve it.
Thus he was not deprived
of the merit of his desired martyrdom
and was spared to be honored in the future
with a **unique** privilege. 1C 57
Thus it came about
that the divine fire
burned still more perfectly in his heart,
so that later it was distilled clearly in his flesh.

O truly blessed man,
whose flesh,
although not cut down by a tyrant's steel,
was yet not deprived
Rv 5:12 of bearing a likeness of *the Lamb that was slain!*
O, truly and fully blessed man, I say,
whose life
"the persecutor's sword did not take away,
and who yet did not lose the palm of martyrdom"![a]

a. *Breviarium Romanum,* antiphon at second Vespers for the feast of Saint Martin of Tours.

Chapter Ten

ZEAL FOR PRAYER
AND THE POWER OF PRAYER

2C 94 [1]Francis,
the servant of Christ,
aware that while *in the body he was away from the Lord,* 2 Cor 5:6, 8
became totally unaware of earthly desires
through love of Christ,
and **strove** to keep **his spirit present** to God
by praying without ceasing 1 Thes 5:17
lest he be without the consolation of the Beloved.
Prayer was a comfort for the contemplative,
even now **a citizen with the angels in the heavenly mansions,**
as *he sought* with burning desire *the Beloved* Sg 3:1-2
2C 94 from whom only the wall of the flesh separated him.
Distrusting his own effort and trusting divine piety,
prayer was a fortress to this worker;
for in everything he did,
he cast his care completely *upon the Lord* Ps 55:23
through his perseverance.
He firmly claimed
that the grace of prayer
must be desired above all else
by a religious,
believing that without it no one could prosper in God's service.
He used whatever means he could
to arouse his brothers
to be zealous in prayer.[a]
1C 71 For whether **walking or sitting,**
inside or outside,
working or resting,
he was so **focused on prayer**
2C 94 that he seemed to have dedicated to it

a. Cf. LMj IV 3.

not only whatever was in **his heart and body,**
but also his effort and time.

[2]**He usually neglected no visitation of the Spirit.** 2C 95
Whenever it was offered, he would follow it;
and for as long as the Lord granted,
he enjoyed the sweetness offered.
When he was occupied with travel
and felt the breathing of the divine Spirit,
while his companions went on ahead,
he would stop in his tracks,
as he turned a new inspiration into something fruitful.
2 Cor. 6:1 **He did not receive grace in vain.**
Many times he was suspended 2C 98
in such an excess **of contemplation,**
that he was carried away above himself and,
experiencing what is **beyond human understanding,**
he was unaware of what went on about him.

For instance, **one time when he was traveling through Borgo San Sepolcro,** a heavily populated town, and **was riding on a donkey** because of physical weakness, crowds rushed to meet him **out of devotion. He was touched** by **them, pulled** and shoved by them, yet he **seemed not to feel any of this,** and **as if he were a lifeless corpse, did not notice** what was going on around him. **Long after** he had passed the town and **left** the crowds, he came **to a dwelling of lepers,** and **the contemplator of heaven,** as if returning **from somewhere else, anxiously** asked **when they would be reaching Borgo.**

His mind was so fixed on heavenly splendors
that he was not aware
of the differences of place, time, and people that he passed.
That this happened to him often was confirmed
by the repeated experience of his companions.

[3]And because he had learned in prayer
that the presence of the Holy Spirit for which he longed
was offered more intimately to those who invoke him,
the more It found them
far from the noise of worldly affairs.

Therefore seeking out **solitary places, he used to go** to deserted 1C 71
and abandoned churches to pray at night. There he often endured 1C 72

horrible struggles with devils who would assault him physically, trying to distract him from his commitment to prayer. But armed with heavenly weapons, the more vehemently he was attacked by the enemy, the more courageous he became in practicing virtue and the more fervent in prayer, saying confidently to Christ: *"Under the* Ps 17:8-9
shadow of your wings, protect me from the face of the wicked who have at-
2C 122 *tacked me."* To the devils he said: "Do whatever you want to me, you malicious and deceitful spirits! For you cannot do anything unless the heavenly hand relaxes its hold on you. And I am ready to endure with delight whatever He decrees." The demons retreated confused, not tolerating such firmness of mind.

2C 95 [4]The man of God
remaining more alone and at peace
would fill the forest with groans,
water the places with tears,
strike his breast with his hand,
and, as if finding a more secret hiding place,
would converse with his Lord.
There he replied to the Judge,
there he entreated the Father,
there he conversed with the Friend.
There too the brothers who were devoutly observing him
heard him on several occasions groan with loud cries,
imploring the divine clemency for sinners,
2C 11 and weeping over the Lord's passion
as if it were before him.
There he was seen praying at night,
with his hands outstretched in the form of a cross,
his whole body lifted up from the ground
and surrounded by a sort of shining cloud,
so that the extraordinary illumination around his body
was a witness to the wonderful light that shone within his soul.
There too,
as is proven by certain evidence,
the *unknown and hidden secrets of* divine *wisdom* Ps 51:6
were opened up to him,
although he never spoke of them outside
except when *the love of Christ urged* him 2 Cor 5:14
and the good of his neighbor demanded.
2C 99 For he used to say:
"It happens that one loses something priceless

for the sake of a small reward,
and easily provokes the giver not to give again."

When he returned from his private prayers, in which he was
1 Sm 10:6 *changed almost into a different man,* he tried his best to resemble the
others, lest what he might show outwardly, the breeze of favor
Sir 2:8 would *deprive* him *of a reward* inwardly. When he was suddenly over- 2C 94
Lk 1:68 come in public by *a visitation of the Lord,* he would always place
something between himself and bystanders, so that he would not
cheapen the sight of the Bridegroom's intimate touch. When he
prayed with the brothers, he completely avoided coughs, groans,
hard breathing, or external movement, either because he loved to
keep secrecy or because he had withdrawn into his interior and was
totally carried into God.

2 Chr 24:9 Often he would say to those close to him: "When a servant of 2C 99
God is praying and is visited by the divine, he must say: 'Lord, you
have sent this consolation from heaven to me, an unworthy sinner,
and I entrust it to your keeping, because I feel I am a thief of your
treasure.' When he returns from his prayer, he should appear as a
poor man and a sinner, as if he had not obtained any new grace."

[5]Once when the man of God was praying in the place of the 2C 100
Portiuncula, the bishop of Assisi happened to come to him, as he
often did. As soon as he entered the place, he went more abruptly
than he should have to the cell where Christ's servant was praying,
knocked on the door, and was about to barge in, when he stuck his
Jb 21:6 head inside and saw the saint praying. Suddenly *struck with trembling,* his limbs froze, and he lost his voice. By the divine will, he
was quickly pushed outside by force and dragged backwards a
long way. Stunned, the bishop hurried to the brothers, and, when
God had restored his speech, at the first word he confessed his fault
as best he could.

One time the abbot of the monastery of San Giustino in the dio- 2C 101
cese of Perugia happened to meet Christ's servant. When he saw
him, the devout abbot quickly dismounted from his horse to show
reverence to the man of God and to converse with him a bit about
the salvation of his soul. Finally, after a pleasant conversation, the
abbot, as he left, humbly asked him to pray for him. The dear man of
God replied: "I will willingly pray." When the abbot had ridden
away a short distance, the faithful Francis said to his companion:
"Wait a little, brother, because I want to pay the debt I promised."
Rom 8:5 As he prayed, suddenly the abbot *felt in spirit* unusual warmth and

sweetness like nothing he felt before, and rapt in ecstasy, he totally fainted away into God. This lasted for a short time, and then he returned to his senses and realized the power of Saint Francis's prayer. From that time on, he always burned with ever greater love for the Order, and told many about this miraculous event.

2C 96 [6]The holy man was accustomed to fulfill the canonical hours with no less reverence than devotion. Although he was suffering from diseases of the eyes, stomach, spleen, and liver, he nevertheless did not want to lean against a wall or partition while he was chanting the psalms. He always fulfilled the hours standing up straight and without a hood, without letting his eyes wander about and without dropping the syllables.

If he were on a journey, he would stop at the right time and never omitted this reverent and holy practice because it was raining. For he would say: "If the body calmly eats its food, which along with itself will be food for worms, should not the soul receive the food of life in great peace and tranquillity?"

2C 97 He also thought that he had committed a serious offense if, while he was at prayer, he was distracted by empty imaginings. When such a thing would happen, he did not fail to confess it and immediately make amends. He had made such a habit of this carefulness, that he was rarely bothered by this kind of "flies."

One Lent he had been making one small cup to occupy any spare time so that it would not in any way be wasted. When he was saying terce, it came to his mind and distracted him a little. Moved by fervor of spirit, he burned the cup in the fire, saying: "I will sacrifice it to the Lord, whose sacrifice it had interrupted!"

He used to say the psalms with such attention of mind and spirit, as if he had God present. When the Lord's name occurred in the psalms, he seemed to lick his lips because of its sweetness.

1C 82; 1C 45 He wanted to honor with special reverence the Lord's name not only when thought but also when spoken and written. He once persuaded the brothers to gather all pieces of paper wherever they were found and to place them in a clean place so that if that sacred name happened to be written there, it would not be trodden underfoot.[a] When he pronounced or heard the name Jesus, he was filled with an inner joy and seemed completely changed exteriorly as if some honey-sweet flavor had transformed his taste or some harmonious sound had transformed his hearing.

a. FA:ED I 252a.

7 It happened, **three years prior to his death,** that he decided to celebrate **at the town of Greccio the memory of the birth of the Child Jesus** with the greatest possible solemnity, in order to arouse devotion. So that this would not be considered a type of novelty, he petitioned for and obtained permission from the Supreme Pontiff. 1C 84

He had **a manger** prepared, 1C 85
hay carried in and an ox and an ass led to the spot.
The brethren are summoned,
the people arrive,
the forest amplifies with their cries,
and that venerable **night** is rendered
brilliant and solemn
by a multitude of bright lights
and by **resonant** and harmonious hymns of praise. 1C 86
The man **of God stands before the manger,** 1C 85
filled **with piety,**
bathed in tears, **and overcome with joy.**
A solemn Mass is celebrated over the manger,
with Francis, a levite of Christ, chanting **the** holy **Gospel.**
Then he preaches to the people standing around him 1C 86
about the birth of the poor King,
whom, **whenever he means to call him,**
he called in his tender love, LJS 54
the Babe from Bethlehem.
A certain virtuous and truthful knight,
Sir **John** of Greccio, 1C 84
who had abandoned worldly military activity out of love of Christ
and had become an intimate friend of the man of God,
claimed that **he saw** a beautiful **little child** asleep **in** that **manger** 1C 86
whom the blessed father Francis embraced in both of his arms
and **seemed to wake it from sleep.**
Not only does the holiness of the witness
make credible
the vision of the devout knight,
but also the truth it expresses
proves its validity
and the subsequent miracles confirm it.
For Francis's example,
when considered by the world,
is capable of arousing
the hearts of those who are sluggish in the faith of Christ.
The hay from the crib 1C 87

was kept by the people
LJS 55 and miraculously cured sick animals
and drove away different kinds of pestilence.
Thus God glorified his servant in every way
and demonstrated the efficacy of his holy prayer
by the evident signs of wonderful miracles.

Chapter Eleven

THE UNDERSTANDING OF SCRIPTURE
AND
THE SPIRIT OF PROPHECY

[1]Unflagging zeal for prayer
with a continual exercise of virtue
had led the man of God to such serenity of mind that,
although he had no expertise in Sacred Scripture through learning, 2C 102
his intellect, nevertheless
enlightened by the splendor of eternal light,
Jb 28:11 *probed the depths* of Scripture
with remarkable incisiveness.[a]
For **his genius, pure and unstained,**
Col 1:26 **penetrated** ***hidden mysteries,***
and where the knowledge of teachers stands **outside,**
the passion of the lover entered.
Whenever he read the Sacred Books,
and something struck his mind
he imprinted it tenaciously **on his memory,**
because[b] he did not grasp in vain
what his attentive mind heard,
for he would mull over it
with affection and constant devotion.

Once, when the brothers asked him whether he was pleased that the learned men, who, by that time, had been received **into the Order,** were devoting **themselves to the study of Sacred Scripture, he replied:**[c] "I am indeed pleased, as long as, after the example of Christ, of whom we read that he prayed more than he read, they do

a. For an in-depth consideration of Bonaventure's appreciation for this aspect of Francis's spiritual life, see his Prologue to the *Breviloquium*. See *Bonaventure: Mystic of God's Word*, introduced and edited by Timothy Johnson (Hyde Park: New City Press, 1999), 31-46.

b. Cf. 2C 102, supra, 314 a.

c. The following section is a collage of similar passages from 2C 102, 163, 189, 194, 195.

not neglect zeal for prayer;[a] and, as long as they study, not to know what they should say, but to practice what they have heard and, once they have put it into practice, propose it to others. I want my brothers," he said, "to be Gospel disciples and so progress in knowledge of the truth that they increase in pure simplicity without separating the simplicity of the dove from the wisdom of the serpent which our eminent Teacher joined together in a statement from his own blessed lips."[b] Mt 10:16

2C 103 [2]**At Siena,** a religious, **who was a Doctor of Sacred Theology,** once **asked him** about certain questions that were difficult to understand. He brought to light the secrets of divine wisdom with such clarity in teaching, that the learned man was absolutely dumbfounded. With admiration he responded: "Truly **the theology** of this holy father, borne aloft, as it were, on the wings **of purity and contemplation, is** ***a soaring eagle;*** **while our learning** ***crawls on its belly on the ground."*** Jb 9:26; Gn 3:14

2C 102 For although he was *unskilled in word,* 2 Cor 11:6
nevertheless, full of knowledge,
he often untangled the ambiguities of questions
and brought the hidden into light. Jb 28:11
Nor is it inconsistent!
If the holy man had received from God
an understanding of the Scriptures,
it is because,
through his imitation of Christ
he carried in his activity the perfect truth described in them and,
through a full anointing of the Holy Spirit, 1 Jn 2:20
held their Teacher in his heart.

a. A thorough presentation of Bonaventure's theology of a prayer based on Scripture can be found in Timothy Johnson, *Iste Pauper Clamavit: Saint Bonaventure's Theology of Prayer* (Frankfurt am Main, Bern, New York, Paris: Peter Lang, 1990). See also Charles Carpenture, *Theology as the Road to Holiness in St. Bonaventure,* Theological Inquiries (New York/Mahwah: Paulist Press, 1999), 13-38.

b. An appropriate commentary on this passage can be found in Bonaventure's *Letter in Response to an Unknown Master,* 10: ". . . [T]hat you might appreciate how much the study of Holy Scripture delighted him, let me tell you what I myself heard from a brother who is still living. Once a New Testament came into Francis's hands, and since so many brothers could not all use it at once, he pulled the leaves apart and distributed the pages among them. Thus each one could study and not be a hindrance to the others. Moreover, the clerics he received into the Order he held in greatest reverence, and at his death he ordered the brothers to venerate the teachers of Sacred Scripture as those from whom they receive the words of life." *Writings Concerning The Franciscan Order,* Works of Saint Bonaventure V, introduction and translation by Dominic Monti, (St. Bonaventure, NY: Franciscan Institute Publications, 1994), 51.

Rv 19:10 [3]*The spirit of prophecy,* too, so shone forth in him 2C 27
that he foresaw the future,
1 Cor 14:25 contuited the secrets of the heart,
knew of events from afar as if they were present,
and miraculously appeared present to those who were absent.[a]

For at the time when the Christian army was besieging 2C 30
Damietta,[b] the man of God was there, armed not with weapons, but
Prv 21:31 with faith. When Christ's servant heard that the Christians *were pre-*
paring for war on the day of the battle, he sighed deeply and said to his
companion: "If a clash of battle is attempted, the Lord has shown
Jb 16:7 me that it will not go well for the Christians. But if I say this, they
will take me for a fool; if I keep silent, my conscience won't leave
me alone. What do you think I should do?" His companion replied:
1 Cor 4:3 "Brother, don't give *the least* thought *to how people judge you.* This
won't be the first time people took you for a fool. Unburden your
Acts 5:29 conscience, and *fear God rather than men."*

When he heard this, the herald of Christ leapt to his feet, and
rushed to the Christians crying out warnings to save them, forbid-
Tb 3:4 ding war, and threatening disaster. But they took the truth *as a*
Ex 4:21; Jn 12:40 *joke. They hardened* their *hearts* and refused to turn back. The whole
Christian army charged, attacked, and retreated fleeing from the
battle carrying not triumph but shame. The number of Christians
was diminished by such a great massacre, that about six thousand
were either dead or captured.

From this
it was abundantly clear
that the wisdom of the poor man was not to be scorned;
Sir 37:18 since *sometimes the soul of a just man will declare truths*
more clearly than seven sentinels
searching the horizon from a height.

[4]At another time, after his return from overseas, he went to 2C 31; 3C 41
Celano to preach; and a certain knight invited him very insistently,
with humble devotion, to dine with him. So he came to the knight's
home and the whole family delighted at the arrival of the poor

a. In this accentuation of the perfect truth contained in Scripture, Bonaventure is laying the foundation for his consideration of Francis's gift of prophecy. "The Prophet does not give assent to what is foretold, because of itself," he teaches, "but because of the Truth enlightening and teaching him." *III Sent,* D. 23, art. 1, q. 2, concl. (III, 514). Furthermore he maintains that "It belongs to a prophet to recognize the truth." Cf. *Commentary on the Gospel of John* I, coll. 7:3 (VI, 544).

b. Cf. FA:ED I 231b.

guests. Before they took any food, the man offered prayers and praise to God as was his custom, standing with his eyes raised to heaven. When he finished his prayer, he called his kind host aside and confidentially told him: "Look, brother host, overcome by your prayers, I have entered your home to eat. Now heed my warnings quickly because you shall not eat here but elsewhere. *Confess your* 1 Jn 7:44
sins right now, contrite with the sorrow of true repentance; and leave nothing in you unconfessed that you do not reveal in a true confession. The Lord will reward you today for receiving His poor with such devotion." The man agreed to the saint's words without delay; and telling all of his sins in confession to his companion, *he* Is 38:1
put his house in order and did everything in his power to prepare for death. Then they went to the table; and while the others began to eat, suddenly their host breathed forth his spirit, carried away by sudden death according to the words of the man of God.

In recompense for the kindness of his hospitality,
it happened according to the word of Truth that
because he had received a prophet, Mt 10:41
he received a prophet's reward.
Through the prophetic warning of the holy man,
that devout knight prepared himself for a sudden death
so that, protected by the armor of repentance,
he escaped perpetual damnation
and entered into *the eternal dwellings.* Lk 16:9

2C 41 [5]At the time, while the holy man lay sick in Rieti, a canon named Gedeone, a lustful and worldly man, was seized by a grave illness and was bedridden. When he had himself carried to him, he, together with those present, tearfully begged to be marked by him with that sign of the cross. "How can I sign you with the cross," he asked, "when you once lived according to the desires of the flesh, with no fear of *the judgments of God?* Because of the devout requests Sir 17:24
of those pleading for you, however, I will sign you with the sign of the cross in the name of the Lord. But you must know you will suffer worse things, if, once set free, you return to *your vomit.* Because Prv 26:11
of the sin of ingratitude *things worse than the first* are always in- Mt 12:45
flicted. When he made the sign of the cross over him, immediately the man who was lying crippled got up restored to health, and bursting with praise of God cried: "I am free!" Many people there heard the bones of his hips cracking as when someone snaps dry twigs with his hands. But after a short time, the canon, *forgetting* Jgs 3:7
God, turned his body back to its unchaste ways.

One evening he dined at the house of a canon, and slept there that night. Suddenly the roof of the house collapsed on all of them. Others who were there escaped with their lives, only that wretch was trapped and killed.

Therefore,
by a just judgment of God,
Mt 12:45 *the last state of that man became worse than the first*
because of his vice of ingratitude
and his contempt for God.
Since gratitude must be shown for forgiveness received,
an offense repeated doubles displeasure.

[6]Another time, a noble woman, devoted to God, came to the saint to explain her trouble to him and ask for help. She had a very cruel husband whom she endured as an antagonist to her service of Christ. So she begged the saint to pray for him so that God in his goodness would soften his heart. When he heard this, he said to her: "Go in peace, and without any doubt be assured that you will soon have consolation from your husband." And he added: "You may tell him for God and for me, that now is the time of clemency, and later it will be the time of justice." 2C 38

After receiving his blessing, the lady returned home, found her
Acts 10:44 husband and relayed the message. *The Holy Spirit came upon* him
and he was changed from the old to the new man, prompting him
Jos 22:27; Gn 19:19 to reply very meekly: "My lady, *let us serve the Lord* and *save our souls.*" At the suggestion of his holy wife, they lived a celibate life for many years. On the same day, they both departed to the Lord.

The power of the prophetic spirit in the man of God
was certainly extraordinary,
which restored vigor to dried up limbs
and impressed piety on hardened hearts.[a]
The transparency of his spirit
was no less wondrous;
for he could foresee future events

a. "Piety," Bonaventure teaches, "is contrary to hardness of heart." Cf. *III Sent*, D. 35, au., q. 6, concl., ad 1, 2, 3, 4 (III, 786b). The same teaching can be found in a more poetic manner: "O human heart, you are harder than any hardness of rocks, if at the recollection of such great expiation you are not struck with terror, nor moved with compassion, nor shattered with compunction, nor softened with piety." Cf. *The Tree of Life* 29, in *Bonaventure: The Soul's Journey Into God, The Tree of Life, The Life of Saint Francis*, introduction and translation by Ewert H. Cousins (New York, Ramsey, Toronto: Paulist Press, 1978), 154.

and even probe obscurity of conscience,
as if another Elisha rivaling *the two-fold spirit* of Elijah. 2 Kgs 2:9

[7]On one occasion he told a friend at Siena what would happen to him at the end of his life. Now when the learned man mentioned above, who consulted him at one time about the Scriptures, heard of this, he asked the holy father in doubt whether he had really said what the man had claimed. He not only confirmed that he had said this but, besides, foretold to this learned man, who was so eager to know another's future, the circumstances of his own end. To impress this with greater certainty on his heart, he miraculously revealed to him a certain secret scruple of conscience that the man had and which he had never disclosed to any living person; and he relieved him of it by his sound advice. The truth of all this was confirmed by the fact that this religious eventually died just as Christ's servant had foretold.

2C 31 [8]When the holy man was returning from overseas, with brother
Leonard of Assisi as his companion, he happened to climb on a
donkey for a while, because he was weak and tired. But his companion walked behind, and was also quite tired. *Thinking in human* Rom 6:19
terms, he *began to say to himself*: "His parents and mine did not so- Lk 7:39
cialize as equals,[a] and here he is riding while I am on foot leading
his donkey." *As he was thinking this,* the holy man immediately got Mt 1:20
off the donkey. "No, brother," he said. "It is not right that I should
ride while you go on foot, for in the world you were more noble and
influential than I." The brother was *completely astonished,* and *over-* Est 7:6; Nm 12:14
come with embarrassment: he knew he had been caught. He fell Est 8:3
down at his feet and, *bathed* in tears, he exposed his naked thought Lk 7:38, 44
and begged forgiveness.

1C 49 [9]A certain brother, devoted to God and to Christ's servant, frequently turned over in his heart the idea: whomever the holy man
embraced with intimate affection would be worthy of divine favor.
Whomever he excluded, on the other hand, he would not regard
among God's chosen ones. He was obsessed by the repeated pressure
of this thought and intensely longed for the intimacy of the man of
1C 50 God, but never revealed the secret of his heart to anyone. The devoted father called him and spoke gently to him in this way: "Let no
thought disturb you, my son, because, holding you dearest among
those very dear to me, I gladly lavish upon you my intimacy and

a. Cf. 2C 31, p. 281 a.

love." The brother was amazed at this and became even more devoted. Not only did he grow in his love of the holy man, but, through the grace of the Holy Spirit, he was also filled with still greater gifts.

While he was secluded in a cell on Mount La Verna, one of his 2C 49
companions was yearning with great desire to have something of the Lord's words commented on and written with his own hand. He believed that by this means he would be set free from—or at least could bear more easily—a serious temptation which oppressed him, not in the flesh but in the spirit. Though growing weary with such a desire, he was in a state of inner anxiety because, overcome with embarrassment, he did not dare to disclose it to the
1 Cor 2:10 venerable father. But what man did not tell him, *the Spirit revealed.*
He ordered that brother to bring him paper and ink. And he wrote PrsG; BlL
down with his own hand the *Praises of the Lord* according to the
Gn 28:2 brother's desire, and, at the end, a blessing for him, saying: *"Take*
this paper *for yourself* and keep it carefully until your dying day." The brother took the gift he so much desired and his temptation disappeared immediately. The letter was preserved and, since later it worked wonders, it became a witness to the virtues of Francis.

[10]There was a brother who, to all appearances, led a life of ex- 2C 28
1 Cor 7:5 traordinary holiness, but who stood out for his singular ways. *He*
spent all his time in prayer and kept such strict silence that he used to make his confession by gestures instead of words. It happened that the holy father came to that place to see and hear the brother, and to have a word with the other brothers about him. While everyone was commending and praising him highly, the man of God replied: "Brothers, stop! Do not sing me the praises of his devilish
Mt 22:16 allusions. *You should know the truth.* This is a diabolical temptation
and a fraudulent deception." The brothers took this very hard, judging that it was impossible that contrivances of fraud could paint themselves over with so many signs of perfection. But a few days later, after he left religion, the brilliance of the interior insight with which the man of God perceived the secrets of his heart became abundantly clear.

Foretelling with unchanging truth 1C 48
the ruin of many who seemed to stand firm,
but also the conversion to Christ of many who were perverse,
he seemed to have approached
the mirror of eternal light
for contemplation,

in whose marvelous brilliance
the gaze of his mind perceived
the physically absent as if they were present.

[11]Once while his vicar was holding a chapter, he was praying in his cell, as *the go-between and mediator* between the brothers and God. Dt 5:5 One of them, hiding behind the mantle of some excuse, would not submit himself to the discipline of obedience. Seeing this in spirit, 2C 34 the holy man called one of the brothers and said to him: "Brother, I saw the devil perched on the back of that disobedient brother holding him tightly by the neck. With a rider like that on him, he spit out the bit of obedience, and gave free rein to his own will. But when I prayed to God for the brother, the devil retreated suddenly confused. Go, therefore, and tell the brother to submit his neck to the yoke of holy obedience without delay!" Warned by means of a messenger, the brother immediately was converted to God and, with humility, cast himself at the feet of the vicar.

2C 45 [12]Another time it happened that two brothers came from far away to the hermitage of Greccio to see the man of God and to receive his blessing which they had desired for a long time. When they arrived, *they did not find him,* because he had already left the common area for a cell; so they went away saddened. Lk 2:45

And behold,
as they were leaving,
although he could not have known anything
of their arrival or departure through any human means,
he came out of his cell contrary to his custom,
called after them
and blessed them in Christ's name with the sign of the cross,
just as they had desired.

2C 39 [13]Once two brothers were traveling from the Terra di Lavoro, and the older one had seriously scandalized the younger one. When they reached the father, he asked the younger how his companion had behaved toward him during the trip. The brother replied: "Well enough." "Be careful, brother," he added, "don't lie under the pretext of humility. I know, I know. But wait a bit and you'll see." The brother was quite amazed that he knew *through the* Acts 21:4 *Spirit* such far away events. *Just a few days later,* the one who *had* Lk 15:13; Rom 14:13; Mt 5:22 *scandalized his brother,* having turned against religion in contempt, left. He did not ask the father's forgiveness nor accept the discipline of correction that was due. In that single fall, two things shone forth clearly: the equity of the divine judgment and the penetrating power of the spirit of prophecy.

14How he appeared as present to the absent,
through divine power,
is evidently clear from the above,
if it is recalled to mind how he appeared to the brothers,
although absent,
transfigured in a fiery chariot, LMj IV 4
and how he presented himself at the Chapter of Arles LMj IV 10
in the image of a cross.
It should be believed that this was done by divine providence
so that from his miraculous appearance in bodily presence
it might clearly shine forth
how present and open his spirit was
Wis 7:24, 27 to the light of *eternal wisdom,*
which is mobile beyond all motion.
Reaching everywhere because of its purity,
spreading through the nations
into holy souls,
it makes them prophets and friends of God.

For the exalted Teacher
is accustomed to opening his mysteries
Prv 3:32; Mt 11:25 *to the simple* and the *little ones*
as first appeared in David, the best of the prophets,
and then in Peter, the prince of the apostles,
and finally in Francis, the little poor man of Christ.
Acts 4:13 For when these simple men were unskilled in letters,
Jn 16:23; Acts 13:9 they were made illustrious by the teaching of the Holy Spirit.
One was a shepherd
Jn 21:15; 1 Pt 5:2 that he would *pasture the Synagogue,*
1 Sm 16:11-12; 2 Sm 5:2 *the flock* God had led out of Egypt;
the other was a fisherman
Mt 13:47-48 that he would *fill the net* of the Church
with many kinds of believers;
Mt 13:44-46 the last was *a merchant*

that he would *purchase the pearl* of the Gospel life,
selling and giving away *all he had*
for the sake of Christ.[a]

a. This passage echoes an autobiographical comment in Bonaventure's *Letter in Response to an Unknown Master*, 13: "I confess before God that what made me love Saint Francis's way of life so much was that it is exactly like the origin and the perfection of the Church itself, which began first with simple fishermen and afterwards developed to include the most illustrious and learned doctors. You will find the same thing in the Order of Saint Francis; in this way God reveals that it did not come about through human calculations but through Christ." "A Letter in Response to an Unknown Master," in *Works of Saint Bonaventure: Writings Concerning the Franciscan Order*, introduction and translation by Dominic Monti (St. Bonaventure, NY: Franciscan Institute Publications, 1994), 54.

Chapter Twelve

THE EFFECTIVENESS OF PREACHING AND THE GRACE OF HEALINGS

[1]The truly faithful servant and minister of Christ,
Francis,
in order to do everything faithfully and perfectly,
directed his efforts chiefly
to the exercise of those virtues which,
by the prodding of the sacred Spirit,
he knew pleased his God more.

In this matter it happened that he fell into a great struggle over a doubt which, after he returned from many days of prayer, he proposed for resolution to the brothers who were close to him.

"What do you think, brothers, what do you judge better? That I should spend my time in prayer, or that I should travel about preach-
2 Cor 11:6 ing? I am a poor little man, simple and *unskilled in speech;* I have received a greater grace of prayer than of speaking. Also in prayer there seems to be a profit and an accumulation of graces, but in preaching a distribution of gifts already received from heaven.

"In prayer there is a purification of interior affections and a unit-
ing to the one, true and supreme good with an invigorating of virtue; ER XXIII 9
Lk 10:11 in preaching, there is a dust on our spiritual feet, distraction over many things and relaxation of discipline.

"Finally, in prayer we address God, listen to Him, and, as if living an angelic life, we associate with the angels. In preaching, it is necessary to practice great self-emptying for people and, by living humanly among them, to think, see, speak, and hear human things.

"But there is one thing to the contrary that seems to outweigh all these considerations before God, that is, the only begotten Son of
1 Cor 1:24, 30; Jn 1:18 God, who is the highest wisdom, came down from *the bosom of the Father* for the salvation of souls in order to instruct the world by His example and to speak the *word* of salvation to people, whom He would
Eph 5:26 redeem by the price of His sacred blood, *cleanse with* its *washing* and sustain with its draught, holding back for Himself absolutely nothing that He could freely give for our salvation. And because we should do

everything according to *the pattern* shown to us in Him as *on the heights* Ex 25:40
of the mountain, it seems more pleasing to God that I interrupt my
1C 35 quiet and go out to labor."

When he had mulled over these words for many days with his brothers, he could not perceive with certainty which of these he should choose as more acceptable to Christ. Although he understood extraordinary things through the spirit of prophecy, this question he could not resolve with clarity on his own.

But God's providence had a better plan, that the merit of preaching would be shown by a sign from heaven, thus preserving the humility of Christ's servant.

[2]He was not ashamed to ask advice in small matters from those under him, true Lesser Brother that he was, though he had learned
1C 91 great things from the supreme Teacher. He was accustomed to search with special eagerness **in what manner, and in what way** he could serve **God more perfectly** according to His good pleasure.

As long as he lived,
this was his highest philosophy,
this his highest desire:
to ask
from the wise and the simple,
the perfect and the imperfect,
the young and the old,
how he could more effectively arrive
at the summit of perfection.

Choosing, therefore, two of the brothers, he sent them to Brother
LMj III 5 Sylvester, who **had seen the cross** coming out from his **mouth,** and, at that time, spent his time in continuous prayer on the mountain above Assisi. He was to ask God to resolve his doubt over this matter, and to send him the answer in God's name. He also asked the holy virgin Clare to consult with the purest and simplest of the virgins living under her rule, and to pray herself with the other sisters in order
to seek *the Lord's will* in this matter. Through a miraculous revelation Lk 12:47
of the Spirit, the venerable priest and the virgin dedicated to God came to the same conclusion: that it was the divine good will that the herald of Christ should preach.

When the two brothers returned and told him God's will as they
had received it, he rose at once, *girded himself* and without the slight- Jn 21:7
est delay took to the roads. He went with such fervor to carry out the

2 Kgs 3:15 divine command, just as he ran along so swiftly as if *the hand of God*
were upon him, giving him new strength from heaven.

[3]When he was approaching Bevagna, he came upon a place 3C 20
where a large flock of birds of various kinds had gathered. When
the holy one of God saw them, he swifty ran to the spot and greeted LJS 37
them as though they had human reason. They all became alert and
turned toward him, and those perched in the trees bent their heads
as he approached them and in an uncommon way directed their attention to him. He approached them and intently encouraged them 3C 20
all to hear the word of God, saying: "My brother birds, you should
greatly praise your Creator, who clothed you with feathers, gave
you wings for flight, confided to you purity of the air, and governs
you without your least care." While he was saying this and similar
things to them, the birds fluttered about in a wonderful way. They 1C 58
began to stretch their necks, spread their wings, open their beaks,
and look at him. He passed through their midst with amazing fervor of spirit, touching them with his tunic. Yet none of them left the 3C 20
place until the man of God made the sign of the cross and gave
them a blessing and permission to leave; then they all flew away to- 1C 58
gether. His companions waiting along the way contuited all these
things.[a] Upon returning to them, the pure and simple man began to 3C 20
accuse himself of negligence because he had not previously
preached to the birds.

[4]From there he went preaching through the neighboring districts 3C 21
and came to a village called Alviano. When the people were gathered, he called for silence, but he could scarcely be heard above the 1C 59
shrieking made by the swallows that were nesting there. In the 3C 21
hearing of all the people, the man of God addressed them and said:
"My sister swallows, it is now time for me to speak, because you
have already said enough. Hear the word of God and stay quiet until the word of the Lord is completed." As if they had been able to
understand him, they suddenly became silent, and did not leave
that place until the whole sermon was over. All who saw this were
Acts 3:10; Mt 9:8 *filled with amazement* and *gave glory to God.* News of this miracle
spread around everywhere, enkindling reverence for the saint and
devotion for the faith.

---

a. In this instance, Bonaventure uses only three words of 1C 58, *socii* [companions] and *in via* [along the way]. It is significant that once again he uses the verb *contuere* to underscore the conviction arising in those companions from the evidence supplied by the effect Francis had on those birds, effects whose presence can only be accounted for by divine intervention.

3C 22 [5]**In the city of Parma, a scholar,** an excellent young man, was diligently studying with his companions when **he was so annoyed by the bothersome chattering of a swallow. He began to say** to his companions: **"This swallow is one of those** that kept bothering the man of God **Francis when he was preaching one time, until he imposed silence on them." And turning to the swallow, he said confidently: "In the name** of God's servant **Francis, I command you** to come **to me** and to be silent at once." When it heard the name of Francis, it immediately became silent, as if it really had been trained by the teaching of the man of God, and entrusted itself **to his hands** as if to safe keeping. **The surprised scholar** immediately **gave it back its freedom** and **heard its chattering** no more.

[6]Another time when God's servant was preaching on the seashore at Gaeta, out of devotion, crowds rushed upon him in order to touch him. Horrified at people's acclaim, the servant of Christ jumped alone into a small boat that was drawn up on the shore. The boat began to move, as if it had both intellect and motion of itself, and, without the help of any oars, glided away from the shore, to the wonderment of all who witnessed it. When it had gone out some distance into the deep water, it stood motionless among the waves, as long as the holy man preached to the attentive crowd on the shore. When, after hearing the sermon, seeing the miracle, and receiving his blessing, the crowd went away and would no longer trouble him, the boat returned to land on its own.

Who, then, would be
so obstinate and lacking in piety
as to look down upon the preaching of Francis?
By his remarkable power,
not only creatures lacking reason learned obedience,
but even inanimate objects served him
when he preached, as if they had life.

[7]*The Spirit of the Lord,* Is 61:1; Lk 4:18
who had *anointed and sent* him,
and also *Christ,* 1 Cor 1:24
the power and the wisdom of God,
were with their servant Francis *wherever he went* Ru 1:16
so that he might abound with words of sound teaching
and shine with miracles of great power.
1C 23 **For his word was like a blazing fire,**
reaching the deepest parts of the heart,

and filling the souls of all with wonder,
since it made no pretense
at the elegance of human composition,
but exuded the breath of divine revelation.

Once when he was to preach **before the pope and cardinals at the suggestion of the lord of Ostia,** he memorized a sermon which he had carefully composed. When he stood in their midst to offer his edifying words, he went completely blank and was unable to say anything at all. This he admitted to them in true humility and directed himself to invoke the grace of the Holy Spirit. Suddenly he began to overflow with such effective eloquence and to move the minds of those high-ranking men to compunction with such force and power that it was clearly evident it was not he, but *the Spirit* of the Lord who *was speaking.* 1C 73

Acts 6:10

[8]**Because he first convinced himself by action and then convinced others by** word, **he did not fear rebuke, but spoke the truth boldly. He did not encourage, but struck at the life of sin with a sharp blow, nor did he smooth over, but** struck **at the faults of sinners with harsh reproaches. He spoke with the same constancy of mind** to the great and the small, **and would speak with the same** joy of spirit **to the few as to the many.** 1C 36 LJS 58

People of all ages and both sexes hurried 1C 36
to see and hear this **new** man
given to the world by heaven.
Moving about through various regions,
he preached the Gospel ardently,
Mk 16:20 *as the Lord worked with* him
and confirmed his preaching with the signs that followed.[a]
For in the power of His name
Francis, the herald of truth,
Lk 11:15; 9:2 *cast out devils and healed the sick,*
and, what is greater,
he softened the obstinate minds of sinners
and moved them to penance,
restoring at the same time health to their bodies and hearts,

a. In his commentary on the missionary mandate, Lk 9:2, Bonaventure clearly reiterates that with the authority to preach the Lord also conferred the power of healing, cf. *Commentary on Luke's Gospel* IX 3 (VII, 217). The following paragraphs 9-11 touch on some of the miracles performed by Francis while he lived.

as his miracles prove,
a few of which we will cite below as examples.

LJS 48; 1C 65 [9]In the city of Toscanella he was warmly taken in as a guest by a
3C 175, 176 knight whose only son had been crippled since birth. At the father's
insistent entreaties, he lifted the child up with his hand and cured
him instantly, so that all the limbs of his body *at once got back their* Acts 3:7
LJS 48 *strength* in view of all. The boy became healthy and strong and immediately rose, *walking and leaping, and praising God.* Acts 3:8

LJS 48; 3C 176 In the city of Narni, at the request of the bishop, he made the
sign of the cross from head to foot over a paralytic who had lost the
use of all his limbs, and restored him to perfect health.

3C 174 In the diocese of Rieti a boy was so swollen for four years that he
could not in any way see his own legs. When the boy was presented
to Francis by his tearful mother, he was cured the moment the holy
man touched him with his sacred hands.

3C 178 At the town of Orte a boy was so twisted that his head was bent
to his feet and some of his bones were broken. When Francis made
the sign of the cross over him at the tearful entreaty of his parents,
he was cured on the spot and stretched out immediately.

3C 177 [10]There was a woman in the town of Gubbio whose both hands
were so withered and crippled that she could do nothing with them.
When he made the sign of the cross over them in the name of the
Lord, she was so perfectly cured that she immediately went home
LJS 48; 3C 177 and prepared with her own hands food for him and for the poor, like
Peter's mother-in-law. Mt 8:14-15

3C 124 In the village of Bevagna he marked the eyes of a blind girl with
his saliva three times in the name of the Trinity and restored the
sight she longed for.

1C 67 A woman of the city of Narni, afflicted with blindness, received
the sign of the cross from him and recovered the sight she longed
for.

At Bologna a boy had one eye covered over with an opaque film so
that he could see nothing at all with it nor could he be helped by any
treatment. After God's servant had made the sign of the cross from
his head to his feet, he recovered his sight so completely that, having
later entered the Order of Lesser Brothers, he claimed that he could
see far more clearly with the eye that had been previously ill than
with the eye that had always been well.

1C 69 In the village of San Gemini, God's servant received hospitality
from a devoted man whose wife was troubled by a demon. After
LJS 50 praying, he commanded the devil to leave by virtue of obedience,

and by God's power drove him out so suddenly that it became evident that the obstinacy of demons cannot resist the power of holy
obedience.

In **Città di Castello,** an evil spirit, which had taken possession of a 1C 70
certain woman, departed **furious** when commanded under **obedience** by the holy man, and left the woman who had been **possessed**
free in body and mind.

[11]**A brother** was suffering from such **a terrible affliction** that 3C 195
many were convinced it was more a case of possession **by a demon** LJS 49
than a natural sickness. **For he was often completely cast down and** 3C 195
rolled about foaming at the mouth, with his limbs now contracted, 1C 68
now stretched out, now bent, now twisted, now rigid and hard.
Sometimes, when he was stretched out and rigid, with his feet
level with his head, he would be lifted into the air and then would
fall down horribly. Christ's servant was **full of pity** for him in such a
miserable and incurable illness, and he sent him a morsel of the
bread he was eating. When he tasted the bread, the sick man received such strength **that** he never **suffered** from that **illness** again.

In the district **of Arezzo, a woman had been in labor for several** 1C 63
days and was already near death; there was no cure left for her in her
desperate state except from God. Christ's servant **was passing** LJS 51; 3C 108
through that region, riding **on horseback because of physical illness**. It happened that when the animal was being returned to its
owner, it was led **through the village where the woman was suffering. When the men of the place saw the horse on which the holy** 1C 63; 3C 108
man had been mounted, they took off the reins and placed them **on**
the woman. As soon as the reins touched her, **all danger** miraculously **passed,** and **the woman gave birth safely.**

A man from Città della Pieve, who was religious and God-fearing, 1C 64; LJS 52
had in his possession a cord which our holy father **had used as a belt.**
Since many **men** and **women in that** town **suffered from various**
diseases, he went to the houses of the sick and gave the sufferers
water to drink which had been touched by the cord. In this way
many were cured.

Sick persons who **ate** bread touched by the man of God were 1C 63; 3C 19
quickly restored to health by divine power.

[12]Since the herald of Christ
in his preaching
brilliantly shone with these and many other marvelous miracles,
people paid attention to what he said
Jgs 2:4 as if *an angel of the Lord were speaking.*

For excelling in him were:
a privilege of virtues,
a *spirit of prophecy,* Rv 19:10
a proficiency for miracles,
a sign given by heaven to preach,
an obedience of creatures lacking reason,
a powerful change of hearts at the sound of his words,
an erudition by the Holy Spirit beyond human teaching,
an authority to preach
granted by the Supreme Pontiff guided by a revelation,
moreover,
a Rule confirmed by that same Vicar of Christ
in which the manner of preaching is described, and,
as a seal, the marks of the Supreme King imprinted on his body.
These are like ten witnesses
affirming to the whole world without any doubt
that Francis, the herald of Christ,
celebrated in mission,
authentic in teaching,
admirable in holiness,
because of all this
truly preached the Gospel of Christ
as a messenger of God.

Chapter Thirteen

THE SACRED STIGMATA

[1]It was a custom for the angelic man Francis 1C 91
never to rest from the good,
Gn 28:12 rather, like the heavenly spirits *on Jacob's ladder,*[a]
he either *ascended* into God
or *descended* to his neighbor.
For he had so prudently learned
to divide the time given to him for merit,
that **he spent some of it working for his neighbor's benefit**
and dedicated **the rest**
to the tranquil excesses of contemplation.
Therefore,
when he emptied himself
according to the demand of times and places
to gain the salvation of another,
leaving the restlessness **of the crowds,**
he would **seek the** secrets **of solitude and a place of quiet,**
where freeing himself more freely for the Lord,
he would shake off the dust that might have clung to him
from the time spent with the crowds.

Therefore, 1C 94
two years **before he returned his spirit to heaven,** LJS 61
after a variety of many labors,
he was led by divine providence
to *a high* place *apart* called Mount La Verna.[b] Mt 17:1

a. The image of Jacob's ladder, Gn 28:12, appears frequently in Bonaventure's writings. It refers to the stages of prayer (*Regula Novitiorum* II 8), understanding Scripture (*Breviloquium*, Prol 3), progressing in virtue (*Breviloquium* V 6), ascending into God from the sensible to the mystical (*Itinerarium* I 9), a life of contemplation (*Collationes in Hexaëmeron* XXII 24). Above all, it refers to Christ (*Christus Unus Omnium* 14) and, in light of Francis's life, to Francis himself (Itin VII 3): "He [Saint Francis] is set forth as an example of perfect contemplation, just as previously he had been of action, like a second Jacob-Israel. And thus, through him, more by example than by word, God would invite all truly spiritual men to this passing over and this transport of soul."

b. In order to appreciate the depth of this image of Mount La Verna as a "high place apart," it is helpful to read Bonaventure's commentary on the Transfiguration in his *Commentary on Luke's Gospel* IX 46-60 (VII, 23-235). The mountain is seen as the summit of an excellent life, as ideal for prayer and contemplation, for divine apparitions, instructions, and for resting in God.

When according to his usual custom
he had begun to fast there for forty days
in honor of Saint Michael the Archangel,
he experienced more abundantly than usual
an overflow of the sweetness of heavenly contemplation,
was on fire with an ever intense flame of heavenly desires,[a]
and began to be aware more fully of the gifts of heavenly entries.
He was carried into the heights,
not as a curious *searcher of the supreme majesty* Prv 25:27
crushed by its glory,
but as a *faithful and prudent servant,* Mt 24:45
exploring God's good pleasure,
to which, with the greatest ardor, he desires
to conform himself in every way.

1C 92 [2]Through a divine sign from heaven he had learned that in opening the book of the Gospel, Christ would reveal to him what God con-
1C 93 sidered most acceptable in him and from him. After completing his **prayer** with much devotion, he took **the book of the sacred Gospels from the altar** and had his companion, a holy man dedicated to God, **open** it three times in the name of the Holy Trinity. All three times,
1C 92; 1C 93 when **the book was opened, the Lord's passion** always met his eyes. **The man filled with God understood that,** just as he had imitated Christ in the actions of his life, so he should be conformed to him in the affliction and sorrow of his passion, before *he would pass out of this* Jn 13:1
world.

And although his body was already weakened
by the great austerity of his past life
and his continual carrying of the Lord's cross,
he was in no way terrified,
but was inspired even more vigorously
to endure martyrdom.
The unconquerable enkindling of love in him
for the good Jesus
had grown into *lamps and flames of fire,* Sg 8:6-7
that *many waters could not quench so* powerful a *love.*

---

a. This passage is reminiscent of the Prologue to Bonaventure's *Soul's Journey into God.* "No one is in any way disposed for divine contemplations that lead to spiritual transports unless like Daniel, he is also a man of desire." Worthy of note is the footnote explaining this text. Cf. *The Journey of the Mind to God,* translated by Philotheus Boehner, edited, with introduction and notes by Stephen F. Brown (Indianapolis/Cambridge: Hackett Publishing Company, 1993), 2, 42-43, note 16.

[3]With the seraphic ardor of desires,
therefore,
he was being borne aloft into God;
and by compassionate sweetness
he was being transformed into Him
Who chose to be crucified out of
Eph 2:4 *the excess of His love.*

On a certain morning about the feast of the Exaltation of the Cross, while Francis was praying on the mountainside, **he saw a Ser- 1C 94
aph having six wings,** fiery as well as brilliant, descend from the grandeur of heaven. And when in swift flight, it had arrived at a spot in the air near the man of God, there appeared between the wings the likeness of a man **crucified,** with **his hands and feet extended** in the form of a cross and **fastened to a cross. Two of the wings were 3C 4
raised above** his **head, two were extended for flight, and two covered his whole body. Seeing this, he was overwhelmed and his heart was flooded with a mixture of joy and sorrow. He rejoiced at the gracious way** Christ looked upon him under the appearance of
Lk 2:35 **the Seraph, but** the fact that **He was fastened to a cross** *pierced his soul with a sword* of compassionate sorrow.

He marveled exceedingly 1C 94
at the sight of so unfathomable **a vision,**
knowing that the weakness of Christ's **passion**
was in no way compatible
with the immortality of the seraphic spirit.
Eventually he understood from this,
through the Lord revealing it,
that Divine Providence had shown him a vision of this sort so that
the friend of Christ might learn in advance
that he was to be totally transformed
into the likeness of Christ crucified,[a]
not by the martyrdom of his flesh,
but by the enkindling of his soul.[b]
As the vision was disappearing,
it left in his heart a marvelous fire

a. For the theology behind this statement, see supra, 515 a.

b. Bonaventure uses the term *incendium mentis,* literally *the conflagration of his soul.* The term *incendium* appears in the alternate title of Bonaventure's treatise on the three stages of the spiritual life: *De triplici via seu Incendium amoris, On the Triple Way* or *The Fire of Love.* On Francis's desire for martyrdom, cf. LMj IX, 5-9.

and imprinted in his flesh a likeness of signs
no less marvelous.

3C 4 **For immediately the marks of nails began to appear in his hands and feet** just as he had seen a little before in the figure **of the man crucified. His hands and feet seemed to be pierced through the center by nails, with the heads of the nails appearing on the inner side of the hands and the upper side of the feet and their points on the opposite sides. The heads of the nails in his hands and his feet were round and black; their points were oblong and bent as if driven back with a hammer, and they emerged from the flesh and stuck out beyond it. Also his right side,** as if pierced with a lance, **was marked with a red wound from which his sacred blood often flowed,** moistening **his tunic and underwear.**

2C 135 [4]As **Christ's servant** realized that he could not conceal from his **intimate companions the stigmata** that had been so visibly imprinted on his flesh, he feared to make public the Lord's *sacrament*[a] Tb 12:7 and was thrown into an agony of doubt whether to tell what he had seen or to be silent about it. He called some of the brothers and, speaking in general terms, presented his doubt to them and sought their advice. One of the brothers, Illuminato, by name and by grace,[b] understanding that Francis had seen something marvelous that made him seem completely dazed, said to the holy man: "Brother, you should realize that at times divine sacraments are revealed to you not for yourself alone but also for others. You have every reason to fear that if you hide what you have received for the profit of many, you will be blamed for *burying* that *talent.*" Although the holy man Mt 25:25 used to say on other occasions: *"My secret is for myself,"* he was moved Is 24:16 by Illuminato's words. Then, with much fear, he recounted the vision in detail, adding that the one who had appeared to him had told him some things which he would never disclose to any person as long as he lived. We should believe, then, that those utterances of that sacred Seraph marvelously appearing to him on the cross were so *secret* that *people are not permitted to speak of them.* 2 Cor 12:4

a. Cf. 2C 9, supra, 248 a. While Bonaventure's use of the *sacramentum* [sacrament] parallels that of Thomas, he uses the word more frequently in reference to the stigmata.

b. Earlier, LMj IX 8, Bonaventure referred to Illuminato as *viro utique luminis et virtutis* [without doubt a man of light and virtue]. In this instance, LMj XIII, he writes of him as *gratia Illuminatus et nomine* [Illuminatus—enlightened—by grace and by name], obviously underscoring his unique qualities and role in the key events of Francis's life. Thomas of Celano, 3C 123, describes the miracle through which he overcame blindness and his entrance into the Order, to which Bonaventure adds by highlighting his growth in holiness, cf. LMj Mir VII 6.

[5]After **true love of Christ** 2C 135
2 Cor 3:18 ***transformed* the lover *into His image,***
when the forty days were over that he spent in solitude
as he had desired,
and the feast of St. Michael the Archangel
had also arrived,
the angelic man Francis
Ex 19:1 *came down from the mountain,*
bearing with him
the likeness of the Crucified,
Dt 4:13 depicted not on *tablets of stone* or on panels of wood
carved by hand,
but engraved on parts of his flesh
Dt 9:10; Jn 11:27 *by the finger of the living God.*
Tb 12:7 And because *it is good to keep hidden*
the sacrament of the King,
the man aware of the royal secret
would then hide from men those sacred signs.
Since it is for God to reveal what He does for his own great glory,
the Lord himself,
who had secretly imprinted those marks,
openly revealed some miracles through them
so that the hidden and marvelous power of the stigmata
would display a brilliance of signs.

[6]**In the province of Rieti a very serious plague broke out and so cruelly took the lives of cattle** and sheep that no remedy could be found. **A certain Godfearing man** was told **in a vision at night to hurry to the hermitage of the brothers and get the water in which** God's servant Francis, **who was staying there at that time, had washed his hands and feet, and to sprinkle it** on all the animals. **He got up in the morning, came to the place,** secretly got the water from the companions of the holy man, and **sprinkled** it on the sheep and cattle. Marvelous to say, the moment that water touched the animals, which were weak and lying on the ground, they immediately recovered their former vigor, stood up and, as if they had had nothing wrong with them, hurried off to pasture. Thus through the miraculous power of that water, which had touched his sacred wounds, the plague ceased and deadly disease fled from the flocks. 3C 18

[7]About the time the holy man stayed on Mount La Verna,
clouds would form over the mountain,
and violent hailstorms would devastate the crops.

But after that blessed apparition
the hail stopped,
to the amazement of the inhabitants,
so that the unusually serene face of the sky proclaimed
the excellence of that heavenly vision
and the power of the stigmata imprinted there.

In wintertime because of his physical weakness and the rough roads, he was once riding on a donkey belonging to a poor man. It happened that he spent the night at the base of an overhanging cliff to try to avoid the inconveniences of a snowfall and the darkness of night that prevented him from reaching his place of lodging. When, however, the saint heard his helper tossing and turning, grumbling and groaning, since, as he had only thin clothing, the biting cold would not let him sleep; burning with the fire of divine love, he stretched out his hand and touched him. A marvelous thing happened! At the touch of his sacred hand, which bore the burning *coal of the Seraph,* the cold fled altogether and the man felt great heat within and without, as if he had been hit by a fiery blast from the vent of a furnace. Comforted in mind and body, he slept until morning more soundly among the rocks and snow than he ever had in his own bed, as he later used to say. Is 6:6-7

Thus it is obvious to certain witnesses
that those sacred marks were imprinted
by the power of Him Who,
through a seraphic activity,
purifies, illumines, and inflames.[a]
Outwardly,
by purifying from pestilence,
with a marvelous effect,
they brought health, serene skies,
and warmth to bodies.
As after his death
this was demonstrated
by even more evident miracles
as we will later record in the proper place.

a. A reference to the three hierarchical acts presented by the Pseudo-Dionysius, *The Celestial Hierarchy* III 2. Cf. supra, 526 a; also, *Pseudo-Dionysius: The Complete Works*, trans by Colm Luibheid and Rene Roques, foreword, preface, and notes by Rene Roques, introductions by Jaroslav Pelikan, Jean Leclercq, and Karlfried Froehlich (New York, Mahwah: Paulist Press, 1987), 154-155.

Mt 13:44 [8]Although **he tried** his best **to hide** the *treasure found in the field,* he 2C 135
could not prevent at least some from seeing **the stigmata in his** 2C 136
hands and feet, although he always kept **his hands** covered and
from that time on always wore shoes.

A number of the brothers saw them **while he was still alive.** Al- 3C 5
though they were men of outstanding holiness and so completely
trustworthy, nevertheless to remove all doubt they confirmed under
oath, touching the most sacred Gospels, that this was so and that
they had seen it.

Also some of the cardinals saw them because of their close friendship with the holy man; and they inserted praises of the sacred stigmata in the hymns, antiphons, and sequences which they composed
Jn 5:33 in his honor, and thus by their words and writings *gave testimony to the*
truth.[a]

Even the Supreme Pontiff Lord Alexander,[b] in a sermon preached
to the people at which many of the brothers and I myself were present, affirmed that he had seen the sacred stigmata with his own eyes
while the saint was still alive.

More **than fifty brothers** with the virgin Clare, who was most de- 3C 5
voted to God, and her sisters, as well as **innumerable laymen,** saw
them after his death. Many of them kissed the stigmata out of devotion and **touched** them **with their own hands** to strengthen their
testimony, as we will describe in the proper place.

But the wound in his side he so **cautiously** concealed that as long 2C 138
as he was alive no one could see it except by stealth. One brother 1C 95
who used to zealously take care of him induced him with a pious care
to take off **his tunic to shake it out. Watching closely, he saw the** 2C 136; 2C 138
wound, and he even quickly touched it with three of his fingers de-
termining the size of the wound by both sight and **touch.** The brother 1C 95
who was his vicar at that time also managed to see it by similar care.
A brother who was **a companion** of his, a man of marvelous simplic- 2C 138
ity, when he was one day **rubbing his shoulders that were weak** 1C 95
from illness, put his hand under his hood and accidentally touched
the sacred **wound, causing him great pain.** As a result, from that
time on, he always wore underclothes made so that they would reach

a. Gregory IX (Cardinal Hugolino) composed the hymn *Proles de caelo*, the response *De paupertatis borreo*, the antiphons *Sancte Francisce propere* and *Plange turba paupercula*, and the sequence *Caput draconis ultimum;* Cardinal Thomas of Capua, the hymns *Deus morum* and *In caelesti collegio*, the response *Carnis spicam*, the antiphon *Salve sancte Pater*, and the sequence *Laeteabundus Francisco;* Cardinal Rainerio Capoci of Viterbo, the hymn *Plaude turba;* Cardinal Stefano di Casa Nova, the antiphon *Caelorum candor splenduit.* Most of these were incorporated into the rhymed office composed by Julian of Speyer.

b. Alexander IV, pope 1254-1261, who made the same affirmation in his bulls: *Benigna operatio* (October 19, 1255) and *Quia longum esset* (June 28, 1259).

up to his armpits to cover the wound on his side. Also the brothers
who washed these or shook out his tunic from time to time, since
3C 5 they found these **stained with blood,** were convinced without any
doubt from this evident sign of the existence of the sacred wound,
3C 5 **which, after his death,** they along with many others contemplated
and venerated *with unveiled face.* 2 Cor 3:18

[9]Come now,
most vigorous knight of Christ,
bear the arms of your invincible Leader!
Visibly shielded with these,
you will overcome all adversaries.
Carry the standard of the Most High King,
by Whose gaze
all combatants of the divine army
are aroused to courage.
Carry the seal of Christ, the Supreme Pontiff,
by which your words and deeds
will be rightly accepted by all
as authentic and *beyond reproach.* Ti 2:8

For now,
because of *the stigmata of the Lord Jesus* Gal 6:17
which you *carry in* your *body,*
no one must *trouble you;*
rather every servant of Christ
must show you with all intensity greater devotion.

Now
through these most certain signs,
corroborated
not by the sufficient testimony *of two or three witnesses,* Dt 19:15
but by the superabundant testimony of a whole multitude,
God's *testimony* about you and through you
has been made overwhelmingly credible, Ps 92:5
removing completely from unbelievers
the veil of excuse,
while they confirm believers in faith,
raise them aloft with confident hope
and set them ablaze with the fire of charity.

[10]Now Dn 9:24; 4:6
the first *vision you saw* is truly *fulfilled,*

that is, that you should be 1C 5
a future leader in the militia of Christ
and bear heavenly arms
emblazoned with the sign of the cross.

Now 3C 2
the vision that you saw **at the outset of** your **conversion**
must undoubtedly be believed as true,
that is, of the Crucified
Lk 2:35 *piercing* your soul *with a sword* of compassionate sorrow,
but also the sound of the voice **from the cross,**
Nm 7:89 as if proceeding *from* the throne of the lofty Christ
and the secret *mercy seat,*
as you confirmed with your own sacred utterance.

Now 3C 3
in the unfolding of your conversion,
the cross Brother Sylvester saw
marvelously coming from your mouth;
and the swords the holy **Pacifico saw**
piercing your body in the form of a cross;
and the figure of you **lifted up in the air** in the form of a cross
the angelic **man Monaldo** saw
while Saint **Anthony was preaching**
about the inscription on the cross:
these must be truly believed and affirmed
not as an imaginary vision,
but as a celestial revelation.

Now,
finally, near the end,
you were shown at the same time
the sublime similitude of the Seraph
and the humble likeness of the Crucified,
inwardly inflaming you and outwardly signing you
Rv 7:2 as *the other Angel ascending from the rising of the sun*
that *you might have* in you *the sign of the living God:*
this both gives strength of faith to the previous ones
Jn 5:33-34 and *receives* from them *the testimony of truth.*

Behold,
you have arrived
with seven apparitions of the cross of Christ

wondrously apparent and visible in you or about you
following an order of time,
like six steps leading to the seventh
where you finally found rest.[a]
For
the cross of Christ,
both offered to and taken on by you
at the beginning of your conversion
and carried continuously from that moment
throughout the course of your most proven life
and giving example to others,
shows with such clarity of certitude
that you have finally reached
the summit of Gospel perfection
that no truly devout person
can reject this proof of Christian wisdom
ploughed into the dust of your flesh.
No truly believing person can attack it,
no truly humble person can belittle it,
since it is truly divinely expressed
and *worthy of complete acceptance.* 1 Tm 1:15; 4:9

a. Note the similarity between the seven stages of *The Soul's Journey into God*, prol., 3; I, 1-7; VII, 1.

Chapter Fourteen

HIS PATIENCE
AND
PASSING IN DEATH[a]

Gal 2:19 [1]*Now fixed with Christ to the cross,*
in both body and spirit,
Francis
not only burned with a seraphic love into God
Jn 19:28 but also *thirsted* with Christ crucified 1C 98
for the multitude of those to be saved.

Since **he could not walk** because of the nails protruding from his
Lk 8:1 feet, **he had his half-dead body carried** ***through the towns and villages*** LJS 64
Lk 9:23 to arouse others to *carry the cross* of Christ. He used to say to the broth- 1C 103
ers: **"Let us begin, brothers, to serve the Lord** our God, **for up** to now
Nm 11:4; Mt 2:10 **we have done little."** *He burned with a great desire* **to return to the hu-**
mility he practiced at the beginning; to nurse **the lepers as** he did at
the outset and to treat like a slave once more his body that was already in a state of collapse from his work.

With the Christ as leader,
he resolved "to do great deeds,"
and although his limbs **were weakening,**
he hoped
for victory over the enemy in a new struggle
with a brave and burning spirit.
For there is no room for apathy and laziness 2C 209
where the goad of love
always urges to greater things.
There was in him such harmony of flesh with spirit, 1C 97
such readiness **of obedience,**
that, when he strove to attain **all holiness,**

a. The Latin word here is *transitu* [passing]. It appears on many levels of Bonaventure's thought: that of creation which has a passage through time; that of the People of God and, most especially, of Jesus, i.e., the biblical connotations; and that of every Christian called to journey or pass over into God. Cf. André Ménard, "Spirituaté du *Transitus*," in *S. Bonaventura 1274-1974*, vol. IV (Grottaferrata, Rome: Collegio S. Bonaventura, 1974), 607-635.

not only **did the flesh not resist,**
it even tried to **run ahead.**

[2]In order that his merits might increase,
for these are brought to perfection *in patience,* Jas 1:4
1C 105 the man of God **started** to suffer from various **illnesses,**
so seriously that scarcely **the rest of his body**
1C 107 **remained without** intense **pain and suffering.**
Through varied, long-lasting, and continual illness
he was brought to the point
where **his** ***flesh was*** already ***all consumed,*** Jb 19:20
as if **only skin** ***clung to his bones.*** Lam 4:8
2C 212 But when he was tortured by harsh bodily suffering,
he called his tribulations not by the name of "pains"
but of "Sisters."

2C 213 Once **when** he was suffering **more intensely than usual,** a certain
brother in his simplicity told him: "Brother, *pray to the Lord* that he Sir 38:9
treat you more mildly, for he seems to *have laid* his *hand* on you more
heavily than he should." At these words, the holy man wailed and Ps 31:4; 2 Cor 1:8
cried out: "If I did not know your simplicity and sincerity, then I
would from now on shrink from your company because you dared to
judge God's judgments upon me as reprehensible." Even though he
was completely worn out by his prolonged and serious illness, he
threw himself on the ground, bruising his weakened bones in the
hard fall. Kissing the ground, he said: *"I thank you,* Lord *God,* for all Lk 18:11
these sufferings of mine; and I ask you, my Lord, if it pleases you, to
increase them a hundredfold. Because it will be most acceptable to
me, *that you do not spare me, afflicting me with suffering,* since the fulfill- Jb 6:10
ment of your will is an overflowing consolation for me."

So it seemed to the brothers, therefore,
that they were almost seeing another Job,
for whom, as the weariness of his flesh was increasing,
so too was the vigor of his soul.
He knew **long in advance the time of his death,**
and as the day of his passing **grew near,**
he told the brothers that
laying aside the tent of his body was at hand, 2 Pt 1:14
1C 108 **as it had been revealed** to him by Christ.

1C 109 [3]For two years after the imprinting of the sacred stigmata
that is, in the twentieth **year of his conversion,**

under the many blows of agonizing illness,
he was squared like a stone to be fitted
into the construction of the heavenly Jerusalem,
and like a work of malleable metal 2C 214
he was brought to perfection
under the hammering blows of many tribulations.

He asked to be taken to Saint Mary of the Portiuncula LJS 69
Gn 6:17 so that he might yield up *the spirit of life* 1C 106
Heb 10:29 where he had received *the spirit of grace.*

When he had been brought there, he showed by the example of 2C 214
Truth that he had nothing in common with the world. In that grave
illness that ended all suffering, he threw himself in fervor of spirit
totally naked on the naked ground so that in that final hour, when
the enemy could still rage, he might wrestle naked with the na-
Jb 20:4 ked.[a] Lying like this *on the ground* stripped of his sackcloth garment,
Jb 11:15 *he lifted up his face to heaven* in his accustomed way, and wholly intent upon that glory, he covered with his left hand the wound in his
right side, so that no one would see it. And he said to his brothers: "I
1 Kgs 19:20; Eph 4:21 *have done what is mine;* may *Christ teach you* yours."

4Pierced with the spear of compassion, the companions of the 2C 215
saint wept streams of tears. One of them, whom the man of God
used to call his guardian, knowing his wish through divine inspiration, quickly got up. He took the tunic with a cord and underwear,
and offered them to the little poor man of Christ, saying: "I am lending these to you as to a poor man, and you are to accept them with
the command of holy obedience." At this the holy man rejoiced and
Sg 3:11 *was delighted in the gladness of his heart,* because he saw that he had
2 Chr 6:13 kept faith until the end with Lady Poverty. *Raising his hands to* 2C 216
heaven, he magnified his Christ, that now set free from all things, he
was going to him free. For he had done all of this out of zeal for pov- 2C 215
erty, not wanting to have even a habit unless it were borrowed
from another.

In all things
he wished without hesitation
to be conformed to Christ crucified,
who hung on the cross poor, suffering, and naked.

a. Cf. FA:ED I 194 a.

Naked he lingered before the bishop
at the beginning of his conversion;
and, for this reason,
at the end of his life,
he wanted to leave this world naked.

2C 217 And so he charged **the brothers** assisting him,
under the obedience of love,
that **when they saw** he was dead,
they should allow **him to lie naked on the ground**
for as long as it takes to walk a leisurely mile.

O truly the most Christian of men,
who strove by perfect imitation to be conformed
while living to Christ living,
dying to Christ dying,
and dead to Christ dead,
and deserved to be adorned
with an expressed likeness!

2C 216 [5]When the hour of his passing was approaching, **he had all the**
brothers staying in the place **called to him and, comforting them**
about his death with *words of consolation,* **he exhorted them to di-** Zec 1:13
vine love with fatherly affection. He spoke at length about preserv-
ing poverty and patience and the faith of the holy Roman Church,
placing the holy Gospel ahead of other observances. As all the
1C 108 **brothers sat around him,** *he stretched his hand over* them, **crossing** Gn 48:14
his arms in the form of a cross, for he always loved this sign. And he
1C 109 **blessed all the brothers, both present and absent,** in the name and
power of the Crucified. Then he added: **"Good bye, all my sons,** *in the* Tb 2:14
fear of the Lord! Remain in Him always! **Because a** *trial* **and** *tribulation* Sir 27:6
is coming in the future, happy are they who will persevere in those
things they have begun. I am hurrying to God, to whose grace I en-
2C 217 **trust all of you."** When he finished this gentle admonition, the man
most beloved of God ordered **the Book of the Gospels brought** to
him and asked that the Gospel according to John be read to him
from the place that begins: *Before the feast of Passover.* **He, as best he** Jn 13:1
could, broke out in this psalm: *With my voice I cried to the Lord; With* Ps 142:2
my voice I beseeched the Lord; and he finished it to the end. *The just,* he Ps 142
said, *will await me until you have rewarded me.*

[6]At last,
2C 117 **when all of the mysteries were fulfilled in him**

and that most holy soul was released from the flesh 1C 110
and absorbed into the abyss of the divine light,
Acts 7:60 the blessed man *fell asleep in the Lord.*
One of his brothers and followers saw that blessed soul
under the appearance of a radiant star
Rv 14:14 carried up on *a shining cloud*
to be borne aloft straight to heaven over many waters,
as if shining with the brightness of sublime sanctity,
and filled with the abundance of heavenly wisdom and grace,
by which the holy man merited to enter
the place of light and peace
where he rests with Christ forever.

At that time the minister of the brothers in Terra di Lavoro was 2C 218
Brother Augustine, a man both holy and upright, who was in his
last hour and had already for some time lost his speech. In the
Acts 23:4; Lk 9:39 hearing of those *who were standing about*: *he suddenly cried out*: "Wait
for me, father, wait! Look, I'm coming with you!" The amazed
brothers asked him to whom he was speaking so boldly. And he
replied: "Don't you see our father Francis going to heaven?" And
immediately his holy soul, leaving the flesh, followed the most holy
father.

At that time the bishop of Assisi had been at the shrine of Saint 2C 220
Michael on Monte Gargano because of a pilgrimage. Blessed Fran-
Jn 16:28 cis appeared to him on the night of his passing and said: "Behold, *I*
Gn 24:54 *am leaving the world and am going to* heaven." When he *rose in the*
morning, the bishop told his companions what he had seen, and returning to Assisi, he carefully inquired and found out with certainty
that the blessed father had departed this world at the very hour
when he appeared to him in this vision.

Larks are birds, 3C 32
friends of the light dreading the shadows of dusk.
At the hour of the holy man's passing,
when it was already twilight of the falling night,
they gathered in a great flock over the roof of the house
and, circling around for a long time with unusual joy,
Jn 1:7 *they offered testimony,*
giving delight as well as confirmation,
of the glory of the saint,
who so often had invited them to divine praise.

Chapter Fifteen

HIS CANONIZATION
AND
THE TRANSFERAL OF HIS BODY

[1]Francis,
1C 95 **the servant and friend of the Most High,**
the founder and leader of the Order of the Lesser Brothers,
the practitioner of poverty, the model of penance,
the herald of truth,
2C 26 **the mirror of holiness,**
2C 161 and **the exemplar** of all Gospel **perfection,**
foreordained by grace from heaven,
in an ordered progression
from the lowest level arrived at the very heights.

The Lord made incomparably more brilliant in death
this marvelous man,
whom He had made marvelously bright in life:
rich in poverty, exalted in humility,
vigorous in mortification,
prudent in simplicity,
distinguished in the integrity of his life.
For after this blessed man left the world,
that sacred spirit,
entering a *home of eternity,* Eccl 12:5
and made glorious by a full draught from *the fountain of life,* Ps 36:9
left certain signs *of future glory* imprinted on his body; Rom 8:18
so that,
his most holy flesh,
which *crucified along with its vices,* Gal 5:24
had already passed into a new creature, 2 Cor 5:17
bore the likeness of Christ's passion
by a singular privilege
and would offer by the newness of a miracle
C 112, 114; 3C 5 **a glimpse of the resurrection.**

3C 5 [2]In his blessed hands and feet could be seen **the nails** that had been marvelously fashioned by divine power out of his flesh, and

thus embedded in the flesh. From whatever point **they were**
pressed, simultaneously, as if by a continuous and tough tendon,
they pulsed at the opposite end. Also **the wound** in his side could be IC 113
clearly seen, which was not inflicted on his body nor produced by human means; it was like the wound in the Savior's side, which
brought forth in our Redeemer the mystery of the redemption and
regeneration of the human race. **The nails were as black as iron;** the LJS 71
wound **in his side was red,** and because it was drawn into a kind of IC 113
circle by the contraction of the flesh looked like a most beautiful rose.
The rest of his **skin, which before** was inclined to be **black** both natu- IC 112
rally and from his illness, **now shone white in its beauty, prefigur-** LJS 71
ing the beauty of that glorious second stole.[a]

[3]**His limbs** were so supple and **soft** to the touch that they seemed LJS 71
to have regained the tenderness of childhood and to be adorned IC 113
with clear signs **of innocence. The nails** appeared black **in his shin-**
Sir 50:8 **ing skin,** and the wound in his side was red *like a rose* in springtime so
that it is no wonder the onlookers were amazed and overjoyed at the
sight of such varied and miraculous beauty.

His sons were weeping at the loss of so lovable **a father** but were LJS 71
filled with **no little** joy while **they kissed the seal marks** of the su- IC 113
preme King in him. **The newness of the miracle turned their grief into** IC 112
joy and transported **into amazement** their attempts at comprehending
it. So unique and so remarkable was the sight to all who observed it
that it confirmed their faith and incited their love. It was a matter of
amazement to those who heard of it and aroused their desire to see it.

[4]When the people heard of the passing of our blessed father and
news of the miracle had spread, they hurried to the place to see with
their own eyes so that they could dispel all doubt and add joy to their
love. A great number of the citizens of Assisi **were admitted** to con- IC 113
template those **sacred marks** with their own eyes and **to kiss** them
with their lips. One of them, a knight who was educated and prudent, Jerome by name, a distinguished and famous man, had doubts
Jn 20:27 about these sacred signs and *was unbelieving* like Thomas. Fervently
and boldly, in the presence of the brothers and the citizens, he did
1 Jn 1:1 not hesitate to move the nails and *to touch with his hands* the saint's
hands, feet, and side. While he was examining with his hands these
authentic signs of Christ's wounds, he completely healed the wound

a. That is, the glory of the body in heaven. Bonaventure, *Breviloquium* VII, 7 and *The Tree of Life*, 44. (The double stole refers to the two rewards of paradise: the beatific vision and the glorification of the body.)

of doubt in his own heart and the hearts of others. As a result, later along with others, he became a firm witness to this truth that he had come to know with such certainty; and he swore to it on the Gospel.[a]

1C 116 [5]**His brothers and sons, who** had been called to their father's
passing, **with** ***the whole multitude of people,*** **spent that night in which** Ez 27:33
the blessed confessor of Christ departed, in the divine praises. They
did this in such a way that **it seemed to be a vigil of angels,** not a
wake for the dead. ***When day was breaking, the crowds that had assembled*** Jn 21:4; Jn 12:13; Mt 21:8
took branches from the trees and carried **his sacred body to the city** of
Assisi, with a blaze of **many candles and hymns** and songs. As they
passed **the church of San Damiano, where** the noble virgin Clare,
now glorious in heaven, was then living enclosed **with the virgins,**
they stopped for awhile so that those holy nuns could see and **kiss**
1C 117; 1C 118 his sacred body, adorned with its heavenly **pearls. Finally reaching**
the city with great rejoicing, with all reverence they placed the pre-
LJS 72 cious treasure they were carrying in the church of Saint George.

There **as a boy he learned his letters,**
there he later preached for the first time,
and there, finally, he received his first place of rest.

LJS 73 [6]**The venerable father left the shipwreck of this world in the one thousandth, two hundredth, twenty-sixth year of the Incarnation of the Lord, on the fourth day of the nones of October,** a Saturday evening, **and was buried on Sunday.**

1C 88 Immediately,
the holy man **began**
to reflect the light radiating from the face of God
and to glitter with many great miracles.
Thus the sublimity of his holiness
which, while he was still in the flesh,
had been familiar to the world as a guide for conduct
through examples of perfect justice,
was approved from heaven
while he is now *reigning with Christ* Rv 20:4

a. Bonaventure quotes a phrase from Gregory the Great in his interpretation of the doubt of knight Jerome: "he completely healed the wound of doubt in his own heart and in the hearts of others." In his Twenty-Ninth Homily on the Gospels, Gregory comments on the slowness of the disciples to believe and comments, in particular, on Thomas "who remained so long in doubt." "While doubting," Gregory comments, "he touched the scars of the wounds, and cut out of our hearts the wounds of doubt." Cf. Gregory the Great, *Forty Gospel Homilies*, trans. Dom David Hurst (Kalamazoo, MI: Cistercian Publications, 1990), 226.

as a confirmation of faith
through miracles performed by the divine power.

In different **parts** of the world, 1C 120
his glorious **miracles**
and the abundant benefits obtained through him, 1C 121
inflamed many to devotion to Christ
and incited them to reverence for his saint.
The wonderful things
which God was working
through his servant Francis
—acclaimed by word of mouth
and testified to by facts—
came to the ears
of the Supreme Pontiff, Gregory IX.

7 That **shepherd of the Church** was fully convinced of Francis's re- 1C 121
markable holiness: not only from hearing of **the miracles** after his
1 Jn 1:1 death, but also from his own experience **during his life.** *Having seen* 1C 124
with his own eyes and *touched with his own hands,* he had no doubt that
Francis was **glorified in heaven by the Lord.** In order to act in confor- 1C 126
mity with Christ, whose vicar he was, after prayerful consideration
he decided to glorify him on earth by proclaiming him worthy of all
veneration. In order to certify to the whole world the glorification of
this most holy man, he had the known miracles recorded and attested to by appropriate witness. These he submitted to the examination of those cardinals who seemed less favorable to his cause. This
material was examined carefully and approved by all. He decreed, 1C 126
with the unanimous **advice** and assent **of** his **brothers and of all the** LJS 74
prelates who were then in the curia, that he should be canonized. He
came **personally** to the city of Assisi **in the one thousandth, two** 1C 126; LJS 74
hundredth, twenty-eighth year of the Incarnation of the Lord, on
the seventeenth day of the calends of August, a Sunday, and en-
rolled the blessed father **in the catalog of the saints, in a great and**
solemn ceremony that would be too long to describe.

8 In the year of one thousand, two hundred and thirty, **when the** LJS 75
brothers had assembled **to celebrate a general chapter** at Assisi, his
body, dedicated to God, **was translated on the eighth of the calends** LJS 76
of June to the basilica constructed in his honor.

While that sacred treasure was being carried,
marked with the seal of the Most High King,
He whose likeness he bore
deigned to perform many miracles,
Sg 1:3 **so that through his saving** *fragrance*

the faithful in their love
might *be drawn to run after* Christ.
It is truly fitting
that *the blessed bones* of one who, Sir 46:14
through the grace of contemplation,
was pleasing to God, beloved by Him in life,
and borne by Him into paradise
like Enoch, Gn 5:24
and of one who,
through the zeal of love,
was snatched up into heaven in a fiery chariot 2 Kgs 2:11
like Elijah,
that these blessed bones,
already blossoming among those *heavenly flowers* Sir 50:8
of the garden of an eternal spring,
should flower again Sir 46:14
with a wonderful permeating fragrance
from their place of rest.

LJS 76 [9]Just as that blessed man
had shone in his life with marvelous signs of virtue,
so from the day of his passing until the present,
in different parts of the world,
he shines with outstanding examples of miracles
through the divine power that glorifies him.
Remedies for all sicknesses, necessities, and dangers
are conferred
through his merits
on the blind and the deaf,
the mute and the crippled,
the paralytic and the dropsical,
the possessed and the leper,
the shipwrecked and the captive.
But also many dead are miraculously brought back to life
through him.
Thus the magnificence
of the power of the Most High Lk 1:35
doing wonders for his saint Ps 4:3
shines forth to the faithful.
To Him be honor and glory Rom 16:27
for endless *ages of ages.*

Amen.

HERE ENDS THE LIFE OF BLESSED FRANCIS.

HERE BEGIN SOME OF THE MIRACLES SHOWN AFTER HIS DEATH

Chapter I
IN THE FIRST PLACE THE POWER OF THE SACRED STIGMATA

[1]To the honor of almighty God
and the glory of our Blessed Father Francis,
as I begin to write down
some of the approved miracles
worked by our Blessed Father
after his glorification in heaven,
it seems to me that I ought to begin by that one
which manifests most clearly the power of Jesus' cross
and by which its glory is newly shown forth.
Eph 4:24 For *the new man,* Francis, 3C 2
became famous for a new and stupendous miracle.
By a singular privilege, not granted in previous ages,
he appeared marked,
adorned with the sacred stigmata,
Phil 3:10, 21; Rom 7:24 and *conformed in this body of death*
to the body of the Crucified.
Whatever human speech can say about this will be less than the praise it deserves.
1 Sm 9:6 Indeed, all the striving of the *man of God,*
whether in public or in private,
revolved around the cross of the Lord.
So that the mark of the cross 1C 90
stamped on his heart at the beginning of his conversion
might mark his body externally
he enclosed himself in the cross itself
when he put on the habit of a penitent,
bearing the image of the cross.
Gal 3:27 Just as, internally, his mind *had put on* the crucified Lord,
so, externally, his body also put on the arms of the cross;
and, in the sign by which God had vanquished the powers of the air
his army would battle for the Lord.[a]

a. The term *arma crucis* could mean both "the armor of the Cross" and "the insignia of the Cross," as in the coat of arms on a shield. Both senses fit the context, and both were probably intended by Bonaventure.

From the very first moment
in which he began to do battle for the Crucified,
the mysteries of the cross began to shine forth in him
in manifold and diverse ways,
as will be clear to anyone who considers the events of his life.
For by the sevenfold apparitions of the Lord's cross
which he experienced,
he became an image of the Crucified in his thoughts,
in his feelings and in his actions,
being transformed by his ecstatic love of Christ.
The mercy of the Supreme King toward those who love Him,
something beyond anything humans can imagine,
stamped the banner of His cross upon his body,
3C 3 **that one who so wonderfully excelled in love of the cross**
should also wonderfully become a wonder in honor of the cross.

[2]The unassailable certainty of this stunning miracle is supported
not only by the witness
—which is in every way *worthy of our trust*— Ps 92:5
of those who *saw these wounds, and touched them,* Lk 24:39
but also by the wondrous apparitions and miracles
which have shone forth after his death
1C 101 to drive away every cloud from our minds.

Indeed, before he had inscribed this standard-bearer of the cross in the catalog of the saints, the Lord Pope Gregory the Ninth, of happy memory (about whom this holy man had prophetically foretold that he would be raised up to the apostolic dignity) carried a certain scruple of doubt in his heart about whether he had really received a wound in his side. But one night—as that blessed pontiff himself used to tell with tears in his eyes—blessed Francis *appeared to* Mt 1:20; 2:13,19
him in a dream with a certain show of sternness in his face. Reproving him for his inner uncertainty, blessed Francis raised up his right arm, uncovered the wound on his side, and asked him for a vial in which to gather the spurting blood that flowed from it. In the dream the Supreme Pontiff brought him the vial requested, and it seemed to be filled to the brim with the blood which flowed abundantly out of the side. From that day he began to feel such devotion towards this sacred miracle, and to burn with such a zeal for it, that he would not allow anyone to obscure these signs with arrogant presumption without striking him with a severe rebuke.[a]

a. Three declarations of Gregory IX, promulgated in 1237, praise the Stigmata of Francis, and defend their genuineness against those who attacked it. The texts of these declarations are in BFr I, 211-214.

[3]A certain brother, Lesser by Order, preacher by office, and a 3C 10
man of outstanding virtue and reputation, was firmly convinced of
the holy stigmata. But, as he tried to examine the reason for this
miracle by the light of human understanding, he began to be irritated by a scruple of doubt. As he struggled for many days over these
questionings, which grew stronger as he turned them over in his
mind, one night, as he slept, Saint Francis appeared to him with
muddy feet, humbly stern, and patiently irritated. And he spoke,
"Why all these conflicting struggles in you? Why these filthy
Jn 20:27 doubts? *See my hands* and my feet!" He saw the pierced hands, but
he did not see the stigmata on the muddy feet. "Remove the mud
Jn 20:25 from my feet," he said, "and examine *the place of the nails.*" As the
brother devoutly took hold of the feet, it seemed to him the mud
1 Jn 1:1 washed away, and *he touched with* his *hands the places of the nails.*
Then suddenly, as the brother awoke, he was flooded with tears,
and he cleansed himself of his earlier muddy feelings both with the
flow of his tears and by public confession.

[4]In the city of Rome a certain matron of upright life and noble 3C 8
Jdt 8:5 family chose Saint Francis for her advocate, and kept his image *in*
Mt 6:6 *the secluded chamber,* where she prayed to the Father in secret. One
day as she gave herself to prayer, she noticed that the Saint's image
did not show the sacred marks of the stigmata. She was very sad
and surprised. No wonder they were not in the painting: the
painter left them out! For several days she wondered anxiously
about the reason for this lack, when suddenly, one day those wonderful signs appeared in the picture, just as they are usually
painted in other images of the Saint. The woman, shaken, quickly 3C 9
called her daughter, who was devoted to God, inquiring whether
the image before then had been without the stigmata. The daughter affirmed and swore that before it had been without the stigmata, but now truly appeared with the stigmata. But, since the
human mind sometimes stumbles over itself, and calls the truth
into doubt, harmful doubts again entered the woman's heart: per-
Acts 8:10 haps the image had those marks from the beginning. So the *power*
of God added a second, so that the first would not be denied. Suddenly the marks disappeared, and the image remained denuded of
those privileged signs. Thus the second sign became proof of the
first.

3C 11 [5]In the city of Llerda[a] in Catalonia **a certain man** called Juan, **who was devoted to blessed Francis, happened to pass by** one evening **on the road where there was concealed a deadly ambush**—not for him, actually, for he harbored no **hostilities**, but for another man who looked like him and who often was in his company. One of the men who lay in ambush leaped out of hiding and, taking him for his enemy, **stabbed him with deadly blows**, wounding him repeatedly, so there was no hope of his recovery. Indeed, the first blow he struck practically lopped off the man's arm and shoulder, and another thrust just below the man's nipple left such a gaping wound that his breath came out through the opening strongly enough to put out the flames of six candles at once.

3C 12 The physicians pronounced his healing to be impossible, for gangrene had begun to set in his wounds, giving out such an unbearable stench that even his own wife could not bear it. So, since he was beyond all human aid, he turned with all possible devotion to beg the protection of the blessed Father Francis, on whom (as well as on the blessed Virgin) he had called with great trust even in the middle of the ambush. And behold, as the poor man lay all alone on his bed, unable to sleep and moaning Francis' name over and over, it seemed to him that someone dressed in the habit of a Lesser Brother came in through the window and approached him. This person *called him by* Is 40:26
name and said: "Since you have placed your trust in me, behold, the Lord will deliver you." When the wounded man asked him who he was, he answered that he was Francis. And as soon as he said this, he approached the man's wounds, undid the bandages, and seemed to anoint all **the wounds** with an ointment. No sooner did he feel the gentle **touch** of those sacred hands, which had the capacity to heal by the power of the Savior's stigmata, than the gangrene was driven out, the flesh was restored and the wounds were closed, so that he was once again in perfect health. After doing this, the blessed Father disappeared. The man, feeling himself **healed**, burst out exultantly into shouts of praise to God and Saint Francis, and cried out for his wife. She hurried in at a run, and, as she saw the man standing up whom she had expected to bury the next day, she was utterly

a. A cathedral city and capital of the province of the same name; also known by the Castilian name of Lérida. There are significant differences between this miracle account and that in 3C 11-13. It is possible that two similar events may be involved. While both miracles take place in Spain, in 3C the event occurs "in the kingdom of Castile;" here it takes place in Catalonia. The nature and location of the victim's deadly wounds in both accounts are carefully described, but differ completely, as do the circumstances of his cure. However, if the accounts describe two different events, a certain amount of contamination must have affected the narratives early on, since the words of the cured man in 3C fit better with Bonaventure's narrative here. Cf. also AF III, 191-3 for another allusion to this miracle, and where the man is further identified as "Ioannes de Castris."

terrified and stunned, so that by her screams she gathered the whole neighborhood.

The people of the household hurried in, and tried to force him 3C 13
back into bed, thinking he was in delirium, while he fought them off, insisting that he was cured, and showing them that this was so. At this they were stupefied, **struck with such amazement that they all seemed out of their minds. They thought what they were seeing a fantastic vision**, since they saw the man who just a while ago had been mangled with frightful wounds, and practically withered away, now standing before them in the pink of health and in high spirits. **But the one who was healed said, "Do not be afraid! Do not believe that what you see is false, because Saint Francis has just left this place and has cured me completely of every wound by the touch of those sacred hands."** As the news of this miracle spread, the whole town hastened there. Seeing the power of blessed Francis's stigmata by means of such an obvious miracle, they were at the same time filled with wonder and with joy, and extolled **Christ's standard** 3C 149
bearer with loud cries of praise.

It was fitting indeed that the blessed Father,
now already dead in the flesh, and living with Christ,
should give health to a mortally wounded man
by the wonderful manifestation of his presence
and the gentle touch of his sacred hands,
Gal 6:17 since *he bore upon his body the brand marks*
of the One who,
by His merciful death and wondrous resurrection,
had healed the human race
Lk 10:30 —which had been wounded and *left half alive*—
healing us by the power of His wounds.

[6]**In Potenza, a city of Apulia, there was a cleric named Ruggero,** 3C 6
an honorable man and a canon of its major church. He was weakened by illness, and one day he entered a church to pray. In the church there was a painted image of blessed Francis, showing the glorious stigmata. He began to doubt that exalted miracle, thinking it was an altogether unprecedented and impossible thing. As, inwardly, his wounded mind **thought useless things, he instantly** felt himself **struck** painfully **in the palm of his left hand** under his glove **as he heard the noise** of a shot, like that **of an arrow from a bow. In-**
2 Mc 14:45 **stantly, as he was injured by the wound and stunned by the noise, he took off the glove from his hand,** to verify by sight what he sensed through touch and hearing. **Though there had previously**

been no mark in his palm, he now saw a wound in mid-hand, like
that from the shot of an arrow. So much heat was coming from it
that he thought he would pass out because of it. What a wonder!
There was no mark on the glove, so the pain of the hidden wound
inflicted on him corresponded to the hidden wound of his heart.
[7]He cried out and roared, afflicted with severe pain for two days,
and unveiled his unbelieving heart to all. He declared that he believed that the sacred stigmata were truly in Saint Francis, and
swore to affirm that all shadow of doubt was gone. He humbly
prayed *the holy one of God* to come to his aid through his sacred stig- Mk 1:24
mata, and he seasoned his many prayers with an abundance of
tears. Amazing! His unbelief discarded, bodily healing followed
the healing of the spirit: all the pain calmed, the fever cooled, and
no sign of the wound remained. Everything worked in such a way
that the hidden illness of the spirit was by God's mercy healed by
means of a manifest cautery of the flesh and, as the spirit was healed,
the flesh was at the same time also cured. He became a man humble
before God, devoted to the saint, and subject in lasting friendship
to the brothers of the Order. The miraculous nature of this incident
was attested by a signed oath, fully corroborated by a document
bearing the seal of the bishop, by which the news of it has come to us.

Concerning the sacred stigmata
let there be no room for ambiguity;
let *no one's eye* be clouded Mt 20:15
because God *is good;*
as if the granting of such a gift
were incompatible with the outpouring of everlasting goodness!
If only *the many members* were joined 1 Cor 12:12
in that same seraphic love *to Christ their head!* Eph 1:22
If only they were to be found worthy of such *armor* in a similar battle, Eph 6:11
and be raised to the same glory in the Kingdom! Rv 1:9
No one of sane mind would not attribute this to the glory of Christ.[a] Mk 5:15

Chapter II
THE DEAD RAISED TO LIFE

3C 40 [1]There was a woman in Monte Marano near Benevento who
Jos 23:14 clung to Saint Francis with special devotion, and she went *the way of*

a. The meaning of this obscure passage seems to be: there is no need to be shocked that God should allow a human being to bear the wounds of Christ, since the members of the Body are one with Christ their Head, and will share in His glory.

all flesh. The clergy came at night with their psalters to sing the
wake and vigils. Suddenly, in the sight of all, the woman sat up in
bed and called to one of them, a priest who was her godfather, "I
want to confess, Father, hear my sin! I have indeed died, and was
destined for a harsh prison because I had never confessed the sin I
will reveal to you. But Saint Francis prayed for me as I served him
with a devout spirit while I was alive. I have now been permitted to
return to my body so that after confessing my sin I might merit eternal life. So now, as all of you watch, after I reveal that to you I will
hurry off to my promised rest." She then shakily confessed to the
shaken priest, and after receiving absolution, composed herself
Acts 7:60 peacefully on the bed and happily *fell asleep in the Lord*.

[2]In the village of Pomarico, in the mountains of Apulia, a 3C 46
mother and father had an only daughter, tender of age and tenderly
loved. When she became seriously ill and close to death, her parents
considered themselves dead with her, as they did not expect any
future offspring. Relatives and friends gathered for a very sad funeral. The unhappy mother lay grief stricken, and the depth of her
sorrow kept her from noticing what was going on. In the meantime, Saint Francis with one companion kindly appeared to visit
the desolate woman, whom he knew was devoted to him, and
Lk 7:13 spoke these pious words, "*Do not weep*, for the quenched light of
your lamp, which you mourn, will be restored to you through my intercession!" The woman jumped up immediately, and told everyone what Saint Francis had told her, and would not allow the body
of the deceased to be removed, but with great faith, invoking the
name of Saint Francis, took hold of her dead daughter, and lifted
her up safe and sound, to the wonder of all the bystanders.

[3]The brothers of Nocera [Umbra] asked a man named Peter for 3C 43
a certain cart that they needed for a short time. He foolishly replied
by hurling insults at them in place of what they asked, and for the
alms requested in honor of Saint Francis he spat out blasphemy at
his name. The man immediately regretted his foolishness, as the
fear of God came upon him, a fear that the vengeance of the Lord
would follow, and it did come soon after. His firstborn son soon
took sick and after a short time gave up his spirit. The unhappy father rolled about on the ground and called out to Saint Francis
2 Sm 24:17 again and again, shouting tearfully, "*It is I who have sinned*; I spoke
evil; you should have punished me personally. Give me back, dear
saint, the one you took from this wicked blasphemer, for now I
have repented. I surrender myself to you; I promise you lasting ser-
Ps 50:14 vice, and will always offer to Christ a devout *sacrifice of praise* in honor

of your name." Amazing! At these words the boy arose, called for a halt to the wailing, and said that as he was dying, he was led forth from his body, led along by blessed Francis, and led back by him.

3C 42 [4]The barely seven-year-old son of a notary of the city of Rome
wanted in his childish way to follow his mother who was going to
the church of San Marco. Forced by his mother to stay at home, he
threw himself from the window of the building and, shaking with a
last tremor, he immediately breathed his last. The mother had not
gone far, and the sound of someone falling made her suspect the
fall of her treasure. She quickly turned back and discovered her son
taken from her by that miserable fall. She turned avenging hands
on herself; and with her cries of anguish moved the neighbors to
tears. A certain brother named Rao, of the Order of Lesser Brothers,
was on his way to preach there. He approached the boy and, full of
faith, spoke to the father. "Do you believe that Francis, the saint of
God, is able to raise your son *from the dead* because of the love he al- Acts 17:31
ways had for Christ, who was crucified to give life back to all?" The
father replied that he firmly believed it and faithfully confessed
that he would forever be the servant of the saint, if only he could receive such a great favor through his merits. That brother knelt with
his companion in prayer and urged the others present there to pray.
With that the boy began to yawn a little, to open his eyes, lift his
arms and sit up. In the sight of all, the boy, unharmed, immediately began walking, restored to life and health through the amazing power of the Saint.

3C 44 [5]In the city of Capua a lad was playing carelessly with his
friends on the bank of the river Volturno. From the bank of the river
he fell into the deep. The *force of the river* quickly swallowed him up Ps 46:5
and buried him, dead, beneath the sand. The children who had
been playing near the river with him shouted, and a large crowd
gathered there. All the people were humbly and devoutly invoking
the merits of blessed Francis, that he might look upon the faith of
the boy's parents, who had a great devotion to him, and save their
child from the danger of death. Some distance away a swimmer
heard their cries and approached them. After some searching, and
having invoked the help of blessed Francis, he found the place
where mud had covered over the boy's cadaver like a tomb. He dug
and dragged him out, and was saddened to find him dead. Even
though the crowd saw that the youth was dead, they still wept and
cried out, "Saint Francis, give the father back his child!" The same
phrase was also said by the Jews who had come, moved by natural
piety: "Saint Francis, give the father back his child!" The boy got

up immediately, unharmed, as all marveled and rejoiced, and begged to be led to the church of blessed Francis, so that he could give thanks to him devoutly, because he knew it was thanks to his power that he had been wondrously revived.

6 In the city of Sessa, in the neighborhood called "Le Colonne," a 3C 45
house suddenly fell, trapping a youth and instantly killing him. Men and women heard the crash of the house and came running from all around. Raising beams and stones here and there, they succeeded in restoring the dead son to his poor mother. She sobbed bitterly, and cried out in a pain-filled voice, "Saint Francis, Saint Francis, give me back my son!" She was not alone: all there implored the help of the blessed father. But since there was no sign of speech or feeling, they placed the cadaver on a bed, waiting to bury him the following day. The mother however, having faith in the Lord through the merits of His saint, made a vow to cover the altar of blessed Francis with a new altar cloth, if he would bring her son back to life. About the hour of midnight the young man began to yawn; warmth returned to his limbs; and he got up alive and well and burst into shouts of praise, and urged the clergy and all the people gathered there to give praise and thanks to God and to blessed Francis with joyful hearts.

7 In Sicily, a young man named Gerlandino, from Ragusa, went 3C 47
out with his parents to the vineyard at harvest time. He crawled into a wine vat beneath the press to fill some skins. The wooden supports shifted, and the huge stones instantly struck his skull a lethal blow. The father quickly hurried over to his son, but he could not help him; he left him under the weight where it had fallen. Other vineyard workers rushed to the scene when they heard the loud wail and cry. Filled with great sorrow for the boy's father, they pulled the young man from the ruin already dead. But the father fell at the feet of Jesus, and humbly prayed that he give him back his only son through the merits of Saint Francis, whose solemnity was coming soon. He groaned his prayers, he promised works of piety, and promised to visit the holy man's body with his son, if he were raised from the dead. What a wonderful thing! Suddenly the boy whose body had been completely crushed stood up rejoicing in front of everyone, restored to life and perfect health. He told them to stop crying, and declared that he had been brought back to life through the help of Saint Francis.

8 He raised up another dead person in Germany: the Lord Pope 3C 48
Gregory recounted this event in his apostolic letter on the occasion of the translation of the Saint. Through it he informed and gladdened

all the brothers who had gathered for the translation and the chapter. I did not write the account of this miracle because I did not know of it, believing that papal testimony is a proof that surpasses any other assertion.[a]

Chapter III

THOSE HE DELIVERED FROM THE DANGER OF DEATH

3C 49 [1]In the vicinity of the City a nobleman named Rodolfo and his wife, who was devoted to God, had given hospitality to Lesser Brothers as much out of hospitality as out of love and reverence for blessed Francis. That same night the castle guard was sleeping at the very top of the tower. He lay upon a pile of wood on the top edge of the wall. Its fastening came loose, and he fell onto the roof of the palace, and then to the ground. The loud crash of his fall awoke the whole family and, learning of the guard's fall, the lord and lady of the castle, together with the brothers, ran outside. But the one who had fallen from that height was so deeply asleep that he did not wake, either at his double fall nor at the loud noise of the family running to him and shouting. Finally he was awakened by the hands of those pushing and pulling him, and began to complain about being deprived of pleasant rest, declaring that he had been sleeping sweetly in the arms of blessed Francis. When he learned from the others about his fall, and he saw himself on the ground, not up above where he was lying, he was amazed that he had not felt what had happened. He then promised before everyone there to do penance out of reverence for God and blessed Francis.

3C 50 [2]In the town of Pofi, located in Campagna, a priest named Tommaso went with many others to repair a mill belonging to his church. He carelessly walked along the edge of the channel, where there was a deep gorge filled with rapidly flowing water, and suddenly fell and was thrust against the wooden blades whose force turned the mill. There he remained, pinned against the wood, unable to move at all. Because he was lying face down, the flow of water flooded his mouth. But with his heart he called plaintively on Saint Francis, since he could not do so with his voice. He remained there a long time, and his companions despaired of his life. With a struggle they turned the mill in reverse, and they saw the trembling priest thrown into the water's current. Suddenly there ap-

a. Oddly enough, Bonaventure's text here copies verbatim Thomas of Celano's personal excuse for not writing an account of this miracle.

peared a Lesser Brother in a shining tunic bound with a cord. With great gentleness he drew him by the arm out of the water, and said, "I am Francis, the one you called." The man was stunned to be freed in this way and wanted to kiss his footprints. He ran here and there, anxiously questioning his companions, "Where is he? Where did the saint go? Which way did he go?" But they were terrified:
Nm 14:5 they *fell prostrate to the ground,* extolling the glorious deeds of the great God and the powerful merits of His humble servant.

[3]Some young people from the town of Celano went out together 3C 51
to cut grass in some fields where an old well lay hidden, its opening covered with plant growth, holding water with a depth of almost four paces. While the children ran about, each going a different direction, one accidentally fell into the well. As the deep pit was swallowing his body, his soul's spirit rose up to call on the aid of blessed Francis, calling out with faith and confidence even as he was falling,
1 Kgs 18:45 "Saint Francis, help me!" The others *turned around this way and that,*
Gn 37:30 and when they noticed that the other *boy was missing* they went in search of him, shouting and crying. When they discovered that he had fallen into the well, they ran crying back to the town, explained what had happened and begged for help. They returned with a large crowd of people, and a man was lowered by a rope into the well. He found the boy floating on the surface of the water totally unharmed. When the boy was lifted out of the well, the boy said to all the bystanders, "When I suddenly fell, I called for Saint Francis's protection, and he instantly arrived while I was still falling. He reached out his hand and gently held me and did not leave until, along with you, he pulled me from the well."

[4]While the Lord Bishop of Ostia, who later became the Supreme Pontiff Alexander,[a] was preaching in the Church of Saint Francis at Assisi in the presence of the Roman curia, a large and heavy stone carelessly left above the raised stone pulpit was pushed out by the strong pressure, and fell onto a woman's head. Since the bystanders assumed that she was definitely dead, with her head completely crushed, they covered her with the mantle she was wearing, intending to take the pitiful corpse out of the church when the sermon ended. She, however, commended herself with faith to Saint Francis, before whose altar she lay. And behold, when the sermon was finished, the woman rose up in the sight of everyone, unharmed, not

a. This miracle is not found in any of the texts of Thomas of Celano. Rinaldo dei Conti de Segni, a nephew of Gregory IX, was made Cardinal Bishop of Ostia in 1234, and elected pope as Alexander IV in 1254. As a young cleric he was privileged to see the wounds of Francis while the saint still lived, as he affirmed in a public sermon in the presence of Bonaventure (LMj XIII 8) and in the bulls *Benigna operatio* (October, 1255) and *Quia longum esset* (June, 1259).

showing the least trace of a wound. And, what is even more amazing, she had for many years and up to that very hour suffered from almost uninterrupted headaches, but now was completely freed from them, as she herself later attested.[a]

3C 54 [5]Some devout men gathered in the brothers's place at Corneto for the casting of a bell. An eight-year-old boy named Bartolomeo carried to the brothers a gift for those who were working. All of a sudden a *great wind came up and shook the house;* with great force it Jb 1:19
blew down the large, heavy door of the entrance onto the boy. It was feared that such a great weight pressing upon him had crushed him to death. He was so completely buried under its weight that nothing of him could be seen from the outside. Everyone present ran to him, calling on the strong right hand of blessed Francis. The father of the boy, however, could not move, his limbs frozen *from grief*. Vowing out loud, he offered his son to Saint Fran- Is 65:14
cis. Finally, the deadly weight was lifted off the boy, and there he was! The one they thought was dead appeared cheerful, like someone waking from sleep, with no sign of injury on him at all. When he reached the age of fourteen he became a Lesser Brother and later became a learned man and a famous preacher.

3C 57 [6]Some men of Lentini cut a huge stone from a mountain. It was to be set over the altar of the church of blessed Francis which was soon to be consecrated. A good forty men strained to load that stone on a cart, but after several attempts the stone fell on one man and covered him like a tomb. In their mental confusion they did not know what to do: most of the men left in despair. But ten who remained plaintively invoked Saint Francis not to allow this man who was in his service to die so horribly. With renewed courage, those men then so easily lifted the stone that no one doubted that the power of Francis was involved. The man stood up, unharmed in all his limbs. What is more he recovered his clear eyesight, which earlier had been dimmed: further proof to all that the merits of blessed Francis have great power in desperate cases.

3C 58 [7]A similar incident took place at Sanseverino in the Marches of Ancona. While a very large stone, brought from Constantinople, was being transported to the basilica of blessed Francis by the efforts of many, it suddenly tipped over on top of one of those pulling it. It appeared he was not just dead, but totally crushed too, but

a. There is no other extant written source for this incident. Bonaventure would not have been present, since he was in Paris as a student or young professor during the whole period in which Alexander was Cardinal of Ostia, but he may have heard it from one of the friars or members of the Curia who witnessed it.

blessed Francis helped him, lifting the stone, and he jumped out without any injury, healthy, and unharmed.

[8]Bartolomeo, a citizen of Gaeta, was very hard at work on the 3C 59
construction of the church of blessed Francis. A beam, in an unsteady position, crashed down, and he was severely crushed, pinned down by the neck. Sensing that his death was imminent, and being a faithful and pious man, he asked one of the brothers for Viaticum. The brother was not able to bring it that quickly, and thinking he would die at any moment, quoted to him the words of blessed Augustine, "Believe, and you have eaten."[a] That night blessed Francis appeared to him with eleven brothers; he carried a
Gn 4:17 little lamb between his breasts. He approached the bed, *called him*
Jer 1:19 *by name,* and said, "Do not fear, Bartolomeo, because the enemy *will not prevail against you*. He wanted to keep you from my service. Here is the lamb you asked for: you have received it because of your good desire. What is more, by His power you will also obtain health in body and spirit." Then drawing his hand across the wounds, he told him to return to the work he had begun. The man got up very early the next morning, and the workers who had left him half-dead were shocked and amazed when he appeared, unharmed and happy, inspiring their spirits to love and respect for blessed Francis as much by his example as by the miracle of the Saint.

Jgs 15:18 [9]A man named Niccolò from the town of Ceprano one day *fell* 3C 56
into the hands of cruel enemies. With beastly cruelty they struck him with blow upon blow, and did not stop their cruelty until they thought him dead or soon to die. When the first blows fell on him, Niccolò called out in a loud voice, "Help me, Saint Francis! Save me, Saint Francis!" Many heard his voice from far away even though they could not help him. When he had been carried home
Lk 2:26 drenched with his own blood, he confidently affirmed that *he would not see death* as a result of those wounds, and that he did not feel any pain, because Saint Francis had come to his aid and begged the
Mk 6:12 Lord that he be allowed *to do penance*. So, cleansed of blood and contrary to any human hope, he was rescued.

[10]The son of a nobleman of Castel San Gimigniano suffered 3C 61
from a severe illness; all hope was abandoned and he seemed near the end. A stream of blood trickled from his eyes, like the flow of blood from the severed vein of an arm. Other signs of death's approach appeared in the rest of his body, so he was considered as

a. Cf. Augustine, *In Joh. Evang*. 25:12, (PL 35, 1602).

good as dead. Because of the weakness of his breathing and strength,
lack of feeling or movement, he seemed already completely gone.
His friends and family, as is usual, gathered for mourning and all
that remained was the burial. His father, having faith in the Lord,
rushed off to the church of blessed Francis, which had been built in
that same town. With a cord hanging around his neck he humbly
threw himself on the ground. He *made a vow* and *prayed repeatedly*. With Jdt 10:23; 1 Sm 1:11; Jb 40:27
sighs and groans, he gained Saint Francis as his patron with
Christ. As the father returned quickly to his son and found him restored to health, his *mourning turned into joy*. Lam 5:15

[11]*The Lord worked* similar things by the merits of the saint for a girl Prv 16:4
3C 52 in the town of Tamarit in Catalonia, and for another girl of Ancona.
Both of them were at their last breath because of grave illness, but
blessed Francis, whom their parents had faithfully invoked, restored them to perfect health at once.

3C 187 [12]A cleric from Vicalvi named Matteo *drank* some *deadly poison*. Mk 16:18
He was so afflicted that he could not speak at all; he awaited only
his end. Even a priest who encouraged him to confess could not
pry a single word from him. But he humbly prayed to Christ *in his* Ps 14:1
heart, to deliver him from the jaws of death through the merits of
blessed Francis. Soon after, strengthened by the Lord, he spoke out
the name of blessed Francis with faithful devotion, and with witnesses present, he vomited up the poison, and gave thanks to his
deliverer.

Chapter IV
THOSE DELIVERED FROM SHIPWRECK

3C 81 [1]Some sailors were placed in grave danger at sea when a fierce
storm came up while they were ten miles out from the port of
Barletta. Anxious for their lives, they let down the anchors. But the
stormy wind swelled the sea more violently, breaking the ropes and Ps 11:6
releasing the anchors. They were tossed about the sea on an unsteady and uncertain course. Finally at God's pleasure the sea was
calmed, and they prepared with all their strength to recover their
anchors, whose ropes were floating on the surface. As they were
unable to achieve this by their own efforts they invoked the help of
many saints and were worn down by their exertion, but could not
recover even one after a whole day. There was one sailor named
Perfetto, though he was anything but perfect in his behavior, who
scoffed and said to his companions, "Look, you have invoked the
aid of all the saints, and as you see not one of them has helped.

Let's call that Francis. He's a new saint; let him somehow dive into
the sea and get our anchors back." The others agreed, seriously,
not scoffing, with Perfetto's suggestion. Rebuking his scoffing
words, by common agreement they made a vow with the saint. At
that very moment the anchors were suddenly floating on the water
with no support, as if the nature of iron had been changed into the
lightness of wood.

[2]A pilgrim, feeble in body, from the symptoms of an acute fever 3C 82
he had recently suffered, was traveling from regions overseas[a] on
board a ship. This man also had a special feeling of devotion for
blessed Francis, and had chosen him as his advocate before the heavenly King. As he was not completely free of his illness, he was tormented by a burning thirst. As the water had run out, he began to
shout loudly, "Go confidently, pour me a cup! Blessed Francis has
filled my flask with water!" What a wonder! The flask that had
Gn 1:2 been left *void and empty* they now found filled with water. Some
Mt 8:24 days later a storm came up and the boat was being *swamped by the
waves* and shaken by strong winds so that they feared they would
be shipwrecked. That same sick man suddenly began to shout
around the ship, "Get up, everyone, come to meet blessed Francis.
Jn 9:38 He is here to save us!" And with a loud voice and tears he *bowed
down to worship*. As soon as he had seen the saint the sick man re-
Mt 8:26 covered his full health; and, on *the sea, calm* ensued.

[3]Brother Giacomo of Rieti was crossing a river in a little boat 3C 83
with some other brothers. At the shore, his companions disembarked first, and he prepared to get out last. But that little craft accidentally overturned, and while the pilot swam, the brother was
Mt 18:6 plunged *into the depths*. The brothers on shore with tender cries
called on blessed Francis and with tearful sobs begged that he save
his son. The drowning brother too, in the belly of a great whirlpool,
could not call with his mouth, but called out from his heart as well
as he could, imploring the aid of his pious father. See! With the help
of his blessed father's presence he walked across the depths as if on
dry land. He caught hold of the overturned little boat and reached
the shore with it. More wonderful still, his clothes were not wet:
not a drop of water clung to his tunic.

[4]A brother named Bonaventure was crossing a lake with two 3C 86
men when a side of the boat split, and, with the force of the water
rushing in, he sank into the depths along with his companions and
Ps 40:3 the boat. From the *pit of misery* they called on the merciful father

a. That is, from a pilgrimage to the Holy Land. Cf. 3C 82, supra 434 a.

Francis with great faith. Shortly the water-filled boat floated up to the surface and, with the saint guiding it, safely reached the shore with them in it.

Similarly a brother from Ascoli was saved by the merits of Saint Francis when he fell into a river.

3C 84 Also some men and women who were in similar danger on the Lake of Rieti safely escaped a dangerous shipwreck in the midst of *many waters* by calling on the name of Saint Francis. Ps 32:6

3C 85 [5]Some sailors from Ancona were caught in a violent storm and knew they were in danger of sinking. In desperation for their lives, they humbly invoked Saint Francis. A great light appeared on the ship,[a] and with the light a heaven-sent calm, as if the holy man, through his admirable power, could *command the winds and the sea.* Mt 8:26

I do not believe it possible to tell one by one
all the outstanding miracles
by which this holy Father has been and is still glorified
on the sea,
or how often he has brought help
to those in desperate straits there.
But it is not surprising
that authority over the waters has been granted to him
now reigning in heaven,
when, even while he was in this mortal life,
all earthly creatures served him marvelously,
restored to their original condition.[b]

Chapter V

THOSE SET FREE FROM CHAINS AND IMPRISONMENT

3C 88 [1]In Romania[c] it happened that a Greek servant of a certain lord was falsely accused of theft. His lord ordered him to be shut in a narrow prison and heavily chained. The lady of the household, however, *had pity on the servant,* for she had no doubt that he was innocent of the crime of which he stood accused, and with devout prayers entreated her husband to free him. But her husband remained firm and rejected her request. The lady turned humbly to Mt 18:27

a. 3C 85 has "on the sea" (*in mari*).

b. That is, to the harmony of creation before human sin. Cf. 1C 61; 2C 166.

c. The "Empire of Romania," (1204-1261) established in parts of Greece (Macedonia, Thrace, and coastal regions) taken by Latin crusaders, whose subjects referred to themselves as "Romans" (*Romaioi*).

Saint Francis and, by a vow, commended the innocent man to his compassion. Quickly the helper of the afflicted was present, and
Mt 25:36,42 mercifully *visited the imprisoned* man. He loosened the chains, broke open the jail, took the innocent man by the hand, and led him out. "I am the one to whom your mistress devoutly commended you," he said. The man shook with fear as he wandered at the edge of a precipice, looking for a way to descend from the very high cliff. Suddenly he found himself on level ground through the power of his deliverer. He went back to his lady and told her his miraculous story, all in order. He inspired his devout lady to the even greater love for Christ and reverence for his servant Francis.

[2]In Massa San Pietro[a] a poor fellow owed a certain knight a sum 3C 89
of money. Since he had no means of paying the debt, the knight had him confined as a debtor. He humbly asked for mercy and, interjecting prayers, requested a deferral for love of Saint Francis. The knight haughtily scorned his prayers; he stupidly mocked the love of the saint as something stupid. He obstinately replied, "I
Gn 41:10 will lock you up in such a place and *put you in* such a *prison* that neither Francis nor anyone else will be able to help you." And he attempted to do what he said. He found a dark prison and threw the chained man into it. A short time later Saint Francis arrived and broke open the prison; he shattered the man's leg-irons and led him to his own home unharmed.

Thus the strength of Francis plundered the proud knight
Mt 6:13; 2 Tm 4:18 and *delivered from evil*
the captive who had made himself his subject,
and turned the knight's impudence into meekness
by an amazing miracle.

[3]Alberto of Arezzo was being held tightly in chains for debts un- 3C 91
justly charged to him. He humbly placed his innocence before Saint Francis. He greatly loved the Order of the Lesser Brothers and venerated Francis with special affection among all the saints. His creditor had made the blasphemous statement that neither God
Dn 3:17 nor Francis would be *able to deliver him from his hands.* On the vigil of the feast of Saint Francis, the bound man had eaten nothing, but out of love for the saint had given his meal to someone in need. As night fell, Saint Francis appeared to him during his vigil.[b] At the

a. Also known as Massa Trabaria.

b. Fasting and keeping night-vigil were common observances on the eve of great feasts; Franciscan tertiaries fasted on the eve of Saint Francis as late as the mid-twentieth century.

saint's entry, the *chains fell from his hands* and his feet. The doors Acts 12:7
opened by themselves and the boards on the roof fell down; the man Acts 12:10
got away free and returned to his home. From then on he kept his vow to fast on the vigil of Saint Francis and, as a sign of his increasing devotion, each year to add an extra ounce to the candle he usually offered annually.

3C 93 [4]When the Lord Pope Gregory IX was occupying the See of blessed Peter there arose an inevitable persecution of heretics. A certain Pietro from Alife was among those accused of heresy, and he was arrested in Rome. By order of the same Pontiff he was handed over to the bishop of Tivoli for safekeeping. The bishop took him, under threat of losing episcopal office, and so that he would not escape, bound him in leg irons and had him confined in a
dark jail cell, providing him food *by weight* and drink *by measure*. But Ez 4:16
that man, with much weeping and praying, began to call on blessed Francis to take pity on him, as he had heard that the vigil of his solemnity was near. And since in purity of faith he had renounced every error of perverse heresy, and clung wholeheartedly to Christ's most faithful servant Francis, he merited to be heard by God through the intercession of blessed Francis's merits. So, on the night before his feast, around dusk, blessed Francis mercifully came down into the prison, called him by name, and ordered him to
stand up. The man asked *in great fear* who was calling him, and 1 Chr 10:4
heard that it was blessed Francis. He saw the chains on his feet break and fall suddenly to the ground by the powerful presence of the holy man; he saw the timbers of the cell opened with their nails sprung outward: there was a clear path for his escape. But once free, he was so astounded that he did not know enough to flee. Instead, he let out a cry and frightened all the guards. When the bishop was told that the man had been freed from his chains, once he understood what had happened, that pontiff devoutly went to
the prison, and openly *acknowledging the power of God*, he there *wor-* Mk 5:30; Gn 24:26
shiped the Lord. The chains were sent to the Lord Pope and the Cardinals: on *seeing what had happened*, with much wonder *they blessed* Lk 23:47; Dn 13:60
God.

3C 94 [5]Guidalotto of San Gimignano was falsely accused of poisoning a man, and further of intending to kill the man's son and the whole family with the same deadly means. He was arrested by the local podestà, who had him heavily chained and confined in a tower. But since he knew that he was innocent, he placed his trust in the Lord, and committed the defense of his cause to the patronage of blessed Francis. The podestà thought about what punishment he

could inflict on him, and through torture to make him confess his
crime. He was to be lead to punishment in the morning, but that
night he was visited by the presence of Saint Francis. He was surrounded by an immense bright light, and he remained in its light
Ps 126:20 until morning, *filled with joy* and great confidence, sure of being rescued. In the morning the executioners arrived, took him out of the
cell, and suspended him from a revolving rack, weighing him down
with weights of iron. Several times he was let down and raised up
again, so that with one torment after another he would be forced
more quickly to confess his crime. But the man's face seemed joyful in an innocent way, showing no sign of sorrow in his pain.
Then a rather large fire was lit beneath the man, but not a hair of
his head was harmed even though his head hung toward the
ground. Finally, burning oil was poured over him, but by the power
of the patron to whom he had entrusted his defense, he overcame
all these things. Therefore he was set free, and went away unharmed.

Chapter VI
ON THOSE WHO WERE DELIVERED FROM THE DANGERS OF CHILDBIRTH

[1]A certain countess of Slavonia, illustrious in nobility and a 3C 95
friend of goodness, had an ardent devotion to Saint Francis and a
sincere affection for the brothers. She suffered severe pains at the
time of childbirth; she was so afflicted with pain that it appeared
that the expected birth of the child would mean the demise of the
mother. She seemed incapable of bringing the child into life unless
she departed from life; and, by this effort, not to give birth but to
Rv 19:1 perish. But the fame of blessed Francis, his *glory and might*, sustained her heart. Her faith aroused, her devotion kindled, she
turned to the effective helper, the trusted friend, the comforter of
those devoted to him, the refuge of the afflicted. "Saint Francis,"
Ps 35:10 she said, "*all my bones* cry out to your mercy, and I vow in spirit what
I cannot say aloud." O the speed of mercy! The end of her speaking
was the end of her suffering, and the end of her labor was the beginning of giving birth. Just as soon as the pains ceased, she safely
gave birth to a child. Nor did she forget her vow or run away from
her promise. She had a beautiful church built and, once it was
built, donated it to the brothers in honor of the saint.

[2]A certain woman named Beatrice from the region of Rome was 3C 96
close to giving birth. For four days she had been carrying a dead fetus in her womb. She was much distressed and beset by deadly

pain. The dead fetus was causing the mother's death, and the abortive offspring, still not brought to light, was an obvious threat to the mother. The help of doctors proved fruitless; every human
remedy *labored in vain*. Thus did the ancient curse fall heavily upon Ps 127:1
the unfortunate woman. Her *womb became a grave*, and she certainly Jer 20:17
awaited the grave soon. Finally, by means of messengers, she en- Jb 3:21,22
trusted herself with great devotion to the Lesser Brothers. She humbly asked in great faith some relic of Saint Francis. By divine consent a piece of a cord was found, one that the saint had once worn. As soon as the cord was placed on the suffering woman, all her pain was relieved with ease. The dead fetus, cause of death, was released and the woman was restored to her former health.

3C 97 [3]Giuliana, wife of a nobleman of Calvi, passed a number of years in mourning over the death of her children: she constantly mourned those unhappy events. All the children she had carried with pain, after a short time, and with even greater anguish, she had
carried to the grave. So when she was four months *with child*, be- Mt 1:23
cause of her earlier experiences, she was more concerned for the death of the offspring she had conceived than about its birth. She faithfully prayed to the blessed father Francis for the life of her un-
born fetus. Then one night as she slept, a woman *appeared* to her *in* Mt 1:20
a dream. The woman carried a beautiful infant in her hands and joyfully offered him to her. But she was reluctant to accept something that she feared she would soon lose. So that woman added, "Take this child confidently; the one that Holy Francis sends to
you, out of compassion for your grief, *shall surely live* and enjoy good Ez 18:9,19
health." The woman immediately awoke and understood from the heaven-sent vision that the help of Saint Francis was with her, and from that moment was filled with more abundant joy. She increased her prayers and offered vows for having a child, according to the
promise. The time for delivery arrived and the woman *gave birth* to a Lk 1:57
son. He thrived in the vigor of youthful age and, as he had received the kindling of life through the merits of blessed Francis, he offered his parents a stimulus for more devoted affection for Christ and His saint.

3C 99 The blessed father did something similar to this in the city of Tivoli. A woman had borne several daughters. She was worn out by the desire for male offspring, and groaned prayers and vows before saint Francis. The woman then conceived through his merits, and the one she had implored allowed her to bear twin boys, even though he had been asked for only one.

[4]A woman was near to childbirth in Viterbo, but considered 3C 98 nearer to death. She had severe abdominal pains and suffered the misfortunes that befall women. As her natural strength was collapsing, and all the efforts of medicine failed, the woman called upon the name of blessed Francis. She was immediately healed and gave birth in good health. But when she got what she wanted, she forgot the favor she received, not returning it to the honor of the Prv 31:20; Lv 23:7 saint, and she *stretched out her hand* to *servile work* on his birthday.[a] Suddenly she was unable to draw back the right arm she had extended to work; it remained rigid and withered. When she tried to pull it back with the other arm, it too withered with a similar pun- Acts 10:4 ishment. *Struck with fear* of God the woman reaffirmed the vow, and through the merits of the merciful and humble saint to whom she vowed herself again, deserved to regain the use of her limbs, which she had lost because of ingratitude and contempt.

[5]A woman from the region of Arezzo bore the pains of labor 3C 106 through seven days, and was turning black. As people had despaired of her, she made a vow to blessed Francis and began calling on his aid as she was dying. But when she had made her vow, she Gn 28:12 quickly fell asleep, and *saw in a dream* blessed Francis. He spoke sweetly to her and inquired whether she recognized his face, and if she could recite that antiphon of the glorious Virgin, the *"Salve, Regina misericordiae"* in honor of the same glorious Virgin. When she answered that she recognized both, the saint said, "Start the holy antiphon, and before you finish you will safely give birth." At this cry, the woman woke up and anxiously began "Salve regina *misericordiae*." When she reached the words *"illos misericordes oculos,"* and *"fructum,"* commemorating the fruit of the virgin's womb, she was immediately freed from all her labor pains, and gave birth to a lovely child, giving thanks to the *"Regina misericordiae,"* who through the merits of blessed Francis was kind enough to have mercy on her.

Chapter VII

THE BLIND WHO RECEIVED SIGHT

[1]A brother named Roberto of the convent of the Lesser Brothers 3C 116 in Naples had been blind for many years. Excess flesh grew in his eyes and impeded the movement and use of his eyelids. Many brothers from other places had gathered there on their way to different parts of the world. Blessed father Francis, that mirror and

a. The *dies natalis* of a saint is the anniversary of death, "birth" into eternal life: in this case, October 4.

exemplar of holy obedience, in order to encourage them on their journey with a new miracle, cured the aforesaid brother in their presence in this way. One night the aforesaid Brother Roberto lay deathly ill and his soul had already been commended, when suddenly the blessed father appeared to him along with three brothers, perfect in holiness, Saint Anthony, Brother Agostino, and Brother Giacomo of Assisi. Just as these three had followed him perfectly in their lives, so they readily accompanied him after death. Saint Francis took a knife and cut away the excess flesh, restored his sight and snatched him from the jaws of death, saying, "Roberto, my son, the favor I have done for you is a sign to the brothers on their way to distant countries that I go before them and *guide their steps*. May they go forth joyfully and fulfill the charge of obedience with enthusiasm!" Ps 40:3

3C 118 [2]A blind woman of Thebes in Romania, spent the vigil of Saint Francis fasting on bread and water, and was led by her husband at early dawn of the feast to the church of the Lesser Brothers. During the celebration of the Mass, at the elevation of the Body of Christ, she opened her eyes, saw clearly, and devoutly adored. In the very act of adoration she broke into a loud cry, "Thanks be to God and to his saint," she cried, "I see the Body of Christ!" All those present broke *into cries of gladness*. After the Mass the woman *returned to her home* with joy of spirit and the sight of her eyes. The woman rejoiced, indeed, not only because she had recovered the sight of bodily light, but also because, by the merits of blessed Francis, helped by the power of faith, the first thing that she saw was that wonderful sacrament which is the true and living light of souls. Ps 47:2; Lk 1:56

3C 119 [3]A fourteen-year-old boy from the village of Pofi in Campania suffered a sudden attack and completely lost use of his left eye. The acuteness of the blow thrust the eye out of its socket so that it hung over the cheeks for eight days, by a loose muscle an inch long, and had nearly dried up. Cutting it off seemed the only choice when medical remedies proved hopeless. Then the boy's father turned his *whole mind* to the help of blessed Francis. The tireless helper of the afflicted did not fail the prayers of his petitioner. He marvelously returned the dried eye to its socket and former vigor with the rays of light so longed for. Mk 12:30

3C 120 [4]In the same province, at Castro, a beam of great weight fell from a high place and crushed the skull of a priest, blinding his left eye. Flat on the ground, he began to cry out mournfully to Saint Francis, "Help me, holy father, so that I can go to your feast as I promised your brothers!" It was the vigil of the saint's feast. He quickly got up fully recovered and broke into shouts of praise and joy. And all the bystanders who were mourning his accident were amazed and jubilant. He went to the feast and there told everyone how he had experienced the power and mercy.

[5]A man from Monte Gargano was working in his vineyard and 3C 122
while he was cutting wood with a blade struck his own eye and sliced it in half, so that almost half of it was hanging out. Since the danger was desperate and he despaired that human help could save him, he promised that he would fast on the feast of Saint Francis if the saint would help him. Right then the saint of God replaced the man's eye to its proper place, closed the wound and restored his earlier sight in such a way that there remained no trace of the wound.

Jn 9:1 [6]The son of a nobleman was born blind and obtained the sight 3C 123
he longed for through the merits of Saint Francis. He was called Illuminato,[a] named for the event. When he was old enough he joined the Order of blessed Francis, not ungrateful for the gift he received, and made such progress in the light of grace and virtue that he
Jn 1:9; Eph 5:8 showed himself *a son of the true light* and fulfilled a holy beginning
with an even holier ending.

[7]In Zancato, a village near Anagni, a knight named Gerardo had 3C 117
entirely lost his sight. Now it happened that two Lesser Brothers arriving from abroad sought out his home for hospitality. The whole household received them devoutly out of reverence for Saint Francis and treated them with every kindness. Giving thanks to God and their host, they went on to the brothers' place nearby. One
Mt 2:13 night blessed Francis *appeared* to one of the brothers *in a dream* saying, "*Get up*, hurry with your companion to the home of your host. He received Christ and me through you. I want to repay the gift of his piety. He has become blind, which he deserves for the offenses he has not tried to wash away by confession." When the father had gone, the brother got up and hurried with his companion to carry out the command quickly. Arriving at the home of their host, the
Est 15:9 one related what he had seen *all in order*. The man was quite astonished as he confirmed the truth of all that was said. He broke out in tears, and freely made his confession. He promised amendment and, as soon as the inner man was thus renewed, he immediately regained his outer eyesight. The news of this miracle not only

a. "Enlightened," cf. LMj XIII 4, supra, 633 b.

encouraged many to reverence for the saint, but also to humble confession of their sins and to the gift of hospitality.[a]

Chapter VIII
THOSE FREED FROM VARIOUS ILLNESSES

3C 125 [1]In Città della Pieve there was a young man, a beggar who was
deaf and mute *from birth*. His tongue was so short and thin that, to Jn 9:1
those who many times examined it, it seemed to be completely cut
out. A man named Marco received him as a guest for God's sake.
The youth, sensing the good will shown him, stayed on with him.
One evening that man was dining with his spouse while the boy
stood by. He said to his wife, "I would consider it the greatest miracle if blessed Francis were to give back to this boy his hearing and
speech. I vow to God," he added, "that if Saint Francis in his good- Ps 132:2
ness will do this, for the love of him I will support this boy as long
as he lives." A marvelous promise indeed! Suddenly the boy's
tongue grew, and he spoke, saying, "Glory to God and Saint Fran- Gn 8:15
cis, who granted me speech and hearing!"

3C 109 [2]Brother Giacomo of Iseo, when he was a tender youth in his parental home, suffered a serious rupture of his body. Inspired by the heavenly Spirit, though he was young and ill he devoutly entered the Order of Saint Francis without revealing to anyone the infirmity that troubled him. It happened that when the body of blessed Francis was transferred to the place where the precious treasure of his sacred bones is now kept, this same brother was in the joyful celebrations of the translation in order to show due honor to the most

a. This account was inserted in the text by order of the general minister, Jerome of Ascoli, later Pope Nicholas IV. "In Assisi a man falsely accused of theft was blinded through the severity of secular justice; the knight Ottone, by means of the public executioners, put into effect the sentence of the judge Ottaviano, that the eyes of the accused should be torn out. His eyes were therefore dug out of their sockets and his optic nerves cut with a knife, and thus disfigured he was led to the altar of Saint Francis. There he implored the Saint's clemency and proclaimed his innocence of the crime of which he had been accused. And by the Saint's merits within three days he received new eyes—smaller than the ones of which he had been deprived, but no less clear in their capacity to see. This amazing miracle was attested under oath by the aforementioned knight Ottone before Lord Giacomo, abbot of San Clemente, on the authority of Lord Giacomo, bishop of Tivoli, who held an inquest on this miracle. A further witness to the miracle was Brother Guglielmo of Rome, who was obliged to tell the truth as he knew it by Brother Jerome, minister general of the Order of Lesser Brothers, under obedience and under pain of excommunication. Being thus compelled, he affirmed this in the presence of many provincial ministers of the same Order, and of other brothers of great merit. While he was still a layman, he had seen the man when he still had his eyes, and later had seen him as his eyes were being torn out — indeed, he himself out of curiosity had pushed around the eyes of the blinded man with a stick as they lay on the ground — and later on had seen the same man seeing very clearly with the new eyes he had received by divine power." Jerome also wrote a letter to the friars of Assisi about this miracle. See *The Chronicle of the Twenty-four General Ministers*, in AF III, 358, note 1.

holy body of the father who was already glorified.[a] Approaching the tomb in which the sacred bones were placed, out of devotion of spirit he embraced the holy grave. His inner parts suddenly and wonderfully returned to their proper place and he felt himself healed. He laid aside his truss and was from then on totally free of his pain.

Through the mercy of God and the merits of Saint Francis, the fol- 3C 110-115
lowing, as well as many others, were miraculously healed from similar infirmities: Brother Bartolo of Gubbio; Brother Angelo of Todi; Niccolò, a priest of Ceccano; Giovanni of Sora; a man from Pisa; and another from the town of Cisterna; Pietro from Sicily; and a man from the town of Spello near Assisi.

[3]A woman in the Marittima had lost her mind for five years and 3C 152
was unable to see or hear. She tore her clothes with her teeth and had no fear of the dangers of fire or water. And lately she suffered terribly from falling sickness she had contracted. But one night, as divine mercy prepared to show her mercy, she was brilliantly illuminated by the brightness of a healing light. She saw blessed Fran-
Is 6:1 cis *seated on a* high *throne,* and prostrate before him she humbly asked for her health. As he still had not granted her request, she made a vow, promising for love of God and the saint never to refuse alms, as long as she had them, to anyone who asked. The saint immediately recognized the same pact he had once made with the Lord,[b] and signing her with the sign of the cross he restored her to full health.

A truthful source reports that the Saint of God Francis mercifully 3C 153-154
delivered from similar afflictions a girl from Norcia and the son of a nobleman, among others.

[4]Pietro of Foligno went one time to visit the shrine of blessed 3C 150
Michael, but he was not making the pilgrimage very reverently. He drank from a fountain and was filled with demons. From then on he was possessed for three years, he was physically run down, vile in speech, and dreadful in expression. But as he had some lucid moments, he humbly called on the power of the blessed man, which he heard was effective in driving away the powers of the air. On reaching the tomb of the pious father, as soon as he touched it, he was marvelously delivered from the demons that cruelly tormented him.

In a similar way the mercy of Francis came to the aid of a woman 3C 151
of Narni who was possessed by a devil, and of many others, but the

---

a. May 25, 1230; see above, LMj XV 8.

b. Cf. 1C 17; 2C 5.

details of their sufferings and the different ways in which they were cured would be too long to tell one-by-one.[a]

3C 147 [5]**A man, named Buonuomo, from the city of Fano, a leper and paralytic, was brought by his parents to the church of blessed Francis, and there he recovered his health completely from both illnesses.**

A young man named Atto from **San Severino was covered with**
3C 146 **leprosy. Having made a vow,** and brought to the tomb of the saint, **he was cleansed of his leprosy** through the saint's merits.

This saint, furthermore, had an outstanding power for curing this disease because, out of love for humility and piety, he had humbly dedicated himself to the service of lepers.

[6]**A noblewoman named Rogata, from the diocese of Sora, had**
3C 148 **been troubled by** ***hemorrhages*** **for twenty-three years,** and had suffered as many kinds of pain as there were doctors. **The illness was so** Mt 9:20
great that it often appeared that the woman would soon breathe her last, and whenever the flow of blood was stopped, her whole body swelled up. But one day **she heard a boy singing in Roman dialect a song about the miracles that God** had performed **through blessed Francis. Sadness overwhelmed her, and as she broke into tears her faith moved her** *to say within herself*:**"O blessed father Francis, so many miracles radiate from you: if you would see fit to** Lk 11:38
free me of my illness it would add to your glory, because **you have not yet done such a great miracle." What happened?** After saying this **she felt herself freed through the merits of blessed Francis.**

Also, **her son Mario, who had a withered arm, after** he made a **vow, was cured by Saint** Francis.

Christ's blessed standard bearer also healed a woman from Sic-
3C 149 **ily who was worn out by suffering a flow of blood for seven years.**

[7]**In the city of Rome** there was a woman named **Prassede known**
3C 181 **for her religiosity. From her tender infancy she had, for love of her eternal Spouse, withdrawn for nearly forty years to a narrow cell. She earned the favor of a special friendship with** blessed **Francis. One day in the course of her tasks, she went up to the attic of her cell and, under some imaginary impulse, fell, breaking her foot and leg, and her shoulder was totally separated from its** place. **The kindly father** appeared to her, **clothed in white,** ***in glorious garments,***
and began speaking to her in sweet words, "Get up, ***beloved daugh-*** Is 52:1
ter, get up and do not fear**!** ***He took her hand, lifted her up,*** **and disap-** Ru 3:10; Lk 6:8; 1:30
peared. Turning here and there in the cell, she still thought she Mk 9:27
was *seeing a vision*. When, at her cries, a lamp was brought, feeling

a. Several more accounts of these miracles are in 3C 155-156.

Acts 12:9 completely healed through the servant of God Francis, **she recounted *in order all* that had happened.**

Est 15:9

Chapter IX

THE PUNISHMENT OF THOSE WHO WOULD NOT KEEP HIS FEAST OR HONOR HIM AS A SAINT

[1]In the village of Le Simon, which is in the region of Poitiers, there was a priest called Renaud who had a great devotion to Saint Francis, and who taught his parishioners to keep his feast day as a holy day. But one among the people, who did not realize the Saint's power, held his priest's command in contempt.[a] *He went out* into his field to
Lk 22:62 chop some wood, but as he prepared himself to start the work, he three times *heard a voice that said:* "Today is a holy day; it's a sin to
Acts 9:4 work!" But since neither the priest's command nor the words of a voice from heaven were enough to curb the serf's audacity, without delay the power of God added a miracle and a scourge to vindicate his Saint's honor. The man already had his forked stick[b] in one hand, and was raising up an iron tool with the other one, when the divine power stuck his hands to both tools so that he was not able to open his fingers and let go of either.

He was utterly amazed at this, and had no idea what to do, so he hastened to the church, where many people gathered from all around to see the miracle. There he went before the altar, pierced to the heart by repentance, and at the suggestion of one of the priests—for many priests had been invited and had come to the celebration—he humbly consecrated himself to Saint Francis, and *made*
1 Sm 1:11 three *vows* to him, because of the three times that he had heard the warning voice. First, that he would always keep his feast day, then that on that feast he would always come to this church in which he now was present, and finally that he would personally go on pilgrimage to the Saint's tomb.[c] (During this, the great crowd which had gathered was imploring the Saint's mercy with great devotion.) Wonderful to tell, as he made his first vow, one of his fingers was set free; as he vowed the second one, another finger became unstuck; and as he vowed the third one, the third finger was freed, as well as

a. The Middle Ages saw a great proliferation of holy days, to the point that the precept to abstain from servile work became a real burden, since in an economy based on fruits rather than wages, a day without work necessarily meant a day without earnings. Hence new holy days were often resisted by the laity.

b. Presumably used to hold a high branch steady while it was being cut down with a long-handled ax.

c. "Personally," because it was not uncommon for persons who had vowed pilgrimages to do so vicariously by paying the expenses of another person, who would go as a proxy.

the whole hand, and also the other one. And so the man was brought back to his original freedom of movement and put down the tools by himself, while everyone *praised God* and the miraculous power of his Saint, which could so wonderfully strike and also heal. The actual Lk 2:13 tools were hung as a memorial before the altar that was raised there in honor of Saint Francis, and hang there to this day.[a]

Many other miracles,
worked there and in nearby places,
show that this Saint is outstanding in heaven
and that his feast should be kept on earth
with great veneration.

[2]**Also in the city of Le Mans a woman** *put her hand* **to the distaff,**
3C 100 *her fingers plied the spindle*. Then **her hands stiffened with pain and** Prv 31:19
her fingers began **to burn. The pain** taught her, and she recognized the power of the saint, and with a contrite heart **hurried to the brothers. As the** devout **sons** begged for the mercy **of the holy Father she was immediately healed, and** no wound **remained on her hands**, except for just **a trace of the burn** as a reminder of the event.

Likewise **a woman in Campania**, another **in the town of Olite**
3C 101-103 and a third one in the **town of Piglio** disdained to celebrate the blessed Father's **feast** and were at first punished for their wrongdoing. But once they had repented they were miraculously delivered by the merits of **Saint Francis.**

[3]**A knight from Borgo in the province of Massa shamelessly dis-**
3C 129 **missed the works and miraculous signs of blessed Francis. He taunted the pilgrims on their way to observe the saint's feast, and he publicly babbled foolishness against the brothers.** One time, however, as he was mocking the glory of the Saint of God, **he added** to his other **sins** a detestable **blasphemy. "If it's true that this Francis is a saint,"** he said, **"let my body fall by the sword today, and if he's not a saint, I'll be unharmed!"** *The anger of God rose* to inflict a fitting punishment, and *his prayer was turned to sin*. After a short time, Ps 78:21,31
the blasphemer **insulted his nephew, and the latter drew his sword** Ps 109:7
and bloodied it with his uncle's bowels. The accursed man died the same day and became a slave of hell and a *son of darkness*. Thus others might learn not to attack Francis's wonderful works with 1 Thes 5:5
words of blasphemy, **but honor them with devout praises.**

a. This miracle does not appear in any previous source; Bonaventure may have heard about it during his stay at Paris, or during his visitation of the French friaries as General Minister.

3C 128

[4]A judge named Alessandro, who led away as many as he could from devotion to blessed Francis, was deprived of speech by divine judgment, and for six years was mute. Wis 11:16 *Tormented by the very things through which he sinned,* great repentance overcame him, and he was sorry that he had ridiculed the saint's miracles. So the merciful saint's anger did not last, and he restored his favor by repairing the man's speech, since he was repentant and humbly invoked him. From then on the judge dedicated his blasphemous tongue to praise of the saint, accepting both discipline and devotion instead of suffering.

Chapter X
Some other miracles of different kinds

3C 16

[1]In the town of Gagliano in the diocese of Valva a woman named Maria subjected herself devoutly to the service of Christ Jesus and Saint Francis. One day during the summer she went out to acquire with her own hands the food she needed. The heat was unbearable and she began to faint from thirst, having nothing to drink, since she was alone on a mountain that was totally deprived of water. Lying nearly lifeless on the ground, she began intently to call upon her patron, Saint Francis, with pious spiritual feeling. As the woman persevered in humble and deeply-felt prayer, in her exhaustion from work, thirst, and heat, she drifted off to sleep. And there was Saint Francis, Is 40:26 who *called her by name*. "Get up," he said, "and drink the water that is provided by divine gift for you and for many!" On hearing the sound the woman, strengthened, got up from her sleep. She grabbed a fern next to her and plucked it from the earth. Digging around it with a Est 10:6 twig, she found living water and what first seemed a *little* drop *grew into a spring* through divine power. The woman drank, and when she had had enough, she washed her eyes, which earlier had been clouded by a long illness, and from that moment she felt them flooded with new light. The woman ran home and told everyone Mt 9:26 about the great miracle, to the glory of Saint Francis. At the *news* of the miracle many came running from every direction, and learned by their own experience the marvelous power of this water. For on contact with it, after confession, many were freed of the affliction of their illnesses. That clear spring still flows, and a chapel in honor of blessed Francis has been built there.

3C 189

[2]In the Spanish town of San Facondo against all hope he marvelously restored leaves, blossoms, and fruit to a man's dried up cherry tree.

3C 190

He freed the people of an area near Villesilos by his miraculous help from an infestation of worms that were destroying the nearby vineyards.

3C 191 He also completely cleansed the grain barn of a priest near Palencia, which annually used to be full of grain worms, after the priest faithfully commended himself to his care.

3C 192 He also preserved unharmed from a plague of locusts the land of a lord of Pietramala in the kingdom of Apulia who humbly put himself under his care while that pestilence devoured *all its surroundings.* Jer 21:14

3C 183 3 A man named Martino led his oxen far from home to find pasture. The leg of one ox was accidentally broken so badly that Martin could think of no remedy for it. He was concerned about getting the hide, but since he had no knife for skinning it he returned home and left the ox in the care of Saint Francis, and faithfully entrusted it to the custody of the faithful saint lest wolves devour it before his return. Early next morning he returned to the ox with his skinning knife, but found the ox grazing peacefully, unharmed. He could not
distinguish its broken leg from the other. He thanked *the good shep-* Jn 10:11
herd who *took* such loving *care* of him, and procured the remedy. Lk 10:34

This humble Saint
knows how to help *all those who call* on him, Ps 85:5; 144:18
nor does he consider it beneath his dignity
to help men in their needs,
small though they may be.
3C 184 To a man of Amiterno
he restored a stolen donkey;
3C 185 for a woman of Antrodoco
he repaired a new dish
which had been accidentally shattered;
and he re-joined the plowshare
3C 186 of a man of Monte dell'Olmo in the Marches
when it had broken in pieces.

3C 182 4 In the diocese of Sabino there was an eighty-year-old woman whose daughter died, leaving behind her nursing baby. The poor old woman was full of poverty but empty of milk, and there was no other woman who would give a drop of milk to the thirsty little child as necessity demanded. The poor old woman did not know where to turn at all. As the baby grew weaker, one night, deprived of any human help, she turned her whole mind to the blessed father Francis begging for help with an outpouring of tears. The lover of the age of innocence was immediately there. "Woman," he said, "I am Francis whom you called with so many tears. Put your breasts in the baby's mouth, for the Lord will give you milk in abundance." The old woman did what she was told, and straightaway her eighty-year-old breasts filled with milk. The marvelous gift of the saint became known to all, and many came, both men and women hurrying to see. Their tongues could not call into doubt what their eyes had seen, and they encouraged all to praise God in the wondrous power and loving piety of His saint.[a]

[5]At Scoppito a man and wife had but one son, but he was the cause of daily lament, a sort of disgrace to their family line. His forearms were joined to his neck, his knees to his chest, and his feet joined to his buttocks, he appeared to be a monster, not the offspring of humans. The wife, overcome with greater sorrow over this, called to Christ, invoking the help of Saint Francis, to see fit to lift her from her unhappy and shameful condition. One night, while she was overcome with sad sleep because of her sad state, Saint Francis appeared to her and kindly addressed soothing words to her. He urged her to carry the boy to the place nearby dedicated to his name, so that once bathed *in the Lord's name* with water from the well of that place he would be completely healthy. She failed to carry out the saint's command, so Saint Francis repeated it a second time. He appeared to her a third time and, walking ahead as guide, took the woman together with the boy, to the door of that place. Some noble matrons were arriving at that place out of devotion, and when the woman carefully explained to them about the vision, they along with her presented the boy to the brothers. Drawing some water from the well, the noblest among them washed the infant with her own hands. The boy instantly appeared healthy, with all his limbs in their proper place. The greatness of this miracle aroused wonder in them all.[b]

3C 158

Ps 19:8

a. Cf. Ps 150:1 and 68:36. Where modern translations say "Praise the Lord in His *sanctuary*" and "God is wonderful in His *sanctuary*," the Vulgate has "in His *saints*."

b. At this point Jerome of Ascoli made another addition to the text: "A young man from Rivarolo Canavese called Ubertino joined the Order of Friars Minor in Susa. But during the time of his novitiate he suffered a horrible fright, as a result of which he lost his wits, became paralyzed on his whole right side, and became so seriously ill that he lost his speech and hearing as well as feeling and movement. When he had been confined to his bed in such a miserable state for quite a few days, to the great sorrow of the other brothers, the solemnity of blessed Francis arrived. On the eve of this solemnity he had a lucid interval, and called upon his merciful Father the best he could, with a barely intelligible voice, but with a faith-filled heart. "That night at the hour of matins, while all the brothers were in church intent on singing God's praises, the blessed Father, dressed in the habit of the brothers, appeared to this novice in the infirmary, and *a* great *light shone in that room* (Acts 12:7). *Stretching out his hand* (Mk 7:33), he gently ran it over the novice's right side, touching it from head to toes, then *he put his fingers into his ears*, and impressed a certain mark upon his right thigh. 'This,' he said, 'will be a sign to you that God has fully restored you to health through me, since you entered the religious life led by my example.' Then he tied a cord around his waist—he was lying in bed without a cord—and said to him: 'Get up and go into the church, and with your brothers return the praises due to God!' When he had said this, as the boy tried to touch him with his hands and kiss his footprints in gratitude, the blessed Father disappeared from his sight. And the young man, having recovered physical health and the use of reason, along with lively feeling and speech, went into the church to the great amazement of the brothers and of the laity who were present there, and who had seen the young man paralyzed and witless. He joined in the divine praises and then narrated the miracle from beginning to end, thus kindling in many people devotion towards Christ and Saint Francis."

3C 159 [6]In the village of Cori of the diocese of Ostia, a man had so totally lost the use of a leg that he could not walk or move at all. He was thus confined in bitter agony and had lost hope in any human assistance. One night he began to spell out his complaint to blessed Francis as if he saw him there present. "Help me, Saint Francis! Think of all my service and devotion to you. I carried you on my donkey; I kissed your holy hands and feet. I was always devoted to you, always gracious, and, as you see, I am dying of the torture of this harsh suffering." Moved by his complaint and recalling his good deeds and devotion gratefully he came immediately and, with one brother, appeared to the man keeping vigil. He said that he had come at his call, and that he carried the means of healing. He touched the source of the pain with a small stick bearing the figure of the "Tau." The abscess healed quickly, as he gave him perfect health. What is even more amazing, he left the sacred sign of the "Tau" stamped on the spot of the healed ulcer as a reminder of the miracle. Saint Francis signed his letters with this sign whenever charity or necessity led him to send something in writing.

[7]But see now how our mind,
wandering about through the diverse miracles
of the glorious Father Francis,
and distracted by the variety of the stories,
comes at last,
by the merits of that glorious standard bearer of the cross,
and not without divine guidance,
to the Tau,
the symbol of salvation.
From this we can understand that,
just as while he was among *the militant* following Christ, 2 Tm 2:4
the Cross was the peak of merit for his salvation
so also, now that he is triumphant with Christ,
the Cross has become the foundation of *testimonies* for his glory. Ps 93:5

[8]Indeed, in this great and awesome mystery of the cross,
the *charisms* of graces, 1 Cor 12:31
the merits of virtue,
and the *treasures of wisdom and of knowledge* Col 2:3
are concealed in such profound depths
as to be hidden

Mt 11:25; Lk 10:21 *from the wise and the prudent* of this world.
But it is *revealed* in such fullness *to the little one* of Christ,
that in his whole life
1 Pt 1:21 *he followed* nothing except *the footsteps* of the cross,
he tasted nothing except the sweetness of the cross,
and he preached nothing except the glory of the cross.
In the beginning of his conversion
he could truly say with the Apostle:
Gal 6:14 *Far be it from me to glory*
except in the cross of our Lord Jesus Christ.
In the course of his life
he could more truly add:
Gal 6:16 *Whoever follows this rule,*
peace and mercy be upon them.
In the finishing of his life
he could most truly conclude:
Gal 6:17 *I bear in my body*
the brand marks of the Lord Jesus.
As for us,
our daily wish is to hear him say:
Gal 6:18 *May the grace of our Lord Jesus Christ*
be with your spirit, brothers. Amen.

Gal 6:14 9 Now, therefore, safely glory in the glory of the cross,
glorious standard-bearer of Christ!
For you began from the cross;
you went forward according to the rule of the cross,
and in the end you finished on the cross.
By the evidence of the cross
you make known to all believers
how great is your glory in the heaven.
Now too you may be safely followed
Ps 114:1 by those who *come forth from Egypt.*
Ps 136:13 With *the sea parted* by the staff of Christ's cross,
Ps 68:8 *they shall cross the desert;*
Dt 27:3 *crossing the Jordan* of mortality,
Acts 7:5 they shall enter *the promised land,*
Ps 142:6 *the land of the living,*
by the wonderful power of the cross.
May we be brought there

by the true Leader and Savior of the people,
Christ Jesus crucified, Gal 3:1
through the merits of His servant Francis,
to the praise and glory of God,
One and Three,
who lives and reigns forever and ever. Rv 10:6; 11:15

Amen.

HERE END THE MIRACLES OF SAINT FRANCIS
SHOWN FORTH AFTER HIS PASSING.

The Minor Legend of Saint Francis

(1260-1263)

Chapter I
HIS CONVERSION

First Lesson

Ti 2:11 *The grace of God, our Savior, has appeared in these last days* **in his ser-** LMj prol 1
vant Francis. *The Father of mercy and light*[a] came to his assistance with LMj I 1
such an abundance of **blessings of sweetness** that, as it clearly appears in the course of Francis's life, God not only led him out from
the darkness of the world into light, but also made him renowned for
his merits and the excellence of his virtues. He also showed that he
was notably illustrious for the remarkable mysteries of the cross displayed in him. Francis was born **in the city of Assisi** in the regions **of** 1C 1
Lk 1:60 **the Spoleto valley.** First *called John* **by his** *mother,* and then **Francis** 2C 3
by his father, he held on to the name his father gave him, but did not
abandon the meaning of the name given by his mother. **At a young** LMj I 1
**age he lived in vain pursuits among the idle sons of men, and after
acquiring a little knowledge of reading and writing he was assigned to work in a lucrative merchant's business; yet with God's
protection, neither did he give himself over to the drives of the**
Sir 31:18 **flesh among wanton youths, nor did he** *put his hope in money or in
treasures* **among greedy merchants.**

a. The reference to the Father of light found in Jas 1:17, which is not found at the beginning of LMj, underscores the liturgical aspect of LMn. Jas 1:17 is among the most frequently cited biblical texts in Bonaventure's writings. The imagery of light at the opening of LMn takes on particular significance in the context of liturgical worship. Medieval art and architecture favored an aesthetic-practical appreciation of light in liturgical space and medieval theologians like Bonaventure considered light symbolic of divine grace sought and experienced in prayer.

Second Lesson

LMj I 1 **For there was to be sure a generous care for the poor** together
with kindness and gentleness **implanted in the heart of the youthful
Francis. Increasing in him from early childhood, it had filled his
heart with such kindness that, even at that time, he resolved not to
be a deaf hearer of the Gospel, but to give an alms to everyone who**
1C 89 **begged, especially if he asked out of divine love.** From the **first
flower of his youth** he bound himself to the Lord by a firm promise
LMj I 1 that, **if it were possible, he would never refuse those who begged
from him for the love of God.** Since he did not cease to fulfill so noble
a promise **until death,** he attained **forevermore abundant increase
of grace and love for God.** Even though a small flame of God's fiery
love flourished constantly in his heart, as a young man involved with
Mj II 1; LMj II 5 worldly concerns, **he was ignorant** of the **mystery of the divine elo-
LMj II 1 quence.** *When the hand of the Lord was upon him,* he was chastened ex- Ez 1:3
teriorly by a long and severe illness and enlightened interiorly **by the
anointing of the Holy Spirit.**

Third Lesson

LMj I 2 After Francis's **strength of body was** somehow **restored** and his
mental attitude changed for the better, he had an unexpected meeting **with a knight who was of noble birth** but **poor** in possessions.
He was reminded of Christ, the poor and noble king. He was moved
toward this man with such **piety** that he removed the fine garments
which he **had just acquired** for himself and **immediately dressed**
LMj I 3 the soldier, leaving **himself** without clothes. **The following night,
when he had fallen asleep,** a worthy revelation **showed him a large
and splendid palace with military arms emblazoned with the insignia of the cross.** He was promised with earnest certitude that **all
these things were for him and his soldiers,** if he constantly bore the
LMj I 4 standard of the cross of Christ. **From that time as he was removing
himself from the pressure of public business, he began to seek out
solitary places favorable for grieving, where, with unutterable
groans, he concentrated incessantly on meriting to be heard by the
Lord after the long perseverance of his prayers** during which he
begged the Lord that the way to perfection be shown to him.

Fourth Lesson

LMj I 5 **One of those days, withdrawn in this way, while he was praying, Christ Jesus, appeared to him as fastened to a cross and repeated for him** so efficaciously **this Gospel text:** *if you wish to come* Mt 16:24

after me, deny yourself, and take up your cross, and follow me.[a] Inwardly, this both kindled his heart with the fire of love and filled it with the painfulness of compassion. **His soul melted at the sight, and the memory of Christ was so impressed on the innermost recesses of his heart,** that with the eyes of his mind he continually, as it were, discerned interiorly the wounds of his **crucified** Lord and **could scarcely contain his tears and sighs.** When now for the love of
Sg 8:7 Christ Jesus *he despised all the goods of his house* by considering them *as*
Mt 13:44, 45 *nothing,* he felt that he had found the *hidden treasure* and the brilliant *pearl* of great price. Moved by the desire to possess it, he arranged to leave all his possessions, and by a divine method of commerce, he exchanged the business of the world for the business of the Gospel.

Fifth Lesson

Gn 24:63 One day when *he went out to meditate in the fields,* **he walked near** LMj II 1
the church of San Damiano, which was threatening to collapse because of age. Impelled by the Spirit, he went inside to pray. Prostrate before an image of the Crucified, he was filled with no little consolation as he prayed. When his tear-filled eyes were gazing at the Lord's cross he heard in a marvelous way **with his bodily ears a voice coming from that cross, telling him three times: "Francis, go, rebuild my house which, as you see, is all being destroyed!"** At the wonderful suggestion of this **astonishing** voice the man of God first was indeed thoroughly terrified, then filled with joy and admiration. **Coming back to himself, he arose** immediately **to carry out the command of repairing the material church; although the principal**
Acts 20:28 **intention of the voice referred to that Church which Christ** *pur-chased by* **precious exchange with** *his own blood,* **just as the Holy Spirit taught him, and as he revealed later** to his close companions.

Sixth Lesson

Soon afterwards Francis, for the love of Christ, put aside all the things he could and offered **money to the poor priest of that church** LMj II 1
for the repair of his church and for the use of the poor. He humbly asked the priest that he be allowed to stay there for a short time. The priest agreed to his staying there, but out of fear of Francis's

a. This encounter with the Crucified Christ, which is not present in Thomas of Celano's account of Francis's life, has a heightened sense of immediacy compared with LMj I 5, where Francis appears to grasp the personal import of Mt 16:24 later. Subsequent reference to vision and memory has a narrative function, as prelude to the San Damiano event, and anticipate the stigmata. Heard in a liturgical context, however, these same terms encourage meditation on the image of the Crucified Christ prominent in early Franciscan churches.

parents he refused the money. But Francis, now a true scorner of wealth, threw a large number of coins on a windowsill, valuing it no
LMj II 2 more than if it were dust. Hearing this had enraged his father, and wanting to leave room for his anger, he hid himself for some days in a dark cave where he fasted, prayed and wept. Finally, filled with
a spiritual joy and *clothed with power from on high,* he confidently came Lk 24:29
forth from the cave and calmly entered the city. When the young people saw his unkempt face and his changed mentality, they thought that he had gone out of his senses. They considered him a fool. They threw mud from the street and shouted insults at him. But this Lord's servant was neither broken nor changed by any wrong. He passed through it as though he were deaf to it all.

Seventh Lesson

LMj II 2 His father, raging and fuming because of all this, seemed as if he were forgetful of natural pity. He began to torment with blows and chains the son who had been dragged home. By wearing down Francis's body with physical abuse, he hoped to turn his mind to the
LMj II 3 attractions of the world. Finally Francis's father learned by experience that this servant of God was most willing to bear any harsh
LMj II 4 treatment for Christ and that he could not restrain him. He began to insist vehemently that Francis go with him to the bishop of the city and renounce into the bishop's hands his hereditary right to all his father's possessions. The servant of the Lord was determined to carry this out further, and as soon as he came before the bishop, he did not delay nor hesitate or speak or listen to a word. He took off all his clothes instead and, in the presence of those standing around him, discarded even his undergarments. Drunk in spirit,[a] he was
LJS 9 not afraid to stand naked out of love for Him who for us hung naked on the Cross.[b]

Eighth Lesson

LMj II 5 Released now from the chains of all earthly desires, this scorner of the world left the town. While free and in a carefree mood, he was singing praises to the Lord in French in the middle of woods when robbers came upon him. As the herald of the great King he

a. Liturgy is conducive to the ecstasy of spiritual intoxication. Francis was often *spiritu ebrius* after receiving the Eucharist, see: LMj IX 2 (VIII, 530b). Spiritual intoxication is also linked with love and mystical union in prayer, as Christ was inebriated out of love for his bride in *The Collations on the Six Days*, coll. 14, n. 19 (V, 396b) and the bride, or soul, is intoxicated as well with Christ in *On the Perfection of Life*, c. 5, n. 9 (VIII, 119b-120a).

b. See LMj II 4, supra, 538 b.

was not afraid nor did he stop singing, inasmuch as a half-naked and
2 Cor 7:4 penniless wayfarer he, like the apostles, *rejoiced in tribulation.* **Then as** LMj II 6
a lover of total humility he gave himself to the service **of lepers,** so
that while he was subjecting himself to miserable and outcast people
under the yoke of servitude, he could first learn perfect contempt of
himself and of the world before he would teach it to others. Surely,
since he used to fear lepers more than any other group of people,
grace was given to him in more abundance. He **moved to the lepers** LMj I 6
and gave himself up to their service with such a humble heart that **he**
washed their feet, bandaged their sores, drew the puss from
wounds, and wiped the filth from them. In an excess of unheard of
fervor, he would fall down to kiss their ulcerous sores, putting his
Lam 3:29, 30 *mouth to the dust,* so that, *filled with reproaches,* he might efficaciously
subject the **pride of the flesh to the** *law of the spirit* and, once the enemy within him was subdued, possess peaceful dominion over himself.

Ninth Lesson

Thereafter, Francis **was grounded in the humility of Christ** and LMj II 7
made rich in his poverty.[a] Even though he possessed absolutely
nothing, he, nevertheless, began to turn his careful attention to **re-**
building the church according to the **command given to him from** LMj II 1; LMj II
the cross. Although his **body was weakened by fasting** and bore the
burdens of the stone, he did not shrink from earnestly begging the
help of alms even from those among whom he had been accustomed
to live as a rich man. **With the devoted assistance** of the faithful,
who now began to realize the remarkable virtue this man of God possessed, he restored not only the church of San Damiano, but also the
abandoned and ruined churches of the **Prince of the Apostles** and of
the glorious Virgin. **He mysteriously foreshadowed, by an exteri-**
orly perceptible work, what the Lord disposed to do **through him in**
the future. For according to the likeness of the threefold buildings
he built up under the guidance of the holy man himself, the Church
was to be renewed in three ways according to the form, rule, and
teaching of Christ. The voice from the Cross, which repeated three
times the command concerning the rebuilding of the house of God,
stands out as a prophetic sign. **We recognize now that it is fulfilled**
in the three Orders established by him.

---

a. Humility and poverty are integral dimensions of the poverty of spirit which is the summation of the evangelical perfection espoused by the Franciscan community, see: *The Commentary on the Gospel of Luke* VII 41 (VII, 175).

Chapter II

THE INSTITUTION OF THE RELIGION AND THE EFFICACY OF PREACHING

First Lesson

LJS 15 After the work on the three churches was finished, he [1C 21]
stayed at the church dedicated to the Virgin. By the merits and
prayers of her who gave birth to the price of our salvation, he merited
LMj III 1 to find the way of perfection through the spirit of evangelical truth
LJS 15 infused into him by God. One day during the solemnity of the Mass,
LMj III 1 that part of the Gospel was read in which the evangelical norm for
living was prescribed for the disciples who were sent to preach;
namely, *do not keep gold, or silver, or money in your girdles, no wallet for* Mt 10:9-10
LJS 15 *your journey, nor two tunics nor sandals, nor staff.* Hearing such words,
he was soon anointed and adorned by the Spirit of Christ with such
power that it transformed him into the described manner of living
not only in mind and heart, but also in life and dress. He immediately
LMj III 1 took off his shoes, put down his staff, and discarded his wallet and
its money. He was satisfied with one tunic; he rejected his leather
belt and put on a piece of rope for his belt. He directed all his
heart's desire to carry out what he had heard and to conform in every way to the rule of right living given to the apostles.

Second Lesson

LMj III 2 Inflamed totally by the fiery vigor of the Spirit of Christ, he began, as another Elias, to be a model of truth. He also began to lead some to perfect righteousness and still others to penance. His statements were neither hollow nor ridiculous; they were, instead, filled with the power of the Holy Spirit, and they penetrated to the marrow of the heart. They moved his listeners with great amazement, and their powerful efficacy softened the minds of the obstinate. As his holy and sublime purpose became known to many through the truth of his simple teaching and life, some began to be moved to penitence by his example.[a] After they left all things, they joined

a. Bonaventure's theology of preaching is evident in Francis who united word and example in a compelling invitation to follow Christ. While the power of the spoken word is not to be overlooked, example is crucial if the import of the message is to be effectively conveyed and received. When the two come together, there is a forceful witness to the Gospel, see: *The Sermon for the Second Sunday after Easter* (1), (IX, 294b).

him in habit and life. That humble man decided that they should be called "Lesser Brothers."

Third Lesson

When at the calling of God the **number of brothers reached six,** LMj III 4
their devoted father and shepherd found a **place for solitude** where, LMj III 6
in bitterness of heart, **he deplored** his life as a youth which he had
not lived without sin. He also begged for pardon and grace for him-
1 Cor 4:15 self and for his offspring which *he had begotten in Christ.* **When an ex-**
cessive joy filled his being, he was assured of complete forgiveness
1 Cor 1:24 *to the last penny* of all his debt. **Then caught up above himself and en-**
gulfed totally in a vivifying **light he saw clearly what the future held**
for him and his brothers. He disclosed this later in confidence for the
Lk 12:32 encouragement *of his little flock,* when he foretold the Order would
soon expand and grow through the clemency of God. After a very few
days had passed, certain others joined him, and their number in- LMj III 7
creased to twelve. **This servant** of the Lord **decided, therefore, to ap-** LMj III 8
proach the presence of the Apostolic See. Together with that band
of simple men, he wished to beg earnestly and humbly that the way
of life, shown to him by the Lord and **written down by him in a few** LJS 21
words, be confirmed by the full authority of that same most Holy
See.

Fourth Lesson

According to his proposal, he hurried with his companions to
come **into the presence of the Supreme Pontiff, Lord Innocent III.** LMj III 9
1 Cor 1:24 *Christ, the power and wisdom of God,* arrived in his clemency before him.
By means of a vision, it was communicated to the **Vicar that he**
should agree to listen calmly to this poor little suppliant and give
Gn 28:12 **him a favorable assent. For** *in a dream* the Roman Pontiff himself LMj III 10
saw **that the Lateran basilica was almost ready to fall down, and a**
poor little man, small and scorned, was propping it up with his
own bent back so that it would not fall. While the wise bishop was
contemplating the **purity of the simple mind in this servant of God,** LMj III 9
his contempt of the world, his love of poverty, the **constancy** of his
perfect **proposal,** his zeal for souls, and the **enkindled fervor of his**
will, he said: "Truly, this is he who will hold up Christ's Church by LMj III 10
what he does and what he preaches." As a result, the pope from
that time on held a special **devotion** toward this man. **He bowed to**
the request in all things, the pope approved the Rule, gave him the

mandate to preach penance, granted everything he asked, and promised generously to concede even more in the future.

Fifth Lesson

LMj IV 1 Strengthened then by grace from on high and by the authority of the Supreme Pontiff, Francis with great confidence took the road to the Spoleto valley. He wanted to teach by word and carry out by deed the truth of the evangelical perfection which he had conceived in his mind and solemnly vowed to profess. When the question was
LMj IV 2 raised with his companions whether they should live among the people or go off to solitary places, he sought the pleasure of the divine will by the fervor of prayer.[a] Enlightened by a revelation from heaven, he realized that he was sent by the Lord to win for Christ souls which the devil was trying to snatch away. Discerning, there-
LMj IV 3 fore, he chose to live for everyone rather than for himself alone, he went to an abandoned hut near Assisi to live with his brothers according to the norm of holy poverty in every hardship of religious life and preach the word of God to the people whenever and wherever
LMj IV 5 possible. Having been made a herald of the Gospel, he went about
the cities and towns *proclaiming the kingdom of God not in* such *words* Lk 9:60; 1 Cor 1:13
taught by human wisdom, but in the power of the Spirit with the Lord directing him by revelations as he spoke *and confirming the preaching by* Mk 16:20
the signs that followed.

Sixth Lesson

LMj IV 4 Once, as was his custom, he was spending the night in prayer apart from his sons. Around midnight, while some of them were resting and others were praying, a fiery chariot of wonderful brilliance came through the little door of the brothers' dwelling. Over this chariot, which moved here and there three times throughout the little house, there rested a bright ball of light which resembled the sun. Those who were awake were stunned at this remarkable, brilliant sight. Those who were asleep were terrified and dumfounded. They experienced a brightness with their hearts as much as with their bodies, while the conscience of each was laid bare to the others by the power of that marvelous light. With one accord,

a. Bonaventure holds that constant prayer proffers divine illumination, see: *The Commentary on the Gospel of Luke*, c. 18, n. 3 (VII, 449a-b). Francis's decision to forgo a strictly contemplative life, which was reinforced for the friars and laity in the depiction of his preaching activities in frescoes and panel paintings, mirrors Bonaventure's theological methodology. Bonaventure maintains the end of theology is found in the moral realm, not in contemplation alone, see: *The Commentary on the First Book of Sentences*, proëm, q. 3, concl. (I, 13b).

they all understood, as they looked into each other's hearts, that it was their holy father Francis who had been transfigured in such an Lk 1:17 image. Shown to them by the Lord as one coming *in the spirit and* 2 Kgs 2:12 *power of Elias*, and *as Israel's chariot and charioteer*, he had been made leader for spiritual men. When the holy man rejoined his brothers, he began to comfort them concerning the vision they had been shown from heaven, probe the secrets of their consciences, predict the future, and radiate with miracles. In this manner, he revealed 2 Kgs 2:9, 15 that the *twofold spirit* of Elias *rested* upon him in such plenitude that it was absolutely safe for all to follow his life and teaching.

Seventh Lesson

At that time a religious of the Order of the Crosiers, whose name LMj IV 8 was Morico, was suffering in a hospital near Assisi from an illness so serious and so prolonged that it was believed that he was very close to death. Through a messenger he solicited the man of God, earnestly asking him to be willing to intercede for him with God. The holy man kindly assented to his request. After first praying, he took some bread crumbs and mixed them with oil taken from a lamp that burned before the altar of the Virgin. He made a kind of pill out of them and sent it to the sick man through the hands of his brothers, saying: "Take this medicine to our brother Morico. By means of it Christ's power will not only restore him to full health, but also will make him a sturdy warrior and enlist him in our forces permanently." When the sick man took the medicine which had been prepared under the inspiration of the Holy Spirit, he was cured immediately. God gave him such strength of mind and body, that when a little later he entered the holy man's religion, he wore only a single tunic, under which for a long time he wore a hair shirt next to his skin. He neither drank wine nor tasted anything that was cooked.

Eighth Lesson

At that time there was a priest from Assisi, whose name was LMj III 5 Sylvester, who was certainly a man of an upright way of life and Gn 28:12 possessed dove-like simplicity. *In a dream he saw* that whole region encircled by a huge dragon whose loathsome and frightful image, it seemed, threatened imminent destruction to different areas of the world. After this, he contuited a glittering golden cross issuing Gn 28:12 from Francis's mouth. The top of the cross *reached the heavens*. Its arms, stretched wide, seemed to extend to the ends of the world, and the glittering sight of it put that foul and hideous dragon to flight forever. While this vision was being shown to Sylvester for the third time, this pious man, who was devoted to God, understood that Francis was destined by the Lord to take up the standard of the glorious cross, to shatter the power of the evil dragon, and to enlighten the minds of the faithful with the glorious and splendid truths of both life and teaching. Not long after he gave an account of all this to the man of God and his brothers, he left the world. In accord with the example of his blessed father, he clung to the footsteps of Christ with such perseverance that his life in the Order confirmed the authenticity of the vision which he had in the world.

Ninth Lesson

When he was still living the secular life, a certain brother whose
LMj IV 9 name was Pacifico, found the servant of God at San Severino where
he was preaching in a monastery. *The hand of the Lord came upon* Ez 1:3
him, and he saw Francis marked with two bright shining swords intersecting in the shape of a cross. One of them stretched from his head to his feet, and the other across his chest from one hand to the other. He did not know the man by sight, but once he had been pointed out by such a miracle, he recognized him immediately. He was exceedingly amazed, frightened, and goaded by the power of his words. Pierced as it were by a spiritual sword coming from his mouth, he completely despised worldly displays and joined himself to his blessed father by profession. Afterwards, he made progress in every moral aspect of religion. Before he became minister in France, as indeed he was the first to hold the office of minister
there, he merited to see a great *Tau* on Francis's *forehead,* which Ez 9:4
displayed a variety of different colors that caused his face to glow with wonderful beauty. The man of God venerated this symbol with great affection.[a] He often spoke of it with eloquence and used it at the beginning of any action. In those letters which out of charity he sent, he signed it with his own hand. It was as if his whole
desire were, according to the prophetic text, *to mark with a Tau the* Ez 9:4
foreheads of those moaning and grieving, of those truly converted to Jesus Christ.

a. The symbol of the Tau, together with every other representation of the cross, is a reminder of the most assured path to Christ. Bonaventure preached that those seeking the Lord need only look to the cross, cf. *Sermon on Saint Andrew* (1) (IX, 465b).

Chapter III
THE PREROGATIVES OF THE VIRTUES

First Lesson

As a loyal follower of the crucified Jesus, Francis, that man of
Gal 5:24 God, *crucified his flesh with its passions* **and desires** from the very be- LMj V 1
ginning of his conversion **with such rigid discipline,** and checked
his **sensual** impulses according to such a strict law of moderation,
that he would scarcely take what was necessary to sustain nature.
When he was in good health he hardly and rarely allowed cooked
food. When he did, however, **he made the food** bitter by either mixing **ashes** with it or **made it as insipid as possible** by pouring **water**
Eccl 2:3 over it. *Withdrawing his flesh from wine in order to turn his mind to the light*
of wisdom, he preserved such strict control over drinking that we can
clearly understand that **when he was suffering from a burning**
thirst, he scarcely would dare to drink enough cold water to satisfy
himself. He often used the naked ground as his bed for his weary
body, a stone or a piece of wood for his head. The **clothes** covering LMj V 2
him were simple, wrinkled, and rough. **Established experience had**
taught him that malignant spirits are put to flight by using things
difficult and harsh, but they are more **strongly animated to tempt-**
ing by things luxurious and delicate.

Second Lesson

Is 21:8 **Unbending in discipline,** he kept an exceedingly attentive *watch* LMj V 3
over himself. **He took** particular **care** in guarding the priceless trea-
2 Cor 4:7; 1 Thes 4:4 sure *in a vessel of clay,* that is, chastity, which he strove *to possess in* holiness and *honor* through the virtuous **purity of both body and soul.**
For this reason, **around the beginning of his conversion during the**
winter cold, he would plunge himself many times, strong **and fer-**
vid in spirit, into a ditch filled with icy water or snow. **He did this to**
subjugate the enemy within and to preserve the white robe of
modesty from the flames of voluptuousness. Practices such as these
enabled him to use **his bodily senses** in an appealing, modest manner. His mastery over the flesh was now so complete that he seemed
Jb 31:1 *to have made a covenant with his eyes;* he would not only flee far away
from carnal sights, but also totally avoid even the curious glance at
anything vain.

Third Lesson

LMj V 8 Truly, **even though he had attained purity of heart and body,** and
in some manner was approaching the height of sanctification, **he did
not cease to cleanse the eyes of his soul with a continuous flood of
tears.** He longed for the sheer brilliance of the heavenly light and disregarded the loss **of his bodily eyes. When he had incurred a very serious eye illness from his continuous weeping, a doctor advised
him to restrain his tears if he wanted to avoid losing his sight.** He,
however, would not assent to this. **He asserted that he preferred to
lose sight than repress the devotion of the spirit and impede the
tears which cleansed his interior vision so that he could see God.**[a]
He was a man devoted to God, who, drenched in spiritual tears, displayed a serenity in both mind and face. The luster of a pure con-
science anointed him with such joy that his *mind was* forever *caught* 2 Cor 5:13; Dt 14:29; Ps 91:5
LMj IX 1 *up* in *God,* and *he rejoiced* at all times *in the works of his hands.*

Fourth Lesson

LMj VI 1 **Humility, that guard and embellishment of all virtues, had by
right so filled the man** of God that, although a manifold privilege of
virtues was reflected in him, nevertheless, it sought its special do-
main in him as though in the least of the lesser ones. **In his own
LMj VI 6 opinion,** by which he accounted himself the **greatest of sinners,** he
LMj VI 1 was really nothing more than some dirty *earthen vessel,* **while in truth** Jer 22:28
he was an elect *vessel of sanctification,* set apart by sanctity and glittering with the adornment of many kinds of virtue and grace. Moreover, **he strove to regard himself as worthless in his own eyes and
LMj VI 2 in those of others,** to reveal by public confession his **hidden faults,**
LMj VI 3 and to keep the Giver's gifts hidden **in the secrecy of his heart.** He
did this so that he would in no way **be subject to praise which could
LMj VI 4 be an occasion for his downfall.** Certainly, in order that he might *ful-* Mt 3:15
fill all justice regarding perfect humility, he so strove to subject himself not only to superiors but also even to inferiors, that he was
accustomed to promise obedience even to his companion on a journey, no matter how simple he was. As a result, he did not give orders
as a **prelate** with authority. **In his humility, he would** rather **obey**
those subject to him as their **minister and servant.**

---

a. Spiritual tears are indicative of conversion and a salient feature of prayer as contemplation, cf. supra, 565 b. Bonaventure's debt to Hugh of Saint Victor's *On the Sacraments* is evident in the reference to the physical eye and inner eye. While the physical eye is capable of sight, the inner or contemplative eye requires cleansing because of the blinding influence of sin, see: *The Collations on the Six Days,* coll. 5, n. 24 (V, 358a). On Francis's tears and medieval spirituality, see: Keith Hanes, "The Death of Saint Francis of Assisi" in *Franciscan Studies* 58 (1976): 43-45.

Fifth Lesson

Jer 31:3 This perfect follower of Christ **was so eager** ***in everlasting love*** **to** LMj VII 1
espouse poverty, the companion of humility, to himself that **he not**
Gn 2:22; Mk 10:7 **only** ***left his father and mother*** **for her, but also scattered everything**
he could have. No one coveted gold as he coveted poverty; nor was
anyone as careful in guarding of a treasure as he was of the pearl of
the Gospel. Since from the beginning of the Religion until his
death, his wealth was a tunic, a cord, and breeches, it would seem
that **he gloried** in want and rejoiced in need. **If at any time he saw** LMj VII 7
anyone dressed poorer than himself, he would criticize himself im-
mediately and set out to be similar. It seemed as if he were contending with a rival and feared that he would be conquered by the
spiritual nobility of that man. Since the **pledge of his** eternal **inheri-** 1C 74
tance, he had preferred poverty to everything perishable, **counting** LMj VII 7
as nothing riches which are granted to us as a fief the false riches
granted for only an hour. He loved poverty more than great wealth,
and he, who had learned from it to regard himself inferior to all, LMj VII 6
hoped to surpass all in its practice.

Sixth Lesson

Through the love of the most sublime poverty, the man of God LMj VII 1
prospered and grew rich in holy simplicity. Although he certainly possessed nothing of his own in this world, he seemed to possess all good things in the very Author of this world. With the steady gaze of a dove, that is, the simple application and pure consideration of the mind, he referred all things to the supreme Artisan and recognized, loved, and praised their Maker in all things.[a] It came to pass, by a heavenly gift of kindness, that he possessed all things in God and
God in all things. **In consideration of the primal origin of all things,** LMj VIII 6
he would call all creatures, however insignificant, **by the names of brother and sister** since they come forth with him **from the one source. He embraced** those, however, **more tenderly and passion-**

a. Bonaventure's usage of literary and artistic terminology in his theology of God bears consideration in the context of liturgy. As the book of Creation, the world speaks eloquently of the divine Author. Learning to read the book of Creation parallels the process of learning how to read the Psalter, as both activities are synonymous with prayer; see: *The Commentary on the Gospel of Luke*, c. 18, n. 16 (VII, 470b-471a) and *The Rule for Novices*, c. 1 (VIII, 475a-476b). The supreme Artisan's activity in the world offers insight into the ultimate significance of the religious art. Just as creatures are visual expressions reflecting the divine Artist's creativity, so, too, is liturgical art a visual reminder of God's presence in the world, see: *The Commentary on the First Book of Sentences*, d. 3, art. unicus, q. 2, concl. (I, 72b) and *The Commentary on the Fourth Book of Sentences*, d. 9, art. 1, q. 2, concl. (III, 203b). Bonaventure likens God's presentation of saints to the Church to the actions of a master painter who offers students models to reproduce in their own paintings. By attempting to depict these models, they themselves will become masters, see: *The Sermon on the Birth of John the Baptist* (1), (IX, 539a).

ately, who portray by a natural likeness the gracious gentleness of
Christ and exemplify it in the Scriptures. It came to pass by a supernatural influx of power that the nature of brute animals was moved
LMj VIII 7-9 in some gracious manner toward him. Even inanimate things
obeyed his command, as if this same holy *man,* so *simple and upright,* Jb 2:3
had already returned to the state *of innocence.*

Seventh Lesson

The source of piety pervaded the servant of the Lord with such
fullness and abundance that he seemed to possess a mother's heart
LMj VIII 5 for relieving the misery of suffering people. He had an inborn kindness doubled by the piety of Christ poured out on him. His soul
melted for the poor and infirm, and to those to whom he could not
extend a hand he extended his affection. With tenderness of a pious heart, he referred to Christ anyone he saw in need or depriva-
tion. In all the poor he saw before him a portrait of Christ. He not
only freely gave to those he met the necessities of life if these had
been given to him, but he also resolved they should be returned as
if they truly belonged to them. He spared nothing at all, neither
mantles nor tunics, neither books nor even appointments of the altar; all these he gave to the poor when he could to fulfill his obligation of piety, even *to the utter privation of himself.* 2 Cor 12:15

Eighth Lesson

His zeal for fraternal salvation, which emerged from the furnace
of love, pierced the inmost parts of this man like a *sharp* and *flaming* Rv 1:16
LMj VIII 1 *sword.* Aflame with the ardor of imitation and stricken with the sorrow of compassion, this man seemed to be completely consumed.
Whenever he became aware that souls redeemed by the precious
blood of Jesus Christ were stained by the filth of sin, he would be
pierced by a remarkable sting of sorrow. He grieved with such tender care that he seemed like a mother who was daily bringing them
to birth in Christ. For this reason, he struggled to pray, was active in
preaching, and outstanding in giving good example. He did not
think that he was a friend of Christ unless he cherished the souls
which Christ redeemed. Although his innocent flesh subjected itself
freely to his spirit, it had no need of the lash due to offenses. Nevertheless, for the sake of example, he kept on subjecting it to pain and
burdens, *keeping the difficult ways* because of others, so that he per- Ps 16:4
fectly followed the footsteps of He who *in death handed over his life* for Is 53:12
the salvation of others.

Ninth Lesson

Given **the fire of his charity** which carried the friend of the Spouse LMj IX 5
into God, one is able to perceive that he thoroughly desired **to offer to**
Rom 12:1 **the Lord his own life as a** ***living sacrifice*** **in the flames of martyrdom.**
It was for this reason that he attempted on **three** occasions **to jour-** LMj IX 7
ney to the territory of the **non-believers.** Twice he was restrained by
the will of God. On the third attempt, after much abuse, **many** LMj IX 8
chains, floggings, and innumerable hardships, **he was led** with the
1 Cor 2:4; Acts 5:12 help of God into the presence of the **Sultan of Babylon.** *He preached*
Jesus with such an efficacious *demonstration of spirit and of power* that
the **Sultan was overflowing with admiration,** and became docile by
the will of God and granted Francis a kind audience. Recognizing in
him a **fervor of spirit, a constancy** of mind, a **contempt** for this present life, and the efficacy of God's word, the Sultan **conceived** such a
devotion toward **him** that he deemed him worthy of great honor. **He**
offered him precious gifts and **earnestly invited him to prolong his**
stay with him. This true **despiser** of himself and **of the world**
spurned as dirt all that was offered to him. When he realized that he LMj IX 9
was **not able to accomplish his purpose** after he had truly done all
that he could to obtain it, he made his way back to **the lands of the**
faithful as he was advised by a revelation. So it was that this friend
of Christ with all his strength sought to die for him and yet could
not achieve it. He did not lack the merit of his desired martyrdom,
and he was spared to be honored in the future with a unique privi-
lege.

Chapter IV

THE ZEAL FOR PRAYER AND THE SPIRIT OF PROPHECY

First Lesson

LMj X 1 Since he was made totally insensible to earthly desires through
his *love of Christ,* aware that while in the body he was exiled from 2 Cor 5:14
the Lord, the servant of Christ strove to keep his spirit present to
God, *by praying without ceasing,* and thus he would not be without 1 Thes 5:17
the consolation of his Beloved. For whether walking or sitting,
inside or outside, working or resting, he was so focused on prayer
that he seemed to have dedicated to it not only whatever was in his
LMj X 2 heart and body but also his effort and time. Many times he was
suspended in such an excess of contemplation that he was carried
away above himself and, experiencing what is beyond human
understanding, he was unaware of what went on about him.

Second Lesson

That he might receive the infusion of spiritual consolations more
LMj X 3 quietly, he went at night to pray in solitary places or abandoned
churches. Although even there he experienced horrible struggles
1C 72; LMj X 3 with demons who, fighting as it were hand to hand with him, tried
to distract him from his commitments to prayer.[a] After these de-
LMj X 4 mons retreated from the unrelenting power of his prayers, the man
of God, remaining alone and at peace, and, as if finding a more secret hiding place, would fill the forest with groans, water the places
with tears, strike his breast with his hand. Now he entreated the
2 C 95; LMj X 4 Father; now he played with the Spouse; now he conversed with
the Friend. There he was seen praying at night, with his hands and arms outstretched in the form of a cross, his whole body lifted up from the ground and surrounded by a sort of shining cloud, so that the extraordinary illumination around his body together with its elevation, was a witness to the wonderful light and elevation within his soul.

a. Francis demonstrated a predilection for solitary sites such as abandoned churches and wilderness areas where he could seek divine consolation. Nevertheless, these same places often served as sanctuary for demons, giving rise to spiritual combat, a common theme in the monastic tradition and medieval hagiography. The struggle with demons is essential to the development of virtue, see: Thomas Heffernan, *Sacred Biography: Saints and Their Biographers in the Middle Ages* (New York: Oxford University Press, 1988): 152-153.

Third Lesson

By the supernatural power of such ecstatic experiences, as has been LMj III 4; LMj X 4
Ps 50:8 proven by certain evidence, the *unknown and hidden secrets of* divine *wisdom were opened to him unless* his zeal for fraternal welfare urged him and the impulse of heavenly revelation forced him. His unflag- LMj XI 1
ging zeal for prayer with his continual exercise of virtues had led the man of God to such serenity of mind that, although he had no expertise in Sacred Scripture which comes through study in human learning, nevertheless, enlightened by the splendor of eternal light, he probed the depths of Scripture with a clear, remarkable incisive-
Is 11:2 ness. The manifold *spirit* of the prophets also *rested* upon him with a LMj XI 3
plenitude of various graces. By its wonderful power, the man of God was present to others who were absent, had certain knowledge of those far distant, saw the secrets of hearts, and also foretold future events, as the evidence of many examples prove, some of which are included below.

Fourth Lesson

At one time the holy man, Anthony, then an outstanding LMj IV 10
preacher but now a glorious confessor of Christ, was preaching eloquently to the brothers at a provincial chapter at Arles on the title
Jn 19:19 of the Cross: *Jesus of Nazareth, King of the Jews.* The man of God, Francis, who at that time was busy faraway, appeared lifted up in the air at the door of the chapter. With his hands extended as if on a cross blessing the friars, he filled their spirits with such manifold consolation that it was certain to them that this wonderful appari- LMj XI 14
tion had been endowed by the power of heaven. Furthermore, that this did not lie hidden from the blessed father is evidently clear from
Wis 7:25, 27 how open his spirit was to the light of *eternal wisdom which is mobile beyond all motion, reaching everywhere because of its purity, spreading through the nations into holy souls, it makes them prophets and friends of God.*

Fifth Lesson

At one time when the friars were entering the chapter according LMj XI 11
to custom at St. Mary of the Portiuncula, one of them, hiding behind the mantle of some excuse, would not submit himself to the discipline. The holy one, who was then praying in his cell as a mediator between those same brothers and God, saw all this in spirit. He had one of the brothers called to him and said: "Brother, I saw the devil perched on the back of that disobedient brother, holding him

tightly by the neck. Constrained by such a rider and having spurned the reins of obedience, the brother was being impelled to follow the devil's reins. Go, therefore, and tell the brother to submit to the yoke of obedience without delay because he, at whose earnestness in prayer this demon left in confusion, suggests that this be done." The brother, warned by the messenger, perceived the light of truth and conceived the spirit of compunction. *He fell forward* (Mt 26:39) *on his face* before the vicar of the holy man, recognized that he was culpable, sought pardon, accepted and bore the discipline, and from then on humbly obeyed in all things.

Sixth Lesson

LMj XI 9 While he was secluded in a cell on Mount La Verna, one of his companions was yearning with great desire to have something of the Lord's words commented on and written with his own hand. This companion was being plagued by a serious temptation, not of the flesh but of the spirit, and he believed that by this means he would be set free from, or at least could bear more easily, the temptation. Though growing weary with such a temptation, he was in a state of anxiety because he was humble, modest, and simple. He was overcome by embarrassment and did not dare to disclose it to the venerable father. But what man did not tell him, *the Spirit re-* (1 Cor 2:10) *vealed*. He ordered the brother to bring him paper and ink. And, he wrote down with his own hand the *Praises of the Lord* according to the brother's desire. He graciously gave the brother what he had written, and the entire temptation vanished immediately. This little note, preserved for posterity, brought healing to a great number of people. This made it clear to all how much merit before God this writer had whose writing left such efficacious power in a small leaf of paper.

Seventh Lesson

LMj XI 6 At another time, a noble woman, devoted to God, went confidently to the holy man and implored him with all her strength to intercede with the Lord on behalf of her husband, so that his hard heart might be softened by a plentiful infusion of his grace. The husband was very cruel to her and opposed her service of Christ. After listening to her, the holy and pious man confirmed her in her good intention with holy words, assured her that consolation would shortly be hers, and finally ordered her to declare to her husband on the part of God and of himself that now is the time for clemency;

later it will be the time for justice. The woman put her trust in the words which the servant of the Lord had spoken to her, **received his blessing,** and in haste returned home. There she met her husband and told him about the conversation she had with that man, and without any doubt, she waited for the hoped for promise to be fulfilled. Without any delay, as soon as [Francis's] words reached his ears, the **spirit** of grace **fell upon him** and softened his heart in such a way that from that time on he permitted his devoted wife **to serve God freely** and offered himself to serve the Lord with her. **At the suggestion of the holy wife, they lived a celibate life for many years,**
Ps 140:2 **and then departed to the Lord on the same day;** she in the morning
as a *morning* **sacrifice,** and he in the evening as an *evening sacrifice.*

Eighth Lesson

At the time when the servant of the Lord **was lying ill at Rieti, a** LMj XI 5
certain canon named Gedeon, who was deceitful and worldly, was seized with a serious illness. Lying on a stretcher, he was brought to him, and with tears in his eyes, he, together with the bystanders, asked that he bless him with the sign of the cross. [Francis] said to
Sir 17:4 **him: "Since you once lived according to the** ***desires of the flesh*** **and**
Gal 5:16 **not in fear of the** ***judgment of God,*** **I will sign you with the sign of the**
cross. This is not for your own sake **but because of the devout petitions of those interceding for you. I do this with the provision** that I let you know, from this moment on, that certainly **you will suffer more serious things if, when you are free, you return to your vomit." After the sign of the cross was made** from his head to his feet, **the bones of his loins resounded and it sounded to all as though dry wood was being broken by hand. Immediately, he who had been lying there constricted, arose cured, and, bursting forth in praise of God said: "I have been freed." Then a short time elapsed when, forgetful of God, he returned his body to impurity, and on a certain evening dined in the lodging of a canon and slept there that night. The roof of the house collapsed suddenly on all but killed only him, while all the others escaped death.** In this one event it was made manifest how strict is **God's** zeal **for justice with**
Rv 19:10 **ungrateful people,** and how true and certain was the *spirit of prophecy*
which had filled Francis.

Ninth Lesson

At that time after his return from overseas, he went to Celano to LMj XI 4
preach. A knight with humble devotion invited him to dinner, and

with great insistence, forced him, as it were, to come. **Before they took any food, the devout man, who offered according to his custom, praise and prayers to God,** saw in spirit that this man's judgment was imminent. He stood there, lifted up in spirit, *with his eyes* Jn 17:1
raised to heaven. Finally, **when he completed his prayer,** he drew his **kind host aside,** predicted that his death was near, admonished him **to confess his sins,** and encouraged him to do as much good as he could. The soldier agreed to what **the blessed man** had said and **in confession, he revealed all his sins to his companion, put his house in order,** committed himself to the mercy of God, and **prepared as much as he could to accept death.** While the others were taking refreshment for their bodies, **the soldier,** who seemed strong and healthy, **suddenly breathed forth his spirit according to the word of the man of God.** Even though this soldier **was carried off by a sudden death,** nevertheless, he was so **protected by the armor of repentance** through the spirit's **prophetic warning** that **he escaped perpetual damnation, and according to the** promise of the Gospel, **entered into the eternal dwellings.**

Chapter V
THE OBEDIENCE OF CREATURES AND THE DIVINE CONDESCENSION

First Lesson

Lk 4:18; 1 Cor 1:24 Surely, the *Spirit of the Lord* who *had anointed* him and also *Christ, the power and the wisdom of God,* were with the servant, Francis. It LMj XII 7
Ps 50:8 was this grace and power that brought it about that not only did *uncertain and hidden things* become evident to him, but even the elements of this world obeyed him. At one time doctors advised him, LMj V 9
and the brothers strongly urged him, to allow his eye affliction to undergo the process of cauterization. The man of God humbly agreed because this would be not only a remedy for a bodily weakness, but also a means for practicing virtue. Given the sensitivity of the flesh, he was struck with panic at the sight of the still-glowing iron. The man of God addressed the fire as a brother, admonishing it in the name and in the power of its Creator to temper its heat that he might be strong enough to bear its gentle burning. When the hissing iron was sunk into his tender flesh and the burn was extended from the ear to the eyebrow, the man filled with God, exulted in spirit and said to the brothers: "Praise the Most High, because I confess what is true; neither the heat of the fire troubled me, nor did pain in the flesh afflict me."

Second Lesson

While the servant of God was suffering from a very serious ill- LMj V 10
ness at the hermitage of Saint Urban he felt a natural weakness. He requested a drink of wine but was told that there was no wine to give him. He then ordered some water brought to him, and, with the sign of the Cross, he blessed it. What had been pure water, immediately became excellent wine, and what the poverty of this deserted place could not provide, the purity of the holy man obtained. At the taste of it, he recovered so easily that it became evidently clear that the desired "drink" was given to him by a bountiful Giver not as much to please his sense of taste as to be efficacious for his health.

Third Lesson

LMj VII 12 At another time, the man of God wanted to go to a certain hermitage to spend some time in contemplation.[a] He rode on a donkey belonging to a poor man because he was weak. While this man followed the servant of God and climbed into mountainous country on a hot day, he became worn out from the journey over a rather rough and long road. When he became weakened from a burning thirst, he began to cry out urgently and say that unless he had a little something to drink, he would die immediately. The man of God leaped down from the donkey without delay, knelt on the ground, raised his hands to heaven, and did not cease praying until he understood that he had been heard. When he finally finished his prayer, he told the man: "Hurry to the rock over there, and there you will find running water, which Christ in his mercy has produced from a rock for you to drink at this very hour." The thirsty man ran to the place pointed out to him and drank the *water* pro- Ps 77:16
duced *from the rock* by the power of another's prayer, and he consumed the drink furnished for him by God *from the most solid rock.* Dt 32:13

Fourth Lesson

LMj XII 6 At one time, when the servant of Lord was preaching on the seashore at Gaeta, he wished to escape the adulation of the crowd, which in its devotion was rushing upon him. He jumped alone into a small boat that was drawn upon the shore. The boat, as though it were guided by an internal source of power, moved itself rather far from land without the help of any oars. All who were present saw this and marveled. When it had gone out some distance into the deep water, it stood motionless among the waves as long as, with the crowd waiting on the shore, it pleased the man of God to preach. After listening to the sermon, witnessing the miracle, and receiving the blessing they asked for, the crowd went away. By the influence of no other command but a heavenly one, the boat reached the shore; it subjugated itself without rebellion, as if it were *a creature* Wis 16:24
serving its Maker, to the perfect worshiper of the Creator and obeyed him without hesitation.

---

a. This account of Francis bringing water from the rock through prayer and the sermon to the birds in the sixth lesson are depicted above the main doors inside the Upper Basilica of Saint Francis in Assisi. The juxtaposition of these stories indicates a reliance on LMn, instead of LMj, at this point in the Giotto cycle. The resultant architectronic-artistic diptych serves as an arresting reminder, to those in the choir area as well as those departing the church, of the necessary synthesis of the contemplative-active dimensions of life.

Fifth Lesson

Once while he was staying in the hermitage of Greccio, the peo- LMj VIII 11
ple of that place were burdened by many disasters. Every year hailstorms destroyed their wheat fields and vineyards while a pack of
raging wolves devoured not only animals but even people. The servant of the all powerful Lord was filled with a benevolent compassion for those sorely afflicted people. He promised and guaranteed
them personally in a public sermon that the entire pestilence would
Mt 3:8 vanish if they would confess their sins and be willing *to bring froth*
fruits worthy of repentance. From the very time that the people began
doing penance at his exhortation the disasters ceased, the dangers
Dn 3:50 vanished, and neither the wolves nor the hail caused *any more trou-*
ble. And even more remarkable, whenever the hail, falling on
neighboring fields, reached the boundaries of these people, either
it would stop or move off in a different direction.

Sixth Lesson

At another time the man of God was journeying around the valley
of Spoleto in order to preach. As he was approaching Bevagna, he LMj XII 3
came upon a place where a very large flock of birds of various kinds
Jude 14:6 had gathered. Looking at them with affection, the *Spirit of the Lord*
came upon him, and he hurriedly ran to the spot, eagerly greeted
them, and commanded them to be silent, so that they might attentively listen to the word of God. While he recounted many things
about the benefits of God to these creatures, who were gathered together, and about the praises that should be returned to him by
them, they began to flutter about in a wonderful way; they
stretched their necks, spread out their wings, opened their beaks,
and looked attentively at him, as if they were trying to experience
Gn 41:38 the marvelous power of his words. It was only proper that this *man,*
full of God, was led by a humane and tender affection to such irrational creatures. For their part, those birds were drawn to him so remarkably that they listened to him when he was instructing them,
obeyed him when he commanded them, flocked to him without fear
when he bid them welcome, and, without distress, remained with
him.

Seventh Lesson

When he had tried to go overseas to pursue the palm of martyr- LMj IX 5
dom, he was impeded by storms at sea from accomplishing his purpose. The Director of all things remained with him to such an extent

that His providence snatched him, together with many others, from the **dangers of death** and showed forth his wonderful works on his behalf **in the depths** of the sea. When he was proposing to return from Dalmatia to Italy and had **boarded a ship** without any provisions at all, a man **sent from God came,** as Francis stepped aboard, **with necessary food for Christ's little poor man.** Then this man gave the provisions to a God-fearing man whom he called from the ship, that **he might administer them** at the proper time to those who had absolutely nothing. **When the crew were unable to land anywhere because of the force of the winds, they used up all their food.** All that remained was a **small portion of the alms which was given from above** to the blessed man. Because of his prayers, merits, and the **power** of heaven, **these alms were multiplied so much that for many days, as the storm at sea continued, they fully supplied their needs until the ship reached the** desired port of Ancona.

Eighth Lesson

LMj V12 **At another time when the man of God was on a preaching journey with a brother companion between Lombardy and the Marches of Treviso, the darkness of night overtook them on the banks of the Po River. The road was exposed to many great dangers because of the river, the marshes, and the darkness. His companion insisted that he should implore, in such a necessity, divine assistance. The man of God replied with great confidence: "*God is* Lk 3:5 *powerful*. If it pleases him, he will make light for us by putting the darkness of night to flight."** What followed was marvelous! **He had scarcely finished speaking when, behold, by the power of God such a great light began to shine around them that, while the darkness of night remained in other places, they could see in clear light not only the road but also many other things** on the other side of the river.

Ninth Lesson

The brightness of heavenly splendor went before them amid the dense darkness of the night in a fitting manner indeed. This proved that those who follow the light of life on a straight path are not able to be overwhelmed by the shadow of death. By the remarkable splen-
LMj V 12 dor of such a light, **they were led physically and comforted spiritually. Singing hymns of praise to God, they arrived safely at their lodging, which was quite a stretch of road away.** He was a truly outstanding and admirable man, **for whom fire tempers its burning
LMj VII 13 heat, water changes its taste, a rock provides abundant drink,**

inanimate things obey, wild animals become tame, and to whom irrational creatures direct their attention eagerly. In his benevolence the Lord of all things listens to his prayer, as in his liberality he provides food, **gives guidance** by the brightness **of light, so that every** creature is subservient **to him as a man** of extraordinary **sanctity,** and even the Creator of all condescends to him.[a] LMj V 12

a. This nuanced transition from self-emptying to the stigmata, with reference to the theme of light, is not found in LMj where the account of the stigmata in Chapter XIII is preceded by accounts of preaching and miracles. The theme of condescension or *condescensio*, which is woven through Bonaventure's thought, sets the stage for the stigmatization of Francis. Divine condescension, witnessed in the incarnation of Christ and manifested in stigmata, is rooted in God's love for humanity. Self-emptying presupposes the radical poverty of created reality which looks to the Creator for redemption.

Chapter VI
THE SACRED STIGMATA

First Lesson

LMj XII 1; LMj XIII 1 The truly faithful servant and minister of Christ, Francis, two years before he returned his spirit to heaven, began a forty day fast in honor of the Archangel Michael in a high place apart called Mount La Verna. Steeped more than usual in the sweetness of heavenly contemplation and on fire with an ever intense flame of heavenly desires, he began to be aware more fully of the gifts of
LMj XIII 3 heavenly entries. With the seraphic ardor of desires, therefore, he was being borne aloft into God; and by compassionate sweetness he was being transformed into Him Who was pleased to be crucified out of the excess of His love. While he was praying one morning on the mountainside around the Feast of the Exaltation of the Holy Cross, he saw the likeness of a Seraph, which had six fiery and glittering wings, descending from the grandeur of heaven. He came in swift flight to a spot in the air near to the man of God. The Seraph not only appeared to have wings but also to be crucified. His hands and feet were extended and fastened to a cross, and his wings were arranged on both sides in such a remarkable manner that he raised two above his head, extended two for flying, and with the two others he encompassed and covered his whole body.

Second Lesson

LMj XIII 3 Seeing this, he was overwhelmed. His mind flooded with a mixture of joy and sorrow. He experienced an incomparable joy in the gracious way Christ appeared to him so wonderful and intimate, while the deplorable sight of being fastened to a cross *pierced* his Lk 2:35
soul with the sword of compassionate sorrow. He understood, as the one whom he saw exteriorly taught him interiorly,[a] that the weakness of suffering was in no way compatible with the immortality of the seraphic spirit; nevertheless, such a vision had been presented to his sight, so that this friend of Christ might learn in advance that he had to be transformed totally, not by a martyrdom of the flesh

a. Christ is the teacher who speaks to the inner spirit through the exterior senses, cf. Bonaventure, *Christ, The One Teacher of All*, 11-14 (V, 570-571), in *What Manner of Man: Sermons on Christ by St. Bonaventure*, translated with introduction and commentary by Zachary Hayes (Chicago: Franciscan Herald Press, 1974), 30-34.

but by the enkindling of his soul, into the manifest likeness of Christ Jesus crucified. The vision, which disappeared after a secret and intimate conversation, inflamed him interiorly with a seraphic ardor and marked his flesh exteriorly with a likeness conformed to the Crucified; it was as if the liquefying power of fire preceded the impression of the seal.

Third Lesson

The marks of nails began to appear immediately in his hands LMj XIII 3
and feet. The heads of these appeared on the inner side of the hands and the upper side of the feet and their points on the opposite sides. The heads of the nails in his hands and feet were round, and their points, which were hammered and bent back, emerged and stuck out from the flesh. The bent part of the nails on the bottom of his feet were so prominent and extended so far out that they did not allow the sole of his feet to touch the ground. In fact, the finger of a hand could be put easily into the curved loop of the points, as
I heard from those who saw them with their own eyes. His right LMj XIII 8, LMj XI
side also appeared as though it were pierced with a lance. It was covered with a red wound from which his sacred blood often flowed. His tunic and underwear were soaked with such a quantity
of blood that his brother-companions, when they washed these LMj XIII 8
clothes, undoubtedly observed that the servant of the Lord had the impressed likeness of the Crucified in his side as well as in his hands and feet.

Fourth Lesson

Gn 41:38 The man, *filled with God,* realized that the stigmata which was im- LMj XIII 4
pressed so splendidly on his flesh, could not be concealed from his intimate companions; nevertheless, he feared making public the
Tb 12:7 Lord's sacrament. He was thrown into an agony of doubt as to
whether to tell what he had seen or be silent about it. Forced by the sting of conscience, he finally recounted with great fear the vision in detail to some of the brothers who were closer to him. He added that He who appeared to him told him some things which he would never disclose to any person as long as he lived. After the
2 Cor 3:18 true love of Christ *transformed* the lover into his *image,*[a] the forty

a. The transformative power of love is an ubiquitous current in Bonaventure's works and an example of his appropriation of the Pseudo-Dionysian heritage, see: *The Commentary on the First Book of Sentences,* d. 15, dubia 5 (I, 275b) and *The Sermon on the 14th Sunday after Pentecost* (1), (IX, 408a).

days on that mountain of solitude were completed and the feast of St. Michael the Archangel arrived. The angelic man, Francis, *came down from the mountain* bearing the likeness of the Crucified, depicted not on *tablets of stone* or on panels of wood, but engraved on parts of his flesh by the *finger of the living God*. Mt 17:9 Ez 31:18

Fifth Lesson

LMj XIII 5 This holy and humble man tried afterwards with all diligence to conceal these sacred marks; nevertheless, it pleased the Lord to reveal through them certain marvelous things for his glory. Their hidden power, therefore, could be made manifest by clear signs and irradiate like a bright star amid the dense darkness of a darkened age. LMj XIII 7 For about the time the holy man stayed on Mount La Verna, for example, dark clouds would form over the mountain and violent hailstorms would devastate the crops. Truly, after that blessed apparition, the normal hail stopped to the amazement and joy of the inhabitants. The very aspect of the sky, tranquil beyond usual, proclaimed the supreme worth of that vision from heaven and the power of the stigmata impressed there.

Sixth Lesson

LMj XIII 6 At that time a very serious plague swept through the province of Rieti and began to afflict the sheep and the cattle to such an extent that almost all of them seemed to languish under an incurable illness. A God-fearing man was admonished by a vision one night to hurry to the brothers' hermitage where the blessed father was then staying and to request from his companions the water he used to wash his hands and feet. He was then to sprinkle this water on the suffering animals and, thereby, put the plague to an end. After the man diligently completed this task, God gave great power to the water which had touched the sacred wounds. Even a little of the water completely drove out the plague from the suffering animals it touched. Once they recovered their former vigor, they ran to their fodder as if they had nothing wrong with them earlier.

Seventh Lesson

LMj M I 5 Finally, from that time on, those hands attained such marvelous power that their saving touch returned both robust health to the sick and living sensation to limbs now dry and paralytic. What is greater, they restored unimpaired life to those who had been mortally wounded. I will anticipate and recall briefly to mind for you two of his many miracles. Once at Lerida, a man, whose name was John and who was devoted to blessed Francis, was so cut and savagely wounded one night that one could hardly believe that he would survive until the next day. Our holy father appeared marvelously to him and with his sacred hands touched those wounds. At the very same hour John was so restored to full health that all the region proclaimed that this wonderful standard bearer of the cross was most worthy of all veneration. Who would not be surprised to look upon a person he knew well, who, at almost the same moment of time, was mangled by the most cruel wounds and then rejoiced in unimpaired health? Who would be able to recall this without giving thanks? Finally, who could ponder in a spirit of faith such a tender, virtuous, and remarkable miracle without experiencing devotion?

Eighth Lesson

At Potenza, a city of Apulia, a cleric named Ruggero was thinking LMj M I 6
foolish things about the sacred stigmata of our blessed father. He received a blow to his left hand under his glove, as though from an arrow shot from a bow. His glove, however, remained untouched. He was subject to the sting of excruciating pain for three days. Feeling remorseful, he called upon and entreated Francis earnestly to help him by means of those glorious stigmata. He received such perfect health that all the pain disappeared and not a trace of a blow remained. From this it seems perfectly clear that those sacred marks of his were impressed by a power and provided with the strength of Him whose characteristic it is to inflict wounds, to provide remedies,
Lk 4:18 to strike the obstinate, and *to heal the contrite.*

Ninth Lesson

This blessed man certainly appeared worthy to be marked with LMj M I 1
this singular privilege since his whole endeavor, both public and private, centered around the cross of the Lord. What else than his wonderful gentleness, the austerity of his life, his profound humility, his prompt obedience, his extreme poverty, his unimpaired chastity; what else than the bitterness of his compunction, his flow of tears, his heartfelt compassion, his zeal for emulation, his desire for martyrdom, his outstanding charity, and finally the privilege of the many virtues[a] that made him Christ-like: what else stood out in him

a. This concise compendium of virtues is a meditation on the remarkable conformity of Francis with Christ as preamble and confirmation of the stigmata. These virtues, which are developed in LMn III, are key to understanding Bonaventure's hagiographical hermeneutic. Literary consideration of the virtues was accompanied by their artistic depictions in liturgical books and churches, see: Adolph Katzenellenborgen, *Allegories of the Virtues and Vices in Medieval Art* (Toronto Press: University of Toronto Press, 1989).

than these similarities to Christ, these preparations for the sacred stigmata? For this reason, the whole course of his life, from the time of his conversion, was adorned with the remarkable mysteries of the cross of Christ. Finally, at the sight of the sublime Seraph and the humble Crucified, he was transformed totally by a fiery, divine power into the likeness of the form which he saw. Those who saw them, touched them, and kissed them testified to this; and after having touched these most sacred wounds, they confirmed them with greater certitude by swearing that they saw them and that they were exactly as reported.

Chapter VII
THE PASSING OF DEATH

First Lesson

Gal 2:19 The man of God was **now,** *fixed to the cross* **in both body and spirit.** LMj XIV 1
Just as he **was being born aloft into God** by the fire of seraphic love, LMj XIII 3
he was also being transfixed by a fervid zeal for souls. **He thirsted** LMj XIV 1
with the crucified Lord for the deliverance of all those **to be saved**[a].
Since **he could not walk because of the nails protruding from his**
Lk 8:1 **feet, he had his half-dead body carried** *through the towns and villages,*
Rv 7:2; Lam 2:3 so that like *another angel ascending from the rising of the sun,*[b] he *might*
Lk 1:79 *kindle* the hearts of the servants of God with a divine *flame of fire, direct*
Rv 7:3 their *feet into the way of peace,* and *seal* their *foreheads* with the sign *of* the
living *God.* **He burned with a great desire to return to the humility
he practiced at the beginning, so that he might, just as he did at the
outset, nurse lepers and treat his body once more like a slave that
was already in a state of collapse from his work.**

Second Lesson

With Christ as leader, he resolved to do great deeds, and al- LMj XIV 1
**though his limbs were weakening, he was strong and fervid in
spirit, and he hoped for a victory over the enemy in a new struggle.
In order that his merits might increase, for these are** brought to per- LMj XIV 2
**fection in patience, the little one of Christ started to suffer from var-
ious illnesses.** The painful agony of **suffering** was diffused
Jb 19:2; Lam 4:8 **throughout his limbs, his *flesh was all consumed,* as if only skin clung
to his bones. While he was tortured by harsh bodily suffering, he
called those punishing conditions not by the name of "pains" but
rather "sisters."** He gave such praise and **thanks to the Lord** in the
joyful bearing of them, that **it seemed to the brothers** taking care of
him that they were looking upon Paul in his joyful and humble glory-
ing, and that they were seeing another Job in the vigor of his imper-
turbable spirit.

---

a. Francis's thirst for the salvation of others is indicative of the fourth and highest degree of love described by Richard of Saint Victor, see: Jean Châtillon, "Richard of Saint Victor," *Dictionnaire de Spiritualité Ascétique et Mystique, Doctrine et Histoire* XIII (Paris: Beauchesne, 1937-1995), 646. The return to evangelization after the stigmata demonstrates the *reductio* of Franciscan mysticism whereby the ecstatic experience of God in prayer leads back into the world. This is evident in Francis's decision to return to preaching and ministering to lepers.

b. The literary identification of the stigmatized Francis with the angel of the apocalypse bearing the seal of Rv 7:2 was mirrored in Franciscan liturgical art, as evidenced in an angel bearing the stigmata in the Lower Basilica of Saint Francis in Assisi.

Third Lesson

LMj XIV 2 He knew long in advance the time of his death. As this day grew
near, he told the brothers that *laying aside the tent* of his body was at 2 Pt 1:14
LMj XIV 3 hand, as it had been pointed out to him by Christ. Two years after the
imprinting of the sacred stigmata and in the twentieth year of his
conversion, he asked to be brought to Saint Mary of the Portiuncula.
He wished to pay his debt to death and arrive *at the prize* of eternal *rec-* Phil 3:14; Col 3:24
ompense there where he had conceived the spirit of perfection and
grace through the Virgin Mother of God. After he was brought to the
above mentioned place, he showed by a true example that there was
nothing in common between him and the world. In that grave illness
that ended all suffering, he placed himself in fervor of spirit totally
naked on the naked ground, so that in that final hour, when the enemy could still rage, he might wrestle naked with the naked. Lying
thus on the ground and in the dust, this naked athlete covered with
his left hand the wound in his right side, lest it be seen. With his serene *face raised* in the customary manner *toward heaven* and his atten- Jb 11:15
LMj XIV 4 tion directed entirely toward that glory, he began to praise the Most
High because, released from all things, he was now free to go to Him.

Fourth Lesson

LMj XIV 5 Finally, when the hour of his passing was approaching, he had all
the brothers staying in the place called to him. Consoling them in
preparation for his death with comforting words, he exhorted them
with fatherly affection to divine love. Then leaving them their rightful
inheritance, the possession of poverty and peace, he charged them to
strive toward things eternal and fortify themselves against the dangers
of this world. He carefully admonished them and persuaded them
with all the efficacy of speech he could muster to follow perfectly the
footsteps of Jesus crucified. As his sons were sitting around him, the
Mass II patriarch of the poor, whose *eyes had been dimmed* not *by age* but by Gn 48:10
LMj XIV 5 tears; the holy man, blind and now near death, crossed his arms and
stretched his hands over them in the form of the cross, for he always Gn 48, 14
loved this sign. He then blessed all the brothers, both present and
absent, in the name and in power of the Crucified.

Fifth Lesson

LMj XIV 5 After this he ordered the Gospel according to John be read to him
2 C 94 from the place that begins: *Before the feast of the Passover*. He wished to Jn 13:1
hear the *voice of the Beloved* knocking, from whom only the wall of flesh Sg 5:2
LMj XIV 6 now separated him. Finally, when all the mysteries were fulfilled in
him, the blessed man, praying and singing psalms, *fell asleep in the* Acts 7:60

Lord. His most holy soul, released from the flesh, was absorbed into the abyss of eternal light. At that very hour one of his brothers and disciples, a man certainly famous for his sanctity, saw that happy soul
Ps 28:31 in the likeness of a brilliant star, borne aloft by a *little cloud over many waters* straight to *heaven*. This soul, glittering with the clear luster of his conscience and glistening with the sure sign of his merits, was being raised on high so effectually by an abundance of graces and divine virtues that nothing would be able to detain it at all from its vision of heavenly light and glory.

Sixth Lesson

The minister of the brothers at that time in Terra di Lavoro was LMj XIV 6
Augustine, a man who was certainly dear to God, and in his last hour.
Lk 9:39 For a long time he had been without the power of speech, but now *he*
Acts 23:4 *called out* to those listening *who were standing about* and said: "Wait for me, father, wait! Look, I am coming with you!" The amazed brothers asked him to whom he was speaking, he asserted that he saw blessed Francis going to heaven. As soon as he said this, he also happily went to his rest. At the same time the Bishop of Assisi had gone to the shrine of Saint Michael at Monte Gargano. Blessed Francis, filled with delight, appeared to him in the hour of his *transitus*, and said that he was leaving the world and passing exultantly into heaven. Arising in the morning, the bishop told his companions what he had seen. Then, after returning to Assisi, he carefully inquired and found out for certain that the blessed father had departed from this life at the very hour when he appeared to him in this vision.

Seventh Lesson

The immensity of celestial goodness deigned to show, by many LMj XV 9
outstanding examples of miracles after his death, just how remarkable this man was for outstanding sanctity. Because of his merits and at his intercession, the power of almighty God restored sight to the blind, hearing to the deaf, speech to the mute, walking to the lame, and feeling and movement to the paralyzed; he gave robust health, moreover, to those who were withered, shriveled, or ruptured, and effectively snatched away those who were in prison; he brought the shipwrecked to the safety of port, granted an easy delivery to those in danger during childbirth, and put demons to flight from those possessed. Finally, he restored those hemorrhaging and lepers to wholesome cleanliness, those mortally wounded to a perfectly sound condition, and what is greater than all these, he restored the dead to life.

Eighth Lesson

Because of him innumerable benefits from God do not cease to abound in different parts of the world, [LMj Prol 3] **as even I myself who wrote** the above have experienced in my own life. When I was just a child and very seriously ill, my mother made a vow on my behalf to the blessed father Francis. I was snatched from the very jaws of death and restored to the vigor of a healthy life. Since I hold this vividly in my memory, I now publicly proclaim it as true, lest keeping silent about such a benefit I would be accused of being ungrateful. Accept, therefore, blessed father, my thanks however meager and unequal to your merits and benefits.[a] As you accept our desires, excuse, too, our faults through prayer, so that you may both rescue those faithfully devoted to you from present evils, and lead them to everlasting blessings.

Ninth Lesson

[LMj XII 12] It is fitting, therefore, that these words be concluded with a brief recapitulation of everything that has been written. Whoever has read thoroughly the things above should ponder carefully these final considerations: the conversion of the blessed father Francis which took place in a marvelous way; **efficacy** in the divine word; **privilege** of exalted **virtues**; *spirit of prophecy* [Rv 19:10] together with an **understanding** of the Scriptures; **obedience of creatures lacking reason**; the impression of the sacred stigmata; and his celebrated **passage** from this world to heaven. These seven **testimonies** clearly attest and show **to the whole world** that he, the glorious **herald of Christ,** *having in himself the seal of the living God,* [Rv 7:2] **should be venerated** by reason of his accomplishments, and for the fact that he was **authentic in his teaching and admirable in his holiness.** [LMj M X 9] So let those who *are leaving Egypt* [Ex 13:17; Ps 113:1] **feel secure in following him. With the** *sea divided* [Acts 7:5] **by the staff of the cross of Christ,** *they will traverse the desert* [Ps 135:13; 67:8; Dt 27:3] **and in crossing the Jordan of mortality, they will enter, by the wonderful power of that cross,** *into the promised land of the living.* [Acts 7:5] **Through the prayers of our blessed father may they, there, be conducted to that glorious Savior and leader, Christ, to whom with the Father and the Holy Spirit, in perfect Trinity be all praise,** ***honor, and glory forever. Amen.*** [Rom 16:27]

THE END OF THE MINOR LIFE OF SAINT FRANCIS.

---

a. In addition to justifying his efforts to recount the life of Francis, Bonaventure's boyhood memory of healing becomes an invitation to the friars gathered in liturgical prayer to seek assistance from the Poor Man of Assisi. The intercession of Francis lies at the heart of prayer as *oratio*, see: *The Journey of the Mind into God*, prol. 1 (V, 295a).

The Evening Sermon on Saint Francis
Preached at Paris, October 4, 1262

According to Sophronius Clasen this dates from October 4, 1258, and was the only sermon preached before the *Major Legend,*[a] and according to John F. Quinn it was preached on October 4, 1269.[b] However, on the basis of the content of this sermon, several passages of which correspond almost literally to the *Major Legend,* Ignatius C. Brady established that this sermon was preached at Paris in the evening of October 4, 1262.[c]

Mt 24:30 *Then will appear the sign of the Son of Man in heaven*

Introduction

Eccl 11:6 *In the morning sow your seed and at evening withhold not your hand; for you do not know which will prosper, this or that: and if both together, it shall be the better.*

The wise Ecclesiastes addresses these words to the preacher of God's truth, that he should not rest content with having preached in the morning, but should preach and go on preaching at every hour in
2 Tm 4:2 the evening, as Saint Paul admonishes Timothy: *Preach the word; be urgent in season and out of season, convince, rebuke, and exhort; be unfailing in patience and in teaching.*

Today the cardinal preached to you and I trust that with God's help the seed he sowed will bear fruit in you.[d] If now I also can say something that will bear fruit in you, that will be excellent.

Of course, some may say: "What is the point of so many sermons, when they have become occasions of boredom and ridicule?" But that is not true. A person with a well-disposed heart does not get bored; on the contrary, he listens willingly at any time to words

a. Cf. Srm1 Introduction, supra, 508.

b. John F. Quinn, "Chronology of St. Bonaventure's Sermons" AFH 67 (1974) 161, 183.

c. Ignatius C. Brady, "The Writings of Saint Bonaventure Regarding the Franciscan Order," *San Bonaventura Maestro di vita francescana e di sapienza cristiana.* Atti del Congresso Internazionale per il VII Centenario di San Bonaventura I (Roma, 1976) 101-102; "Saint Bonaventure's Sermons on Saint Francis," *Franziskanische Studien* 58 (1976), 132-137.

d. A reference to the sermon of Eudes of Châteauroux, Chancellor of the University of Paris from 1238-1244, preached on the morning of October 4, 1262, cf. infra, 811-818.

about his God and Creator. A person with a mind eager to learn will attend lectures at any time of the day in order to grow in knowledge. Nor will he miss hearing a lecturer in the afternoon because he heard a professor in the morning. Rather, he will attend it willingly.

The same applies to a person with a heart well-disposed to hear God's word. He will not miss an evening sermon because he heard one in the morning but will go willingly to the evening sermon. And even if he does not profit by it or sometimes gets little of it, nevertheless, if he was pleased to attend and listened willingly to the sermon about his Creator, there is great merit in that. Among the accepted customs here, it is one of the better ones that the students of this city come eagerly to hear the Word of God.

So, the Word of God is to be preached and sown in the morning and the evening; and just as a natural seed will produce little or nothing unless rain pours down to make it germinate and bear fruit, so the seed of my word will bear little fruit unless the rain of God's blessing comes down upon it. Here at the outset, therefore, let us ask Him who, according to the Psalm, shed rain in abundance and restored His heritage, to grant me to say something in His honor, to the praise and commendation of Saint Francis and for the consolation of our souls. Ps 68:9

I

We began with the text: *Then will appear the sign of the Son of Man in heaven.* Mt 24:30

LMj XIII 3; XV 2 Among all the gifts which God bestowed on this humble and poor little man, Saint Francis, there was one special and if I dare to say, unique privilege: that he bore on his body the stigmata of our Lord Jesus Christ, for two years before he died. His side was pierced and blood flowed from it, and on his hands he had wounds in which there were black nails bent over at the back. This is certain, as certain as anything in this world can be. Many saw the stigmata on his body, some of whom are still alive. The Lord himself imprinted this sign on that most humble and poor little man, who in his humility made himself a servant of lepers, as you heard today. In praise of this special or, as I would rather say, unique, privilege, I have quoted the text from Saint Matthew's Gospel. Gal 6:17 LMj XIII 8

In its literal sense and according to its historical meaning this text refers to the Lord's sign, that is the cross, which will appear on the Day of Judgment; in its allegorical meaning, it refers to the marks of the cross which will be seen then on Christ's body, put on it at the crucifixion; and in its tropological or moral meaning, it refers to the stigmata of the Lord Jesus which appeared on the body of Saint Francis.

In the literal sense "the heavens" refer to the reality we see above us. Understood in this sense, the sign of the cross will appear in the
Rv 1:7 heavens on Judgment Day as a sign of the Judge's severity, so that *all*
Hb 3:11 *tribes of the earth will wail on account of him* and as Habakkuk says: *The*
1 Sm 17:41-51 *sun and moon . . . shall speed in the brightness of your glittering spear.* This spear by which David brought down Goliath, namely, the Devil, is the cross of Christ. Saint John Chrysostom remarks that it will appear on Judgment Day more splendid than all the stars.[a]

The sign of the cross appeared in heaven which can be understood allegorically; that is, it appeared on the body of our Lord Jesus Christ
Is 11:43 on the day of the crucifixion. We read in Isaiah: *In that day the root of Jesse shall stand as an ensign to the peoples,* that is, as a sign of mercy. The cross which Christ carried and on which he suffered is a sign of mercy to all peoples and to every nation, as Isaiah continues: *him shall the nations seek and his tomb shall be glorious.* The Jews who refuse to recognize and accept Christ ought to consider all this carefully and acknowledge its truth. Let them search to see if the tomb of any other man is as glorious.

This sign also appeared in the mystical body of Christ and it will be
Gal 5:24 seen on his members, as Saint Paul says: *Those who belong to Christ Jesus have crucified the flesh with its passions and desires.* Only those who bear his sign belong to Christ's army, that is, the sign of Christ's cross. Therefore, everyone will have to bear this sign. God revealed the sign of the cross, however, in a special way to two members of Christ's mystical body: to Emperor Constantine I and to Saint Francis.

For many generations up to the time of Constantine, kings and emperors had been pagans and there had been war and dissension among the peoples of the earth. It was as though the blessings of Christ's cross had been consigned to oblivion. Then the sign of the cross appeared in the heavens to Constantine when he had to go to war against Maxentius. It appeared as a sign of victory for Constantine was told: τούτῳ which means "in this sign, conquer" or "In this sign you will be victorious."[b] At that moment he acknowledged the Crucified One and made the sign of the cross on his forehead. From then onwards the cross was transformed from being a gibbet for brigands into a sign on the foreheads of emperors. After this Constantine sent his mother, Saint Helen, to Jerusalem to search for the wood of the cross. She found it and sent it to Jerusa-

a. Saint John Chrysostom, *Homilia II de Cruce et Latrone*, n. 4, (PG 49, 414).

b. Eusebius, *De vita Constantini*, Lib. 2, c. 28, (PG 20, 943).

lem. From it all the relics of the wood of the cross which are found throughout the whole world have been taken.

It was the Lord's good pleasure at the time of Constantine that he willed to put an end to wars and tribulations through the sign of victory, that is, the sign of the cross, which appeared to Constantine. As he willed to imprint the sign of victory on Constantine, so he chose to imprint the sign of penance on Saint Francis. In so doing he chose a simple, poor, and humble man to be the model of penance to all who were to come after him. Therefore, the text from Revelation can be
understood of him: *I saw another angel ascend from the rising of the sun* Rv 7:2
with the seal of the living God, and this that he might *put a mark upon the* Ez 9:4
foreheads of the men who sigh and groan.

There are two elements in the text quoted at the beginning. The first concerns the privilege of a special grace which Saint Francis received by being conformed to Christ, as the text says: *Then will appear the sign of the Son of Man*; the second touches on his surpassing merits, as the text continues: *in heaven*, for the Holy Spirit fills the heavens—that is, heavenly men—with his gifts.

II

You will know that the heavens possess numerous characteristics. Leaving aside many others, I want to concentrate on these: their very presence above us, their vast extent which encompasses everything, and their effects on the earth.

First, then, they stand above us in lofty heights which may be taken as referring to the exalted poverty embraced by holy people, and by Saint Francis in particular; they are adorned with splendor, which may be understood as unblemished purity; and they remain unalterable in their position, which I take as referring to Saint Francis's humble obedience.

Saint Francis was like the heavens in their lofty heights because
of his exalted poverty. We read in Isaiah: *Heaven is my throne and the* Is 66:1-2
earth my footstool, and a little later: *To whom shall I look but to him who is poor and little contrite in spirit and trembles at my words.* O Lord God, how do you bring together in the same passage *a poor little man* and *heaven*? Of which heaven are you speaking? In which heaven is the Lord pleased to place his throne? Beyond doubt *in the poor little man* who
may be called a *heaven*. I will prove this by the Psalm which says: *The* Ps 10:4
Lord is in his holy temple, the Lord's throne is in heaven, and then adds: *His* Ps 10:5
eyes behold the poor man. To the avaricious, poverty is a detestable thing, but not so in the eyes of God. For though in appearance it is most base, in truth it is exalted and most high. Saint Paul writes to

2 Cor 8:2 the Corinthians: *Their extreme poverty has abounded to the riches of their simplicity.* As the heavens are arranged in spheres of high, higher, and highest heavens, so there is a poverty borne in patience that is good, a poverty that is desired and longed for which is better, and poverty embraced with joy in which a person glories and rejoices, which is best of all. Poverty, therefore, is the reason why a person can be likened to the heavens, because it leads to the kingdom of heaven. Our
Mt 5:3 Lord says: *Blessed are the poor in spirit, for theirs is the kingdom of heaven.* Poverty excludes those who do not love it, or who malign it, from the
Mt 19:24 kingdom of heaven, as Scripture says: *It is easier for a camel to go through the eye of a needle than for a rich man to enter the kingdom of God,* that is, for a rich man who has set his heart on riches and placed his
1 Tm 6:9 trust in them. Avarice drags a person down because *those who desire to be rich fall into temptation, into a snare, into many senseless and hurtful desires that plunge men into ruin and destruction.* Take note that avarice casts a person into the depths. Poverty, on the other hand, uplifts a person to the state of heavenly life and, above all, that poverty in which a person glorifies and rejoices.

You will not find anyone who embraced poverty like Saint Fran- LMj VII 1-3
cis, nor who gloried in it as he did. He refused to possess anything at all, either personally or in common, nor did he want his brothers to own anything. The cross of Christ is the sign of poverty because on it he was reduced to the utmost poverty, not having had even an old rag with which to cover his nakedness. Saint Francis also chose the highest poverty. It is fitting, therefore, that the sign of the Son of Man, namely, Christ's cross, should be found on Saint Francis.

At this point someone may remark that self-praise is distasteful, and so I ought not to be saying these things in praise of ourselves, of our own Orders and of our holy father Saint Francis. But really one should not remain silent about these things by which the Holy Spirit himself approved and confirmed the life of poverty by the sign of the
cross. For at the very time Saint Francis sought approval of his Order LMj IV 11
from the pope, the stigmata of our Lord were imprinted on his body. This was God's approval, not man's, for men can be deceived. And so not only did a human being issue a bull approving poverty, the Lord himself issued his own bull approving poverty by imprinting the stigmata of his passion on the poor and humble Saint Francis. It is not granted to everybody to observe such poverty or to choose it, but it is given to all to admire it. And it ought to be a source of joy to anyone who cannot be poor like this, that such poverty was embraced by someone.[a]

a. Saint Bonaventure may well be excusing himself here.

We noted also that the heavens are adorned with splendor. Saint Francis can be compared to this aspect of the heavens because of his unblemished purity. We read in the book of Sirach: *The firmament on* [Sir 43:1] *high is his beauty, the beauty of heaven with its spectacle of glory.*

The firmament which is arrayed with beauty may be likened to a soul that is marked by purity, as an impression is made by a seal in wax. It says in Exodus that the elders of Israel *saw the God of Israel; and* [Ex 24:9-10] *there was under his feet as it were a pavement of sapphire stone, like the very heaven for clearness.* The latter words may be understood of a soul that has been cleansed of every impurity, of all stain and corruption of sins of the flesh. Such as this were the souls of the Nazarites of whom the Book of Lamentations says: *Her Nazarites were whiter than snow,* [Lam 4:7] *purer than milk, more ruddy than coral, fairer than sapphire*. These words are said of men who had been consecrated to the Lord and were obliged to observe chastity. The Nazarites are described as *whiter than snow,* which is rightly said of people vowed to chastity because of their bodily purity, *purer than milk,* because of the integrity of their desires and the uprightness of their thoughts; *more ruddy than coral,* because all these virtues blend into a unity; and *fairer than sapphire,* which is to say, fairer than the serene blue heavens, because the sapphire has the same color as the clear sky.

Saint Francis, then, can be compared to the heavens adorned with splendor on account of his utter purity. He made himself a eunuch [Mt 19:12] for the sake of the kingdom of heaven, by chastising, severely punishing, and mortifying his flesh so that it would not bring forth [Gn 3:18] thorns and thistles, that is, the passions of unchaste thoughts and desires. Saint Benedict did likewise. At the beginning of his conversion he was so troubled for a short time by temptation of the flesh "that he almost considered abandoning his solitary retreat. Then suddenly God graciously looked upon him and he flung himself naked upon stinging thorns and burning nettles. In so doing he changed his lust to pain, and from that time on he never again experienced a sensation like that."[a]

[LMj V 3] Saint Francis also in the early days of his conversion suffered temptations of the flesh. As he wrestled with these temptations one winter's night, he threw himself naked into the snow and mastered them thoroughly. From that time he scarcely needed to go to such lengths because of the other penance he endured which were quite

a. Gregory the Great, *Dialogues* II 2 (PL 77, 132).

sufficient to conquer such temptations. His desire was to overcome completely both the lust of the flesh and evil thoughts and desires of the heart. This man was totally possessed of bodily purity, or better, heavenly purity. And I would remind you, dear brothers, that purity enhances the other virtues, it adorns and ennobles them all. When we hear it said of someone that he leads an honorable life and is chaste and pure, that means in fact that he has honor and glory in the sight of God. The cross of Christ is the sign of chastity, of bodily mortification, and of lamb-like simplicity and purity. Therefore, how right it is that this sign should have been found on Saint Francis.

I pointed out, finally, that the heavens remain unalterable in their position. They suffer no disturbance and everything they contain is fixed according to an order. Saint Francis can be compared to this characteristic of the heavens on account of his humble obedience. Jb 38:33 We read that Job was asked: *Do you know the order of the heavens?* And we may ask: "What is the order of the heavens?" We know that the higher sphere draws all the other spheres by its movement. Though these move in their course by their own power, nevertheless they move with the higher sphere which draws them all with itself in such a way that in the heavens there is no toil, disorder, or hardship.

There is a similar order in the ranks of heaven where the activity of the highest determines all the rest. And who established that order? Beyond doubt its origin is this: the highest order of angels, the supreme spirits, conforms to the eternal law, and the lower ranks of angels, in their turn, are subject to the higher ranks. If you were to ask an angel of one of the lower ranks: "Why do you obey the higher angels when you, like them, were created directly by God?" he would reply: "Why should it be strange that I obey an angel of a higher rank? He commands nothing of himself, but only what has been entrusted to him by God. And I must needs obey my Creator." According to this pattern there is an established order both in God's Church, where the lower ranks are subject to the higher and should obey them, and in the soul of the just man, where the lower faculties are subject to the higher and should obey them.

Why then does the flesh rebel against the spirit? This was not the case at the beginning, for it is unthinkable that God should have created humanity in such disorder. If humanity had remained in original innocence our lower nature and the desires of the flesh would never have rebelled against reason, and we should not have been ignorant of the truths we ought to know. All this was the result of original sin. There lies the reason why our highest spiritual powers are not obedient to God, why our senses do not submit to reason, and why our lower faculties are not subject to the higher. But these disorders can be set right by humble obedience. A person lives by the obedience born of humility when he submits to God's law without any resistance or hesitation, and guides his life by the truth. Anyone who conducts himself in this way can be compared to the heavens where the lower spheres are unconditionally obedient to the further and higher spheres.

LMj II 7-8 Saint Francis possessed true humility and it was his desire that both he himself and his Order should be named from it. Therefore, his Order is called simply "the Order of Lesser Brothers." He was, or
LMj IV 9 at all events he reckoned himself, the least of all men. The first provincial minister of the brothers in France was a brother named Pacifico.[a] He was a companion of Saint Francis who was sent by him
LMj VI 6 to establish the Order in France. One day in a dream it seemed to him that he was taken up into paradise. He saw there a large number of thrones which were all occupied, and higher than the rest a more august throne which was unoccupied. On inquiring whose throne it might be, he was told it was reserved for Saint Francis. Sometime later he asked Saint Francis how he saw himself and what he thought of himself. He answered: "It seems to me I am the greatest sinner in the world. Yes, beyond question, that is what I think of myself." Pacifico protested: "How can you say that? Aren't there numerous thieves, fornicators, and murderers in the world?" Saint Francis replied: "Listen. There is no one in the world who, if God has bestowed on him so many and such great graces as he has on me, would not be more pleasing to God than I am. That is the reason I consider myself the worst of sinners. Saint Paul said the same of himself: *I am the first of sinners.*" He did not mean first in time, for 1 Tm 1:15
there had been many sinners before him, but the first in the sense of foremost. And Saint Paul was a most humble and lowly man as his name reveals. In fact, he was a most humble and lowly lesser brother.

A great burden has been placed on us by the name we bear: *Lesser Brothers*, because it obliges us to account ourselves worse and more sinful than others. If it causes us displeasure to find a brother of our

a. Cf. AC, supra, 65.

own Order who is proud, how much more must it be displeasing to God. All this is abundantly clear from the fact that Christ's cross is
Phil 2:8 above all the sign of humility. Listen to Saint Paul: *Christ humbled himself and became obedient unto death, even death on a cross.* Christ's cross is the sign of the most perfect humility and self-abasement because on the cross he humbled and abased himself to such an extreme for our sake. So again, how right it is to find this sign on Saint Francis who possessed the greatest humility and reckoned himself the lowest and meanest of sinners. He used to implore in prayer: "Why, O LMj VIII 3
Lord, have you laid this burden on me? Why have you made a simple, unlettered, despicable creature like me the head of this Order?" And the Lord would reply: "I have placed you over this Order so that what I achieve in you may be attributed to my grace and not to man's ingenuity."

Second, we admire the heavens because of their vast extent. They contain all things. Saint Francis can be likened to this feature of the heavens because of his all-embracing love which went out to every-
Sir 24:8 one. We read in the Book of Sirach: *I alone have compassed the circuit of heaven.* This can be said of the love that is in God and in us for it also has compassed the heavens which contain everything. Yet only the righteous dwell in heaven. Love embraces all that love commands, but such love is found only in the virtuous. It was through love that the divine nature was united to flesh and through love that Christ humbled himself and underwent death. The Book of Sirach tells us:
Sir 43:12 *Look upon the rainbow and praise him who made it.* What is this rainbow except the cross of Christ? Therefore, the sign of Christ's cross had to be found on this man of heavenly virtue, Saint Francis, whose love was boundless. He had love without limit for everyone. Love spends itself for sinners without counting the cost. Saint Francis was not content with preaching God's word only to the Christian faithful who listen with glad hearts and accept it willingly. He even went to LMj IX 5-8
the Saracens to proclaim the Gospel in the hope that he might be put to death for his faith in Christ and so become a martyr.

How is it that we, wretched as we are, have such cold hearts that we are not prepared to endure anything for our Lord's sake? Our hearts neither burn nor glow with love. Ardent love is a quality of the heart and the stronger this love burns in a person's heart, the more heroic and virtuous are his deeds. Do you desire to imprint Christ crucified on your heart? Do you long to be transformed into him to

the point where your heart is aflame with love? Just as iron when heated to the point where it becomes molten can take the imprint of any mark or sign, so a heart burning fervently with love of Christ crucified can receive the imprint of the Crucified Lord himself or his cross. Such a loving heart is carried over to the Crucified Lord or
LMj XIII 1-5 transformed into him. That is what happened with Saint Francis.

Some people express surprise that when the stigmata of Christ's passion were to be imprinted on Saint Francis, a Seraph was sent to him. Surely none of the Seraphim was crucified! But the Seraphim are the angels whose name comes from "burning flame."[a] Thus, what this detail tells us is that Saint Francis was aflame with love when the Seraph was sent to him. The cross or sign of the cross imprinted on his body symbolized his love of Christ crucified and by the flame of that love he was totally transformed into Christ.

I want to tell you something that happened in the province of
LMj XIII 6 Rieti which confirms what I have been saying. There was a fatal epidemic which had attacked the animals of the region so that they could not take food. Suddenly, all the animals were dying and the people did not know what to do to save them. One of the local people went to see a devout man and told him how the animals were dying and asked his advice. The devout man advised him to get some of the water in which Saint Francis had washed his hands and feet, sprinkle it over the animals and they would be cured. He did this and the animals came running for their food. I was told this by someone who saw it happen.

So, because Saint Francis had a love as vast as the heavens, and the cross is the sign of the greatest love in the world, it is to be expected that we should find this sign on him.

Moreover, the heavens contain mysteries. The Latin word for heaven, *caelum*, is derived from the verb *celare* meaning to keep secret or conceal.[b] Saint Francis can be compared to this feature of the heavens because he reached the heights of contemplation. It says in
the Psalms: *You stretched out the heavens like a tent and covered its higher* Ps 103:2-3
rooms with waters. Waters are indeed limpid, refreshing, and shimmering with light and are a symbol of contemplation. There where the waters meet a man sees the reflection of his own image and the

a. Gregory, *Homilia in evangelia* I, 34, nn. 10, 12, (PL 76, 1251, 1254); *Gregory the Great: Forty Gospel Homilies*, Cistercian Studies Series 123, translated by David Hurst (Kalamazoo: Cistercian Publications, 1990), 289, 291.

b. *Isidore, Etymologae*, XIII, c. 4, n. 1, (PL 82, 474).

splendor of God's light. Saint Francis reached such heights of contemplation that he foretold the future, saw the secrets of people's hearts, and appeared to those who were absent, just like Saint Anthony the Hermit of whom Saint Augustine speaks in the prologue to his work *On Christian Doctrine.*[a] The cross of Christ is the sign of wisdom and of the revelation of God's mysteries. This is clear from the Book of Revelation where we are told that *the Lamb who was slain opened the scroll sealed with seven seals,* which means he unveiled by his cross all the mysteries of Holy Scripture. The cross of Christ is the key of David; Christ is the Holy One *who opens and no one shall shut, who shuts and no one opens.* Because Saint Francis soared to such heights of contemplation and wisdom, we should expect yet again to find on him the sign of Christ's cross. LMj XI 3-14

Rv 5:12, 9, 2

Rv 3:17

Mt 10:16

The Gospel tells us: *Be simple as doves.* We should love simplicity and innocence of heart if we desire God to enlighten us with the brilliant light of wisdom. When the moon is directly opposite the sun, it is all lit up and appears radiant; when it is in eclipse with the sun neither its light nor radiance can be seen. But in fact the nearer it is to the sun and the closer it draws to it, the more light it receives. For in truth it has more light then than it receives when directly opposite the sun. Similarly, with us: the more a person parades his wisdom and wants to appear wise, so much the less is he enlightened. But when a person flees human company, enters into himself and reflects on his union with God, then is he so much the more enlightened. Though someone may appear enlightened, to be truly so it is utterly necessary to draw close to God in the greatest humility and simplicity of heart. I will give you an example. Students at the University of Paris went to Praepositivus the Chancellor and asked him: "What do you believe? Tell us what we ought to believe." So Praepositivus called in a simple man who was passing in the street and the question was put to him. With simplicity he replied: "I believe in God the Father Almighty and in his Son and in their Spirit and likewise that there is one God." "Excellent," answered Praepositivus, "that is how I want to believe, in simplicity and humility."[b]

a. Augustine, *De doctrina christiana*, prol., n. 4; *Teaching Christianity*, translated with introduction and notes by Edmund Hill, edited by John Rotelle (Hyde Park: New City Press, 1991), 102.

b. See G. Lacombe, "Prevostin de Cremone," in *Dictionnaire de Theologie Catholique* xm, 1 Part., 162-69; J.N. Garvin, "Praepositinus of Cremona," in *New Catholic Encyclopedia* XI (Washington, 1967), 660. His dates are 1130/5-1210. He was Chancellor of Paris from 1206 to 1209. His name is found in various forms: Praepositus, Praepositinus, Praepositivus.

Lastly, the heavens encompass everything, they contain all things, yet they are contained by nothing. Saint Francis can be likened to this aspect of them because he was filled with God's sevenfold grace. We read that God said to Abraham: *Look toward heaven and* Gn 15:5 *number the stars, if you are able to number them . . . so shall your descendants be.* There is no star however small whose immensity would not fill the earth and give it light. Though the light and rays of each star coalesce in the atmosphere, they are found to be distinct when we look up at the stars themselves.[a] It is something similar with devout souls whom the Holy Spirit enlightens with divine radiance. These Gn 1:11 are the posterity of the Holy Spirit and his posterity is as the stars of heaven, for the Holy Spirit brings forth devout souls in an altogether wondrous way. The Book of Job says: *His Spirit has adorned the heav-* Jb 26:13 *ens*—that is, men of heavenly virtue—*and with a midwife's skill his hand brought forth the winding serpent.* The marvel of Holy Scripture is how it brings together ideas which appear disparate but in fact are not. What is this hand of God whereby his works are wrought? As regards the creation of the world the Son can be called the hand of God Jn 1:1-5 through whom he made all things; as regards the variety of gifts, the Holy Spirit is God's hand who distributes the diverse gifts of grace *and apportions to each one individually as he wills.* Therefore, the Holy 1 Cor 12:11 Spirit is the hand of God which bestows the manifold gifts of grace. How many are the graces placed in our hands? They are fourteen. The winding serpent will only be brought out of us if this hand of God, that is, the Holy Spirit, showers down on us his sevenfold grace: the four cardinal virtues and the three theological virtues, so that we can set out on the path of holiness and persevere to the end. The seven gifts of the Holy Spirit are given to us that we may do good works with zeal. Christ's cross is the sign of God's boundless grace because from the cross, that is, from Christ's sufferings, flow all the gifts of grace. So, once again, we should expect to find the sign of the Son of man, the cross of Christ, on Saint Francis who was filled with the gifts of the Holy Spirit.

Finally, I wish to say a word about the four effects the heavens have on the earth. They light up the earth by their luster, moisten it with rain from the clouds, bestow warmth on it from their heat and give it brilliance in flashes of lightning. In a similar way these effects of the heavens may be attributed to Saint Francis. He shed light on his neigh-

a. Cf. *II Sent.*, d. XIII, a. III, q. 2 (II, 327).

bors, less advanced on the way of perfection, by his manifest virtue; refreshed them with ardent love by his devout prayers; and filled them with wonder by the miracles wrought through his holiness and goodness. The cross of Christ is the sign of God's perfect works and of all his wonderful deeds. And because Saint Francis may be likened to the heavens in all that he did, we should expect to find the cross imprinted on him, so that by this sign he would be raised on high. The Lord regards the lowly and therefore he looked upon this humble and poor little man, Saint Francis, and imprinted on him the sign of the cross; but
Ps 138:6 the haughty and proud he knows from afar. As Saint James reminds
Jas 4:6 us: *God opposes the proud, but gives grace to the humble.*

Therefore, let us ask God to grant us so to humble ourselves in this life like Saint Francis, that by his merits and prayers we may be exalted in the next. May the Lord Jesus Christ who loves and lifts up the humble, hear our prayer. Amen.

Sermon on Saint Francis
Preached at Paris , October 4, 1266

Three opinions exist regarding the date of this sermon. John F. Quinn maintains that it was delivered as early as October 4, 1254.[a] Sophronius Clasen, on the other hand, maintains that it was delivered after the composition of the *Major Legend.*[b] While sympathetic to an early date, Ignatius C. Brady concurs with Clasen and offers as his proof the text of Revelation 7:2, the angel bearing the seal of the living God. In light of a sermon Bonaventure delivered to the General Chapter of the Friars in 1266,[c] Brady proposes October 4, 1266 as the day on which Bonaventure delivered this sermon.[d]

I will take you, O Zerubbabel my servant, the son of Shealthiel, and make you like a seal, for I have chosen you Hg 2:23

This text from the Book of Haggai can be applied to Saint Francis. For as Zerubbabel, whose name means "leader of the exodus," led the people out of Babylon and rebuilt the Temple, so Saint Francis brought many people from the disorder of sin to Christ, and he founded a religious order. The saint is commended in this text on three accounts: for his worthy service which was pleasing to God: *I will take you . . .* for the seal of his outstanding holiness: *and make you like a seal;* and for the privilege of having been chosen by God: *for I have chosen you.*

I

As regards the first, we should take note that his service was pleasing to God because he was humble, for he spurned worldly honors. As the Apostle Paul says: *For though I am free from all, I have made* 1 Cor 9:19

a. John F. Quinn, "Chronology of St. Bonaventure's Sermons" AFH 67 (1974) 177.

b. Sophronius Clasen, *Franziskus Engel des Sechsten Siegels. Sein Leben nach den Schriften des heligen Bonaventura* (Werl/West, 1962), 153.

c. Clasen, *Franziskus Engel,* 156, 180, n. 239; Brady "The Writings," 102, n. 52; S. Bihel, "S. Franciscus fuitne angelus sexti sigilii?" *Antonianum* 2 (1927) 66, 73.

d. Ignatius C. Brady, "Saint Bonaventure's Sermons on Saint Francis," *Franziskanische Studien* 58 (1976), 130-131.

myself a slave to all that I might win the more. In this way Saint Francis
Phil 2:6, 7 imitated Christ *who though he was in the form of God emptied himself, taking the form of a servant.* And indeed, the service of God begins with humility. In this connection Saint Gregory says: "The person who
acquires other virtues but not humility, is like someone carrying dust
against the wind; he becomes all the more blinded by what he is seen
to be carrying."[a]

Saint Francis was so humble that he also served lepers. Because of LMj I6; II 6
his great humility he was taken to the heights of knowing divine
Is 52:13 mysteries. We read in Isaiah: *Behold my servant shall understand, he
shall be exalted, and shall be exceeding high,* and in Saint Matthew's Gos-
Mt 11:25 pel: *You have hidden these things from the wise and revealed them to babes.*

Furthermore, he was pleasing to God because of his steadfastness
Ps 115:4, 6 through mortification of the flesh. The Psalm says: *I will lift up the cup
of salvation . . . O Lord, for I am your servant.* The cup signifies mortifica-
Rom 6:6 tion of the flesh. Saint Paul writes: *Our old self was crucified with him so
that the sinful body might be destroyed, and we might no longer be enslaved to
sin.* By this kind of mortification we serve God as Saint Paul makes
Rom 6:19 clear: *I am speaking in human terms . . . For just as you once yielded your
members to serve impurity and greater and greater iniquity, so now yield your
members to serve righteousness for sanctification.*

That is precisely what Saint Francis did. Even in the severest win- LMj V 3
ter he rolled himself in the snow to curb temptations of the flesh. On
account of his self-denial he was found worthy to receive divine con-
Lk 12:35 solations. Commenting on the text of Saint Luke's Gospel: *let your
loins be girt,* Saint Gregory explains: "We gird our loins when we curb
the lusts of the flesh by continence."[b] Saint Luke goes on to say that
Lk 12:37 when the Lord finds servants such as these *he will gird himself and
make them sit down,* that is, be consoled. All the unchaste will be ex-
Rv 22:15 cluded from this consolation, as the Book of Revelation testifies: *Outside are the dogs and sorcerers and unchaste.*

Third, Saint Francis was pleasing to God because he was faithful
by having renounced all earthly desires. We read in the Book of
Nm 12:17 Numbers: *My servant Moses is the most faithful in all my house.* A faithful
servant is one who does not look for human praise, as we learn from
Gal 1:10 the text of Saint Paul: *If I yet pleased men, I should not be the servant of
Christ.* On this Saint Bernard writes: "You are indeed a faithful ser-

---

a. Gregory, *Homilia in evangelia* I, hom. 7, n. 4, (PL 76, 1103); *Gregory the Great: Forty Gospel Homilies,* Cistercian Studies Series 123, translated by David Hurst (Kalamazoo: Cistercian Publications, 1990), 27.

b. Gregory, *Homilia in evangelia* I, hom. 13, n. 1, (PL 76, 1123); *Gregory the Great: Forty Gospel Homilies,* Cistercian Studies Series 123, translated by David Hurst (Kalamazoo: Cistercian Publications, 1990), 151.

vant when nothing of the Lord's abundant glory remains clinging to your hands. That glory comes not from you, it is channeled through you."[a]

More faithful still is the servant who does not seek bodily rest. In Saint Matthew's Gospel the Lord asks: *Who then is the faithful and wise servant, whom his master has set over his household to give them their food at the proper time?* He continues: *Blessed is that servant whom his master when he comes will find so doing.* The Lord comes to us at our death and prior to that we must not rest from our labors. Of the Prophet Samuel Scripture says: *And all Israel from Dan to Beersheba knew that Samuel was a faithful prophet of the Lord,* and again, *money, or anything, even to a shoe, he had not taken of any man and no man did accuse him.*

Mt 24:45 Mt 24:46 1 Sm 3:20 Sir 46:22

LMj VII 1-3 Saint Francis observed all this literally for he fulfilled the gospel law perfectly. He had *neither money in his belt nor sandals on his feet.* In this way he imitated the Lord Jesus, for as Saint Jerome remarks: "The Lord could not himself possess what he had forbidden to his servants."[b] Because of his fidelity Saint Francis was found worthy to be raised to regal honors as the Gospel says: *Well done, good and faithful servant; enter into the joy of your master.* The covetous will not be taken into this joy, as Saint Paul tells us: *No immoral or impure man or one who is covetous, that is, an idolater, has any inheritance in the kingdom of Christ and of God.* Therefore, anyone who proclaims that we should love earthly goods is a blasphemer. Saint Jerome wrote to Bishop Nepotian: "You are the priest of a crucified Lord, one who lived in poverty and on the bread of strangers, and it is a shameful thing for a consul's attendants and bodyguards to keep watch before your door."[c] And we should note well that *a servant is not greater than his master.*

Mk 6:8; Mt 10:9 Mt 25:21 Eph 5:5 Jn 13:16

Lastly, Saint Francis was pleasing to God because he was devoted in carrying out God's commands in a way similar to Job: *Have you considered my servant Job, that there is none like him on the earth, a blameless and upright man, who fears God and turns away from evil?* Of the service of God Scripture says: *Serve him only and he will deliver you.* Jesus himself tells us: *No one can serve two masters,* that is, no one can serve the devil and God, except by some such agreement as Nahash the Ammonite wanted to make with the sons of Israel when he proposed: *On this*

Jb 1:8 1 Sm 7:3 Mt 6:24 1 Sm 11:2

a. Bernard of Clairvaux, Sermon 13:3, *On the Song of Songs*, translated by Kilian Walsh, introduction by M. Corneille Halflants (Spencer, MA: Cistercian Publications, 1971), 90.

b. Jerome, *Epistula XXII ad Eustochium*, n. 19, in *Corpus Scriptorum Ecclesiasticorum Latinorum*, Vienna (Collected Works of Latin Church Writers) (hereafter CSEL), 168; *Select Letters of Saint Jerome*, Loeb Classical Library, translated by Frederick Wright (London: Heinemann, 1975), 95.

c. Jerome, *Epistula LII ad Nepotianum Presbyterum*, n. 11, CSEL, 433; *Select Letters of Saint Jerome*, Loeb Classical Library, translated by Frederick Wright (London: Heinemann, 1975), 217.

condition I will make a treaty with you, that I gouge out all your right eyes, and thus put disgrace upon all Israel. The right eye is the one fixed on eternal things, the left on earthly things. The devil wants his servants to lose their longing for eternal things even when they do something good.

In everything he did Saint Francis had his right eye fixed on eternal things, for he was *blameless and upright.* And because he possessed
Mt 6:22 a blameless eye, the *whole body* of his actions was *full of light.* He was found worthy to be raised to the heavenly dwelling place on account
Is 42:1 of his devoted service of God. We read in Isaiah: *Behold my servant, whom I uphold, my chosen in whom my soul delights; I have put my spirit upon him.* Whoever refuses to carry out God's commands is not fit to enter this heavenly dwelling place, as it is written in Saint Matthew's
Mt 25:30 Gospel: *Cast the worthless servant into the outer darkness.*

Saint Francis, then was a servant pleasing to God because he was humble, steadfast, faithful, and devoted. That is to say, he resisted vainglory, the lusts of the flesh, worldly desires, and the powers of evil.

II

Hg 2:23 We come now to the second part of the text: *and make you like a seal.* Saint Francis is commended here for the seal of his outstanding holiness. The marks of the passion imprinted on his body bear eloquent LMj XIII 1-10
witness to this.

First of all it should be noted that he was like a seal that has been refashioned, made new, through lament and sorrow for the sins of his
Jb 38:14 past life. The Book of Job says: *The seal shall be restored as clay and shall stand as a garment.* A fallen angel who once bore the seal of God cannot be restored to his original state, because there can be no repentance for an angel. But for human beings it is quite different. The first half of Job's text says: *The seal shall be restored as clay.* That takes place by the waters of sorrow and the earth of humility. The text continues: *and shall stand as a garment.* A garment does not stand of itself but only when it clothes a body. Saint Francis was like a seal restored like clay through sorrow for his sins, and he stood like a garment of the Holy Spirit.

Second, he was like a seal transformed by the fire of love. The Song of
Sg 8:6 Solomon says: *Set me as a seal upon your heart.* Speaking of God's love Hugh of Saint Victor writes: "I feel, O my soul, such is the power of love, that you are being transformed into the likeness of him you love."[a]

a. Hugh of St. Victor, *De arrha animae,* (PL 176, 954); *Soliloquy on the Earnest Money of the Soul,* translated with introduction by Kevin Herbert (Marquette: Marquette University Press, 1956), 16.

Third, he was like a seal that has been imprinted, through being
an example of perfect virtue. For this there is a text in Romans: *He re-* Rom 4:11
ceived circumcision as a sign or seal of the righteousness he had by faith. Saint
Paul is referring of course to spiritual not bodily circumcision.

Lastly, he was like a declaratory seal by his ardent desire for the
salvation of others. We read in the Book of Revelation: *Then I saw an-* Rv 7:2
other angel ascend from the rising of the sun, with the seal of the living God.
This seal is the ardent desire for the salvation of all people. Then
there is this text in Ezechiel: *And the Lord said to him: "Go through the* Ez 9:4
city, through Jerusalem, and mark Tau upon the foreheads of the those who
sigh and mourn over all the abominations that are committed in it." So it is Ex 12:29
that God smote those in the land of Egypt who did not bear this sign.

In summary, Saint Francis was like a seal refashioned, transformed, imprinted, and declaratory.

III

In the third part of the text: *for I have chosen you,* Saint Francis is
commended for the privilege of having been chosen by God. It
should be emphasized at the outset that no other cause of divine
election can be assigned except the will of him who has said: *I will be* Ex 33:19
gracious to whom I will be gracious and will show mercy on whom I will show
mercy. However, signs of divine election can be discerned and they
are chiefly seven.

The first is reverence for God's name. Scripture tells us: *The fear of* Sir 1:16
the Lord is the beginning of wisdom, and was created with the faithful in the
womb, it walks with chosen women, that is, with souls, and is known with the
just and faithful. A few verses earlier we read: *With him that fears the* Sir 1:13
Lord, it shall go well at the end, and on the day of his death he will be blessed.
And in the same chapter: *For he who is without fear, cannot be justified: for* Sir 1:28
the wrath of his high spirits is his ruin. The whole of Sacred Scripture is
directed toward arousing in us reverence for the Lord, as Ecclesiastes
teaches: *Fear God, and keep his commandments; for this is the whole duty of* Eccl 12:13
a human being.

The second is love of bodily purity. Saint Paul tells us that *God . . .* Eph 1:4
chose us in him before the foundation of the world, that we should be holy and
blameless before him, and Saint Peter says: *You are a chosen race, a royal* 1 Pt 2:9
priesthood, a holy nation, God's own people.

The third is the graciousness of natural compassion. As the Apos-
tle writes: *Put on then as God's chosen ones, holy and beloved, compassion.* Col 3:12
In another text he shows Timothy that this is a sign of divine elec-
tion: *Godliness is of value in every way, as it holds promise for the present life* 1 Tm 4:8
and also for the life to come. We read, on the one hand, in the Book of

Jb 31:18 Job: *For from my infancy mercy grew up with me: and it came out with me*
Sir 3:27 *from my mother's womb.* On the other hand, Sirach warns: *A hard heart shall fear evil at the last;* and Saint Bernard advises: "If you want to
Ex 7:13, 21 know what a hard heart is, ask Pharaoh."[a]

The fourth is joy in voluntary poverty whether the poverty was
Is 48:10 chosen or inflicted initially. As Scripture tells us: *I have chosen you in*
Jas 2:5 *the furnace of poverty,* and in another place: *Has God not chosen the poor in this world, rich in faith, and heirs of the kingdom which God has promised to*
Mt 5:3 *those who love him;* and again: *Blessed are the poor in spirit, for theirs is the kingdom of heaven.*

The fifth is the humility of a devoted heart. As Saint Paul writes to
1 Cor 1:26-27 the Corinthians: *For consider your call, brethren; not many of you were wise according to worldly standards, not many were powerful, not many were of noble birth, but God chose what is foolish in the world to shame the wise, God chose what is weak in the world to shame the strong.* This in fact, on the one
2 Sm 6:21-22 hand, was a sign of divine election in David who said to Michaël: *It was before the Lord, who chose me above your father . . . and I will make merry before the Lord. I will make myself yet more contemptible than this, and*
Lk 16:15 *I will be abased in your eyes.* On the other hand, Jesus told the Pharisees: *What is exalted among humans is an abomination in the sight of God.*

The sixth is the humanity of inherent gentleness. As Sirach says:
Sir 45:4 *He sanctified him in his faith and meekness and chose him out of all flesh.* On
Prv 6:16, 19 the other hand, Proverbs warns: *There are six things which the Lord hates and the seventh his soul detests: a man who sows discord among brothers.*

The seventh is the help of heavenly grace. As the Book of Wisdom
Wis 4:15 says: *God's grace and mercy are with his elect.* Here God's grace and mercy signify his providence over us. Saint John records the words of Jesus:
Jn 15:16 *You did not choose me, but I chose you and appointed you that you should go and bear fruit and that your fruit should abide.*

Therefore, because these seven signs were plainly found in Saint Francis, they show that he was chosen by God.

a. Bernard of Clairvaux, *Five Books on Consideration: Advice to a Pope*, The Works of Bernard of Clairvaux, vol. 13, translated by John Anderson and Elizabeth Kennan (Kalamazoo: Cistercian Publications, 1976), 28.

Sermon on the Feast of the Transferal of the Body of Saint Francis

Probably preached at Paris, May 25, 1267

Bonaventure preached this sermon on the thirty-seventh anniversary of the transferal of Saint Francis's body from its temporary resting place in the church of San Giorgio in Assisi to the newly built basilica in his honor. The occasion was the Vigil of the Solemnity of the Ascension.[a]

Friend, go up higher Lk 14:10

Introduction

You who dwell in the gardens, my companions listen for your voice; deign to let me hear it. Sg 8:13

This text tells us why the word of God must be preached often. One reason that should inspire us to preach is love of Christ, and another is love of our neighbor. The words of Holy Scripture provide spiritual nourishment for our neighbor, just as material food sustains the body.

In the same way that a person listens to news of a friend, and a sick person pays close heed to the advice of the doctor, so those who love God listen attentively to his word. By the mouth of the contemplative soul dwelling in the gardens of Holy Scripture, because of the consolations to be found there, the Lord, the Holy Spirit says: I will come to listen.

A third reason that ought to inspire us to preach is that the Lord desires to be honored. He wishes to be praised in our prayers, homilies, and sermons, and he wishes our neighbor to be edified by all these. As it is written: *Let us praise the Lord and he will be glorified.* We learn in lectures to distinguish essential and related purposes. The essential purpose of our sermons ought to be to praise God and the I Thes 3:1

a. The friars of Quaracchi had published this sermon, cf. S. Bonaventurae, (IX 534-535). A more complete edition can be found in a manuscript in Munich, Staatsbibliothek, Clm 23372, ff. 119v-24r. It was published by R.E. Lerner, "A Collection of Sermons given in Paris c. 1267, including a new text by Saint Bonaventure on the Life of Saint Francis," *Speculum* 49 (1974): 466-98. Because of internal evidence, the sermon has not been called into question.

related purpose to edify our neighbor. No man of himself can intend or achieve these purposes, but only with the help of God. So here at the beginning ask the Lord to grant me the grace to be able to say something to his praise, in commendation of Saint Francis, and for our edification. Let each one say an *Our Father* and *a Hail Mary*.

I

I began with the *text: Friend, go up higher.* These are Christ's words inviting to the wedding feast those guests found to be humble whom the Lord exalts and desires to exalt. Immediately before these words, the Lord advises: *When you are invited, go and sit in the lowest place.* Saint Francis, having been invited to Christ's wedding feast, sat in the lowest place. That is to say, he clothed himself in a shabby habit and he founded the Order of Lesser Brothers. He did not qualify the word "Lesser" in any way, but simply and unconditionally called his Order the Order of Lesser Brothers. The Lord said to the humble guest, the one who had taken a lower place, *Friend, go up higher.* Notice the Lord calls the humble his friends, and this text may be taken as addressed to the holy confessor Francis who so humbled himself that he wanted to be a lesser brother and *sit in the lowest place.* To this man who made himself humble and lowly for Christ's sake, the Lord says:
Ps 113:7 *Friend, go up higher,* raising, as it were, *the poor from the dust.*

The wisdom of God draws the mind to three noteworthy features in this text, which correspond to its three component parts. First, it indicates the presence of grace by the idea of friendship, and so the text says: *Friend.* Second, it signifies "glory" by the spatial adverb *higher.* And third, it symbolizes "pass over from grace to glory" by the verb *go up.* Therefore, in saying *Friend* it means: because you are endowed with grace *go up higher,* that is, come to heavenly glory.

Grace, then, is rightly symbolized by the first word *Friend.* The word refers to the power of grace and eternal wisdom in devout souls, which has been bestowed on many saints for generation after generation. In these latter times grace was given to this holy man, making him a model of repentance to us all.

Jesus calls Saint Francis his friend for a number of special reasons. First, due to his truly humble spirit in all that was committed to him, he was a faithful friend of the Lord. Second, because of his utter purity of heart in everything he pledged himself to do, he was a congenial friend of the Lord. Third, on account of the serenity of his contemplative soul, he was an intimate friend of the Lord. And fourth, because the marks of Christ's cross were imprinted on his body, he
became, as Christ's friend, conformed to his likeness. The word LMj XIII 3

Friend, therefore, is addressed to Saint Francis because he was a faithful, congenial and intimate friend of the Lord, conformed to him by the marks of the stigmata on his body.[a]

First, he was a faithful friend on account of his true humility. We read in Sirach: *There is nothing so precious as a faithful friend.* The Lord greatly loves his faithful friends, and that is because he has few faithful ones; and though many nominal friends, few true ones. Saint Gregory advises: "In God's service we must beware of two things: deceit and negligence."[b] Excessive love of self leads to deceit; minimal love of our neighbor leads to negligence, and reduces the love of God to less than it ought to be. A faithful friend possesses a truly humble heart. He observes all God's commandments and attributes nothing to his own glory that is accomplished by God. Saint Bernard writes: "You are indeed a faithful servant of the Lord when nothing of the Lord's abundant glory, which does not come from you but is channeled through you, remains clinging to your hands."[c] Sir 6:15

Many achieve nothing for God, because when they see that something of his glory is being channeled through them, they desire to be praised and honored themselves. And who is there these days who does not seek to steal this glory and have it attributed to himself, even from good works which he has not performed? Many are frauds and deceivers. Dear brothers, Saint Francis made himself subject to everyone and was obedient even to the tiniest commandment of God. If anyone ordered him to do anything he was ready to carry it out and be obedient to all.

Moreover, he sought no glory for himself in this world. On the contrary, he always acknowledged himself the greatest and vilest sinner. We read in the account of his life that he used to ask the Lord in prayer: "Why, O Lord, have you put me, wretched and stupid as I am, in charge of this Order?" And the Lord answered: "Have you not considered that I am above you in governing and caring for the Order? Since I am above you, you can put me in your place in governing and directing the Order." For the Lord's sake he attributed everything to the glory of God. Dear brothers, we should learn to be faithful like this ourselves. LMj V 3

Second, he was a congenial friend in everything he pledged himself to do, due to his utter purity of heart. We read in Proverbs: *He who* Prv 22:11

a. The Latin text is: *amicus conformis in ornamento corporis per Christi corpore ad exemplum conformitatem,* literally translated, a friend conformed in the adornment of body by conformity to the example of Christ's body.

b. Gregory I, *Moralia in Job* IX, c.34, n. 53, CCSL 143, 494.

c. Bonaventure had quoted this passage of Bernard of Clairvaux in his sermon of October 4, 1266, cf. supra 732-733.

loves purity of heart and whose speech is gracious will have the king as his friend, and not merely an earthly king, but the everlasting King of glory whose friendship ensures that we will arrive at the eternal
Wis 7:26 kingdom. For the Son of God who is *the reflection of eternal light and untarnished mirror of God's active power,* loves only the pure of heart. As the
Wis 1:4 Book of Wisdom tells us: *Wisdom will never make its way into a crafty soul nor stay in a body enslaved to sin.* Saint Francis cherished innocence and purity and so he won the friendship of the everlasting King. Dear brothers, anyone who desires to preserve innocence and purity of heart has to fulfill two necessary conditions. First, he must do penance by willingly undertaking afflictions; and second, he must have patience in tribulations inflicted by others. These are two refining virtues which purify the soul: the first as by water, the second as by
Ps 66:12 fire. We read in the Psalms: *We went through fire and water and you have brought us out to a place of rest.* Just as it is impossible to clean dirty clothes without washing them, so the soul cannot be purified without passing through the refining fire of penance and patience. Be-
Prv 17:17 cause a friend is *a friend at all times,* he has to be pure of heart. Sirach
Sir 34:30 reflects: *If a man washes after touching a corpse, and then touches it again, what is the good of his washing?*

Saint Francis was purified through penance in fasting, abstinence and afflictions. There is a remarkable similarity between him and Saint Benedict. Once when Saint Benedict was troubled by temptations of the flesh, he flung himself naked upon thorns and stinging
nettles to drive the temptations away.[a] Saint Francis also when he LMj V 3-4
was once in the Alps threw himself into thorns and freezing snow to curb temptations of the flesh.

Dear brothers, if from your earliest years, you have subdued the flesh, you will withstand its temptations all the more easily and be free of its lusts. I have an example to tell you about a young man who joined the Order of Lesser Brothers.[b] After he had been in the Order for a short time, he became troubled with temptations of the flesh. He was so aroused by lust that he was convinced he could neither withstand nor control it. He went to his provincial minister who was staying in the friary at that time, and confided to him how tormented he was with lust, and told him that he felt he ought to leave the friary, he was so plagued by the flesh. The provincial spoke many words of comfort to him, but to no avail. Subsequently, another brother told him how Saint Francis had overcome temptations of the flesh,

a. Gregory, *Dialogue* II 2.

b. Bonaventure may well have heard of this incident from one of the brothers. There is no written account of it.

and that once in the Alps he had flung himself stark naked into the snow and upon stinging nettles. So the young man decided that the best thing for him to do was subdue his flesh. So, for many days he fasted and abstained from tasty foods and undertook much discipline and for a long period severely scourged his flesh. The result was that whenever he was roused in one part of his flesh by lust or unchaste desires, some other part became so terrified with the scourges it had received, that his whole body began to tremble, even as soon as a thought about lust and sins of the flesh came into his head. He succeeded in chastising his flesh to the point where it was completely under control, and he became so chaste that he lived on in the Order untroubled and died in it a good and holy man. That is one way of safeguarding purity of heart.

A second refining virtue is patience in tribulations. When we are beset with sorrow and adversity caused by others, patience enables us to bear them willingly and joyfully and in this way to purify the soul. Saint Francis desired to undergo tribulations for Christ's sake
LMj IX 5-8 and to suffer in order to do something for him. Indeed, so much did he want to bear trials on behalf of his neighbor that he offered himself to the pagan Sultan, that he might be put to death on account of Christ. He used to say: "The Lord chose to undergo death for our justification and I earnestly desire to be put to death for purity of heart."

Dear brothers, when temptations of the flesh come upon you, be mindful of the sufferings and chastisements of the flesh. When tribulations assail you have patience in mind and strength of soul. Saint Jerome tells of a young man who was tempted by lust and greatly troubled. He advised him: "Chastise your body."[a] Then he told another: "Go to the young man, chastise him, torment him with harsh words and cover him with insults." Then in front of their brethren he made accusations against the young man and said such terrible things to him, that the young man was covered with such confusion that he did not know what to do. First, one accused him; then another. Finally, his superior said to him: "My friend, how do you feel?" He replied: "So many scornful and such awful things have been said to me, that I cannot go on living. How could I take pleasure in fornication?" You see, through the reproaches he suffered, the young man lost the desire to commit fornication. There are some, even a great number of people nowadays, who say they want to be chaste; yet, they take on no purifying penance. Without these, I tell

a. The complete text may be found in Jerome, *Epistula CXXV ad Rusticum,* (PL 22, 1079-1080); *Select Letters of Saint Jerome,* Loeb Classical Library, trans. by Frederick Wright (London, Cambridge, Boston: Harvard University Press, 1933), 396-438.

you, we cannot be chaste. Moreover, we ought to practice these purifying penances at all times, unlike so many who choose to do penance only during one period of the year, for example, in Lent. Afterwards, they fall away again. Dear brothers, that is simply not enough. We ought rather to be stamped with these purifying penances as with a seal.

Third, Saint Francis was an intimate friend of the Lord because of
Jn 3:29 the serenity of his contemplative soul. *The friend of the bridegroom,* that
is, of Christ, *who stands and hears him, rejoices greatly when he hears the*
Ex 2:10 *bridegroom's* voice. We read in the Book of Exodus that Moses, whose
name means "drawn out of the water," spoke with the Lord as with a
Ex 33:11 friend: *the Lord used to speak to Moses face to face, as a man speaks to his*
Ex 2:5-7; 15 friend. Moses was rescued from the river, and he had to flee from
Pharaoh, that is to say, he was poor. The Lord gave him nothing other than a staff; no riches, just a staff with which to make his way in the desert. Later he came to be on such intimate terms with the Lord that
Ex 3:1 he spoke with him as a friend. Moses was a shepherd and tended
flocks. What we read of Moses can be said of Saint Francis: the Lord spoke with him as a friend. As Moses was rescued from the river, so Saint Francis was saved from the dangerous currents of a worldly life. God gave him the staff of the cross to lead the people out of the Egypt of vice into the desert of the Order of Lesser Brothers. He carried in his hand nothing other than the staff of Christ's cross at the beginning of his conversion, during his life, and at its end. The Lord does not make his call through riches and learning, but through the
Ex 5:1; 14:26-29 cross. Exodus tells us that God called Moses to lead his people
through the desert into the Promised Land. Likewise, the Lord calls his chosen ones to the cross to lead others into the desert of repentance and at the end of this life into the Promised Land, that is, to the glory of the heavenly kingdom.

Moses received heavenly grace because the Lord invited him to a
Ex 19:3-6; 18-24 unique companionship with himself. We read in Exodus that he
spoke with God and God spoke with Moses and gave him the Law. The same, I tell you, happened to Saint Francis. He was called by the
Lord to a unique grace of friendship. Through his prayers he found LMj III 8
the *Rule* of the Lesser Brothers, and when he lost it he returned to the
mountain where he had found it and prayed again. And there once LMj IV 11
more by divine revelation and through the power of his prayers he found the lost rule. Then it was confirmed for him.

After this the stigmata of Christ crucified were imprinted on his LMj XIII 3
body. The Lord revealed himself to Saint Francis in the likeness of a Seraph. God appeared to him in the form of a Seraph. He appeared to him as the Crucified Lord so that he could speak with him as with a

friend. Perhaps you might ask: "How could this happen?" But it
surely did. Saint Paul was so caught up that he saw God's glory. Yet 2 Cor 12:1-4
early in his life he had been a most cruel persecutor of God's Church Acts 7:58
and he had been present at the stoning of Saint Stephen. I assure you, if we are true and faithful friends of Christ, he will still speak to us.

Fourth, as Christ's friend, he was made like him in appearance by having the marks of the crucified body of Christ imprinted visibly on his own. The text from the Book of Maccabees about Alexander and
Jonathan can be applied to Saint Francis: *he sent him a purple robe and* 1 Mc 10:20
a golden crown and you are to take our side and keep friendship with us. Alexander, that is, Christ, dispelling the darkness sent Saint Francis *a purple robe,* namely, the marks of his passion. He imprinted on him the stigmata of his own wounds. Hence Saint Paul's saying applies to
him: *I bear on my body the marks of Jesus.* Gal 6:17

LMj IV 4 What was the *purple robe?* I tell you that among the wondrous and well-nigh unheard of things we read about Saint Francis, there is one of a transfiguration when he appeared to his brothers in a burning chariot in the garden of the canons where he prayed for a whole night. While the brothers watched, the door opened and the burning chariot came in and went round the whole of the little house and they saw Saint Francis like a horseman in the chariot. He told his brothers that this happened for their consolation. Furthermore, he used to tell his brothers their own thoughts and the temptations they had. Thus, the Lord sent him the *purple robe* when he enlightened his mind.

He also sent him a *crown* on the feast of the Exaltation of the Cross when the golden sign appeared to him and within its wings the likeness of the Crucified Lord. He sent him first a chariot, then a likeness of the Seraph and the marks of the stigmata. So, I tell you, the passion of Jesus Christ was renewed in Saint Francis. He used to say that
LMj XIII 3 everyone who loved the Crucified Christ was his brother. He bore the stigmata of our Lord Jesus Christ on his hands, feet, and side. On his hands and feet what looked like nails with the points bent over at the back appeared, and they were made of what seemed like dark, sinewy skin. The points under his feet were bent back in such a way that you could put your middle finger into the ring they made. None of
LMj XIII 8 this is ancient history. I have seen and been in the company of some one who saw all this and told it to me.[a]

a. Alexander IV saw the stigmata while Saint Francis was still alive.

Dear brothers, God could truly call Saint Francis his friend and so he said to him: *Friend, go up higher.* What we have said so far provides the first reason why he was named God's friend.

II

Second, the text adds: *go up higher.* He addresses Saint Francis in these words as if to say to him on the feast of the Ascension,[a] "*Go up* with my help by calling on me in prayer. *Go up* after me, by following my example in your life. *Go up* to God's presence by contemplating the divine splendor. *Go up* because of me whom you shall see at last in glory."

The Lord says to him: *Go up* with my help, for I am the ladder on which you can ascend. This is signified by the ladder which Jacob
Gn 28:12 saw: *set up on the earth, and the top of it reached to heaven.* What is this ladder other than our Lord Jesus himself, the Son of God who through his humanity is set up on earth and by his divinity transcends the heavens? The flesh of Christ, though transformed, remains in union with our earth, and his divinity unites him to the Father who is in
Gn 28:12 heaven. On that ladder, Genesis tells us, *the angels of God were ascending and descending.* They were descending to the humanity of Christ who came in the flesh for us; and, sighing after divine wisdom, they were ascending to heaven. So the Lord says: *Go up* with my help. How is this achieved? By calling on God the Father through the Lord Jesus Christ. In that way you ought to ascend so that it may be said of you
Sg 3:6 what is said of the devout soul in The Song of Solomon: *Who is this that is going up from the desert, like a column of smoke, breathing of myrrh and frankincense, and every perfume the merchant knows?* The desert signifies penance; myrrh, which is bitter, the hardship of sorrow and tears; frankincense, devotion to God; and the perfumes, the spectrum of the virtues. Saint Francis followed Christ by praying con- LMj X 1-4
stantly and by shedding tears for his sins. He was always at prayer, and he wept so much that he lost his sight. He told those who asked him why he wept so much, as many rebuked him for it: "I do not consider my own sight more precious than the light the angels see."

Then the Lord says to him: *Go up* after me by following my example
1 Sm 14:13 perfectly in your life. We read in the Book of Samuel: *Then Jonathan climbed up on his hands and feet and his armor-bearer after him.* Jonathan may be taken here as a figure of Christ who was crucified through his hands and feet, and the armor bearer as Saint Francis, filled with the Holy Spirit, who carried the arms of Christ, namely,

a. The sermon was delivered on the vigil of the Ascension.

the cross, the nails, and the spear. These were the arms of our Re-
LMj VII 1; XV 9 deemer and Saint Francis bore them as second nature to him. He taught us to observe poverty like Christ, and he left this world naked
LMj VI 2 just as Christ did. After he had become famous and was sick with fever, he was told to eat some meat, and he did so. Then on Laetare Sunday he preached on the slave and the free woman,[a] and after- Gal 4:22
LMj VII 1-6 wards stripped himself naked [because he had eaten meat]. Both in his life and preaching he desired to be poor and to be seen to be poor.
LMj XIV 3-5 When he was dying he ordered his brothers to lay him completely naked on the ground with his arms outstretched in the form of a cross, and even to be buried like that. And so, I tell you, he was made utterly Christ-like and configured to him. Stretched out as it were on the cross on high, he went up higher. He was totally obedient to the command: *Go up* after me by following me literally.

Third, the Lord said to him: *Go up* to God's presence by contemplating the divine splendor. Moses was told by the Lord: *Ascend this* Dt 32:49
mountain, that is, the established mountain which is Christ. For the Lord himself is the established mountain. And standing before the people I will show you *the holy city Jerusalem.* Rv 21:10

We read in the Book of Job: *he hides the light in his hands.* It is a char- Jb 36:32
acteristic of light that no one can claim it as his own. Light is given only to spiritual men. As you know, as long as matter is devoid of form, it can have no ability to receive spiritual light.[b] In a similar way,
LMj VII 1-2 when a person is tied to temporal possessions which waste away and are dark and tainted, he cannot perceive the brilliance of divine light. That was the kind of advice Saint Francis gave to his brothers, having in mind the words of the Psalm: *fire has fallen on them,* that is, the fire Ps 58:9
of avarice and possessiveness, *and they shall not see the sun* of justice. The fire of avarice and possessiveness causes blindness, whereas the fire of poverty gives brightness and solace. As you know yourselves, an eagle untied and set free soars gracefully on high; but when the leaden ball is tied to its foot, it can neither fly nor soar on high, but falls to the ground. Likewise, when the soul of a Christian is shackled by the things of this earth, it cannot rise up to contemplate God. For this reason the Lord tells us: *Do not lay up for yourselves treasures on earth* Mt 6:19, 21
. . . for where your treasure is, there will your heart be also. I assure you that love of earthly possessions can no more be harmonized with love of heavenly treasures than the earth can be united to the heavens. All this is the teaching of our Lord Jesus Christ. However, I am not con-

a. Gal 4:22. This text occurred in the epistle for that Sunday.

b. Cf. *In II Sent.*, d. XII, dub. 2, (II, 307).

demning those who have riches, but have not set their hearts on them.

Fourth, the Lord said to him: *Go up* because of me whom you shall contemplate at last and in that you will be glorified. We read in The
Sg 7:8 Song of Solomon: *I will climb the palm tree and lay hold of its branches.*
The palm tree has a trunk whose lower part is very narrow. The section nearest the ground is thinner than the higher section of the trunk, which is not the case with any other tree. The palm tree is a
Ps 8:7 figure of Jesus Christ, who in his humanity was made *a little less than the angels,* and was small and weak in this world, and in his divinity is Lord and Creator of the angels and of all things. The fruit of this tree is nothing less than the joys of eternal sweetness and everlasting glory which consists in the vision, possession, and enjoyment of God. The Lord Jesus Christ, the Son of God, led our patron, Saint Francis, to eternal glory. So it is that the Son of God could say to him: *Friend, go up higher* to my presence that with me and in me you may be glorified forever. The miracles that he performed during his life prove that he was and remains the friend of God. There is a text about Mordecai
Est 6:7-8 in the Book of Esther that we may apply to Saint Francis: *The man whom the king desires to honor is to be clothed with the king's apparel and set upon the horse which the king has ridden and to have the royal crown upon his head.* During his life he bore the stigmata of our Lord Jesus Christ. At his death he rode upon the king's horse, that is, on the cross of Christ, when a cloud appeared on which he was taken to heaven. We can say
Acts 1:9 of him what Scripture says of Christ: *a cloud took him out of their sight.*
Furthermore, the royal crown was put upon his head when he was LMj XV 1-9
canonized and taken to heaven to be in the company of the saints. I tell you, they consider themselves blessed who were able to touch his body.

1 Kgs 19:19 His glory has been made great on earth. The Lord honored shepherds, prophets, and lawgivers. He gave his love to fishermen and made them princes. God loved all these and finally, after them, he set his love on merchants. He greatly loved Saint Francis who was a merchant. He made him a true merchant which Saint Francis became Mt 13:44-46
when he found the pearl of heavenly glory. He teaches us also to purchase the pearl.

Let us ask the Lord to give us in this life the grace to buy that pearl so that together with Saint Francis we may obtain the reward of the heavenly kingdom. May he grant us this who lives and reigns forever and ever. Amen.

The Morning Sermon on Saint Francis
Preached at Paris, October 4, 1267

The reference to the "Sisters of Saint Clare," enables us to date this sermon at a point after October 18, 1263, when Pope Urban IV changed the title of the Order of Saint Damian to that of the Order of Saint Clare.[a] A manuscript found in Troyes dates the sermon at October 4, 1267.

Behold my servant whom I uphold, Is 42:1
my chosen in whom my soul delights;
I have put my spirit upon him, he will bring forth justice to the nations.

Introduction

Who, do you think, is a faithful and wise servant, whom his master has set over his household, to give them their food at the proper time? These words from Saint Matthew's Gospel tell us how difficult it is to find a man fit to preach God's word, for such a man must be faithful and wise. Mt 24:45

Who, do you think, is faithful? We read in Proverbs: *Many men are called merciful; but who shall find a faithful man?* A faithful man is one who seeks nothing but God's glory in everything that he does. He seeks nothing to his own advantage, no praise, no favor, his only concern is God's glory and the salvation of others. It is indeed difficult to find a faithful man. Prv 20:6

Nor is it easy to find a wise man. According to Scripture, a wise man is one who gives *them their food at the proper time;* or as Saint Luke has it, who gives *them their portion of food at the proper time.* It is a great art in preaching to gauge wisely the mental range of the hearers, so as not to speak at too great a length or in words too condensed, nor too far beyond them or in words patronizingly simple. And who can achieve this? If a preacher manages it once, he fails in it often. I must confess, when I think about the standard required in a preacher of Lk 12:42

a. Clare was canonized in 1255. The change in name was made by Urban IV on Oct. 18, 1263, see Ignatius C. Brady, "St. Bonaventure's Sermons on Saint Francis," *Franziskanische Studien* 58 (1976): 132.

God's word, that I am getting old,[a] and I acknowledged I am hardly fit to do it. However, it is God who speaks in preaching. A preacher believes that sometimes he has preached well and thought out many fine ideas; sometimes he may have said nothing, for we read in Proverbs: *It is a human's part to prepare the soul; it is the Lord's to govern the tongue.*

Prv 16:1

I am afraid that if I preach with too much restraint, God will be angry with me. On the other hand, if I set myself to speak at great length on the glories of Saint Francis, I fear that some may think that in praising him I am really seeking praise for myself. It is difficult for me to speak on this matter. My aim, however, is to describe to you a holy and perfect man so that each of you may strive to imitate him. And in doing this I wish to put before you the example of Saint Francis, adhering all the while to the truth. At the beginning let us pray to the Lord that he will grant me to say and you to hear what is to his praise and glory and for our salvation.

We began with the text from Isaiah: *Behold my servant* . . . The meaning of these words refers primarily to our Lord Jesus Christ. However, what is true of the head may be applied to the members on account of their likeness and closeness to the head. Thus, these words may fittingly be understood of any holy and perfect person. But they highlight in a pre-eminent way the unique and perfect holiness of Saint Francis with regard to its root, its loftiness, and its radiance.

The root of perfect holiness lies in deep humility, its loftiness in well tried virtue, and its radiance in consummate love. Endowed with deep humility we are sustained by God; by well tried virtue we are made pleasing to him; and in consummate love we are taken up to God and brought closer to our neighbor. Consequently, in this text Saint Francis is commended for his deep humility, for which he was sustained by God, as its opening words say: *Behold my servant whom I uphold.* Then he is commended for his well tried virtue which made him pleasing to God, as the text continues: *my chosen, in whom my soul delights.* Third, he is commended for his consummate love whereby he passed over into God and opened his heart to his neighbor, as the text concludes: *I have put my spirit upon him* . . .

a. The Latin text has *senex* [old]. The Quaracchi editor questioned the word, (IX, 575). Saint Bonaventure was about fifty when he preached this sermon, 1267. According to his own words this puts him in the fifth age of man, since "*senectus*" suggests the period that runs from fifty to seventy. See *IV Sent.*, d. XL, q.3, dub. III (IX, 854): "*quarta, iuventus usque ad quinquagesimum; quinta, gravitas sive senectus usque ad septuagesimum; sexta, senium sive aetas decrepita usque in finem* [the fourth, youth until the fiftieth year; the fifth, dignity or maturity until the seventieth; the sixth, old age or failing age until the end]."

Who, then is such a perfect saint? Listen well. It is the person endowed with deep humility, well tried virtue, and consummate love. The root of holiness begins in humility, develops through well tried virtue, and is crowned in consummate love. Humility moves God to sustain us, well-tried virtue makes us pleasing to Him, but consummate love brings us to be totally rapt in God and to share what we have with others.

I

First of all, Saint Francis is commended here by the mouth of God for his deep humility: *Behold my servant whom I uphold.* What the Lord
says in Haggai may be applied to him: *In that day I will take you, O* Hg 2:23
Zerubbabel my servant, and make you like a seal, for I have chosen you. This text says: *I will make you like a seal* and that by the signs and marks of the passion impressed on you by the Word of the Almighty. And why does he say this? Because Saint Francis was a servant of God, humble in his reverence for Him, more humble still in caring for his neighbor, and most humble of all in despising himself. I admire the humility of Saint Francis more than all his other virtues.

He was a humble servant of God in the reverence he had toward Him. For this reason what the Lord says in the Book of Job may be
applied to Saint Francis: *Have you considered my servant Job, that there is* Jb 1:8
none like him on the earth, a blameless and upright man, who fears God and turns away from evil?

God calls Job his servant on account of his humility. He was committed to God's service and reckoned a *servant* of outstanding reverence for God because he was blameless in his motives, *upright* in what he chose, *God-fearing* in his feelings, and *turned away* from evil in his actions. In all that he did and suffered he praised God. Moreover,
we read of Job that *there were born to him seven sons and three daughters.* Jb 1:2
The name Job is interpreted "sorrowing," and this truly describes
LMj X 4 Saint Francis, because his life was filled with sorrow. He was always
LMj III 7 in tears weeping over his own sins or the sins of others. Looking back
to the very early days of the Order, we find that Saint Francis had seven friars and he was the eighth. At the Lord's bidding he sent them out two by two in the four directions of the compass, and in accordance with his desire the Lord brought them back together again.

LMj II 7-8 Saint Francis also had three "daughters." At the outset of his religious life he repaired three churches: one dedicated to Saints Cosmas and Damian, another dedicated to Saint Peter the Apostle and another to the Blessed Virgin Mary. It was in the last mentioned church that the Lord revealed to him the form of life he was to lead. Besides

this, he founded three religious Orders: the first, the Order of Friars
Minor; the second, the Order of Sisters of Saint Clare. Earlier these
had been called the Poor Ladies of Saints Cosmas and Damian, but
now, with Saint Clare having been canonized, they are called the Sisters of Saint Clare. The third is called the Order of Penitents, known
as the Penitent Brethren. These Orders may be understood as his LMj IV 6
three "daughters," and they were founded for the purpose of honoring God. We see, then, that Saint Francis revered God and was his
Ps 116:16 humble servant. With the Psalmist he could say: *O Lord I am your servant, I am your servant, the son of your handmaid.* We should follow the
example of Saint Francis and serve God with reverence.

Mt 10:28 Scripture admonishes us that we should *fear him who can destroy
both body and soul in hell.* We ought to revere God and submit ourselves
Mal 1:6 to His will. Otherwise, He will reproach us, saying: *If I am a father,
where is my honor? And if I am the Lord, where is my fear?* And likewise
Jb 19:16 those words from Job: *I called my servant, and he gave me no answer.* The
Lord calls us through interior inspirations, through preaching,
through chastisements, blessings, and the good example of holy people. Yet we remain unmoved despite what is written in Saint Luke's
Lk 12:47 Gospel: *That servant, who knew his master's will but did not make ready or
act according to his will, shall receive a severe beating.* Let us recall once
more that Saint Francis was a humble servant of God through the
reverence he bore Him.

Second, this servant of God was humbler still in caring for his
1 Cor 9:19 neighbor. As Saint Paul writes to the Corinthians: *For though I am free
from all men, I have made myself a slave to all.* Our holy Father Francis became all things to all men and the servant of everybody. He wanted
even to be the servant of the most despised. And once, walking along LMj VI 4
the road, he promised obedience to one of his brothers. When he was Test 1-3
still in the world he had a great loathing for lepers. But after his con- LMj II 6
version he devoted himself to taking care of them. He washed their
feet, bandaged their ulcers and sores, cleaned away the pus and rot-
ten blood, and kissed their feet. He cared for his neighbor to this extent in order to make himself contemptible and to implore God's
Gal 5:13 grace. Saint Paul tells the Galatians: *For you were called to freedom,
brethren; only do not use your freedom as an opportunity for the flesh, but
through love be servants of one another.* Such should our freedom be.

Someone might object that while it is true we must serve our
neighbor, we are not obliged to serve lepers. But God himself did not
disdain this kind of service. He bent down to wash the dirty feet of
Jn 13:13-16 his disciples, and then said to them: *You call me Teacher and Lord; and
you are right, for so I am. If I then, your Lord and Teacher, have washed your
feet, you also ought to wash one another's feet. For I have given you an*

example, that you also should do as I have done to you. Truly, truly, I say to you, a servant is not greater than his master; nor is he who is sent greater than he who sent him. Commenting on this passage Saint Augustine remarks: "Let us with humility do to one another what in humility was done by the Most High. Great is this commendation of humility. And in fact the brethren do this to one another even literally when they receive one another as guests. And among the brethren where this custom of washing the feet is not practiced, they do in their hearts what they do not do with their hands. But it is much better that it should be done with the hands, for what Christ did, the Christian ought not to disdain to do. When the body stoops down to the feet of a brother, then in the heart itself the affection of humility is either enkindled or, if it is already there, confirmed."[a]

Pope Gregory the Ninth, who was a man full of wisdom, because of his great friendship with Saint Francis, followed his example closely. He kept a leper in his room and, dressed in the habit of a friar, looked after him. One day the leper said to him: "Has the Supreme Pontiff no one but an old man like you, to look after me?" The Pope was exhausted.[b] We do good in serving our neighbor. This is why Saint Paul tells us: *I pommel my body and subdue it,* and the Book of I Cor 9:27
Lamentations says: *It is good for a man that he has borne the yoke from his* Lam 3:27
youth.

We have seen, then, that Saint Francis was humble through his reverence for God, and humbler still in taking care of his neighbor. Coming now to the third point, we find him humblest of all despising himself, and he did so in order to follow him of whom it is written: *He* Phil 2:7
emptied himself, taking the form of a servant. Christ was conceived in the form of a servant and, therefore, He could say of Himself: *I am small* Ps 119:141; 22:6
and despised. I am a worm and no man; scorned by men, and despised by the people. The Lord revealed His glory in heaven, and for coveting it, Lucifer and the angels who copied him came to perdition. Together with himself, Lucifer brought down humanity, created in God's image. Gn 1:27-3:24
Christ did not reveal His humility in heaven, but desiring to show us the root of wisdom, He humbled Himself. Anyone who desires to possess the wisdom of Christ must begin at the root of holiness, just as
LMj II 2 Saint Francis did. When he first changed his way of life the townsfolk pelted him with mud from the streets and threw stones at him, he
LMj II 4 went naked in front of the bishop and all the people announcing

a. Augustine, *In Iohannis Evangelium tractatus* CXXIV, tr. 58, CCSL 36, 399-400; *St. Augustine: Tractates on the Gospel of John* 55-111, The Fathers of the Church, vol. 90 (Washington: The Catholic University of America Press, 1994), 21-22.

b. It seems clear enough from this passage that the leper did not know that it was the pope who was serving him.

that he had given up all his worldly goods. Later, after he had become LMj VI 2
a man of outstanding holiness, he had himself dragged naked through mud. He could not bear to hear himself praised. From all this we see that he reached the summit of perfect holiness and humility. Saint Bernard writes: "The truly humble man wants to be considered despicable rather than to be proclaimed a humble man;"[a] and Saint Gregory writes: "As the proud glory in their superiority, so the humble rejoice in being despised."[b] Where does humility have its source? Most surely in the depths of the heart.

Brother Pacifico, who first introduced the Order of Lesser LMj IV 9
Brothers into France, was a man of great holiness. One day while LMj VI 6
praying in a church with Saint Francis, he fell asleep. In his sleep he saw heaven opened and there in heaven a glorious throne. When he asked whose throne it might be, he was told it was the throne which Lucifer had lost because of his pride, and it was now reserved for Saint Francis because of his humility. When he woke up he asked Saint Francis: "What do you think of yourself?" Saint Francis answered: "I think I am the greatest sinner in the world." Pacifico rejoined: "But there are murderers and robbers and all kinds of wicked people." "Even the greatest sinner in the world," replied Saint Francis, "would be holier than I am if he had received so many graces."

We should take careful note of this remarkable fact. Of everything that can cause us to wonder, it is among the greatest wonders that of all the figures in the Old and New Testaments, God has exalted only those who were humiliated and despised.

In the Old Testament the Lord firmly exalted three men. Saul was not among them because he was not steadfast in virtue. These three were Joseph, Moses, and David. What do we read of Joseph? The
Ps 105:17, 18 Psalmist says: *He sent a man before them: Joseph who was sold for a slave.* The text goes on to say that he was imprisoned and bound with fetters; and he served his fellow prisoners. Then afterwards Pharaoh
Ps 105:21 *made him lord of his house.*

Ex 3:1 Moses was adopted as son by Pharaoh's daughter. The Lord did not promise him exaltation in the land of Egypt, but when Pharaoh's anger blazed against him and he had become a shepherd in the desert, then the Lord appeared to him and revealed to him his judgments.

And what is said about David, what do we read of him? He himself
Ps 78:70-71 tells us: *And he chose his servant David, and took him from the sheepfolds;*

a. Bernard of Clairvaux, Sermon 16:10, *On the Song of Songs*, translated by Kilian Walsh, introduction by M. Corneille Halflants (Spencer, MA: Cistercian Publications, 1971), 121.

b. Gregory, *Dialogue* I 5.

from tending the ewes that had young he brought him to be shepherd of Jacob, his people, and Israel his inheritance. We find also in the New Testament that [all Christ's disciples] humbled themselves, and Christ greatly cherishes the humble.

If someone owned a precious gem which the more worthless it was considered, the more precious it became, how willingly he would show it to those who disparage it. Strength of spirit increases through reproaches; what folly it is, therefore, to seek praise. The Saints wanted to be despised by others in order to be pleasing to God. As Saint Gregory says: "If holy people who achieve so much, reckon themselves as practically worthless, what is to be said of those puffed up with pride, yet devoid of virtue?"[a] Saint Anselm tells us that there are six degrees of humility, and he who succeeds in arriving at the sixth, possesses the fulness of grace.[b] The first degree of humility is to account oneself despicable; the second is to speak of oneself as despicable; the third, to convince others that one is despicable; the fourth, to want to be judged despicable; the fifth, to want to be spoken of as despicable; and the sixth, to want to be treated as despicable. At this point one is close to God and is his humble servant. Saint Francis himself says: "What a man is before God, that he is and no more." A man is worth no more than God reckons him. It is extraordinary that we want to find favor with other people whose approval does nothing for us, and we care little to be pleasing to him whose favor is the summit of holiness. So it is that Saint Francis is commended in this text for his deep humility.

Adm XX; LMj VI 1

For his humility Saint Francis was sustained by a threefold mercy of God. We read in the Psalms: *Uphold your servant for good: let not the proud calumniate me. Deal with your servant according to your mercy.* This humble servant who revered God, took care of his neighbor and despised himself, and was found worthy to be sustained by God's mercy. Because he despised himself he was sustained by God's forgiving mercy; then because he took care of his neighbor, he was sustained by God's protecting mercy; and third, because he so revered God, he was sustained by God's liberating and uplifting mercy.

Ps 119: 122, 124

First, Saint Francis despised himself and for that he was sustained by God's forgiving mercy. Mary says in the Magnificat: *He has put down the mighty from their thrones and exalted the humble. He has helped his servant Israel, in remembrance of his mercy.* Israel, also named Jacob, struggled with the angel and was crippled. But he was sus-

Lk 1:52, 53

Gn 32:24-25

a. Gregory I, *Homiliarum in evangelia* I, hom. 7, n. 4, (PL 76, 1103); *Gregory the Great: Forty Gospel Homilies*, Cistercian Studies Series 123, translated by David Hurst (Kalamazoo: Cistercian Publications, 1990), 27.

b. Pseudo-Anselmus, *De Similitudo*, c. 100-109, (PL 159, 665-68); cf also *Epistola* 75, (PL 159, 112).

tained by God's mercy because from his stock the Son of God was to
Gn 32:25 be born, through whom all sins were to be forgiven. It was first of all
necessary for the sinew of his thigh to shrink, which may be interpreted as "to mortify the flesh." In the Book of Daniel the three
Dn 3:38-39 young men prayed: *And at this time there is no prince . . . no place to make an offering before you or to find mercy. Yet with a contrite heart and a humble spirit may we be accepted* by the Lord. If you desire to be sustained by God's forgiving mercy, you must first struggle with the angel in
Ps 50:17 prayer in order to curb evil desires, and then you can offer the sacrifice of a contrite heart. Here on earth the soul is set on fire by evil desires and objects enticing the senses, as if it were burning in a fiery furnace. But if the angel comes down into the furnace and penetrates our spirit with God's grace, then we will humble ourselves and begin to mortify the flesh and so be pleasing to God. As the Book of Daniel
Dn 3:50 records, the angel will make *the midst of the furnace like the blowing of wind bringing dew,* and so the young will not feel the flame of sensual desires, and should they feel them, they will do them no harm.

Saint Francis did not cease from weeping for his sins from the mo- LMj III 6
ment of his conversion to the time the Lord appeared to him and as-
Lk 7:47; Mt 5:26 sured him that his *many sins were forgiven him down to the last farthing.* I would like to have this assurance more than anything else in the
Lk 7:36-50 world. It was given also to Mary Magdalene. And so, because Saint Francis despised himself, he was sustained by God's forgiving mercy.

Second, because he took care of his neighbor he was sustained by
Is 41:9-10 God's protecting mercy. We read in Isaiah: *You are my servant. I have chosen you and not cast you away. . . . I have strengthened you and helped you*
Lk 9:62 *and the right hand of my Just One has upheld you.* Saint Francis did not turn back; after putting his hand to the plough, he did not look back. He was chosen and not cast away. He avoided not only mortal sin,
Is 41:10 but also venial sin, as far as this is humanly possible. *The right hand of my Just One has upheld you,* says Isaiah. Who is this Just One? Saint
1 Jn 2:1 John gives us the answer: *We have an advocate in heaven with the Father, Jesus Christ the just. The right hand of my Just One* is the right hand of Almighty God who kept him safe from all his enemies. When demons attacked him and thrashed him bodily, he always had recourse to
Ps 63:7-8 God's help. He was able to make his own the words of the Psalm: *In the shadow of your wings I sing for joy. My soul clings to you; your right hand upholds me.* Anyone who seeks protection must place himself under God's right hand.

Third, Saint Francis revered God and for this he was sustained by
Ps 72:24 God's liberating mercy. As the Psalm says: *You have held me by the right hand; and by your will you have guided me and with your glory you have*

received me. Moreover, we read in the Book of Proverbs: *Humiliation follows the proud: and glory shall uphold the humble of spirit.* So it is that the Lord himself says: *For those who honor me I will honor . . . For great is the power of God alone and he is honored by the humble.* Prv 29:23 1 Sm 2:30; Sir 3:20

Only those who honor God will be honored and glorified by him. Since only the humble honor God, only the humble will be glorified. Therefore, if you desire to be sustained by this threefold mercy, be a humble servant by despising yourself, taking care of your neighbor, and revering God. This is the first stage of the Christian philosophy of his life. When Dioscorus asked Saint Augustine what the Christian philosophy of his life chiefly consists of, Saint Augustine replied: "If you were to ask me what is the most important factor in rhetoric, I would answer: eloquence. If you were to ask me a second or third time or even a hundred times, I would still reply: eloquence. This is how I would answer your question. If you ask me what is the essence of the Christian philosophy of life, I answer: humility. And were you to ask me a second or a third time, or even a hundred times, I would still reply: humility."[a] The Gospel also teaches this and there is not a page nor a line in Holy Scripture which does not proclaim humility. If we are proud, we fall from true wisdom, as Saint Paul remarks: *Claiming to be wise they become fools.* True wisdom was that of the Prophets and Apostles. Rom 1:22

From these reflections Saint Francis's deep humility will now be apparent to everyone.

II

We pass now to say something about the well tried virtue of this man. Let us recall the words: my chosen, in whom my soul delights. The word "election" signifies eminence, which raises the person higher than others. Saint Francis was chosen not merely to be taken from among sinners, but also to be raised high among the virtuous. Hence a text from Sirach about wisdom can be applied to him: *In the multitude of the elect she shall have praise, and among the blessed she shall be blessed.* There are three reasons why Saint Francis is to be accounted as chosen by God and of well tried virtue: his perfect observance of the Law and Gospel, his indomitable zeal for the Christian faith, and his exceedingly fervent love of the Crucified Savior. Sir 24:4

First of all, Saint Francis was chosen because of his perfect observance of the Law and Gospel. We read in Isaiah: *Behold, I have refined* Is 48:10

a. Augustine, *Epistola 118*, n. 22, (PL 33, 442); *Saint Augustine: Letters*, vol. 2, The Fathers of the Church, vol. 18, translated by Wilfrid Parsons (New York: Fathers of the Church, 1953), 282.

you, but not like silver; I have chosen you in the furnace of poverty. Poverty is a furnace which consumes some and refines others. It consumes those whose poverty is coupled with impatience and covetousness Sir 13:24 for worldly goods. As the Book of Sirach says: *Poverty is evil in the opinion of the ungodly.* On the other hand, voluntary poverty which carries with it imitation of Christ and conformity to him, is a furnace which purifies God's chosen ones. The three young men mentioned in the Book of Daniel were in a furnace of this kind. Commenting on this Chrysostom says: "And as one like the Son of God appeared in the midst of the fiery furnace with the three young men, so in a similar way the Son of God appears in the world among the poor." The Lord Lk 14:33 Jesus says: *Whoever of you does not renounce all that he has cannot be my disciple.* Having spoken earlier about the need to hate one's very life in Lk 14:27 order to be his disciple, he adds: *Whoever does not bear his own cross and come after me, cannot be my disciple.* That poverty which is inseparable from bearing one's own cross, is like a refining furnace, and is an integral part of gospel discipleship. Life according to the Gospel consists in self-denial, purity, simplicity, and every form of kindness. Self-denial eradicates greed; purity, lust; simplicity, inquisitiveness; humility, pride; and kindness drives away anger. By keeping these virtues, a person is a follower of the naked Christ in the furnace of poverty. If I choose to be greedy, unchaste, or proud, this is not to be in the furnace which refines, but in that which destroys.

Saint Francis was like pure gold, refined in the furnace of poverty. How wretched are those who go into this furnace and then jump out again. They are not worthy to be purified. Dear brothers, it is a noble Dn 3:50 thing to enter this furnace, for as we said earlier: *The angel made the midst of the furnace like the blowing of a wind bringing dew.*

A brother who stayed with Saint Francis at Montepulciano near Siena, related how one day they could find only some stale bread to eat.[a] They went to the entrance of a church where they ate the bread and drank water. When they had finished eating they went into the church where Saint Francis was filled with great joy. He stood there for a whole hour and this tired the other friar. Afterwards, he asked Saint Francis what he had experienced. He told him that he had never felt such sweetness from the time of his conversion. How pleasing to God is poverty combined with self-denial, purity, simplicity, humility, and kindness. Afterwards, he went to Saint Peter's in Rome so that the Apostle might be his surety that he never deflected from his promise to observe poverty. Anyone who seeks

a. Unknown until this point, the incident was afterwards transcribed in the *Actus Beati Francisci et Sociorum eius*. Ed. Paul Sabatier in *Collection d'Etudes et de Documents* IV (Paris, 1902).

earthly comfort, forfeits heavenly consolation, as when God *rained* Ps 78:24; Wis 16:20; Nm 11:5
down upon the sons of Israel manna to eat, a food having in it all that is deli-
cious and the sweetness of every taste, not sensing its sweetness, they pined after
the melons and garlic. Furthermore, God made streams come out of the Nm 20:8-13; Ps 78:16; 105:41
rock for the Jews. Therefore, to everyone in the furnace of poverty observing self-denial, purity, simplicity, humility, and kindness, God will give his grace and make them like pure gold.

Second, Saint Francis was chosen by God because of his indomi-
table zeal for the Christian faith. Of Saint Paul it is written: *He is a cho-* Act 9:15
sen instrument of mine to carry my name before the Gentiles and kings and the sons of Israel. The Apostle Paul was endowed with this zeal because he was consumed with desire to spread faith in Christ among the Jews, then the Greeks, and afterwards among the Romans. Saint Francis wanted to be poor for Christ's sake, and because of his zeal for the
LMj IX 6-8 faith he became God's chosen instrument. He journeyed into many countries to spread the Christian faith. On three occasions, he attempted to go overseas but was prevented by shipwreck. He travelled to Miramamolin in Spain and then to Morocco, where later our friars were martyred.[a] On a third occasion, he went to the Sultan of Egypt and proclaimed the Christian faith to him, longing to be torn to pieces for the faith. The Sultan said to him: "Let us bring in our wise men so that we can debate our faith and yours." Saint Francis replied: "Our faith is beyond human reason and reason anyway is of no use except to a believer. Besides, I cannot argue from Holy Scripture because your wise men do not believe the Scriptures. Instead, make a fire of wood, and I will go into it together with your wise men. Whichever of us is burnt, his faith is false." On hearing this the Sultan's wise men withdrew. The Sultan began to smile and said: "I don't think I will find anybody to go into the fire with you." "Then," answered Saint Francis, "I will go into the fire alone, and if I am burnt, account it to my sins; if I am not, then embrace the Christian faith." The Sultan replied: "I could not dare do that, for fear my people would stone me. But I believe that your faith is good and true." And from that moment the Christian faith was imprinted on his heart.

Third, Saint Francis was chosen by God on account of his exceedingly fervent love of Christ crucified. He could make his own the
words of The Song of Solomon: *My beloved is all radiant and ruddy, cho-* Sg 5:10
sen out of thousands. Christ himself was *radiant* in the incarnation be-
LMj X 7; I 5 cause of his sinlessness and *ruddy* in his passion. Saint Francis had

a. AF III, 579-96; La *scimitarra del Miramolino: Relazione dei primi martiri francescani del Marrocco (1220)*, translated by A. Ghinato (Roma, 1962).

the greatest devotion to the incarnation and the cross of Christ. On
account of his love of the cross, his skin became a dark reddish color,
he was interiorly crucified and transformed into Christ. Because of LMj XIII 3
his love of the Virgin's Son he was transformed, even while still alive,
into the Crucified, by the Seraph with six wings that appeared to
him. He was pierced with huge, strong nails, the points of which
were bent over under the soles of his feet, and there was a wound in
Sg 4:9 his side. In the words of the Song of Solomon he could say: *You have
wounded my heart.* He was dark-skinned, which was accentuated because of his austerities. Yet at his death his flesh became radiant LMj XV 2
white and ruddy. He asked the brothers to let him lie naked on the LMj XIV 4
ground, when he was dead, for the length of time it takes to walk a
Gal 2:20; 6:14 mile. With Saint Paul he could say: *I have been crucified with Christ . . .
Far be it from me to glory except in the cross of our Lord Jesus Christ.*

It is evident then that Saint Francis was chosen by God. Let us ask God to hear our prayers.

The Evening Sermon on Saint Francis
Preached at Paris, October 4, 1267

Behold my servant whom I uphold . . .

Earlier today we said in praise of Saint Francis that he was perfect and holy. He is commended in the text we began with for the root, loftiness, and radiance of his perfect holiness. The root of perfect holiness lies in deep humility, its loftiness in well tried virtue, and its radiance in consummate love. For these three graces Saint Francis is worthy of the highest praise. He was sustained by God because of his deep humility, pleasing to God for his well tried virtue, and through his consummate love he opened his heart to his neighbor. I showed how his deep humility is commended in this text: *Behold my servant whom I uphold. . . .* This servant was humble because of his reverence for God; humbler still in caring for his neighbor; and humblest of all in despising himself. Thus he was sustained by God's forgiving mercy because he despised himself; by his protecting mercy because of his care for his neighbor; and by his liberating mercy because of the reverence he bore him. I pointed out, further, that he was chosen by God on three accounts: his perfect observance of the Law and Gospel, his indomitable zeal for the Christian faith, and his deep love of Is 42:1
the Crucified Christ. Now it remains for me to explain how he was pleasing to God, how God put his *spirit upon him* and how Saint Francis brought *forth justice to the nations.*

Let us ask God, then, that in the remainder of this sermon he may grant me to say something worthwhile and you to draw inspiration from it, to his honor and glory. Amen.

Behold my servant whom I uphold . . .

As we said earlier, deep humility is the condition of our being sustained by God. Likewise, well tried virtue is the chief condition of our being pleasing to God. When God utters those words to a person: *My chosen, in which my soul delights,* how lovely they are in the hearing. It pleases God's gracious will to guide our souls. The divine will is drawn toward the Son in whom God delights uniquely, for in him is found the perfection of every virtue. Therefore, it is through well tried virtue that a person is made pleasing to God, the Lord of all virtues. The leader of an army delights in none other than a valiant soldier.

To speak now of Saint Francis, we should take note that he was pleasing to God because of his unquestioning obedience, his passion for righteousness, and the refinement of his devotion to God. Among the virtues these three are especially efficacious to make us pleasing
Is 62:4 to God. And if we are endowed with them God will delight in us.

First of all, we will be pleasing to God by unquestioning obedience. Thus Isaiah says: *You shall no more be termed Forsaken, and your land shall be no more termed Desolate; but you shall be called My delight is in her . . . for the Lord delights in you.*

Our land will never be deserted by the Lord through his abandoning it; most surely not, but only through our abandoning him. When God is far from us, then we must become as desolate land. In uttering those words: *You shall be called My delight is in her,* the Lord is speaking to the obedient soul, that is, to one who does nothing other than
Jn 8:29 what pleases God, one utterly obedient to the divine will. Saint Francis strove with all his powers to imitate Christ and in truth he could say: "I will not forsake you; I will not forsake him who sent me, for *I do what is pleasing to him.* And if I am sick, then I freely will that I be LMj II 1
sick."

The Lord showed his delight in Saint Francis by choosing to speak to him not as a stranger, but as an intimate friend, for the crucifix spoke to him, which is now preserved by the Sisters at San Damiano.

Lk 1: 28 Perhaps you may ask: "What really happened there?" Then I in
Lk 1:11 turn will ask you: "What took place when the angel said to the Virgin Mary: *'Hail Mary, full of grace?'* " or "What did Zechariah experience when the angel, *standing on the right side of the altar of incense,* spoke to
Rom 12:2 him?"

If we are ready to do what pleases God He will make His will known to us. As the Apostle Paul says: *Do not be conformed to this world, but be transformed by the renewal of your mind, that you may prove what is the will of God, what is good and acceptable and perfect.* God, who is Cre- LMj XI 1-9
ator, Sanctifier, and Glorifier, wills only what is good.

Saint Francis was once in doubt whether he should give himself to a life of prayer or to a life of preaching. For a whole week he brooded over the matter because it was not entirely clear to him what he ought to do. When at last he recognized that he should devote himself to preaching, he girded himself and went for six miles around preaching to the people. He came upon a field full of birds
Sir 45:23; Nm 25:8 and the birds listened to him.

Second, Saint Francis was pleasing to God because of his passion for righteousness. We read in Scripture that *Phinehas in the goodness and readiness of his soul appeased God for Israel* when he pierced with his spear both the fornicator and his mistress. Sir 44:16; 2 Kgs 2:11 No sacrifice is more pleasing to God than zeal for souls. 1 Kgs 8:23 This zeal brought Christ down to earth and led him to endure many sufferings; it caused Enoch and Elijah to LMj IV 9 be taken up into heaven. The Lord will save the just and condemn the wicked.

As a result of this same zeal Saint Francis became rapt in ecstasy and was raised to the heights. Brother Pacifico had a vision in which LMj IV 4 he saw Saint Francis marked with the sign of the cross formed by two radiant swords, the one stretching from his head to his feet, the other from hand to hand across his chest. Likewise, because of his zeal, he was found worthy to be rapt in ecstacy in the church of San Rufino, where later he was to preach. His brothers were in a little shelter, about a mile away, that is, according to the measurements in this country, about half a league away.[a] Saint Francis appeared to them in a fiery chariot, and their minds were so filled with light that each could see into the consciences of the others. Saint Francis was taken up with Elijah and made pleasing to God. God's delight was in him because of his passion for righteousness. Few people nowadays worry about the wickedness the devil causes. Saint Francis, however, wept daily over his own sins and those of others. Ps 69:30-31

Third, he was pleasing to God because of the refinement of his devotion. As the Psalm says: *I will praise the name of the Lord,* and continues: Ps 50:23 *this will please the Lord more than an ox or a bull with horns and hoofs* and as another Psalm tells us: *He who brings thanksgiving as his sacrifice honors me.*

Saint Francis was so carried away with the praise of God that he went into ecstasy while reciting the Divine Office, as his companion related. As he felt the ecstasy coming over him, he said to the brother: "Leave me." The brother suggested: "Wouldn't it be better to recite the Office first?" Saint Francis replied: "I cannot experience LMj X 5 this kind of visitation at any time just as I decide, for that is not in my power; but I can begin the Divine Office whenever I like. I prefer to say the office later rather than forfeit this visitation." One day a Cistercian abbot met Saint Francis and asked him to pray for him. When Saint Francis did so, the abbot experienced a consolation he had never known before.

We see, then, Saint Francis is commended in this text for his deep humility and well tried virtue.

---

a. No doubt it was the cosmopolitan character of his listeners that prompted Bonaventure to give this explanation.

III

Finally, he is commended for his consummate love as the text concludes: *I have put my spirit upon him, he will bring forth justice to the*
Rom 5:5 *nations.* Saint Paul writes to the Romans: *God's love has been poured into our hearts through the Holy Spirit who has been given to us.* When we receive grace, we receive the Holy Spirit. The Lord put his *Spirit* into Saint Francis, and afterwards *he brought forth justice.* Thus we read in
Mt 10:20 the Gospel of Saint Matthew: *For it is not you who speak, but the Spirit of your Father speaking through you.* Our text asserts that God *put* his *spirit upon him.* What spirit is this? It is the spirit who is enabled to teach others, that is to say, God put the hierarchical spirit upon him.[a]
Jb 26:13 Scripture says: *By his Spirit the heavens were made fair,* and Saint Gregory writes: "The virtues of preachers are the adornment of heaven."[b] I maintain, then, that God gave him the spirit of purification, enlightenment, and perfection, because the Spirit of the Lord first purified him, then enlightened him, and finally brought him to perfection.[c]

First, the Lord endowed him with the spirit of purification of
Ez 3:14 which Ezechiel speaks: *The Spirit also lifted me and took me up, and I went away in bitterness in the heat of my spirit; for the hand of the Lord was with me, strengthening me.*

Our spirit is purified when it has lost the desire for earthly things. As light makes the air purer, so the soul becomes pure when it is united with the Eternal God. When the soul is united by love to a
Ez 3:12 creature, it takes on that creature's likeness. Ezechiel's text says: *The*
Jb 7:15 *Spirit lifted me,* and Job writes: *My soul would choose to be suspended.* When the soul is lifted up to God it must needs experience bitterness and conceive a distaste for created things past, present and future. As
Is 38:15 King Hezekiah lamented: *All my sleep has fled because of the bitterness of my soul.*

Saint Francis was raised on high by this purifying, strengthening, LMj III 8
and uplifting spirit. When he went to Rome a priest saw him lifted a few feet from the ground into the air to about the height of a barrel, and the brothers often saw him lifted from the ground. All this happened because of his utmost purity. The angels lifted him into the air;

---

a. "Hierarchical spirit" is clumsy, but it is so technical that the editors could find no other expression, cf. supra, 526 a.

b. Gregory, *Homiliarum in evangelia* II, hom. 30, n. 7, (PL 76, 1224); *Gregory the Great: Forty Gospel Homilies*, Cistercian Studies Series 123, translated by David Hurst (Kalamazoo: Cistercian Publications, 1990), 243.

c. Pseudo-Dionysius, *The Celestial Hierarchy*, c. 3, n. 2, in *Pseudo-Dionysius: The Complete Works*, translated by Colm Luibheid and Paul Rorem, The Classics of Western Spirituality (New York: Paulist Press, 1987), 154; Saint Bonaventure is referring here to the classical three ways: *via purgativa, illuminativa, unitiva*; See *De triplici via* (VIII, 3-23).

as it is recorded, they lifted Saint Mary Magdalene while she was at prayer.[a] Such graces are given only to those who have set themselves above worldly desires.

Second, the Lord endowed Saint Francis with the spirit of enlightenment. Therefore the text of Sirach may be said of him: *In the midst* Sir 15:5
of the church wisdom shall open his mouth and fill him with the spirit of wis-
LMj XI 1-2 *dom and understanding.* Saint Francis was not an educated man, nor
did he have a teacher. Yet he preached without ever uttering a word
deserving of rebuke. The same is true of Saint Anthony.[b] The Apos- Acts 4:13
tles themselves were uneducated men, yet they were filled with wisdom; they preached, and they taught others.

LMj XII 7 Saint Francis once had to preach in the presence of Pope Honorius. With guidance from Pope Gregory, who was then cardinal bishop of Ostia, he prepared his sermon. When the time came to deliver it, his mind went blank, so he explained: "Someone, namely Pope Gregory IX, drew up for me a very learned sermon which I was going to preach, but now I've forgotten it completely. Wait a while and I'll ask the Lord to give me something to say." And after he had prayed, he preached a splendid sermon. We can apply to him the
words of the Psalm: *I understand more than the aged.* He was a great Ps 119:100
teacher. He spoke accurately about creation and the simplicity of eternal truths. But he did not have the required competence from himself, he was enlightened entirely from on high. He unraveled hidden mysteries and he appeared to those absent. He possessed the spirit of enlightenment. If we want to receive the light of this wisdom, we must not rest content with earthly things.

Third, the Lord endowed Saint Francis with the spirit of perfection, which makes a person firm and unshakeable and brings completion and fulfillment. Of this spirit Sirach says: *Come over to me all* Sir 24:26-27
you that desire me, and be filled with my fruits. For my spirit is sweet above honey and my inheritance above honey and the honeycomb. The Lord filled him with this spirit and gave him its savor and solid food, as Hebrews
says: *Solid food is for the perfect.* This spirit leads a person to perform Heb 5:14
humble tasks which are of the essence of perfect virtue. As Saint Augustine remarks: "Love has the right to flourish so that flourishing it

a. Surius in *Vita B. Mariae Magdalenae*, secund. Silvestr. Prierat., par. 10; *De probatis sanctorum historiis ab A. Lipomano conscriptis nunc primum a Laurent. Surio emandatis et auctis*, 6 vols. (Coloniae Agrippinae, 1570-1577).

b. That is, Saint Anthony the Abbot. He had no schooling, yet he was able to instruct the wise: Athanasius, *The Life of St. Antony and the Letter to Marcellinus*, The Classics of Western Spirituality, translated with introduction by Robert Gregg (New York: Paulist Press, 1980), 30.

may reach fulfillment."[a] With the Apostle Paul Saint Francis could
Phil 1:23 say: *My desire is to depart and be with Christ.* On the spirit of perfection
Ps 51:12 the Psalmist says: *Restore to me the joy of your salvation and strengthen me*
Acts 1:8 *with a perfect spirit.* The Lord said to the Apostles: *You shall receive the power of the Holy Spirit coming upon you.*

Being endowed with this threefold spirit Saint Francis brought forth justice as a model of God-like virtue, by the utter certainty of all he foretold and by the awe-inspiring nature of the miracles he performed.

First, *he brought forth justice* as a model of God-like virtue. When we come across someone in whom there is nothing blameworthy, who is without anger and deceit, we account such a person upright and an
Jb 36:6 ambassador of God. According to Job, *the Lord does not save the wicked, he gives judgment to the poor.* Saint Francis proclaimed the commands of God, his promises, and his judgments. Job's text says: *He gives judg-*
Mt 19:28 *ment to the poor,* and so the Lord told his Apostles: *Truly I say to you, in the new world, when the Son of Man shall sit on his glorious throne, you who have left all things and followed me will also sit on twelve thrones, judging the twelve tribes of Israel.* According to the text quoted at the beginning of the sermon, God's chosen servants *will bring forth justice.* To each
Ez 3:17 shepherd of his Church God has said: *I have made you a watchman.* You, therefore, ought to live in a way that your very life is a sermon to everyone. Saint Gregory writes: "To speak virtuously and to live wickedly is to condemn oneself out of one's own mouth."[b] And another writer says: "Those who live in sin and preach virtue, give God instructions on how he ought to punish them."[c] We read in the Book
Rv 7:2, 4 of Revelation: *I saw another angel ascend from the rising of the sun; he sealed out of every tribe of the sons of Israel* the servants of God. Those sealed by the angel are in heaven living a life conformed to Christ.

Second, Saint Francis *brought forth justice* by the utter certainty of everything he foretold. There was a hunchback who lived in de- LMj XI 5
bauchery and greed, and some people asked Saint Francis to pay him a visit. He replied: "Because you ask I will do so willingly. But this
Prv 26:11 man should know that *if he goes back to his vomit,* it will be all the worse for him." So Saint Francis touched him, and with a creaking of his bones, the man who had previously been bent over, now stood

a. Augustine, *Epistola 186*, c.3, n. 10, (PL 33, 819); *Saint Augustine: Letters*, vol. 4, The Fathers of the Church, vol. 30, translated by Wilfrid Parsons (New York: Fathers of the Church, 1955), 198; also, *Tractatus Decem in Epistolam Iohannis ad Parthos*, tr. 5, n. 4, SC 75, 353; *Tractates on the First Epistle of John*, The Fathers of the Church, vol. 92, translated by John Retting (Washington: The Catholic University of America Press, 1995), 188.

b. Gregory, *Moralia in Job* XV, c. 14, n. 17, CCSL 143 A, 757.

c. *Opus imperfectum in Matthaeum* (once attributed to Saint John Chrysostom), hom. 43, (PG 56, 876).

upright on his limbs. After some time he began to forget the warning Saint Francis had given and he went back to his vomit. Then one day while at a meal with some canons, the house fell in and they all escaped but him.

Finally, Saint Francis brought forth justice by the awe-inspiring nature of the miracles he performed. The Apostles had the power of working miracles: *As in their life they did wonders, so in death they wrought* Sir 48:14
miracles. Likewise, Saint Francis worked miracles both during his life and after his death.

You should recall, then, how Saint Francis cultivated profound humility, well tried virtue, and consummate love, so that you may arrive at eternal life, to which may He lead us Who lives and reigns with the Father and the Holy Spirit for ever. Amen.

RELATED DOCUMENTS

(1237–1272)

Introduction

Besides Francis's own writings and the hagiographic materials which focus specifically on him, there are a wide variety of other sources which provide a good amount of additional data and interesting perspectives on the life of Saint Francis and the early years of the evangelical movement he began. The following section contains several shorter Franciscan pieces which are of significant historical interest. The remainder of these related documents come from outside the Order, and are similar to those contained in the first volume; we have divided these into papal documents, portrayals of Francis by Dominican authors, and other chronicles. Some of these witnesses were captivated by the new Order, others were threatened or indifferent. But taken together, they form a rich tapestry of impressions, letting us see how contemporaries viewed Francis and his Order of Lesser Brothers as they moved to a prominent position in the life of Christendom during these middle decades of the thirteenth century.

Miscellaneous Franciscan Sources

Witnesses to the Stigmata (1237-50)

The following entry was discovered in a parchment folio contained in the communal archives of Assisi early in the twentieth century.[a] Although strictly speaking it did not emanate from within the Franciscan Order itself, it represents an attempt on the part of the commune of Assisi and no doubt the friars at the Sacro Convento to authenticate the description of Francis's stigmata as reported in *The Life of Saint Francis* by Thomas of Celano.[b] The process for Francis's canonization was not as extensive as that used for Saint Clare a quarter of a century later.[c] So in light of Francis's growing cult, it was important to secure evidence of the reality of the stigmata from unimpeachable witnesses, most of whom were leading citizens of the commune.[d]

> In the name of the Lord, Amen! These are persons who saw the stigmata of blessed Francis while he was living in the flesh and after his death: Giovanni, son of Simone; Bonaccurso, son of Ugono de Leto; and Giovanni Deoteaiute. The Lord Jacopo, a canon of the bishop, saw the stigmata of the saint only while he was living. Alberico, notary.
>
> The following are those who saw the stigmata after his death: Messer Tommaso, son of Rainerio, who was then chamberlain of the commune; Messer Girolamo;[e] Messer Giovanni, son of Guarnerio; Offreduccio; Scalla; Alberico, the notary; Messer Masseo, son of Andrea del Prete; Bartolo, son of Lady Fantina; Giovanni di Guittolo; Baliero; Giovanni of Greccio.[f]
>
> On the inside of the hands these marks were round, on the outside they were oblong, and a little piece of flesh was apparent, like the top of nails which were hammered and bent back and were higher than the rest of the flesh. His right side also was as if pierced with a lance and covered with a scab, which often shed blood, so that

a. Francesco Pennacchi, "Saggio del Processo per la canonizzatione di S. Francesco: Le stimmate," *Miscellanea Franciscana* 15 (1914): 129-137; Michael Bihl, "De Quodam Elencho Assisiano Testium Oculatorum s. Francisci Stigmatum," AFH 19 (1926): 931-36. the text is included in *Testimonia Minora*, ed. by Leonardus Lemmens (Ad Claras Aquas, Quaracchi: Collegium S. Bonaventurae, 1926), 41.

b. 1C 95. The list of signatories have been largely identified by Fortini using other contemporary Assisi documents [*Nova Vita* 2: 448-51]. For a summary, see Octavian Schmucki, *The Stigmata of St. Francis: A Critical Examination in Light of Thirteenth Century Sources*, trans. Canisius Connors (St. Bonaventure: The Franciscan Institute, pp. 83-84).

c. Cf. *Clare of Assisi, Early Documents*, pp. 132-85.

d. For the background, see André Vauchez, "The Stigmata of St. Francis and its Medieval Detractors," GR 13 (1999): 61-89.

e. This is the Jerome mentioned by Bonaventure, cf. LMj XV 4, supra, 646.

f. Cf. 1C 84.

his tunic together with his drawers was many times splattered with his sacred blood.

Giovanni di Magnolo, Messer Giacomo di Pellipario di Margarita of Nocera.

Encyclical Letter of John of Parma and Humbert of Romans (1255)

By the 1250's, the new mendicant orders were facing increased opposition in the church. Under Papal protection, the brothers had gained almost unlimited freedom of action for their pastoral mission, bringing them into strong competition with local pastors. The discontent of many clergy found an articulate voice in some of the secular masters of the University of Paris, who, beginning in 1253, launched an attack on the whole theological basis of the brothers' life and ministry.[a] To complicate the situation, the Dominicans and Franciscans had become increasingly jealous rivals, as they competed for potential recruits and benefactors. Strong partisans from both orders claimed that theirs was a more authentic expression of the "apostolic life."

In the midst of this critical situation, the leaders of the two Orders, Humbert of Romans and John of Parma,[b] issued a lengthy joint encyclical letter to their friars, urging cooperation rather than conflict, especially in face of a common threat. What is especially notable about this letter is its striking use of apocalyptic imagery, much of it reflecting the writings of the visionary abbot, Joachim of Fiore (+ 1202). Joachite ideas were especially prominent among the Franciscans, and John of Parma himself was a key figure in their dissemination; this selection certainly reflects his convictions.[c]

This letter was written in the midst of much apocalyptic speculation: the year before it appeared, a young student brother at Paris, Gerardo of Borgo San Donnino, published a book which interpreted Joachim's major works in a radical way, seeming to predict the demise of the present institutional church. Gerardo's work was condemned by a Papal commission later in 1255, and the scandal helped bring about the resignation of John of Parma in 1257.

To the Friars Preacher and Lesser throughout the world, most dear and beloved in Christ Jesus: Brother Humbert, Master General

---

a. The fullest account of the conflict at Paris is M.-M. Dufeil, *Guillaume de Saint-Amour et la polémique universitaire parisienne 1250-59* (Paris: A. et S. Picard, 1972). A shorter account is provided by Decima Douie, *The Conflict between the Seculars and the Mendicants at the University of Paris in the Thirteenth Century* (London: Blackfrairs, 1954).

b. Humbert of Romans was master general of the Order of Preachers from 1254 to 1263; John was general minister of the Friars Minor from 1247 to 1257.

c. In the 1240's, increasing attention was given to an inauthentic work attributed to Joachim, the *Commentary on Jeremiah*, which emphasized the imminence of the coming third age of the Holy Spirit and the critical role of two orders of "spiritual men" in this period of crisis. John of Parma was apparently the first to identify Francis with the Angel of the Sixth Seal of Revelation 7:2. See Marjorie Reeves, *The Influence of Prophecy in the Later Middle Ages* (Oxford: Oxford at The Clarendon Press, 1969), pp. 145-190; this letter is discussed on pp. 146-148. See also E. Randolph Daniel, "A Re-examination of the Roots of Franciscan Joachitism," *Speculum* 43 (1968): 671-76. The Latin text of this letter is in Luke Wadding, *Annales Minorum*, vol. 3 (Ad Claras Aquas, Quaracchi: Collegium S. Bonaventurae, 1931-1951), 380-381.

of the same Preachers, and Brother John of Parma, Minister General of the same Lesser Brothers, send greetings to all. May you walk worthily and laudably in your holy calling.

The Savior of the world, who loves souls and wishes none of them to perish, has ceaselessly applied various remedies through different ministers in each generation to repair the human race after its primal fall. In these last days, which without any doubt we believe to be the end of the world, he has raised up our two orders to the ministry of salvation; he has called many men to join them and enriched them with celestial gifts through which they might be able to work salvation effectively by words and example, not only for themselves, but also for others. These two orders are, to speak of God's glory and not
Gn 1:16 our own, *the two great lights,* which by celestial light shine upon and
Lk 1:79; Nm 10:2 minister to those *who sit in darkness and in the shadow of death.* These are the *two trumpets* of the true Moses, of Christ our God, by whose ministry a multitude of peoples has already been called back to their
Ex 25:17-22 source. These are the *two cherubim* full of knowledge, facing one another while they gaze at the same object, spreading out their wings to the people while they protect them by word and example, and flying about on obedient wings over the whole people to spread saving
Sg 4:5 knowledge. These are the *two breasts* of the spouse from which Christ's little ones suck the milk by which they are nourished and receive saving increase. These are *the two olive trees* of the Son of splen-
Zec 4:3, 14 dor that *stand by the Ruler of the whole earth,* ready for his command
Rv 11:3 wherever his will might lead them to fulfill his mission. These are the *two witnesses* of Christ who, *clad in sackcloth,* are already preaching and bearing testimony to the truth. These are the two shining stars that according to the Sibylline prophecy[a] have the appearance of the four animals and in the last days will cry out in the name of the Lamb in the way of humility and voluntary poverty . . .

. . . O what an example of mutual love and peace our Fathers Francis and Dominic and the other early brothers left us! They willingly obliged themselves to this in their lifetime: they would manifest to each other the tokens of sincere love by seeing each other as angels of God, by receiving each other as if he were Christ, by anticipating each other with honor, by rejoicing mutually over successes, by exalting each other with praise, by promoting their mutual advantage, and by bewaring of mutual scandals and quarrels with the greatest diligence and prudence . . .

a. A reference to a pseudo-Joachimist work, the supposed oracles of the Erythraean Sybil (Reeves, *Influence*, 147).

Inscription of Brother Leo (1257-60)

This inscription by Brother Leo is at the beginning of the so-called Breviary of St. Francis, which is still preserved today in the protomonastery of St. Clare in Assisi.[a] It appears to have been written at the time he donated the breviary to the community, with whom he had a close connection.[b] This can be dated with some precision from the inscription itself: the Sister Benedetta mentioned in the letter succeeded Clare as abbess of San Damiano in 1253, but she would not have been the "Abbess of the monastery of St. Clare" until 1257, when the Poor Ladies obtained possession of the former church of San Giorgio, where Clare's body had been buried, and thus could initiate their plans of moving their community to that location. Benedetta herself died in 1260, shortly after the dedication of the new basilica of St. Clare.[c]

> Blessed Francis acquired this breviary for his companions Brother Angelo and Brother Leo, and when he was well he wished always to say the Office, as is stated by the Rule.[d] At the time when he was sick and not able to recite it, he wished to listen to it. And he continued do this for as long as he lived. He also had the Book of the Gospels copied, and whenever he would be unable to hear Mass due to infirmity or any other manifest impediment, he had that Gospel read to him, which on that day was read at Mass in Church. And he continued to do this until his death. For he used to say: "When I do not hear Mass, I adore the Body of Christ in prayer with the eyes of my mind, just as I adore It when I see it during Mass." After blessed Francis read the Gospel or listened to it, he always kissed the Gospel out of the greatest reverence for the Lord. For this reason Brother Angelo and Brother Leo, as much as they can, humbly beg Lady Benedetta, the abbess of the Poor Ladies of the Monastery of Saint Clare, and all the abbesses of the same monastery who are to come after her, that in memory of and out of devotion to our holy Father they always preserve in the Monastery of Saint Clare this book out of which he so many times read.

---

a. *Testimonia Minora Saeculi XIII de S. Francisco Assisiensi*, compiled and edited by Leonardus Lemmens (Ad Claras Aquas: Collegium S. Bonaventurae, 1926), 61.

b. When Bonaventure wrote a letter to "the Abbess of the Poor Ladies of Assisi in the monastery of St. Clare" in 1259, he mentioned that Leo had informed him of the devotion of the community to Franciscan ideals. See *Clare of Assisi: Early Documents*, p. 340.

c. *Clare of Assisi: Early Documents*, p. 179.

d. Cf. Test 29.

Papal Documents

Ordinem vestrum of Innocent IV (1245)

As the pastoral ministries of the Lesser Brothers continued to expand dramatically throughout the 1230's, many brothers increasingly viewed some provisions of their *Rule* as being too restrictive. The minister general, Crescentius of Jesi, who succeeded to that office in 1244, appears to have been one of those who favored further relaxation of certain prescriptions. Shortly after his accession he obtained the following declaration from Innocent IV who, like his predecessor Gregory IX, strongly favored the work of the mendicant orders in the church, but unlike him did not know Francis personally and cared little for his distinctive values.[a] This document was the second major papal declaration on the Franciscan *Rule;* although it claimed the modest role of further clarifying Gregory IX's *Quo elongati* of 1230, it actually went far beyond it in a number of respects.[b]

This document was to prove controversial in the Order and contributed to the growing division among the brothers over their interpretation of Francis's ideals.[c] The party opposed to Innocent's relaxation of the poverty standards triumphed at the General Chapter of Genoa in 1251 under the new general minister, John of Parma, when the assembly decided not to utilize the new privileges, but remain under the stricter standards of *Quo elongati.*[d] This remained the official position of the Order throughout the generalates of John of Parma and Bonaventure.[e] Despite this principled stand, many local superiors viewed the refusal to use this papal privilege as unrealistic in light of the pressing ministerial duties the Order had assumed, and both John and Bonaventure had to contend with many violations of the official standards.

---

a. Innocent also issued a new Rule for the Order of San Damiano in 1247 which ignored the values of Franciscan poverty. Cf. *Clare of Assisi: Early Documents*, pp. 113-128.

b. For the text of *Quo elongati*, see FA: ED 1 570-575. For a full discussion of the background and significance of *Ordinem vestrum*, see Malcolm Lambert, *Franciscan Poverty*, revised edition (St. Bonaventure University: Franciscan Institute Publications, 1998), 93-107.

c. For example, 2C 69 and 130 might well be viewed as a reaction against perceived abuses justified by *Ordinem Vestrum*'s allowance of "useful" items as well as those which were strictly "necessary"(cf. section 4 below, infra, 776).

d. Eccleston, 55. The author of this chronicle gives maximum credit to the delegates of his own country in effecting this change.

e. The decision of the chapter of Genoa was re-affirmed at the chapter of Metz in 1254 and at Narbonne in 1260. The latter chapter decreed: "As was decided in the chapter of Metz, the declaration of the Lord Pope Innocent shall remain suspended, and we strictly forbid anyone to use it in those points in which it contradicts the declaration of the Lord Pope Gregory" Cf. *Writings Concerning the Franciscan Order*, Works of Saint Bonaventure V, introduction and translation by Dominic Monti (St. Bonaventure, NY: Franciscan Institute Publications, 1994), 47, 82, 180. The controversy seems to have been only in regard to the poverty provisions. For a full discussion, see Lambert, *Franciscan Poverty* pp. 109-131.

[1]We have tended your Order with affection, and in that spirit we fervently desire that it make continual progress through praiseworthy increase. And so, in our paternal solicitude, we are happy to obtain for you the things through which it might receive the support of suitable buttresses.

Now there are certain doubtful and obscure things contained in your Rule, which only catch your spirits up in entangled complexities and knotty intricacies that impede your understanding. Thus Pope Gregory, our predecessor of happy memory, expounded and declared the meaning of some of these, although incompletely. We, therefore, wish to remove entirely all obscurity from these passages by a complete declaration of their meaning and to excise totally all scruples of anxiety from your minds by means of the certainty of a fuller exposition. We therefore declare to you that when your *Rule*
LR I 1 imposes on you the observance of the holy Gospel,[a] you are bound only to those Gospel counsels which are expressly contained in that same Rule by way of precept or prohibition.

LR II 1 [2]Moreover, it is lawful for the provincial ministers, with the advice of some of the more discreet brothers, to entrust the reception of those entering the Order to their vicars as well as to other circumspect brothers for their provinces. However, they should not receive indiscriminately all who present themselves, but only those candidates whose learning and other praiseworthy qualities recommend them, and who thus can be of benefit to the Order and to themselves by a meritorious life and to others by a good example.[b] The provincial ministers may also receive back those who have left the Order when they return and expel brothers once received in certain cases as determined by your general chapter.

LR III 1 [3]The aforesaid *Rule* also states that "the clerical brothers are to recite the Divine Office according to the rite of the holy Roman Church excepting the psalter, for which reason they may have breviaries." However, when they attend the Divine Office celebrated by other clergy, this suffices to fulfill their obligation and thus they are not bound to recite their own Office.[c]

---

a. This one sentence in Innocent's bull summarizes the sense of *Quo elongati* 4.

b. Cf. LR II 1. This declaration on the provision of the *Later Rule* represents a liberalization of *Quo elongati*, 9, which did not allow the provincial ministers to delegate this faculty. This restriction represented a grave inconvenience in light of the large numbers of candidates seeking to enter the Order, and so in 1241, Gregory allowed such delegation, at the same time emphasizing that only men suitable to the Order's pastoral mission should be so received [*Gloriantibus vobis*, June 19, 1241 (BFr, 1: 298, no. 344)]. Legislation restricting the admission of non-clerical candidates to the Order dates from about the same time. Cf. Lawrence Landini, *The Causes of the Clericalization of the Order of Friars Minor 1209-1260* (Chicago: Franciscan Herald Press, 1968), pp. 66-69.

c. This provision repeats the provisions of the bull *Pio vestro collegio* of Gregory IX, June 6, 1241. BFr 1: 342.

[4]Furthermore, it states in the same *Rule* that the brothers are forbidden "to receive coins or money in any way, either personally or through an intermediary." However, if the brothers want to buy something necessary or useful for themselves or to make payment for something already purchased, they may present to those persons who wish to give them a [monetary] alms either an agent of the person from whom the purchase is being made or someone else, unless perchance these donors prefer to make payment themselves or through agents of their own. The person presented by the brothers in this manner is not their agent, even though he may have been designated by them; rather, he is the agent of the person on whose authority he makes the payment, or of the one who is receiving it. And, once payment has been made for such [specified] goods, if this agent still has alms remaining in his possession, it is permissible for the brothers to have recourse to him for other necessary or beneficial items. If, however, someone is named or presented by them for other necessary or useful items, this person can keep the alms committed to him as though they were his own, or with a spiritual friend or familiar acquaintance of the brothers, who may or may not be designated by them, and through such a one, dispense the alms as deemed expedient by the brothers according to the circumstances and time of their needs or benefit, and even transfer such alms to another person or place. The brothers may also in good conscience have recourse to such agents for necessary and useful items, especially if they are negligent of or simply unaware of their needs. And the person so named or designated by the brothers is not their agent or treasurer, but of those persons who have entrusted their alms and donations to them. And when the brothers have recourse to such appointed or presented persons they are not "receiving coins or money in any form either personally or through intermediaries," since it is not their intention to have such coins or money held by these persons on their own authority nor are they drawing from what has been deposited with them in their own name: they are simply entrusting such agents or depositors with providing for their necessary or useful items.[a] LR IV 1

[5]And since in the same *Rule* it says that "the ministers and custodians alone may take special care through their spiritual friends to provide for the needs of the sick and the clothing of the other brothers," [we say that] other brothers may also diligently take up this LR IV 2

a. This passage represents a great extension of the permission granted by Gregory IX in *Quo elongati*, 5. The friars are now authorized to employ an agent to receive monetary alms not only for "imminent necessities," but for whatever the superiors might deem as "useful," "thus giving *carte blanche* to superiors to use agents to take money alms whenever they wished" Lambert, *Franciscan Poverty*, 101.

care, which falls upon the said ministers and custodians by precept of the Rule, whenever it has been committed to them by the latter.[a]

LR VI 1 [6]Furthermore, since that *Rule* clearly states that "the brothers shall not appropriate anything as their own, neither a house nor a place nor anything at all," it is not lawful for them to possess property either individually nor in common. However, the Order may have the use of places, houses, equipment, books, and other such moveable property as is permitted, and individual brothers may use these things at the discretion of the general and provincial ministers. But places, houses, or moveable goods which have been or are to be given, sold, or exchanged for the use of the brothers by any persons whatsoever, may not be sold, exchanged, or alienated outside the Order by any person in any way, unless the Apostolic See or Cardinal of the Roman Church who for the time being is the governor of the brotherhood authorizes the transaction or gives approval for it to the general or provincial ministers.[b] For the right, ownership, and dominion of such immobile and mobile goods belong immediately to the [Roman] church itself, except for those cases where the donors or grantors have expressly reserved these property rights and dominion to themselves. The houses and places of this Order, along with the churches and other things pertaining to them, we receive as the property and possession of blessed Peter, to which [Roman church] these brothers are acknowledged to be totally and immediately subject in both spiritual and temporal matters.[c] However, it is lawful for the brothers to give away moveable items of low cost and little value to people outside the Order, for the sake of piety or devotion or for any other proper or reasonable cause, having first obtained the permission of their superiors.

---

a. This provision reflects the growing size of the Order and the increased involvement of provincial superiors in administrative and pastoral concerns.

b. The inconvenience of having to receive the permission of the Pope or cardinal protector to alienate the houses or major moveable goods of the Order was removed by Innocent two years later in the bull *Quanto studiosus* of August 19, 1247 (BFr 1: 487). By this privilege the friars received the right of appointing apostolic syndics or procurators who could "ask for, sell, exchange, alienate, manage, and spend any things given, or to be given for the use of the friars, for their necessities or advantages." Such syndics, although technically acting on behalf of the Papacy as the legal owner of the friars' property, were entirely under the control of the friars. Thus, in practice the former functions of the 'spiritual friends' mentioned in the Later Rule and the *ad hoc* 'agents' permitted by *Quo elongati* and *Ordinem Vestrum* were absorbed into this new office. This privilege was an extension of one which Innocent had already granted the Sacro Convento in Assisi in 1240 (BFr 1: 288).

c. Through this prescription, the Holy See clearly became the technical owner of the friars' dwellings and other belongings. Actually, through this bull the friars were conforming to the same pattern as many of the early houses of the Poor Clares, which were received as Papal property by Cardinal Hugolino in 1217-19, cf. *Clare of Assisi: Early Documents*, 87-88. A further precedent was set by Gregory IX's assumption of ownership of the basilica of San Francesco in Assisi and its attached friary in 1229, see FA: ED 1 564-65. Innocent is assuming that the friars' exemption from local church authority is taken for granted.

LR VII 1

[7]Another chapter of the aforesaid *Rule* says: "If any of the brothers, at the instigation of the enemy, sin mortally in regard to those sins about which it may have been decreed among the brothers to have recourse only to the provincial ministers, such brothers must have recourse to them as soon as possible, without delay." We declare that the chapter in question refers only to manifest public sins. Furthermore, these same ministers, in order to avoid great effort and hazardous travel, if it seems expedient to them, may entrust such cases to the custodians and other discreet brother priests in their places. We also wish that these same ministers appoint, or have appointed, from among the more mature and discreet priests, as many confessors as they deem suitable for their provinces. Let these priests hear the confessions for the private sins of the brothers, unless they choose instead to confess to their ministers or custodians who happen to be visiting their places.

LR VIII 2

[8]Again, the *Rule* states that "upon the death of the general minister, the election of a successor should be made by the provincial ministers and custodians at the Pentecost chapter." We say that the custodians of the several provinces should designate one of their number to send along with their provincial minister to represent them at the general chapter, commissioning him to vote in their place.

LR IX 2

[9]Furthermore, it is also the sense of the aforesaid *Rule* that it is not lawful for any brother to preach to the people "unless he has been examined and approved by the general minister and received from him the office of preaching." The general minister can delegate these matters to the provincial ministers and their vicars. Thus, in his absence, these same provincials or their vicars together with the definitors at their provincial chapters might examine and approve the brothers of their provinces, conferring on them the office of preaching, as it seems best to them in the sight of God.[a] Now, if these candidates do not require an examination, on the basis of having had training both at a school of theology and in the office of preaching; and if they are of mature age; and if they possess all those other qualities that are expected of such men, then they may receive permission from the general or their provincial ministers to preach to the people in the approved manner.

---

a. This provision represents a considerable relaxation of the provisions of *Quo elongati* 8 on the same subject. There Gregory IX required that preachers be licensed by the general minister. The rapid expansion of the friars' ministries quickly made this unrealistic, however, and in 1240 Gregory granted the privilege of licensing preachers to the provincial ministers as well [*Prohibente regula*, December 12, 1240 (BFr, 1: 287, no. 325)].

LR XI 2 [10]Finally, the *Rule* says that "the brothers should not enter the monasteries of nuns, except those to whom special permission has been granted by the Apostolic See." We say that this prohibition affects especially the cloistered nuns of the Order of San Damiano, to whom no one has access without the express permission of the Apostolic See. And by the term monastery we mean the cloister, the living quarters, and workshops. But in regards to the other areas of the monastery, those brothers to whom the superiors have granted permission by virtue of their maturity and suitability may enter there, just as other religious, in order to preach or beg alms or for some other proper and reasonable cause.

It is forbidden, therefore, for anyone to tamper with this decree which we have confirmed, or rashly dare to oppose it. If anyone presumes to attempt this, let him know that he shall incur the anger of almighty God and of his blessed apostles Peter and Paul.

Given at Lyons, the fourteenth day of November, in the third year of our pontificate.

Benigna operatio of Alexander IV (1255)

The increasing criticism of the ministry of the mendicant orders not surprisingly once again raised questions about the authentic holiness of their founders. In particular, the alleged miracle of the stigmata of St. Francis, which for Franciscans was a divine confirmation of the saint's life and mission, came under special attack. In 1237, Gregory IX directed no fewer than three Papal documents to certain individuals and groups in central Europe who were denying the authenticity of the stigmata of St. Francis.[a] The election of the long-time cardinal protector of the Order, Cardinal Raynald di Jenne,[b] to the Papacy as Alexander IV late in 1254 came at a particularly critical time for the Franciscans, as the anti-mendicant movement was gaining strong theological support from the secular masters at the University of Paris. To demonstrate his unswerving support of the friars, Alexander retained his role as Protector of the Order even after his election to the Papacy. Over the next five years he directed four different letters which upheld the authentic-

a. André Vauchez, "The Stigmata of St. Francis and its Medieval Detractors," GR 13 (1999): 66-68.

b. Although most literature in the English-speaking world still identifies Cardinal Raynald as belonging to the same family (the Conti of Segni) as Gregory IX, the research of A. Paravacini Vagliani, *Cardinali di Curia e 'familiae' cardializie dal 1227 al 1254*, I (Padua, 1972), pp. 41-53, has shown that Raynald belonged to the family of the counts of Jenne, one of the major feudal lords in the southern part of the Papal States, near Mount Subiaco. He was named cardinal protector by Gregory IX in 1227 upon the latter's election as pope. Apparently, he was related to Gregory in some way, perhaps through one of their mothers. Cf. Raoul Manselli, "Allesandro IV," *Dizionario biografico degli italiani* (Rome: Ed. A. M. Ghisalberti, 1960-), 2: 189-193.

ity of the stigmata.[a] The fullest of these is the declaration, *Benigna operatio,* which was addressed to all the bishops of the church, obliges the faithful to believe in the truth of the stigmata; it is especially interesting for the Pope's own eye-witness testimony.[b]

> . . . While he was still among the Church Militant and later when he was triumphant in the ranks of the saints, the divine power deigned to glorify Francis with many miracles. Pope Gregory, our predecessor of happy memory, caused these miracles to be subjected to the most careful investigation and to be shown as most evident by the most trustworthy documents, lest either evil, which is jealous of sanctity, pervert them, or the finger of oblivion, which quickly erases deeds, destroy them. By adding this same confessor's name to the catalogue of the saints, the Pontiff caused these miracles to be entrusted to everlasting memory for the glory of God, for a proof of faith, and for the salutary instruction of both those now living and of even those to come.
>
> It would take too long to describe each single miracle or even to outline in a brief report the evident prodigies of divine power, which provided both in works of healing and in other remarkable evidence that this confessor holds a place of glory with the saints in heaven. Therefore, we wish at least to set before your eyes those gratifying insignia of the Lord's Passion which should be frequently recalled and greatly admired, and which the hand of divine operation impressed on the body of this saint while he was still alive. Eyes looking closely saw, and touching fingers became most sure, that in his hands and feet a truly formed likeness of nails grew out of the substance of his own flesh or was added from some newly created material. While he was still living, the Saint zealously hid these from the eyes of men whose praise he shunned.
>
> After he had died, a wound in his side, which was not inflicted or made by man, was clearly seen in his body. It was something like the side of our Savior, which revealed in our Redeemer the mystery of the redemption and salvation of mankind. This wound had existed for a long time while he was still alive. It could not be hidden from certain brothers who were his close companions, because it exuded fluid.

a. Vauchez, 68-69. The reasons for the attacks on the stigmata are discussed on pp. 70-89.The text of the bull is in *BF* 2: 85-87, no.120. We are indebted to the translation of Canisius Connors, in Octavian Schmucki, *The Stigmata of St. Francis of Assisi: A Critical Examination in Light of the Thirteenth Century Sources* (St. Bonaventure, NY: Franciscan Institute Publication, 1991), 276-77.

b. According to Bonaventure, Alexander also testified in a sermon that he had personally seen the stigmata. Cf. LMj XIII 8.

While we declare these things about the Saint with a rather great confidence, we are not depending upon foolish fables or the absurdities of an inane imagination. For a long time now we have had great assurance about this. When we held lesser positions and were applying ourselves for service in the house of our aforementioned predecessor, by a gift of God we merited at that time to have an intimate knowledge of this confessor.[a] Therefore, let no one attack this Saint who carried in his body the triumphant Stigmata of Christ.

Given at Anagni, on the twenty-ninth day of October [1255], in the first year of our pontificate.

a. As a young cleric, Raynald became a member of the household of Cardinal Hugolino in 1221, accompanying him on his legations throughout Tuscany and Lombardy and at the Papal Court.

Dominican Hagiography and Sermons

Bartholomew of Trent (c. 1240-45)

Bartholomew (+1251), a native of the city of Trent, entered the Dominican Order in Bologna around 1220. He traveled widely in Italy, France, and Germany—for example, he knew Anthony of Padua and was present at the translation of St. Dominic's body in 1233. Politically astute, Bartholomew was often in attendance at both the Papal and Imperial courts; in particular, he was employed as an envoy by Pope Innocent IV in his negotiations with Emperor Frederick II. He is most famous for his *Liber epilogorum in gesta sanctorum,* written in the 1240's, which did much to set a new style in hagiography. In it he interspersed concise lives of the saints with ascetic and moral reflections for a popular audience.[a] The following are brief selections from it concerning St. Francis.[b] In his account, Bartholomew clearly follows the order of Thomas of Celano's First Life, but concentrates on the marvels worked by the saint.

Francis, who was born in the city of Assisi, possessed such vanity that, while he was a merchant, he wanted to become a soldier. In a dream he saw many weapons that were to be prepared for himself and his comrades, but he did not understand what this meant. Finally, goaded by pangs of conscience at Foligno, he sold whatever he was able to get hold of. He attached himself to the priest of San Damiano, threw the money into the window there, and hid in a cave for several days. At length, he left the cave and was made captive by his father, but his mother freed him. Then he came before the bishop, returned his money and even his very clothes to his father, his naked body being covered by the bishop's cloak. He ran through the woods, praising God. When asked by robbers who he was, he answered: "The herald of God." But the robbers threw him into a pile of snow and said: "Lie there, O uncouth herald." Afterwards he went to work in the kitchen of certain monks; wearing only a ragged shirt, he was scarcely sustained on broth. He went to Gubbio where he accepted a tunic from a man and then began to take care of lepers. He next repaired the Church of San Damiano where he established the Order of Ladies; he repaired another church near Assisi, and then a third one dedicated to Saint Mary of the Portiuncula, at which he decided to remain because of his devotion to the Mother of God.

At first he wore the habit of a hermit, but after he heard the Gospel of Christ, how the Lord sent his disciples out to preach, he took on

a. Cf. Thomas Kaeppeli, *Scriptores Ordinis Praedicatorum Medii Aevi*, 4 vols. (Rome: Istituto Storico Domenicano, 1970-93), 1: 172-74; D. Frioli, *Bartolomeo da Trento: domenicano e agiografo medievale* (Trent, 1990).

b. *Testimonia Minora*, 63-65.

the habit which is now that of the Lesser Brothers and began to gather brothers together. It was revealed to him that his sins had been forgiven and that people of many different languages would come together to join him. He also predicted that in the beginning of his Order pleasant things would be experienced, then those which would be less pleasant, and lastly, things that would be bitter. He wrote a Rule, had it confirmed, and wished that it be called the Order of Lesser Brothers.

Once his soul appeared to his brothers as a resplendent globe of light in a fiery chariot. Another time, while Saint Anthony was preaching to the brothers in Provence and was speaking of "Jesus of Nazareth, King of the Jews," a Brother Monaldo saw Saint Francis with his hands extended in the form of the Cross. In spirit he knew many deeds of his absent brothers. Longing for martyrdom he went to preach to both the Miramamolin and the Sultan. He came to the sailors' assistance during storms and by his prayers had their provisions increased. In the vicinity of Bevagna he preached to the birds and walked here and there among them, but they did not fly away until he gave them leave. At Alviano he imposed silence on swallows who were impeding him in his preaching. A hare, a small rabbit, and fish obeyed him. At the hermitage of San Urbano he converted water into wine, which, when drunk, cured a sick man. At Ascoli, Arezzo, and other places he performed many miracles, so that even the things he touched benefited a woman giving birth in pain and many other people besides. In the city of Toscanella he raised up a cripple; he healed a paralytic at Narni; he cured a blind woman, a shriveled woman and those having epilepsy; he expelled demons and did many remarkable things.

Francis was filled with compassion for all creatures. He so venerated the name of Jesus that when it was written down, he would not allow it to be trampled upon by anyone. At that time Lord William, the bishop of the church of Sabina was teaching, just as even now he is accustomed to do, that this name should be magnified above all things. On the day of the Nativity of our Lord Jesus Christ Saint Francis out of devotion caused a manger to be built at a village called Greccio. He had an ox with an ass and some hay placed there, and Mass was celebrated. He himself read the Gospel and preached to the people. A boy appeared there, as if lifeless, and the Saint was seen to approach him and arouse the boy as if from a deep sleep. Afterwards that hay was beneficial toward the health of many people; and in that place there is now a church dedicated in honor of Saint Francis.

It is recorded in the writings that he had seen the form of a seraph affixed to a cross, and while he was wondering what this vision meant, it is said that the marks of the wounds of Jesus Christ appeared in his hands, feet, and side. He was not puffed up by all this, but now proven in all perfection, he gave his blessing to his brothers, and just as it had been revealed to Brother Elias by a messenger at Foligno, Francis passed over to heaven while the Passion of the Lord according to John was being read in his presence. One of the brothers saw his soul, in the form of a star as large as the moon and with the brilliance of the sun, arising from the place in a straight path. The image of the Crucified showed forth in him, his flesh was dazzlingly white, and the members of his body attractively composed. He was buried at Assisi, canonized by the Lord Pope Gregory with the Lord Rayner of Viterbo explaining his life and miracles to the people.

After his death he performed many miracles; we read that the withered, the crippled, the blind, and many others were cured at his tomb. At the tomb a young brother appeared to a crippled boy from Montenero; he offered a pear to the boy and the boy ate it. And while he was stretching out his hand for another pear, the youth lifted the boy, led him out cured, and then disappeared. In like manner, Francis cured a woman from Coccorano, who had lost the use of all her members except the tongue; a boy of Gubbio, who due to shriveled limbs, was brought in a basket; and Bartholomew, a beggar from Narni, and many others whom he cured from various maladies.

The second selection is from his treatment of St. Dominic, and notes the friendship between the two saints.[a]

In those days Saint Francis, who founded the Order of Lesser Brothers, was renowned; Saint Dominic was joined to him with a love such that what each one wished or did not wish were the same.

Constantine of Orvieto (1246-48)

Constantine, a native of Orvieto, entered the Brothers Preacher at an unknown date. Noted for his eloquence, in 1246 he was commissioned to revise the Order's official Legenda of St. Dominic. The circumstances of this work bear a close parallel to those which surrounded the writing of Thomas of Celano's *Remembrance of the Desire of a Soul* at virtually the same time. In 1245 the Dominican general chapter had requested that provincial superiors should submit to the following year's chapter any and all reports which testified to the holiness and intercessory power of Saint Dominic. John 'the Teuton,' Master General of the Order, then turned these materials over to Constantine, who presented his work to the general chapter of 1248 where it

a. *Testimonia Minora*, 70. The same point of the friendship between Francis and Dominic is made by the virtually contemporaneous 2C 148-50.

was adopted as the official biography of the saint.[a] The following selection from Constantine's Legenda does not mention St. Francis, but it is given here to illustrate how both Dominicans and Franciscans were beginning to circulate similar miraculous stories about the origins of their Orders about the same time.[b]

Constantine himself was eventually chosen as Bishop of Orvieto in 1250. In 1256, he was sent by Alexander IV on an embassy to the Byzantine Emperor Theodore II; he died in Constantinople not long afterwards.[c]

He [Dominic] went to Innocent, the Supreme Pontiff, and asked him to confirm for himself and his followers, an Order which would be called and which would in fact be an Order of Preachers. But the Pope at first seemed to show himself to be a little unyielding to a petition of this kind. Nevertheless, he eventually agreed to it, but not without a divine command. For it was surely as a result of the following revelation that the Vicar of Jesus Christ came to know just how necessary for the universal church, over which he presided, would be this Order which Dominic, the divinely inspired man of God, desired. For it has been made known by many trustworthy people that one night,[d] this same Supreme Pontiff, through divine revelation, saw in a dream the Church of the Lateran suddenly threatening to collapse, as though its very structure was buckling. As he looked at this sight, trembling and lamenting, Dominic, the man of God, suddenly appeared before him and with his shoulders propped up the whole building which was about to tumble down. As he marveled over this most unusual vision, the Pope prudently recognized its meaning, and without any delay commended the man of God's proposal and joyfully accepted his petition. The Pope counseled him to return to his brothers and, after deliberating with them, to choose by unanimous consent some approved Rule, which could serve as a basis on which to build up this new undertaking. They then could return to him at their leisure and take back with them his confirmation of their Order.

---

a. Edward T. Brett, *Humbert of Romans: His Life and Views of Thirteenth-Century Society* (Toronto: Pontifical Institute of Mediaeval Studies, 1984), 93.

b. This incident is a remarkable parallel to 2C 17.

c. *Testimonia Minora*, 67-68; Kaeppeli, 1: 292-94.

d. Simon Tugwell, in a study of the sources of the life of St. Dominic, mentions that some manuscripts attribute this story to the authority of Cardinal Rainerio Capocci, who would have been well placed to know what Innocent III had said in 1215. It is possible that in the 1240's Capocci was telling a story about the pope's dream; as a supporter of both orders of friars, he may have felt that the vision was being fulfilled in both of them. Tugwell believes that it is "almost certain the Franciscan version is closer to the original way in which the story was told," as in Thomas of Celano's account the Pope had simply said that he had seen an unidentified "small and despicable-looking man" propping up the Lateran basilica. Cf. "Notes on the Life of St. Dominic," *Archivum Fratrum Praedicatorum* 65 (1995): 10-11.

Gerard de Frachet (1257-60)

Gerard de Frachet [de Fracheto] was born near Limoges c. 1205 and took the Dominican habit in Paris in 1225. Over the years he served in a variety of positions of responsibility in his Order, attaining the post of prior provincial of Provençe from 1251 to 1259. While he was serving in that office, the Master General, Humbert of Romans, asked him to compile a book of edifying anecdotes about the early brothers of the Order, which Gerard entitled the *Lives of the Brethren (Vitae fratrum)*. The material Gerard drew upon for this work had been submitted by local superiors in response to a request of the general chapter of 1256. This collection, from which the following selection is taken, provides an invaluable portrait of Dominican life during the first generation. Gerard also wrote a number of chronicles later in his life. He died at Limoges in 1271.[a] The following story from *The Lives of the Brethren* places the first meeting of Dominic and Francis in Rome at the time of the Fourth Lateran Council.

> A Lesser Brother, who was both a religious and trustworthy man, and who for a long time was a companion of blessed Francis, told the following incident to some brothers, one of whom wrote it down for the Master of our Order. When Saint Dominic was at Rome and was urging God and the Lord Pope to confirm his Order,[b] he had a vision one night when he was at his customary prayers. It seemed to him that he saw our Lord Jesus Christ standing in the air, brandishing three lances against the earth. His Virgin Mother, falling on her knees, asked him to temper justice with mercy and to show pity on those whom He had redeemed.
>
> Her Son said to her: "You see, do you not, how great are the injuries done to me? My justice will not allow such evils to go unpunished." Then his Mother said: "You who know all things, know this: there is a way by which you will lead those people back to you. I have a faithful servant whom you will send into the world to proclaim your word. The people will be converted and will seek you, the Savior of all. I will also give him another servant to work as a fellow laborer in the same way." Then the Son said to his Mother: "Behold, I am now appeased and I accept your offer; nevertheless show me the one whom you wish to destine for such an office." Then the Lady Mother offered blessed Dominic to the Lord Jesus Christ. The Lord said to her: "He will carry out well and zealously what you have said." She offered Saint Francis also, and the Savior commended him in a similar manner.

a. *Testimonia Minora*, 70-71; Kaeppeli, 2: 35-38. For a description of the *Lives of the Brethren*, see William Hinnebusch, *The History of the Dominican Order*, 2 vols. (New York: Alba House, 1965-73), 2: 281-82.

b. That is, at the time of the Fourth Lateran Council, 1215.

Blessed Dominic then carefully studied his companion in that vision, for he did not know him previously. The next day, however, encountering Francis in the church,[a] Dominic recognized him as the one he had seen during the night. He ran up and tenderly embraced him with a kiss, saying: "You are my comrade and will run together with me; let us stand together, and no adversary will prevail against us." He recounted to Francis his vision; and from that time on they became but one heart and one mind in God. They also enjoined their posterity to foster this fellowship for all time.

Stephen of Bourbon (1250-61)

Stephen, born in Belleville-sur-Saône (c. 1185-90), was a student at Paris (c. 1217-22), where he became acquainted with the newly-founded Order of Preachers, which was just becoming established there at the time. He was attached to the priory in Lyons in 1223, where he appears to have been based for the rest of his life. Stephen was a noted preacher and traveled widely; he was named to the office of inquisitor in 1235. He is best known for his vast collection of sermon aids, one of the first of its kind, the *Tractatus de diversis materiis praedicabilis,* which was still incomplete at the time of his death in 1261.[b] Arranged around the theme of the seven gifts of the Holy Spirit, Stephen's work featured many illustrative anecdotes or *exampla,* which preachers might find useful in composing their own sermons.[c] Several of his *exampla* concern St. Francis; the first of these is an account of Francis's showing reverence to a sinful priest.[d]

. . . I have heard that once, while Saint Francis was traveling through Lombardy, he entered into a church to pray, when a certain man ran up to him. Now this man, who was a Patarine or a Manichean,[e] was aware of the reputation for holiness that blessed Francis had among the people, and so he decided to take advantage of his visit to attract people to his own sect, subvert their faith, and bring the priestly office into contempt. For the parish priest there was notorious for his immoral life, it being known throughout the district that he kept a concubine. And so this man said to the saint: "Look, should we believe what a priest says and reverence the sacraments

a. The Lateran basilica.

b. An incomplete edition of this work was published by A. Lecoy de la Marche, *Anecdotes historiques tirés d'Etienne de Bourbon* (Paris, 1877), from which the texts in *Testimonia Minora* are taken.

c. Kaeppeli, 3: 354-55. Cf. D. L. d'Avray, *The Preaching of the Friars* (Oxford: Clarendon Press, 1985), 67-69.

d. *Testimonia Minora*, 93-94. 2C 201 speaks of Francis's reverence for priests, but this is a much more elaborate story.

e. That is, a Cathar.

he administers, when he maintains a concubine and his hands are polluted from touching the flesh of a whore?"

The holy man, realizing the evil intent of the heretic, went up to the priest in the presence of all the parishioners, knelt down before him and said: "I do not know whether these hands are such as this man says they are. But even if they were, I know that they can in no way lessen the power and the efficacy of the sacraments of God. These hands remain the means through which many of God's benefits and graces flow to the people. That is why I kiss them, out of respect for the things they administer and out of reverence for Him by whose authority they do so." Having said this, he knelt down in front of that priest and kissed his hands, to the confusion of the heretics and their adherents who were present.

Further on, Stephen gives another version of the same story:[a]

I have heard that one day blessed Francis entered a certain village in Lombardy where the fame of his holiness preceded him. Now a certain heretic, knowing him to be a simple man, wanted to demonstrate the truth of his own sect and increase those who believed in it, for all the people had run out to meet Francis. Therefore, seeing that the priest of the village was also hurrying out to greet Francis, the heretic called out: "Look, good man, what do you think about this fellow who has the care of this parish? He keeps a concubine, and it is clear to all of us that he is guilty of many sins. Can such a man administer or do anything which is not tainted?"

The Saint, realizing the heretic's malice, said: "Is this man here the priest of this village about whom you are saying such things?" When they said: "It is," Francis fell down on his knees in the dust and, kissing the priest's hands, said: "These hands have touched my Lord. No matter what kind of hands they may be, they are not able to make Him impure nor lessen His power. For the honor of the Lord, I will honor his servant. For himself, this man might be evil, but he is good for me." And at this the heretics were confounded.

In the same tract Stephen tells about a sermon which Francis gave in the presence of the prelates:[b]

a. *Testimonia Minora*, 94.

b. *Testimonia Minora*, 94-95. There is a story in 1C 73, about Francis preaching before the pope and cardinals, but it does not mention a prepared text which Francis had memorized and then forgot. Bonaventure, following Stephen, includes this detail in LMj XII 7.

I have heard from one of our brothers, a priest, that once some prominent prelates were gathered together in a certain place and were hearing that Saint Francis was preaching to both the birds and people. Now they knew that Francis was a simple man as far as letters were concerned, so they summoned him and told him that they wanted to hear him preach—a man who had usurped that office for himself. So they assigned a day on which he was to come before them to preach a sermon. Then, a very high-ranking bishop, who was a friend of the saint, fearing that the holy man would be confounded, had him come secretly to his house and confided to him the words of a soundly composed and well ordered sermon.

Now when the holy man arrived at the designated place, he tried to preach the text that had been prepared for him and which he had spent a long time memorizing, but he was not able to say a word. Pausing for a moment, he was wondering what he should do, and then, placing his confidence in God, he opened his Psalter, and this passage met his eyes: *All day long my disgrace is before me: my face is cov-* Ps 43:15
ered with shame. Using this text and speaking in the common dialect, he said many things about the arrogance and bad example of prelates, and how the entire Church becomes disordered by this. He told them they were the countenance of the Church, on which all its beauty should be reflected, for as Augustine says: "A beautiful countenance ought to have regular proportions, be properly adorned, and of a good complexion." But he told them how this countenance was covered with shame because of their bad example. For the more prominent, the more visible, the more beautiful, and the more worthy a part of the body is, all the more unsightly is any blemish on it.

And he told them many other things along these lines which were sufficiently able to embarrass them in a healthy way and profitably edify them.

Again, Stephen repeats this story later on in a more concise fashion:[a]

I heard that when Francis was preaching at Rome, some important clerics said to him: "We want you to preach to us tomorrow." A compassionate cardinal, fearing that Francis would become confused since he was a man of very little learning, called for him and promised him a prepared sermon to give, which he spent the entire night memorizing. However, when it was time for him to give the sermon, whatever he had firmly in his mind escaped him. Not knowing what to say, he opened the psalter and this verse stood out: *All day* Ps 43:15

a. *Testimonia Minora*, 95.

long my disgrace is before me: my face is covered with shame. Then he beautifully pointed out how they, in whom the beauty of the Church should be reflected, as in the face of a woman, were defiling it by their shameful deeds and rendering it detestable to all.

Jacopo de Voragine c. 1255-1267

The following selection is from the famous *Golden Legend,* which was far and away the most popular collection of saints' lives in the later Middle Ages. Its author was a Dominican brother, Jacopo [James] of Varazze, commonly referred to by the Latin form of his name and birthplace, Jacobus de Voragine. Born in the small town of Varazze on the Ligurian Riviera about 1228, Jacopo entered the Dominican Order in 1244. Over the course of the next five decades he became a noted teacher and administrator, serving as Prior Provincial of Lombardy for almost twenty years. In 1292, over his protests, he was elected Archbishop of Genoa, where he was esteemed as a reconciler and a friend of the poor. He died in 1298 and is venerated as "Blessed" in the Dominican Order.

Jacopo called his massive work simply *Legenda sanctorum,* and organized his material around the format of the liturgical year. Although he most likely intended it to provide material for preachers, it also was ideal as daily spiritual reading for the growing number of literate lay people, and this fact led to its translation into every European vernacular language over the next several centuries. Jacopo did not claim originality; he essentially wove together earlier legends. His purpose was to show that the individual concerned was truly a saint: one whose life was characterized by the practice of heroic virtue and the performance of miracles. These are certainly the elements which come through in the following depiction of Francis. Jacopo also interlarded his narrative with moral reflections from patristic sources; we have included one of these sections to give an appreciation of his style. Because of the tremendous diffusion of this work, Jacopo's portrayal of Francis would have been the one most widely shared by medieval Western Christians outside the Franciscan orders.[a]

[1]Francis was first named John, but later was called Francis. It 2C 3
seems that there were many reasons for this change. First, it was to
call attention to a miracle, because it is known that he miraculously
received from God [the ability to speak] the French language. For in 2C 13
his Legend it is related that whenever he was filled with the ardor of
the Holy Spirit, he would burst out with ardent words in French. The
second reason was to make manifest to all Francis's purpose in life.
For his Legend says that divine Providence caused this name to be 2C 3

a. See *The Golden Legend, Readings on the Saints*, trans. William Granger Ryan, 2 vols. (Princeton: University Press, 1993); A. Boureau, *Le legende dorée* (Paris: Editions du Cerf, 1984). The Latin text was edited by Th. Graese (Leipzig, 1850).

given to him, so that by means of such a distinctive and unusual name the report of his ministry would more quickly become known to the whole world. The third reason was to indicate the effects that would follow, for by this name all would understand that through his own ministry and that of his many sons he would set free and enfranchise[a] many slaves of sin and of the devil. The fourth reason was to indicate his magnanimity of heart. For the Franks get their name from the Latin *ferocitas*, or fierceness, because in the French there is a natural truthfulness and greatness of soul. The fifth reason was because of his skill in speech, for his preaching, like a battle ax, would cut into vices. Sixth, by reason of their fear when he would put the demons to flight. Seventh, by reason of his security in virtue, the perfection of his works, and his honorable dealings with others. For it is said that the term *franciscae* is used for the ax-shaped insignia which at Rome was carried before the consuls, and which generated terror and a sense of security and honor.

2C 3; LCh 2 [2]Francis, the servant and friend of the Most High, was born in the city of Assisi. He became a merchant and, up to the time he was
2C 3 twenty years old, passed his time in vain living. Then the Lord reproved him with the scourge of illness, and suddenly changed him into a different person, so that he now began to excel in the spirit of prophesy. Once he and many others had been captured by the Perugians and cast into a horrid prison, where the others bemoaned their fate, while Francis alone was exuberant. When he was questioned about this by his fellow prisoners, he replied: "Know that I am rejoicing now because eventually I will be venerated for all time."

2C 8; LMj I 6 [3]Another time he went to Rome for reasons of devotion, and there he put off his own fine clothing and donned the garb of a certain poor man. Then he sat among the beggars in front of the Church of St. Peter, and he eagerly ate among them as one of them; he would have done this more often, if he were not inhibited by shame before those who knew him.

2C 9 [4]The ancient enemy tried to turn Francis away from his salutary purpose, and put into his mind the image of a woman of Assisi who was monstrously hunchbacked, threatening to make Francis like her unless he came back to his senses from what he had begun to do. But he was encouraged by the Lord when he heard these words: "Francis, choose the bitter over the sweet and despise yourself, if you wish to acknowledge me." Then he happened to come across a leper, and although he had a very natural abhorrence for such persons, he remembered the Lord's utterance, and so rushed up and kissed the

a. There is a play on the Latin words *Franciscus* and *francus*, cf. FA:ED I 290 b.

man. The leper vanished instantly. Then Francis hastened to the
abode of the lepers and, after devoutly kissing their hands, he gave
them alms.

5 He went into the Church of San Damiano to pray, and the image 2C 10
of Christ miraculously spoke to him. "Francis," He said, "Go, repair
my house, which as you see, is fallen into ruins." From that hour his 2C 11
soul melted, and compassion for the Crucified became marvelously 2C 10
fixed in his heart. He then applied himself solicitously to the repairing of churches. He sold all he possessed, and when he offered the LCh 2
money to a priest, he refused to accept it out of fear of Francis's parents. Francis thereupon threw the money in front of him, as though
he valued it no more than dust.

6 For this reason his father seized him and held him bound, 2C 12; LMj II 4
whereupon Francis gave back the money to his father and in like
manner returned his clothing as well; thus naked he came swiftly to
the Lord and clothed himself with a hair shirt. Moreover, the servant
of God summoned a simple man whom he took in place of his father,
and he asked this man to bless him whenever his father verbally
abused him. Also during the winter, Francis's blood brother, seeing 2C 12
him at prayer clothed in rags and shivering with cold, said to someone: "Ask Francis whether he would sell you a penny's worth of his
sweat!" When Francis heard this, he quickly retorted: "In fact, I sell
it to my Lord."

7 Another day, hearing what the Lord said to his disciples when He LCh 3
sent them out to preach, he rose up at once to carry out all these
things with all his might. He took the shoes from his feet, clothed
himself with a single cheap tunic, and exchanged his belt for a rope.
Then, walking through the woods during the winter, he was cap- LMj II 5
tured by robbers. When they asked who he was, he declared that he
was the herald of God. So they seized him and threw him into the
snow, saying: "Lie there, you bumpkin, herald of God!"

8 Many people, of both noble and humble birth, clerics as well as LCh 4
lay people, spurned the pomp of the world and followed Francis's
footsteps. Their holy Father taught them how to strive for the fulfillment of evangelical perfection, to embrace poverty, and to walk in
the way of holy simplicity. Furthermore, for himself and for his present and future followers, he wrote an evangelical Rule which Pope
Innocent confirmed. From then on, he began with even greater fer- 2C 17
vor to sow the seeds of the word of God, making the rounds of the cities and towns.

9 Now there was a brother who seemed from the outside to possess 2C 28; LMj XI 10
remarkable sanctity, but he was nevertheless very peculiar. He used to
observe silence with such strictness that in making his confession he

used signs, not words. While he was being praised by all as a saint, the man of God came along and said: "Let that be enough, brothers! Don't praise his diabolical illusions to me! Let him be admonished to confess his sins once or twice a week. If he does not, it is all a temptation from the devil and a fraudulent deception." So the brothers admonished this brother, but he placed a finger over his lips, and shaking his head, he indicated that he would not confess his sins. Not many days later he returned to his vomit, and ended his life in evil deeds.

2C 31 [10]Once when the servant of God, worn out from a journey, was riding an ass, his companion, Brother Leonard of Assisi, who was also tired, began to think and say within himself: "This man's parents and mine were not of equal birth." At that moment the man of God dismounted from the ass and said to the brother: "It is not right for me to ride and you go on foot, because you are of nobler stock than I." The brother, astounded at this, threw himself at his Father's feet and begged his pardon.

2C 38 [11]Another time Francis was traveling along a road when a certain noble woman, almost running, caught up to him. Seeing how tired and out of breath she was, he felt compassion for her and asked her if she wanted something. "Father," she answered, "pray for me! I am not keeping the salutary resolution which I made because my husband is impeding me. He is very much opposed to my serving Christ." Then Francis said to her: "Go home, my daughter, because you will very soon be consoled concerning your husband. Tell him in the name of Almighty God and me, that now is the time of salvation; later it will be time for justice!" After she conveyed this message, her husband changed his attitude, and promised to live in continence.

2C 46 [12]By his prayers Francis procured a spring of water for a peasant who lived in a wilderness and was fainting for thirst.

2C 52 Under the inspiration of the Holy Spirit, Francis disclosed this secret to a brother who was very close to him: "Today on earth there is a certain servant of God, for whose sake, the Lord will not permit famine to rage among the people as long as he lives." And it is said that
2C 53 indeed such was the case throughout the saint's own lifetime. But once he was taken away, the whole condition of things was changed. For after his happy death, he appeared to that brother and said: "See, the famine is now upon you which, as long as I was living, the Lord did not permit to come upon the earth."

2C 61 [13]On the feast of the Resurrection the brothers in the hermitage at Greccio prepared the table more elaborately than usual with white coverings and glassware. When the man of God saw this, he retraced his steps immediately, placed on his head the hood of a beggar who was present there, took a staff in his hand, went outside and stood at the door. While the brothers were eating, he made a clamor at the door, that for the love of God they should give an alms to a poor, weak stranger. Invited, the poor man entered, and sitting alone on the floor, he placed his dish on the ashes. When the brothers saw this, they were filled with great amazement. Francis then said to them: "I saw a table set and made ready, and I know that it is not the table of poor men begging from door to door."

14 He so loved poverty in himself and in others, that he would al- 2C 70
ways call poverty his Lady. If he saw someone poorer than himself, 2C 83
he would immediately envy him, and would be afraid that he was being surpassed by him. For after he came across a poor little man one 2C 84
day, he said to his companion: "His neediness has put us to shame, and he censures our poverty very much. For my riches I have chosen my Lady Poverty, and look, she is reflected more in him . . ."

15 Saint Augustine[a] testifies: "Such is the beauty of divine justice, such is the joy of eternal light that, if it were not allowed to live more than a day in it, for this alone countless years of this life would rightly and justly be considered of very little worth. And so it is said
Ps 84:11 with not a little feeling: *I had rather one day in your courts than a thousand elsewhere.*"[b] It must also be realized that God especially regards one when He allows him to be afflicted. Hence Saint Augustine writes to Vincent the Donatist: "Not everyone who spares is a friend, nor is everyone, who uses the lash, an enemy; for better are the wounds of a friend than the voluntary kisses of an enemy. It is better to love with severity than to deceive with leniency. It is more beneficial to take bread from a hungry man if with no worry about food he neglects justice, than to break bread with the hungry man and who thus seduced gives in to injustice. Who ties up a mad man and arouses a lethargic one, is troublesome to both, yet he loves both. Who can love us more than God? And yet He not only does not cease to teach us lovingly, but He also does not cease to put fear into us profitably. Even the most pungent medicine of tribulation is often joined to the warm lotions by which we are soothed."[c] Ambrose also says: "A father is not always kissing his son; sometimes he chastises him. Therefore, when he chastises whom he loves, he is then exercising what is his duty towards him. For, love possesses its own wounds which are sweeter when they are inflicted most bitterly. Kinder is dutiful correction than flattering relaxation."[d]

a. This paragraph is missing in many manuscripts, possible due to its more ascetical nature.

b. Augustine, *De libero arbitrio* III 26, n. 77 (PL 32, 1308).

c. Augustine, *Epistola* 93, c.2, n.4 (PL 33, 323).

d. Ambrose, *Sermo* 44, n. 2 (PL 17, 690).

2C 85 [16]Once a certain poor man walked by him, and the man of God was moved with heartfelt compassion, but his companion said to him: "Even if this man is poor, yet perhaps in the whole province there is no one richer than he would like to be." The man of God replied: "Quick, take off your tunic and give it to that poor man and,
LMj VIII 5 prostrate at his feet, cry out that you are at fault." The brother immediately obeyed him.

2C 93; LMj VII 6 [17]One day three women, entirely alike in features and finery, met Francis and greeted him with the words: "Welcome to Lady Poverty!" Thereupon they vanished immediately and were seen no more.

2C 108 [18]Once when he came to the city of Arezzo and found that civil strife had erupted there, he looked down from a high point above the town and saw demons exulting over it. Summoning Sylvester, his companion, he said: "Go to the city gate, and on the part of Almighty God command the demons to leave the city!" The brother hurried to the gate and shouted out in a loud voice: "In the name of Almighty God and by command of our Father Francis, all you demons depart!" And in a short time all the citizens returned to tranquillity.

2C 109; LMj III 5 Now, this Brother Sylvester, when he was still a secular priest, saw in a dream a golden cross coming forth from the mouth of Francis. The top of the cross touched the heavens; its arms stretched wide and enclosed both parts of the world in its embrace. The priest, smitten with self-reproach, promptly left the world and became a perfect imitator of the man of God.

2C 116; LMj V 4 [19]While the man of God was at prayer, the devil called him three times by his given name. When the saint answered, the devil said: "There is no one in the whole world who is such a sinner that the Lord would not forgive if he repents. But whoever kills himself by harsh penances, he will never experience mercy." By a revelation, the servant of God immediately recognized the enemy's deceit: how the devil was trying to seduce him to cool his ardor to tepidity. So the ancient enemy, seeing that he did not prevail, aroused in Francis a serious temptation of the flesh. The man of God, realizing this, took off his clothes and beat himself with a very hard lash, saying: "Come now, brother ass, it is right that you remain subject to the whip."

2C 117 But when the temptation refused to depart, he went outside and plunged himself naked into a snowdrift. Then he took seven handfuls of snow which he shaped into balls. Setting these before himself, he began to address his body: "Look here," he said, "this larger one is your wife, these next four are your two sons and two daughters, and the last two are a manservant and a maidservant. Hurry up and clothe them all, for they are dying of cold. Or, if it bothers you to give them so much attention, then be solicitous in serving the one Lord!" The devil was immediately confounded and went away, and the man of God returned to his cell, glorifying God.

[20]Once Francis was invited by Lord Leo, Cardinal of [the church 2C 119
of] the Holy Cross, to be his guest for a little while. One night demons
came and gave him a severe beating. He called his companion and re- 2C 120
lated his experience, saying: "The demons are our Lord's police,
whom He designates to punish excesses. I truly do not recall an offense which through the providence of God I have not washed away LMj VI 10; 2C 12
by making satisfaction. But perhaps He has permitted his police to attack me because I am staying in the courts of the powerful, and this might not be making a good impression on my poor brothers, who may think that I am lolling here in luxury." So he arose very early the next morning and left that house.

[21]One time when Francis was praying, he heard troops of demons 2C 122
running about noisily on the roof of the house. Provoked by this, he went outside, made the sign of the cross over himself and said: "On the part of Almighty God I tell you demons, whatever you are permitted to do to my body, do it! I will gladly bear everything, because I have no greater enemy than my body. So you will be freeing me from my adversary when you are taking vengeance upon it instead of upon me." The demons, confounded, vanished.

[22]Once a certain brother, a companion of the man of God, was rapt 2C 123; LMj VI 6
in ecstasy. Among the thrones in heaven he saw one that was particularly distinguished and that shone forth with a remarkable glory. While he was wondering for whom such a glittering throne was reserved, he heard: "This throne belonged to one of the fallen princes, and is now being made ready for the humble Francis." Leaving his prayer, the brother asked the man of God: "Father, what is your opinion of yourself?" Francis said to him: "It seems to me that I am the greatest of sinners." And immediately the Holy Spirit spoke in the heart of the brother: "Know by this that the vision you saw was true, since humility has raised this humblest of men to the throne which was lost through pride."

[23]In a vision the servant of God saw a crucified seraph above him, LCh 11
who so graphically impressed the marks of the Crucifixion upon him that he himself seemed to have been crucified; his hands, feet, and side were marked with the sign of the cross. But with diligent zeal he hid these stigmata from the eyes of all. Certain people, however, saw them during his lifetime, and very many more saw them when he was dead.

[24]It has been demonstrated by many miracles that these stigmata were real. It may suffice to insert here two of these miracles which

3C 6 happened after his death. In Apulia a man named Rogero, while standing before an image of Saint Francis, began to ask himself: "Is this true? Had he been so illustrious for such a miracle? Or was this a pious illusion or even a fraud contrived by his brothers?" While he was turning this over in his mind, he suddenly heard a sound like that of a arrow being shot from a crossbow, and felt that he was seriously wounded in his left hand. But when he saw that his glove was not torn, he pulled it from his hand, and there he saw in the palm of his hand a serious wound such as an arrow would make. From this wound such a powerful burning heat came forth that he felt he would faint with the pain and the burning. Then Rogero repented his doubt and testified that he firmly believed in the stigmata of blessed
3C 7 Francis. And after he petitioned the holy man of God by his stigmata for two days, he was suddenly healed of the heat and the pain.

3C 11 [25]And the following happened in the kingdom of Castile. A man who was devoted to Saint Francis was on his way to compline, when he was ambushed by mistake in a trap set for another man and was left half dead of a lethal wound. Then the cruel murderer thrust a sword into the man's throat, but he could not pull it out, and so went
3C 12 away. From all sides a great crowd came running and loudly bewailed the man for dead. Then, when at midnight the bell of the brothers was rung for Matins, the man's wife began to cry out: "My lord, arise and go to Matins. The bells are calling you!" He immediately raised his hand as if to summon someone to extract the sword; but, as all looked on, the sword, as if brandished by the hand of a brawny fighter, leaped out and fell at a distance. Immediately the
3C 13 man was perfectly cured, and raising himself up, he said: "Blessed Francis came to me and touched his stigmata to my wounds, and by their soothing power he treated all my wounds and wondrously healed them by their contact with the stigmata. And when he was about to leave, I indicated to him that he should withdraw the sword, because otherwise I would not be able to speak. He immediately grasped it and vehemently pulled it out, and at once, by touching my wounded throat with his holy stigmata, he cured it perfectly."

2C 148 [26]In the city of Rome those brilliant luminaries, blessed Dominic and blessed Francis, were in the presence of the Lord of Ostia who later became the Supreme Pontiff. The Bishop asked them: "Why do we not make bishops and prelates out of your brothers, since they have distinguished themselves above others by their teaching and example?" A long discussion took place between the two saints as to who would give the response. Finally, humility conquered Francis, lest he put himself before Dominic, and it also conquered Dominic so that he would humbly obey by answering first. Blessed Dominic therefore said: "My lord, my brothers have already been raised to a high status, if they only knew it; even if it were in my power, I would not permit them to attain any other type of honor." Then Francis responded by saying: "My brothers are called Lesser so that they will not presume to become greater."

27 Full of dove-like simplicity he exhorted all creatures to the love LCh 7; 1C 59
of their Creator. He preached to the birds and was understood by them. They were touched by him, nor did they leave him without his permission. When some swallows were chattering while Francis was preaching, they all became silent at his command. A cricket, living in 2C 171
a fig tree near his cell at the Portiuncula, would frequently sing. Once the man of God extended his hand and called to it: "My Sister Cricket, come to me!" The obedient cricket immediately flew up to his hand. He said to it: "Sing, Sister Cricket, and praise your Lord!" This she immediately did, nor did she leave without permission.

28 He spared lights, lamps and candles for he did not wish to dim 2C 165
their brightness with his hand. He walked on rocks reverently out of
1 Cor 10:4 respect for Him who is called *the Rock*. He would pick up worms from
the road lest they be trampled underfoot by those passing by, and during the winter cold he commanded that the best wine and honey be put out for the bees lest they perish from want of food. He called all animals "brothers" and "sisters." Because of the love of the Cre- 1C 80
ator he was filled with a remarkable and ineffable love, whenever he looked upon the sun, the moon, and the stars, and he invited them to 1C 81
love their Creator. He did not allow a large tonsure be made for him. 2C 193
He said: "I want my simple brothers to have a share in my head."

29 A certain man of the world heard the servant of God, Francis, 2C 106; LMj IV 9
preaching at San Severino, and by divine revelation saw that Saint Francis was pierced through by two gleaming swords in the form of a cross, one of them passing from his head to his feet, and the other passing through his breast from one outstretched hand to the other. Since he had never seen Francis, this man nevertheless recognized him by such a sign. With a change of heart he entered the Order, and completed his life happily.

30 When Francis incurred a weakness of the eyes from his constant LMj V 8
weeping, he gave this answer to those who were persuading him to desist from crying: "The visitation of eternal light should not be rejected because of the love of the light which we have here in common with flies." When he was urged by his brothers that he allow a rem- LMj V 9; 2C 166
edy to be applied to his failing eyes, and the surgeon held in his hands an iron instrument glowing with fire, he said: "My Brother Fire, at this hour be kind to me and helpful! I pray to the Lord who LMj V 9
created you that you temper your ardor for me." And saying this, he

made the sign of the cross over the searing iron. It is related that when the instrument was applied to his tender flesh, from his ear to his eyebrow, he felt no pain.

LMj V 10 31 When the servant of God was suffering from a very serious illness at the hermitage of Sant'Urbano and realized his strength was failing, he asked for a cup of wine, but there was none there. Yet he made the sign of the cross over water that was brought to him, and soon it was turned into excellent wine. Thus what the poverty of that solitary place could not provide, this holy man's purity accomplished, and when he tasted the wine, he suddenly felt better.

LMj VI 1 32 Francis preferred to hear himself reviled rather than praised, so when people extolled the merits of his sanctity, he would order a brother to fill his ears with abusive words. And when that brother, though unwilling, called him a peasant and an unskilled and useless merchant, he would rejoice and say: "May God bless you, because you are saying what is very true, and I should hear such things!"

LMj VI 4 33 The servant of God did not wish to rule, but to be subject to authority; not to give orders, but to obey. Therefore, he resigned his office as general, and asked for a guardian, to whose will he would be subject in everything. To the brother with whom he was accustomed to travel he also always promised obedience and kept this promise.

LMj VI 11; 2C 154 34 Once a certain brother had done something against the law of obedience but then gave indications of repentance. Still, the man of God to the fright of all, commanded that this brother's capuche be thrown into the fire. And when the capuche had been in the middle of the fire for a while, he commanded that it be retrieved from the fire and restored to the brother. The capuche was snatched from the middle of the flames and showed no trace of burning.

LMj VIII 9 35 Once, when he was walking through the Venetian marshes, he came upon a great multitude of birds singing, and said to his companion: "Our sister birds are praising their Creator; let us go among them and recite the canonical Hours to the Lord." When they entered that part of the marsh, the birds did not move away, but since the brothers could not hear one another because of their great chattering, Francis said: "My Sister Birds, stop your singing, until we have finished our praises which are due to the Lord!" The birds immediately became silent and, after the praises were finished, he gave them permission to sing, and immediately they resumed their song in their accustomed manner.

LMj XI 4 36 Once, when Francis was courteously invited to dinner by a knight, he said to him: "Brother Host, take my advice and confess your sins, because you will soon be dining elsewhere!" The soldier quickly followed his advice: he put his house in order and accepted a salutary penance. Then as they went into dinner, the host suddenly expired.

[37]Francis came upon a great many birds and saluted them as though they had the use of reason, saying: "My brother birds, you ought to give great praise to your Creator, who clothes you with feathers, furnishes you with wings to fly, gives you air that is pure, and governs you and makes you carefree." The birds began to stretch their necks toward him, spread their wings, open their beaks, and fix their eyes on him. And as he walked through their midst, his tunic would touch them, but not one of them moved until, after he gave them permission, they all flew away at once . . . LMj XII 3

[38]Since we do not know whether the justice which we exhibit in our works is genuine, we have one remedy: we can take refuge in a humble confession, and call upon the court of divine mercy. As St Bernard says: "We are not able to have sufficient influence with the
Jas 3:2; Ps 43:22 Lord since *in many things we all offend,* nor is deception of any use, for He *knows the secrets of the heart,* the more the works are made manifest;
Jb 21:15 nor can He be resisted by strength, because He is *the Almighty.* What, then, is left for us, except that with our whole mind we take refuge in the remedies of humility, so that what we find wanting in other things, we can supply from those remedies."[a] Therefore, he also says: "Humility, however great, simply should not be feared; however, one should tremble at and be greatly frightened at even the least bit of pride, rashly taken for granted. Therefore, O man, do not compare yourself to those who are greater; do not compare yourself to those who are lesser; do not compare yourself to someone, not even to one."[b]

Also Saint Augustine wrote in the fourteenth chapter of his *City of God;* "Humility is especially recommended now in the city of God in this time of our sojourn and it is especially preached in its king who is Christ. The opposite to this virtue is the vice of pride. It is especially found in His adversary, who is the devil and who has dominion in this regard as is taught by the Sacred Scriptures."[c]

Christ taught humility by His example in His birth, in His death, in His preaching, and in His performing miracles. It should be noted that humility is recommended in every type of person.

When King Xerxes saw his army before him, an innumerable multitude of soldiers, and thinking that this whole army would be

---

a. Bernard, *De gradibus humilitatis* IV 14 (PL 182, 949).

b. Bernard, *On the Song of Songs*, 37:7, translated by Kilian Walsh, introduction by Jean Leclercq (Kalamazoo, London, Oxford: Cistercian Publications, 1976), 186.

c. Augustine, *The City of God* XIV 6.

turned to dust within one hundred years, he is reported to have said: "People say that I am the commander-in-chief of a great and brave army. But I confess that I am going to be the king of dust."

Ambrose says: "Humility is the guardian of virtue."[a] Gregory says something similar: "Everything you do will perish if it is not carefully protected in humility."[b] The devil said to Macharius: "It is your humility alone that conquers me."[c] In a section of *De Moralibus,* Gregory states: "In order that anyone's deeds be considered more worthy, it is necessary that to him they always seem unworthy."[d] And Jerome says: "How does he become proud who always carries humility with him?"[e]

LMj XII 4 [39]When Francis was preaching at Alviano, he was not able to be heard because of the chirping of the swallows who were nesting there. So he said to them: "My sister swallows, it is now time for me to speak. You have spoken enough. Keep silent, until the Word of God is completed!" The swallows, with prompt obedience, were suddenly silent.

2C 68; LMj VII 5 [40]Once the man of God was passing through Apulia and came upon a large purse bursting with coins, lying on the road. When his companion saw it, he wanted to take it and distribute the money to the poor. But Francis would not allow him to do so. He said to his companion: "It is not right, my son, to take what belongs to someone else." When his companion insisted vehemently, Francis prayed a little and then commanded his companion to pick up the purse, which now contained a snake instead of money. When the brother saw the snake, he began to be afraid, but wishing to fulfill the obligation of obedience, he took the purse in his hands, and from the purse a huge serpent sprang out. The holy man said: "For a servant of God money is nothing else but the devil and a poisonous snake."

2C 49; LMj XI 9 [41]Once there was a brother who had a serious temptation. He began to think that if he had something written by the hand of his father, the temptation would immediately be put to flight, but he would in no way dare to reveal the temptation to the saint. But then one time the man of God called him and said: "My son, bring me pen and paper, because I want to write down some Praises of God!" After he wrote the Praises, he said: "Take this paper and guard it diligently

a. Ambrose, *Expositio Evangelium secundum Lucam* VIII 41 (PL 15, 1777).

b. Gregory, *Morals* XXXIV 51(PL 76, 747).

c. *Vitis Patrum* V, XV, 26 (PL 73, 959).

d. Gregory, *Morals* V 17 (PL 75, 688).

e. Jerome, *In Epistola ad Ephesios* II 3, 3 (PL 26, 493).

until the day of your death." All temptation immediately left the brother.

When the holy man was lying ill, this same brother began to think: "Look, our father is approaching his death, and how very much consoled I would be, if after his death I had my father's tunic." A little while later, the holy man called him and said: "I give you this tunic and after my death you may have full right to it." 2C 50

[42]When Francis was the guest of a upright man at Alessandria in Lombardy, he was asked by him to observe the Gospel by eating whatever was placed before him. When Francis assented to his devotion, the host prepared a fine seven-year-old capon for him to eat. While they were eating, an unbeliever came and asked for an alms for the love of God.[a] The man of God, hearing that blessed name, sent the man a piece of the capon. The wretched man kept what was given to him, and on the next day, while the holy man was preaching, held it up and said: "Look at what kind of meat this man Francis eats, whom you honor as a saint. He gave this to me last evening." But the piece of capon now appeared like a fish, and so all the people jeered at him as a madman. The man was ashamed and sought pardon, and, once he had come to his senses, the meat returned to its own species. 2C 78 2C 79

[43]One time when Francis was seated at table and a comparison was being made concerning the poverty of the Blessed Virgin and her Son, the man of God immediately rose from the table and, with repeated sorrowful sobs and tears, he ate the rest of his bread sitting on the bare ground. 2C 200

[44]In his *Letter on the Sacraments of the Church,*[b] Anselm tells how great was Christ's poverty and how much he was despised, and then
1 Pt 2:21 says: "*Christ suffered for us, leaving us an example, that we might follow in his footsteps.* He gave us in these things an example of enduring incomparable contempt and poverty for the sake of justice. For he was held in such contempt and was judged so accursed that he was deemed unworthy to die in any human habitation, nor even among human beings except those who were accursed, nor under any shelter but the sky, from beneath which he could not be ejected. Thus, ac-
Ps 22: 7 cording to the prophet, he was regarded as *one scorned by others and the outcast of the people.* Moreover, he was so poor that when he came into the world, he was born not in his own house but in another's. And once he was born he was placed, for lack of a room, in the manger of
Mt 8:20 brute animals. And living in the world, he had *nowhere to lay his head.* And dying, he had nothing with which to cover his nakedness. And

a. A Cathar heretic.

b. Anselm, *Epistola de diversitate Sacramentorum Ecclesiae*, Responsio 3 (PL 158, 554).

dead, he had nothing with which to be enshrouded; and he had neither a sepulcher nor a place where His corpse could be buried."

And Jerome in his *Letter to Eustochium* says:[a] "The Son of God for our salvation became the son of man. For nine months in the womb he awaits his birth, undergoes the most revolting conditions, and comes forth covered with blood, to be swathed in rags and mocked with caresses. He who encloses the world in his fist is confined in the narrow limits of a manger. I say nothing of the thirty years during which he lives in obscurity, content with the poverty of his parents. When he is scourged he holds his peace; when He is crucified, He
prays for those who crucified Him. *What, then, shall I return to the Lord* Ps 115:3
for all the things he has given me?"

2C 201 [45]Francis wished that great reverence be shown to the priestly order, to whom the power has been given to confect the sacrament of the Body of Christ. He often said: "If I happened to meet a saint from heaven on a road and some poor priest, I would straight-away hurry to kiss the hands of the priest and would say to the saint: "Wait for me, St. Lawrence, because the hands of this priest handle the Word of life, and therefore he possesses something that is beyond what is human."

1Ch 9 [46]During his lifetime Francis was famous for many miracles.
Bread brought to him to be blessed brought health to many who
Ch 10; LMj V 9 were sick. He turned water into wine. A sick person who tasted this
wine was immediately cured. And he performed many other miracles.

2C 214 [47]When he was worn out by long infirmity and his last days were
2C 216 approaching, he had himself placed naked on the bare ground, and
then had all the brothers assisting there called to him. He laid his
2C 217 hands on each one and blessed all who were present. And then, after
the manner of the Lord's Supper, he divided small pieces of bread
among each one. As was his custom he invited all creatures to praise
God; he even encouraged death itself, hateful and detestable as it is
to all, to join in praise. Happily hastening towards it, he invited it to
LMj XIV 6 be his guest, saying: "Welcome, my Sister Death!" Thus he came to
his last hour and fell asleep in the Lord.

2C 217a [48]A brother saw Francis's soul in the form of a star, as large as the
2C 218 moon and as brilliant as the sun. The minister of the brothers in the
Terra di Lavoro, Augustine by name, was also in his last hour of life, and although he had long since lost his power of speech, he nevertheless suddenly cried out: "Wait, Father, wait for me! See, I am coming with you." When the brothers asked what he meant, he said:

a. Jerome, *Epistola ad Eustochium* 39 (PL 22, 423).

"Don't you see our Father Francis who is on his way to heaven?" Then suddenly dying in peace, he followed his father.

[49]A lady who had been devoted to blessed Francis had gone the 3C 40
way of all flesh, and the priests and clerics were present in great numbers at the bier to celebrate the funeral rites. Suddenly, the woman sat up erect on her bier and called to one of the attending priests, saying: "Father, I want to go to confession. I had died, and I was about to be committed to a horrid prison, because I had not yet confessed the sin I shall now declare to you. But St. Francis prayed for me to be allowed to return to my body, in order that by confessing this sin I might merit pardon. As soon as I declare this sin, I will rest in peace as all of you will see." As soon as she confessed her sin and received absolution, she fell asleep in the Lord.

[50]When the brothers of Nocera asked a man for the loan of a cart, 3C 43
he replied indignantly: "I would rather skin two of you alive, and Saint Francis with you, than let you use my cart." But when he calmed down, he contradicted himself and was sorry for his blasphemous words, for he feared the wrath of God. Soon his son became ill and died. When the man saw his son dead, he rolled around on the ground in grief, and weeping, invoked Saint Francis, saying: "It is I who have sinned! You ought to be scourging me! O Saint, give back to the one devoutly beseeching you what you have taken from the one who unjustifiably blasphemed you!" His son arose and held his laments in check. "When I was dead," he said, "St. Francis led me along a long, dark road and finally brought me to a very beautiful garden. Then he said to me: 'Return to your father! I do not wish to detain you any longer.' "

[51]A poor man owed a sum of money to a rich man and he asked 3C 89
the rich man to extend the time of payment out of love for Saint Francis. But the rich man responded arrogantly: "I will shut you up in a place where neither Francis nor anyone else will be able to help you." Then he chained the poor man and locked him up in a dark prison. A short time later Saint Francis came there, broke into the prison, smashed the chains, and brought him home safe and sound.

[52]There was a knight who belittled the works and miracles of 3C 129
Saint Francis. One time when he was playing at dice, he was filled with incredulity and folly and he said to those watching: "If Francis is a saint, let the dice turn up eighteen!" On his first throw, three sixes turned up. Then he cast the dice nine more times, and each time three sixes appeared. But even then, compounding his madness, he said: "If it is true that this Francis is a saint, may my body fall today to the sword! But if he isn't a saint, may I escape unharmed." In order that his prayer be to no avail, when he was finished with the dice and

was beating his nephew, the latter grasped a sword, pierced his uncle's vital parts and killed him instantly.

3C 159 [53]A certain man whose leg was so consumed with disease that he was unable to move called upon Saint Francis in these words: "Help me, Saint Francis! Be mindful of the devotion and the service I have rendered you! For I have transported you upon my donkey, I have kissed your holy hands and feet, and look! I am dying from this most excruciating pain." Soon Saint Francis appeared to him carrying a small staff on which was the figure "Tau," and touched the source of the pain. The abscess broke and he immediately was cured, but the sign of the 'Tau' always remained over the spot. Saint Francis used to sign his letters with this symbol.

LMj M II 2 [54]In the town of Pomereto in the mountain region of Apulia, a young girl, the only child of her mother and father, had died. The mother, who was devoted to Saint Francis, was overcome with very great grief. But the saint appeared to her and said: "Do not weep! The light of your lamp, which you mourn as extinguished will be restored to you through my intercession." The mother, therefore, with her confidence restored, did not allow the corpse to be carried out for burial, but calling upon the name of Saint Francis, she took hold of her dead daughter, and raised her in good health.

LMj M II 4 [55]In the city of Rome, a little boy fell from the window of a palace and was killed, but when St. Francis was invoked, the child was immediately restored to life.

LMj M II 6 [56]And in the city of Suessa a house collapsed and crushed a young man to death. His corpse had already been placed on a bier for burial, and the mother invoked blessed Francis with all the devotion she could. Then about midnight the boy yawned, arose sound in body, and broke out into words of praise.

LMj V M 3 [57]Brother James of Rieti had crossed a river with some brothers in a small boat and he had already left his companions on the bank. He was preparing to step ashore himself when the boat capsized and he was plunged into the depths of the river. His brothers called upon blessed Francis to save the drowning man, and he himself, as best he could, implored the saint's aid. And what happened? This brother began to walk on the river bed as though on dry land! He took hold of the submerged boat, and brought it to the shore. His clothing was not even wet, not so much as a drop of water had touched his tunic.

Chronicles

Philippe Mousket (c. 1238-43)

Born into a middle-class family in the region of Tournai, Philippe was one of the more celebrated composers of vernacular lyric narratives in the first half of the thirteenth century.[a] He is best known for his rhymed "History of the French Kings," composed in old French, a lengthy work which traces their lineage from mythological beginnings during the Trojan Wars. The work ends with events in 1243, so it is generally thought that Philippe died shortly afterwards.[b]The following brief entry under the events of the year 1228 is particularly interesting for its description of the Stigmata.

Behold, another advances,
Coming from Rome, Saint Francis.
At Perugia lies his holy body;
When he died, his hands and feet
Were not sound, but pierced through
With nails hammered by God.
When he prayed, God heard,
And his holy body rejoiced much in it.
He died, and wrought marvels,
For he was patient in suffering.
He was humble, so God exalted him.
He was the one who initiated
The Order of Lesser Brothers
Those who renounce both land and honors.

Passion of San Verecondo (c. 1250-70)

The Benedictine monastery of San Verecondo was located just south of Gubbio, on the road from Assisi. According to tradition, this is the monastery Francis stopped at briefly shortly after the break with his father. Although Francis met a harsh reception there, he apparently later had good relationships with the community.[c]

This "passion" of the titular saint of the monastery, written by an unknown monk of the abbey in the third quarter of the thirteenth century, incorporates some data on the monastery's history.[d] Especially interesting are two incidents about St. Francis reported by eyewitnesses.

---

a. On this genre, see VL, introduction in FA: ED I 423-37.

b. Cf. D. Hoeges, "Mousket, Philippe," *Lexicon des Mittelalters* 6: 875; text taken from *Historia Regum Francorum*, *Monumenta Germaniae Historiae*, *Scriptores*, XXVI, p. 816.

c. Cf. 1C 16.

d. See M. Faloci-Pulignani, "San Francesco e il monastero di San Verecondo," *Miscellanea Franciscana* 10 (1906): 6-7. The Latin text is taken from *Testimonia Minora*, pp. 10-11. The numbers in parentheses are those used in the text itself.

[1]Among more recent events, [it should be mentioned that] the blessed Francis, that little poor man, was offered hospitality quite often at the Monastery of San Verecondo, where the devoted abbot and the monks received him graciously. It was here that he performed the miracle concerning the sow that had devoured a little lamb.[a]

[2]It was also in the vicinity of this monastery that Blessed Francis held a chapter of three hundred of the first brothers, and the abbot and the monks graciously provided them, as best they could, with the necessities of life. Signore Andrea, now a very elderly man, who was there at the time, testified that there was plenty of barley and wheat bread, as well as millet and sorghum, pure water to drink, and apple wine diluted for the infirm. They had also ample supplies of beans and peas.

[3]Now Blessed Francis was wasted and weakened from frequently chastising his flesh, from nocturnal vigils, from praying and fasting, and thus quite unable to walk about; especially after he was marked with the wounds of our Savior he was not well enough to travel on foot, so he rode about on a little donkey. One evening when it was almost dark, Francis was on this donkey, traveling with his companion along the road to San Verecondo, his shoulders and upper arms covered with a rough sackcloth mantle, when some field laborers called out to him: "Brother Francis, stay with us here. Do not go any farther. Ferocious wolves are roaming about in this area. They will devour your little donkey and do you harm." Then Brother Francis replied: "I have done no injury to Brother Wolf, that he would attempt to harm our Brother Ass. Farewell, my sons, and fear God." And so Brother Francis continued on his way unharmed. This incident was reported to me by a farmer who was present at the time.

Thomas of Split (1250-65)

Thomas was born (c. 1200) in Split (called Spalato by the Italians), on the Dalmatian coast of Croatia. As a young man he studied arts and law in Bologna; returning to his native city, he became a canon of the cathedral church. Appointed archdeacon of Split in 1230, Thomas played a prominent role in church affairs in the region; he was elected archbishop in 1242 but resigned in order to devote himself to his scholarly career. He is best known for his Historia Salonitana, one of the major sources for medieval Croatian history, from which the following vivid incident is taken. Thomas died in 1268 and was buried in the Franciscan church in Split.[b]

---

a. Cf. 2C 111; LMj VIII 6.

b. The Latin text can be found in *Historia Pontificia Salonitanorum et Spalatensium*, in *Monumenta Germaniae Historica* 29, 580; *Testimonia Minora*, 10. See "Thoma v. Split," *Lexicon der Mittelalters* 8: 852-53.

In the same year (1222) on the feast of the Assumption of the Mother of God, when I was residing at the Studium in Bologna, I saw Saint Francis preaching in the square in front of the town hall, where almost all the inhabitants of the city had assembled.[a] The theme of his sermon was: "Angels, People, Demons." He spoke so well and so clearly about these three kinds of rational creatures that this unlettered man's sermon became the source of not a little amazement for the many educated people who were present. He did not, however, hold to the usual manner of preaching, but spoke like a political orator.[b] The whole tenor of his words concerned itself with abolishing hostilities and renewing agreements of peace. His habit was filthy, his whole appearance contemptible, and his face unattractive; but God gave his words such efficacy that many factions of the nobility, among whom the monstrous madness of long-standing enmities had raged uncontrollably with much bloodshed, were led to negotiate peace. There was such great popular reverence and devotion towards him, that a mob of men and women crowded in upon him, jostling about either to touch the fringe of his habit or even tear off a shred of his ragged clothing.

Richer of Sens (1255-1264)

Richer, a Benedictine monk of the abbey of Sens in northern France, wrote a chronicle of his archdiocese, in which he describes the rise of the new mendicant orders.[c] His description reflects the secular-mendicant controversy then raging in northern France, and the hostility towards the friars by many in the church establishment there.

[1]About thirty years before these things, there lived in the lower parts of Germany, a certain enclosed nun by the name of Hildegard, who led a extremely holy way of life. Among the other graces God bestowed upon her she enjoyed the gift of prophecy . . .[d] She wrote and

a. We possess another testimony of this same event. Federico Visconti, Archbishop of Pisa, said in a sermon given in 1265: "Blessed are those who saw this Saint, namely Francis. Through God's grace we ourselves saw him and even touched him with our hand in the town square of Bologna, in the midst of a great throng of people." Cf. Michael Bihl, "E sermonibius Friderici de Vicecomitibus, archiepiscopus Pisani, de S. Francisco," AFH 1 (1908): 652-655.

b. The genre of speech specified here by Thomas is a *contio,* the type of political speech or harangue characteristic of the assemblies of the Italian communes. In his *Rhetorica novissima* , Boncompagno da Signa [cf. FA:ED 1 590] gives a disdainful description of this popular *ars concionandi* (Book XIII, ed. A. Gaudentius, *Bibliotheca iuridica Medii Aevi. Scripta Anecdota glossatorum*, II [Bologna, 1892]), pp. 296-97. See C. Delcorno, "Origini della predicazione francescana," in *Francesco d'Assisi e francescanesimo dal 1216 al 1226* (Assisi, 1977), 125-60 (description of the *contio* on p. 151).

c. "Gesta Senonensis Ecclesiae," *Monumenta Germaniae Historicae, Scriptores*, XXV, 306-307. The prophecy of St. Hildegard is lacking in the selection in *Testimonia Minora*, 32-33.

d. On Hildegard, see FA:ED I 595.

prophesied about the orders which would arise in the future, that is to say, of the Preachers and the Lesser Brothers, who have arisen in our own times. For she spoke clearly that certain brothers would arise with a large tonsure, in a novel type of religious habit, who in the beginning would be received by all the people as they would receive God himself. She predicted that they would not have any property of their own, but would live solely on the alms of the faithful, nor would they keep any of these alms for the next day's needs. Rather, satisfied with this poverty, they would go through towns and villages and countryside, preaching everywhere. In these early years they would be much loved by their God and by all the people. But in a short time, they would become lukewarm in their commitment, and their reputation would become cheapened. This is what Hildegard predicted about the brothers, the Preachers and the Minors, and what she said was later proven correct.

[2]And so it was during the time of Innocent III that a man called Dominic, from the region of Tuscany,[a] began his Order of Preachers, just as about the same time, a certain Francis, of whom we shall speak shortly, began the Order of the Lesser Brothers . . .

[3]Francis, the first of the Lesser Brothers of whom we spoke of earlier, was born in Assisi, a city in the valley of Spoleto. He was the son of a wealthy citizen of that city, who was accustomed to send Francis frequently to France for business purposes. In fact, it is reported that he was called Francis because of this connection with France. While exhibiting good native ability and wisdom as a young man, as merchants usually do, he pursued the quest of worldly things; yet he most liberally dispersed to churches and the poor some of the merchandise entrusted to him by his father. It happened one time that Francis returned to his native place. Welcomed cheerfully by his father, he remained with him for a few days. But one day when his father was celebrating a feast day in great style, Francis, a truly praiseworthy young man, entered a room and completely undressed. Then he clothed himself with a tunic, made of cheap cloth, to which a capuche had been sewn, and he girt himself with a knotted cord. And so, barefoot and with his hair shorn, he went out to his father, and bidding his father farewell he asserted that he *wished to serve God rather than mammon.* (Mt 6:24) While traveling around that region he gathered many brothers to himself and to his Order. Going to Pope Gregory,[b] they were authorized as preachers by him. And so they were located throughout various regions.

a. An error of the author.

b. Another error; the permission to preach was first granted by Innocent III.

[4]Francis, traveling around through cities and towns, with a few of his brothers, is reported once to have come to a certain city to preach. He wanted to preach the word of God there, but the citizens of that place, considering him and his companions to be fools because of their habit, expelled them from their city. But standing outside the city gate next to a public road, he saw various kinds of birds feeding in a field. As if he were speaking to people, he called them to come to him, and immediately at his words such a multitude of different birds flocked around him that it is said that never had so many been seen in that area.

Blessed Francis admonished the birds that since human beings, who possessed intelligence and feeling, disdained to listen to the word of God, at least they, who lacked discernment, should not fail to listen to God's decrees. Those birds, raising their necks, extended their heads and faces toward him, as if they understood him. Then he exhorted them that with their voices and their songs they should praise and glorify God, who created and nourishes them. He spoke to them in this manner for a long time, as if he were discussing the word of God with them as though with rational creatures.

Now the people, passing by and seeing an unknown man in such strange clothes, preaching to birds as if he were preaching to people, told all this in the city. The whole city came out to Francis and were in admiration over the miracle of the birds. Then they asked him to pardon their city for expelling him. But he blessed the birds and ordered them to leave. Then turning towards the people, he reproached them, because a people with intelligence and reason refused to hear the word of God, while birds, who lacked reason, received it with great joy. After he spoke to the people for a long time and finished his sermon, he blessed them, and then left the area.

[5]It is said that he had even sailed across the sea and had come to Babylonia, and there had obtained permission to preach from the ruler of that land. Therefore blessed Francis, seeing that he had gained the favor of the ruler and the people of that land, left a few of his brothers there and returned to his own country, because he wanted to direct more of his brothers to that place to preach. But because it is not proper to the laborer or traveler, but to the will of God to direct the course of a person, he was detained by some obstacle or other and did not return to Babylonia. After he spread more of his brothers abroad everywhere and became illustrious by more miracles in his life, he returned to the city of Assisi, and detained there by infirmity, by means of a good death he went to sleep in the Lord, and was buried there.

Annals of Santa Giustina (1260-1270)

Yet another monastic chronicle, that of the abbey of Santa Giustina in Padua, also gives an account of the rise of the mendicants.[a] The unknown author, unlike many other chroniclers from traditional orders, was highly positive in his estimation of the friars. This is perhaps not surprising, given the fact that his city boasted the shrine of a popular Franciscan saint, Anthony of Padua. It is interesting to see how the author has appropriated some of the same Biblical imagery used by John of Parma in his encyclical letter.

> [1]At this time in the month of November a general council was held in Rome under Pope Innocent III, a truly magnificent and prudent man, who excelled all others in his magnanimity and constancy.
>
> [2]It was about this time that divine providence out of the treasury of its mercy produced *two great lights*, that is the Order of Preachers and the Lesser Brothers, which God *set in the firmament* of the church. Gn 1:16-17 By means of their clear teaching and by the clarity and splendor of their holy way of life they have in a wondrous way illuminated the whole world which was wrapped in the darkness of error. The founders of these orders were two most upright men, adorned with the splendor of many virtues, namely Dominic and Francis. They were like the *two trumpets* of Moses, for the awe-inspiring sound of their Nm 10:2 preaching roused a world which had fallen asleep in its vices and sins to do battle against the three-fold foe.[b] *Their voice has gone out through* Ps 19: 4 *all the earth* and in a brief time their venerable religion has spread *to the ends of the world*. Thus, in consideration of their most holy life, their many demonstrated miracles, as well as their heavenly teaching which has watered the hearts of people, they have deservedly been numbered among the saints of the church triumphant and militant . . .
>
> [3]In the year 1231, in the month of June, the blessed Anthony of the Order of Lesser Brothers, whose holiness illumined all of Italy, passed to heaven.

Eudes of Châteauroux (Paris, October 4, 1262)

Eudes of Châteauroux, Chancellor of the University of Paris from 1238 to 1244, was named a cardinal and bishop of Tusculum, Frascati, in 1246, the successor of Jacques de Vitry. A papal legate to the Crusades, an articulate theologian, and a confidant of King Louis IX of France, Eudes directed in 1255 the commission established to study Gerard of Borgo San Donino's

a. "Annales S. Justinae Patavini," in *Monumenta Germaniae Historicae, Scriptores*, XIX, 151-154.

b. A reference to "the world, the flesh, and the devil" (1 Jn. 1:16).

Introduction to the Eternal Gospel. Not only did he assist at the dedication of La Sainte Chapelle in Paris, he was also involved in the dedication of the Basilica of Saint Clare in Assisi. After preaching this sermon to the friars, Eudes spoke as papal legate of Urban IV to the prelates on the opposition of the barons and bishops of King Henry III in England. He died in 1273.[a]

Gn 1:27, 26 *God created man in his own image and likeness.*

I

Before I come to speak on this text I want to answer a puzzling question that some of you, and perhaps many of you, may have in your minds. The question is the one the angels asked as the Lord ascended into heaven: "*Who is this that comes from Edom, in crimsoned garments from Bozrah?* Many of you may well be asking about me: Who is this that comes from a distant land?" for the word "Edom" means distant. Who is this that has taken it upon himself to speak in the presence of so many distinguished people and prelates of the Church, in front of so many revered, wise, and learned men? (Is 63:1)

In reply to these questions I can tell you that there are two reasons which moved and led me to present a few words to such an exalted company, though I am ill-equipped in knowledge and unworthy by my life. The first which moved me to this was a command of the Lord Pope, or the obedience I owe him, for the pope is to be obeyed and never defied. It is his good pleasure that I say a few words to you, which I shall do at the end of my sermon. There then is the first reason that led me to speak to you, though I am unworthy and ill-equipped. The second is audacity, springing from a deep personal love I have for Saint Francis and have had for a long time, for I have found him gracious to me in my needs. The boldness of love has led me to say a few words to you on this the feast of Saint Francis. Those are the reasons that have given me the courage to come before you and preach this sermon.

At the beginning ask Saint Francis in his kindness to pray for me to the Lord Jesus Christ who *gave speech to the dumb and made the tongues of babes speak clearly,* that is, the inexperienced and less advanced. May I preach God's word to his own glory, in praise of Saint Francis, and for our edification and comfort. (Mk 7:37; Wis 10:21)

Let us recall the text from Genesis *God created man in his own image and likeness.* (Gn 1:27, 26)

a. Cf. Marie-Madeleine Lebreton, "Eudes de Châteauroux," *Dictionnaire de Spiritualité Ascétique et Mystique, Doctrine et Histoire* IV (Paris: Beauchesne, 1961): 1675-1678.

As you well know there are two kinds of creation, one which
brings nature into being, the other whereby grace comes into being.
The first creation gives existence to natural life, the second to the life
of grace. About the first it is written: The *Lord created man out of earth?* Sir 17:1
and this that he might have being. Of the second we read: *When you* Ps 106:30
send forth your Spirit, they are created, that is, endowed with the life of
grace, so that they may be virtuous. The first manner of being is to be
understood of Adam, the second of Saint Francis and the other saints
who were established in grace, and were called and glorified by God.
There are two things to be said of Saint Francis: first, he was created
in the image of the Godhead, and second, he was made in the likeness of Christ's humanity.

First, he was created in the image of the Godhead, and this by virtue of a definite likeness he bore to the Divine Nature which exists in Three Persons.

He bore a likeness to the Father, or to the Person of the Father, in
his power. Power is attributed to the Father and is manifested by his
sovereign authority and his creative activity. The Father possesses
the power of sovereign authority for he is *the King of kings and Lord of* 1 Tm 6:15
lords, and he has the power to create because he is the Almighty Creator
of all things: *He has made all things as he willed,* and he can do all Ps 114:3
things.

Saint Francis bore a resemblance to the Father in his creative
power because he worked many miracles. He cured lepers, raised the
dead, healed the sick, and restored speech to the dumb. Saint Francis
also resembled the Father is his sovereign authority, for he had authority
not only over people, but also *over the fish of the sea and over birds* Gn 1:26
of the air and over the cattle of the earth. We read in his *Life* that once,
when going from one city to another, he was walking through a
wood, and the deer took flight as he and his companion approached.
He called out to one of them: "Why are you running away? Stay
there." At his command the deer stood still. Then he went up to it
and patted it on the shoulder and said: "Go now, and give praise to
58-61; 2C 166-171 God." The birds of the air were obedient to him in the same way.
Again we read in his *Life* that one time he was on a journey and came
upon a flock of birds singing in a field, making too much noise in
their song. He ordered them to be quiet and together they all fell silent.
After a while he ordered them to start singing again, and once
more they resumed their song. Similarly, he had authority over fish,
as his *Life* also relates.

Second, Saint Francis bore a likeness to the Son in his wisdom.
Wisdom consists in two qualities: knowledge of hidden things and
foreknowledge of the future, as it says in the Book of Sirach *The eyes of* Sir 23:19

the Lord are ten thousand times brighter than the sun; they look upon all the ways of men. Saint Francis had knowledge of hidden things; indeed, he knew many hidden things, and he foretold future events. I heard 1C 100
from Pope Alexander that Saint Francis predicted the death of Honorius III and the election of Gregory IX, who at that time was Cardinal Bishop of Ostia. He foretold there would be an earthquake on a certain day and at a definite time, and it happened just as he said.

Third, Saint Francis bore a likeness to the Holy Spirit by his good-
Rom 5:5 ness. Goodness reveals itself in love, as we read in Romans: *God's love has been poured into our hearts through the Holy Spirit who has been given to us.* Saint Francis had a wondrous love of God and of his neighbor. So great indeed was his love of Christ and his attraction toward him, that he went into total ecstasy at the mere mention of his name. And LMj III 4
not only he, but also another brother who had been his companion for a long time, and had been taught by his example to revere God and to love him. At the mention of Christ he too went into ecstasy and became rigid like a block of wood.[a] Saint Francis had great love for Christ and wanted to follow him and imitate his love. Christ gave us all these earthly goods we see around us that we might use them well, but not set our hearts on them. And so, when he was a rich merchant, Saint Francis gave up all his worldly possessions for God's sake and distributed them to the poor. Again, as God gave his angels to help sinners, so Saint Francis sent his brothers and sons to bear the burden of people's sins. Lastly, as the Lord Christ chose to undergo his passion and death out of his love for us, so Saint Francis wanted to undergo suffering for Christ and for his faith in him. He longed so much to die for Christ that he went among infidels to preach the Christian faith and even to the cruel Sultan, in the hope of having to suffer for Christ. But when the Sultan realized this, he refused to make him a martyr in order to deprive him of so great a glory.[b]

Furthermore, Saint Francis had a wonderful love for his neighbor. He and his brothers ministered to the sick and looked after them; they begged food for them and took care of them with their own hands. They lived in hospitals, leper houses, and the homes of the deprived, and took care of them, and served them. Without doubt the
Ps 111:5 words of the Psalmist may be said of Saint Francis: *Acceptable is the man who shows* mercy. A lawyer with a good case to defend goes confi-

a. This is Brother Giles, see *The Life of Blessed Brother Giles* 6, in *Scripta Leonis, Rufini et Angeli Sociorurn S. Francisci*, edited and translated by Rosalind B. Brooke (Oxford: Oxford at The Clarendon Press, 1970), 326-27.

b. The Cardinal here obviously is making a somewhat unwarranted interpretation of the facts.

dently before the judge because he knows his case will be treated fairly. In the same way an upright man will appear confidently before the Supreme Judge. Saint Francis was able to say to the Lord: "You were sick and I visited you; naked, and I clothed you," and so on. Then he heard that favorable and gracious sentence pronounced on him *Come, 0 blessed of my Father . . .* Mt 25:34-40

We ought to give a good deal of thought to all this. Woe to those who at that moment will not know what to say, who will not be able to reply: "I gave you food, I gave you drink, I visited you" when the Lord says: "I was hungry, thirsty, and sick." These will await God's judgment against them, the judgment wherein he will say *Depart from me, you cursed, into the eternal fire . . .* Mt 25:41-46

II

Second, Saint Francis was made in the likeness of Christ's humanity in three ways: his form of life, his passion, and his resurrection.

First, with regard to his form of life, for the Lord Jesus lived in poverty and humility. His poverty is proved from the Gospel where we read: *Foxes have holes, and birds of the air have nests; but the Son of Man has nowhere to lay his head.* At his birth he was laid *in a manger, because there was no place for them in the inn.* Saint Francis also lived in poverty and humility. For the Lord's sake he gave up everything he possessed and distributed it to the poor and it was his wish that his sons and brothers do likewise. He refused to live according to the pleasures and delights of the flesh because, as the Apostle Paul writes: *Those who are in the flesh cannot please God,* and the Book of Wisdom teaches: *The Holy Spirit of discipline will flee from deceit and will rise and depart from foolish* thoughts. Such thoughts have their source in sensuality, not in the judgments of right reason. (Mt 8:20; Lk 2:7; Rom 8:8; Wis 1:5)

There are many dangers involved in possessing worldly goods, and it would be better neither to possess them nor to desire them. We ought not to strive after worldly possessions because they are vain as Ecclesiastes says: *Vanity of vanities. All is vanity . . . I saw in all things vanity . . . and that nothing was lasting under the sun.* Riches fade like dreams. As the Psalmist tells *us: They have slept their sleep and all the men of riches have found nothing in their hands.* Furthermore, earthly goods are perishable. They do not last, but disappear like shadows. As Saint John writes: *The world passes away, and the lust of it,* and Saint Paul says: *For the form of this world is passing away.* and we read in the Book of Wisdom: *All those things have vanished like a shadows.* We may instance the rich man in the Gospel who thought he could enjoy his possessions. (Eccl 1:2; 2:11; Ps 75:5; 1 Jn 2:17; 1 Cor 7:31; Wis 5:9)

Lk 12:20 He was told that he would lose everything one night: *Fool! This night your soul is required of you; and the things you have prepared, whose will they be?*

Finally, earthly possessions cause much anxiety. Great toil is involved in acquiring them, and once possessed there comes fear that thieves and robbers will steal them, and there is sadness when they are lost. Take merchants, for example. They expend such efforts to acquire riches. They traverse so many lands, sail the seas, and go to foreign countries. When they possess their riches they have fears, and are sorely grieved and miserable when they lose them. These aspects should lead us to despise earthly goods, or at least not to pine after them or set our hearts on them. As Saint Gregory advises: "We ought to despise this world even when it coaxes the heart with its attractions. For after battering us with so many sorrows, wearying us with so many misfortunes, and daily increasing our anxieties, what else does the world cry out to us other than not to set our hearts on it, but rather to flee from it?"[a] How wretched they are who crave and long for earthly possessions that they know they will not be able to enjoy for long.

Second, Saint Francis was made like Christ in his passion. He would have been glad to undergo and embrace martyrdom for Christ's sake, but this was denied him. Yet he did not rest content with that: he longed to follow Christ and carry Christ's cross. And so while he was at prayer one of the Seraphim appeared to him and as a result the marks of the passion of our Lord Jesus Christ were made visible on his body, that is, on his hands and feet. Thus he could make
Gal 6:17 his own those words of Saint Paul: *I bear on my body the marks of Jesus.* It was truly said and can be said now that he was made in the image and likeness of Christ in his sufferings.

Third, he was made like Christ in his resurrection, and this in two senses. First in a literal sense, because he mortified his flesh to such an extent that it turned black; then at his death, his flesh became so radiant and shining as though he had been raised from the dead. Second, he was made like the risen Christ because he rose from the death of sin by the grace of his Creator, as the Lord rose from the
death of the body by His divine power. The Lord granted Saint Fran- 1C 26
cis the remission of all his sins. While he still lived in this world, he received a revelation and a word assuring him of this. The forgiveness of sins is a kind of resurrection from the dead because sinners are as it were dead, without feeling and movement. The words of
Prv 23:35 Proverbs can be applied to sinners: *They struck me but I sensed no pain;*

a. Gregory, *Dialogue II*, 38 (PL 77, 316).

they beat me, but I did not feel it. Sinners are without feeling. Likewise
they are without the movement of virtuous actions, as the Psalm
says: *There is no one does good, no, not* one. In this sense, Saint Francis Ps 14:3
was raised from the dead, as the Apostle Paul tells us: *Awake, O sleeper* Eph 5:14
and arise from the dead, and Christ shall give you light.

But how does one rise from the death of sin? Every sinner should
consider this well in order to judge and accuse himself first, before he
is judged by God. We should keep in mind that if we offend Christ,
we will be judged by him unless we judge ourselves first. Now we
judge ourselves by being contrite of heart and by having remorse for
our sins. As we read in the Psalm: *The things you say in your hearts, be* Ps 4:4-5; 66
sorry for them on your bed, and each night I flood my bed with tears, that is, I
cleanse my heart and my conscience with my tears, tears of sorrow
and remorse. And as another Psalm says: *A contrite and humbled heart,* Ps 51:17
O God, you will not despise.

Further, we judge ourselves by confessing our sins. Job says: *If I* Jb 9:20
would justify myself, my own mouth shall condemn me, that is, because I
will confess my sins by my own mouth. Isaiah advises us: *Put forth* Is 43:26
what you have to confess that you may be justified, and Proverbs teaches:
He who conceals his transgressions will not prosper, but he who confesses and Prv 28:13
forsakes them will obtain mercy.

Third, we judge ourselves by doing penance for our sins. Saint
Francis mortified his flesh to an astonishing degree. He fasted, went
barefoot, and endured many other forms of penance. Hence he could
say with Saint Paul: *I pommel my body and subdue it.* In doing this he 1 Cor 9:27
sought to make satisfaction for his sins in this life so that he would
have nothing to fear in the next.

There are some people, however, who refuse to judge themselves through contrition because, observing the lives of others and their evil ways, they argue: "That famous man acts like this, so I can do the same. I needn't worry about it." This is a vicious argument, for we will not burn any the less in hell just because a pope or a cardinal or our own superior is guilty of the same sins. You may not do evil because they do. Rather, *practice and observe whatever they tell you, but not* Mt 23:3
what they do.

Another reason why people do not do penance is because they
promise themselves a long life: "I'm young and healthy; I'll live a
long time, so I can do as I please. I'll do penance at the end." These
people are pitiable. The Lord tells us in Isaiah: Cry *aloud, spare not . . .* Is 40:6
And I said: "What shall I cry?" All flesh is grass, and all its beauty is like the
flower of the field. Grass which is green in the morning, by sunset is as
dry as hay. It is the same for all humanity. As Job reflects: *The days of* Jb 12:5, 1
man are short and the number of his months is with you, and you have ap-

pointed his bounds that he cannot pass, and again: *Man that is born of a woman is of few days and full of trouble.* If you are born only to live for a brief time, how can you look forward to a long life? As Scripture Sir 9:12; Jb 14:2 warns: *Man knows not his own end. He comes forth like a flower, and withers; he flees like a shadow and continues not.* It is therefore strange and astonishing how anyone can convince himself that he will surely live a Jer 1:52 long life. Jeremiah says that he *saw a rod watching. The rod is* always watching; it is the judgment of God that will be pronounced against us unless we are watchful over ourselves.

A third reason why people do not do penance is because they pre- Ps 32:5 sume on Christ's mercy. They say: "The *earth is full of the mercy of the Lord.* That mercy is as great as he who created me in his own image and likeness, and he will have mercy on me to the same extent." It is true that the earth is full of God's mercy and that his mercy is as great as himself, but not so great that there is no hell. Therefore, if you were to die without mercy and go to hell, you could never know mercy after that. However, if I seek God's mercy while I am still living in this world, I will obtain it. If I go from this world without his mercy, I will never find mercy again, but will weep and gnash my Mt 8:12 teeth, as the Lord says: *There men will weep and gnash their teeth.*

Again, other people say: "I will confess my sins in my last illness." But how will anyone be able to think clearly about his sins in that condition, when he is exhausted by sickness and incapable of turning his mind to anything else, when he is weighed down with so many sorrows and so greatly preoccupied about the separation of soul and body? We should not rate this kind of sorrow highly, nor, however, should we disparage it. Saint Augustine says: "I will neither praise nor censure this kind of sorrow."[a] The reason is that we cannot know the motive: whether it is fear of death that brings great sorrow, or love of righteousness and God. If it comes from love of God it is praiseworthy, because at whatever moment a sinner repents, Is 43:25 God says to him: *I will not remember your sins* any longer.

Those, then, are four obstacles which prevent us from judging ourselves. Saint Francis never behaved in any of these ways. On the contrary, he judged himself so that he would not be judged by God. We can say of him in truth: God *created* this *man in his own image and likeness,* in the image of the Godhead and the likeness of Christ.

Let us then implore the Lord to give us the grace of being conformed and configured to himself after the pattern of Saint Francis, and that so configured, we may be found worthy through his merits and prayers to see the Lord in glory. May Christ grant us this. Amen.

---

a. Pseudo-Augustine, Sermon 253, (PL 39, 2216).

Rhymed Austrian Chronicle (1268-1272)

One of the many popular rhymed narratives of the time,[a] this chronicle was written by an unknown author who had fled from Hungary into Austria. This following brief poetic description focuses on the external appearance and popular impact of the new orders of friars.

In the seventh year (1207) arise the Jacobites,[b]
Wearing a black cape, sowing the word of life.
And under Gregory the Ninth, the Cordbearers
As true Israelites preach barefoot the naked Christ.
For these brothers, all are filled with compassion,
And moved to piety through these servants of Christ.
Wisdom appears, error put to flight.
Through these two orders, Beguines take the veil.
They make their abode only in cities,
And live by the Gospel, winning many;
Those without hope receive the Good News.

a. "Anonymi Chronicon Rhytmicum Austriacum," *Monumenta Germaniae Historicae, Scriptores*, XXV, 357-58.

b. The Dominicans; this popular nickname came from their general house of study in Paris, St. Jacques.

APPENDIX

Explanation of Maps

This geographic supplement is designed to orient the reader—especially those unfamiliar with European geography—to the world of Francis. At its heart is a series of maps, but equally important is the gazetteer, or index of geographic place names, which will allow the reader to find specific locations.

Map one illustrates the European political world in which Francis lived. The political geography of this world was fundamentally different from that of Europe today. That there are many recognizable names of places is deceptive; even though a region may have the same name in the thirteenth century as it does today, its overall political structure was completely different. Nation-states as we know them did not exist in the Middle Ages. Western Europe at this time was organized under a feudal social-political system. Land was controlled by local nobility in the name of a king, or regional ruler. The local nobility swore oaths of fealty to the king, who depended on the cooperation of his nobility to carry out his wishes. No boundaries between regions in Western Europe are shown on Map 1 because they would tend to communicate the notion of a stable, demarked and defended border as is found in Europe today.

Map two illustrates some of these new social realities of the High Middle Ages. The population of Europe had fallen considerably after the fall of Rome and the Germanic invasions, and only began to recover and grow after the tenth century. All population estimates of the Middle Ages can be considered educated guesses at best because the historical data is fragmentary. Geographers estimate that the population between the ninth and fourteenth century doubled, from approximately 45 to 90 million. This increase was not uniformly distributed over the continent, and was frequently interrupted by invasions, wars, plagues, or famines.

The two regions of Europe having the greatest agricultural productivity and the most rapid population increase were the Northern Italian Peninsula and the lowlands of Northwest Europe (modern Belgium, Netherlands, and the Rhine Valley). It is important to distinguish between these regions, however. Although they had suffered a long period of decline in sophistication and population since the fall of the Roman Empire, Northern Italian cities had perdured, and because of their location, when trade with Byzantium and the East began to increase, they were uniquely positioned to become thriving commercial centers. Located at the southern edge of Western Europe and surrounded by the Mediterranean Sea, the cities of Lombardy, the Po Valley, Tuscany and to a lesser extent, the Duchy of Spoleto, had merchants who traded with Byzantium in the east and the rest of Europe in the north. The port cities of Venice, Genoa, and Pisa were some of the largest and wealthiest cities in Europe at this time.

The population growth in Northwest Europe was furthered primarily by the wool industry. The climate and soils are not well suited for crop production, so the region began to specialize in the production of wool and woolen cloth. From the twelfth century onward, agricultural specialization increased, which in turn led to the revival of fairs as a place to exchange goods. These were huge gatherings of merchants from all over Europe lasting about thirty days each. Eventually a pattern of rotation evolved between the various fairs in the two main geographic areas, Flanders (today's Belgium) and Champagne (northern France). The economies of Northern and Southern Europe linked up at these fairs, which fulfilled commercial functions similar to that of the Italian cities.

Map three shows the region of Italy during Francis's era. What we understand to be the modern country of Italy did not exist until the end of the 19th century. During Francis's era, Italy would have been understood to be the area south of the Alps but not extending beyond Rome (on map 3 this is shown as the Holy Roman Empire, Peter's Patrimony and the Papal States). Strong regional contrasts and variations have characterized the Italian Peninsula. Some of these contrasts can be attributed to physical geography, and some to cultural history. Since the fall of Rome, the Italian Peninsula had been divided into numerous political configurations, and there was little expectation that the whole peninsula could be politically united. Extending 700 miles into the Mediterranean and divided into sub-regions by mountains, the peninsula's population identified much more with a local region than with the political aspirations of political leaders. During the Middle Ages, the Byzantine Empire, Moslems, Normans, and the Holy Roman Empire alternately controlled the southern peninsula and the island of Sicily. Lying at the crossroads of the Mediterranean, the Kingdom of Sicily was one of the richest and most civilized states of Europe.

Lombardy and Tuscany grew to be among the most populous and wealthy regions in Europe during the High Middle Ages. The cities in this region benefited from the fertility of the Po Valley, their location as a natural sea-land transfer point for goods between Northern Europe and Byzantium, and the protection of the Alps.

Map four demonstrates how climate and geology combined to impose sharp natural divisions on the Italian Peninsula. The Alps forms a natural barrier to the North, one impenetrable as much as half the year. Over two-thirds of the peninsula may be classified as hill or mountain, and along most of the 100-mile wide peninsula, these are jumbled together in the Apennines. In Lombardy alone there are more variations of elevation, climate, soil and vegetation than in the whole of Germany. The Po Valley is the only expansive fertile plain; in peninsular Italy, fertile lowlands are limited. The ruggedness of the landscape, the unevenness of soil fertility, and the ease of access to the sea led the residents of the Italian Peninsula to become proficient mariners. Trade was much more easily accomplished along the peninsula by sea than by land. There are several physical regions of the northern Italian Peninsula: the greater Po Valley (including Lombardy, Romagna and Venice), the Arno Valley and Tuscany, the more isolated eastern coast of the Marche, Abruzzi (which has historically been the wildest part of the Apennines), the Duchy of Spoleto and Latium (the upper and lower watershed of the Tiber River, respectively).

Map five describes the transportation, religious and social geography of the northern Italian Peninsula at the time of Francis. There is no reliable way to determine the population of cities during the Middle Ages. Map 5 shows Venice, Milan, Genoa and Florence to be larger than other towns. Historians generally agree that Venice was the largest town, and estimate that it had a population of between 50,000 and 100,000. The other three large towns had slightly fewer residents, and overall, the population density in Lombardy and the Po Valley was twice that of the rest of the Italian Peninsula. Rome's population is estimated to have been 30,000. Assisi is estimated to have between 10,000 and 20,000 people at this time, with Perugia about twice as large.

The rise of the city-states and the movement toward urbanization coincided with the heretical movements that began to appear in Western Europe. A proper geography of medieval religious dissent has yet to be undertaken, and a thorough job may be impossible because of the scattered historical record. At the onset of the thirteenth century, there were several heretical movements in Lombardy and the Italian Peninsula, the most significant being the Waldensians, and the Cathars (they were called several other names, including Albigensians and Patarines). The Catholic hierarchy perceived these movements as grave threats because they challenged the official Church authority. Map 5 shows the cities with established communities of these two groups. Other heretical groups may have been present, and these two groups almost certainly had followers in many other cities, but the historical evidence is missing.

Map six details the regions of the Duchy of Spoleto and the Marche of Ancona. The first Franciscans did much of their preaching in the towns and villages shown on this map. Maps 6-9 show all the towns and villages that Francis or the early friars are reported by the early sources to have visited on the Italian Peninsula. There are, of course, many other villages that existed, but in the interest of clarity, they are not shown on the maps. The spine of the Central Apennines separate the Duchy of Spoleto and the Marche of Ancona, with much of Marche oriented toward the Adriatic Sea. Map 6 can be seen as having three sub-regions: the lower Spoleto Valley, where Assisi and Perugia are located, the Rieti Valley, where Francis spent considerable time, and the less-densely settled region of the Marche of Ancona.

Map seven shows the physical relief of the Rieti Valley and the location of the several places of the friars in that region. This map is a good illustration of the geographic relationship between early Franciscan hermitages and an emerging urban center. Francis spent a considerable amount of time in this region.

Map eight illustrates the territories of Assisi and Perugia, its neighbor to the west. Perugia became a papal city and the empire claimed Assisi. Tensions between the two cities dated back centuries, with the Tiber River forming a historical boundary between peoples. Sometime during the eleventh century, Perugia had occupied a strip of land on the east bank near an area called Collestrada. Violence escalated after 1200, resulting in the Battle of Collestrada in 1202. Francis fought in this battle, and when Assisi lost, he was imprisoned in Perugia (2C 4). It seems that Francis's father, Pietro Bernardone, owned some land near the site of the battle.

Map nine shows the first places of the brothers as well as the first two temporary residences of Clare. Also shown are the approximate location of most of the lands which archival records show as belonging to Francis's father, Pietro Bernardone.

Maps ten and eleven show what the city of Assisi looked like at the time of Francis. The walls on this map are essentially the same as those built by the ancient Romans. The locations of the four most important social powers in Assisi are all shown on this map. The Rocca Maggiore was the symbol of Imperial authority, and it dominated the landscape until it was torn down by the Assisians in 1198. The bishop's palace was the seat of Church power, and it was in the Santa Maria Maggiore Piazza (plaza) that Francis shed his clothes, spurning his father and embracing his vocation in a deeper way. Trade and commerce had grown remarkably in the century before Francis's birth and the Market in the town's center became increasingly important. With the emergence of the *commune*, the lesser nobility and merchants organized themselves and established the *Palazzo del Consoli*, or city hall, across from the Basilica of San Rufino. The *Palazzo del Consoli* moved in 1212 to the Tempio di Minerva.

Although Arnaldo Fortini confidently asserts that the paternal house of Francis lies in between the churches of San Paolo and San Nicolo (site #1), the evidence is circumstantial. Other scholars argue that his family home lay on the site now occupied by the Chiesa Nuova (site #2), or the church of San Francesco Piccolo (site #3).

Gazetteer

Place Name	General Location	Type of Feature	Map	Co-ord
Abruzzi	C Italian Peninsula	Region	5	5F
Acquapendente	Tuscany	Town	5	5D
Acquasparta	Sabina	Village	7	1B
Acre	Holy Land	Kingdom/City	1	5H
Adriatic Sea	N Mediterranean	Sea	3	3E
Alessandria	Lombardy	Town	5	2A
Alexandria	Egypt	City	1	6G
Alife	Kingdom of Sicily	Town	5	6F
Almería	Iberian Peninsula	Town	2	4A
Alps	C Europe	Mountains	4	1D
Alviano	SW Duchy of Spoleto	Village	6	7B
Amiterno	Abruzzi	Village	5	5F
Ancona	Marche of Ancona	Town	6	2F
Antioch	Asia Minor	City	1	5H
Antrodoco	Sabina	Village	7	4G
Apennines	Italian Peninsula	Mountains	4	3D
Apulia	S Italian Peninsula	Region	3	5F
Aquitaine	France	Region	1	3B
Aragon	Iberian Peninsula	Kingdom	1	3B
Arezzo	E Tuscany	City	6	3A
Arles	S France	Town	1	3C
Armenia	Asia Minor	Kingdom	1	5G
Ascoli	S Marche of Ancona	Village	6	5F
Assisi	Duchy of Spoleto	Town	6	4C
Asti	Lombardy	Town	5	2A
Atlantic Ocean	W Europe	Ocean	1	2A
Augsburg	Holy Roman Empire	Town	1	2D
Austria	Central Europe	Region	1	2E
Bagnara	Duchy of Spoleto	Village	6	4D
Bagnolo	Lombardy	Town	5	1C
Bagnoregio	Peter's Patrimony	Village	6	7A
Baltic Sea	N Europe	Sea	1	1E
Barcelona	Iberian Peninsula	Town	1	3B
Bari	Apulia	Town	3	4F
Barletta	Apulia	Town	5	6H
Basel	Holy Roman Empire	Town	2	3D
Bastia	Lower Spoleto Valley	Village	9	2A
Bavaria	Holy Roman Empire	Region	1	2D
Benvento	Kingdom of Sicily	Town	3	5D
Bergamo	Lombardy	Town	5	1C
Bettona	Spoleto Valley	Village	8	5E
Bevagna	Spoleto Valley	Village	8	7G
Biscay, Bay of	Atlantic Ocean	Bay	1	2B
Bishop Guido's Palace	Assisi	Bishop's palace	11	5C
Black Sea	W Asia	Sea	1	3G
Bobbio	Lombardy	Monastery	5	2B
Bologna	Romagna	City	5	3D
Bolsena, Lake	Peter's Patrimony	Lake	4	4E
Bordeaux	France	Town	1	3B
Bovara	Spoleto Valley	Village	6	5C
Bracciano, Lake	Peter's Patrimony	Lake	4	4E
Brenner Pass	Alps	Mountain pass	4	1E
Brescia	E Lombardy	Town	5	1C
Brindisi	Kingdom of Sicily	Town	3	5F
Bruges	Low Countries	Town	1	1C

Place Name	General Location	Type of Feature	Map	Co-ord
Buda Petsch	E Europe	Town	1	2E
Bulgaria	Balkan Peninsula	Kingdom	1	3F
Burgundy	France	Region	1	2C
Cadiz	Iberian Peninsula	Town	2	4A
Cairo	Egypt	City	1	6G
Calvi	Sabina	Village	7	5B
Camaldoli	N Marche of Ancona	Monastery	5	3D
Camerino	W Marche of Ancona	Village	6	4D
Campagna	Peter's Patrimony	Region	5	6E
Campiglia	N Tuscany	Village	5	4C
Candia	Cyprus	Town	1	5F
Cannara	Lower Spoleto Valley	Village	8	6F
Canterbury	England	Town	1	1C
Capua	Kingdom of Sicily	Town	5	6F
Carceri	Monte Subasio	Friars' place	9	2E
Carpathians	Eastern Europe	Mountains	2	2E
Castile	Iberian Peninsula	Kingdom	1	3A
Celano	Abruzzi	Village	5	5F
Celle di Cortona	E Tuscany	Friars' place	8	1A
Cerea	Lombardy	Town	5	1D
Cetona	E Tuscany	Friars' Place	6	5A
Champagne	France	Region	1	2C
Chiascio	Lower Spoleto Valley	River	9	1A
Chiusi	E Tuscany	Castle	6	2A
Città della Pieve	W Duchy of Spoleto	Town	6	5A
Città di Castello	N Duchy of Spoleto	Town	6	3B
Cività Castellana	Sabina	Village	7	6A
Civitavecchia	Peter's Patrimony	Town	5	5D
Collestrada	Lower Spoleto Valley	Battle site	8	4F
Collevecchio	Sabina	Village	7	6B
Cologne	Holy Roman Empire	Town	1	2D
Concorezo	Lombardy	Town	5	1B
Constantinople	Asia Minor	City	1	4F
Contigliano	Rieti Valley	Village	7	5D
Coppito	Abruzzi	Village	6	8E
Córdoba	Iberian Peninsula	Town	2	4A
Cori	Peter's Patrimony	Village	5	6E
Corsica	Central Mediterranean	Island	1	3C
Cortona	E Tuscany	Village	8	1A
Cremona	Lombardy	Town	5	2C
Cremona	S Lombardy	City	5	1C
Cyprus	E Mediterranean	Island	1	5F
Dalmatia	E Europe	Region	1	3E
Damascus	Holy Land	City	1	5H
Damietta	Egypt	City	1	6G
Danube	Hungary	River	2	3E
Denmark	N Europe	Kingdom	1	1D
Dijon	France	Town	2	2C
Durazzo	Bulgaria	Town	1	4E
Egypt	NE Africa	Region	1	6G
Emilia	N Italian Peninsula	Region	5	2B
England	NW Europe	Kingdom	1	1B
Erfurt	Holy Roman Empire	Town	2	2D
Faenza	Romagna	Town	5	3D
Fano	Marche of Ancona	Town	6	1D
Farfa	Peter's Patrimony	Monastery	5	5E
Farneto	Duchy of Spoleto	Friars' Place	8	3F
Fermo	E Marche of Ancona	Village	6	4F
Ferrara	Lombardy	Town	5	2D
Flanders	N Europe	Region	1	1C
Florence	N Tuscany	City	5	3D
Foggia	Kingdom of Sicily	Town	5	6G
Foligno	Duchy of Spoleto	Town	8	6H
Fondi	Kingdom of Sicily	Town	5	6F
Fonte Columbo	Rieti Valley	Friars' place	7	5E
Forano	Marche of Ancona	Friars' place	6	3E
France	W Europe	Kingdom	1	2C
Gaeta	S Italian Peninsula	Town	5	6F
Geneva	Central Europe	Town	2	3C

Place Name	General Location	Type of Feature	Map	Co-ord
Genoa	N Italian Peninsula	City	5	3B
Georgia	W Asia	Region	1	3H
Giano	Duchy of Spoleto	Village	6	6C
Granada	Iberian Peninsula	Town	2	4A
Greccio	Rieti Valley	Friars' place	7	4D
Gualdo Tadino	N Duchy of Spoleto	Village	8	2H
Gubbio	NE Duchy of Spoleto	Town	6	3C
Hispania	Iberian Peninsula	Region	1	3A
Hochtor Pass	Alps	Mountain Pass	4	1E
Holy Roman Empire	N Europe	Empire	1	2D
H. of Bernardo di Quintivale	Assisi	House	11	4A
House of Clare	Assisi	House	10	2G
H. Pietro B. (Chiesa Nuova)	Assisi	House	11	3D
H. Pietro B. (Fortini)	Assisi	House	11	2A
H. Pietro B. (S.F. Piccolo)	Assisi	House	11	3D
Hungary	E Europe	Kingdom	1	3E
Iesi	Marche of Ancona	Town	6	2E
Imola	Romagna	Town	5	3D
Ireland	NW Europe	Kingdom	1	1B
Isola Maggiore	Lake Trasimeno	Friars' place	8	3B
Isola Romana	Lower Spoleto Valley	Village	9	2A
Jerusalem	Holy Land	Town	1	6H
Kiev	Russia	Town	1	2G
La Foresta	Rieti Valley	Friars' place	7	4E
La Verna	N Marche of Ancona	Friars' place	6	2A
Languedoc	France	Region	1	3C
Leon	N Iberian Peninsula	Kingdom	1	3A
Limoges	Touraine	Town	2	3C
Lisbon	W Iberian Peninsula	Town	1	4A
Lisciano	NW Duchy of Spoleto	Village	8	1B
Lombardy	N Italian Peninsula	Region	5	1C
London	England	Town	1	1C
Lubeck	N Germany	Town	1	1D
Lucca	NW Tuscany	City	5	3C
Lugano	Lombardy	Town	5	1A
Lyons	France	Town	1	3C
Machilone	Abruzzi	Village	7	3G
Magliano	Sabina	Village	7	5A
Málaga	Iberian Peninsula	Town	2	4A
Mantova	Lombardy	Town	5	2C
Marche of Ancona	C Italian Peninsula	Region	5	4E
Market (P.d. Commune)	Assisi	Piazza	11	2C
Marseilles	S France	Town	2	3C
Massa Trabaria	N Marche of Ancona	Region	6	2B
Mediterranean Sea	S Europe	Sea	1	4C
Messina	Island of Sicily	Town	3	7E
Milan	Lombardy	City	5	1B
Modena	Lombardy	Town	5	2C
Mogliano	Marche of Ancona	Friars' place	6	4F
Mont Cenis Pass	Alps	Mountain pass	4	2B
Monte Cassino	S Italian Peninsula	Monastery	5	6F
Monte Castrilli	Sabina	Village	7	1B
Monte Gargano	N Apulia	Monastery	5	5H
Monte San Vicino	Marche of Ancona	Friars' place	6	3D
Monte Subasio	Duchy of Spoleto	Mountain	9	3F
Montecasale	W Marche of Ancona	Friars' place	6	2B
Montefalco	Duchy of Spoleto	Village	6	5C
Montefeltro	N Marche of Ancona	Castle	6	1B
Monteluco	Duchy of Spoleto	Friars' place	6	6D
Montenero	Duchy of Spoleto	Village	6	6B
Montenero	Duchy of Spoleto	Village	6	6B
Montepulciano	Tuscany	Town	5	4D
Monteripido	Duchy of Spoleto	Friars' place	8	3D
Monterubbiano	Marche of Ancona	Friars' place	6	4F
Montpellier	Languedoc	Town	2	3C
Morocco	NW Africa	Region	1	5A
Mount Alverna	see: La Verna			
Naples	S Italian Peninsula	Town	3	5D
Narbonne	S France	Town	1	3C

Place Name	General Location	Type of Feature	Map	Co-ord
Narni	Duchy of Spoleto	Village	7	3B
Navas de Tolosa	Iberian Peninsula	Town	1	4A
Nera	Duchy of Spoleto	River	7	4A
Nicea	Asia Minor	Kingdom	1	4G
Nocera Umbra	N Duchy of Spoleto	Village	8	4H
Norcia	S. Marche of Ancona	Village	6	6E
North Sea	N Europe	Sea	1	1C
Nottiano	Duchy of Spoleto	Village	8	4G
Orte	Sabina	Village	7	4A
Orvieto	Duchy of Spoleto	Town	6	6A
Osimo	E Marche of Ancona	Village	6	2F
Ostia	Peter's Patrimony	Town	5	5E
Oxford	England	Town	2	1C
Padua	Lombardy	Town	5	1D
Padua	N Italian Peninsula	City	5	1D
Palazzo dei Consoli	Assisi	Council hall	11	1E
Palermo	Island of Sicily	City	3	7D
Panzo	see: Sant'Angelo di Panzo			
Papal States	Italian Peninsula	Region	5	4E
Paris	France	City	2	2C
Parma	Emilia	Town	5	2C
Pavia	Lombardy	Town	5	2B
Penne	Abbruzzi	Town	5	5F
Perugia	Duchy of Spoleto	Town	6	4B
Peter's Patrimony	C Italian Peninsula	Region	5	5E
Petrella	Sabina	Village	7	6G
Piacenza	Lombardy	Town	5	2B
Piazza del Commune	Assisi	Piazza	11	2C
Piglio nella Campania	Peter's Patrimony	Village	5	5E
Pisa	NE Tuscany	City	5	4C
Po	N Italian Peninsula	River	4	2C
Pofi	Kingdom of Sicily	Village	5	6F
Poggibonsi	Tuscany	Town	5	4C
Poggio Bostone	Rieti Valley	Friars' place	7	3F
Poland	NE Europe	Kingdom	1	1E
Ponte dei Galli	Lower Spoleto Valley	Bridge	9	1D
Ponte San Vettorino	Lower Spoleto Valley	Bridge	9	2C
Porta Antica	Assisi	Gate	10	3C
Porta del Parlascio	Assisi	Gate	10	2H
Porta del Sementone	Assisi	Gate	10	5E
P. Murorupto Inferiore	Assisi	Gate	10	3A
P. Murorupto Superiore	Assisi	Gate	10	2A
Porta Moiano	Assisi	Gate	10	4F
P. qua itur in Marchiam	Assisi	Gate	10	1G
Porta San Giorgio	Assisi	Gate	10	3G
Porta San Rufino	Assisi	Gate	10	3G
Porta Sant'Antimo	Assisi	Gate	10	4D
Portiuncula, S. Maria A.	Spoleto Valley	Friars' place	9	3B
Portugal	W Iberian Peninsula	Kingdom	1	3A
Potenza	Kingdom of Sicily	Town	5	5E
Prague	Holy Roman Empire	Town	1	2D
Preggio	Duchy of Spoleto	Friars' place	8	2C
Provence	France	Region	1	3C
Provins	France	Town, Fair	2	2C
Ragusa	Balkan Peninsula	Town	1	4E
Ratisbon	Holy Roman Empire	Town	2	2D
Ravenna	Lombardy	Town	5	3D
Recanati	Marche of Ancona	Village	6	3F
R. Canons of San Rufino	Assisi	Church residence	10	2G
Rhine	Germany	River	2	2D
Rhone	France	River	2	3C
Rieti	Sabina	Town	7	5E
Rieti Valley	Sabina	Region	7	4E
Rimini	SE Romagna	Town	5	3E
Rivo Torto	Spoleto Valley	Stream	9	3D
Rivotorto	Spoleto Valley	Friars' place	9	3D
Rocca	Sabina	Village	7	6F
Rocca Maggiore	Assisi	Castle	10	1D
Romagna	N Italian Peninsula	Region	5	3D

Place Name	General Location	Type of Feature	Map	Co-ord
Rome	C Italian Peninsula	City	5	5E
Russia	E Europe	Kingdom	1	1G
Sabina	C Italian Peninsula	Region	5	5E
San Bartolomeo	Lower Spoleto Valley	Priory	9	2C
San Benedetto	Mt. Subasio	Abbey	9	4F
San Bernardo Pass	Alps	Mountain Pass	4	2B
San Damiano	Spoleto Valley	Friars' place	9	2D
San Gemini	Duchy of Spoleto	Village	7	2B
S. Giacomo Murorupto	Assisi	Church	10	2A
San Gimignano	Tuscany	Town	5	4C
San Giorgio	Assisi	Church	10	4G
San Giorgio	Assisi	Piazza	10	4G
San Gottardo	Alps	Mountain pass	4	1C
San Gregorio	Assisi	Church	11	3A
San Gregorio	Assisi	Piazza	11	3A
San Lorenzo	Assisi	Church	10	1G
San Masseo	Lower Spoleto Valley	Church	9	2C
San Nicolo	Assisi	Church	11	2B
San Paolo Abbadesse	Lower Spoleto Valley	Monastery	9	2A
San Paolo di Assisi	Assisi	Church	11	2A
San Pietro della Spina	Lower Spoleto Valley	Church	9	4C
San Quirico	Tuscany	Village	5	4D
San Rufino	Assisi	Basilica	10	2G
San Rufino	Assisi	Piazza	11	1E
San Rufino del Arce	Lower Spoleto Valley	Church	9	3C
San Severino	Marche of Ancona	Village	6	4E
San Stefano	Assisi	Church	10	3D
San Stefano	Marche of Ancona	Village	6	2A
San Verecondo	Duchy of Spoleto	Monastery	8	1G
San Vettorino	Lower Spoleto Valley	Monastery	9	1C
Sansepolcro	E Tuscany	Town	6	2A
Sant' Agata	Assisi	Church	11	2C
Sant' Angelo di Panzo	Spoleto Valley	Church	9	3E
Sant' Annessa	Lower Spoleto Valley	Monastery	9	2D
S. Eleuterio Contigliano	Sabina	Friars' place	7	5D
Sant' Elia	Rieti Valley	Village	7	5E
Sant' Urbano	Sabina	Friars' place	7	4C
S. Maria degli Episcopi	Lower Spoleto Valley	Monastery	9	2D
Santa Maria Maggiore	Assisi	Church	11	4C
Santa Maria Maggiore	Assisi	Piazza	11	4C
Santiago de Compostela	W Iberian Peninsula	Pilgrimage Site	1	3A
Sardinia	C Mediterranean	Island	1	4C
Sarteano	E Tuscany	Friars' place	6	5A
Satriano	Duchy of Spoleto	Village	8	3G
Saxony	N Germany	Region	1	1D
Sclavonia	E Europe	Region	1	3E
Serbia	Balkan Peninsula	Region	1	3E
Seville	Iberian Peninsula	Town	1	4A
Sicily	C Mediterranean	Island	3	8D
Siena	Tuscany	Town	5	4D
Sirolo	NE Marche of Ancona	Friars' place	6	2F
Soffiano	Marche of Ancona	Friars' place	6	5E
Sora	Kingdom of Sicily	Village	5	6F
Spello	Duchy of Spoleto	Village	8	6G
Spoleto	Duchy of Spoleto	Town	6	6C
Spoleto Valley	Duchy of Spoleto	Valley	9	2B
Spoleto, Duchy of	C Italian Peninsula	Region	5	4D
Subiaco	Peter's Patrimony	Monastery	5	6E
Syracuse	Island of Sicily	Town	3	8E
Syria	Asia Minor	Region	1	5H
Tarano	Sabina	Village	7	5B
Tempio di Minerva	Assisi	Roman temple	11	2B
Terni	Duchy of Spoleto	Village	7	2C
Tescio	Lower Spoleto Valley	River	9	2B
Tiber	C Italian Peninsula	River	4	4E
Tivoli	Campagna	Village	5	5E
Todi	Duchy of Spoleto	Village	6	6B
Toledo	Iberian Peninsula	Town	1	4A
Topino	Spoleto Valley	Stream	9	3B

Place Name	General Location	Type of Feature	Map	Co-ord
Torino	Lombardy	Town	5	2A
Torre del Pozzo	Assisi	Tower	11	2D
Toscanella	Sabina	Village	6	8A
Toulouse	S France	Town	2	3C
Touraine	France	Region	1	2B
Tours	France	Town	2	2B
Trapani	Island of Sicily	Town	3	7C
Trasimeno, Lake	Duchy of Spoleto	Lake	8	3B
Trave Bonate	Marche of Ancona	Friars' place	6	4D
Trevi	Spoleto Valley	Village	6	5C
Treviso	N Italian Peninsula	Town	5	1D
Tripoli	Holy Land	Town	1	5H
Tripoli	N Africa	City	1	6D
Troyes	France	Town	2	2C
Tunis	N Africa	Town	2	5D
Tuscany	Central Italian Peninsula	Region	5	4C
Tyrrhenian Sea	C Mediterranean	Sea	4	5D
Valencia	Iberian Peninsula	Town	2	4B
Valfabbrica	Duchy of Spoleto	Monastery	8	3F
Vallombrosa	Tuscany	Monastery	5	4D
Venetian Territories	E Mediterranean	Captured lands	1	5E
Venice	N Italian Peninsula	City	3	1E
Venosa	Kingdom of Sicily	Town	3	5E
Verina	Sabina	River	7	3D
Verona	N Italian Peninsula	Town	5	1C
Via Aemilia	Lombardy	Roman road	4	3E
Via Antica	Lower Spoleto Valley	Road	9	4E
Via Appia	S Italian Peninsula	Roman road	4	5G
Via Aurelia	C Italian Peninsula	Roman road	4	4D
Via Capobove	Assisi	Street	11	1A
Via d. Ceppo della Catena	Assisi	Street	11	3D
Via dell'Abbadia	Assisi	Street	11	3C
Via di Murorupto	Assisi	Street	10	3B
Via di San Rufino	Assisi	Street	11	2D
Via di Spello	Lower Spoleto Valley	Road	9	4E
Via Flaminia	C Italian Peninsula	Roman road	4	4E
Via Francesca	Lower Spoleto Valley	Road	9	4E
Via per il Collis Infernus	Assisi	Street	10	3B
Via Portica	Assisi	Street	10	3D
Via Sabina	Sabina	Roman road	7	5F
Vicenza	Lombardy	Town	5	1D
Vienna	Holy Roman Empire	Town	2	2E
Viterbo	Peter's Patrimony	Town	6	8A
Volterra	Tuscany	Town	5	4C
Ypres	France	Town, Fair	2	2

MAP ONE
EUROPE & THE MEDITERRANEAN
POLITICAL REGIONS, c. 1220
Latin Christians Lands
Eastern Orthodox Christian Lands
Muslim Lands
Non-Christian Lands
0 150 300 miles
0 200 400 km
Atlantic Ocean
North Sea
Baltic Sea
Bay of Biscay
Black Sea
Adriatic Sea
Tyrrhenian Sea
Mediterranean Sea
Red Sea
IRELAND
ENGLAND
Oxford
London
Canterbury
Bruges
Flanders
FRANCE
Paris
Champagne
Touraine
Burgundy
Aquitaine
Bordeaux
Provence
Languedoc
Lyons
Arles
Marseilles
Narbonne
DENMARK
Lubeck
Saxon
HOLY ROMAN EMPIRE
Cologne
Erfurt
Prague
Augsburg
Bavaria
Vienna
Austria
Milan
Lombardy
Venice
Genoa
Pisa
Florence
Assisi
Rome
Naples
Sicily
Palermo
Messina
Corsica
Sardinia
POLAND
RUSSIA
Kiev
Approximate Boundary
Buda Pestsh
HUNGARY
Slavonia
Dalmatia
Serbia
Ragusa
Durazzo
BULGARIA
LATIN EMPIRE
Constantinople
X1202
Venetian Territories
Candia
NICAEA
GEORGIA
ARMENIA
SYRIA
Antioch
Principality of Antioch-Tripoli
Cyprus
Tripoli
Damascus
Kingdom of Acre
Acre
Jerusalem
HOLY LAND
Damietta
X1219-1221
Alexandria
Cairo
EGYPT
Santiago de Compostela
Leon
Portugal
Castile
Aragon
HISPANIA
Lisbon
Toledo
Barcelona
Valencia
Navas de Tolosa 1212
Seville
MOROCCO
MUSLIM
Tunis
Tripoli
AFRICA
A B C D E F G H
1 2 3 4 5 6

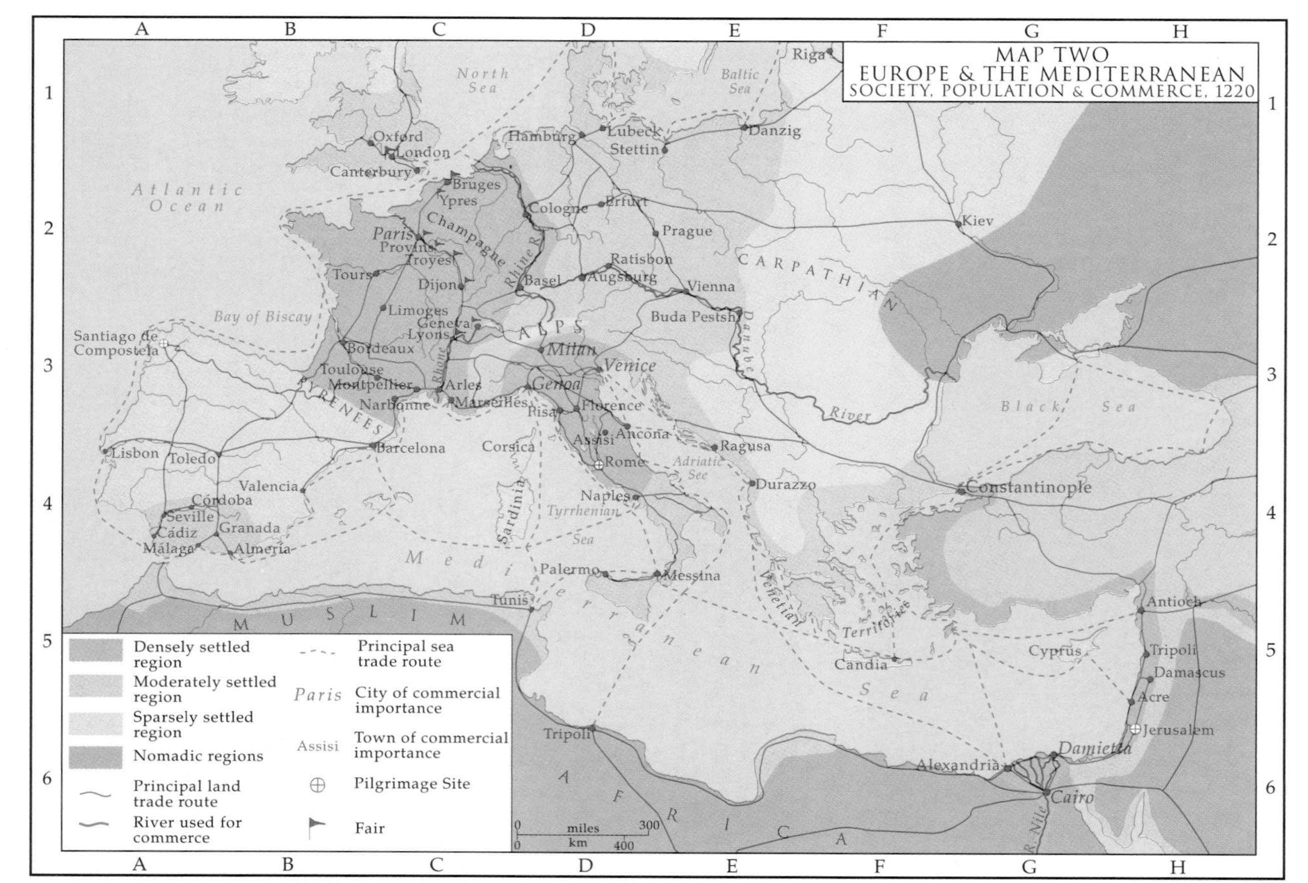
MAP TWO
EUROPE & THE MEDITERRANEAN
SOCIETY, POPULATION & COMMERCE, 1220
Atlantic Ocean
North Sea
Baltic Sea
Bay of Biscay
Black Sea
Adriatic Sea
Tyrrhenian Sea
Mediterranean Sea
CARPATHIAN
ALPS
PYRENEES
MUSLIM
AFRICA
Champagne
Rhine R.
Rhone
Danube River
R. Nile
Venetian Territories
Riga
Oxford
London
Canterbury
Bruges
Ypres
Hamburg
Lubeck
Stettin
Danzig
Cologne
Erfurt
Prague
Kiev
Paris
Provins
Troyes
Tours
Dijon
Basel
Augsburg
Ratisbon
Vienna
Buda Pestsh
Limoges
Geneva
Lyons
Bordeaux
Toulouse
Montpellier
Narbonne
Arles
Marseilles
Milan
Venice
Genoa
Pisa
Florence
Ancona
Assisi
Rome
Ragusa
Durazzo
Constantinople
Santiago de Compostela
Lisbon
Toledo
Barcelona
Valencia
Córdoba
Seville
Cádiz
Málaga
Granada
Almeria
Corsica
Sardinia
Naples
Palermo
Messina
Tunis
Tripoli
Candia
Cyprus
Antioch
Tripoli
Damascus
Acre
Jerusalem
Damietta
Alexandria
Cairo
Densely settled region
Moderately settled region
Sparsely settled region
Nomadic regions
Principal land trade route
River used for commerce
Principal sea trade route
Paris City of commercial importance
Assisi Town of commercial importance
Pilgrimage Site
Fair
0 miles 300
0 km 400
A B C D E F G H
1 2 3 4 5 6

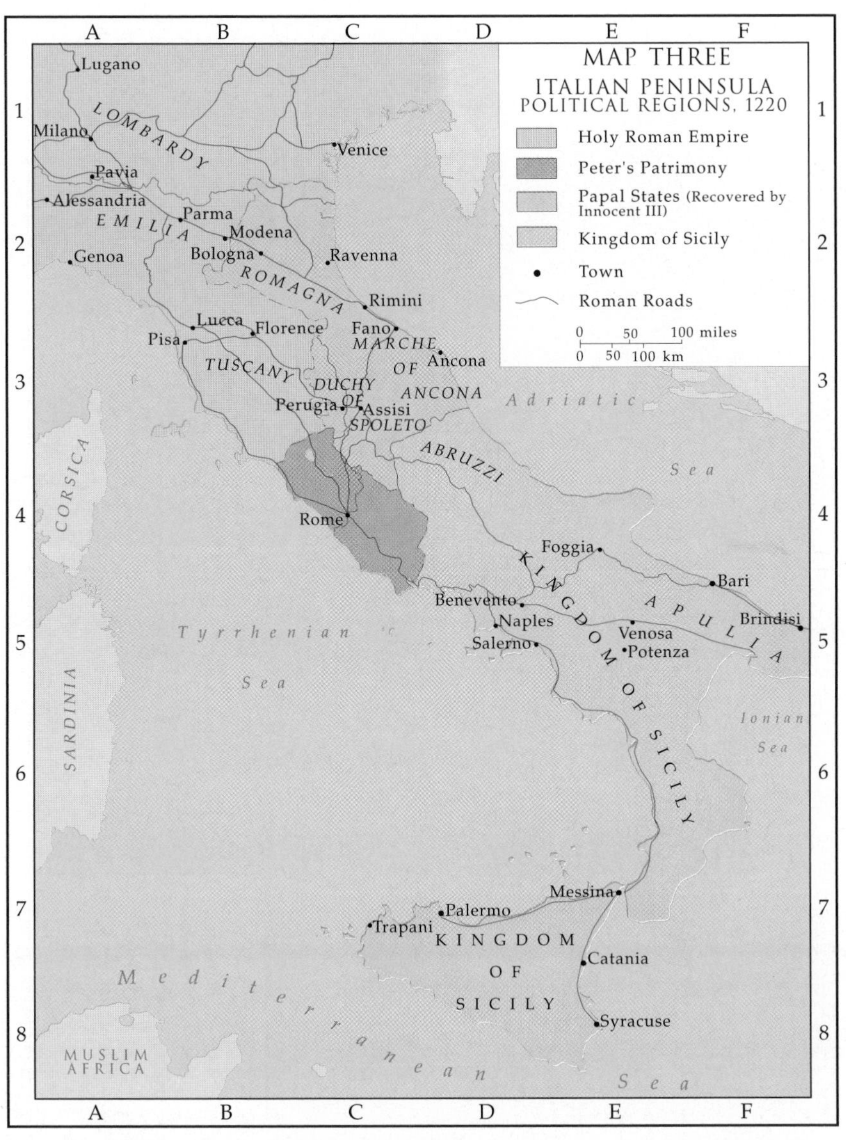
MAP THREE
ITALIAN PENINSULA
POLITICAL REGIONS, 1220
Holy Roman Empire
Peter's Patrimony
Papal States (Recovered by Innocent III)
Kingdom of Sicily
Town
Roman Roads
0 50 100 miles
0 50 100 km
A B C D E F
1 2 3 4 5 6 7 8
Lugano
LOMBARDY
Milano
Venice
Pavia
Alessandria
Parma
EMILIA
Modena
Bologna
Genoa
Ravenna
ROMAGNA
Rimini
Lucca
Florence
Fano
Pisa
MARCHE
Ancona
OF
ANCONA
TUSCANY
DUCHY
OF
SPOLETO
Perugia
Assisi
Adriatic
Sea
ABRUZZI
CORSICA
Rome
Foggia
KINGDOM OF SICILY
Bari
APULIA
Benevento
Brindisi
Naples
Venosa
Potenza
Salerno
Tyrrhenian
Sea
Ionian
Sea
SARDINIA
Messina
Palermo
Trapani
KINGDOM
OF
SICILY
Catania
Syracuse
Mediterranean
Sea
MUSLIM
AFRICA

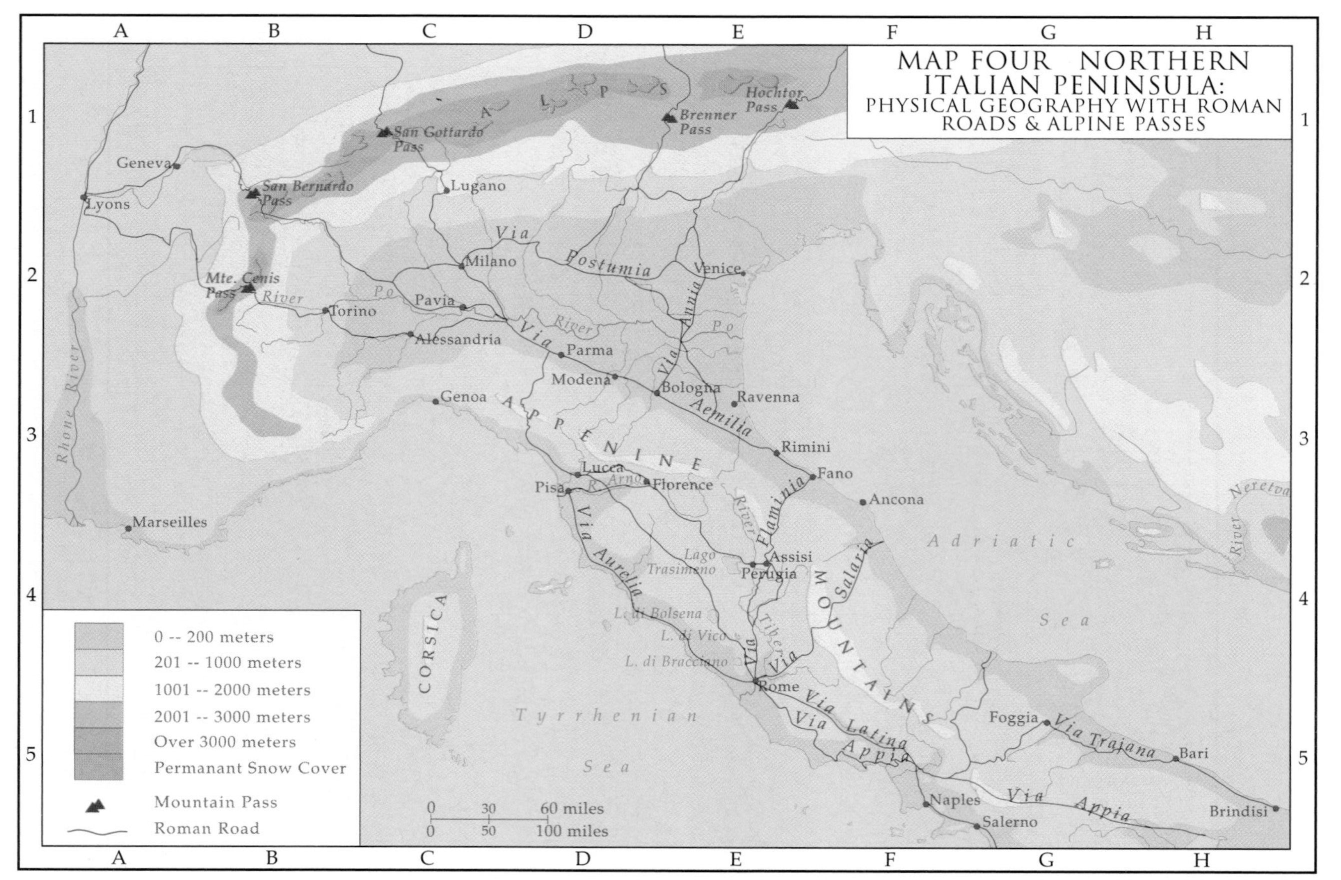
MAP FOUR NORTHERN ITALIAN PENINSULA:
PHYSICAL GEOGRAPHY WITH ROMAN ROADS & ALPINE PASSES
A B C D E F G H
1 2 3 4 5
A L P S
San Gottardo Pass
Brenner Pass
Hochtor Pass
San Bernardo Pass
Mte. Cenis Pass
Geneva
Lyons
Lugano
Milano
Venice
Torino
Pavia
Alessandria
Parma
Modena
Bologna
Ravenna
Genoa
Rimini
Fano
Ancona
Lucca
Pisa
Florence
Marseilles
Assisi
Perugia
Rome
Foggia
Bari
Brindisi
Naples
Salerno
Via Postumia
Via Annia
Via Aemilia
Via Flaminia
Via Aurelia
Via Salaria
Via Latina
Via Appia
Via Trajana
Via
A P P E N I N E
M O U N T A I N S
Po River
Rhone River
R. Arno
Tiber River
Neretva River
Lago Trasimeno
L. di Bolsena
L. di Vico
L. di Bracciano
CORSICA
Adriatic Sea
Tyrrhenian Sea
0 -- 200 meters
201 -- 1000 meters
1001 -- 2000 meters
2001 -- 3000 meters
Over 3000 meters
Permanant Snow Cover
Mountain Pass
Roman Road
0 30 60 miles
0 50 100 miles

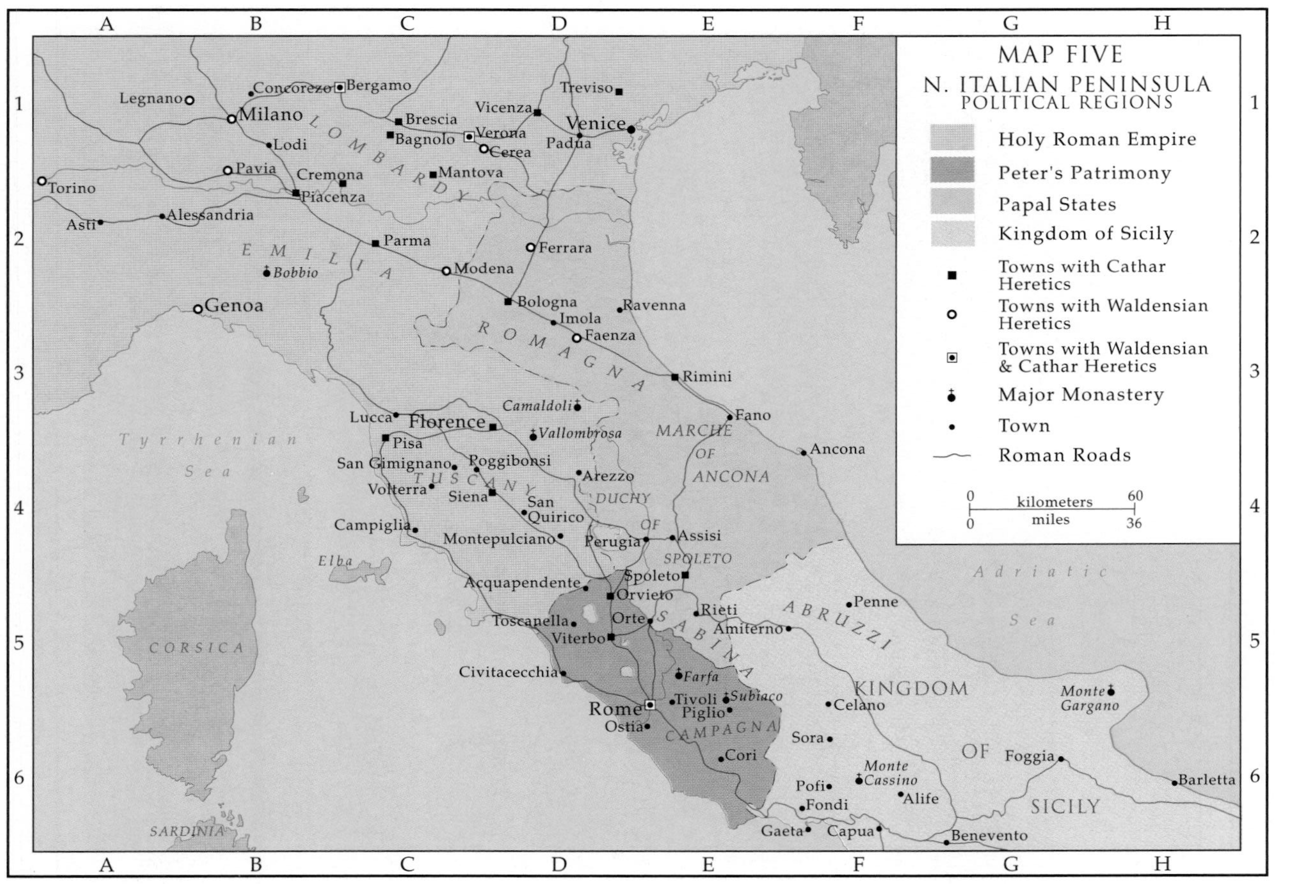
MAP FIVE
N. ITALIAN PENINSULA
POLITICAL REGIONS
Holy Roman Empire
Peter's Patrimony
Papal States
Kingdom of Sicily
Towns with Cathar Heretics
Towns with Waldensian Heretics
Towns with Waldensian & Cathar Heretics
Major Monastery
Town
Roman Roads
0 kilometers 60
0 miles 36
A B C D E F G H
1 2 3 4 5 6
Legnano
Concorezo
Bergamo
Milano
LOMBARDY
Lodi
Pavia
Torino
Cremona
Piacenza
Brescia
Bagnolo
Mantova
Verona
Cerea
Vicenza
Treviso
Venice
Padua
Asti
Alessandria
EMILIA
Bobbio
Parma
Modena
Ferrara
Genoa
Bologna
Imola
Faenza
Ravenna
ROMAGNA
Rimini
Fano
Ancona
Camaldoli
Lucca
Florence
Vallombrosa
Pisa
MARCHE OF ANCONA
Tyrrhenian Sea
San Gimignano
Poggibonsi
Arezzo
TUSCANY
Volterra
Siena
San Quirico
DUCHY OF SPOLETO
Campiglia
Montepulciano
Perugia
Assisi
Elba
Spoleto
Acquapendente
Orvieto
Rieti
Penne
ABRUZZI
Adriatic Sea
Toscanella
Orte
SABINA
Amiterno
CORSICA
Viterbo
Civitacecchia
Farfa
KINGDOM OF SICILY
Monte Gargano
Rome
Tivoli
Subiaco
Piglio
Celano
Ostia
CAMPAGNA
Sora
Cori
Foggia
Monte Cassino
Barletta
Pofi
Alife
Fondi
SARDINIA
Gaeta
Capua
Benevento

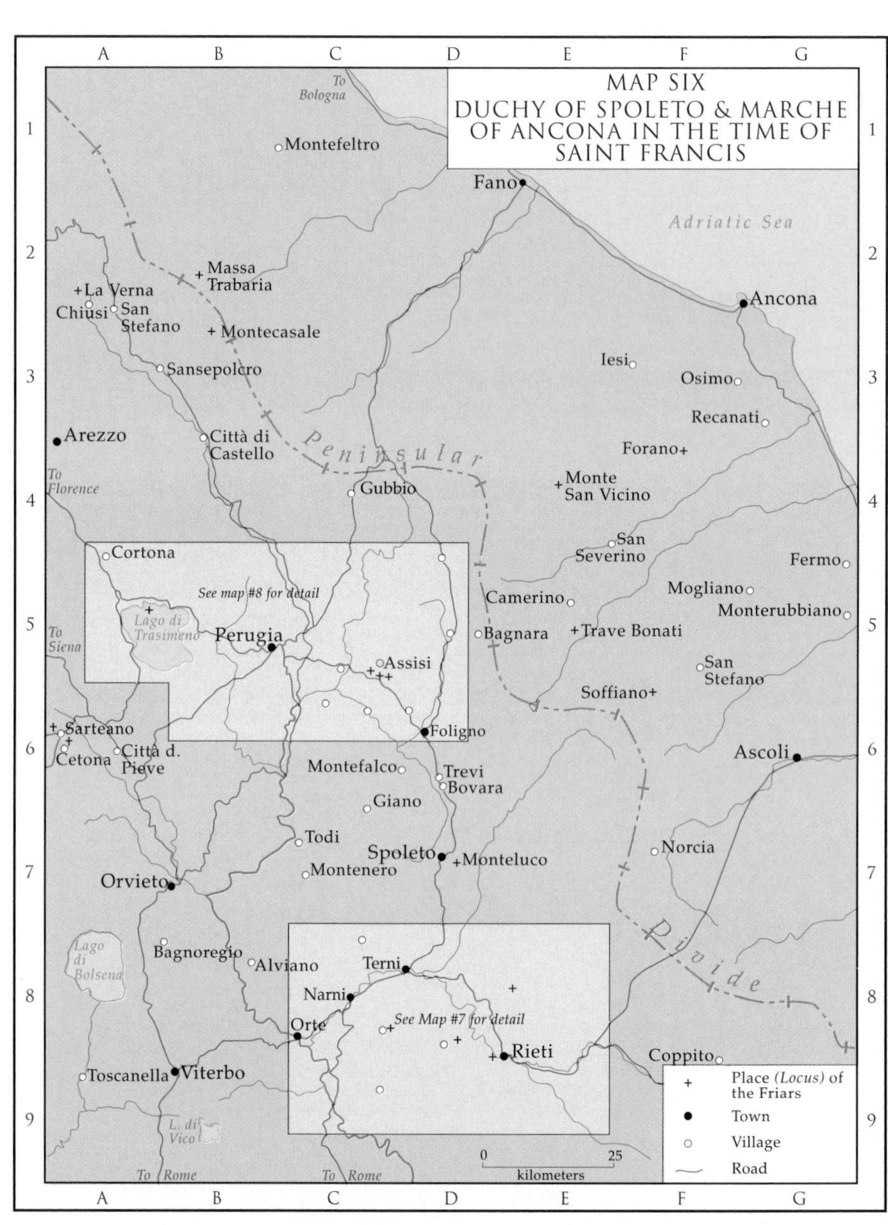
MAP SIX
DUCHY OF SPOLETO & MARCHE OF ANCONA IN THE TIME OF SAINT FRANCIS
A B C D E F G
1 2 3 4 5 6 7 8 9
To Bologna
Montefeltro
Fano
Adriatic Sea
Massa Trabaria
La Verna
Chiusi
San Stefano
Montecasale
Ancona
Sansepolcro
Iesi
Osimo
Recanati
Arezzo
Città di Castello
Peninsular Divide
Forano
To Florence
Gubbio
Monte San Vicino
Cortona
San Severino
Fermo
See map #8 for detail
Camerino
Mogliano
Lago di Trasimeno
Monterubbiano
To Siena
Perugia
Bagnara
Trave Bonati
Assisi
San Stefano
Soffiano
Sarteano
Foligno
Cetona
Città d. Pieve
Ascoli
Montefalco
Trevi
Bovara
Giano
Todi
Spoleto
Monteluco
Norcia
Orvieto
Montenero
Lago di Bolsena
Bagnoregio
Alviano
Terni
Narni
Orte
See Map #7 for detail
Rieti
Coppito
Toscanella
Viterbo
L. di Vico
To Rome
To Rome
0 25 kilometers
Place (Locus) of the Friars
Town
Village
Road

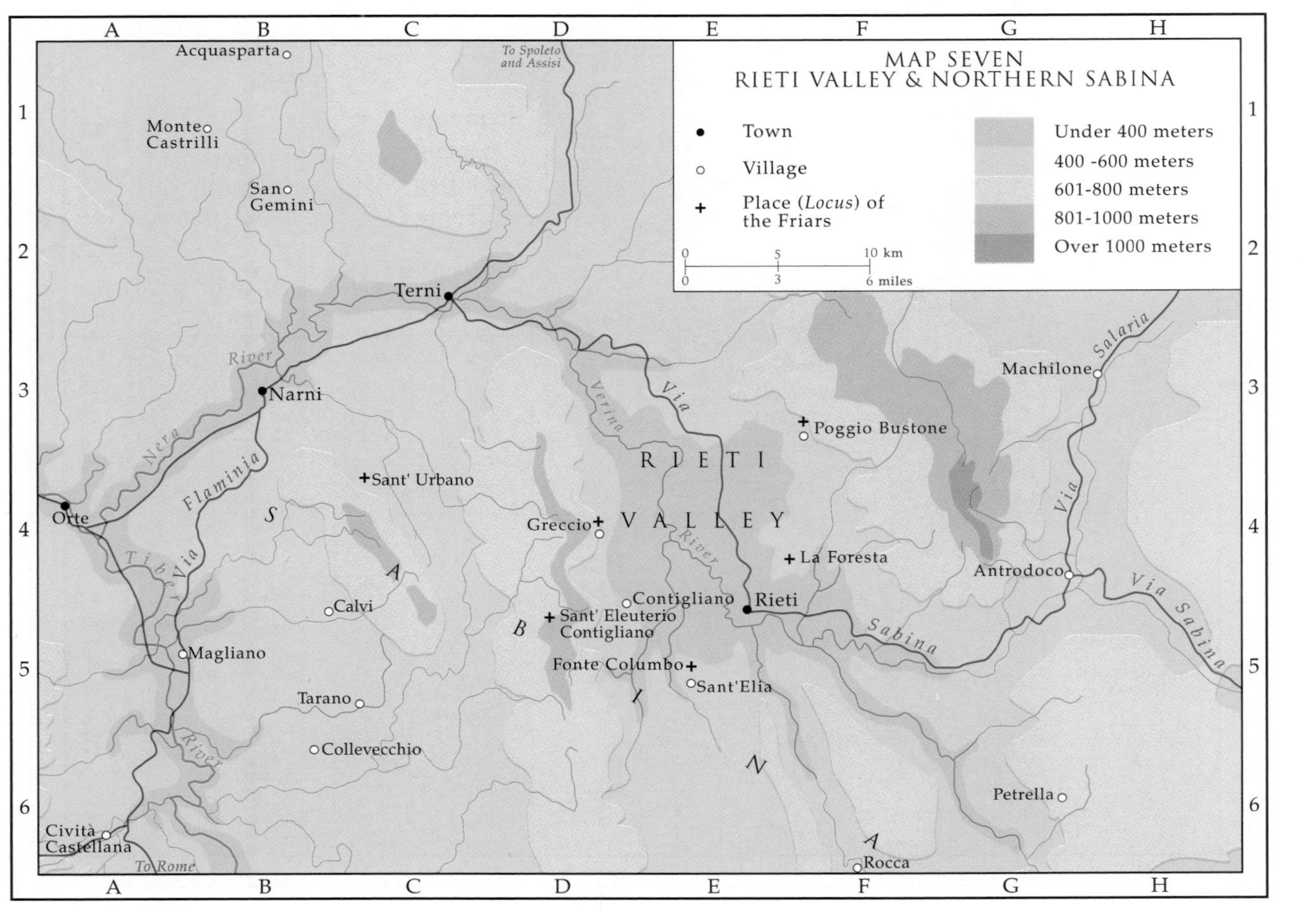
MAP SEVEN
RIETI VALLEY & NORTHERN SABINA
Town
Village
Place (Locus) of the Friars
Under 400 meters
400 -600 meters
601-800 meters
801-1000 meters
Over 1000 meters
0 5 10 km
0 3 6 miles
Acquasparta
To Spoleto and Assisi
Monte Castrilli
Sano Gemini
Terni
Narni
Nera River
Via Flaminia
Orte
Tiber River
Sant' Urbano
Calvi
Magliano
Tarano
Collevecchio
Cività Castellana
To Rome
Greccio
Verina
Via
RIETI VALLEY
River
Poggio Bustone
La Foresta
Contigliano
Rieti
Sant' Eleuterio Contigliano
Fonte Columbo
Sant'Elia
SABINA
Via Sabina
Machilone
Via Salaria
Antrodoco
Petrella
Rocca

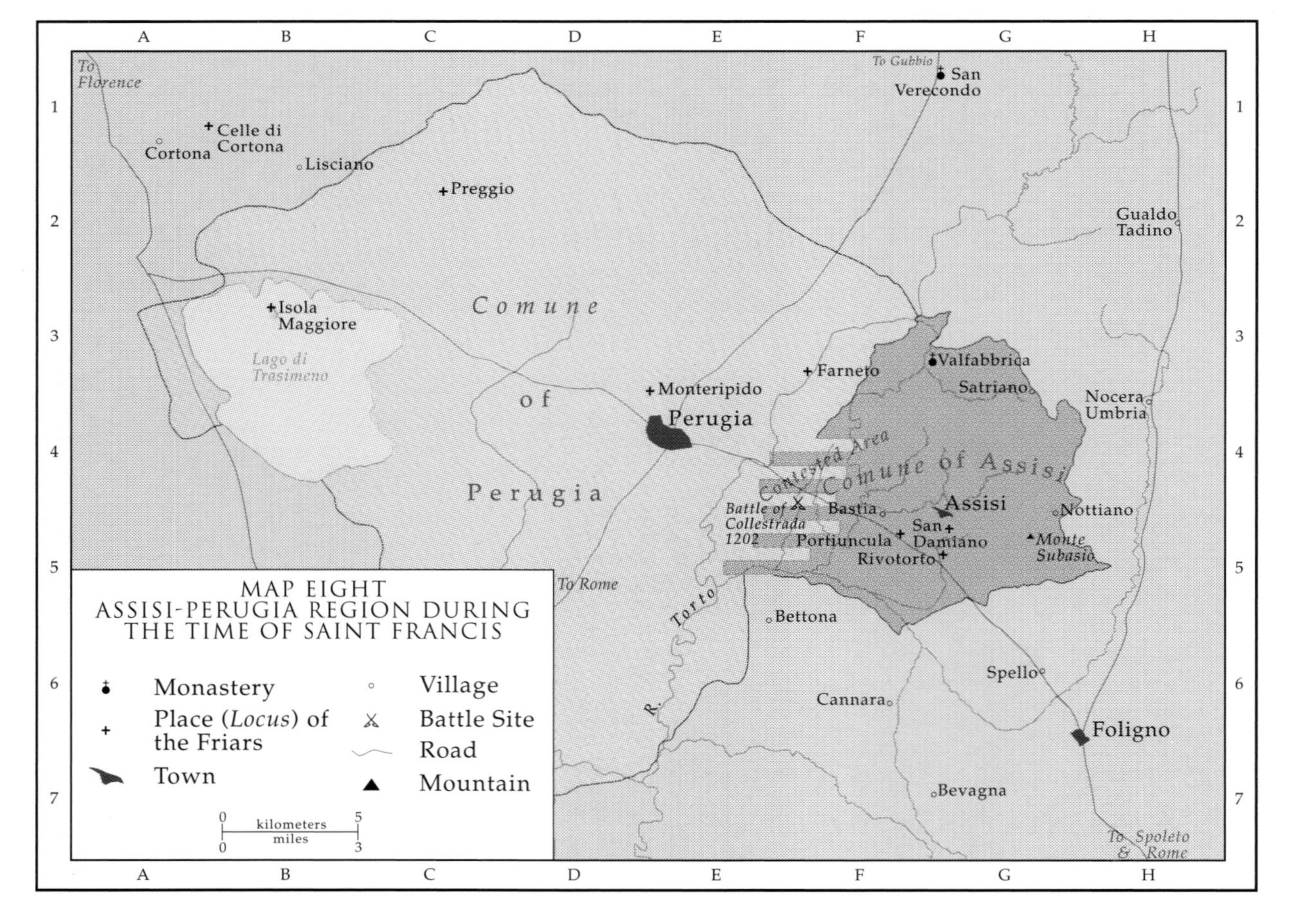

MAP EIGHT
ASSISI-PERUGIA REGION DURING THE TIME OF SAINT FRANCIS
Monastery
Place (Locus) of the Friars
Town
Village
Battle Site
Road
Mountain
kilometers
miles
0
5
0
3
A
B
C
D
E
F
G
H
1
2
3
4
5
6
7
To Florence
Cortona
Celle di Cortona
Lisciano
Preggio
Isola Maggiore
Lago di Trasimeno
Comune of Perugia
Monteripido
Perugia
To Rome
R. Torto
To Gubbio
San Verecondo
Gualdo Tadino
Farneto
Valfabbrica
Satriano
Nocera Umbria
Contested Area
Comune of Assisi
Battle of Collestrada 1202
Bastia
Assisi
San Damiano
Portiuncula
Rivotorto
Nottiano
Monte Subasio
Bettona
Spello
Cannara
Foligno
Bevagna
To Spoleto & Rome

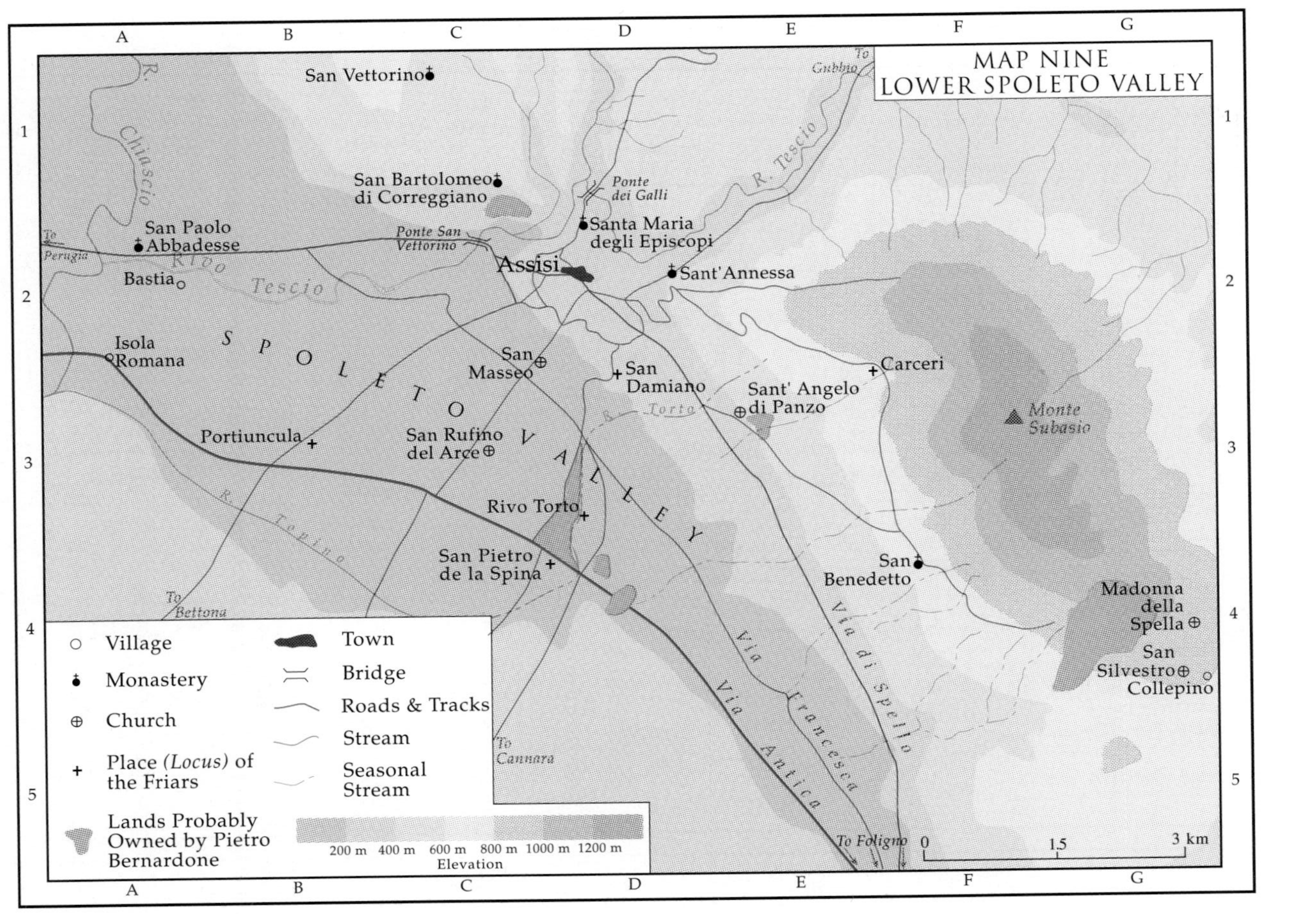

MAP NINE
LOWER SPOLETO VALLEY
San Vettorino
San Bartolomeo di Correggiano
San Paolo Abbadesse
Bastia
Isola Romana
R. Chiascio
Rivo Tescio
To Perugia
Ponte San Vettorino
Ponte dei Galli
Santa Maria degli Episcopi
Assisi
Sant'Annessa
R. Tescio
To Gubbio
SPOLETO VALLEY
San Masseo
San Damiano
Sant' Angelo di Panzo
Carceri
Monte Subasio
R. Torto
Portiuncula
San Rufino del Arce
Rivo Torto
San Pietro de la Spina
R. Topino
To Bettona
To Cannara
San Benedetto
Via Antica
Via Francesca
Via di Spello
To Foligno
Madonna della Spella
San Silvestro
Collepino
Village
Monastery
Church
Place (Locus) of the Friars
Lands Probably Owned by Pietro Bernardone
Town
Bridge
Roads & Tracks
Stream
Seasonal Stream
200 m 400 m 600 m 800 m 1000 m 1200 m
Elevation
0 1.5 3 km

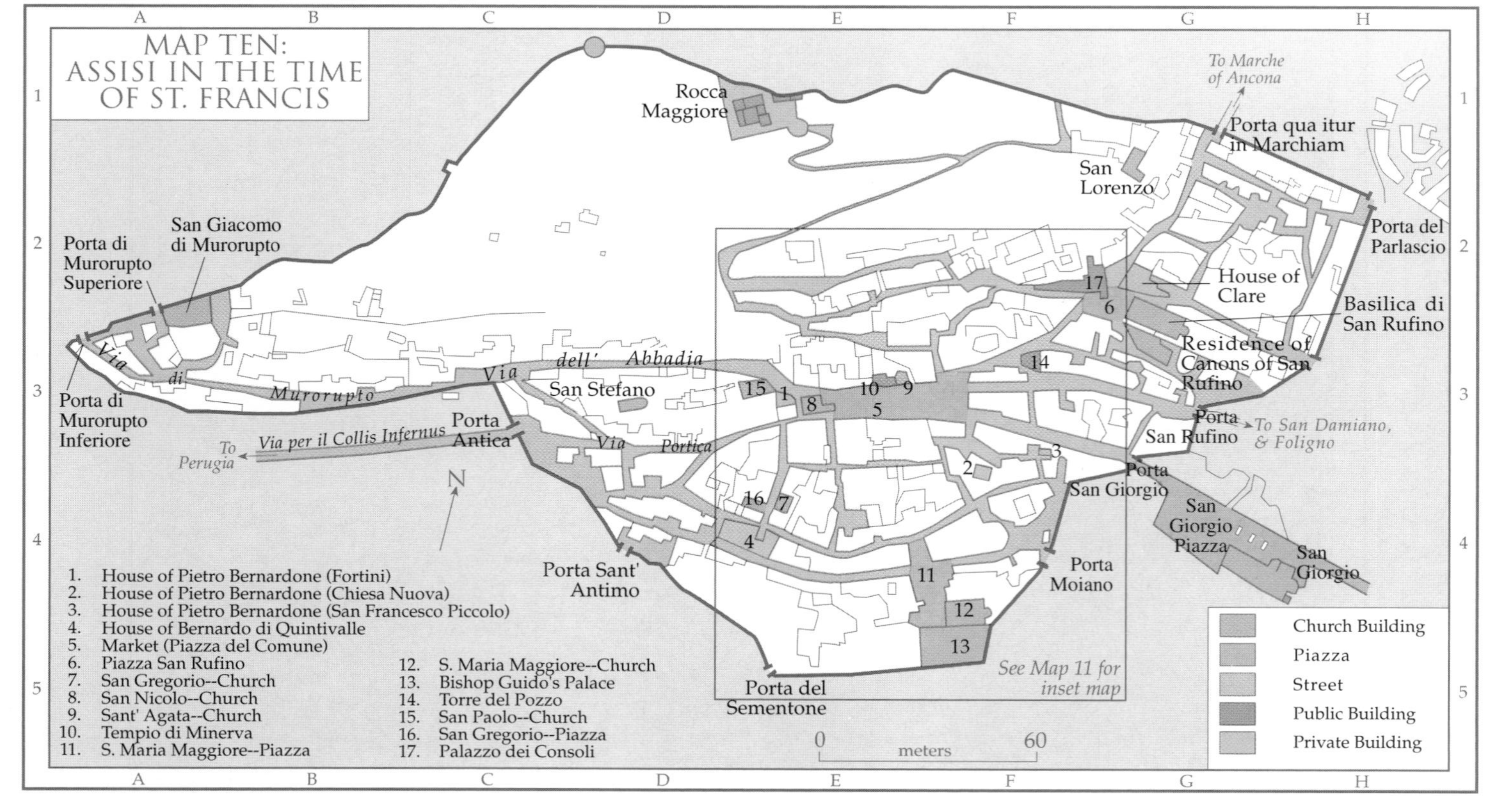
MAP TEN:
ASSISI IN THE TIME
OF ST. FRANCIS
Rocca Maggiore
To Marche of Ancona
Porta qua itur in Marchiam
San Lorenzo
Porta del Parlascio
House of Clare
Basilica di San Rufino
Residence of Canons of San Rufino
Porta San Rufino
To San Damiano, & Foligno
Porta San Giorgio
San Giorgio Piazza
San Giorgio
Porta Moiano
Porta del Sementone
Porta Sant' Antimo
Porta Antica
Via per il Collis Infernus
To Perugia
Via Portica
Via dell' Abbadia
San Stefano
Via di Murorupto
San Giacomo di Murorupto
Porta di Murorupto Superiore
Porta di Murorupto Inferiore
N
See Map 11 for inset map
0 meters 60
Church Building
Piazza
Street
Public Building
Private Building
1. House of Pietro Bernardone (Fortini)
2. House of Pietro Bernardone (Chiesa Nuova)
3. House of Pietro Bernardone (San Francesco Piccolo)
4. House of Bernardo di Quintivalle
5. Market (Piazza del Comune)
6. Piazza San Rufino
7. San Gregorio--Church
8. San Nicolo--Church
9. Sant' Agata--Church
10. Tempio di Minerva
11. S. Maria Maggiore--Piazza
12. S. Maria Maggiore--Church
13. Bishop Guido's Palace
14. Torre del Pozzo
15. San Paolo--Church
16. San Gregorio--Piazza
17. Palazzo dei Consoli

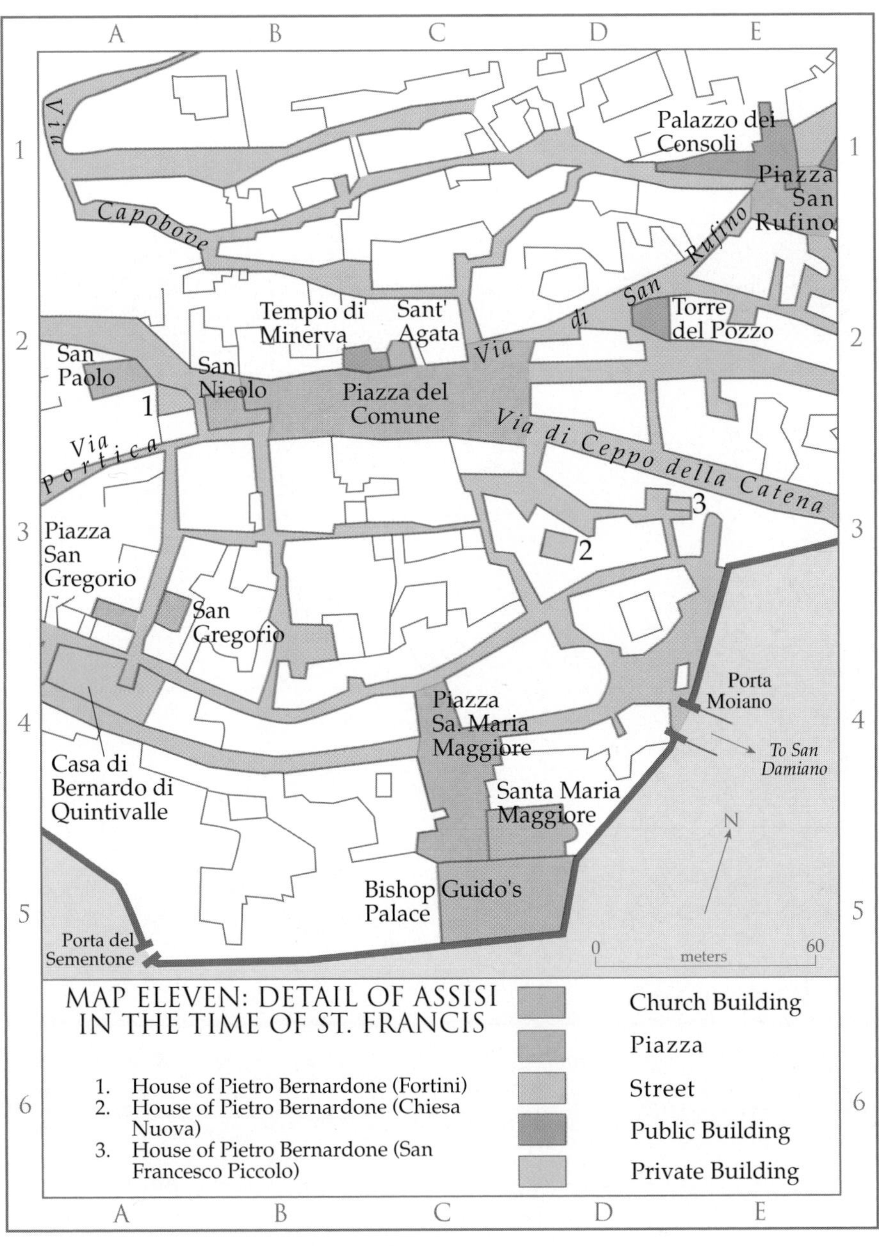
A
B
C
D
E
1
2
3
4
5
6
Via Capobove
Palazzo dei Consoli
Piazza San Rufino
Via di San Rufino
Tempio di Minerva
Sant' Agata
Torre del Pozzo
San Paolo
San Nicolo
Piazza del Comune
1
Via Portica
Via di Ceppo della Catena
3
2
Piazza San Gregorio
San Gregorio
Porta Moiano
To San Damiano
Piazza Sa. Maria Maggiore
Casa di Bernardo di Quintivalle
Santa Maria Maggiore
N
Bishop Guido's Palace
Porta del Sementone
0
meters
60
MAP ELEVEN: DETAIL OF ASSISI IN THE TIME OF ST. FRANCIS
1. House of Pietro Bernardone (Fortini)
2. House of Pietro Bernardone (Chiesa Nuova)
3. House of Pietro Bernardone (San Francesco Piccolo)
Church Building
Piazza
Street
Public Building
Private Building